NFL Head Coaches

ALSO BY JOHN MAXYMUK

Strong Arm Tactics: A History and Statistical Analysis of the Professional Quarterback (McFarland, 2008)

Uniform Numbers of the NFL: All-Time Rosters, Facts and Figures (McFarland, 2005)

NFL Head Coaches

A Biographical Dictionary,
1920–2011

JOHN MAXYMUK

McFarland & Company, Inc., Publishers
Jefferson, North Carolina, and London

Everyone could use a coach;
mine is Suzanne, and
she is a champion every year.

LIBRARY OF CONGRESS CATALOGUING-IN-PUBLICATION DATA

Maxymuk, John.
NFL head coaches : a biographical dictionary, 1920–2011 / John Maxymuk.
p.   cm.
Includes bibliographical references and index.

ISBN 978-0-7864-6557-6
softcover : acid free paper ∞

1. Football coaches — United States — Biography — Dictionaries.
I. Title.   II. Title: National Football League head coaches.
GV939.A1M39 2012   796.3320922 — dc23   [B]   2012026520

BRITISH LIBRARY CATALOGUING DATA ARE AVAILABLE

On the cover: New England Patriots head coach Bill Belichick
on the sidelines in a game against the Dallas Cowboys in
Foxboro, Massachusetts, on November 16, 2003
(Associated Press/Elise Amendola)

Manufactured in the United States of America

McFarland & Company, Inc., Publishers
Box 611, Jefferson, North Carolina 28640
www.mcfarlandpub.com

CONTENTS

ACKNOWLEDGMENTS

At the top, I would like to thank esteemed sports historian David Neft for helping with several knotty problems. Thanks also to Jeff Miller, Ken Crippen and John Steffenhagen who assisted with some Western New York issues. Numerous archivists and librarians provided invaluable research aid with information on coaches from the 1920s. They include Alan Aimore, West Point; Dina Allen, University of Illinois; Raymond Butti, Brown University; Lynn Conway, Georgetown University; Bradley D. Cook, University of Indiana; Paul Dyzak, Penn State University; Tom Frusciano, Rutgers University; Erin George, University of Minnesota; Theresa Gray, Vanderbilt University; Kevin C. Haire, Ohio State University; Craig A. Holbert, University of Akron; Marianne Kasica, University of Pittsburgh; Angela Kindig, Notre Dame; Kae Kirkwood, Geneva College; Betty Menges, New Albany Floyd County Public Library; Judy Miller, Valparaiso University; Nancy R. Miller, University of Pennsylvania; Mary O'Brien, Syracuse University; Catriona Schlosser, West Point; Pamela L. Speis, Mahoning Valley Historical Society; Susan Stawicki, Marquette; Gyorgy Toth, University of Iowa; Beth Swift, Wabash College; as well as the staff at the Public Library of Cincinnati & Hamilton County and Joe Di Bari of the Fordham Athletic Department. Thank you to all.

PREFACE

The 466 men who have held the increasingly demanding and prestigious position of head coach in the National Football League and the two leagues that merged into it (the All America Football Conference of the 1940s and the American Football League of the 1960s) form an exclusive club. At times lauded, at other times cursed and second-guessed, they live and work in a very public world. However, aside from current coaches, we rarely hear about the complete historical roster of the NFL coaching brethren. In this book, we look at every head coach and attempt to answer three questions about each one: (1) Who was he?; (2) What was his coaching approach and style, both in terms of leadership and gridiron tactics?; (3) How successful was he?

In the process of answering these questions, we run across some remarkable stories. Who was the first coach to win four NFL titles? Which coach died during the landing on Iwo Jima? Which coach's brother-in-law won a Nobel Prize? Which coach died on New Year's Eve when his coal stove extinguished in remote Alaska? Which coach backed up Babe Ruth and roomed with Lou Gehrig? Which coach appeared in more than 150 movies? Who was the first Packers coach? Who were the last NFL player-coaches? Which former coach founded the NFL Pro Bowl? Who was the last coach to simultaneously coach an NFL team and a college team? Who coached in the NFL, WFL, USFL, CFL and college ranks? And that is just a sampling of the facts, twists and connections of these coaches' lives.

I have divided the listings into two sections. The first contains the 358 men who have served as NFL/AAFC/AFL head coaches in the modern game from 1933 to the present. I did not include acting coaches who fulfilled their bosses' duties in the event of illness (such as Dante Scarnecchia for Dick MacPherson in 1992, Elijah Pitts for Marv Levy in 1995 and Rich Brooks for Dan Reeves in 1998) or brief absence (such as Walt Michaels for Red Conkright who was off scouting during one game in 1962). The second section contains the 108 coaches who coached solely in the NFL's early days from 1920 to 1932. The nine men who coached in both eras are listed in section one with cross-references to those names in section two. In that early period, so much was dissimilar in pro football that I felt those coaches belonged in their own subset. The duties of the head coach were minimal, the game on the field was played in a now-unrecognizable style, and the league was run within vastly different parameters. Those differences to which I alluded are more fully explained in the introduction, but suffice to say here that the job of professional head football coach has evolved and expanded tremendously over time.

Each entry begins with a standard set of information categories. Name, birth/death dates, college attended and position(s) played/professional teams represented are all self-explanatory. "Apprenticeship" breaks down the years the coach spent as a college coach, head coach in another professional league or professional assistant coach before he landed his first NFL head coaching job. "Roots" lists the coaches he worked under before his first full-year job as head coach; "Branches" lists his assistants who went on to their first professional head coaching job after serving on his staff. "Coordinators/Key Coaches" provides the names of the most important coaches on the staff. The job titles and duties of assistant coaches also have evolved over time. Teams began using "offensive coordinator" and "defensive coordinator" as job titles in the 1970s as staffs expanded, but the practice of assistants being in charge of the whole offense or whole defense dates earlier than that. In the 1950s, offensive coach Vince Lombardi and defensive coach Tom Landry were the clearest example under the Giants and chief delegator head coach Jim Lee Howell. However, when Lombardi went to Green Bay, he hired Phil Bengtson as his defensive coach and handled the offense himself. Meanwhile, Landry ran both sides of the ball at first in Dallas before beginning to delegate responsibility more. The next categories of "Hall of Fame Players" and "Primary Quarterbacks" are also self-explanatory.

Along with each coach's yearly regular season and postseason coaching record, the next item notes whether the coach was a player-coach, owner-coach, co-coach or solely an interim coach. In this book, I have expanded the definition of "interim" to include not only coaches promoted to finish out a season for a fired coach, but also those, such as Bobby Petrino in Atlanta in 2007, who failed to complete a single full season as head coach. Interim coaches are noted with an (i) in the Roots and Branches sections. Any league championships won are indicated here as well as the entrant's Hall of Fame status as either a player or coach. For Hall of Fame coaches, a second table is inserted that shows that coach's head-to-head record against other Hall of Fame coaches.

The final item at the top of the entries is "Tendencies," which contains some additional statistics of interest for all full season coaches. These numbers are not provided for interim coaches because their data sample is too small. The elements of Tendencies include Average Points Scored and Allowed; the percentage of running plays called and how that compares to the league average at the time; the percentage of starts given to primary quarterbacks; the number rookie starters he used over his career; and the ratio of full-year winning seasons to full-year losing ones.

The entries for the earlier coaches in Section II are briefer. The coaching tree and key coaches categories are eliminated because there were virtually no full-time assistant coaches in that time. In fact, most coaches were player-coaches, and sometimes they had player-assistant-coaches too. Instead, I have listed the college coach these early coaches played under because that college mentor was often the greatest influence on these early NFL coaches. No teams ran a modern T formation offense so the primary quarterback category was dropped as well. Furthermore, the record section is different because there was no postseason in that time period. I have substituted yearly points scored and allowed for the playoff game data in the annual record. Finally, the tendencies item is eliminated because the data for that period is either unavailable or of much less significance.

In the Appendix, I take a stab at ranking coaches according to a formula of my own design that is explained in the text. Also in the back of the book, a bibliography lists the works and resources consulted to assemble this reference work. Finally, for those "quiz" questions at the top of the preface, consult these entries for more details: Guy Chamberlin; Jack Chevigny; George Gibson; Hal Griffen; Hinkey Haines; Dutch Hendrian; Joe Hoeffel; Johnny Blood, Dutch Clark and Art Lewis; Paul Schissler; Aldo Donelli; and Jack Pardee. Take a look.

INTRODUCTION

The essential duties of an NFL head coach have remained constant for decades. He must assist in acquiring talent, develop the skill level of that talent, motivate that talent to work as a team and utilize that talent in the optimal way, putting players in their best position to help the club win. However, there are a number of duties that have evolved as the job of head coach has expanded over time, such as crafting creative game plans, making game time adjustments, interacting constructively with the front office, the media and fans, coordinating with scouts and management on the draft and free agency, recruiting free agents and dealing with salary cap issues.

By contrast, 1920s tackle John Alexander provided Jim Campbell a good overview of how the job of coach was different during the early, "dead ball" days of pro football in a 1995 article in *Coffin Corner*:

"The coach, during the game, was really not much of a factor in those days. There was no coaching from the sidelines—you couldn't yell instructions, you couldn't even signal in plays. That would have been a fifteen-yard penalty if you got caught. The game was really played on the field by the eleven men you had out there. The captain was the key man on game day. He called the signals. He kept order and discipline. Not the coach. Coaches worked with us in practice and when the game came around they'd say, 'I did all I could. Now, you go out and play. I'm going to watch and enjoy the game.' There was a lot of truth to that. There were few timeouts. When there were, we didn't go to the sideline to discuss the upcoming plays. There were even rules in effect that kept the game on the field rather than on the sidelines. Did you know that if a substitute came into the game—and there weren't many times that happened—an official went right into the huddle with him to make sure he didn't convey any messages from the coach to his teammates?"

Furthermore, Robert Peterson pointed out in *Pigskin* a number of additional differences from the earliest days. Coaches did not produce playbooks. There was no weekly film study of previous games. Players played both offense and defense; most were 60-minute men. Rosters consisted of just 16 men so substitutions were limited, and if a player came out of the game, he had to stay out until the next quarter. Huddles were just beginning to become widely accepted. There were no hashmarks on the field, so the next play began where the last ended. If a team ran wide and got tackled near the sideline, six linemen might be on one side of the center on the next snap because the ball was spotted so close to the sideline. The ball was fatter and harder to throw and several punitive passing rules made throwing the ball risky and a rarity. Overall, the game was a slow, low-scoring, ground-and-pound affair in which punting and turnovers played a key role in determining the field position that most contributed to victory.

It wasn't until the 1932 de facto championship game that things began to change significantly. Up to 1932, the NFL had no divisions. Instead, its champion was determined by which team had the highest winning percentage. In 1932, the Bears finished the scheduled season 6–1–6 and the Portsmouth Spartans finished 6–1–4 (obviously, teams didn't even necessarily play the same number of games at that time). The two teams agreed to a showdown two weeks later in Chicago, but a blizzard intervened, so George Halas arranged for the game to be played indoors in Chicago Stadium. Because the field was narrower and only 60 yards long, special ground rules were established including putting hashmarks on the field so plays would not start from either sideline and placing the goal posts at the goal line. The Bears won the game 9–0, but Lions coach Potsy Clark was incensed because he felt that on the Bears' touchdown pass from Bronko Naguski to Red Grange Nagurski was not thrown from five yards behind the line of scrimmage as the rules then required.

The upshot was that the game generated so

much interest that NFL owners made several rules changes for 1933. The league was divided into east and west divisions with the champion to be determined in a playoff game. The goal posts were placed on the goal line. Hashmarks were instituted permanently. Passing was permitted anywhere behind the line of scrimmage, and the diameter of the ball was decreased, making it easier to throw. Moreover, all of these changes made a clear distinction between the pro and college games for the first time. Pro football was growing up, and coaches began to assume a greater role in the success or failure of their teams.

Who coaches were also changed. There were fewer owners who doubled as coaches and fewer co-coach arrangements. There were four co-coaching arrangements in the 1940s, and just two since — a trio of Cardinal interim co-coaches in 1961 and a pair of co-coaches for the last game of the Patriots' 1978 season. Player-coaches essentially vanished during the 1930s. From 1920 until 1932, there were 117 different men who served as NFL head coaches. Eighty-two of them, 70%, were player-coaches at least part of that time. From 1933 on, only 10 of the 358 NFL coaches, 2.8%, have been player-coaches in that time. In the 1930s, Al Jolley, Algy Clark, Jap Douds, Milan Creighton, Dutch Clark, Art Lewis and Johnny McNally were the last of the player-coaches. After McNally was fired in 1939, the only player-coaches were a trio of Chicago Rockets who led that All America Football Conference team on an interim basis for a half-dozen games in 1946.

Coaches also got older. All but one of the championship coaches from 1920 to 1932 were under 30, with 1932's Ralph Jones being the lone exception. Since 1933, 15% of championship coaches have been under 40; 24% have been between 40 and 44; 31% have been between 45 and 49; 19% have been between 50 and 54; and 11% have been 55 or over. The percentages for the runners up, the coaches of the teams that lost in the title game, are roughly the same. The youngest coach to win a championship was George Halas at 26 (with apologies to his 26-year-old co-coach Dutch Sternaman); the oldest was George Halas at 68. Among championship coaches, Bill Cowher went the longest without winning his first title at 14 years, although a number of Hall of Fame coaches had longer careers without ever winning a championship.

Another indication of the growth of the stakes of pro football and the stature of the head coach has been the growth of coaching staffs. In the 1920s, some teams had a player double as a line or backfield coach, but the first full time assistant coaches began in 1933 with Laurie Walquist of the Bears — although there are some indications that Dim Batterson was a full time assistant coach for Buffalo in 1925 and 1926. In 1934, Walquist was joined by J.P. Rooney and Cad Reese in Pittsburgh. In 1935, Curly Lambeau added Red Smith as his line coach, but his entire staff in the remaining 15 years of his Green Bay tenure never exceeded three: assistants for the backfield, line and either ends or defense. By this point in the late 1940s, Paul Brown introduced year-round assistant coaches in Cleveland. In the 1950s, the trend began to have one assistant in charge of one side of the ball, with the head coach in charge of the other, but the New York Giants took that a step further when administrative head coach Jim Lee Howell appointed Vince Lombardi the offensive coach and Tom Landry the defensive coach; there were still no coordinator positions.

In 1960, Buck Shaw became the last part-time head coach to win a championship. Buck only worked for the Eagles six months a year, spending the rest of his time with his cardboard box company. In the next decade, some coaches would begin sleeping in their offices they were putting in so many hours at work. Staffs continued to grow. Vince Lombardi's staff reached six by his last title in 1967: assistants for ends, backs, offensive line, defensive line, linebackers and defensive backs with the linebackers' coach doubling as the defensive coach. George Allen hired Dick Vermeil as the league's first special teams coach in 1969, the term coordinator began to flourish in the 1970s and staffs continued to increase. Mike Holmgren's first Packers staff in 1992 included a baker's dozen of assistant coaches. When Mike McCarthy won the Super Bowl in 2011, he was assisted by 20 assistant coaches. Moreover, coaches increasingly have begun to look upon their profession as the family business, bringing their sons to work with them. Marty Schottenheimer, Buddy Ryan, Mike Shanahan, Gregg Williams and many others have given a staff position to their sons and put them on a fast track to coordinator position. With so much emphasis on film study in the modern game, there is some sense to this nepotism. Expertise in analyzing film is a skill that can be passed on; working with players, though, is another question.

With all of this extra manpower, the game also has advanced in strategy. We have evolved from the days of 60-minute men who played both offense and defense to pre-war teams like the Giants and Redskins platooning squads by quarter to the emergence of two-platoon football in the post-war era to the play-by-play extensive situational substitution prevalent today. Similarly, roster sizes have risen from 16 players in the 1920s to 53 in the new century.

On offense, we have gone from the single wing to the T formation to the pro set with two wide receivers to the shotgun to one-back sets and H-backs, to the run-and-shoot and on to a variety of five-receiver spread formations. Add in variations in motion, spacing and alignment for offensive players, and the possibilities are infinite. The passing game has been pushed forward by Paul Brown's set of timing patterns, Sid Gillman's down-the-field approach, Al Davis' vertical deep passing game, Red Hickey's shotgun, Don Coryell's mix of timing and deep routes, Bill Walsh's ball-control West Coast offense, Mouse Davis' run-and-shoot and Bill Belichick's spread experiments. With all of this planning, it is no surprise that in the 1970s and 1980s, the practice of a quarterback calling his own plays on the field began to vanish. From Paul Brown's messenger guards to Tom Landry's messenger quarterbacks and ends to sideline signaling in the 1970s and 1980s to radio helmets in the mid–1990s (although Paul Brown first tried them in 1956), coaches have become the signal callers in pro football.

On defense, every offensive advance must be countered. We have gone from the five-man-line Eagle defense of the 1940s to the Umbrella that opened into the 4–3 standard alignment in the 1950s to the 3–4 in the 1970s to a plethora of flexible variants, including nickel defenses, Buddy Ryan's 46, the zone blitz and a host of amorphous configurations of shifting defenders with masked intentions.

In conclusion, NFL coaches are in more control of the game today than they ever have been and are under more scrutiny from ownership, players, the media and fans. NFL coaches, in large measure, have built the great game we have today. Some in particular have advanced the game a great deal. Throughout this book, I refer at times to some coaches as being among the best as to their influence or effectiveness. To put these judgments in perspective, let me close by listing in alphabetical order who I consider from my research to be the top coaches in the league's history.

Top Ten Offensive Assistants

Joe Bugel — built the Hogs, the most celebrated offensive line in history

Blanton Collier — ran the Browns passing offense and pass defense until 1954

Luke Johnsos — unheralded eye in the sky who ran the offense for the 1940s Monsters of the Midway from the press box

Vince Lombardi — Used option blocking and the power sweep to Run to Daylight

Ted Marchibroda — tutored a series of top quarterbacks and explosive offenses for over 30 years

Mike Martz — the heir to Gillman and Coryell; designed the Greatest Show on Turf

Tom Moore — Peyton Manning's tutor; spent over a dozen seasons each with the Colts and the Steelers

Hampton Pool — designed the modern Pro Set with flanker

Clark Shaughnessy — drew up counter plays and other moves to expand the T

Bill Walsh — created the misnamed West Coast Offense in Cincinnati, a ball control passing attack

(Honorable mention to Mouse Davis, Ron Erhardt, Joe Gibbs, Jim Hanifan, Red Hickey, Mike Holmgren, Red Miller, Sean Payton, Mike Shanahan, Norv Turner and Sam Wyche)

Top Ten Defensive Assistants

Hunk Anderson — father of the blitz and the safety blitz; drove the big bad Bear defenses of the 1940s

Bill Arnsparger — his 53 defense experimented with the 3–4; Miami's No Name and Killer B's defenses were his

Bill Belichick — creates an original scheme each week

Phil Bengtson — built the 1960s Packers impregnable pass defense with rangy, swift linebackers dropping into coverage

Dom Capers — used blitzing linebackers from New Orleans to Blitzburgh to Green Bay

Bud Carson — designed the Cover 2 for the back end of the Steel Curtain

Joe Collier — directed the 4–3 1960s Bills and the 3–4 1970s and 1980s Orange Crush Broncos

Dick LeBeau — perfected the Zone Blitz, with constantly changing pressure points

Tom Landry — drew up the 4–3 base defense in the

1950s and the Flex variation in the 1960s; his style was read and react

Buddy Ryan — devised the 46 defense, bunch at the line and meet at the quarterback

(Honorable mention to George Allen, Marion Campbell, Tony Dungy, Jim Johnson, Marvin Lewis, Monte Kiffin, Wade Phillips, Rex Ryan, George Seifert and Fritz Shurmur)

Top Ten Most Influential Head Coaches

George Allen — the Future Is Now; the Over the Hill Gang; the nickel defense and complex zone packages

Bill Belichick — the most complete technical coach since Tom Landry

Paul Brown — the supreme organizer and innovator

Don Coryell — Air Coryell, the pass route tree, a fast-paced timing passing offense

Sid Gillman — father of the modern passing game and of the attack first attitude

George Halas — father of pro coaches, founder of the Bears, stabilizing force of the NFL for over 60 years

Tom Landry — supreme engineer on both sides of the ball, the motion offense and the Doomsday Defense

Vince Lombardi — the ultimate motivator; winning isn't everything, it's the only thing; blocking, tackling and execution

Hank Stram — designed the floating pocket, offset defensive alignment and the stack defense

Bill Walsh — devised the most emulated offense of the past 30 years, plus scripting plays and wholesale situational substitution

(Honorable mention to Al Davis, Tony Dungy, Joe Gibbs, Jimmy Johnson, Ralph Jones, Curly Lambeau, Greasy Neale, Steve Owen, Bill Parcells and Don Shula.)

Look them all up in the following pages.

I. The Coaching Roster, 1933–2011

ALBERT, FRANK C. (FRANKIE) 1/27/1920–9/5/2002. Stanford. Played QB for the San Francisco 49ers from 1946 to 1952. *Apprenticeship:* Pro asst.—1 year. *Roots:* Red Strader. *Branches:* Red Hickey, Phil Bengtson, Bill Johnson. *Coordinators/Key Assistants:* Bill Johnson helped with the offense and Phil Bengtson ran the defense. *Hall of Fame Players:* John Henry Johnson, Hugh McElhenny, Leo Nomellini, Joe Perry, Bob St. Clair, Y. A. Tittle. *Primary Quarterbacks:* Y.A. Tittle. *Tendencies:* • His teams scored 20.8 points and allowed 24.2 per game • His teams ran 51.4% of the time, which was 90% of the league average • Three starting quarterbacks in three years; 69% of starts to primary quarterback • 14 rookie starters in three years • Winning Full Seasons to Losing Full Seasons: 1:1.

Had it not been for World War II, Chicago-native Frankie Albert would have been the first left-handed T-formation quarterback in the NFL. In 1942, he was the top draft pick of the league champion Bears who already had Sid Luckman at quarterback. Instead, Albert spent four years in the Navy and became the 49ers' first quarterback when the All America Football Conference started in 1946. The 5'10" 166-pound Albert was a crafty deceptive ball handler who excelled at the bootleg play. He learned the T from legendary strategist Clark Shaughnessy who came to Stanford when Frankie was a junior. Stanford was coming off a one-win 1939 season with Albert as a desultory single wing tailback when Shaughnessy brought in former Bears' quarterback Bernie Masterson to tutor Frankie in the intricacies of T quarterbacking. Stanford's "Wow Boys" then went undefeated in 1940 and won the Rose Bowl. Albert became so famous that he played himself in his own Columbia Pictures movie, *The Spirit of Stanford* in 1942.

After the war, Frankie was an instant star with San Francisco in the All America Football Conference. For four years, he drew All League recognition, and he led the AAFC in touchdown passes in 1948 and 1949. Under easy-going coach Buck Shaw, Albert was the team's inspirational leader. Halfback Hugh McElhenny claimed that Albert even ended team practice at times with Shaw calmly acquiescing. The only thing Frankie couldn't do was lead the 49ers past the Browns. By the time he got to the NFL in 1950 when the two leagues merged, Albert was 30 and starting to slip. A year later, the 49ers obtained Y.A. Tittle who took over as the team's starting quarterback within a year. Albert spent one final season playing in Canada before retiring in 1954. He missed football, though, and in 1955 was hired by owner Tony Morabito as backfield coach for new 49ers' head coach Red Strader. However, Frankie spent most of the year as a scout because he did not get along with Strader.

Most of the players did not get along with Strader either, so Morabito replaced him after just one season with Albert, his old favorite. Tony even sold Frankie five percent of the team for $5,000 at the time. At his opening press conference, Albert asserted, "I intend to put a colorful representative team on the field." The 36-year-old claimed his team would be more "self-disciplined," and he would not attempt to be as controlling as his predecessor. He also stressed the importance of the draft in bringing in new talent. Indeed, San Francisco was an aging team, and Albert introduced several new starters during his tenure. His biggest downfall was his defense that continually ranked at the bottom of the league from 1956 to 1958, giving up over 24 points a game. Still, the 49ers did tie for the Western Conference title in 1957 and played a memorable playoff game against the Lions on December 22 at San Francisco. The 49ers took a 24–7 halftime lead and then lengthened it to 27–7 in the opening minutes of the third quarter, but still lost 31–27 in an epic collapse. Afterwards, Albert cited "too many mistakes" and also too conservative play-calling as the team's downfall. Ironically, after the second game of

Albert, Frank C. (Frankie)									
Year	Team	Games	Wins	Losses	Ties	%	P Wins	P Losses	P %
1956	49ers	12	5	6	1	.458	0	0	.000
1957	49ers	12	8	4	0	.667	0	1	.000
1958	49ers	12	6	6	0	.500	0	0	.000
3 years		36	19	16	1	.542	0	1	.000

the 1957 season, Frankie told *Sports Illustrated*, "You get real conservative when you start coaching. When I was playing, I never thought about a play failing."

Ultimately, Albert was not emotionally cut out for the pressures of coaching. In 1958, he started flipping back and forth between Y. A. Tittle and second-year pro John Brodie at quarterback and the team slipped back to .500. He resigned at the end of the season, saying, "It got so that my wife and daughters had to run out of the supermarkets; they couldn't shop without being insulted." Frankie got out of football and led a long and happy life. And that 1956 investment of $5,000 investment? He sold it in the 1980s to Eddie DeBartolo for close to a million dollars.

ALLEN, GEORGE H. 4/29/1922–12/31/1990. Marquette, Alma and Michigan. Did not play professionally. *Apprenticeship:* College head coach — 9 years; pro assistant — 8 years. *Roots:* Sid Gillman; George Halas. *Branches:* Mike McCormack, Marion Campbell, Howard Schnellenberger, Jack Pardee, Ted Marchibroda, Dick Vermeil, Jack Patera, Marv Levy, Pete McCulley (i), Fred O'Connor (i), Joe Walton, Richie Petitbon. *Coordinators/Key Assistants:* For the Rams, Ted Marchibroda handled the offense and Tom Catlin the defense; for the Redskins, Marchibroda and then Charlie Waller handled the offense and Torgy Torgeson the defense. *Hall of Fame Players:* Bob Brown, Bill George, Chris Hanburger, Ken Houston, Deacon Jones, Sonny Jurgensen, Tom Mack, Merlin Olsen, John Riggins, Charley Taylor. *Primary Quarterbacks:* Roman Gabriel, Billy Kilmer. *Record:* **Hall of Fame Coach.** *Tendencies:* • His teams scored 22.1 points and allowed 15.1 per game • His teams ran 53% of the time, which was 98% of the league average • Four starting quarterbacks in 12 years; 85% of starts to primary quarterbacks • Eight rookie starters in 12 years • Winning Full Seasons to Losing Full Seasons: 12:0.

George Allen was in many ways the first modern coach in the NFL. So determined to win that he once

said, "Every time you win, you're reborn; when you lose, you die a little." Allen obsessed over the smallest details, routinely worked 16-hour days and often slept in his office. On the field, he hired the NFL's first Special Teams coach with Dick Vermeil in 1969 and was an early proponent of the zone defense. He never had a losing season in the league, was twice awarded Coach of the Year honors (1967 and 1971) and was elected to the Hall of Fame in 2002, a dozen years after his death. Still, after he was fired by the Rams for the *fourth* time in 1978, he had burned so many bridges that he was never seriously considered for another coaching position in the NFL. He ended his coaching career with Long Beach State, a lower division school that dropped football a year after his death.

Hailing from Grosse Point Woods, Michigan, Allen got his start as an assistant to Fritz Crisler on the JV team at Michigan where George earned his Master's degree in 1947. Moving on to Morningside College in Iowa, he posted a 16–11–2 mark there in three years as head coach and then went 32–22–5 in six leading the Whittier Poets (Richard Nixon's alma mater). Finally, Sid Gillman hired Allen as offensive end coach for the Rams in 1957. Unfortunately, George was fired a year later in a staff shakeup, but

Head-to-Head:		
Hall of Fame Opponent	Regular Season	Postseason
Paul Brown	0–1	0–0
Weeb Ewbank	1–0	0–0
Bud Grant	4–2	0–3
George Halas	2–1	0–0
Tom Landry	8–8	1–0
Vince Lombardi	1–2	0–1
John Madden	0–1	0–0
Chuck Noll	0–1	0–0
Don Shula	4–3–1	0–1
Hank Stram	0–1	0–0
Total	20–20–1	1–5

Allen, George H.

Year	Team	Games	Wins	Losses	Ties	%	P Wins	P Losses	P %
1966	Rams	14	8	6	0	.571	0	0	.000
1967	Rams	14	11	1	2	.786	0	1	.000
1968	Rams	14	10	3	1	.714	0	0	.000
1969	Rams	14	11	3	0	.786	0	1	.000
1970	Rams	14	9	4	1	.643	0	0	.000
1971	Redskins	14	9	4	1	.643	0	1	.000
1972	Redskins	14	11	3	0	.786	2	1	.667
1973	Redskins	14	10	4	0	.714	0	1	.000
1974	Redskins	14	10	4	0	.714	0	1	.000
1975	Redskins	14	8	6	0	.571	0	0	.000
1976	Redskins	14	10	4	0	.714	0	1	.000
1977	Redskins	14	9	5	0	.643	0	0	.000
12 years		168	116	47	5	.690	2	7	.222

was hired as a consultant by George Halas to scout the Rams for the Bears in 1958. The next year, Halas hired Allen as a full-time assistant coach and head of player personnel. Allen handled the Bears' drafts for the next six years and selected three Hall of Famers in Mike Ditka, Dick Butkus and Gale Sayers.

During the 1962 season, Halas had Allen take over the defensive coaching responsibilities from cranky legend Clark Shaughnessy who was unpopular with the players for his stodgy and overly complicated defensive schemes. Allen switched the Bears to a blitzing zone defense, and the next season Chicago gave up a record 144 points in winning the NFL championship. The players gave the game ball from that title game to Allen and could be heard on the televised locker room coverage affectionately serenading him, "Hooray for George; he's got a lot of class; hooray for George; he's a horse's ass."

Halas promised Allen the head coaching position, but with the old man showing no signs of leaving in 1966, Allen signed a contract with the Rams owner Dan Reeves to be their new head coach. Halas took Allen to court for breach of contract and won, but then abruptly dropped the suit and let Allen leave. Halas never forgave Allen for being "disloyal."

Allen took over the 4–10 Rams and immediately started making trades to upgrade the roster. In his five years in Los Angeles, George made 50 trades, giving up many draft picks for veterans and declaring the "future is now." In that first year, he brought in linebackers Bill George, Maxie Baughan and Myron Pottios as well as cornerback Irv Cross while settling on Roman Gabriel as his starting quarterback over Bill Munson. The team improved to 8–6 in 1966 and then to 11–1–2 and the playoffs in 1967. Allen's defense was superb led by the renowned Fearsome Foursome defensive line; his ball control offense took few risks and owed more to his time with Halas than his year with Sid Gillman, but Gabriel blossomed in this basic attack. George's approach to his players was corny, and he liked to lead them in cheers after wins. Most Rams bought into Allen's rah-rah attitude and fully supported him, although Hall of Fame tackle Bob Brown was a noticeable exception. However, Dan Reeves was not happy with Allen's plodding offense and his lack of deference to the owner, so he fired the coach the day after Christmas 1968 following a 10–3–1 season. The next day, a dozen Rams banded together to call a press conference and announce they did not want to play for Los Angeles without Allen. Eleven days later, Reeves reinstated George to fulfill his original five-year contract, but then fired him again at the end of that deal. At one point, Reeves indicated that losing was more fun than winning with Allen.

Edward Bennett Williams of the 6–8 Redskins promptly came calling in 1971 and signed George to a seven-year contract for $125,000 a year and near au-tonomy in running the club. With Washington, Allen increased his deal making. He brought in veterans Billy Kilmer, Roy Jefferson, Boyd Dowler, John Wilbur, Ron McDole, Diron Talbert, Verlon Biggs, Jack Pardee, Myron Pottios, Richie Petitbon and Speedy Duncan in the first year and made 81 trades in his seven-year tenure in DC. He even traded one draft pick to two different teams and was fined by the league for that negligence. Washington did not have a first round draft pick in any of Allen's years with the club or for the two years after he left. Only once did they even have a second round pick. The Redskins were tagged the "Over-the-Hill Gang," but instantly became winners who went to the playoffs five times in seven years. Despite having great receivers and a Hall of Fame quarterback in Sonny Jurgensen, though, Allen was clearly more comfortable having the more conservative Kilmer hand off to workhorse runner Larry Brown. During his career, Allen's teams were in the top 10 in turnover ratio and point margin all but the last three years, while his defense finished in the top 10 in points allowed all but one year.

Inevitably, the team began to decline by the conclusion of his contract, and George signed on once again in 1978 with the Rams, now owned by Carroll Rosenblum. Allen became frustrated by his lack of control, and his new players were not buying into the program. The sad end of Allen's NFL career came quickly after just two preseason games when George was replaced by assistant Ray Malavasi on the day the moving vans arrived from Washington with the Allen family's things. George's intense intractability and propensity to spend money, scared away owners, and Allen never coached in the NFL again. He tried contacting Halas about the Bears opening in 1981 but was rebuffed. Allen surfaced in the USFL and led the Chicago Blitz to a 12–6 record in 1983 and the Arizona Wranglers to a 10–8 record and a trip to the USFL title game in 1984, but that was his last coaching job in the pros.

In 12 NFL seasons, Allen's teams made the playoffs seven times, and he led the Redskins to a Super Bowl appearance in 1972. However, that year was the only time Allen ever won a postseason game. His teams' other six playoff runs were all one-and-done. His overly cautious style was not successful in the playoffs so he did not have an easy passage to the Hall of Fame. Allen's greatest legacy was his four children who all became successful in their own fields: George Jr. served Virginia as governor and senator, Greg became a doctor, Bruce worked in the front office of the Raiders and Bucs before becoming the Redskins' general manager in 2010, and Jennifer became a writer who movingly explored her feelings about her passionately-driven father in an insightful memoir called *Fifth Quarter*.

ANDERSON, HEARTLEY W. (HUNK) 9/22/1898–4/24/1978. Notre Dame • Played G/C for the Chicago

Bears from 1922 to 1925. *Apprenticeship:* College coach —13 years (8 as head coach); pro asst.— 3 years. *Roots:* George Halas. *Branches:* None. *Coordinators/Key Assistants:* Co-coach Luke Johnsos ran the offense, while Anderson handled the defense. *Hall of Fame Players:* Dan Fortmann, Sid Luckman, George McAfee, George Musso, Bronko Nagurski, Joe Stydahar, Bulldog Turner. *Primary Quarterbacks:* Sid Luckman. *Record:* **Co-Coach** (with Luke Johnsos); NFL Championship 1943. *Tendencies:* • His teams scored 26.4 points and allowed 16.1 per game • His teams ran 66.1% of the time, which was 104% of the league average • Three starting quarterbacks in four years; 68% of starts to primary quarterback • Nine rookie starters in four years • Winning Full Seasons to Losing Full Seasons: 3:1.

The candid, brusque and salty Hunk Anderson knew what he did best. In his autobiography, *Notre Dame, Bears and Hunk*, he said of himself as an assistant coach, "My disposition wasn't molded for public relations, which is a prime requirement for a head coach, and realizing that I was really doing 'my thing' as a journeyman...being on the field of play teaching everything I had ever learned, I felt that I was thereby fulfilling my desires and destinies." George Halas and Knute Rockne both referred to him as the greatest line coach they had ever seen, and, as a defensive coach, he claimed to have invented the blitz.

Anderson was recruited from Calumet, Michigan to Notre Dame in 1918 by his boyhood friend George Gipp. Hunk was a 190-pound guard who learned everything he could about leverage and technique. After four years playing for Notre Dame, where he also excelled at hockey and basketball, Anderson joined the Chicago Bears in 1922. For the next four years, Hunk played for the Bears on Sundays while coaching the Fighting Irish line Monday through Saturday. As a guard for Chicago, Anderson was part of the NFL's All-Decade team of the 1920s; for Notre Dame, he coached the Seven Mules and later trained future Hall of Fame coach Frank Leahy. Hunk also worked at the South Bend Iron Works firm of fellow Notre Dame alumnus Cap Edwards.

Anderson spent two seasons as the head coach of St. Louis University from 1927 to 1928 with a 9–9–1 record and then returned to Notre Dame to assist Rockne again in 1930. When Rockne died in a plane crash in 1931, Hunk succeeded him at Notre Dame

for three years with a 16–9–2 mark, but produced no undefeated seasons and was fired. Anderson moved on to become head coach at North Carolina State in 1934, but after three years of 11–17–1 football, he was relieved, leaving his eight-year head coaching record at 36–35–4. Hunk coached the line at Michigan and Cincinnati for one year each before Gus Henderson hired him to do the same for the Detroit Lions in 1939. It was here that Anderson says he invented the blitz by creating a scheme that sent linebacker Fred Vanzo rushing the quarterback. He also taught his Lions' defense the best way to compete with the rugged Bears by having all his linemen start the game by slugging their opposing Bear linemen on each of the game's first three plays, earning three penalties but also deference and respect.

When Henderson was fired a year later, George Halas swooped in to rehire Anderson as line and defensive coach. With the Bears, Hunk claimed that he invented the safety blitz using George McAfee. He was also very proud of his defense's work in the 1940 73–0 title game massacre of the Redskins because they intercepted eight passes that day and returned three for touchdowns. When Halas entered the Navy in October 1942, he turned over his franchise to his two top coaches: Anderson on defense and Luke Johnsos on offense. Since 1933, there have been seven instances of co-coaches in the NFL and just three for a whole season. The Anderson-Johnsos pairing was the only one that truly worked. The two respected each other and focused on their own responsibilities. Under Anderson/Johnsos, the Bears lost the title game to the Redskins in 1942, but won the title back in 1943.

Anderson spent a dozen years coaching the Bears line and defense. However, when Halas hired Clark Shaughnessy as an assistant in 1951, Hunk was ready to quit. He considered the legendary Shaughnessy to be a "charlatan" and a "grandstander" and could not abide working with him. Early in that season, George Marshall fired the Redskins head coach and offered the job to Anderson, but Halas blocked the move, saying that Hunk was still under contract to him. Anderson finished the season with the Bears and then retired from football to work as a manufacturer's representative for Production Steel. His only subsequent coaching foray was in the 1950s to coach the line for the College All Stars in their annual showdown with the NFL champions. He died at 79 of respiratory failure.

Anderson, Heartley W. (Hunk)									
Year	*Team*	*Games*	*Wins*	*Losses*	*Ties*	*%*	*P Wins*	*P Losses*	*P %*
1942	Bears	6	6	0	0	1.000	0	1	.000
1943	Bears	10	8	1	1	.850	1	0	1.000
1944	Bears	10	6	3	1	.650	0	0	.000
1945	Bears	10	3	7	0	.300	0	0	.000
4 years		36	23	11	2	.667	1	1	.500

ARMSTRONG, NEILL F. 3/9/1926– Oklahoma State. Played E for the Philadelphia Eagles from 1947 to 1951. *Apprenticeship:* College asst.— 7 years; CFL head coach — 6 years; pro asst.—10 years. *Roots:* Pop Ivy, Bud Grant. *Branches:* Buddy Ryan, Hank Kuhlmann (i). *Coordinators/Key Assistants:* Ken Meyer, then Ted Marchibroda handled the offense; Buddy Ryan handled the defense. *Hall of Fame Players:* Dan Hampton, Alan Page, Walter Payton, Mike Singletary. *Primary Quarterbacks:* Mike Phipps, Vince Evans. *Tendencies:* • His teams scored 17.4 points and allowed 17.4 per game • His teams ran 58.3% of the time, which was 112% of the league average • Three starting quarterbacks in four years; 77% of starts to primary quarterbacks • Seven rookie starters in four years • Winning Full Seasons to Losing Full Seasons: 1:3.

Neill Armstrong was not suited to be a head coach, but was an excellent assistant coach for many years. With his roots in Tishomingo, Oklahoma, Armstrong was the number one draft choice of the Philadelphia Eagles in 1947 out of Oklahoma State. The 6'2" 189-pound end and defensive back played for two championship teams in his five years in Philadelphia. Ironically, Armstrong was outshone in 1951 by rookie Bud Grant who would play a large role in Neill's subsequent career. Armstrong jumped to Winnipeg in the CFL in 1952 and spent three years as a Blue Bomber, two of them as a teammate of Grant who also had left the NFL to play in Canada. Neill retired in 1955 and accepted an assistant coaching job at his alma mater. After seven years at Oklahoma State, Armstrong was hired by Pop Ivy, another former NFL end and CFL coach, as an Oiler assistant in 1962. Two years later, Neill was named head coach of the Edmonton Eskimos of the CFL. While Bud Grant was winning Grey Cups coaching Winnipeg, though, Armstrong struggled in Edmonton, attaining a 37–56–3 record in six seasons.

The Eskimos fired Neill in 1970, and he joined Bud Grant's staff in Minnesota. When Vikings' defensive coordinator Bob Hollway became head coach of the Cardinals a year later, Armstrong ascended to defensive coordinator for the next seven seasons. In 1976, he brought in a vocal defensive line coach who had played under him at OSU, Buddy Ryan. After Jack Pardee surprisingly quit the Bears to coach the Redskins in 1978, former Vikings' GM Jim Finks hired Neill as the Bears coach, and Armstrong brought along Ryan to handle the defense. As a head coach, Armstrong could not generate any offense. While his defense gave up just 17 points per game, that's all the offense was scoring. With Bob Avellini, Mike Phipps and Vince Evans at quarterback, the Bears sole offensive weapon was Walter Payton; they ran the ball nearly 60% of the time, 12% more than the average team. Chicago managed to sneak into the playoffs in Neill's second season, but was destroyed by Dallas in the playoffs. As the vultures began to circle Armstrong in 1981, his old friend Buddy Ryan began politicking for the job and did manage to secure an extension as defensive coordinator before Neill was fired. Armstrong made no public complaints about any of this and moved on to Dallas where he coached under Tom Landry and then Jimmy Johnson until retiring in 1990.

ARNSPARGER, WILLIAM S. (BILL) 12/16/1926– Miami (OH). Did not play professionally. *Apprenticeship:* College asst.–14 years; pro asst.—10 years. *Roots:* Don Shula. *Branches:* John McVay, Marty Schottenheimer. *Coordinators/Key Assistants:* Hunter Enis and Ted Plumb handled the offense; Arnsparger directed his own defense. *Hall of Fame Players:* Harry Carson, Larry Csonka. *Primary Quarterbacks:* Craig Morton. *Tendencies:* • His teams scored 13.9 points and allowed 22 per game • His teams ran 54.5% of the time, which was the league average • Three starting quarterbacks in three years; 80% of starts to primary quarterback •

Armstrong, Neill F.									
Year	*Team*	*Games*	*Wins*	*Losses*	*Ties*	*%*	*P Wins*	*P Losses*	*P %*
1978	Bears	16	7	9	0	.438	0	0	.000
1979	Bears	16	10	6	0	.625	0	1	.000
1980	Bears	16	7	9	0	.438	0	0	.000
1981	Bears	16	6	10	0	.375	0	0	.000
4 years		64	30	34	0	.469	0	1	.000

Arnsparger, William S. (Bill)									
Year	*Team*	*Games*	*Wins*	*Losses*	*Ties*	*%*	*P Wins*	*P Losses*	*P %*
1974	Giants	14	2	12	0	.143	0	0	.000
1975	Giants	14	5	9	0	.357	0	0	.000
1976	Giants	7	0	7	0	.000	0	0	.000
3 years		35	7	28	0	.200	0	0	.000

Nine rookie starters in three years • Winning Full Seasons to Losing Full Seasons: 0:2.

Bill Arnsparger came to the Giants in 1974 with an impressive resume. He played high school football under Blanton Collier in Paris, Kentucky and college football at Miami of Ohio under Woody Hayes. After graduating from Miami in 1950, the World War II vet spent the next 14 years coaching at Miami, Ohio State, Kentucky and Tulane, mostly under Hayes and Collier again. In 1964, he joined the staff of the Baltimore Colts under Don Shula, whom Arnsparger met when both worked on Collier's staff at Kentucky. Bill spent 10 years on Shula's staff, half of it as defensive coordinator. From 1964–1969, they were together in Baltimore and from 1970 to 1973 in Miami. Arnsparger was the architect of the underrated No-Name Defense that led the Dolphins to three straight Super Bowls, two championships and one undefeated season from 1971 to 1973. Furthermore, his experiments with the so-called "53 Defense" using Bob Matheson as a sometime linebacker and sometime defensive end directly foreshadowed the development of the 3–4 defense that became prevalent in the 1970s.

To show how much trust the Giants had in their new hire, GM Andy Robustelli introduced Arnsparger to the press in January 1974 by saying, "Bill's going to run the draft, he's going to be the influence." Robustelli went on to list New York's needs as, "offensive linemen, a young quarterback, a blistering fullback and defensive ends." Indeed, that 1974 draft was a key element in Arnsparger's ultimate failure. New York selected guards John Hicks and Tom Mullen in the first two rounds, and neither amounted to much, even though Hicks was highly touted from Ohio State. They picked Rich Dvorak in the third round as a defensive end, but he was a bust. They tried for a young quarterback in round four with Carl Summerell, but Danny White was the only solid quarterback to come out of that draft. Despite the availability of Wilbur Jackson, Delvin Williams and John Cappelletti, they never found a fullback worth picking. Meanwhile Pittsburgh, drafting well after New York, came up with four Hall of Famers in that draft. The offense was so bad that first season that the Giants gave Dallas their first pick from 1975 to obtain battered Craig Morton as their franchise quarterback. Not only did Morton struggle, New York's top pick in the 1975 draft

was a second rounder, lineman Al Simpson — another bust.

So Arnsparger inherited a terrible team and missed his best opportunity to turn things around with the draft. As the team floundered especially on offense, Bill seemed to become less sure of himself and lose control of the team. By nature a professorial man — he wrote two primers on defensive football and his nickname was "One More Reel" for all the game film he studied — Arnsparger was over his head in New York. Two days after Bill was fired in 1976, Don Shula rehired him in Miami. The Dolphins defense had slipped in his absence, so Bill went about to create a new defense, the Killer B's, that took Miami back to the Super Bowl in 1982. Arnsparger left Miami for the head job at LSU in 1983 and managed a 26–8–2 record in Batoan Rouge in three years. He then spent seven years as athletic director at the University of Florida, where he hired Steve Spurrier as coach before capping his football career by coaching the defense for Bobby Ross in San Diego. His last game as a coach was Super Bowl XXIX that the outgunned Chargers lost to the 49ers.

AUSTIN, WILLIAM L. (BILL) 10/18/1928– Oregon State. Played G for the New York Giants from 1949 to 1950 and 1953–1957. *Apprenticeship:* College asst.— 1 year; pro asst. 7 years. *Roots:* Vince Lombardi. *Branches:* Mike McCormack. *Coordinators/Key Assistants*: For the Steelers, Don Heinrich handled the offense and Torgy Torgeson the defense; for the Redskins, Austin ran the offense and Harland Svare handled the defense. *Hall of Fame Players:* Chris Hanburger, Sonny Jurgensen, Charley Taylor. *Primary Quarterbacks:* Dick Shiner, Kent Nix, Sonny Jurgensen. *Tendencies:* • His teams scored 20.5 points and allowed 24.6 per game • His teams ran 47.8% of the time, which was 94% of the league average • Six starting quarterbacks in four years; 66% of starts to primary quarterbacks • Nine rookie starters in four years • Winning Full Seasons to Losing Full Seasons: 0:4.

The pride of San Pedro, California, Bill Austin played under two Hall of Fame coaches in New York, Steve Owen and Vince Lombardi, and was succeeded by Hall of Fame coaches, Chuck Noll and George Allen, in both his head coaching stops, but Bill was no Hall of Famer on the sidelines. In 1959, Vince Lom-

Austin, William L. (Bill)									
Year	Team	Games	Wins	Losses	Ties	%	P Wins	P Losses	P %
1966	Steelers	14	5	8	1	.393	0	0	.000
1967	Steelers	14	4	9	1	.321	0	0	.000
1968	Steelers	14	2	11	1	.179	0	0	.000
1970	Redskins	14	6	8	0	.429	0	0	.000
4 years		56	17	36	3	.330	0	0	.000

bardi hired Austin, his former star guard, as line coach — a crucial job in Lombardi's offense. In Bill's six years in Green Bay, the Packers ran the ball at will behind his well-drilled line. His work was so impressive that Austin's name was bandied about as a potential hire when the Browns fired Paul Brown in 1962 and when the Colts fired Weeb Ewbank in 1963. Austin left Green Bay to coach the line for old teammate Harland Svare in Los Angeles in 1965 (while Rams line coach Ray Wietecha, another former Giant, joined the Packers). A year later, Austin was the first coaching hire of new Steelers' President Dan Rooney. Years later, Rooney noted in his autobiography that Austin interviewed well, and that Dan's dad, Art, mistakenly decided the team did not need to go any further with interviews.

Austin promised a disciplined, hustling team, and he generally delivered that. He did not produce a winner in three seasons in Pittsburgh, however. He tried too hard to imitate his mentor, Lombardi, even reciting Vince's pep talks nearly verbatim. Bill's offensive coach, Don Heinrich (another former Giant) could not get along with the only decent quarterback, Bill Nelsen, on the team, so Austin traded Nelsen to Cleveland in 1967 where he led the Browns to two division titles. After the Steelers cut Bill loose, he teamed up with Lombardi once more, this time in Washington. When Vince died a year later, Austin succeeded him for one disappointing year. Bill spent the next 15 years as the line coach with the Bears, Cardinals, Redskins (rehired by his successor George Allen), Giants, the USFL Generals and the Jets before retiring in 1986.

BACH, JOSEPH A. (JOE) 1/17/1901–10/24/1966. Carleton and Notre Dame. T; did not play professionally. *Apprenticeship:* College coach — 8 years (1 as head coach). *Roots:* None. *Branches:* Keith Molesworth. *Coordinators/Key Assistants:* In Bach's first stint, Johnny McNally was an assistant; in his second stint, Walt Kiesling coached the line and Chuck Cherundolo the defense. *Hall of Fame Players:* Jack Butler, Cal Hubbard, Ernie Stautner. *Primary Quarterbacks:* Jim Finks. *Tendencies:* • His teams scored 14.8 points and allowed 19.4 per game • His teams ran 55.9% of the time, which was 94% of the league average • Two starting quarterbacks in two T formation years; 88% of starts to primary quarterback • 28 rookie starters in four years • Winning Full Seasons to Losing Full Seasons: 0:2.

Originally from Tower, Minnesota, Joe Bach began his college career at Carleton College before transferring to Notre Dame in 1922. At Notre Dame, Joe was a tackle, one of the Seven Mules who blocked for the famed Four Horsemen backfield. Like practically everyone on that great Knute Rockne team, Bach went immediately into coaching upon graduation. After three years as line coach at Syracuse, Joe worked under former teammate Elmer Layden at Duquesne from 1928 to 1933 before succeeding him to produce an 8–2 mark in 1934. Bach was an inspirational holler guy as a coach and became Pittsburgh's third head coach in 1935. Despite being outscored nearly two-to-one, he overhauled the team and improved their record to .500 in his second season. Joe then left Pittsburgh for Niagara University in 1937 and coached there for five years with a 23–14–3 record until the school dropped football in 1942. He then spent a year coaching a service team at Fort Knox before Lions' coach Gus Dorais, another Notre Dame alumnus, hired Bach as line coach in 1943. When Dorais was fired, still another former Irish star, Clipper Smith, hired Joe as line coach for the Boston Yanks in 1948. The Yanks became the New York Bulldogs in 1949 with a new coach, Charley Ewart, but with Bach still coaching the line.

Joe returned to a head coaching position in 1950 with St. Bonaventure, where he was hired by the Bonnies athletic director, Father Silas Rooney, Art's brother. There, Bach coached future Steelers Jack Butler and Ted Marchibroda to a 12–6 record until the school dropped football in 1952. Art Rooney then brought Joe back to the Steelers where again he had limited success. He is best remembered as installing the T formation at last in Pittsburgh; the Steelers were the last team still running the single wing in the NFL by 1951. By this time, though, Bach had developed diabetes and lacked the energy he once possessed. After being replaced by Walt Kiesling in 1954, Joe coached the line at Columbia and then found work as a labor mediator in Pennsylvania. He died from a heart attack at the age of 65 just minutes after being inducted into the Curbstone Coaches Hall of Fame in Pittsburgh. Bach had accepted the honor by reading from the original Grantland Rice newspaper story where Rice im-

Bach, Joseph A. (Joe)										
Year	Team	Games	Wins	Losses	Ties	%	P Wins	P Losses	P %
1935	Pirates (Steelers)	12	4	8	0	.333	0	0	.000
1936	Pirates (Steelers)	12	6	6	0	.500	0	0	.000
1952	Steelers	12	5	7	0	.417	0	0	.000
1953	Steelers	12	6	6	0	.500	0	0	.000
4 years		48	21	27	0	.438	0	0	.000

mortalized Notre Dame's backfield as the Four Horsemen in a poem.

BALL, HERMAN 4/9/1910–1/12/1998. Davis & Elkins. G; did not play professionally. *Apprenticeship:* College asst.— 3 years; pro asst.— 4 years. *Roots:* John Whelchel (i). *Branches:* Dick Todd (i). *Coordinators/ Key Assistants*: Wilbur Moore and then Dick Todd coached the backs. *Hall of Fame Players:* Sammy Baugh, Bill Dudley. *Primary Quarterbacks:* Sammy Baugh. *Tendencies:* • His teams scored 18.5 points and allowed 29.6 per game • His teams ran 55.6% of the time, which was 101% of the league average • Two starting quarterbacks in three years; 50% of starts to primary quarterback • 20 rookie starters in three years • Winning Full Seasons to Losing Full Seasons: 0:1.

Herman Ball coached quarterback Tommy Mont at three levels, high school, college and the pros. Ball, a West Virginia native, began coaching high school football right out of college and had three undefeated seasons from 1935 to 1942. Mont was the quarterback of the 1940 team and entered Maryland the next year. Ball was hired by Maryland in 1943 as an assistant to Doc Spears for two years and then stayed on when Bear Bryant coached the team in 1945. 1946 was a transitional year for Ball. He was still coaching at Maryland part-time under Clark Shaughnessy (with Tommy Mont back from the war and on the team), while doing more and more scouting and coaching for the Redskins.

Ball continued with Washington where Mont played in the post-war years, assisting Turk Edwards through 1948 and then John Whelchel in 1949. Whelchel clashed with meddling Redskins' owner George Preston Marshall and was fired seven games into the season with a 3–3–1 record and replaced by Ball. Herman went just 1–4 for the rest of the season, but was rehired in 1950 and 1951. After winning only four of 20 games overall, Marshall fired Ball in week four of 1951. He tried to hire Hunk Anderson to replace Herman, but was blocked by George Halas, so he turned to assistant Dick Todd instead. Todd took the 0–3 team and went 5–4 with it to finish the year. Thus, in both of Ball's partial seasons, the team performed markedly better when not coached by him. Most notably, Ball's teams gave up almost 30 points per game.

Ball then had a long career as an assistant in the NFL. He actually stayed in Washington for three more years as a scout and coach, and then spent a year in Pittsburgh, seven in Baltimore, one in Buffalo and five in Philadelphia before landing the Player Personnel job with the Eagles in 1969. He retired from the Eagles in 1977 but continued to serve as a consultant with the team for another decade.

BATES, JAMES I. (JIM) 5/31/1946– Tennessee • Did not play professionally. *Apprenticeship*: College asst.— 13 years; Arena League asst.—1 year; USFL coach — 3 years (1 as head coach); pro asst.—14 years. *Roots:* Bill Belichick, June Jones, Barry Switzer, Chan Gailey, Dave Campo, Dave Wannstedt. *Branches:* None. *Coordinators/Key Assistants*: Chris Foerster ran the offense; Bates was promoted from defensive coordinator. *Hall of Fame Players:* None. *Primary Quarterbacks:* A.J. Feeley. *Record:* **Interim Coach.**

Jim Bates exemplifies the itinerant football coach. After graduating from Tennessee, the Pontiac, Michigan native coached high school football from 1969 to 1971 before jumping to the college ranks. From 1972–1982, Jim coached at Southern Mississippi, Villanova, Kansas State, West Virginia and Texas Tech. He joined the USFL's San Antonio Gunslingers as an assistant in 1984 and became their head coach in 1985. He then resigned from the 3–9 Gunslingers 12 weeks into the season because neither he nor his players were getting paid. Bates spent another season in the USFL and one in the Arena League before moving back to the college ranks with Tennessee in 1989. A year later, Steve Spurrier made him defensive coordinator at Florida.

In 1991, Bill Belichick brought Bates into the NFL. Jim spent 1991–1993 and 1995 in Cleveland, 1994 in Atlanta, 1996–1999 in Dallas, 2000–2004 in Miami, 2005 in Green Bay, 2007 in Denver (where his son Jeremy coached) and 2009 in Tampa, serving as defensive coordinator in Atlanta, Miami, Green Bay,

Ball, Herman

Year	Team	Games	Wins	Losses	Ties	%	P Wins	P Losses	P %
1949	Redskins	5	1	4	0	.200	0	0	.000
1950	Redskins	12	3	9	0	.250	0	0	.000
1951	Redskins	3	0	3	0	.000	0	0	.000
3 years		20	4	16	0	.200	0	0	.000

Bates, James I. (Jim)

Year	Team	Games	Wins	Losses	Ties	%	P Wins	P Losses	P %
2004	Dolphins	7	3	4	0	.429	0	0	.000
1 yr		7	3	4	0	.429	0	0	.000

Denver and Tampa. He was scapegoated after just one year by June Jones with the Falcons and by Mike Shanahan with the Broncos. Most recently, Raheem Morris demoted him after just 10 games in 2009. Bates generally ran a standard 4–3 defense. When Jim was with Miami, he told *Sports Illustrated*, "My philosophy is just to play sound football. I don't rely on gimmicks. You can steal a game with gimmicks, but also might get into trouble if you do a lot of exotic things. We want to play within our schemes and make people beat us at what we do best." Bates' one shot as an NFL head coach took place in 2004 when the 1–8 Dolphins fired Dave Wannstedt. Jim made the Dolphins competitive with mediocre A. J. Feeley at quarterback, but Miami hired Nick Saban as coach at the end of the year.

BATTLES, CLIFFORD F. (CLIFF) 5/1/1910–4/28/1981. West Virginia Wesleyan. Played RB for the Boston/Washington Redskins from 1932 to 1937. *Apprenticeship*: College/military asst.—8 years. *Roots:* None. *Branches:* None. *Coordinators/Key Assistants*: End coach Steve Hokuf was with Battles for both seasons. *Hall of Fame Players:* None. *Primary Quarterbacks:* Bob Hoernschemeyer, Glenn Dobbs. *Record:* **Hall of Fame Player.** *Tendencies:* • His teams scored 13.6 points and allowed 25.6 per game • His teams ran 60.9% of the time, which was 97% of the league average • Three starting quarterbacks in two years; 95% of starts to primary quarterbacks • Two rookie starters in two years • Winning Full Seasons to Losing Full Seasons: 0:1.

Hailing from Akron, Ohio, Cliff Battles lettered in five sports in college while being selected Phi Beta Kappa for his studies at West Virginia Wesleyan. A Hall of Fame halfback, he signed with the brand new Boston Braves franchise in 1932 and led the NFL in rushing as a rookie. The Braves became the Redskins in 1933 and then moved to Washington in 1937, when they won the championship with Battles again leading the league in rushing. However, Redskins' owner George Preston Marshall refused to give Cliff a raise in the offseason, so Battles took a job coaching the backfield for Colum-

bia in 1938. In December 1940, he got some measure of revenge by watching his one-time pupil at Columbia, Sid Luckman, lead the Chicago Bears over Marshall's Redskins 73–0 in the NFL title game.

Cliff coached at Columbia through 1942, but then joined the Marines. He worked as an assistant coach to Dick Hanley from 1943 to 1945 with the powerful El Toro service team in California. Meanwhile, the All America Football Conference began playing in 1946. Mal Stevens, former Yale and NYU coach, led the Brooklyn Dodgers' franchise, but abruptly quit before the team's seventh game, leaving rookie assistant Tom Scott in charge of the team for that game with Miami. Team owner William Cox announced that he would replace Stevens with his former assistant at Yale, Fred Linehan. Then, Linehan backed out so Cox had to scramble to find Battles ready to take the job for the second half of the season.

Unfortunately, the Dodgers were a terrible team whose only gate attraction was triple threat tailback Glenn Dobbs, the AAFC's long and lanky answer to Sammy Baugh. After a 3–10–1 initial season, though, Battles traded his star in a three-way deal that sent Dobbs to Los Angeles, Angelo Bertelli to Chicago and Bob "Hunchy" Hoernschemeyer to Brooklyn at the beginning of the 1947 season. Battles defended the decision by citing Dobbs' "strategical mistakes" and the fact that Hunchy was five years younger. Ultimately, the effect was nil as the Dodgers finished the season with a second straight 3–10–1 record. Battles was fired and left football. He went on to work as an executive for GE for several years and died at age 70 as a member of both the College and Pro Football Halls of Fame.

BAUGH, SAMUEL A. (SAMMY) 3/17/1914–12/17/2008. Texas Christian. Played TB/QB for the Washington Redskins from 1937 to 1952. *Apprenticeship*: College head coach—5 years. *Roots:* None. *Branches:* Bones Taylor. *Coordinators/Key Assistants*: Baugh ran his own offense; for the Titans, John Dell Isola handled the defense, while Red Conkright han-

Battles, Clifford F. (Cliff)									
Year	Team	Games	Wins	Losses	Ties	%	P Wins	P Losses	P %
1946	Dodgers (AAFC)	7	1	6	0	.143	0	0	.000
1947	Dodgers (AAFC)	14	3	10	1	.250	0	0	.000
1 Year		21	4	16	1	.214	0	0	.000

Baugh, Samuel A. (Sammy)									
Year	Team	Games	Wins	Losses	Ties	%	P Wins	P Losses	P %
1960	Titans (Jets)	14	7	7	0	.500	0	0	.000
1961	Titans (Jets)	14	7	7	0	.500	0	0	.000
1964	Oilers (Titans)	14	4	10	0	.286	0	0	.000
3 years		42	18	24	0	.429	0	0	.000

dled it for the Oilers. *Hall of Fame Players:* George Blanda, Don Maynard. *Primary Quarterbacks:* Al Dorow, George Blanda. *Record:* **Hall of Fame Player.** *Tendencies:* • His teams scored 23.6 points and allowed 27.2 per game • His teams ran 42.4% of the time, which was 93% of the league average • Four starting quarterbacks in three years; 95% of starts to primary quarterbacks • 24 rookie starters in three years • Winning Full Seasons to Losing Full Seasons: 0:1.

Sammy Baugh of Temple, Texas was the best passer in the NFL for over a decade, but was also one of the greatest all around players of all time. The best evidence for that is the 1943 season when Baugh led the NFL in passing, punting and, on defense, interceptions. He took the Redskins to five NFL championship games and won two of them in his record-setting 16-year career. Sammy learned his approach to the game from the wide-open style of his coach at TCU, Dutch Meyer. Meyer employed a spread offense that relied heavily on passing in an aggressive offensive attack. Three years after Baugh retired as a player, he took the head coaching job with nearby Texas college Hardin-Simmons and ran the program that way for five years.

Although Sammy only went 23–28 at Hardin-Simmons, he was hired as the first coach of the New York Titans in the new American Football League in 1960. Titans' owner Harry Wismer was a former Redskins' announcer and was disastrously under-capitalized. Forced to play in the decrepit Polo Grounds, the team could not draw fans even with the exciting offense Baugh put on the field, featuring former Redskins' quarterback Al Dorow throwing to fleet wide receivers Don Maynard and Art Powell. The Titans scored nearly 24 points per game with their wide-open attack. Unfortunately, they were giving up nearly

28, and it was remarkable the team finished at .500 both seasons with a defense that leaky.

Tensions between Baugh and Wismer mounted throughout the 1961 season, with Wismer instigating a series of sniping remarks between the two. Wismer didn't want to pay Sammy for the third year of his contract, so he tried to goad the coach into quitting. Wismer hired Bulldog Turner as head coach in 1962 and demoted Baugh to backfield coach then consultant then coach of the kickers. Sammy refused to quit because he was owed another year of salary. Wismer was eventually forced to give in and pay Baugh his money.

Sammy spent 1963 as an assistant to his 1940s All America Football Conference doppelganger, Glenn Dobbs, at Tulsa, and then returned to the AFL as the head coach of the Houston Oilers in 1964. The same pattern emerged on the field with the Oilers — an explosive offense and an ineffective defense, so Baugh resigned in December to spend more time on his ranch. His Oilers' assistant and former Redskins' teammate, Bones Taylor was named head coach, and Bones reflexively hired Sammy as backfield coach in 1965. Baugh spent one more season in Houston and then one in Detroit under another former teammate, Harry Gilmer, before retiring for good to his beloved ranch where he spent the next 40 years until dying at age 94.

BELICHICK, WILLIAM S. (BILL) 4/16/1952– Wesleyan. C/TE; did not play professionally. *Apprenticeship:* Pro asst.—16 years. *Roots:* Ted Marchibroda, Rick Forzano, Tommy Hudspeth, Red Miller, Ray Perkins, Bill Parcells. *Branches:* Rick Venturi (i), Al Groh, Jim Bates (i), Nick Saban, Romeo Crennell, Eric Mangini, Josh McDaniels, Jim Schwartz. *Coordinators/Key Assistants:* For the Browns, Belichick was

Belichick, William S. (Bill)										
Year	*Team*	*Games*	*Wins*	*Losses*	*Ties*	*%*	*P Wins*	*P Losses*	*P %*
1991	Browns	16	6	10	0	.375	0	0	.000
1992	Browns	16	7	9	0	.438	0	0	.000
1993	Browns	16	7	9	0	.438	0	0	.000
1994	Browns	16	11	5	0	.688	1	1	.500
1995	Browns	16	5	11	0	.313	0	0	.000
2000	Patriots	16	5	11	0	.313	0	0	.000
2001	Patriots	16	11	5	0	.688	3	0	1.000
2002	Patriots	16	9	7	0	.563	0	0	.000
2003	Patriots	16	14	2	0	.875	3	0	1.000
2004	Patriots	16	14	2	0	.875	3	0	1.000
2005	Patriots	16	10	6	0	.625	1	1	.500
2006	Patriots	16	12	4	0	.750	2	1	.667
2007	Patriots	16	16	0	0	1.000	2	1	.667
2008	Patriots	16	11	5	0	.688	0	0	.000
2009	Patriots	16	10	6	0	.625	0	1	.000
2010	Patriots	16	14	2	0	.875	0	1	.000
2011	Patriots	16	13	3	0	.813	2	1	.667
17 years		272	175	97	0	.643	17	7	.708

assisted in the offense by Gary Tranquil and Steve Crosby, while Nick Saban then Rick Venturi handled the defense; for the Patriots, Charlie Weis, Josh Mc-Daniels and Bill O'Brien have handled the offense, while Romeo Crennell, Eric Mangini and Dean Pees have handled the defense. *Hall of Fame Players:* None. *Primary Quarterbacks:* Vinny Testaverde, Tom Brady. *Record:* Super Bowl Championships 2001, 2003, 2004 *Tendencies:* • His teams scored 24 points and allowed 18.4 per game • His teams ran 44.4% of the time, which was the league average • Nine starting quarterbacks in 17 years; 70% of starts to primary quarterbacks • 44 rookie starters in 17 years • Winning Full Seasons to Losing Full Seasons: 12:5.

Born in Nashville, Tennessee, Bill Belichick learned the intricacies of football on the field, in the film room and in the classroom from his father Steve, a longtime coach and scout at the Naval Academy. After graduating from Wesleyan with a degree in economics, Bill eschewed Wall Street to work his way up from a "gofer" on Ted Marchibroda's Colts' staff in 1975 to defensive coordinator on the Giants in 1985, with brief stops in Detroit and Denver. Belichick was hired on Ray Perkins' Giants' staff in 1979 and continued in New York under Bill Parcells in 1983. The two Bills worked together on the Giants for the next eight years, sharing an acute attention to detail, a demanding, competitive intensity and an affinity for tough defense.

In his time in New York, Belichick was called "Doom" by the players for his relentless, abrasive personality, while the writers referred to him as "Captain Sominex" for his dull and monotonous responses to all questions. That persona has changed only slightly in the decades since. Belichick's focus was on designing new, creative defenses each week to exploit that opponent's weaknesses through the best usage of the talents of his defenders. His own weakness was his aloof personality. After the Giants won a second Super Bowl in 1991, Belichick was a hot coordinator in demand. Although Parcells retired for the first time in the spring, Art Modell already had hired Bill to run the Browns.

Belichick's time in Cleveland was marked by controversy. He made no connection with the Browns' rabid fan base, and they complained about his plodding offense and his conflicts with fan-favorite Bernie Kosar, a hometown hero. Increasingly, Belichick favored his imported quarterback Vinny Testaverde over Kosar, who was less likely to follow Bill's game plan. The culmination came when Testaverde got hurt in November 1993; Belichick then cut Kosar and went with the execrable Todd Philcox at quarterback. Vinny did lead Cleveland to a 11–5 playoff season in 1994, but everything fell apart the next year when word got out in midseason that the Browns were moving to Baltimore.

Upon being fired by Cleveland, Belichick returned to Parcells' staff in New England in time for another Super Bowl run in 1996. When Parcells forced his way out of New England in the offseason, Belichick followed him to the Jets, even briefly becoming the nominal Jets coach while a deal for compensation for Parcells leaving New England was worked out. Parcells rebuilt the Jets in three years and then decided to step down. He named Belichick his successor, but at the official press conference for the announcement the next day, Belichick scrawled a note reading "I resign as HC of the NYJ" for Parcells and turned his inaugural press conference into a resignation speech. Rather than continue as Parcells' acolyte on a team that was up for sale, Belichick signed with the Patriots in 2000 to everyone's surprise. In New England, he found a more stable front office situation where he has enjoyed control over personnel and found his own voice with remarkable success.

The Patriots were coming off an 8–8 season and were over the cap and on a downward trend. That first year, New England sunk to 5–11 as Belichick decided how to rebuild the team. In 2001, he and personnel man Scott Pioli focused on the lower end of the free agent market, signing 17 role-players for a combined $2.7 million in signing bonus money — less than the signing bonus garnered by mediocre Patriots' defensive end Chad Eaton in Seattle that year. The team struggled at the outset of the season and then franchise quarterback Drew Bledsoe was lost to injury against the Jets in week two. In stepped untried seventh round draft choice Tom Brady and the team of the decade was born. The unsung Pats upset the Rams in the Super Bowl that year and then won back-to-back Super Bowls in 2003 and 2004. New England did not feature the biggest stars, but wholly embraced the team concept under Belichick, winning an NFL record 21 consecutive games in the latter two years.

Belichick hired good coaches, but ultimately he controlled both sides of the ball. On offense, the Pats evolved into a wide open spread passing offense over the years, while on defense, the schemes changed weekly. In the years Belichick has been running defenses since being named defensive coordinator of the Giants in 1985, only five of his 27 defensive units has given up an average of 20 points or more per game over a season. Even injuries did not derail his teams. New England employed 42 different starters in 2003 and 45 in 2005. When Brady himself was injured on opening day in 2008, Belichick plugged in Matt Cassell, who had not started a game since high school, and finished 11–5.

With such a reliable history, it came as a shock when the unflappable Patriots blew a 21–3 lead to their archrival Colts in the 2006 playoffs. Belichick went on a mission the following year. The Patriots made big changes to improve their squad by bringing in receivers Randy Moss, Wes Welker and Donte Stall-worth as well as All Pro linebacker Adalius Thomas on defense. In view of their 2006 playoff collapse, Belichick spurred the team to play all out for 60 minutes each game. What's more, Jets' coach Eric Mangini, a former Patriots' assistant coach, charged New England with filming opponents' sideline defensive signals in violation of league rules. The resultant Spygate scandal, for which Belichick was fined $500,000, diminished the Patriots' three Super Bowl wins of the decade in the eyes of many and motivated the Patriots even more. Not only would they play each game the full 60 minutes, they would bury their opponents. Eight of their first 10 wins were by 20 points or more before back-to-back struggles against the tough Eagles and Ravens defenses gave teams a blueprint on how to slow the New England offensive juggernaut. 2007 was a watershed year in which the Pats set new records for team points with 589, touchdown passes (Tom Brady's 50) and touchdown receptions (Randy Moss' 23). The Patriots went 16–0 in the regular season but then fell to the Giants in a monumental upset in the Super Bowl. Belichick revamped the team over the next few years and drove it to a 14–2 record in 2010 and 13–3 in 2011 despite defensive deficiencies and lost a second Super Bowl in 2011.

BELL, DeBENNEVILLE (BERT) 2/25/1895–10/11/1959. Pennsylvania. QB; did not play professionally. *Apprenticeship:* College asst.—10 years. *Roots:* None. *Branches:* None. *Coordinators/Key Assistants:* Bell brought in Heine Miller in 1940 to take over the Eagles in 1941, but then sold the team. *Hall of Fame Players:* Bill Hewitt. *Primary Quarterbacks:* Davey O'Brien. *Record:* **Hall of Fame Commissioner.** *Tendencies:* • His teams scored 9.1 points and allowed 17 per game • His teams ran 59.4% of the time, which was 88% of the league average • 18 starters in six years • Winning Full Seasons to Losing Full Seasons: 0:5.

De Benneville "Bert" Bell was born into privilege. His maternal grandfather was a U.S. congressman. His father was district attorney of Philadelphia and then Attorney General for the state of Pennsylvania. His brother John was elected Pennsylvania's lieutenant governor, served briefly as governor and was named as a

justice to the state's Supreme Court. While his father insisted, "He'll go to Penn or he'll go to hell," Bert still followed his own path. He did go from prep school in Haverford to playing quarterback for the University of Pennsylvania in 1916 when the Quakers lost the Rose Bowl to Oregon. But then Bell took a year off to serve with a hospital unit in World War I before returning to Penn, first as a player and then as backfield coach under John Heisman and then Lou Young from 1920 to 1928. Finding himself increasingly at odds with the harsh coaching styles of head coach Lou Young and line coach and former teammate Lud Wray, he left Penn in 1928.

Bert was the black sheep of the family, a charming rascal who loved to drink, play cards and the ponies and celebrate life. By 1929, he found himself in debt from lavish spending and frenzied gambling, in addition to having lost $50,000 in the stock market decline. His father bailed him out one last time, and Bert gave up gambling and the stock market. While running his family's luxury hotels, he also returned to football by becoming the line coach for Temple under another former Penn teammate Heine Miller from 1930 to 1932. Concurrently in 1932, he fell in love with Ziegfield Follies star Frances Upton who insisted Bert give up drinking if he wanted to be with her. With a grand gesture, he did and married her in 1934. He still had the football habit, though. In 1933, Bell reconciled with Wray, gathered some investors, made good on the debts of the dissolved, bankrupt Frankford Yellow Jackets and paid the NFL franchise fee to form the Philadelphia Eagles.

From the start, the Eagles were a low-budget operation: for their first road trip to Green Bay, the team traveled by bus and would stop at empty fields along the way to practice. To avoid a small gate, Bert once postponed a game due to "inclement weather" on a day that baseball's Philadelphia Athletics played a doubleheader in town. By 1936, the franchise had lost $80,000, but Bell bought out the other investors for $4,500. For the Eagles first three years, he had served as general manager, ticket seller, and public relations agent. In 1936, he forced out his old friend Wray and added head coach to his responsibilities, but would only win more than two games in one season from

Bell, DeBenneville (Bert)									
Year	Team	Games	Wins	Losses	Ties	%	P Wins	P Losses	P %
1936	Eagles	12	1	11	0	.083	0	0	.000
1937	Eagles	11	2	8	1	.227	0	0	.000
1938	Eagles	11	5	6	0	.455	0	0	.000
1939	Eagles	11	1	9	1	.136	0	0	.000
1940	Eagles	11	1	10	0	.091	0	0	.000
1941	Steelers	2	0	2	0	.000	0	0	.000
6 years		58	10	46	2	.190	0	0	.000

1936 to 1940. His biggest star was 5'6" passing tailback Davey O'Brien who had to run for his life behind Philadelphia's porous line. Almost always playing from behind, Bell's Eagles threw the ball 12% more than the league average, but not very effectively. Bell's biographer, Robert Lyons, notes that some contemporary press accounts even indicated that Heine Miller, former Temple coach brought in by Bell to "learn the ropes" in 1940, was actually the coach or co-coach that season.

Bert's strengths were in ticket sales, promotions and innovations. Bell was the owner who proposed and sold the idea of an NFL draft, and he indefatigably kept the struggling team going. His weaknesses were in selecting and coaching players. Seeing no other way to improve the floundering Philadelphia and Pittsburgh teams in 1941, Bell and his friend Art Rooney ended up as co-owners of the Pittsburgh franchise in a complicated franchise transaction that brought Lex Thompson to Philly as the owner of the new Eagles.

For five years in Pittsburgh, Bell was only marginally more successful than in Philadelphia. He began as the Steelers' coach in 1941, but only lasted two games, both losses, until Rooney hired Duquesne's Buff Donelli to simultaneously coach both Steel City teams. Pittsburgh just barely eked through the war years, merging with Philadelphia in 1943 and the Cardinals in 1944. However, when Bert was named commissioner in 1946, he finally found his niche. The gravel-voiced Bell worked 18-hour days enthusiastically selling pro football and the notion that the success of the league as a whole came first, deftly handling the owners' rampaging egos and prickly personalities. He ran the NFL from a small office in the suburbs of Philadelphia and did almost everything over the telephone, racking up $10,000 annual phone bills throughout the 1950s. Bert was always available to the press and always good for a comment. As with the Eagles, he tended to do everything himself as commissioner. For example, each year he would spend weeks working laboriously by hand on the league schedule using a set of labeled dominos. During his time, he guided the NFL through difficult waters. In his first year in charge, he faced a serious challenge from the fledgling All America Football Conference and had to deal with a gambling scandal in that year's championship game. Throughout the fifties there were court proceedings, competitive balance concerns and

dealings with Congress over antitrust issues. Bell presided over these affairs and the development of league-wide television policies, including the local blackout rules, in a way that enabled the league to grow significantly during the decade. In essence, Bert laid the foundation for Pete Rozelle's amazing successes in the 1960s and 1970s.

As the fifties drew to a close, Bell was thinking of retiring, buying back the Eagles and letting his sons run the team. His older son John already was business manager for Baltimore, while his younger son Upton would go on to serve as director of player personnel for the Colts and general manager of the Patriots. However, Bert Bell did not get to live out that dream because he suffered a fatal heart attack at Franklin Field in 1959 watching a game between his two former teams, the Eagles and Steelers, on the field where he had played quarterback for Penn 40 years before. Bell was an improbable character out of a Frank Capra movie — a rich, smoothie to the manor born, but truly a man of the people. While he was an utter failure as a coach, he was a vital figure in league history.

BENGTSON, JOHN P. (PHIL) 7/17/1913–12/18/1994. Minnesota. T; did not play professionally. *Apprenticeship:* College asst.—17 years; pro asst.—16 years. *Roots:* Buck Shaw, Red Strader, Frankie Albert, Vince Lombardi. *Branches:* Forrest Gregg. *Coordinators/Key Assistants:* Zeke Bratkowski and Bob Schnelker handled the offense, while Bengtson ran his own defense in Green Bay. *Hall of Fame Players:* Herb Adderley, Willie Davis, Forrest Gregg, Henry Jordan, Ray Nitschke, Bart Starr, Willie Wood. *Primary Quarterbacks:* Bart Starr. *Tendencies:* • His teams scored 17.6 points and allowed 19 per game • His teams ran 54.7% of the time, which was the 107% of league average • Three starting quarterbacks in four years; 66% of starts to primary quarterback • Eight rookie starters in four years • Winning Full Seasons to Losing Full Seasons: 1:2.

When the Packers hired Vince Lombardi in 1959, he remembered Phil Bengtson from a game in 1957 during which Bengtson's 49er defense unleashed a surprising tactic on Lombardi's Giant offense — blitzing linebackers. The 49ers called it the Red Dog defense, and they hit Giant quarterback Charlie Conerly repeatedly, causing him to fumble five times to help San

Bengtson, John P. (Phil)									
Year	Team	Games	Wins	Losses	Ties	%	P Wins	P Losses	P %
1968	Packers	14	6	7	1	.464	0	0	.000
1969	Packers	14	8	6	0	.571	0	0	.000
1970	Packers	14	6	8	0	.429	0	0	.000
1972	Patriots	5	1	4	0	.200	0	0	.000
4 year		47	21	25	1	.457	0	0	.000

Francisco to beat New York that day. By 1959, Bengtson had just finished a seven-year stint with the 49ers and quickly signed on in Green Bay. Before coming to the 49ers, Phil had coached only in the college ranks. He was an All-American tackle at Minnesota in 1934, blocking for quarterback Bud Wilkinson, and then found steady employment as line coach for 17 years at Missouri, Minnesota and Stanford under such talented coaches as Don Faurot, Bernie Bierman, Clark Shaughnessy and Marchy Schwartz.

A native of Rousseau, Minnesota, Bengtson ran the Packer defense for nine years under Lombardi and then succeeded him as head coach in Green Bay. In those 12 years with Phil pacing the sidelines chain smoking cigarettes, the Packers gave up an average of just 15.9 points a game. During that time, they finished first in fewest points allowed three times, second four times and third twice. They finished first in fewest yards allowed twice, second twice, and third four times. His pass defense was especially effective, allowing the fewest yards in the league six times (1962 and from 1964 to 1968). The combination of a consistent offense and a ball hawking defense allowed the Packers of those 12 years to be an amazing +124 in turnover ratio. Over those dozen years, the defense also scored 20 touchdowns on interceptions and six on fumble recoveries. In his autobiography, *Packer Dynasty*, Bengtson stressed, "In the modern game of football, the defense attacks. The defense has plays, formations, strategies, and it can even produce points by making touchdowns and safeties. Most important, the aggressive defensive squad must have a morale of its own." Phil put a great deal of emphasis on pride, and his defenses responded.

Bengtson's first Packer defenses featured a lot of blitzing, but as Lombardi brought in more quality players, the blitzes decreased dramatically. Despite that 49ers-Giants game in 1957, neither Lombardi nor Bengtson were strong advocates of the tactic. Phil preferred a much more patient defense that reflected Lombardi's simple offense. His defense was a 4–3 arrangement that primarily relied on man-to-man coverage. The defensive tackles were pinched toward the center to allow middle linebacker Ray Nitschke the freedom

to pursue the ball. Blitzing was rare and was that much more effective because it was unexpected. Usually the pass rush was generated by the small and quick front line, while the large, fast, athletic linebackers were expected to cover short passes underneath and to stay with backs coming out of the backfield all the way down the field. The inside deep passing game was funneled to safety Willie Wood in "centerfield," while the quick and rangy cornerbacks took the outside routes.

Bengtson taught his players their responsibilities, and his scheme allowed them to succeed. His calm, quiet personality was diametrically opposed to Lombardi's volatile one, but he got results through more measured corrections, and his players loved and respected him for it. In fact, both Ray Nitschke and Willie Wood had Phil present them for induction into the Pro Football Hall of Fame. As head coach, though, he found that following a legend is a near impossible task, especially when the offense is rapidly aging and cannot generate points. After three mediocre seasons, Bengtson was fired. He briefly ran the Chargers' defense in 1971 before taking a leave of absence as the Patriots' interim head coach in 1972. He later served in the Pats' front office before settling in San Diego in retirement.

BENNETT, LEEMAN 6/20/1938– Kentucky. QB; did not play professionally. *Apprenticeship:* College asst.—7 years; pro asst.—7 years. *Roots:* Charley Winner, Bob Hollway, Joe Schmidt, Chuck Knox. *Branches:* Jerry Glanville. *Coordinators/Key Assistants:* For the Falcons, John North handled the offense, while Bennett ran the defense with Jerry Glanville's help; for the Bucs, Jimmy Raye handled the offense, while Doug Shively then Jim Stanley handled the defense. *Hall of Fame Players:* Steve Young. *Primary Quarterbacks:* Steve Bartkowski, Steve Young. *Tendencies:* • His teams scored 19 points and allowed 21.5 per game • His teams ran 50.2% of the time, which was 99% of the league average • Five starting quarterbacks in eight years; 79% of starts to primary quarterbacks • 30 rookie starters in eight years • Winning Full Seasons to Losing Full Seasons: 3:4.

Paducah's Leeman Bennett was Blanton Collier's

Bennett, Leeman									
Year	Team	Games	Wins	Losses	Ties	%	P Wins	P Losses	P %
1977	Falcons	14	7	7	0	.500	0	0	.000
1978	Falcons	16	9	7	0	.563	1	1	.500
1979	Falcons	16	6	10	0	.375	0	0	.000
1980	Falcons	16	12	4	0	.750	0	1	.000
1981	Falcons	16	7	9	0	.438	0	0	.000
1982	Falcons	9	5	4	0	.556	0	1	.000
1985	Buccaneers	16	2	14	0	.125	0	0	.000
1986	Buccaneers	16	2	14	0	.125	0	0	.000
8 years		119	50	69	0	.420	1	3	.250

starting quarterback at Kentucky for three seasons before joining his staff upon graduation. Bennett coached at his alma mater for three years sandwiched around a two-year stint in the military from 1963 to 1964. Leeman moved on to the University of Pittsburgh in 1966 and the University of Cincinnati in 1967 before reaching the NFL in 1970 on Charley Winner's staff in St. Louis. After two years in St. Louis and one in Detroit, he joined Chuck Knox's first staff in Los Angeles as the Rams' receivers coach. Four years with a perennial playoff team brought him to the attention of the Falcons who hired Bennett as head coach in 1977.

Leeman brought an aggressive style of play to Atlanta, especially on defense with the "Grits Blitz" that pressured the quarterback on every play by sending up to nine men at a time to rush the quarterback. That defense gave up 129 points, the fewest ever for a 14-game season. They went from 22nd in defense to first in one year. On offense, Bennett got the floundering Steve Bartkowski established as a young star at quarterback so that in Leeman's second year the Falcons had their first-ever winning season and took their first trip to the postseason. Two years later, Atlanta won its first division title with a 12–4 record before losing a heartbreaker in the playoffs to Dallas After two mediocre years and one more trip to the playoffs, Bennett was shocked to be fired; he was the first Falcons coach to leave Atlanta with an overall winning record. The team would not reach the playoffs again for ten years until Bennett's defensive coach Jerry Glanville was hired as head coach.

Leeman spent two years out of football, selling RV's, until Hugh Culverhouse hired him in 1985 to take over the woeful Tampa Bay Bucs from the retiring John McKay. Tampa was an unmitigated disaster for Leeman. Despite the presence of Steve DeBerg and inexperienced Steve Young at quarterback, the Bucs could neither generate points nor prevent them. The only memorable thing from those two years was the 1985 Snow Bowl game played in a blizzard in Green Bay when Young was nearly suffocated after being sacked headfirst into a snowdrift. Bennett's football career ended with the crash of back-to-back 2–14 seasons. In the years since, he has owned a car dealership, worked for a Christian school and founded a local bank.

BERGMAN, ARTHUR J. (DUTCH) 2/23/1895–8/18/1972. Notre Dame. HB; did not play professionally. *Apprenticeship:* College coach — 20 years (14 as

head coach). *Roots:* None. *Branches:* Turk Edwards. *Coordinators/Key Assistants:* Turk Edwards coached the line. *Hall of Fame Players:* Sammy Baugh. *Primary Quarterbacks:* Sammy Baugh. *Tendencies:* • His team scored 22.9 points and allowed 13.7 per game • His team ran 55.8% of the time, which was 89% of the league average • One starting quarterback in one year; 100% of starts to primary quarterback • One rookie starter in one year • Winning Full Seasons to Losing Full Seasons: 1:0.

Before and after his service as an airman in World War I, Dutch Bergman was a 150-pound halfback for Notre Dame, one of three brothers from Peru, Indiana to play for the Irish. Dutch finished at South Bend in 1919 as George Gipp's roommate on Rockne's first undefeated team. After graduating, he spent some time as a coal miner in West Virginia while wooing his future wife before getting a job as coach and athletic director at New Mexico State. After a three year record of 15–5–1 as head coach in New Mexico, he spent three years in Dayton coaching football and track and then three at Minnesota coaching football and baseball. That led him to Catholic University in D.C. in 1930. Bergman coached Catholic for 11 years, amassing a 59–31–4 record that included a victory in the 1936 Orange Bowl and a tie in the 1940 Sun Bowl. When Catholic deemphasized football in 1941, Dutch worked as an NFL official and a scout for the Redskins during the next two years. At that time, Washington's coach Ray Flaherty went into the service, so George Preston Marshall hired Bergman as Redskins' coach in 1943.

Dutch installed his version of the Notre Dame Box offense and led the Redskins to a 6–0–1 start by Thanksgiving. Unfortunately, that was followed by three straight losses to conclude the season. Although Washington's last two losses were to the Giants, the Redskins won a playoff between the two teams one week later in New York after Dutch fired the team up by castigating them for quitting on the season. In the championship game against the Bears, though, Sammy Baugh was kicked in the head early in the game and was ineffective in a 41–21 loss. Bergman left the team after just one year, but he continued as a D.C. institution. The founder of the Washington Touchdown Club, Dutch managed the Armory and later RFK Stadium from 1948 until his death in 1972.

BERRY, RAYMOND E. 2/27/1933– Southern Methodist. Played WR for Baltimore Colts from 1955

Bergman, Arthur J. (Dutch)									
Year	Team	Games	Wins	Losses	Ties	%	P Wins	P Losses	P %
1943	Redskins	10	6	3	1	.650	1	1	.500
1 year		10	6	3	1	.650	1	1	.500

to 1967. *Apprenticeship:* Pro asst.—11 years; college asst. 3 years. *Roots:* Tom Landry, Don McCafferty, Rick Forzano, Forrest Gregg, Dick Modzelewski (i), Chuck Fairbanks, Ron Erhardt, Les Steckel (in training camp). *Branches:* Rod Rust. *Coordinators/Key Assistants:* Berry brought in his friend Les Steckel to help with the offense, while Rod Rust handled the defense. *Hall of Fame Players:* John Hannah, Andre Tippett. *Primary Quarterbacks:* Tony Eason, Steve Grogan. *Record:* **Hall of Fame Player.** *Tendencies:* • His teams scored 21.2 points and allowed 19.9 per game • His teams ran 49.3% of the time, which was 106% of the league average • Six starting quarterbacks in six years; 74% of starts to primary quarterbacks • 12 rookie starters in six years • Winning Full Seasons to Losing Full Seasons: 4:1.

Although his father coached Paris High School in Texas for 30 years, when scrawny Raymond Berry came out for the team he didn't earn a starting slot until his senior season. After a nondescript career at Southern Methodist, Berry was drafted in the 20th round by Baltimore in 1954. Raymond was slow and not particularly big, but he worked harder than anyone else on the fundamentals of pass catching, route running and blocking. He devised his own series of drills to rehearse every movement and would go through them every day on the practice field, before and after practice. When Johnny Unitas joined the team, Berry had someone with whom to practice, and the two workaholics forged a partnership based on a mutually held diligent work ethic. Each partner went on to retire as the all time leader at his position and go into the Hall of Fame.

The methodical, analytical Berry went into coaching immediately upon retirement, joining Tom Landry's Cowboys' staff in 1968. Raymond spent two years in Dallas, three at the University of Arkansas, three in Detroit, two in Cleveland and then four in New England before dropping out of football in 1982

when Ron Meyer took over as the Pats' coach. Berry helped his friend Les Steckel during the Vikings' training camp in 1984 and then was hired as interim coach for New England after Meyer was fired in a dispute with ownership. The ultra slick Meyer was not very popular with his players either. Running back Tony Collins said at the time, "Raymond Berry earned more respect in one minute than Ron Meyer earned in three years."

Berry was soft-spoken, self-effacing and, above all, sincere. He favored a ball-control offense that ran the ball much more than the league as a whole. He stabilized the Patriots in 1984 and led them to a surprising Super Bowl appearance a year later. Still, Raymond was a committed Christian who kept all things in perspective. He said of NFL coaching during Super Bowl week, "It's all consuming. It's always been this way. As a coach, you don't take a day off until the season ends. It's not a particularly good arrangement. It's not healthy. It's not balanced. It's too much work. But that's the nature of the business, and there isn't anything you can do about it." The Patriots were mauled by the Bears that week, but continued as a contender for the next four years, with Berry's calm leadership style holding the team together through a storm of drug use issues. On the heels of his first losing season in 1989, Raymond was fired after refusing to hire an offensive coordinator. Berry subsequently coached the quarterbacks in Detroit in 1991 and in Denver in 1992 before retiring from the game.

BETTIS, WILLIAM T. (TOM) 3/17/1933– Purdue. Played LB for the Green Bay Packers, Pittsburgh Steelers and Chicago Bears from 1955 to 1963. *Apprenticeship:* Pro asst.—12 years. *Roots:* Hank Stram, Paul Wiggin. *Branches:* None. *Coordinators/Key Assistants:* Bob Schnelker handled the offense; Bettis was promoted from defensive coordinator. *Hall of Fame Players:* Willie Lanier, Jan Stenerud, Emmitt Thomas. *Primary*

Berry, Raymond E.

Year	Team	Games	Wins	Losses	Ties	%	P Wins	P Losses	P %
1984	Patriots	8	4	4	0	.500	0	0	.000
1985	Patriots	16	11	5	0	.688	3	1	.750
1986	Patriots	16	11	5	0	.688	0	1	.000
1987	Patriots	15	8	7	0	.533	0	0	.000
1988	Patriots	16	9	7	0	.563	0	0	.000
1989	Patriots	16	5	11	0	.313	0	0	.000
6 years		87	48	39	0	.552	3	2	.600

Bettis, William T. (Tom)

Year	Team	Games	Wins	Losses	Ties	%	P Wins	P Losses	P %
1977	Chiefs	7	1	6	0	.143	0	0	.000
1 yr		7	1	6	0	.143	0	0	.000

Quarterbacks: Mike Livingston. *Record:* **Interim Coach.**

The Packers' number one draft pick in 1955, Tom Bettis was a solid, dependable linebacker on championship teams in Green Bay and his hometown of Chicago during his nine-year playing career. Bettis retired from the 1963 championship Bears and went into advertising. In 1966, he returned to pro football as the defensive backs coach for Kansas City where he would spend the next 12 years and win a Super Bowl ring for the Chiefs win over the Vikings in 1970. Bettis was popular with his players and stayed on staff after Hank Stram was replaced by Paul Wiggin in 1975. In fact, Stram refused the Oilers permission to interview Tom for their head coaching vacancy in 1971. When Wiggin himself was fired midseason in 1977, Bettis took over to finish the year. Under Tom, the Chiefs won their first game and then lost the next six. Bettis was let go at the end of the year, but continued as an assistant in the league for two more decades: 1978–1984 with the Cardinals; 1985 with the Browns; 1986–1987 with the Oilers; 1988 back with the Chiefs; 1989–1990 with the Eagles; 1992 with the Rams; and 1993–1994 back with the Oilers. After an NFL career that spanned 40 years, Tom retired to the Houston area in 1995.

BEZDEK, HUGO F. 4/1/1884–9/19/1952. Chicago. Did not play professionally. *Apprenticeship:* College head coach — 23 years. *Roots:* None. *Branches:* Art Lewis (i). *Coordinators/Key Assistants*: Art Lewis coached the line. *Hall of Fame Players:* None. *Primary Quarterbacks:* Bob Snyder. *Tendencies:* • His teams scored 7.9 points and allowed 19.8 per game • His teams ran 68.8% of the time, which was 98% of the league average • Two starting quarterbacks in two years; 71% of starts to primary quarterback • 14 rookie starters in two years • Winning Full Seasons to Losing Full Seasons: 0:1.

A Bohemian immigrant from Prague, Hugo Bezdek is the only man to both manage a major league baseball team and coach an NFL squad. He got his start as a second basemen and All-American fullback for the University of Chicago under Amos Alonzo Stagg in 1905. The next year Bezdek set out on his own as the football and basketball coach for Oregon. Hugo then spent five years at Arkansas, where he initiated the Razorback team nickname, as the football and baseball coach before returning to Oregon in 1913

as the football, baseball and basketball coach for the next five years. Bezdek led the Ducks to a Rose Bowl win over Penn in 1917 and then won the Rose Bowl again the next year coaching the Mare Island Service team to a wartime win over Camp Lewis.

By this time, Bezdek had taken over as the manager of the last place Pittsburgh Pirates midway through the 1917 season. The Pirates remained in last place that year, but Bezdek's football-style workouts inspired Pittsburgh to a winning record and fourth place finish in each of the next two seasons. While rowdy Pirate pitcher Burleigh Grimes got into a fistfight with Hugo on a train, outfielders Casey Stengel and Billy Southworth both cited Bezdek as an influence on their own managing style in later years. Hugo took over as football, basketball and baseball coach at Penn State in 1918 and stuck with football and baseball there through 1929–30. He made a third trip to the Rose Bowl in 1923, although Penn State lost to USC after Bezdek and Trojans' coach Gus Henderson got into a pre-game fight. In 1930, Bezdek became athletic director and stepped down from coaching. As a football coach, he was credited by early college football historian Allison Danzig with being an innovator who developed the screen pass, spinner plays, the roving center and the staggering of ends on defense according to. His overall college coaching record was 127–58–16. Bezdek served as athletic director at Penn State through 1936, but his belligerent style alienated alumni and led to the deterioration of the football program.

In 1937, the new Cleveland Rams hired Hugo as their first coach, but he managed just one victory in a little over a year until he was fired and replaced by player/line coach Art Lewis. Bezdek's NFL experience ended with 12 straight losses after the Rams upended Bert Bell's low-flying Eagles in the second game of 1937. Lewis achieved a 4–4 record for the remainder of the 1938 season. Hugo retired to chicken farming, although he returned to coach National Agricultural College (later called Delaware Valley) in 1949 before retiring for good.

BILES, EDWARD G. (ED) 10/18/1931– Miami (OH). Did not play professionally. *Apprenticeship:* College coach —13 years (7 as head coach); pro asst.— 11 years. *Roots:* Tom Fears, Weeb Ewbank, Sid Gillman, Bum Phillips. *Branches:* Chuck Studley (i), Jim Shofner (i). *Coordinators/Key Assistants*: Jim Shofner

Bezdek, Hugo F.									
Year	Team	Games	Wins	Losses	Ties	%	P Wins	P Losses	P %
1937	Rams	11	1	10	0	.091	0	0	.000
1938	Rams	3	0	3	0	.000	0	0	.000
2 years		14	1	13	0	.071	0	0	.000

then O. Kay Dalton handled the offense, while Dick Nolan then Biles then Chuck Studley ran the defense. *Hall of Fame Players:* Elvin Bethea, Earl Campbell, Dave Casper, Bruce Matthews, Mike Munchak. *Primary Quarterbacks:* Ken Stabler, Gifford Nielsen. *Tendencies:* • His teams scored 17 points and allowed 25 per game • His teams ran 46.1% of the time, which was 95% of the league average • Four starting quarterbacks in three years; 77% of starts to primary quarterbacks • 10 rookie starters in three years • Winning Full Seasons to Losing Full Seasons: 0:2.

The college playing career for 5'6" Ed Biles ended in injury and hastened the beginning of his coaching career. After two years coaching high school, the Cincinnati native became the freshman coach at Xavier in 1956; six years later, he took over the varsity position. In his seven years as Xavier's head coach, Ed attained a 40–27–3 record before leaving to join the Saints staff in 1969. When Tom Fears was fired in 1970, Biles moved on to the Jets for three years until fellow Miami of Ohio alumnus Weeb Ewbank retired in 1973. Ed then connected with another Miami alumnus in 1974, Sid Gillman in Houston. One year later, Bum Phillips was promoted to Oilers' head coach, and he named Biles as his defensive coordinator. Over the next six years, the "Luv Ya Blue" Oilers were a perennial contender that simply was unable to get past Pittsburgh's Steel Curtain. Biles' defenses were consistently good, but lacked the overwhelming talent of the Steelers.

Ed's head coaching opportunity came in 1981 when Phillips unexpectedly was fired. Bum quickly got another job as the head coach in New Orleans, while Biles was named coach of the Oilers. Ed optimistically declared, "There are no major problems. It's just a situation where a few minor adjustments have to be made." Unfortunately that was not the case. The team was aging and slipping. All but two members of Phillips' staff followed him to New Orleans, while Biles hired former Saints coach Dick Nolan to run his 3–4 defense even though Nolan had only coached a 4–3. Furthermore, the league was investigating Oiler quarterback Ken Stabler over his alleged gambling ties. After falling out of the playoffs in 1981, Biles' Oilers won just one game in the strike-shortened 1982 season and dropped the first six games of 1983 before Ed resigned. His team had lost 13 straight games, and his exasperated comment was, "I felt like I've been the eye of the hurricane, the center of controversy and sometimes the punching bag. It hasn't been much fun the last 2½ years." Indeed, Ed never coached in the NFL again. He coached a little Arena football, but mostly has worked as a color commentator on college games in Texas in the intervening decades.

BILLICK, BRIAN H. 2/28/1954– Brigham Young. TE; did not play professionally. *Apprenticeship:* College asst.—11 years; pro asst.—7 years. *Roots:* Dennis Green *Branches:* Marvin Lewis, Jack Del Rio, Mike Nolan, Mike Smith, Mike Singletary, Rex Ryan. *Coordinators/Key Assistants:* Matt Cavanaugh then Jim Fassel then Rick Neuheisel handled the offense, while Marvin Lewis then Mike Nolan then Rex Ryan handled the defense. *Hall of Fame Players:* Deion Sanders, Shannon Sharpe, Rod Woodson. *Primary Quarterbacks:* Kyle Boller, Steve McNair. *Record:* Super Bowl Championship 2000. *Tendencies:* • His teams scored 20 points and allowed 17.3 per game • His teams ran 46.2% of the time, which was 105% of the league average • 12 starting quarterbacks in nine years; 44% of starts to pri-

Biles, Edward G. (Ed)

Year	Team	Games	Wins	Losses	Ties	%	P Wins	P Losses	P %
1981	Oilers (Titans)	16	7	9	0	.438	0	0	.000
1982	Oilers (Titans)	9	1	8	0	.111	0	0	.000
1983	Oilers (Titans)	6	0	6	0	.000	0	0	.000
3 years		31	8	23	0	.258	0	0	.000

Billick, Brian H.

Year	Team	Games	Wins	Losses	Ties	%	P Wins	P Losses	P %
1999	Ravens	16	8	8	0	.500	0	0	.000
2000	Ravens	16	12	4	0	.750	4	0	1.000
2001	Ravens	16	10	6	0	.625	1	1	.500
2002	Ravens	16	7	9	0	.438	0	0	.000
2003	Ravens	16	10	6	0	.625	0	1	.000
2004	Ravens	16	9	7	0	.563	0	0	.000
2005	Ravens	16	6	10	0	.375	0	0	.000
2006	Ravens	16	13	3	0	.813	0	1	.000
2007	Ravens	16	5	11	0	.313	0	0	.000
9 years		144	80	64	0	.556	5	3	.625

mary quarterbacks • 22 rookie starters in nine years • Winning Full Seasons to Losing Full Seasons: 5:3.

The irony of Brian Billick's career is that he made his assistant coaching reputation as an offensive genius but any success he had as a head coach was due almost entirely to his defense; in nine years, he never managed to find a reliable quarterback in Baltimore. That deficiency does not reflect his roots. After being cut by the 49ers and Cowboys as a free agent tight end in 1977, the Fairborn, Ohio, native spent a year as a graduate assistant at his alma mater before serving two years as a public relations assistant under Bill Walsh in San Francisco in 1979 and 1980. Working with Walsh was an influential experience for Billick, and his PR experience has been evident ever since with his smart, smooth and sometimes smug interactions with the public.

Billick spent five years at San Diego State and three at Utah State before landing the assistant head coach job at Stanford under Dennis Green in 1989. Brian had first met Green when Dennis worked as an assistant on Bill Walsh's 49ers' staff while Billick was there. Green got the Vikings job in 1992 and brought Billick along as tight ends coach, but promoted Brian to offensive coordinator in 1994. The Vikings changed their quarterbacks almost annually, but always scored points. In 1998, with a revitalized Randall Cunningham throwing bombs to rookie Randy Moss and glue-fingered Cris Carter, Minnesota stormed to a 15–1 season and scored more points than any team in history doing it. They did not reach the Super Bowl, but Billick was the league's hottest coordinator. In 1999, he turned down the Cleveland Browns job to accept the position in Baltimore.

Brian inherited a terrific defense but struggled to score with Tony Banks at quarterback through more than a season. In fact, the Ravens went five weeks without scoring a touchdown in 2001, forcing Billick to demote Banks for backup Trent Dilfer. While Dilfer did not have the skill to light up the scoreboard, he did a much more consistent job of managing the game and minimizing mistakes. Meanwhile, the Ravens' record-setting defense allowed just 165 points in 16 games and took the team to a Super Bowl title. Despite appreciating what Dilfer had done, Billick and GM Ozzie Newsome realized they had to get better at quarterback so they let Dilfer leave as a free agent and signed Elvis Grbac to replace him once former Viking Brad Johnson signed with the Redskins. Billick is often pilloried for this decision since the Ravens never returned to the Super Bowl and he continued to search for a quarterback for the remainder of his tenure in Baltimore. Dilfer himself was understandably bitter and commented years later that his teammates "will go to their graves swearing to God that we could have won two, three Super Bowls if they would have kept me."

However, Billick knew that the defense would never be this good again and the offense had to improve. While the defense was still excellent, it was no longer so otherworldly that the team could afford inadequate quarterback play; the Ravens allowed 100 more points in 2001 to drop to fourth in that category. As a second illustration, 2006 was Billick's last hurrah in Baltimore. That season, the defense gave up just 201 points, again first in the league, and finished 13–3 behind imported veteran quarterback Steve McNair. Still, they were one-and-done in the playoffs. If Steve McNair, admittedly banged up, couldn't take the Ravens back to the Super Bowl that year, what chance would Trent Dilfer have had to duplicate his good fortune of 2001? The decision to move on was sound; the decision on who to sign was flawed.

The remainder of Billick's tenure in Baltimore was an up and down one, and Brian eventually wore out his welcome with players, fans and ownership. Since being fired in 2008, Billick has written a book on football and worked as a generally respected football broadcaster for Fox and the NFL Network. It is no secret that he would like to coach again.

BLACKBOURN, LISLE W. (LIZ) 6/3/1899–6/14/1963. Lawrence. T; did not play professionally. *Apprenticeship:* College coach — 6 years (4 as head coach). *Roots:* None. *Branches:* Scooter McLean, Lou Rymkus. *Coordinators/Key Assistants:* Scooter McLean coached the backs and Lou Rymkus the line. *Hall of Fame Players:* Forrest Gregg, Paul Hornung, Jim Ringo and Bart Starr. *Primary Quarterbacks:* Tobin Rote. *Tendencies:* • His teams scored 20.3 points and allowed 24.6 per game • His teams ran 48.3% of the time, which was 85% of the league average • Three starting quarterbacks in four years; 73% of starts to primary quarterback • 15 rookie starters in four years • Winning Full Seasons to Losing Full Seasons: 0:3.

Blackbourn, Lisle W. (Liz)									
Year	Team	Games	Wins	Losses	Ties	%	P Wins	P Losses	P %
1954	Packers	12	4	8	0	.333	0	0	.000
1955	Packers	12	6	6	0	.500	0	0	.000
1956	Packers	12	4	8	0	.333	0	0	.000
1957	Packers	12	3	9	0	.250	0	0	.000
4 years		48	17	31	0	.354	0	0	.000

Lisle Blackbourn was a lifelong Wisconsin resident who coached at all levels in the state. Born in Beetown, he attended college at Lawrence in Appleton, where he captained the football, baseball and wrestling teams. In 1926, he became football coach at Washington High School in Milwaukee and stayed there for 22 years, attaining a 141–30–6 record. In 1948, he took a job coaching the line at the University of Wisconsin and moved on to coach the line at Marquette the next year. In 1950, he was named head coach of the struggling Marquette Golden Eagles and went 18–17–4 in four years, which was a step up for the school.

In 1954, Blackbourn ascended to the top level coaching job in the state by taking over the floundering Packers. In conjunction with Green Bay's scouting and personnel director, Jack Vainisi, Blackbourn assembled a wealth of talent; unfortunately, he did not always employ that talent in the optimal way. For example, he tried Paul Hornung at each backfield position, but the future Hall of Famer had no success at any of them. Blackbourn did see Bart Starr's potential when few others did, but after three losing years out of four, there were whispers that Clark Shaughnessy would replace the coach in 1957. Instead, Blackbourn was replaced by backfield coach Scooter McLean and moved on to coach at Carroll College in Waukesha, Wisconsin. Marquette brought Blackbourn back in 1959, but after two years, the school pulled the plug on the financially-draining football program altogether. Among the players on that final 1960 team were future Cowboy George Andrie and future Viking Karl Kassulke. Blackbourn commented at the time, "I think it's regrettable that the largest Catholic university in the nation will not have a well-rounded intercollegiate sports program." He died in Lancaster, Wisconsin three years later. His overall college coaching record was 30–32–4.

BOLAND, PATRICK H. (PAT) 10/12/1906–7/2/1971. Minnesota. T; did not play professionally. *Apprenticeship:* College asst.—11 years. *Roots:* Dick Hanley (i). *Branches:* None. *Coordinators/Key Assistants:* None. *Hall of Fame Players:* Elroy Hirsch. *Primary*

Quarterbacks: Bob Hoernschemeyer. *Record:* **Interim Coach.**

Duluth's Pat Boland played tackle at Minnesota alongside All-American guard Biggie Munn under Fritz Crisler in 1931. When Bernie Bierman replaced Crisler in 1932, Boland was named line coach. Five years later, Pat moved on to Iowa as line coach and stayed there until joining the Navy in 1943. When the Chicago Rockets of the new All America Football Conference hired Dick Hanley as their first coach in 1946, Hanley signed Boland as line coach and Ernie Nevers as backfield coach. From the outset, Hanley struggled to get along with meddlesome owner John Keeshin, a trucking magnate, and either quit or was fired (they disagreed about that, too) on September 25, the date of the Rockets' third game. Hanley and his two assistants watched from the stands as the Rockets, directed by the player-coach triumvirate of Bob Dove, Ned Mathews and Willie Wilkin, beat Buffalo for its first victory. Keeshin left the player-coach trio in charge for the next month, but kept Boland and Nevers on the payroll while he tried to persuade Sid Luckman to coach the team. On October 29 with the Rockets at 3–3–2, Keeshin brought back Boland as head coach with Nevers as his assistant, and Pat finished out the season. The 5–6–3 record that year would prove to be the franchise's best, but of the 1946 ownership and coaching staff, only Bob Dove was still with the team a year later. Boland returned to the college ranks and worked for several years as a recruiter for Iowa and Miami before his death at age 64.

BOWLES, TODD R. 11/18/1963– Temple. Played S for the Redskins and 49ers from 1986 to 1993. *Apprenticeship:* College asst.—3 years; pro asst.—12 years *Roots:* Al Groh, Butch Davis, Terry Robiskie (i), Bill Parcells, Wade Phillips, Tony Sparano. *Branches:* None. *Coordinators/Key Assistants:* Brian Daboll ran the offense and Mike Nolan handled the defense. *Hall of Fame Players:* None. *Primary Quarterbacks:* Matt Moore. *Record:* **Interim Coach.**

Born in Elizabeth, New Jersey, Todd Bowles was a four-year letterman at Temple University through 1985. Although he went undrafted, he signed as a free

Boland, Patrick H. (Pat)									
Year	Team	Games	Wins	Losses	Ties	%	P Wins	P Losses	P %
1946	Rockets (AAFC)	6	2	3	1	.400	0	0	.000
1 year		6	2	3	1	.400	0	0	.000

Bowles, Todd R.									
Year	Team	Games	Wins	Losses	Ties	%	P Wins	P Losses	P %
2011	Dolphins	3	2	1	0	.667	0	0	.000
1 year		3	2	1	0	.667	0	0	.000

agent with the Redskins in 1986 and played on special teams as a rookie and was part of a Super Bowl champion that year. Bowles moved into the starting lineup at free safety the next year. Bowles played for Washington through 1990, spent one year with the 49ers and then finished his career with the Redskins from 1992 to 1993.

Bowles scouted for the Packers in 1995 and 1996 before beginning his coaching career at Morehouse State in 1997 as secondary coach. Todd moved on to Grambling in 1998 and jumped to the NFL in 2000 with the Jets. After just one year in New York, Bowles joined Butch Davis' staff in Cleveland in 2001 and then became a "Parcells Guy" in Dallas in 2005. Todd stayed on the Cowboys' staff in 2007 when Wade Phillips replaced Parcells and then left for Miami in 2008 after Bill Parcells took control of that franchise. Bowles was named assistant head coach/secondary coach for the Dolphins under Tony Sparano.

In his years under Sparano, Todd earned respect throughout the league and interviewed for several head coaching jobs. In December 2011, he was promoted to interim head coach when the Dolphins fired Sparano with three games to play. Team owner Stephen Ross emphasized that those three games would serve as an audition for Bowles in his quest to be named permanent head coach of the team. After Ross hired Joe Philbin as head coach, Todd moved on to Philadelphia as the secondary coach for 2012.

BRIDGES, FRANK D. 7/4/1890–6/10/1970. Harvard. Did not play professionally. *Apprenticeship:* College coach —14 years; pro asst.— 2 years. *Roots:* Pete Cawthon. *Branches:* None. *Coordinators/Key Assistants:* None. *Hall of Fame Players:* Bruiser Kinard. *Primary Quarterbacks:* None. *Record:* **Interim Co-Coach** with Ed Kubale.

While Bruiser Kinard was the only Canton inductee who was coached by Savannah's Frank Bridges, he was not the only Hall of Famer. Bridges' first claim to fame was as the football, basketball and baseball coach at Baylor in the early 1920s where he coached pitcher/outfielder Ted Lyons. Frank got Lyons a tryout with the Chicago White Sox during their 1923 spring training stay in Texas, and Lyons pitched for 21 seasons in Chicago to earn a spot in the Baseball Hall of Fame. As for Bridges, the Harvard-educated coach is a member of the Texas Sports Hall of Fame. He coached football at Baylor from 1920 to 1925 and led the Bears to two Southwest Conference championships and a 35–

18–6 record; the school would not win another conference title until 1974. Reportedly, Bridges gave Baylor President Samuel Brooks an ultimatum in 1925 to give him a raise or else, and Brooks succinctly replied, "Your resignation is accepted. Good luck and good day." However, Bridges' version was that he asked Brooks for $10,000, and the President replied, "I only receive $10,000." Frank retorted, "Don't worry, Doc. I'll get you a raise." Either way, he was no longer the football coach, but continued as Baylor's baseball coach through 1927 when he was hired by Hardin-Simmons as football coach. He would have a three-year record there of 16–13–4 and later coached football, baseball and basketball at St. Mary's in Texas from 1935 to 1939.

Bridges was an acerbic and clever man who is credited with such gridiron innovations as the spread formation, the hidden ball play, the end around, the tackle around and the quick kick. In 1943, another Texas coach, Pete Cawthon, brought Frank to Brooklyn as his end coach and scout. After Brooklyn dropped the first five games of the 1944 season, Cawthon resigned. His two assistants, Bridges and line coach Ed Kubale, were named co-coaches for the remainder of the season. Oddly, Bridges had been Kubale's high school coach in 1919 in Fort Smith, Arkansas. The two announced they would be adding the spread formation and some T formation plays to the offense, but the team was just awful. Scoring just 13 points, Brooklyn lost the last five games of the season, finished the season 0–10 and vanished from the NFL. Afterwards, Bridges worked as a baseball scout for the White Sox and Athletics.

BROOKS, RICHARD L. (RICH) 8/10/1941– Oregon State. DB; did not play professionally. *Apprenticeship:* College coach — 27 years (18 as head coach); pro asst.— 4 years. *Roots:* Dick Nolan, Tommy Prothro. *Branches:* Mike Martz. *Coordinators/Key Assistants:* Jack Reilly handled the offense and Willie Shaw ran the defense. *Hall of Fame Players:* Jackie Slater. *Primary Quarterbacks:* Chris Miller; Tony Banks. *Tendencies:*
• His teams scored 19.1 points and allowed 25.8 per game • His teams ran 40.9% of the time, which was 94% of the league average • Four starting quarterbacks in two years; 81% of starts to primary quarterbacks • Seven rookie starters in two years • Winning Full Seasons to Losing Full Seasons: 0:2.

A native of Forest, California, Rich Brooks spent 34 of his 44 years as a coach in the college ranks. For

Bridges, Frank D.									
Year	*Team*	*Games*	*Wins*	*Losses*	*Ties*	*%*	*P Wins*	*P Losses*	*P %*
1944	Brooklyn Tigers	5	0	5	0	.000	0	0	.000
1 year		5	0	5	0	.000	0	0	.000

Brooks, Richard L. (Rich)

Year	Team	Games	Wins	Losses	Ties	%	P Wins	P Losses	P %
1995	Rams	16	7	9	0	.438	0	0	.000
1996	Rams	16	6	10	0	.375	0	0	.000
2 years		32	13	19	0	.406	0	0	.000

25 years he was a head coach for two universities, Oregon and Kentucky, not known as football powers, but managed to lead each to four bowl games. On the whole, though, Brooks had a losing record at both schools, amassing a 128–154–4 college coaching record.

Brooks played with Heisman Trophy winner Terry Baker at Oregon State under Coach Tommy Prothro in the early 1960s and later worked as an assistant to Prothro at Oregon State, UCLA and the Los Angeles Rams. After leaving the Rams when Prothro was fired after the 1972 season, Rich coached the defense at Oregon State for a year, spent two years coaching the defensive backs for the 49ers under Dick Nolan, then one year coaching the linebackers at UCLA before becoming head coach of the Oregon Ducks in 1977.

When the St. Louis Rams hired Brooks as head coach in 1995, he announced, "After 18 years [at Oregon], I felt a change would be good for me. I really believe the ultimate in the coaching profession is the NFL. The challenge of being a head coach in that league is very intriguing." Rich took over a 4–12 franchise after Chuck Knox's failed second stint as Rams' coach. While the team showed some improvement the first year, Brooks made the monumental mistake of trading running back Jerome Bettis for draft picks in the offseason because, "I wanted a little more speed at the position. Jerome is an outstanding player and the Pittsburgh scheme will suit him more than my scheme will." Thus while the 1996 Rams sunk to 6–10 behind the skittish quarterbacking of Tony Banks and Steve Walsh and no running game, Bettis rushed for over 1,400 yards for the Steelers. That very obvious mistake in talent evaluation did as much as the Rams' losing record to seal Brooks' fate after just two seasons.

In 1997, Rich was hired by Dan Reeves in Atlanta as defensive coordinator, and even stepped in to run the team for the last two games of the 1998 season when Reeves had heart surgery. Reeves came back for the playoffs, and the Falcons ended up in the Super Bowl that year. Brooks resigned from Atlanta after the 2000 season and spent two years out of football before coming back as Kentucky's head coach from 2003 to 2009 until he retired for good.

Brown, Paul E. 9/7/1908–8/5/1991. Ohio State and Miami of Ohio. QB; did not play professionally. *Apprenticeship:* College head coach — 3 years. *Roots:* None. *Branches:* Weeb Ewbank, Red Conkright (i), Blanton Collier, Rick Forzano, Bill Johnson, Bill Walsh, Chuck Studley (i). *Coordinators/Key Assistants:* For the Browns, Blanton Collier was Brown's key lieutenant on both offense and defense and Howard Brinker handled the defense after Collier left; for the Bengals, Bill Walsh ran the offense, while Tom Bass and then Chuck Weber handled the defense. *Hall of Fame Players:* Doug Atkins, Jim Brown, Willie Davis, Len Dawson, Len Ford, Frank Gatski, Otto Graham, Lou Groza, Gene Hickerson, Charley Joiner, Henry Jordan, Dante Lavelli, Mike McCormack, Bobby Mitchell, Marion Motley and Bill Willis. *Primary Quarterbacks:* Otto Graham, Milt Plum, Ken Anderson. *Record:* **Hall of Fame Coach; Owner-coach** in Cincinnati; AAFC Championship 1946, 1947, 1948, 1949; NFL Championship 1950, 1954, 1955. *Tendencies:* • His teams scored 24 points and allowed 16.7 per game • His teams ran 58.1% of the time, which was 106% of the league average • 17 starting quarterbacks in 25 years; 71% of starts to primary quarterbacks • 87 rookie starters in 25 years • Winning Full Seasons to Losing Full Seasons: 20:4.

Although the Super Bowl Trophy is named after Vince Lombardi, Paul Brown is arguably the greatest coach of all time. In fact, these two great coaches shared certain similarities. Both emphasized precise execution of basic plays rather than flashy trick plays. Both stressed the importance of blocking and tackling and always had solid defenses even though they were primarily offensive coaches. Finally, while Lombardi ran the ball 12% more than the league average, in Cleveland, Brown ran the ball nine percent more than

Head-to-Head:

Hall of Fame Opponent	Regular Season	Postseason
George Allen	1–0	0–0
Weeb Ewbank	2–6	0–0
Ray Flaherty	5–0–1	2–0
Sid Gillman	2–5	1–0
Bud Grant	1–0	0–0
George Halas	3–1	0–0
Curly Lambeau	8–0	0–0
Tom Landry	4–2	0–0
Vince Lombardi	0–1	0–0
John Madden	3–4	0–1
Greasy Neale	2–0	0–0
Chuck Noll	4–8	0–0
Steve Owen	4–4	1–0
Don Shula	0–2	0–1
Hank Stram	4–4	0–0
Total	43–37–1	4–2

the mean —13% more in the Jim Brown years. Of course, their personalities were diametrically opposed, but the cool, aloof Brown got along well with the volatile Lombardi. Their players shared one other trait: they hoped to avoid either Lombardi's rants or Brown's icy stare and cutting sarcasm.

One thing that sets Brown apart is that he won championships at every level. After starring at quarterback for Massillon High, the Norwalk, Ohio native enrolled at Ohio State, but then transferred to Miami of Ohio. After graduation, he began his coaching career going 16–1–1 in two years at Severn Prep in Ohio from 1930 to 31. Then from 1932 to 1940, Paul coached Washington High School in Massillon, Ohio and amassed an 80–8–2 record. In his last six years in Massillon, Brown went 58–1–1 and won six straight state championships. In 1941, he moved up to Ohio State (18–8–1 in three years) and won the National Championship in his second season in Columbus. After two years of wartime service at the Great Lakes Naval Station where his team went 15–5–2, Paul was named the first coach of the Cleveland Browns of the new All America Football Conference in 1946; in fact, the team was named after him. The Browns dominated the new league, finishing 52–4–3 with four straight championships, before they were brought into the NFL in 1950. From 1950–1955, Brown led Cleveland to six straight Eastern Division crowns and won three NFL titles.

Those early Browns were built by the greatest organizer the game has ever known. Most of the early Browns were players that Paul had either coached or coached against in high school and college. When Cleveland joined the NFL, Brown also finessed the allocation of former AAFC players to obtain such stalwarts as Len Ford, Abe Gibron and Rex Bumgardner. As time went on, it became clear that Paul also had a real affinity for the college draft, and he used it to supplement his roster with fresh talent each year. He brought in so many great players that he ended up dealing Lombardi three-fourths of Vince's first championship defensive line with Willie Davis, Henry Jordan and Bill Quinlan.

Paul's advances on the field and in the classroom became standard throughout the league. He introduced the taxi squad, the quarterback radio helmet, calling plays from the sidelines, the 40-yard dash, intelligence and psychological testing, game plan tests, graded playbooks and having a year round staff. He popularized the facemask, grading game films and charting tendencies. His practices were short and focused. He was an early advocate of the draw play and a primary developer of the pass pocket. His passing attack relied on timed patterns that could change by the quarterback and receiver reading the defense and altering the pattern during the play.

Cleveland under Brown led the league in points

Brown, Paul E.

Year	Team	Games	Wins	Losses	Ties	%	P Wins	P Losses	P %
1946	Browns	14	12	2	0	.857	1	0	1.000
1947	Browns	14	12	1	1	.893	1	0	1.000
1948	Browns	14	14	0	0	1.000	1	0	1.000
1949	Browns	12	9	1	2	.833	2	0	1.000
1950	Browns	12	10	2	0	.833	2	0	1.000
1951	Browns	12	11	1	0	.917	0	1	.000
1952	Browns	12	8	4	0	.667	0	1	.000
1953	Browns	12	11	1	0	.917	0	1	.000
1954	Browns	12	9	3	0	.750	1	0	1.000
1955	Browns	12	9	2	1	.792	1	0	1.000
1956	Browns	12	5	7	0	.417	0	0	.000
1957	Browns	12	9	2	1	.792	0	1	.000
1958	Browns	12	9	3	0	.750	0	1	.000
1959	Browns	12	7	5	0	.583	0	0	.000
1960	Browns	12	8	3	1	.708	0	0	.000
1961	Browns	14	8	5	1	.607	0	0	.000
1962	Browns	14	7	6	1	.536	0	0	.000
1968	Bengals	14	3	11	0	.214	0	0	.000
1969	Bengals	14	4	9	1	.321	0	0	.000
1970	Bengals	14	8	6	0	.571	0	1	.000
1971	Bengals	14	4	10	0	.286	0	0	.000
1972	Bengals	14	8	6	0	.571	0	0	.000
1973	Bengals	14	10	4	0	.714	0	1	.000
1974	Bengals	14	7	7	0	.500	0	0	.000
1975	Bengals	14	11	3	0	.786	0	1	.000
25 years		326	213	104	9	.667	9	8	.529

four times, and seven times finished first or second in scoring. Defensively, they were even better. Nine times the Browns allowed the fewest points in the league, and three more years finished second. Six times, the team led the league in turnover differential and 12 times finished in the top three.

Once quarterback Otto Graham retired, though, Brown never won another championship; in fact, he never won another postseason game. While he was still an excellent coach, he also was inflexible, so the better teams found ways to beat the Browns. With quarterbacks Tommy O'Connell, Jim Ninowski and Milt Plum, Brown's options were more limited. At the same time, though, Paul failed to develop young quarterbacks Len Dawson and Frank Ryan, and that failure led to his downfall.

In 1957, Paul drafted Jim Brown from Syracuse, and during Paul's remaining six years as Cleveland's coach, the two very proud men named Brown often failed to see eye-to-eye. Jim was adamant that the play calling was too conservative. He said of Paul to the *New York Times*, "The man's ego was such that when other coaches stole his ideas and added new twists, he simply would not or could not change and adapt to the new styles of play. We players saw this. Our professional lives were involved. We happened not to be the brainless automatons he wanted his players to act like." Still, Jim once told reporter Ray Didinger, "I always respected Paul and was grateful for the opportunity he gave me to showcase my talents. Even when we disagreed, we disagreed respectfully."

Storm clouds loomed when Art Modell bought the team in 1961. Brown looked on the neophyte Modell with disdain. Rebuffed, Modell grew close to Jim Brown and to gentle assistant coach Blanton Collier. When Modell fired Paul Brown in 1963, though, it was a shock to the rest of the league and most of all to Paul himself. He vowed he would get back in the league, but only with complete franchise control. For six years, Brown played golf and traveled with his wife but deeply missed football. He told *Sports Illustrated* of his years in the wilderness, "It was terrible. I had everything a man can want: leisure, enough money, a wonderful family. Yet, with all that, I was eating my heart out."

Finally, in 1968 Brown received an AFL expansion team in Cincinnati and was back in the game. As a talent evaluator, he was still highly skilled, coming up with quarterbacks Greg Cook from the University of Cincinnati and then Ken Anderson from tiny Augustana College as well as All Pro middle line-

backer Bill Bergey from Arkansas State. By the Bengals' third season, they had reached the playoffs, but they never reached the heights of Paul's Browns. When Brown decided to step aside as coach and retreat to the front office, the Bengals were coming off an 11-win season in 1975. Unfortunately, he bungled the coaching handoff by choosing fiery line coach Tiger Johnson whom he had know for thirty years rather than the team's dynamic, innovative offensive coach for the past eight seasons, Bill Walsh. In fact, Walsh's famous West Coast Offense was developed in Cincinnati to accentuate the limited positives of quarterback Virgil Carter in 1970.

Sadly, though, there was also a rather small side to this great coach. Blanton Collier was not only Brown's chief assistant from 1946 to 1953, but also a close family friend. Collier returned to the Browns in 1962 but was shunted aside when he drew some publicity for trying to empower the quarterbacks to change Paul's play calls at the line of scrimmage. When Modell fired Paul, he offered the job to Collier, but Blanton insisted on getting Brown's blessing first. Paul gave that to him, but that ended their relationship. A dozen years later when Bill Walsh wanted to strike out on his own after being passed over in Cincinnati, Brown tried to sabotage Walsh by talking him down to each team that showed any interest. Eventually, Paul got to see two Bengal teams reach the Super Bowl while he owned the team, but both times, with poetic justice, they lost to Bill Walsh's 49ers. Brown ran the team until his death in 1991; under his son, Mike, the Bengals haven't been the same since.

BRUNEY, FREDERICK K. (FRED) 12/30/1931– Ohio State. Played DB for the 49ers, Steelers, Rams and Patriots from 1953 to 1962. *Apprenticeship:* Pro asst.— 23 years. *Roots:* Mike Holovak, Joe Kuharich, Norm Van Brocklin, Marion Campbell and Dick Vermeil. *Branches:* Tom Coughlin and Frank Gansz. *Coordinators/Key Assistants:* None. *Hall of Fame Players:* None. *Primary Quarterbacks:* None. *Record:* **Interim Coach**.

A home-state hero who starred at halfback for Ohio State under Woody Hayes, Fred Bruney had a journeyman's ten-year NFL playing career as a defensive back for the 49ers, Steelers, Rams and Patriots. In his final season as a player, 1962, Bruney doubled as the defensive backs coach of the Pats and stayed on in that capacity for another year. In 1964, Fred moved on to the Eagles for five years and then spent eight seasons with Atlanta before returning to Philadelphia in

Bruney, Frederick K. (Fred)									
Year	*Team*	*Games*	*Wins*	*Losses*	*Ties*	*%*	*P Wins*	*P Losses*	*P %*
1985	Eagles	1	1	0	0	1.000	0	0	.000
1 year		1	1	0	0	1.000	0	0	.000

1977 under Dick Vermeil. In both Atlanta and his second stint in Philly, Bruney worked with his old teammate from the Patriots, Marion Campbell. Campbell replaced Vermeil as the Eagles' head coach in 1983, but after a disappointing three-year run, he was fired with one game to go in 1985. Bruney was named interim coach and announced he was interested in making the interim job permanent and emptied the playbook in the season finale against the Viking with trick plays and a wide open offense that pulled out a 37–35 victory in the closing seconds. Both Campbell and Bruney were given game balls by the players, but both coaches were in Atlanta the next year — once again with Bruney as the loyal assistant to Campbell. Not surprisingly, Campbell failed again in Atlanta, and Bruney moved on in 1990 to Tampa, then after two years with the Giants, he finished his 44-year NFL career as an assistant in Indianapolis from 1993 to 1996.

BUGEL, JOSEPH J. (JOE) 3/10/1940– Western Kentucky. G/LB; did not play professionally. *Apprenticeship:* College asst.—11 years; pro asst.—15 years. *Roots:* Rick Forzano, Tommy Hudspeth, Bum Phillips, Joe Gibbs. *Branches:* None. *Coordinators/Key Assistants:* For the Cardinals, Jerry Rhome handled the offense, while Joe Pascale then Fritz Shurmur ran the defense; for the Raiders, Ray Perkins handled the offense and Fred Whittingham ran the defense. *Hall of Fame Players:* None. *Primary Quarterbacks:* Chris Chandler, Timm Rosenbach and Jeff George. *Tendencies:* • His teams scored 17 points and allowed 22 per game • His teams ran 43.1% of the time, which was 95% of the league average • Five starting quarterbacks in five years; 65% of starts to primary quarterbacks • 11 rookie starters in five years • Winning Full Seasons to Losing Full Seasons: 0:5.

Pittsburgh's Joe Bugel was one of the most famous and effective assistant coaches in NFL history, but as a head coach he never had a winning season. After earning a master's degree in counseling from his alma mater, Western Kentucky, Bugel began his coaching career there in 1964. Over the next 11 years, Joe worked on the staffs at Western Kentucky, Navy, Iowa State and Ohio State before being named the line coach for Rick Forzano's Detroit Lions' staff. Despite having such talented assistant coaches on hand as Raymond Berry, Bill Belichick and Jerry Glanville,

the Lions struggled and Forzano was fired in 1976. Bugel moved on to Houston to coach the line under Bum Phillips for four years. When Phillips got the "bum's rush" in 1980, Bugel was hired by Joe Gibbs in Washington as the coach of the offensive line and the nominal offensive coordinator. It was here that Bugel created the Hogs, a quick and massive offensive line that powered the Redskins' offense for more than a decade as the team won three Super Bowls.

The energetic and effusive Bugel became a hot coaching commodity. He turned down the Raiders' head job in 1988 and then finished second to Jerry Glanville for the Falcons' job before landing in Arizona as the Cardinals head coach in 1990. The Cardinals had long been dysfunctional franchise that served as a coaching graveyard, and it proved the same for Bugel. After three losing seasons, owner Bill Bidwill told Bugel he had one last chance to produce a winning team. Even though the Cards won their last three games in 1993, they still finished just 7–9, and Bugel was fired.

Joe was hired a year later as Mike White's line coach in Oakland. After two mediocre seasons, White was fired, but the players went to owner Al Davis to plead for the popular Bugel. Davis had been planning to go outside the organization for a new coach, but promoted Bugel instead because, "There was overwhelming support from our players, and I was shocked by it." A players' coach is not necessarily a winning one, however. A 4–12 season with coach-killer Jeff George at quarterback resulted in Bugel being replaced by Jon Gruden as the Raider's coach. Joe spent the next four years as the Chargers' line coach and retired. When Joe Gibbs came out of retirement to return to Washington in 2004, though, Bugel came with him and stayed on under Jim Zorn and Mike Shanahan before retiring for good in 2011.

BULLOUGH, HENRY C. (HANK) 1/24/1934– Michigan State. Played G and LB for the Packers in 1955 and 1958. *Apprenticeship:* College asst.—11 years; pro asst.—15 years; USFL head coach —1 year. *Roots:* Don McCafferty, John Sandusky (i), Chuck Fairbanks, Forrest Gregg and Kay Stephenson. *Branches:* Dick Jauron. *Coordinators/Key Assistants:* For the Bills, Jim Ringo handled the offense and Herb Patera ran the defense. *Hall of Fame Players:* Joe Delamielleure, Jim

Bugel, Joseph J. (Joe)									
Year	Team	Games	Wins	Losses	Ties	%	P Wins	P Losses	P %
1990	Cardinals	16	5	11	0	.313	0	0	.000
1991	Cardinals	16	4	12	0	.250	0	0	.000
1992	Cardinals	16	4	12	0	.250	0	0	.000
1993	Cardinals	16	7	9	0	.438	0	0	.000
1997	Raiders	16	4	12	0	.250	0	0	.000
5 years		80	24	56	0	.300	0	0	.000

Kelly and Bruce Smith. *Primary Quarterbacks:* Jim Kelly. *Record:* Began as **Interim Co-Coach** (with Ron Erhardt in 1978). *Tendencies:* • His teams scored 15 points and allowed 23.1 per game • His teams ran 43% of the time, which was 93% of the league average • Four starting quarterbacks in three years; 41% of starts to primary quarterback • Eight rookie starters in three years • Winning Full Seasons to Losing Full Seasons: 0:1.

Sandwiched around two years of military service, Scranton, Pennsylvania's Hank Bullough spent two seasons playing in the NFL before returning to his alma mater as an assistant on Duffy Daugherty's staff for 11 years. Bullough was the defensive coordinator for the legendary mid–Sixties Spartan teams that featured All-Americans Bubba Smith and George Webster on defense. In 1970, Hank joined Don McCafferty's staff in Baltimore as linebackers coach and won a Super Bowl ring a year later. After McCafferty was fired in 1972, Bullough became Chuck Fairbanks' defensive coordinator in New England where he helped develop the 3–4 defense that was just coming to the NFL in 1973. Hank coached the Patriot defense through the 1979 season, and then took over the Bengals' defense in 1980 under Forrest Gregg. When Gregg was fired after the 1983 season, Bullough got his first head coaching job with the Pittsburgh Maulers of the USFL, but could produce only a 3–15 record in 1984, the Maulers only season.

Kay Stephenson then hired Hank as defensive coordinator in Buffalo. After the Bills lost the first four games of 1985, Bullough was named head coach. Unfortunately, Hank could only win two games the rest of 1985 and two in the first half of 1986 before owner Ralph Wilson hired Marv Levy to usher in the Bills' golden era. Bullough was a loquacious man given to malaprops such as, "I have to teach these guys the work ethnic" or "We keep beating ourselves, but we're getting better at it." The main criticism leveled at him

as a head coach was that his offense was too conservative and didn't take advantage of the Bills' new quarterback, Jim Kelly. Hank then spent two years in Green Bay and five in Detroit before finishing his 36-year coaching career by running the defense at Michigan State one last year in 1994.

BURNS, JEROME M. (JERRY) 1/24/1927– Michigan. QB; did not play professionally. *Apprenticeship:* College coach —14 years (5 as head coach); pro asst.— 20 years. *Roots:* Vince Lombardi, Bud Grant and Les Steckel. *Branches:* Pete Carroll. *Coordinators/Key Assistants:* Bob Schnelker then Tom Moore ran the offense; Floyd Peters then Monte Kiffin handled the defense. *Hall of Fame Players:* Chris Doleman, Randall McDaniel, John Randle and Gary Zimmerman. *Primary Quarterbacks:* Wade Wilson, Tommy Kramer and Rich Gannon. *Tendencies:* • His teams scored 22.6 points and allowed 18.4 per game • His teams ran 47.2% of the time, which was 102% of the league average • Four starting quarterbacks in six years; 97% of starts to primary quarterbacks • Seven rookie starters in six years • Winning Full Seasons to Losing Full Seasons: 4:1.

Detroit's Jerry Burns apprenticed under some legendary coaches after graduating from Michigan. After a year at the University of Hawaii, Burns spent a year under George Allen at Whittier, seven under Forrest Evashevski at Iowa, two under Vince Lombardi at Green Bay and 17 under Bud Grant in Minnesota. He also spent five years as Iowa's head coach in the early 1960s and went 16–27–2. When Bud Grant first retired in 1984, Burns was passed over as Grant's replacement despite the fact that he had been Grant's offensive coordinator for 16 years and, before that, had worked with Grant during training camps when Bud coached in Canada. Instead, end coach Les Steckel was promoted to head coach and then was replaced

Bullough, Henry C. (Hank)

Year	Team	Games	Wins	Losses	Ties	%	P Wins	P Losses	P %
1978	Patriots	1	0	1	0	.000	0	0	.000
1985	Bills	12	2	10	0	.167	0	0	.000
1986	Bills	9	2	7	0	.222	0	0	.000
3 years		22	4	18	0	.182	0	0	.000

Burns, Jerome M. (Jerry)

Year	Team	Games	Wins	Losses	Ties	%	P Wins	P Losses	P %
1986	Vikings	16	9	7	0	.563	0	0	.000
1987	Vikings	15	8	7	0	.533	2	1	.667
1988	Vikings	16	11	5	0	.688	1	1	.500
1989	Vikings	16	10	6	0	.625	0	1	.000
1990	Vikings	16	6	10	0	.375	0	0	.000
1991	Vikings	16	8	8	0	.500	0	0	.000
6 years		95	52	43	0	.547	3	3	.500

by Grant a year later. When Bud retired for good in 1986, Jerry at last got the Vikings' position.

Burns had run a freewheeling offense in Minnesota with quarterbacks Fran Tarkenton and Tommy Kramer and that continued when Jerry became head coach. In many ways, Burns was not a typical NFL head coach. He did not wear a headset on the sidelines; he did not sleep in his office; and he did not have his own TV or radio program. Jerry once told *Sports Illustrated*, "You can't take yourself too seriously in this business. The thing I see that amuses me is coaches who take credit for the development of this guy and that guy. I don't know how much development you can ever do with a player. I'm never going to say I developed Fran Tarkenton." Tarkenton, for his part, said, "Working with him was the most enjoyable eight years of my career." The closest the Vikings ever got to the Super Bowl in Burns' six-year tenure was the 1987 NFC Championship game in which Darrin Nelson dropped a fourth down game-tying touchdown in the closing minute against the Redskins. Burns also was the coach when the Vikings made their ill-fated trade with Dallas for Herschel Walker. Most memorable was how he came to the defense of his beleaguered offensive coordinator Bob Schnelker after a win in 1989. Despite the victory, Burns went on a blistering tirade against the media at the treatment given to his assistant coach. At the end of the 1991 season, Jerry retired from football.

CABLE, THOMAS L. (TOM) 11/26/1964– Idaho. G; did not play professionally. *Apprenticeship:* College coach —14 years (4 as head coach); pro asst.— 3 years. *Roots:* Jim Mora, Jr., Lane Kiffin. *Branches:* Hue Jackson. *Coordinators/Key Assistants:* Ted Tollner then Hue Jackson handled the offense, while John Marshall ran the defense. *Hall of Fame Players:* None. *Primary Quarterbacks:* Jamarcus Russell, Jason Campbell. *Tendencies:* • His teams scored 18 points and allowed 23.6 per game • His teams ran 46.7% of the time, which

was 107% of the league average • Five starting quarterbacks in three years; 66% of starts to primary quarterbacks • Eight rookie starters in three years • Winning Full Seasons to Losing Full Seasons: 0:1.

While Tom Cable demonstrated some ability as a head coach for the Raiders, his story was clouded by a number of unseemly violent incidents off the field. Hailing from Merced, California, Cable blocked for quarterback Scott Linehan at Idaho when both future NFL coaches were college players under Dennis Erickson, and Tom moved directly onto the coaching staff in 1987. Cable worked mostly as a line coach from 1987 to 1999 for Idaho, San Diego State, Fullerton State, UNLV, California and Colorado before becoming head coach at his alma mater in 2000. Over the next four years, the Vandals won just 11 of 46 games. Next, Tom spent two years as UCLA's offensive coordinator and then joined the Falcons as Jim Mora, Jr.'s line coach in 2006.

After Mora was fired, Lane Kiffin hired him in Oakland in 2007. A year later, Kiffin was jettisoned four games into the season, and Cable took over. In three years, Cable's Raiders showed steady progress, reaching 8–8 in 2010, but Al Davis took great umbrage at Cable celebrating a .500 season and fired him. When Davis announced the hiring of Hue Jackson as Tom's replacement, he spent more time running down Cable than talking about Jackson. Although Davis was well aware of Cable's alleged violence towards women and of his mysterious role in the breaking the jaw of assistant coach Randy Hanson, he claimed that he had had enough of paying for Cable's legal problems. Tom took a job on the Seattle staff in 2011.

CALDWELL, JAMES (JIM) 1/16/1955– Iowa. DB; did not play professionally. *Apprenticeship:* College coach — 24 years (8 as head coach); pro asst.— 8 years. *Roots:* Tony Dungy. *Branches:* None. *Coordinators/Key Assistants:* Tom Moore and Clyde Christiansen ran the offense, while Larry Croyer then Mike Murphy handled the defense. *Hall of Fame Players:* None yet. *Pri-*

Cable, Thomas L. (Tom)									
Year	Team	Games	Wins	Losses	Ties	%	P Wins	P Losses	P %
2008	Raiders	12	4	8	0	.333	0	0	.000
2009	Raiders	16	5	11	0	.313	0	0	.000
2010	Raiders	16	8	8	0	.500	0	0	.000
3 years		44	17	27	0	.386	0	0	.000

Caldwell, James (Jim)									
Year	Team	Games	Wins	Losses	Ties	%	P Wins	P Losses	P %
2009	Colts	16	14	2	0	.875	2	1	.667
2010	Colts	16	10	6	0	.625	0	1	.000
2011	Colts	16	2	14	0	.125	0	0	.000
3 years		48	26	22	0	.542	2	2	.500

mary Quarterback: Peyton Manning. *Tendencies:* • His teams scored 22.8 points and allowed 23.4 per game • His teams ran 37.8% of the time, which was 88% of the league average • Four starting quarterback in three years; 67% of starts to primary quarterback • 15 rookie starters in three years • Winning Full Seasons to Losing Full Seasons: 2:1.

When Beloit, Wisconsin's Jim Caldwell was a defensive back at Iowa in the 1970s, he played against a Minnesota quarterback who would have a major influence on his career, Tony Dungy. Caldwell had a long rise in the profession and has worked for several top coaches. After a year at Iowa and three at Southern Illinois, Caldwell spent one season under Denny Green at Northwestern, three under Bill McCartney at Colorado, one under Howard Schnellenberger at Louisville and seven under Joe Paterno at Penn State. After helping to develop Kerry Collins at Penn State, Jim was named head coach at Wake Forest in 1993, but went just 26–63 over the next eight seasons before being fired. Dungy then hired him as quarterbacks coach in Tampa in 2001 and brought him to Indianapolis a year later. Peyton Manning said of his longtime position coach, "There's no question that he's taken my game to the next level.... The discipline he's brought to the drills; every quarterback should have a coach like that."

With the Colts, Caldwell carried the additional title of Assistant Head Coach and took over the team when Dungy retired after the 2008 season. Caldwell generated controversy in his first season when the Colts rested their starters at the end of the season with a 14–0 record, just as Jim's mentor Dungy had done in prior seasons. The Colts then lost the last two games of the regular season and were upset in the Super Bowl against the Saints. Still, it was a successful rookie season for Caldwell. The Colts began to slip a bit in 2010; only the inspired leadership of Manning led them back to the playoffs, where Caldwell lost more fan support with clock management problems in their postseason loss to the Jets. Despite winning 24 of his first 32 games as an NFL coach, Caldwell found himself under increasing scrutiny as fans and the media expressed doubts as to his ability to think on his feet and inspire respect. When Manning was lost to injury in 2011, the Colts collapsed to a 2–14 year and finished in the bottom five both in points scored and allowed. Team architect Bill Polian and his GM son Chris were fired while Caldwell was dismissed soon after. Jim signed to coach the Ravens' quarterbacks for 2012.

CALLAHAN, WILLIAM E. (BILL) 7/31/1956– Benedictine. QB; did not play professionally. *Apprenticeship:* College asst.—15 years; pro asst.—7 years. *Roots:* Ray Rhodes, Jon Gruden. *Branches:* Jim Harbaugh. *Coordinators/Key Assistants:* Marc Trestman handled the offense, while Chuck Bresnahan ran the defense. *Hall of Fame Players:* Jerry Rice and Rod Woodson. *Primary Quarterback:* Rich Gannon. *Tendencies:* • His teams scored 22.5 points and allowed 21.3 per game • His teams ran 40.7% of the time, which was 92% of the league average • Three starting quarterbacks in two years; 72% of starts to primary quarterback • Three rookie starters in two years • Winning Full Seasons to Losing Full Seasons: 1:1.

For 15 years, Chicago's Bill Callahan worked his way up the college coaching ranks from Illinois to Northern Arizona to Southern Illinois and finally to Wisconsin. For the Badgers, Callahan was the offensive line coach under Barry Alvarez and got to know Packers' assistant Jon Gruden. When the youthful Gruden was named offensive coordinator of the Eagles under new head coach Ray Rhodes in 1995, he brought in Callahan to coach Philadelphia's patchwork line. After three years, the very visible Gruden was named head coach in Oakland and brought along Callahan as his offensive coordinator. Gruden took the Raiders to the brink of the Super Bowl in four years, but wore out his welcome with owner Al Davis. Davis traded Gruden's rights to Tampa and elevated Callahan to head coach in 2002. As fate would dictate, both teams made the Super Bowl that year, and the Raider players made sure that everyone understood how much nicer it was to play under the low key Callahan than the intense Gruden. However, it turned out to be a Super Bowl mostly memorable for the extent to which Gruden outcoached his former pupil, as the Bucs dominated the Raiders from start to finish.

Despite winning 11 of 16 games in 2002 and reaching the Super Bowl, Callahan's star was greatly diminished by the championship meltdown. The Raiders were the third-oldest team in the league in 2003, and things quickly fell apart. Dissension rapidly spread in the Oakland locker room as Callahan lost control of the team. Due to this decline, Al Davis replaced him with generally unsuccessful Norv Turner at the end of the year. Bill returned to the college ranks, winning the coveted head coaching job at Nebraska, but he could manage just a 27–25 record in four years in Lincoln. That was not good enough for

Callahan, William E. (Bill)									
Year	Team	Games	Wins	Losses	Ties	%	P Wins	P Losses	P %
2002	Raiders	16	11	5	0	.688	2	1	.667
2003	Raiders	16	4	12	0	.250	0	0	.000
2 years		32	15	17	0	.469	2	1	.667

football-frenzied Husker alumni. Callahan had tried to turn the traditional power running team into a passing team and was excoriated. Even former coach and athletic director Tom Osborne commented, "We used to be a team people hated to play because they felt it for two or three weeks." Still a fine line coach, Callahan was hired by the Jets' Rex Ryan in 2008 as Assistant Head Coach in charge of the line and was responsible for New York employing a punishing ground attack to support young quarterback Mark Sanchez. Callahan moved on to Dallas as line coach for 2012.

CAMERON, MALCOLM (CAM) 2/6/1961– Indiana. QB; did not play professionally. *Apprenticeship:* College coach —16 years (5 as head coach); pro asst.— 8 years. *Roots:* Norv Turner and Marty Schottenheimer. *Branches:* None. *Coordinators/Key Assistants*: Cameron ran his own offense, while Dom Capers handled the defense. *Hall of Fame Players:* None. *Primary Quarterback:* Cleo Lemon. *Tendencies:* • His team scored 16.7 points and allowed 27.3 per game • His team ran 39.3% of the time, which was 90% of the league average • Three starting quarterbacks in one year; 44% of starts to primary quarterback • Five rookie starters in one year • Winning Full Seasons to Losing Full Seasons: 0:1.

Of the ten NFL coaches who won no more than one game in a season since the schedule was expanded to 16 games in 1978, only three survived that performance to remain in charge of the team: Jimmy Johnson, Steve Spagnuolo and Mike Riley. Cam Cameron was not so lucky in Miami; a change in management at the end of 2007 hastened his demise after his only season as an NFL coach. Born in Chapel Hill, North Carolina, Cameron began his career as a two-sport athlete at the Indiana University in the early 1980s, playing guard under Bobby Knight and quarterback

under Lee Corso. His first coaching position was as a graduate assistant under Bo Schembechler at Michigan in 1983, and he spent 11 years in Ann Arbor. In 1994, Norv Turner hired Cam as the quarterbacks coach in Washington, where he worked with Heath Shuler, Gus Frerotte and a third-stringer from Indiana, Trent Green. After three years with the Redskins, Cameron was named head coach at his alma mater, but produced a sickly 18–37 record from 1997 to 2001.

Marty Schottenheimer hired Cam as offensive coordinator in San Diego in 2002, and Cameron got the opportunity to prove he could run an effective offense when surrounded by talented players. The Chargers finished third, fifth and first in points scored from 2004 to 2006. Despite coming off a 14–2 season, Chargers' management slowly forced out Schottenheimer as coach after both Cameron and defensive coordinator Wade Phillips left for head coaching jobs in Dallas and Miami. With the Dolphins though, everything went wrong from his wasted first round draft choice of slight speedster Ted Ginn to his sorry quarterback choices of banged-up Trent Green, Charger retread Cleo Lemon and 26-year-old rookie John Beck. Miami lost the first 13 games of the season before upsetting the Ravens in overtime to stave off a winless campaign. Cameron was fired four days after the end of the season, but was hired as the Ravens offensive coordinator just three weeks later. Cam has done a good job improving the Baltimore offense and tutoring Joe Flacco, but Flacco expressed anger when quarterbacks coach Jim Zorn was fired in 2011. Cameron is viewed by some as being overly intransigent and inflexible, so his performance in Baltimore will be monitored closely by the media and fans.

CAMPBELL, FRANCIS M. (MARION) 5/25/1929– Georgia. Played DE and DT for the 49ers and Eagles

Cameron, Malcolm (Cam)									
Year	Team	Games	Wins	Losses	Ties	%	P Wins	P Losses	P %
2007	Dolphins	16	1	15	0	.063	0	0	.000
1 year		16	1	15	0	.063	0	0	.000

Campbell, Francis M. (Marion)									
Year	Team	Games	Wins	Losses	Ties	%	P Wins	P Losses	P %
1974	Falcons	6	1	5	0	.167	0	0	.000
1975	Falcons	14	4	10	0	.286	0	0	.000
1976	Falcons	5	1	4	0	.200	0	0	.000
1983	Eagles	16	5	11	0	.313	0	0	.000
1984	Eagles	16	6	9	1	.406	0	0	.000
1985	Eagles	15	6	9	0	.400	0	0	.000
1987	Falcons	15	3	12	0	.200	0	0	.000
1988	Falcons	16	5	11	0	.313	0	0	.000
1989	Falcons	12	3	9	0	.250	0	0	.000
9 years		115	34	80	1	.300	0	0	.000

from 1954 to 1961. *Apprenticeship:* Pro asst.—13 years. *Roots:* Mike Holovak, Norm Van Brocklin and George Allen. *Branches:* Fred Bruney (i), Frank Gansz, Tom Coughlin and Al Groh. *Coordinators/Key Assistants:* For the Falcons, John Rauch and Bill Nelsen ran the offense in Campbell's first stint, and Rod Dowhower did so in his second stint; for the Eagles, Dick Wood then Ted Marchibroda ran the offense. Campbell ran his own defense in all sites along with the help of Fred Bruney. *Hall of Fame Players:* Deion Sanders, Reggie White. *Primary Quarterbacks:* Steve Bartkowski, Ron Jaworski and Chris Miller. *Tendencies:* • His teams scored 15 points and allowed 21.6 per game • His teams ran 41.5% of the time, which was 86% of the league average • Ten starting quarterbacks in nine years; 73% of starts to primary quarterbacks • 26 rookie starters in nine years • Winning Full Seasons to Losing Full Seasons: 0:7.

Of the 88 coaches who have coached at least 100 games in the NFL, Marion Campbell's winning percentage of .300 is the lowest; coaches with this poor a record do not usually last nine seasons in the league. Granted, the three teams that Campbell was hired to coach were not good, but he did little to improve any of these teams. He was an excellent defensive coach of the "bend-don't-break" style, of whom Eagles' coach Dick Vermeil once said, "There was no better football coach in America than Campbell. When we went to the Super Bowl, I got the credit because I was the head man; but we never would have gotten there without Marion and his staff." As a head coach, though, Campbell never had a winning season; three times his team was last in scoring and five times finished in the bottom three in the category.

Marion Campbell was known as "Swamp Fox" ever since a University of Georgia PR man began referring to him by that name, mistakenly assuming that Campbell was named after the famous officer from the Revolution, Francis Marion, a fellow South Carolina native. After an eight-year NFL career as a tough defensive lineman and team leader, Campbell was hired by Mike Holovak in Boston to coach the Patriots' defensive line in 1962. Two seasons later, Marion joined the Vikings' staff of former Eagle quarterback Norm Van Brocklin and put together the forerunner of the famous Purple People Eater front four. After Van Brocklin was fired in 1967, Campbell worked on George Allen's staff in Los Angeles for two years. However, when Van Brocklin got a second chance as the

Falcons' coach, he brought in Marion to coach the defense in 1969. By 1974, Atlanta grew tired of the ineffectual, ranting Van Brocklin, and Campbell was promoted to head coach in mid season. Despite winning just one of six games, that year he was rehired in January, one month before new Atlanta GM Pat Peppler was hired. Peppler watched the team go 4–10 in 1975 and wanted to fire Campbell to hire his own man, but owner Rankin Smith insisted on retaining Campbell. Smith grew so tired of Peppler's complaints about the coach that five games into the 1976 season he ordered Peppler to name himself head coach.

Campbell landed in Philadelphia in the off-season as Vermeil's defensive coach and built one of the best defenses in the league over the next several years. When Vermeil tearfully stepped aside from coaching burnout in 1983, the Eagles promoted Campbell. Philadelphia was plagued with aging players and an unstable, financially-strapped owner who sold the team in 1985 to Norman Braman, a car dealer focused on the bottom-line. The 1985 Eagles were saddled with 11 holdouts during training camp and a quarterback controversy between veteran Ron Jaworski and rookie Randall Cunningham; with the 6–9 team clearly in disarray, Braman fired Campbell with one game still to play.

Marion landed on his feet with Atlanta again the following season. Falcons' coach Dan Henning was on the brink of being fired after 1985, but persuaded Rankin Smith to give him one more chance if he hired the well-respected Campbell as defensive coach. The Falcons' defense did improve in 1986, but the team still posted a losing record, so Smith fired Henning and, for the second time, promoted Campbell to head coach in 1987. In the midst of the third losing season of his second stint in Atlanta, Marion resigned with four games to go in 1989 and was replaced by line coach Jim Hanifan. It was the end of a 28-year NFL coaching career—perhaps the most extensive example of a skilled assistant coach unable to fulfill the more demanding requirements of head coach.

CAMPBELL, HUGH T. 5/21/1941– Washington State. Played WR in the Canadian Football League. *Apprenticeship:* College coach—8 years (7 as head coach); CFL head coach—6 years; USFL head coach—1 year. *Roots:* None. *Branches:* Jerry Glanville. *Coordinators/Key Assistants:* Kay Dalton then Joe Farugalli ran the offense, while Jerry Glanville handled the

Campbell, Hugh T.									
Year	Team	Games	Wins	Losses	Ties	%	P Wins	P Losses	P %
1984	Oilers (Titans)	16	3	13	0	.188	0	0	.000
1985	Oilers (Titans)	14	5	9	0	.357	0	0	.000
2 years		30	8	22	0	.267	0	0	.000

defense. *Hall of Fame Players:* Earl Campbell, Bruce Matthews, Warren Moon and Mike Munchak. *Primary Quarterback:* Warren Moon. *Tendencies:* • His teams scored 16.2 points and allowed 26.2 per game • His teams ran 43.8% of the time, which was 93% of the league average • Two starting quarterbacks in two years; 93% of starts to primary quarterback • Six rookie starters in two years • Winning Full Seasons to Losing Full Seasons: 0:2.

"Gluey Hughy" was a sure-handed record-setting receiver for Washington State in the early 1960s. Drafted in the fourth round by San Francisco, the San Jose native was cut in training camp for being too slow. Campbell went north and caught on with the Saskatchewan Roughriders of the Canadian Football League in 1963. Hugh played for Saskatchewan for six of the next seven years, twice being named a CFL All-Star. In 1970, he retired from playing to become head coach of Whitworth, a small college in Washington, and stayed there for seven years with a 30–30 record. In 1977, Campbell returned to the CFL as head coach of the Edmonton Eskimos. With Warren Moon at quarterback, Hugh's Eskimos went to the Grey Cup finals for six years in a row and won the championship the last five. Campbell attained a sterling 79–22–5 record with Edmonton and began looking for a new challenge. He was named head coach of the Los Angeles Express of the brand new USFL in 1983, but led the team to only a mediocre 8–10 record. The team was then sold, and Hugh was let go.

The Houston Oilers, who were in the running to sign new free agent quarterback Warren Moon, named Campbell as their head coach in January 1984. Moon signed with Houston one month later to reunite the successful CFL pair. Campbell was an understated, relaxed coach who treated his players like men. When signed by Houston, he promised an explosive offensive attack, but both Moon and the Oilers struggled right from the start. Meanwhile, Campbell was under increasing pressure from GM Ladd Herzeg to make changes to his staff. After less than two seasons, Hugh was fired and replaced by his defensive coordinator, Jerry Glanville. Campbell returned to Edmonton as the GM for 10 years, and from 1998 to 2007, served as the Eskimos' team president. Edmonton won two more championships with Campbell as GM and two with him as president. In 2007, he retired after having been part of 10 Grey Cup champions, including one as a player.

CAMPO, DAVID C. (DAVE) 7/18/1947– Central Connecticut State. DB; did not play professionally. *Apprenticeship:* College asst.—18 years; pro asst.—11 years. *Roots:* Jimmy Johnson, Barry Switzer and Chan Gailey. *Branches:* None. *Coordinators/Key Assistants:* Jack Reilly then Bruce Coslet ran the offense, while Mike Zimmer handled the defense. *Hall of Fame Players:* Troy Aikman and Emmitt Smith. *Primary Quarterbacks:* Quincy Carter and Troy Aikman. *Tendencies:* • His teams scored 15.8 points and allowed 21.4 per game • His teams ran 48.9% of the time, which was 112% of the league average • Seven starting quarterbacks in three years; 54% of starts to primary quarterbacks • 13 rookie starters in three years • Winning Full Seasons to Losing Full Seasons: 0:3.

Dave Campo's won-lost records for the Cowboys represented perfect consistency in that the team finished 5–11 every season. However, the offense declined each season as the heroes of the great 90's teams aged and retired. Once Troy Aikman retired in 2001, Campo ran through Quincy Carter, Chad Hutchinson, Ryan Leaf, Clint Stoerner and Anthony Wright at quarterback. While Campo's temperament clearly was that of an assistant coach, the primary reason for the Cowboys' collapse was owner Jerry Jones acting as the team's GM — mismanaging the salary cap, drafting poorly and making a series of bad free agent signings. In this environment, Campo was in a difficult situation with his players. One player told the *New York Times* in 2001, "I used to think Coach Campo was the stand-in until Jerry hired the next stooge." In the same article, Dave told the *Times,* "This is the first time since Jimmy [Johnson] that only the coach, and not Jerry has spoken to the players in team meetings during the season."

Born in New London, Connecticut, Campo was a lifelong assistant coach, having worked at Central Connecticut State, Albany, Bridgeport, Pittsburgh, Washington State, Boise State, Oregon State, Weber State, Iowa State, Syracuse and Miami from 1971 to 1988 and then in the pros with the Cowboys from 1989 to 1999. His tenure as head coach is memorable for two things. First, in the 2000 opener, his team was totally unprepared and shocked by Andy Reid's Eagles beginning the season with an onside kick en route to beating Dallas 41–14. Second, Campo's 2002 squad was the second team featured in NFL Films' now-annual training camp show, "Hard Knocks." After being

Campo, David C. (Dave)									
Year	Team	Games	Wins	Losses	Ties	%	P Wins	P Losses	P %
2000	Cowboys	16	5	11	0	.313	0	0	.000
2001	Cowboys	16	5	11	0	.313	0	0	.000
2002	Cowboys	16	5	11	0	.313	0	0	.000
3 years		48	15	33	0	.313	0	0	.000

fired by Dallas, Campo spent two years on Butch Davis' Browns' staff and three in Jacksonville before returning to the Cowboys as secondary coach in 2008.

CAPERS, ERNEST D. (DOM) 8/7/1950– Mount Union. LB; did not play professionally. *Apprenticeship:* College asst.—12 years; USFL asst.—2 years; pro asst.—9 years. *Roots:* Jim Mora, Sr., Bill Cowher. *Branches:* None. *Coordinators/Key Assistants*: For the Panthers, Joe Pendry then Gil Haskell ran the offense, while Chris Palmer handled the offense for the Texans. Vic Fangio ran the defense for both teams. *Hall of Fame Players:* None. *Primary Quarterbacks:* Kerry Collins and David Carr. *Tendencies:* • His teams scored 17.9 points and allowed 21.7 per game • His teams ran 45.5% of the time, which was 102% of the league average • Six starting quarterbacks in eight years; 86% of starts to primary quarterbacks • 26 rookie starters in eight years • Winning Full Seasons to Losing Full Seasons: 1:7.

Dom Capers is one of three men (with Paul Brown and Lud Wray) to be the first coach of two new franchises; Capers is the only one of the three who did so without having any ownership stake in either franchise. The Cambridge, Ohio native is a coaching lifer, having worked as an assistant at Kent State, Washington, Hawaii, San Jose State, California, Tennessee and Ohio State from 1972 to 1983, before joining Jim Mora's staff with the Philadelphia Stars of the USFL in 1984. When the USFL went under before the 1986 season, Capers followed Mora to New Orleans where he was secondary coach for six years. In 1992, Bill Cowher hired Dom as defensive coordinator for the Steelers, and Capers huddled with secondary coach Dick LeBeau for three years developing and polishing an array of zone blitz schemes in which defensive linemen dropped into coverage and linebackers or defensive backs blitzed the quarterback from unexpected places. The Steelers' defensive success led to Capers' first head coaching assignment with the expansion Carolina Panthers in 1995.

Capers emphasized planning and dedication at his opening news conference in Carolina, "I believe that a head coach has to have knowledge and control of all phases of the game. I assure you that I will know as much about what's going on with the offense and the kicking game as I will the defense." Dom could not be outworked. Panthers' tackle Blake Brockermeyer once told *Sports Illustrated* after a game with the division rival 49ers, "We out-prepared them. Our coaches spent the night here during the week and looked at everything they've ever done on film." The Panthers spent wisely in the free agent market and won a record seven games in their initial season. The next season, Capers had them in the NFC Conference championship with a 12–4 record. Just as quickly, though, everything unraveled. Quarterback Kerry Collins had an alcohol problem and made some impolitic racial comments that tore the team apart. Linebacker Kevin Greene had a meltdown with an assistant coach on the sidelines. Capers lost control of his aging team as it dropped back to seven wins in year three and to just four in year four.

Fired in 1999, Dom was hired as Tom Coughlin's defensive coordinator in Jacksonville for two years before he was named head coach of the expansion Houston Texans in 2001. Once again, he tried to accumulate a strong veteran presence, and once again, he quickly went with a young quarterback (David Carr this time). However, it took him three years to get to seven wins this time, and he was fired, once again, after four seasons. Since Houston, Capers spent two years as an assistant in Miami and one in New England under Bill Belichick before Mike McCarthy hired him as defensive coordinator in Green Bay in 2009. In two years, Dom transformed the leaky Packer defense into one that equaled their explosive offense. Super Bowl XLV turned into a zone blitz clinic as Capers' Packers matched up with Dick Lebeau's Steelers in a memorable showdown that won Capers a Super Bowl ring at long last.

CARROLL, PETER C. (PETE) 9/15/1951– Pacific. S: did not play professionally. *Apprenticeship:* College asst.—6 years; pro asst.—10 years. *Roots:* Bud Grant, Jerry Burns and Bruce Coslet. *Branches:* None. *Coordinators/Key Assistants*: For the Jets, Ray Sherman ran the offense and Foge Fazio handled the defense; for

Capers, Ernest D. (Dom)									
Year	*Team*	*Games*	*Wins*	*Losses*	*Ties*	*%*	*P Wins*	*P Losses*	*P %*
1995	Panthers	16	7	9	0	.438	0	0	.000
1996	Panthers	16	12	4	0	.750	1	1	.500
1997	Panthers	16	7	9	0	.438	0	0	.000
1998	Panthers	16	4	12	0	.250	0	0	.000
2002	Texans	16	4	12	0	.250	0	0	.000
2003	Texans	16	5	11	0	.313	0	0	.000
2004	Texans	16	7	9	0	.438	0	0	.000
2005	Texans	16	2	14	0	.125	0	0	.000
8 years		128	48	80	0	.375	1	1	.500

the Patriots, Larry Kennan then Ernie Zampese ran the offense, while Steve Sidwell handled the defense; for the Seahawks, Jeremy Bates then Darrell Bevell ran the offense, while Casey Bradley handled the defense. *Hall of Fame Players:* Ronnie Lott, Curtis Martin and Art Monk. *Primary Quarterbacks:* Boomer Esiason, Drew Bledsoe, Matt Hasselbeck, Tarvaris Jackson. *Tendencies:* • His teams scored 19.8 points and allowed 20.3 per game • His teams ran 41.7% of the time, which was 95% of the league average • Seven starting quarterbacks in six years; 92% of starts to primary quarterbacks • 14 rookie starters in six years • Winning Full Seasons to Losing Full Seasons: 2:3.

While Pete Carroll has always been seen as a smart technician as a coach, his youthful enthusiasm generally has been viewed with disdain in the NFL despite his great success as a college coach. San Francisco's Carroll worked as a college assistant from 1978 to 1983 at Iowa State, Ohio State, North Carolina State and Pacific before landing his first NFL job as the secondary coach of the Bills in 1984. Pete held the same position for the Vikings from 1985 to 1989, and then took over as Bruce Coslett's defensive coordinator for the Jets from 1990 to 1993. When Coslett was dumped in 1994, Carroll was promoted to head coach.

All went well for the 1994 Jets at first. The team got off to a 6–5 start and was competing for the playoffs until the infamous fake spike "clock play" by Dan Marino pulled out a Dolphins' win in week 12. The Jets lost their last five games, and Carroll was replaced by Rich Kotite because, ironically, octogenarian Jets' owner Leon Hess insisted he wanted to win *now*. George Seifert hired Carroll as defensive coordinator in San Francisco in 1995, and the team won the Super Bowl that year. After a second season with the 49ers, Pete was a hot coordinator in the league; for his second chance as head coach, he replaced the confrontational but effective Bill Parcells who grumbled his way out of New England in 1997 after a Super Bowl appearance.

Patriot players reacted as if they had been freed from prison. Quarterback Drew Bledsoe told *Sports Illustrated,* "There's give-and-take [now]. Before, there was just take." Tight end Ben Coates told the same magazine, "Bill's yelling and screaming had worn itself out. I don't think his leaving will affect us. Once we're

on the field, things will be the same, just quieter." Defensive back Willie Clay told the press, "This is the New England Patriots, coached by Pete Carroll. It's our team. Last year, we were just players on Bill's team." While New England did reach the playoffs in 1997 and 1998, the team won fewer games in each of Carroll's three years there. The team was neither as good nor as tough, and ultimately, Pete was seen as too soft for the NFL.

After a season out of coaching, Carroll was named head coach of USC in 2001. In nine seasons in Los Angeles, Pete restored the Trojans to national prominence. From 2001 to 2009, USC went 83–19, won 34 straight games in one stretch, turned out an army of future NFL players and won two national championships. Carroll told the *New York Times* in 2003, "I would really like to grow old doing this. I'm just going to keep having fun, enjoying my work and listening to my songs." However, right before the USC program was hit in 2010 with heavy sanctions from the NCAA for infractions committed during Carroll's reign; Pete left LA and was named head coach and executive Vice-President of the Seattle Seahawks.

With Seattle, it was the same old Pete, jumping up and down on the sidelines and exhorting his players with high fives and by telling them how "jacked up" he was. While the Seahawks sported a losing record in 2010, they did reach the postseason and upset New Orleans before being ousted by Chicago. A second 7–9 season, though, produced a third place finish in 2011 with Carroll's legacy looking less like that of a great coach than just a great *college* coach.

CARSON, LEON H. (BUD) *4/28/1931–12/7/2005.* North Carolina. DB; did not play professionally. *Apprenticeship:* College coach—15 years (5 as head coach); pro asst.—17 years. *Roots:* Chuck Noll, Ray Malavasi, Frank Kush, John Mackovic and Joe Walton. *Branches:* Jim Shofner (i). *Coordinators/Key Assistants:* Marc Trestman then Jim Shofner ran the offense, while Dan Radakovich then Jim Vechiarella handled the defense. *Hall of Fame Players:* Ozzie Newsome. *Primary Quarterbacks:* Bernie Kosar. *Tendencies:* • His teams scored 18.5 points and allowed 19.6 per game • His teams ran 40.2% of the time, which was

Carroll, Peter C. (Pete)									
Year	Team	Games	Wins	Losses	Ties	%	P Wins	P Losses	P %
1994	Jets	16	6	10	0	.375	0	0	.000
1997	Patriots	16	10	6	0	.625	1	1	.500
1998	Patriots	16	9	7	0	.563	0	1	.000
1999	Patriots	16	8	8	0	.500	0	0	.000
2010	Seahawks	16	7	9	0	.438	1	1	.500
2011	Seahawks	16	7	9	0	.438	0	0	.000
6 years		96	47	49	0	490	2	3	.400

88% of the league average • Two starting quarterbacks in three years; 96% of starts to primary quarterback • Seven rookie starters in two years • Winning Full Seasons to Losing Full Seasons: 1:0.

Hailing from Brackenridge, Pennsylvania, Bud Carson was one of the most influential assistant coaches in NFL history, but he had to wait until he was 59 years old until he got his brief opportunity as head coach in the league. Bud's long road to NFL head coach began as a defensive back for North Carolina from 1949 to 1951. Subsequently, Carson never played pro ball. Instead, he spent four years in the Marines and then coached high school ball for three more years. In 1957, he was hired as an assistant at his alma mater and stayed with the Tarheels for nine years. After a season at South Carolina and one at Georgia Tech, Bud replaced Bobby Dodd as Tech's head coach in 1967. While the Yellow Jackets did win the Sun Bowl in 1970, their five-year record during Carson's tenure was a so-so 27–27, and Bud was fired in 1972. Chuck Noll hired him that year as the Steelers' defensive backs coach, and promoted Bud to defensive coordinator in 1973.

Carson's six years in Pittsburgh coincided with the glory years of the Steel Curtain defense. With the Steelers, Bud perfected the Cover 2 defense that was later popularized by Tony Dungy; Dungy learned the intricacies of the scheme firsthand from Carson as a Pittsburgh defensive back and later took it to Minnesota, Tampa and Indianapolis. The Cover 2 is a zone defense that requires an active, effective front four that can pressure the quarterback without blitzes, a small, fast and smart linebacker corps that can drop into pass coverage, physical bump-and-run corners and clever, wide-ranging safeties to cover the deep pass. The 1970s' Steelers had all of that and ran Carson's exacting schemes to suffocating perfection. While the players respected Carson, he was a bit gruff and hard to know. Years later, Pittsburgh safety Mike Wagner told Tom Danyluk in *The Super 70's*, "A lot of us never showed Carson our appreciation, probably because his temperament sometimes didn't blend well with our personalities. He wasn't the type of guy who said 'great job' or 'good effort' to the players." In particular, Bud had a running battle with proud cornerback Mel Blount, but Blount ended up in the Hall of Fame after being coached by Bud Carson.

In 1978, Carson moved on and spent the next decade as itinerant defensive coordinator with the Rams (1978–1981), the Colts (1982), the Chiefs (1983) and the Jets (1985–1988), bumping heads with his superiors from time to time. Finally in 1989, Bud was named head coach of the Cleveland Browns in the wake of Marty Schottenheimer. His tenure opened with a bang — beating the Steelers 51–0 in the opener — although Carson was embarrassed by having beaten his mentor, Noll, so badly. While the aging Browns were on the decline, they did go to the playoffs in Bud's first year. His second year was a different story. Carson changed offensive coordinators, but the team fell apart on both sides of the ball. After losing 42–0 to Buffalo and dropping to 2–7 on the season, Bud was fired. Browns receiver Brian Brennan said afterwards of Carson, "Bud was an eccentric guy that we respected very much and as a result we played hard because we liked Bud." Carson himself summed up his experience to *Sports Illustrated* years later, "To be a successful head coach, you have to be a great communicator. I'm not that. I'm a teacher."

Rich Kotite, who knew Bud from the Jets, hired him as the Eagles defensive coordinator in 1991. Carson took over Buddy Ryan's fearsome Eagle defense and improved it, allowing 3.5 fewer points per game over the next couple of years. When Kotite was fired after the 1994 season, Bud retired. Despite the fact he had heart problems and was battling emphysema, Carson made two coaching comebacks with the Rams — in 1997 under Dick Vermeil and in 2000 under Mike Martz — before retiring for good. Although Carson died in 2005, his legacy lives on through the choking Cover 2 defense prevalent throughout the NFL.

CASEY, EDWARD L. (EDDIE) 5/16/1894–7/26/1966. Harvard. Played WB for the Buffalo All Americans in 1920. *Apprenticeship:* College coach — 15 years (10 as head coach). *Roots:* None. *Branches:*

Carson, Leon H. (Bud)

Year	Team	Games	Wins	Losses	Ties	%	P Wins	P Losses	P %
1989	Browns	16	9	6	1	.594	1	1	.500
1990	Browns	9	2	7	0	.222	0	0	.000
2 years		25	11	13	1	.460	1	1	.500

Casey, Edward L. (Eddie)

Year	Team	Games	Wins	Losses	Ties	%	P Wins	P Losses	P %
1935	Redskins	11	2	8	1	.227	0	0	.000
1 year		11	2	8	1	.227	0	0	.000

None. *Coordinators/Key Assistants:* None. *Hall of Fame Players:* Cliff Battles and Turk Edwards. *Primary Quarterbacks:* None. *Tendencies:* • His team scored 5.9 points and allowed 11.2 per game • His team ran 71.9% of the time, which was the league average • Three rookie starters in one year • Winning Full Seasons to Losing Full Seasons: 0:1.

Eddie Casey of Natick, Massachusetts, had a big year in 1920. He helped Harvard beat Oregon in the Rose Bowl, appeared in one APFA game as a 160-pound wingback for the Buffalo All-Americans and began his college coaching career with Mount Union College in Ohio. Casey spent two years coaching Mount Union to a 7–9–1 record and then four posting a 15–16–2 mark at Tufts University before returning to his alma mater as an assistant in 1926. After five years, he succeeded his old backfield mate Arnie Horween as the Crimson head coach in 1931. From 1931 to 1934, Eddie led Harvard to a 20–11–1 record, but could only beat Yale once. Faced with dissension on his staff and grumbling from alumni, Casey resigned.

Meanwhile, George Preston Marshall, bellicose owner of the Boston Redskins, was looking for his third coach in four years. After being refused by prominent college coaches Dick Harlow, Dick Hanley and Biff Jones, Marshall offered the job to the soft-spoken Casey. Eddie signed a two-year contract, but not surprisingly lasted only one. Tackle Jim Barber later recalled, "We won our first game and the coach we had [Casey] said, 'Fellas, if you never win another game, you're a great bunch of guys.' And we didn't win another game." Barber's memory was a little fuzzy. Boston won its opener, lost the next eight games and then finished with a second win and a tie, but Casey was fired nonetheless.

For the next five years, Eddie became the regional director of the National Youth Administration and then returned to coaching briefly with the Boston Bears of the third American Football League in 1940. The Bears went 5–4–1, but folded. Casey was a Lt. Commander in the Naval Reserve during World War II (he had previously served in the Navy during World War I) and later worked as an IRS agent and a middle school principal.

CAWTHON, PETER W. (PETE) 3/24/1898–12/31/1962. Southwestern. HB; did not play profes-sionally. *Apprenticeship:* College coach—16 years (15 as head coach). *Roots:* None. *Branches:* Frank Bridges (i) and Ed Kubale (i). *Coordinators/Key Assistants:* Frank Bridges coached the ends and Ed Kubale coached the line. *Hall of Fame Players:* Bruiser Kinard. *Primary Quarterbacks:* None. *Tendencies:* • His teams scored 8.1 points and allowed 21 per game • His teams ran 62.6% of the time, which was 93% of the league average • Six rookie starters in two years • Winning Full Seasons to Losing Full Seasons: 0:1.

Now forgotten, Houston's Pete Cawthon was famous in the 1940s as "Football's Whirling Dervish," as a *Saturday Evening Post* profile from 1944 phrased it. The article's accompanying photographs depicted Cawthon on the sidelines with his head in hands, gesturing wildly and rolling around on the ground. He was referred to as the "world's worst loser" who regularly had to take sedatives to sleep because, in his own accented words, "I just caint face anybody. I cain't sleep. I caint eat. I just gotta get out of town. It nearly kills me to lose." Although Cawthon did a lot of losing in the pros, he was very successful in the college ranks.

Pete lettered in baseball, football and basketball at Southwestern University and began his baseball coaching career while still a student during World War I. After college, Cawthon coached high school and also the baseball team at Rice Institute. His first football coaching job was with Austin College from 1923 to 1927 and he compiled a 21–20–4 record. During that time, Pete met Knute Rockne and adopted the Notre Dame Shift as his own offense. Frenetically, he worked himself to the point of exhaustion and resigned following the 1927 season for health reasons. After two years as a Southwest Conference official, Cawthon was named head coach at Texas Tech in 1930 and went 76–32–6 over the next 11 years. With the Red Raiders about to deemphasize football in 1941, Pete resigned. He spent one year as the line coach at Alabama under Frank Thomas and then was named head coach of the Brooklyn Dodgers in 1943.

Dodgers' owner Dan Topping had requested suspending operations of his team due to the war in 1943, but was refused permission by the league, so Cawthon was hired late in the off season and was not given much material with which to work. Pete continued using the Notre Dame system in the pros and emphasized hidden ball plays. One player told Roger Godin for

Cawthon, Peter W. (Pete)									
Year	Team	Games	Wins	Losses	Ties	%	P Wins	P Losses	P %
1943	Brooklyn Dodgers (defunct)	10	2	8	0	.200	0	0	.000
1944	Brooklyn Tigers (defunct)	5	0	5	0	.000	0	0	.000
2 years		15	2	13	0	.133	0	0	.000

The Brooklyn Football Dodgers that Cawthon's offense, "wasn't much of a football system compared to the Chicago Bears and Clark Shaughnessy and those people. It was just off tackle, around end ... reverse ... up the middle, and that was about the size of the offensive plan." The Dodgers were shut out in their first four games in 1943 and finished just 2–8. The next year was even worse. After opening the year with five straight defeats, Cawthon resigned. His biographer Etta Lynch told the story in *Tender Tyrant* that Pete cashed his settlement check at a local bank, stuffed the cash in his suitcase and took the train out of town that night. Cawthon spent 1945–1947 as an assistant to Gus Dorais in Detroit and later served as the athletic director at Alabama in the 1950s. Upon leaving the game, Pete operated his own summer youth camp and did quite well in the oil business.

CHILDRESS, BRAD 6/27/1956– Eastern Illinois. QB; did not play professionally. *Apprenticeship:* College asst.—20 years; pro asst.—8 years. *Roots:* Andy Reid. *Branches:* Mike Tomlin and Leslie Frazier. *Coordinators/Key Assistants:* Darrell Bevell ran the offense, while Mike Tomlin then Leslie Frazier handled the defense. *Hall of Fame Players:* None yet. *Primary Quarterbacks:* Brett Favre and Tarvaris Jackson. *Tendencies:* • His teams scored 22.5 points and allowed 20.4 per game • His teams ran 46.8% of the time, which was 106% of the league average • Six starting quarterbacks in five years; 61% of starts to primary quarterbacks • 10 rookie starters in five years • Winning Full Seasons to Losing Full Seasons: 2:1.

The inspiration for the frustrated fan web site firechilly.com, Brad Childress had some success in Minnesota, but ultimately became the focus of public disappointment with Vikings' football. While the team showed slow and steady improvement in their record during his tenure, Childress' mental sideline stumbles with clock management, odd substitutions and dull play calling left fans feeling the team could have achieved more with a sharper coach.

Hailing from Aurora, Illinois, Childress played quarterback and wide receiver downstate at Eastern Illinois and went immediately into college coaching upon graduation in 1978. Seven years at Illinois, mostly under Mike White, four at Northern Arizona,

one at Utah and eight at Wisconsin under Barry Alvarez culminated with Brad joining Andy Reid's staff in Philadelphia in 1999 to work with offensive coordinator Rod Dowhower (who had hired Childress for his only other pro experience in 1985 with the Colts). In 2003, Childress replaced Dowhower as offensive coordinator and began to be mentioned as a potential head coach even though Reid called all the plays for the Eagles and petulant star receiver Terrell Owens refused to speak to Childress.

With the Vikings reeling from off-the-field scandals in 2006, new owner Zygi Wilf saw the stolid Childress as just the man to instill discipline in the team. Childress did steady the team and get it moving in the right direction, but his inability to find an effective quarterback was the team's main weakness. Enter free agent Brett Favre whom Childress courted and even chauffeured from the airport in 2009. Minnesota rode a rejuvenated Favre to a 12–4 record and the NFC Championship game until a typical Favre interception cost the team the game. From that point on, everything went downhill for the team and Childress. He had struggled to get along with the balky Favre in good times; in 2010, after dispatching three players to jet to Favre's Mississippi home and beg him to return, the two bickered in the press all year. Childress squabbled with other players as well and then traded a third round pick to acquire Randy Moss only to cut him four games later without consulting the owner. With the 3–7 Vikings in complete disarray, Wilf fired Childress in November. In the end, Childress was seen as incommunicative, stubborn, inflexible and unable to get the best out of his players. In 2012, he was hired as offensive coordinator for the Browns under Pat Shurmur who was the Eagles' quarterback coach when Brad was in Philadelphia.

CHRISTIANSEN, JOHN L. (JACK) 12/20/1928– 6/29/1986. Colorado State. Played DB for the Detroit Lions from 1951 to 1958. *Apprenticeship:* Pro asst.—5 years. *Roots:* Red Hickey. *Branches:* Bill Johnson and Jim Shofner (i). *Coordinators/Key Assistants:* Bill Johnson ran the offense, while Christiansen handled the defense with help from Dick Voris. *Hall of Fame Players:* Jim Johnson, Leo Nomellini, Joe Perry, Bob St. Clair and Dave Wilcox. *Primary Quarterbacks:* John

Childress, Brad									
Year	Team	Games	Wins	Losses	Ties	%	P Wins	P Losses	P %
2006	Vikings	16	6	10	0	.375	0	0	.000
2007	Vikings	16	8	8	0	.500	0	0	.000
2008	Vikings	16	10	6	0	.625	0	1	.000
2009	Vikings	16	12	4	0	.750	1	1	.500
2010	Vikings	10	3	7	0	.300	0	0	.000
5 years		74	39	35	0	.527	1	2	.333

Brodie. *Record:* **Hall of Fame Player.** *Tendencies:* • His teams scored 20.9 points and allowed 25.3 per game • His teams ran 46.7% of the time, which was 93% of the league average • Four starting quarterbacks in five years; 69% of starts to primary quarterback • 12 rookie starters in five years • Winning Full Seasons to Losing Full Seasons: 1:3.

The defensive secondary of the champion Lions' teams of the 1950s were known as "Chris' Crew" for their leader, Hall of Fame defensive back and punt returner Jack Christiansen, a Kansas native who starred at Colorado State. Jack went directly from playing for the Lions in 1958 to coaching the defense for the 49ers in 1959 under Red Hickey. The talented 49ers never won more than seven games for Hickey, and he was fired three games into the 1963 season with Christiansen being elevated to head coach. Unfortunately for Jack a day after he was hired, star quarterback John Brodie was sidelined for the rest of the year with a broken arm. After two losing seasons, Christiansen led the team back to mediocrity with another seven-win season in 1965.

Jack was a players' coach. Halfback John David Crow told *Sports Illustrated* in 1965, "He's the easiest coach I ever played for. Oh, he may get mad and chew you out if you need it, but he's been a player recently and he knows how to treat players. He doesn't humiliate you, and he doesn't talk it up too much. This is a game for professionals and we don't need pep talks, and here we don't get them." After two more mediocre seasons, though, an anonymous player told the same magazine, "I think the real trouble is that we're not a mentally tough club. I hate to say that, but I think that may be it."

Bouncing from Brodie to George Mira to Steve Spurrier and back at quarterback, the offense was inconsistent, but spectacular at times. Christiansen's defense, though, never allowed fewer than 23 points per game in any season. After being fired, Jack stayed in the Bay area by joining John Ralston's staff at Stanford in 1968. Four years later, he was named the school's head coach after offensive coach Mike White turned the job down. From 1972 to 1976, Stanford went 30–22–3 but Jack gained a reputation for being too easy on the players and too tough on the alumni. Christiansen was replaced by Bill Walsh and subsequently returned to the pros, coaching in Kansas City in 1977, in Seattle from 1978 to 1982 and in Atlanta in 1983 before cancer sidelined him and ultimately killed him.

CLARK, EARL H. (DUTCH) 10/11/1906–8/5/1978. Colorado College. Played QB/TB for the Portsmouth Spartans from 1931 to 1932 and the Detroit Lions from 1934 to 1938. *Apprenticeship:* College coach — 2 years (1 as head coach). *Roots:* None. *Branches:* None. *Coordinators/Key Assistants:* None. *Hall of Fame Players:* None. *Primary Quarterbacks:* None. *Record:* **Hall of Fame Player; Player-Coach** for 2 years. *Tendencies:* • His teams scored 14.1 points and allowed 15.4 per game • His teams ran 64.3% of the time, which was 98% of the league average • 22 rookie starters in six years • Winning Full Seasons to Losing Full Seasons: 2:3.

Dutch Clark was a charter member of both the College and Pro Football Halls of Fame as a player; as a coach, though, he was no immortal. Born in Fowler, Colorado, Dutch began his career as an All-American at the University of Colorado, graduating in 1930. He stayed on as an assistant coach for a year before signing with the Portsmouth Spartans in 1931.

Christiansen, John L. (Jack)

Year	Team	Games	Wins	Losses	Ties	%	P Wins	P Losses	P %
1963	49ers	11	2	9	0	.182	0	0	.000
1964	49ers	14	4	10	0	.286	0	0	.000
1965	49ers	14	7	6	1	.536	0	0	.000
1966	49ers	14	6	6	2	.500	0	0	.000
1967	49ers	14	7	7	0	.500	0	0	.000
5 years		67	26	38	3	.410	0	0	.000

Clark, Earl H. (Dutch)

Year	Team	Games	Wins	Losses	Ties	%	P Wins	P Losses	P %
1937	Lions	11	7	4	0	.636	0	0	.000
1938	Lions	11	7	4	0	.636	0	0	.000
1939	Rams	11	5	5	1	.500	0	0	.000
1940	Rams	11	4	6	1	.409	0	0	.000
1941	Rams	11	2	9	0	.182	0	0	.000
1942	Rams	11	5	6	0	.455	0	0	.000
6 years		66	30	34	2	.470	0	0	.000

After two All Pro seasons in Portsmouth, Clark retired to become the head coach of the Colorado School of Mines in 1933, but the team won just one game that year. In 1934, Clark returned to the former Spartans who since had moved to Detroit to become the Lions. He continued to star on the field, leading the Lions to an NFL title in 1935 and winning All Pro honors four more years.

When head coach Potsy Clark left the Lions in 1937, Dutch seemed the natural successor. Under Dutch, Detroit won seven games and finished second both in 1937 and 1938. He resigned after 1938 because he felt he was "coach number two" behind meddlesome owner George Richards. Just days later, the Rams signed Dutch as their head coach after they were unable to acquire Cliff Battles from Washington. Clark spent four seasons in Cleveland, but never produced a winning season. One reason was that he couldn't draw on his own considerable playing talents. He requested permission to play for the Rams in 1939, but the Lions refused to relinquish his rights as a player. Detroit finally released Clark as a player in 1941, but he never did appear in a game for the Rams.

By his final year as a coach, Clark had the team running out of a modified T formation, but he was not much of a strategic innovator. Hall of Fame center Alex Wojciechowicz told Richard Whittingham years later for *What a Game They Played* that Dutch did not impress Alex as a coach, "A lot of people did not like him, and I was one of them. No personality. No charisma. He never taught me a thing, neither did his assistants. He just played the basics, running, running, running, running. It's a good thing to be basic, but, my God, you need a lot more in the pros." Dutch went into the army in 1943 and coached Seattle in the Pacific Coast Football League in 1944 to a 5–5–1

mark. Later, he served as head coach and athletic director of the University of Detroit without much success His Titans went 13–17 from 1951 to 1953.

CLARK, GEORGE M. (POTSY) 3/20/1894– 11/8/1972. Illinois. QB; did not play professionally. *Apprenticeship:* College coach —12 years (9 as head coach). *Roots:* None. *Branches:* None. *Coordinators/Key Assistants:* Clark had Jerry Allard and Bob Rosen on his staff in 1938, George Christensen in 1939 and Clare Randolph in 1940. *Hall of Fame Players:* Dutch Clark, Bruiser Kinard, Ace Parker and Alex Wojciechowicz. *Primary Quarterbacks:* Dutch Clark and Ace Parker. *Record:* NFL Championship 1935. *Tendencies:* • His teams scored 13.1 points and allowed 10.3 per game • His teams ran 74.4% of the time, which was 106% of the league average • 48% of starts to primary quarterbacks • 44 rookie starters in ten years • Winning Full Seasons to Losing Full Seasons: 6:2.

Potsy Clark was a personable man of many talents. Raised on an Illinois farm in Carthage, he was given his odd nickname by a local veterinarian. At the University of Illinois, Potsy quarterbacked Bob Zuppke's first undefeated Fighting Illini teams in 1914 and 1915, while also playing shortstop on the baseball team well enough to be offered a contract by the Giants' John McGraw and the Senators' Clark Griffith. Instead, Clark took an assistant coaching job at Kansas in 1916 and then coached service football during the war. In 1919, he returned to his alma mater as an assistant before getting his first head coaching assignment leading Michigan Agricultural (now Michigan State) to a 4–6 mark in 1920. From there he moved on to Kansas (16–17–6 from 1921 to 1925), Minnesota (1926 as an assistant) and Butler (14–9–1 from 1927 to 1929). He also coached baseball at each stop.

Clark, George M. (Potsy)									
Year	*Team*	*Games*	*Wins*	*Losses*	*Ties*	*%*	*P Wins*	*P Losses*	*P %*
1931	Portsmouth Spartans (Lions)	14	11	3	0	.786	0	0	.000
1932	Portsmouth Spartans (Lions)	12	6	2	4	.667	0	0	.000
1933	Portsmouth Spartans (Lions)	11	6	5	0	.545	0	0	.000
1934	Lions	13	10	3	0	.769	0	0	.000
1935	Lions	12	7	3	2	.667	1	0	1.000
1936	Lions	12	8	4	0	.667	0	0	.000
1937	Brooklyn Dodgers (defunct)	11	3	7	1	.318	0	0	.000
1938	Brooklyn Dodgers (defunct)	11	4	4	3	.500	0	0	.000
1939	Brooklyn Dodgers (defunct)	11	4	6	1	.409	0	0	.000
1940	Lions	11	5	5	1	.500	0	0	.000
10 years		118	64	42	12	.593	1	0	1.000

Potsy spent 1930 selling insurance and then was named head coach of the Portsmouth Spartans. He stayed with that franchise through 1936 even after it moved to Detroit to become the Lions. Clark's teams were a continual challenger to the domination by the league powers, the Packers and Bears. Four times they finished second in scoring and five times finished in the top three in points allowed. The 1932 Spartans tied the Bears for the NFL lead and the two squared off in the first NFL playoff game, held indoors on a shortened field at Chicago Stadium because of a blizzard. The game was controversial and later ushered in league rules changes as to where a pass can be thrown as well as the initiation of hashmarks on the field to eliminate sideline scrimmages. The 1934 Lions won their first 10 games, the first seven by shutouts, but then lost the last three games to the Packers and Bears (each time by three points) and finished second in the west. While the 1935 Lions won three fewer games than the previous season and shutout just three opponents, they stormed to the NFL title — Clark's only championship team.

Potsy was a fiery guy who favored pep talks. Dutch Clark said of him, "He was a great handler of men. He had a way that was different and could always get that little extra out of you." Dutch's teammate Glenn Presnell told NFL Films, "We called Potsy 'the Little General' because he was a strict disciplinarian. He worked us real hard. He was a stickler for conditioning. I think we were always in better shape than most of the teams we played." Brooklyn half back Joe Maniaci recalled to Roger Godin in *The Brooklyn Football Dodgers*, "Potsy Clark was in my mind a great football coach, but he was very selfish. When it came to playing the game, when it came to defense work or anything, what he says goes. You had to play it ... his way ... if you had the ability in football and ... had something to say, it was against his principals. You carried out everything he said or you didn't stay in Brooklyn."

In conflict with Detroit management, Clark was fired a year after the championship, despite going 8–4 in 1936. He immediately was signed by the struggling Brooklyn Dodgers. Three mediocre years in Brooklyn led to Potsy returning to Detroit, under new ownership, in 1940, but he left a year later to coach the University of Grand Rapids to a 6–2 season with future President Gerald Ford as his line coach. After serving as a Commander in the Navy during World War II, Clark coached Nebraska for one year and then returned to Grand Rapids for two years before jumping back to Nebraska in 1948 where he spent five years as athletic director. His tally at Nebraska was a disappointing 6–13. At the time he retired from football, only Hall of Famers George Halas, Curly Lambeau, Steve Owen, Jimmy Conzelman, Ray Flaherty and Paul Brown had won more games in the NFL than Potsy. In retirement, Clark kept busy as a stockbroker into his seventies.

CLARK, MONTE D. 1/24/1937–9/16/2009. Southern California. Played T for the 49ers, Cowboys and Browns from 1959 to 1969. *Apprenticeship:* Pro asst.— 6 years. *Roots:* Don Shula. *Branches:* Marty Schottenheimer. *Coordinators/Key Assistants:* For the 49ers, Doug Gerhart handled the offense and Floyd Peters ran the defense; for the Lions, Bob Schnelker then Ted Marchibroda then Bill Nelsen handled the offense, while Marty Schottenheimer then Maxie Baughan then Ed Beard ran the defense. *Hall of Fame Players:* Jim Johnson. *Primary Quarterbacks:* Jim Plunkett, Eric Hipple and Gary Danielson. *Tendencies:* • His teams scored 19.5 points and allowed 19.5 per game • His teams ran 51.5% of the time, which was 101% of the league average • 12 starting quarterbacks in eight years; 68% of starts to primary quarterbacks • 23 rookie starters in eight years • Winning Full Seasons to Losing Full Seasons: 3:4.

Monte Clark from Fillmore, California, was an imposing figure on the field and on the sidelines at 6'6". Clark was co-captain of the football team as a senior at USC and then was drafted in the fourth round by San Francisco in 1959. After three years as a 49ers' defensive tackle, Monte was traded to Dallas and shifted to offense in 1962. The following year, he was traded to Cleveland for All Pro guard Jim Ray Smith who wanted to play closer to his Texas home. With the Browns, Clark's career took off at last as he

Clark, Monte D.									
Year	Team	Games	Wins	Losses	Ties	%	P Wins	P Losses	P %
1976	49ers	14	8	6	0	.571	0	0	.000
1978	Lions	16	7	9	0	.438	0	0	.000
1979	Lions	16	2	14	0	.125	0	0	.000
1980	Lions	16	9	7	0	.563	0	0	.000
1981	Lions	16	8	8	0	.500	0	0	.000
1982	Lions	9	4	5	0	.444	0	1	.000
1983	Lions	16	9	7	0	.563	0	1	.000
1984	Lions	16	4	11	1	.281	0	0	.000
8 years		119	51	67	1	.433	0	2	.000

became a starter on one of the two best offensive lines in the NFL in the 1960s (along with Green Bay's). Clark retired after the 1969 season and was hired as line coach of the Dolphins by Don Shula solely on the strong recommendation of Browns' coach Blanton Collier.

With Miami, Clark took five castoffs from other teams and molded them into the best offensive line of the decade as the Dolphins steamrolled to back-to-back Super Bowl titles. In 1976, Monte was named head coach and director of player personnel for the woeful 49ers. In a controversial move, Clark traded three number one draft picks and a number two to the Patriots for a shopworn Jim Plunkett. However, the team improved by three games in 1976. The next year, new owner Eddie DeBartolo brought in scorched-earth GM Joe Thomas to run the team. Well aware of Thomas' abrasive and abrupt style, Clark refused to give up his personnel duties, so he was fired in the off-season. However, Thomas would last just two seasons by the Bay.

A year later, Monte was hired as head coach of the Lions. He would spend seven years in Detroit, but make just two playoff appearances in that time. Clark was very much a players' coach. All Pro defensive end Bubba Baker said of Monte after his death from cancer in 2009, "Like a good teacher, he said you can be good and have a long career, and man he got in my face about it. He had higher expectations of me than I did of myself." After a 4–11–1 1984 season, Clark was fired and dropped out of football for five years. In the 1990s, though, Clark filled many roles. He spent a year as Miami's director of player personnel, worked as a broadcaster, coached an American-football team in Russia (the Minsk Belarus Zubers), and worked as line coach for the Dolphins, Stanford and the University of California. In 1999, Monte returned to Detroit as a special consultant, working with incompetent GM Matt Millen for most of the next 10 years.

CLARK, MYERS A. (ALGY) 1903–Deceased. Ohio State. Played HB for the Brooklyn Dodgers, Cleveland Indians, Boston Braves, Cincinnati Reds and Philadelphia Eagles from 1930 to 1934. *Apprenticeship:* None. *Roots:* None. *Branches:* None. *Coordinators/Key Assistants:* None. *Hall of Fame Players:* None. *Primary Quarterbacks:* None. *Record:* **Player Coach.** *Tendencies:* • His team scored 1.2 points and allowed 30.4 per game • His team ran 69.1% of the time,

which was 94% of the league average • One rookie starter in one year • Winning Full Seasons to Losing Full Seasons: 0:1.

Ohio native Algy Clark graduated from Ohio State in 1927 and embarked on an anonymous NFL career as a blocking back and kicker that took him to five cities in five years. Clark began playing professionally in 1930 with the Brooklyn Dodgers, moved on to the Cleveland Indians in 1931, played for the Boston Braves in 1932 and returned to Ohio with the Cincinnati Reds in 1933. Each of these four teams was a first year expansion franchise, and each was named after a major league baseball team. Only Brooklyn achieved a winning record.

The 1933 Reds finished 3–6–1 and were outscored 110–38. Their player-coach, former Giant Mike Palm, quit after that first year, and Clark was promoted to replace him. Algy told the press that the Reds would be, "the hardest fighting club in the league ... I guarantee my eleven will be there fighting every minute of the game and will play heads-up football all the time."

However, the season started out bad and then turned disastrous. The Reds lost their first six games by a collective score of 141–10 and followed that by losing game number seven to Detroit 38–0 and game number eight to lowly Philadelphia 64–0. Fighting every minute and playing heads-up ball will take you only so far. Years later, fullback Red Corzine told *Pro!* That Clark's offense had "no deception whatever" and lacked imagination. The Eagles, who would finish 4–7, scored more than half their season's points in that one game. The bankrupt 0–8 Reds were sold that week to the owner of the semipro St. Louis Gunners who took in five Reds players (not Clark) and finished out Cincinnati's 1934 schedule. Oddly enough, Algy then caught on with Philadelphia for the last game of his forgettable five-year pro football career.

COLLIER, BLANTON L. 7/2/1906–3/22/1983. Georgetown (KY). Did not play professionally. *Apprenticeship:* Pro asst.— 9 years; college head coach — 8 years. *Roots:* Paul Brown. *Branches:* Dick Modzelewski (i). *Coordinators/Key Assistants:* Dub Jones then Nick Skorich handled the offense; while Howard Brinker ran the defense. *Hall of Fame Players:* Jim Brown, Lou Groza, Gene Hickerson, Leroy Kelly, Tommy McDonald and Paul Warfield. *Primary Quarterbacks:* Frank Ryan and Bill Nelsen. *Record:* NFL

Clark, Myers A. (Algy)									
Year	*Team*	*Games*	*Wins*	*Losses*	*Ties*	*%*	*P Wins*	*P Losses*	*P %*
1934	Cincinnati Reds (defunct)	8	0	8	0	.000	0	0	.000
1 year		8	0	8	0	.000	0	0	.000

Championship 1964. *Tendencies:* • His teams scored 25.8 points and allowed 20.3 per game • His teams ran 53.8% of the time, which was 107% of the league average • Six starting quarterbacks in eight years; 94% of starts to primary quarterbacks • 18 rookie starters in eight years • Winning Full Seasons to Losing Full Seasons: 7:0.

Much like Tony Dungy, Kentucky-native Blanton Collier was a quiet, studious gentleman who inspired his players by his intelligence, composure, dignity and decency. The respected Collier began his career at Paris (Kentucky) High School in 1928 and coached various sports there for the next 15 years. During World War II, Blanton was stationed at Great Lakes Naval Reserve where he got to know Paul Brown who was coaching the base football team. The two became friends and colleagues over the next couple of years, and Brown hired Collier as his top assistant when Paul formed the Browns in 1946.

Brown came to rely on Blanton's astute study and teaching, with Collier being particularly active in coaching both the offensive and defensive backs. For his part, Blanton was happy, telling the *Saturday Evening Post* in 1949, "I'd rather work under Paul Brown than coach a national champion. Besides, if I ever left here I'd look for a high school job. I couldn't take the headaches that alumni and trustees and faculty and students give a college coach." And he was effective in Cleveland. Tony Grossi in *Tales from the Browns' Sideline* quoted star quarterback Otto Graham on Collier, "He was the brains of our offense. He did most of the coaching with me, frankly. Without him, we wouldn't have been as great as we were."

With his reputation, Collier had several opportunities to coach elsewhere, but always removed himself from consideration. He told his family that the only three places he ever wanted to work were Paris High School, the University of Kentucky and the Cleveland Browns. In 1954, Kentucky offered Blanton his dream job and he accepted. With the Wildcats, Collier was following in the footsteps of Paul "Bear" Bryant who was moving on to Texas A&M. Although Collier assembled a top flight coaching staff that included at various times future NFL coaches Don

Shula, Chuck Knox, Bill Arnsparger, Howard Schnellenberger and John North, the team recorded just a 41–36–3 mark from 1954 to 1961 before Blanton was fired. Collier was never comfortable with the dishonest dance of college recruiting and ultimately it cost him his job.

Paul Brown brought Blanton back to Cleveland in 1962 to coach the backfield again. However, when Collier began to draw favorable notice by setting up a system to allow Cleveland quarterbacks to audible out of Paul Brown's ironclad play calls, he was relegated to intense film study. Film study suited Collier, though, and it even brought him closer to owner Art Modell who watched film with Blanton since Paul Brown had rebuffed both of them. Brown stubbornly refused to alter his ways to meet changing times and in 1962 was fired by the owner he foolishly snubbed. Modell offered Collier the head coaching job, but Blanton insisted on getting his old friend's blessing. Even though, Paul gave Collier the okay, he was angry that Blanton would agree to take the job and ended their friendship.

One of Paul Brown's biggest failings was relating to proud star fullback Jim Brown. Jim chafed under Paul's inflexibility, but came alive under the patient Collier. He told Terry Pluto for *When All the World Was Browns Town*, "I loved talking to that man. He had a way of making you feel important. He allowed you to breathe, to grow." Blanton consulted with Jim daily in practice and memorably defended him with a Kentucky twist to *Sports Illustrated* against the criticism that Jim didn't block, "Man o' War was a fabulous racehorse. Undoubtedly, he could have pulled a plow, too, but his greatest talent was running." Collier also had to defuse some racial tension on the Browns during his first year, but in 1964 Cleveland reached the NFL title game against the heavily favored Colts coached by Blanton's protégé, Don Shula. Not only did the Browns upset the powerful Colts that day, but they did so by shutting out the Johnny Unitas–led offense to win the first Browns' championship in nine years.

The Browns remained contenders throughout Collier's eight years as head coach. In addition to de-

Collier, Blanton L.

Year	Team	Games	Wins	Losses	Ties	%	P Wins	P Losses	P %
1963	Browns	14	10	4	0	.714	0	0	.000
1964	Browns	14	10	3	1	.750	1	0	1.000
1965	Browns	14	11	3	0	.786	0	1	.000
1966	Browns	14	9	5	0	.643	0	0	.000
1967	Browns	14	9	5	0	.643	0	1	.000
1968	Browns	14	10	4	0	.714	1	1	.500
1969	Browns	14	10	3	1	.750	1	1	.500
1970	Browns	14	7	7	0	.500	0	0	.000
8 years		112	76	34	2	.688	3	4	.429

veloping castoffs Frank Ryan and Bill Nelsen into winning quarterbacks, Blanton also ensured the team transitioned smoothly from Jim Brown to Leroy Kelly when Jim unexpectedly retired after the 1965 season. Collier introduced option blocking to the Browns, giving the backs greater freedom in finding a hole. Five times the Browns were in the top three in scoring and three times in the top three in turnover ratio during Collier's reign. Throughout his career, Blanton had a severe hearing problem that continued to worsen with time. Eventually, that and his approaching 65th birthday hastened his retirement in 1971. Five years later, he came back briefly to assist new head coach Forrest Gregg with the backfield, but then retired for good. He and Paul Brown never reconciled.

COLLIER, JOEL D. (JOE) 6/7/1932– Northwestern. WR; did not play professionally. *Apprenticeship:* College asst.—3 years; pro asst.—6 years. *Roots:* Lou Saban. *Branches:* John Mazur. *Coordinators/Key Assistants:* John Mazur ran the offense and Dick McCabe handled the defense. *Hall of Fame Players:* Billy Shaw. *Primary Quarterbacks:* Jack Kemp. *Tendencies:* • His teams scored 20.3 points and allowed 20.1 per game • His teams ran 46% of the time, which was 99% of the league average • Three starting quarterbacks in three years; 83% of starts to primary quarterbacks • Seven rookie starters in three years • Winning Full Seasons to Losing Full Seasons: 1:1.

Rock Island's Joe Collier spent 26 years as a defensive coordinator in professional football and was known as one of the ablest strategists in the game. Bills' Hall of Fame guard Billy Shaw told Bob Carroll for *When the Grass Was Real*, "What Coach Collier can do with Xs and Os is matchless." However, his brief tenure as a low key head coach early in his career taught him that not everyone is cut out to be a head coach.

Collier was an All-American end at Northwestern in 1952 and was drafted in the 22nd round of the 1954 NFL draft. However, he also was drafted by Uncle Sam that year and spent the next three years in the army. Upon his discharge, Joe began his coaching career on Lou Saban's Western Illinois staff in 1957. When Saban was hired to be the first coach of the Boston Patriots in 1960, he brought his staff with him. Saban was fired midseason in 1961, but landed in Buffalo the following year and hired Collier as the Bills' defensive coach.

Saban built the Bills to be similar to Vince Lombardi's Packers. They featured a basic but effective run-oriented offense backed by a punishing, unyielding defense. Collier fashioned the AFL's best defense by utilizing the Bills' athletic talent with his imaginative schemes. In the 1965 AFL title game against the high-powered Chargers, for example, Collier had defensive linemen dropping off into pass coverage — anticipating the zone blitz schemes of the future — and at times had the entire front seven standing upright at the snap, with no one in a three-point stance. After back-to-back AFL titles, the mercurial Saban quit in 1966 after conflicts with owner Ralph Wilson, and the 34-year-old Collier was appointed his successor.

Joe drove the Bills back to the AFL title game in 1966, but they were stomped by Kansas City and missed the chance to play in the first Super Bowl that year. One key mistake of Collier's was never finding a reliable placekicker. A second mistake the next year was trading underutilized quarterback Daryle Lamonica to Oakland for a washed up Art Powell. The team slipped to 4–10 in 1967, and the bottom fell out in 1968. After losing a sloppy preseason game in 1968, an angry Collier ordered a full-pads scrimmage the next day and starting quarterback Jack Kemp had his leg broken. Buffalo would go through four more quarterbacks that year, but Collier wasn't around to see it; he was fired after week two.

Lou Saban resurfaced as Denver's head coach in 1969 and once again hired Collier to run the defense. This time Joe would not only outlast Saban, but the three coaches who succeeded him as well. Collier served as Denver's defensive coordinator from 1969 to 1988, under Saban, Jerry Smith, John Ralston, Red Miller and Dan Reeves and made four fruitless Super Bowl trips. Joe sought intelligent, small, quick players as he switched from a 4–3 to a 3–4 defense, and the vaunted Bronco defense became known as the "Orange Crush." He told Larry Zimmer for *Denver Broncos: Colorful Tales of the Orange and Blue*, "We were a four-man line team and then one year we lost Lyle Alzado on the first play of the first game with a knee injury, so we decided to switch over to the 3–4. We had more good linebackers than we had linemen. We had been playing a 3–4 a little bit, but now we went to it full-time. We put in more variations and the players played it for a while. You could just see it coming together. The key was that we kept that group together."

Collier, Joel D. (Joe)									
Year	Team	Games	Wins	Losses	Ties	%	P Wins	P Losses	P %
1966	Bills	14	9	4	1	.679	0	1	.000
1967	Bills	14	4	10	0	.286	0	0	.000
1968	Bills	2	0	2	0	.000	0	0	.000
3 years		30	13	16	1	.450	0	1	.000

In 1989, Dan Reeves felt the defense was too insular from the rest of the team and fired Collier. Two years later, Joe returned to the Patriots, where his career had begun, as defensive coordinator under former Broncos' assistant Dick MacPherson for two years until he retired. His son Joel has worked as a secondary coach for 15 years in the NFL.

CONKRIGHT, WILLIAM F. (RED) 4/17/1914–10/1/1980. Oklahoma. Played C and LB for the Bears, Rams, Redskins and Dodgers from 1937 to 1944. *Apprenticeship:* Pro asst.— 6 years; college coach — 7 years (3 as head coach). *Roots:* Adam Walsh, Paul Brown, Red Dawson, Cecil Isbell, Walt Driskill, Eddie Erdelatz, Marty Feldman. *Branches:* Walt Michaels. *Coordinators/Key Assistants:* Walt Michaels coached the defense. *Hall of Fame Players:* Jim Otto. *Primary Quarterbacks:* Cotton Davidson. *Record:* **Interim Coach.**

Born in Beggs, Oklahoma, Red Conkright captained the Oklahoma Sooners in 1936 and was drafted in the fifth round of the very first NFL draft that year by the Bears. Conkright played center in the league for eight years: two with Chicago, five with the Cleveland Rams and one split between Brooklyn and Washington. In 1945, he retired from the Rams as a player, but joined their coaching staff for the team's championship season. When the Rams moved to Los Angeles the next year, Red stayed in Cleveland as an assistant coach and advance scout for the new Browns' franchise in the All America Football Conference that also won a title. In 1947, he moved on to Buffalo for two years and then the Colts for one. When the AAFC folded, Conkright got a job as line coach for Mississippi State. Throughout the 1950s' Red worked at MSU and the University of Houston before being named head coach at Stephen F. Austin in 1959. After compiling a 6–25–1 record over the next three years at Austin, Conkright was fired.

The Oakland Raiders hired Red as defensive coach and director of player personnel in April 1962. After the Raiders dropped the first five games of the season (11 losses in a row going back to 1961), Conkright replaced Marty Feldman as head coach. Red announced that the team would employ the "running gun" offense and the "monster" defense." The Running Gun was a shortened shotgun formation designed to keep pressure off the quarterback; the Monster was a blitzing defense that might send as many as eight pass rushers at a time. Despite this opening fanfare, Oakland lost the next eight games under Conkright, bringing their season record to 0–13 and the losing streak to 19 games. For the week 13 game, both Conkright and line coach Ollie Spencer were off scouting, leaving defensive backfield coach Walt Michaels as the only coach on the sidelines to oversee a 38–20 loss to Houston. Conkright returned the next week as the Raiders knocked off the Patriots 20–0 at home to end the losing streak at last. The Patriots had been eliminated from contention the day before and clearly exhibited that they had little for which to play. Conkright was let go and replaced by Al Davis who ushered in a reign of Raider excellence. Red went on to work as a scout.

CONZELMAN, JAMES G. (JIMMY) 3/6/1898–8/5/1970. Washington (MO). Played B for the Decatur Staleys, Rock Island Independents, Milwaukee Badgers, Detroit Panthers and Providence Steam Roller from 1920 to 1929. *Apprenticeship:* None. *Roots:* None. *Branches:* Phil Handler and Buddy Parker. *Coordinators/Key Assistants:* For the Cardinals, Buddy Parker coached the backs, Phil Handler the line and Dick Plasman the ends. *Hall of Fame Players:* Ed Healey, Fritz Pollard and Charley Trippi. *Primary Quarterbacks:* Paul Christman. *Record:* **Hall of Fame Coach**; began as **Player-Coach; Owner-Coach** (in Detroit); NFL Championships 1928, 1947. *Tendencies:*
• His teams scored 13.8 points and allowed 11.4 per game • His teams ran 60.4% of the time in his post–1932 career, which was the 97% of the league average • Three starting quarterbacks in three T formation years; 80% of starts to primary quarterback • 48 rookie starters in 16 years • Winning Full Seasons to Losing Full Seasons: 8:6.

Garrulous and gregarious, Jimmy Conzelman was a gridiron renaissance man. Not only did he play and coach football, but also boxed, played minor league baseball, composed songs, played the piano, painted, wrote, gave speeches, published a newspaper

Head-to-Head:		
Hall of Fame Opponent	Regular Season	Postseason
Guy Chamberlin	1–1	0–0
Ray Flaherty	0–2	0–0
George Halas	5–13–3	0–0
Curly Lambeau	7–11–2	0–0
Greasy Neale	2–2	1–1
Steve Owen	2–3	0–0
Total	17–32–5	1–1

Conkright, William F. (Red)									
Year	Team	Games	Wins	Losses	Ties	%	P Wins	P Losses	P %
1962	Raiders	9	1	8	0	.111	0	0	.000
1 year		9	1	8	0	.111	0	0	.000

and, finally, worked as a broadcaster, sports executive and business manager. One speech that he gave during World War II, "A Young Man's Mental and Physical Approach to War," was required reading at West Point and was read into the *Congressional Record* twice.

Conzelman was born in St. Louis and attended Washington University in his hometown in 1916. He went into the Navy in 1917 and was stationed at the Great Lakes Naval Base where he was middleweight boxing champion and played quarterback on the base football team. Jimmy and teammate George Halas led the 1918 Great Lakes team to a Rose Bowl victory and were discharged in January 1919. Returning to Washington University for his final year of college in 1919, Conzelman then reconnected with Halas on the newly formed Decatur Staleys of the fledgling APFA in 1920. He moved on to Rock Island the next year and in the

middle of the team's second game was named the team's new player-coach after mercurial team owner Walter Flanigan fired player-coach Frank Coughlin in between plays. He also served as a player-manager for the Rock Island minor league baseball team that summer. In the NFL, Jimmy worked as a player-coach for the rest of the 1920s with five different teams. He even owned the Detroit Panthers' franchise, but turned it back to the league as unprofitable in 1926. His greatest success came with the Providence Steam Roller that he led to the NFL title in 1928, three years before the franchise folded. A knee injury ended his playing career in 1929, but he continued as the Providence coach through 1930.

In 1931, Conzelman was hired to coach an independent team just starting in his hometown, the St. Louis Gunners, and led them to a 5–2–1 record. The

Conzelman, James G. (Jimmy)

Year	Team	Games	Wins	Losses	Ties	%	P Wins	P Losses	P %
1921	Rock Island Independents (defunct)	5	4	1	0	.800	0	0	.000
1922	Milwaukee Badgers (defunct)	3	0	3	0	.000	0	0	.000
	Rock Island Independents (defunct)	7	4	2	1	.643	0	0	.000
1923	Milwaukee Badgers (defunct)	12	7	2	3	.708	0	0	.000
1925	Detroit Panthers (defunct)	12	8	2	2	.750	0	0	.000
1926	Detroit Panthers (defunct)	12	4	6	2	.417	0	0	.000
1927	Providence Steam Roller (defunct)	14	8	5	1	.607	0	0	.000
1928	Providence Steam Roller (defunct)	11	8	1	2	.818	0	0	.000
1929	Providence Steam Roller (defunct)	12	4	6	2	.417	0	0	.000
1930	Providence Steam Roller (defunct)	11	6	4	1	.591	0	0	.000
1940	Cardinals	11	2	7	2	.273	0	0	.000
1941	Cardinals	11	3	7	1	.318	0	0	.000
1942	Cardinals	11	3	8	0	.273	0	0	.000
1946	Cardinals	11	6	5	0	.545	0	0	.000
1947	Cardinals	12	9	3	0	.750	1	0	1.000
1948	Cardinals	12	11	1	0	.917	0	1	.000
16 years		167	87	63	17	.572	1	1	.500

following year, Jimmy returned to his alma mater as head football coach and stayed there for the rest of the decade, winning three Missouri Valley Conference titles and compiling a 40–35–2 record. In 1940, Charley Bidwill brought him back to the NFL as the head coach of the woeful Cardinals. Conzelman had even penned a team fight song, "It's in the Cards to Win," but in three years Chicago could not manage a winning season. Jimmy left the Cardinals for baseball's St. Louis Browns in 1943. As assistant to the team president, he presided over the only American League pennant the team would ever win in 1944.

After three years in baseball, Conzelman was lured back to the Cardinals by Bidwill who opened up his wallet, enabling Jimmy to build a post-war juggernaut with the Dream Backfield of All-Americans Paul Christman, Charley Trippi, Elmer Angsman and Pat Harder. In his first stint with the Cards, Conzelman had relied on the Notre Dame system for his offense. In his second go-round, though, he converted to the T formation, and the team finished in the top three in scoring all three years. 1946 brought the Cardinals' first winning season in 11 years, while 1947 delivered a championship. Conzelman was a players' coach, a fun-loving storyteller and prankster. Marshall Goldberg told David Cohen for *Rugged and Enduring*, "Jimmy Conzelman was a wonderful guy, and he was very imaginative. He was quite a personality and very clever, and he got the most out of his boys."

The Cardinals played in back-to-back title games against the Philadelphia Eagles in 1947 and 1948, and both were in bad weather. In Chicago in 1947, the field was covered with ice and the Cardinals burst through Philadelphia's eight-man line for long touchdown runs of 44, 70 and 70 yards, in addition to having a 75-yard punt return touchdown. The Eagles later complained that they were forced to take off their spikes by the officials, rendering the footing too slick. The following year it was Chicago's turn to complain as the 1948 championship in Philadelphia was played in a blizzard. The only touchdown came after backup quarterback Ray Mallouf fumbled at his own 17, leading to a short touchdown drive for the Eagles in the 7–0 game.

Unfortunately, the Cardinals were also a team with a black cloud following them. Owner Charley Bidwill died suddenly in April 1947. In October 1947, rookie punter Jess Burkett perished in a plane crash. Most shocking of all, star tackle Stan Mauldin died in the locker room from a heart attack following an opening day victory over the Eagles on September 24, 1948. With these deaths weighing on Conzelman, as well as his desire to spend more time with his young son, Jimmy left coaching for good after the season. He told reporters, "I am very tired. This is a helluva grind." Conzelman worked in public relations for an advertising firm in St. Louis until retirement. He was elected to the Hall of Fame in 1964 and was presented for induction by his lifelong friend, Supreme Court Justice William O. Douglass.

CORYELL, DONALD D. (DON) 10/17/1924– 7/1/2010. Washington. DB; did not play professionally. *Apprenticeship:* College coach —16 years (15 as head coach). *Roots:* None. *Branches:* Ray Perkins, Jim Hanifan, Joe Gibbs, Rod Dowhower, Al Saunders, Jim Mora, Jr. *Coordinators/Key Assistants*: For the Cardinals, Joe Gibbs and Jim Hanifan were the key offensive coaches, while Ray Willsey ran the defense. For the Chargers, Joe Gibbs then Dave Levy then Ernie Zampese were the key offensive coaches, while Jackie Simpson then Jack Pardee then Tom Bass then Dave Adolph then Ron Lynn ran the defense. *Hall of Fame Players:* Fred Dean, Dan Dierdorf, Charlie Joiner, Don Maynard, Jackie Smith, Roger Wehrli and

Coryell, Donald D. (Don)									
Year	*Team*	*Games*	*Wins*	*Losses*	*Ties*	*%*	*P Wins*	*P Losses*	*P %*
1973	Cardinals	14	4	9	1	.321	0	0	.000
1974	Cardinals	14	10	4	0	.714	0	1	.000
1975	Cardinals	14	11	3	0	.786	0	1	.000
1976	Cardinals	14	10	4	0	.714	0	0	.000
1977	Cardinals	14	7	7	0	.500	0	0	.000
1978	Chargers	12	8	4	0	.667	0	0	.000
1979	Chargers	16	12	4	0	.750	0	1	.000
1980	Chargers	16	11	5	0	.688	1	1	.500
1981	Chargers	16	10	6	0	.625	1	1	.500
1982	Chargers	9	6	3	0	.667	1	1	.500
1983	Chargers	16	6	10	0	.375	0	0	.000
1984	Chargers	16	7	9	0	.438	0	0	.000
1985	Chargers	16	8	8	0	.500	0	0	.000
1986	Chargers	8	1	7	0	.125	0	0	.000
14 years		195	111	83	1	.572	3	6	.333

Kellen Winslow. *Primary Quarterbacks:* Jim Hart and Dan Fouts. *Tendencies:* • His teams scored 24.5 points and allowed 22.3 per game • His teams ran 47.9% of the time, which was 93% of the league average • Six starting quarterbacks in 14 years; 91% of starts to primary quarterbacks • 31 rookie starters in 14 years • Winning Full Seasons to Losing Full Seasons: 8:3.

Probably one of the ten most influential coaches in NFL history, Seattle's Don Coryell left a legacy that lives on today in the pass-oriented offenses of the wide-open contemporary NFL. Ironically, he began his coaching career as a proponent of the I-formation before developing an up-tempo, downfield passing attack built on timing patterns and the pass route tree he established. His offense was simple in its basics and complex in its details; when run correctly, it was unstoppable.

Coryell was a paratrooper in World War II and went to college after the war. He played defensive back for the University of Washington from 1949 to 1951 and then coached in Canada and high school for the next three years. In 1955, he moved up to Wenatchee Junior College and produced an undefeated season. A year later he coached the service team at Fort Ord. In 1957, he succeeded George Allen as the head coach of the Whittier Poets and went 25–5–1 from 1957 to 1959 running the offense out of the I formation. After a season as an assistant to John McKay at USC, Don was named coach at San Diego State in 1961. Because San Diego could not compete with larger schools such as USC and UCLA in garnering the top recruits, Coryell began developing his radical Air Coryell passing offense with San Diego State in order to level the playing field. From 1961 to 1972, the airborne Aztecs went 104–19–2. Coryell regularly turned out pro quarterbacks (Brian Sipe, Don Horn, Dennis Shaw) wide receivers (Gary Garrison, Haven Moses, Isaac Curtis) and future NFL coaches (John Madden, Joe Gibbs, Jim Hanifan and Rod Dowhower).

After 12 years in San Diego, Coryell finally got his chance in the NFL with the preternaturally malfunctioning St. Louis Cardinals in 1973. He announced his intentions from the start, "I believe in a wide open style of play. I like to throw the ball. I believe in attacking the defense." Don quickly turned around the Cardinals, driving them to division titles in 1974 and 1975 as well as three straight double-digit-win seasons. Throughout his career, Coryell was a players' coach who inspired devotion and respect from his players and staff. Notorious Cardinals' guard Conrad Dobbler said on Coryell's death, "Don Coryell actually taught me that football is supposed to be fun. Yeah, it's a business, but it's a game." He did not find such support from the Cardinals' front office, though. At the end of the 1978 season, Don was so frustrated by his lack of say in the draft and personnel matters with his star scatback Terry Metcalf jumping to the CFL

that he made it known he wanted out. By "mutual agreement" with owner Bill Bidwill, Coryell left St, Louis.

By the fifth game of the 1978 season, Coryell was back in the NFL with the Chargers, replacing Tommy Prothro as coach. Over the next five years, the Chargers had the most explosive, trend-setting offense in the game with Dan Fouts passing to Charlie Joiner, John Jefferson, Wes Chandler and Kellen Winslow and with Chuck Muncie and James Brooks running the ball as a change of pace. As Marv Levy told *Sports Illustrated* after a Chiefs' loss to San Diego, "Don was in low cuts when the rest of the world was in high tops." Coryell spent nine seasons in San Diego, but the team declined over the last few years, and he quit in the middle of the 1986 season because the losing was getting to him, "I figured I'd die if I didn't get out of football." He never coached again.

Upon his death in 2010, Coryell was widely eulogized by all who knew him. Chargers' quarterback Don Fouts told *Sports Illustrated*, "He was one of a kind: a major contributor, a person who changed the game. There aren't many men in the Hall of Fame you can actually point to and say that the game changed because of them." At a memorial service for Coryell in San Diego, John Madden commented, "You know, I'm sitting down in front, and next to me is Joe Gibbs and next to him is Dan Fouts, and the three of us are in the Hall of Fame because of Don Coryell. There's something missing."

Indeed, Coryell, who is the only coach to win 100 games in both the pros and college, is in the College Hall of Fame, but did not make the Pro Football Hall before his death. Why? Ultimately, he never won a championship. In fact, his postseason won-lost record is a paltry 3–6 because his teams were always flawed — essentially, Coryell only put half a team on the field. While his teams led the league in points three times, seven times they were in the bottom five in points allowed. Moreover, against the toughest competition, they folded. In those nine postseason games, Coryell's teams averaged 21 points scoring but gave up 27 points a game. They turned the ball over on offense 35 times (almost four per game) and took it away just 17 for a –18 postseason turnover ratio. For his massive impact on the game, Coryell may be elected to the Hall someday, but it won't be for his teams' won/lost records.

COSLET, BRUCE N. 8/5/1946– Pacific. Played TE for the Bengals from 1968 to 1976. *Apprenticeship:* Pro asst.—10 years. *Roots:* Bill Walsh, Forrest Gregg and Sam Wyche. *Branches:* Pete Carroll, Dick LeBeau. *Coordinators/Key Assistants*: For the Jets, Coslet ran his own offense, and Pete Carroll handled the defense; for the Bengals, Ken Anderson handled the offense, while Larry Peccatielo then Dick LeBeau ran the defense. *Hall of Fame Players:* Ronnie Lott. *Primary Quarter-*

backs: Ken O'Brien, Boomer Esiason, Jeff Blake. *Tendencies:* • His teams scored 18.2 points and allowed 22.6 per game • His teams ran 46.1% of the time, which was 101% of the league average • Eight starting quarterbacks in nine years; 73% of starts to primary quarterbacks • 20 rookie starters in nine years • Winning Full Seasons to Losing Full Seasons: 0:5.

Bruce Coslet was no Jim Mora as a coach, but he did have one post-game comment that ranks with Mora's set of postgame exasperated declarations. After a 1997 loss to the Jets, Bengals coach Coslet summed up the performance with, "Emotionally, we suck." It was not an unusual feeling for Bruce as a coach. When he coached the Jets a few years before, he complained to reporters about quarterback Ken O'Brien, "You know my quarterback sucks. I know my quarterback sucks. Everyone knows my quarterback sucks."

Born in Oakdale, California, Coslet was signed as an undrafted free agent on the first Bengals' team in 1968. Bruce spent eight years as tight end Bob Trumpy's backup, mostly under Paul Brown and offensive coach Bill Walsh, before retiring to run a deli in 1977. Walsh brought Coslet into coaching in 1980 as the 49ers' special teams coach. A year later, Coslet returned to Cincinnati on Forrest Gregg's staff and stood on the losing sidelines in Super Bowl XVI, watching Walsh's 49ers win the championship. Coslet served as an assistant in Cincinnati for nine years, the last four as Sam Wyche's offensive coordinator, and got to watch Walsh beat the Bengals in Super Bowl XXIII as well.

By 1990, Coslet was a highly ranked coordinator after the Bengals had finished in the top five in points three out of four years. The 4–12 Jets, by contrast were 26th in points in 1989, presenting Bruce with a challenge when they named him their new head coach. Coslet came across as arrogant to the media and that was clear from the start. The day after a 30–7 loss to Buffalo in Bruce's third game as coach, he held his weekly press conference over speaker phone sitting in his office one floor above where the reporters were gathered. Over the next four years, the Jets were never better than mediocre and made the playoffs just once

after an 8–8 1991 season. In 1993, the team started 7–4 but then lost four of their last five, scoring just three touchdowns in the last six weeks, to finish 8–8. Coslet, who had been under fire for refusing to hire an offensive coordinator, was fired and returned to Cincinnati as David Shula's offensive coordinator in 1994.

Two years later, the Bengals got off to a 1–7 start so Shula was canned and replaced by Coslet. After Cincinnati finished on a 7–2 run, Bruce won a new contract. However, being the Bengals, the team could not win more than seven games in any of the following seasons with Coslet. At quarterback, Coslet was forced to rely on Jeff Blake and an aging Boomer Esiason in bad times and Neil O'Donnell, Akili Smith and Paul Justin in worse ones. Coslet later served two years as the Cowboys' offensive coordinator under the not-so-illustrious Dave Campo. He has been out of football since 2003.

COUGHLIN, THOMAS R. (TOM) 8/31/1946– Syracuse. WB; did not play professionally. *Apprenticeship:* College coach — 18 years (7 as head coach); pro asst.— 7 years. *Roots:* Marion Campbell, Fred Bruney (i), Forrest Gregg, Bill Parcells. *Branches:* Kevin Gilbride, Chris Palmer, Dick Jauron, Lane Kiffin, Tony Sparano, Bobby Petrino, Steve Spagnuolo, Perry Fewell (i). *Coordinators/Key Assistants:* For the Jaguars, Kevin Gilbride then Chris Palmer then Coughlin then Bobby Petrino ran the offense, while Dick Jauron then Dom Capers then Gary Moeller then John Pease ran the defense; for the Giants, John Hufnagel then Kevin Gilbride ran the offense, while Tim Lewis then Steve Spagnuolo then Bill Sheridan then Perry Fewell handled the defense. *Hall of Fame Players:* None. *Primary Quarterbacks:* Mark Brunell, Eli Manning. *Record:* Super Bowl Championship 2007 and 2011. *Tendencies:* • His teams scored 22.8 points and allowed 21 per game • His teams ran 44.7% of the time, which was 102% of the league average • 10 starting quarterbacks in 16 years; 90% of starts to primary quarterbacks • 37 rookie starters in 16 years • Winning Full Seasons to Losing Full Seasons: 9:5.

A multisport star in high school in Waterloo,

Coslet, Bruce N.									
Year	*Team*	*Games*	*Wins*	*Losses*	*Ties*	*%*	*P Wins*	*P Losses*	*P %*
1990	Jets	16	6	10	0	.375	0	0	.000
1991	Jets	16	8	8	0	.500	0	1	.000
1992	Jets	16	4	12	0	.250	0	0	.000
1993	Jets	16	8	8	0	.500	0	0	.000
1996	Bengals	9	7	2	0	.778	0	0	.000
1997	Bengals	16	7	9	0	.438	0	0	.000
1998	Bengals	16	3	13	0	.188	0	0	.000
1999	Bengals	16	4	12	0	.250	0	0	.000
2000	Bengals	3	0	3	0	.000	0	0	.000
9 years		124	47	77	0	.379	0	1	.000

New York, Tom Coughlin wore number 44 in honor of Syracuse star Ernie Davis who died the year before Coughlin himself matriculated at Syracuse. Tom was a starter at wingback alongside future pro Hall of Famers Floyd Little and Larry Csonka, but went right into coaching after graduation, first as a grad assistant and then as the 24-year-old head coach at Rochester Institute of Technology where the team went 16–15–2 from 1970 to 1973. Coughlin returned to his alma mater in 1974 as an assistant and stayed until head coach Frank Maloney was fired following the 1980 season. Tom was hired by Boston College to be Doug Flutie's quarterback coach in 1981 and stayed at BC for three years. In 1984, he moved up to the NFL with Philadelphia where sarcastically he was called "Technical Tom" by the players. Following two years in Philly and two in Green Bay, Coughlin was added to Bill Parcells' Giants' staff in 1988. After New York's Super Bowl triumph over the Bills in January 1991, Parcells retired for health reasons, and Tom replaced Jack Bicknell as Boston College's head coach. Two years later, the Giants fired Ray Handley as head coach and offered the job to Coughlin, but he opted to stay at BC for another year.

Tom left BC just a year later after the 1993 season with a 21–13–1 record to become the first head coach and general manager of the new Jacksonville Jaguars franchise slated to begin in 1995. Coughlin sought out two other coaches who started franchises for advice, Tom Landry and John McKay, for their advice. He told Ray Didinger in *Game Plans for Success*, "Just because you are starting a new team doesn't mean you have to start with zero background. I've always believed in doing my homework." That homework allowed the Jags to advance to the AFC Championship game in just their second season. That was followed

by three consecutive double-digit-win seasons and a second trip to the AFC title game, but there were no Super Bowl trips for Jacksonville.

Along the way, Coughlin gained a reputation as one of the most intense and toughest coaches in the league. As both GM and coach, he was a disciplinarian who brooked no dissent. Tom insisted his players play by his demanding rules. Being on time for meetings brought a fine for being five minutes late. Wearing a hat was forbidden as was crossing your legs — both feet on the floor for film sessions. While the team was winning, this approach worked. After four straight losing seasons, though, it was time for a change. Coughlin made some personnel mistakes and mismanaged the salary cap, so after the Jags third consecutive 6–10 season in 2002, Tom was fired.

A year later, the Giants hired Coughlin to bring discipline to a team that had gotten away from his predecessor Jim Fassel. Coughlin instituted an autocratic atmosphere in New York, but met public resistance from such stars as Tiki Barber and Jeremy Shockey. After three years of talented Giants' teams getting off to good starts every year and then fading badly each season, Coughlin was on the verge of being fired. Tom softened his approach a bit and hired dynamic new defensive coordinator Steve Spagnuolo to turn things around in 2007. In addition, Barber retired and Shockey was injured. In the playoffs that year, the Giants at last played as a team, with few turnovers and penalties, all units contributing equally and without finger-pointing and selfish emotional displays. With the team's recent history, no one expected that to last for a four-game road playoff run, but Coughlin took this underrated team all the way to the NFL championship over the undefeated New England Patriots. Defensive end Michael Strahan marveled to *Sports Il-*

Coughlin, Thomas R. (Tom)

Year	Team	Games	Wins	Losses	Ties	%	P Wins	P Losses	P %
1995	Jaguars	16	4	12	0	.250	0	0	.000
1996	Jaguars	16	9	7	0	.563	2	1	.667
1997	Jaguars	16	11	5	0	.688	0	1	.000
1998	Jaguars	16	11	5	0	.688	1	1	.500
1999	Jaguars	16	14	2	0	.875	1	1	.500
2000	Jaguars	16	7	9	0	.438	0	0	.000
2001	Jaguars	16	6	10	0	.375	0	0	.000
2002	Jaguars	16	6	10	0	.375	0	0	.000
2004	Giants	16	6	10	0	.375	0	0	.000
2005	Giants	16	11	5	0	.688	0	1	.000
2006	Giants	16	8	8	0	.500	0	1	.000
2007	Giants	16	10	6	0	.625	4	0	1.000
2008	Giants	16	12	4	0	.750	0	1	.000
2009	Giants	16	8	8	0	.500	0	0	.000
2010	Giants	16	10	6	0	.625	0	0	.000
2011	Giants	16	9	7	0	.563	4	0	.000
16 years		256	142	114	0	.555	12	7	.632

lustrated, "You expect somebody to change a little bit here and there, but the changes he's made have exceeded anything I ever expected to see as long as I've played for him. The guy is actually a personality now." Since that game, the Giants remained contenders but without playoff success until going on an another unexpected four-game postseason run that once again ended with a victory over the favored Patriots in the Super Bowl to conclude the 2011 season. Coughlin's second NFL championship put him in the conversation for Canton.

Cowher, William L. (Bill) 5/8/1957– North Carolina State. Played LB for the Eagles and Browns in 1980 and from 1982 to 1984. *Apprenticeship:* Pro asst.—7 years. *Roots:* Marty Schottenheimer. *Branches:* Dom Capers, Chan Gailey, Jim Haslett, Dick Lebeau, Marvin Lewis, Mike Mularkey and Ken Whisenhunt. *Coordinators/Key Assistants*: Ron Erhardt then Chan Gailey then Ray Sherman then Kevin Gilbride then Mike Mularkey then Ken Whisenhunt ran the offense, while Dom Capers then Dick LeBeau then Jim Haslett then Tim Lewis handled the defense. *Hall of Fame Players:* Dermonti Dawson, Rod Woodson. *Primary Quarterbacks:* Neil O'Donnell, Kordell Stewart and Ben Roethlisberger. *Record:* Super Bowl Championship 2005. *Tendencies:* • His teams scored 21.3 points and allowed 17.6 per game • His teams ran 50.3% of the time, which was 113% of the league average • Nine starting quarterbacks in 15 years; 73% of starts to primary quarterbacks • 23 rookie starters in 15 years • Winning Full Seasons to Losing Full Seasons: 11:3.

"The Chin," as Crafton, Pennsylvania's Bill Cowher is known for his jutting jaw, knows how far effort can take a player. Cowher was a lowly free agent out of North Carolina State who was the last

linebacker cut in 1979 by Eagles' coach Dick Vermeil. The following year, he hooked on with Cleveland and became the captain of the Browns' special teams. He injured his knee and missed the entire 1981 season, but returned frothing at the mouth in 1982. The next season, the Eagles spent a ninth round draft pick to reacquire Cowher for depth at inside linebacker. Bill was not very quick or fast, but was a very physical player who was tough, hard-nosed and disciplined. He also had an aggressive attitude that was demonstrated within weeks of his arrival in Philadelphia by his taunting of the All Pro Lawrence Taylor in a game against the Giants in 1983. Named the special teams' captain in 1984, he went down to a knee injury after four games and never played again. Marty Schottenheimer hired him to coach the Browns special teams in 1985, promoted him to secondary coach in 1987 and brought him to Kansas City as defensive coordinator in 1989. Three years later, he was the head coach of his hometown Pittsburgh Steelers and stayed there for 15 years before leaving on his own terms.

Cowher was all about toughness. Bill was interviewed for Dan Rooney's autobiography and described his approach with the Steelers, "I think the bottom line was I wanted it to be tough football team. I wanted to be able to run the football and I wanted to be able to play defense. I knew you had to score points and I knew you had to throw the ball. But I always thought that being a tough football team was important." Still, receiver Hines Ward told the local press, "Everyone thinks he's tough — he is — but he's a players' coach. His door is always open if you have a problem or just want to talk."

Cowher was fortunate to work for an organization that drafted as well as the Steelers so that there was always a steady flow of fresh talent arriving. However, he also had to deal with continually losing es-

Cowher, William L. (Bill)									
Year	Team	Games	Wins	Losses	Ties	%	P Wins	P Losses	P %
1992	Steelers	16	11	5	0	.688	0	1	.000
1993	Steelers	16	9	7	0	.563	0	1	.000
1994	Steelers	16	12	4	0	.750	1	1	.500
1995	Steelers	16	11	5	0	.688	2	1	.667
1996	Steelers	16	10	6	0	.625	1	1	.500
1997	Steelers	16	11	5	0	.688	1	1	.500
1998	Steelers	16	7	9	0	.438	0	0	.000
1999	Steelers	16	6	10	0	.375	0	0	.000
2000	Steelers	16	9	7	0	.563	0	0	.000
2001	Steelers	16	13	3	0	.813	1	1	.500
2002	Steelers	16	10	5	1	.656	1	1	.500
2003	Steelers	16	6	10	0	.375	0	0	.000
2004	Steelers	16	15	1	0	.938	1	1	.500
2005	Steelers	16	11	5	0	.688	4	0	1.000
2006	Steelers	16	8	8	0	.500	0	0	.000
15 years		240	149	90	1	.623	12	9	.571

tablished starters to free agency because the Steelers could not afford to pay the bonuses that larger market teams could. He also had to deal with a continual loss of coaching talent as his successful coordinators moved up within the league. After having lost Dick LeBeau and Dom Capers who built the Blitzburgh defense, Bill accurately told *Sports Illustrated* in 1997, "This defense will continue to be strong because there's one person who was responsible for it when Dick LeBeau was here, and it's the same person who oversaw it when Dom Capers was here. There's one guy who has been here all along, and you're looking at him."

The Steelers made the playoffs in each of Cowher's first six seasons in Pittsburgh and 10 times in 15 years, but a Super Bowl ring eluded him for the first 13 years. Cowher's Steelers won eight division titles, went to six AFC Championship games and lost four of them — all four losses occurring at home. His teams always featured a strong defense, even in losing years, finishing five times in the top three in fewest points allowed. However, his offense was dependent on such mediocre quarterbacks as Neil O'Donnell, Mike Tomczak, Kent Graham, Kordell Stewart and Tommy Maddox for his first 12 years. Perhaps that's why Bill always had such a proclivity towards gadget plays on offense. It wasn't until Ben Roethlisberger was drafted in 2004 that Pittsburgh finally had a franchise quarterback to support his power running attack.

Pittsburgh went 15–1 in 2004 with Big Ben as a rookie, but lost at home to the Patriots in the playoffs. The next year, the season was slipping away with the team at 7–5 and on the verge of dropping out of playoff contention when Cowher promised his team they would not lose another game. Four straight regular season wins got them the sixth seed in the playoffs. Three straight road wins over the Bengals, Colts and Broncos took them to the Super Bowl where they defeated the Seahawks in fullback Jerome Bettis' hometown of Detroit despite an ugly game by Roethlisberger.

Cowher came back for another season, but the team seemed to lack some fire after finally winning the franchise's fifth Vince Lombardi Trophy. Roethlisberger began to chafe under Cowher's direction, and Bill decided to step down after an 8–8 season. While many observers expected Cowher to return to football in a year or two, he moved to North Carolina and has eschewed coaching for broadcasting and watching his daughters

grow up for over five years now. In 2010, his wife died from skin cancer, and it remains to be seen how that might influence his potential return to coaching.

CREIGHTON, MILAN S. 1/21/1908–5/16/1998. Arkansas. Played E for the Cardinals from 1931 to 1937. *Apprenticeship:* None. *Roots:* None. *Branches:* Phil Handler. *Coordinators/Key Assistants*: Phil Handler coached the line. *Hall of Fame Players:* None. *Primary Quarterbacks:* None. *Record:* **Player-Coach**. *Tendencies:* • His teams scored 9.1 points and allowed 12.5 per game • His teams ran 71.7% of the time, which was 102% of the league average • 13 rookie starters in four years • Winning Full Seasons to Losing Full Seasons: 1:2.

If Milan Creighton is remembered at all today, it is through an amusing anecdote in which the Cardinals are penalized five yards and Creighton asks for an explanation. Referee Jim Durfee than tells Creighton it's for coaching from the sidelines, which was not permitted in the 1930s, and that even though that is a 15-yard penalty, the mouthy Creighton's coaching isn't worth that much yardage. Creighton was frequently combative with the officials. Jim Dent relates another story in *Monster of the Midway* that Bears' coach George Halas became so frustrated by Creighton's complaints in a 1937 game that he walked over and punched him in the nose, beginning a brawl. A year later, Milan charged the field to protest a holding call on October 26 and slugged referee Tommy Hughitt.

Creighton was one of the last player-coaches in the NFL, having been elevated to head coach in his fifth year with the Cardinals at age 27. In that first year, he kept the Cardinals in contention to the end, but that 6–4–2 record was his coaching high point. Milan stressed blocking and tackling, but was unable to turn around the Cardinals. By 1938, he was no longer a player himself and was getting desperate. With the Cards at 1–4 on October 11, he cut five players, saying, "This is only the beginning. We are not running a rest haven for athletes. I have no quarrel with men who play to win, but lose. But I am convinced that we have a better football team than the standing indicates and the players will prove it starting Sunday against the Bears or they will be given a chance to do their loafing in some other line of endeavor." Unfortunately, that was only the beginning of the end as the team lost the next five games before winning

Creighton, Milan S.

Year	Team	Games	Wins	Losses	Ties	%	P Wins	P Losses	P %
1935	Cardinals	12	6	4	2	.583	0	0	.000
1936	Cardinals	12	3	8	1	.292	0	0	.000
1937	Cardinals	11	5	5	1	.500	0	0	.000
1938	Cardinals	11	2	9	0	.182	0	0	.000
4 years		46	16	26	4	.391	0	0	.000

the season finale. Milan resigned the day after the season ended.

The Gothenberg, Nebraska native had played end under Francis "Close the Gates of Mercy" Schmidt at Arkansas. Creighton was elected to the school's Hall of Honor for his football, basketball and track heroics as a Razorback. He later coached Hot Springs High School and worked in real estate.

CRENNEL, ROMEO 6/18/1947– Western Kentucky. DL/OL; did not play professionally. *Apprenticeship:* College asst.—11 years; pro asst.— 24 years. *Roots:* Bill Parcells, Ray Handley, Chris Palmer and Bill Belichick. *Branches:* Mel Tucker (i). *Coordinators/Key Assistants*: Maurice Carthon then Jeff Davidson then Rob Chudzinski ran the offense, while Todd Grantham then Mel Tucker handled the defense. *Hall of Fame Players:* None. *Primary Quarterbacks:* Derek Anderson, Charlie Frye. *Tendencies:* • His teams scored 17.1 points and allowed 21.2 per game • His teams ran 42.9% of the time, which was 97% of the league average • Seven starting quarterbacks in five years; 70% of starts to primary quarterbacks • Ten rookie starters in five years • Winning Full Seasons to Losing Full Seasons: 1:3.

After a 35-year apprenticeship, respected assistant coach Romeo Crennel finally got an opportunity to be a head coach in the NFL in 2005, but really had no chance in Cleveland. When your job depends upon a parade of quarterbacks like Charlie Frye, Derek Anderson, Brady Quinn, Ken Dorsey and Bruce Gradkowski, you can expect to have a short tenure.

Crennel's father was a career military man, and Romeo intended on following the same path, but was overweight with flat feet. Rejected by the Army, the Lynchburg, Virginia native began his coaching career at his alma mater while earning his master's degree. From 1970 to 1980 Crennel coached the defensive line at Western Kentucky, Texas Tech (under defensive coordinator Bill Parcells), Mississippi and Georgia Tech.

In 1981, Ray Perkins hired him in New York as special teams coach, and he was reunited with Parcells. Romeo stayed with the Giants through 1992 and then followed Parcells to the Patriots in 1993 and the Jets in 1997. When Parcells quit the Jets, Crennel became the Browns defensive coordinator under another former Parcells assistant, Chris Palmer. Palmer was fired a year later, and Romeo returned to the Patriots as Bill Belichick's defensive coordinator for three Super Bowls in four years.

That success brought him back to Cleveland as head coach, but, aside from some fluky 10–6 success in 2007 with the team, the Browns failed dismally on both sides of the ball. After a year out of football, Crennel and former Patriots' offensive coordinator Charlie Weis both returned to the NFL as coordinators under the latest Parcells protégé, Todd Haley, in Kansas City in 2010. Although Weis left after one season, Romeo was on hand to replace the churlish Haley as head coach with three games to go in 2011. After the Chiefs rallied to win two of those games — one against the undefeated Packers — Crennel was named permanent head coach in January.

CROWE, CLEM F. 10/18/1903–4/13/1983. Notre Dame. E; did not play professionally. *Apprenticeship:* College coach —16 years (15 as head coach); pro asst.— 4 years. *Roots:* Red Dawson. *Branches:* Wayne Millner (i). *Coordinators/Key Assistants*: For the Colts, Wayne Millner coached the ends, Rocco Pirro the line and Joel Hunt the backs. *Hall of Fame Players:* Art Donovan and Y.A. Title. *Primary Quarterbacks:* George Ratterman and Y.A. Title. *Tendencies:* • His teams scored 17.9 points and allowed 30.1 per game • His teams ran 42% of the time, which was 76% of the league average • Three starting quarterbacks in two years; 83% of starts to primary quarterbacks • 10 rookie starters in two years • Winning Full Seasons to Losing Full Seasons: 0:1.

Clem Crowe had six younger brothers who

Crennel, Romeo

Year	Team	Games	Wins	Losses	Ties	%	P Wins	P Losses	P %
2005	Browns	16	6	10	0	.375	0	0	.000
2006	Browns	16	4	12	0	.250	0	0	.000
2007	Browns	16	10	6	0	.625	0	0	.000
2008	Browns	16	4	12	0	.250	0	0	.000
2011	Chiefs	3	2	1	0	.667	0	0	.000
5 years		67	26	41	0	.388	0	0	.000

Crowe, Clem F.

Year	Team	Games	Wins	Losses	Ties	%	P Wins	P Losses	P %
1949	Bills (AAFC)	6	4	1	1	.750	0	1	.000
1950	Colts (defunct)	12	1	11	0	.083	0	0	.000
2 years		18	5	12	1	.306	0	1	.000

played sports at Notre Dame, but Clem was the most accomplished. A two-time All-American in football under Knute Rockne, Crowe was team captain and played end on the "Seven Mules" line that blocked for the famous "Four Horsemen" backfield; he also starred on the basketball team in South Bend. The Lafayette, Indiana native summed up his time at Notre Dame by noting, "I don't think anyone could play under Knute Rockne without learning a lot. And mainly, I think we learned how to handle men."

Crowe went directly into coaching both football and basketball upon graduation. From 1926 to 1931, he led Saint Vincent to a 23–27–3 record; from 1936 to 1943, he led Xavier to a 46–32–2 record; and in 1945 coached Iowa to a 2–7 finish. After an overall 71–66–5 record in the college ranks, Clem was hired as scout, line coach and defense coach for the Buffalo Bills of the new All America Football Conference in 1946 under Red Dawson and even signed the team's two biggest stars: Chet Mutryn and George Ratterman. With the Bills off to a 1–4–1 start in 1949, Dawson was fired and Crowe was promoted to head coach. The team reversed its record in the second half of the season to finish at .500, but the league was merged into the NFL, with Buffalo dissolved in 1950.

Crowe was hired to coach the Baltimore Colts, one of three surviving AAFC teams, that year, but the Colts were the worst team in the league. Clem optimistically said in training camp that, "In nearly 25 years of coaching, I've never had a bunch of boys who have worked as hard. They've given me all the cooperation in the world and if hustle and desire to win mean anything, I don't think the outlook's bad." In the 1–11 season that followed, Baltimore four times gave up more than 50 points in a game, including 70 to the Rams (who also had scored 70 on the Colts in the preseason), and folded. Crowe went to Canada and won a Grey Cup championship in 1951. However, his overall coaching record at Ottawa and British Columbia from 1951 to 1958 was 31–55–1. He finished his coaching career as the freshman coach at the University of Buffalo in 1959 and scouted for Buffalo in the AFL before going into the freight business. He had 10 children.

CROWLEY, JAMES H. (JIM) 9/10/1902–1/15/1986. Notre Dame. Played HB for the Packers and the Providence Steam Roller in 1925. *Apprenticeship:* College coach —16 years (13 as head coach). *Roots:* None. *Branches:* Hampton Pool. *Coordinators/Key Assistants:*

Hampton Pool coached the line. *Hall of Fame Players:* Elroy Hirsch. *Primary Quarterbacks:* Sam Vacanti. *Record:* **Owner-Coach.** *Tendencies:* • His team scored 18.8 points and allowed 30.4 per game • His team ran 54% of the time, which was 86% of the league average • Three starting quarterbacks in one year; 57% of starts to primary quarterback • Five rookie starters in one year • Winning Full Seasons to Losing Full Seasons: 0:1.

Sleepy Jim Crowley is the direct link between Packer legends Curly Lambeau and Vince Lombardi. Crowley played under Lambeau at Green Bay East High School and, on his urging, matriculated at Notre Dame where Curly had attended. Under Knute Rockne in South Bend, Jim was a member of the renowned backfield dramatically compared to the Four Horsemen of the Apocalypse by sportswriter Grantland Rice — Jim waggishly maintained that he was Pestilence. Upon graduation, Crowley appeared in a couple of NFL games for Green Bay and Providence in 1925 before going into coaching like so many of Rockne's players. Jim spent three years in Georgia as an assistant to George Woodruff and then to former teammate Harry Mehre until taking over as head coach at Michigan State in 1929. The Spartans went 22–8–3 in four years under Crowley, after having achieved just one winning season in the previous decade. Jim moved on to Fordham in 1933 where he built a powerhouse team centered on the Rams' impregnable "7 Blocks of Granite" line; one of those blocks of granite was guard Vince Lombardi. From 1933 to 1941, Fordham went 56–13–7 and appeared in the Cotton Bowl and the Sugar Bowl. During the war, Crowley served as a commander in the Navy from 1942 to 1945.

Throughout his career, Jim was a favorite of reporters because he was ever-ready with a quip or colorful comment. When the All America Football Conference began in 1946, the personable Crowley was drafted as the league's first commissioner, standing as a stark contrast to the NFL's dour commissioner Elmer Layden, another former member of the Four Horsemen. The AAFC had been organized by *Chicago Tribune* Sports Editor Arch Ward and was based in Chicago. The flagship Chicago Rockets franchise was a dud on the launch pad, however, and volatile trucking magnate John Keeshin sold the team in 1947 to a group headed by Crowley who resigned as commissioner. After Notre Dame alum Ed McKeever turned

Crowley, James H. (Jim)									
Year	Team	Games	Wins	Losses	Ties	%	P Wins	P Losses	P %
1947	Rockets (AAFC)	14	1	13	0	.071	0	0	.000
1 year		14	1	13	0	.071	0	0	.000

down the Rockets' coaching job, Jim stepped in, but nothing went right all year. The team was terrible, and Crowley was lost. Halfback Elroy Hirsch later told Stuart Leuthner for *Iron Men*, "Sleepy Jim Crowley didn't know one of us from the other anyhow. He'd grab a tackle and send him into the backfield." After an 0–8 start, rumors circulated that Crowley would be fired by the majority owner and replaced by assistant coach Hampton Pool. Indeed, two football encyclopedias list Crowley as having coached only the first 10 games of 1947 before being replaced by Pool. However, contemporary news accounts continue to talk about Crowley as the coach until his resignation in Los Angeles after the Rockets last game in December. He was replaced in 1948 by Ed McKeever who also went 1–13 with the woebegone Rockets.

In fact, Crowley not only resigned from coaching but from football altogether. He worked in the insurance business from 1948 to 1952, then took over a TV station in Scranton, Pennsylvania for two years. Jim also served as the Industrial Commissioner of Lackawanna County and then chaired the Pennsylvania Athletic Commission until 1972 when he retired.

CUNNINGHAM, GUNTHER 6/19/1946– Oregon. LB; did not play professionally. *Apprenticeship:* College asst.—12 years; CFL asst.—1 year; pro asst.—17 years. *Roots:* Don Coryell, Al Saunders, Dan Henning, Art Shell, Marty Schottenheimer,. *Branches:* None. *Coordinators/Key Assistants:* Jimmy Raye ran the offense, and Kurt Schottenheimer handled the defense. *Hall of Fame Players:* Warren Moon and Derrick Thomas. *Primary Quarterbacks:* Elvis Grbac. *Tendencies:* • His teams scored 23.3 points and allowed 21.1 per game • His teams ran 44.1% of the time, which was 102% of the league average • Two starting quarterbacks in two years; 97% of starts to primary quarterback • Four rookie starters in two years • Winning Full Seasons to Losing Full Seasons: 1:1.

Born in Munich shortly after V-E Day to an American serviceman and German mother, Gunther Cunningham didn't move to the U.S. until he was 10, but quickly took to American football. Cunningham was a linebacker and kicker at the University of Oregon for three years and upon graduation immediately began his coaching career at his alma mater in 1969. Three years at Oregon, one at Arkansas under Frank Broyles, four at Stanford under Jack Christiansen and then four at California as defensive coordinator brought Gunther to the Hamilton Tiger-Cats in the CFL in 1981 under Frank Kush. When Kush was hired by the Colts a year later, he brought Cunningham to the NFL with him. Kush was fired in 1985, but Gunther caught on with the Chargers under Don Coryell and then Al Saunders from 1985 to 1990. After another coaching change, Cunningham landed on Art Shell's Raiders' staff from 1991 to 1994 and then was named defensive coordinator under Marty Schottenheimer in Kansas City in 1995. Employing a blitz-heavy approach that made the most of edge linebacker Derrick Thomas, Cunningham's defense was the strength of the team. The Chiefs allowed the fewest points in the NFL in 1995 and 1997 and were always among the league leaders in takeaways.

When Schottenheimer stepped down in 1999, Cunningham was named head coach after his 30-year apprenticeship. Having never served as a head coach before, Gunther tended to be a micromanager, involved in too many things, and the team's record was mediocre. Oddly, Cunningham's more wide open offense improved to the top 10 in points scored, while his aggressive defense slipped, especially following Derrick Thomas' accidental death in 2000. After two middling seasons, Cunningham was replaced by Dick Vermeil. Gunther worked in Tennessee from 2001 to 2003, returned to Kansas City as Vermeil's defensive coordinator from 2004 to 2008 and then joined Jim Schwartz in Detroit in 2009, again as defensive coordinator.

DAVIS, ALLEN (AL) 7/4/1929–10/8/2011. Syracuse. Did not play professionally. *Apprenticeship:* College asst.—10 years; pro asst.—3 years. *Roots:* Sid Gillman.

Cunningham, Gunther

Year	Team	Games	Wins	Losses	Ties	%	P Wins	P Losses	P %
1999	Chiefs	16	9	7	0	.563	0	0	.000
2000	Chiefs	16	7	9	0	.438	0	0	.000
2 years		32	16	16	0	.500	0	0	.000

Davis, Allen (Al)

Year	Team	Games	Wins	Losses	Ties	%	P Wins	P Losses	P %
1963	Raiders	14	10	4	0	.714	0	0	.000
1964	Raiders	14	5	7	2	.429	0	0	.000
1965	Raiders	14	8	5	1	.607	0	0	.000
3 years		42	23	16	3	.583	0	0	.000

Branches: John Rauch. *Coordinators/Key Assistants:* John Rauch on offense and Charlie Sumner on defense. *Hall of Fame Players:* Fred Biletnikoff, Jim Otto. *Primary Quarterbacks:* Tom Flores. *Record:* **Hall of Fame Owner.** *Tendencies:* • His teams scored 23 points and allowed 20.7 per game • His teams ran 41.2% of the time, which was 93% of the league average • Three starting quarterbacks in three years; 64% of starts to primary quarterback • Eleven rookie starters in three years • Winning Full Seasons to Losing Full Seasons: 2:1.

Combative, litigious, triumphal Al Davis was one of the most significant figures in the history of the NFL. Although he was born to a comfortable, stable home in Brooklyn, he cultivated a street fighter's persona of "Just Win, Baby" throughout his long career in football. Never afraid to make enemies, he led the Raiders for nearly 50 years, established their "Pride and Poise" style and marked the Black and Silver team with the Bad Ass brand.

Davis graduated from Syracuse, where he never played on any varsity team, but was able to talk himself into a job as freshman coach at Adelphi College in 1950. Drafted into the army in 1952, Al wrangled a coaching spot at Fort Belvoir in Virginia and even drew the attention of Colts' coach Weeb Ewbank who attended some of the team's games looking for players. Upon his discharge, Davis did some scouting for the Colts before being hired as line coach by The Citadel in 1955. Two years later, Al was named the end coach at USC and coached there through 1959. When the American Football League started in 1960, Los Angeles Chargers' coach Sid Gillman didn't have to look far to find an ends coach since the Chargers, Rams and Trojans all played in the LA Coliseum. Gillman's downfield passing offense meshed well with Davis' ideas, and Al would develop his own style of Vertical Offense when he was hired to coach the dreadful Oakland Raiders in 1963. Gillman once memorably said of Davis, "Al thinks he's the smartest guy in football. He isn't. But he is going to be."

The Raiders played on a glorified high school field and were coming off of a 19-game losing streak when Davis took over as coach and general manager in 1963. Principal owner Wayne Valley once told the *New York Times* the reason he hired Davis was, "Because everyone hated his guts. Al Davis wants to win, and he'll do anything to win. And after losing all those games, I wanted to win any way I could." After winning just three games in the two previous years, Oakland went 10–4 in Al's first year, and he was named Coach of the Year. Davis completely remade the squad, bringing in castoffs such as receiver Art Powell and runner Clem Daniels to power his explosive offense. He told *Sports Illustrated,* "Some people talk about the bad things that can happen when you put the ball in the air, but I know one good thing that can happen. You can get six

points in a matter of seconds from anywhere on the field." Years later he succinctly explained his approach to Paul Zimmerman of the same magazine, "Attack, fear, pressure. Don't take what they give you. You're going deep and they're not going to stop you by design or location. They have to do it on the field. Screw it. You say you can stop us. Prove it."

While the club slipped in the standings in 1964, they rebounded to another second place finish in 1965. All the while, Davis was building a winner for the long term. A fellow AFL coach told *Sports Illustrated*, "Al Davis is a great listener. He'll talk to some top offensive coaches about a play, and then mull it over and take the best of what they said and present it as his own theory. He can synthesize it beautifully." Bill Walsh later told Tom LaMare for *Oakland Raiders: Colorful Tales of the Silver and Black,* "Had he chosen to remain in coaching, he would be considered one of the great coaches of all time."

Walsh was hired as a Raiders assistant in 1966, but not under Davis. Instead, Al was drafted by the league to serve as its commissioner as the competition with the NFL heated up. Davis took the charge seriously and instituted an aggressive stance, advocating a policy of raiding the older league of its stars, particularly quarterbacks. Unbeknownst to Davis, though, backchannel negotiations between Lamar Hunt and Tex Schramm brought about a merger of the two leagues in 1967. Davis felt betrayed and never has relinquished his animus toward the older league, feeling that the AFL should have maintained its own distinct identity.

Davis returned to the Raiders and purchased a 10-percent stake in the club. On the field, he built a Super Bowl team in 1967 through astute deals that brought stars Daryle Lamonica, George Blanda and Willie Brown to Oakland and then built on that success to maintain the Raiders as a perennial contender for the next 20 years. Off the field, Davis manipulated the other Raider owners to force out Valley by 1976 and to enforce his will as the managing general partner and voice of the franchise despite the fact that Davis did not own a majority of team shares until 2005.

Along the way, he repeatedly ensnared the league in legal proceedings. Davis sued the NFL for the right to move the Raiders to Los Angeles in 1980 before moving the team in 1982, only to move them back to Oakland in 1995. He sided with the upstart USFL in its legal battle with the NFL in 1985 and sued the league again in 1995 over its alleged undermining of his efforts to build a stadium in Inglewood. Furthermore, former players and coaches have discovered severing ties with Davis can be an ugly thing. Super Bowl hero Marcus Allen found himself labeled a cancer for questioning Davis. Coaches Mike Shanahan and Lane Kiffen found Davis reneging on contractual pay arrangements after they were fired. When Davis named Hue Jackson the Raiders' latest coach in 2011, he spent much more time lambasting fired coach Tom Cable than talking about Jackson. Meanwhile, the Raiders became a league joke in the last 15 years of Al's life (aside from the four-year period in which Jon Gruden rebuilt the franchise). The aging Davis continually overpaid for overrated free agents like Super Bowl MVPs Larry Brown and Desmond Howard, and his drafting acumen also turned into a caricature with his misguided search for speed at the expense of real talent. Despite all that, Al Davis, a Hall of Famer himself, will be remembered best as the presenter of nine Raiders' Hall of Famers and the one who most embodied the lengthy glory days of the franchise.

DAVIS, PAUL H. (BUTCH) 11/17/1951– Arkansas. DE; did not play professionally. *Apprenticeship:* College coach—16 years (6 as head coach); pro asst.— 6 years. *Roots:* Jimmy Johnson, Barry Switzer. *Branches:* Todd Bowles (i), Chuck Pagano. *Coordinators/Key Assistants*: Bruce Arians then Terry Robiskie ran the offense, while Foge Fazio then Dave Campo handled the defense. *Hall of Fame Players:* None. *Primary Quarterbacks:* Tim Couch. *Tendencies:* • His teams scored 18.3 points and allowed 20.2 per game • His teams ran 44% of the time, which was 99% of the league average •Three starting quarterbacks in four years; 66% of starts to primary quarterback • Seven rookie starters in four years • Winning Full Seasons to Losing Full Seasons: 1:3.

Like his mentor Jimmy Johnson, Butch Davis played his college ball at Arkansas. A knee injury cut short Butch's playing career, though, and hastened his entry into coaching. The Tahlequah, Oklahoma native coached high school football from 1973 to 1978 before landing on Johnson's Oklahoma State staff in 1979. When Jimmy left OSU for the University of Miami in 1984, Davis followed along, and when Johnson left the Hurricanes for Dallas in 1989, Butch continued

to serve as Jimmy's defensive line coach. After defensive coordinator Dave Wannstedt was named head coach of the Bears in 1993, Davis was given charge of the Cowboys' defense for their second Super Bowl championship and then stayed for one more year under new coach Barry Switzer.

In 1995, Davis was named head coach at Miami in the wake of Dennis Erickson's lax reign. Miami was placed under heavy sanctions by the NCAA for various violations during the Erickson years, and Butch was given the job of restoring the program to its place of prominence in college football. Davis accomplished that mission and his Hurricanes went 51–20 with four bowl victories in six years. On that record, Butch was named head coach of the Cleveland Browns in 2001.

In Davis' four years in Cleveland, the Browns had just one winning season and played in just one playoff game, which they lost. Butch's tenure as an NFL head coach was marred by poor drafting, including first round busts William Green and Gerard Warren, some drug problems and a pair of quarterback controversies. First, it was Tim Couch versus Kelly Holcomb, with Couch being booed by Cleveland fans even when he got injured, and then there was free agent Jeff Garcia versus draft pick Luke McCown. The trouble was that none of the four was very good. Moreover, veteran front office wise man Ron Wolf was brought in by ownership as a personnel consultant, but was shut out by Davis and left the team in short order. After being fired in 2005, Butch returned to the college ranks with North Carolina in 2007 and guided the Tar Heels to a 28–23 record in four years before he was dismissed in 2011 with the school placed on NCAA probation for improper payments made to players by agents during his tenure.

DAWSON, LOWELL P. (RED) 12/20/1906–6/10/1983. Tulane. Did not play professionally. *Apprenticeship:* Col-

Davis, Paul H. (Butch)									
Year	Team	Games	Wins	Losses	Ties	%	P Wins	P Losses	P %
2001	Browns	16	7	9	0	.438	0	0	.000
2002	Browns	16	9	7	0	.563	0	1	.000
2003	Browns	16	5	11	0	.313	0	0	.000
2004	Browns	10	3	7	0	.300	0	0	.000
4 years		58	24	34	0	.414	0	1	.000

Dawson, Lowell P. (Red)									
Year	Team	Games	Wins	Losses	Ties	%	P Wins	P Losses	P %
1946	Bisons (AAFC)	14	3	10	1	.250	0	0	.000
1947	Bills (AAFC)	14	8	4	2	.643	0	0	.000
1948	Bills (AAFC)	14	7	7	0	.500	1	1	.500
1949	Bills (AAFC)	6	1	4	1	.250	0	0	.000
4 years		48	19	25	4	.438	1	1	.500

lege coach — 14 years (6 as head coach). *Roots:* None. *Branches:* Clem Crowe, Red Conkright (i). *Coordinators/Key Assistants*: Clem Crowe and John Scafide were with Dawson all four years in Buffalo. *Hall of Fame Players:* None. *Primary Quarterbacks:* George Ratterman. *Tendencies:* • His teams scored 22.3 points and allowed 24.4 per game • His teams ran 64% of the time, which was 104% of the league average • Five starting quarterbacks in four years; 67% of starts to primary quarterback • 17 rookie starters in four years • Winning Full Seasons to Losing Full Seasons: 1:1.

Lowell "Red" Dawson is not to be confused with William "Red" Dawson who took over as coach of Marshall University in 1970 after a plane crash wiped out the entire team. Lowell Dawson was long retired from football when that tragedy occurred. Lowell played quarterback for Tulane under Bernie Bierman from 1929 to 1931 and led the undefeated Green Wave to the 1932 Rose Bowl where they lost to USC. Bierman left Louisiana for Minnesota in 1932, taking over the Golden Gophers, with Dawson on hand as backfield coach in his Minneapolis hometown. Dawson's best backfield pupil was quarterback Bud Wilkinson who helped lead Minnesota to three straight national championships from 1934 to 1936. By the third one, Dawson had returned to Tulane as head coach. Red compiled a 36–19–4 record in six years at Tulane, including a trip to the 1940 Sugar Bowl. He was an early proponent of using two 11-man platoons that alternated by quarter to keep everyone fresh.

After a couple of .500 seasons, Dawson left Tulane and returned to Minnesota as an assistant for the duration of World War II. When the All American Football Conference began in 1946, Dawson was named head coach of the Buffalo Bisons. That first year, Dawson mixed his offense between the single wing and T formation, but in 1947, the rechristened Bills signed Notre Dame's George Ratterman as quarterback and switched to the T fulltime. The team improved by five games in 1947, but still finished second. In 1948, Buffalo's record declined to 7–7 but they tied Baltimore for first place in the East and defeated the Colts in a playoff to advance to the title game. Dawson's Bills were no match for Paul Brown's Cleveland Browns, though, and Buffalo lost 49–7 in the championship game.

Ratterman held out in 1949, and the Bills only

won one of their first six games. At that point, Dawson was replaced by his assistant Clem Crowe. Halfback Joe Sutton recalled Dawson to Ken Crippen in *The Original Buffalo Bills* as, "a bit of a curmudgeon [who] didn't know how to communicate with the players." Under Crowe, Buffalo finished out the season 5–5–2, but once again lost to Cleveland in the playoffs. Dawson coached the backfield for Michigan State in 1950 and 1951 and then was named head coach at Pitt in 1952. Three games into his third year with the Panthers, however, heart problems forced him to quit the game with a 9–11–1 mark at Pitt. Red moved to Ocala, Florida where he took over a Gulf Oil distributorship and did quite well over the next 30 years till his death.

DeGroot, Dudley S. 11/20/1899–5/5/1970.

Stanford. Did not play professionally. *Apprenticeship:* College coach — 21 years (19 as head coach). *Roots:* None. *Branches:* Turk Edwards, Mel Hein (i), Ted Shipkey (i). *Coordinators/Key Assistants*: Edwards was his only fulltime assistant in Washington; Hein and Shipkey were joined by Merl Condit as DeGroot's Los Angeles assistants. *Hall of Fame Players:* Sammy Baugh, Wayne Millner. *Primary Quarterbacks:* Sammy Baugh, Charley O'Rourke and Glenn Dobbs. *Tendencies:* • His teams scored 22.5 points and allowed 18.8 per game • His teams ran 60.7% of the time, which was 96% of the league average • Five starting quarterbacks in four years; 96% of starts to primary quarterbacks • 18 rookie starters in four years • Winning Full Seasons to Losing Full Seasons: 3:0.

Chicago's Dudley DeGroot was an all-around athlete who played basketball and water polo and was a champion swimmer as well as a member of the U.S. Olympic Rugby team in 1924. In football, he was an All-American center under Pop Warner at Stanford, and that is where he began his coaching career as an assistant in 1923 while earning his doctorate in education. From 1925 to 1931, DeGroot coached at Santa Barbara and Menlo Junior College until he was named head coach at San Jose State in 1932. Dudley coached there for the rest of the 1930s and compiled a 59–19–8 record. After an undefeated 1939 season, DeGroot moved on to the University of Rochester in 1940 and went 24–6 in four years there.

In 1944, George Preston Marshall, owner of the Redskins, persuaded Dudley to take over as coach in

DeGroot, Dudley S.									
Year	Team	Games	Wins	Losses	Ties	%	P Wins	P Losses	P %
1944	Redskins	10	6	3	1	.650	0	0	.000
1945	Redskins	10	8	2	0	.800	0	1	.000
1946	Dons (AAFC)	14	7	5	2	.571	0	0	.000
1947	Dons (AAFC)	11	5	6	0	.455	0	0	.000
4 years		45	26	16	3	.611	0	1	.000

Washington. Marshall had a reputation for meddlesome interference, and DeGroot addressed that with humor at his opening press conference, "Mr. Marshall has assured me that whenever he comes to the bench next season he will bring a touchdown play, and I want to go on record right now that whenever we fail to score while he is on the bench, the responsibility will be Mr. Marshall's and not mine." Two years later, Dudley was not laughing anymore; he soon found that the players answered to the owner, not to the coach. In addition, having learned at the feet of Warner, the inventor of the single and double wing offenses, DeGroot's preference was the single wing. However, the Redskins were installing the T formation with special advisor Clark Shaughnessy, and there were friction and sparks between the head coach and his appointed special advisor.

Still, the Redskins reached the title game in 1945, but lost to the Rams 15–14 on an icy field when a safety was awarded after a Sammy Baugh pass from his own end zone hit the goal post, as was the rule at the time. At halftime, Marshall was furious that his team would not don sneakers to improve their footing because DeGroot had made a gentleman's agreement with Rams' coach Adam Walsh to eschew tennis shoes since the Rams did not have them. DeGroot resigned a month later, and an anonymous "confidant" told the *Washington Post*, "In the two years he had the title of head coach, DeGroot never actually was more than a subordinate, always trying to adjust himself to everybody else's way of doing things."

Two days after his resignation, Dudley was named head coach of the Los Angeles Dons of the new All America Football Conference. Unfortunately, DeGroot did not get along much better with management in Los Angeles. After a 7–5–2 first season, DeGroot won a power struggle with general manager Slip Madigan who resigned. Madigan's responsibilities were assumed by owner Ben Lindheimer. Lindheimer felt that his coach was not keeping him informed during his second season with the Dons, so the owner's daughter Marge began sitting in on team meetings and practices. Needless to say, DeGroot had trouble maintaining control of the team in this atmosphere.

For the 11th game of the year against the Yankees, Marge ordered DeGroot to the stands, while she went on the field with the team and had assistant coaches Ted Shipkey and Mel Hein make all substitutions and game decisions. Not surprisingly, Dudley quit when the team returned to Los Angeles. To his great dismay, though, his assistants refused to walk out with him on principle because they needed the money.

DeGroot moved on to coach West Virginia from 1948 to 1949 with a 13–9–1 record and New Mexico from 1950 to 1952 with a 13–17 mark. Fired after a 7–2 season with the Lobos, Dudley strangely applied for the vacant line coach job with the Redskins, but was turned down. He then was named Sports Coordinator for the Army's European Theater in 1953 and held that job until he retired.

Del Rio, Jack 4/4/1963– Southern California. Played LB for the Saints, Chiefs, Cowboys, Vikings and Dolphins from 1985 to 1996. *Apprenticeship:* Pro asst.—6 years. *Roots:* Mike Ditka, Brian Billick, John Fox. *Branches:* Mike Smith, Mel Tucker (i). *Coordinators/Key Assistants*: Bill Musgrave then Carl Smith then Dirk Koetter ran the offense, while Mike Smith then Gregg Williams then Mel Tucker handled the defense. *Hall of Fame Players:* None. *Primary Quarterbacks:* David Garrard and Byron Leftwich. *Tendencies:* • His teams scored 19.9 points and allowed 20.3 per game • His teams ran 47.8% of the time, which was 108% of the league average • Seven starting quarterbacks in nine years; 83% of starts to primary quarterbacks • 27 rookie starters in nine years • Winning Full Seasons to Losing Full Seasons: 3:3.

Looking at Jack Del Rio's record over nine seasons raised one main question: how did he keep his job so long? He made the playoffs just twice in that time and generally bobbed around .500 each year. Moreover, Del Rio's teams scored and allowed the same 20.5 points per game for his first eight years of his mediocre tenure. The one thing he is best remembered for was the wooden stump and ax he put in the locker room in 2003 that punter Chris Hanson demonstrated by gashing open his leg and ending his season.

Del Rio, Jack

Year	Team	Games	Wins	Losses	Ties	%	P Wins	P Losses	P %
2003	Jaguars	16	5	11	0	.313	0	0	.000
2004	Jaguars	16	9	7	0	.563	0	0	.000
2005	Jaguars	16	12	4	0	.750	0	1	.000
2006	Jaguars	16	8	8	0	.500	0	0	.000
2007	Jaguars	16	11	5	0	.688	1	1	.500
2008	Jaguars	16	5	11	0	.313	0	0	.000
2009	Jaguars	16	7	9	0	.438	0	0	.000
2010	Jaguars	16	8	8	0	.500	0	0	.000
2011	Jaguars	11	3	8	0	.273	0	0	.000
9 years		139	68	71	0	.489	1	2	.333

After Jack's All-American college career at USC, the Castro Valley, the California native played linebacker in the NFL for 11 years with moderate success. Upon retirement Del Rio went directly into coaching, first with the Saints from 1997 to 1998, then with the Ravens for three years and finally for one season as defensive coordinator for Carolina in 2002. In 2006, Ravens' coach Brian Billick praised him to the *New York Times*, "Jack was totally committed from the beginning. He's articulate, he's bright, he relates to players and they relate to him. Those are qualities you want in a coach."

Del Rio's first draft choice in 2003 was Brian Leftwich. Four years later, he tired of Leftwich's shortcomings, cut him right before the start of the 2007 season and switched to backup David Garrard. Garrard, like Leftwich, had his moments, but also had his weaknesses. Jack then tired of Garrard in 2011 and cut him five days before the season for retread Luke McCown and then unprepared rookie Blaine Gabbert. Disaster ensued.

Del Rio's teams ran much more than the league average and his offense tended toward the dull side. More important, his defenses slid in effectiveness towards the bottom of the league during the second half of Jack's tenure. While his players really seemed to like Del Rio, Jags' outgoing owner Wayne Weaver eventually ran out of patience late in 2011 when it was clear the team had not made a significant leap forward. John Fox rehired Jack as defensive coordinator in Denver for 2012.

DEVINE, DANIEL J. (DAN) 12/22/1924–5/9/2002. Minnesota-Duluth. QB; did not play professionally. *Apprenticeship:* College coach — 21 years (16 as head coach). *Roots:* None. *Branches:* Bart Starr, Hank Kuhlmann (i). *Coordinators/Key Assistants:* Bob Schnelker, Bart Starr and Perry Moss were the key offensive coaches; Dave Hanner handled the defense. *Hall of Fame Players:* Ted Hendricks, Ray Nitschke, Bart Starr, Willie Wood. *Primary Quarterbacks:* Scott Hunter. *Tendencies:* • His teams scored 17.7 points and allowed 17.7 per game • His teams ran 62.9% of the time, which was 114% of the league average • Seven starting quarterbacks in four years; 52% of starts to primary quarterback • Ten rookie starters in four years • Winning Full Seasons to Losing Full Seasons: 1:3.

Dan Devine was a fine college coach who earned a spot in the College Hall of Fame; in the pros, he had considerably less success. A native of Augusta, Wisconsin and a veteran of the Army Air Corps, Devine attended Minnesota-Duluth after the war and captained both the football and baseball teams. Following two years of coaching high school, Dan joined the staff of Biggie Munn at Michigan State in 1950. In 1955, Devine was named head coach at Arizona State and compiled a 27-3-1 record over the next three years. He left for Missouri in 1958 and was succeeded at ASU by his assistant Frank Kush. Devine indirectly was following a legend at Missouri, Don Faurot, the father of the Split T, but created his own legacy by leading the Tigers to a 93-37-7 record including four Bowl wins in six appearances over the next 13 years.

In 1971, the Packers hired the well-regarded Devine to replace Phil Bengtson and bring the glory days back to Green Bay. However, Dan's tenure got off to an inauspicious start when he was run over on the sidelines during his first league game and had his leg broken by former Packer Bob Hyland. Both Devine and the Pack limped through the 1971 season, but came out strong in 1972. Dan's drafts were very thin, but he did pick John Brockington and Scott Hunter in 1971 and Willie Buchanan, Jerry Tagge and Chester Marcol in 1972. Coupled with a trade for Macarthur Lane, Green Bay was fortified enough to win the division title that year. The twin battering rams of Brockington and Lane powered an offense that ran an astounding 23% more than the league average in a run-oriented league, while Marcol provided a reliable field goal kicker at last. In the playoffs, though, the Redskins' George Allen countered with a five-man line, daring the Packers to pass. Offensive coach Bart Starr urged Devine to open up the offense, but Devine refused, and the team lost 16-3. Starr quit at the end of the year.

Even with that success, Devine did not win much loyalty from his players. One anonymously told the *Washington Post* that year, "Let's just say a lot of us respect Devine more as a leader of men than as a football coach. But I will say this. The man is a hell of an organizer." His main problem on the field was quarterback because neither Hunter nor Tagge panned out. Devine started making questionable trades to fill the gap: two second rounders for Miami third stringer Jim

Year	Team	Games	Wins	Losses	Ties	%	P Wins	P Losses	P %
1971	Packers	14	4	8	2	.357	0	0	.000
1972	Packers	14	10	4	0	.714	0	1	.000
1973	Packers	14	5	7	2	.429	0	0	.000
1974	Packers	14	6	8	0	.429	0	0	.000
4 years		56	25	27	4	.482	0	1	.000

Devine, Daniel J. (Dan)

Del Gaizo; a fifth rounder for Jack Concannon; and third rounder for Dean Carlson; and finally two firsts, two seconds and a third for an aging John Hadl. Not only did none of the quarterbacks work out, the team's future drafts were decimated. Dan became increasingly unpopular both in the locker room and in the stands. Some disgruntled players reportedly tried to organize a boycott of the 1974 season finale. To make matters worse, Devine complained about his mistreatment by the town to *Time Magazine*, even asserting that some-one went so far as to kill his dog. Years later, Devine admitted that his dog, that was allowed to run free, was accidentally shot by a chicken farmer trying to scare the dog away from his chickens.

On the verge of being fired at the end of 1974, Dan pulled an ace out of his sleeve and quit to accept the head coaching job at Notre Dame, following Ara Parseghian. In South Bend, Devine led the Irish to a 53–16–1 record and a national championship, but he was never especially well liked. Even today, he is more remembered for his mishandling of Joe Montana than anything else. After leaving Notre Dame in 1981, Dan spent four years as a fundraiser for Arizona State and then returned to Missouri as athletic director from 1985 to 1992. In retirement, Devine wrote an autobiography in 2000, while in 1995 he told the *Milwaukee Journal Sentinel*, "I'd be about 10 times better as a coach today than I was in 1972. I probably should have followed Lombardi's pattern a little more, the way he emphasized blocking and tackling. I thought football at that level wasn't the same as college football. It is."

DEVORE, HUGH J. 11/25/1910–12/8/1992. Notre Dame. E; did not play professionally. *Apprenticeship:* College coach — 20 years (14 as head coach); pro asst. —1 year. *Roots:* Gene Ronzani. *Branches:* None. *Coordinators/Key Assistants*: Charley Gauer handled the offense, and Steve Owen ran the defense. *Hall of Fame Players:* Chuck Bednarik, Sonny Jurgensen, Tommy McDonald, Jim Ringo. *Primary Quarterbacks:* Bobby Thomason. *Tendencies:* • His teams scored 13.3 points and allowed 20.2 per game • His teams ran 62% of the time, which was 104% of the league average • Five starting quarterbacks in three years; 65% of starts to primary quarterback • 13 rookie starters in three years • Winning Full Seasons to Losing Full Seasons: 0:2.

Hugh Devore was a born assistant whose head coaching career essentially was book ended by two sea-

sons as interim coach at his alma mater, Notre Dame, 7–2 in 1945 and 2–7 in 1963. The Newark, New Jersey native played end for the Irish under Hunk Anderson from 1931 to 1933 and then took over as the freshman coach in South Bend for a year. From 1935 to 1937, Hugh was line coach for Notre Dame alumnus Jim Crowley at Fordham, then took his first head coaching job at Providence in 1938. Four years later, after a 12–19–2 run, Providence discontinued football, so Devore moved on to Holy Cross as an assistant coach. Hugh returned to Notre Dame as ends coach under Frank Leahy in 1943 and replaced interim coach Ed McK-eever in 1945 with Leahy in the Navy.

After the war, Devore was named head coach at St. Bonaventure in 1946 and posted a 25–9–1 record in four years, the only coaching assignment where he had a winning record. Hugh then took over the NYU program in 1950 and coached the last three NYU teams to a 4–17–2 mark until that school discontinued football after 1952. He then spent one season under Gene Ronzani in Green Bay, and when Ronzani was fired late in the year, Devore and Scooter McLean coached the Packers' season ending West Coast road trip. In 1954, Devore was named head coach at Dayton and led the Flyers to a 8–11–1 record until he was lured to the Eagles in 1955. The only thing memorable about his two-year stay in Philadelphia was that he hired illustrious former Giants' coach Steve Owen as his defensive coach. He returned to Notre Dame as freshman coach in 1958 and then bridged the wide gap between the Joe Kurarich and Ara Parseghian eras by helming the Irish in 1963. Hugh worked in the Irish athletic department for a couple of years before spend-ing five years as an assistant coach for the Oilers from 1966 to 1970. From 1971 to 1986, Devore finished his career by serving as the Promotions Director for the Astrodome. Throughout his career in pros and the college ranks, Hugh was known as a kind and amiable man popular with both players and the press.

DIETZ, WILLIAM H. (LONE STAR) 8/17/1884–7/20/1964. Carlisle Indian Industrial School. T; did not play professionally. *Apprenticeship:* College coach —19 years (15 as head coach). *Roots:* None. *Branches:* None. *Coordinators/Key Assistants*: None. *Hall of Fame Players:* None. *Primary Quarterbacks:* None. *Tendencies:* • His teams scored 8.8 points and allowed 8 per game • His teams ran 78.3% of the time, which was 107% of the

Devore, Hugh J.									
Year	Team	Games	Wins	Losses	Ties	%	P Wins	P Losses	P %
1953	Packers	2	0	2	0	.000	0	0	.000
1956	Eagles	12	3	8	1	.292	0	0	.000
1957	Eagles	12	4	8	0	.333	0	0	.000
3 years		26	7	18	1	.288	0	0	.000

league average • Eleven rookie starters in two years • Winning Full Seasons to Losing Full Seasons: 0:0.

Although his Indian heritage was later questioned, Lone Star Dietz attended the Carlisle Indian School with Jim Thorpe and began his coaching career there as an assistant to the celebrated Glenn "Pop" Warner in 1913 and 1914. Dietz struck out on his own in 1915 as the head coach at Washington State and racked up two undefeated seasons in his 17–2–1 tally from 1915 to 1917. Lone Star was a showman who often coached in full Indian regalia on the sidelines and was very popular with the students. He led the Cougars to a victory in the 1916 Rose Bowl, coaching the game in a top hat and tails to commemorate the New Year. However, school President Ernest Holland did not share that enthusiasm for Dietz; in fact, Lone Star's biographer Tom Benjey quotes a letter from Holland's personal secretary in *Keep A'Goin'* that alleges Holland felt Indians should not be integrated with white society. Holland fired Dietz when his contract ran out, and Lone Star surfaced as the coach of the Mare Island Marines in 1918, guiding them to the 1919 Rose Bowl.

The next two years were difficult ones for Dietz. His estranged wife died in the 1919 Flu epidemic, and he was charged with dodging the draft during the war on the basis of having falsely registered as a "Non-Citizen Indian" even though both his Pine Ridge, South Dakota parents were white. Dietz's mother testified that Lone Star actually was adopted, and the trial ended in a hung jury. However, the government retried the case. Dietz pled "Nolo Contendere" to avoid more legal fees and was sentenced to a month in jail. Putting that incident behind him, he continued his coaching career in 1921 leading Purdue to a 1–6 mark. He then moved on to Louisiana Tech in 1922 (5–1–1) and Wyoming in 1924. After a 10–13–2 record in three years with the Cowboys, Lone Star spent 1927 and 1928 as an assistant to Pop Warner once again, this time at Stanford. In 1929, Dietz took over the program at the Haskell Indian School in Kansas and stayed for four years, compiling a 26–16–1 record.

George Preston Marshall came calling in 1933, hiring Dietz to coach his pro team in Boston. Having played 1932 in the home of baseball's Boston Braves, the football team carried the same name. With Marshall moving the team to Fenway Park in 1933, the team was renamed the Redskins. Some say that was done in honor of Dietz who brought along four Indian players from Haskell to Boston. Ever the promoter, Marshall made a big splash by having the whole team wear "war paint" for the home opener that year. With the Redskins, Lone Star was most remembered by his players for having a strong predilection for trick plays, continually using the fake fumble play or the broken shoelace play. The only trick play that players recalled as having been effective, though, was the "Squirrel Cage" kickoff return in which all the Redskins raced towards the kicked ball and huddled around it, hiding who was actually going to emerge with the ball. In both of Lone Star's years, Boston won as many games as it lost and no more.

Out of work in 1935, Dietz again signed on as Warner's assistant, this time for two years at Temple University. His final head coaching job was from 1937 to 1942 at Albright College in Reading, Pennsylvania, where he went 31–23–2; his overall college record was 96–63–7. Lone Star was also a fine artist, having provided the illustrations for Pop Warner's *Football for Coaches and Players* in 1927 and having designed the logo for the Redskins' team. From 1943 to 1946, he worked at a New York advertising agency and later ran his own art school. Sadly, he died penniless and forgotten, though, from cancer at the age of 79 in Reading in 1964.

DIMEOLO, ALBERT (LUBY) 10/27/1903–6/17/1966. Pittsburgh. G; did not play professionally. *Apprenticeship:* College asst.—1 year. *Roots:* None. *Branches:* None. *Coordinators/Key Assistants:* Cad Reese and J.P. Rooney were among the first assistant coaches in the NFL. *Hall of Fame Players:* Johnny Blood McNally. *Primary Quarterbacks:* None. *Tendencies:* • His team scored 4.3 points and allowed 17.2 per game • His team ran 69.2% of the time, which was 93% of the league average • Five rookie starters in one year • Winning Full Seasons to Losing Full Seasons: 0:1.

Dietz, William H. (Lone Star)

Year	Team	Games	Wins	Losses	Ties	%	P Wins	P Losses	P %
1933	Redskins	12	5	5	2	.500	0	0	.000
1934	Redskins	12	6	6	0	.500	0	0	.000
2 years		24	11	11	2	.500	0	0	.000

DiMeolo, Albert (Luby)

Year	Team	Games	Wins	Losses	Ties	%	P Wins	P Losses	P %
1934	Pirates (Steelers)	12	2	10	0	.167	0	0	.000
1 year		12	2	10	0	.167	0	0	.000

Youngstown, Ohio's Luby DiMeolo played guard and captained the 1929 Pitt Panthers. After graduation, Luby coached the line at NYU under Chick Meehan in 1931 and under Howard Caan in 1932 and 1933. One of his teammates at Pitt was Jim Rooney whose brother Art founded the Pittsburgh Pirates NFL team in 1933 after having run a semipro football team in the Steel City for many years. When the Pirates' coach that first season, Jap Douds, elected to return to being just a player in 1934, Art offered the job to West Virginia coach Greasy Neale. Instead, Greasy took a job as backfield coach at Yale, so Art hired DiMeolo as head coach who in turn hired Art's brother Jim as his backfield coach.

Luby quickly proved that he was no head coach. The untested DiMeolo was more one of the boys and instilled no team discipline, much like his predecessor. He got into an argument with Rooney once about whether football players or boxers were tougher, and the two of them decided to settle it right in Rooney's office. Art was a former boxer and pummeled Luby to prove his point. DiMeolo was fired after one year, but remained a lifelong friend of the Rooneys. Luby later coached the line at Westminster College in 1935 and Carnegie Tech in 1936. During the war, he served in the Navy and then worked in state government before being named a U.S. Marshall in 1955. DiMeolo subsequently worked security for U.S. Steel in the 1960s until dying from a heart attack following a squash match at age 62 in 1966.

DITKA, MICHAEL K. (MIKE) 10/18/1939– Pittsburgh. Played TE for the Bears, Eagles and Cowboys from 1961 to 1972. *Apprenticeship:* Pro asst.— 9 years. *Roots:* Tom Landry. *Branches:* Buddy Ryan, Hank Kuhlmann (i), Vince Tobin, Dave McGinnis, Jeff Fisher, Jack Del Rio. *Coordinators/Key Assistants:* For the Bears, Ed Hughes then Greg Landry ran the of-

fense, while Buddy Ryan then Vince Tobin handled the defense; for the Saints, Dan Abramowicz ran the offense, while Zav Yaralian handled the defense. *Hall of Fame Players:* Richard Dent, Dan Hampton, Walter Payton, Willie Roaf, Mike Singletary. *Primary Quarterbacks:* Jim McMahon, Jim Harbaugh, Mike Tomczak. *Record:* **Hall of Fame Player**; Super Bowl Championship 1985. *Tendencies:* • His teams scored 20.2 points and allowed 18.6 per game • His teams ran 50.5% of the time, which was 110% of the league average • 20 starting quarterbacks in 14 years; 66% of starts to primary quarterbacks • 26 rookie starters in 14 years • Winning Full Seasons to Losing Full Seasons: 7:6.

On the football field, they don't come any tougher than Mike Ditka. Raised in the Western Pennsylvania region of coal mines and steel mills, Ditka became an All-American at the University of Pittsburgh and was the first round draft pick of the Chicago Bears in 1961. Ditka expected to play linebacker for the Bears, but instead was put on offense where he revolutionized the tight end position. He and the Packers' Ron Kramer were the first tight ends able to block like a tackle and catch passes downfield like an end. Mike was the Bears' primary offensive weapon for his first four years until his body started to deteriorate from the weekly pounding. Furthermore, he got into hot water with George Halas when he was quoted as saying that the Bears' owner "throws around nickels like manhole covers." Halas did not appreciate being called cheap and traded Ditka to the lowly Eagles, where Mike was suspended in his second year by coach Joe Kuharich for making negative comments about "the team" (really Kuharich). Traded again in 1969, Ditka spent the last four years of his career on the Cowboys, even catching a touchdown pass in Super Bowl VI against Miami.

Mike retired a year after that and joined Tom

Ditka, Michael K. (Mike)

Year	Team	Games	Wins	Losses	Ties	%	P Wins	P Losses	P %
1982	Bears	9	3	6	0	.333	0	0	.000
1983	Bears	16	8	8	0	.500	0	0	.000
1984	Bears	16	10	6	0	.625	1	1	.500
1985	Bears	16	15	1	0	.938	3	0	1.000
1986	Bears	16	14	2	0	.875	0	1	.000
1987	Bears	15	11	4	0	.733	0	1	.000
1988	Bears	16	12	4	0	.750	1	1	.500
1989	Bears	16	6	10	0	.375	0	0	.000
1990	Bears	16	11	5	0	.688	1	1	.500
1991	Bears	16	11	5	0	.688	0	1	.000
1992	Bears	16	5	11	0	.313	0	0	.000
1997	Saints	16	6	10	0	.375	0	0	.000
1998	Saints	16	6	10	0	.375	0	0	.000
1999	Saints	16	3	13	0	.188	0	0	.000
14 years		216	121	95	0	.560	6	6	.500

Landry's coaching staff in 1973. Ditka spent nine years coaching special teams and tight ends in Dallas before reconciling with Halas and coming home as Bears' head coach in 1982. The good news was that outgoing GM Jim Finks had acquired a solid talent base with which to work; the bad news was that Mike had no say over the defensive side of the ball with Halas' retention of Bears' belligerent defensive coordinator Buddy Ryan. Ditka and Ryan clashed from the start, and things would only worsen in the four years the two shared the Chicago sideline. Hall of Fame linebacker Mike Singletary got along with both coaches and noted to the *Washington Post*, "I don't see a whole lot of difference in Buddy Ryan and Mike Ditka. I think, basically, maybe that's why they didn't get along very well." However, Hall of Fame defensive end Dan Hampton told Bob McGinn in *The Ultimate Super Bowl Book*, "Ditka had great strengths. Motivation was number one, and talent evaluation. It was great playing for Ditka, and I love him to death. But as far as like an offensive genius? No. Well, Buddy didn't respect Ditka because of that. He didn't understand why our offense was always so, you know, rudimentary, when our defense was so high-tech."

For his part, Ditka embraced the basics; his teams ran the ball 10% more than the league average. He told the Hall of Fame in 2001, "We had a great defense — hardnosed — got after people. And offensively, we challenged people. We ran the ball — we had enough of the good plays, the passing plays and all that — but we had a great running game because we had Walter Payton. It was that simple." On top of his feud with Ryan, Ditka had a fiery relationship with his punky quarterback Jim McMahon, but these three outsized personalities coexisted long enough to breeze through the 1985 season with one of the fiercest defenses in NFL history and stomp their way to a Super Bowl victory that year. Tellingly, Ryan was given a ride off the field on the shoulders of defensive ends Hampton and Richard Dent, while defensive tackles Steve McMichael and William Perry carted off Ditka. Ryan left for Philadelphia in 1986, while McMahon spent the next few seasons getting hurt and causing friction before Ditka traded him in 1989. Ditka's Bears rolled on for several seasons with weak quarterbacking and an aging defense but still winning because they played in a very weak division.

The most indelible image for the post Super Bowl Bears' was Ditka raging at quarterback Jim Harbaugh on the sidelines after an interception on Monday Night Football in 1992. By this point, Ditka had become a self-caricature, the pugnacious face of the Bears in decline, and was fired at the end of the year. Five years later, the Saints named Mike their new head coach, but his three-year tenure in New Orleans was particularly ugly and pointless. Ditka's drafts were terrible, and he compounded that weakness by trading all his 1999 draft picks for the rights to running back Ricky Williams. Moreover, a distasteful training camp hazing incident confirmed the out-of-control nature of the team. Finally, the quarterback situation in New Orleans was even weaker than it had been in Chicago. After three losing seasons, Mike was fired in 2000. However, despite hip replacements, knee problems and a heart attack, Ditka continues on as a popular broadcaster and restaurateur.

DONELLI, ALDO T. (BUFF) 7/22/1907–8/9/1994. Duquesne. HB; did not play professionally. *Apprenticeship:* College coach —13 years (4 as head coach). *Roots:* None. *Branches:* None. *Coordinators/Key Assistants*: Walt Kiesling coached the line in Pittsburgh. *Hall of Fame Players:* None. *Primary Quarterbacks:* None. *Tendencies:* • His teams scored 15.7 points and allowed 24.7 per game • His teams ran 66.3% of the time, which was 104% of the league average • Eleven rookie starters in two years • Winning Full Seasons to Losing Full Seasons: 0:1.

Aldo Donelli was called Buff for his affection for Buffalo Bill as a kid in Western Pennsylvania. As an athlete, he starred both in soccer and football and was named to the National Soccer Hall of Fame in 1944. He played on the 1934 U.S. World Cup team and was the only American to score a goal that year. While he continued to play soccer into the war years, he became more famous as a football coach. In particular, he was the only man since 1933 to serve as a head coach of both a pro and college team at the same time.

Donelli played halfback at Duquesne under Elmer Layden from 1927 to 1929 and then served as the school's freshman coach for the next nine years. In 1939, Buff took over as Duquesne's head coach and produced an undefeated team in his first season. Two years later, Art Rooney convinced him to replace Bert Bell two games into the 1941 season and coach the Steelers on the side. Donelli set up a crazy schedule where he coached the Steelers from 8 A.M. to noon and then went to Duquesne from 1 to 6 P.M. After din-

Donelli, Aldo T. (Buff)

Year	Team	Games	Wins	Losses	Ties	%	P Wins	P Losses	P %
1941	Steelers	5	0	5	0	.000	0	0	.000
1944	Rams	10	4	6	0	.400	0	0	.000
2 years		15	4	11	0	.267	0	0	.000

ner, he would return to the Steelers for night meetings. Donelli, who was also the Dukes' Athletic Director, was listed as the "Advisory Coach" with assistant Steve Sinko the official Coach during this time. However, Donelli was on the Duquesne bench for each game. Despite his previous relationship with Donelli, NFL commissioner Elmer Layden was displeased with this farce. When the Dukes were scheduled to play St. Mary's in California on the same weekend that the Steelers would be playing in Philadelphia, Layden told Donelli he had to choose which job to keep. With the Steelers at 0–5 and the Dukes at 6–0, it really was no choice at all. Buff was replaced in Pittsburgh by Walt Kiesling for the rest of 1941, but spent just one more year at Duquesne before football was discontinued for the war. His four year record was 29–4–2.

Donelli signed on as Pete Cawthon's line coach for the Dodgers in 1943 and then was named head coach of the Rams in 1944. He told the press, "It won't be any joyride in Cleveland, but I believe the teams have leveled off, even in the professional ranks." Donelli used his own version of the T formation, which combined the Notre Dame Box he learned from Layden and the Split T, but was let go after just one year. Buff returned to the college ranks, assisting Lou Little at Columbia in 1945 until landing the head coaching job at Boston University in 1947. He spent ten years at BU with a 46–36–4 mark and then succeeded Lou Little at Columbia in 1957. While the good-natured Donelli only posted two winning seasons in 11 at Columbia, he did lead the Lions to a share of the Ivy League title in 1961, but his cumulative mark was 30–67–2. He retired after the 1967 season with an overall college coaching record of 105–107–8.

DOOLEY, JAMES W. (JIM) 2/8/1930–1/8/2008. Miami. Played E for the Bears from 1952 to 1954 and 1957–1961. *Apprenticeship:* Pro asst.—6 years. *Roots:* George Halas. *Branches:* Abe Gibron, Jim Ringo. *Coordinators/Key Assistants*: Dooley handled his own offense, while Joe Fortunato then Jim Carr then Abe Gibron ran the defense. *Hall of Fame Players:* Dick Butkus, Gale Sayers. *Primary Quarterbacks:* Jack Concannon. *Tendencies:* • His teams scored 16.1 points and allowed 21.6 per game • His teams ran 48.9% of the time, which was 94% of the league average • Four starting quarterbacks in four years; 50% of starts to primary quarterback • Nine rookie starters in four years • Winning Full Seasons to Losing Full Seasons: 0:3.

In the *Chicago Tribune*, George Halas once said of Jim Dooley, "If I had a choice of any other coach in the country, I would go to Jim because he was a great assistant coach. [He] wasn't much of a head coach on account of a lot of things we won't get into." Dooley was a very clever assistant whose one opportunity as head coach was laden with bad luck and the bizarre just as Halas intimated.

Born in Missouri but raised in Miami, Dooley was an All-American end at the University of Miami. He was picked in the first round of the 1952 NFL draft by the Bears and began on the defensive side, but switched to offense after a year. His ten years playing with the Bears was interrupted by military service from 1955 to 1956 and a knee injury in 1958. Jim retired after the 1961 season and immediately joined Halas' coaching staff as the ends coach. Four years later once George Allen left for Los Angeles, Dooley assumed control of the Bears' defense in 1966. In that role, he popularized the Nickel Defense in 1967 with his regular practice of substituting a defensive back for a linebacker in passing downs being called the "Dooley Shift." When Halas retired from coaching for good at the end of that season, he named his able assistant as his successor.

After a 7–7 first season, everything went wrong in 1969. Despite Gale Sayers leading the NFL in rushing for the second time, the Bears won just won game and finished in a tie for the top drafting slot with the Steelers. During that season, Brian Piccolo was diagnosed with cancer, while quarterback Virgil Carter called Dooley "gutless and a liar" for replacing him with rookie Bobby Douglass at halftime in week 13. To top it all off, Pittsburgh won the coin toss for the number one pick and selected Terry Bradshaw; the Bears traded the number two pick to Green Bay for three washed up Packers. In 1970, Carter was traded to Cincinnati, Piccolo died during training camp and Sayers suffered a second knee injury that essentially ended his career. Still, the Bears rebounded to 6–8 by allowing six fewer points per game. Dooley tried to turn the offense over to scatter-armed Bobby Douglass in 1971, but found Bobby so irresponsible that Jim actually moved in to Douglass' bachelor quarters at one

Dooley, James W. (Jim)									
Year	Team	Games	Wins	Losses	Ties	%	P Wins	P Losses	P %
1968	Bears	14	7	7	0	.500	0	0	.000
1969	Bears	14	1	13	0	.071	0	0	.000
1970	Bears	14	6	8	0	.429	0	0	.000
1971	Bears	14	6	8	0	.429	0	0	.000
4 years		56	20	36	0	.357	0	0	.000

point during the year, trying to keep his playboy quarterback focused. It did not work, and Dooley was fired after another 6–8 year.

Jim spent 1972 as an assistant in Buffalo and the next year out of football before resurfacing as an assistant with the Southern California Sun of the ill-fated WFL. Unfortunately, Dooley's financial state at this point mirrored the WFL; he was bankrupt and deep in debt. Sid Luckman came to Dooley's rescue, giving him a position at Sid's packaging firm and helping him erase his debts over the next half dozen years. In 1981, Halas brought Dooley back as an assistant for Neill Armstrong's staff, although he answered directly to Halas and was considered a stoolie for the boss. When Mike Ditka was hired in 1982, he kept Dooley on staff and made use of him as a film scout of upcoming opponents for the next decade. Jim died from Lou Gehrig's disease in 2008.

DORAIS, CHARLES E. (GUS) 7/2/1891–1/3/1954. Notre Dame. QB; did not play in the NFL. *Apprenticeship:* College coach — 28 years (27 as head coach). *Roots:* None. *Branches:* None. *Coordinators/Key Assistants:* Pete Cawthon, Joe Bach and Bob Winslow were his only assistants. *Hall of Fame Players:* Alex Wojciechowicz. *Primary Quarterbacks:* Roy Zimmerman. *Tendencies:* • His teams scored 18.2 points and allowed 22.2 per game • His teams ran 53.9% of the time, which was 86% of the league average • Three starting quarterbacks in one T formation year; 58% of starts to primary quarterback • 19 rookie starters in five years • Winning Full Seasons to Losing Full Seasons: 2:3.

Since his name was pronounced the same as that of 19th century French engraver Gustave Dore, Charles Dorais' friends began calling him "Gus." The 5'7" 145-pound quarterback from Chippewa Falls, Wisconsin was a four-year starter at Notre Dame where he and end Knute Rockne were the first great passing combination in college football. In fact, Dorais is sometimes credited with being the first passer to master the spiral. After graduation, both Dorais and his friend Rockne played some pro football while they began their coaching careers. Dorais played for the Fort Wayne Friars in 1915 and 1916 and the Massillon Tigers in 1918 and 1919.

Meanwhile, Gus coached Dubuque College to a

17–9–2 record from 1914 to 1917 before returning to Notre Dame in 1918 to coach the basketball team and the backfield for Rockne. Future coach Dutch Bergman later told the *Washington Post*, "Gus was rough on us as a coach. A real tough guy, but I learned a lot under him in my last year at school and we grew to be great friends." In 1920, Dorais took on the head coaching assignment at Gonzaga where he coached future Hall of Fame coach Ray Flaherty. Gonzaga went 20–13–3 in five years under Gus who moved on to the University of Detroit in 1925. Dorais coached the Titans for 18 years and compiled a 113–48–7 mark in that time. He became such a part of the community that he also served multiple terms on the Detroit City Council. Lions' owner Fred Mandel unsuccessfully tried to convince Gus to take over the pro team in Detroit in 1940, but finally wore Dorais down in 1943 — the same year that Gus fractured his skull in a fall.

Dorais used a combination of the Notre Dame Box and Spread formations with the Lions and had some success during the war with ace tailback Frankie Sinkwich calling signals. In 1946, he signed a five-year extension with Detroit, but after 1–10 and 3–9 seasons, he was fired in 1948. In his last season, he began to experiment with the T formation, but did not have the talent on hand to run it. Gus did some scouting and ran an automobile dealership over the next few years. In 1952, he returned to the NFL as backfield coach for fellow Notre Dame alumnus Joe Bach in Pittsburgh. The two, along with assistant Keith Molesworth, installed the T formation for the Steelers, and then Dorais retired for good in 1953.

DOUDS, FORREST M. (JAP) 4/21/1905–8/16/1979. Washington and Jefferson. Played T for the Providence Steam Roller, Portsmouth Spartans, Chicago Cardinals and Pittsburgh Pirates from 1930 to 1934. *Apprenticeship:* None. *Roots:* None. *Branches:* None. *Coordinators/Key Assistants:* None. *Hall of Fame Players:* None. *Primary Quarterbacks:* None. *Record:* Player-Coach. *Tendencies:* • His teams scored 6.1 points and allowed 18.9 per game • His teams ran 63.3% of the time, which was 88% of the league average • Nine rookie starters in one year • Winning Full Seasons to Losing Full Seasons: 0:1.

Jap Douds of Rochester, Pennsylvania was a

Dorais, Charles E. (Gus)									
Year	Team	Games	Wins	Losses	Ties	%	P Wins	P Losses	P %
1943	Lions	10	3	6	1	.350	0	0	.000
1944	Lions	10	6	3	1	.650	0	0	.000
1945	Lions	10	7	3	0	.700	0	0	.000
1946	Lions	11	1	10	0	.091	0	0	.000
1947	Lions	12	3	9	0	.250	0	0	.000
5 years		53	20	31	2	.396	0	0	.000

three-time All-American tackle for Washington & Jefferson and captained the team as a senior. His remaining claim to fame is that Art Rooney hired him as player-coach for the expansion Pittsburgh Pirates in 1933. Art's brother Jim who had starred on Art's semi-pro teams for years later said simply of Douds, "He was no coach." Indeed, Jap was eager to give up coaching at the end of the season because the added worries of coaching were not earning him any additional money. One of the players on Pittsburgh was former Duquesne tackle Ray Kemp. Kemp and the Cardinals Joe Lillard were the last two black players in the NFL before the color line was drawn in 1934. The two faced each other in Pittsburgh's second game of the season and at halftime, Douds implored his team, "We have to stop that nigger." On the way back to the field, Douds apologized to Kemp for the comment, but two weeks later, Kemp was cut, perhaps because he and Douds competed for the same position. In need of players at the end of the season, Kemp was brought back for the 1933 season finale, but it would be 19 years before another black player played for Pittsburgh.

DOVE, ROBERT L.P. (BOB) 2/21/1921–4/19/2006. Notre Dame. Played E for the Chicago Rockets, Chicago Cardinals and Detroit Lions from 1946 to 1954. *Apprenticeship:* None. *Roots:* None. *Branches:* None. *Coordinators/Key Assistants:* None. *Hall of Fame Players:* None. *Primary Quarterbacks:* None. *Record:* **Interim Player-Coach and Co-Coach** (with Ned Mathews and Willie Wilkin).

Youngstown, Ohio's Bob Dove was a two-time All-American end with Notre Dame in 1941 and 1942 before entering the Marines during World War II. In the service, he played for the famed El Toro Marine team under Coach Dick Hanley from 1943 to 1945. Hanley subsequently strong-armed many of his best players, including Dove, to join him on the fledgling Chicago Rockets in the new All America Football Conference in 1946. When Hanley had a rancorous falling out with intrusive owner John Keeshin after just the second game of the year, Keeshin appointed a player-coach triumvirate of Dove, halfback Ned Mathews and lineman Wee Willie Wilkin to run the team until he hired a fulltime coach. Six games later, Keeshin appointed former Rockets' line coach Pat Boland to finish out the year with the team, and the triumvirate went back to just playing. Dove had a long career in both the AAFC and NFL, mostly as a defensive end. Upon retiring from the Lions at the end of the 1954 season, he began his coaching career as an assistant coach. He spent 1953–1957 with the University of Detroit, 1958–1959 with the Lions, 1960–1961 with the Bills before being named head coach at Hiram College where he posted a 22–34 mark from 1962 to 1968. In 1969, Dove went home, joining the staff at Youngstown State and staying there as an assistant through 1987. Even in retirement, Bob continued at Youngstown for four more years as an emeritus coach.

DOWHOWER, RODNEY D. (ROD) 4/15/1943– San Diego State. QB; did not play professionally. *Apprenticeship:* College coach —13 years (1 as head coach); pro asst.— 5 years. *Roots:* Don Coryell, Red Miller, Jim Hanifan. *Branches:* Rick Venturi. *Coordinators/Key Assistants:* Billie Matthews helped with the offense, and George Hill handled the defense. *Hall of Fame Players:* None. *Primary Quarterbacks:* Mike Pagel, Jack Trudeau. *Tendencies:* • His teams scored 16.1 points and allowed 25 per game • His teams ran 43.9% of the time, which was 95% of the league average • Four starting quarterbacks in two years; 86% of starts to primary quarterbacks • Seven rookie starters in two years •

Douds, Forrest M. (Jap)									
Year	Team	Games	Wins	Losses	Ties	%	P Wins	P Losses	P %
1933	Pirates (Steelers)	11	3	6	2	.364	0	0	.000
1 year		11	3	6	2	.364	0	0	.000

Dove, Robert L.P. (Bob)									
Year	Team	Games	Wins	Losses	Ties	%	P Wins	P Losses	P %
1946	Rockets (AAFC)	6	3	2	1	.583	0	0	.000
1 year		6	3	2	1	.583	0	0	.000

Dowhower, Rodney D. (Rod)									
Year	Team	Games	Wins	Losses	Ties	%	P Wins	P Losses	P %
1985	Colts	16	5	11	0	.313	0	0	.000
1986	Colts	13	0	13	0	.000	0	0	.000
2 years		29	5	24	0	.172	0	0	.000

Winning Full Seasons to Losing Full Seasons: 0:2.

Born in Ord, Nebraska, Rod Dowhower spent 35 years coaching college and pro football but only five as a head coach. Dowhower was an acolyte of Don Coryell, having played quarterback for him at San Diego State from 1963 to 1965. He then spent seven years on Coryell's Aztec staff and followed Don to St. Louis as a Cardinals' assistant in 1973. Rod moved on to UCLA under Dick Vermeil in 1974, Boise State in 1976 and Stanford under Bill Walsh in 1977. When Walsh took the 49ers' job, Dowhower succeeded him as head coach at Stanford. After just one 5–5–1 year, though, Rod quit to work as offensive coordinator in Denver under Red Miller for two years. At the time, Stanford's assistant athletic director Gary Cavalli commented, "Rod is oriented toward the technical side of football. Offensive tactics and strategy are what he enjoys most. He wasn't comfortable with the peripheral responsibilities of a head coach — the time-consuming work with the media, alumni, donors, faculty and others — but he was trying." Mostly, Rod kept moving. In 1983, Dowhower joined another Coryell alumnus, Jim Hanifan, in St. Louis, and spent two years as offensive coordinator molding quarterback Neil Lomax before taking the head coaching job with the Colts in 1985.

On taking the Colts' job, Dowhower announced, "I've been with systems where we throw the ball a lot, and that's the type of offense I want here. I'm prone to the forward pass." Rod made a full commitment to Art Schlichter in training camp, but then benched him after an opening day loss in 1985, and both the coach and the quarterback felt betrayed. With quarterbacks like Mike Pagel and Jack Trudeau, though, Dowhower's offense was DOA. Things turned from bad to worse in 1986, with Dowhower even hyperventilating and collapsing on the sidelines after a key play against the Dolphins in week eight. Mercifully, he was fired after week 13. Rod moved on as an assistant in Atlanta from 1987 to 1989, then with the Redskins from 1990 to 1993 before trying head coaching once more with Vanderbilt, resulting in a 4–18 record for 1995 and 1996. Dowhower finished his coaching career with a season on the Giants' staff under Jim Fassel and three with Andy Reid in Philadelphia as offensive coordinator from 1999 to 2001.

DRISCOLL, JOHN L. (PADDY) 1/11/1896– 6/29/1968. Northwestern. Played TB for the Decatur Staleys, Chicago Cardinals and Chicago Bears. *Apprenticeship:* None. *Roots:* None. *Branches:* None. *Coordinators/Key Assistants*: For the Bears, Clark Shaughnessy and Luke Johnsos were the key assistants. *Hall of Fame Players:* Doug Atkins, George Blanda, Bill George, Stan Jones. *Primary Quarterbacks:* Ed Brown. *Record:* **Hall of Fame Player**; began as a **Player-Coach**. *Tendencies:* • His teams scored 15.7 points and allowed 11.4 per game • His teams ran 63.4% of the time in 1956–57, which was 106% of the league average • Two starting quarterbacks in two T formation years; 83% of starts to primary quarterback • 23 rookie starters in five years • Winning Full Seasons to Losing Full Seasons: 3:1.

Although listed at 5'11" in most encyclopedias, Evanston, Illinois-native Paddy Driscoll was probably closer to 5'8" and weighed no more than 160 pounds, but was one of the biggest stars of the early days of pro football. Driscoll starred as an All-American halfback at Northwestern from 1914 to 1916 and then played some second base for the Chicago Cubs in 1917, batting a feeble .107. In 1918, he went into the service and teamed with George Halas on the Great Lakes Naval Station that won the 1919 Rose Bowl. After his discharge, Paddy spent 1919 playing minor league baseball before joining the Hammond Pros football team that fall. With the start of the APFA in 1920, Driscoll signed on as player-coach with Chris O'Brien's Chicago Cardinals and also appeared in one game as a ringer for Halas' Decatur Staleys late in the year. Paddy served as the team's coach for three years, but starred on the field for six with the Cardinals. While he was a fine runner and passer, Paddy was especially noted as a punter and drop-kicker, which were vital parts of the game in the 1920s. Halas continually tried to pry Driscoll loose from the Cardinals and finally succeeded in 1926 when O'Brien was struggling financially and facing an additional competitor that year with Joey Sternaman's Chicago Bulls in Red Grange's new American Football League.

Sold to the Bears for the 1926 season, Driscoll spent four years starring in the backfield and cemented his lifelong friendship with George Halas. Retiring at the end of the 1929 season, Paddy was a six-time All Pro and

Year	Team	Games	Wins	Losses	Ties	%	P Wins	P Losses	P %
1920	Cardinals	10	6	2	2	.700	0	0	.000
1921	Cardinals	8	3	3	2	.500	0	0	.000
1922	Cardinals	11	8	3	0	.727	0	0	.000
1956	Bears	12	9	2	1	.792	0	1	.000
1957	Bears	12	5	7	0	.417	0	0	.000
5 years		53	31	17	5	.632	0	1	.000

Driscoll, John L. (Paddy)

later was named to the NFL's All-Decade team. He had begun coaching high school football at St. Mel's in Chicago in 1924 and continued there through 1937, also coaching the basketball and baseball teams. In 1937, Driscoll took over as head coach at Marquette, but only compiled a 10–23–1 record in four years before returning to the Bears in 1941 as an assistant coach. He would stay with Chicago in various capacities until his death 27 years later. The quiet, soft-spoken Driscoll served as go-between defensive coach Hunk Anderson and offensive coach Luke Johnsos when they co-coached the Bears in Halas' absence during World War II, but mostly had a minor role in the coaching. Therefore, it was a surprise when Halas named Paddy head coach when George stepped down for a "younger man" in 1956. According to Jeff Davis in *Papa Bear*, Halas told Luke Johnsos he was going to be named coach, but Johnsos made the mistake of telling the press ahead of time. So Halas switched to Driscoll, who returned to head coaching after a 34-year gap. Fullback Rick Caseras told Davis, "Paddy Driscoll was one of the sweetest guys who ever lived. But Paddy was just a figurehead. He didn't say 10 words."

Chicago went to the NFL title game in 1956 but lost to the New York Giants in a second "sneakers game" on an icy field. However, Halas was still calling the shots and dissension on the staff, especially between Johnsos and defensive coach Clark Shaughnessy, was rife. The Bears dropped to 5–7 in 1957, bringing about Halas' final return to the head coaching reigns. Driscoll was given a golden parachute for his loyal service. He was named an administrative vice-president with the title of Director of Research and Planning, which meant he would scout game film. He remained in that position till his death at the age of 73.

DRISKILL, WALTER S. 9/20/1913–7/25/1998. Colorado. T; did not play professionally. *Apprenticeship:* College asst.—7 years. *Roots:* None. *Branches:* Red Conkright (i). *Coordinators/Key Assistants:* None. *Hall of Fame Players:* Y.A. Title. *Primary Quarterbacks:* None. *Record:* **Interim Coach.**

As a senior, Walter Driskill played tackle for Colorado through 1935 when All-American Whizzer

White was a sophomore. Driskill stayed at Colorado to earn his master's degree in history and worked as an assistant coach on the football team from 1937 through 1940. He coached at Wyoming in 1942 and then served in the Navy from 1943 to 1945. Upon his discharge, Walter joined the staff of Split T advocate Jim Tatum at Oklahoma in 1946 and followed Tatum to Maryland in 1947, where Driskill also served as athletic director. A year later, he was enlisted as the GM and President of the AAFC's Baltimore Colts even though he had agreed previously to join Bud Wilkinson's staff at Oklahoma. The Colts, under Cecil Isbell, tied for the Eastern Division crown that year, but floundered in 1949 while Driskill pushed heavily for a merger of the two leagues. With the team at 1–7 the club's board of directors met and Isbell was dismissed. Walter actually voted against firing Isbell. He told the press, "I got out of coaching two years ago, and I didn't want to get back in." Driskill took over "reluctantly" and led the Colts to four straight losses to close out the year. With the Colts under new ownership and merged into the NFL in 1950, Driskill continued as GM for a second consecutive one-win season before the Colts franchise folded. Walter left football entirely at this point. He became Director of Marketing for Ruppert Brewing and then Vice President of Gunther Brewing before joining Miller Brewing as Director of Marketing in 1961. Along the way in 1967, he formed Dribeck Importers, an import beer distributorship that he later sold for $28-million.

DRULIS, CHARLES J. (CHUCK) 3/8/1918–8/23/1972. Temple. Played G for the Bears and Packers in 1942 and from 1946 to 1950. *Apprenticeship:* Pro asst.—11 years. *Roots:* Gene Ronzani, Ray Richards, Pop Ivy. *Branches:* None. *Coordinators/Key Assistants:* None. *Hall of Fame Players:* Larry Wilson. *Primary Quarterbacks:* None. *Record:* **Interim Co-Coach** with Ray Prochaska and Ray Willsey.

Hailing from Girardville, Pennsylvania, Chuck Drulis played guard for Temple University and had a six-year NFL career despite not being drafted. He played for the Bears in 1942 and then went into the Marines for three years. After the war, Drulis returned

Driskill, Walter S.

Year	Team	Games	Wins	Losses	Ties	%	P Wins	P Losses	P %
1949	Colts (AAFC)	8	1	7	0	.125	0	0	.000
1 year		8	1	7	0	.125	0	0	.000

Drulis, Charles J. (Chuck)

Year	Team	Games	Wins	Losses	Ties	%	P Wins	P Losses	P %
1961	Cardinals	2	2	0	0	1.000	0	0	.000
1 year		2	2	0	0	1.000	0	0	.000

to Chicago for four years before finishing his career in 1950 with the Packers. Green Bay was coached by former Bear Gene Ronzani at the time, and he added Chuck to his staff in 1951. When Ronzani was fired, Drulis joined the staff of the Eagles in 1954 and subsequently returned to Chicago with the Cardinals in 1956. Chuck would remain with the Cardinals for the rest of his life, a fixture on the defensive side of the ball under five head coaches in two cities.

In 1961, Pop Ivy suddenly resigned as the Cardinals' coach with two games left in the season, so owner Walter Wolfner appointed Drulis, offensive line coach Ray Prochaska and backfield coach Ray Willsey co-coaches. St. Louis won both remaining games, but hired Wally Lemm as the new head coach for 1962, although Drulis continued to coach the defense.

In his 17 years with the Cards, Drulis gained both positive and negative notoriety. On the plus side, he is widely credited with popularizing the safety blitz, first with Jerry Norton and then with Larry Wilson. Cornerback Pat Fischer also gave Drulis credit for instituting bump-and-run coverage techniques in St. Louis in 1965, before the Raiders became famous for it.

To his detriment, though, Drulis was accused of racial insensitivity in 1968 as the Cardinals were riven by racial problems. Head Coach Charley Winner described Chuck to *Sports Illustrated* as "a rough tough character…. He's a straight talker. He doesn't give you any window dressing." Meanwhile, black cornerback Bobby Williams told *Sports Illustrated* Drulis' gruff name-calling detracted from his talent, "That's one reason it hurts so much when he treats you so bad because as a defensive football coach he's the greatest." To his credit, Drulis worked through his problems with the black players on the team and was still the defensive coach in 1972 when he suffered a fatal heart attack on the team plane traveling to an exhibition game in July. Chuck's wife Dale was an artist who created the façade for the Pro Football Hall of Fame in 1963.

DUNGY, ANTHONY K. (TONY) 10/6/1956– Minnesota. Played DB for the Steelers and 49ers from 1977 to 1979. *Apprenticeship:* College asst.—1 year; pro asst.—14 years. *Roots:* Chuck Noll, Marty Schottenheimer and Dennis Green. *Branches:* Herman Edwards, Lovie Smith, Rod Marinelli, Mike Tomlin, Jim Caldwell, Leslie Frazier. *Coordinators/Key Assistants*: For the Bucs, Mike Shula then Les Steckel then Clyde Christiansen ran the offense, while Monte Kiffin handled the defense; for the Colts, Tom Moore ran the offense, and Ron Meeks handled the defense. *Hall of Fame Players:* Randall McDaniel. *Primary Quarterbacks:* Trent Dilfer, Peyton Manning. *Record:* Super Bowl Championship 2006. *Tendencies:* • His teams scored 23.2 points and allowed 18.3 per game • His teams ran 45.6% of the time, which was 103% of the league average • Five starting quarterbacks in 13 years; 82% of starts to primary quarterbacks • 32 rookie starters in 13 years • Winning Full Seasons to Losing Full Seasons: 11:1.

The title of Tony Dungy's autobiography, *Quiet Strength*, reflects the unique style that took him to the top of the coaching profession, overcoming all obstacles. The son of two teachers, Dungy hails from Jackson, Michigan and was a four-year starter at quarterback for the University of Minnesota. However, in that era, it was standard practice for black college quarterbacks to switch positions in the NFL. Undrafted, Tony signed as a free agent with the Steelers in 1977 and played safety for analytical Chuck Noll for two seasons, winning a Super Bowl ring in 1978. Dungy did appear in one game at quarterback for Pittsburgh when both Terry Bradshaw and backup Mike Kruczek were hurt against the Oilers in 1977. Tony was the emergency quarterback but could not stave off a 27–10 defeat; in the game, he both intercepted a pass on defense and threw two on offense.

In 1979, Dungy was traded to the 49ers and spent a season under cerebral Bill Walsh. A year later, Tony began his coaching career at his alma mater as

Year	Team	Games	Wins	Losses	Ties	%	P Wins	P Losses	P %
1996	Buccaneers	16	6	10	0	.375	0	0	.000
1997	Buccaneers	16	10	6	0	.625	1	1	.500
1998	Buccaneers	16	8	8	0	.500	0	0	.000
1999	Buccaneers	16	11	5	0	.688	1	1	.500
2000	Buccaneers	16	10	6	0	.625	0	1	.000
2001	Buccaneers	16	9	7	0	.563	0	1	.000
2002	Colts	16	10	6	0	.625	0	1	.000
2003	Colts	16	12	4	0	.750	2	1	.667
2004	Colts	16	12	4	0	.750	1	1	.500
2005	Colts	16	14	2	0	.875	0	1	.000
2006	Colts	16	12	4	0	.750	4	0	1.000
2007	Colts	16	13	3	0	.813	0	1	.000
2008	Colts	16	12	4	0	.750	0	1	.000
13 years		208	139	69	0	.668	9	10	.474

Dungy, Anthony K. (Tony)

defensive backs coach. Chuck Noll then brought him back to Pittsburgh as the youngest assistant coach in the league in 1981; three years later, the 28-year-old Dungy became the youngest coordinator in league history when Noll turned over the Steeler defense to him. Four years after that, Tony left Pittsburgh to join the staff of Marty Schottenheimer in Kansas City, again coaching the defensive backs. In 1992, he left Kansas City and was named defensive coordinator in Minnesota under Dennis Green. Over the next few years, Dungy was the subject of numerous articles asking when he was going to get his chance as a head coach, intimating that Dungy had not yet been offered a head coaching job because of racial prejudice.

While his race may have been a factor in his failure to land a head coaching position, other factors weighed more heavily. Dungy was a soft-spoken evangelical Christian who was as committed to coaching his players' character as their football skills. Most teams were looking for a coach more expressly devoted to winning games at all costs. Years later, Tony told the *New York Times*, "I really wanted to show people you can win all kinds of ways. I always coached the way I've wanted to be coached."

Finally in 1995, Rich McKay hired Dungy in Tampa as the Buccaneers head coach. Within a year, Tony had the woeful Bucs headed in the right direction. Through astute player evaluation and development, he elevated the overall talent base of the Bucs with his clampdown Cover 2 defense serving as the team's strength. Dungy first learned the Cover 2 scheme from Bud Carson in Pittsburgh, developed it in Minnesota and perfected it in Tampa along with coordinator Monte Kiffin whom he brought with him from Minnesota. Dungy's Bucs had unprecedented success for Tampa, making the playoffs in four of six seasons. However, a chronically weak offense always sunk the team in the postseason. Tony changed offensive coordinators three years in a row, but when the offense did not respond, Dungy was fired in 2002.

Within two weeks, Dungy was named head coach in Indianapolis, a team with a powerful offense led by quarterback Peyton Manning and offensive coordinator Tom Moore who had coached with Tony in Pittsburgh. By contrast, the Colts' defense was porous. Dungy set about building the defense and slowly improved Indianapolis on that side of the ball. Ultimately, the Colts twice finished in the top three

in points allowed — and five times in the top three in points scored. The Colts won at least 10 games and made the playoffs in each of Tony's seven seasons with the team, but after four years, still hadn't reached the Super Bowl. In three of those years they lost in the playoffs to the eventual Super Bowl champions, the Patriots twice and then the Steelers.

In 2006, though, everything came together on the field despite Tony having to come to grips with his oldest son's suicide that December. The Colts rallied around Dungy, overcame the Patriots in a thrilling postseason comeback victory and defeated the Bears in the Super Bowl to win the NFL title. Not only was Dungy the first black coach to win the Super Bowl, but opposing coach Lovie Smith was an African American coach who was mentored by Tony on his Tampa staff. Commissioner Roger Goodell told the *New York Times*, "He has changed the way you coach. You can be a quiet and effective leader and a man of principles and values."

After two more years coaching the Colts, Dungy retired in 2009. In his 13 years as a head coach, his teams only experienced one losing season and made the playoffs 11 times. Dungy's calm rectitude and coaching excellence inspired his players to treat him with love and respect and to attribute Tony as a major influence on their lives. Dungy has continued to write best selling books on his approach to life and has worked with the league to improve its mentoring of players, with Tony taking a special interest in rehabilitating troubled Mike Vick. In addition, he has become a respected broadcaster who is unafraid to speak out when prominent league figures such as Bill Belichick or Rex Ryan fail to demonstrate good sportsmanship or act as worthy role models for youth.

EDWARDS, ALBERT G. (TURK) 9/28/1907–1/12/1973. Washington State. Played T for the Redskins from 1932 to 1940. *Apprenticeship:* Pro asst.— 6 years. *Roots:* Ray Flaherty, Dutch Bergman, Dud DeGroot. *Branches:* Wayne Millner (i). *Coordinators/Key Assistants:* Wilbur Moore and Wayne Millner were the key assistants. *Hall of Fame Players:* Sammy Baugh. *Primary Quarterbacks:* Sammy Baugh. *Record:* **Hall of Fame Player.** *Tendencies:* • His teams scored 21.6 points and allowed 24.1 per game • His teams ran 55.8% of the time, which was 92% of the league average • Three starting quarterbacks in three years; 80% of starts to primary

Edwards, Albert G. (Turk)									
Year	Team	Games	Wins	Losses	Ties	%	P Wins	P Losses	P %
1946	Redskins	11	5	5	1	.500	0	0	.000
1947	Redskins	12	4	8	0	.333	0	0	.000
1948	Redskins	12	7	5	0	.583	0	0	.000
3 years		35	16	18	1	.471	0	0	.000

quarterback • Nine rookie starters in three years • Winning Full Seasons to Losing Full Seasons: 1:1.

A native of the state of Washington, Turk Edwards was a teammate of Mel Hein at Washington State University, where both were named All American after the undefeated 1930 season. Edwards finished his eligibility the following year and signed with the expansion Boston Braves franchise that would become the Washington Redskins five years later. At 255 pounds, Turk was very big for that era and received some All Pro notice in each of his first eight seasons. In 1940, he took on the role of player-coach, but only appeared in two games. Edwards started the season opener, but the next week when he went out to kick off to start game two, he freakishly injured his leg just from turning around. He tried to return three weeks later against the Cardinals, but aggravated the same injury and never played again.

Turk spent the next five years coaching the line under head coaches Ray Flaherty, Dutch Bergman and Dudley DeGroot, as the Redskins appeared in four NFL championship games. However, Flaherty was the only coach that was ever able to control meddlesome owner George Preston Marshall at all. After Ray joined the Navy during the war, Marshall went quickly through Bergman and DeGroot before turning to Edwards in 1946. By this time, the team was beginning to slip and never would reach the postseason again while Marshall was running the team. Turk was too nice a man to succeed in that environment. Center Al DeMao told Thom Loverro in *Hail Victory*, "Turk was a hell of a football player and a good line coach, but he never did make a good head coach." Edwards was not able to stand up to Marshall and even took orders from the owner by telephone during the games according to end Joe Aguirre who jumped to the Los Angeles Dons in 1946. Marshall kicked Turk upstairs as a team executive in 1949, but Edwards left for good a year later, opening a sporting goods store in Spokane that he ran for several years. He was elected to both the College and Pro Football Halls of Fame.

EDWARDS, HERMAN 4/27/1954– San Diego State. Played DB for the Eagles, Falcons and Rams from 1977

to 1986. *Apprenticeship:* College asst.—3 years; pro asst.—9 years. *Roots:* Marty Schottenheimer, Tony Dungy. *Branches:* None. *Coordinators/Key Assistants:* For the Jets, Paul Hackett then Mike Heimerdinger ran the offense, while Ted Cottrell then Donnie Henderson handled the defense; for the Chiefs, Mike Solari then Chan Gailey ran the offense, while Gunther Cunningham handled the defense. *Hall of Fame Players:* Curtis Martin. *Primary Quarterbacks:* Vinny Testaverde, Chad Pennington. *Tendencies:* • His teams scored 18.5 points and allowed 20.6 per game • His teams ran 45% of the time, which was 101% of the league average • Eight starting quarterbacks in eight years; 53% of starts to primary quarterbacks • 32 rookie starters in eight years • Winning Full Seasons to Losing Full Seasons: 4:4.

Herman Edwards was recruited out of high school by Dick Vermeil for UCLA, but chose to enroll at Berkeley instead. Despite setting a University of California record with four interceptions in one game, Edwards eventually transferred to San Diego State to finish his college eligibility. Vermeil signed him to the Eagles as an undrafted free agent in 1977, and Herman led the team with six interceptions as a rookie. In Philadelphia, Edwards was an all-around cornerback who played both the pass and the run well. He was not blazing fast, but was smart, disciplined, tough and a durable player who started all 135 games over his nine-year Eagle career. He's most famous for the "Miracle of the Meadowlands," when he scored the game-winning touchdown in the closing seconds on a Joe Pisarcik fumble after the Giants bungled an opportunity to run out the clock in 1978.

Buddy Ryan was never one for sentiment, but went out of his way to praise Edwards when he cut him in August 1986. Ryan told the *Philadelphia Inquirer*, "He had all the things I look for in a player. I told him this morning, 'I've been trying to find a way to make it work where you can stay.' He was a positive leader; he enjoyed practice and the games. But he just got old and can't do it anymore. I had to make that decision. That's all. I hated to do it." Herm spent one last season in the NFL and then went into coaching at San Jose State from 1987 to 1989. In 1990, Marty

Edwards, Herman

Year	Team	Games	Wins	Losses	Ties	%	P Wins	P Losses	P %
2001	Jets	16	10	6	0	.625	0	1	.000
2002	Jets	16	9	7	0	.563	1	1	.500
2003	Jets	16	6	10	0	.375	0	0	.000
2004	Jets	16	10	6	0	.625	1	1	.500
2005	Jets	16	4	12	0	.250	0	0	.000
2006	Chiefs	16	9	7	0	.563	0	1	.000
2007	Chiefs	16	4	12	0	.250	0	0	.000
2008	Chiefs	16	2	14	0	.125	0	0	.000
8 years		128	54	74	0	.422	2	4	.333

Schottenheimer hired him to coach the defensive backs in Kansas City. Tony Dungy then brought Herm to Tampa as Assistant Head Coach in 1996, and in 2001 the Jets hired him as head coach.

Edwards had some success with the Jets, getting to the playoffs three times in four years, but became better known for his dramatic motivational pronouncements on football and life. For example, "The game is not hard. Sometimes coaches make it hard," he opined at his opening press conference in New York. Of course, the most famous Edwards remark came when a reporter asked him whether the Jets were good enough to win after a midseason loss in 2002, "You play to win the game. Hello? You play to win the game. You don't play it just to play it." Ironically, the main criticism of Edwards as a coach–aside from his dreadful clock management skills — was that his conservative style resulted in his teams seeming to play not to lose rather than to win.

After five years in New York, Edwards forced his way out of town to sign on as Dick Vermeil's replacement in Kansas City. However, the grass was not greener in the Midwest. The Chiefs were a team in decline. In his final year, Herm made a commitment to play his young players, and they took a beating. Late in 2008, a reported asked him if he was interested in the San Diego State coaching opening, and he replied, "I've got a college team right now." A month later he was fired, but with his verbal skills has remained active as a broadcaster.

EDWARDS, WILLIAM M. (BILL) 6/21/1905–6/12/1987. Ohio State and Wittenberg. C; did not play professionally. *Apprenticeship:* College head coach — 6 years. *Roots:* None. *Branches:* Bull Karcis (i). *Coordinators/Key Assistants*: Roy Miller and Bull Karcis were his only assistants. *Hall of Fame Players:* Alex Wojciechowicz. *Primary Quarterbacks:* None. *Tendencies:* • His teams scored 9.1 points and allowed 17.9 per game • His teams ran 65.9% of the time, which was 102% of the league average • Six rookie starters in two years • Winning Full Seasons to Losing Full Seasons: 0:1.

Massillon, Ohio's Bill Edwards provides a direct link between coaching legends Paul Brown and Bill Belichick. Edwards dropped out of high school at 14 to work in the mines, but returned three years later to become the star center on the Massillon team that boasted Paul Brown as its quarterback. Both Edwards

and Brown enrolled at Ohio State in 1926, rooming together and playing on the freshman team. Neither was happy in Columbus, though, and each transferred out: Brown to Miami of Ohio and Edwards to Wittenberg. In 1929, Bill was called the "best center in the nation" by sportswriter Grantland Rice and went directly into high school coaching upon graduation.

In 1935, Edwards was hired as an assistant coach at Western Reserve, but when head coach Sam Willaman suddenly died that summer, Bill was promoted to head coach. In six years at the school, Edwards compiled a 49–6–2 record. Detroit Lions' owner Fred Mandel took note and hired Bill as head coach in 1941. Edwards brought one of his players, Steve Belichick, with him to act as trainer, but when they saw the quality of the Lions' backfield, Steve was upgraded to player. Steve enlisted in the Navy in 1942, and Edwards was fired when Detroit lost the first three games of the season, scoring just seven points. Edwards spent 1943–1945 in the Navy and 1946 as a salesman before returning to football in 1947 as the tackles coach for Cleveland under Paul Brown. After two years with the Browns, Bill was hired as head coach by Vanderbilt in 1949. A year later, faithful Steve Belichick joined the Commodores' staff. Edwards enjoyed only modest success with Vanderbilt, a 21–19–2 record in four years, but gained a legacy when Steve Belichick's son Bill was born in Nashville in 1952 and named after his godfather, Bill Edwards.

Edwards moved on to North Carolina as an assistant in 1953, as did Steve Belichick, but then the two parted company: Edwards took over as head coach at his alma mater, and Belichick was hired as an assistant at Annapolis. Edwards' Wittenberg squads went 98–20–4 from 1955 to 1968 when he retired. Edwards was elected to the College Football Hall of Fame in 1986, a year before he died. His overall college record was 168–45–8.

ERDELATZ, EDWARD J. (EDDIE) 4/21/1913–11/10/1966. Saint Mary's College. E; did not play professionally. *Apprenticeship:* College coach —18 years (9 as head coach); pro asst.— 2 years. *Roots:* Buck Shaw. *Branches:* Marty Feldman, Red Conkright (i). *Coordinators/Key Assistants*: Tom Kalamanir coached the backs, and Marty Feldman coached the line. *Hall of Fame Players:* Jim Otto. *Primary Quarterbacks:* Tom Flores. *Tendencies:* • His teams scored 19.9 points and allowed 30.4 per game • His teams ran 46.8% of the

Edwards, William M. (Bill)									
Year	Team	Games	Wins	Losses	Ties	%	P Wins	P Losses	P %
1941	Lions	11	4	6	1	.409	0	0	.000
1942	Lions	3	0	3	0	.000	0	0	.000
2 years		14	4	9	1	.321	0	0	.000

time, which was 98% of the league average • Two starting quarterbacks in two years; 88% of starts to primary quarterback • 16 rookie starters in two years • Winning Full Seasons to Losing Full Seasons: 0:1.

San Francisco-native Eddie Erdelatz was an aggressive All-American end at St. Mary's College in California and his head took a pounding. He played football without a helmet and also boxed and wrestled. Later, as a coach, he would joke that his cauliflower ears were a result of "the hard pillows in my dormitory." He was a good-natured man and a players' coach who said in 1950, "I treat the boys just like I wanted to be treated when I was a player."

Although Eddie was drafted by the Cardinals in the third round of the very first NFL draft in 1936, he opted to forego the pros to serve as an assistant coach to Slip Madigan at his alma mater for two years. In 1938, he moved on to the University of San Francisco and then jumped back to St. Mary's in 1940 under Red Strader. From 1942 to 1944, Erdelatz served as a Lieutenant Commander in the Navy before joining the coaching staff at Annapolis in 1945 for three years. In 1948, Eddie returned to the West Coast, coaching the 49ers' defense under Buck Shaw for two years until he was offered the head job at Navy.

In nine years at Navy, Erdelatz compiled a 50–26–8 record that included a 5–3–1 mark against West Point. Under Eddie, Navy won the 1955 Sugar Bowl and the 1958 Cotton Bowl. He also uttered one of the most famous lines in football history on November 9, 1953 after Navy and Duke battled to a 0–0 tie. Erdelatz's piquant spontaneous reaction was, "A tie is like kissing your sister." After a series of clashes with the athletic director at Annapolis, though, Eddie resigned as coach after the 1958 season. Although courted by USC, the New York Giants and the Washington Redskins, he stayed out of football in 1959.

In 1960, Erdelatz turned down the head coaching job with the Los Angeles Chargers, but later accepted the Oakland Raiders' job closer to home. There were

bad omens about this from the start. Eddie and his top assistant Ernie Jorge got into an auto accident in June, Jorge suffered a heart attack in September and Eddie was diagnosed with ulcers in October. Still, he managed to fulfill the modest goal he set for the team in 1960 after seeing the quality of players assembled for him by Oakland's management — they finished third in a four-team division. Erdelatz blamed himself for the team's losing record. He told the press in 1961, "We used standard defenses all season and would line up like ducks on a pond. It was my fault. I'd just returned to the pros from college and was getting my feet wet." Babe Parilli, one of the Raiders' starting quarterbacks, was less charitable years later when he reminisced about Eddie to Jeff Miller in *Going Long*, "Eddie really didn't know pro football. We had 10 plays. All we did was run. We had two teams. [Tom] Flores on one team and me on the other. We'd run on the field in practice, run a play, and sprint off the field. Eddie and I didn't get along too well."

The year 1961 was worse. Some key starters were gone, and the mismanaged Raiders only signed one of their draft picks. After losing the first two games 55–0 to the champion Oilers and 44–0 to the runner-up Chargers, Erdelatz was fired and replaced by assistant Marty Feldman. The team would finish 1961 2–12 and 1962 1–13 before Al Davis took charge in 1963. Eddie talked to the Cardinals about their coaching vacancy in 1962, but instead remained as a vice president at a California finance company until his death from stomach cancer in 1966 at the age of 53.

ERHARDT, RON 2/27/1931– Jamestown College. QB; did not play professionally. *Apprenticeship:* College coach —10 years (7 as head coach); pro asst.— 6 years. *Roots:* Chuck Fairbanks. *Branches:* Raymond Berry, Bill Parcells. *Coordinators/Key Assistants:* Erhardt handled his own offense, and Hank Bullough then Fritz Shurmur ran the defense. *Hall of Fame Players:* John Hannah, Mike Haynes. *Primary Quarterbacks:*

Erdelatz, Edward J. (Eddie)

Year	Team	Games	Wins	Losses	Ties	%	P Wins	P Losses	P %
1960	Raiders	14	6	8	0	.429	0	0	.000
1961	Raiders	2	0	2	0	.000	0	0	.000
2 years		16	6	10	0	.375	0	0	.000

Erhardt, Ron

Year	Team	Games	Wins	Losses	Ties	%	P Wins	P Losses	P %
1978	Patriots	1	0	1	0	.000	0	0	.000
1979	Patriots	16	9	7	0	.563	0	0	.000
1980	Patriots	16	10	6	0	.625	0	0	.000
1981	Patriots	16	2	14	0	.125	0	0	.000
4 years		49	21	28	0	.429	0	0	.000

Steve Grogan. *Record:* Began as **Interim Co-Coach** (with Hank Bullough in 1978). *Tendencies:* • His teams scored 24 points and allowed 21.3 per game • His teams ran 53.2% of the time, which was 105% of the league average • Three starting quarterbacks in four years; 73% of starts to primary quarterback • Eight rookie starters in four years • Winning Full Seasons to Losing Full Seasons: 2:1.

The road from Mandan, North Dakota to NFL coach is a long one that Ron Erhardt skillfully traversed to complete a 25-year tenure in the league. Upon graduation from college, Erhardt fulfilled a two-year service commitment before beginning a seven-year stint as high school coach in North Dakota from 1956 to 1962. Ron moved up to North Dakota State as an assistant in 1963 and took over as head coach there in 1966. As coach and athletic director from 1966 to 1972, Erhardt compiled a 61–7–1 record that included two national championships. In 1973 when Chuck Fairbanks became head coach of the Patriots, he hired Ron to coach the backfield. Coincidentally, one of Erhardt's players from North Dakota, Steve Nelson, was a star linebacker in New England. When Red Miller left to become the Broncos head coach in 1977, Ron was promoted to offensive coordinator.

Things began to get strange for New England in 1978. Fairbanks grew tired of management interference and accepted the coaching job at the University of Colorado in December. Owner Billy Sullivan then suspended Fairbanks and replaced him with coordinators Erhardt and Hank Bullough for the season finale, which the Patriots lost. Sullivan next brought back Fairbanks as coach for the playoffs, but the unfocused Pats lost to Houston by 17 points. Sullivan continued to fight Colorado over Fairbanks for three more months before accepting a cash buyout from the school.

Finally, Sullivan named Erhardt as Fairbanks' replacement in April. Ron confidently announced, "I've never been a loser in football and I don't intend to start now." Problems with management continued, though. In 1979, disgruntled All Pro tackle Leon Gray was traded, and in 1980 the team was distracted by several holdouts, including stars Mike Haynes and Sam Cunningham. Erhardt was an outgoing players' coach who gave quarterback Steve Grogan the freedom to call his own plays. New England recorded winning seasons in those two years, but failed to make the play-offs. Eventually everything came apart in 1981 as the Pats dropped to 2–14, so Sullivan fired Erhardt, saying, "He was just too nice a guy. What we really need and what we will be looking for is more of a disciplinarian."

Erhardt took his run-oriented approach to the Giants where he served, mostly as offensive coordinator, from 1982 to 1991 under former Pats' offensive assistant Ray Perkins, former Pats' linebacker coach Bill Parcells and then Ray Handley. His most famous accomplishment came in Super Bowl XXV when he followed Bill Parcells' succinct directive to "shorten the game" to enable the smash mouth Giants to upset the high flying Bills and win the championship. Ron moved on to Pittsburgh under Bill Cowher from 1992 to 1995 and then followed free agent Steelers' quarterback Neil O'Donnell to the Jets in 1996. Erhardt spent one year there under Rich Kotite and one last year under Bill Parcells before retiring in 1998.

ERICKSON, DENNIS 3/24/1947– Montana State. QB; did not play professionally. *Apprenticeship:* College coach — 26 years (14 as head coach). *Roots:* None. *Branches:* Jim Mora, Jr., Jim Zorn. *Coordinators/Key Assistants:* For the Seahawks, Bob Bratkowski ran the offense, while Greg McMakin handled the defense; for the 49ers, Greg Knapp then Ted Tollner ran the offense, while Jim Mora, Jr., then Willy Robinson handled the defense. *Hall of Fame Players:* Cortez Kennedy and Warren Moon. *Primary Quarterbacks:* Warren Moon, Rick Mirer, Jeff Garcia. *Tendencies:* • His teams scored 21.5 points and allowed 22.9 per game • His teams ran 43.9% of the time, which was 99% of the league average • Eight starting quarterbacks in six years; 61% of starts to primary quarterbacks • 12 rookie starters in six years • Winning Full Seasons to Losing Full Seasons: 0:3.

Everett, Washington's Dennis Erickson has led one of the most restless careers in all of coaching. The son of a high school coach, Erickson played quarterback at Montana State for three years and began his coaching career there in 1969. Then, he spent one year as a high school coach, three more years at Montana State, two at Idaho, three at Fresno State and three at San Jose State (under Jack Elway). Finally in 1982, Dennis was named to his first college head coaching

Erickson, Dennis									
Year	Team	Games	Wins	Losses	Ties	%	P Wins	P Losses	P %
1995	Seahawks	16	8	8	0	.500	0	0	.000
1996	Seahawks	16	7	9	0	.438	0	0	.000
1997	Seahawks	16	8	8	0	.500	0	0	.000
1998	Seahawks	16	8	8	0	.500	0	0	.000
2003	49ers	16	7	9	0	.438	0	0	.000
2004	49ers	16	2	14	0	.125	0	0	.000
6 years		96	40	56	0	.417	0	0	.000

position at Idaho where he coached from 1982 to 1985. Then, his head coaching relay began: 1986 at Wyoming, 1987–1988 at Washington State; and 1989–1994 at the University of Miami, including national championships in 1989 and 1991. Erickson left Miami right before the NCAA sanctions hit in 1995 and landed with the Seattle Seahawks. On December 27, 1994, Dennis denied rumors he was going to the Seahawks, saying, "I'm staying. I have no interest in the NFL right now." Two weeks later, he signed with Seattle.

By this time, Erickson seemed a bit jaded. In *Steve Raible's Tales from the Seahawks Sidelines*, Raible recounted Dennis addressing a fan club banquet soon after he was hired by remarking, "You're standing and clapping now, but wait until I lose a few games. We'll see if you're still cheering." He must have had a premonition because the Seahawks had no winning seasons and did not make the playoffs in Erickson's four years. To be fair, it should be pointed out that a terrible official's call at the end of the season finale against the Jets in 1998 cost Seattle the game and a playoff slot, and that cost Dennis his job. That phantom touchdown scored by New York's Vinny Testaverde was so egregious a mistake that it was a contributing factor to the reinstatement of instant replay the next year.

In 1999, Erickson took over Oregon State and turned around that long dormant program in four years before being lured back to the NFL with the 49ers in 2003. Erickson took over from Steve Mariucci and essentially dropped the West Coast Offense that San Francisco had used for the last quarter of a century. Dennis generally ran a more wide-open offense, but after two losing seasons, he was fired again. He resurfaced in 2006 with Idaho and then jumped to Arizona State in 2007. In 23 years as a college head coach, Erickson has compiled an impressive 179–96–1 record through 2011, but his laxity on details and discipline were his undoing as a pro coach.

Ewart, Charles D. (Charley) 10/16/1915–4/30/1990. Yale. QB; did not play professionally. *Apprenticeship:* College asst.—2 years; pro asst.—3 years. *Roots:* Greasy Neale. *Branches:* None. *Coordinators/Key Assistants:* Joe Bach coached the line and Ray Nolting coached the backs. *Hall of Fame Players:* Bobby Layne. *Primary Quarterbacks:* Bobby Layne. *Tendencies:* • His team scored 12.8 points and allowed 30.7 per game •

His team ran 47.5% of the time, which was 83% of the league average • One starting quarterback in one year; 100% of starts to primary quarterback • Three rookie starters in one year • Winning Full Seasons to Losing Full Seasons: 0:1.

Born in Lynn, Massachusetts, Charley Ewart was a three-year starter at quarterback for Yale from 1935 to 1937, calling signals for an Eli team that boasted back-to-back Heisman Trophy winners Larry Kelly in 1936 and Clint Frank in 1937. Backfield coach Greasy Neale later said, "Charley was the smartest quarterback I ever had at Yale." Ewart went on to earn his master's degree at Yale while beginning his coaching career as backfield coach at Wesleyan in 1940 and at Dartmouth in 1941. Charley joined the FBI in 1942 and spent the war years working on espionage cases and security assignments, including the Manhattan Project.

In 1946, Eagles' head coach Greasy Neale hired Ewart as the team's backfield coach. Charley also served as Philadelphia's scouting director, and in 1948 was named GM by team owner Alexis Thompson, a fellow Yalie. Ewart became the youngest GM to ever a championship when Philadelphia won it all that year. In the meantime, Charley was shopping the team for Thompson who was losing money in the NFL's fight against the AAFC. Ewart presciently commented, "If I had the money, I'd buy it myself. You could hardly call it speculation. It's actually an investment."

Instead, Ewart left the Eagles in 1949 to become head coach for entertainment impresario Ted Collins' dismal New York Bulldogs whose only asset was second-year quarterback Bobby Layne. Behind a porous line and with no scoring weapons, Layne spent most of the season being driven into the dirt. Years later, Bobby told Myron Cope for *The Game That Was*, "Charley Ewart was a nice young guy who had been coaching over in Philadelphia, and he believed in that Steve Van Buren type of football. But the trouble was we didn't have any Steve Van Burens. 'Run it!' Ewart would tell me. He liked the running game. But Collins would tell me, 'Throw it!'" Layne listened to the owner; he also reported that Collins would tell Ewart not even to come to practice or to do any coaching at times, but turn the team over to his assistants. At the end of a frustrating 1–10–1 season, Ewart resigned and said, "I am planning not only to leave the Bulldogs but pro football as well. It is my plan to consider a more certain future in college football coaching, athletic adminis-

Ewart, Charles D. (Charley)									
Year	Team	Games	Wins	Losses	Ties	%	P Wins	P Losses	P %
1949	New York Bulldogs (defunct)	12	1	10	1	.125	0	0	.000
1 year		12	1	10	1	.125	0	0	.000

tration or possibly in the business world." He chose business, working as Marketing Director for General Foods, vice president in a Chicago advertising firm and Vice President of American Bakeries until retirement.

EWBANK, WILBUR (WEEB) 5/6/1907–11/17/1998.

Miami (Ohio). QB; did not play professionally. *Apprenticeship:* College coach — 3 years (2 as head coach); pro asst.— 5 years. *Roots:* Paul Brown. *Branches:* Charley Winner, Clive Rush, Don McCafferty, John Sandusky (i), Joe Thomas (i), Ken Meyer, Walt Michaels, Ed Biles, Buddy Ryan. *Coordinators/Key Assistants*: For the Colts, John Sandusky and Don McCafferty were the key offensive coaches, and Charley Winner ran the defense; for the Jets, Clive Rush then Ken Meyer were the key offensive coaches, while Walt Michaels then Charley Winner ran the defense. *Hall of Fame Players:* Raymond Berry, Art Donovan, Gino Marchetti, Don Maynard, Lenny Moore, Joe Namath, Jim Parker, Joe Perry, John Riggins, John Unitas. *Primary Quarterbacks:* John Unitas, Joe Namath. *Record:* **Hall of Fame Coach;** NFL Championships 1958, 1959, Super Bowl Championship 1969. *Tendencies:* • His teams scored 22.2 points and allowed 21.7 per game • His teams ran 50.5% of the time, which was 96% of the league average • 13 starting quarterbacks in 20 years; 65% of starts to primary quarterbacks • 58 rookie starters in 20 years • Winning Full Seasons to Losing Full Seasons: 7:9.

At Weeb Ewbank's funeral, his former defensive tackle Art Donovan, a Hall of Famer, volunteered, "I think Weeb is the greatest coach ever. He took two of the worst teams ever, the Colts and the Jets, and built them into champions. He took Unitas and Namath as rookies and developed them into Hall of Famers. You can't do any better than he did." Indeed, Ewbank himself is in the Hall of Fame for the reasons Donovan detailed. For his career, though, Weeb is just one game over .500 and had more losing seasons than winning ones. While he was a master builder, he was not able to maintain what he built for very long in either Baltimore or New York.

Born in Richmond, Indiana, Ewbank attended Miami University (Ohio) where his competitor for the quarterback position was Paul Brown who would play a major role in Weeb's career. Upon graduation, Ewbank went directly into coaching at the high school level, spending 1928–1929 at Van Wert High School and then from 1930 to 1942, he coached football, base-

Head-to-Head:			
Hall of Fame Opponent	Regular Season	Postseason	
George Allen	0–1	0–0	
Paul Brown	6–2	0–0	
Sid Gillman	9–13–2	0–0	
Bud Grant	1–0	0–0	
George Halas	9–9	0–0	
Tom Landry	1–1	0–0	
Vince Lombardi	4–4	0–0	
John Madden	0–3	0–0	
Chuck Noll	0–2	0–0	
Don Shula	1–7	1–0	
Hank Stram	5–7	0–1	
Total	36–49–2	1–1	

Ewbank, Wilbur (Weeb)

Year	Team	Games	Wins	Losses	Ties	%	P Wins	P Losses	P %
1954	Colts	12	3	9	0	.250	0	0	.000
1955	Colts	12	5	6	1	.458	0	0	.000
1956	Colts	12	5	7	0	.417	0	0	.000
1957	Colts	12	7	5	0	.583	0	0	.000
1958	Colts	12	9	3	0	.750	1	0	1.000
1959	Colts	12	9	3	0	.750	1	0	1.000
1960	Colts	12	6	6	0	.500	0	0	.000
1961	Colts	14	8	6	0	.571	0	0	.000
1962	Colts	14	7	7	0	.500	0	0	.000
1963	Jets	14	5	8	1	.393	0	0	.000
1964	Jets	14	5	8	1	.393	0	0	.000
1965	Jets	14	5	8	1	.393	0	0	.000
1966	Jets	14	6	6	2	.500	0	0	.000
1967	Jets	14	8	5	1	.607	0	0	.000
1968	Jets	14	11	3	0	.786	2	0	1.000
1969	Jets	14	10	4	0	.714	0	1	.000
1970	Jets	14	4	10	0	.286	0	0	.000
1971	Jets	14	6	8	0	.429	0	0	.000
1972	Jets	14	7	7	0	.500	0	0	.000
1973	Jets	14	4	10	0	.286	0	0	.000
20 years		266	130	129	7	.502	4	1	.800

ball and basketball at the high school affiliated with his college alma mater. In 1943, Weeb went into the Navy and reconnected with Paul Brown, working as his assistant at the Great Lakes Naval Station for three years. After the war, Ewbank spent one year as the backfield coach at Brown University and two as head coach of Washington University in St. Louis, compiling a 14–4 record. There, his star halfback was Charley Winner who went on to marry Weeb's daughter.

Paul Brown reached out to Ewbank again in 1949, bringing him to Cleveland as the team's tackles coach. Weeb told the St. Louis press, "The only man who could take me away from this job said he needed me." The avuncular Ewbank spent five years coaching the line and scouting for the Browns as they made their yearly trips to the championship game. In that winning atmosphere, Brown had a powerful hold on his coaches, emotionally and professionally. When the Colts tried to hire Blanton Collier as their coach in 1954, Brown blocked the move, but when Baltimore next asked about Ewbank, he let him go. Weeb inherited a one-year old team that had finished 3–9 in its initial season, but he promised a championship in five years. Ewbank had a sharp eye for talent and was very methodical in his approach to things; slowly the team came into focus as Ewbank acquired talent and developed it, while fending off annual scares that his job was in jeopardy. Weeb built a powerhouse team led by the greatest and most daring quarterback in the game, Johnny Unitas, whom he rescued from the oil-soaked fields of Western Pennsylvania semipro football. Finally, the Colts won their first championship in the famous Sudden Death title game of 1958 — the culmination of Weeb's five-year plan. Baltimore repeated as champions in 1959, but the team started to slip after that. Three successive mediocre finishes cost Ewbank his job in 1963.

With fortuitous timing at that point, the bedraggled and bankrupt New York Titans in the American Football League were sold to a group led by agent Sonny Werblin who swooped in and hired Ewbank on the same day he announced the team was changing its name to the Jets. Weeb later said that the Jets' building job was the tougher of the two; although he again announced a five-year plan, it took him six years to reach the top this time. Ewbank later told the *New York Times* that the secret to his success was threefold, "I think I've been able to recognize talent and see the potential in a young guy; I've had the patience to stick with players and I've been able to place them in positions where they do the team the most good. I also feel I've been able to instill confidence in players, and that's very important. For the most part, players have given me all they've had." Jets' line coach Joe Spencer, who had played for Ewbank in Cleveland, once described the respect Weeb engendered for his calm tolerance of players' eccentricities as, "It's like working for your dad."

Of course, when the Joe Namath-led Jets reached the Super Bowl after the 1968 season they found the heavily-favored Colts coached by Weeb's successor Don Shula waiting. Given no chance by the press as an 18-point underdog, Joe Namath responded by guaranteeing a victory. He explained his braggadocio to a scolding Ewbank by pointing out that Weeb had given him the utmost confidence in their team. In a total team effort, the Jets backed up that guarantee in perhaps the greatest upset in pro football history that legitimized the AFL for good. Ewbank told *Sports Illustrated*, "If I had to isolate my greatest satisfaction as a coach, it would have to be this: I gave the American Football League a Super Bowl winner for the first time, and it was over Baltimore."

Once again, though, his championship team faded rather quickly. With the Jets, the process was accelerated by Namath's frequent injuries that left the team without an offense, which was Ewbank's specialty. Seven times in Weeb's career his teams finished in the top three in scoring. The Jets did not have a winning season in Weeb's last four years with the club. He retired in 1974 and turned the club over to his son-in-law Charley Winner, but that was a failure as the team continued its descent. Ewbank lived on till the age of 91. At the funeral, Joe Namath summed up his former coach, "Great is not enough to describe what he meant to people. Not just individually. He meant a great deal to so many people. It sounds a little corny saying that pro coaches were like fathers, but it's true. Not only Weeb, but his wife Lucy. They cemented relationships. You saw all these guys with an outpouring of love. That's because people loved Weeb and Weeb loved people."

FAIRBANKS, CHARLES L. (CHUCK) 6/10/1933–

Michigan. E; did not play professionally. *Apprenticeship:* College coach —15 years (6 as head coach). *Roots:* None. *Branches:* Red Miller, Sam Rutigliano, Ray Perkins, Ron Erhardt, Raymond Berry, Hank Bullough. *Coordinators/Key Assistants:* Red Miller then Ron Erhardt ran the offense, while Hank Bullough handled the defense. *Hall of Fame Players:* John Hannah, Mike Haynes. *Primary Quarterbacks:* Steve Grogan, Jim Plunkett. *Tendencies:* • His teams scored 22 points and allowed 19.6 per game • His teams ran 59% of the time, which was 105% of the league average • Three starting quarterbacks in six years; 98% of starts to primary quarterbacks • 20 rookie starters in six years • Winning Full Seasons to Losing Full Seasons: 3:2.

Steve Zabel played for Chuck Fairbanks at both Oklahoma and New England and accurately described the coach to Stephen Norwood for *Real Football*, "He was a great, great disciplinarian. He was a good motivator. But his strong suit was that he could really delegate authority. Chuck had great assistant coaches who were great teachers. And he let those guys run their own program."

Detroit's Chuck Fairbanks played end for Biggie Munn and Duffy Daugherty at Michigan State before beginning his coaching career at Ishpeming High School in 1955. When another former Spartan, Frank Kush, got the head coaching position at Arizona State in 1958, Fairbanks moved up to the college ranks as an ASU assistant. In 1962, Chuck moved on to the University of Houston under former Michigan State assistant Bill Yeoman who ran the Veer offense. Four years later, Fairbanks was hired as an assistant to Jim Mackenzie at Oklahoma in 1966. Mackenzie died in April 1967, and Fairbanks was appointed as his successor. On his staff during his tenure were Barry Switzer who introduced the Sooners to the Wishbone (replacing Fairbanks' Veer) a few years later and Jimmy Johnson. Although Fairbanks returned Oklahoma to national prominence, it was Switzer and Johnson who turned out to be championship coaches. In Chuck's six seasons in Norman, the Sooners finished 52–15–1. Meanwhile in that same 1967–1972 period, the New England Patriots went 22–61–1.

Understandably, the Patriots were looking for a new head coach. After being turned down by renowned college coaches Joe Paterno and Bob Devaney, owner Billy Sullivan hired Fairbanks as head coach and general manager. Chuck told the press, "I realize there are many things about professional football I have to learn, but I do know something about winning." While Fairbanks' ultimate legacy in New England was mixed, his talents as a team builder are undeniable. Decades later, Bill Belichick brought in Fairbanks to talk to his 2007 undefeated team and praised Chuck's accomplishments in New England at a press conference, "Chuck really is a great football coach. He had tremendous success at Oklahoma and of course he came here and for six years built this team into one of the best teams in the National Football League and acquired, in my opinion, talent that was … it was really a rare acquisition of talent. I mean, not only did he get it between '73 and '78, but then the core of that team was really the core of the Super Bowl team in '85." In one lopsided deal, Fairbanks traded quarterback Jim Plunkett to San Francisco for three first round and one second round draft picks as well as backup quarterback Tom Owen. Plunkett was expendable because the quarterback Fairbanks drafted

in the fifth round, Steve Grogan, was a better fit for the team.

However, once Fairbanks rebuilt the Patriots, each year there was disappointment. In 1976, the Patriots lost to the Raiders in the playoffs after the phantom roughing the passer penalty on Sugar Bear Hamilton. In 1977, ownership meddling exacerbated the joint holdout of All Pro linemen Leon Gray and John Hannah. In 1978, Darryl Stingley was paralyzed during an exhibition game, but the team was still headed to the postseason when it was revealed in December that Chuck had signed a secret deal with Colorado to coach the Buffalos in 1979. Billy Sullivan suspended Fairbanks for the season finale and then reinstated him for the playoffs. Linebacker Steve Nelson recalled to Jim Donaldson for *Stadium Stories: New England Patriots* that the Fairbanks' situation, "totally knocked the team for a loop because Chuck was such a strong, dominant leader. It was demoralizing. We had such faith in him. We depended on him."

The Patriots lost to the Oilers 31–14 in the playoffs, but the soap opera continued for four more months as Sullivan threatened legal action and extracted a $200,000 buyout from Colorado before moving on and promoting offensive coordinator Ron Erhardt to head coach. Admittedly, Fairbanks' sense of timing was terrible, but in his defense, he had grown completely dissatisfied with the interference of ownership, particularly of the owner's son Chuck Sullivan, that detracted from the welfare of the team. It turned out to be effectively the end of his coaching career, though. In three years, Colorado went 7–26 under Fairbanks. Chuck got another coaching shot in the USFL when he was named coach and team president for the New Jersey Generals in 1983; he even owned a part of the team. After one 6–12 season though, Donald Trump bought the team, and Chuck was out of football. In subsequent years, Fairbanks focused on developing golf courses and his auto dealership. His football reputation forever was ruined by how he destroyed the Patriots 1978 season and inspired the memorable headline, "Win One for the Quitter."

FASSEL, JAMES E. (JIM) 8/31/1949– Long Beach State. QB; did not play professionally. *Apprenticeship:* College coach —14 years (5 as head coach); pro asst. —

Fairbanks, Charles L. (Chuck)									
Year	Team	Games	Wins	Losses	Ties	%	P Wins	P Losses	P %
1973	Patriots	14	5	9	0	.357	0	0	.000
1974	Patriots	14	7	7	0	.500	0	0	.000
1975	Patriots	14	3	11	0	.214	0	0	.000
1976	Patriots	14	11	3	0	.786	0	1	.000
1977	Patriots	14	9	5	0	.643	0	0	.000
1978	Patriots	15	11	4	0	.733	0	1	.000
6 years		85	46	39	0	.541	0	2	.000

8 years. *Roots:* Ray Handley, Wade Phillips, Vince Tobin. *Branches:* John Fox, Sean Payton, Eric Studesville (i). *Coordinators/Key Assistants:* Jim Skipper then Sean Payton then Fassel handled the offense, while John Fox then Johnnie Lynn ran the defense. *Hall of Fame Players:* None. *Primary Quarterbacks:* Kerry Collins *Tendencies:* • His teams scored 18.6 points and allowed 19.3 per game • His teams ran 44.2% of the time, which was the league average • Four starting quarterbacks in seven years; 61% of starts to primary quarterback • 20 rookie starters in seven years • Winning Full Seasons to Losing Full Seasons: 3:3.

A native of Anaheim, California, Jim Fassel played quarterback at Long Beach State and was a seventh round draft pick of the Bears in 1972. Fassel washed out of training camp with the Bears, Oilers and Chargers in 1972 and served as an assistant coach at Fullerton College in 1973. In 1974, he served as a part-time coach and sometime player with the World Football League's Hawaiians, even throwing the last pass in WFL history before the league folded in October 1975. Fassel caught on as an assistant with Utah in 1976, moved on to Weber State in 1977 and Stanford in 1979. After five years in Palo Alto, Jim was named offensive coordinator for the New Orleans Breakers of the USFL in 1984. When that troubled franchise moved to Portland the next year, Fassel was named head coach at the University of Utah. From 1985 to 1989, the Utes were just 25–33 under Jim. Fassel then was hired by the Giants for the first time as offensive coordinator under Ray Handley who had worked with him at Stanford. From 1991 to 1996, Fassel spent two years in New York, two in Denver, one in Oakland and one in Arizona as a quarterback specialist working with Phil Simms, John Elway, Jeff Hostetler and Boomer Esiason.

The Giants brought him back in 1997 as head coach, but Fassel's years as the Giants' coach were inconsistent and up-and-down, with the team compiling a so-so 58–53–1 record. New York surprisingly made the playoffs with Danny Kanell at quarterback in Jim's first season, but stumbled to mediocrity the next two years with Giants' defensive players openly questioning Fassel's decisions. With his job in jeopardy, Fassel changed his own destiny by rescuing the career of troubled quarterback Kerry Collins. Fassel got the best out of Collins, and, with a simple forceful statement the day before Thanksgiving 2000, Jim Fassel defined that season for the Giants: "This is a poker game. I'm shoving my chips to the center of the table. I'm raising the ante. This team is going to the playoffs." That statement of assurance and purpose seemed to have a visceral effect on the team; the players became more focused and determined and swept into the postseason. The Giants then tore apart the favored Vikings 41–0 in the NFC Championship Game; it was the high point of Fassel's tenure in New York. In the Super Bowl that year, the Ravens overwhelmed the Giants, and the team stumbled to a losing record again in 2001. 2002 seemed to be a new start, but an awful fourth quarter collapse blowing a 24-point lead to the 49ers in the playoffs that year carried over to 2003 when Fassel lost control of a team that finished 4–12.

After being fired by New York, Fassel signed on as offensive coordinator for his old friend Brian Billick in Baltimore while waiting for another head coaching position in 2004. Instead, he suffered the humiliation of having Billick take over the stagnant offense halfway through the season in 2006. Jim went into broadcasting for a few years before resurfacing as the head coach of the Las Vegas Locomotives in the developmental United Football League in 2009, still hoping for another shot in the NFL. He led Las Vegas to a 14–7 record from 2009 to 2011, winning league championships in the first two seasons.

FAULKNER, JACK T. 4/4/1926–9/28/2008. Miami (Ohio). LB; did not play professionally. *Apprenticeship:* College asst.—6 years; pro asst.—7 years. *Roots:* Sid Gillman. *Branches:* Mac Speedie, Ed Hughes, Red Miller, Ray Malavasi. *Coordinators/Key Assistants:* Mac Speedie and Red Miller were the key offensive coaches, while Dale Dodrill then Ray Malavasi ran the defense. *Hall of Fame Players:* Willie Brown. *Primary Quarterbacks:* Frank Tripucka. *Tendencies:* • His teams scored 21.9 points and allowed 29.5 per game • His teams ran 38.9% of the time, which was 88% of the league average • Four starting quarterbacks in three years; 47% of starts to primary quarterback • 14 rookie starters in three years • Winning Full Seasons to Losing Full Seasons: 0:1.

Fassel, James E. (Jim)									
Year	Team	Games	Wins	Losses	Ties	%	P Wins	P Losses	P %
1997	Giants	16	10	5	1	.656	0	1	.000
1998	Giants	16	8	8	0	.500	0	0	.000
1999	Giants	16	7	9	0	.438	0	0	.000
2000	Giants	16	12	4	0	.750	2	1	.667
2001	Giants	16	7	9	0	.438	0	0	.000
2002	Giants	16	10	6	0	.625	0	1	.000
2003	Giants	16	4	12	0	.250	0	0	.000
7 years		112	58	53	1	.522	2	3	.400

Youngstown, Ohio's Jack Faulkner played linebacker at Miami University under Sid Gillman in 1947, and when Gillman became coach at the University of Cincinnati in 1949, he hired the newly graduated Faulkner as an assistant. Jack spent six years coaching under Gillman at Cincinnati, five more coaching the Rams' defense under Sid from 1955 to 1959 and then two coaching the Chargers' defense for Gillman from 1960 to 1961. In 1962, Faulkner finally stepped out of Gillman's shadow by taking over as coach and general manager of the lackluster, second class Denver Broncos.

Jack got off to a great start, changing the teams colors, burning the hideous vertically-striped socks that came with the uniforms the team had acquired cheaply as surplus property in 1960 and leading the Broncos to a 7–2 record by November 1962. From that point on though, everything collapsed quickly. The Broncos lost the final five games that season to begin the slide that led to a 2–20–1 record for Faulkner's last 23 games. He even lost his friendship with his mentor. Denver beat San Diego twice in 1962 and also in the teams' first meeting in 1963. When the teams met in the 1963 season finale, Gillman took out his frustration on the field with the Chargers winning 58–20. Faulkner accused Sid of running up the score by going for a two-point conversion and trying an onside kick in the fourth quarter.

The 1962 Coach of the Year was fired after four games in 1964, but not before he made a highly unusual trade with Houston to "borrow" quarterback Jacky Lee for two seasons. He spent 1965 coaching defense in Minnesota under former Ram Norm Van Brocklin, 1966 scouting for the Rams, 1967–1969 coaching New Orleans' defense under former Ram receiver Tom Fears and 1970 as the Saints' Player Personnel Director. Finally in 1971, Faulkner returned to the Rams for good — as a scout from 1971 to 1972, as an assistant coach and advance scout from 1973 to

1979 and as the Director of Football Operations from 1980 to 1993. At that point, he retired rather than follow the Rams to St. Louis in 1994. In all, Jack spent 14 years with Sid Gillman and 28 with the Rams.

FEARS, THOMAS J. (TOM) 12/3/1922–1/4/2000. Santa Clara and UCLA. Played E for the Rams from 1948 to 1956. *Apprenticeship:* Pro asst. — 8 years. *Roots:* Bob Waterfield, Vince Lombardi, Norb Hecker. *Branches:* J.D. Roberts, Ed Khayat, Jerry Smith (i), Ed Biles. *Coordinators/Key Assistants:* Don Heinrich was the key offensive coach, while Jack Faulkner and Ed Khayat were the key defensive coaches. *Hall of Fame Players:* Doug Atkins, Jim Taylor. *Primary Quarterbacks:* Bill Kilmer. *Tendencies:* • His teams scored 17.9 points and allowed 25.6 per game • His teams ran 43.5% of the time, which was 86% of the league average • Four starting quarterbacks in four years; 82% of starts to primary quarterback • 16 rookie starters in four years • Winning Full Seasons to Losing Full Seasons: 0:3.

Tom Fears was born in Guadalajara, Mexico, but grew up in Los Angeles. His father was a mining engineer who married a Mexican woman. Fears ultimately would become the NFL's first Hispanic assistant coach, head coach and Hall of Famer. In college, he played at Santa Clara under Buck Shaw from 1941 to 1942 and then joined the Army Air Corps from 1943 to 1945 while his father was a Japanese prisoner of war in the Philippines. He was drafted by the Rams that year, but chose to complete his college eligibility with UCLA in 1946 and 1947. Fears joined the Rams in 1948 and led the league in receptions for his first three seasons.

After a nine-year playing career, Fears retired in 1957 and dropped out of football. He returned as Vince Lombardi's end coach for the Packers in 1959, performed the same function for former teammate Bob Waterfield on the Rams from 1960 to 1961 and then

Faulkner, Jack T.										
Year	Team	Games	Wins	Losses	Ties	%	P Wins	P Losses	P %	
1962	Broncos	14	7	7	0	.500	0	0	.000	
1963	Broncos	14	2	11	1	.179	0	0	.000	
1964	Broncos	4	0	4	0	.000	0	0	.000	
3 years		32	9	22	1	.297	0	0	.000	

Fears, Thomas J. (Tom)										
Year	Team	Games	Wins	Losses	Ties	%	P Wins	P Losses	P %	
1967	Saints	14	3	11	0	.214	0	0	.000	
1968	Saints	14	4	9	1	.321	0	0	.000	
1969	Saints	14	5	9	0	.357	0	0	.000	
1970	Saints	7	1	5	1	.214	0	0	.000	
4 years		49	13	34	2	.286	0	0	.000	

returned to Green Bay in 1962. In 1966, Tom followed fellow Packers' assistant Norb Hecker to the expansion Atlanta Falcons when Hecker was named head coach. A year later, Fears was named head coach of the next expansion team, the New Orleans Saints. Tom told the press, "I'm not predicting anything, but I'll be satisfied if we stay in there, show progress, show that we're starting to jell." He indicated he planned to build the team with young players through the draft, but eventually traded three of his first four first round draft picks for a beat-up Jim Taylor, an overrated Gary Cuozzo and limited possession receiver Dave Parks. Still, the Saints showed slow progress from three to four to five wins in the first three years. After winning just one game in the first half of 1970, though, Fears was fired.

Tom spent 1971–1972 as the Eagles' offensive coach, was out of football in 1973 and then returned as the head coach of the WFL's Southern California Sun in 1974. Featuring Pat Haden, Daryle Lamonica and Anthony Davis, the Sun was 20–12 in two years, but the league folded in October 1975. Fears returned to pro football once more as an executive with the Los Angeles Express of the USFL from 1983 to 1985. Tom was a loner, blunt and outspoken; it was not surprising that he never worked in the NFL again after 1972. He expressed some bitterness in 1975 to the *Los Angeles Times*, "There are probably 50 Vince Lombardi's on pro coaching staffs today, who, because of luck, will never get the chance to prove it." Over the years, Fears was prosperous in business with holdings in restaurants, condominiums and even an avocado farm. He died of complications from Alzheimer's disease in 2000 at the age of 77.

FELDMAN, MARTIN (MARTY) 9/12/1922– Stanford. G; did not play professionally. *Apprenticeship:* College asst.—11 years; junior college head coach—1 year; pro asst.—2 years. *Roots:* Eddie Erdelatz. *Branches:* Red Conkright (i), Walt Michaels. *Coordinators/Key Assistants:* Tom Kalamanir coached the backs, while Walt Michaels and Red Conkright handled the defense. *Hall of Fame Players:* Jim Otto. *Primary Quarterbacks:* Tom Flores. *Tendencies:* • His teams scored 18.6 points and allowed 30.7 per game • His teams ran 42.8% of the time, which was 95% of the league average • Three starting quarterbacks in two years; 71% of starts to primary quarterback • Ten rookie starters in two years • Winning Full Seasons to Losing Full Seasons: 0:1.

While this Marty Feldman was not the bug-eyed British comic who starred in *Young Frankenstein*, his Raiders played as if they belonged in a Mel Brooks movie. Feldman was born in Los Angeles and attended the University of Oregon as a freshman in 1940. When the war broke out, Marty joined the Marines and won three Purple Hearts in his five years of service. After the war, Feldman enrolled at Stanford where he played guard on the football team from 1946 to 1947, but made his biggest impact on the rugby field. In fact, he is in the Stanford Athletic Hall of Fame for his rugby exploits.

Marty began his coaching career at Stanford as an assistant under Marchy Schwartz in 1948. In 1955, Feldman moved on to New Mexico for a year, and then took over as head coach at Valley Junior College in 1956. After just one year, he joined the staff of Bob Titchenal at San Jose State from 1957 to 1959. In 1960, Eddie Erdelatz hired Feldman to coach the offensive and defensive lines for the brand new Oakland Raiders franchise. Erdelatz was fired two games into the 1961 season after being outscored 99–0, and Marty took over the Raiders. He told the press, "I think the club is absolutely salvageable, despite two major setbacks in two weeks. It's too late to make any major changes in personnel now. We'll go with what we have and try to jell it into a representative ballclub." Oakland managed to win two of their first six games under Feldman, but then lost the next 11 games in a row, including the first five games in 1962, before Marty was fired. In 1962, starting quarterback Tom Flores was lost to a lung ailment so Feldman brought in Don Heinrich and then Cotton Davidson to replace him. Hunter Enis, Chon Gallegos and M.C. Reynolds were also tried at quarterback to no avail. Hall of Fame center Jim Otto recalled to Jeff Miller in *Going Long*, "Marty Feldman got very close to the owners and made them think he knew something about football. He was not a football coach. He was a rugby coach." Later, Feldman scouted for the Rams, Cowboys and Toronto Argonauts.

FEWELL, PERRY 9/7/1962– Lenoir-Rhyne DB; did not play professionally. *Apprenticeship:* College asst.—13 years; pro asst.—12 years. *Roots:* Tom Coughlin, Mike Martz, Lovie Smith, Dick Jauron. *Branches:* Eric Studesville (i). *Coordinators/Key Assistants:* Turk Schonert ran the offense and Fewell handled his own defense. *Hall of Fame Players:* None. *Primary Quarterbacks:* Ryan Fitzpatrick. *Record:* **Interim Coach.**

Feldman, Martin (Marty)									
Year	Team	Games	Wins	Losses	Ties	%	P Wins	P Losses	P %
1961	Raiders	12	2	10	0	.167	0	0	.000
1962	Raiders	5	0	5	0	.000	0	0	.000
2 years		17	2	15	0	.118	0	0	.000

Born in Gastonia, North Carolina, Perry Fewell attended college 30 miles away at Lenoir-Rhyne where he played defensive back. After graduation, Perry moved across state to start his coaching career at the University of North Carolina from 1985 to 1986. Fewell subsequently coached at West Point in 1987, Kent State from 1988 to 1991, West Point again from 1992 to 1994, and Vanderbilt from 1995 to 1997. In 1998, Perry got his NFL break when Tom Coughlin hired him as the defensive backs coach in Jacksonville. After five years with the Jags, Fewell moved on to the Rams in 2003, the Bears in 2005 and the Bills in 2006. With the Bills, Perry was named defensive coordinator and was reunited with Dick Jauron who had been the Jacksonville defensive coordinator in 1998. Jauron was fired half way through the 2009 season, and Fewell did a creditable job as interim coach but new GM Buddy Knox hired Chan Gailey as the Bills' coach for 2010. Perry then returned to Tom Coughlin as the Giants defensive coordinator, replacing Bill Sheridan who had a disastrous one-year tenure in New York. Fewell improved the Giants defense from 30th to 17th in points allowed that first year with Fewell's self-described "disciplined, attacking, aggressive, eleven hats to the football" approach. After 2011's Super Bowl title, Perry may very well earn another shot at a head coaching position in the league.

FILCHOCK, FRANK J. 10/8/1916–6/20/1994. Indiana. Played TB for the Pirates, Redskins, Giants and Colts from 1938 to 1941, 1944 to 1946 and 1950; also played in Canada from 1947 to 1953. *Apprenticeship:* Canada head coach — 9 years. *Roots:* None. *Branches:* None. *Coordinators/Key Assistants:* Jim Cason and Ken Carpenter were the key offensive coaches, while Dale Dodrill handled the defense. *Hall of Fame Players:* None. *Primary Quarterbacks:* Frank Tripucka. *Tendencies:* • His teams scored 20 points and allowed 29.5 per game • His teams ran 39.4% of the time, which was 85% of the league average • Two starting quarterbacks in two years; 86% of starts to primary quarterback • 28 rookie starters in two years • Winning Full Seasons to Losing Full Seasons: 0:2.

A native of Crucible, Pennsylvania, Frank Filchock had a 25-year career in pro football in two countries. A single wing tailback at the Indiana University, Frank was picked in the second round of the 1938 NFL draft by Pittsburgh, but was sold to Washington in midseason when Art Rooney had financial problems. In Washington, Flingin' Frank teamed with Slingin' Sammy Baugh to give the Redskins the best pair of passing tailbacks in the league. Also like Baugh, Filchock played some minor league baseball on the side and would be one of the first coaches in the American Football League years later. Washington coach Ray Flaherty alternated two distinct backfields by quarter to provide a different look to opposing defenses — Baugh's passing game and Filchock's running game. Filchock spent 1942–1943 in the Navy, but returned to Washington in 1944 when the Redskins switched to the T formation. Filchock actually took to the switch quicker than Baugh who struggled for a year before mastering the quarterback position. In 1946 with young backups Jim Youel and Jack Jacobs on hand, Washington traded the 30-year-old Filchock to New York where he led the Giants to the Eastern Division crown that season.

That 1946 championship game proved to be Frank's NFL downfall. Commissioner Bert Bell heard that Filchock and halfback Merle Hapes were offered bribes to play against the point-spread rather than the Bears. Hapes admitted not reporting the bribe attempt and was suspended, but Filchock denied even being approached and was allowed to play. In the game, Frank played valiantly through a broken nose but threw six interceptions as the Bears beat the Giants by 10 points, exactly the point spread. In the speedy trial the next month, it came out that Filchock had indeed been approached as well as Mapes and both were suspended indefinitely by Bell immediately after the trial. Ironically, the next publicly reported bribe attempt in the NFL occurred in 1971 when lineman Jerry Sturm reported being approached by gamblers in Houston — Sturm had played for Filchock in Calgary and Denver.

Locked out of the NFL, Filchock was courted by

Fewell, Perry									
Year	Team	Games	Wins	Losses	Ties	%	P Wins	P Losses	P %
2009	Bills	7	3	4	0	.429	0	0	.000
1 year		7	3	4	0	.429	0	0	.000

Filchock, Frank J.									
Year	Team	Games	Wins	Losses	Ties	%	P Wins	P Losses	P %
1960	Broncos	14	4	9	1	.321	0	0	.000
1961	Broncos	14	3	11	0	.214	0	0	.000
2 years		28	7	20	1	.268	0	0	.000

two Canadian teams and signed with the Hamilton Tigers for 1947. The Canadian league initially disallowed the contract because of his NFL suspension, but then switched their rationale to the fact that he was a professional since Canadian football at the time was posing as an amateur league. Hamilton forfeited several games at the beginning of the year for using the "professional" Filchock before his contract was finally approved in October, by which time Frank was the player-coach and had instituted a single wing offense. The Tigers dropped out of the league in 1948 and played in a minor league. By 1949, Filchock was back in the main Canadian league, playing for Montreal. Finally in 1950, Bell reinstated Filchock, and Frank returned to play in one game for the Baltimore Colts once the Montreal season ended, but returned to the Great White North the next year.

Filchock finished his career as a player-coach with Edmonton and then Saskatchewan from 1951 to 53 and then coached Saskatchewan through 1957. His coaching record in Edmonton and Saskatchewan was 50–41–5, but he lost his only Grey Cup appearance in 1952 with the Eskimos. He then spent one year coaching the Sarnia Golden Bears to a league championship in a Canadian minor league before catching on as an assistant in Calgary in 1959.

When Frank was hired by former Calgary GM Dean Griffing as the initial coach of the Denver Broncos of the American Football League in 1960, he brought his old Saskatchewan quarterback Frank Tripucka with him as an assistant coach. Once the two saw the sorry Bronco quarterbacks, though, Tripucka came out of retirement as a player. Filchock ran a very loose ship as a coach, finished just 7–20–1 in two years and was fired. Tripucka told *Sports Illustrated* in 1962, "We always had the talent, but we never had the organization. We used to make up plays in the huddle. 'OK, who wants to run out for a pass?' And on blocking assignments at the line of scrimmage, I was up there at the line of scrimmage pointing to the guys on the other team." Filchock coached high school in 1963 and served as quarterbacks coach for Quebec in the semipro United Football League as his gridiron swan song in 1964. In succeeding years, Frank drove a beer truck, ran an asphalt company, operated a restaurant, opened a custard stand, directed a cookie company, sold insurance and headed a food distribution company. He died in 1994 at the age of 77.

FISHER, JEFFREY M. (JEFF) 2/25/1958– Southern California. Played DB for the Bears from 1981 to 1984. *Apprenticeship:* Pro asst.—10 years. *Roots:* Mike Ditka, Buddy Ryan, John Robinson, George Seifert, Jack Pardee. *Branches:* Gregg Williams, Jim Schwartz, Mike Munchak. *Coordinators/Key Assistants:* Jerry Rhome then Les Steckel then Mike Heimerdinger then Norm Chow then Heimerdinger again ran the offense, while Steve Sidwell then Gregg Williams then Jim Schwartz then Chuck Cecil handled the defense. *Hall of Fame Players:* Bruce Matthews. *Primary Quarterbacks:* Steve

Fisher, Jeffrey M. (Jeff)									
Year	Team	Games	Wins	Losses	Ties	%	P Wins	P Losses	P %
1994	Oilers (Titans)	6	1	5	0	.167	0	0	.000
1995	Oilers (Titans)	16	7	9	0	.438	0	0	.000
1996	Oilers (Titans)	16	8	8	0	.500	0	0	.000
1997	Oilers (Titans)	16	8	8	0	.500	0	0	.000
1998	Oilers (Titans)	16	8	8	0	.500	0	0	.000
1999	Titans	16	13	3	0	.813	3	1	.750
2000	Titans	16	13	3	0	.813	0	1	.000
2001	Titans	16	7	9	0	.438	0	0	.000
2002	Titans	16	11	5	0	.688	1	1	.500
2003	Titans	16	12	4	0	.750	1	1	.500
2004	Titans	16	5	11	0	.313	0	0	.000
2005	Titans	16	4	12	0	.250	0	0	.000
2006	Titans	16	8	8	0	.500	0	0	.000
2007	Titans	16	10	6	0	.625	0	1	.000
2008	Titans	16	13	3	0	.813	0	1	.000
2009	Titans	16	8	8	0	.500	0	0	.000
2010	Titans	16	6	10	0	.375	0	0	.000
17 years		262	142	120	0	.542	5	6	.455

McNair, Vince Young, Kerry Collins. *Tendencies:* • His teams scored 21.6 points and allowed 21 per game • His teams ran 47.7% of the time, which was 108% of the league average • Nine starting quarterbacks in 17 years; 80% of starts to primary quarterbacks • 31 rookie starters in 17 years • Winning Full Seasons to Losing Full Seasons: 6:5.

Derisively referred to by some disgruntled Titans' fans as "Coacho Ocho" for his preponderance of five 8–8 years in 16 full seasons, Jeff Fisher is widely respected throughout his profession for getting the most out of his players, even the difficult ones like moody defensive tackle Albert Haynesworth. Fisher kept his equanimity and his team focused through multiple rebuilding terms in his long tenure in Houston and Tennessee, but never rose to take the ultimate prize of winning the Super Bowl.

Fisher was born in Culver City, California, and played defensive back at USC with Hall of Famer Ronnie Lott and All Pros Dennis Smith and Joey Browner. Jeff was drafted in the seventh round in 1981 by the Bears and had a four-year career as a punt returner and backup defensive back. Placed on Injured Reserve in 1985 with a bad ankle, Fisher began his coaching career as a defensive assistant to coordinator Buddy Ryan. Jeff followed Ryan to Philadelphia in 1986 and ascended to defensive coordinator for the Eagles in 1988. When Ryan was fired at the end of 1990, the Eagles' management interviewed the team's two coordinators, but made the poor choice of hiring offensive coordinator Rich Kotite instead of the dynamic 33-year-old Fisher.

Jeff spent a year with the Rams as defensive coordinator under his former USC coach John Robinson and then coached the defensive backs for San Francisco from 1992 to 1993. In 1994, Jack Pardee hired Fisher to replace the pugilistic Buddy Ryan as defensive coordinator of the Oilers. With the team at 1–9, Pardee was fired and Jeff was promoted to interim coach. Over the next 17 years, he coached the Houston Oilers, the Tennessee Oilers and the Tennessee Titans. Like most defensive-oriented coaches, Fisher emphasized a strong rushing attacking (running 8% more than the league average) and stopping the run on defense. He was a players' coach of whom tackle Brad Hopkins once said, "You know why players really like him? He never lies to you. He never tells you a load of garbage. He communicates well. He'll go out and say, 'Kick that player in the crotch or smack him in the mouth.' He's not politically correct. Players love that."

Fisher held the team together as they moved from Houston to Memphis to Nashville and established a great rapport with quarterback Steve McNair, allowing him to develop into a star. While Fisher's defenses were consistently good, he went through a series of offensive coordinators trying to spice up his conservative

attack. What he was best at was preparation. That was most evident with the Music City Miracle in 1999 when Fisher called a trick kickoff return play, the "Home Run Throwback," that the Titans had practiced, and that play went for the winning touchdown in the closing seconds in the playoffs against Buffalo. That year the Titans went all the way to the Super Bowl and battled the favored Rams right to the final play of the game, one yard short of the goal line.

After McNair left Tennessee, the Titans brought in heralded rookie Vince Young, but Fisher and Young never connected; Jeff felt more comfortable with stolid veteran Kerry Collins at quarterback. By 2010, there was an outright showdown between Fisher and Young. When the team announced in January 2011 that Young would no longer be a Titan, it appeared that Fisher had won. However, three weeks later, Jeff resigned. Supposedly, one of the main differences between Fisher and owner Bud Adams was that Adams would not let Fisher hire his son as an assistant. More significant, though, was Jeff's comment at the closing press conference, "I've been coaching for 25 years and I think I'm tired. I need a rest." After a one-year respite, Fisher was pursued by both Miami and St. Louis in January 2012 before signing to coach the Rams.

FLAHERTY, RAYMOND P. (RAY) 9/1/1903–7/19/1994. Gonzaga. Played E for the Yankees and Giants from 1927 to 1929 and from 1931 to 1935. *Apprenticeship:* College head coach—1 year; pro asst.—three years. *Roots:* Steve Owen. *Branches:* Turk Edwards, Red Strader, Wayne Millner. *Coordinators/Key Assistants:* Turk Edwards coached the line and Ray Baker the backs. *Hall of Fame Players:* Cliff Battles, Sammy Baugh, Turk Edwards, Bruiser Kinard, Wayne Millner, Ace Parker, Arnie Weinmeister. *Primary Quarterbacks:* Sammy Baugh. *Record:* **Hall of Fame Coach**; NFL Championships 1937, 1942. *Tendencies:* • His teams scored 18.6 points and allowed 14 per game • His teams ran 63.8% of the time, which was 98% of the league average • Six starting quarterbacks in 11 years; 51% of starts to primary quarterback • 31 rookie starters in 11 years • Winning Full Seasons to Losing Full Seasons: 9:1.

Spokane's Ray Flaherty was an innovative Hall

Head-to-Head:		
Hall of Fame Opponent	Regular Season	Postseason
Paul Brown	0–5–1	0–2
Jimmy Conzelman	2–0	0–0
George Halas	2–3	1–1
Curly Lambeau	1–4	0–1
Greasy Neale	4–0	0–0
Steve Owen	5–8–1	0–0
Total	14–20–2	1–4

of Fame coach in the NFL in the 1930s and 1940s who is little remembered today because he made himself obsolete in the prime of his coaching career by sticking with an outmoded offense. Playing end at Gonzaga from 1923 to 1925, Flaherty was friends with classmate Bing Crosby and teammates with Houston Stockton, the grandfather of NBA star John Stockton. Ray joined the Los Angeles Wildcats of Red Grange's American Football League in 1926 and once the AFL collapsed, he joined Grange's New York Yankees in the NFL from 1927 to 1928. Ray moved on to the Giants at the end of 1928 and was All Pro in 1929. In 1930, he coached the University of Georgia to a 1–7–1 record and then returned to the Giants in 1931, when he led the league in receptions. He also played minor league baseball during this time. Flaherty was again All Pro in 1932 and was team captain and playing assistant coach from 1933 to 1935. It was his idea for the Giants to hunt down some sneakers to improve their footing in the 1934 NFL title game since known as the "Sneakers' Game."

Flaherty was the original hot assistant coach and was hired by George Preston Marshall to coach the Redskins in 1936. Flaherty handled the meddling Marshall better than any other coach ever would and lasted seven years, longer than any other head coach under Marshall. Ray later said, "I never had any trouble with Mr. Marshall. He came down to the bench one day and I sent him back to the stands. He never came down again." When you win 72% of your games, go to four championship games and win two NFL titles, you gain a little leeway, even from abrasive busybodies. He was also popular with his Washington players. Tackle Jim Barber said at Flaherty's funeral, "He knew football, but his biggest asset was in knowing how to handle players. He knew when to chew a fanny or pat somebody on the back. The players liked him, but he was no patsy." With the Redskins, Flaherty began using a two platoon system where he would alternate quarters with Sammy Baugh or Frank Filchock at tailback, using the different skills of the

two stars to present different looks to the opposing defense. He also popularized the behind the line of scrimmage screen pass in order to lessen the pass rush on Baugh, beginning with the 1937 championship game in which Sammy threw three touchdown passes. While those Redskins lost the 1940 title game to Chicago 73–0, they attained sweet revenge two years later, beating the Bears 14–6 right before Flaherty left football to go into the Navy in 1943.

When Flaherty returned to football after the war, it was not to Washington, but to the new All America Football Conference. Originally, it was reported that he would coach Gene Tunney's Baltimore team in the AAFC, but that team did not materialize so Flaherty signed with Dan Topping's New York Yankees instead. With his league jump, Ray was getting more money, New York exposure and no further Marshall interference. For the first two years of the AAFC, Flaherty had a powerhouse team whose only fault was that they could not defeat the Cleveland Browns. The Browns beat the Yankees in both the 1946 and 1947 title games. After the 1946 championship loss, several Yankee stars, including tailback Ace Parker, tackle Bruiser Kinard and fullback Pug Manders, surprisingly complained about Flaherty's strategy. In the second meeting of the Yankees and Browns in 1947, New York built a 28–0 lead only to end up with a 28–28 tie. The rivalry with unbeatable Browns' coach Paul Brown was intense. Flaherty derided Brown as a "high school coach," while Brown referred to Ray as "Ray Flattery."

In 1948, the AAFC attempted to prop up some of its weaker teams by having the stronger teams send them some players. The Yankees lost Dick Barwegan to Baltimore and Eddie Prokop and Nate Johnson to Chicago. When the weakened Yankees got off to a 1–3 start, Flaherty resigned "under pressure" from the club. A year later, Flaherty returned as head coach of the Chicago Hornets who were coming off back-to-back 1–13 seasons as the Chicago Rockets. The renamed Hornets improved to 4–8 under Flaherty. There was some question when Ray was hired whether

Flaherty, Raymond P. (Ray)									
Year	Team	Games	Wins	Losses	Ties	%	P Wins	P Losses	P %
1936	Redskins	12	7	5	0	.583	0	1	.000
1937	Redskins	11	8	3	0	.727	1	0	1.000
1938	Redskins	11	6	3	2	.636	0	0	.000
1939	Redskins	11	8	2	1	.773	0	0	.000
1940	Redskins	11	9	2	0	.818	0	1	.000
1941	Redskins	11	6	5	0	.545	0	0	.000
1942	Redskins	11	10	1	0	.909	1	0	1.000
1946	Yankees (AAFC)	14	10	3	1	.750	0	1	.000
1947	Yankees (AAFC	14	11	2	1	.821	0	1	.000
1948	Yankees (AAFC	4	1	3	0	.250	0	0	.000
1949	Hornets (AAFC)	12	4	8	0	.333	0	0	.000
11 years		122	80	37	5	.676	2	4	.333

he would at last switch from the single wing to the T formation, but he told the press, "We've got a new spirit, but the same old single wing. I'll stick with that until somebody shows me a better formation — which isn't the T."

Because of Flaherty's devotion to the single wing, his coaching career ended with the merging of the AAFC into the NFL in 1950. Baltimore considered hiring him as their new coach, but wanted to run the T. By 1950, the only NFL team running the single wing was the Steelers, and they would switch to the T when they changed coaches again in 1952. Flaherty was a great coach who stressed the fundamentals of blocking and tackling over all else to build balanced teams. Five times his teams were in the top three in scoring and five times they were in the top three in fewest points allowed. Upon his early retirement from football, Ray returned to his hometown of Spokane, ran a beverage distributorship and enjoyed the great outdoors. He died at age 90 in 1994.

FLORES, THOMAS R. (TOM) 3/21/1937– Pacific. Played QB for the Raiders, Bills and Chiefs from 1960 to 1961 and from 1963 to 1969. *Apprenticeship:* College asst.—1 year; pro asst.—8 years. *Roots:* Harvey Johnson, John Madden. *Branches:* Art Shell, Terry Robiskie (i). *Coordinators/Key Assistants*: For the Raiders, Larry Kennan was the key offensive coach, while Charley Sumner then Bob Zeman ran the defense; for the Seahawks, Larry Kennan handled the offense, and Rusty Tillman ran the defense. *Hall of Fame Players:* Marcus Allen, Dave Casper, Mike Haynes, Ted Hendricks, Cortez Kennedy, James Lofton, Howie Long, Art Shell, Gene Upshaw. *Primary Quarterbacks:* Jim Plunkett, Marc Wilson, Rick Mirer. *Record:* Super Bowl Championships 1980, 1983 *Tendencies:* • His teams scored 20.4 points and allowed 20.1 per game • His teams ran 47.5% of the time, which was the league average • Nine starting quarterbacks in 12 years; 74% of starts to primary quarterbacks • 21 rookie starters

in 12 years • Winning Full Seasons to Losing Full Seasons: 6:5.

Sanger, California's Tom Flores was the first Hispanic coach to win a Super Bowl. Flores came from the humble roots of the fruit fields of the San Joaquin Valley, and as a boy he worked in the icehouse where the picked fruit was preserved. That job earned Tom the lifelong nickname of the "Ice Man," but the name was just as apt for his cool, low-key personality both as a player and coach.

Flores transferred to the College of the Pacific from Fresno City College in 1957 and broke Eddie LeBaron's passing records despite hurting his arm. Undrafted, Tom was cut by Calgary in the CFL in 1958 and by the Washington Redskins in 1959 and spent the year coaching the freshmen at his alma mater. When the AFL opened in 1960, he hooked on with the Raiders and won the starting job. Although Flores was sidelined in 1962 by a lung ailment, he returned under new coach Al Davis in 1963 to share the quarterbacking with Cotton Davidson. Tom was traded to Buffalo in 1967 in the Daryle Lamonica deal and was picked up by Kansas City in their stretch run in 1969, winning a Super Bowl ring as a backup quarterback.

In 1971, Flores returned to Buffalo as quarterbacks coach, but then came back to the Raiders as receivers' coach in 1972. He served for seven years under John Madden and then replaced him when Madden stepped aside in 1979. In Flores' second season, the Raiders won the Super Bowl as a wild card team, with Hispanic quarterback Jim Plunkett running the offense. Flores reacted to the *Washington Post* by saying, "I got the happiest feeling being a head coach rather than as a player. It's the team you molded and put together. I have the control of our design and practices, and I enjoy the relationship with the players." Like Madden before him, Flores had to contend with whispers that Al Davis was really in charge and that the coach was merely a puppet, but Flores led the Raiders to a second Super Bowl win over the Redskins three

Flores, Thomas R. (Tom)

Year	Team	Games	Wins	Losses	Ties	%	P Wins	P Losses	P %
1979	Raiders	16	9	7	0	.563	0	0	.000
1980	Raiders	16	11	5	0	.688	4	0	1.000
1981	Raiders	16	7	9	0	.438	0	0	.000
1982	Raiders	9	8	1	0	.889	1	1	.500
1983	Raiders	16	12	4	0	.750	3	0	1.000
1984	Raiders	16	11	5	0	.688	0	1	.000
1985	Raiders	16	12	4	0	.750	0	1	.000
1986	Raiders	16	8	8	0	.500	0	0	.000
1987	Raiders	15	5	10	0	.333	0	0	.000
1992	Seahawks	16	2	14	0	.125	0	0	.000
1993	Seahawks	16	6	10	0	.375	0	0	.000
1994	Seahawks	16	6	10	0	.375	0	0	.000
12 years		184	97	87	0	.527	8	3	.727

years later. By then according to the *Los Angeles Times*, even some anonymous players were questioning Tom's minimalist leadership and strategy. After two more seasons of double-digit victories, the team began to slip as Plunkett gave way to Marc Wilson at quarterback. After a 5–10 1987 season, Flores resigned, saying, "I'm not burned out, but I am tired — this is an all consuming job — and it is time to move on."

After one year in the Raiders' front office, Flores was hired in 1989 as president and GM of the Seattle Seahawks. Three years later, he took over as coach. In those six years, though, the Seahawks went from mediocre to bad, and Flores reputation took a hit. When Paul Allen bought the Seahawks, Flores was out. Since then, he has worked as a Raiders' radio broadcaster in addition to running a beer distributorship and an auto dealership.

FONTES, WAYNE 2/2/1940– Michigan State. Played DB for the New York Titans in 1962. *Apprenticeship:* College asst.—11 years; pro asst.—13 years. *Roots:* John McKay, Darryl Rogers. *Branches:* None. *Coordinators/Key Assistants*: Mouse Davis then Dave Levy then Dan Henning then Tom Moore ran the offense, while Woody Widenhofer then Hank Bullough then Herb Patera then Jim Eddy handled the defense. *Hall of Fame Players:* Barry Sanders. *Primary Quarterbacks:* Rodney Peete, Scott Mitchell. *Tendencies:* • His teams scored 20.8 points and allowed 21.2 per game • His teams ran 44% of the time, which was 98% of the league average • Ten starting quarterbacks in nine years; 65% of starts to primary quarterbacks • 19 rookie starters in nine years • Winning Full Seasons to Losing Full Seasons: 4:4.

Of Portuguese roots, Wayne Fontes was born in New Bedford, Masachusetts, but grew up in Canton, Ohio. He played halfback for Duffy Daugherty at Michigan State and spent 1962 with the New York Titans as a defensive back until he blew out his knee. Fontes returned to Michigan State as an assistant in 1963 before coaching high school for two years. From 1966 to 1971, he worked as an assistant at Dayton and Iowa and then talked himself into a job with John

McKay at USC in 1972. When McKay took over as the first head coach of the Tampa Bay Bucs in 1976, Fontes came with him, eventually rising to defensive coordinator in Tampa. McKay retired in 1985, and Fontes moved on to Detroit as the Lions' defensive coordinator under another former college coach, Darryl Rogers. Like so many Lions' coaches, Rogers was a flop and was replaced by Fontes 11 games into 1988.

Over the next nine years, Fontes would win more games than any other Lions' coach — and lose more as well. With Fontes, though, there was always a bit of buffoonery going on, a sense that nothing was serious. Fontes was a joyful, emotional, demonstrative, personable coach who described himself as a hugger. Hall of Fame runner Barry Sanders said, "He proves that a coach can show affection and appreciation [and still win.]" Fontes told the *New York Times*, "My office is like a bus station. The players come in and sit down, sometimes just to talk, but other times with problems. They know I'm right here and the door is open."

Meanwhile, Fontes' indecisive quarterback carousel was divisive and nonproductive. He went back and forth through Bob Gagliano, Eric Hipple, Rodney Peete, Andre Ware, Erik Kramer, Scott Mitchell, and Dave Krieg. He had those quarterbacks running a modified version of the Run-and-Shoot called the Silver Stretch, but the team's performance was up and down. After one benching, Mitchell showed up at team function dressed like Fontes in Mickey Mouse ears. Fontes did not seem to realize he had lost the respect of his team by 1996. Star receiver Herman Moore told the *New York Times* that Fontes characterization of the failing offense as sputtering was wrong, "It's more than sputtering. He's the head coach and that's the only answer he can come up with. I'm just fed up with this. It's time for Wayne to stop fooling himself, fooling the media and fooling the fans." By 1996, Fontes was fooling no one but himself. Even at the press conference announcing his firing, Fontes was in Wayne's World, showing up during owner William Ford's remarks and bellowing, "Fired?! What do you mean I'm fired?" He then gave Ford a big awkward hug. Two years later, Fontes filed a dis-

Fontes, Wayne									
Year	Team	Games	Wins	Losses	Ties	%	P Wins	P Losses	P %
1988	Lions	5	2	3	0	.400	0	0	.000
1989	Lions	16	7	9	0	.438	0	0	.000
1990	Lions	16	6	10	0	.375	0	0	.000
1991	Lions	16	12	4	0	.750	1	1	.500
1992	Lions	16	5	11	0	.313	0	0	.000
1993	Lions	16	10	6	0	.625	0	1	.000
1994	Lions	16	9	7	0	.563	0	1	.000
1995	Lions	16	10	6	0	.625	0	1	.000
1996	Lions	16	5	11	0	.313	0	0	.000
9 years		133	66	67	0	.496	1	4	.200

ability claim for alleged injuries incurred while coaching, but the claim was refused. He never coached again.

FORZANO, RICHARD E. (RICK) 11/20/1928– Kent State. Did not play professionally. *Apprenticeship:* College coach —14 years (6 as head coach); pro asst.— 4 years. *Roots:* Paul Brown, Charley Winner, Don McCafferty. *Branches:* Raymond Berry, Jerry Glanville, Bill Belichick, Joe Bugel. *Coordinators/Key Assistants:* Bob Gibson handled the offense, while Jim Carr ran the defense. *Hall of Fame Players:* Lem Barney, Charley Sanders. *Primary Quarterbacks:* Bill Munson *Tendencies:* • His teams scored 17.2 points and allowed 18.3 per game • His teams ran 50.4% of the time, which was 92% of the league average • Three starting quarterbacks in three years; 44% of starts to primary quarterback • Two rookie starters in three years • Winning Full Seasons to Losing Full Seasons: 0:0.

Born in Akron, Ohio, Rick Forzano's playing career ended in high school due to an eye injury suffered in a game. He attended Kent State and then went directly into coaching high school from 1951 to 1955. In 1956, Rick moved up to the college ranks as an assistant at Wooster for a year and then two at his alma mater before joining Wayne Hardin's staff at Annapolis in 1959. Rick's most significant accomplishment at the Naval Academy was convincing Cincinnati's highly touted schoolboy athlete Roger Staubach to play for Navy.

In 1964, Forzano was named head coach at the University of Connecticut and went 7–10–1 in two years before leaving to become the backfield coach for the St. Louis Cardinals in 1966. Along the way, Forzano got to know Paul Brown, and Brown promised him a job when he got back into pro football. When Brown started the Bengals in 1968, Rick was his backfield coach, but stayed for just one year because Navy hired him as its head coach in 1969. Forzano told the *Washington Post* at the time, "I used to go to all [Brown's] coaching clinics when I was coaching in Ohio. As far as I'm concerned, Paul Brown is one of the greatest men who ever walked the earth. He's the greatest friend I ever had."

When Forzano assumed control of the Navy football program, times were hard for the service academies. In four years, Rick went 10–33 overall and 1–3 to Army, although the program was improving.

Forzano resigned in 1973 to join Don McCafferty's staff with the Lions. He knew McCafferty from when the two of them coached at Kent State in the 1950s. After a mediocre 6–7–1 finish in 1973, McCafferty, the "Easy Rider," dropped dead from a heart attack during training camp in 1974. Forzano replaced his friend, saying, "As a football staff, we have to dedicate ourselves to Mac, and we're going to do the job for him."

With the Lions, though, Forzano came to be known as "Rigid Rick," a disciplinarian who would run five hour practices with just one water break according to *Charlie Sanders' Tales from the Detroit Lions*. He did have a top flight coaching staff that included future NFL coaches Raymond Berry, Joe Bugel, Jerry Glanville and Bill Belichick. Belichick recalled Forzano for Terry Pluto's *Things I've Learned from Watching the Browns*, "Many of Rick's methods came from Paul [Brown] and I observed them in Detroit, and later put them into my own coaching style: discipline, preparation, practice schedules, situation football, and projects for assistant coaches."

Forzano did a better job with his coaches than his players. The team finished at .500 twice and then got off to a slow start in 1976. Rick resigned in October 1976 and never coached again. Instead he ran his own company and did some broadcasting of Big Ten games. Still, in 1977, he told the *Baltimore Sun*, "I just want to be a head coach again." And in 1981, he told the same paper, "Well, I enjoy broadcasting, but I still miss coaching. I can't kid anybody about it. You get it in your system, and it's something you love. It's something my wife misses, my children miss, but I'm a manufacturer's rep now too, in business. But you're always looking to see if that door might be open for one more shot." It never was.

FOX, JOHN 2/8/1955– San Diego State. DB; did not play professionally. *Apprenticeship:* College asst.— 9 years; pro asst.—12 years. *Roots:* Chuck Noll, Bobby Ross, Art Shell, Mike White, Jim Fassel. *Branches:* Jack Del Rio, Dennis Allen. *Coordinators/Key Assistants:* For the Panthers, Dan Henning then Jeff Davidson ran the offense, while Mike Trgovic then Ron Meeks handled the defense; for the Broncos, Mike McCoy ran the offense, while Dennis Allen handled the defense. *Hall of Fame Players:* None. *Primary Quarterbacks:* Jake Delhomme, Tim Tebow. *Tendencies:* • His teams

Forzano, Richard E. (Rick)									
Year	Team	Games	Wins	Losses	Ties	%	P Wins	P Losses	P %
1974	Lions	14	7	7	0	.500	0	0	.000
1975	Lions	14	7	7	0	.500	0	0	.000
1976	Lions	4	1	3	0	.250	0	0	.000
3 years		32	15	17	0	.469	0	0	.000

scored 19.4 points and allowed 20.6 per game • His teams ran 48.4% of the time, which was 110% of the league average • 11 starting quarterbacks in ten years; 63% of starts to primary quarterback • 25 rookie starters in ten years • Winning Full Seasons to Losing Full Seasons: 3:4.

"A punt is not a bad play," according to Virginia Beach's John Fox, one of the most conservative, defensive-oriented coaches in the NFL. Fox pursued a winding path to the NFL, coaching at eight different universities before reaching the league in 1989. In college, he played in the San Diego State defensive backfield with Herman Edwards in 1976. Fox, who was called "Crash" then, finished his eligibility in 1977 and went right into coaching at his alma mater in 1978. From there, he worked at U.S. International University under Sid Gillman in 1979, Boise State in 1980, Long Beach State in 1981, Utah in 1982, Kansas in 1983 and Iowa State in 1984. In 1985, Fox was the defensive backs coach for the Los Angeles Express in the USFL before returning to the college ranks with Pittsburgh as defensive coordinator from 1986 to 1988 under Mike Gottfreid who was also Fox's head coach at Kansas.

Finally in 1989, Fox made the NFL when Chuck Noll hired him as the Steelers' defensive backs coach. He spent three years there, two in San Diego under Bobby Ross and then was named defensive coordinator of the Raiders under Art Shell in 1994. Fox did an effective job with the Raiders, but during training camp in 1996, he got into a contentious discussion with owner Al Davis about the defense, and Fox abruptly quit. He has remained quiet about the incident that caused him to spend 1996 doing some scouting for the Rams before Jim Fassel hired him as Giants defensive coordinator in 1997. Over the next five years, Fox had the Giants in the top ten in points allowed three times, with his masterwork being the 2000 NFC Championship game when his defense shut out the favored Vikings in a 41–0 rout.

A year later, Fox took over as head coach of the 1–15 Carolina Panthers and invoked Chuck Noll when he was hired, "Chuck Noll told me early that you have to be able to stop the run and you better be able to run. That's not all, but I want to be able to do those things." Two years later when the Panthers were in the midst of making a Super Bowl run, Fox cited another coaching hero to the *New York Times*, "Coaches in my background, from 1966 when I was a Green Bay Packers fan watching Vince Lombardi — to me, he was the essence of football. The toughness and the mentality of running and stopping the run to me is kind of where it all starts."

Despite being a tough talking, brutally honest disciplinarian, Fox is known for his warm, personable nature and is, in essence, a players' coach. Panther defensive end Michael Rucker said of Fox, "You know Coach Fox is going to be in there swinging until the end. That's why guys play so hard for him, because they see what he puts into it. He works like we work." Fox emphasized teamwork and fundamentals. His run-oriented offense was simple but did take Carolina to one Super Bowl where it took Tom Brady's heroics to defeat Fox's impassioned team.

Overall, Fox's record in Carolina was up-and-down almost every year, but for the first eight years that meant alternating between excellent and mediocre. In 2010, the bottom fell out, and the Panthers won just two games, relying on two rookies and two backups at quarterback. He was fired, but was quickly rehired by new Denver GM John Elway as the new Broncos' head coach for 2011. With the Broncos, Fox dumped conventional quarterback Kyle Orton for Tim Tebow early in the season and revamped the offense to institute "Tebowmania" in Denver. Although the run-oriented offense got the team to an 8–8 season and a division title, the oddly talented Tebow was traded at season's end.

FRAZIER, LESLIE A. 4/3/1959– Alcorn State. Played CB for the Bears from 1981 to 1985. *Apprenticeship:* College coach —11 years (9 as head coach); pro asst.—12 years. *Roots:* Andy Reid, Marvin Lewis, Tony Dungy, Brad Childress. *Branches:* None. *Coor-*

Fox, John									
Year	Team	Games	Wins	Losses	Ties	%	P Wins	P Losses	P %
2002	Panthers	16	7	9	0	.438	0	0	.000
2003	Panthers	16	11	5	0	.688	3	1	.750
2004	Panthers	16	7	9	0	.438	0	0	.000
2005	Panthers	16	11	5	0	.688	2	1	.667
2006	Panthers	16	8	8	0	.500	0	0	.000
2007	Panthers	16	7	9	0	.438	0	0	.000
2008	Panthers	16	12	4	0	.750	0	1	.000
2009	Panthers	16	8	8	0	.500	0	0	.000
2010	Panthers	16	2	14	0	.125	0	0	.000
2011	Broncos	16	8	8	0	.500	1	1	.500
10 years		160	81	79	0	.506	6	4	.600

dinators/Key Assistants: Bill Musgrave ran the offense, while Fred Pagac handled the defense. *Hall of Fame Players:* None. *Primary Quarterbacks:* Christian Ponder. *Tendencies:* • His teams scored 20.4 points and allowed 26 per game • His teams ran 45.6% of the time, which was 106% of the league average • Five starting quarterbacks in two years; 45% of starts to primary quarterbacks • Seven rookie starters in two years • Winning Full Seasons to Losing Full Seasons: 0:1.

Born in Columbus, Mississippi, Leslie Frazier attended little Alcorn State, an historically black college in the state where he teamed with Roynell Young at cornerback. While Young was a first round draft choice of the Eagles in 1980, Frazier went undrafted the following year, signing with the Bears as a free agent. In Chicago, Frazier was a four-year starter who intercepted 20 passes, just three fewer than Young had in his nine-year career. Frazier was never an All Pro; instead, his defensive coach, Buddy Ryan, once referred to him and fellow cornerback Mike Richardson as "the sorriest corners in the league." Playing in Ryan's 46, Frazier and Richardson played under more pressure than any other corners because they often had no safety help with everyone bunched at the line of scrimmage.

Frazier tore up his knee returning a punt in Super Bowl XX and never played again. Two years later, Leslie became the first-ever head coach of Trinity College, a Christian college near Chicago, and in nine years took a startup team to two conference titles and a 33–36–3 record. In 1997, Frazier moved up the ladder to the University of Illinois as an assistant for two years. In 1999, he joined Andy Reid's staff in Philadelphia as defensive backs coach and then was hired by Marvin Lewis as defensive coordinator of the Bengals in 2003. In 2005, Leslie joined Tony Dungy's staff in Indianapolis and won a Super Bowl ring as defensive backs coach a year later. Frazier then was named defensive coordinator of the Vikings in 2007 under Brad

Childress, with whom Leslie had worked in Philadelphia.

Frazier built a run-stuffing defense that was the strength of the team, while Childress' bristly personality and coaching shortcomings got him fired 10 games into 2010 and replaced by Frazier. Childress had lost the team. Star runner Adrian Peterson greeted the change of head coaches by saying of Leslie, "When he talks, guys ears are pinned up. It's a feeling of being sure about the words that are coming out of his mouth and trusting them." For his part, Frazier promised a run-first offense and stabilized the team in the closing weeks to earn a contract as the permanent head coach in 2011. A protégé of Tony Dungy, Frazier is known for his honesty and integrity. However, the Vikings gave up the second most points in the league in 2011, and the team won just three games behind free agent flop Donovan McNabb and rookie Christian Ponder at quarterback.

GAILEY, THOMAS C. (CHAN) 1/5/1952– Florida. QB; did not play professionally. *Apprenticeship:* College coach —12 years (3 as head coach); pro asst.— 10 years; WLAF head coach — 2 years. *Roots:* Dan Reeves, Bill Cowher. *Branches:* Dave Campo, Jim Bates. *Coordinators/Key Assistants:* For the Cowboys, Gailey ran his own offense, while Dave Campo handled the defense; for the Bills, Curtis Modkins ran the offense, while George Edwards handled the defense. *Hall of Fame Players:* Troy Aikman, Michael Irvin, Deion Sanders and Emmitt Smith. *Primary Quarterbacks:* Troy Aikman, Ryan Fitzpatrick *Tendencies:* • His teams scored 21.7 points and allowed 22 per game • His teams ran 45% of the time, which was 104% of the league average • Five starting quarterbacks in four years; 84% of starts to primary quarterbacks • 14 rookie starters in four years • Winning Full Seasons to Losing Full Seasons: 1:2.

In his nearly forty year coaching career, Chan Gailey has served four NFL teams as offensive coor-

Frazier, Leslie A.

Year	Team	Games	Wins	Losses	Ties	%	P Wins	P Losses	P %
2010	Vikings	6	3	3	0	.500	0	0	.000
2011	Vikings	16	3	13	0	.188	0	0	.000
2 years		22	6	16	0	.273	0	0	.000

Gailey, Thomas C. (Chan)

Year	Team	Games	Wins	Losses	Ties	%	P Wins	P Losses	P %
1998	Cowboys	16	10	6	0	.625	0	1	.000
1999	Cowboys	16	8	8	0	.500	0	1	.000
2010	Bills	16	4	12	0	.250	0	0	.000
2011	Bills	16	6	10	0	.375	0	0	.000
4 years		64	28	36	0	.438	0	2	.000

dinator and two, with an 11-year gap, as head coach. Hailing from Gainesville, Georgia, Gailey played quarterback in Gainesville, Florida for the University of Florida under Doug Dickey from 1971 to 1973 before advancing directly into coaching as a graduate assistant at his alma mater from 1974 to 1975. He began on the defensive side of the ball as defensive backs coach at Troy State from 1976 to 1978 and held the same position at the Air Force Academy in 1979. In 1981, Air Force promoted Chan to defensive coordinator, and Troy State brought him back as head coach in 1983. A 19–5 two-year record at Troy got Gailey hired by Dan Reeves in Denver as special teams/tight ends coach. In his six years with the Broncos, Chan worked himself up to offensive coordinator.

In 1991, he was named head coach of the Birmingham Fire in the developmental World League of American Football and went 12–7 in two seasons. After one 5–6 year as head coach of Samford University in Alabama, Gailey returned to the NFL as receivers coach for Pittsburgh in 1994. Two years later, he replaced Ron Erhardt as the Steelers' offensive coordinator. While Gailey is generally known to favor a run-oriented attack, his Pittsburgh offense took full advantage of the multiple gifts of Kordell "Slash" Stewart and showed great imagination.

In 1998, Jerry Jones hired Gailey as head coach of the fading Cowboys, replacing Barry Switzer. Quarterback Troy Aikman told the *New York Times*, "Chan presents us with a fresh start. Usually when you get a new head coach you tend to be in a rebuilding mode. This football team is not going to be like that. We expect great things." Early in the season, Jones told *Sports Illustrated*, "If I had it to do all over again, I'd have made the change [to Gailey] after the '95 Super Bowl. The way [Switzer] was critiqued after that wasn't good for him. At the time I thought not making a change was our best chance to keep winning. But watching Chan work, the wisdom of making a change has been reinforced time and again this year. His attention to every detail, his work ethic, what he's done with our offense — he's better than I could have ever imagined."

By the end of 1999, Jones was complaining about the unimaginative play calling and the inordinate amount of dump off passes, while Gailey had stopped attending quarterback meetings at all because Aikman and backup Jason Garrett questioned his play-calling so vociferously. Refusing to hire an offensive coordi-

nator, Chan was mercifully fired after two years, and Dallas continued its descent in the league. Gailey moved on to Miami as offensive coordinator in 2000, and then was hired as head coach for Georgia Tech in 2002. At Tech, Gailey had a winning team each year, but never posted fewer than five losses in six seasons. He was fired with an overall 44–32 record in 2008. Hired by Herm Edwards as the Chiefs' offensive coordinator that year, Chan stayed on when Edwards was replaced by Todd Haley in 2009. However, he and rookie head coach Haley clashed early, and Gailey was fired during the preseason.

Gailey resurfaced the next year when he was hired as head coach in Buffalo, also in the process winning a recommendation from Jerry Jones who now regretted having fired him a decade before. Gailey told the press, "I've been around enough winning programs that when I walk on the field I expect to win. I don't just hope to win. But the bottom line is we've got to do it on the field." After a 4–12 first season, Gailey drove the Bills to a 5–2 start in 2011 before the team collapsed soon after awarding bearded Harvard quarterback Ryan Fitzpatrick a rich contract extension.

GANSZ, FRANCIS V. (FRANK) 11/22/1938–4/27/2009. Navy. C; did not play professionally. *Apprenticeship:* College asst.—13 years; pro asst.—9 years. *Roots:* Pete McCully (i), Fred O'Connor (i), Homer Rice, Forrest Gregg, Marv Levy, Marion Campbell, Fred Bruney (i), John Mackovic. *Branches:* Rod Rust. *Coordinators/Key Assistants:* Homer Smith then George Sefcik ran the offense, while John Paul Young then Rod Rust handled the defense. *Hall of Fame Players:* None. *Primary Quarterbacks:* Bill Kenny, Steve De-Berg. *Tendencies:* • His teams scored 17 points and allowed 22.8 per game • His teams ran 45.2% of the time, which was 95% of the league average • Six starting quarterbacks in two years; 77% of starts to primary quarterbacks • Five rookie starters in two years • Winning Full Seasons to Losing Full Seasons: 0:2.

Born in Altoona, Pennsylvania, Frank Gansz attended the Naval Academy from 1956 to 1959 before serving as a jet pilot in the Air Force for nearly seven years. Reportedly, Gansz told his players stories of having flown dangerous missions during that time and was called "Crash" by them in tribute. When Gansz was named head coach of the Chiefs, however, it came out that he had never been in combat. Despite the ap-

Gansz, Francis V. (Frank)									
Year	Team	Games	Wins	Losses	Ties	%	P Wins	P Losses	P %
1987	Chiefs	15	4	11	0	.267	0	0	.000
1988	Chiefs	16	4	11	1	.281	0	0	.000
2 years		31	8	22	1	.274	0	0	.000

parent exaggerations, Gansz was beloved by his players as one of the top special teams coaches in pro football.

He began his coaching career as an assistant at the Air Force Academy from 1964 to 1966. Frank was on the staff of the ill-fated Long Beach Admirals that played just one game in the Continental Football League in 1967 and folded two days later. He then worked at Colgate in 1968, the Naval Academy from 1969 to 1972, Oklahoma State in 1973, West Point in 1974, back at Oklahoma State in 1975 and at UCLA from 1976 to 1977. In 1978, Frank moved up to the NFL in San Francisco as special teams coach under former Navy assistant coach Pete McCulley. From there, he worked in Cincinnati from 1979 to 1980, in Kansas City from 1981 to 1982 and in Philadelphia from 1983 to 1985. He returned to Kansas City in 1986 with the unique title of Assistant Head Coach/Special Teams under John Mackovic. That year, his unit blocked 10 kicks and scored five touchdowns. Gansz told *Sports Illustrated*, "Special teams requires a lot of discipline. Every situation unfolds differently. It takes a great deal of practice and a great deal of study." The Chiefs won 10 games and went to the playoffs in 1986, but the unpopular Mackovic was dismissed anyway, and a group of Chief players met team president Jack Steadman at kicker Nick Lowery's house to advocate for Gansz.

The Chiefs hired Frank as head coach later that week, but Gansz proved a disappointment, winning just eight games in two years. In the second season, he suspended running back Paul Palmer after Palmer commented to a coach that he might fumble the ball on purpose to ensure Gansz be fired. Predictably, both Gansz and Palmer were working elsewhere in 1989. Gansz moved on to Detroit from 1989 to 1993, Atlanta from 1994 to 1996, the Rams from 1997 to 1999 and the Jaguars from 2000 to 2001. He subsequently retired, but returned in 2008 at age 70 as the special teams coach at Southern Methodist under June Jones, his former boss in Atlanta. Gansz died a year later. His son, Frank Jr., followed in his father's footsteps to become a respected special teams coach for several colleges and for the Raiders, Chiefs and Ravens in the NFL.

GARRETT, JASON 3/28/1966– Princeton. Played QB for the Cowboys and Giants from 1993 to 2000. *Apprenticeship:* Pro asst.— 6 years. *Roots:* Nick Saban,

Wade Phillips. *Branches:* None. *Coordinators/Key Assistants:* Garrett ran his own offense, while Paul Pasqualoni then Rob Ryan handled the defense. *Hall of Fame Players:* None. *Primary Quarterbacks:* Tony Romo. *Tendencies:* • His teams scored 25.1 points and allowed 23 per game • His teams ran 43.2% of the time, which was the league average • Three starting quarterbacks in two years; 67% of starts to primary quarterback • Five rookie starters in two years • Winning Full Seasons to Losing Full Seasons: 0:0.

Jason Garrett hails from Abington, Pennsylvania and a family of football coaches. His father Jim coached in both college and the pros and Jim's sons Jason, John and Judd have followed suit. Jason began his college playing career at Princeton, but when his dad got the head coaching position at Columbia, he transferred there. Jim subsequently resigned after one 0–10 season, so Jason and his brothers transferred back to Princeton. John was a wide receiver at Princeton in 1986 and 1987; Judd was a running back there from 1987 to 1989; and Jason was the Tigers' quarterback from 1986 to 1988.

Coming from the Ivy League, there was no great demand for Jason's services from the NFL. Garrett worked his way on the Saints' taxi squad in 1989 and 1990 and played in the developmental World League in 1991 and the CFL in 1992 before catching as the Cowboys' third quarterback in 1993. Garrett's one day of NFL heroics came on Thanksgiving 1994, when he quarterbacked Dallas over Green Bay by passing for 311 yards and two touchdowns. By 1999, Jason was the Cowboys' backup and then he moved on to the Giants in 2000 as their backup. He was on the Giants' roster for three more years as well as splitting 2004 between the Bucs and Dolphins, but never appeared in another league game after 2000.

Garrett was hired as quarterbacks coach in Miami by Dave Wannstedt in 2005, and in 2007 returned to the Cowboys as the highest paid assistant coach in the league — even before Jerry Jones hired Wade Phillips as head coach. Jason ran the Cowboys' high-powered offense in the style of his mentors, Norv Turner and Ernie Zampese, and the team lit up the scoreboard. When the lax Phillips inevitably lost control of the team in 2010, Jones made the long-anticipated move to promote Garrett at midseason. Although the team had struggled on offense for the first half of the year with Jason as coordinator, when he took over as head coach, the offense improved with

Garrett, Jason									
Year	Team	Games	Wins	Losses	Ties	%	P Wins	P Losses	P %
2010	Cowboys	8	5	3	0	.625	0	0	.000
2011	Cowboys	16	8	8	0	.500	0	0	.000
2 years		24	13	11	0	.542	0	0	.000

a renewed emphasis on the running game with backup quarterback Jon Kitna. Rookie cornerback Bryan Mc-Cann told *Sports Illustrated*, "Coach Garrett added a little spark, a little more intensity in practice, and it showed up in the game. Teams carry the personality of their coach, and he's fiery and feisty."

Jones made Garrett the permanent head coach after the season. However, the Cowboys' 2011 season was disturbingly inconsistent with the team making a regular practice of losing games in bizarre ways in the fourth quarter. Dallas missed the playoffs for the second year in a row under their favorite son. The Cowboys employed Jason's dad as a scout from 1987 to 2004, and his brother Judd works in the front office, while brother John is the team's tight ends' coach.

GETTO, MICHAEL J. (MIKE) 9/18/1905– 8/27/1960. Pittsburgh. T; did not play professionally. *Apprenticeship:* College asst.—11 years; pro asst.—2 years. *Roots:* Jock Sutherland. *Branches:* Mike Nixon. *Coordinators/Key Assistants*: Bill Hargiss coached the line and Mike Nixon the backs. *Hall of Fame Players:* Bruiser Kinard. *Primary Quarterbacks:* None. *Tendencies:* • His team scored 9.1 points and allowed 15.3 per game • His team ran 73.1% of the time, which was 114% of the league average • One rookie starter in one year • Winning Full Seasons to Losing Full Seasons: 0:1.

A native of Jeannette, Pennsylvania, Mike Getto was an All American tackle for the University of Pittsburgh in 1928, despite playing as a starter for only one year under Pitt coach Jock Sutherland. In fact, the previous season, Mike was the only Panther not taken on the cross-country trip to the Rose Bowl because he was so nonessential. After graduation, Getto went directly into coaching with the University of Kansas. Reportedly, he was recommended to Jayhawks' coach Phog Allen by Notre Dame's Knute Rockne, but that connection is curious. At any rate, Getto coached the Kansas line from 1929 to 1939.

In 1940, Mike was summoned back east by Jock Sutherland who wanted him to coach the line for the Brooklyn Dodgers. Getto spent two years with Sutherland in Brooklyn before Jock left for the Navy during the war. Owner Dan Topping made inquiries with the league to see if Brooklyn could drop out of the NFL during the war, but was turned down. Two weeks before training camp, Topping hired Getto as head

coach, noting, "A strong factor in dictating the selection of Getto was the unqualified endorsement given him by Sutherland." Sutherland actually returned to watch Mike conduct his first practice in August. The Dodgers were thinned out by injuries and losses to the military during the 1942 season. They won their first two games under Getto, but only one more the rest of the year. In the second half of the year, they scored just 10 points and lost all six games. By the end of the year, Getto was forced to use assistant coach Mike Nixon in the backfield because manpower was so scarce. End Don Eliason told Roger Godin for *The Brooklyn Football Dodgers*, "Mike knew his football, but he was not [as] strict as Jock Sutherland was. He was a little bit easier going. Only once did I ever hear Mike really get mad."

Mike quit the Dodgers at the end of the year and returned to Kansas to run his in-laws' hotel during the war. In 1947, he was rehired as line coach by Kansas and stayed through 1950 before going back to the hotel business from 1951 until his death in 1960 from a heart attack.

GIBBS, JOE J. 11/25/1940– San Diego State. TE/LB; did not play professionally. *Apprenticeship:* College asst.—9 years; pro asst.—8 years. *Roots:* Don Coryell, John McKay. *Branches:* Dan Henning, Joe Bugel, Richie Petitbon, Emmitt Thomas (i). *Coordinators/Key Assistants*: In his first stint, Dan Henning then Joe Bugel then Rod Dowhower were the key offensive assistants, while Richie Petitbon and Larry Peccatiello ran the defense; in Gibbs' second stint, Don Breaux then Al Saunders handled the offense, while Gregg Williams ran the defense. *Hall of Fame Players:* Darrell Green, Russ Grimm, Art Monk, John Riggins. *Primary Quarterbacks:* Joe Theismann, Mark Rypien, Mark Brunell. *Record:* **Hall of Fame Coach**; Super Bowl Championships 1982, 1987, 1991. *Tendencies:* • His teams scored 22.9 points and allowed 19.1 per game • His teams ran 49.2% of the time, which was 106% of the league average • Ten starting quarterbacks in 16 years; 66% of starts to primary quarterbacks • 34 rookie starters in 16 years • Winning Full Seasons to Losing Full Seasons: 12:3.

Joe Gibbs coped well with change. Very few coaches have ever won as many as three Super Bowls. Joe is the only coach to do so with three different starting quarterbacks. A native of North Carolina, his fam-

Getto, Michael J. (Mike)									
Year	Team	Games	Wins	Losses	Ties	%	P Wins	P Losses	P %
1942	Brooklyn Dodgers (defunct)	11	3	8	0	.273	0	0	.000
1 year		11	3	8	0	.273	0	0	.000

ily moved to California when Joe was 14, and he went on to attend San Diego State where he played tight end and linebacker for Don Coryell. After graduation, Gibbs pursued his master's degree at San Diego while joining Coryell's coaching staff as line coach from 1964 to 1966. Joe moved on to coach the line at Florida State under Bill Peterson in 1967 and moved back west in 1969 to be John McKay's line coach at USC for two years. John Madden, who coached with Gibbs on Coryell's staff, noted years later to the *Washington Post*, "He's solid [as a tactician] because he started as an offensive line coach. Before he draws pass patterns, he draws how to protect [the passer]. So many guys don't understand. They draw all these fancy plays, but they don't know how to block for them."

In 1971, Gibbs shifted gears to become the backfield coach for Frank Broyles at Arkansas because he thought it would increase his chance of getting a head coaching job. Two years later, Gibbs reunited with Coryell as his running backs coach with the St. Louis Cardinals. Gibbs stayed with the Cards until Coryell left in 1978. Gibbs landed with John McKay that year as the Bucs offensive coordinator, working with rookie quarterback Doug Williams. When Coryell was hired by the Chargers, he hired Gibbs for a third time, this

time as offensive coordinator. With Joe overseeing the Chargers' offense, they finished second and fourth in scoring in 1979 and 1980.

That impressive record brought Gibbs to the Redskins in 1981. When he was hired, Joe told the *Washington Post*, "Offensively, I want to dictate to the defense. I don't want to slow down offensively and adjust to what the defense is doing. I want an offense that is fast-paced and aggressive, that makes the defense keep up with us." While that sounds like Don Coryell speaking, Gibbs' approach was really a hybrid of Coryell's wide-open passing attack and John McKay's power running game. Joe's teams actually ran six percent more than the league average. Gibbs hired a top flight staff, in particular, offensive line coach Joe Bugel who built the massive Redskin line known as the Hogs into the most consistent strength of the team. The defense, Gibbs left up to holdover defensive coach Richie Petitbon. Gibbs was a master at designing clever plays, and popularized the one-back set, the versatile H-back position and the "Trips" or "Bunch" formation in Washington. However, the team's signature play during his era, the Counter Trey, was actually borrowed from the University of Nebraska. Gibbs relied on an ever-changing mix of backs with differing skills. His quarterbacks changed every few years, while his receivers evolved from the relatively anonymous Fun Bunch to the more memorable trio of Art Monk, Gary Clark and Thomas Sanders. Five times Joe's Redskins would finish in the top five in points scored.

Still, Gibbs got off to a very slow start in 1981 as the team lost its first five games getting familiar with his system. From 0–5, though, they stabilized to 8–8 that year and won 30 of 36 games over the next couple of years in making back-to-back trips to the Super Bowl. Washington beat Miami in Super Bowl XVII,

Head-to-Head:			
Hall of Fame Opponent	Regular Season	Postseason	
Bud Grant	0–0	1–0	
Tom Landry	7–8	1–0	
Marv Levy	2–0	1–0	
Chuck Noll	3–0	0–0	
Don Shula	1–3	1–0	
Bill Walsh	1–4	1–0	
Total	14–15	5–0	

Gibbs, Joe J.

Year	Team	Games	Wins	Losses	Ties	%	P Wins	P Losses	P %
1981	Redskins	16	8	8	0	.500	0	0	.000
1982	Redskins	9	8	1	0	.889	4	0	1.000
1983	Redskins	16	14	2	0	.688	2	1	.667
1984	Redskins	16	11	5	0	.688	0	1	.000
1985	Redskins	16	10	6	0	.625	0	0	.000
1986	Redskins	16	12	4	0	.750	2	1	.667
1987	Redskins	15	11	4	0	.733	3	0	1.000
1988	Redskins	16	7	9	0	.438	0	0	.000
1989	Redskins	16	10	6	0	.625	0	0	.000
1990	Redskins	16	10	6	0	.625	1	1	.500
1991	Redskins	16	14	2	0	.875	3	0	1.000
1992	Redskins	16	9	7	0	.563	1	1	.500
2004	Redskins	16	6	10	0	.375	0	0	.000
2005	Redskins	16	10	6	0	.625	1	1	.500
2006	Redskins	16	5	11	0	.313	0	0	.000
2007	Redskins	16	9	7	0	.563	0	1	.000
16 years		248	154	94	0	.621	17	7	.708

and the 14–2 Redskins were upset by the Raiders in Super Bowl XIX the next year. By the time, Washington returned to the Super Bowl following the 1987 season, the quarterback had changed from Joe Theismann to veteran Doug Williams, but the Redskins pounded the Broncos with 35 unanswered points in the second quarter alone. Gibbs made one last trip to the Super Bowl following the 1991 season, now with Mark Rypien at quarterback, when they outplayed the Buffalo Bills for Gibbs' third championship. Joe came back for one more year and then resigned after the 1992 season.

While Gibbs is an openly devout Christian, he is also an openly devout competitor. Over the next decade and a half after his retirement, Joe set up his own NASCAR racing team and in fact won three NASCAR Cup Series Championships in the new century. Gibbs was also part of a group that tried to buy the Redskins when they went up for sale in 1999. Gibbs' group was beaten out by computer mogul Daniel Snyder who repeatedly tried to lure Joe back as the team's head coach. Finally, in 2004, Gibbs agreed to come back as head coach and team president. As with many attempts to rekindle past glories, Gibbs' second term in Washington was nowhere nearly as successful as the first. Joe was less involved and didn't even call the plays anymore. On the plus side, though, he did reorganize the team and manage to get the Redskins to the playoffs twice in four years. In the 11 years that Gibbs was away, Washington only had two winning seasons and one postseason berth. Joe retired from coaching for good in January 2008, but remained with the team as a special advisor. His NASCAR team is now run by his son J.D.

Gibbs was elected to the Pro Football Hall of Fame in 1996, and told the *Washington Post* at the time, "The most fun in coaching was the personalities of the assistant coaches and players, all of us almost living together for six months and trying to build something. Those are the things you remember as great." Gibbs was a great organizer and goal setter. He kept firm control of his team, but he also knew how to get the best out of his coaches and players in a humanistic fashion.

GIBRON, ABRAHAM (ABE) 9/22/1925–9/23/1997. Valparaiso and Purdue. Played G for the Bills (AAFC), Browns, Eagles and Bears from 1949 to 1959. *Appren-*

ticeship: Pro asst.—12 years. *Roots:* Mike Nixon, Bill McPeak, George Halas, Jim Dooley,. *Branches:* Jim Ringo. *Coordinators/Key Assistants:* Zeke Bratkowski was the key offensive coach, while Bill George then Jim Carr ran the defense. *Hall of Fame Players:* Dick Butkus. *Primary Quarterbacks:* Bobby Douglass. *Tendencies:* • His teams scored 13.6 points and allowed 21.1 per game • His teams ran 59% of the time, which was 106% of the league average • Three starting quarterbacks in three years; 69% of starts to primary quarterback • Nine rookie starters in three years • Winning Full Seasons to Losing Full Seasons: 0:3.

As a player, guard Abe Gibron was wide, squat and powerful but surprisingly fast and nimble on his feet. As a head coach, he was wider and more noted for having trouble keeping his pants up on the sideline than for nimble game plans. Born in Michigan City, Indiana, Gibron served in the military, attended Valparaiso as a freshman and then transferred to Purdue. He was a sixth round pick of the Giants in 1949, but chose to sign with Buffalo in the All America Football Conference instead. When that league merged with the NFL a year later, Gibron was obtained by Paul Brown in the dispersal of AAFC players. Gibron started as one of Brown's messenger guards, shuttling in plays on alternate snaps, but that stopped when he proved himself the best guard on the team — Abe went to four Pro Bowls with Cleveland.

In 1956, Brown traded the 31-year-old Gibron to Philadelphia. Two years later, Abe moved to the Bears and would finish his playing career with them in 1958 and 1959. Upon retirement in 1960, he immediately was hired by Mike Nixon as the Redskins' line coach and continued in that role under Bill McPeak. Five years later, he returned to the Bears in the same capacity, although he later switched to coaching the Bears' defense. The loquacious and earthy Gibron was popular with players, fans and the media, but when he was named head coach in 1972, he was over his head. Abe announced at his opening press conference, "I'm a Halas man. I'm a Bears man. I'm a Gibron man. But I'm not a yes man. I will control all the physical end of the game and be contacted before any personnel decisions are made. I will put the game plan in, and take the blame for it. I will make the decisions, and the guys are going to have to earn the right to play."

In some ways, Abe was perfect for the Bears and

Gibron, Abraham (Abe)									
Year	Team	Games	Wins	Losses	Ties	%	P Wins	P Losses	P %
1972	Bears	14	4	9	1	.321	0	0	.000
1973	Bears	14	3	11	0	.214	0	0	.000
1974	Bears	14	4	10	0	.286	0	0	.000
3 years		42	11	30	1	.274	0	0	.000

their fans. In 1973, the 300-pound coach told the *Chicago Tribune*, "Football is a hitting game. It's a violent game. That's why people like it. There's a bit of sadist in all of us." However, that purely physical approach can only take a team so far without enough good players. Under Gibron, the Bears' defense was mediocre and the offense, behind quarterbacks Bobby Douglass and Gary Huff, was awful. Abe was fired after three disappointing seasons. He briefly caught on as the coach of the Chicago Wind in the WFL in 1975, but the entire league folded at midseason with the Wind at 1–4. Abe then joined John McKay's staff in Tampa in 1976. Gibron knew McKay from when they played together in 1946 at Purdue before McKay transferred to Oregon. Abe coached the defensive line during his nine years with the Bucs. When McKay retired in 1985, Gibron signed on as a scout in Seattle for a few years until he had brain surgery in 1989. A year later, he finished his career working on projects for Bucs' coach Sam Wyche.

GILBRIDE, KEVIN 8/27/1951– Southern Connecticut. QB/TE; did not play professionally. *Apprenticeship:* College coach 13 years (5 as head coach); pro asst.— 8 years; CFL asst.— 2 years. *Roots:* Jerry Glanville, Jack Pardee, Tom Coughlin. *Branches:* None. *Coordinators/Key Assistants:* Mike Sheppard was the key offensive coach, while Joe Pascale ran the defense. *Hall of Fame Players:* None. *Primary Quarterbacks:* Stan Humphries, Craig Whelihan *Tendencies:* • His teams scored 15.3 points and allowed 24 per game • His teams ran 39.9% of the time, which was 90% of the league average • Four starting quarterbacks in two years; 68% of starts to primary quarterbacks • Five rookie starters in two years • Winning Full Seasons to Losing Full Seasons: 0:1.

While Kevin Gilbride's work with Eli Manning as the Giants' offensive coordinator helped him win a Super Bowl ring, he might still be in San Diego with the record of a successful NFL head coach if he had been lucky enough to end up with Eli's brother Peyton rather than Ryan Leaf in 1998 when he was head coach of the Chargers. Instead, his one shot as head coach was a complete ugly failure.

Born in New Haven, Connecticut, Gilbride played both quarterback and tight end at Southern Connecticut State and then began his coaching career as a graduate assistant at Idaho State from 1974 to 1975. He then spent two years at Tufts as linebackers'

coach and two as defensive coordinator at American International University before returning to his alma mater as head coach in 1980. Kevin spent five years coaching Southern Connecticut and compiled a 35–14–2 record. He left in 1985 for an assistant's job with the Ottawa Rough Riders in the CFL. After two years there and two at East Carolina, Gilbride finally reached the NFL in 1989 as the Houston Oilers quarterbacks coach. A year later, he was promoted to offensive coordinator under Jack Pardee, running a variation of the Run-and-Shoot offense that Buddy Ryan sneeringly called the "Chuck-and-Duck."

When Pardee hired Ryan as defensive coordinator in 1993, sparks were sure to fly. Gilbride and Ryan verbally sparred all season, but things got out of hand as halftime approached in the nationally televised season finale against the Jets when Ryan threw a punch at Gilbride on the sidelines for not running out the clock to protect the defense. The two were quickly separated, and Kevin later commented, "It's a daily, ongoing thing—the comments, the sarcasm, the denigrating and disparaging remarks toward the offense. We just try to survive it." The Oilers lost two weeks later in the playoffs, and Ryan departed for Arizona. Quarterback Warren Moon also left Houston and the team fell apart in 1994. Gilbride then moved on to become the Jaguars first offensive coordinator under Tom Coughlin in 1995.

Two years later, Kevin was named head coach of the Chargers. He had a reputation as a quarterback specialist, but could do little with washed up veterans Stan Humphries and Jim Everett who both finished their careers in 1997 or with inaccurate, immobile Craig Whelihan. As the 1998 draft approached, San Diego held the second overall pick. With two highly rated quarterbacks, Peyton Manning and Ryan Leaf, it seemed Gilbride would have a quarterback of the future to mold. As it turned out, the Colts took Manning who was better than advertised, but the Chargers took the booby prize. Leaf was an immature head case who flamed out of San Diego within three years. The Chargers had the NFL's top ranked defense in 1998, but would only win five games because of the awful quarterbacking. Gilbride only saw two of those victories. He was fired after six games, having lost control of the team.

Gilbride moved on to Pittsburgh as offensive coordinator in 1999, but failed to connect with the Steelers' emotionally fragile quarterback Kordell Stewart

Gilbride, Kevin									
Year	Team	Games	Wins	Losses	Ties	%	P Wins	P Losses	P %
1997	Chargers	16	4	12	0	.250	0	0	.000
1998	Chargers	6	2	4	0	.333	0	0	.000
2 years		22	6	16	0	.273	0	0	.000

and was gone in two years. After a year in broadcasting, Gilbride spent two years as the Bills' offensive coordinator before returning to Tom Coughlin's staff as the Giants' quarterbacks coach in 2004. Three years later, offensive coordinator John Hufnagel was let go when he had trouble getting through to Eli Manning, and Gilbride was promoted to New York's top offensive job where he has thrived in helping direct the team to two Super Bowl titles.

GILLMAN, SIDNEY (SID) 10/26/1911–1/3/2003. Ohio State. Played E for the Cleveland Rams of the second American Football League in 1936. *Apprenticeship:* College coach — 21 years (10 as head coach). *Roots:* None. *Branches:* Bob Waterfield, Lou Rymkus, Jack Faulkner, Al Davis, Bones Taylor, George Allen, Chuck Noll, Charlie Waller, Joe Thomas, Bum Phillips, Ed Biles, Richie Petitbon. *Coordinators/Key Assistants:* Gillman always ran the offense. For the Rams, Jack Faulkner handled the defense; for the Chargers, Faulkner, then Chuck Noll then Tom Bass

then Bum Phillips handled the defense; for the Oilers, Burnie Miller then Bum Phillips handled the defense. *Hall of Fame Players:* Lance Alworth, Elvin Bethea, Tom Fears, Elroy Hirsch, Larry Little, Ollie Matson, Ron Mix, Les Richter, Andy Robustelli and Norm Van Brocklin. *Primary Quarterbacks:* Bill Wade, Norm Van Brocklin, Jack Kemp, John Hadl, Dan Pastorini. *Record:* **Hall of Fame Coach**; AFL Championships 1963. *Tendencies:* • His teams scored 23.6 points and allowed 22.2 per game • His teams ran 48.9% of the time, which was 93% of the league average • 11 starting quarterbacks in 18 years; 85% of starts to primary quarterbacks • 71 rookie starters in 18 years • Winning Full Seasons to Losing Full Seasons: 10:3.

Sid Gillman, the stocky, chain smoker wearing the dapper bow tie on the sidelines, was arguably the most influential offensive mind in NFL history. Three times his teams led the league in points scored and nine times finished in the top three in that category. Charger tackle Ron Mix pointed out to Jeff Miller in *Going Long*, "Lately, they talk about Don Coryell, about Bill Walsh, but it started with Sid." Al Davis, once a Charger assistant and one of 12 former Gillman assistants who became NFL head coaches, said on Sid's death, "Sid Gillman was the father of modern-day passing. It had been thought of as vertical, the length of the field, but Sid also thought of it as horizontal. Sid used the width of the field."

Born in Minneapolis, Gillman played end for Ohio State and won honorable mention notice as an All American in 1932 and 1933. When the legendary, mercurial Francis "Close the Gates of Mercy" Schmidt brought his bold, flashy offense to OSU as head coach in 1934, Gillman stuck around Columbus helping out

Head-to-Head:

Hall of Fame Opponent	Regular Season	Postseason
Paul Brown	5–2	0–1
Weeb Ewbank	13–9–2	0–0
Bud Grant	0–1	0–0
George Halas	2–8	0–0
Vince Lombardi	1–1	0–0
John Madden	0–4	0–0
Chuck Noll	1–3	0–0
Hank Stram	10–13–1	0–0
Total	32–41–3	0–1

Gillman, Sidney (Sid)

Year	Team	Games	Wins	Losses	Ties	%	P Wins	P Losses	P %
1955	Rams	12	8	3	1	.708	0	1	.000
1956	Rams	12	4	8	0	.333	0	0	.000
1957	Rams	12	6	6	0	.500	0	0	.000
1958	Rams	12	8	4	0	.667	0	0	.000
1959	Rams	12	2	10	0	.167	0	0	.000
1960	Chargers	14	10	4	0	.714	0	1	.000
1961	Chargers	14	12	2	0	.857	0	1	.000
1962	Chargers	14	4	10	0	.286	0	0	.000
1963	Chargers	14	11	3	0	.786	1	0	1.000
1964	Chargers	14	8	5	1	.607	0	1	.000
1965	Chargers	14	9	2	3	.750	0	1	.000
1966	Chargers	14	7	6	1	.536	0	0	.000
1967	Chargers	14	8	5	1	.607	0	0	.000
1968	Chargers	14	9	5	0	.643	0	0	.000
1969	Chargers	9	4	5	0	.444	0	0	.000
1971	Chargers	10	4	6	0	.400	0	0	.000
1973	Oilers	9	1	8	0	.111	0	0	.000
1974	Oilers	14	7	7	0	.500	0	0	.000
18 years		228	122	99	7	.550	1	5	.167

the new coach and learning what he could from Schmidt's frenzied experience. In 1935, Sid got an assistant's job at nearby Denison University and coached there for three years — even while playing end for the American Football League's Cleveland Rams in 1936; the Rams would join the NFL a year later, but Gillman stayed with Denison. In 1938, Schmidt got the funding to hire Gillman as his assistant, and the two were together for three years. When Schmidt was replaced by Paul Brown in 1941, Gillman returned to Denison for a year.

In 1942, Stu Holcomb hired Gillman as his line coach at Miami of Ohio. Holcomb and Gillman had played together on the Buckeyes in 1931. Two years later, Holcomb left Miami to serve as an assistant coach on Red Blaik's staff at West Point, and Sid was promoted to head coach at Miami. In four years running the Miami program, Gillman used a mix of straight T formation and spread formation to attain a 31–6 record before leaving to serve as Blaik's line coach for Army in 1948 where he explored option blocking. One year after that, Gillman was named head coach at the University of Cincinnati; Vince Lombardi replaced him on Army's staff.

At Cincinnati, Gillman experimented with situational substitution and the Split-T and compiled a 50–13–2 record from 1949 to 1954. Two of his assistants, Joe Madro and Jack Faulkner, would continue with Sid right through San Diego; in fact, Madro stayed with Gillman all the way to his tenure in Houston. With the Bearcats, Sid was ultra competitive and not above bending rules. When he left Cincinnati to become the head coach of the Los Angeles Rams in 1955, Cincinnati was sanctioned by the NCAA for recruiting violations.

Sid took the Rams to the NFL championship game in his first year, but they were humbled by Paul Brown's Cleveland team 38–14 in Otto Graham's final game. 1955 turned out to be Gillman's high point in Los Angeles — it was the only year his defense finished in the top half of the league in points allowed. Gillman and volatile quarterback Norm Van Brocklin clashed repeatedly, especially once Sid tried to switch to Bill Wade in 1956. After the 1957 season, Van Brocklin threatened to quit if he weren't traded, so he was dealt to Philadelphia. Behind Wade, the Rams went 8–4 in 1958, but then collapsed to 2–10 the following year. Sid had also had problems with other veterans like Andy Robustelli and made some questionable personnel moves. Former Ram receiver Tom Fears told the *Los Angeles Times*, "He doesn't know how to get the men to play for him." Fears accused Gillman of "tearing down a dynasty which had been carefully erected."

The Rams fired Sid at the end of 1959, but the brand new Los Angeles Chargers of the startup American Football League hired him as their first head coach a few weeks later. It was with the Chargers that Gillman fully developed his wide open passing attack where the Chargers spread out the defense and then used quick quarterback reads, precision timed mid-length pass routes, and swift, lightning bolt deep strikes to score nearly at will. The Chargers went to the AFL title game in both 1960 and 1961, but lost both years to the Oilers. Injury problems sunk the team in 1962, so Gillman tried a new approach in 1963. He took the team to a desert ranch called Rough Acres for a brutal training camp that year and also brought in Alvin Roy as strength coach; Roy was an early proponent of steroids. The pumped and toughened Chargers rolled through the league in 1963, both scoring the most points and allowing the fewest in the AFL. The season culminated in a championship game pummeling of the Patriots 51–10. Gillman challenged NFL commissioner and former Ram GM Pete Rozelle for a game with the NFL champion Bears by sending him a telegram saying, "Pete — Even Pope John recognized the other league." Rozelle responded, "Sid — Yes, but it took two thousand years." Many observers consider the 1963 Chargers one of the greatest professional teams of all time.

The Chargers won the Western Division for the next two years, but lost the title to the defense-oriented Bills both times. After that, San Diego remained a very good team, but could not compete with Hank Stram's Chiefs and Al Davis' Raiders in the West. Plagued by a stomach ulcer and a chest hernia, Gillman stepped down as head coach nine games into the 1969 season and was succeeded by assistant Charlie Waller. By 1971, Gillman was feeling better and returned as head coach of the team. Ten games into the season, though, Gillman resigned again due to a number of personnel-related disputes with owner Gene Klein and left San Diego for good. In the wake of a lawsuit by former Charger defensive lineman Houston Ridge against the team and the league a couple years later, Pete Rozelle rebuked Sid for the overly free dispensation of drugs during his San Diego tenure.

Gillman next was hired by Tom Landry as a quality control coach in 1972. With Sid's lifelong obsession with game film (he even brought a film projector with him on his honeymoon in the 1930s), it seemed like a good fit but lasted just one year. Bud Adams hired Sid as the Oilers' GM in 1973, and he took over as head coach six games into that season. The next year, he lifted those 1–13 Oilers to 7–7 and won Coach of the Year honors. At the end of 1974, though, he stepped down as both coach and GM after conflicts with Adams over expenditures on scouting. Gillman returned to the NFL as the Bears' offensive coordinator under Jack Pardee in 1977, but he left because he thought Pardee's offensive approach was too conservative. In 1978, he helped grow the football program at United States International University in San Diego and then joined Dick Vermeil's staff with the Eagles in 1979. He subsequently retired in 1981, but came back to Philadelphia in 1982. In 1983, Sid got involved with the USFL, serving as Oklahoma's GM that year and as a special assistant to head coach — and former Chargers' quarterback — John Hadl of the Los Angeles Express in 1984. Sid spent one last season with Philadelphia in 1985 and finally finished his career by helping Mike Gottfried at the University of Pittsburgh in 1987.

Gillman was elected to the Pro Football Hall of Fame in 1983 and the College Football Hall of Fame in 1989. Bum Phillips, the assistant who succeeded Sid in Houston, told Tom Danyluk for *The Super 70s* that the game was central for Gillman, "If you liked football, he liked you. If you didn't like football, Sid had no use for you." Gillman emphasized the importance of the game to *Sports Illustrated*, "With some [players], football is a vocation. With some it's an avocation. You know what football is to me? It's blood." Gillman died in 2003 at age 91, still studying game films.

GILMER, HARRY V. 4/14/1926– Alabama. Played QB for the Redskins and Lions from 1948 to 1952 and from 1954 to 1956. *Apprenticeship:* Pro asst. — 8 years. *Roots:* Buddy Parker, Norm Van Brocklin. *Branches:* Joe Schmidt. *Coordinators/Key Assistants*: Sammy Baugh was a key offensive coach and Carl Brettschneider was a key defensive coach. *Hall of Fame Players:* Dick Lane, Dick LeBeau, Joe Schmidt. *Primary Quarterbacks:* Milt Plum. *Tendencies:* • His teams scored 16.5 points and allowed 21.9 per game • His teams ran 48.7% of the time, which was 98% of the league average • Three starting quarterbacks in two years; 61% of starts to primary quarterback • Four rookie starters in two years • Winning Full Seasons to Losing Full Seasons: 0:2.

Birmingham's Harry Gilmer was a local hero as an All-American and Rose Bowl MVP at Alabama before being picked first overall in 1948 NFL draft as the bonus choice of the Washington Redskins. Not a big man, Gilmer was known for his jump passes in college, but that did not work very well in the pros. Washington compounded its mistake by trading the rights to Charley Conerly to New York in order to keep Gilmer, But Harry never was going to beat out or succeed Sammy Baugh. The Redskins also tried Gilmer at halfback and defensive back before trading him in 1955 to Detroit where he backed up Bobby Layne for two years.

When Lions' coach Buddy Parker quit in 1957 and relocated to Pittsburgh, he brought Gilmer with him as an assistant coach. Harry was on Parker's staff from 1957 to 1960 and then joined the expansion Vikings in 1961 as Norm Van Brocklin's defensive coach. Gilmer gained respect throughout the league for his work in Minnesota and was hired in 1965 to replace George Wilson in Detroit. Van Brocklin said of his departing assistant, "Harry Gilmer, besides being a great football coach, is about the finest person I've met in football." Harry told the press in his thick Southern drawl that the Lions were "very, very close to what we all are after, and that, of course, is the championship."

In Detroit, however, Gilmer was taking over a clique-ridden team of underachievers who had just gotten George Wilson fired with their complaints to the owner. The defense was aging and the quarterbacking consisted of mediocre Milt Plum and substandard George Izo and Karl Sweetan. Harry, who cut a striking figure on the sideline in a ten-gallon hat and cowboy boots, made a series of bad personnel moves such as drafting Tom Nowatzke in the first round and trading for malcontent Joe Don Looney whom he then suspended and traded to Washington. He also had trouble getting along with some of his stars like defensive tackle Alex Karras and receiver Gail Cogdill with overly authoritarian moves such as ordering a full-pads scrimmage in midseason. In the off season, Cogdill told a women's club that "Gilmer doesn't know how to handle men, and he's not ready for a coaching job." He added, "You can't talk to the guy. The men are afraid of him. How would you like to work for someone you can't trust? Some say he won't last a year."

Gilmer suspended and fined Cogdill in the off season, but by the end of 1966, the fans were pelting Harry with snowballs and serenading him with choruses of "Good Bye, Harry." Gilmer was fired in January, and his grouchy line coach Lou Rymkus commented then, "Harry has a wonderful intellect for the game. His only fault is that he expects grown men to behave like grown men and not like babies."

Harry worked as an assistant in St. Louis from 1967 to 1969 and then reunited with Van Brocklin in Atlanta from 1970 to 1974. In 1975 he returned to the Cardinals as a scout and continued with those duties into the 1980s.

Gilmer, Harry V.									
Year	*Team*	*Games*	*Wins*	*Losses*	*Ties*	*%*	*P Wins*	*P Losses*	*P %*
1965	Lions	14	6	7	1	.464	0	0	.000
1966	Lions	14	4	9	1	.321	0	0	.000
2 years		28	10	16	2	.393	0	0	.000

GLANVILLE, JERRY M. 10/14/1941– Northern Michigan. LB; did not play professionally. *Apprenticeship:* College asst.— 9 years; pro asst.—12 years. *Roots:* Rick Forzano, Tommy Hudspeth, Leeman Bennett, Kay Stephenson, Hugh Campbell. *Branches:* June Jones, Kevin Gilbride, Nick Saban. *Coordinators/Key Assistants:* For the Oilers, Dick Jamieson then June Jones then Kevin Gilbride handled the offense, while Glanville ran his own defense; for the Falcons, Tom Rossley then June Jones handled the offense, while Glanville again ran his own defense. *Hall of Fame Players:* Eric Dickerson, Bruce Matthews, Warren Moon, Mike Munchak, Deion Sanders. *Primary Quarterbacks:* Warren Moon, Chris Miller. *Tendencies:*
• His teams scored 21.7 points and allowed 23.4 per game • His teams ran 44.8% of the time, which was 97% of the league average • Ten starting quarterbacks in nine years; 81% of starts to primary quarterbacks • 23 rookie starters in nine years • Winning Full Seasons to Losing Full Seasons: 4:4.

Jerry Glanville made a name for himself in coaching, but it was as much for his public persona as for his accomplishments. Glanville had a whole shtick going of dressing all in black, leaving tickets at the box office for some dead celebrity such as Elvis Presley or James Dean or Buddy Holly and, in general, of creating a circus atmosphere around his teams. His teams had talent, but were much longer on swagger and talk than discipline and results. Atlanta defensive end Tim Green wrote in *The Dark Side of the Game*, "His locker rooms and sidelines were a hysterical mix of celebrities and music and singing and hand-slapping high fives." For his players, it was fun while it lasted, but it didn't last long.

Glanville was born in Perrysburg, Ohio, and played linebacker at Northern Michigan University. He began his coaching career the next year by working as an assistant at his alma mater from 1965 to 1966. He spent 1967 at Western Kentucky and from 1968 to 1973 at Georgia Tech. In 1974, Jerry moved up to the NFL with the Lions for three years. In 1977, he moved to Leeman Bennett's staff in Atlanta and helped develop the all-out Grits Blitz package for the Falcons. Glanville was in Atlanta for six years and then spent 1983 with Buffalo before being named defensive coordinator for Houston in 1984. When head coach Hugh Campbell was fired with two games to play in 1985, Jerry was named interim coach. Glanville was made permanent in 1986 and brought in June Jones the following year to install the Run-and-Shoot offense. Playing in the AFC's Central Division, Glanville rubbed some of his coaching competitors the wrong way. He openly feuded with Chuck Noll, who accused Glanville's team of dirty tactics, and Sam Wyche, who considered him a punk. After one game, Noll held on to Glanville at midfield to lecture him about his boorishness. Wyche took the opportunity in 1989 to have his Bengals run up the score in a 61–7 beating of the Oilers, adding, "They're the dumbest, most undisciplined, stupid football team we've ever played." Houston made the postseason that year for the third straight season, but Glanville dismissed at the end of the year.

Jerry landed back in Atlanta as head coach. He quickly switched the team's uniforms to all black and installed his version of the Run-and-Shoot, the Red Gun. He took the Falcons to the NFC Championship game in his second season, but they lost to Washington and spiraled into an unruly disaster the next year. His defense finished in the bottom three in points allowed three times in Atlanta. Furthermore, in his most significant and short-sighted move, Glanville insisted the team dump young Brett Favre in 1992. Jerry memorably described the impermanence of his profession, "If you're a pro coach, NFL stands for 'Not For Long.'" Indeed, he was fired by Atlanta after the 1993 season. Like Joe Gibbs, Jerry took a detour from football and established a NASCAR team from 1995 to 1999. In the new century, Glanville returned to football, both as a broadcaster and coach. June Jones brought him to Hawaii as defensive coordinator in 2005. Jerry finished his coaching career as the head coach at Portland State from 2007 to 2009, attaining a 9–24 record at the birthplace of the Run-and-Shoot.

Glanville, Jerry M.

Year	Team	Games	Wins	Losses	Ties	%	P Wins	P Losses	P %
1985	Oilers (Titans)	2	0	2	0	.000	0	0	.000
1986	Oilers (Titans)	16	5	11	0	.313	0	0	.000
1987	Oilers (Titans)	15	9	6	0	.600	1	1	.500
1988	Oilers (Titans)	16	10	6	0	.625	1	1	.500
1989	Oilers (Titans)	16	9	7	0	.563	0	1	.000
1990	Falcons	16	5	11	0	.313	0	0	.000
1991	Falcons	16	10	6	0	.625	1	1	.500
1992	Falcons	16	6	10	0	.375	0	0	.000
1993	Falcons	16	6	10	0	.375	0	0	.000
9 years		129	60	69	0	.465	3	4	.429

Graham, Otto E. 12/6/1921–12/17/2003. Northwestern. Played QB for the Browns from 1946 to 1955. *Apprenticeship:* College head coach — 7 years. *Roots:* None. *Branches:* Ed Hughes, Mike McCormack. *Coordinators/Key Assistants:* Graham ran his own offense, while Mike Scarry handled the defense. *Hall of Fame Players:* Chris Hanburger, Sam Huff, Stan Jones, Sonny Jurgensen, Paul Krause, Bobby Mitchell, Charley Taylor. *Primary Quarterbacks:* Sonny Jurgensen. *Record:* **Hall of Fame Player.** *Tendencies:* • His teams scored 22.5 points and allowed 25.4 per game • His teams ran 42.1% of the time, which was 84% of the league average • Two starting quarterbacks in three years; 95% of starts to primary quarterback • Nine rookie starters in three years • Winning Full Seasons to Losing Full Seasons: 0:2.

As a player, there never was a greater winner than Otto Graham, who appeared in 10 championship games in ten years as a pro, winning seven of them. As a coach, he did not have the same drive. Redskins' middle linebacker Sam Huff told Thom Loverro for *Hail Victory,* "He would spend a lot of time during the week working on trick plays, rather than fundamentals ... Otto loved to play tennis. He loved to play golf. He wore hush puppies and athletic socks. The dedication just didn't seem to be there. He didn't pay attention to a lot of little things, and it just didn't click."

Graham was born in Waukegan, Illinois, and played football and basketball for Northwestern. As a single wing tailback, he led the Wildcats over Paul Brown's Ohio State Buckeyes in both 1941 and 1943. Brown took notice and signed Graham for Cleveland during the war before there was even a Browns' team. Graham played for Bear Bryant while in the Navy and then played on the National Basketball League champion Rochester Royal in 1945–46 before reporting to Browns' training camp.

After Otto's Hall of Fame playing career as the best quarterback in football, he took on the annual assignment of coaching the College All Stars in the yearly preseason game against the NFL's reigning champions. Otto had played in two of these games when in college and three more with the Browns. From 1956 to 1965 and again from 1969 to 1970 he coached the All Stars, sometimes making enemies of players he left sitting on the bench. In 1959, the Coast Guard Academy hired Graham as athletic director and

head coach. To him this job was ideal. He later told the *New York Times,* "I had the best college football job in the country. I didn't want the big time in college ball because of the tremendous pressures such as recruiting."

In 1966, high-powered Washington attorney Edward Bennett Williams assumed control of the Redskins and persuaded Graham to take over as head coach. Otto's interest was primarily offense. Right at the start, he announced, "I'd rather risk losing some games by say 35–28 and have the fans up off their seats with excitement. I think the players would have more fun, too." Graham got what he wished for. His offense, driven by quarterback Sonny Jurgensen and receivers Bobby Mitchell, Charley Taylor and Jerry Smith, was dynamic, with the three receivers being in the league's top ten in receptions in 1966 and in the top four in 1967. Graham's offense passed the ball 16% more than the league average. However, his defense was porous, and he never had a winning season. His decisions were a mixed bag. Moving Charley Taylor from runner to receiver was a success, but trying to switch Bobby Mitchell back to being a runner was a failure. He was another foolhardy coach who traded for the lunatic Joe Don Looney, traded away Hall of Fame safety Paul Krause and drafted poorly.

Replaced by Vince Lombardi in 1969, Otto returned to the Coast Guard as athletic director from 1969 to 1984, even serving as head coach again for 1974–1975. His overall coaching record at the Coast Guard was 44–32–1. He died in 2003 at the age of 82.

Grant, Harry P. (Bud) 5/20/1927– Minnesota. Played E for the Eagles in 1951–1952 and in the CFL from 1953 to 1956. *Apprenticeship:* CFL head coach — 10 years. *Roots:* None. *Branches:* Bob Hollway, Jack Patera, Neill Armstrong, Les Steckel, Jerry Burns, Buddy Ryan, Pete Carroll. *Coordinators/Key Assistants:* Jerry Burns ran the offense, while Bob Hollway then Neill Armstrong then Hollway again ran the defense. *Hall of Fame Players:* Dave Casper, Chris Doleman, Carl Eller, Paul Krause, Jim Langer, Alan Page, Jan Stenerud, Fran Tarkenton, Ron Yary. *Primary Quarterbacks:* Fran Tarkenton, Tommy Kramer, Joe Kapp *Record:* **Hall of Fame Coach.** *Tendencies:* • His teams scored 20.6 points and allowed 16.9 per game • His teams ran 50% of the time, which was 96% of the

Graham, Otto E.									
Year	*Team*	*Games*	*Wins*	*Losses*	*Ties*	*%*	*P Wins*	*P Losses*	*P %*
1966	Redskins	14	7	7	0	.500	0	0	.000
1967	Redskins	14	5	6	3	.464	0	0	.000
1968	Redskins	14	5	9	0	.357	0	0	.000
3 years		42	17	22	3	.440	0	0	.000

league average • Ten starting quarterbacks in 18 years; 79% of starts to primary quarterbacks • 18 rookie starters in 18 years • Winning Full Seasons to Losing Full Seasons: 12:4.

With his stone face, crew cut and steely, pale blue eyes, Bud Grant did not necessarily give off the appearance of the practical joker he was. This devoted family man was taciturn and hid his personality from public view. Coaching football was just part of his life. He also had six children and was an avid hunter and fisherman. Thus, he explained his first retirement in a newspaper piece, "A good coach needs a patient wife, a loyal dog and a great quarterback, but not necessarily in that order. I happen to have been blessed with all three. And when I did happen to have extra time, I didn't spend it with the quarterback."

Grant was born in Superior, Wisconsin, and during the war was stationed at the Great Lakes Naval Training Station, where he was exposed to coaches Paul Brown, Blanton Collier and Weeb Ewbank. After his discharge, Bud starred in football, basketball and baseball at the University of Minnesota and in 1951 was drafted both the Eagles in the NFL and the Minneapolis Lakers in the NBA. He played two seasons as a reserve forward for the Lakers and won a championship with them. At the same time, he played end for the Eagles—1951 on defense and 1952 on offense. Ironically, Grant lobbied to play offense although most of his success as a coach was due to his defense.

In 1953, Bud felt the Eagles weren't offering him enough money so he jumped to Winnipeg in Canada. He played for the Blue Bombers for four seasons under Allie Sherman and then was offered the head coaching job in 1957 a few months before his 30th birthday. Grant coached Winnipeg for the next ten years and led the team to a 102–56–2 record, six Grey Cup games and four CFL championships. When the Vikings started up in 1961, they offered the coaching position first to Bud who opted to stay in Canada. Six years later, he accepted the Vikings offer to replace Norm Van Brocklin as head coach and brought down quarterback Joe Kapp from Canada as well. After one season to sort things out, Grant built a vaunted Vikings team that won the Central Division 10 out of 11 years and went to four Super Bowls.

The Vikings were a defensive-oriented team whose strength was its pass rushing front four, the Purple People Eaters. The team's defensive scheme relied on the front four getting pressure on the quarterback and forcing mistakes that Minnesota's slow sec-

Head-to-Head:		
Hall of Fame Opponent Postseason		Regular Season
George Allen	2–4	3–0
Paul Brown	0–1	0–0
Weeb Ewbank	0–1	0–0
Joe Gibbs	0–0	0–1
Sid Gillman	1–0	0–0
George Halas	0–1–1	0–0
Tom Landry	4–4	1–3
Marv Levy	0–1	0–0
Vince Lombardi	1–1	0–0
John Madden	1–2	0–1
Chuck Noll	3–2	0–1
Don Shula	2–4–1	0–2
Hank Stram	3–0	0–1
Bill Walsh	2–1	0–0
Total	19–22–2	4–9

Grant, Harry P. (Bud)									
Year	Team	Games	Wins	Losses	Ties	%	P Wins	P Losses	P %
1967	Vikings	14	3	8	3	.321	0	0	.000
1968	Vikings	14	8	6	0	.571	0	1	.000
1969	Vikings	14	12	2	0	.857	2	1	.667
1970	Vikings	14	12	2	0	.857	0	1	.000
1971	Vikings	14	11	3	0	.786	0	1	.000
1972	Vikings	14	7	7	0	.500	0	0	.000
1973	Vikings	14	12	2	0	.857	2	1	.667
1974	Vikings	14	10	4	0	.714	2	1	.667
1975	Vikings	14	12	2	0	.857	0	1	.000
1976	Vikings	14	11	2	1	.821	2	1	.667
1977	Vikings	14	9	5	0	.643	1	1	.500
1978	Vikings	16	8	7	1	.531	0	1	.000
1979	Vikings	16	7	9	0	.438	0	0	.000
1980	Vikings	16	9	7	0	.563	0	1	.000
1981	Vikings	16	7	9	0	.438	0	0	.000
1982	Vikings	9	5	4	0	.556	1	1	.500
1983	Vikings	16	8	8	0	.500	0	0	.000
1985	Vikings	16	7	9	0	.438	0	0	.000
18 years		259	158	96	5	.620	10	12	.455

ondary could lay back and capitalize on. The problem was that in each of the Vikings four Super Bowl appearances they were outplayed along both offensive and defensive lines. Their defensive line shrunk in going against the powerful offensive lines of the Chiefs, Dolphins, Steelers and Raiders; similarly, Minnesota's relatively small offensive line was overrun by the massive front fours of their opponents. In addition, even as the Vikings' offense evolved from a plodding, pounding running game featuring Bill Brown and Dave Osborn to a more versatile passing attack led by Fran Tarkenton, Sammy White and Chuck Foreman, the defense did not evolve. Tom Flores told Bob McGinn for *The Ultimate Super Bowl Book*, "Minnesota did not change since the Super Bowl when I played for Kansas City other than they had Fran Tarkenton."

For his part, Grant advised his team after their fourth Super Bowl loss, "You don't look back after any losing game. Life goes on. I don't want to sound mercenary, but we have earned more money from playoffs than any other team. We have never lost a [conference] championship; we have never lost when a Super Bowl berth was on the line." He was the opposite of George Allen who claimed to die a little with each loss. Grant started Vikings training camp late each year, worked his team lightly in practice and liked to be home for dinner. While that approach may be admirable, it never resulted in a championship.

The Vikings had the advantage of playing in a weak division in the weaker conference during the 1970s. From 1973 to 1976, no other Central Division team ever had a winning record. In the ten years up to 1976, Grant's Vikings finished in the top ten in scoring seven times and in the top ten in fewest points allowed nine times. In fact, they finished first in fewest points allowed three times and in the top three seven times. After 1976, though, Minnesota under Grant was never again in the top ten in either category. His Vikings' run-pass ratio changed from 56% runs through 1977 (three percent greater than the league average) to 41.4% runs from 1978 on (17% less than the league). Grant retired after the 1983 season, but his successor, Les Steckel, was such a disappointment that Grant returned to stabilize the team in 1985. At the end of that season, he retired for good. As he put it at his first retirement two years before, "I want to get out and do things that I might not be able to do when I'm 65: walk through the woods, wade through a trout stream, climb a mountain."

Bud was the first man elected to both the Pro Football Hall of Fame and CFL Hall of Fame. His son Mike has coached Eden Prairie High School for the last 20 years, with six state championships.

Green, Dennis 2/17/1949– Iowa. Played HB in the CFL in 1971. *Apprenticeship:* College coach —16

years (8 as head coach); pro asst.— 4 years. *Roots:* Bill Walsh. *Branches:* Tony Dungy, Brian Billick, Mike Tice, Emmitt Thomas (i). *Coordinators/Key Assistants:* For the Vikings, Jack Burns then Brian Billick then Ray Sherman then Sherman Lewis ran the offense, while Tony Dungy then Foge Fazio then Emmitt Thomas handled the defense; for the Cardinals, Alex Wood then Keith Rowen ran the offense, while Clancy Pendergast handled the defense. *Hall of Fame Players:* Chris Doleman, Randall McDaniel, Warren Moon, John Randle, Emmitt Smith, Gary Zimmerman. *Primary Quarterbacks:* Warren Moon, Brad Johnson, Josh McCown. *Tendencies:* • His teams scored 22.3 points and allowed 21.2 per game • His teams ran 42% of the time, which was 95% of the league average • 15 starting quarterbacks in 13 years; 44% of starts to primary quarterbacks • 30 rookie starters in 13 years • Winning Full Seasons to Losing Full Seasons: 8:4.

Born in Harrisburg, Pennsylvania, Dennis Green lost both his parents by the time he was 13 and then was raised by his grandparents. Dennis was a starting halfback for three years at Iowa and was among 16 black players who boycotted spring practices in 1969 protesting racial issues. Green was one of seven players reinstated that fall and played for the Hawkeyes through 1970. Upon graduation, he gave pro football a try in Canada, but then returned to Iowa as a graduate assistant in 1972 to start his coaching career. He spent 1973 at Dayton, 1974–1976 back at Iowa again and 1977–1978 at Stanford under Bill Walsh. Walsh brought Green with him when he took over the 49ers in 1979, but Dennis returned to Stanford a year later as offensive coordinator under Paul Wiggin.

After a one-year stint in Palo Alto, Green was hired as the head coach of Northwestern in 1981. In five years in Evanston, Dennis never won more than three games, but told the *New York Times* that Northwestern was "where I learned to take my ego completely out of it. You weren't going to a bowl game every year and you weren't going to win as many games as you would like. But you could graduate kids and leave every game with 100% pride." His five-year record with the Wildcats was 10–45 before Walsh brought him back to San Francisco to mentor him for a pro head coaching job. Green coached the 49ers' wide receivers for three years and left after winning a Super Bowl ring for the 1988 season. He was named head coach at Stanford in 1989 and went 16–18 in his three-year tenure, but took the Cardinal to a bowl game in 1991.

In 1992, Dennis was named head coach of the Vikings, just the second black coach in the modern NFL. Seeing that the division rival Packers and Bucs were coached by West Coast Offense proponents (Mike Holmgren and Sam Wyche), Green forged his own path by bringing in Jack Burns from the Redskins to install a more run-oriented offense. Dennis cleared

Green, Dennis

Year	Team	Games	Wins	Losses	Ties	%	P Wins	P Losses	P %
1992	Vikings	16	11	5	0	.688	0	1	.000
1993	Vikings	16	9	7	0	.563	0	1	.000
1994	Vikings	16	10	6	0	.625	0	1	.000
1995	Vikings	16	8	8	0	.500	0	0	.000
1996	Vikings	16	9	7	0	.563	0	1	.000
1997	Vikings	16	9	7	0	.563	1	1	.500
1998	Vikings	16	15	1	0	.938	1	1	.500
1999	Vikings	16	10	6	0	.625	1	1	.500
2000	Vikings	16	11	5	0	.688	1	1	.500
2001	Vikings	15	5	10	0	.333	0	0	.000
2004	Cardinals	16	6	10	0	.375	0	0	.000
2005	Cardinals	16	5	11	0	.313	0	0	.000
2006	Cardinals	16	5	11	0	.313	0	0	.000
13 years		207	113	94	0	.546	4	8	.333

out the deadwood on the team and set about instilling a team-oriented winning attitude on a chronically underachieving team. Despite changing starting quarterbacks almost every year, Green built a winning program that made the playoffs in eight of his first nine years.

It wasn't until his fifth trip to the playoffs, though, that Green recorded his first postseason win. Bad luck, questionable play calling and a suspect defense led to annual postseason disappointment. Even after the 1998 team went 15–1 and set a league record for points scored, the Vikings found a way to lose in the NFC championship against Atlanta. In 2000, Minnesota was favored in the NFC championship again and lost 41–0 to the Giants. The combination of that devastating loss, Randy Moss' antics and the 2001 training camp death of tackle Korey Stringer led to the team's complete meltdown the following year, and Green was fired before the season finale.

Even with the success, there was controversy. Two members of the Vikings' ownership board tried to have Green fired and replaced with Lou Holtz in 1996. Green responded with a book entitled *No Room for Crybabies* in which he threatened to sue the Vikings and force them to sell him 30% of the team. After all that drama, Dennis was out of football for a couple of years before resurfacing as the Cardinals head coach in 2004. In the Arizona desert, the tragic anxiety of the Minnesota years was repeated as farce. Green again moved from quarterback to quarterback and again tried desperately to instill a winning attitude in the team, but everything came to a head on a Monday Night game pitting the 1–4 Cardinals against the undefeated Bears. The Cardinals blew a 20-point lead to the Bears in the final 20 minutes by giving up two touchdowns on fumble returns and one on a punt return. An incensed Green went on an impassioned post game rant that immediately went viral on YouTube, snarling, "The Bears are who we thought they were! That's why we took the damn field. Now if you want to crown them, then crown their ass! But they are who we thought they were! And we let 'em off the hook!" Green was fired at the end of the year. He did some broadcasting for a couple of years, and then returned to football as a head coach in the developmental United Football League in 2009.

GREGG, ALVIS F. (FORREST) 10/18/1933– Southern Methodist. Played T for the Packers and Cowboys in 1956 and from 1958 to 1971. *Apprenticeship:* Pro asst.— 5 years. *Roots:* Phil Bengtson, Harland Svare, Nick Skorich. *Branches:* Dick Modzelewski (i), Hank Bullough, Raymond Berry, Frank Gansz, Lindy Infante, Bruce Coslet, Tom Coughlin, Dick LeBeau, Dick Jauron. *Coordinators/Key Assistants*: For the Browns, Blanton Collier helped with the offense, while Rich McCabe then Dick Modzelewski handled the defense; for the Bengals, Lindy Infante then George Sefcik ran the offense, while Hank Bullough handled the defense; for the Packers, Bob Schnelker then George Sefcik handled the offense, while Dick Modzelewski ran the defense. *Hall of Fame Players:* James Lofton, Anthony Munoz, Paul Warfield. *Primary Quarterbacks:* Brian Sipe, Ken Anderson, Lynn Dickey, Randy Wright. *Record:* **Hall of Fame Player.** *Tendencies:* • His teams scored 20 points and allowed 21 per game • His teams ran 48.5% of the time, which was 97% of the league average • 13 starting quarterbacks in 11 years; 76% of starts to primary quarterbacks • 32 rookie starters in 11 years • Winning Full Seasons to Losing Full Seasons: 3:5.

Not only a Hall of Famer, but also a member of the NFL's 75th Anniversary All-Time Team, Forrest Gregg was called by his coach Vince Lombardi, "the finest player I ever coached" in *Run to Daylight*. Tough as nails, he is a multiple cancer survivor. As a coach, though, Gregg was never able to approach the legacy of Lombardi despite trying harder than any of Vince's former players.

Born in Birthright, Texas, Gregg attended Southern Methodist and was drafted by the Packers in the second round in 1956; the tall Texan played 14 years in Green Bay and one last year as a backup in Dallas, with his playing career interrupted by military service in 1957. A seven-time All-Pro, he was part of six championship teams as a player, but none as a coach. Forrest's coaching career started in earnest in 1972 as the Chargers' line coach, although he originally had tried to retire in 1964 to take a coaching job at the University of Tennessee before changing his mind and had served as a player/assistant coach for his last two years as a Packer. After two years coaching in San Diego, Gregg joined Nick Skorich's staff in Cleveland, again as line coach. Skorich was fired at the end of 1974, and Forrest was named the Browns' head coach.

Gregg was quiet but very tough and a clear disciple of Vince Lombardi. In each of his three NFL stops as a coach, he was hired as much for his attitude as for anything else. Forrest tried too hard to live up to that tough guy reputation at the expense of his coaching. In both Cleveland and Cincinnati, Gregg's best season was his second as he turned around losing teams, but then did not adjust his style; Forrest's belligerent practice of cursing players as "yellow sons of bitches" quickly grew very stale to his players. Cleveland fullback Mike Pruitt told Jonathan Knight in *Kardiac Kids*, "Gregg was more of your military-type coach, a screamer." Defensive back Tony Peters recalled an incident to Steven Norwood in *Real Football* when Gregg caught a front office person named Bob Nussbaumer appearing to spy on him. According to Peters, Gregg grabbed Nussbaumer, shook him up and threw him into a chair. With his relationship fully deteriorating with owner Art Modell, Gregg resigned from the Browns with one game to play in 1977.

Gregg spent a year in the business world and then was named head coach of the Toronto Argonauts of the CFL in 1979. After a disappointing 5–11 first season, though, Forrest begged out of his three-year contract to become the head coach of the Bengals in 1980.

Quarterback Ken Anderson praised Gregg to Bob McGinn for *The Ultimate Super Bowl Book*, "We were a team that wasn't disciplined, wasn't necessarily in great physical shape and wasn't very strong. Forrest grabbed us by the back of the neck and shook us and made us a tough football team, physically and mentally." The Bengals went to the Super Bowl in Gregg's second year, losing to Bill Walsh's 49ers and then went 7–2 in the strike-shortened 1982 season. 1983 was a disaster on many fronts. Pete Johnson and defensive end Ross Browner were suspended for drug use, 10 players signed with the USFL, offensive coordinator Lindy Infante signed a head coaching contract for 1984 with the USFL and was abruptly fired for disloyalty by Paul Brown before the 1983 season. The team unraveled, and Forrest was fired.

His next job brought him back to Green Bay to follow the failed nine-year stint of former teammate Bart Starr. Gregg succeeded in toughening the Packers a bit, but could do no better than Starr with an 8–8 record in his first two seasons. Once he cut quarterback Lynn Dickey in 1986, the team collapsed. After two losing seasons, Gregg was fired again. Fortunately for Forrest, his alma mater was planning on reinstating football after having had the NCAA completely shut down the program a few years before for flagrant abuses of recruiting regulations. The upright Gregg coached SMU for two years going 3–19 and then stayed on as athletic director into 1994 when he returned to coaching with the Shreveport Pirates of the CFL. Gregg coached Shreveport for two years and went 8–28, leaving him with losing records as a college coach, CFL coach and NFL coach.

GROH, ALBERT (AL) 7/13/1944– Virginia. DE; did not play professionally. *Apprenticeship:* College coach — 20 years (6 as head coach); pro asst.—12 years. *Roots:* Marion Campbell, Bill Parcells, Ray Handley, Bill Belichick. *Branches:* Mike Nolan, Ken Whisenhunt, Todd Bowles (i). *Coordinators/Key Assistants:* Dan Henning ran the offense, while Mike Nolan han-

Gregg, Alvis F. (Forrest)									
Year	Team	Games	Wins	Losses	Ties	%	P Wins	P Losses	P %
1975	Browns	14	3	11	0	.214	0	0	.000
1976	Browns	14	9	5	0	.643	0	0	.000
1977	Browns	13	6	7	0	.462	0	0	.000
1980	Bengals	16	6	10	0	.375	0	0	.000
1981	Bengals	16	12	4	0	.750	2	1	.667
1982	Bengals	9	7	2	0	.778	0	1	.000
1983	Bengals	16	7	9	0	.438	0	0	.000
1984	Packers	16	8	8	0	.500	0	0	.000
1985	Packers	16	8	8	0	.500	0	0	.000
1986	Packers	16	4	12	0	.250	0	0	.000
1987	Packers	15	5	9	1	.367	0	0	.000
11 years		161	75	85	1	.469	2	2	.500

dled the defense. *Hall of Fame Players:* Curtis Martin. *Primary Quarterbacks:* Vinny Testaverde. *Tendencies:* • His team scored 20.1 points and allowed 20.1 per game • His team ran 38.9% of the time, which was 89% of the league average • One starting quarterbacks in one year; 100% of starts to primary quarterback • One rookie starter in one year • Winning Full Seasons to Losing Full Seasons: 1:0.

Al Groh coached for 32 years before getting his shot as an NFL coach and then walked away from the league after just one year. Groh was a New Yorker who played defensive end at Virginia. After coaching high school, Groh joined the staff at West Point in 1968 where he first met his wife and fellow Cadet assistant coach Bill Parcells. Al spent two years at Army, three at his alma mater, five at North Carolina, two at Air Force (where he again crossed paths with Parcells) and one at Texas Tech (again with Parcells) before landing a head coaching job at Wake Forest in 1981.

In six years at Wake Forest, Groh compiled a 26–40 record and then was named special teams coach for the Atlanta Falcons in 1987. A year later, he returned to the college ranks as the offensive coordinator for South Carolina. A year after that, he reunited with Parcells as the Giants linebackers coach in 1989. In 1990, New York won the Super Bowl, and Parcells stepped down as head coach afterwards. Groh stayed on in New York for a year under Ray Handley and then spent a year in Cleveland under Bill Belichick. When Parcells returned to coaching in 1993 with the Patriots, Groh joined him as defensive coordinator. After four years and another Super Bowl berth, Parcells quit New England and took the Jets' job. Groh followed him as linebackers coach again.

Three years later, Parcells was ready to step down again and pass the head coaching job to Bill Belichick, but Belichick got cold feet and resigned at the press conference announcing his appointment. Three weeks later, Groh was hired as Parcells' replacement, telling the press, "The best way to replace Bill Parcells is with a Parcells guy. There's been a firm hand on the rudder of every team that Bill's been on. The players are used to being coached and prepared in a particular way." By the end of the season, though, players viewed "tough guy Al" as "phony Al." His long-winded speeches were widely ignored, and he seemed out of place as a pro head coach. Groh was a Parcells guy, having coached with Bill for 13 years over a 30-year span, but he was not Parcells. When Groh's alma mater offered him a head coaching position in 2001, he jumped at the chance. Al coached the Cavaliers for nine years and attained a 59–53 record before he was fired in 2009. While two Parcells alums (Tony Sparano in Miami and Bill Belichick in New England) were interested in hiring Groh in 2010, he preferred the college life and joined Georgia Tech as their defensive coordinator instead.

GRUDEN, JON D. 8/17/1963– Dayton. QB; did not play professionally. *Apprenticeship:* College asst.—5 years; pro asst.—7 years. *Roots:* Mike Holmgren, Ray Rhodes. *Branches:* Bill Callahan, Rod Marinelli, Mike Tomlin, Raheem Morris. *Coordinators/Key Assistants:* For the Raiders, Bill Callahan handled the offense, while Willie Shaw then Chuck Bresnahan ran the defense; for the Bucs, Bill Muir was Gruden's key offensive assistant, while Monte Kiffin ran the defense. *Hall of Fame Players:* Jerry Rice. *Primary Quarterbacks:* Rich Gannon, Brad Johnson. *Record:* Super Bowl Championship 2002 *Tendencies:* • His teams scored

Groh, Albert (Al)

Year	Team	Games	Wins	Losses	Ties	%	P Wins	P Losses	P %
2000	Jets	16	9	7	0	.563	0	0	.000
1 year		16	9	7	0	.563	0	0	.000

Gruden, Jon D.

Year	Team	Games	Wins	Losses	Ties	%	P Wins	P Losses	P %
1998	Raiders	16	8	8	0	.500	0	0	.000
1999	Raiders	16	8	8	0	.500	0	0	.000
2000	Raiders	16	12	4	0	.750	1	1	.500
2001	Raiders	16	10	6	0	.625	1	1	.500
2002	Buccaneers	16	12	4	0	.750	3	0	1.000
2003	Buccaneers	16	7	9	0	.438	0	0	.000
2004	Buccaneers	16	5	11	0	.313	0	0	.000
2005	Buccaneers	16	11	5	0	.688	0	1	.000
2006	Buccaneers	16	4	12	0	.250	0	0	.000
2007	Buccaneers	16	9	7	0	.563	0	1	.000
2008	Buccaneers	16	9	7	0	.563	0	0	.000
11 years		176	95	81	0	.540	5	4	.556

21.1 points and allowed 18.7 per game • His teams ran 44% of the time, which was 99% of the league average • 13 starting quarterbacks in 11 years; 46% of starts to primary quarterbacks • 23 rookie starters in 11 years • Winning Full Seasons to Losing Full Seasons: 6:3.

Jon Gruden has been one of the most visible coaches in football in the new century, despite winning just one championship. On the sidelines, he was known for his demonstrative gestures, full throated screams and wide portfolio of scowls. Those angry facial expressions earned him the nickname of "Chucky" after the main character in the 1988 horror movie *Child's Play*, a red-headed homicidal doll. Working as a broadcaster on Monday Night Football since 2009, Gruden has become even more prominent a personality in the game.

Born in Sandusky, Ohio, Gruden grew up a coach's son, with his father most famously being an assistant coach under Dan Devine at Notre Dame. Jon was an undersized quarterback who graduated from Dayton after spending three years there as a backup. He then went into coaching as a graduate assistant at Tennessee in 1986, moving on to Southeast Missouri State in 1988 and Pacific in 1989. By 1990, Gruden's dad was working as a scout for the 49ers and got Jon an interview with offensive coordinator Mike Holmgren who then hired Jon as quality control coach. One year later, Gruden returned to the college ranks as the receivers coach for Pitt. When Holmgren was named head coach in Green Bay in 1992, though, he hired Gruden for his staff. Three years later, Ray Rhodes, who had served as defensive coordinator for both the Packers and 49ers, was named head coach of the Eagles in 1995; he hired the 32-year-old Gruden to run the offense.

While Philadelphia succeeded in signing star 49ers runner Ricky Watters as a free agent, the offense as a whole was a patchwork of spare parts quarterbacked by Rodney Peete and Ty Detmer. Gruden fashioned his own run-oriented version of the West Coast Offense that led the NFC in passing and was second in rushing in his second season. Philadelphia made the playoffs two years in a row, and Gruden started to be mentioned as a possible head coach. In 1998, Al Davis named Gruden the Raiders' head coach in something of a surprise because Gruden's style of attack ran counter to Davis' preference for a deep passing game. Jon brought in heady Rich Gannon as his quarterback and turned around the flailing Raider franchise. Gruden became known for working 16-hour days, going in to work at 4 A.M. every day, and out-preparing everyone else. After two 8–8 seasons, Oakland made the playoffs in 2000 and 2001. Receiver Tim Brown told the *New York Times*, "Players love Jon because he works hard and he treats us with respect. I like his intensity." Gannon added, "There isn't a better play caller in the league right now."

Nearing the end of his contract, Gruden began looking for a contract extension. Al Davis thought Gruden was about to become overpriced. Even though Gruden led the Raiders to the AFC conference championship after the 2001 season, Davis balked at rewarding his coach. That year, Oakland lost the title game to New England in the infamous "Tuck Rule" game in which an apparent fourth quarter fumble was negated in a controversial decision. It was the last game Gruden would coach for the Raiders. Davis dealt his coach to the Bucs for two first round draft choices, two second round choices and $8-million in 2002, an astronomical price.

In Tampa, Gruden was replacing a beloved coach, Tony Dungy, who was fired for not going deep enough in the playoffs. Gruden did nothing to change the Bucs' fearsome defense, but the workaholic set about constructing an offense behind quarterback Brad Johnson good enough to help that defense win a title. Tampa upset the Eagles in the NFC title game in Philadelphia — a major step for a team that had never won a cold weather game before — only to find their Super Bowl opponent to be the Raiders coached by Gruden's former assistant Bill Callahan. Tampa fullback Mike Alstott praised his coach in the *New York Times*, "Gruden put us over the top. He came in; he was a motivator." However, Jon's former players on the Raiders unloaded on him as, "the kind of coach who didn't like to listen as much as he liked to start a conversation and end it." Gruden prepared his defense to understand exactly what to expect from Gannon and the Raiders, even playing scout team quarterback in practice to demonstrate the quarterback's rhythm, tendencies and manner. In the Super Bowl, the Bucs picked off five Gannon passes and blasted Oakland 48–21. Gruden had built Gannon and then destroyed him.

While the media began calling Gruden a genius, he only made the playoffs two more times in the next six years and lost in the first round both times. Thus, Gruden's star lost a bit of its luster, especially when you consider what a great situation he was presented with in that Super Bowl, knowing the complete play book of his rivals and knowing every tendency of all its players. The Bucs defense essentially knew every play that the Raiders were running. The Glazers, who owned Tampa, certainly got their money's worth in that Gruden gave them the franchise's only championship. By contrast, Al Davis reaped little from the heavy price he extracted for Gruden, with no winning seasons for the Raiders while Jon coached Tampa. Gruden was fired at the end of 2009 after having dropped the last four games of the season to miss the playoffs. He has prospered as a broadcaster, but is continually linked with every major college or professional job opening that comes along.

HALAS, GEORGE S. 2/2/1895–10/31/1983. Illinois. Played E for the Bears from 1920 to 1929. *Apprenticeship:* None. *Roots:* None. *Branches:* Ralph Jones, Hunk Anderson, Luke Johnsos, Clark Shaughnessy, Gene Ronzani, George Wilson, Bulldog Turner, George Allen, Jim Dooley, Abe Gibron. *Coordinators/Key Assistants:* Longtime assistants included end coach Luke Johnsos, line coaches Hunk Anderson and Phil Handler, quarterbacks coach Sid Luckman, backs coach Paddy Driscoll and strategy coach Clark Shaughnessy. In Halas' final stint, Clark Shaughnessy then George Allen then Jim Dooley ran the defense. *Hall of Fame*

Players: Doug Atkins, George Blanda, Dick Butkus, Guy Chamberlin, George Connor, Jimmy Conzelman, Mike Ditka, Paddy Driscoll, Dan Fortmann, Bill George, Red Grange, Ed Healey, Bill Hewitt, Stan Jones, Walt Kiesling, Bobby Layne, Sid Luckman, Link Lyman, George McAfee, George Musso, Bronko Nagurski, Gale Sayers, Joe Stydahar, George Trafton and Bulldog Turner. *Primary Quarterbacks:* Sid Luckman, Bernie Masterson, Carl Brumbaugh, Ed Brown, Bill Wade. *Record:* **Hall of Fame Owner-Coach**; began as **Player-Coach**; NFL Championships 1921, 1933, 1940, 1941, 1946, 1963. *Tendencies:* • His teams

Halas, George S.										
Year	*Team*	*Games*	*Wins*	*Losses*	*Ties*	*%*	*P Wins*	*P Losses*	*P %*	
1920	Decatur Staleys	13	10	1	2	.846	0	0	.000	
1921	Chicago Staleys	11	9	1	1	.864	0	0	.000	
1922	Bears	12	9	3	0	.750	0	0	.000	
1923	Bears	12	9	2	1	.792	0	0	.000	
1924	Bears	11	6	1	4	.727	0	0	.000	
1925	Bears	17	9	5	3	.618	0	0	.000	
1926	Bears	16	12	1	3	.844	0	0	.000	
1927	Bears	14	9	3	2	.714	0	0	.000	
1928	Bears	13	7	5	1	.577	0	0	.000	
1929	Bears	15	4	9	2	.333	0	0	.000	
1933	Bears	13	10	2	1	.808	1	0	1.000	
1934	Bears	13	13	0	0	1.000	0	1	.000	
1935	Bears	12	6	4	2	.583	0	0	.000	
1936	Bears	12	9	3	0	.750	0	0	.000	
1937	Bears	11	9	1	1	.864	0	1	.000	
1938	Bears	11	6	5	0	.545	0	0	.000	
1939	Bears	11	8	3	0	.727	0	0	.000	
1940	Bears	11	8	3	0	.727	1	0	1.000	
1941	Bears	11	10	1	0	.909	2	0	1.000	
1942	Bears	5	5	0	0	1.000	0	0	.000	
1946	Bears	11	8	2	1	.773	1	0	1.000	
1947	Bears	12	8	4	0	.667	0	0	.000	
1948	Bears	12	10	2	0	.833	0	0	.000	
1949	Bears	12	9	3	0	.750	0	0	.000	
1950	Bears	12	9	3	0	.750	0	1	.000	
1951	Bears	12	7	5	0	.583	0	0	.000	
1952	Bears	12	5	7	0	.417	0	0	.000	
1953	Bears	12	3	8	1	.292	0	0	.000	
1954	Bears	12	8	4	0	.667	0	0	.000	
1955	Bears	12	8	4	0	.667	0	0	.000	
1958	Bears	12	8	4	0	.667	0	0	.000	
1959	Bears	12	8	4	0	.667	0	0	.000	
1960	Bears	12	5	6	1	.458	0	0	.000	
1961	Bears	14	8	6	0	.571	0	0	.000	
1962	Bears	14	9	5	0	.643	0	0	.000	
1963	Bears	14	11	1	2	.857	1	0	1.000	
1964	Bears	14	5	9	0	.357	0	0	.000	
1965	Bears	14	9	5	0	.643	0	0	.000	
1966	Bears	14	5	7	2	.429	0	0	.000	
1967	Bears	14	7	6	1	.536	0	0	.000	
40 years		497	318	148	31	.671	6	3	.667	

scored 19.4 points and allowed 13.9 per game • His teams ran 59.7% of the time, which was 104% of the league average • 17 starting quarterbacks in 30 T formation years; 75% of starts to primary quarterbacks • 122 rookie starters in 40 years • Winning Full Seasons to Losing Full Seasons: 34:6.

Papa Bear George Halas was not only the founder of the Bears, but essentially the founding father of the NFL — the man most responsible for the league's stability and game's growth over six decades. Halas spent 63 years as an owner and 40 as head coach. He was the youngest coach to win an NFL title at 26 in 1921 and the oldest at 68 in 1963. He introduced daily practices, film study and assistant coaches analyzing the game from the press booth. His Bears set up the first training camp in 1933 on the campus of Notre Dame. He won six championships and revolutionized the game in 1940 with the modern T formation that continues to be the base pro set over which myriad variations are run even today.

Halas was so cantankerous that he and early rival Curly Lambeau never shook hands after a Bears-Packers game, but he served as one of Curly's pall bearers in 1965. George was so tight in negotiating salaries that Mike Ditka got himself banished from Chicago for remarking, "He throws around nickels like manhole covers." Yet, there are countless stories are private, personal generosity that Halas bestowed on players or ex-players in need. He was so competitive that he regularly lobbied referees for every edge, was not above tripping an opposing player who came to near the Bear sideline and would steal signals at every opportunity. At the same time, he worked hard to help Green Bay win the funding for a new City Stadium in 1957 and was great friends with Vince Lombardi despite striving desperately to beat the Packers.

Born in Chicago, Halas played football, baseball and basketball at the University of Illinois. However,

his football career under Bob Zuppke was abbreviated by injuries. George broke his jaw in 1915 and broke his leg in 1916. Only in 1917, his senior season, did Halas get to play extensively. George went into the service in 1918 and played football for the Great Lakes Naval Station team that won the 1919 Rose Bowl. Halas was MVP of the game by scoring two touchdowns. He went to spring training in 1919 with the Yankees, but hurt his hip sliding and that robbed him of his speed. That summer he appeared in 12 games for the Yankees, but batted just .091. Sticking to football, George played that fall for the Hammond Pros.

When the NFL, or American Professional Football League as it was first called, started in 1920, Halas was right there sitting on the running board at Ralph Hay's Hupmobile showroom as the league by-laws were established. George was representing his Staley Starch Company-sponsored Decatur Staleys as one of the charter franchises of the league. The team lost money that first year, so A.E. Staley decided to get out of football. However, Staley made a deal with Halas that he would give him $5,000 seed money to take the team to Chicago and maintain the Staley name for one more year. The Chicago Staleys won the league title that year, but in order to keep going in 1922 as the renamed Chicago Bears, Halas took on Dutch Sternaman as a full partner. His first choice for a partner was old friend Paddy Driscoll, but Paddy was signed to the Cardinals. Sternaman had been Halas' teammate at both Illinois and with the Staleys. For the next nine years, Halas and Sternaman combined to own and operate the team, but as time went on, the arrangement became increasingly prickly. When Dutch's brother Joey, who was the Bears quarterback, jumped to Red Grange's rival league as the owner of the Chicago Bulls in 1926, Halas saw Dutch's loyalty leaning toward his brother. By 1929, Dutch and Halas were so completely at odds in coaching the team that the two agreed on hiring Ralph Jones as the Bears coach. Jones had coached both men in football, baseball and basketball at Illinois. So Halas, who had retired as a player a year before, stepped aside as Bears coach (or co-coach, really) for the first time, having gone 84–31–19 with one championship between 1920 and 1929.

In the ensuing three years, Jones reworked Zuppke's T formation and opened it up, winning a championship in the process. Sternaman ran into financial problems and asked Halas to buy him out. George borrowed heavily to do so, but acquired full control of the Bears in July 1932 and returned to the sidelines as coach that fall. Over the next ten years, Halas led the Bears to five NFL championship games and won three of them: in 1933, 1940 and 1941. In 1939, he acquired Sid Luckman to be his quarterback, and brought in Clark Shaughnessy the following year to further develop the T formation. The culmination was

Head-to-Head:		
Hall of Fame Opponent	Regular Season	Postseason
George Allen	1–2	0–0
Paul Brown	1–3	0–0
Guy Chamberlin	3–5	0–0
Jimmy Conzelman	13–5–3	0–0
Weeb Ewbank	9–9	0–0
Ray Flaherty	3–2	1–1
Sid Gillman	8–2	0–0
Bud Grant	1–0–1	0–0
Curly Lambeau	30–17–2	1–0
Tom Landry	2–1	0–0
Vince Lombardi	5–13	0–0
Greasy Neale	5–1	0–0
Steve Owen	8–5	3–1
Don Shula	4–5	0–0
Total	93–70–6	5–2

the 1940 championship game in which the Bears unleashed the full power of the T and whipped the Redskins 73–0, throwing just 10 passes.

In midseason 1942, Halas went into the Navy and left his team in the capable co-coaching hands of Luke Johnsos for the offense and Hunk Anderson for the defense. Chicago won another title in 1943 under this pair. Halas' second coaching stint resulted in a 84–22–4 record, and he returned in 1946 for his third term. In that first season back, Halas led Chicago to another title, but over the next decade the Eagles, Browns, Rams and Lions were more dominant. The Bears remained a rugged and competitive team, but were no longer the Monsters of the Midway. With a 10-year mark of 75–42–4, George decided to step down for a "younger man" in 1956, promoting longtime aide Paddy Driscoll as head coach in 1956. Unexpectedly, the Bears reached the title game that season, but lost to the Giants. 1957 brought a losing record, and Halas could not contain himself. He returned for his final 10-year stint as coach in 1958.

Not only was George getting older by this time, but so was his staff. Halas was extremely loyal to old friends, essentially making them coaches for life, but men like Shaughnessy, Luckman and Driscoll were adding little to the team. Halas began to bring in some new coaching blood in the early 1960s with Chuck Mather, Jim Dooley and, especially, George Allen. With fresh talent brought in by scouting head Allen, the 1963 Bears roared to the NFL title behind a ferocious defense coached by Allen. Allen even drafted Gale Sayers and Dick Butkus in 1965 right before he left to coach the Rams, and Chicago remained fairly strong throughout Halas' last years as coach, going 75–53–6 over the last decade. George retired from coaching after the 1967 season, saying, "I knew it was time to stop coaching. I started to go after an official walking along the sideline and I couldn't keep up with him."

Over his full 40-year career, the Bears led the league in scoring seven times and finished in the top three 19 times. On defense, the team gave up the fewest points in the league five times and ten times finished in the top three. Fourteen times Chicago was in the top three in turnover differential. Although never to return to the sidelines, Halas continued to run the Bears for the next 15 years. Those years were a far cry from the days when Halas was young. It wasn't until prodigal son Mike Ditka came back to coach the team that the Bears returned to greatness. Unfortunately, their 1985 Super Bowl season came two years after Halas' death in 1983 at the age of 88. Vince Lombardi said of Halas, "There is only one man I embrace when we meet and only one I call Coach." George Halas established the parameters of being an NFL coach, but there will never be another one like him.

HALEY, TODD 2/28/1967– North Florida. Did not play in college or professionally. *Apprenticeship:* Pro asst.—13 years. *Roots:* Bill Parcells, Dick Jauron, Ken Whisenhunt. *Branches:* None. *Coordinators/Key Assistants:* Haley first ran his own offense, then Charlie Weis took over then Bill Muir, while Clancy Pendergast then Romeo Crennel handled the defense. *Hall of Fame Players:* None. *Primary Quarterbacks:* Matt Cassell. *Tendencies:* • His teams scored 18.5 points and allowed 23.4 per game • His teams ran 47.5% of the time, which was 110% of the league average • Three starting quarterbacks in three years; 87% of starts to primary quarterback • Nine rookie starters in three years • Winning Full Seasons to Losing Full Seasons: 1:1.

Todd Haley is the son of former Steeler defensive back Dick Haley who had a 30-year career in scouting and player personnel in the NFL. Todd was born in Atlanta, but grew up in the Pittsburgh area. He played on the golf squads for both Miami and Florida before graduating from Northern Florida in 1991. Four years later, his father brought him to the Jets as a scout in 1995. A year after that, he joined the staff of Rich Kotite and stayed on under both Bill Parcells and Al Groh. In 2001, he moved on to the Bears as receivers coach under Dick Jauron for three years before reuniting with Parcells in Dallas in 2004. For the Cowboys, Haley coached both the wide receivers and the passing game. In 2007, Parcells retired, and Haley moved on to the Cardinals as offensive coordinator under new head coach Ken Whisenhunt. When the Cardinals made a surprise trip to the Super Bowl behind their explosive passing game in 2008, Haley gained a great deal of notoriety. In the off season, he was hired as Chiefs' head coach by their new GM Scott Pioli, who was Bill Parcells' son-in-law.

Haley is an emotional and volatile figure on the sidelines who has been known to get into confronta-

Haley, Todd									
Year	Team	Games	Wins	Losses	Ties	%	P Wins	P Losses	P %
2009	Chiefs	16	4	12	0	.250	0	0	.000
2010	Chiefs	16	10	6	0	.625	0	1	.000
2011	Chiefs	13	5	8	0	.385	0	0	.000
3 years		45	19	26	0	.422	0	1	.000

tions with players such as receiver Anquan Boldin in Arizona during the NFC championship game. In Kansas City, he also has clashed with some players and even coaches. Originally, Haley retained incumbent offensive coordinator Chan Gailey, but then fired him in the 2009 preseason and took over the play-calling himself. On Pioli's recommendation, Haley brought in two former Patriot coordinators Charlie Weis and Romeo Crennel in 2010, and the rebuilt Chiefs won the division and went to the playoffs. Weis left to become offensive coordinator of the Florida Gators at the end of the year. Reportedly, his relationship with Todd was rocky. With the team struggling in 2011, the belligerent Haley was replaced by Romeo Crennel with three games to play. Seen as more a Parcells imitator than the real deal, Todd was hired as offensive coordinator by Pittsburgh in 2012.

HANDLER, PHILIP J. (PHIL) 7/21/1908–
12/8/1968. Texas Christian. Played G for the Cardinals from 1930 to 1936. *Apprenticeship:* Pro asst.— 6 years. *Roots:* Milan Creighton, Ernie Nevers, Jimmy Conzelman. *Branches:* Buddy Parker. *Coordinators/Key Assistants*: Buddy Parker coached the backs for Handler and later co-coached the team with him in 1949; Handler co-coached the Card-Pitts with Walt Kiesling in 1944. *Hall of Fame Players:* Charley Trippi. *Primary Quarterbacks:* None. *Record:* Co-Coach (with Walt Kiesling in 1944, Buddy Parker in 1949 and Cecil Isbell in 1951). *Tendencies:* • His teams scored 12.5 points and allowed 25.3 per game • His teams ran 58% of the time, which was 91% of the league average • 12 rookie starters in five years • Winning Full Seasons to Losing Full Seasons: 0:3.

A native of Fort Worth, Texas, Phil Handler spent most of his life in Chicago, employed by either of two pro football teams. Handler played guard for Texas Christian from 1927 to 1929 under Francis "Close the Gates of Mercy" Schmidt and signed with the Chicago Cardinals in 1930. Phil played for the Cards for seven years and doubled as line coach in 1935 and 1936. When he retired in 1937, he became the line coach full time under Milan Creighton then Ernie Nevers and then Jimmy Conzelman.

Conzelman left the team in 1943, and Handler was promoted to head coach and remained in that po-

sition throughout the very lean War years. The Cardinals had finished 1942 with six straight losses and then lost the next 23 games under Handler until finally beating the Bears in October 1945. Over two years, 11 months and 27 days, the Cardinals had lost 29 straight games. That one victory over the Bears would be the only win of the year for the team. Phil's one accomplishment as head coach was the introduction of the T formation in 1945. The year before, the Cardinals had even combined forces with the Steelers to form a merged team officially known as the Card-Pitts, but more popularly called the "Carpets" because everyone walked all over them. Handler was co-coach of that team with Walt Kiesling, the Steelers' coach. Those two horse players got along famously, enjoying their days at the track more than their days on the gridiron sidelines.

Before that team's season finale, tailback Johnny Grigas, who had been on the losing side in each of the 19 games he had played as a pro, trailed only the Giants' Bill Paschal in rushing. The day of the game, though, he disappeared and left a florid note on the disheartening effects of losing: "The human mind is the faculty of the soul, which is influenced by the human body. When your mind is changed because of the physical beating, week in week out, your soul isn't in the game. My mind has been influenced this past week, and I tried to stick it out, but it has reached the stage where the mind is stronger than the will. In all justice to the management and to myself, I am leaving because I couldn't play the whole game."

Conzelman returned as head coach in 1946, and Handler went back to coaching the line through the best three-year run in Chicago Cardinal history. When Conzelman surprisingly stepped down after 1948, both Phil and backfield coach Buddy Parker were promoted to co-head coach. This awkward arrangement lasted for the first half of the season before Parker was named coach and Handler kicked upstairs as vice president of scouting. Parker left for Detroit in 1950, and Curly Lambeau was hired as the new Cardinals' coach, with Phil returning to the sidelines to coach the line. When Lambeau was fired with two games to go in the 1951 season, Handler and backfield coach Cecil Isbell assumed the co-coaching role to close out the season.

Handler had enough of the Cardinals' yo-yo

Handler, Philip J. (Phil)									
Year	*Team*	*Games*	*Wins*	*Losses*	*Ties*	*%*	*P Wins*	*P Losses*	*P %*
1943	Cardinals	10	0	10	0	.000	0	0	.000
1944	Card-Pitts	10	0	10	0	.000	0	0	.000
1945	Cardinals	10	1	9	0	.100	0	0	.000
1949	Cardinals	6	2	4	0	.333	0	0	.000
1951	Cardinals	2	1	1	0	.500	0	0	.000
5 years		38	4	34	0	.105	0	0	.000

effect in 1952 and moved cross-town to coach the Bears' line once Hunk Anderson quit football. Phil stayed on the Bears' staff through the 1967 season. He retired in 1968 after suffering a serious heart attack. Handler died on December 8, 1968 from a second heart attack that occurred while he watched on TV as the Bears beat the Rams 17–16 in Los Angeles.

HANDLEY, ROBERT R. (RAY) 10/8/1944– Stanford. HB; did not play professionally. *Apprenticeship:* College asst.—16 years; pro asst.—7 years. *Roots:* Bill Parcells. *Branches:* Jim Fassel, Al Groh, Romeo Crennel. *Coordinators/Key Assistants*: Ron Erhardt then Jim Fassel handled the offense, while Al Groh then Rod Rust ran the defense. *Hall of Fame Players:* Lawrence Taylor. *Primary Quarterbacks:* Jeff Hostetler. *Tendencies:* • His teams scored 18.3 points and allowed 20.8 per game • His teams ran 50.1% of the time, which was 110% of the league average • Three starting quarterbacks in two years; 66% of starts to primary quarterback • One rookie starter in two years • Winning Full Seasons to Losing Full Seasons: 0:1.

Giants' GM George Young called the hiring of Ray Handley to replace Bill Parcells in 1991 as "my worst decision." He would get no argument from New York fans about that.

Handley was born in Artesia, New Mexico, and was a history major at Stanford where he also played halfback. In 1966, he was in the Chargers' training camp, but did not last long. He began his coaching career in 1967 as an assistant at his alma mater and moved on to West Point in 1968 where he coached with Bill Parcells for two years. Ray was out of football in 1970, but returned to Stanford as an assistant in 1971. From 1971 to 1974, he worked on the staffs of John Ralston and then Jack Christiansen before moving on to the Air Force Academy in 1975. He stayed there for four years and was reunited with Parcells there in 1978. Both coaches left in 1979; Handley returned to Stanford for the fourth time, working under Rod Dowhower and Paul Wiggin from 1979 to 1983.

In 1984, Handley joined Parcells' staff on the Giants as the running backs coach. By 1991, Ray was getting restless and was considering leaving football for law school when he was promoted to offensive coordinator in February. Three months later, Parcells decided he needed to step down for health reasons, and Handley was promoted to head coach. Ray told the press that he would give backup quarterback Jeff

Hostetler an opportunity to win the starting job in training camp and planned to open up the offense. As for Parcells, Handley said, "Bill can be a little more volatile than I can." He added, "I'm hoping I can get the same amount out of the players using a different approach."

Handley was promoted as a man with a genius-level IQ who was so sharp that he was banned from casinos in Reno as a card counter. However, his short reign as head coach was beset by problems. His defense was growing old for one thing, and he brought in a defensive coordinator, Rod Rust, whose style ran completely counter to how the defense was accustomed to play. Second, he created a quarterback controversy by giving the job to Hostetler and announcing that the decision was final but then did not stick to it. He said, "Hostetler will not be looking over his shoulder for Phil Simms to come in if he throws an incomplete pass." However, Handley bounced back and forth between the two quarterbacks, unable to make a truly final decision. Third, he did not communicate well with his team and ended up in shouting matches with some players. Finally, his media relations were extremely poor and embarrassed team ownership. In one instance, he walked out on the media after refusing to answer a question about which quarterback would start. He also curtailed media access to the coach and to the practice field.

Former Giants' offensive coordinator Ron Erhardt summed it up best when he left the Giants for the Steelers in 1992, "It was really bad. It was a guy who worked for me for seven years and when he got the job, he wanted to be coordinator. What it boiled down to was the guy was insecure." Handley was fired after two seasons and retreated to Nevada, never to be seen in the NFL again.

HANIFAN, JAMES M. (Jim) 9/21/1933– California. Played E in the CFL. *Apprenticeship:* College asst.—10 years; pro asst.—7 years. *Roots:* Don Coryell. *Branches:* Rod Dowhower. *Coordinators/Key Assistants*: Dick Jamieson then Rod Dowhower handled the offense, while Tom Bettis then Floyd Peters ran the defense. *Hall of Fame Players:* Dan Dierdorf, Deion Sanders, Roger Wehrli. *Primary Quarterbacks:* Jim Hart, Neil Lomax. *Tendencies:* • His teams scored 20.5 points and allowed 24.1 per game • His teams ran 46.8% of the time, which was 97% of the league average • Four starting quarterbacks in seven years; 99%

Handley, Robert R. (Ray)									
Year	Team	Games	Wins	Losses	Ties	%	P Wins	P Losses	P %
1991	Giants	16	8	8	0	.500	0	0	.000
1992	Giants	16	6	10	0	.375	0	0	.000
2 years		32	14	18	0	.438	0	0	.000

of starts to primary quarterbacks • 19 rookie starters in seven years • Winning Full Seasons to Losing Full Seasons: 3:3.

Born in Compton, California, Jim Hanifan starred at end for California under Pappy Waldorf from 1952 to 1954, making All-American as a senior. Jim played for Toronto in the CFL in 1955 and then was called into the military. In the service, Hanifan played for Fort Ord coached by Don Coryell in 1956 before spending 1957 in Europe. After his discharge, Hanifan coached junior college and high school football through 1965. The next year he joined the staff at Utah and stayed through 1969. In 1970, he returned to his alma mater under Ray Willsey for two years before reuniting with Coryell at San Diego State in 1972. When Coryell was named head coach of the Cardinals, he brought Jim with him as line coach.

In St. Louis, Hanifan quickly built a reputation as one of the best line coaches in football and was named the NFL's Assistant Coach of the Year in 1977. Jim's Hall of Fame tackle Dan Dierdorf said of him for Hanifan's book *Beyond Xs and Os*, "If you loved the game and had a passion for the game, you were his kind of player. If you weren't a very good player, but still had a passion for it, you had a friend for life in Jim Hanifan." Hanifan's line kept the pressure off slow-footed quarterback Jim Hart and allowed Coryell's offense to work. Hanifan stayed with the Cardinals through 1978, even after Coryell was fired, and then followed him to San Diego in 1979. In 1980, Jim returned to St. Louis as the Cardinals' head coach, optimistically telling the press, "My relationship with [owner] Bill Bidwill is going to be a smooth-working relationship."

Hanifan did last six years as Cardinals' head coach. He put two 5–11 seasons on either end of four mediocre seasons right around .500, and that was fairly good work for the Cardinals' franchise. Hanifan's

biggest move was switching from veteran Jim Hart to rookie Neil Lomax at quarterback midway through the 1981 season. Lomax rewarded Jim's faith by playing well, but the team was never quite good enough. The Cards came within a missed field goal in the 1984 season finale of winning the East Division, but missed the playoffs entirely instead.

After being fired by St. Louis, Hanifan worked as line coach for Atlanta from 1987 to 1989 — serving the last four games as interim head coach for Marion Campbell who was fired. In 1990, Hanifan replaced Joe Bugel as line coach of the Redskins, and the Hogs didn't miss a beat. Ironically, Bugel had left Washington to become head coach of the Cardinals. Jim won a Super Bowl ring for the 1991 season in D.C. and stayed there through 1996 under three coaches. In 1997, Dick Vermeil returned to the sidelines after a 15-year hiatus and recruited the best staff of veteran coaches he could find, including Hanifan for the line. Jim spent seven years with the Rams and then moved into local broadcasting in St Louis after his retirement from coaching. Defensive line coach Floyd Peters once aptly described the affable Hanifan to the *Washington Post*, "Give him a cigarette and a beer and he can talk forever. He's one of those guys whose battery is charged forever."

HANLEY, RICHARD E. (DICK) 11/19/1894–12/16/1970. Washington State. Played HB for the Racine Legion in 1924. *Apprenticeship:* College head coach —13 years. *Roots:* None. *Branches:* Pat Boland (i). *Coordinators/Key Assistants:* Ernie Nevers and Pat Boland were Hanley's assistants. *Hall of Fame Players:* Elroy Hirsch. *Primary Quarterbacks:* None. *Record:* **Interim Coach.**

Dick Hanley was a rough-and-tumble kind of guy from Cloquet, Minnesota. Dick played halfback for Washington State from 1915 to 1917 until joining

Hanifan, James M. (Jim)									
Year	*Team*	*Games*	*Wins*	*Losses*	*Ties*	*%*	*P Wins*	*P Losses*	*P %*
1980	Cardinals	16	5	11	0	.313	0	0	.000
1981	Cardinals	16	7	9	0	.438	0	0	.000
1982	Cardinals	9	5	4	0	.556	0	1	.000
1983	Cardinals	16	8	7	1	.531	0	0	.000
1984	Cardinals	16	9	7	0	.563	0	0	.000
1985	Cardinals	16	5	11	0	.313	0	0	.000
1989	Falcons	4	0	4	0	.000	0	0	.000
7 years		93	39	53	1	.425	0	1	.000

Hanley, Richard E. (Dick)									
Year	*Team*	*Games*	*Wins*	*Losses*	*Ties*	*%*	*P Wins*	*P Losses*	*P %*
1946	Rockets (AAFC)	2	0	1	1	.250	0	0	.000
1 year		2	0	1	1	.250	0	0	.000

the Marines in World War I. While in the service, Hanley also was light heavyweight boxing champion of the Marines. After his discharge, he returned to Washington State and was team captain in 1920. Dick then coached high school in Pendleton, Oregon in 1921 and took over as head coach at the Haskell Indian Institute in 1922. From 1922 to 1926, Haskell finished 52–4–9. During that time, Hanley also managed to play in one NFL game for the Racine Legion in 1924.

Dick left Haskell in 1927 and was appointed head coach at Northwestern. Hanley built the Wildcats into conference champs in 1930 and 1931, but then the program started to slip. In 1934, Dick resigned after opposition from the faculty made it clear his contract would not be renewed despite an overall 36–26–4 record. While he was at Northwestern, Hanley employed African American star Fritz Pollard as his unofficial backfield coach from 1927 to 1928, an unusually open minded appointment for that time period. At this point, Dick gave up football and sold insurance in Chicago for six years. After Pearl Harbor though, Hanley, who had been in the Marine Reserves since 1927, returned to active duty.

For Dick, that duty was coaching the football team on the El Toro, California Marine base. The El Toro Marines were one of the best service teams in the nation from 1941 to 1945. Hanley was even featured in a short film called *Marines in the Making* in 1942 that showed different training techniques. When the war ended, John Keeshin, who owned the Chicago Rockets of the new All America Football Conference, hired Hanley as his head coach. Predictably, Dick stocked the Rockets with 17 players from El Toro, including Elroy Hirsch, Willie Wilkin and Bob Dove.

Keeshin and Hanley clashed repeatedly, and Dick spent the third game of the year in the stands as Wilkin, Dove and Ned Mathews led the team as player-co-coaches. They were put in charge by Keeshin who asserted that Hanley had quit, while Hanley insisted he had been fired. Dick told reporters, "For someone who knows nothing about football, Keeshin has more coaching advice than anybody I ever knew." And then it turned uglier. When Keeshin told the *Chicago Tribune* on September 27 that 32 of 33 Rocket players voted that Hanley should be fired, Hanley sued him for libel. The case dragged on for seven years, but in January 1953, Hanley was awarded $100,000 in damages for malicious libel when multiple players testified that there had been no vote and that several players indeed had a high regard for Hanley.

By 1953, he was long out of football (so was Keeshin). Dick continued in his insurance business from 1947 to 1959 before retiring to California. He died in 1970 from pneumonia and emphysema.

HARBAUGH, JAMES J. (JIM) 12/23/1963– Michigan. Played QB for the Bears, Colts, Ravens and Chargers from 1987 to 2000. *Apprenticeship:* Pro asst.— 2 years; college head coach — 7 years. *Roots:* Bill Callahan. *Branches:* None. *Coordinators/Key Assistants:* Greg Roman ran the offense, while Vic Fangio handled the defense. *Hall of Fame Players:* None. *Primary Quarterbacks:* Alex Smith. *Tendencies:* • His team scored 23.8 points and allowed 14.3 per game • His team ran 50.1% of the time, which was 117% of the league average • One starting quarterback in one year; 100% of starts to primary quarterback • Two rookie starters in one year • Winning Full Seasons to Losing Full Seasons: 1:0.

Jim Harbaugh became famous as a player, but is from a family of coaches. His father Jack worked as an assistant to Bo Schembechler at Michigan until getting a head coaching job at Western Michigan when Jim enrolled at Ann Arbor in 1982. Over 21 years at Western Michigan and Western Kentucky, Jack compiled a 117–94–3 record. Jim's brother John has coached the Baltimore Ravens since 2008 and his brother-in-law Tom Crean has headed the basketball programs at Marquette and Indiana.

Born in Toledo, Ohio, Jim was a three-year starter at quarterback for Michigan from 1984 to 1986 before being drafted in the first round by the Bears. While Harbaugh is known as being competitive and emotional, he found his match in Chicago coach Mike Ditka. Harbaugh had an up-and-down tenure with the Bears. The lowest point came when he threw an interception on an audible in a nationally televised game against the Vikings. Ditka, who had specifically told Jim not to call an audible because of the noise level in the Metrodome, was livid and unloaded a blistering tirade on Harbaugh when he came to the sidelines. Jim proved to have a tough hide and later told Lew Freedman for *Game of My Life: Chicago Bears,* "Even when I was playing, I watched Coach Ditka, how he handled situations and the passion he brought to the game. I tried to pick up on just the football knowledge it takes to become a coach. It was always in my mind when he would be in front of the team giving a talk."

Harbaugh's most memorable years were with the

Harbaugh, James J. (Jim)									
Year	Team	Games	Wins	Losses	Ties	%	P Wins	P Losses	P %
2011	49ers	16	13	3	0	.813	1	1	.500
1 year		16	13	3	0	.813	1	1	.500

Indianapolis Colts from 1994 to 1997 when he became known by Roger Staubach's nickname, Captain Comeback, for his late game heroics. The undermanned Colts came within a dropped Hail Mary pass in the 1995 AFC championship against Pittsburgh of going to the Super Bowl. Also while in Indianapolis, the volatile Harbaugh cracked a bone in his hand when he punched former Buffalo quarterback Jim Kelly for calling him a "baby" who "overdramatized" injuries on a TV broadcast. On the side, Harbaugh worked as an official unpaid coaching volunteer for his father at Western Kentucky for the last seven years of his playing career.

Harbaugh went into coaching for real when his playing career ended as a member of Bill Callahan's Raiders' staff in 2002 and 2003. In 2004, Jim took over the struggling University of San Diego program and led the team to a 29–6 record from 2004 to 2006. Hired by Stanford in 2007, Harbaugh transformed that flagging program and brought the Cardinal to the Bowl Championship Series in 2010 with a 12–1 mark that capped his cumulative Palo Alto record at 29–21. His highly regarded Stanford quarterback Andrew Luck told *Sports Illustrated*, "He's not your average football coach. He is very hands-on. It's almost like he's playing a little."

Harbaugh returned to the NFL in 2011, taking over the 49ers, a once-proud franchise that has not had a winning season in eight years. In his first year, Jim led San Francisco back to the playoffs on the strength of an imposing defense that allowed the second fewest points in the league and a run-oriented yet imaginative offense piloted by resurrected draft bust Alex Smith at quarterback. Harbaugh's effervescent positive leadership style established a new winning tradition in San Francisco in his biggest coaching challenge yet.

HARBAUGH, JOHN 9/23/1962– Miami (OH). DB; did not play professionally. *Apprenticeship:* College asst.—14 years; pro asst.—10 years. *Roots:* Andy Reid. *Branches:* Rex Ryan, Hue Jackson, Chuck Pagano. *Coordinators/Key Assistants*: Cam Cameron ran the offense, while Rex Ryan then Greg Mattison then Chuck Pagano handled the defense. *Hall of Fame Players:* None. *Primary Quarterbacks:* Joe Flacco. *Tendencies:* • His teams scored 23.6 points and allowed 16.3 per game • His teams ran 48.6% of the time, which was 111% of the league average • One starting quar-

terbacks in four years; 100% of starts to primary quarterback • Four rookie starters in four years • Winning Full Seasons to Losing Full Seasons: 4:0.

While both John and Jim Harbaugh were the sons of a college coach, John's long journey to become a head coach was much more typical than that of star quarterback Jim. John played defensive back for Miami of Ohio, but the Toledo-native's career was derailed by multiple knee injuries. However, he did win the school's Football Scholar Award for his high grades in the classroom. Upon graduation, Harbaugh went to work with dad in the family business in 1984. John spent three years as an assistant at Western Michigan under his father, Jack, before setting out on his own in 1987 as the tight ends coach for Pitt. A year later, he served as Morehead State's special teams coach, and then moved to the University of Cincinnati in the same capacity in 1989. He stayed with the Bearcats for eight years until reaching the Big Ten in 1997 as Indiana's special teams coach.

Meanwhile in Philadelphia, Ray Rhodes had struggled with special teams for three years. In 1998, he hired Harbaugh who quickly straightened out that unit while the rest of the team collapsed. Rhodes was fired, but new coach Andy Reid retained John for his staff. For the next eight years, the Eagles regularly had one of the best special teams' units in the NFL, but Harbaugh was getting restless. He felt pigeonholed as a special teams coach and felt he needed to become a position coach to ever have a chance at a head coaching position. Reid switched John to defensive backs coach in 2007, and the Ravens hired him as their head coach in 2008. According to *Sports Illustrated*, one factor in Baltimore selecting Harbaugh was that Ravens' owner Steve Bisciotti received an unsolicited recommendation of John from New England coach Bill Belichick who was impressed with his work and his manner.

With the Ravens, Harbaugh was taking over a veteran team known for its tough and headstrong defense that would have preferred defensive coordinator Rex Ryan to be promoted to head coach. John won over Ryan and the defense with his dedication to winning, competitive personality and command of the game. His most important decision was how to handle the quarterback position, long a hole on the Baltimore depth chart. Harbaugh decided to play rookie Joe Flacco right from the start, while supporting the young

Harbaugh, John									
Year	Team	Games	Wins	Losses	Ties	%	P Wins	P Losses	P %
2008	Ravens	16	11	5	0	.688	2	1	.667
2009	Ravens	16	9	7	0	.563	1	1	.500
2010	Ravens	16	12	4	0	.750	1	1	.500
2011	Ravens	16	12	4	0	.750	1	1	.500
4 years		64	44	20	0	.688	5	4	.556

quarterback's growth with a ground-heavy approach that saw the Ravens running 11% more than the league average. Flacco's mature yet limited play led the Ravens to four straight playoff appearances. Baltimore finally got past the arch rival Steelers in 2011 only to lose in the final seconds to New England in the AFC Championship.

Haslett, James D. (Jim) 12/9/1955– Indiana University of Pennsylvania. Played LB for the Bills from 1979 to 1985 and the Jets in 1987. *Apprenticeship:* College asst.— 3 years; pro asst.— 7 years; WLAF asst.— 2 years. *Roots:* Art Shell, Jim Mora, Sr., Rick Venturi (i), Bill Cowher. *Branches:* Mike McCarthy. *Coordinators/Key Assistants*: For the Saints, Mike McCarthy then Mike Sheppard ran the offense, while Ron Zook then Rick Venturi handled the defense; in Haslett's interim stint for the Rams, Al Saunders ran the offense and Venturi handled the defense. *Hall of Fame Players:* Willie Roaf. *Primary Quarterbacks:* Aaron Brooks. *Tendencies:* • His teams scored 20.7 points and allowed 23.6 per game • His teams ran 43% of the time, which was 97% of the league average • Four starting quarterbacks in seven years; 85% of starts to primary quarterback • 15 rookie starters in seven years • Winning Full Seasons to Losing Full Seasons: 2:3.

Pittsburgh-native Jim Haslett is a linebacker through-and-through — tough and full of bluster. His coaching friend Jim Mora, Jr., told Jeff Duncan in *Tales from the Saints Sideline*, "He'll say anything if he thinks it helps him. He's like the Iraqi Minister of Propaganda."

Haslett played linebacker at Indiana University of Pennsylvania and was drafted in the second round by Buffalo in 1979. Jim played for the Bills from 1979 to 1985. He missed 1986 with a broken leg and then finished his career with the Jets as a replacement player for three games in 1987. The next year he began his coaching career as an assistant coach with the University of Buffalo. After three years, Jim moved on to the Sacramento Surge of the developmental World League of American Football in 1991 and 1992. In 1993, Art Shell brought him in as the Raiders' linebackers coach. He moved to New Orleans as linebackers coach in 1995 and was promoted to defensive coordinator by Jim Mora, Sr., the next year.

After Mora was fired in 1997, Haslett replaced Dick LeBeau as defensive coordinator in Pittsburgh under Bill Cowher. The Steelers defensive rankings slipped a bit, particularly against the run, over the next three years, but Jim interviewed for a number of head coaching positions and was hired by the Saints. Haslett brought a burst of energy to New Orleans that lifted the team into the playoffs and even to the first postseason win in franchise history, but that did not last. The team dropped back to mediocrity, going 32–32 over the next four years and never returning to the playoffs. Jim's Saints were an undisciplined bunch led by flashy but inconsistent quarterback Aaron Brooks and finished in the bottom five in points allowed three times. Haslett was on the hot seat going into 2005 to start with and then the city was hit by Hurricane Katrina, and the bottom fell out for the city and the team. Jim told *Sports Illustrated*, "It's going to be a hard year. We are going to be gypsies." The road warrior Saints barely struggled through a 3–13 season, and Haslett was fired.

After leaving the Saints, Jim served as Scott Linehan's defensive coordinator with the Rams for two-plus years until Linnehan was fired and Haslett replaced him. The Rams went 2–10 under Haslett that year and his bid to continue on as head coach was rejected. He did land another head coaching position in 2009, but it was with the Florida Tuskers of the developmental United Football League. In 2010, Jim returned to the NFL as Mike Shanahan's defensive coordinator in Washington. As with Pittsburgh and St. Louis, the Redskins defense under Haslett trended downward in rankings, especially in rushing yardage allowed.

Hecker, Norbert E. (Norb) 5/26/1927–3/14/2004. Baldwin-Wallace. Played S for the Rams from 1951 to 1953 and the Redskins from 1955 to 1957. *Apprenticeship:* Pro asst.— 8 years. *Roots:* Vince Lombardi. *Branches:* Tom Fears. *Coordinators/Key Assistants*: Tom Fears then Lew Carpenter were his key offensive assistants, while Hal Herring ran the defense. *Hall of Fame Players:* Tommy McDonald. *Primary Quarterbacks:* Randy Johnson. *Tendencies:* • His teams scored 13.5 points and allowed 31 per game • His teams ran 47.2% of the time, which was 96% of the league av-

Haslett, James D. (Jim)									
Year	Team	Games	Wins	Losses	Ties	%	P Wins	P Losses	P %
2000	Saints	16	10	6	0	.625	1	1	.500
2001	Saints	16	7	9	0	.438	0	0	.000
2002	Saints	16	9	7	0	.563	0	0	.000
2003	Saints	16	8	8	0	.500	0	0	.000
2004	Saints	16	8	8	0	.500	0	0	.000
2005	Saints	16	3	13	0	.188	0	0	.000
2008	Rams	12	2	10	0	.167	0	0	.000
7 years		108	47	61	0	.435	1	1	.500

erage • Four starting quarterbacks in three years; 84% of starts to primary quarterback • Nine rookie starters in three years • Winning Full Seasons to Losing Full Seasons: 0:2.

Norb Hecker was the direct connection between two dissimilar Super Bowl coaches — Vince Lombardi and Bill Walsh. Hecker won three NFL titles coaching the Packers' secondary for Lombardi and two Super Bowls coaching the 49ers' linebackers for Walsh. As a head coach, though, Hecker won fewer games than he won championship rings under those two great coaches.

A native of Berea, Ohio, Norb spent two years in the Army after graduating high school. After the war, he lettered in football, baseball, basketball and track at Baldwin-Wallace College in his hometown. Norb was a two-time Little All-American and was selected in the sixth round of the 1951 NFL draft by the Rams. Hecker played safety for Los Angeles from 1951 to 1953, picking off 11 passes. He spent 1954 with Toronto of the CFL and then the next three years with the Redskins, for whom he nabbed 17 interceptions. Norb also was involved in organizing the NFL Players' Association before returning to the CFL in 1958 as a player/assistant coach for the Hamilton Tiger Cats.

Hecker then joined Lombardi's first Green Bay staff in 1959 and stayed through the 1965 season, as the Packers won titles in 1961, 1962 and 1965. Hecker went from first to worst in 1966 when the expansion Falcons named him as their first head coach in a bit of a surprise. Most observers were expecting Atlanta to hire Cowboys' assistant Red Hickey. Norb told the press, "You cannot have a team in the NFL without discipline, And I will follow Lombardi in this." He also noted, "Some of the players we get will be from championship clubs, some from chronic losers. The players from championship clubs will have to help instill this desire in the losers and the kids." That hope didn't materialize.

Hecker's tenure was dominated by poor personnel decisions. He drafted Randy Johnson as his franchise quarterback in 1966 and that did not pan out. Worse still, he completely whiffed on the 1967

draft, with none of his 16 draft picks that year spending any appreciable time in the NFL. Three games into the 1968 season, Norb was fired and replaced by an old Ram teammate, Norm Van Brocklin. Hecker subsequently served as the defensive coach for the Giants from 1969 to 1971 before jumping to Stanford in 1972. Hecker coached for five years under Jack Christiansen in Palo Alto and then was retained on the staff when Bill Walsh took over in 1977. Two years later when Walsh moved to the 49ers, Hecker came with him. Norb coached in San Francisco from 1979 to 1986 and then worked in the front office until 1991. Four years later, he briefly came out of retirement to coach and manage the Amsterdam Admirals of the developmental World League.

HEFFERLE, ERNEST E. (ERNIE) 1/12/1915– 8/8/2000. Duquesne. E; did not play in the NFL. *Apprenticeship:* College coach —15 years (2 as head coach); pro asst.— 6 years. *Roots:* Mike Nixon. *Branches:* None. *Coordinators/Key Assistants:* None. *Hall of Fame Players:* None. *Primary Quarterbacks:* None. *Record:* **Interim Coach.**

Born in Herminic, Pennsylvania, Ernie Hefferle once summed up his simple football philosophy to Mike Ditka at Pitt as, "Beat the crap out of the guy across from you." Another former Pitt end, Joe Walton, said at Ernie's funeral, "He was the type of guy who was your friend and confidant except during practice. At practice, he was a taskmaster, a wonderful teacher of basic skills. He was a real tough guy with a great heart." Hefferle starred at end for Duquesne from 1934 to 1936 and caught the game-winning 72-yard touchdown pass in the 1937 Orange Bowl against Mississippi State. Ernie spent the next 14 years, aside from three in the Navy during the war, coaching high school football in Western Pennsylvania. In 1951, he moved up to the college ranks at Pitt and worked as line coach for three different Panther coaches through 1958. In 1959, he joined his friend Mike Nixon's Redskins' staff and then a year later was named head coach of Boston College in 1960. Hefferle only attained a 7–

Hecker, Norbert E. (Norb)

Year	Team	Games	Wins	Losses	Ties	%	P Wins	P Losses	P %
1966	Falcons	14	3	11	0	.214	0	0	.000
1967	Falcons	14	1	12	1	.107	0	0	.000
1968	Falcons	3	0	3	0	.000	0	0	.000
3 years		31	4	26	1	.145	0	0	.000

Hefferle, Ernest E. (Ernie)

Year	Team	Games	Wins	Losses	Ties	%	P Wins	P Losses	P %
1975	Saints	8	1	7	.000	.125	0	0	.000
1 year		8	1	7	.000	.125	0	0	.000

12–1 record at BC, despite uncovering scrambling quarterback Jack Concannon. By 1962, Ernie was back at Pitt, working as an assistant for three more years. Then in 1965, he again joined the staff of his friend Mike Nixon, this time for the Steelers.

When Nixon was fired after one year, Hefferle caught on with George Wilson's first staff in Miami from 1966 to 1969 until Don Shula took over in 1970. Ernie returned to Pitt for the third time that year for two more seasons as the Panthers' line coach. Then in 1973, Hefferle joined the front office of the New Orleans Saints as their personnel director. Two years later with the Saints at 1–5, Ernie relieved John North as coach, saying, "I accept the challenge.... Whether we accomplish it or not, there's going to be one hell of a try." New Orleans won Hefferle's debut as head coach, beating Atlanta 23–7. Quarterback Archie Manning said that the coach "gave us a Knute Rockne speech before the game. I saw Derland Moore with tears in his eyes and I had goose bumps." The stirring speech wore off quickly when New Orleans played tougher competition, and the Saints lost their last seven games of 1975. Ernie returned to the front office the next year and stayed on as personnel director until he retired from football in 1983.

Hein, Melvin J. (Mel) 8/22/1909–1/31/1992. Washington State. Played C for the Giants from 1931 to 1945. *Apprenticeship:* College head coach — 3 years; pro asst.—1 year. *Roots:* Dudley DeGroot. *Branches:* None. *Coordinators/Key Assistants:* Hein was an interim co-coach with Ted Shipkey. *Hall of Fame Players:* None. *Primary Quarterbacks:* None. *Record:* **Hall of Fame Player; Interim Co-Coach** (with Ted Shipkey).

Fifteen-year 60-minute man Mel Hein once claimed, "I can't prove this with any statistics, but I may have played more minutes than anybody in pro football history." A center on offense and linebacker on defense, Hein was an All-American teammate of Turk Edwards at Washington State and played in the 1931 Rose Bowl before turning pro. He signed first with the Providence Steam Roller but quickly recalled that letter and signed with the Giants instead. With New York, Hein was an eight-time All Pro and even was named league MVP in the Giants' championship season of 1938.

Mel first tried to retire from playing in 1943 when he accepted the head coaching position at Union College in Schenectady, but then Union cancelled football

that year due to the war. Union reinstated football in 1944, so Hein at last began his coaching career. However, with the lack of available manpower during the war, the Giants still needed him as a player. Mel spent that year taking the train to New York on Sundays to play pro football, while coaching college ball the rest of the week. Union dropped football again in 1945, so Hein continued playing through the 1945 season until retiring. Mel retired from playing after the 1945 season and spent one more year coaching Union, posting an overall 3–10 record, before returning to the West Coast as the line coach for Dudley DeGroot on the Los Angeles Dons of the rival All America Football Conference in 1947.

As it turned out, the relationship between De-Groot and team owner Ben Lindheimer deteriorated to the point where Ben had his daughter Marge begin sitting in on team meetings and practices. The culmination came in the 11th game of the year against the Yankees. Marge ordered DeGroot to the stands, while she went on the field with the team and had assistant coaches Hein and Ted Shipkey make all substitutions and game decisions. Predictably, DeGroot quit when the team returned to Los Angeles and his assistants were named as the team's co-coaches.

Hein remained on staff under new coach Jimmy Phelan in 1948, but then came east again in 1949 as Red Strader's line coach on the Yankees of the AAFC. When the two leagues merged in 1950, Hein went back west as Joe Stydahar's line coach on the Rams. One year later, Mel moved to a different office in the Coliseum as USC's line coach and stayed there for 15 years — mirroring the time he spent with the Giants. At Southern California, he met Al Davis who was the Trojans' end coach in the late 1950s. Several years later, Davis was named American Football League Commissioner in 1966 and hired Hein as supervisor of the AFL's officials. Mel continued in the job when it evolved into head of the AFC officials after the NFL-AFL merger. He retired in 1975 as the patriarch of an athletic family. Hein's son Mel Jr. once set a world indoor pole vault record, and his grandson Gary was a World Cup rugby player. Mel died in 1992 from stomach cancer, sadly having wasted away from 230 to 130 pounds before he died.

Henderson, Elmer C. (Gus) 3/10/1889– 12/16/1965. Oberlin. Did not play professionally. *Apprenticeship:* College head coach —17 years; AFL II

Hein, Melvin J. (Mel)									
Year	Team	Games	Wins	Losses	Ties	%	P Wins	P Losses	P %
1947	Los Angeles Dons (AAFC)	3	2	1	0	.667	0	0	.000
1 year		3	2	1	0	.667	0	0	.000

head coach —1 year. *Roots:* None. *Branches:* None. *Co-ordinators/Key Assistants*: Hunk Anderson coached the line. *Hall of Fame Players:* Alex Wojciechowicz. *Primary Quarterbacks:* None. *Tendencies:* • His team scored 13.2 points and allowed 13.6 per game • His team ran 64.1% of the time, which was 99% of the league average • Three rookie starters in one year • Winning Full Seasons to Losing Full Seasons: 1:0.

Gloomy Gus Henderson received his nickname for his tendency to poormouth his team's chances in the next game, no matter how weak a future opponent was. However, Gus was one of the game's early offensive innovators, and his teams were explosive and dangerous. His coaching career began because he took a proactive approach by coaching the Oberlin high school team while he was playing as an undergraduate at Oberlin College in 1910 and 1911. Henderson was an Oberlin native and graduated from his hometown college in 1912. That year, he coached the Chamberlin Military Academy in New York and then coached high school football in Seattle for the next six years until joining the Navy in 1918.

After World War I, Henderson was named head coach of Southern California and elevated the Trojans to national prominence between 1919 and 1924 with a 45–7 record. It was at USC that Gus first became noted for his wide open spread formation, ideal for passing and laterals — not to mention double laterals and reverses. He led USC to the 1923 Rose Bowl where his team defeated Penn State 14–3 after the two head coaches, Henderson and Hugo Bezdek, got into a fist fight prior to the game. Despite Henderson's great success in Los Angeles — he still has the highest winning percentage of any USC coach — the university bought out the remaining year of Gus' contract after the 1924 season because he could not beat California. Five of USC's seven losses under Henderson were to the Golden Bears.

He took his creative spread offense to Tulsa in 1925 and led the Golden Hurricane to a 70–25–5 record from 1925 to 1935, elevating a second college program to national prominence. Gus subsequently returned to LA in 1936 as head coach of an independent pro team, the Los Angeles Bulldogs. In 1937, the Bulldogs joined the second American Football League and finished first with an 8–0 record. When the league folded, the Bulldogs returned to independent status in 1938. Over the three years that Gus coached the team, the Bulldogs unofficially went 44–5.

Hired by the Lions in 1939, Henderson got the

team off to a 6–1 start, averaging 16.5 points per game and allowing just 10 per game. At that point, Henderson and his defensive assistant Hunk Anderson had a rancorous falling out that divided the whole team. Detroit dropped the last four games of the season, averaging just 7.5 points per game while giving up 20 per game. What really did Gus in, though, was the 1940 NFL draft. Owner Dick Richards explicitly instructed Henderson to select center Bulldog Turner in the first round, but Gus decided he preferred USC quarterback Doyle Nave and picked him instead. Richards then fired Henderson, so Gus told acting NFL president Carl Storck that Richards had made improper pre-draft payments to Turner. Storck then fined Richards, but the Detroit owner sold the team instead. Parenthetically, Nave never played in the NFL, but Turner was a Hall of Famer with the Bears.

Henderson again returned to Los Angeles in 1940, this time to coach Occidental College. In three years at the school, Henderson went 11–10–2 before the football program was discontinued for the war. Gus coached the Los Angeles Wildcats to a 2–4–2 record in the third American Football League in 1944 and then retired from coaching and eventually moved to the desert.

HENNING, DANIEL E. (DAN) 6/21/1942–
William & Mary. Played QB for the Chargers in 1966. *Apprenticeship:* College asst.— 6 years; pro asst.— 8 years. *Roots:* Bill Peterson, Lou Holtz, Walt Michaels, Don Shula, Joe Gibbs. *Branches:* Gunther Cunningham, Jim Mora, Jr. *Coordinators/Key Assistants*: For the Falcons, Bob Fry helped coach the offense, while Jim Marshall then Marion Campbell ran the defense; for the Chargers, Henning ran the offense, while Ron Lynn handled the defense. *Hall of Fame Players:* None. *Primary Quarterbacks:* Steve Bartkowski, David Archer, Billy Joe Tolliver. *Tendencies:* • His teams scored 18.5 points and allowed 21.6 per game • His teams ran 48.4% of the time, which was 104% of the league average • Eight starting quarterbacks in seven years; 72% of starts to primary quarterbacks • 31 rookie starters in seven years • Winning Full Seasons to Losing Full Seasons: 0:7.

When Dan Henning was hired for his second head coaching job, he tried to defend his .352 winning percentage to San Diego reporters by saying, "Take Bill Walsh's first 35 games in San Francisco and someone might have said he's not a good football coach." It's true that Walsh was 9–26 (.257) in his first 35 games, but at this point Henning had coached 64

Henderson, Elmer C. (Gus)									
Year	*Team*	*Games*	*Wins*	*Losses*	*Ties*	*%*	*P Wins*	*P Losses*	*P %*
1939	Lions	11	6	5	0	.545	0	0	.000
1 year		11	6	5	0	.545	0	0	.000

games; when Walsh reached 64 games, he had already won a Super Bowl and his winning percentage was nearing .500. Henning was one of the very best offensive coordinators in the game, but failed miserably as a head coach in two cities.

The Bronx-born Henning starred at quarterback at William & Mary in the early 1960s and earned a tryout with the Chargers in 1964. After Sid Gillman cut Dan, he played in the Continental League for two years before winning a spot as a backup quarterback for San Diego in 1966. The following year he was beaten out as backup in San Diego by Kay Stephenson and returned to the Continental League for one last year as a player.

Henning began his coaching career in 1968 with Florida State under Bill Peterson. He spent three years there and one with Virginia Tech before reuniting with Peterson as an assistant in Houston in 1972. Returning to the college ranks a year later, Dan worked at Virginia Tech again in 1973 and Florida State again in 1974. By 1975, he was out of football, working for a security firm at the World Trade Center. Dan got back in the NFL in 1976, working under Lou Holtz and Walt Michaels for the Jets through 1978, under Don Shula in Miami during 1979 and 1980 and then under Joe Gibbs in 1981 and 1982. After the Redskins won the Super Bowl, Henning was hired by Atlanta as head coach on the same day that his old quarterback rival Kay Stephenson was hired as head coach by the Bills.

With the Falcons, Dan established the same one-back set that Washington ran, but without the same success. He was popular with the players, but could not manage a winning record. The only reason he got extended for a fourth season in Atlanta was that he convinced Marion Campbell to come south and take over the defense in 1986. As it turned out, Campbell did such a nice job with the defense that he was named head coach in 1987, while Henning went back to Washington and won another Super Bowl as an assistant. Just two years later, he got his second chance as head coach with San Diego.

The Chargers were a better overall team than the Falcons, but in three years, Dan completely lost control of the team. Defensive end Burt Grossman told the *New York Times* later, "It was like prisoners running

the ship. Did what we wanted. Under Henning, guys lay down on practice dummies, talking on their cellular phones or playing Nintendo." Fired by the Chargers in 1992, Dan worked for two years on the Lions' staff before being named head coach at Boston College in 1994, succeeding Tom Coughlin. Henning lasted three years, but the combination of BC's 16–19–1 record and an embarrassing betting scandal involving several players led to his resignation in 1997. Since then, he has worked for Buffalo in 1997, the Jets from 1998 to 2000, Carolina from 2002 to 2006 and Miami from 2008 to 2010.

Two of his most celebrated bosses sung his praises. Joe Gibbs told the *Washington Post*, "I feel like he's got as sharp and as quick a mind as there is in football." Bill Parcells, who Henning has known since Florida State, once told the *New York Daily News*, "I love the guy. If I needed an offensive coordinator, he'd be the first guy I'd go to." In short, Henning won the respect of his peers as one of the best assistant coaches in football; as an NFL head coach, he never had a winning season.

HICKEY, HOWARD W. (RED) 2/14/1917–3/30/2006. Arkansas. Played E for the Steelers and Rams in 1941 and from 1945 to 1948. *Apprenticeship:* Pro asst.—10 years. *Roots:* Clark Shaughnessy, Joe Stydahar, Hampton Pool, Red Strader, Frankie Albert. *Branches:* Jack Christiansen, Bill Johnson. *Coordinators/Key Assistants:* Bill Johnson helped with the offense, while Jack Christiansen ran the defense. *Hall of Fame Players:* Jim Johnson, Hugh McElhenny, Leo Nomellini, Joe Perry, Bob St. Clair, Y.A. Tittle. *Primary Quarterbacks:* John Brodie. *Tendencies:* • His teams scored 20.7 points and allowed 20.6 per game • His teams ran 55.1% of the time, which was 105% of the league average • Two starting quarterbacks in five years; 75% of starts to primary quarterback • 17 rookie starters in five years • Winning Full Seasons to Losing Full Seasons: 3:1.

Red Hickey was born in Clarksville, Arkansas, and played both football and basketball for the Razorbacks. He began his NFL career with the Steelers in 1941, but was dealt to the Rams that same year. Hickey spent the next three years in the Navy during the war before returning to the Rams for their cham-

Henning, Daniel E. (Dan)									
Year	Team	Games	Wins	Losses	Ties	%	P Wins	P Losses	P %
1983	Falcons	16	7	9	0	.438	0	0	.000
1984	Falcons	16	4	12	0	.250	0	0	.000
1985	Falcons	16	4	12	0	.250	0	0	.000
1986	Falcons	16	7	8	1	.469	0	0	.000
1989	Chargers	16	6	10	0	.375	0	0	.000
1990	Chargers	16	6	10	0	.375	0	0	.000
1991	Chargers	16	4	12	0	.250	0	0	.000
7 years		112	38	73	1	.344	0	0	.000

pionship season of 1945. His best year as a player was his last, catching 30 passes in 1948 opposite Tom Fears. In 1949, Red moved onto the Rams' coaching staff, and he coached two Hall of Fame receivers for the next six years, Fears and Elroy Hirsch. In December 1954, Hickey and three other assistants resigned in bitter conflict with head coach Hamp Pool. Pool himself resigned two weeks later, but Hickey traveled up the coast to join Red Strader's 49ers' staff in 1955. Strader was replaced by Frankie Albert one year later, and then Albert himself resigned, and Red was promoted to head coach in 1959.

Today, Hickey is remembered for two innovations that arose in San Francisco. First, was the "Alley Oop" play that came about by accident in practice in 1957 when Red was coaching the offense. Essentially, this play was a Hail Mary jump ball thrown high to former basketball player R.C. Owens who would leap above the defenders to snag the ball. The second innovation was the Shotgun offense that Hickey implemented late in the 1960 season to defeat a superior Colts team. Hickey first called the offense simply a spread formation, but with prodding from sportswriters he gave it the snazzier name of the Shotgun. Red was so confident in his new offense that he traded veteran quarterback Y.A. Tittle during the 1961 preseason so that he could spread the snaps among his three young quarterbacks — John Brodie, Billy Kilmer and Bob Waters.

San Francisco won four of its first five games in 1961 and was scoring 36 points a game alternating those three quarterbacks play by play. Then the Bears came in and shut down the Shotgun with strong pressure up the middle. The 49ers did not win again for five weeks and fell out of the division race. Hickey insisted that it was the team that failed and not the Shotgun, but he basically junked the offense by the end of the year. Red had his first losing season in 1962 and then lost both Brodie and Kilmer to car accidents by the start of 1963. With the team also riddled by dissension, Hickey quit

after losing the first three games of the season, saying, "In this game you either win or move on."

Red joined Tom Landry's staff in Dallas for the next two years and was the favorite to become the first coach of the expansion Falcons in 1966, but Atlanta surprised everyone by picking Norb Hecker instead. Hickey retired from coaching altogether at this point and became the Cowboys top scout from 1966 until he retired in 1982. Red did return to the sidelines briefly in 1975 to install the Shotgun in Dallas with Roger Staubach. 14 years after the Shotgun's short lived debut, Staubach and the Cowboys employed the offense so effectively on passing downs that it has since become a staple in most offenses. The Shotgun remains Red Hickey's legacy in the NFL.

HOLLWAY, ROBERT (BOB) 1/29/1926–3/13/1999. Michigan. E; did not play professionally. *Apprenticeship:* College asst.—15 years; pro asst.— 4 years. *Roots:* Bud Grant. *Branches:* Leeman Bennett. *Coordinators/ Key Assistants:* Lew Carpenter handled the offense, while Dick Voris ran the defense. *Hall of Fame Players:* Dan Dierdorf, Jackie Smith, Roger Wehrli, Larry Wilson. *Primary Quarterbacks:* Jim Hart. *Tendencies:* • His teams scored 15.1 points and allowed 20.8 per game • His teams ran 49.4% of the time, which was 90% of the league average • Four starting quarterbacks in two years; 43% of starts to primary quarterback • 12 rookie starters in two years • Winning Full Seasons to Losing Full Seasons: 0:2.

Ann Arbor's own Bob Hollway got to play in two Rose Bowls while playing end for Michigan from 1946 to 1949 He began his coaching career a year later at the University of Maine from 1951 to 1952 and then moved on to Eastern Michigan in 1953. Bob returned to his alma mater in 1954 and coached there for the next dozen years under Bennie Oosterbaan and Bump Elliott. After a year out of football in private business, Hollway joined the staff of new Vikings' coach Bud

Hickey, Howard W. (Red)

Year	Team	Games	Wins	Losses	Ties	%	P Wins	P Losses	P %
1959	49ers	12	7	5	0	.583	0	0	.000
1960	49ers	12	7	5	0	.583	0	0	.000
1961	49ers	14	7	6	1	.536	0	0	.000
1962	49ers	14	6	8	0	.429	0	0	.000
1963	49ers	3	0	3	0	.000	0	0	.000
5 years		55	27	27	1	.500	0	0	.000

Hollway, Robert (Bob)

Year	Team	Games	Wins	Losses	Ties	%	P Wins	P Losses	P %
1971	Cardinals	14	4	9	1	.321	0	0	.000
1972	Cardinals	14	4	9	1	.321	0	0	.000
2 years		28	8	18	2	.321	0	0	.000

Grant in 1967. Bob's expertise was defense, and he built the Purple People Eaters front four that was the strength of Minnesota's defense for the next decade.

After four years of running the Vikings defense, Hollway was named head coach of the St. Louis Cardinals in 1971. At this time, the Cardinals were divided by a front office battle for control between the Bidwill brothers. All of the finalists for the job were actually given psychological tests as part of the hiring procedure. At his hiring, Bob told the press, "My observations of the Cardinals are that they are a team with great speed. Because of this, we may not have to be quite as conservative as we were much of the time in Minnesota." Indeed, the Cardinals passed the ball 10% more than the league average under Hollway. However, the coach seemed to have trouble sorting through his skill players. Runner Macarthur Lane and receiver John Gilliam were dealt away after one year. Young speed receiver Mel Gray was underutilized, while Hollway had interpersonal issues with rookie Bobby Moore (later known as Ahmad Rashad) who regularly questioned his coach's moves. While he was brusk like Grant, Bob lacked Bud's personal touch with the players. Furthermore, Hollway could not decide on a quarterback, shuffling between, Jim Hart, Pete Beathard, Gary Cuozzo and Tim Van Galder in two seasons.

Hollway had been Stormy Bidwill's choice. Once Bill Bidwill won the brothers' ownership battle, it was just a matter of time till Bob was fired. To put special emphasis on the move, Bidwill had the locks of the coach's office changed when he fired Holloway. Bob had no trouble catching on as defensive line coach with Detroit from 1973 to 1974, with San Francisco in 1975 and with Seattle from 1976 to 1977. Seattle's head coach was Jack Patera who had coached with Bob in Min-

nesota. When Hollway returned to Minnesota as defensive coordinator in 1978, the jilted Seahawks accused the Vikings of tampering. Bob served as Minnesota's defensive coordinator from 1978 to 1985 and then was appointed personnel director in 1986. When he was forced to retire in 1993, the 67-year-old Hollway filed suit on age discrimination grounds. He returned to the sidelines in 1995 to help out his son Mike, head coach of Ohio Wesleyan University. While Bob passed away in 1999, Mike has coached the Battling Bishops since 1988, having won over 130 games through 2010.

HOLMGREN, MICHAEL G. (MIKE) 6/15/1948– Southern California. QB; did not play professionally. *Apprenticeship:* College asst.— 5 years; pro asst.— 6 years. *Roots:* Bill Walsh, George Seifert. *Branches:* Ray Rhodes, Steve Mariucci, Jon Gruden, Dick Jauron, Andy Reid, Mike Sherman, Marty Mornhinweg, Jim Zorn. *Coordinators/Key Assistants*: Holmgren ran his own offense with Sherm Lewis as offensive coordinator for the Packers, and Mike Sherman then Gil Haskell for the Seahawks; Ray Rhodes then Fritz Shurmur handled the defense for the Packers, while Shurmur then Steve Sidwell then Rhodes then John Marshall handled the Seahawks defense. *Hall of Fame Players:* Cortez Kennedy, John Randle, Jerry Rice, Reggie White. *Primary Quarterbacks:* Brett Favre, Matt Hasselbeck. *Record:* Super Bowl Championship 1996. *Tendencies:* • His teams scored 23 points and allowed 19.8 per game • His teams ran 43.7% of the time, which was 99% of the league average • Nine starting quarterbacks in 17 years; 78% of starts to primary quarterbacks • 30 rookie starters in 17 years • Winning Full Seasons to Losing Full Seasons: 14:3.

Packer GM Ron Wolf wrote of his coach Mike

Holmgren, Michael G. (Mike)									
Year	Team	Games	Wins	Losses	Ties	%	P Wins	P Losses	P %
1992	Packers	16	9	7	0	.563	0	0	.000
1993	Packers	16	9	7	0	.563	1	1	.500
1994	Packers	16	9	7	0	.563	1	1	.500
1995	Packers	16	11	5	0	.688	2	1	.667
1996	Packers	16	13	3	0	.813	3	0	1.000
1997	Packers	16	13	3	0	.813	2	1	.667
1998	Packers	16	11	5	0	.688	0	1	.000
1999	Seahawks	16	9	7	0	.563	0	1	.000
2000	Seahawks	16	6	10	0	.375	0	0	.000
2001	Seahawks	16	9	7	0	.563	0	0	.000
2002	Seahawks	16	7	9	0	.438	0	0	.000
2003	Seahawks	16	10	6	0	.625	0	1	.000
2004	Seahawks	16	9	7	0	.563	0	1	.000
2005	Seahawks	16	13	3	0	.813	2	1	.667
2006	Seahawks	16	9	7	0	.563	1	1	.500
2007	Seahawks	16	10	6	0	.625	1	1	.500
2008	Seahawks	16	4	12	0	.250	0	0	.000
17 years		272	161	111	0	.592	13	11	.542

Holmgren in *The Packer Way*, "He fills a room with a presence that you can't manufacture. He has that Bill Walsh type of confidence where you feel he just knows what he does is right.... His personality was far different from Bill Walsh's — he's much more outgoing and loquacious — but he had the same cockiness." For his part, Walsh told David Harris in *The Genius*, "Mike and I exchanged openly and he had a better feel for football than anyone I knew. It wasn't difficult to hire him. He was obviously the man."

For someone with such obvious qualities, it took a long while for Mike Holmgren to get noticed. The 6′5″ San Francisco native was one of the top quarterbacks in California in high school and attended Southern California at the same time as O.J. Simpson, but watched from the sidelines as the backup to quarterback Steve Sogge for two years and then to Jimmy Jones as a senior in 1969. Still, Mike was drafted in the eighth round by the Cardinals in 1970. After washing out of training camp with both the Cards and Jets, though, Holmgren tried selling real estate and cars during 1970. In 1971, he took an assistant coaching job at his alma mater, Lincoln High School in San Francisco. Throughout the decade of the 1970s, Mike coached at three different California high schools before moving up to San Francisco State in 1981 as an assistant coach. One year later, he was hired as quarterbacks coach at pass-happy BYU where he tutored Steve Young and Robbie Bosco — as well as a studious offensive tackle named Andy Reid — over the next four years. That brought Mike to Bill Walsh's attention, and Bill hired him as quarterbacks coach with the 49ers in 1986.

In San Francisco, Holmgren learned the West Coast Offense from the master and coached two of the greatest quarterbacks in NFL history, Joe Montana and Steve Young. In particular, Mike developed and polished Young, his BYU confederate, and Young appreciated it. He told Brad Adler in *Coaching Matters*, "Mike is one of the best coaches ever, because he understands people. He can sit down and have a conversation with somebody and know what kind of football player they are." Holmgren won his first Super Bowl ring as the 49ers' quarterbacks coach in Walsh's last year, 1988. When George Seifert succeeded Walsh, he promoted Mike to offensive coordinator. Mike won a second ring that year and began to be mentioned in connection with NFL coaching vacancies. Holmgren remained in San Francisco until Ron Wolf offered him the Packers job in 1992.

At that time, Green Bay had recorded just four winning seasons in the 25 years since Vince Lombardi retired from coaching the team, and there was growing doubt of the continued viability of the franchise in the modern NFL. Wolf and Holmgren turned that perception and attitude completely around to the point that the Packers have had just two losing seasons in the 19 years since 1992. The excellence established

by Wolf and Holmgren has continued on long since they both left Wisconsin in the late 1990s. Wolf made three critical moves in transforming the Packers: hiring Holmgren in 1992, trading for Brett Favre the same year and signing Reggie White as a free agent in 1993. Holmgren took the pieces Wolf was supplying and put together a winning team in his first year. While Favre was raw and undisciplined, Mike worked with him and transformed Brett into a Hall of Fame quarterback. Holmgren's Packers advanced a new step almost every year — a winning team in 1992, the playoffs in 1993, 11 wins and the NFC championship game in 1995, 13 wins and a Super Bowl win in 1996, 13 wins and a repeat Super Bowl trip in 1997. However, Green Bay was upset by Denver in that second Super Bowl appearance largely because Holmgren refused to adjust to the Broncos extensive blitz scheme, and it was a great missed opportunity — the chance to mark the team as something truly special. Green Bay slipped back to 11 wins in 1998, and Holmgren made it clear he wanted more responsibility for obtaining the players.

With his Packers' contract up, Mike signed with Seattle as head coach and general manager in 1999. After four years holding both jobs, though, Holmgren's record in Seattle was 31–33 — the same achieved by previous Seahawks' coach Dennis Erickson. At that point, owner Paul Allen took away Holmgren's GM responsibilities, leaving him to concentrate fully on coaching. The team went 51–29 over the next five years, including five straight trips to the playoffs and one to the Super Bowl. The Seahawks were led by former Packers' backup quarterback Matt Hasselbeck, whom Holmgren had obtained in 2001 and molded into an NFL quarterback. In 2008, Mike turned 60 and announced he would not coach beyond the end of his contract that year; defensive coach Jim Mora, Jr., was named as his successor. Predictably, Holmgren's lame duck year was a 4–12 disappointment. After one year out of the game, Mike rekindled his competitive fire and returned in 2010 as the team president in Cleveland, trying to turn around another sorry franchise.

Above all, Holmgren as coach was known as a teacher who got the most out of his players and coaches and made them better in turn. Indeed, eight of Mike's assistants in Green Bay and Seattle became NFL coaches themselves. Holmgren's accomplishments were substantial. He helped the West Coast Offense evolve in San Francisco, Green Bay and Seattle, trained three Hall of Fame quarterbacks and took two different downtrodden franchises to the Super Bowl.

HOLOVAK, MICHAEL J. (MIKE) 9/19/1919–1/27/2008. Boston College. Played FB for the Rams and Bears from 1946 to 1948. *Apprenticeship:* College coach — 11 years (9 as head coach); pro asst. — 2 years. *Roots:* Lou Saban. *Branches:* Marion Campbell, Fred Bruney (i). *Coordinators/Key Assistants:* Holovak ran his own offense, while a succession of three former Eagles coached the defense: Marion Campbell, Chuck Weber and Jess Richardson. *Hall of Fame Players:* Nick Buoniconti, Joe Namath. *Primary Quarterbacks:* Babe Parilli. *Tendencies:* • His teams scored 22 points and allowed 22.7 per game • His teams ran 47.4% of the time, which was 103% of the league average • Eight starting quarterbacks in nine years; 75% of starts to primary quarterback • 19 rookie starters in nine years • Winning Full Seasons to Losing Full Seasons: 5:3.

Mike Holovak was a coal miner's son from Lansford, Pennsylvania who played fullback for Boston College under Frank Leahy and Denny Myers and was drafted in the first round by the Rams in 1943. However, the Rams did not field a team that year, and Mike spent the next three years in the Pacific Ocean as a Lieutenant Commander on a PT boat. Oddly, one of his shipmates was another future NFL coach, Wally Lemm. Holovak joined the defending champion Rams in 1946 and then was obtained by the defending champion Bears in 1947. Unfortunately, those two seasons were the closest Mike ever came to being part of a championship team in his 42 years in pro football.

After two years in Chicago, Holovak retired to become the freshman coach at his alma mater in 1949. Two years later, he replaced Myers as BC's head coach. In nine years from 1951 to 1959, the Eagles were 49–29–3 under Mike, but he was forced to resign after the 1959 season due to conflicts with school administrators. Two weeks later, though, the fledgling Boston Patriots of the new American Football League hired Holovak as a scout. By the Patriots' first training camp in 1960, head coach Lou Saban added Mike to his staff as backfield coach. Five games into 1961, Saban was fired, and Holovak took over the struggling team. Receiver/kicker Gino Cappelletti later told the *Boston Globe,* "From that day, the morale went sky high among the players. As a coach, he had the ability to really have you believe in yourself. Having been a player himself, and a good one, he just seemed to know how to get the most out of his players."

Holovak at first experimented with alternating veteran quarterbacks Babe Parilli and BC's Butch Songin, but eventually settled on Parilli. Babe called his own plays because, as Mike told *Sports Illustrated,* "All I would do by sending in plays from the sideline would be to destroy the continuity of his thinking. He knows more of what is going on from the field than I do from the bench." The heavy blitzing Patriots finished in the top three in points allowed four times. That defense combined with Boston's strong passing attack to fashion four second place finishes in the decade. In 1963, Holovak led the Pats to the AFL championship game, but they were blasted 51–10 by the Chargers in that mismatch. Mike stressed unity, camaraderie and family to his team and got the best effort from his players. The two-time AFL Coach of the Year told *Sports Illustrated,* "If I have any secret, it's that we work hard and this team is gifted with fellows who stick together and believe in themselves. We can play anybody to a standstill, and we know it."

By 1968, though, the team was aging and a series of poor drafts had depleted their talent level. Holovak was fired and moved on as an assistant in San Francisco in 1969 and 1970 and in Oakland in 1971. Mike returned to scouting in 1972 with the Jets, but then joined their coaching staff for the next two years. In 1975, he returned to New York's front office, but was enlisted to coach the last game of 1976 after Lou Holtz resigned. The next year, Holovak came back to the Patriots as head scout and stayed through 1980. In 1981, Bud Adams hired Mike for the Oilers' front office, and he was promoted to GM in 1989 at the age of 70. Five years later in 1994, Holovak returned to scouting for Houston until he retired in 1998 at 79. He died ten years later and was recalled by longtime Oiler/Titan lineman Bruce Matthews, "I can't tell you how much I respected Mike. Not only was he a great personnel man who played a big role in our success with the Oilers and Titans, but he was such a kind man, a devoted family man."

HOLTZ, LOUIS L. (LOU) 1/6/1937– Kent State. LB; did not play professionally. *Apprenticeship:* College coach—16 years (7 as head coach). *Roots:* None. *Branches:* Walt Michaels, Dan Henning. *Coordinators/*

Holovak, Michael J. (Mike)									
Year	*Team*	*Games*	*Wins*	*Losses*	*Ties*	*%*	*P Wins*	*P Losses*	*P %*
1961	Patriots	9	7	1	1	.833	0	0	.000
1962	Patriots	14	9	4	1	.679	0	0	.000
1963	Patriots	14	7	6	1	.536	1	1	.500
1964	Patriots	14	10	3	1	.750	0	0	.000
1965	Patriots	14	4	8	2	.357	0	0	.000
1966	Patriots	14	8	4	2	.643	0	0	.000
1967	Patriots	14	3	10	1	.250	0	0	.000
1968	Patriots	14	4	10	0	.286	0	0	.000
1976	Jets	1	0	1	0	.000	0	0	.000
9 years		108	52	47	9	.523	1	1	.500

Key Assistants: Holtz ran his own offense, while Walt Michaels handled the defense. *Hall of Fame Players:* Joe Namath. *Primary Quarterbacks:* Joe Namath. *Tendencies:* • His team scored 12.8 points and allowed 26.2 per game • His team ran 50% of the time, which was 89% of the league average • Two starting quarterbacks in one year; 54% of starts to primary quarterback • Six rookie starters in one year • Winning Full Seasons to Losing Full Seasons: 0:1.

It's hard to picture the 5'10" 150-pound Lou Holtz as a linebacker, but that's what he played at Kent State from 1956 to 1957. Clever and wiry, Holtz was better suited to coaching. He had a 45-year career coaching, 36 of it as head coach, and racked up a 249–132–7 record in the college ranks. He led six different programs to bowl games, four schools to a top 20 ranking and one, Notre Dame, to a national championship. As a college coach, he was elected to the College Football Hall of Fame in 2008. As a pro head coach, though, he was an admitted complete failure.

Holtz began his coaching career at Iowa in 1960 under Forrest Evashevski, then worked under Jim Drewer at William & Mary from 1961 to 1963, under Rick Forzano at Connecticut from 1964 to 1965, under Paul Dietzel at South Carolina from 1966 to 1967 and under Woody Hayes at Ohio State in 1968. He got his first head coaching job in 1969 with William & Mary, succeeding Marv Levy. Lou went 13–20 in three years at William & Mary then went 33–12–3 from 1972 to 1975 at North Carolina State running the Veer offense.

Despite the fact that Holtz's teams did not run a pro style offense, the Jets hired him in 1976 as the offensive wizard that would resurrect the franchise. Lou was hopelessly out of place in the pro game and made one misstep after another. He wrote a team fight song for the Jets and tried to get the reticent players to sing it. He drafted the undersized Buckey twins who he had coached at NC State and tried to use them running the Veer. He delayed the development of rookie quarterback Richard Todd by having him pointlessly run the Veer. He took the play-calling away from Joe Namath and repeatedly flip-flopped his quarterbacks. On top of his being so small in stature, these amateurish decisions ensured that Holtz never engendered any respect from his players. By December, rumors circulated that Lou was looking for a way out. On the fifth of the month, he insisted that he would not quit; four days later, he resigned before the end of his first season and bolted for Arkansas just like Bobby Petrino would three decades later. In announcing his resignation, Holtz said, "God did not put Lou Holtz on this earth to coach pro football." That was clear to all Jets' fans.

After leaving pro football, Holtz coached Arkansas from 1977 to 1983, Minnesota from 1984 to 1985, Notre Dame from 1986 to 1996 and South Carolina from 1999 to 2004. His greatest success was at Arkansas where he went 60–21–2 and Notre Dame where he went 100–30–2; he posted losing records at Minnesota (10–17) and South Carolina (33–37). Known for his wit and for his chronic poor mouthing of his own team's chances, Holtz was a natural fit for ESPN's college football coverage and has worked regularly as a broadcaster since leaving coaching.

HOWELL, JAMES LEE (JIM LEE) 9/27/1914–1/4/1995. Arkansas. Played E for the Giants from 1937 to 1942 and from 1946 to 1947. *Apprenticeship:* College coach — 9 years (7 as head coach); pro asst.— 5 years. *Roots:* Steve Owen. *Branches:* Vince Lombardi, Tom Landry, Allie Sherman, Harland Svare. *Coordinators/Key Assistants:* Vince Lombardi then Allie Sherman ran the offense, while Tom Landry then Harland Svare handled the defense. *Hall of Fame Players:* Rosey Brown, Frank Gifford, Sam Huff, Don Maynard, Andy Robustelli, Emlen Tunnell. *Primary Quarterbacks:* Charley Conerly *Tendencies:* • His teams scored 22.4 points and allowed 17 per game • His teams ran 58.5% of

Holtz, Louis L. (Lou)

Year	Team	Games	Wins	Losses	Ties	%	P Wins	P Losses	P %
1976	Jets	13	3	10	0	.231	0	0	.000
1 year		13	3	10	0	.231	0	0	.000

Howell, James Lee (Jim Lee)

Year	Team	Games	Wins	Losses	Ties	%	P Wins	P Losses	P %
1954	Giants	12	7	5	0	.583	0	0	.000
1955	Giants	12	6	5	1	.542	0	0	.000
1956	Giants	12	8	3	1	.708	1	0	1.000
1957	Giants	12	7	5	0	.583	0	0	.000
1958	Giants	12	9	3	0	.750	1	1	.500
1959	Giants	12	10	2	0	.833	0	1	.000
1960	Giants	12	6	4	2	.583	0	0	.000
7 years		84	53	27	4	.655	2	2	.500

the time, which was 106% of the league average • Four starting quarterbacks in seven years; 76% of starts to primary quarterback • 12 rookie starters in seven years • Winning Full Seasons to Losing Full Seasons: 7:0.

Giants' receiver Kyle Rote told the story of walking down the hall in training camp and seeing defensive coach Tom Landry studying film in one room and offensive coach Vince Lombardi running the projector in another, while Head Coach Jim Lee Howell sat in a third room reading the newspaper. Comfortable in his own skin, the self-deprecating Howell often joked, "I just blow up the footballs and keep order." Actually, Jim Lee's organizational structure was one forerunner of the contemporary game; he was the supreme delegator, not a master strategist, but he was very successful in that style. Under him, the Giants never had a losing season and three times went to the championship game, winning it all in 1956.

Born in Lonoke, Arkansas, Howell was the epitome of the 1950s' company man. After graduating from the University of Arkansas where he had also starred in basketball, Jim Lee spent 1936 as an assistant coach at his alma mater. The 6'5" Howell signed with the Giants in 1937 and spent the rest of his working life commuting between his Arkansas cattle ranch and New York. Howell was a starting end under Coach Steve Owen from 1937 through 1947, aside from three years in the Pacific as a Marine company commander during World War II. He became the Giants' first end coach in 1948 and then succeeded the legendary Owen as head coach in 1954. Jim Lee already had gained some coaching experience by serving as an assistant at Manhattan College in 1940 and as the head coach at Wagner College from 1947 to 1953, with a 24–30–1 record. He also found time during the 1940s to serve in the Arkansas State Legislature.

As the Giants' coach, Howell was a disciplinarian with a booming voice who liked to perform his own bed checks, but he gave a lot of freedom to his celebrated assistant coaches. He liked to say that making fourth down decisions was his responsibility. No wallflower, Jim Lee rode star runner Frank Gifford mercilessly as a "California hotshot." Linebacker Sam Huff told Baker and Corbett for *The Most Memorable Games in Giants History,* "He did very little coaching. But he managed. He had Lombardi and Landry. He managed the coaches, which I later learned that head coaches do. That's what Jim Lee Howell did. He was an administrator." By contrast, African American defensive tackle Rosey Grier remembered him to Baker and Corbett as "the fairest coach I ever played for." Even if some stars like Huff and Frank Gifford did not care much for him, Howell was successful because of the team's talented players who were so ably directed by Lombardi and Landry.

As one of his first acts, Jim Lee talked quarterback Charlie Conerly out of retiring by promising him better pass protection, and the Giants' line did get better. In New York, Lombardi developed the offense he later would perfect in Green Bay, featuring option blocking, the power sweep and the half back option pass. Landry developed the 4–3 defense that would become the standard NFL base defense from that point forward and made a star out of his middle linebacker Huff by funneling all the action his way. Five times that defense finished in the top three in points allowed. In Howell's third year, the Giants swept to the NFL title by overwhelming the Bears 47–7 in the championship game.

Two years later, New York made a late-season drive to catch the Browns in the East and forced a playoff game. They won that game on a 49-yard Pat Summerall field goal ordered by Howell despite the driving snow. The Giants returned to the title game in 1958, but were defeated by the brilliance of Colts' quarterback Johnny Unitas in the first sudden death overtime game in NFL history. Perhaps appropriately, the day after the last-minute heroics of Unitas, Howell was photographed in his office shrugging his shoulders with a sheepish grin on his face. Lombardi left soon after that. New York and Baltimore met again for the championship in 1959; once again Baltimore rallied in the fourth quarter and won the title. Landry left shortly afterwards.

After six seasons, Howell announced that 1960 would be his last as coach. He told the press, "I am not sick, my wife didn't tell me to quit. I'm not mad at anyone, and I'm not unhappy, but there are other reasons. Defeat became more and more unbearable last year, although we had a pretty good season. My eyes were beginning to twitch from looking at so many football films that I now need glasses. Whenever I'd eat, my stomach would burn. I was not sleeping nights and I found myself becoming edgy, cantankerous and getting to arguing with everyone." Predictably, the 1960 season was anticlimactic with a lame duck coach and with Allie Sherman and Harland Svare running the offense and defense respectively. As an early victim of coaching burnout, Jim Lee moved up to the front office. Howell was the Giants' director of personnel from 1961 through 1979 and then served as a roving scout until 1986 when at last he retired, having spent 50 years with the Giants.

HUDSPETH, TOMMY JOE 9/14/1931– Tulsa. DB; did not play professionally. *Apprenticeship:* College coach—14 years (10 as head coach); CFL asst.—3 years; WFL asst.—1 year. *Roots:* None. *Branches:* Jerry Glanville, Joe Bugel, Bill Belichick. *Coordinators/Key Assistants:* Hudspeth handled his own offense, while Jim Carr then Fritz Shurmur ran the defense. *Hall of Fame Players:* Lem Barney, Charley Sanders. *Primary Quarterbacks:* Greg Landry *Tendencies:* • His teams scored 16.5 points and allowed 17.4 per game • His teams ran 53.6% of the time, which was 94% of the league average • Three starting quarterbacks in two years; 88% of starts to primary quarterback • Seven rookie starters in two years • Winning Full Seasons to Losing Full Seasons: 0:1.

Born in Cherryvale, Kansas, Tommy Hudspeth has been closely associated with Tulsa, Oklahoma throughout his life. Tommy was a three-year starter at defensive back for the Tulsa Golden Hurricane from 1950 to 1952. During the next four years, Hudspeth spent two years in the military and two coaching high school. In 1957, he returned to his alma mater as an assistant coach under Tulsa's legendary Glenn Dobbs. After four years, Tommy moved to Canada to serve on the Calgary Stampeders' staff of Bobby Dobbs, Glenn's brother. Three years in Calgary led to his getting the job of head coach at Brigham Young in 1964. Hudspeth coached BYU from 1964 to 1971, compiling a 39–42–1 record. Although his sideline temper tantrums were frowned on in Utah, Tommy opened up the BYU offense, and his best years came with national passing leader Virgil Carter in 1965 and 1966. Followed by his defensive coach LaVell Edwards, Hudspeth helped usher in a new era of BYU football.

Named offensive coordinator at Texas El Paso in 1972, Tommy took over as head coach with the team at 0–7 and finished 1–3 that year. Rehired in 1973, UTEP went 0–11 and Hudspeth was fired. He caught on as the backfield coach of the Chicago Fire in the WFL in 1974, coaching Virgil Carter again. The team went bankrupt by the end of the year, but Tommy landed the scouting director's job with the Lions in 1975. When Rick Forzano resigned as Detroit's coach four game into the 1976 season, Hudspeth replaced him, saying, "I will be demanding of our football team. We will work a lot harder. I will sit down with the staff and, like men, we will talk the situation over and see what needs to be done." Still, at the end of the year, the Lions made a strong push to hire Chuck Knox as head coach. Only when Knox decided to stay in Los Angeles, was Tommy rehired as head coach. His one memorable contribution to the NFL was that he gave assistant Bill Belichick his first position coaching assignment as tight ends coach in 1977. In fact, Belichick still calls the double tight end set that Hudspeth designed with the Lions "Detroit." After another year of Detroit mediocrity, Hudspeth was fired.

Tommy moved back across the border in 1979, becoming the GM of the Toronto Argonauts of the CFL. Two years later, he once again left the front office to take over a struggling team. Hudspeth fired Coach

Willie Wood with the team at 0–10 and finished the season 2–4 before losing his job as coach and GM as well. From 1984 to 1989, Hudspeth was the Director of Development for Northeastern Oklahoma Junior College and also served as the vice president of the local chamber of commerce. While Tommy had been a candidate for the open head coaching job at his alma mater in 1985, he came home in 1990 when Tulsa named him executive director of its Golden Hurricane Club. He stepped down in 1993 to become sales manager of Sagebrush Pipeline. Since 2006, though, Hudspeth has been back at Tulsa as an assistant athletic director and fundraiser for the school.

HUGHES, EDWARD D. (ED) 10/23/1927–6/23/2000. North Carolina State and Tulsa. Played DB for the Rams and Giants from 1954 to 1958. *Apprenticeship:* College asst.—1 year; pro asst.—11 years. *Roots:* Hank Stram, Jack Faulkner, Bill McPeak, Otto Graham, Dick Nolan. *Branches:* None. *Coordinators/Key Assistants:* King Hill helped on offense, while Walt Schlinkman was the key defensive assistant. *Hall of Fame Players:* Elvin Bethea, Ken Houston, Charley Joiner. *Primary Quarterbacks:* Dan Pastorini. *Tendencies:* • His team scored 17.9 points and allowed 23.6 per game • His team ran 44.3% of the time, which was 83% of the league average • Three starting quarterbacks in one year; 57% of starts to primary quarterback • Two rookie starters in one year • Winning Full Seasons to Losing Full Seasons: 0:1.

Buffalo native Ed Hughes began his career as a lineman ... climbing poles for the phone company after high school and before college. After graduating from Tulsa, he played defensive back for the Rams from 1954 to 1955 before being traded to the Giants in 1956. Ed spent three years in the New York secondary under defensive coach Tom Landry and alongside Dick Nolan, two men who would play a big role in his future career. Hughes retired as a player in 1959 and served as an assistant coach at his alma mater that year. In 1960, he joined Hank Stram's staff as the secondary coach for the AFL's Dallas Texans. Ed continued working as a defensive coach in Denver in 1963 and in Washington from 1964 to 1967. The following year, Hughes' brother-in-law and former teammate, Dick Nolan, hired Ed as the 49ers offensive coach, and by his third season in San Francisco, the team topped the league in scoring.

On the strength of that record, Bud Adams signed Hughes to a five-year contract to coach the Oilers in

Hudspeth, Tommy Joe									
Year	Team	Games	Wins	Losses	Ties	%	P Wins	P Losses	P %
1976	Lions	10	5	5	0	.500	0	0	.000
1977	Lions	14	6	8	0	.429	0	0	.000
2 years		24	11	13	0	.458	0	0	.000

1971. However, Ed only lasted one turbulent year in Houston. At the outset, he announced, "I'm not thinking about a building program. I'm thinking about winning this year." With that, Hughes set out to remake the Oilers through several trades. While he did bring in future star receiver Ken Burrough in one deal, most of his trades did not work out, with Houston giving up such players as Doug Wilkerson, Bobby Maples, Glen Ray Hines and Roy Gerela and receiving little in return. Ed inconclusively juggled three quarterbacks, veteran Charley Johnson and rookies Dan Pastorini and Lynn Dickey, but Elvin Bethea wrote in his autobiography *Smashmouth* that the coach's biggest problem was "He was so quiet that he was completely ineffective at motivating players. Coach Hughes was a relaxed, easy-going, almost catatonic nonentity who was doomed to fail. Coach Hughes had no passion or fire at all."

The killing blow though was getting into a series of strange squabbles with management. In November, GM John Breen promoted King Hill from scout to quarterback coach and had offensive line coach Ernie Zwahlen dismissed without Hughes' consent. At the end of the season, the owner insisted that Hughes reinstate the equipment manager he had fired and instead fire the trainer. Hughes refused. In Bud Adams' view that meant that Ed resigned, while Hughes declared that he had been fired. A hearing with Pete Rozelle eventually was required to settle the rancorous contract dispute. A year later, former Oiler lineman Jerry Sturm added an odd postscript to Hughes' short tenure in Houston by claiming that he had been offered a bribe by gamblers toward the end of the 1971 season.

Ed moved on as an offensive assistant for the Cardinals in 1972, the Cowboys under Tom Landry from 1973 to 1976, the Lions in 1977, the Saints under Dick Nolan from 1978 to 1980, the Eagles in 1981, the Bears from 1982 to 1988 and the Eagles again in 1989. He briefly worked as the defensive coach for Lake Forest College in 1990 and then retired. He won his only Super Bowl ring in 1985 as the offensive coordinator for the Bears.

HUNTER, HAROLD (HAL) 6/3/1934– Pittsburgh.
Did not play professionally. *Apprenticeship:* College coach — 23 years (4 as head coach); CFL asst. — 1 year; pro asst. — 3 years. Roots: Frank Kush. *Branches:* Rick Venturi (i). *Coordinators/Key Assistants:* None. *Hall of Fame Players:* None. *Primary Quarterbacks:* None. *Record:* **Interim Coach.**

A native of Canonsburg, Pennsylvania, Hal Hunter spent nearly 50 years in football, mostly as a line coach at several stops. Hunter was co-captain of the Pitt Panthers in his senior season of 1956, but was undrafted by the NFL although he tried to catch on as a free agent with the hometown Steelers. He began his coaching career in 1958 at Washington and Jefferson and then worked as the line coach at Richmond from 1959 to 1961, West Virginia from 1962 to 1963, Maryland from 1964 to 1965, Duke from 1966 to 1970, Kentucky from 1971 to 1972 and Indiana from 1973 to 1976. Finally, in 1977, Hal was named head coach of California State College of Pennsylvania, a Division II school. Despite compiling just a 9–30–1 record in four seasons, Hunter landed on his feet in 1981 when Frank Kush hired him as offensive coordinator of the Hamilton Tiger-Cats in the CFL. Kush was trying to rehabilitate his name after being fired from Arizona State due to an incident with a player and called on Hunter as an old friend. As Hal told reporters, "I coached Frank's brother at West Virginia and I helped him through some personal problems. Frank got word of this and he contacted me to say thanks and ever since we've kept in touch."

One season later, Kush was named head coach of the Colts and brought Hunter with him as line coach. Three years later, Kush resigned to take on the coaching job at the USFL's Arizona Wranglers, and Hal replaced him in Indianapolis for the season finale, a 16–10 loss to the Patriots. While Hunter hoped to stay on as head coach, the Colts hired Rod Dowhower in 1985, and Hal moved on to Pittsburgh as Chuck Noll's line coach for the next four years. In 1989, he switched to Cleveland under Bud Carson and was retained in 1991 when Bill Belichick was hired as head coach. At the end of the 1992 season, though, Hunter resigned, saying, "I don't think I could live through another year with [Belichick]." Hal spent a year as a scout for San Francisco and then joined the expansion

Hughes, Edward D. (Ed)									
Year	Team	Games	Wins	Losses	Ties	%	P Wins	P Losses	P %
1971	Oilers (Titans)	14	4	9	1	.321	0	0	.000
1 year		14	4	9	1	.321	0	0	.000

Hunter, Harold (Hal)									
Year	Team	Games	Wins	Losses	Ties	%	P Wins	P Losses	P %
1984	Colts	1	0	1	0	.000	0	0	.000
1 year		1	0	1	0	.000	0	0	.000

Carolina Panthers in 1995 as a scout. From 1998 to 2006, he served as the Panthers' personnel coordinator before retiring. Following in Hunter's footsteps, his son Hal Jr. has made ten stops as a line coach, mostly in the college ranks over the past 30 years.

INFANTE, GELINDO (LINDY) 5/27/1940– Florida. TB; did not play professionally. *Apprenticeship:* College asst.—11 years; WFL asst.—1 year; pro asst.— 7 years; USFL head coach—2 years. *Roots:* John McVay, Forrest Gregg, Marty Schottenheimer,. *Branches:* Dick Jauron. *Coordinators/Key Assistants*: For the Packers, Infante ran his own offense, while Hank Bullough handled the defense; for the Colts, Infante again ran the offense, while Jim Johnson handled the defense. *Hall of Fame Players:* Richard Dent, Marshall Faulk. *Primary Quarterbacks:* Don Majkowski, Jim Harbaugh. *Tendencies:* • His teams scored 18.5 points and allowed 21.5 per game • His teams ran 39.4% of the time, which was 87% of the league average • Seven starting quarterbacks in six years; 69% of starts to primary quarterbacks • Eleven rookie starters in six years • Winning Full Seasons to Losing Full Seasons: 2:4.

Miami's Lindy Infante starred at tailback for Ray Graves at Florida and was team captain in 1962. After graduation, Infante coached high school football until returning to his alma mater in 1966 as an assistant. In Gainesville, Lindy coached under Graves and Doug Dickey through 1971. In 1972, he was named offensive coordinator at Memphis State. Three years later, he joined the coaching staff of Charlotte in the WFL, but the league folded at midseason. Infante then coached at Tulane in 1976 and 1979, spending 1977–1978 as the receivers coach of the New York Giants. In 1980, Forrest Gregg made him offensive coordinator for the Bengals, and a year later the team went to the Super Bowl. However, good feelings in Cincinnati ended in 1983 when Paul Brown fired Lindy because Infante had signed a contract to serve as head coach of Jacksonville in the USFL in 1984.

Infante's first head coaching job did not go well; the USFL's Bulls finished 15–21 in two seasons under Lindy. When Jacksonville merged with Denver in 1986, Denver coach Mouse Davis was named coach, so Lindy took the job of offensive coordinator in Cleveland, sued the Bulls and won the lawsuit. Infante's de-

velopment of young quarterback Bernie Kosar in 1986 and 1987 made him a hot commodity, and he was named head coach of the Packers in 1988. He asserted to the press, "We'll be a winner or it's time to find something else to do." In four years in Green Bay, though, Lindy managed just one winning season, 1989, when he was named Coach of the Year. That was an exciting but very flukey season as it turned out. The team wasn't very strong, but managed to pull out six close victories with late-game drives led by quarterback Don "Majik Man" Majkowski. The magic and luck wore off in 1990, although Infante did not acknowledge it. He told the *Milwaukee Journal- Sentinel* in 2009, "Quarterbacks can make or break you. I would have liked to have had another year in Green Bay and had Brett [Favre], a quarterback I've admired for a long time." Instead, Packer GM Ron Wolf fired Infante after a wretched 4–12 1991 season. Wolf wrote in *The Packer Way* that Lindy was deluding himself, "Because he put in many long hours and gave so much of himself to his job, he thought that meant he was succeeding—that he was owed something because of his conscientiousness."

Infante, who had studied architecture at Florida, spent the next few years building his retirement beach house in the Sunshine State. In 1995, he returned to football as Ted Marchibroda's offensive coordinator in Indianapolis. As usual, Lindy struck up a nice rapport with the team's quarterback, this time Jim Harbaugh, and the Colts shocked everyone by coming within a dropped Hail Mary pass of landing in the Super Bowl. Marchibroda then quit after the Colts made him a lowball offer to return, and Infante got a second chance as an NFL head coach. The Colts snuck back into the playoffs in 1996, but completely collapsed in 1997, giving up over 400 points and winning just three games. That ended Infante's football career and landed him on the beach. As a coach, the pass-happy Infante was very scheme-driven to the point were players found him distant and isolated. He was very successful as a coordinator, but as a head coach he was a "loser" as Colts' defensive tackle Tony Siragusa said of him to *Sports Illustrated.*

ISBELL, CECIL F. 7/11/1915–6/23/1985. Purdue. Played TB for the Packers from 1938 to 1942. *Apprenticeship:* College coach—4 years (3 as head coach).

Infante, Gelindo (Lindy)									
Year	Team	Games	Wins	Losses	Ties	%	P Wins	P Losses	P %
1988	Packers	16	4	12	0	.250	0	0	.000
1989	Packers	16	10	6	0	.625	0	0	.000
1990	Packers	16	6	10	0	.375	0	0	.000
1991	Packers	16	4	12	0	.250	0	0	.000
1996	Colts	16	9	7	0	.563	0	1	.000
1997	Colts	16	3	13	0	.188	0	0	.000
6 years		96	36	60	0	.375	0	1	.000

Roots: None. *Branches:* Red Conkright. *Coordinators/Key Assistants:* For the Colts, Tom Stidham then Mike Michalske coached the line. *Hall of Fame Players:* Y.A. Tittle, Charley Trippi. *Primary Quarterbacks:* Y.A. Tittle, Bud Schwenk. *Record:* **Interim Co-Coach** in 1951 (with Phil Handler) *Tendencies:* • His teams scored 17.1 points and allowed 25.7 per game • His teams ran 57.8% of the time, which was 95% of the league average • Three starting quarterbacks in four years; 88% of starts to primary quarterbacks • 14 rookie starters in four years • Winning Full Seasons to Losing Full Seasons: 0:1.

Houston's Cecil Isbell is a long forgotten contemporary and near equal of Hall of Famers Sammy Baugh and Sid Luckman. In fact, in Isbell's short five-year career as a single wing tailback for the Packers, he threw the most touchdown passes and had the lowest interception percentage of those three skilled early passers. Isbell also rushed for 1,522 yards on 422 attempts and had 9 interceptions as a defensive back. His coach Curly Lambeau once said that Isbell was the best passer he ever saw, "Isbell was the master at any range. He could throw soft passes, bullet passes, or feathery lobs. He was the best with Sid Luckman of the Bears a close second and Sammy Baugh of the Redskins a long third. Luckman wasn't as versatile and Baugh couldn't compare on the long ones."

Furthermore, Isbell was as fine a passer as there was in the league despite being severely limited by a chronically bad shoulder. Cecil had dislocated his left shoulder several times in college so he started wearing a chain that went from his arm to his torso to keep him from raising his arm too high and damaging the shoulder. Still, from 1940 through 1942, Cecil threw a touchdown pass in 23 straight games, a league record that Johnny Unitas would break in 1958 en route to an ultimate total of 47 straight. Isbell twice was All-League and three times was second team All-League, but was determined to quit on his own time and not be cut like so many veterans. When his alma mater, Purdue, offered him a coaching job at a pay cut in 1943, he signed on as Elmer Burnham's assistant. A year later, Burnham left for Rochester, and Isbell was named head coach. The Boilermakers went 14–14–1 from 1944 to 1946, before Cecil left to become head coach of the expansion Baltimore Colts in the All America Football Conference in 1947, admitting.

"Sure it's going to be a rugged grind. We might not be able to get far this year, but by '48 I'm sure the Colts will be up there."

Isbell's prediction came true. Behind quarterback Bud Schwenk in 1947, the Colts won only two games, but with rookie Y.A. Tittle as signal caller in 1948, Baltimore tied for the Eastern Division with a so-so 7–7 record, although they lost the playoff game that followed. Tittle recalled in his autobiography, *I Pass* that "I suppose I gained self-confidence quickly under Cecil because he believed that you should put the ball in the air. Even though I was a rookie, Cecil did not second guess me." Unfortunately, the Colts' success was short-lived. When the team got off to an 0–4 start in 1949, Isbell was forced to resign. He told the press, "Quitting is the nice way to put it," then added wistfully, "My future was in Baltimore. I raised this ball club; it was my baby."

Cecil's former Packers' coach Curly Lambeau hired him as an assistant on the Cardinals in 1950, and Isbell and Phil Handler took over the team when Lambeau first resigned and then was fired with two games to go in 1951. Isbell then spent 1952 as the backfield coach for the woeful Dallas Texans and for LSU in 1953 before leaving football for the business world. He worked as the public relations director for a manufacturing firm in Michigan, then as a sales manager for a Milwaukee manufacturer and finally as a transportation executive in Milwaukee in the 1960s. Although he is a member of the College Football Hall of Fame, his illustrious NFL career was too short to merit Canton. Three of his brothers also played college football and his younger brother Larry later became a star in the CFL.

IVY, FRANK (POP) 1/25/1916–5/17/2003. Oklahoma. Played E for the Pittsburgh Pirates and the Cardinals from 1940 to 1942 and 1945–1947. *Apprenticeship:* College asst.—6 years; CFL head coach—4 years. *Roots:* None. *Branches:* Wally Lemm, Chuck Drulis (i), Ray Prochaska (i), Ray Willsey (i), Neill Armstrong. *Coordinators/Key Assistants:* For the Cardinals, Ivy ran his own offense, while Chuck Drulis handled the defense; for the Oilers, Ivy again ran the offense, while Neill Armstrong then Red Conkright handled the defense. *Hall of Fame Players:* George Blanda, Dick Lane, Larry Wilson. *Primary Quarterbacks:* King Hill, John Roach, George Blanda *Tenden-*

Isbell, Cecil F.									
Year	*Team*	*Games*	*Wins*	*Losses*	*Ties*	*%*	*P Wins*	*P Losses*	*P %*
1947	Colts (AAFC)	14	2	11	1	.179	0	0	.000
1948	Colts (AAFC)	14	7	7	0	.500	0	1	.000
1949	Colts (AAFC)	4	0	4	0	.000	0	0	.000
1951	Cardinals	2	1	1	0	.500	0	0	.000
4 years		34	10	23	1	.309	0	1	.000

cies: • His teams scored 22.4 points and allowed 23.8 per game • His teams ran 49.4% of the time, which was 97% of the league average • Nine starting quarterbacks in six years; 66% of starts to primary quarterbacks • 25 rookie starters in six years • Winning Full Seasons to Losing Full Seasons: 2:4.

Born in the Tulsa suburb of Skiatook, Oklahoma, Frank Ivy was part American Indian and played end for Oklahoma from 1937 to 1939. Called Pop for his prematurely bald head, he was selected in the 1940 NFL draft by Pittsburgh but was traded to the Cardinals in October of his rookie year. Pop played for the Cards through 1942 when he entered the service. He returned to Chicago at the end of the 1945 season and remained with the team through its championship season of 1947. At the age of 32, Ivy retired from playing and returned to his alma mater as an assistant to Bud Wilkinson for six years.

In 1954, Pop set out on his own, taking on the head coaching job for the Edmonton Eskimos. He was not afraid to try new things in Canada, such as the "lonesome quarterback" formation that was a precursor to today's Shotgun, and won three straight Grey Cups. After four years in Canada with a 50–14 record, Ivy was lured back to Chicago to take over the fumbling Cardinals franchise in 1958. The team's managing director Walter Wolfner told the press, "We thought about him quite a while. We knew he was a taskmaster who demands perfection and gets it or else. And he's the best organizer of any coach we ever had."

Again with the Cardinals, Pop took an innovative approach, unveiling two new offensive formations. The first was generally called the Double Wing T in which both halfbacks lined up as wingbacks to the outside of the ends. The second scheme Ivy called his "Jack and Jill" formation, but others called it a Triple Wing T. In this one, both halfbacks and the fullback lined up as wingbacks, but inside the two split ends. In both formations, the running game was generated mostly from lateral motion of the backs. Essentially, Pop was experimenting with four and five receiver sets, although he was using running backs to do so. The upshot was that the team improved to mediocrity in his four-year tenure, but no better. With two games to go in the 1961 season, Ivy resigned, saying "My feeling is a coach can only work for so long. Then if he

does not get the desired results, it is in the best interest of everyone concerned that a change be made." Three months later after Oilers' coach Wally Lemm took over the Cardinals, Ivy was named head coach of Houston, the AFL's two-time defending champion.

In Houston, Pop tried some of the same formations he had pioneered at previous coaching stops, and the team did reach the title game again in 1962, but lost in sudden death overtime to the Dallas Texans. The next year, the Oilers' defense fell apart, and Ivy lost control of the team. In one game in 1963, Pop sent in backup quarterback Jacky Lee after George Blanda was sacked roughly, but Blanda angrily waved him back to the bench while Ivy did not respond. Pop was dismissed in June of 1964 with owner Bud Adams brutally commenting, "This town just doesn't go for losers." That year, he was hired as a scout by the Giants and would spend the next 21 years working for New York. He coached the Giants' defense in 1965, 1966 and 1971 and spent the rest of his time with the team as a scout. He retired from football in 1984.

JACKSON, HUE 10/22/1965– Pacific. QB; did not play professionally. *Apprenticeship:* College asst.—14 years; WLAF asst.—1 year; pro asst.—10 years. *Roots:* Marty Schottenheimer, Steve Spurrier, Marvin Lewis, Bobby Petrino, Emmitt Thomas (i), John Harbaugh, Tom Cable. *Branches:* None. *Coordinators/Key Assistants:* Al Saunders ran the offense, while Chuck Bresnahan handled the defense. *Hall of Fame Players:* None. *Primary Quarterbacks:* Carson Palmer. *Tendencies:* • His team scored 20.8 points and allowed 24.7 per game • His team ran 45.4% of the time, which was 107% of the league average • Three starting quarterbacks in one year; 56% of starts to primary quarterbacks • Three rookie starters in one year • Winning Full Seasons to Losing Full Seasons: 0:0.

Los Angeles native Hue Jackson played quarterback at Pacific just like a previous Raiders' coach, Tom Flores. However, Jackson never played professionally. Rather, he embarked on a long coaching apprenticeship that ultimately led him into the cauldron of working for Al Davis.

Jackson began his coaching career at his alma mater in 1987, before moving on to Cal State Fullerton in 1990. In 1991, he spent a season in London as an assistant in

Ivy, Frank (Pop)									
Year	Team	Games	Wins	Losses	Ties	%	P Wins	P Losses	P %
1958	Cardinals	12	2	9	1	.208	0	0	.000
1959	Cardinals	12	2	10	0	.167	0	0	.000
1960	Cardinals	12	6	5	1	.542	0	0	.000
1961	Cardinals	12	5	7	0	.417	0	0	.000
1962	Oilers (Titans)	14	11	3	0	.786	0	1	.000
1963	Oilers (Titans)	14	6	8	0	.429	0	0	.000
6 years		76	32	42	2	.434	0	1	.000

the developmental World League of American Football before returning to the college ranks in 1992 with Arizona State. Hue coached at ASU through 1995, spent 1996 at California and from 1997 to 2000 at USC. Marty Schottenheimer gave Jackson his NFL start as running backs coach with the Redskins in 2001, and his successor Steve Spurrier promoted Hue to offensive coordinator in 2003. Jackson was the receivers coach for the Bengals from 2004 to 2006, offensive coordinator for Atlanta in 2007 and quarterbacks coach for the Ravens from 2008 to 2009. Al Davis brought him to Oakland in 2010 to be Tom Cable's offensive coordinator and then fired Cable at year's end to promote Jackson.

Davis poetically introduced Jackson by saying, "The fire in Hue will set a flame that will burn for a long time in the hearts and minds of the Raider football team and the Raider Nation." Davis then spent more of the new coach's introductory press conference running down the old coach (Cable) in Al's inimitable surly fashion. In accepting the head coaching job of the Raiders, Hue took on one of the most challenging and impermanent positions in the NFL, but forged a close relationship with Davis before Al died in October 2011. Oakland seemed headed to the playoffs when the team acquired veteran quarterback Carson Palmer six games into the season, but went just 4–6 down the stretch while setting a new NFL record for team penalties to fall short of the postseason. Jackson blasted his team after the game and insisted he would take a more assertive role throughout the organization in the future. He didn't run that by Davis' son Mark, however, who had other ideas. Mark Davis immediately brought in longtime Packers' player personnel director (and former Raider linebacker) Reggie McKenzie as GM, and the loquacious Jackson was fired.

JAURON, RICHARD M. (DICK) 10/7/1950– Yale. Played DB for the Lions and Bengals from 1973 to 1980. *Apprenticeship:* Pro asst.—14 years. *Roots:* Kay Stephenson, Hank Bullough, Forrest Gregg, Lindy Infante, Mike Holmgren, Tom Coughlin. *Branches:* Todd Haley, Perry Fewell (i), Eric Studesville (i). *Coordinators/Key Assistants*: For the Bears, Gary Crowton then John Shoop ran the offense, while Greg Blache handled the defense; for the Bills, Steve Fairchild then Turk Schonert ran the offense, while Perry Fewell handled the defense. *Hall of Fame Players:* None. *Primary Quarterbacks:* Jim Miller, J.P. Losman, Trent Edwards. *Tendencies:* • His teams scored 17.6 points and allowed 20.9 per game • His teams ran 43.4% of the time, which was 98% of the league average • 13 starting quarterbacks in ten years; 57% of starts to primary quarterbacks • 29 rookie starters in ten years • Winning Full Seasons to Losing Full Seasons: 1:8.

The son of a coach, Dick Jauron was born in Peoria, Illinois, and succeeded Calvin Hill as the star halfback at Yale, running for a school record of over 2,900 yards from 1970 to 1972. He was drafted as a shortstop by the St. Louis Cardinals in baseball and in the fourth round of the NFL draft by Detroit. The Lions switched him to safety, where he started for five years, while also returning punts. In 1978, Jauron joined the Bengals and played with them for three years before spending 1981 on Injured Reserve and then getting cut in 1982. He made one last attempt to extend his playing career in 1983 by going to training camp with the Boston Breakers of the USFL, but did not make the team. After going into business in Cincinnati, Jauron returned to football in 1985, coaching the secondary for Bills' defensive coordinator Hank Bullough who had coached him on the Bengals. A year later, Dick moved on to Green Bay, where he coached the sec-

Jackson, Hue									
Year	Team	Games	Wins	Losses	Ties	%	P Wins	P Losses	P %
2011	Raiders	16	8	8	0	.500	0	0	.000
1 year		16	8	8	0	.500	0	0	.000

Jauron, Richard M. (Dick)									
Year	Team	Games	Wins	Losses	Ties	%	P Wins	P Losses	P %
1999	Bears	16	6	10	0	.375	0	0	.000
2000	Bears	16	5	11	0	.313	0	0	.000
2001	Bears	16	13	3	0	.813	0	1	.000
2002	Bears	16	4	12	0	.250	0	0	.000
2003	Bears	16	7	9	0	.438	0	0	.000
2005	Lions	5	1	4	0	.200	0	0	.000
2006	Bills	16	7	9	0	.438	0	0	.000
2007	Bills	16	7	9	0	.438	0	0	.000
2008	Bills	16	7	9	0	.438	0	0	.000
2009	Bills	9	3	6	0	.333	0	0	.000
10 years		142	60	82	0	.423	0	1	.000

ondary from 1986 to 1994 under Forrest Gregg, Lindy Infante and Mike Holmgren.

Jauron left Green Bay to become defensive coordinator of the expansion Jaguars in 1995, and his success there under Tom Coughlin won him the Bears' head coaching job in 1999 although he was not Chicago's first choice. The Bears intended on hiring Dave McGinnis as head coach, but mismanaged the job offer and lost out on McGinnis. As a fallback, team owner Michael McCaskey favored Green Bay's Sherman Lewis while GM Mark Hatley wanted to hire Kansas City's Joe Pendry. As a compromise, the two agreed on Jauron.

As a coach, Jauron was patient and extremely cautious, pretty much how one would expect a compromise choice to act. Bears' quarterback Jim Miller had high praise to *Sports Illustrated* for Dick's stolid personality, "Like Tom Landry, the guy does not waver. And we've taken on his personality." Bears linebacker Roosevelt Colvin claimed to the same magazine, "He's the type of leader you want to play for. In three years here I've only seen him yell at a guy one time." While it is clearly more pleasant to play for a calm presence like Jauron, that steadiness produced only one flukey winning season in five years in Chicago.

Jauron was fired in 2004, but caught on immediately as the defensive coordinator for the Lions. A year later, he replaced Steve Mariucci as Detroit's coach with five games to play. Unexpectedly, Dick got a second chance at head coach when Marv Levy hired him in Buffalo in 2006. Three straight mediocre 7–9 seasons were followed by a 3–6 start in 2009, and Jauron was fired again. To be fair, Dick has never had the opportunity to work with a quality quarterback — even the high draft picks he was given were underachieving flops Cade McNown and J.P. Losman — and four times his teams finished in the bottom five in scoring. Still, he lacked the boldness to break out of the losing situations he inherited. Jauron spent 2010 as the Eagles secondary coach before signing on as Cleveland's defensive coordinator in 2011.

JOHNSON, HARVEY P. 6/22/1919–8/8/1983. William & Mary. Played T, G, LB for the New York Yankees from 1946 to 1949 and the New York Yanks in 1951. *Apprenticeship:* Canadian football coach — 7 years; pro asst. — 4 years. *Roots:* Buster Ramsey. *Branches:* Tom Flores. *Coordinators/Key Assistants:* John Mazur then Tom Flores were the key offensive coaches, while Dick McCabe then Doc Urich ran the defense.

Hall of Fame Players: O.J. Simpson. *Primary Quarterbacks:* Dennis Shaw. *Tendencies:* • His teams scored 14.2 points and allowed 26.8 per game • His teams ran 44.6% of the time, which was 85% of the league average • Six starting quarterbacks in two years; 46% of starts to primary quarterbacks • Eleven rookie starters in two years • Winning Full Seasons to Losing Full Seasons: 0:2.

A native of Bridgeton, New Jersey, Harvey Johnson played with All-American Buster Ramsey at William & Mary in 1941 and 1942 before going into the service during World War II. In 1946, Johnson joined the powerful New York Yankees of the new All America Football Conference as a lineman, but made his mark as the team's reliable place kicker who had a noteworthy streak of 133 consecutive points after touchdown at one point. When the AAFC merged into the NFL in 1950, Harvey was assigned to the New York Yanks (formerly known as the Bulldogs), but stayed out of pro football that year and instead coached high school. He returned to play for the Yanks in 1951 before retiring as a player.

A year later, Johnson moved north to serve as the backfield coach of the Hamilton Tiger-Cats in Canada under his William & Mary coach Carl Voyles. After one season, Harvey was named head coach of Kitchener in a Canadian minor league and led that team to four straight titles from 1954 to 1957. Johnson then coached the backfield for the CFL's Montreal Alouettes for two years until his old college teammate Buster Ramsey hired him to coach the secondary for the Buffalo Bills of the new American Football League. He would remain with Buffalo for the rest of his life in a variety of capacities.

When Ramsey was replaced with Lou Saban in 1962, Johnson moved into the front office as the director of player personnel. Saban resigned after producing back-to-back AFL championships with the players Harvey signed and was succeeded by defensive coach Joe Collier in 1966. By 1968, the team was in chaos and Collier was dismissed just two games into the season. Johnson took over in a disastrous year in which the Bills would go through five starting quarterbacks, ending with receiver/defensive back Ed Rutkowski for the last four games. Not surprisingly, the team was awful and Johnson did little to help. Rookie quarterback Dan Darragh recalled to Jeffrey Miller in *Rockin' the Rockpile*, "In 12 games as head coach, Harvey learned maybe one offensive play. We started every game with the same play. It wasn't really

Johnson, Harvey P.									
Year	*Team*	*Games*	*Wins*	*Losses*	*Ties*	*%*	*P Wins*	*P Losses*	*P %*
1968	Bills	12	1	10	1	.125	0	0	.000
1971	Bills	14	1	13	0	.071	0	0	.000
2 years		26	2	23	1	.096	0	0	.000

sophisticated; it was called a '46.' And all it was was a halfback off-tackle to the right." Receiver Elbert Dubenion remembered Johnson's "stirring" halftime speeches to Sal Maiorana for *Buffalo Bills: The Complete Illustrated History*," We'd be getting beat bad at the half, and Harvey would come in and say, 'Look, I don't want to go back out there either, but we have to finish the game.'"

The Bills lost their last eight games of 1968, which won them the right to draft O.J. Simpson first overall that year. While no one else had much positive to say about Harvey's coaching, Simpson did in 1971. Simpson had chafed under abrasive coach John Rauch who was determined not to rely on O.J. as a runner during his two years in Buffalo. Right before training camp of 1971, owner Ralph Wilson tired of Rauch, fired him and appointed loyal soldier Johnson to take over again. According to *Sports Illustrated*, Johnson told Simpson, "We now have a new offense. It is called O.J. left, O.J. right and, occasionally, O.J. up the middle." For his part Simpson told the same magazine, "Harvey has made the game fun again. We work hard when we work, but he gives us a lot of free time. He's done away with much of the senseless stuff and the boredom." He also did away with any chance of winning with the offense continuing to rely more on the pass than the run because the defense was so bad. The Bills lost the first ten games of the season, extending Harvey's personal losing streak to 18 games, and won just one game all year.

Lou Saban returned in 1972 and rebuilt the Bills around O.J. Simpson. Johnson spent the next dozen years as either the team's chief scout or general manager until his death in 1983 from a heart attack.

Johnson, James W. (Jimmy) 8/19/1943– Arkansas. DL; did not play professionally. *Apprenticeship*: College coach — 23 years (10 as head coach). *Roots*: None. *Branches*: David Shula, Dave Wannstedt, Norv Turner, Dave Campo, Butch Davis. *Coordinators/Key Assistants*: For the Cowboys, David Shula then Norv Turner ran the offense, while Dave Wannstedt then Butch Davis handled the defense; for the Dol-

phins, Gary Stevens then Kippy Brown ran the offense, while George Hill handled the defense. *Hall of Fame Players*: Troy Aikman, Michael Irvin, Dan Marino, Emmitt Smith, Rayfield Wright. *Primary Quarterbacks*: Troy Aikman, Dan Marino. *Record*: Super Bowl Championships 1992, 1993. *Tendencies*: • His teams scored 20.1 points and allowed 19 per game • His teams ran 44.5% of the time, which was 99% of the league average • Nine starting quarterbacks in nine years; 86% of starts to primary quarterbacks • 33 rookie starters in nine years • Winning Full Seasons to Losing Full Seasons: 6:2.

Jimmy Johnson never lacked for confidence and made a specialty of following legendary coaches. When he took the head coaching job at the University of Miami, he was replacing the coach of the Hurricanes first national championship team, Howard Schnellenberger. When he left Miami, he replaced Tom Landry, the only coach the Cowboys ever had. For his final head coaching position, he replaced Don Shula, the NFL's winningest coach of all time, on the Dolphins. As for his own legacy, Johnson told the *New York Times* that it was a good thing for a coach to follow him because he left a lot of talent at each team, "Ask Pat Jones who took over at Oklahoma State. Or ask Dennis Erickson, who won a couple of championships at Miami. Or ask Barry Switzer, who won a Super Bowl at Dallas. So it wasn't the worst thing in the world to follow me."

Johnson was born and raised in Port Arthur, Texas, where he was classmate of ill-fated rock singer Janis Joplin. He played defensive line for the University of Arkansas and was a member of the 1964 Razorback national championship team along with future partner and nemesis Jerry Jones, with Barry Switzer on the coaching staff. After graduation, Jimmy went immediately into coaching, working as an assistant at Louisiana Tech in 1965, at the high school level in 1966, at Wichita State in 1967, at Iowa State under Johnny Majors from 1968 to 1969, at Oklahoma under Chuck Fairbanks from 1970 to 1972, at his alma mater under Frank Broyles from 1973 to 1976 and at Pittsburgh under Jackie Sherrill from 1977 to 1978. Finally

Johnson, James W. (Jimmy)									
Year	Team	Games	Wins	Losses	Ties	%	P Wins	P Losses	P %
1989	Cowboys	16	1	15	0	.063	0	0	.000
1990	Cowboys	16	7	9	0	.438	0	0	.000
1991	Cowboys	16	11	5	0	.688	1	1	.500
1992	Cowboys	16	13	3	0	.813	3	0	1.000
1993	Cowboys	16	12	4	0	.750	3	0	1.000
1996	Dolphins	16	8	8	0	.500	0	0	.000
1997	Dolphins	16	9	7	0	.563	0	1	.000
1998	Dolphins	16	10	6	0	.625	1	1	.500
1999	Dolphins	16	9	7	0	.563	1	1	.500
9 years		144	80	64	0	.556	9	4	.692

in 1979, Johnson was offered his first head coaching job at Oklahoma State, forever number two in the Sooner state. Jimmy took the Cowboys to two bowl games in five years and compiled a 29–25–3 record. He then succeeded Schnellenberger at Miami in 1984 and went 52–9 in five years. In his last three years at the "U," Miami went 34–2, winning one national championship and finishing number two the other two years. Johnson's Hurricanes were loved by some and reviled by others for their outrageous and audacious attitude on and off the field. By this time, the man with the helmet hair that never moved had gained quite a reputation as a motivational coach, and Johnson's players were devoted to him.

Meanwhile, former Razorback teammate Jerry Jones took the millions he had made in oil and bought the Dallas Cowboys in 1989. While Jones made more of his friendship with Johnson than Jimmy did, Jones later told *Texas Monthly* that Jimmy was a natural at coaching, "He was intelligent and focused. Even in college, you could tell that he had what I call 'people skills.' His positive attitude was infectious. He had the ability to make hard work seem pleasant." Jones fired Tom Landry and hired Johnson, unleashing a storm of protest from Dallas fans. However, the Cowboys had sunk to 3–13 in 1988 under Landry so it was understandable that Jones wished to nudge the elderly pair of Landry and GM Tex Schramm out the door.

Even though Jones liked to take co-credit on personnel moves, it was Johnson who built the Cowboys—as the post–Johnson two decades in Dallas will attest. Four games into 1989, Johnson decided he needed to be bold to improve a terrible team. His one asset was runner Herschel Walker who the Vikings saw as the one missing piece to their Super Bowl puzzle. In an 18-man deal that involved six players and 12 draft picks, Dallas parted with Walker and a handful of mid to late round draft picks for five Vikings, a 1992 first round pick and six conditional picks. What Johnson really wanted were the draft picks and at the end of the season he started waiving the Viking mediocrities he had received in order to activate the conditional picks. Johnson worked from those picks on draft day to make a series of deals in the coming years that eventually involved 15 teams and 55 players all told and remade the Cowboys with young, fast, hungry players who would win back-to-back Super Bowls for the 1992 and 1993 seasons. While he was lucky to have former Miami receiver Michael Irvin on the team already, Johnson drafted Troy Aikman and Emmitt Smith to form the Hall of Fame "triplets" that powered the team for the next decade. Johnson also drafted his former Miami quarterback Steve Walsh as a hedge against Aikman being a flop and then traded him to New Orleans for three more draft picks—a one, a two, and a three.

Despite his exuberant coaching style (whooping

"How 'bout them Cowboys!" in the locker room), Johnson held a firm hand on the team and was not hesitant to cut a lesser player who was not following orders. With success, though, came ego problems, both among the players and the front office. As Jones tried more and more to horn in on the credit for the Cowboys' triumphs, Johnson began to resent his all-too-visible boss. Ultimately, Jimmy missed out on the chance to go for a third straight Super Bowl when he and Jones mutually agreed to part ways in 1994.

Jimmy went into broadcasting for two years, but still wanted to coach. In 1996, he had two options close to his Florida home—the Dolphins and the Bucs were both courting him. Even though the Dolphins team was older and in trouble with the salary cap, he chose Miami, telling *Sports Illustrated*, "But I just can't get past one thing, Dilfer and Marino." Ironically, while Miami's future Hall of Famer Dan Marino would never win a Super Bowl, Tampa's mediocre Trent Dilfer would win one with Baltimore the year after both Johnson and Marino would both retire from the game.

While Don Shula had not left the cupboard as bare as Tom Landry did in Dallas, the Dolphins were not a serious Super Bowl contender. As in Dallas, Johnson built a fast and hungry defensive unit, but unlike Dallas was never able to supplement his Hall of Fame quarterback's strong arm with a reliable, punishing running game. As a result, Miami made the playoffs three times in four years, but never was a threat to advance. In the last playoff game for both Johnson and Marino in January 2000, the Dolphins were embarrassed 62–7 by the cross-state Jacksonville Jaguars. A day later, Johnson stepped down as coach, leaving the team to his longtime loyal assistant Dave Wannstedt. While the team remained a contender for the next four years, they never reached the Super Bowl—of course, neither did the Cowboys. Linebacker Robert Jones who played for Johnson at both pro stops told *Sports Illustrated*, "Jimmy was more intense in Dallas. Maybe it's because of the type of players he had there. The players in Dallas responded positively to him, but here it's different." It was no secret that Johnson and Marino never built much rapport, and the Dolphins probably were more Dan's team than Jimmy's—at least on offense.

Johnson returned to the broadcast booth and the fishing boat in 2000 and has remained happily in both ever since. He gained further notoriety in 2010 when he was a 67-year-old contestant on the popular reality television series *Survivor* although he was voted out on day 8.

JOHNSON, WILLIAM L. (BILL OR TIGER) 9/14/1926–1/7/2011. Texas A&M and Tyler Junior College. Played C for the 49ers from 1948 to 1956. *Apprenticeship:* Pro asst.—19 years. *Roots:* Red Strader, Frankie Albert, Red Hickey, Jack Christiansen, Paul

Brown. *Branches:* Homer Rice, Chuck Studley (i). *Coordinators/Key Assistants:* Boyd Dowler was a key offensive coach, while Howard Brinker ran the defense. *Hall of Fame Players:* None. *Primary Quarterbacks:* Ken Anderson. *Tendencies:* • His teams scored 19.4 points and allowed 16.9 per game • His teams ran 54.4% of the time, which was 96% of the league average • Two starting quarterbacks in three years; 85% of starts to primary quarterback • Eleven rookie starters in three years • Winning Full Seasons to Losing Full Seasons: 2:0.

Bill Johnson spent 37 of his 43 years in professional football in two cities: San Francisco and Cincinnati. Today, the native of Tyler, Texas is remembered solely as the man Paul Brown chose to succeed himself as coach of the Bengals, the man chosen instead of Bill Walsh, but he was a fine player and coach who was widely admired by his teammates and players.

Johnson was chosen in the 11th round of the 1948 All America Football Conference draft by the 49ers and had a nine-year career as a center and linebacker with the team. Upon retirement, the two-time Pro Bowler transferred seamlessly onto the coaching staff as the offensive line coach in 1957. Bill worked under four successive 49ers head coaches and pretty much ran the offense under the last, Jack Christiansen. When Dick Nolan was hired to replace Christiansen in 1968, Bill signed on as the line coach of the expansion Cincinnati Bengals. Coach Paul Brown remembered Johnson from his playing days in the AAFC when San Francisco was the chief rival of Brown's Cleveland Browns. While Johnson coached the offensive line, backfield coach Bill Walsh ran the offense with a scheme that would become known as the West Coast Offense when Walsh took over the 49ers.

Walsh expected to succeed Brown as the Bengals' head coach, but when Brown decided to step down in 1976, he looked instead to Johnson. The story was reported that Johnson was being courted as Dick Nolan's

successor in San Francisco and that Brown didn't want to lose the assistant to whom he had promised his job. Walsh felt he deserved the job and was devastated. Moreover, when Walsh resigned from the Bengals, Brown bitterly tried to blacklist him from getting other jobs in the league. While Walsh went on to have a Hall of Fame coaching career with the 49ers a few years later, the choice of Johnson was not a terrible one. Tiger was eminently qualified and posted winning seasons in his first two years. Center Bob Johnson said of Tiger, "He's a motivating type. He's a very intense guy with an aptitude to inspire people." Guard Dave Lapham recalled Johnson upon his death, "He was a man's man in every sense of the word. He was tough, hard-nosed, the epitome of the old-school. He was as honest as the day is long. His word was important to him. Players loved him because there was no B.S. or hidden agendas." Line coach Jim McNally remembered him as being fond of trick plays, and even Bill Walsh credited Tiger with innovative uses of putting the tight end in motion.

Johnson's downfall came in the final preseason game of 1978 when he made the ill-advised decision to send starting quarterback Ken Anderson back out for the second half. Anderson promptly broke his hand in the meaningless game, and Paul Brown was extremely upset. After the Bengals dropped their first five games of 1978, Brown fired Johnson. Tiger worked as line coach of the Bucs from 1979 to 1982 and the Lions in 1983 and 1984, but in 1985 Brown recommended to Bengals coach Sam Wyche to bring Johnson back to Cincinnati. Tiger finished his coaching career by coaching the tight ends under Wyche from 1985 to 1990. His son, William, rose to become president and CEO of the H.J. Heinz Corporation.

JOHNSOS, LUKE A. 12/9/1905–12/10/1984. Northwestern. Played E for the Bears from 1929 to 1936. *Apprenticeship:* Pro asst.—6 years. *Roots:* George Halas.

Johnson, William L. (Bill or Tiger)									
Year	Team	Games	Wins	Losses	Ties	%	P Wins	P Losses	P %
1976	Bengals	14	10	4	0	.714	0	0	.000
1977	Bengals	14	8	6	0	.571	0	0	.000
1978	Bengals	5	0	5	0	.000	0	0	.000
3 years		33	18	15	0	.545	0	0	.000

Johnsos, Luke A.									
Year	Team	Games	Wins	Losses	Ties	%	P Wins	P Losses	P %
1942	Bears	6	6	0	0	1.000	0	1	.000
1943	Bears	10	8	1	1	.850	1	0	1.000
1944	Bears	10	6	3	1	.650	0	0	.000
1945	Bears	10	3	7	0	.300	0	0	.000
4 years		36	23	11	2	.667	1	1	.500

Branches: None. *Coordinators/Key Assistants:* Paddy Driscoll coached the backs. *Hall of Fame Players:* Dan Fortmann, Sid Luckman, George McAfee, George Musso, Bronko Nagurski, Joe Stydahar, Bulldog Turner. *Primary Quarterbacks:* Sid Luckman. *Record:* **Co–Coach** (with Hunk Anderson); NFL Championship 1943. *Tendencies:* • His teams scored 26.4 points and allowed 16.1 per game • His teams ran 66.1% of the time, which was 104% of the league average • Three starting quarterbacks in four years; 68% of starts to primary quarterback • Nine rookie starters in four years • Winning Full Seasons to Losing Full Seasons: 3:1.

Chicago's Luke Johnsos teamed with Hunk Anderson during World War II in the only NFL co-coaching arrangement that was wholly a success. The two respected each other's abilities, did not interfere in the other man's responsibilities and relied on likeable assistant Paddy Driscoll as a liaison to promote harmony. While Anderson had served as a head coach in the college ranks, Johnsos never was an individual head coach on any level despite the quality of his work throughout his decades with the Bears.

Johnsos spent his entire pro career with the Bears, but that was almost by accident. Chicago wanted to sign star runner Walter Holmer out of Northwestern in 1929, but Holmer insisted his teammate Johnsos come, too. Luke also signed a contract with the Cincinnati Reds as a shortstop, but poor vision ended his baseball career. With the Bears, Johnsos was a two-time All Pro end from 1929 to 1936. Upon retirement, George Halas hired Luke as an assistant coach; he would remain on the coaching staff for the next 33 years.

Johnsos liked to sit in the press box where he could see the whole field as plays developed. In 1940, he had Halas install a phone to the bench and thus instituted the practice of eye-in-the-sky coaching in the NFL. When Halas joined the Navy midseason in 1942, he turned over his team to Johnsos and Anderson. The pair led the Bears to the title game that year and to the championship in 1943. One thing that united the two co-coaches was their mutual resentment of Clark Shaughnessy, regarded by both Halas and the press as the genius of the T formation. While Halas tried to foist Shaughnessy upon them, Johnsos and Anderson even went so far as to lock him out of practice so he wouldn't be able to claim credit for their work to Halas.

Johnsos drew interest from other teams in the league as a head coaching prospect. He was a candidate for the Cardinals job in both 1943 and 1949 and was offered the Rams job in 1945. Luke was reluctant to leave the Bears, though. In 1949, he told reporters, "I've got a wife and five children, and any chance I have to better myself I'm going to take it. But it will have to be a good offer before I leave the Bears. I became a stockholder in the Bears' club last year. I want to stay in Chicago." Jeff Davis reported in *Papa Bear* that Halas told Johnsos he was going to promote him to head coach in 1956, but when word leaked to the press, presumably through Luke, Halas announced Paddy Driscoll as his successor instead.

Despite feeling betrayed, Johnsos stayed with the Bears. And when Sid Luckman's packaging company undercut Johnsos' printing company for the Kraft Foods account the following year, Luke continued running the Bears' offense. He was still running the offense for Halas' final championship season in 1963 and retired six years later. Upon Johnsos' death, former tight end Mike Ditka said, "He was a good football man. He taught practical football. He was the man on the phone up in the stadium, who can be tremendously important if you have confidence in him."

JOLLEY, ALVA J. (AL) 9/29/1899–8/26/1948. Marietta, Tulsa and Kansas State. Played T for the Akron Pros, Dayton Triangles, Oorang Indians, Buffalo Bisons, Brooklyn Dodgers and Cleveland Indians from 1922 to 1923 and from 1929 to 1931. *Apprenticeship:* None. *Roots:* None. *Branches:* Mike Palm (i). *Coordinators/Key Assistants:* Mike Palm coached the backs. *Hall of Fame Players:* None. *Primary Quarterbacks:* None. *Record:* Began as **Player-Coach; Interim Coach** in 1933.

Al Jolley was an American Indian from Onaga, Kansas, who had a sporadic playing career for six teams in the pre–1933 NFL. Most notably, he played with Jim Thorpe and several other Native Americans on the Oorang Indians in 1923. After that, he dropped out of the league. He was coaching high school football in 1929 when the Buffalo Bisons hired him as player-coach, but the team won only its season finale. In fact, he made his coaching debut on his 30th birthday, a 9–3 loss to the Cardinals. Al then played a season with Brooklyn and a season with Cleveland before retiring from playing.

In 1933, the expansion Cincinnati Reds hired Jolley in July as their first head coach. He immediately took a road trip through the Ohio and Kentucky region searching for players. Although the player limit

Jolley, Alva J. (Al)									
Year	Team	Games	Wins	Losses	Ties	%	P Wins	P Losses	P %
1929	Buffalo Bisons	9	1	7	1	.125	0	0	.000
1933	Cincinnati Reds	6	0	5	1	.083	0	0	.000
2 years		15	1	12	2	.133	0	0	.000

at that time was just 30, Jolley reportedly went through at least 79 players in the team's preseason practices and preseason games against local independent teams. Jolley had the Reds running the Notre Dame Box Offense, but not very well; they would score only three points in six games with him as the coach, managing a field goal in a 17–3 loss to the expansion Pittsburgh franchise. In game two, volatile lineman Les Caywood was ejected along with the Cardinals black halfback Joe Lillard after the two got into a slugfest.

Although Jolley is credited with coaching the Reds for just three games in the ESPN and MacMillan football encyclopedias, he actually lasted twice as long. After the fourth game, he brought in linemen Jim Mooney and Cookie Tackwell as well as back Jim Bausch. That influx of talent brought a 0–0 tie with Pittsburgh in the fifth game, but after a 6–0 loss to Philadelphia in game six, Jolley resigned "in the best interests of the team"— and actually it was, since the team finished 3–1 under former assistant Mike Palm who junked the Notre Dame Box. After leaving pro football, Al coached high school football and worked in insurance. He was involved in Washington County, Ohio politics and also chaired the local board of education.

JONES, JUNE S. 2/9/1919– Oregon, Hawaii and Portland State. Played QB for the Falcons from 1977 to 1979 and 1981. *Apprenticeship:* College asst.—1 year; USFL asst.— 2 years; CFL asst.—1 year; pro asst.— 7 years. Roots: Jerry Glanville. *Branches:* Jim Bates (i). *Coordinators/Key Assistants*: For the Falcons, Mouse Davis helped Jones run the offense, while Joe Haering then Rod Rust handled the defense. *Hall of Fame Players:* Chris Doleman. *Primary Quarterbacks:* Jeff George. *Tendencies:* • His teams scored 20 points and allowed 24.7 per game • His teams ran 36.3% of the time, which was 83% of the league average • Four starting quarterbacks in four years; 60% of starts to primary quarterback • Eight rookie starters in four years • Winning Full Seasons to Losing Full Seasons: 1:2.

Born in Portland, Oregon, June Jones spent two years at the University of Oregon and two at Hawaii before coming home to play quarterback at Portland State in 1975 for new coach Mouse Davis. Davis had attained a great deal of success coaching the Run-and-Shoot offense at Oregon high schools for 15 years and made Jones his first starting quarterback at PSU. Jones

showcased the passing offense by throwing for over 3,500 yards in 1976. June was succeeded by Neil Lomax at PSU and signed with Atlanta as a free agent in 1977. After completing just 45% of his passes during a four-year stint as a backup quarterback in the NFL, Jones spent one final season quarterbacking the Toronto Argonauts in Canada before beginning his coaching career as an assistant coach for Hawaii in 1983.

The following year, Jones was hired as the wide receivers coach for the Houston Gamblers of the USFL; Mouse Davis was the team's offensive coordinator, and he had Jim Kelly direct a potent version of the Run-and-Shoot. A year later, Davis became head coach of the USFL's Denver Gold, with Jones serving as the team's offensive coordinator. When that league folded, June was named offensive coordinator for the Ottawa Roughriders of the CFL in 1986. A year later he moved up to the NFL as the quarterbacks coach for Jerry Glanville's Houston Oilers as they were instituting the Run-and-Shoot. In 1989, Jones left Houston to reunite with Mouse Davis, who by then was the Lions' offensive coordinator. Both Davis and Jones left Detroit in 1991: Davis went to the World League of American Football, while June became Jerry Glanville's offensive coordinator in Atlanta.

By 1993, the Glanville carnival came crashing to the ground, and the Falcons turned to Jones to restore the franchise. The team traded for strong armed and strong willed Jeff George to run June's Run-and-Shoot offense and the two teamed to put on an aerial show for in 1994 and 1995, with Atlanta making the playoffs in Jones' second season. Jones' Falcons astoundingly threw the ball 17% more than the league average. Things completely came apart in year three, however. George and Jones clashed with the two getting into a screaming match on the sidelines during week three of the season. George was suspended and then released. Meanwhile the defense dropped nearly to the bottom of the league, allowing 461 points. Defensive end Chuck Smith complained after game 15, "We need a head coach who is going to be a defensive man. Right now that's not the case. Until we play defense, we will always be losers." Smith was suspended for the season finale, but Jones was fired soon after.

A year later, Jones took the job of quarterbacks coach for the San Diego Chargers under Kevin Gilbride. Gilbride was fired after just six games, largely due to

Jones, June S.									
Year	Team	Games	Wins	Losses	Ties	%	P Wins	P Losses	P %
1994	Falcons	16	7	9	0	.438	0	0	.000
1995	Falcons	16	9	7	0	.563	0	1	.000
1996	Falcons	16	3	13	0	.188	0	0	.000
1998	Chargers	10	3	7	0	.300	0	0	.000
4 years		58	22	36	0	.379	0	1	.000

the failures of quarterback Ryan Leaf. Jones finished out the 1998 season as the interim head coach and then left the continental U.S., taking over the football program at Hawaii that had lost 18 games in a row. Beginning in 1999, Jones posted seven winning seasons in nine years in the Aloha state, with Run-and-Shoot offenses that featured one record-setting passer after another. By 2008, June grew tired of the perceived lack of support for his program by the university where he had posted a 76–41 record and took over the woeful program at SMU that had been down since 1987 when the NCAA shut down SMU football for a year, the "death penalty" of college sports. While his first Mustangs team won just one game, Jones took SMU to consecutive bowl games from 2009 to 2011, using his passing offense as the great equalizer against stronger programs and attained a 24–28 mark through 2011. Although none of Jones' record setting college passers has yet made a success in the NFL, June has established his niche in the college ranks where he has won 100 games.

KARCIS, JOHN (BULL) 12/3/1908–9/4/1973. Carnegie Tech. Played FB for the Brooklyn Dodgers, Pittsburgh Pirates and the New York Giants from 1932 to 1939 and in 1943. *Apprenticeship:* Pro asst.—1 year. *Roots:* Bill Edwards. *Branches:* None. *Coordinators/Key Assistants:* None. *Hall of Fame Players:* Alex Wojciechowicz. *Primary Quarterbacks:* none. *Record:* **Interim Coach.**

A product of Monaca, Pennsylvania, Bull Karcis starred at tackle and fullback for Carnegie Tech from 1928 to 1930 and then played for Pittsburgh's independent J.P. Rooneys in 1931. In 1932, Bull joined the NFL by signing with the Brooklyn Dodgers. The 5'9" 223-pound rugged fullback banged out a nine-year NFL career at fullback. He first retired after the 1939 season with the Giants and spent the next two years coaching high school football. He returned to the league in 1942 as Bill Edwards' assistant in Detroit. After the Lions lost the first three games by a combined 55–7 score, though, Edwards was fired and Karcis promoted. Bull told the press, "I still think we can win some games. I like this job even though it's the toughest one I've ever had. There's only one way to stay here — by winning — and we'll cause some trouble in this league." Unfortunately for Karcis, the team lost the last eight games of the season and was outscored in that stretch 208–31. In only one game did the Lions lose by fewer than 12 points. Bull returned to the Giants in 1943 as a fullback in the depleted NFL before retiring for good. In the ensuing years, Karcis was a longtime high school coach in Pennsylvania.

KHAYAT, EDWARD M. (ED) 9/14/1935– Millsaps and Tulane. Played DT for the Redskins, Eagles and Patriots from 1957 to 1966. *Apprenticeship:* Pro asst.— 5 years. *Roots:* Tom Fears, Jerry Williams. *Branches:* None. *Coordinators/Key Assistants:* Tom Fears and John Rauch were his key offensive coaches, while Jess Richardson was his key defensive coach. *Hall of Fame Players:* None. *Primary Quarterbacks:* Pete Liske. *Tendencies:* • His teams scored 13.7 points and allowed 21.8 per game • His teams ran 48.8% of the time, which was 89% of the league average • Three starting quarterbacks in two years; 56% of starts to primary quarterback • Eight rookie starters in two years • Winning Full Seasons to Losing Full Seasons: 0:1.

Pugnacious Ed Khayat of Moss Point, Mississippi was the state's Golden Glove heavyweight champion in 1953–54 before starring on the line for Tulane in 1955 and 1956. Not drafted by the NFL, Khayat caught on as a free agent in Washington in 1957. Traded to the Eagles in 1957, Ed got to play for a championship team in 1960 before being traded back to the Redskins in 1962. In his second term in Washington, Ed played with his brother Bob, who eventually would go on to become chancellor of the University of Mississippi in 1995. That second stint with the Redskins is more memorable for the time that Giants' coach Allie Sherman charged at Khayat after the game and shook his finger at him while the two had a shouting contest over Ed's playing style. It was a scene repeated 40 years later when another Coach Sherman, Packers coach Mike Sherman, confronted Buccaneer Warren Sapp after Sapp delivered a cheap shot to Packer tackle Chad Clifton. Giant defensive

Karcis, John (Bull)									
Year	*Team*	*Games*	*Wins*	*Losses*	*Ties*	*%*	*P Wins*	*P Losses*	*P %*
1942	Lions	8	0	8	0	.000	0	0	.000
1 year		8	0	8	0	.000	0	0	.000

Khayat, Edward M. (Ed)									
Year	*Team*	*Games*	*Wins*	*Losses*	*Ties*	*%*	*P Wins*	*P Losses*	*P %*
1971	Eagles	11	6	4	1	.591	0	0	.000
1972	Eagles	14	2	11	1	.179	0	0	.000
2 years		25	8	15	2	.360	0	0	.000

tackle Dick Modzelewski was quoted in the *Washington Post* the next day saying Khayat was, "dirty. He's no good. He can't play well.... He did a lot of punching in New York, and he was punching out there today." Khayat returned to the Eagles in 1964 and then concluded his playing career with a final season with the Patriots in 1966.

Upon retirement, Eddie moved directly into coaching, joining the staff of Tom Fears in New Orleans in 1967 as the defensive line coach. When Fears was fired in 1971, both he and Khayat joined Jerry Williams' staff in Philadelphia. Williams had coached Khayat on the 1960 Eagles as defensive coach and was in the midst of his third straight losing season in Philadelphia. After losing the first three games of the 1971 season by a combined score of 110–24, Williams was fired by owner Leonard Tose and Ed Khayat was hired as interim coach. The Eagles dropped their next two games when Khayat got the inspired notion that what was holding back the team was its facial hair and ordered the players to shave that off. "Good grooming is one of the many facets of discipline," he said at the time. The Eagles won their next game in the rain against the Giants and went on a 6–2–1 tear for the rest of the season. They concluded the year with a four-game winning streak. Khayat and GM Pete Retzlaff both got two-year contract extensions. The key to the team's improvement was the defense led by middle linebacker Tim Rossovich and free safety Bill Bradley who paced the NFL in interceptions in 1971.

In 1972, though, Ed Khayat folded under the strain of being head coach. As an assistant coach, he was a positive, happy-go-lucky motivator who was big on communication. As an interim head coach of a team that was 0–5, he was under absolutely no pressure to succeed. Linebacker Steve Zabel recalled to Steven Norwood in *Real Football*, "Eddie had a way of keeping the guys pretty loose and pretty focused. His whole approach was a maul 'em attitude. Just go out and knock the hell out of somebody. Don't worry about the outcome. Just play as hard as you can." After the stirring turnaround in 1971, however, increased expectations led to increased pressures, and Khayat seemed to tighten up. Bad things started in training camp when Rossovich and Bradley staged a holdout. Rossovich was traded, and outside linebacker Zabel was asked to move over to the middle where he felt unfamiliar and uncomfortable. With the linebacking corps weakened, the other holes in the defense became more pronounced. As for the offense, the starting quarterbacking was split between rag-armed incumbent Pete Liske and overmatched and untutored rookie John Reaves. The Eagles lost their first five games for the second consecutive year, but this year also lost the last five games to finish 2–11–1. The lowest point came on November 26th when the Birds lost to the Giants 62–10. It was the team's worst loss for the decade, and Khayat accused his team of the ultimate sin, quitting. Three weeks later, Khayat was fired and Retzlaff resigned.

Khayat resumed his career as a popular defensive line coach in the league in 1973 with the Lions. In 1975 he moved on to the Falcons, then to the Colts in 1977, back to the Lions in 1982 on to the Patriots from 1985 to 1989. Ed was named head coach again in 1991 of the New Orleans Night of the Arena Football League, but returned to the NFL as the Bucs defensive line coach from 1992 to 1993. Khayat then took over the Arena League's Nashville Kats in 1997 and led them to back-to-back championship game appearances in 2000–2001. His last coaching stop was the Carolina Cobras from 2003 to 2004, also in the Arena League. His overall Arena League coaching record was 25–24.

KIESLING, WALTER A. (WALT) 5/3/1903–3/2/1962. St. Thomas (MN). Played G for the Duluth Eskimos, Pottsville Maroons, Chicago Cardinals, Chicago Bears, Green Bay Packers and Pittsburgh Pirates from 1926 to 1938. *Apprenticeship:* Pro asst.— 2 years. *Roots:* Johnny Blood McNally. *Branches:* Jim Leonard, Bill McPeak, Nick Skorich. *Coordinators/Key Assistants:* In his first stint, Wilbur Sortet was his as-

Kiesling, Walter A. (Walt)									
Year	Team	Games	Wins	Losses	Ties	%	P Wins	P Losses	P %
1939	Pirates (Steelers)	8	1	6	1	.188	0	0	.000
1940	Pirates (Steelers)	11	2	7	2	.273	0	0	.000
1941	Steelers	4	1	2	1	.375	0	0	.000
1942	Steelers	11	7	4	0	.636	0	0	.000
1943	Steagles	10	5	4	1	.550	0	0	.000
1944	Card-Pitts	10	0	10	0	.000	0	0	.000
1954	Steelers	12	5	7	0	.417	0	0	.000
1955	Steelers	12	4	8	0	.333	0	0	.000
1956	Steelers	12	5	7	0	.417	0	0	.000
9 years		90	30	55	5	.361	0	0	.000

sistant; in his second stint, Jim Leonard was his assistant; in his third stint, Nick Skorich coached the line, while Chuck Cherundolo ran the defense. *Hall of Fame Players:* Jack Butler, Bill Dudley, Marion Motley, Ernie Stautner. *Primary Quarterbacks:* Jim Finks. *Record:* **Hall of Fame Player; Co-Coach** (in 1942 with Greasy Neale) and (in 1943 with Phil Handler). *Tendencies:* • His teams scored 15 points and allowed 21.3 per game • His teams ran 60.8% of the time, which was 101% of the league average • Three starting quarterbacks in three T formation years; 67% of starts to primary quarterback • 29 rookie starters in nine years • Winning Full Seasons to Losing Full Seasons: 2:6.

St. Paul's Walt Kiesling was a giant 260-pound guard in a time of much smaller players and may be the most questionable member of the Pro Football Hall of Fame. Despite being named All Pro only once in 1930, Walt was named to the NFL's All Decade team for the 1920s. Kiesling is listed as a Steeler in Canton since he both played and coached there. However, he played longest for the Cardinals, five years. He also played two years for the Duluth Eskimos who then ceased operations, one for the Pottsville Maroons who then went out of business, one for the Chicago Bears, two for the Packers and two for Pittsburgh when he also served as player-coach Johnny Blood McNally's assistant coach. No Hall of Famer whose career began after the formation of the NFL in 1920 played for as many teams as Kiesling

After retiring from playing in 1939, Walt took over as Pittsburgh's head coach in game five and coached the team through the 1940 season. Art Rooney went through Bert Bell and Buff Donelli as coaches in 1941 before bringing back Kiesling for his second stint as head coach in the Steel City with two games to play that year. Walt stayed on in 1942 and led the Steelers to their first winning season that year. Pittsburgh merged with the Eagles for 1943, and Kiesling and Greasy Neale were co-coaches who did not get along at all. Rooney told Myron Cope for *The Game That Was,* "Kies was a great coach, but everything with Kies was that nobody knew football like Kies." The next year, Pittsburgh merged with the Cardinals and Kiesling co-coached the team with fellow horse player Phil Handler. The two coaches got along well, especially at the race track, but the team did not win a single game.

Walt was let go after the season and spent 1945–

1948 as Curly Lambeau's line coach in Green Bay. He returned to Pittsburgh as line coach from 1949 to 1953. When Joe Bach was forced out as head coach due to his failing health, Rooney once again turned to Kiesling as head coach in 1954. Walt's third stint as Steeler head coach lasted three years and is remembered mostly for his plodding offense, his problems with star players and his cutting of Johnny Unitas. Three times Kiesling's Steelers finished last in scoring and six times were in the league's bottom three. The Steeler offense was so dull that the fans had a saying, "Hey Diddle Diddle, Rogel up the middle," since each game began with the same fullback dive play. Rooney ordered Kiesling to begin one game with a pass, which went for a big gain, but Walt had sabotaged the play by ordering one of his linemen to go offside so that Rooney would stop interfering in play calling. Halfback Lynn Chandnois recalled to Jim Wexell in *Pittsburgh Steelers: Men of Steel,* "Here's a guy [Kiesling] who didn't know anything about the T-formation; he was a single-wing coach. And he'd only talk to certain players. He never talked to me."

Rooney said that the gruff Kiesling responded to any problems by insisting the player was dumb. When Johnny Unitas was in the 1955 Steelers' training camp, he could not remember the plays so Walt thought he must be too dumb for the pro game and cut him. In 1957, Buddy Parker left the Lions and was named coach of the Steelers. Kiesling went back to being the team's line coach again. Ole Haugsrud, who knew Walt since he began his career in 1926 playing for Ole's Duluth Eskimos, once said, "The thing about Walt was that he preferred to be an assistant. He was available whenever the Steelers needed somebody, yet he would much rather be an assistant than the boss." He continued as an assistant on Parker's staff through 1961 when heart problems forced him to retire. He died a year later. Kiesling was elected to the Hall posthumously in 1966; he was represented by his friend Johnny Blood and presented for induction by Supreme Court Justice Byron "Whizzer" White, a Pittsburgh teammate from 1938.

KIFFIN, LANE M. 5/9/1975– Fresno State. QB; did not play professionally. *Apprenticeship:* College asst.— 9 years; pro asst.—1 year. *Roots:* Tom Coughlin. *Branches:* Tom Cable. *Coordinators/Key Assistants:* Greg Knapp handled the offense, while Rob Ryan ran the defense. *Hall of Fame Players:* None. *Primary Quar-*

Kiffin, Lane M.

Year	Team	Games	Wins	Losses	Ties	%	P Wins	P Losses	P %
2007	Raiders	16	4	12	0	.250	0	0	.000
2008	Raiders	4	1	3	0	.250	0	0	.000
2 years		20	5	15	0	.250	0	0	.000

terback: Josh McCown. *Tendencies:* • His teams scored 18.3 points and allowed 25 per game • His teams ran 51.5% of the time, which was 117% of the league average • Five starting quarterbacks in two years; 45% of starts to primary quarterback • Five rookie starters in two years • Winning Full Seasons to Losing Full Seasons: 0:1.

Born when his father Monte was defensive coordinator of the Nebraska Cornhuskers, Lane Kiffin grew up on the football field. Only a backup quarterback at Fresno State, he gave up his eligibility as a senior to begin his coaching career as an assistant while he finished his education in 1997 and 1998. He spent the following year as the line coach at Colorado State before joining Tom Coughlin's Jacksonville staff in 2000. From 2001 to 2006, Lane worked on Pete Carroll's staff at USC, working his way up to offensive coordinator by 2005. He was lured back to the pros by former USC assistant Al Davis who hired Kiffin as the Raiders' head coach in 2007.

Kiffin was just 31 at the time, but since Davis himself was just 34 when he was named the Raiders' head coach in 1963, he has hired a series of young head coaches, including John Madden, Mike Shanahan and Jon Gruden. Davis announced the hiring by saying, "Thirty-one years old. Wow, that's young. But you don't have to be old to be great." However, the honeymoon period for Davis and Kiffin was extremely short. Kiffin was against drafting immense quarterback Jamarcus Russell with the first overall pick in 2007, but Davis picked him and told Kiffin to just coach the team. Conflicts continued over high salaried players and disgruntled receiver Randy Moss as the season ground on to 4–12 result.

In the offseason, the two clashed over whether Rob Ryan would continue as defensive coordinator and the composition of the roster. By training camp, the media awaited the firing or resignation of Kiffin, but Davis let him dangle in the wind while he accumulated a paper trail of reasons. Finally, after four games of the 2008 season, Davis fired Kiffin "for cause," meaning he had no intention of paying off the rest of Kiffin's contracted salary. Al told the media, "I didn't hire the person I thought I was hiring. I think he conned me like he conned all you people." Kiffin filed a grievance for his missing salary, but ultimately lost the case as many did when they entered a legal matter with Al Davis.

Two months later, Kiffin was named head coach of the University of Tennessee, bringing his father with him as defensive coordinator. Lane's mouth got him into a series of jams in Knoxville, including a dustup in which he accused Florida coach Urban Meyer of recruiting violations. After one 7–6 season, Kiffin shocked Volunteer followers by bolting from his six-year contract to succeed Pete Carroll as USC's head coach (with father Monte in tow), making some observers think that maybe Al Davis wasn't far off in his negative characterizations of the Raiders' former carpet bagging coach. Through 2011, Kiffin's USC record was 18–7.

KNOX, CHARLES R. (CHUCK) 4/27/1932– Juniata. T; did not play professionally. *Apprenticeship:* College asst.— 5 years; pro asst.—10 years. *Roots:* Weeb Ewbank, Joe Schmidt. *Branches:* Leeman Bennett, Ken Meyer, Ray Malavasi, Kay Stephenson, Mike Martz, Joe Vitt (i). *Coordinators/Key Assistants:* In his first stint with the Rams, Ken Meyer then Ray Prochaska handled the offense, while Ray Malavasi ran the defense; for the Bills, Ray Prochaska handled the offense, while Tom Catlin ran the defense; for the Seahawks, Ray Prochaska then Steve Moore then John Becker handled the offense, while Tom Catlin ran the defense; in his second stint with the Rams, Ernie Zampese handled the offense, while George Dyer ran the defense. *Hall of Fame Players:* Joe Delamielleure, Franco Harris, Cortez Kennedy, Steve Largent, James Lofton, Tom Mack, Joe Namath, Merlin Olsen, Jackie Slater, Jack Youngblood. *Primary Quarterbacks:* Dave Krieg, Joe Ferguson, James Harris, Jim Everett. *Tendencies:* • His teams scored 20.5 points and allowed 18.1 per game • His teams ran 52% of the time, which was 105% of the league average • 17 starting quarterbacks in 22 years; 73% of starts to primary quarterbacks • 47 rookie starters in 22 years • Winning Full Seasons to Losing Full Seasons: 13:7.

The pride of Sewickley, Pennsylvania, Chuck Knox was known as "Ground Chuck" for his devotion to the running game. That devotion brought him great success in the regular season — he was the first NFL coach to lead three different franchises to division titles — but little success in the postseason. He grew up valuing hard work, laboring for the railroad in high school and at a steel mill in college, and ultimately would donate over a million dollars to his alma mater.

Knox was a 190-pound tackle at Juniata College in the early 1950s. He immediately went into coaching at Juniata in 1954. From 1955 to 1958, Chuck coached high school football in Pennsylvania before joining the staff at Wake Forest in 1959. In 1961, Knox moved on to Blanton Collier's Kentucky staff as offensive line coach, forcing Bill Arnsparger to move to the defensive line. Chuck stayed on under new head coach Charley Bradshaw in 1962 and then became Weeb Ewbank's line coach for the Jets in 1963. Chuck built a strong line in New York to protect Joe Namath, but left before the Jets' epic Super Bowl upset. Instead, Knox coached the Lions' line from 1968 to 1972 under Joe Schmidt.

After 10 years as a celebrated line coach in the league, Chuck was hired as the Rams' head coach in 1973. Over the next five years, Los Angeles would go 54–15–1 and win five division titles with five different

Knox, Charles R. (Chuck)

Year	Team	Games	Wins	Losses	Ties	%	P Wins	P Losses	P %
1973	Rams	14	12	2	0	.857	0	1	.000
1974	Rams	14	10	4	0	.714	1	1	.500
1975	Rams	14	12	2	0	.857	1	1	.500
1976	Rams	14	10	3	1	.750	1	1	.500
1977	Rams	14	10	4	0	.714	0	1	.000
1978	Bills	16	5	11	0	.313	0	0	.000
1979	Bills	16	7	9	0	.438	0	0	.000
1980	Bills	16	11	5	0	.688	0	1	.000
1981	Bills	16	10	6	0	.625	1	1	.500
1982	Bills	9	4	5	0	.444	0	0	.000
1983	Seahawks	16	9	7	0	.563	2	1	.667
1984	Seahawks	16	12	4	0	.750	1	1	.500
1985	Seahawks	16	8	8	0	.500	0	0	.000
1986	Seahawks	16	10	6	0	.625	0	0	.000
1987	Seahawks	15	9	6	0	.600	0	1	.000
1988	Seahawks	16	9	7	0	.563	0	1	.000
1989	Seahawks	16	7	9	0	.438	0	0	.000
1990	Seahawks	16	9	7	0	.563	0	0	.000
1991	Seahawks	16	7	9	0	.438	0	0	.000
1992	Rams	16	6	10	0	.375	0	0	.000
1993	Rams	16	5	11	0	.313	0	0	.000
1994	Rams	16	4	12	0	.250	0	0	.000
22 years		334	186	147	1	.558	7	11	.389

quarterbacks, but go just 3–5 in the playoffs. Knox believed in discipline, the fundamentals of blocking and tackling, organization and preparation. His defenses finished in the top three in the league five times in fewest points allowed. He was a taskmaster, but was well liked for his approachable personality. Chuck was especially noted for his "Knox-isms," offbeat clichés that he often repeated, like, "Work will win. Wishing won't." or "What you do speaks so well there's no need to hear what you say." While fans criticized him for being a dull coach, Knox's response was, "I'll tell you what's dull — losing." Still, Rams' halfback Lawrence McCutcheon reflected on Knox with Tom Danyluk in *The Super 70s*. "If Chuck had a shortcoming, it would be that he was very stubborn in trying to accomplish his main goal, and that was to run the football. When you get in playoff games, teams have a week or two to evaluate and study your team. They can put together a defense that will take away your strengths."

After five years in Los Angeles, Knox and owner Carroll Rosenbloom mutually agreed it was time for Chuck to move on. Each year brought a new quarterback controversy, and Rosenbloom made it clear that he wanted to see a more exciting brand of football. Knox turned down the Lions who were looking for a new coach and instead took over the Bills, a team that had won just five games in the last two seasons. Chuck took Buffalo to the playoffs twice in his first four seasons, but missed out on postseason in the strike season of 1982. When he and owner Ralph Wilson could not

agree on a contract extension, Knox quit and one day later signed with the Seahawks.

With Seattle, Knox opened up his offense a bit, bringing more balance. For the first time, Knox's team actually called more passing plays than rushing plays with the Seahawks. While the team did not have the sustained excellence of the Ram years, Seattle did make the playoffs four times, win a division title and reach one AFC Championship game. Quarterback Dave Krieg told *Sports Illustrated*, "There's no doubt about it, Chuck's overall presence, his intensity, his toughness, play a big factor in helping us to win." Knox told the same magazine that key for him was, "Consistency of approach. I take the same basic premise I took when I coached high school football in Pennsylvania. Hard work will win. I take the same professional approach every day and set expectations high."

After nine years in the Great Northwest, Knox resigned and returned to Los Angeles in 1992 to coach the Rams a second time and also serve as team vice president. For the first time in his career, Chuck came up empty, winning just 15 games in his second stint with the Rams. After three years, Knox was fired and retired from the game.

KOPF, HERBERT M. (HERB) 6/25/1901–3/22/1996. Washington & Jefferson. Played E for the Hartford Blues. *Apprenticeship:* College coach.—18 years (5 as head coach). *Roots:* None. *Branches:* None. *Coordinators/Key Assistants:* John Dell Isola coached the line. *Hall of Fame Players:* Ace Parker. *Primary*

Kopf, Herbert M. (Herb)

Year	Team	Games	Wins	Losses	Ties	%	P Wins	P Losses	P %
1944	Boston Yanks (defunct)	10	2	8	0	.200	0	0	.000
1945	Boston Yanks (defunct)	10	3	6	1	.350	0	0	.000
1946	Boston Yanks (defunct)	11	2	8	1	.227	0	0	.000
3 years		31	7	22	2	.258	0	0	.000

Quarterbacks: George Cafego, Paul Governali. *Tendencies:* • His teams scored 12.7 points and allowed 23.1 per game • His teams ran 63.4% of the time, which was the league average • Six starting quarterbacks in three years; 65% of starts to primary quarterbacks • 12 rookie starters in three years • Winning Full Seasons to Losing Full Seasons: 0:3.

From New Britain, Connecticut, Herb Kopf came to Washington & Jefferson College to play baseball like his brother Larry who had a 10-year career in the big leagues, primarily as a shortstop with the Cincinnati Reds. Larry was a starter in the 1919 World Series later made infamous for the Black Sox gambling scandal. Herb switched to football when Washington & Jefferson dropped baseball and, as a freshman, played end on the Presidents' surprising 1922 Rose Bowl team coached by another Cincinnati Red, Greasy Neale. In that Rose Bowl, the fearless and feisty Kopf went up to California's stout star end Brick Muller at the beginning of the game and smeared mud all over the front of his uniform. Herb was just 150 pounds, but Neale later said of him, "All his weight was brains."

That brainy nature led Kopf into coaching immediately upon his graduation in 1925, although he did appear briefly with the independent Hartford Blues that year. Herb worked as an assistant to Lou Little at Georgetown from 1925 to 1929 while attending law school there and then worked as Little's assistant at Columbia from 1930 to 1937. He got his first head coaching position with Manhattan College in 1938 and led the Jaspers to a 18–24–1 record over the next five years until the school dropped football in 1943. That year, he was asked by the *New York Times* how he was doing and replied, "It's been kind of tough — this inactivity — but there's no complaint from me."

In 1944, Kopf was hired to coach the expansion Boston Yanks owned by entertainment impresario Ted Collins. Collins had planned on hiring Jim Crowley as coach, but he was in the Navy so turned to Herb as a temporary replacement. As it turned out, though, when Crowley returned from the war, he was hired as Commissioner of the new All America Football Conference, so Kopf ended up coaching the Yanks for their first three difficult seasons. His offense was of his own design from Manhattan College, and he called it the "QT," a combination of the T and the single wing. He told the *Times,* "I can run a quick-opening to the inside, the man-in-motion, flanker sweeps and pass, all from the QT, which has the quarterback line up behind the center, two backs in the T and one on the wing." However, the Yanks were an awful team that won just seven games in three years, so Kopf was fired after the 1946 season.

In 1948, Kopf returned to coaching as an assistant at Boston College under Denny Myers. When Myers was fired in 1951, Kopf was let go as well. Herb later resurfaced as Benny Friedman's assistant at Brandeis College from 1953 to 1960 until the school dropped football.

KOTITE, RICHARD E. (RICH) 10/13/1942– Wagner. Played TE for the Giants and Steelers from 1967 to 1969 and from 1971 to 1972. *Apprenticeship:* College asst.— 4 years; pro asst.—14 years. *Roots:* Hank Stram, Sam Rutigliano, Joe Walton, Buddy Ryan. *Branches:* None. *Coordinators/Key Assistants:* For the Eagles, Zeke Bratkowski helped Kotite run the offense, while Bud Carson handled the defense; for the Jets, Bratkowski then Ron Erhardt ran the offense, while Jim Vechiarella handled the defense. *Hall of Fame Players:* James Lofton, Reggie White. *Primary Quarterbacks:* Randall Cunningham, Boomer Esiason. *Tendencies:* • His teams scored 18.3 points and allowed 20.3 per game • His teams ran 42.4% of the time, which was 95% of the league average • 12 starting quarterbacks in six years; 48% of starts to primary quarterbacks • 14 rookie starters in six years • Winning Full Seasons to Losing Full Seasons: 2:3.

Born in Brooklyn, Rich Kotite was a New Yorker through and through and had the worst 39-game stretch of any coach in NFL history. Other coaches have had longer losing streaks, but no one has sustained a .103 winning percentage for a stretch as long as 39 games aside from Kotite, whose Eagles and Jets went 4–35 from midseason 1994 through the end

Kotite, Richard E. (Rich)

Year	Team	Games	Wins	Losses	Ties	%	P Wins	P Losses	P %
1991	Eagles	16	10	6	0	.625	0	0	.000
1992	Eagles	16	11	5	0	.688	1	1	.500
1993	Eagles	16	8	8	0	.500	0	0	.000
1994	Eagles	16	7	9	0	.438	0	0	.000
1995	Jets	16	3	13	0	.188	0	0	.000
1996	Jets	16	1	15	0	.063	0	0	.000
6 years		96	40	56	0	.417	1	1	.500

of the 1996 season. Kotite's closest competitor was Phil Handler who went 4–34 for his career as a sometime coach of the woeful Cardinals, mostly during World War II.

Although he was selected in the 18th round of the 1965 draft, Kotite did not stick in the league till 1967 as a backup tight end for the Giants. In his lackluster five-year career with the Giants and Steelers, Rich grabbed just 17 passes and retired after the 1972. He immediately began his coaching career as an assistant under former Giants' teammate Joe Morrison at the University of Tennessee-Chattanooga from 1973 to 1976. In 1977, Kotite returned to the NFL on Hank Stram's staff in New Orleans. The following year, he moved on to Cleveland, working under Sam Rutigliano from 1978 to 1982. In 1983, new Jets' coach Joe Walton, who had first scouted Kotite for the Giants many years before, hired Rich as receivers coach. Three years later, Kotite took over as offensive coordinator. After Walton was fired, Kotite was hired by Eagles' GM Harry Gamble as offensive coordinator for Buddy Ryan in 1990. Ryan had little use for management and did not think much of Kotite. However, when the Eagles crashed in the playoffs for the third straight season, Kotite was rewarded with the head coaching job after management-irritant Ryan was dumped by owner Norman Braman.

Star quarterback Randall Cunningham went down in Kotite's first game as head coach, but the Eagles managed a 10–6 record in 1991 anyway. Kotite began to reveal his tense and threatened nature that season by closing practices to the media. 1992 was a tumultuous year marked by the death of defensive tackle Jerome Brown, the benching of Cunningham and a series of outbursts by such outspoken players as linebacker Seth Joyner who for years brutally criticized Rich's decisions, questioned his guts and called the coach a puppet. Kotite's biggest problem in Philadelphia was that he was neither loved nor respected by the bulk of his players. Still, the team went 11–5 and won one playoff game before ultimately losing to Dallas. Things went downhill rapidly from there. Defensive end Reggie White left as a free agent, and Kotite seemed to make no effort to convince management to try to sign him. Keith Jackson and Keith Byars both headed to Miami. Cunningham went down again to

injury, and the team struggled to finish 8–8 by winning its last three games.

The team's top picks in Kotite's first three drafts all proved to be disappointments. Somehow the Eagles got off to a 7–2 start under new owner Jeffrey Lurie in 1994, and Kotite began to make noises about a contract extension with his career record standing at 36–21 at that point. Lurie wisely put that off till the end of the season because the Birds went completely into the tank by losing their last seven games of the year. Kotite had a terrible relationship with the Philadelphia media, relying entirely on aggravating coach-speak to respond to real concerns. "Without question" was one common expression; after losses, another was "the players left nothing in the locker room." Perhaps his biggest hapless fiasco was when he misread a rain-smudged 2-point conversion chart in the fourth quarter of a 1994 loss to Dallas. In four years, he let a very talented team assembled by his predecessor crumble steadily under his direction.

He was fired the day after Christmas in 1994 and hired 10 days later by Jets' octogenarian owner Leon Hess, who famously said he hired Rich because, "I want to win now." With a 36–28 record, the national press still looked at Kotite as a good coach. The New York media in particular refused to believe how incompetent he was and thought it was a case of a Philadelphia media feeding frenzy. One headline from the *New York Times* saw Kotite as, "A Tough Guy Takes Over a Marshmallow Team." In reality, Kotite was an easy-going players' coach who made few demands on his players. Intense Super Bowl winning linebacker Bill Romanowski recalled in his autobiography *Romo* that he was underwhelmed by Rich's ambitions for the team, "'Our goal,' Coach Kotite told us in our first meeting, 'is to hopefully make the playoffs.'"

The Jets experience was a disaster from the start. The Jets were coming off a 6–10 season under Pete Carroll, but weren't without some talent. Under Kotite's aimless leadership, though, the team dropped to 3–13 in 1995 and 1–15 in 1996. Kotite brought in a number of high-priced free agents who flopped, his starting wideouts Keyshawn Johnson and Wayne Chrebet were at each other's throats, and he completely lost control of his team for some of his mindless moves. In a game against Oakland, he started converted quarterback Vance Joseph at cornerback and assigned him to cover star receiver Tim Brown without help. In another, he gave undrafted free agent tackle Everett McIver his first NFL start against Hall of Fame defensive end Bruce Smith. The final bizarre touch came the last week of the 1996 season when Kotite announced he would be stepping down at the end of the year, quizzically adding, "I wasn't fired; I didn't quit." The next season Bill Parcells took over and turned that 1–15 team into a 9–7 one. Kotite never coached in the NFL again.

KUBALE, EDWIN A. (ED) 11/22/1899–2/4/1971. Centre. C; did not play professionally. *Apprenticeship:* College coach —17 years (13 as head coach); pro asst.—1 year. *Roots:* Pete Cawthon. *Branches:* None. *Coordinators/Key Assistants*: His co-coach Frank Bridges handled the backs. *Hall of Fame Players:* Bruiser Kinard. *Primary Quarterbacks:* None. *Record:* **Interim Co-Coach.**

Ed Kubale was the center for the Centre College team that upset mighty Harvard in 1921. Born in South Bend, Indiana, Kubale went into coaching right out of college, serving as the line coach for Texas Christian from 1925 to 1928. He then returned to Centre in 1929 as head coach of the football team. From 1929 to 1937, Kubale's football squads compiled a 50–32–4 record, while Ed also coached basketball and track in addition to being the school's athletic director. In 1938, he moved on to Southwestern College in Memphis, where he attained a 16–16–4 record through 1941 when the school dropped football. Kubale was a contender for the Yale head coaching position that year, but lost out. He resurfaced in July 1944 when he was hired as Brooklyn's line coach by Pete Cawthon; the backfield coach was Frank Bridges who had been Ed's high school coach in Fort Smith, Arkansas.

Brooklyn was on its last legs as a franchise and changed its name in 1944 from Dodgers to Tigers to mask the decline brought about by depleted manpower. The Tigers lost their first five games and were outscored 56–81, although they did not lose any game by more than seven points. Cawthon resigned and Brooklyn GM Tom Gallery appointed his two assistants as co-coaches, saying, "We won't look for a name coach if Kubale and Bridges can do the job and I don't see why they can't." Kubale said he would change the offense, "We'll give them some spreads and add a sort of modified T, but, of course, that will take time." However, the losing continued with the Tigers producing just 13 points in the next three games. At that point, Ed wondered, "I won't ask any questions about scoring. We'll take all we can get in any way we can get them. Don't you think it's about time our luck turned for us?" Brooklyn was shut out in its last two games, having been outscored 85–13 under Kubale and Bridges. In 1945, Brooklyn was merged into the Boston Yanks and disappeared from the NFL for good. Kubale retired to farming and also served on the Kentucky Turnpike Commission. His son became a Kentucky state legislator.

KUBIAK, GARY W. 8/15/1961– Texas A&M. Played QB for the Broncos from 1983 to 1991. *Apprenticeship:* College asst.— 2 years; pro asst.—12 years. *Roots:* George Seifert, Mike Shanahan. *Branches:* None. *Coordinators/Key Assistants*: Mike Sherman then Kyle Shanahan then Rick Dennison ran the offense, while Richard Smith then Frank Bush then Wade Phillips handled the defense. *Hall of Fame Players:* None. *Primary Quarterbacks:* Matt Schaub. *Tendencies:* • His teams scored 22.6 points and allowed 22.7 per game • His teams ran 44.1% of the time, which was 101% of the league average • Five starting quarterbacks in six years; 67% of starts to primary quarterback • 18

Kubale, Edwin A. (Ed)									
Year	*Team*	*Games*	*Wins*	*Losses*	*Ties*	*%*	*P Wins*	*P Losses*	*P %*
1944	Brooklyn Tigers (defunct)	5	0	5	0	.000	0	0	.000
1 year		5	0	5	0	.000	0	0	.000

Kubiak, Gary W.									
Year	*Team*	*Games*	*Wins*	*Losses*	*Ties*	*%*	*P Wins*	*P Losses*	*P %*
2006	Texans	16	6	10	0	.375	0	0	.000
2007	Texans	16	8	8	0	.500	0	0	.000
2008	Texans	16	8	8	0	.500	0	0	.000
2009	Texans	16	9	7	0	.563	0	0	.000
2010	Texans	16	6	10	0	.375	0	0	.000
2011	Texans	16	10	6	0	.625	1	1	.500
6 years		96	47	46	0	.490	1	1	.500

rookie starters in six years • Winning Full Seasons to Losing Full Seasons: 2:2.

Houston native Gary Kubiak was a smart but undersized quarterback at Texas A&M when he was drafted in the eighth round in 1983 by Denver. The Broncos got their quarterback of the future that year from the draft, but it wasn't Kubiak. Instead, Denver made a trade with the Colts to bring in the first overall pick of the draft, John Elway. Kubiak befriended Elway and became his loyal and reliable backup for nine seasons. The highpoint of Gary's career came in his final game when he replaced an injured Elway in the fourth quarter of the AFC Championship game in January 1992 and nearly led the Broncos to a come-from-behind victory until a fumble by runner Steve Sewell abruptly ended Kubiak's 11 of 12 passing day and Denver's season.

Kubiak returned to Texas A&M in 1992 as running backs coach. Two years later, Mike Shanahan, former Broncos offensive coordinator now coaching in San Francisco, hired Gary as the 49ers' quarterbacks coach for the 1994 Super Bowl year. Shanahan parlayed that championship into the head coaching job at Denver and brought Kubiak along as the Broncos offensive coordinator. Gary worked under Shanahan in Denver from 1995 to 2005 and won two Super Bowl rings coaching his old teammate John Elway.

In 2006, Kubiak returned to his hometown to become the second coach of the Houston Texans. For the first five years, the results were decidedly mixed. After one year with failed quarterback David Carr, Kubiak traded for quarterback Matt Schaub who has brought more professionalism to the position, but both Shaub and the Texan offense tend to be streaky and inconsistent. On the other side of the ball, Houston's defense has ranged from mediocre to terrible. The total collapse of the defense in 2010, just a year after the Texans' first winning season ever, nearly cost Kubiak his job. Owner Bob McNair has been exceedingly patient with the team's mediocre record under Kubiak, but decided to keep the coach for 2011 be-

cause, "One of Gary's strengths, and one of the things that influenced me, is that, in spite of the tough period we went through, Gary was able to hold the team together. That's the sign of a good coach, because it's very difficult to do that." Instead, Houston brought in Wade Phillips as its new defensive coordinator, and he rebuilt that unit to one that allowed the fourth fewest points in the league to help Kubiak produce a playoff team for the first time despite losing its top two quarterbacks to season-ending injuries.

KUHARICH, JOSEPH L. 4/14/1917–1/25/1981. Notre Dame. Played G for the Cardinals from 1940 to 1941 and in 1945. *Apprenticeship:* College coach.—7 years (4 as head coach); pro asst.—1 year. *Roots:* Jock Sutherland. *Branches:* Mike Nixon, Dick Stanfel (i), Fred Bruney (i). *Coordinators/Key Assistants:* For the Cardinals, Mike Nixon was his key offensive coach and Dick Evans handled the defense; for the Redskins, Nixon and Evans again were the key coaches; for the Eagles, Herman Ball was the key offensive coach, while Dick Evans again ran the defense. *Hall of Fame Players:* Bob Brown, Mike Ditka, Ollie Matson, Jim Ringo, Charlie Trippi. *Primary Quarterbacks:* Eddie LeBaron, Norm Snead. *Tendencies:* • His teams scored 19.9 points and allowed 23.7 per game • His teams ran 55.9% of the time, which was 106% of the league average • 11 starting quarterbacks in 11 years; 63% of starts to primary quarterbacks • 47 rookie starters in 11 years • Winning Full Seasons to Losing Full Seasons: 2:8.

Joe Kuharich was born in South Bend, Indiana, and his heart was always with the Fighting Irish. Kuharich was a 195-pound All American at guard for Notre Dame under Elmer Layden from 1935 to 1937 and then served as an assistant coach for the team in 1938 and 1939. In 1940 and 1941, Joe played for the Cardinals before going into the Navy from 1942 to 1945, returning to finish out the 1945 season in Chicago. Kuharich took a job as the Steelers' line coach in 1946 and then moved on to the University of San Francisco in 1947 under former Notre Dame

Kuharich, Joseph L.

Year	Team	Games	Wins	Losses	Ties	%	P Wins	P Losses	P %
1952	Cardinals	12	4	8	0	.333	0	0	.000
1954	Redskins	12	3	9	0	.250	0	0	.000
1955	Redskins	12	8	4	0	.667	0	0	.000
1956	Redskins	12	6	6	0	.500	0	0	.000
1957	Redskins	12	5	6	1	.458	0	0	.000
1958	Redskins	12	4	7	1	.375	0	0	.000
1964	Eagles	14	6	8	0	.429	0	0	.000
1965	Eagles	14	5	9	0	.357	0	0	.000
1966	Eagles	14	9	5	0	.643	0	0	.000
1967	Eagles	14	6	7	1	.464	0	0	.000
1968	Eagles	14	2	12	0	.143	0	0	.000
11 years		142	58	81	3	.419	0	0	.000

coach Ed McKeever. A year later, Joe was named the Dons' head coach, and McKeever undercut him by sending out a letter indicating 18 of his players were ineligible. Despite that, Joe built a juggernaut in four years. His 1951 team went 9–0 and produced 10 NFL players, including Hall of Famers Ollie Matson, Gino Marchetti and Bob St. Clair, in addition to Pro Bowlers Ed Brown and Joe Scudero. Kuharich also got to know the team's student publicist, Pete Rozelle, and produced a 25–14 record — the only time in his career he would leave a team with a winning record.

Kuharich was hired by the Cardinals as head coach in 1952, succeeding Curly Lambeau. In Chicago, he got to coach Ollie Matson again, but the team finished just 4–8. Kuharich was dismissed when he got into a dispute with management over the retention of his assistant coaches. After a year as a scout, Joe was hired by Curly Lambeau as the Redskins' line coach in 1954. However, in training camp, owner George Preston Marshall fired Lambeau over the players drinking beer in the team hotel and promoted Kuharich to head coach. End Joe Tereshinski told Thom Loverro for *Hail Victory*, "He worked hard and respected his players, and they respected him back. You could trust him. He was a man, and the team got behind him." In five years, though, Joe only had one winning season, but his 26–33–1 record still won him a five-year extension and increased powers in 1958. Yet, at the end of the season, he left Washington to return to his alma mater, saying, "I am flattered and proud that Notre Dame decided to give me the opportunity. It always has been my hope and prayer that I could return to Notre Dame." However, from 1959 to 1962, the Fighting Irish did not put up much of a fight, going a paltry 17–23; Kuharich thus was the first Notre Dame coach to leave South Bend with a losing record. He then spent 1963 working in the NFL office under his old associate Pete Rozelle, now league commissioner.

That connection brought Kuharich to the attention of new Eagles' owner Jerry Wolman, and Wolman named Joe head coach and GM in 1964. Trader Joe went right to work and started making deals. Most notably, Kuharich traded away the Eagles two biggest stars to division rivals, the popular receiver Tommy McDonald to the Cowboys and the gun-slinging quarterback Sonny Jurgensen to Washington for stolid Norm Snead who was four years younger than Sonny. While defensive backs Jimmy Carr and Claude Crabb also changed addresses in the deal, this was a blockbuster starting-quarterback-for-starting-quarterback exchange almost never seen in the NFL. Joe was a blustery guy whose true gift was not self-expression, and he said of the trade, "It's quite rare but not unusual." Kuharich became known as a Mr. Malaprop for such odd comments as, "Every coach must view a player with three different eyes. " or "That's a horse of a different fire department." or "We were three points behind, but that's not the same as being even."

More important than his problems with the English language, though, were his problems on the field. Despite being given a 15-year contract by Wolman at the end of his first season, Joe was an incompetent coach and general manager. Other owners in the league were appalled at the contract, but Wolman asserted, "It is our belief that the most expedient way to build a winner in the NFL is to place authority in one knowledgeable individual. The Eagles are fortunate to have such a person in Joe Kuharich." The offensive production of his teams was inconsistent, while the defensive performance was uniformly bad. Five times Kuharich's teams finished in the bottom three in scoring and twice were in the bottom three in points allowed. Although some players like Bob Brown and Ollie Matson thought highly of Joe, many others like Mike Ditka came to despise him. His draft record was poor. His frequent trades were a mixed bag — some worked out and some didn't. The Jurgensen for Snead trade was spectacularly bad. In the next seven seasons, Jurgensen's Redskins would go 9–3–2 against Snead's Eagles. Kuharich made a half-dozen major trades in his first year, and the Eagles did improve, but they never became good.

In fact, Kuharich distrusted stars "whose value goes up and down like the stock market." He battled with exciting all-purpose back Tim Brown and shuffled his starting quarterbacks on a game-by-game basis. He also fought a losing war with the local media that he felt was entirely too negative. Kuharich didn't help himself by insisting to the *New York Times*, "The most stupid approach in the world is to look for reasons. Football is an intangible game you can't pinpoint. We don't expect to play highly efficient football every week." He then added, "This isn't a roulette wheel, it's a profession. You don't lose a game and worry about your job. You coach, seek talent, think, research, develop and plan like any other business, just like General Motors. Anyone who thinks you have to win a title is erroneous."

After four seasons of mostly mediocrity, the bottom fell out in 1968 when the team lost its first 11 games and seemed to be heading for the league's worst record and the chance to draft O.J. Simpson. Franklin Field was filled with "Joe Must Go" banners as well as serenading fans and even airplanes with streamers providing the same message. As expected, Kuharich screwed up in reverse, and the team won two of its last three games to miss out on Simpson. As soon as Leonard Tose bought the Eagles from the financially-strapped Wolman in 1969, he fired Kuharich. Joe had to battle cancer in the 1970s, but lived long enough to collect his salary for the remaining ten years of his contract. He died during the Eagles 1980 Super Bowl appearance and will always be remembered as the man who traded a Hall of Fame quarterback for Norm Snead. His son Lary has coached in college, the USFL, the CFL the NFL and the Arena League over the past 40 years, while his other son Bill has worked in the front offices of the Chiefs and Saints for many years.

KUHLMANN, HENRY N. (HANK) 10/6/1937– Missouri. FB; did not play professionally. *Apprenticeship:* College asst.—13 years; pro asst.—12 years; USFL asst.— 3 years. *Roots:* Dan Devine, Neill Armstrong, Mike Ditka, Gene Stallings. *Branches:* None. *Coordinators/Key Assistants:* Jim Shofner ran the offense, while Jim Johnson was the key defensive coach. *Hall of Fame Players:* None. *Primary Quarterbacks:* None.

St. Louis native Hank Kuhlmann starred at fullback at the University of Missouri for three celebrated coaches from 1956 to 1958. He was a Tiger for Don Faurot's last season, Frank Broyles only one and Dan Devine's first. Three members of Missouri's 1957 backfield were offered contracts to play baseball by the St. Louis Cardinals. While Mike Shannon and Charley James signed with the Cardinals, Kuhlmann stayed for his senior year and met Devine who would have a major role in his coaching career.

After graduation in 1959, though, Kuhlmann signed with the baseball Cardinals for a $30,000 bonus. However, he hit only .235 in four years in the Cardinals minor league chain and was blocked from advancing by Tim McCarver who had signed with the team at the same time and could hit. In 1962, Hank returned to Missouri as an assistant and worked under Dan Devine for the next nine years. Dan once said of his assistant, "Hank is a guy who is very serious on the field. He's all business, no nonsense. Off the field, he's quick to laugh." In 1971, Devine was named head coach of the Packers, but Kuhlmann stayed with Missouri under new coach Al Onofrio. A year later, Devine brought Hank to Green Bay as the franchise's first-ever special teams coach. In his three years with the Packers, the combative Kuhlmann twice got into a fight with defensive back Al Matthews — once, Matthews came at him swinging a tennis racket.

When Devine moved on to Notre Dame in 1975, Kuhlmann came along, but Hank returned to the NFL in 1978 as running backs coach for the Bears. He spent five years in Chicago and got into another in-team fight there, this time with fellow coach Buddy Ryan. Hank moved on to the Birmingham Stallions of the USFL in 1983, serving three years as their offensive coordinator. After the team and league folded, Kuhlmann was hired as running backs coach by the Cardinals in 1986. When the Cardinals dismissed head coach Gene Stallings with five games to go, Kuhlmann was named interim coach. With nothing to lose, Kuhlmann even gave punter and third-stringer Tom Tupa a couple of starts at quarterback, but the team went into a nosedive and lost all five games under Hank.

Kuhlmann spent 1990 scouting for the Cardinals and then was named offensive coordinator for the Bucs in 1991, but that job lasted just one year. He resurfaced in 1994 due to his Missouri connections. Hank was hired as tight ends coach for the Colts whose GM, Bill Tobin, had played for Missouri when Kuhlmann was an assistant there in the 1960s. Hank switched to special teams in 1995 and stayed with the Colts through 1997. In 1998, Tobin's brother Vince, another Missouri alum, hired Hank as tight ends coach back with the Cardinals. Once again, Kuhlmann switched to special teams in 2000 and coached in Arizona through 2003 when he retired. Hank once said movingly of his career, "That's what team sports are about, football or baseball ... when you love each other, and you work together, there's so many things that can happen out of it, and you can see it at the professional level, the college level and the high school level."

KUSH, FRANK J. 1/20/1929– Michigan State. T; did not play professionally. *Apprenticeship:* College coach — 25 years (22 as head coach); CFL head coach —1 year. *Roots:* None. *Branches:* Hal Hunter (i), Bud Carson, Rick Venturi. *Coordinators/Key Assistants:* Zeke Bratkowski ran the offense, while Bud Carson then Kush himself handled the defense. *Hall of Fame*

Kuhlmann, Henry N. (Hank)									
Year	*Team*	*Games*	*Wins*	*Losses*	*Ties*	*%*	*P Wins*	*P Losses*	*P %*
1989	Cardinals	5	0	5	0	.000	0	0	.000
1 year		5	0	5	0	.000	0	0	.000

Kush, Frank J.									
Year	*Team*	*Games*	*Wins*	*Losses*	*Ties*	*%*	*P Wins*	*P Losses*	*P %*
1982	Colts	9	0	8	1	.056	0	0	.000
1983	Colts	16	7	9	0	.438	0	0	.000
1984	Colts	15	4	11	0	.267	0	0	.000
3 years		40	11	28	1	.288	0	0	.000

Players: None. *Primary Quarterbacks:* Mike Pagel. *Tendencies:* • His teams scored 15.2 points and allowed 24.7 per game • His teams ran 54% of the time, which was 114% of the league average • Three starting quarterbacks in three years; 83% of starts to primary quarterback • 18 rookie starters in three years • Winning Full Seasons to Losing Full Seasons: 0:3.

Frank Kush from Windber, Pennsylvania was an undersized, 5'9" 180-pound middle guard at Michigan State who was named All-American in 1952. The son of a coal miner and one of 15 children, he worked for the railroad as a teenager to help support the family. His hardscrabble background molded a tough and determined fighter who achieved great success and wrought much controversy. He was a motivator who once told the *Washington Post*, "Football is football and there are certain fundamental ingredients that must always be there.... I'm not so intrigued with the Xs and the Os. I'm more satisfied if I'm able to change a guy's attitude from a negative attitude to a positive one."

After college, Kush served two years in the military, coaching at Fort Benning. Upon his discharge, he joined the staff of Dan Devine at Arizona State. Devine had been on the Michigan State coaching staff when Frank played there. Kush served as a Sun Devil assistant from 1955 to 1957 and then was promoted to head coach in 1958 when Devine left for Missouri. Over the next 22 years in Arizona, Kush had two undefeated seasons and six with double digit wins, while experiencing just one losing season. Overall, his ASU record was 176–54–1, and his teams were known for their speed and conditioning. Future NFL receivers Charley Taylor, Jerry Smith, John Jefferson, Fair Hooker, J.D. Hill and Ben Hawkins all got their starts under Kush, and Frank even was offered the Philadelphia Eagles' job in 1975.

Kush trained his players extremely hard and was the college equivalent of Vince Lombardi. Players who got on Frank's bad side were disciplined by being ordered to run up and down "Mt. Kush" a steep hill near the practice facility. Kush also was known for getting physical with his players, grabbing their facemasks or slapping their helmets to get their attention and that physicality led to his swift downfall. In 1979, former Sun Devils' punter Kevin Rutledge filed suit alleging that Kush had slugged him during a 1978 game against Washington. When some players and coaches alleged that Kush asked them to lie about the incident and cover it up, Frank was dismissed as coach in October.

The next year was taken up with the trial, so Kush missed out on a chance at the Baltimore Colts' coaching job. Frank claimed that he "never used a closed fist on any young man." Quarterback Danny White testified that Kush had slapped his helmet and berated him, but that it motivated White to improve. Receiver Jerry Smith told the *Washington Post*, "What nobody realized or what usually did not get reported

was that while Kush had us running the mountain, he was running it, too. Frank Kush pushed players harder at that level, but he never asked me to do anything unreasonable." Ultimately, Kush was found not liable in the lawsuit. He and the school agreed on a settlement package, but he was still out of work. With no NFL teams showing interest, Frank accepted the head coaching job of the Hamilton Tiger-Cats in 1981 and led them to an 11–4–1 record that year as he rehabilitated his image. In his mind, Kush was still the same man, telling *Sports Illustrated*, "I still believe in discipline. And the only way to perfect timing is by hitting. That's why we scrimmage a lot. I haven't changed my ideas in 35 years, and I'm not going to change now."

His success in Canada brought him to the NFL a year later. In 1982, the Colts hired Kush as head coach and drafted two quarterbacks: Art Schlichter in round one and Arizona State's Mike Pagel in round four. With Schlichter imploding with his personal gambling problems, Pagel did most of the quarterbacking on the 0–8–1 1982 Colts. The team then drafted John Elway first overall in the 1983 draft, but Elway made clear that neither he nor his father wanted anything to do with Kush and the Colts. While GM Ernie Accorsi tried to smooth over the situation, owner Robert Irsay went ahead and traded Elway to Denver without the coach or GM having any say. Meanwhile, receiver Holden Smith poured either a soda or an entire tray of food (accounts differ) on Frank's head after being cut in training camp. The Colts did improve that season to 7–9 behind Pagel, but then stole out of Baltimore one March night in 1984 to move to Indianapolis. In a new state, things didn't get any better, with the plodding Colts winning just four games behind Pagel and Schlichter in 1984. Ever the diplomat, Kush indicated that he had a team of quitters and that there were just eight legitimate players on the team. In his three years with the Colts, the team finished in the bottom three of the league in scoring all three years and in the bottom four in points allowed twice.

Kush resigned near the end of the 1984 season to return to Arizona — this time as the head coach of the Arizona Wranglers of the USFL. The Wranglers finished 8–10 in 1985, but both the team and the league were finished and that finished Kush's coaching career. Frank did some public relations work and was involved with horse racing in the following years. In 1995, he was named to the College Football Hall of Fame and a year later the playing field at Sun Devil Stadium was renamed "Frank Kush Field." Finally in 2000, Arizona State fully welcomed back the once disgraced coach as a fundraiser in the athletic department.

LAMBEAU, EARL L. (CURLY) 4/9/1898–6/1/1965. Wisconsin and Notre Dame. Played TB for the Packers from 1921 to 1929. *Apprenticeship:* None. *Roots:*

None. *Branches:* Buster Ramsey. *Coordinators/Key Assistants*: For the Packers, the line coaches were Red Smith then George Trafton then Walt Kiesling then Tom Stidham, while ends and backs were coached by Eddie Kotal then Don Hutson then Bob Snyder; for the Cardinals, Cecil Isbell coached the backs, Phil Handler the line and Buster Ramsey the defense; for the Redskins, Herman Ball was the key offensive coach, while Larry Siemering was the key defensive coach. *Hall of Fame Players:* Sammy Baugh, Tony Canadeo, Bill Dudley, Arnie Herber, Clarke Hinkle, Cal Hubbard, Don Hutson, Walt Kiesling, Johnny Blood McNally, Mike Michalske, Charlie Trippi. *Primary Quarterbacks:* Arnie Herber, Cecil Isbell (single wing tailbacks). *Record:* **Hall of Fame Coach**; began as **Player-Coach**; NFL Championships 1929, 1930, 1931, 1936, 1939 and 1944. *Tendencies:* • His teams scored 16.5 points and allowed 12.1 per game • His teams ran 63.5% of the time, which was 102% of the league average • Nine starting quarterbacks in six T

formation years • 84 rookie starters in 33 years • Winning Full Seasons to Losing Full Seasons: 27:6.

Green Bay football is rooted in the tradition of town teams that were annually formed throughout the early years of the twentieth century. Green Bay native Curly Lambeau put his hometown on the national map by building the most unique team in professional

Head-to-Head:			
Hall of Fame Opponent	Regular Season		Postseason
Paul Brown	0–8		0–0
Guy Chamberlin	1–2–1		0–0
Jimmy Conzelman	11–7–2		0–0
Ray Flaherty	4–1		1–0
George Halas	17–30–2		0–1
Greasy Neale	3–2		0–0
Steve Owen	12–14		2–1
Total	48–64–5		3–2

Lambeau, Earl L. (Curly)

Year	Team	Games	Wins	Losses	Ties	%	P Wins	P Losses	P %
1921	Packers	6	3	2	1	.583	0	0	.000
1922	Packers	10	4	3	3	.550	0	0	.000
1923	Packers	10	7	2	1	.750	0	0	.000
1924	Packers	11	7	4	0	.636	0	0	.000
1925	Packers	13	8	5	0	.615	0	0	.000
1926	Packers	13	7	3	3	.654	0	0	.000
1927	Packers	10	7	2	1	.750	0	0	.000
1928	Packers	13	6	4	3	.577	0	0	.000
1929	Packers	13	12	0	1	.962	0	0	.000
1930	Packers	14	10	3	1	.750	0	0	.000
1931	Packers	14	12	2	0	.857	0	0	.000
1932	Packers	14	10	3	1	.750	0	0	.000
1933	Packers	13	5	7	1	.423	0	0	.000
1934	Packers	13	7	6	0	.538	0	0	.000
1935	Packers	12	8	4	0	.667	0	0	.000
1936	Packers	12	10	1	1	.875	1	0	1.000
1937	Packers	11	7	4	0	.636	0	0	.000
1938	Packers	11	8	3	0	.727	0	1	.000
1939	Packers	11	9	2	0	.818	1	0	1.000
1940	Packers	11	6	4	1	.591	0	0	.000
1941	Packers	11	10	1	0	.909	0	1	.000
1942	Packers	11	8	2	1	.773	0	0	.000
1943	Packers	10	7	2	1	.750	0	0	.000
1944	Packers	10	8	2	0	.800	1	0	1.000
1945	Packers	10	6	4	0	.600	0	0	.000
1946	Packers	11	6	5	0	.545	0	0	.000
1947	Packers	12	6	5	1	.542	0	0	.000
1948	Packers	12	3	9	0	.250	0	0	.000
1949	Packers	12	2	10	0	.167	0	0	.000
1950	Cardinals	12	5	7	0	.417	0	0	.000
1951	Cardinals	10	2	8	0	.200	0	0	.000
1952	Redskins	12	4	8	0	.333	0	0	.000
1953	Redskins	12	6	5	1	.542	0	0	.000
33 years		380	226	132	22	.624	3	2	.600

football. As one of his Hall of Fame Packers, Tony Canadeo, said upon Curly's death, "What he's done for Green Bay borders on the miraculous. He brought a small town into the big leagues."

Hometown hero Curly Lambeau was team captain at Green Bay's East High School and graduated in 1917. Lambeau matriculated at the University of Wisconsin that fall, but soon dropped out to work for his father's construction business. In the fall of 1918, Curly enrolled at Notre Dame on a football scholarship and played in the Fighting Irish backfield alongside the fabled George Gipp of "win one for the Gipper" fame. Curly came home in December suffering from tonsillitis and never returned to South Bend. Instead he took a job with the local Indian Packing Company in 1919 and got married to his high school sweetheart. That fall, Curly joined up with the men reorganizing the Green Bay football team. Due to Lambeau's prowess and stature, he was elected captain and he arranged with his boss at Indian Packing, Frank Peck, for the company to sponsor the team by paying for uniforms. The team's coach was Bill Ryan, coach of Green Bay West High School. The Indian Packing Company subsequently was taken over in 1920 by the Acme Packing Company, run by brothers John and Emmett Clair, and Acme continued to sponsor the semipro Packers.

In 1921, at Lambeau's urging, the Clairs successfully applied for a franchise in the American Professional Football Association as the NFL was then called. Joe Hoeffel, Lambeau's high school coach, was named coach and Lambeau was once again captain. At the time, coaches were not permitted to send in plays from the sideline; it was the captain who ran the team on game day. While Hoeffel deserves notice as being the team's first coach, Lambeau still was its vital force. The Packers went 3–2–1 in their first season in the league, but had their franchise revoked at season's end because they had used underclassmen for a game late in the year. Acme Packing then ceased its sponsorship, so Lambeau himself got the franchise reinstated by the league in July 1922. He enlisted the help of *Green Bay Press Gazette* sportswriter George Calhoun, who had served as team manager and publicity agent for the team in 1919, to raise money to stake the team. By the middle of the 1922 season, though, the undercapitalized Packers were in financial turmoil again. Calhoun brought in *Press Gazette* publisher Andrew Turnbull who ultimately used a stock sale to raise money and got the team finally on firm financial footing by converting them into the non-profit publicly-owned corporation they still are today. Lambeau remained in charge of the team on the field.

On the field, Curly was a player-coach. Throughout the NFL's first decade, he threw 24 touchdown passes and scored 110 points, both excellent totals for the 1920s, and was a second team All League

selection three times. As a coach, most notably, he was an early proponent of the forward pass as the great equalizer against bigger and stronger opponents. His teams played a fast and exciting brand of football, emphasizing speed and trickery. In his long career, four times his teams led the NFL in scoring and 16 times finished in the top three; his defense allowed the fewest points three times and finished in the top three 11 times. He was one of the first coaches to hold daily practices and was an early advocate of the use of game films for preparation and planning. Lambeau's Packers were the first team to barnstorm across Hawaii and the first to travel by airplane to a league game.

Of most importance, his teams won. He would endure only three losing seasons in his 29 years in Green Bay. In 1929, he acquired future Hall of Famers Johnny Blood, Cal Hubbard and Mike Michalske and then won three league titles in a row. Only Lombardi's Packers have been able to duplicate the threepeat feat throughout NFL history. When Curly signed swift, elusive end Don Hutson out of Alabama in 1935 that led to winning two more titles in the 1930s and one last championship in 1944 during the war. Only the Bears' George Halas can match Lambeau's six NFL titles, and that is fitting. The Packers-Bears rivalry was based on the personal rivalry of two great competitors, Lambeau and Halas. Their teams would meet on the football field 50 times over three decades, but the two reportedly never once shook hands after any contest. Halas said on Curly's death, "He kept beating the Bears. You know that was the greatest thing that could have happened to us. He kept beating us until he started such a rivalry that I couldn't hope would end."

Curly was sometimes known as the "Bellicose Belgian" for his frequent loud verbal admonitions of his players. Hall of Fame tackle Cal Hubbard once wondered aloud how they would find six men willing to serve as pallbearers when Lambeau were to die. Longtime team photographer Vern Biever felt that Lambeau yelled more than Lombardi, and Curly's fines could be extravagant. He once fined the entire team half their weekly paychecks after a subpar performance in the late 1940s. By then, the Packers were fading. On the field, Lambeau's offensive and defensive schemes were outdated — the Packers were the next to the last team in the league to move to the T formation. His single wing attack had been run by a smooth succession of star passers from Red Dunn to Hall of Famer Arnie Herber to Cecil Isbell until Isbell abruptly retired after 1942. The team had been led by a top passer up to that point, but then the string ended. When Hutson retired in 1946, the decline was swift.

Without a winning team, his domineering, spendthrift ways became intolerable to the Board of Directors. In addition, Green Bay could not compete financially with the rival All America Football Conference in the late 1940s, and the talent level of the team deteriorated precipitously. After an opening game loss to the Bears in 1949, Lambeau shockingly told the press he was stepping down as head coach to focus on his duties as GM and club president. He was leaving the team in the hands of assistants Tom Stidham (line), Bob Snyder (backs) and Charley Brock (defense). In reality, Curly saw that the team was terrible and just didn't want to coach it anymore. However, he was still in charge and still traveled with the team and spoke to them at halftime, so he is credited as being the head coach for the full year.

At year's end Curly offered his resignation and the Board gleefully accepted it. He immediately signed as the new head coach of the Chicago Cardinals, but that would last only two losing seasons. That term was followed by two years coaching Washington where he had a winning record in the second year. However, his two biggest stars (Eddie Lebaron and Gene Brito) left to play in Canada rather than put up with Curly. LeBaron claimed to Stuart Leuthner for *Iron Men* that Lambeau "probably didn't know more than ten offensive plays." Center Al DeMao concluded for Michael Richman in *The Redskins Encyclopedia*, "He wasn't much of a coach when he got here." When Curly got into a shoving match with owner George Preston Marshall over players drinking beer in their hotel during training camp in 1954, he was fired.

Lambeau kept active by coaching the College All Stars in their annual charity tilt with the reigning NFL champion for three summers in a row from 1955 to 1957. By 1959, he was angling to return to the Packers who had won just one-third of their games since he left and who were looking for a new coach again. However, the Packers hired Vince Lombardi, and Curly's coaching career was over. Lambeau died in June 1965 when he had a heart attack while mowing a friend's lawn. In his honor, the team put his picture on the 1965 yearbook and renamed City Stadium "Lambeau Field" in September of that year. Both moves were done over the strenuous objections of Lombardi who harbored some competitive resentment toward the Packer patriarch. Curly was a charter member of the Pro Football Hall of Fame and in his brief acceptance speech in 1963 succinctly summed up his contribution to his town and his sport, "I am deeply grateful and very happy to be honored here today. Forty one years ago I came to Canton to get a franchise for Green Bay, Wisconsin. The franchise was issued by Joe Carr at that time, and it cost fifty dollars. And the last time I looked, the Packers were still in the league. Thank you."

LANDRY, THOMAS W. (TOM) 9/11/1924– 2/12/2000. Texas. Played DB for the New York Yankees and New York Giants from 1949 to 1955. *Apprenticeship:* Pro asst.— 6 years. *Roots:* Steve Owen, Jim Lee Howell. *Branches:* Dick Nolan, Dan Reeves,

Mike Ditka, John Mackovic, Gene Stallings, Jim Shofner. *Coordinators/Key Assistants*: Landry was primarily responsible for both his offense and defense, but Jim Myers then Dan Reeves then Jim Shofner then Paul Hackett were his key offensive coaches, while Dick Nolan then Ernie Stautner were his defensive coordinators. *Hall of Fame Players:* Herb Adderley, Lance Alworth, Mike Ditka, Tony Dorsett, Forrest Gregg, Bob Hayes, Michael Irvin, Bob Lilly, Tommy McDonald, Mel Renfro, Jackie Smith, Roger Staubach, Randy White, Rayfield Wright. *Primary Quarterbacks:* Don Meredith, Roger Staubach, Danny White. *Record:* **Hall of Fame Coach**; Super Bowl Championships 1971, 1977. *Tendencies:* • His teams scored 23.6 points and allowed 19.4 per game • His teams ran 51.6% of the time, which was 101% of the league average • 14 starting quarterbacks in 29 years; 71% of starts to primary quarterbacks • 52 rookie starters in 29 years • Winning Full Seasons to Losing Full Seasons: 20:8.

Tom Landry was an upright, religious, stoic gentleman from Mission, Texas who enrolled at the University of Texas in 1942. He went into the Army Air Corps soon afterwards and flew 30 bombing missions as a co-pilot, even surviving one crash landing when his plane ran out of fuel. After the war, he returned to Austin and shared the Texas backfield with Bobby Layne for two of his three remaining years of eligibility.

Tom signed with the New York Yankees of the AAFC in 1949 and played defensive back for the team as well as serving as its punter. When the AAFC merged into the NFL in 1950, the Yankees' players were assigned to the NFL's two New York teams. Landry and two of his secondary mates, Otto Schnellbacher and Harmon Rowe, were nabbed by the Giants (who had drafted Tom in the 20th round in 1947) and helped the team's defense cut its points allowed in half that year. Landry took a clear leadership role on the defense by helping his teammates understand head

Head-to-Head:

Hall of Fame Opponent	Regular Season	Postseason
George Allen	8–8	0–1
Paul Brown	2–4	0–0
Weeb Ewbank	1–1	0–0
Joe Gibbs	8–7	0–1
Bud Grant	4–4	3–1
George Halas	1–2	0–0
Vince Lombardi	2–3	0–2
John Madden	0–1	0–0
Chuck Noll	3–4	0–2
Don Shula	2–5	1–0
Hank Stram	1–0	0–0
Bill Walsh	2–3	0–1
Total	34–42	4–8

Landry, Thomas W. (Tom)

Year	Team	Games	Wins	Losses	Ties	%	P Wins	P Losses	P %
1960	Cowboys	12	0	11	1	.042	0	0	.000
1961	Cowboys	14	4	9	1	.321	0	0	.000
1962	Cowboys	14	5	8	1	.393	0	0	.000
1963	Cowboys	14	4	10	0	.286	0	0	.000
1964	Cowboys	14	5	8	1	.393	0	0	.000
1965	Cowboys	14	7	7	0	.500	0	0	.000
1966	Cowboys	14	10	3	1	.750	0	1	.000
1967	Cowboys	14	9	5	0	.643	1	1	.500
1968	Cowboys	14	12	2	0	.857	0	1	.000
1969	Cowboys	14	11	2	1	.821	0	1	.000
1970	Cowboys	14	10	4	0	.714	2	1	.667
1971	Cowboys	14	11	3	0	.786	3	0	1.000
1972	Cowboys	14	10	4	0	.714	1	1	.500
1973	Cowboys	14	10	4	0	.714	1	1	.500
1974	Cowboys	14	8	6	0	.571	0	0	.000
1975	Cowboys	14	10	4	0	.714	2	1	.667
1976	Cowboys	14	11	3	0	.786	0	1	.000
1977	Cowboys	14	12	2	0	.857	3	0	1.000
1978	Cowboys	16	12	4	0	.750	2	1	.667
1979	Cowboys	16	11	5	0	.688	0	1	.000
1980	Cowboys	16	12	4	0	.750	2	1	.667
1981	Cowboys	16	12	4	0	.750	1	1	.500
1982	Cowboys	9	6	3	0	.667	2	1	.667
1983	Cowboys	16	12	4	0	.750	0	1	.000
1984	Cowboys	16	9	7	0	.563	0	0	.000
1985	Cowboys	16	10	6	0	.625	0	1	.000
1986	Cowboys	16	7	9	0	.438	0	0	.000
1987	Cowboys	15	7	8	0	.467	0	0	.000
1988	Cowboys	16	3	13	0	.188	0	0	.000
29 years		418	250	162	6	.605	20	16	.556

coach Steve Owen's overriding concepts. When Owen decided to confront the powerful Browns with a 6–1–4 alignment in 1950, he drew the formation on the blackboard and then turned the chalk over to Landry to explain how it would work and what each player's responsibilities would be in this new "Umbrella Defense."

When Owen was forced out after the 1953 season, he was replaced by end coach Jim Lee Howell who recognized Landry's defensive genius and put him in charge of the defense officially even though Tom was still a starting player. Landry retired from playing after the 1955 season (with 32 career interceptions) and became the Giants' fulltime defensive coach; Vince Lombardi was New York's offensive coach, while Howell acted primarily as an administrator. In 1956, Landry opened up the Umbrella to establish the 4–3 alignment that remains today as a base defense in the league. Tom's defense was a read-and-react defense in which the defenders would study the offense for keys to read on each play to direct their movements. The general idea was to keep blockers away from the middle linebacker who became the spearhead of the defense; Sam Huff became a star in this defense. The defense's success inspired the origin of the "DE-FENSE" chant from Giant fans in Yankee Stadium in the late 1950s and led the team to three championship games in Landry's last four years in New York.

The day after the 1959 title game, Landry was named the first head coach of the expansion Dallas Rangers, who would change their name to Cowboys before beginning play in 1960. Tom went through close to 200 players in his first training camp, but the original Cowboys were an awful team that went 0–11–1—they tied the Giants in week 11 to avoid losing all 12 games. By their third year, though, Landry's Cowboys were second in the league in scoring. In fact, his Cowboys led the NFL in scoring five times and finished in the top two 10 times, while his defense finished in the top three for fewest points allowed four times. Industrial engineer Tom Landry proved to be equally facile in designing offense and defense. He later told the *Los Angeles Times*, "When I developed the 4–3 defense in '50s when I was playing with New York, it was based upon a lot of principles I was studying in the engineering and management fields. How to control situations and how to work together, that's the whole 4–3 coordinated defensive concept that we still play today with variations. They call it a flex now because we've moved a little bit to cover up the innovations of offense through the years. But it's still the same idea. Then when I came in as a head coach, I had the chance on the other side of the line to say, 'What kind of offense will attack this best?' So I started the multiple-formation shifting thing."

Landry was not afraid of innovation. As noted, he adjusted his defense to a flex arrangement with half of his defensive lineman just off the line of scrimmage to produce better gap control and easier key reading. On offense not only did he change formations from play to play, but also continually put players in motion and shifted them before becoming set. He had his linemen rise up right before setting to further mask the shifting. Landry, an early advocate of calling the offensive plays from the sideline, also pioneered alternating quarterbacks in 1962 with Eddie LeBaron and Don Meredith. He tried that maneuver again in 1971 while trying to decide on a starting quarterback between Craig Morton and Roger Staubach. Tom also reintroduced the Shotgun formation in the 1970s and perfected it to the point that the formation became part of every team's standard arsenal.

Landry teamed with GM Tex Schramm and player personnel chief Gil Brandt to provide the Cowboys with nearly 30 years of strong and successful direction. Tom's tenure with Dallas can be divided into eras by his starting quarterbacks. In his first decade, the Cowboys were primarily led by Don Meredith, a prodigiously talented and flippantly free spirited leader who had the respect of the players but did not always see eye-to-eye with the more ordered Landry. Those early Cowboys progressed slowly, not having a winning season until 1966, but once Landry finally got all the pieces together, Dallas went to the playoffs in 18 of the next 20 seasons. The Doomsday Defense completely shut down the running game, while the often spectacular offense relied on trick plays and deep passing to score freely. In the early part of that success, though, the team was known as "next year's champions" or the "team that couldn't win the big one" as they kept falling short in the post season.

After Meredith abruptly retired in 1969, Landry went back-and-forth between Morton and Staubach for a couple years before fully committing to "Roger the Dodger." With Staubach, no deficit was insurmountable, and he became known as "Captain Comeback" for his frequent late-game heroics. In the 1970s, Staubach led Dallas to four Super Bowls, won two and nearly pulled out the other two. Although Roger was not quite the pocket passer that Landry envisioned, he embodied Tom's spirit as the quarterback of "America's Team," as the Cowboys became known as in this time.

Staubach retired after the 1979 season, and his place was taken by Danny White. White had been the team's punter and Roger's backup for the last four years

and proved himself an able NFL starter, but lacked the extra dimension of Staubach. White led the Cowboys to three straight NFC championship games in his first three years as a starter, but lost all three. At that point the team started to age, and the team's drafts began to decline in effectiveness. Throughout the 1980s talent on the field steadily deteriorated as the team returned to the level at which it began. After a 3–13 1988, Dallas again qualified for the top spot in the 1989 draft. With an ambitious new owner, Jerry Jones, the team of Landry, Schramm and Brandt would not be around to rebuild the Cowboys. Landry was fired within a week of Jones buying the team in February 1989 and replaced by Jimmy Johnson. While the move was a shock in that the 64-year-old Landry was such a local institution, it clearly was time for new blood in the organization.

Landry's image was often distorted so that outsiders looked at him as an unfeeling, "plastic" man, but he had emotions — he just deliberately kept them hidden. He once said, "Leadership is a matter of having people look at you and gain confidence, seeing how you react. If you're in control, they're in control." As Tom roamed the sidelines with a tight-lipped expression under his fedora, he invited jokes like fullback Walt Garrison's famous reply to the question of whether he'd ever seen Landry smile, "No, but I've only been here nine years." Many of his players did find him too cold and distant and not much of a motivator. There were occasions, however, when Landry displayed emotions on the field, and there were times when he broke down and cried in the locker room, because he felt he had failed his team as a leader.

While Landry believed that God and then family came above all, winning was what mattered to him on the field. He once told *Sports Illustrated*, "If you think winning is not too important, then you are not willing to pay the price to win. Take away winning, and you take away everything that is strong about America." Tom took Dallas to 12 NFC championship games, five Super Bowls and won two NFL titles. He won more regular season games than any coach aside from George Halas and Don Shula, while winning more postseason games than any other coach. He was elected to the Pro Football Hall of Fame in 1990. War hero, devout family man, the greatest technical coach of his time, Tom Landry was a great American.

LeBeau, Charles R. (Dick) 9/9/1937– Ohio State. Played DB for the Detroit Lions from 1959 to 1972. *Apprenticeship:* Pro asst.— 28 years. *Roots:* Mike McCormack, Bart Starr, Forrest Gregg, Sam Wyche, Bill Cowher, Bruce Coslet. *Branches:* None. *Coordinators/Key Assistants*: Ken Anderson then Bob Bratkowski ran the offense, while Mark Duffner handled the defense. *Hall of Fame Players:* None. *Primary Quarterbacks:* Jon Kitna, Akili Smith. *Record:* **Hall of**

LeBeau, Charles R. (Dick)

Year	Team	Games	Wins	Losses	Ties	%	P Wins	P Losses	P %
2000	Bengals	13	4	9	0	.308	0	0	.000
2001	Bengals	16	6	10	0	.375	0	0	.000
2002	Bengals	16	2	14	0	.125	0	0	.000
3 years		45	12	33	0	.267	0	0	.000

Fame Player. *Tendencies:* • His teams scored 15.2 points and allowed 23.3 per game • His teams ran 43.6% of the time, which was the league average • Four starting quarterbacks in three years; 80% of starts to primary quarterbacks • Seven rookie starters in three years • Winning Full Seasons to Losing Full Seasons: 0:3.

Although London, Ohio's Dick LeBeau was drafted by his home state Browns in 1959, he was cut in training camp and instead spent his entire 14-year playing career as a defensive back for the Detroit Lions. At the time, the Lions had a fierce blitzing defense, and their defensive backfield was often cited as the best in the league. LeBeau intercepted 62 passes during his career and set the record for consecutive starts by a defensive back with 171. Upon retirement, he went immediately into coaching and worked for five organizations over nearly 40 years. His first position in 1973 was special teams coach for the Eagles. From there LeBeau served as secondary coach for the Packers from 1976 to 1979, secondary coach and then defensive coordinator of the Bengals from 1980 to 1991, secondary coach and then defensive coordinator of the Steelers from 1992 to 1996 before returning to Cincinnati as defensive coordinator in 1997.

LeBeau was with Cincinnati for both of the team's Super Bowl runs in the 1980s. The innovative late 1980s team was notable for Sam Wyche's introduction of the No Huddle Offense and for the Zone Blitz that was devised by defensive coordinator LeBeau to combat the Oilers' Run-and-Shoot Offense. LeBeau later fine-tuned the Zone Blitz with Dom Capers on the Steelers. What the Zone Blitz aims for is "safe pressure" in the phrase of defensive guru Bill Arnsparger, an early influence on Lebeau's designs. The scheme requires quick and agile lineman able to drop off into short coverage zones to allow the linebackers, corners and safeties to blitz from unexpected areas with no decrease in pass defenders.

Dick second term as coordinator with Bengals was under Bruce Coslet but when Coslet was fired three games into the 2000 season, LeBeau got his first and only chance to be a head coach. However, the Bengals did not have the talent they had when Paul Brown was still alive in the 1980s. Behind the quarterbacking of Akili Smith, Jon Kitna, Gus Frerotte and Scott Mitchell, the team finished in the bottom five in offense all three years. Cincinnati also dropped to last on defense in 2002.

After being fired by the Bengals, LeBeau spent a season in Buffalo before returning to Pittsburgh in 2004 at the age of 67 for his second stint as the defensive coordinator of the Steelers. The personable and loquacious LeBeau has had no trouble relating to his much younger players, and by all reports, they have a fierce loyalty to him. In the most recent decade, Dick won not only two Super Bowl rings but also a groundswell of support for his election to the Hall of Fame. Although listed solely as a player, his election likely was for his 50-year career as a talented player and inventive assistant coach who had an ugly three-year blip as a head coach for a terrible franchise.

LEMM, WALTER H. (WALLY) 10/23/1919–10/2/1988. Carroll (WI). HB; did not play professionally. *Apprenticeship:* College coach —12 years (6 as head coach); pro asst.— 3 years. *Roots:* Ray Richards, Pop Ivy, Lou Rymkus. *Branches:* None. *Coordinators/Key Assistants:* For both Oilers' stints, Walt Schlinkman was the key offensive coach, while Lemm handled the defense; for the Cardinals, Ray Prochaska ran the offense, while Chuck Drulis handled the defense. *Hall of Fame Players:* Elvin Bethea, George Blanda, Ken Houston, John Henry Johnson, Charlie Joiner, Jackie Smith and Larry Wilson. *Primary Quarterbacks:* George Blanda, Charlie Johnson, Pete Beathard. *Record:* AFL Championship 1961. *Tendencies:* • His teams scored 22.5 points and allowed 21.4 per game • His teams ran 48.1% of the time, which was 97% of the league average • 11 starting quarterbacks in 10 years; 77% of starts to primary quarterbacks • 26 rookie starters in 10 years • Winning Full Seasons to Losing Full Seasons: 4:4.

Chicago's Wally Lemm was a senior running back at Carroll College in Wisconsin, planning to go to graduate school for journalism when the Cardinals came to Carroll for training camp in 1942. Working as a waiter in the dining hall, Lemm was so impressed with coach Jimmy Conzelman that he decided that coaching might offer a better future than sports writing. Wally went into the Navy, commanding a PT boat during the war, but on returning to the states got a job as an assistant coach at Notre Dame under Hugh Devore in 1945. He returned to his alma mater as an assistant coach from 1946 to 1947 and then coached high school football in 1948.

In 1949, Lemm's former college coach, John Breen, hired Wally as an assistant at Lake Forest Col-

Lemm, Walter H. (Wally)

Year	Team	Games	Wins	Losses	Ties	%	P Wins	P Losses	P %
1961	Oilers (Titans)	9	9	0	0	1.000	1	0	1.000
1962	Cardinals	14	4	9	1	.321	0	0	.000
1963	Cardinals	14	9	5	0	.643	0	0	.000
1964	Cardinals	14	9	3	2	.714	0	0	.000
1965	Cardinals	14	5	9	0	.357	0	0	.000
1966	Oilers (Titans)	14	3	11	0	.214	0	0	.000
1967	Oilers (Titans)	14	9	4	1	.679	0	1	.000
1968	Oilers (Titans)	14	7	7	0	.500	0	0	.000
1969	Oilers (Titans)	14	6	6	2	.500	0	1	.000
1970	Oilers (Titans)	14	3	10	1	.250	0	0	.000
10 years		135	64	64	7	.500	1	2	.333

lege. From 1949 to 1951, Lemm filled that position while also coaching the school's basketball team. In 1952, Breen left and Lemm replaced him. After going 11–4–1 in two years, Wally left for Montana State in 1954. Lemm went 8–9–1 from 1954 to 1955, and was hired as secondary coach for the Cardinals in 1956; the team led the league in interceptions that year. However, Lemm returned to Lake Forest as head coach the next year and went 11–5 from 1957 to 1958. Wally then came back to the Cardinals as secondary coach again in 1959 under Pop Ivy.

When the American Football League started in 1960, Lemm was hired as the defensive coach of the Houston Oilers under Lou Rymkus. While the Oilers won the first AFL championship, the team did not care for the irritable Rymkus. In the off season, Lemm retired to run a sporting goods store in Libertyville, Illinois. However, when Houston began 1961 0–4–1, Rymkus was fired, and Oilers' GM John Breen brought back Wally as head coach. Receiver Charley Hennigan recalled to Ed Gruver in *The American Football League*, "Wally came over from the defense and let the offense run itself. We ran double and triple wing sets, we'd send out five guys on passes. We had a ball; it was fun." Lemm told *Sports Illustrated*, "Pro football players, like anybody else, do their jobs better when they like their work." Under this atmosphere, the Oilers won their last nine games and swept to a second league championship. Wally modestly commented on the title, "I feel like someone who inherited a million dollars in tarnished silverware. All I did was polish it."

Lemm got into a dispute with management after the season, though, and left the Oilers to become head coach of the Cardinals in 1962; the Oilers then hired the coach the Cards had fired, Pop Ivy, to replace Lemm. Wally continued with his easygoing style in his third stint with the Cardinals. He aimed to keep things simple on offense and told *Sports Illustrated*, "With all these different defenses, the players have enough to think about. The more you give them, the more mistakes they will make, and errors beat you quicker than anything else." Lemm made brainy quarterback Charley Johnson his starter and posted back-to-back nine-win seasons in 1963 and 1964. When Johnson had some injury problems in 1965, both the offense and the team slipped. In fact, the defense had been mediocre at best throughout Lemm's tenure. In January 1966, Lemm and the Bidwill brothers decided it was best for Lemm to leave. The Bidwills wanted a year-round coach, but Lemm preferred to focus on football just six months a year.

Not unexpectedly, Houston was looking to hire a new coach for the sixth time in seven years, so Lemm returned for his third stint with the Oilers. With ancient George Blanda at quarterback, though, the team was ripe for change. Lemm brought in Pete Beathard in his second season in Houston and the team made the playoffs twice in five years with a more defensive approach to the game. Both those postseason trips, though, resulted in thrashings by the Oakland Raiders — 40–7 in 1967 and 56–7 in 1969. After five years, Lemm was having severe stomach problems from tension and stress and retired from coaching for good.

LEONARD, JAMES R. 2/14/1910–12/2/1993. Notre Dame. Played HB for the Eagles from 1934 to 1937. *Apprenticeship:* College coach — 5 years (4 as head coach); pro asst. — 2 years. *Roots:* Walt Kiesling. *Branches:* None. *Coordinators/Key Assistants:* Lud Wray coached the line. *Hall of Fame Players:* Bill Dudley. *Primary Quarterbacks:* None. *Tendencies:* • His team scored 7.9 points and allowed 22 per game • His team ran 68.5% of the time, which was 108% of the league

Leonard, James R.									
Year	Team	Games	Wins	Losses	Ties	%	P Wins	P Losses	P %
1945	Steelers	10	2	8	0	.200	0	0	.000
1 year		10	2	8	0	.200	0	0	.000

average • Six rookie starters in one year • Winning Full Seasons to Losing Full Seasons: 0:1.

Hailing from Pedricktown, New Jersey, Jim Leonard starred at fullback for Notre Dame from 1931 to 1933 before joining Bert Bell's Eagles for a four-year NFL playing career. Jim retired in 1938 to reestablish the football program at St. Francis College in Pennsylvania after a seven-year absence. After winning just one game in Leonard's first two seasons, St. Francis won six in each of the next two, enabling Jim to compile a 13–15–2 record from 1938 to 1941. In 1942, he was hired as Walt Kiesling's assistant on the Steelers, and the team posted the franchise's first winning season that year. The following year, the Steelers merged with the Eagles, so Leonard left to serve on the staff at Holy Cross. The Steelers then merged with the Cardinals in 1944, and Art Rooney brought Jim back as an assistant to keep an eye on the two distracted horse players who were co-coaching the merged team, Kiesling and Phil Handler. After an 0–10 season, Rooney promoted Leonard to head coach for the un-merged Steelers in 1945.

As head coach, Jim used the Notre Dame offensive system with a few T elements, but the team was fully depleted by the war. Star halfback Bill Dudley returned for the last few games, but couldn't do much good for a team that finished last in scoring and within 15 points of last in points allowed. Still, co-owner Bert Bell is quoted in Robert Lyons biography *On Any Given Sun-day*, "Leonard and Wray [line coach] kept plugging away. They worked night and day and, considering the handicaps, I think they did a marvelous job."

Leonard, however, was aware that Bell had been negotiating with the legendary Jock Sutherland to take over the Steelers. Leonard reacted by resigning long distance. From his home in New Jersey, Jim called the *Pittsburgh Press* and told the paper he was quitting, adding, "This probably is the first time an owner has found out that his coach has quit by reading the paper." Art Rooney responded, "Leonard's contract expired with the Steelers last game in Washington, December 2. When he agreed to terms at the last draft meeting I explained to him in the presence of Walt Kiesling, our former coach, that he was to be here for one year only."

Leonard returned to St. Francis in 1947 and led the team to a 4–1 mark. In 1949, he took over the head coaching job at Villanova and went 12–6 in two years. At the age of 40, Jim then gave up football and returned to New Jersey to be an asparagus farmer.

LEVY, MARVIN D. (MARV) 8/3/1925– Coe. Did not play professionally. *Apprenticeship:* College coach.—16 years (11 as head coach); pro asst.—4 years; CFL head coach—5 years. *Roots:* Jerry Williams, George Allen. *Branches:* Frank Gansz, Bobby Ross, Rod Rust. *Coordinators/Key Assistants:* For the Chiefs, Levy handled his own offense, while Rod Rust ran the

Levy, Marvin D. (Marv)									
Year	Team	Games	Wins	Losses	Ties	%	P Wins	P Losses	P %
1978	Chiefs	16	4	12	0	.250	0	0	.000
1979	Chiefs	16	7	9	0	.438	0	0	.000
1980	Chiefs	16	8	8	0	.500	0	0	.000
1981	Chiefs	16	9	7	0	.563	0	0	.000
1982	Chiefs	9	3	6	0	.333	0	0	.000
1986	Bills	7	2	5	0	.286	0	0	.000
1987	Bills	15	7	8	0	.467	0	0	.000
1988	Bills	16	12	4	0	.750	1	1	.500
1989	Bills	16	9	7	0	.563	0	1	.000
1990	Bills	16	13	3	0	.813	2	1	.667
1991	Bills	16	13	3	0	.813	2	1	.667
1992	Bills	16	11	5	0	.688	3	1	.750
1993	Bills	16	12	4	0	.750	2	1	.667
1994	Bills	16	7	9	0	.438	0	0	.000
1995	Bills	16	10	6	0	.625	1	1	.500
1996	Bills	16	10	6	0	.625	0	1	.000
1997	Bills	16	6	10	0	.375	0	0	.000
17 years		255	143	112	0	.561	11	8	.579

defense; for the Bills, Jim Ringo then Ted Marchibroda then Tom Bresnahan then Dan Henning handled the offense, while Herb Patera then Walt Corey then Wade Phillips ran the defense. *Hall of Fame Players:* Jim Kelly, James Lofton, Bruce Smith, Jan Stenerud, Emmitt Thomas, Thurman Thomas. *Primary Quarterbacks:* Steve Fuller, Jim Kelly. *Record:* **Hall of Fame Coach.** *Tendencies:* • His teams scored 20.8 points and allowed 18.9 per game • His teams ran 51.2% of the time, which was 109% of the league average • 11 starting quarterbacks in 17 years; 71% of starts to primary quarterbacks • 37 rookie starters in 17 years • Winning Full Seasons to Losing Full Seasons: 9:6.

Among Hall of Fame coaches, Chicago's Marv Levy has perhaps the weakest case. He is one of only three who never won a championship, and the other two (Bud Grant and George Allen) had much higher regular season winning percentages. In fact, the only two Canton coaches with a lower regular season winning percentage are Weeb Ewbank who won three championships and Sid Gillman who won one AFL title and is one of the most influential offensive minds in league history. Levy was a fine coach and fascinating man, but his most notable coaching achievement was taking Buffalo to four straight Super Bowls — and losing each one.

Levy went into the Army Air Corps out of high school in 1943 and spent three years in the service. He graduated from Coe College in 1950 and then earned a Masters in English History from Harvard in 1951. He also began his coaching career in 1951 at the high school level. In 1953, he returned to Coe as an assistant coach for two years before taking an assistant coaching position at New Mexico in 1954. Four years later in 1958, Marv was named head coach at New Mexico and compiled a 14–6 record in two years. He moved on to California in 1960, but could only manage an 8–29–3 record with the Golden Bears from 1960 to 1963 despite recruiting Craig Morton as his quarterback. In 1964, Levy moved on to William & Mary as head coach. From 1964 to 1968, he led the school to a 23–25–1 record and developed another NFL quarterback, Dan Darragh, although on a lesser scale.

Levy reached the NFL in May 1969 as the kicking team coach of the Eagles under Jerry Williams, only the second special teams coach in league history. George Allen hired Dick Vermeil as the Rams' special teams coach just one month before in April. A year later, Vermeil moved across town to UCLA and Levy replaced him on the Rams. Marv coached special teams for George Allen one year in Los Angeles and then followed him to Washington for two more seasons from 1971 to 1972. Allen later said of Levy, "I liked his organization. He always seemed to be in control of his emotions as well as his team." Marv told the *New York Times,* "George probably had more effect on me as a pro coach than anyone else. His attention to detail was fantastic. He believed the kicking game

Head-to-Head:		
Hall of Fame Opponent	*Regular Season*	*Postseason*
Joe Gibbs	0–2	0–1
Bud Grant	1–0	0–0
John Madden	0–2	0–0
Chuck Noll	2–2	0–0
Don Shula	14–7	3–0
Bill Walsh	0–1	0–0
Total	17–14	3–1

merited the same attention as the offense and defense." John Madden noted in *Hey, I'm Talking Football* that Levy had the same intensity as Allen. However, Marv was more of an even-tempered teacher like Bud Wilkinson rather than embodying Allen's inspirational style.

Levy left the U.S. in 1973 when he was named head coach of the Montreal Alouettes in Canada. In five years from 1973 to 1977, Marv led Montreal to a 43–31–4 record and three Grey Cup games, winning two CFL titles. He returned to the NFL in 1978 as the head coach of the Kansas City Chiefs and slowly tried to rebuild a franchise that had slipped badly since Hank Stram left town. At one point, Levy even dusted off the old Wing T offense that featured the quarterback run-pass option play with big running quarterback Steve Fuller, but the team never rose above mediocrity. He was fired at the end of the 1982 season and was out of football in 1983. He returned in 1984 as head coach of the Chicago Blitz of the USFL, replacing George Allen, who took most of the team's best players and left for Arizona. The depleted Blitz finished 5–13 under Marv in 1984 and folded. Again Levy was out of football in 1985, although he did some work in the Montreal front office and worked as a broadcaster.

In the middle of the 1986 season at the age of 61, Marv landed in Buffalo as the new head coach. With GM Bill Polian, the Bills were in the process of accumulating a lot of talent and over the next decade, Levy put that talent to good use. In general, he favored a balanced attack and ran the ball more than he passed it, running the ball almost 10% more than the league average. As with Kansas City, he was not afraid to try something new that fit the personnel, and he and offensive coordinator Ted Marchibroda installed the Bills' version of the No Huddle offense at the end of the 1980s, the K-Gun, in which quarterback Jim Kelly called his own plays in a hurry-up offense that Buffalo would move into at any time. Four times, Buffalo finished in the top three in scoring. The team was fearless and could never be counted out, as the famous second half comeback from 32 points down to Houston in the 1992 playoffs attested. Levy's Bills were an explosive team that dominated their division, beating the Shula/Marino Dolphins 14 of 21 times and swept to four straight Super Bowls. However, after the first one in which they lost to an inferior but better coached

Giants team in a grinding game that came down to a "wide right" 47-yard field goal attempt, the other three losses were not close. The Bills were outplayed and outcoached each time.

Levy was no motivator. He once told the *New York Times*, "I don't think of myself as a disciplinarian. I'm not a drillmaster." As Buffalo special teams ace Steve Tasker told *Sports Illustrated*, "He's not a strong motivator, and he covers himself by saying, 'if I have to motivate you on game day, then I've got the wrong team.'" Defensive tackle Fred Smerlas appreciated Levy when he came to Buffalo, saying, "Marv has respect for everyone's personality. He doesn't belittle people. He lets them be themselves." A few years later, though, Smerlas looked back and told *Sports Illustrated*, "To see Marv try to give a pep talk is like watching a librarian get all fired up. Your eyes glaze over." Indeed, Levy was known for telling his team inspirational tales from British history or reciting poetry to them. While many appreciated that elevated approach, it didn't go over with everyone.

Levy retired from coaching in 1998 and the Bills have not had a consistent winning team since then. Marv said on his retirement at 73, "The anguish I felt after every loss over the last few years had begun to reach an intensity that the thrill of victory could not overcome." He returned in 2006 as GM for two years to stabilize a reeling franchise, but the team's future remains in doubt.

LEWIS, ARTHUR E. (ART OR PAPPY) 2/18/1911–6/13/1962. Ohio. Played T for the Giants in 1936 and the Rams from 1938 to 1939. *Apprenticeship:* College asst.—1 year; pro asst.—1 year. *Roots:* Hugo Bezdek. *Branches:* None. *Coordinators/Key Assistants:* None. *Hall of Fame Players:* None. *Primary Quarterbacks:* None. *Record:* **Interim Player-Coach.**

Art Lewis was born in Pomeroy, Ohio, and played tackle for Ohio University from 1932 to 1935, gaining Little All-American status. He was drafted in the ninth round by the Giants in 1936 and played for the team that year. In 1937, Art dropped out of the pros and worked as an assistant coach for Ohio Wesleyan and then was traded to Cleveland for Johnny Gildea. Lewis reported to Cleveland as both a player and as the team's line coach under Hugo Bezdek. The Rams went 1–10 record the year before, and Bezdek's club got off to a 0–3 start in 1938, so Hugo was replaced by Lewis. Under Lewis, the Rams ripped off a three-game winning streak, but ultimately ended the season with a 4–7 record.

The Rams brought in star Dutch Clark as coach in 1939, and Lewis returned to just being a player. In 1940 and 1941, he was retired from playing and served as Clark's line coach. Art was hired by Washington & Lee as line coach in January 1942, but joined the Navy in June and served his country for the next four years. After his discharge, Lewis was promoted to head coach of Washington & Lee in 1946. Over the next three years, the school went 11–17, and Art was fired. He spent 1949 as the line coach for Mississippi State and then landed the head coaching job at West Virginia in 1950. In 10 years with the Mountaineers, Lewis went 58–38–2, and the team was nationally ranked three times. In Morgantown, he developed such future NFL stars as Sam Huff, Bruce Bosley and Joe Marconi. Art resigned at the end of the decade and was hired as head scout by the Steelers in 1960. He continued in that position until a heart attack killed him in 1962. Lewis was just 51 years old.

LEWIS, MARVIN 9/23/1958– Idaho State. DB; did not play professionally. *Apprenticeship:* College asst.—12 years; pro asst.—11 years. *Roots:* Bill Cowher, Ted Marchibroda, Brian Billick, Steve Spurrier. *Branches:*

Lewis, Arthur E. (Art or Pappy)									
Year	Team	Games	Wins	Losses	Ties	%	P Wins	P Losses	P %
1938	Rams	8	4	4	0	.500	0	0	.000
1 year		8	4	4	0	.500	0	0	.000

Lewis, Marvin									
Year	Team	Games	Wins	Losses	Ties	%	P Wins	P Losses	P %
2003	Bengals	16	8	8	0	.500	0	0	.000
2004	Bengals	16	8	8	0	.500	0	0	.000
2005	Bengals	16	11	5	0	.688	0	1	.000
2006	Bengals	16	8	8	0	.500	0	0	.000
2007	Bengals	16	7	9	0	.438	0	0	.000
2008	Bengals	16	4	11	1	.281	0	0	.000
2009	Bengals	16	10	6	0	.625	0	1	.000
2010	Bengals	16	4	12	0	.250	0	0	.000
2011	Bengals	16	9	7	0	.563	0	1	.000
9 years		144	69	74	1	.483	0	3	.000

Leslie Frazier, Hue Jackson. *Coordinators/Key Assistants*: Bob Bratkowski then Jay Gruden ran the offense, while Leslie Frazier then Chuck Bresnahan then Mike Zimmer handled the defense. *Hall of Fame Players:* None. *Primary Quarterbacks:* Carson Palmer, Andy Dalton. *Tendencies:* • His teams scored 21.3 points and allowed 22.2 per game • His teams ran 44.3% of the time, which was the league average • Four starting quarterbacks in Nine years; 78% of starts to primary quarterback • 28 rookie starters in nine years • Winning Full Seasons to Losing Full Seasons: 3:3.

From McDonald, Pennsylvania, Marvin Lewis went to Idaho State to play linebacker in the late 1970s. Upon graduation, he went immediately into coaching as the linebackers coach at his alma mater from 1981 to 1984. In the same position, Lewis then coached at Long Beach State from 1985 to 1986, New Mexico from 1987 to 1989 and Pitt from 1990 to 1991. Bill Cowher hired Marvin as the Steelers' linebackers coach in 1992, and four years later, he was hired by Ted Marchibroda to be the first defensive coordinator of the Baltimore Ravens. In four years, Marvin had shaped a top ten NFL defense, and in year five, 2000, his defense had one of the most dominant seasons in league history, leading the Ravens to a Super Bowl victory.

With that on his resume, Lewis was frustrated in not getting any head coaching offers as the league continued to lag behind in promoting African Americans to head coach. After another successful season with the Ravens, Tampa Bay was poised to make an offer to Lewis but pulled away at the last minute. Marvin then made a lateral move to become the defensive coordinator for Steve Spurrier in Washington in 2002. Finally in 2003, Lewis was named head coach of the Cincinnati Bengals, a noted coaching graveyard. From 1991 when owner Mike Brown took control of the team after his father passed away, Cincinnati had gone 55–137 in 12 years. While Lewis' 69–74 record since then has not been stellar, it compares very favorably to the previous dozen years.

Lewis' Bengals have had some stars in Carson Palmer, Chad Johnson and T.J. Houshmandzadeh, but even the play of the stars has been inconsistent. Even more troubling was the Bengals tendency during the decade to lead the league in player arrests, including 8 in 2006. While Cincinnati has twice won its division under Lewis, they lost both first round playoff games. Despite finishing 2010 a disappointing 4–12, Marvin

was rewarded with an unspecified contract extension. Jettisoning those veteran stars and going with a youth movement, the Bengals returned to the postseason in 2011 behind rookie quarterback Andy Dalton, a youthful receiving corps and a challenging defense.

LINEHAN, SCOTT T. 9/17/1963– Idaho. QB; did not play professionally. *Apprenticeship:* College asst.— 13 years; pro asst.— 4 years. *Roots:* Mike Tice, Nick Saban. *Branches:* None. *Coordinators/Key Assistants*: Greg Olson then Al Saunders ran the offense, while Jim Haslett handled the defense. *Hall of Fame Players:* None. *Primary Quarterbacks:* Marc Bulger. *Tendencies:* • His teams scored 18.7 points and allowed 26.8 per game • His teams ran 39.6% of the time, which was 89% of the league average • Five starting quarterbacks in three years; 89% of starts to primary quarterback • Nine rookie starters in three years • Winning Full Seasons to Losing Full Seasons: 0:1.

Scott Linehan, out of Sunnyside, Washington, threw for over 7,000 yards as quarterback for the Idaho Vandals from 1982 to 1986. He tried out for the Cowboys in 1987, but a shoulder injury in training camp ended his playing career. Still, his college coach Dennis Erickson later told the *Seattle Times*, "He had a tremendous passion and knowledge when he played here. But I knew he always wanted to coach, and he had a passion for the game, and he obviously has had great success."

Linehan immediately began coaching high school football in 1987 and got his first break when he returned to his alma mater in 1989 as the receivers coach. Two years later, Scott joined the UNLV staff as the quarterbacks coach, and then again returned to Idaho, this time as offensive coordinator in 1992. Two years later, Linehan came home to Washington to coach on the Huskies staff from 1994 to 1998, working his way up to offensive coordinator. Scott then moved across country to serve as Louisville's offensive coordinator from 1999 to 2001.

Finally, in 2002, Mike Tice brought Linehan to the NFL as the Vikings offensive coordinator. When Tice was fired after the 2004 season, Scott took the offensive coordinator job under new coach Nick Saban in Miami. While Linehan's offense in Minnesota finished in the top 10 in points all three years, his Dolphins' offense behind journeyman quarterback Gus Frerotte was in the middle of the pack. In 2006, Linehan was named head coach of the Rams succeeding Mike Martz and Joe Vitt.

Linehan, Scott T.									
Year	Team	Games	Wins	Losses	Ties	%	P Wins	P Losses	P %
2006	Rams	16	8	8	0	.500	0	0	.000
2007	Rams	16	3	13	0	.188	0	0	.000
2008	Rams	4	0	4	0	.000	0	0	.000
3 years		36	11	25	0	.306	0	0	.000

The Rams had enough talent to get to 8–8 in Linehan's first season, winning four of the last six games after Scott turned over the play calling to co-ordinator Greg Olson. However, the bottom fell out on the aging team in 2007. Linehan lost control of his squad, getting into verbal disputes on the sidelines with runner Steven Jackson and receiver Torry Holt and clashing continually with starting quarterback Marc Bulger. The Rams followed a 3–13 2007 by dropping the first four games of 2008. The team had allowed more than 30 points in each of its last seven games and had been outscored 147–43 in the current year. It came as no surprise that Linehan was fired at that point, although it was odd that defensive coach Jim Haslett was promoted to replace him considering the play of the defense. The next year, Linehan joined new coach Jim Schwartz in Detroit as offensive coordinator and is working to develop promising young quarterback Matthew Stafford into an NFL star. If he can pull that off, he might get another head coaching opportunity at some point and the chance to learn from his mistakes in St. Louis.

LOMBARDI, VINCENT T. (VINCE) 6/11/1913–9/3/1970. Fordham. G; did not play professionally. *Apprenticeship:* College asst.—7 years; pro asst.—5 years. *Roots:* Jim Lee Howell. *Branches:* Bill Austin, Norb Hecker, Tom Fears, Phil Bengtson, Mike McCormack, Jerry Burns. *Coordinators/Key Assistants*: Lombardi ran his own offense, while Phil Bengtson handled the defense for the Packers and Harland Svare did so for the Redskins. *Hall of Fame Players:* Herb Adderley, Willie Davis, Forrest Gregg, Chris Hanburger, Paul Hornung, Sam Huff, Henry Jordan, Sonny Jurgensen, Ray Nitschke, Jim Ringo, Bart Starr, Charlie Taylor, Jim Taylor, Emlen Tunnell, Willie Wood. *Primary Quarterbacks:* Bart Starr, Sonny Jurgensen. *Record:* **Hall of Fame Coach**; NFL Championships 1961, 1962, 1965 Super Bowl Championships 1966, 1967. *Tendencies:* • His teams scored 24.9 points and allowed 16.1 per game • His teams ran 56.8% of the time, which was 112% of the league average • Five

starting quarterbacks in 10 years; 93% of starts to primary quarterbacks • Eleven rookie starters in 10 years • Winning Full Seasons to Losing Full Seasons: 10:0.

It stands to reason that a coach who had the championship trophy of his sport named after himself would have to be a great coach, maybe even the greatest of all. That is where we must begin with Vince Lombardi whose namesake, the Vince Lombardi Trophy, is given to each year's Super Bowl champion. Indeed, Lombardi had a .673 winning percentage coaching against fellow Hall of Fame coaches; only John Madden's has a better head-to-head record at .691. Lombardi's overall winning percentage of .740, though, tops all other coaches, including Madden's .731. Most important of all are those five NFL championships that Vince packed into a seven-year stretch. That separates him from everyone.

Lombardi was born in Brooklyn and played football at Fordham under Sleepy Jim Crowley from 1933 to 1936 as a 5′8″ 180-pound guard. Vince was one of the famous Seven Blocks of Granite line that gave up just 26 points in his senior year. In the next two years, Lombardi played some semipro football with the Brooklyn Eagles and the Wilmington Clippers and attended law school for one semester before dropping out. In 1939, Vince took a job teaching science and coaching sports for St. Cecilia's High School in New

Head-to-Head:		
Hall of Fame Opponent	Regular Season	Postseason
George Allen	2–1	1–0
Paul Brown	1–0	0–0
Weeb Ewbank	4–4	0–0
Sid Gillman	1–1	0–0
Bud Grant	1–1	0–0
George Halas	13–5	0–0
Tom Landry	3–2	2–0
Chuck Noll	1–0	0–0
Don Shula	6–4	1–0
Hank Stram	0–0	1–0
Total	32–18	5–0

Lombardi, Vincent T. (Vince)									
Year	Team	Games	Wins	Losses	Ties	%	P Wins	P Losses	P %
1959	Packers	12	7	5	0	.583	0	0	.000
1960	Packers	12	8	4	0	.667	0	1	.000
1961	Packers	14	11	3	0	.786	1	0	1.000
1962	Packers	14	13	1	0	.929	1	0	1.000
1963	Packers	14	11	2	1	.821	0	0	.000
1964	Packers	14	8	5	1	.607	0	0	.000
1965	Packers	14	10	3	1	.750	2	0	1.000
1966	Packers	14	12	2	0	.857	2	0	1.000
1967	Packers	14	9	4	1	.679	3	0	1.000
1969	Redskins	14	7	5	2	.571	0	0	.000
10 years		136	96	34	6	.728	9	1	.900

Jersey, where he introduced the T formation. In the eight years from 1939 to 1946, Lombardi drove tiny St. Cecilia's to six state championships and won 36 straight games at one point. In 1947, he returned to his alma mater as the freshman football coach for one year until he was offered a chance to join Red Blaik's staff at West Point. Lombardi spent six years under the revered Blaik at Army with the Cadets going 38–13–3 despite the Honor Code scandal that decimated the team in 1951. Under Blaik, Lombardi learned to focus primarily on the handful of things you do the very best and try to hone them to perfection.

In 1954, Lombardi moved up to the NFL when fellow Fordham alumnus Wellington Mara helped bring him to the Giants as the team's offensive coach under new head coach Jim Lee Howell. Howell preferred to delegate responsibilities to his coaches, which works very well indeed if you have Vince Lombardi coaching your offense and Tom Landry running your defense. This group led the Giants to an NFL championship in 1956 and back to the title game in 1958, when the Giants fell to Johnny Unitas' Colts in Sudden Death in Vince's last game for New York. With the Giants, Vince joined a veteran team and had to learn how to communicate with professionals. At first, he tried to force plays on them he thought would work like the Wing T quarterback option, but soon found that grizzled quarterback Charlie Conerly had no interest in running that play and getting creamed by large defensive linemen. Lombardi adjusted his offense and won the respect of his players in New York.

In 1959, he took over the 1–10–1 Green Bay Packers, a team that had not had a winning season since 1947. He told the *New York Times*, "I'll take the Giant offense with me and use it with the Packers as personnel permits." As it turned out, Green Bay had much more talent than was evident, but the team needed direction and a workable system. Lombardi provided that. In building the Packers' offense, Vince only needed to add guard Fuzzy Thurston off the scrap heap and receiver Boyd Dowler from the draft to the existing players; the five Packer Hall of Fame offensive players were already on the roster. The defense wasn't so complete, but Lombardi quickly changed that. At the time, only Vince and Cleveland's Paul Brown were both coach and GM of their teams in the NFL, so Lombardi had complete freedom to improve Green Bay. From Cleveland, he acquired three-fourths of his defensive line in trades, including Hall of Famers Willie Davis and Henry Jordan. He already had four fine linebackers, including Hall of Famer Ray Nitschke, and by bringing in veteran free safety Emlen Tunnell from the Giants, his secondary was decent. Later he would add free agent Willie Wood at safety and cornerbacks Herb Adderley and Bob Jeter through the draft. Wood and Adderley would be Hall of Famers.

Thus while Lombardi added some talent, his

major upgrade was in coaching. He once noted, "Coaches who can outline plays on a blackboard are a dime a dozen. The ones who win get inside their players and motivate them." He told his players, "One can never achieve perfection, but in chasing perfection, one can achieve excellence." He insisted on that pursuit of excellence through repetition and practice. In another of his sayings, "Winning is not a sometime thing; it's an all the time thing. You don't win once in a while; you don't do things right once in a while; you do them right all the time." The offensive system he installed was, on the surface, as simple as possible, and stood in sharp contrast in the 1960s to Tom Landry's shifting, multi-set passing offense in Dallas. His view was that football was in essence blocking and tackling, and his offense was run-based, featuring fewer plays than most teams ran. The complexity was in the multiplicity of options possible off of each basic play. The line took the defenders in the direction they wanted to go, using Lombardi's "option blocking." The running backs then had to read where the hole opened up and cut back into it. *Run to Daylight* was the title of Lombardi's own football book, and his teams ran 12% more than the league average. On pass plays, receivers were expected to read the defense and break off their routes accordingly.

The key to the whole offense was the Power Sweep; it was the lead play that every opponent knew they had to stop. Lombardi told George Flynn for *Vince Lombardi on Football*, "There is nothing spectacular about it, it's just a yard gainer. But on that sideline when the sweep starts to develop, you can hear those linebackers and defensive backs yelling, 'Sweep! Sweep!' and almost see their eyes pop as those guards turn upfield after them. But maybe it's my number 1 play because it requires all 11 men to play as one to make it succeed, and that's what 'team' means." The Packers practiced the play thousands of times and would run it repeatedly in each game.

The play itself dated to the single wing era of Lombardi's college days and owed a lot to the power attack of Jock Sutherland. Lombardi simply updated it for modern football. As with everything else about him, the key was its sophisticated simplicity. Packer players had to be intelligent because each play presented a great many possible options for each player depending on what the defense was doing. In the passing game, not only did quarterback Bart Starr read the defense, but the wide receivers had to read coverages as well and could change their routes in response. The blocking scheme of the Packers was known as option blocking, i.e., take the defensive man in the direction he is leaning. The hole for the runner may open in a different spot than where the play is planned to go ostensibly, so the runner must find the hole, make the right cut, and "run to daylight" as Lombardi phrased it. The sweep itself could be run to either side, and while the sweep was designed to go around the end, the runner would cut back inside if that was where the hole was. The ability of halfback Paul Hornung to throw an accurate pass made the play that much more effective; it was one more option the defense had to defend against. They couldn't come up too fast or Hornung would throw the ball over their heads. Then, once the defense got too comfortable defending the sweep, the Packers would hit them with the "sucker" or influence play which looked like a sweep but was actually a fake and was run as a slant play up the middle.

With this offense, Green Bay twice led the league in scoring and four times were in the top two. On defense, the Packers allowed the fewest points in the NFL three times and eight times in nine years finished in the top three. Beyond all that, Lombardi's teams played nearly error free and six times finished on the top three in turnover differential. What that led to were title game appearances from 1960 to 1962 with championships in 1961 and 1962. In 1963, the team went 11–2–1 but fell short in its quest for a three-peat by losing twice to the Bears who finished 11–1–2. Lombardi's men started a new run in 1965, won the first Super Bowl after the 1966 season and went for the three-peat a second time in 1967. Although the team was aging fast, they put together one last playoff run for the old man culminating with the legendary Ice Bowl and won Super Bowl II going away for their third straight title.

Lombardi retired as coach soon after, but the strain of watching the team lose without being able to do anything about it got to Vince. He resigned as general manager in 1969 and took over the Washington Redskins who had not had a winning season since 1955. Washington did not have the store of untapped talent that Green Bay had in 1959. Lombardi had to build a running game from scratch with rookie late round draft pick Larry Brown and trade acquisition Charley Harraway. All in all, Vince turned over half the roster in 1969, brought in nine new starters and led the Redskins to a 7–5–2 record. In 1970, though, he was diagnosed with cancer and died during training camp. It's interesting to speculate how well Lombardi would have done in Washington, but it's almost certain that it would have been a step down from Green Bay. Even if he would have had as much

success as George Allen had with the Redskins from 1971 to 1977 — a .691 winning percentage, five post-season trips, one Super Bowl appearance, but no championships — that would have been a downgrade for Lombardi and his pristine reputation.

With his death, Lombardi's career consisted almost solely of his spectacular run in Green Bay. Because of that success, there have probably been more poor imitations by Lombardi poseurs at all levels of football than any other coach. Coaches who think they are motivating their players by screaming at them miss the humanity and the magnetism of Lombardi. While there have been many great coaches such as Paul Brown, Don Shula, George Halas and Joe Gibbs, there have been very few with anything like the charisma of Lombardi. Bill Walsh, Bill Parcells and John Madden are three who come to mind, but all pale in comparison to Vince who is still quoted regularly in pop culture, who was featured in a popular series of Nike ads in the 1990s, 25 years after his death, and who was the subject of a sold out Broadway show in 2010, 40 years after his death. Among football coaches, there will never be another Vince Lombardi.

MACKOVIC, JOHN 10/1/1943– Wake Forest. QB; did not play professionally. *Apprenticeship:* College coach —14 years (3 as head coach); pro asst.— 2 years. *Roots:* Tom Landry. *Branches:* Frank Gansz, Bud Carson. *Coordinators/Key Assistants:* Mackovic handled his own offense, while Bud Carson then Dan Daniel then Walt Corey ran the defense. *Hall of Fame Players:* None. *Primary Quarterbacks:* Bill Kenney. *Tendencies:* • His teams scored 21.5 points and allowed 21.5 per game • His teams ran 40.4% of the time, which was 86% of the league average • Two starting quarterbacks in four years; 66% of starts to primary quarterback • 12 rookie starters in four years • Winning Full Seasons to Losing Full Seasons: 1:2.

John Mackovic from Barberton, Ohio was an Academic All-American at quarterback at Wake Forest from 1962 to 1964 but the Demon Deacons won only six games in that time despite having Brian Piccolo in the backfield. Mackovic's coaching career was more successful, but had few real high points.

Mackovic began his coaching career in 1965 as a graduate assistant under Bo Schembechler at Miami of Ohio. He coached high school football the next

Year	Team	Games	Wins	Losses	Ties	%	P Wins	P Losses	P %
1983	Chiefs	16	6	10	0	.375	0	0	.000
1984	Chiefs	16	8	8	0	.500	0	0	.000
1985	Chiefs	16	6	10	0	.375	0	0	.000
1986	Chiefs	16	10	6	0	.625	0	1	.000
4 years		64	30	34	0	.469	0	1	.000

Mackovic, John

year, spent a year as the basketball coach at Fort Knox and another year as the freshman football coach at West Point. He was on the staff at San Jose State from 1969 to 1970 and at Arizona from 1973 to 1976. In 1977, Mackovic made a splash as offensive coordinator at Purdue with record-setting quarterback Mark Herrmann, and that led to his getting his first head coaching opportunity at his alma mater in 1978.

However, in three years at Wake Forest, John only but managed a 14–20 record. In 1981, though, he got his big break when Tom Landry hired him to replace Dan Reeves on the Cowboys staff. That was a dream come true for Mackovic since John had been emulating Landry's offense from the time he was coaching high school in 1966. Two years under Landry brought him to the attention of the Kansas City Chiefs. Kansas City GM Jack Steadman called John "the most outstanding young coach in professional football" when he hired him as the team's head coach in 1983. Years later, Mackovic told Dennis Freeman and Jaime Aron for *I Remember Tom Landry*, "What happens in sports is that people hire someone from an organization in hopes that that person will bring that organization with them to a certain extent. In this particular case, I'm sure Lamar Hunt was very much interested in bringing to the Kansas City Chiefs some of those same things the Cowboys had. And that's what I was trying to do. I wanted to bring the same style of coaching, preparation, good administration."

Ironically, from 1984 to 1986, the Cowboys began to decline, yet Kansas City and Dallas had very comparable records in that period. Both teams ranged from mediocre to good. For Dallas, that was a step down; for Kansas City, a step up. In many ways, Mackovic's fate was decided by his choice for his first round draft pick in 1983, the "year of the quarterback." The Chiefs had the seventh choice in the draft and only John Elway was off the board at that point. With Jim Kelly, Dan Marino, Ken O'Brien and Tony Eason as possibilities, Kansas City selected Todd Blackledge of Penn State, and Blackledge would turn out to be the only one of the six 1983 first rounders to have no NFL success at all. Blackledge ultimately was unable to beat out Bill Kenney, the final overall selection from the 1978 draft. Fate tossed Mackovic another cruel blow when the Chiefs leading runner, Joe Delaney, drowned while trying to save three kids before training camp in 1983. Still, Mackovic did improve the Chiefs on both sides of the ball over his four-year tenure. Even

with Kenney at quarterback, Kansas City could move the ball through the air and threw the ball 14% more than the league average. Furthermore, the Chiefs special teams under assistant Frank Ganz were truly special.

Mackovic, though, was seen as too brusque and too poor a communicator by his players. Former Chiefs' star Otis Taylor noted in his autobiography that Mackovic was stiff, "If you watched him on the sidelines during games, he didn't really know what to do after something happened, good or bad. He didn't know how to react — whether to touch the guy, talk to him soft or hard." So even though Kansas City made the playoffs in 1986 for the first time in 15 years, Mackovic was fired in January. A group of players met with management at kicker Nick Lowery's house after the season and urged the team to replace Mackovic with Ganz, and that's what Lamar Hunt did. Hunt remarked, "The chemistry of an organization is an intangible that is crucial to its success. My evaluation is that our football team is lacking that ingredient." Ganz lasted just two seasons as head coach before he was replaced by Marty Schottenheimer.

Mackovic landed at Illinois and posted a 30–16–1 record in Champaign from 1988 to 1991 behind strong armed quarterback Jeff George and then coached Texas to a 41–28–2 record from 1992 to 1997. The highlight of his time in Austin was a 10–2–1 season in 1995, Ricky Williams' freshman year. By 1997, though, the Longhorns had fallen to 4–7, including a disastrous 66–3 loss to UCLA, and John was fired. For the next few years, Mackovic was active in several national coaching organizations and college football ruling bodies. He returned to the sidelines in 2001 as the head coach at Arizona, but a 10–18 record from 2001 to 2003 ended his college coaching career. Resurfacing in 2007, John coached the U.S. national football team to victory in the American Football World Cup in Japan. Since 2008, he has written a column on football for the *Desert Sun* in Palm Springs.

MacPherson, Richard F. (Dick)

MacPherson, Richard F. (Dick) 11/4/1930– Springfield (MA). C; did not play professionally. *Apprenticeship:* College coach — 26 years (17 as head coach); pro asst. — 7 years. *Roots:* Lou Saban, Sam Rutigliano. *Branches:* None. *Coordinators/Key Assistants:* Dick Coury handled the offense, while Joe Collier ran the defense. *Hall of Fame Players:* Andre Tippett. *Primary Quarterbacks:* Hugh Millen. *Tendencies:* • His

MacPherson, Richard F. (Dick)									
Year	Team	Games	Wins	Losses	Ties	%	P Wins	P Losses	P %
1991	Patriots	16	6	10	0	.375	0	0	.000
1992	Patriots	16	2	14	0	.125	0	0	.000
2 years		32	8	24	0	.250	0	0	.000

teams scored 13 points and allowed 20.9 per game • His teams ran 44.7% of the time, which was 98% of the league average • Four starting quarterbacks in two years; 63% of starts to primary quarterback • Six rookie starters in two years • Winning Full Seasons to Losing Full Seasons: 0:2.

Born in Old Town, Maine, Dick Macpherson went into the Air Force out of high school in 1950 and later attended Springfield College in Massachusetts on the GI Bill from 1954 to 1957. MacPherson then spent one season as a graduate assistant at Illinois before joining the staff at the University of Massachusetts in 1959. Two years later, he moved on to the University of Cincinnati from 1961 to 1965 and then was hired by Lou Saban to coach the secondary for Maryland in 1966. When the peripatetic Saban left to take over the Denver Broncos in 1967, Dick came along to coach the linebackers and defensive backs. After four years in Denver, MacPherson was hired as the head coach at Massachusetts in 1971. Over the next seven years, the Minutemen finished 45–27–1 and went to two bowl games.

Dick returned to the NFL in 1978 as the linebackers coach for Cleveland under Sam Rutigliano who had also worked on Saban's staff in Denver. After three years in Cleveland, MacPherson was hired as head coach at Syracuse in 1981. Over the next decade, Dick led the Orangemen to a 66–46–4 record and four bowl games. Oddly, his greatest player was African American quarterback with a similar name, Don McPherson. After reviving the moribund program, Dick's record over his last four years, 1987–1990, in Syracuse was 36–10–3. At the age of 60 and looking for a new challenge, MacPherson then made the biggest mistake of his career by accepting the offer of the New England Patriots to become their head coach in 1991.

The Patriots were a basket case on the field (1–15 in 1990) and even worse off the field with the team in the process of being sold to James Orthwein who wanted to move the club to St. Louis. Furthermore, the league had just fined three players for sexually ha-

rassing a female reporter in the locker room and penalized two other players for their involvement in a bar fight. At the time, though, MacPherson said, "I can't emphasize to you how much of a joy it is for me to be here. What a great way to make a living." 18 years later on the eve of being inducted into the College Football Hall of Fame, he told the *Syracuse Post-Standard*, "I was very happy to leave New England. I think that I could've gotten another good college job. I'm positive I could've gotten another good college job if I wanted one. But I think it was time. I think I made a huge mistake in going because, see, the thing you ought to make sure is, who the hell are you working for. I don't think it was a good marriage. I've never gotten a divorce before."

In New England, Coach Mac was an outgoing, exuberant presence on the sideline, giving out hugs, pumping his fist, and even playfully tackling his journeyman quarterback Hugh Millen in celebration. Former Syracuse receiver Rob Moore told the *New York Times*, "He's a real emotional and energetic type of coach." And for a short time, that breathed life into a bad team. The Patriots won six games in 1991 and pulled out four of them in the fourth quarter or overtime. The newness wore off in 1992. Not only did the team sink back to 2–14, but MacPherson missed the second half of the season in the hospital with diverticulitis. Although longtime Patriots' assistant Dante Scarnecchia ran the team on the field at the time as acting coach, Dick was still in charge and, as best he could, ran things from his hospital bed. At the end of the dismal season, MacPherson was fired and replaced by Bill Parcells who was given full authority to direct the team. Coach Mac never coached again but worked as a broadcaster of Syracuse football for several years.

MADDEN, JOHN E. 4/10/1936– Cal Poly-San Luis Obispo. T; did not play professionally. *Apprenticeship:* College asst.— 5 years; pro asst.— 2 years. *Roots:* John Rauch. *Branches:* Ray Malavasi, Tom Flores, John Robinson. *Coordinators/Key Assistants:* John Pilonchek and Tom Flores were the key offensive coaches, while

Madden, John E.

Year	Team	Games	Wins	Losses	Ties	%	P Wins	P Losses	P %
1969	Raiders	14	12	1	1	.893	1	1	.500
1970	Raiders	14	8	4	2	.643	1	1	.500
1971	Raiders	14	8	4	2	.643	0	0	.000
1972	Raiders	14	10	3	1	.750	0	1	.000
1973	Raiders	14	9	4	1	.679	1	1	.500
1974	Raiders	14	12	2	0	.857	1	1	.500
1975	Raiders	14	11	3	0	.786	1	1	.500
1976	Raiders	14	13	1	0	.929	3	0	1.000
1977	Raiders	14	11	3	0	.786	1	1	.500
1978	Raiders	16	9	7	0	.563	0	0	.000
10 years		142	103	32	7	.750	9	7	.563

Richie McCabe then Ray Malavasi then Bob Zeman handled the defense. *Hall of Fame Players:* Fred Biletnikoff, George Blanda, Bob Brown, Willie Brown, Dave Casper, Ted Hendricks, Ron Mix, Jim Otto, Art Shell, Gene Upshaw. *Primary Quarterbacks:* Daryle Lamonica, Ken Stabler. *Record:* **Hall of Fame Coach;** Super Bowl Championship 1976. *Tendencies:* • His teams scored 24.1 points and allowed 17.4 per game • His teams ran 57.9% of the time, which was 105% of the league average • Five starting quarterbacks in 10 years; 96% of starts to primary quarterbacks • Eleven rookie starters in 10 years • Winning Full Seasons to Losing Full Seasons: 10:0.

John Madden was born in Austin, Minnesota, but grew up in Daly City, California where his closest boyhood friend was another future NFL coach, John Robinson. Madden not only went on to have a Hall of Fame career as a football coach, but followed that by becoming the most popular TV analyst in the sport's history and lent his name to the one of the most popular video games of the past 25 years, the perennially updated *Madden NFL*. That is not to mention his three bestselling football books in the 1980s. But Madden made his reputation first as a rowdy, rumpled, red headed players' coach for ten years in Oakland, His Raiders' record is rivaled only by Vince Lombardi's in winning percentage, although John was more of a big brother to his players than a Lombardi-like father figure.

Madden began as a tackle at Cal-Poly San Luis Obispo and was drafted in the 21st round by the Eagles in 1958. John injured his knee as soon as training camp began and spent the year rehabbing his knee and soaking up football knowledge from the team's vociferous veteran quarterback Norm Van Brocklin who invited him to watch game films together. Although Madden had an offer to try out with the Chargers in 1960, he instead returned to his alma mater and earned his Master's Degree in Education. He then spent 1961 coaching high school football and attending coaching clinics. Madden later fondly recalled one led by Vince Lombardi in which the Packers' coach spent eight hours talking in detail about his famous power sweep from every conceivable angle. In 1962, John moved up a level as an assistant at Hancock Junior College, and then joined Don Coryell's staff as the defensive coach at San Diego State from 1964 to 1966. Fellow Hall of Famer Joe Gibbs was also on that staff. Madden rose to the pros in 1967 when Raiders' coach John Rauch hired him as the new linebackers coach in Oakland. Two years later, Rauch found he could not get along with Al Davis and resigned. The 32-year-old Madden applied for the job and convinced Davis he was ready. While outsiders were shocked at the appointment, the choice made sense. Davis later said, "The word is passion. What I saw in John is what you still see in John. It's his love of football, his love of friendship, his loyalty, and goal-oriented things."

There has never been a better fit of team to coach than that of Madden to the 1969–1978 Raiders, the "Pride and Poise Boys," aka, the "Badasses" as the team preferred to think of itself. His players weren't always choir boys, but they were talented, and Madden knew how to get the most from them. Linebacker Phil Villapiano told Tom Danyluk for *The Super 70s*, "Coaches like Tom Landry or Chuck Knox, maybe they liked guys who did it by the numbers. John would rather have guys out there reacting and hitting and enjoying themselves." Madden kept things simple by having just three simple team rules: Be on time; Pay attention; and Play like Hell. John told Peter Richmond for *Badasses*, "I liked all my players. I made a point of talking to every player every day. I'd walk up and down the locker room and talk to them as they'd come in, going into the training room, because I liked them. They were my friends. They're people. When you start thinking, 'How do you treat them?' you're thinking about it too much. You just do what's normal." Villapiano added to Danyluk, "John was a great psychologist. He knew how to handle all different types of people very well. He knew when you needed a pat on the back and when you needed to be sat on a little bit. I used to admire John's simplicity and his brain."

At the outset of Madden's coaching career, there were cynical detractors who implied that Al Davis was the real head coach of the Raiders and that John was just his puppet. However, Davis, Madden and his players all vehemently disputed that misguided notion. As time went on, it was easy to see that while Al Davis procured the talent, it was John Madden orchestrating the team on the field. Davis and Madden did get along well, and John felt very comfortable in picking Al's brain on things, but Madden made the decisions on the field. His team was a reflection of him. He had a massive offensive line that overpowered the opposition and favored the deep passing game on an offense that led the league three times in scoring and five times finished in the top three; he employed aggressive

Head-to-Head:		
Hall of Fame Opponent	*Regular Season*	*Postseason*
George Allen	1–0	0–0
Paul Brown	4–3	1–0
Weeb Ewbank	3–0	0–0
Sid Gillman	4–0	0–0
Bud Grant	2–1	1–0
Tom Landry	1–0	0–0
Marv Levy	2–0	0–0
Chuck Noll	4–2	2–3
Don Shula	2–2	2–1
Hank Stram	7–3–2	1–1
Total	30–11–2	7–5

bump-and-run coverage on his defense that twice finished in the top three for fewest points allowed. Like Madden, the Raiders were hard-hitting and intimidating.

Throughout his coaching career, Madden made friends everywhere. Chuck Noll was a friend when both were assistant coaches in San Diego — Madden with San Diego State and Noll with the Chargers. The two became fierce rivals during the 1970s as the league's two black-uniformed teams, Steelers and Raiders, regularly lit into each other for domination of the AFC. The two teams most memorably met in the Immaculate Reception game in the 1972 playoffs and Ice Bowl II in the 1975 playoffs, with the Steelers coming out on top both times. In 1976, though, Madden's Raiders finally upended the Steelers in the AFC championship game to reach the Super Bowl at last. The Raiders subsequently topped off that 13–1 season with the franchise's first Super Bowl victory, 32–14 over the Vikings, and Madden began to think of retirement.

John never liked plane travel and began to have ulcer troubles from the stress of coaching. In the 1978 preseason, he watched Patriots receiver Darryl Stingley be paralyzed from a hard hit by Raiders' safety Jack Tatum and that strongly affected him as well. Above all, John indicated he was just fatigued from the pressures of coaching. Retiring in 1978, he said, "I gave it everything I have and just don't have anything left." He tearfully added, "I'm retiring from football coaching, and I'm never going to coach again in my life."

The surprising thing is that John kept to his no coaching pledge unlike so many other coaches who have walked away only to return a few years later like Bill Parcells–Dick Vermeil even came back after 15 years out of coaching. Instead, Madden went in other directions and was successful at every turn. He worked as a TV broadcaster for 30 years: 1979–1993 on CBS, 1994–2004 on Fox, 2005 on ABC's Monday Night Football and 2006–2008 on NBC's Sunday Night Football. His bestselling books, *Hey, Wait a Minute, One Knee Equals Two Feet* and *One Size Doesn't Fit All,* were written with *New York Times*' columnist Dave Anderson and came out in 1984, 1986 and 1988 respectively. A fourth book, *All Madden,* came out in 1997. By 1988, he had also moved into the video game

market with EA Sports' *Madden NFL.* Largely owing to the brevity of his coaching career, Madden wasn't elected to the Hall of Fame until 2006, but it was long overdue. His regular season winning percentage is second to none as is his head-to-head record against other Hall of Fame coaches. He led the Raiders to one AFL championship game and six AFC championship games, including five in a row. While his Raiders only made it to one Super Bowl, they were annually in the NFL's top echelon, exuding more vitality and personality than any other team and fully mirroring their flamboyant coach.

MALAVASI, RAYMONDO G.G.B. (RAY) 11/8/1930–12/15/1987. Mississippi State. G; did not play professionally. *Apprenticeship:* College asst.— 6 years; pro asst.—13 years; CFL asst.—2 years. *Roots:* Jack Faulkner, Mac Speedie, John Madden, Chuck Knox. *Branches:* Bud Carson. *Coordinators/Key Assistants:* For the Broncos, Red Miller was the key offensive coach, while Malavasi ran the defense; for the Rams, Malavasi then Lionel Taylor handled the offense, while Bud Carson ran the defense. *Hall of Fame Players:* Willie Brown, Tom Mack, Jackie Slater, Ron Yary, Jack Youngblood. *Primary Quarterbacks:* Pat Haden, Vince Ferragamo. *Tendencies:* • His teams scored 20.5 points and allowed 20.7 per game • His teams ran 52.2% of the time, which was 102% of the league average • Nine starting quarterbacks in six years; 74% of starts to primary quarterbacks • 14 rookie starters in six years • Winning Full Seasons to Losing Full Seasons: 3:3.

Jersey boy Ray Malavasi was born in Passaic and raised in Clifton. He entered West Point at the height of its football glory under Red Blaik and was a starting guard for Army until he was implicated in the honor code cheating scandal in 1951 along with 90 other cadets. Malavasi landed at Mississippi State under Murray Warmath, his former line coach at West Point. Ray graduated from there in 1952 and also received his ROTC commission. Drafted in the seventh round by the Eagles, Malavasi was cut in training camp of 1953. For the next two years, Malavasi coached the line at Fort Belvoir in Virginia, where Al Davis had coached for the two prior years. Ray left there in 1956 and again joined Murray Warmath, this time as an as-

Malavasi, Raymondo G.G.B. (Ray)

Year	Team	Games	Wins	Losses	Ties	%	P Wins	P Losses	P %
1966	Broncos	12	4	8	0	.333	0	0	.000
1978	Rams	16	12	4	0	.750	0	1	.000
1979	Rams	16	9	7	0	.563	2	1	.667
1980	Rams	16	11	5	0	.688	0	1	.000
1981	Rams	16	6	10	0	.375	0	0	.000
1982	Rams	9	2	7	0	.222	0	0	.000
6 years		85	44	41	0	.518	2	3	.400

sistant at Minnesota from 1956 to 1957. He then worked at Memphis State from 1958 to 1960 and Wake Forest in 1961.

Malavasi moved up to the pros in 1962 when Jack Faulkner hired him to be the personnel director for the Denver Broncos, and the two would become lifelong friends. A year later, Faulkner added him to the coaching staff as the defensive line coach. When Faulkner was fired in 1963, his successor Mac Speedie kept Malavasi on staff. Two games into the 1966 season, Speedie was fired, and Malavasi was named interim coach. Denver went through five quarterbacks that season and ended up starting rookie Max Choboian who never played again. Malavasi left Denver at year's end and worked as defensive line coach for the Hamilton Tiger-Cats of the CFL from 1967 to 1968. The next two years, he held that same position for the Buffalo Bills before joining John Madden's Raiders' staff in 1971. Again, Malavasi left after two years, but this time under questionable circumstances. Ray said he was frustrated in Oakland; Madden charged the Rams with tampering with his assistant coach.

Chuck Knox hired Malavasi to be his defensive coach in 1973, and Ray worked for five years under him. When Knox resigned in 1978, the Rams hired George Allen as head coach, and he kept Ray as the defensive coach. However, after just two preseason games, owner Carroll Rosenbloom realized he had made a mistake and fired Allen, replacing him with Malavasi. While no one expected Ray to hold that position long, he surprised everyone by leading the team to a 12–4 record in 1978. The following season, the Rams slipped to 9–7, but, behind young quarterback Vince Ferragamo, made an inspired run in the playoffs to reach the Super Bowl where they led the mighty Steelers in the fourth quarter before finally succumbing to a superior team.

Malavasi was popular with his players because, as he told the *Washington Post*, "I'm tough when I have to be, but a while back I began to see you could get a lot more out of the players with a different approach. On this team, I haven't had to get tough." Free spirit defensive end Fred Dryer told the *New York Times*, "Ray's a nice guy. He's happy with himself and he understands what's going on. He lets players be players."

Malavasi led the Rams to another playoff berth in 1980, but then Ferragamo jumped to Canada over a money dispute in 1981, and the team flopped under battered veteran import Dan Pastorini. Ferragamo returned in 1982, but was not the same. Behind him and new battered veteran import Bert Jones, the Rams had a second bad year in a row, so Malavasi was fired. After a year out of football, Malavasi was hired as the offensive line coach for the Oakland Invaders of the USFL in 1984. Two games into the season, though, head coach John Ralston fired him after the line allowed 16 sacks. He was immediately hired as defensive coordinator for the Los Angeles Express of the same league by their coach John Hadl who had played on the Rams when Ray was there. He later worked for a sports management firm for athletes and also coached the Australian national football team in a tour of Europe. He died suddenly of a heart attack at the age of 57 in 1987.

MANGINI, ERIC 1/19/1971– Wesleyan. DT; did not play professionally. *Apprenticeship:* Pro asst.—10 years. *Roots:* Ted Marchibroda, Bill Parcells, Bill Belichick. *Branches:* None. *Coordinators/Key Assistants*: For the Jets, Brian Schottenheimer ran the offense, while Bob Sutton handled the defense; for the Browns, Brain Daboll ran the offense, while Rob Ryan handled the defense. *Hall of Fame Players:* None. *Primary Quarterbacks:* Chad Pennington, Brett Favre. *Tendencies:* • His teams scored 18.8 points and allowed 21.4 per game • His teams ran 46.3% of the time, which was 105% of the league average • Eight starting quarterbacks in five years; 50% of starts to primary quarterbacks • 13 rookie starters in five years • Winning Full Seasons to Losing Full Seasons: 2:3.

Dubbed "Mangenius" by the press after his initial success as Jets' head coach in 2006, Hartford's Eric Mangini has fallen fast since his speedy rise. Mangini played nose tackle at Wesleyan, Bill Belichick's alma mater, in the early 1990s and also coached a semipro team in Australia in 1992 while still a student. Belichick hired him as a public relations intern for the Cleveland Browns in 1994, and Eric remained in the organization when it moved to Baltimore in 1996, advancing onto Coach Ted Marchibroda's staff. Bill Parcells hired him as a defensive assistant on the Jets in

Mangini, Eric									
Year	Team	Games	Wins	Losses	Ties	%	P Wins	P Losses	P %
2006	Jets	16	10	6	0	.625	0	1	.000
2007	Jets	16	4	12	0	.250	0	0	.000
2008	Jets	16	9	7	0	.563	0	0	.000
2009	Browns	16	5	11	0	.313	0	0	.000
2010	Browns	16	5	11	0	.313	0	0	.000
5 years		80	33	47	0	.413	0	1	.000

1997 when he was reunited with Belichick. Mangini followed Belichick to New England in 2000 and was promoted to secondary coach in 2002 and defensive coordinator in 2005. He gained some notoriety in 2004 when he held together a patchwork secondary decimated by injuries to enable the Patriots to win their third Super Bowl in four years.

Although he gave one of his sons the middle name of William in honor of Belichick, Mangini went against Belichick's wishes by accepting the Jets' job in 2006, sparking a bitter feud between the two. Belichick was reportedly upset that Eric was going to a division rival and that he was poaching some key coaches from the Patriots' staff. Mangini's 2006 Jets managed to split the season series with the Patriots to make the playoffs, but lost there to New England. The following season, the Jets fell apart, but Mangini caused a league firestorm by accusing the Patriots of filming his team's defensive signals against league rules. The ensuing Spygate controversy engulfed the Patriots, dented Belichick's reputation and heightened the rivalry between the two former colleagues. New York brought in Brett Favre for 2008, which seemed to be a great move when the team got off to 8–3 start, but a 1–4 collapse behind an ailing Favre in December caused the Jets to miss the playoffs and Mangini to be fired.

Eric was soon hired by Cleveland as the Browns' head coach in 2009. Mangini was even given the power to hand pick the Ravens' George Kokinis as the team's GM. Eric told the press at his signing, "The most important thing to do is to be yourself and that's who I felt I always was. I learned so many things over three years. There's no Dummies guide to head coaching. I've had some great mentors. I worked under Bill for a long time. I worked under Bill Parcells. They were my football parents." The Browns have been a troubled organization since rejoining the NFL in 1999. Under Mangini, things did not get noticeably better. Instead, there was much upheaval between the

coach and the players without any improvement showing on the field. After the team got off to a 1–7 start, Kokinis was fired. The Browns rallied some in the second half of the year to finish 5–11 and buy Mangini some time under new team president Mike Holmgren, but the team's identical 5–11 finish in 2010 allowed Holmgren to fire Mangini and bring in his own coach. Mangini followed the path of ex-coaches in 2011 by becoming an analyst for ESPN while trawling for his next job.

MARCHIBRODA, THEODORE J. (TED) 3/15/1931– St. Bonaventure and Detroit. Played QB for the Steelers and Cardinals in 1953 and from 1955 to 1957. *Apprenticeship:* Pro asst.—14 years. *Roots:* Bill McPeak, George Allen. *Branches:* Pete McCulley (i), Bill Belichick, Vince Tobin, Marvin Lewis, Eric Mangini, Ken Whisenhunt, Jim Schwartz. *Coordinators/Key Assistants:* For his first Colts' stint, Marchibroda ran his own offense, while Maxie Baughan handled the defense; for his second Colts' stint, Nic Nicolau then Lindy Infante ran the offense, while Rick Venturi then Vince Tobin handled the defense; for the Ravens, Marchibroda ran his own offense, while Marvin Lewis handled the defense. *Hall of Fame Players:* Marshall Faulk. *Primary Quarterbacks:* Bert Jones, Jim Harbaugh, Vinny Testaverde *Tendencies:* • His teams scored 19.5 points and allowed 21.2 per game • His teams ran 48.3% of the time, which was 99% of the league average • 15 starting quarterbacks in 12 years; 60% of starts to primary quarterbacks • 18 rookie starters in 12 years • Winning Full Seasons to Losing Full Seasons: 5:6.

Ted Marchibroda from Franklin, Pennsylvania had a long career in football that was filled with dislocation episodes. The 5'10" 175-pound passer captained the St. Bonaventure football team until the school dropped the sport in 1952. Ted moved to the University of Detroit to finish his college eligibility that year and was the first round pick of the local Steel-

Marchibroda, Theodore J. (Ted)									
Year	Team	Games	Wins	Losses	Ties	%	P Wins	P Losses	P %
1975	Colts	14	10	4	0	.714	0	1	.000
1976	Colts	14	11	3	0	.786	0	1	.000
1977	Colts	14	10	4	0	.714	0	1	.000
1978	Colts	16	5	11	0	.313	0	0	.000
1979	Colts	16	5	11	0	.313	0	0	.000
1992	Colts	16	9	7	0	.563	0	0	.000
1993	Colts	16	4	12	0	.250	0	0	.000
1994	Colts	16	8	8	0	.500	0	0	.000
1995	Colts	16	9	7	0	.563	2	1	.667
1996	Ravens	16	4	12	0	.250	0	0	.000
1997	Ravens	16	6	9	1	.406	0	0	.000
1998	Ravens	16	6	10	0	.375	0	0	.000
12 years		186	87	98	1	.470	2	4	.333

ers despite his undersized physique. He played briefly in 1953 and then was called into the Army for the 1954 season. Marchibroda returned in 1955 and won the starting job in 1956 after Jim Finks retired, but completed just 45% of his passes. After one final season as a backup with the Cardinals, Ted retired in 1958 to work for a company that reconditioned old football equipment.

Marchibroda was brought back to the NFL by his former Steeler teammate Bill McPeak who was hired as the Redskins' coach in 1961. Ted was the team's backfield coach and worked extensively with rookie quarterback Norm Snead who the team later traded for Sonny Jurgensen. McPeak was fired after the 1965 season and Ted was hired as the backfield coach of the Rams under George Allen, helping to develop Roman Gabriel into a top flight NFL quarterback. When Allen moved on to take over the Redskins in 1971, he brought Marchibroda along as the team's offensive coordinator, working again with Jurgensen and also with Billy Kilmer. The success of the Over the Hill Gang in Washington brought coaching opportunities to several of Allen's assistants. Ted's turn came in 1975 when he became head coach of the Colts. He generously credited his former bosses at his opening press conference, "I learned Xs and Os from McPeak and organization, preparation and hard work from Allen."

The Colts' turnaround was remarkable under Marchibroda. Baltimore went from 2–12 to 10–4 winning a division title in that first year, 1975. Controversial GM Joe Thomas had completely turned over the aging Colts he had inherited in 1972 with youthful talent, but Marchibroda transformed that talent into a winner. However, the reigning Coach of the Year found his working situation untenable in Baltimore because of constant interference from blustering owner Robert Irsay and his dominant GM, so Ted resigned a week before the season opener. His players rallied to his support just as George Allen's had the first time the Rams fired him. Quarterback Bert Jones crafted a statement that said, in part, "Every player on this team will tell you that Ted Marchibroda is the man responsible for the success of the team and not the front office. You put a pile of lumber on a lot, but it does not make a house, and Ted Marchibroda has made this pile of lumber a house." Two days later, Ted was given full authority to run the team and returned.

Baltimore won two more consecutive division

crowns, but could not advance in the playoffs. Disaster struck in 1978 when Jones suffered the first of a series of shoulder injuries that would shorten his career. The Colts posted back-to-back 5–11 seasons in 1978 and 1979 behind backup quarterbacks Bill Troup and Greg Landry, and Marchibroda was fired and out of football in 1980. In 1981, he was named the Bears' offensive coordinator and then held that job for the Lions from 1982 to 1983 and the Eagles from 1984 to 1985 until again falling out of the league in 1986. Marv Levy, a colleague from Allen's staff in Los Angeles and Washington, hired Ted as quarterbacks coach for Buffalo in 1987 and promoted him to offensive coordinator in 1989. For the Bills, Marchibroda took Sam Wyche's No Huddle Offense and adapted it for quarterback Jim Kelly. The resultant K-Gun offense took Buffalo to four straight Super Bowls in the early 1990s, but Ted was only present for the first two before he earned another NFL head coaching job for his innovative approach. As Bert Jones said of his former coach to Tom Danyluk for *The Super 70s*, "The greatest complement to a coach is that he is able to adjust his strategy to fit the players he has on the field, not to fit the players into a system." Oddly enough, Marchibroda's success in Buffalo brought him back to the Colts for a second stint as head coach, this time in Indianapolis.

Marchibroda took over a 1–15 club and led it to a 9–7 record in 1992. By 1995, he had the Colts in the AFC Championship game, a dropped Hail Mary pass away from the Super Bowl. The Colts then rewarded Ted by low-balling him with a contract offer at the same rate as his old contract. Marchibroda quit and returned to Baltimore in 1996, this time with the new Ravens franchise that had just moved from Cleveland. While Ted had some success working with beleaguered quarterback Vinny Testaverde and laid the groundwork for the Ravens later success, he was fired after the 1998 season. He later returned again to the Colts where he worked as a pre-game broadcaster for the team.

MARINELLI, RODNEY (ROD) 7/13/1949– California Lutheran. T; did not play professionally. *Apprenticeship:* College asst.— 20 years; pro asst.—10 years. *Roots:* Tony Dungy, Jon Gruden. *Branches:* None. *Coordinators/Key Assistants:* Mike Martz then Jim Colletto ran the offense, while Donnie Henderson then Joe Barry handled the defense. *Hall of Fame Play-*

Marinelli, Rodney (Rod)									
Year	Team	Games	Wins	Losses	Ties	%	P Wins	P Losses	P %
2006	Lions	16	3	13	0	.188	0	0	.000
2007	Lions	16	7	9	0	.438	0	0	.000
2008	Lions	16	0	16	0	.000	0	0	.000
3 years		48	10	38	0	.208	0	0	.000

ers: None. *Primary Quarterbacks:* Jon Kitna. *Tendencies:* • His teams scored 19.1 points and allowed 28.3 per game • His teams ran 34.5% of the time, which was 78% of the league average • Three starting quarterbacks in three years; 75% of starts to primary quarterback • Seven rookie starters in three years • Winning Full Seasons to Losing Full Seasons: 0:3.

Rod Marinelli will never live down coaching the Lions to an unprecedented 0–16 season in 2008, but, to his credit, he has never tried. When he was fired, he refused to place any blame on the incompetent GM who hired him, Matt Millen. Instead, the Vietnam vet from Rosemead, California said simply, "I've said all year long, 'It starts with me.'"

Marinelli was a born assistant. After coaching high school football from 1973 to 1975, he embarked on a 20-year stretch as college defensive coach: Utah State from 1976 to 1982, California from 1983 to 1991, Arizona State from 1992 to 1994 and finally USC in 1995. Tony Dungy brought him to Tampa as the Bucs' defensive line coach in 1996 and Rod remained in Tampa for a decade, adding the title of assistant head coach in 2002 under Jon Gruden. In his autobiography, Dungy said of him, "Rod could relate to, teach and motivate each of our linemen, whether they were veterans or rookies, fast learners or not. He inspired all of those guys to play hard, fast and smart."

Showing desperation while trying to hire his third coach during his woeful tenure as Lions' GM, Matt Millen persuaded Marinelli to take the job in 2006. Detroit gave up on draft bust Joey Harrington and brought in journeyman Jon Kitna as quarterback that year in addition to Mike Martz to coach the offense, but without success. In 2007, Marinelli had a 750-pound Michigan fieldstone delivered to the locker room to emphasize his "pound the rock" motto, and Kitna predicted a 10-win season. The Lions got off to a 6–2 start with Kitna passing well and telling the *New York Times,* "Every guy in here will probably fall on a sword for this guy. He has no ego." From that point on, though, Detroit would win just one game out of the next 24.

Millen deserves much of the blame, but Marinelli

was over his head as head coach. He made the mistake of hiring his son-in-law Joe Barry as defensive coordinator and that led to an uncomfortable incident when a reporter jokingly questioned Rod whether he wished his daughter "had married a better defensive coordinator." That and defensive line coach Joe Cullen being arrested for driving nude through a drive-in lane added to the hopeless and pathetic atmosphere surrounding the team. Marinelli was hired immediately by Lovie Smith as the Bears' defensive line coach in 2009 and promoted to defensive coordinator in 2010.

MARIUCCI, STEVEN R. (STEVE) 11/4/1954– Northern Michigan. QB; did not play professionally. *Apprenticeship:* College coach—14 years (1 as head coach); pro asst.—4 years; USFL asst.—1 year. *Roots:* Mike Holmgren. *Branches:* Marty Mornhinweg, Jim Mora, Jr. *Coordinators/Key Assistants:* For the 49ers, Marty Mornhinweg then Greg Knapp ran the offense, while John Marshall then Jim Mora, Jr., handled the defense; for the Lions, Sherman Lewis then Ted Tollner ran the offense, while Kurt Schottenheimer then Dick Jauron handled the defense. *Hall of Fame Players:* Jerry Rice, Steve Young. *Primary Quarterbacks:* Steve Young, Jeff Garcia, Joey Harrington. *Tendencies:* • His teams scored 22 points and allowed 21.9 per game • His teams ran 44.1% of the time, which was the league average • Seven starting quarterbacks in nine years; 95% of starts to primary quarterbacks • 21 rookie starters in nine years • Winning Full Seasons to Losing Full Seasons: 4:5.

Gregarious Steve Mariucci emerged from the salary-cap-hell years of the 49ers with his reputation intact, but could not survive working for Matt Millen's Lions, even though he still has an overall winning record as a head coach. Born in Iron Mountain, Michigan, in the state's Upper Peninsula, Mariucci grew up a fan of Lombardi's Packers and was childhood friends with future Michigan State basketball coach Tom Izzo. He was a Little All-American quarterback at Northern Michigan who led his school to a Division II national championship in 1975 as a sophomore. Attracting no interest from the pros, he

Mariucci, Steven R. (Steve)									
Year	*Team*	*Games*	*Wins*	*Losses*	*Ties*	*%*	*P Wins*	*P Losses*	*P %*
1997	49ers	16	13	3	0	.813	1	1	.500
1998	49ers	16	12	4	0	.750	1	1	.500
1999	49ers	16	4	12	0	.250	0	0	.000
2000	49ers	16	6	10	0	.375	0	0	.000
2001	49ers	16	12	4	0	.750	0	1	.000
2002	49ers	16	10	6	0	.625	1	1	.500
2003	Lions	16	5	11	0	.313	0	0	.000
2004	Lions	16	6	10	0	.375	0	0	.000
2005	Lions	11	4	7	0	.364	0	0	.000
9 years		139	72	67	0	.518	3	4	.429

then began his coaching career at his alma mater from 1978 to 1979. He moved on to California Fullerton from 1980 to 1982 and to Louisville from 1983 to 1984 before coaching the receivers for the Orlando Renegades of the USFL in 1985 and then joining the Rams' staff later that same year. Steve coached at USC in 1986 and then moved to California in 1987, working up to offensive coordinator for the Golden Bears in 1990 and 1991.

Mike Holmgren hired Mariucci as his quarterbacks coach in 1992. For the next four years, Steve helped undisciplined quarterback Brett Favre to develop into the league's MVP. The fun-loving Mariucci grew very close to Favre, even having the quarterback babysit his kids on occasion. Just as the team was on the verge of its first Super Bowl, though, Steve left Green Bay to become head coach at Cal in 1996. Although the Golden Bears finished just 6–6 including a bowl game loss, 49ers GM Carmen Policy made Mariucci an offer to become the offensive coordinator and heir apparent under head coach George Seifert. Seifert, though, decided he didn't want to work in that environment and resigned immediately, so Steve was hired as head coach, not offensive coordinator in 1997.

Both quarterback Steve Young and receiver Jerry Rice were injured in the 1997 season opener. While Young would only miss one start, Rice missed all but one other game that year. Still, Mariucci led the veteran team to the NFC championship game where they lost to the Packers at home. The next year, the 49ers beat Green Bay in the playoffs for the only time in Steve Young's career, but lost to Atlanta in the second round. In 1999 and 2000, the 49ers' spendthrift ways caught up to them, and Bill Walsh returned to the front office to try to straighten out the salary cap mess. Walsh brought with him Jeff Garcia, a quarterback from the CFL who would emerge as the new 49ers quarterback after Steve Young went down to a career-ending concussion early in 1999.

Mariucci held the team together in this transition period, and San Francisco returned to the postseason in 2001, again losing to Favre's Packers. By this time, talented receiver Terrell Owens had bloomed into full divahood, presenting a wealth of problems for Mariucci. Steve suspended Owens after his famous spike-the-ball-on-the-star moment in Dallas and later had to deal with Owens telling the press that Mariucci wasn't dedicated enough to winning and needed to get him the ball more. That offseason the 49ers offered the coach a chance to work out a deal with Tampa to coach the Bucs, but Steve backed off because he wanted to stay in the Bay area.

Mariucci did his best to smooth over his relationship with Owens, and the team returned to the playoffs in 2002. In fact, they staged one of the greatest comebacks in league history in the playoffs, rallying from a 24-point second half deficit to beat the Giants by a point. Two weeks later, though, the coach was out. San Francisco followed that thrilling comeback victory with a loss to Tampa the next week. In the discussion to extend his contract, Mariucci sought more power within the organization. Management decided that he was overstepping his bounds and released him from the final year of his contract. Less than three weeks later, Matt Millen swooped in and brought Steve back to his home state as head coach of the Lions. Because Millen did not follow the guidelines of the Rooney Rule and interview any minority candidates before hiring Mariucci, he was fined. Although his hiring was greeted with optimism by Detroit fans, Steve's time in the Motor City was a major disappointment. He was unable to develop Joey Harrington into an NFL starter and was given little talent by the drafts and acquisitions of his inept GM. Moreover, he was no disciplinarian and his teams tended to lose focus. Despite showing small progress with the talent-poor team, Mariucci was fired following a Thanksgiving loss to Atlanta in 2005

Since leaving Detroit, Mariucci has worked as a popular, demonstrative broadcaster on the NFL Network, even winning as sports Emmy in 2009. His name has been mentioned in connection with occasional head coaching openings, notably the Packers, Redskins and USC, but he has received no offers.

MARTZ, MICHAEL J. (MIKE) 5/13/1951– Fresno State. TE; did not play professionally. *Apprenticeship:* College asst.—18 years; pro asst.—8 years. *Roots:* Chuck Knox, Rich Brooks, Norv Turner, Dick Ver-

Martz, Michael J. (Mike)									
Year	Team	Games	Wins	Losses	Ties	%	P Wins	P Losses	P %
2000	Rams	16	10	6	0	.625	0	1	.000
2001	Rams	16	14	2	0	.875	2	1	.667
2002	Rams	16	7	9	0	.438	0	0	.000
2003	Rams	16	12	4	0	.750	0	1	.000
2004	Rams	16	8	8	0	.500	1	1	.500
2005	Rams	5	2	3	0	.400	0	0	.000
6 years		85	53	32	0	.624	3	4	.429

meil. *Branches:* Lovie Smith, Joe Vitt (i), Perry Fewell (i). *Coordinators/Key Assistants:* Martz then Steve Fairchild ran the offense, while Pete Giunta then Lovie Smith then Larry Marnie handled the defense. *Hall of Fame Players:* Marshall Faulk. *Primary Quarterbacks:* Kurt Warner, Marc Bulger. *Tendencies:* • His teams scored 26.5 points and allowed 23.3 per game • His teams ran 37.9% of the time, which was 85% of the league average • Seven starting quarterbacks in six years; 88% of starts to primary quarterbacks • 13 rookie starters in six years • Winning Full Seasons to Losing Full Seasons: 3:1.

Offensive genius or arrogant know-it-all: Mike Martz has been called both and with some justification in each case. Coming out of Sioux Falls, South Dakota, Martz played tight end for San Diego Mesa Junior College in 1969 and 1970, and transferred to California-Santa Barbara in 1971. When that school dropped its football program the next year, Mike transferred to Fresno State and graduated in 1972. He went directly into high school coaching in 1973 and then returned to San Diego Mesa as an assistant in 1974. Over the next two decades, Martz worked mostly up and down the far west: 1975 at San Jose State, 1976–1977 at San Diego Mesa again, 1978 at Santa Ana College, 1979 at Fresno State, 1980–1981 at the University of the Pacific, 1982 at Minnesota and from 1983 to 1991 at Arizona State.

Finally, in 1992, Martz reached the NFL when Chuck Knox hired him as the Rams quarterbacks coach under noted offensive coordinator Ernie Zampese. Although Knox was fired after the 1994 season, Martz stayed on staff under his successor Rich Brooks as receivers coach in 1995 and 1996. After Brooks was replaced by Dick Vermeil in 1997, Mike was hired as the quarterbacks coach for Norv Turner, another coach mentored by Zampese. Strikingly under Martz's hand, third-string quarterback Trent Green developed into an impressive starting quarterback for the 1998 Redskins.

In 1999, Dick Vermeil signed both Martz and Green to revive the Rams offense with fans and the media volubly maintaining that Vermeil's return after 15 years out of coaching was a mistake. When Green, the hand-picked quarterback, going down to a season-ending injury in the preseason, things looked bleak until unknown backup Kurt Warner stepped in and played like the second coming of Johnny Unitas in Martz's wide open passing attack. Martz's offense emphasized speed, timing and stretching the field, just as Don Coryell and Sid Gillman had in earlier years. Mike told *Sports Illustrated*, "You don't score points running the ball. We're going to be aggressive and throw the ball no matter who we play and what they're doing. That's who we are and that's what we do." Indeed, the Rams passed 15% more than the league average in Martz's tenure as head coach. And they twice

led the league in scoring and finished second another year.

Martz had full control of the offense in 1999, but Vermeil coached the whole team, and the pair led the Rams to an exciting come-from-behind Super Bowl victory that year. With his innovative offense, Mike was drawing attention from teams looking for a new head coach. In order to make sure they hung on to Martz, the Rams' nervous management pushed Vermeil to retire after the Super Bowl and promoted Mike to head coach. The Rams seemed to have the stars in place for a multi-championship run, but that never came to pass. Instead, the "Greatest Show on Turf" was just that, an entertaining show and nothing more. Martz's Rams never repeated as champions despite the glut of talent on offense.

In Martz's first season as head coach in 2000, the Rams returned to the postseason but five turnovers in the opening playoff game led to a season-ending loss to the undermanned Saints. A hallmark of Mike's aggressive style was excessive turnovers, and that failing would plague his team throughout his tenure. 2001 brought an improved team defense, a 14–2 record and a return to the Super Bowl to meet the Bill Belichick's overmatched Patriots. Belichick told *Sports Illustrated*, "You're dealing with a very smart offensive coach. Show him the same stuff, and he'll hurt you." The Patriots lost to the Rams during the regular season by relying heavily on blitzes. However in the Super Bowl, Belichick laid off the blitzes and concentrated on "rerouting" the receivers, especially runner Marshall Faulk, by hitting them at the line of scrimmage so that the offense's timing and rhythm were destroyed. While the Rams superior talent still almost won the game, Martz was outcoached and lost a Super Bowl he should have won. Warner told the *New York Times*, "Mike is a true good guy and a smart leader. From the outside, I think, people have an impression of him that we don't see. We just see him as a great coach."

Warner injured his thumb the next year and would never be the same in St. Louis again. In an awkward transition, Marc Bulger took over as the starting quarterback in 2002, but he was no Warner. The team went 12–4 that year, but at crunch time in the playoffs, Martz was afraid to go for a touchdown to win with Bulger at the controls Instead, Mike settled for a tying field goal and lost to the Panthers in double overtime. From that point on, the Rams went into a steep decline hastened both by a series of bad drafts and by Martz's repeated clashes with management. No longer the undisputed genius, he was increasingly viewed as an inflexible, egotistical egghead who angered opponents by trying onside kicks when comfortably ahead, ignored strategic implications by consistently challenging trivial officials calls, botched the Kurt Warner situation and classlessly blamed backup quarterback Chris Chandler for the team's failings at one low point.

Mike was forced to take a medical leave of absence five games into the 2005 season due to a bacterial infection on his heart, but was barred by management from returning to the team after being cleared by the doctors.

Martz has not been able to land another head coaching job since then. He spent 2006–2007 as the Lions' pass happy offensive coordinator. He was fired at the end of the year and moved on to San Francisco, bringing error prone backup quarterback J.T. O'Sullivan with him. O'Sullivan was a disaster as a starter, leading to head coach Mike Nolan being replaced at midseason by Mike Singletary, a defensive coach who wanted a more ball-control offense. When he didn't get that, he fired Martz at the end of the year. After a season as an analyst for the NFL Network, Martz returned to the sidelines in 2010 as the Bears' offensive coordinator tutoring inconsistent quarterback Jay Cutler. The Bears did reach the NFC championship that year, but it was more due to their defense and special teams than the offense. Head coach Lovie Smith, Martz's one-time defensive coordinator in St. Louis, clamped down on Mike to emphasize the pass less and to highlight the run. Martz had the offense playing more consistently in 2011 until injuries to Cutler and runner Matt Forte derailed the season. He and the Bears severed their relationship in 2012.

MATHEWS, NED A. 8/11/1918–9/18/2002. UCLA. Played HB for the Detroit Lions, Boston Yanks, Chicago Rockets and San Francisco 49ers from 1941 to 1943 and 1945–1947. *Apprenticeship:* None. *Roots:* None. *Branches:* None. *Coordinators/Key Assistants:* Part of a midseason committee of interim player coaches with Bob Dove and Willie Wilkin. *Hall of Fame Players:* Elroy Hirsch. *Primary Quarterbacks:* None. *Record:* **Interim Player Co-Coach.**

In 1939, Ned Mathews was part of the star-studded UCLA backfield with Jackie Robinson, Kenny Washington and Chuck Fenenbock. In the season finale, the undefeated Bruins faced undefeated rival USC for the right to go to the Rose Bowl. The game was still a scoreless tie with 4:54 remaining, but the Bruins were on the Trojan three, facing a fourth and goal. Quarterback Ned Mathews polled his teammates in the huddle whether to go for the touchdown or the field goal. Surprising even for the 1930s, Coach Babe Horrell had no say in the matter. Mathews broke the 5–5 voting deadlock in the huddle by calling for a pass play, but his pass to end Don McPherson was

tipped away and ended the game's last scoring threat. Despite the 0–0 tie, USC went to the Rose Bowl with a 7–0–2 record rather than UCLA's 6–0–4. What is left unexplained is what was wrong with trying for the chip shot field goal to take the lead?

Hailing from Provo, Utah, Mathews spent one more year at UCLA and then joined the Detroit Lions as a wingback in 1941. After three years in the NFL, Ned went into the service, while also playing for the Hollywood Rangers of the Pacific Coast Football League in 1944. He returned to the NFL in 1945 with the Boston Yanks and then jumped to the Chicago Rockets of the new All America Football Conference in 1946. When Coach Dick Hanley was fired after just two games, owner John Keeshin put Hanley's assistants Pat Boland and Ernie Nevers on paid leave, while turning the team over to a triumvirate of player coaches: end Bob Dove, tackle Willie Wilkin and halfback Mathews. The Rockets posted a winning record over the next six weeks, but Keeshin then brought back line coach Boland as head coach. At that point, Mathews was waived, although Dove and Wilkin remained on the team.

Mathews was claimed by the 49ers and even got to score a touchdown against his old team on November 30 when San Francisco beat Chicago 14–0. Ned spent another season as a backup for the 49ers in 1947 and then returned to his alma mater as an assistant coach in 1948. He spent one year there and one as an assistant with Arizona and then got out of coaching. Mathews scouted for the 49ers in later years and was very active in the alumni groups of both UCLA and the NFL.

MAZUR, JOHN E. 6/17/1930– Notre Dame. Played QB in the CFL. *Apprenticeship:* College asst.— 7 years; pro asst.— 9 years. *Roots:* Lou Saban, Joe Collier, Clive Rush. *Branches:* San Rutigliano. *Coordinators/Key Assistants:* Mazur ran his own offense, while Dick Evans was the key defensive coach. *Hall of Fame Players:* None. *Primary Quarterbacks:* Jim Plunkett. *Tendencies:*
• His teams scored 14 points and allowed 27.1 per game
• His teams ran 49.5% of the time, which was 91% of the league average • Two starting quarterbacks in three years; 77% of starts to primary quarterback • Eight rookie starters in three years • Winning Full Seasons to Losing Full Seasons: 0:1.

John Mazur from Plymouth, Pennsylvania played quarterback for Notre Dame from 1949 to 1951 and was the starter in his senior season. In the Fighting

Mathews, Ned A.									
Year	Team	Games	Wins	Losses	Ties	%	P Wins	P Losses	P %
1946	Rockets (AAFC)	6	3	2	1	.583	0	0	.000
1 year		6	3	2	1	.583	0	0	.000

Irish quarterback string of Angelo Bertelli, Johnny Lujack, Frank Dancewicz, Steve Nemeth, George Terlep, George Ratterman, Joe Gasparella, Bob Williams, Ralph Guglielmi and Paul Hornung, Mazur was the only signal caller not to play in the NFL. Instead, he served in the Marines from 1952 to 1953 and played one year for the B.C. Lions in Canada, completing only 42% of his passes and tossing 10 interceptions to just two touchdowns.

Mazur began his coaching career the next year at Tulane where he stayed from 1955 to 1957. In 1958 he moved on to Marquette and then to Boston University from 1959 to 1961. Lou Saban hired John in 1962 as the Buffalo Bills' backfield coach, and he ran the offense in Buffalo from 1962 to 1968, including two championship seasons with quarterbacks Jack Kemp and Daryle Lamonica.

1969 ushered in the new John Rauch regime in Buffalo, so Mazur got a job with the Patriots under new coach Clive Rush. With Rush melting down from mental problems the following year, John replaced him as head coach at midseason in 1970, saying, "I don't have time to change everything. We'll go with what we have." Despite winning just one of seven games, Mazur was rehired for 1971 when the team drafted Jim Plunkett to fill the quarterback slot. Behind Plunkett's heroics, the Patriots rebounded to a 6–8 finish in 1971, but Mazur did not get along with new GM Upton Bell who wanted to fire the coach. Bell made a deal with the board of directors that if the Patriots lost to the defending champion Colts in the season finale, John would be fired. However, the Patriots upset the Colts 21–17 on an 88-yard touchdown pass to Randy Vataha in the last two minutes while Bell fumed in the press box.

Mazur had won himself another year, but no peace. During training camp in 1972, Bell traded halfback Carl Garrett to the Cowboys for malcontent runner Duane Thomas, but that blew up quickly. At Duane's first practice, John was installing the I formation and told Thomas to go into a three-point stance. Thomas refused because he could not see past the fullback in that stance. Thomas remained in a two-point stance, so Mazur banished him from the field. Thomas was returned to Dallas in short order.

While Mazur was in control at that point, it didn't last long. The Patriots got off to a 2–7 start, and John officially resigned after the ninth game, a 52–0 loss to Miami. He announced, "I have always placed uppermost in my mind the best interests of any organization with which I have been associated. In accordance with this long-time personal policy, I am resigning my position." Bell was fired three games (all losses) later. Neither man lasted the full season. Mazur was hired as an assistant by Mike McCormack in Philadelphia in 1973 and continued with the Eagles in 1976 under new coach Dick Vermeil. He then joined the Jets' staff from 1977 to 1980 until he was forced to retire because he was diagnosed with Parkinson's disease. Struggling along on a meager pension in 2005, Mazur sadly told the *Boston Globe*, "I feel like I'm being blitzed every damn time I walk around."

McCAFFERTY, DONALD W. (DON) 3/12/1921–7/28/1974. Ohio State. Played E for the Giants in 1946. *Apprenticeship:* College asst.—11 years; pro asst.—11 years. *Roots:* Weeb Ewbank, Don Shula. *Branches:* John Sandusky (i), Rick Forzano, Hank Bullough, Raymond Berry. *Coordinators/Key Assistants:* For the Colts, John Idzik ran the offense, and Hank Bullough handled the defense; for the Lions, Rick Forzano was the key offensive coach, and Bob Hollway the key defensive coach. *Hall of Fame Players:* Lem Barney, Ted Hendricks, John Mackey, Charlie Sanders, John Unitas. *Primary Quarterbacks:* John Unitas, Bill Munson, Greg Landry. *Record:* Super Bowl Championship 1970. *Tendencies:* • His teams scored 20.8 points and allowed 15.3 per game • His teams

Mazur, John E.

Year	Team	Games	Wins	Losses	Ties	%	P Wins	P Losses	P %
1970	Patriots	7	1	6	0	.143	0	0	.000
1971	Patriots	14	6	8	0	.429	0	0	.000
1972	Patriots	9	2	7	0	.222	0	0	.000
3 years		30	9	21	0	.300	0	0	.000

McCafferty, Donald W. (Don)

Year	Team	Games	Wins	Losses	Ties	%	P Wins	P Losses	P %
1970	Colts	14	11	2	1	.821	3	0	1.000
1971	Colts	14	10	4	0	.714	1	1	.500
1972	Colts	5	1	4	0	.200	0	0	.000
1973	Lions	14	6	7	1	.464	0	0	.000
4 years		47	28	17	2	.617	4	1	.800

ran 54.7% of the time, which was the league average • Five starting quarterbacks in four years; 79% of starts to primary quarterbacks • Five rookie starters in four years • Winning Full Seasons to Losing Full Seasons: 2:1.

Cleveland native Don McCafferty was a 6'4" tackle for Paul Brown's Ohio State national champions in 1942. Drafted by the Giants in 1943, McCafferty did not report till 1946, twice playing for the College All Stars in the interim. With the Giants, Don was switched to end, but played just one NFL season. He spent 1947 working for the recreation department in his hometown and then began his coaching career as an assistant at Kent State in 1948. After 11 years at Kent State, McCafferty accepted a new challenge in 1959 by joining Weeb Ewbank's staff on the reigning champion Colts in 1959 as an offensive coach. The Colts repeated as NFL champs in Don's first season in Baltimore and then began to slip. In 1963, Ewbank was fired and replaced by Don Shula, but McCafferty stayed on board to run the offense. McCafferty readied Tom Matte as the team's emergency quarterback when both Unitas and backup Gary Cuozzo were injured in 1965. He also tutored journeyman Earl Morrall to be a surprisingly effective replacement for an injured Unitas three years later, taking Baltimore to the Super Bowl where they were upset by the Jets. Shula began to wear out his welcome with owner Carroll Rosenbloom after that momentous upset and was fired a year later.

Rosenbloom considered hiring a big name coach like George Allen, Ara Parseghian or Joe Paterno, but instead turned to longtime low-key, loyal assistant McCafferty to take over the veteran Colts. On the team, Don was known as the "Easy Rider" for his calm and quiet approach to coaching. He told *Sports Illustrated*, "I never did like to scream. I never liked to be yelled at when I was a player. If you treat players like men, they'll perform like men. If they don't, then get rid of them. Sometimes you'll lose anyway, but there's no sense dwelling on it." He told the press that Paul Brown was his biggest influence, "I have a lot of respect for him and learned a lot from him. He did as much for pro football as any one man. It's an honor to be coaching in the same league with him."

Just as in his first season as a Colts' assistant, McCafferty's first season as head coach was capped with an NFL championship. Baltimore returned to the Super Bowl that year and in the "Blunder Bowl" defeated the Cowboys on a last second field goal in a horrible, sloppy game featuring 11 turnovers. The team followed that triumph with a 10–4 record in 1971, but was embarrassed 21–0 by Shula's Dolphins in the playoffs. In 1972, Rosenbloom traded his ownership of the Colts to Robert Irsay for the ownership of the Rams. New owner Irsay brought in aggressive GM Joe Thomas who cut a wide swath in trying to rebuild the aging Colts into a youthful contender. When McCafferty refused to bench Johnny Unitas for new quarterback Marty Domres five games into 1972, Thomas fired Don and replaced him with assistant John Sandusky. Many of the veteran Colts were upset. Center Bill Curry said, "Don McCafferty is the finest gentleman I've played for in pro football." He added, "Mac is a decent man and a talented coach and the way he was let go is an injustice to all of us." On the other hand, ornery middle linebacker Mike Curtis contended, "McCafferty was too good natured and it backfired on him. The players took advantage of him." Curtis further concluded, "McCafferty had two good years but I think it was a carryover from Shula and because we had an easy schedule. In 1970, we didn't exactly pound anybody."

McCafferty was named head coach of the Lions in 1973, but the team dropped from 8–5–1 to 6–7–1 that season. After losing to the 1–4 Colts, Don reflected, "If we can't beat the Colts, we can't beat anybody." By the end of the season, McCafferty was avowing, "We've got some losers on this ball club and they won't be around next year." Sadly, it was Don who was not around; he never got the chance to prove he could rebuild the Lions because he died of a heart attack while mowing his lawn at the beginning of training camp in July 1974. He was a popular players' coach who calmed and healed a damaged Colts team and led it to a championship. He is best remembered by how Carroll Rosenbloom gushed at that time, "Here is a man who has no inner sanctum, no pretensions, no assistants — only associates. Everybody gets the credit except McCafferty. He's just a splendid man. What's more, he brought the fun back into the game of football for me"

McCARTHY, MICHAEL J. (MIKE) 11/10/1963–

Baker. TE; did not play professionally. *Apprenticeship:* College asst.— 6 years; pro asst.—13 years. *Roots:* Marty Schottenheimer, Ray Rhodes, Jim Haslett, Mike Nolan. *Branches:* Joe Philbin. *Coordinators/Key Assistants*: Jeff Jagodzinski then Joe Philbin ran the offense, while Bob Saunders then Dom Capers handled the defense. *Hall of Fame Players:* None. *Primary Quarterbacks:* Brett Favre, Aaron Rodgers. *Record:* Super Bowl Championship 2010. *Tendencies:* • His teams scored 26.7 points and allowed 20.1 per game • His teams ran 41.1% of the time, which was 94% of the league average • Three starting quarterbacks in six years; 99% of starts to primary quarterbacks • 20 rookie starters in six years • Winning Full Seasons to Losing Full Seasons: 4:1.

Pittsburgh native Mike McCarthy achieved his ultimate professional goal in the 2010 season at the expense of his boyhood team, the Steelers, when his Packers beat them 31–25 in Super Bowl XLV. McCarthy had not been the first choice of Packer fans when he was hired in 2006, but the underrated coach delivered Titletown's 13th NFL championship.

McCarthy got his start as the tight end for Baker University in Kansas and captained the team in 1985 and 1986. Upon graduation, he worked as a graduate assistant at nearby Fort Hays State from 1987 to 1988. Former Bill Walsh assistant Paul Hackett hired Mike in 1989 as the quarterbacks coach at the University of Pittsburgh and trained him in the West Coast Offense. During his four-year stint with the Panthers, two other future NFL coaches, Jon Gruden and Marvin Lewis, also joined the Pitt staff. McCarthy made the leap to the pros in 1993 by joining Marty Schottenheimer's staff in Kansas City as offensive quality control coach. Two years later, Mike was promoted to quarterbacks coach and served the Chiefs in that capacity from 1995 to 1998. When Schottenheimer resigned in 1999, McCarthy took the quarterbacks coach job with the Packers under Ray Rhodes. However, Rhodes only lasted one year in Green Bay, so Mike was on the move again in 2000, joining the Saints as offensive coordinator. In the off season, McCarthy persuaded New Orleans to obtain the Packers' third string quarterback Aaron Brooks, and the raw Brooks started most of the Saints' games while Mike was in charge of the offense. Although McCarthy was NFC Assistant Coach of the Year in 2000 largely for his work with Brooks, the team and the offense began to slip by 2005 and Mike was let go. He moved on to San Francisco as new head coach Mike Nolan's first offensive coordinator and worked with first round draft choice Alex Smith, who the 49ers selected over Aaron Rodgers, the other top-ranked college quarterback that year.

One year later, McCarthy was hired as head coach of the Packers, where Rodgers had landed. Packer fans were skeptical of a man whose main claims to fame were working with terminally inconsistent Aaron Brooks and draft bust Alex Smith, but Ted Thompson saw a winner, "There are a lot of good Xs and Os guys. To be a head coach, I think you have to be a good people person, know how to push the right buttons. I was hiring the man, not the coach." Green Bay had slipped to 4–12 under previous coach Mike Sherman, but McCarthy led the team back to 8–8 in 2006 by closing the season with four straight wins. Behind a rejuvenated Brett Favre, the Packers swept

to a 13–3 record in 2007 that led all the way to the NFC championship game at Lambeau Field. However, Favre' last pass as a Packer was intercepted in overtime, enabling the Giants to kick a game-winning field goal and reach the Super Bowl. Favre subsequently retired. Then he unretired and wanted his job back. McCarthy and GM Ted Thompson told Favre he could come back as Aaron Rodgers' backup, but Favre wanted to start. After a month of Favre agonistes, Thompson traded Brett to the Jets and the Aaron Rodgers era began.

McCarthy had trained Rodgers well in the past two years. Despite the added pressure, Aaron kept the offense humming at a high level. However, the defense collapsed, resulting in a 6–10 record in 2008. Mike brought in Dom Capers to fix the defense in 2009, and the veteran defensive coordinator did just that. Green Bay went 11–5 but lost the division crown to the Vikings led by Brett Favre who twice beat Rodgers during the regular season. In the playoffs against the Cardinals, Green Bay came back from 21-points down in the third quarter to force overtime, but Rodgers was stripped of the ball in the first series, and his fumble was recovered for the game-winning score.

McCarthy used that defeat to motivate his team in 2010 through a flurry of injuries to key starters that dropped the team to 10–6 and the last wild card spot in the playoffs. Mike led the Packers on the road in the postseason to beat the Eagles, Falcons and Bears in successive weeks to reach the Super Bowl where they outlasted the Steelers. Throughout the entire tumultuous season, Green Bay never trailed in any game by more than a touchdown. In addition, they beat Favre's Vikings twice to vanquish the past forever.

Under McCarthy, Green Bay has featured an aggressive passing attack that relies on three and four wideouts and uses the tight end extensively (at least when starter Jermichael Finley is active.) Four times, his airborne Packers have finished in the NFL's top five in scoring. Mike uses his running attack as a counter to the explosive passing game, but nearly abandoned it against the Steelers because he felt he could pass at will against them. Bringing in Capers to coach the other side of the ball ensured an aggressive, ball hawking defense that mirrored the offense and created a dangerous team that no one wanted to face

McCarthy, Michael J. (Mike)

Year	Team	Games	Wins	Losses	Ties	%	P Wins	P Losses	P %
2006	Packers	16	8	8	0	.500	0	0	.000
2007	Packers	16	13	3	0	.813	1	1	.500
2008	Packers	16	6	10	0	.375	0	0	.000
2009	Packers	16	11	5	0	.688	0	1	.000
2010	Packers	16	10	6	0	.625	4	0	1.000
2011	Packers	16	15	1	0	.938	0	1	.000
6 years		96	63	33	0	.656	5	3	.625

as it rambled through the longest route possible to the championship. Despite the setbacks, McCarthy's team displayed unswerving confidence that Mike exemplified when he had the players measured for their Super Bowl rings before the game. McCarthy has established a clear rapport with his players that was evident in veteran wide receiver Donald Driver's comment about his coach, "It's all about what you stand for, your integrity. Mike has that."

That continued in 2011 when the Packers won their first 13 games and clinched the top seed in the postseason. Although the defense declined to an alarming degree, the hyper efficient offense averaged 35 points per game and led the league in scoring behind NFL MVP Aaron Rodgers. Unexpectedly, the 15–1 team was upset by the Giants in the divisional round of the playoffs, the only home team to lose in the first two rounds of the postseason in 2011.

McCORMACK, MICHAEL J. (MIKE) 6/21/1930–Kansas. Played T for the New York Yanks in 1951 and the Cleveland Browns from 1954 to 1962. *Apprenticeship:* Pro asst.—7 years. *Roots:* Otto Graham, Vince Lombardi, Bill Austin, George Allen. *Branches:* Walt Michaels, Dick LeBeau. *Coordinators/Key Assistants:* For the Eagles, John Mazur ran the offense, while Walt Michaels was the key defensive coach; for the Colts, John Idzik handled the offense, while Chuck Weber ran the defense; for the Seahawks, Jerry Rhome ran the offense, while Jackie Simpson handled the defense. *Hall of Fame Players:* Steve Largent. *Primary Quarterbacks:* Roman Gabriel, Bert Jones, Jim Zorn. *Record:* **Hall of Fame Player.** *Tendencies:* • His teams scored 18.4 points and allowed 23.9 per game • His teams ran 46.1% of the time, which was 87% of the league average • Four starting quarterbacks in six years; 88% of starts to primary quarterbacks • 19 rookie starters in six years • Winning Full Seasons to Losing Full Seasons: 0:4.

Born in Chicago, Mike McCormack starred as a tackle for Kansas before being selected in the third round of the 1951 NFL draft by the New York Yanks. After one season in New York, McCormack was called into military service in 1952 and 1953. In the meantime, the Yanks franchise folded, and the players were transferred to the new Dallas Texans franchise in 1952. Dallas went bankrupt by midseason, so McCormack and the other players on the roster were transferred to the new Baltimore Colts franchise in 1953. Before Mike ever played for the Colts, though, he was included in a 15-player trade with the Browns. McCormack was one of five Colts headed to Cleveland in exchange for ten Browns, including defensive back Don Shula.

With the Browns, McCormack played defensive tackle in 1954 and then moved to offense from 1955 to 1962 and played in six Pro Bowls in eight years. He retired in 1963 to focus on his insurance business in Kansas City, but returned to football in 1966 as the line coach for the Redskins under Otto Graham, his former teammate from Cleveland. Mike spent seven years coaching the line in Washington under not only Graham, but also Vince Lombardi, Bill Austin and George Allen.

When the highly-touted assistant was named head coach and general manager of the Eagles in 1973, he cited his legendary influences, "I spent the longest time with Paul Brown, so I believe more of his philosophy of teaching remains with me, and I hope I can motivate like Lombardi and Allen." Actually McCormack borrowed most heavily from Allen in trading draft picks for veterans. He noted, "We want to win this year. It's going to be tough. But the day of the rebuilding program is over."

His biggest trade was obtaining quarterback Roman Gabriel from the Rams for two players and three high draft choices. A year later, he acquired Bill Bergey from Paul Brown's Bengals for two number ones and a number two. Both of these players were very good, but the price for them was too steep. McCormack continued with several more dubious deals that gutted the Eagles' draft for years to come. Mike gave up high draft picks for the likes of Norm Bulaich, Mike Boryla, Jerry Patton, Wes Chesson, Tom Roussel, John Tarver, Randy Jackson, aged John Niland, James McAlister and Horst Muhlmann. Unlike Allen's Over the Hill Gang, McCormack's acquisitions did not form the foundation of a Super Bowl team. The result was that the Eagles highest draft choices from 1974 through 1978 were: 1974, 3rd round; 1975,

McCormack, Michael J. (Mike)									
Year	*Team*	*Games*	*Wins*	*Losses*	*Ties*	*%*	*P Wins*	*P Losses*	*P %*
1973	Eagles	14	5	8	1	.393	0	0	.000
1974	Eagles	14	7	7	0	.500	0	0	.000
1975	Eagles	14	4	10	0	.286	0	0	.000
1980	Colts	16	7	9	0	.438	0	0	.000
1981	Colts	16	2	14	0	.125	0	0	.000
1982	Seahawks	7	4	3	0	.571	0	0	.000
6 years		81	29	51	1	.364	0	0	.000

7th round; 1976, 5th round; 1977, 5th round; 1978 3rd round. Mike's successor in Philadelphia, Dick Vermeil, didn't have a first round draft pick for four years. Ultimately, McCormack mortgaged the future for a best season of 7–7 in 1974. He convincingly demonstrated that George Allen's trading style is difficult to pull off.

After being fired by the Eagles, McCormack was hired as the Bengals line coach under Bill Johnson and stayed in Cincinnati for four years until he was hired in 1980 to replace another former Allen assistant, Ted Marchibroda, in Baltimore. Marchibroda was popular with his players for the way he stood up to the Colts' erratic management, but two straight seasons of quarterback Bert Jones going down to injury spelled his demise. Jones stayed healthy under Mike, but the team declined. In contrast to Marchibroda, McCormack wilted under pressure from the owner — even allowing Robert Irsay to call some plays in one game — and lost control of the team. Bert Jones later told Tom Danyluk for *The Super 70s*, "He was probably the weakest coach I've ever experienced throughout the NFL. Not so much strategically but in the way he handled the team. Unfortunately, McCormack didn't have the gumption and ability to take the head coaching position and go with it. He was a coach without a whole lot of backbone"

Despite coming off a 2–14 1981 season in Baltimore in which his team gave up a league record of 533 points, 33.3 per game, McCormack immediately landed on his feet in Seattle. He served as interim coach in 1982 and then as president and GM through the 1989 season. From 1990 to 1992, he worked as a consultant for the ownership group seeking an NFL franchise for Carolina and was the team's first team president and GM from 1993 to 1997. In neither Seattle nor Carolina did Mike continue his former reckless trading policy. He retired in 1998.

McCULLEY, PETER (PETE) 1/29/1931–1/25/1992.
Louisiana Tech. QB; did not play professionally. *Apprenticeship:* College asst.—15 years; pro asst.— 5 years. *Roots:* Howard Schnellenberger, Joe Thomas (i), Ted Marchibroda, George Allen. *Branches:* Fred O'Connor (i), Frank Gansz. *Coordinators/Key Assistants:* McCulley handled his offense with Fred O'Connor, while Jimmy Carr ran the defense. *Hall of Fame Players:* O.J. Simpson. *Primary Quarterbacks:* Steve DeBerg. *Record:* **Interim Coach.**

At the end of his career in 1992, Pete McCulley

compared himself to the main character in *Gulliver's Travels* for his wide wanderings in the world of football. "Someone asked me if I was going back to the NFL and I said I've already done that one time. I've been in high school, college, professional football, international football, and now I am going to try a new venture: spring football. It's another move for Gulliver." McCulley had been hired to coach the Miami Tribe of the Professional Spring Football League, but the league never got off the ground, and Pete died later that year.

Hailing from Franklin, Mississippi, McCulley went into the Marines after high school and then played quarterback for Louisiana Tech, graduating in 1956. He began coaching high school before moving up to Stephen F. Austin University from 1957 to 1959. In 1960, he switched to the University of Houston, then coached at Baylor from 1963 to 1969, and worked on Rick Forzano's staff at Navy from 1970 to 1972. McCulley made it to the NFL in 1973 as part of Howard Schnellenberger's staff in Baltimore and worked for the Colts from 1973 to 1976 under three coaches, including GM Joe Thomas at one point.

When Thomas was fired in 1977, McCulley joined the Redskins as George Allen's receivers coach. Thomas landed in San Francisco as the 49ers GM and wanted to hire Pete as his new head coach but couldn't get permission to speak to him from Allen. Thomas hired Ken Meyer instead but fired him a year later after a 5–9 season. He named McCulley the 49ers head coach for 1978, and Pete commented on his plans, "I believe in balance, but I also believe in utilizing the big play when the opportunity presents itself. I like to see some action out there and I want a hard-nosed running attack. But I want the big pass play, too."

The neophyte head coach never had a chance with his undermanned, inexperienced team. Thomas traded five draft picks for a washed-up O.J. Simpson to add excitement, but O.J.'s worn out legs just bogged down the offense. The GM also traded several veterans, including Del Williams, Tommy Hart and Woody Peoples to further deplete the squad. McCulley cut quarterback Jim Plunkett in training camp, and San Francisco kept 15 rookies that year plus eight other players with less than two years experience, including rookie quarterback Steve Deberg. Mistakes were inevitable. Tackle Keith Fahnhorst later recalled, "It was pitiful. Honestly, we didn't have a clue. It was unorganized, unprofessional and such a joke." Assistant

McCulley, Peter (Pete)									
Year	*Team*	*Games*	*Wins*	*Losses*	*Ties*	*%*	*P Wins*	*P Losses*	*P %*
1978	49ers	9	1	8	0	.111	0	0	.000
1 year		9	1	8	0	.111	0	0	.000

coach Mike White related in Bill Walsh's *The Score Takes Care of Itself* that strangely McCulley didn't change his watch when he moved to the West Coast, but stayed on East Coast time instead and scheduled meetings accordingly. Meanwhile, the players saw Pete as cold and militaristic. With the team at 1–8, an inpatient Thomas replaced McCulley with offensive coach Fred O'Connor, but things did not improve in San Francisco until Bill Walsh took over in 1979. Pete commented on his firing with equanimity, "If Billy Martin can be fired after winning a world championship, they could certainly let me go." Asked if he was surprised, McCulley quipped, "I haven't been surprised since I found out ice cream cones weren't filled to the bottom."

McCulley coached for the Jets from 1979 to 1982 and the Chiefs from 1983 to 1986 — memorably telling Kansas City quarterback Bill Kenney, "I'm the best quarterback coach in the world, and if I'm not. It's a very short roll call." Pete scouted for the Chargers from 1987 to 1988 and coached an American football team in Finland from 1989 to 1991, while also running his own quarterback school in Pensacola, Florida until his death at the age of 60.

MCDANIELS, JOSH 4/22/1976– John Carroll. WR; did not play professionally. *Apprenticeship:* College asst.— 2 years; pro asst.— 7 years. *Roots:* Bill Belichick. *Branches:* Eric Studesville (i). *Coordinators/Key Assistants*: Mike McCoy handled the offense, while Mike Nolan then Don Martindale ran the defense. *Hall of Fame Players:* None. *Primary Quarterbacks:* Kyle Orton. *Tendencies:* • His teams scored 20.8 points and allowed 23.5 per game• His teams ran 40.9% of the time, which was 94% of the league average• Two starting quarterbacks in two years; 96% of starts to primary quarterback• Three rookie starters in two years• Winning Full Seasons to Losing Full Seasons: 0:1.

Josh McDaniels was born in Barberton, Ohio, the son of a celebrated local high school coach who won a state championship while Josh was playing wide receiver for John Carroll University as a teammate of future NFL linebacker London Fletcher. Upon graduation, McDaniels subsequently worked as a graduate assistant from 1999 to 2000 for Michigan State under Nick Saban, a former Bill Belichick assistant. McDaniels was hired by Belichick in 2001 as a personnel assistant the same year that Nick Caserio, the Carroll

quarterback who threw passes to McDaniels, joined the Patriots' coaching staff. While Caserio moved into the front office, McDaniels was promoted to defensive coaching assistant in 2002 and quarterbacks coach in 2004. He was named offensive coordinator in 2006, but had unofficially performed those duties in 2005 as well after Charley Weis left.

McDaniels was at the controls of the record-setting Patriots offense in 2007 when both Tom Brady and Randy Moss set new league standards for their positions. Center Dan Koppen told the *New York Times,* "When he got the job, he really took the reins. It's not about age. It's about respect, and the guys have it for him. He feels the game out for what it is and does what's working." However, Josh's slowness to adjust to the Giants' blitzing defensive scheme in the Super Bowl that year resulted in a missing Super Bowl ring for the undefeated Patriots.

A year later, Broncos' owner Patrick Bowlen fired yesterday's genius, Mike Shanahan and hired Josh, hoping he would prove to be the new coaching guru in the NFL. However, McDaniels' head coaching inexperience showed almost immediately when word got out that Josh tried to acquire quarterback Matt Cassell from the Patriots. Immature incumbent Bronco quarterback Jay Cutler responded badly, and McDaniels was not able to quell the situation before it escalated to the point where Denver was forced to deal Cutler to Chicago for little regarded Kyle Orton. McDaniels' relationship with mercurial wide receiver Brandon Marshall also underwent extreme ups and downs throughout 2009.

As it turned out, Orton played well under McDaniels tutelage, and Denver got off to a 6–0 start in 2009. From that high point, though, it was all downhill for Josh and the Broncos. The team finished the season on a 2–6 skid and then began 2010 3–9 before McDaniels was fired. His two drafts did not pan out and neither did his free agent signings. For further embarrassment, McDaniels' director of video operations was caught taping an opponent's walkthrough in an episode reminiscent of the Patriots' Spygate scandal from 2007. While Josh declined to view the tape, he was fined $50,000 by the league for failing to immediately report the misconduct. McDaniels received more unwanted publicity in November when Chiefs coach Todd Haley refused to shake his hand, accusing Denver of running up the score. Haley got his revenge three weeks later when his Chiefs defeated

McDaniels, Josh									
Year	*Team*	*Games*	*Wins*	*Losses*	*Ties*	*%*	*P Wins*	*P Losses*	*P %*
2009	Broncos	16	8	8	0	.500	0	0	.000
2010	Broncos	12	3	9	0	.250	0	0	.000
2 years		28	11	17	0	.393	0	0	.000

the Broncos in McDaniels' last game before being fired.

Josh had no trouble landing on his feet in 2011 as the offensive coordinator for the Rams under Steve Spagnuolo, who was the Giants' defensive coordinator when the Giants upset the Patriots in the Super Bowl. Working with young quarterback Sam Bradford seemed to give McDaniels the opportunity to rebuild his reputation and get a second chance at an NFL head coaching job. With a second chance, he might correct the mistakes he made the first time around, just as his mentor Bill Belichick did in coming to New England after Cleveland. However the Rams finished last in scoring in 2011, and Spagnuolo was fired, so McDaniels returned to the Patriots as offensive coordinator for 2012.

McEWAN, JOHN J. (CAP) 2/18/1893–8/9/1970 Minnesota and West Point. C; did not play professionally. *Apprenticeship:* College coach — 14 years (10 as head coach). *Roots:* None. *Branches:* None. *Coordinators/Key Assistants*: None. *Hall of Fame Players:* None. *Primary Quarterbacks:* Benny Friedman. *Tendencies:* • His teams scored 7.3 points and allowed 9.9 per game • His teams ran 66.8% of the time, which was 92% of the league average • Five rookie starters in two years • Winning Full Seasons to Losing Full Seasons: 1:1.

Born in Alexandria, Minnesota, Cap McEwan enrolled at the University of Minnesota in 1912, but transferred to West Point the following year. Playing center for the Cadets, McEwan was named All-American in 1914 and team captain in 1916. Cap served in World War I after graduation and then returned to West Point in 1919 as the team's line coach. In 1923, he was promoted to head coach and from 1923 to 1925 posted a 18–5–3 record, including 2–0–1 against Navy. At this point, he resigned from his commission in the Army and as coach at West Point to sign a five-year contract to coach Oregon. Oregon compiled a 20–13–2 record from 1926 to 1929 under Cap, who then officially resigned, but did so on condition of accepting a settlement of $6,250 for his unexpired contract. Two months after being forced out at Oregon, McEwan was named head coach at Holy Cross. He coached the Crusaders from 1930 to 1932, achieving

a 21–5–1 record, but he was no stranger to conflict. Cap was suspended by Holy Cross in November of 1932 because of clashes between him and the team trainer as well as college officials. The main incident occurred during a loss to Brown when McEwan attempted to send in a substitute in the closing minutes, but the trainer would not allow it. Cap then tried to have the trainer fired, but found himself suspended instead. In response, McEwan sued the school. After the parties reached an out of court settlement in January, he resigned as coach.

McEwan next took the head coaching job of the Brooklyn Dodgers, a team that was co-owned by Cris Cagle who played under Cap at Army. With Benny Friedman on hand at tailback, the Dodgers posted a winning record in 1933, but the following year, Friedman only appeared in one game and Brooklyn had a losing record. McEwan was an independent thinker and late in that first season employed the famous basketball troupe, the New York Celtics, to help tutor the Dodgers in pass defense. Not that it helped much, but guard Herman Hickman, who became a sportswriter, remembered his old coach as a "brilliant" man. In 1935, Cap was replaced as coach by Paul Schissler who had coached at Oregon State when McEwan coached Oregon. McEwan worked for the WPA in the 1930s, returned to the service in World War II and worked as the head of labor relations for the New York City Transit Authority from 1947 to 1963 when he retired. He was also the longtime president of the New York Touchdown Club.

McGINNIS, DAVID (DAVE) 9/9/1937– Texas Christian. DB; did not play professionally. *Apprenticeship:* College asst. — 12 years; pro asst. — 14 years. *Roots:* Mike Ditka, Dave Wannstedt. *Branches:* None. *Coordinators/Key Assistants*: Rich Olson then Jerry Sullivan handled the offense, while Larry Marnie ran the defense. *Hall of Fame Players:* Emmitt Smith. *Primary Quarterbacks:* Jake Plummer. *Tendencies:* • His teams scored 15.3 points and allowed 25.2 per game • His teams ran 41.4% of the time, which was 94% of the league average • Three starting quarterbacks in four years; 72% of starts to primary quarterback • Nine rookie starters in four years • Winning Full Seasons to Losing Full Seasons: 0:3.

McEwan, John J. (Cap)									
Year	Team	Games	Wins	Losses	Ties	%	P Wins	P Losses	P %
1933	Brooklyn Dodgers (defunct)	10	5	4	1	.550	0	0	.000
1934	Brooklyn Dodgers (defunct)	11	4	7	0	.364	0	0	.000
2 years		21	9	11	1	.452	0	0	.000

Dave McGinnis was born in Independence, Kansas, but raised in Snyder, Texas. He played defensive back for Texas Christian from 1970 to 1972 but went undrafted by the NFL. He began his coaching career the next season at his alma mater and in two years moved on to Missouri from 1975 to 1977. In 1978, he coached at Indiana State before leaving to go into private business in 1979. Dave returned to ISU from 1980 to 1981 and then returned to TCU in 1982. From 1983 to 1985, he concluded his college coaching career as an assistant at Kansas State.

McGinnis was hired as the linebackers coach of the defending champion Bears in 1986 under new defensive coordinator Vince Tobin. Dave spent 10 seasons in Chicago, seven under Tobin, and was popular with the players in his unit. When Tobin was named head coach of the Cardinals in 1996, he hired the genial McGinnis as his defensive coordinator. Unexpectedly, Tobin led Arizona to the playoffs in 1998 behind the scrambling heroics of quarterback Jake Plummer, but the team dropped back to its usual depths after that.

From that high point, Dave was offered the head coaching job with the Bears in 1999, but turned it down because of the clumsy way owner Michael McCaskey negotiated. McCaskey issued a press release naming McGinnis as the new coach before Dave had agreed to anything. Then in the negotiations, McCaskey tried to lowball McGinnis on salary before throwing in the kicker, a buyout clause after two years. According to John Mullin in *Tales from the Chicago Bears Sidelines*, McGinnis told McCaskey he wouldn't be able to attract good assistant coaches with that shaky a framework. McCaskey's response was, "Don't

tell them." In the face of that duplicitous attitude, Dave withdrew his name from consideration and returned to Arizona.

With the Cards sinking at 2–5 in 2000, Tobin was fired and replaced by McGinnis even though Dave's defense had not finished above 24th in points allowed during his time in Arizona. While McGinnis was a popular players coach he had no success on the field over the next three-and-a-half years. His greatest triumph came in his final game as coach. The Cardinals beat the Vikings on a last second touchdown pass to reserve Nate Poole to knock the Vikings out of the playoffs and the grateful Packers in. In the locker room afterwards, McGinnis reportedly told his team, "I've never been afraid to open myself to you because you've got my heart." He was fired a day later and has worked as the linebackers coach for the Tennessee Titans since 2004.

McKay, John H. 7/5/1923–6/10/2001. Purdue and Oregon. HB; did not play professionally. *Apprenticeship:* College coach — 26 years (16 as head coach). *Roots:* None. *Branches:* Joe Gibbs, Wayne Fontes. *Coordinators/Key Assistants:* John Rauch then Joe Gibbs then Bill Nelsen then Boyd Dowler handled the offense, while Abe Gibron then Tom Bass then Wayne Fontes ran the defense. *Hall of Fame Players:* Lee Roy Selmon. *Primary Quarterbacks:* Doug Williams. *Tendencies:* • His teams scored 15.5 points and allowed 20.1 per game • His teams ran 49.8% of the time, which was 97% of the league average • 12 starting quarterbacks in nine years; 50% of starts to primary quarterback • 33 rookie starters in nine years • Winning Full Seasons to Losing Full Seasons: 3:6.

McGinnis, David (Dave)

Year	Team	Games	Wins	Losses	Ties	%	P Wins	P Losses	P %
2000	Cardinals	9	1	8	0	.111	0	0	.000
2001	Cardinals	16	7	9	0	.438	0	0	.000
2002	Cardinals	16	5	11	0	.313	0	0	.000
2003	Cardinals	16	4	12	0	.250	0	0	.000
4 years		57	17	40	0	.298	0	0	.000

McKay, John H.

Year	Team	Games	Wins	Losses	Ties	%	P Wins	P Losses	P %
1976	Buccaneers	14	0	14	0	.000	0	0	.000
1977	Buccaneers	14	2	12	0	.143	0	0	.000
1978	Buccaneers	16	5	11	0	.313	0	0	.000
1979	Buccaneers	16	10	6	0	.625	1	1	.500
1980	Buccaneers	16	5	10	1	.344	0	0	.000
1981	Buccaneers	16	9	7	0	.563	0	1	.000
1982	Buccaneers	9	5	4	0	.556	0	1	.000
1983	Buccaneers	16	2	14	0	.125	0	0	.000
1984	Buccaneers	16	6	10	0	.375	0	0	.000
9 years		133	44	88	1	.335	1	3	.250

A legendary college coach at USC who led the Trojans to four national championships, John McKay was elected to the College Football Hall of Fame in 1988. Over his 16 years at USC, several teams, including the Patriots, Browns and Rams, showed serious interest in hiring McKay, but John always declined. He once told the *Washington Post*, "I'm doing all right at SC. I like what I'm doing. I like the kids. I'm enjoying myself being a college coach. I have everything I need. Why be greedy?"

After all, McKay came up the hard way. Born in Everettville, West Virginia, he had to turn down a football scholarship to Wake Forest in 1941 because his mother was sick. Instead, he spent the year working as an electrician's assistant in a coal mine. During the war, John was a tail gunner on B-29 bombing missions from 1942 to 1945. In 1946, he enrolled at Purdue where one of his teammates was Abe Gibron who would later work as an assistant coach at Tampa Bay. McKay transferred to Oregon in 1947 and played in the backfield with Norm Van Brocklin for two seasons. When Van Brocklin graduated early in 1949, John took over as the Ducks' signal caller.

After graduation, McKay stayed at Oregon as an assistant coach for the next nine years. In 1959, he joined Don Clark's staff at Southern California, and when Clark resigned in 1960, John was promoted to head coach. In 16 years, he led the Trojans to eight Rose Bowls and coached two Heisman Trophy winners. McKay featured a power running game out of the I formation that produced a steady stream of talented tailbacks who became star runners in the NFL. His key play was either Student Body Right or Student Body Left. It was a sweep play similar to Vince Lombardi's power sweep, but operated via a quick toss and thus opened up faster. McKay's Trojans were big, fast and powerful; they sent dozens of players to the pros on both sides of the ball.

McKay finally relented to the pull of the pros and left USC for the NFL in 1976 with the expansion Tampa Bay Bucs. Seeing the lack of talent afforded him at the outset, he must have had serious regrets. The Bucs lost their first 26 games over the first two years, and they did so on merit. The closest they came to a win in 1976 was a 13–10 loss to fellow expansioners, the Seahawks, in game six. That was Seattle's first victory, but it was a horrid game marred by 35 penalties for 310 yards. Always known for his sarcasm, John polished his mordant wit in these years. After the team's first game, he summarized the team's performance, "Well, we didn't block, but we made up for it by not tackling." When asked about his team's execution in one game, McKay replied, "I'm in favor of it." Another time, he was caught by NFL Films on the sidelines, saying, "Can't stop a pass or a run ... otherwise we're in great shape." Some players interpreted that sarcasm as the coach being aloof and unfeeling. Linebacker Richard Wood told the *New York Times*, "He can draw you in, but to me and a bunch of other players, he's a cold person." John's clever response to calls for emotion was, "Emotion is overrated. My wife is very emotional. She can't play worth a damn."

Tampa went through eight terrible quarterbacks in its first three years before number one pick Doug Williams took over in 1978. Williams was the first black quarterback to establish himself as an NFL team's franchise quarterback and exhibited McKay's noteworthy open attitude toward black athletes. Behind Williams and a fast, hard-hitting defense, the Bucs swept to a division title in 1979. 1980 was a setback with rumors of heavy drug use among some players, but Tampa returned to the top of its division in 1981. In 1983, though, the Bucs tried to play hardball on Williams' contract and the quarterback jumped to the USFL. Left with a void on offense, the Bucs returned to the bottom for McKay's last two years as coach. Four times McKay's Bucs finished in the bottom four in scoring in the NFL. In his final game as coach, John rustled feathers in the league by ordering his defense to let the Jets score in the final minute with Tampa leading 41–14 so that runner James Wilder would have a chance to set a new record for combined yards from scrimmage. Wilder did not reach the mark, and McKay was fined $5,000 by the NFL.

McKay was named team president in 1985, but he resigned at the end of the year. His sons both were involved with the Bucs as well. J.K. played wide receiver for his father from 1976 to 1978, while Rich rose to become GM of the team from 1992 to 2003 and then moved on to become president of the Atlanta Falcons in 2004. McKay died in 2001, a year before Tampa at last won the Super Bowl for the first time.

McKEEVER, EDWARD C.T. (ED) 8/25/1910–9/12/1974. Notre Dame and Texas Tech. HB; did not play professionally. *Apprenticeship:* College coach —13 years (4 as head coach). *Roots:* None. *Branches:* Scooter McLean. *Coordinators/Key Assistants:* Scooter McLean

McKeever, Edward C. T. (Ed)									
Year	Team	Games	Wins	Losses	Ties	%	P Wins	P Losses	P %
1948	Rockets (AAFC)	14	1	13	0	.071	0	0	.000
1 year		14	1	13	0	.071	0	0	.000

coached the backs and George Musso the tackles. *Hall of Fame Players:* Elroy Hirsch. *Primary Quarterbacks:* Jesse Freitas, Sr. *Tendencies:* • His team scored 14.4 points and allowed 31.4 per game • His team ran 58.7% of the time, which was the league average • Three starting quarterbacks in one year; 64% of starts to primary quarterback • Two rookie starters in one year • Winning Full Seasons to Losing Full Seasons: 0:1.

San Antonio native Ed McKeever originally enrolled at Notre Dame, but transferred to Texas Tech in 1931. He played quarterback under Pete Cawthon from 1932 to 1934 and then was hired to be the Horned Frogs' part-time backfield coach; Cawthon even got Ed a side job with West Texas Gas to fill out his paycheck. In 1938, Ed worked with Boston College coach Frank Leahy at a coaching clinic, and Leahy offered him an assistant's position at BC in 1939. McKeever served as BC's backfield coach in 1939 and 1940 and then followed Leahy to Notre Dame in 1941. When Leahy went into the Navy in 1944, Ed stepped in as the acting coach of the Irish. Notre Dame went 8–2 in 1944, losing to Navy and getting pummeled by Army 59–0— the school's worst ever defeat.

McKeever resigned from Notre Dame in 1945 and took the head coaching position at Cornell reportedly because it would afford his family more job security. Over the next two seasons, Cornell went 10–7–1, but Ed resigned after the 1946 finale because he felt constricted by the university's stringent recruiting policies. McKeever was courted by both the Baltimore Colts and the Chicago Rockets of the All America Football Conference, but rather signed to be the head coach at the University of San Francisco two months later. He led the team to a 7–3 record in 1947, but then resigned again to sign a three-year deal with the Rockets of the AAFC. Ed and his San Francisco assistant Joe Kuharich had repeatedly clashed in the past year, so when McKeever left, he awkwardly poisoned the waters behind him. Ed sent a letter to the head of athletics at USF as well as to several other college football officials in California alleging that up to 22 of San Francisco's players might be ineligible for football because they were accepting secret payments and may have played at two or three other schools before USF.

Tony Morabito, a loyal San Franciscan and the owner of the AAFC's 49ers, called for the league to investigate McKeever's bizarre ploy, but nothing came of it. Ed got his comeuppance on the field by coaching the dreadful Rockets, despite his assertion that, "I believe the team has a great future or I would not have accepted the job. We are planning to line up a strong group of new talent. On paper, we have the finest backs in football." However, the 1948 Rockets finished with the same 1–13 mark as the 1947 team, and McKeever was let go.

Ed worked as an assistant at LSU from 1949 to 1951 and then went into private industry in a PR firm, which fit with one reporter's claim that McKeever "could sell Florida oranges in California." He returned to football as a scout for the Giants in the 1950s but ended up being sued by New York in 1960. By this time, Ed was the first general manager of the Boston Patriots in the new American Football League. The Giants alleged that the Chargers, whose GM was Frank Leahy, paid McKeever $1,000 to sign Mississippi fullback Charlie Flowers for them even though the Giants had already signed him. The suit eventually was thrown out, and Flowers reported to the Chargers in July. McKeever remained the Pats' GM for two years and then headed the team's meager scouting and personnel operations for the rest of the decade

McLean, Raymond (Scooter)

McLEAN, RAYMOND (SCOOTER) 12/6/1915–3/4/1964. St. Anselm. Played HB for the Bears from 1940 to 1947. *Apprenticeship:* College head coach — 3 years; pro asst.— 7 years. *Roots:* Ed McKeever, Gene Ronzani, Lisle Blackbourn. *Branches:* Nick Skorich. *Coordinators/Key Assistants:* Nick Skorich coached the line, and Ray Richards coached the defense. *Hall of Fame Players:* Len Ford, Forrest Gregg, Paul Hornung, Ray Nitschke, Jim Ringo, Bart Starr, Jim Taylor. *Primary Quarterbacks:* Bart Starr. *Record:* **Co-coach** in 1953 (with Hugh Devore). *Tendencies:* • His teams scored 16 points and allowed 33.1 per game • His teams ran 47.3% of the time, which was 89% of the league average • Three starting quarterbacks in two years; 57% of starts to primary quarterback • Two rookie starters in one year • Winning Full Seasons to Losing Full Seasons: 0:1.

Scooter McLean at 5'10" 168-pound, was a jack of all trades for the Bears throughout the 1940s, catching passes, running the ball, playing defensive back, returning punts and even kicking extra points in his final year in the NFL. The Lowell, Massachusetts native retired in 1948 at age 33 to become the head coach at Lewis College in Illinois where he posted a 19–6 record from 1948 to 1950. In 1951, Scooter returned

McLean, Raymond (Scooter)									
Year	Team	Games	Wins	Losses	Ties	%	P Wins	P Losses	P %
1953	Packers	2	0	2	0	.000	0	0	.000
1958	Packers	12	1	10	1	.125	0	0	.000
2 years		14	1	12	1	.107	0	0	.000

to the NFL as the backfield coach for his former Bears teammate Gene Ronzani in Green Bay. When Ronzani was forced to resign with two games to play in 1953, McLean and Hugh Devore coached the Packers on their season-ending West Coast trip.

Scooter remained the team's backfield coach under Ronzani's successor Lisle Blackbourn from 1954 to 1957 and then was promoted to head coach in 1958. Green Bay first offered the job to Hampton Pool, but he elected to stay in Canada rather than tackle the mess in Wisconsin, the NFL's Siberia. Management turned to McLean because he was a long-time popular assistant and promoting from within was a strong trend in the 1950s. McLean only received a one-year contract, however.

Scooter was a very nice man who was extremely popular with the players. He played cards with them and put them on a naive honor system for training rules. It didn't take long for the team to be completely out of control. On the field the 1–10–1 Packers were a disorganized and undisciplined disaster despite having a great deal of talent on hand that the next coach, Vince Lombardi, would mold into a champion. McLean's only victory came when Green Bay outlasted the Eagles, who would end up 2–9–1, 38–35 in week five. At the end of the season, Scooter remarked, "It's been a long season and I'm glad it's over." Three days later, he resigned and left to coach the backfield for the Lions under another former Bears' teammate, George Wilson. McLean replaced Red Cochran on the Detroit staff; Cochran in turn was hired by Vince Lombardi to coach the Packers' secondary. Sadly, Scooter died of a heart attack in the spring of 1964 after coaching with the Lions for five years and finishing behind the Packers in each one.

McMILLIN, ALVIN N. (BO) 1/12/1895–3/31/1952.
Centre. Played QB for the Milwaukee Badgers and Cleveland Indians from 1922 to 1923. *Apprenticeship:* College head coach — 26 years. *Roots:* None. *Branches:* Buddy Parker, Wayne Millner (i), Jim Trimble, George Wilson. *Coordinators/Key Assistants*: For the Lions, Buddy Parker coached the backs and Aldo Forte the line; for the Eagles, Wayne Millner was the key offensive coach and Jim Trimble the key defensive coach. *Hall of Fame Players:* Chuck Bednarik, Lou Creekmur, Bill Dudley, Pete Pihos, Steve Van Buren,

Doak Walker. *Primary Quarterbacks:* Fred Enke, Bobby Layne. *Tendencies:* • His teams scored 20.9 points and allowed 25.8 per game • His teams ran 49.2% of the time, which was 86% of the league average • Five starting quarterbacks in four years; 76% of starts to primary quarterbacks • 19 rookie starters in four years • Winning Full Seasons to Losing Full Seasons: 0:2.

Bo McMillin came out of Prairie Hill, Texas to lead tiny Centre College in Kentucky to one of the biggest upsets in college football history. McMillin followed his high school coach, Chief Meyers, to Centre in 1917 and then spent 1918 in the Navy. Returning to Centre in 1919, Bo quarterbacked the Praying Colonels to an undefeated season that year, an 8–2 record in 1920 and 10–1 in 1921. The three-time All-American's greatest moment came when he led underdog Centre to an upset of mighty Harvard as a senior and caught the imagination of the nation's football fans.

Upon graduation, McMillin took over as Centre's head coach and led the team to a 26–4 record from 1922 to 1924, while also squeezing in four games playing for Milwaukee and one for Cleveland in the NFL. Bo moved on to coach at Geneva College in Pennsylvania from 1925 to 1927 and brought in star tackle Cal Hubbard, a future Hall of Famer. Geneva went 22–5–1 under McMillin, who then took the head coaching position at Kansas State in 1928. Coaching the Wildcats for the next six years, he posted a 29–21–1 record before leaving for Indiana in 1934.

Indiana had not had a winning season since 1920, but McMillin produced three straight winning seasons before hitting a four-year losing patch from 1938 to 1941. He had his greatest success with the Hoosiers in his last six years in Bloomington, 1942–1947, when the team went 38–16–4, including an undefeated record in 1945 with backfield stars George Taliaferro and Pete Pihos leading the way. Overall, Bo's record at Indiana from 1934 to 1947 was 63–48–11, and he was torn when offered the head coaching job of the Lions in 1948, "Leaving college football after all these years pulls at my heartstrings. Most of my friends down through the years have been college men. I can tell you truthfully I have been sweating blood for ten days now, making my decision to accept this position with the Lions."

McMillin was an inspirational leader as a coach

McMillin, Alvin N. (Bo)									
Year	Team	Games	Wins	Losses	Ties	%	P Wins	P Losses	P %
1948	Lions	12	2	10	0	.167	0	0	.000
1949	Lions	12	4	8	0	.333	0	0	.000
1950	Lions	12	6	6	0	.500	0	0	.000
1951	Eagles	2	2	0	0	1.000	0	0	.000
4 years		38	14	24	0	.368	0	0	.000

and a popular public speaker who averaged 150 speaking dates a year. A religious, prim and proper man, he did not drink, smoke or swear, but was no saint. Edwin Pope quoted an anonymous star player from Indiana on Bo in *Football's Greatest Coaches*, "I never knew him to admit a mistake. He often was unreasonable to his assistants. He seldom took their suggestions and he changed plays right on the practice field without either telling them or consulting them. He liked spectacular football whether it won or not. He just wanted everybody to get a kick out of it." In the pros, his autocratic ways eventually would cause problems in Detroit. At the outset, though, McMillin did an excellent job in rebuilding a toothless Lions team that had recorded just two winning seasons in the 1940s and had won just four games in the last two years before he arrived.

Bo turned over the roster and had a .500 club by his third season, although some saw the disgruntled roster as underachieving in that 1950 season. McMillin found himself at odds with factions of ownership and several of his key players. He submitted a three-page open letter of resignation in December 1950 that said in part, "It has been said and printed that some of my players did not like or respect me. I want you football fans to know that while coaching the Detroit Lions I was not conducting a popularity contest. There might have been others who were doing just that, but not me." Star quarterback Bobby Layne, halfback Doak Walker and end Cloyce Box had gone to management to say, "We can win with Parker," meaning backfield coach Buddy Parker. Layne told the press the problems, "It was McMillin's coaching methods and his handling of personnel." According to Parker, Bo's play-calling terminology was unnecessarily complicated and his practices were too long and wore out the players. After Parker simplified the playbook and shortened practices, the Lions would go to four NFL title games in the 1950s and win three championships with the foundation established by McMillin.

Six weeks later, Bo was hired to replace Greasy Neale in Philadelphia, but would coach just two games for the Eagles before being diagnosed with stomach cancer. He stepped down from coaching and died of a heart attack in March 1952. He was elected to the College Football Hall of Fame shortly before his death.

McNALLY JOHN V. (JOHNNY BLOOD)

11/27/1903–11/28/1985. Wisconsin — River Falls, Notre Dame and St. John's (MN). Played HB for the Milwaukee Badgers, Duluth Eskimos, Pottsville Maroons, Green Bay Packers and Pittsburgh Pirates from 1925 to 1938. *Apprenticeship:* None. *Roots:* None. *Branches:* Walt Kiesling. *Coordinators/Key Assistants:* Walt Kiesling coached the line. *Hall of Fame Players:* Walt Kiesling. *Primary Quarterbacks:* None. *Record:* **Hall of Fame Player; Player Coach.** *Tendencies:* • His teams scored 8.3 points and allowed 14.7 per game • His teams ran 72.6% of the time, which was 106% of the league average • 10 rookie starters in three years • Winning Full Seasons to Losing Full Seasons: 0:2.

John Victor McNally was born into wealth in New Richmond, Wisconsin, where his father ran a flourmill and his uncle published the *Minneapolis Tribune.* His life was a remarkable celebration of the joys of hearty drinking, convivial women and late night carousing. The Vagabond Halfback fought authority at every turn, but always with a smile and not in anger. He was 6'2" and 190 pounds in his prime with jet black hair, a handsome face, and a winning attitude. Furthermore, he was extremely intelligent, ever charming, and never lacking female companionship. McNally graduated from high school at age 14 and according to Arthur Daley in *Pro Football's Hall of Fame* wistfully wrote in his yearbook, "Dear God, how sweet it is in spring to be a boy." Despite his intelligence, John would not finish college till he reached 46; in between he played football.

McNally first attended River Falls College in 1919 but transferred in 1920 to St. John's College in Minnesota, where he lettered in four sports and edited the school newspaper over the next three years. John then tried Notre Dame in 1923 but illustrious Coach Knute Rockne switched him to tackle. When John refused, he was thrown off the team. In the spring, he was suspended from school for 60 days for curfew violations and other transgressions and took off on an adventurous motorcycle trip to the East Coast with an attractive coed sitting right behind him. Upon his eventual return to the Midwest, McNally set type for his uncle's newspaper and joined a local semipro football team with a friend, Ralph Hanson. In order to preserve their collegiate eligibility, they played under assumed names

McNally John V. (Johnny Blood)									
Year	Team	Games	Wins	Losses	Ties	%	P Wins	P Losses	P %
1937	Pirates (Steelers)	11	4	7	0	.364	0	0	.000
1938	Pirates (Steelers)	11	2	9	0	.182	0	0	.000
1939	Pirates (Steelers)	3	0	3	0	.000	0	0	.000
3 years		25	6	19	0	.240	0	0	.000

taken off a movie marquee for the current Rudolph Valentino vehicle "Blood and Sand." From that point forward, John McNally became the more romantic-sounding Johnny Blood. He began his 14-year NFL career in 1925 with the Milwaukee Badgers, and subsequently moved on to Duluth and Pottsville before finding a true home in Green Bay in 1929.

Blood was the best receiver and defensive back of the early days of the NFL. Moreover, he was a touchdown maker in a low scoring era. When he retired in 1939, he had scored more touchdowns (49) than any other NFL player, except his Packer teammate Verne Lewellen who had scored 51. Unofficial counts of interceptions list Johnny as the league record holder with 40 until Emlen Tunnell passed him in 1953. He was perhaps the fastest player of his day with sure hands and great leaping ability. Once he got the ball, he was an elusive runner with a nose for the goal line. On defense, he was a hard and certain tackler. While he was a spectacular talent for Coach Curly Lambeau, though, he was also a spectacular headache to handle. Prompted by too many drunken incidents, Lambeau cut Blood in 1934, so he spent the year with the Art Rooney's Pittsburgh Pirates before returning to Green Bay in 1935 for a final two-year stint.

At 33, Blood returned to Pittsburgh in 1937, but this time as a player-coach. He could still play. In his first game, he returned the opening kickoff 92 yards for a touchdown and also scored on a 44-yard pass reception in a rare Pittsburgh victory. Owner Art Rooney later summed up Blood's coaching with the quip, "On most teams, the coach worries about where the players are at night. Our players worry about the coach." In 1938, Johnny did convince studious and reluctant Colorado football star Byron "Whizzer" White to sign a pro football contract with lowly Pittsburgh. White led the league in rushing that one year before leaving to further his education in Oxford, England, but he maintained a lifetime friendship with the roguish Blood. Whizzer told Sports Illustrated, "He was a great teammate. A cheerful fellow, friendly off the field. Nothing fazed him. Sometimes, although he was player-coach, he might miss a practice and explain next day that he had been to the library." Johnny was present for White's swearing in as a Supreme Court Justice, and White acted as Blood's presenter on Johnny's induction into the Pro Football Hall of Fame in 1963.

The most famous Blood coaching story was that he forgot to attend one game, but that is not quite true. The story goes that Blood was in the press box in Chicago watching a Bears-Packers game in 1938 when Ernie Nevers asked him why he wasn't with Pittsburgh, and Blood replied they weren't playing. However, just then the scoreboard listed the score: Philadelphia 14 Pittsburgh 7. In reality, Blood played

in all but two games in 1938. The first game he missed was a 17–0 loss to the Giants November 6, 1938 while Green Bay indeed played at Wrigley Field. However, Blood is mentioned as being on hand that day in the New York Times post-game story. Pittsburgh then traveled west for two moneymaking exhibition games in Colorado and California before returning east two weeks later. Blood said he missed the train east, so he gave Walt Kiesling control of the team for the game against Philadelphia on November 20, 1938 that oddly was played in West Virginia. The Eagles beat the Steelers 14–7 that day, but the Packers were at New York and the Bears at Brooklyn so the Wrigley Field part of the story is purely fanciful.

A gridiron philosopher, Blood told Sports Illustrated his thoughts deepened in Pittsburgh,

"One question we discussed has been on my mind for years. It was posed to me when I was coaching the Steelers. Just before the start of the season it became necessary to cut four men from the squad. I hated to do it. But I told the boys that I had heard of an independent pro team being organized in St. Louis. I suggested they go there and try out. I persuaded Art Rooney owner of the Steelers to advance the money enough to get them to St. Louis. Well, the boys went out, worked hard to make the team, but all four failed. They sent me a wire after their release. It read simply, 'Where to now, Coach?' I didn't know the answer. In a larger sense, does anybody?"

Blood retired from playing in 1939 and then resigned as Pittsburgh's coach three games into the season. In the next two years, he coached and played semipro ball in Kenosha and Buffalo and also wrote a 150-page manuscript called Spend Yourself Rich that was never published. He enlisted in the Army in 1941 and served as a cryptographer in Asia through the end of the war. As noted in Denis Gullickson's Vagabond Halfback, after a couple of lost years spent drinking, Johnny returned to St. John's in 1948 and at last earned his degree in economics. He then taught the subject at St. John's while also coaching the football team from 1950 to 1952. The team finished 13–9 over that time. As a side note, McNally's replacement in 1953, John Gagliardi, was still there nearly 60 years later having won more games than any other college coach at any level. In the ensuing years, McNally operated a couple of small businesses, ran unsuccessfully for county sheriff on the alleged platform of "Honest Wrestling" and mostly told amusing, puckish stories of a rambunctious life to anyone who would listen as the sport's ancient mariner.

McPeak, William P. (Bill) 7/24/1926–5/7/1991. Pittsburgh. Played DE for the Steelers from 1949 to 1957. *Apprenticeship:* Pro asst.— 5 years. *Roots:* Walt Kiesling, Buddy Parker, Mike Nixon. *Branches:* Ed Hughes, Abe Gibron, Ted Marchibroda. *Coordi-*

nators/Key Assistants: Ted Marchibroda and Abe Gibron were the key offensive coaches, while Ray Willsey and Chuck Cherundolo were the key defensive coaches. *Hall of Fame Players:* Chris Hanburger, Sam Huff, Sonny Jurgensen, Paul Krause, Bobby Mitchell, Charley Taylor. *Primary Quarterbacks:* Norm Snead, Sonny Jurgensen. *Tendencies:* • His teams scored 18.9 points and allowed 25.3 per game • His teams ran 43.5% of the time, which was 86% of the league average • Three starting quarterbacks in five years; 99% of starts to primary quarterbacks • 21 rookie starters in five years • Winning Full Seasons to Losing Full Seasons: 0:5.

Hailing from New Castle, Pennsylvania near Pittsburgh, Bill McPeak was a local hero who starred for the Pitt Panthers from 1945 to 1948 and was selected in the 16th round of the NFL draft by the Steelers. Bill played in three Pro Bowls during his nine-year career as a defensive end with the Steelers from 1949 to 1957. He also served as an assistant coach during his last two years as a player and stayed on staff after he retired in 1958. The next season he joined Mike Nixon's staff in Washington. When Nixon was fired in 1961, the 35-year-old McPeak was promoted to head coach of the Redskins, although he was only given a one-year contract. He told the press, "We hope to generate some kind of offense that's a consistent threat. Basically, I'm going to insist on 100 percent attention on the field and at meetings. This is serious business and the players must treat it accordingly."

Despite winning only one game in his first year, Bill was given the added responsibility of general manager in 1962 and swung the blockbuster deal with Cleveland for star halfback Bobby Mitchell. Mitchell became the first Black player in Redskins' history, and McPeak converted him to flanker where he had a Hall of Fame career. With Mitchell, Bill could open up his playbook. Under McPeak, the Redskins tried to constantly alter its formations and spacing with frequent shifting on offense. They even employed a spread formation at times. Still, they finished in the bottom four in scoring three times as well as three times in the bottom three in fewest points allowed.

McPeak continued to obtain talent for Washington through big trades that brought in quarterback Sonny Jurgensen for Norm Snead and linebacker Sam Huff for disgruntled halfback Dick James, who later told Thom Loverro for *Hail Victory,* "He was not a head coach, he was an assistant, probably a good one." By contrast, McPeak's head scout Bucko Kilroy told the *Washington Post,* "He never really got mad at people. He was a good teacher. He was never insulting." In five years, Bill never produced a winning team, but he did leave the Redskins a much more competitive team than the one he inherited.

After being fired, McPeak took a job as an assistant to Joe Schmidt in Detroit from 1967 to 1972. When Schmidt stepped down in 1973, Don Shula hired Bill as his new offensive coach, replacing Howard Schnellenberger. The Dolphins repeated as Super Bowl champions that year, but the following spring, McPeak suffered a stroke. He returned to work for Miami that June but in such a diminished capacity that line coach Monte Clark ran the offense in 1974. In January 1975, the Dolphins coldly fired McPeak. Bill commented at the time, "What else can I do? I can't ask them to carry me forever. It doesn't do any good to be mad or bitter. They more or less carried me last year."

That year, McPeak worked as an assistant with both the Chicago Wind and the Philadelphia Bell in the collapsing World Football League. From 1976 to 1978, he was out of football and in private business, while continuing to rehabilitate fully from the stroke. Bill returned to the NFL in 1979 when Bucko Kilroy was promoted to GM of the Patriots. Kilroy hired his old boss as the Pats' director of pro scouting. He remained in that position through 1991 when he suffered a fatal heart attack shortly after announcing his retirement.

McVay, John E. 9/9/1937– Miami (Ohio). Did not play professionally. *Apprenticeship:* College coach —11 years (8 as head coach); WFL head coach — 2 years; pro asst.—1 year. *Roots:* Bill Arnsparger. *Branches:* Marty Schottenheimer, Lindy Infante. *Coordinators/Key Assistants*: Bob Gibson ran the offense, while Marty Schottenheimer then Dick Modzelewski handled the defense. *Hall of Fame Players:* Harry Carson, Larry Csonka. *Primary Quarterbacks:* Joe Pisarcik. *Tendencies:* • His teams scored 14.6 points and allowed 17.5 per game • His teams ran 59.2% of the time, which was 105% of the league average • Five starting quarterbacks in three years; 62% of starts to primary

McPeak, William P. (Bill)									
Year	Team	Games	Wins	Losses	Ties	%	P Wins	P Losses	P %
1961	Redskins	14	1	12	1	.107	0	0	.000
1962	Redskins	14	5	7	2	.429	0	0	.000
1963	Redskins	14	3	11	0	.214	0	0	.000
1964	Redskins	14	6	8	0	.429	0	0	.000
1965	Redskins	14	6	8	0	.429	0	0	.000
5 years		70	21	46	3	.321	0	0	.000

quarterback • 10 rookie starters in three years • Winning Full Seasons to Losing Full Seasons: 0:2.

Born in Bellaire, Ohio, John McVay graduated from Miami University, the Cradle of Coaches, where he played center for Woody Hayes and then Ara Parseghian. McVay subsequently coached high school football in Ohio from 1953 to 1961. His biggest star during that time was future Hall of Famer Alan Page who once told Canton's *The Repository*, "He taught you not only what to do, but why you are doing it."

In 1962, McVay moved up a level by becoming an assistant to Duffy Daugherty at Michigan State. After three years with the Spartans, McVay was hired by Dayton as head coach. From 1965 to 1972, McVay's Flyers went 37–41–4 before John kicked himself upstairs as athletic director in 1973. With the start of the World Football League in 1974, McVay was named as head coach of the Memphis Southmen. Memphis had the best record in the league in year one, 17–3, but were knocked out in the playoffs early. The following year, Larry Csonka, Jim Kiick and Paul Warfield jumped from the Miami Dolphins to the Southmen, but Memphis got off to a sluggish 7–4 start before the league folded. As probably the strongest WFL team, the Southmen petitioned to be accepted into the NFL, but that bid was ignored.

Instead, McVay was hired as an assistant to fellow Miami alumnus Bill Arnsparger of the Giants in 1976. He was put in charge of special teams and research and development, i.e., he scouted and evaluated personnel. Halfway through another dismal season in New York, the 1–6 Giants fired Arnsparger and promoted McVay because he was the one coach on staff with head coaching experience. Under McVay, the team did show slow progress over the next two-and-a-half years, but years later he recalled to *The Commercial Appeal*, "It was tough coaching the Giants; I think we had better players in Memphis." After all, McVay's starting quarterbacks in New York were Joe Pisarcik, Jerry Golesteyn and Randy Dean. Furthermore, linebacker Brian Kelley told Baker and Corbett

for *The Most Memorable Games in Giants History*, "His coaching staff was probably the weakest I've ever seen in my life ... John was a great guy, but just didn't have the right people around him at all."

The one unforgettable moment from McVay's tenure in New York ultimately led to his 1978 firing—the "Miracle of the Meadowlands." Leading the Eagles 17–12 with 31 seconds left, all New York had to do was to have Joe Pisarcik take a knee and the game would be over. Instead, offensive coordinator Bob Gibson sent in a play that called for a handoff to fullback Larry Csonka. While several players protested in the huddle against Pisarcik running it, Joe followed orders. He took the handoff gripping the back end of the ball and turned to the right before turning all the way around to find Csonka who was headed to Joe's left. The botched handoff bounced off Csonka's hip as he ploughed into the line. As Csonka turned around, Pisarcik dove for the bouncing ball, but cornerback Herman Edwards scooped it up. Edwards carried the ball triumphantly in his left hand as he sprinted the 26 yards to the end zone; his windmill spike signaled an impossible Giants' loss and the low point for the franchise. Gibson was fired within days, and McVay followed him out the door at the end of the year after the team dropped three of its last four games even as the Eagles made the playoffs. 25 years later, John told the *Sacramento Bee*, "You never forget games like that. I'm down to one nightmare a week."

From those depths, McVay rose to the highest heights. He was hired in 1979 by Bill Walsh in San Francisco as director of football operations to organize the personnel department for the 49ers. From 1979 to 1996, McVay was present for all five 49ers' Super Bowl triumphs. Indeed, Walsh told the *Bee*, "It's quite possible that the San Francisco 49ers would not have won five Super Bowls had it not been for John McVay. He and I worked together as partners in all personnel moves." John retired in 1997, but then returned to the 49ers' front office in 1998 for another six-year stretch. He retired for good in 2004.

McVay, John E.

Year	Team	Games	Wins	Losses	Ties	%	P Wins	P Losses	P %
1976	Giants	7	3	4	0	.429	0	0	.000
1977	Giants	14	5	9	0	.357	0	0	.000
1978	Giants	16	6	10	0	.375	0	0	.000
3 years		37	14	23	0	.378	0	0	.000

Meagher, John F. (Jack)

Year	Team	Games	Wins	Losses	Ties	%	P Wins	P Losses	P %
1946	Miami Seahawks (AAFC)	6	1	5	0	.167	0	0	.000
1 yr		6	1	5	0	.167	0	0	.000

MEAGHER, JOHN F. (JACK) 10/1/1896–11/1968. Notre Dame. Played E for the Chicago Tigers in 1920. *Apprenticeship:* College head coach — 22 years. *Roots:* None. *Branches:* Hampton Pool. *Coordinators/Key Assistants*: Hampton Pool and Hank Crisp were his assistants. *Hall of Fame Players:* None. *Primary Quarterbacks:* None. *Record:* **Interim Coach**.

Chicago's Jack Meagher played end for Notre Dame from 1915 to 1916 when former end Knute Rockne was an assistant coach in South Bend. Jack went into the Marines for World War I and then appeared in four games for the Chicago Tigers in the first year of NFL in 1920. Shortly thereafter, he began his coaching career as the head coach at St. Edward's College in Texas from 1922 to 1928, compiling a 24–21–4 record. Moving up in the college ranks, he was hired by Rice Institute in 1929 and posted a 26–26 record over the next five years. In 1934, Meagher left the state of Texas for Alabama, where he coached Auburn from 1934 to 1942 and went 48–37–10 with the Tigers. Auburn became known for Jack's clever shifting defensive schemes. Meagher later told the *Miami News*, "In certain situations, we'd load up one side of the defensive line; in others, play it quite loose. We'd shoot a backer-up through the line on others, split spaces and do the other things that have become so common it sounds like idle chatter to mention them now." Jimmy Hitchcock, who was Auburn's star quarterback in the years right before Jack arrived, acted as the team's backfield coach under Meagher. He fondly recalled the coach for Phillip Marshall's *Stadium Stories: Auburn Tigers,* "He was something special. He was a tough little guy, and he was smart. Outside, he had a very calm demeanor. I never once heard him raise his voice."

Jack went into the Navy from 1943 to 1945 and succeeded Don Faurot as the coach of the Iowa Pre-Flight team in 1944, leading them to a 10–1 record. After the war, Meagher was named the first head coach of the Miami Seahawks of the new All America Football Conference. Miami had a unique emphasis on its club by solely recruiting players from Southern colleges. With that self-imposed limitation, the Seahawks' roster was exposed as deficient in the league's first game when Cleveland manhandled Miami 44–0. For a further disadvantage, the Seahawks had an odd schedule in which they played seven of their first eight games on the road and finished with a six-game home stand. Unfortunately, by that time, the team was 1–7 and not likely to draw much fan interest. Miami's home opener came in week four, but was de-

layed for two days by a hurricane that passed through on Sunday. The Seahawks lost that game 34–7.

In this bleak situation, Meagher had had enough after six games and resigned. He briefly worked as an assistant under Eddie Anderson at Iowa in 1947 and then retired from football. Instead, Jack moved back to Miami and went into business. Auburn offered their head coaching job to him again in 1950, but he declined and recommended his former assistant at both Auburn and Miami, Shug Jordan, for the job instead. Jordan spent the next 25 years as the popular and successful Tigers coach.

MEYER, KEN 7/14/1926– Denison. QB; did not play professionally. *Apprenticeship:* College asst.—16 years; pro asst.— 9 years. *Roots:* Weeb Ewbank, Chuck Knox, Dick Nolan. *Branches:* Jim Shofner (i). *Coordinators/Key Assistants*: Meyer handled his own offense, and Floyd Peters ran the defense. *Hall of Fame Players:* None. *Primary Quarterbacks:* Jim Plunkett. *Tendencies:* • His team scored 15.7 points and allowed 18.6 per game • His team ran 61.7% of the time, which was 107% of the league average • One starting quarterbacks in one year; 100% of starts to primary quarterback • No rookie starters in one year • Winning Full Seasons to Losing Full Seasons: 0:1.

Born in Erie, Pennsylvania, Ken Meyer grew up in Ashtabula, Ohio and served as a tail gunner on B-17 bombing missions for the Air Force during World War II right out of high school. From 1946 to 1949, he played quarterback for Denison University in Ohio, mostly under Woody Hayes, and led the team to two undefeated seasons. After graduation, Meyer coached high school football for two years prior to returning to his alma mater as an assistant coach from 1952 to 1957. He subsequently worked at Wake Forest from 1958 to 1959 and Florida State from 1960 to 1962 before being hired by Bear Bryant at Alabama to work with highly touted quarterback Joe Namath. Ken stayed in Tuscaloosa through 1967 and tutored Namath's skilled successors Steve Sloan and Ken Stabler until Dick Nolan hired him as the 49ers backfield coach in 1968.

Meyer stayed just one year in San Francisco and then was reunited with Namath on the Jets in 1969. Joe told the *New York Times* that Weeb Ewbank consulted with him before bringing in Meyer as the team's offensive coach and that, "He knows more about the game than I do, and he helped me a lot in college, particularly in developing my football sense in actual game situations." Ken changed jobs again in 1973 and

Meyer, Ken									
Year	Team	Games	Wins	Losses	Ties	%	P Wins	P Losses	P %
1977	49ers	14	5	9	0	.357	0	0	.000
1 year		14	5	9	0	.357	0	0	.000

was named the Rams' offensive coordinator under run-oriented Chuck Knox who Ken knew from when they worked together at Wake Forest. Meyer guided the Rams offense for four seasons and four division championships until San Francisco's volatile new GM Joe Thomas offered Ken his first chance as head coach in 1977 after firing popular incumbent Monte Clark over issues of power and control. Meyer informed *Sports Illustrated*, "People told me Joe Thomas had this reputation or that reputation, but one reputation he definitely has is that he gets good football players. I'd be foolish not to want to be with a man who gets me good football players."

Meyer was doomed from the beginning as the team got off to an 0–5 start. With the coach calling the plays, the running game was nonexistent, and the team was averaging just nine points per game. Ken turned the play calling over to quarterback Jim Plunkett in week six, and the 49ers won four in a row. Plunkett later laughed about Meyer's calls to *Sports Illustrated*, "He'd call the plays from the sidelines by a system of body signals. It was so ridiculous. All the parts of his body referred to certain numbers. It was actually funny." Nearing .500, the 49ers then split the next two games and lost the last three to finish 5–9. Thomas fired Meyer in January and hired the man he originally wanted to hire 1977, Pete McCulley. Ken was disappointed but not bitter, noting, "I have no ill feeling toward anyone in San Francisco, but I didn't feel I got a fair shake."

Meyer landed in Chicago as the Bears' offensive coordinator from 1978 to 1980 and then held the same position at Tulane in 1981 and 1982. In 1983, Chuck Knox hired Ken again, this time as quarterbacks coach in Seattle, where the two remained for nine years. When Knox left the Pacific Northwest in 1992, Meyer worked as an assistant on the New Orleans Night of the Arena Football League for one year and then coached some American football in Finland from 1992 to 1996. Since then, he has worked as a regional scout for the NFL.

MEYER, RONALD S. (RON) 2/17/1941– Purdue. QB; did not play professionally. *Apprenticeship:* College coach — 15 years (9 as head coach). *Roots:*

None. *Branches:* Jim Mora, Sr., Rod Rust, Rick Venturi. *Coordinators/Key Assistants:* For the Patriots, Lew Erber ran the offense, while Jim Mora, Sr., then Rod Rust handled the defense; for the Colts, John Becker then Larry Kennan then Leon Burtnett ran the offense, while George Hill then Bill Muir then Rick Venturi handled the defense. *Hall of Fame Players:* Eric Dickerson, John Hannah, Mike Haynes, Andre Tippett. *Primary Quarterbacks:* Steve Grogan, Jack Trudeau, Jeff George, Chris Chandler. *Tendencies:* • His teams scored 18.6 points and allowed 19.4 per game • His teams ran 50.7% of the time, which was 109% of the league average • Nine starting quarterbacks in nine years; 75% of starts to primary quarterbacks • 22 rookie starters in nine years • Winning Full Seasons to Losing Full Seasons: 3:1.

Miami Beach's Ron Meyer was a smooth talking salesman who always knew all the angles. He had some success in both the college ranks and the pros, but ultimately things tended to blow up around him. In college, he played quarterback and defensive back for Purdue from 1961 to 1962 and went into coaching three years later as an assistant at his alma mater. From 1965 to 1970, Meyer coached future NFL quarterbacks Bob Griese and Mike Phipps for the Boilermakers and then joined the Dallas Cowboys as a scout working with Bucko Kilroy from 1971 to 1972.

In 1973, Meyer took over Nevada-Las Vegas coming off a disastrous 1–10 season. In three years, Ron compiled an impressive 27–8 record in the desert. Moving on to beleaguered Southern Methodist in 1976, Meyer endured four losing seasons before his program took hold in 1980 with the thunderous "Pony Express" rushing attack of Eric Dickerson and Craig James that resulted in an undefeated season in 1981. Ron parlayed that success in 1982 to being named the head coach of the Patriots where Bucko Kilroy was GM, although he was the team's third choice after Joe Paterno and John Robinson turned down the job. Owner Billy Sullivan introduced his new coach by noting, "Ron has rebuilt two college football programs from losers into national powers." What was not known at the time was that Meyer's SMU team was

Meyer, Ronald S. (Ron)

Year	Team	Games	Wins	Losses	Ties	%	P Wins	P Losses	P %
1982	Patriots	9	5	4	0	.556	0	1	.000
1983	Patriots	16	8	8	0	.500	0	0	.000
1984	Patriots	8	5	3	0	.625	0	0	.000
1986	Colts	3	3	0	0	1.000	0	0	.000
1987	Colts	15	9	6	0	.600	0	1	.000
1988	Colts	16	9	7	0	.563	0	0	.000
1989	Colts	16	8	8	0	.500	0	0	.000
1990	Colts	16	7	9	0	.438	0	0	.000
1991	Colts	5	0	5	0	.000	0	0	.000
9 years		104	54	50	0	.519	0	2	.000

headed for having its football program shut down by the NCAA five years later under his successor Bobby Collins for extensive violations of NCAA regulations dating from the mid–1970s to mid–1980s.

In New England, Meyer inherited a talented core of a team that had underachieved in recent years. Many players did not welcome his demanding style or his sweeping personnel changes. One Patriot knew him well; former SMU Mustang Craig James wrote in *Game Day*, "Ron Meyer was a great motivator and knew how to recognize talent." However, Hall of Fame guard John Hannah told Michael Felger for *Tales from the Patriots Sideline*, "He was the biggest joke I've ever been around in my life. He knew nothing about football. He was strictly a public relations guy. He was a liar. He was a fraud. I chased him around the stadium one time trying to kill him. He was degrading our coaching staff— I won't say what it was about, but I found out it was a lie. And the son of a bitch ran from me." Even Meyer's greatest moment in New England is a bit shady — the infamous Snowplow Game when he directed a stadium employee, who was out of prison on work release, to use a snow plow to clear a spot for kicker John Smith to kick the winning field goal in a 3–0 triumph over Miami in a snowstorm. While the team never had a losing year under Meyer, the players did not respect the coach or his skills. The final straw was when he fired popular defensive coach Rod Rust in midseason of 1984. Days later, Ron found himself replaced by Raymond Berry who promptly reinstated Rust as the team's defensive coordinator.

Meyer returned to the NFL in 1986 when he replaced Rod Dowhower as head coach of the 0–13 Colts. In fact, Indianapolis owner Robert Irsay's son Jim had been a walk-on player for SMU under Meyer. Ron led that hopeless 1986 team to three straight wins to close the season and then two straight winning seasons. In 1987, Meyer swung a 10-player three-team deal that netted Indianapolis former SMU Mustang Eric Dickerson who then gave focus to Ron's run-oriented offense. In 1988, the galloping Colts even ran some plays from the Wishbone formation that was popular only at the college level. While some of Meyer's slick program did not appeal to the players, such as the weekly personal goals sheet each player was expected to fill out, receiver Bill Brooks told the *New*

York Times in 1990, "This is my fifth year here, and I can honestly say that there has never been a game that we entered with Ron and his coaching staff and were not fully prepared for that game." That year, Meyer traded with Atlanta for the top pick in the draft and selected Indiana's Jeff George, who he envisioned as his quarterback of the future. When 1991 began with five consecutive losses, though, Ron was fired.

Meyer spent a couple years as a broadcaster and then coached the Las Vegas Posse of the CFL to a 5–13 record in 1994. After that, he worked as an analyst and columnist for CNN and *Sports Illustrated*. He tried coaching again in 2001 with the Chicago Enforcers of Vince McMahon's aborted cartoonish XFL. Meyer also has served as the regional director of a hotel/casino in Dallas and most recently as a football handicapper for the online betting site, Vegas Sports Masters.

MICHAELS, WALTER E. (WALT) 10/16/1929–

Washington & Lee. Played LB for the Packers in 1951, the Browns from 1952 to 1961 and the Jets in 1963. *Apprenticeship:* Pro asst.—15 years. *Roots:* Marty Feldman, Red Conkright, Weeb Ewbank, Mike McCormack, Lou Holtz. *Branches:* Joe Walton, Dan Henning. *Coordinators/Key Assistants:* John Idzik then Pete McCulley then Joe Walton ran the offense, while John Mazur then Joe Gardi handled the defense. *Hall of Fame Players:* None. *Primary Quarterbacks:* Richard Todd. *Tendencies:* • His teams scored 20.6 points and allowed 21.8 per game • His teams ran 53.5% of the time, which was 103% of the league average • Three starting quarterbacks in six years; 83% of starts to primary quarterback • 17 rookie starters in six years • Winning Full Seasons to Losing Full Seasons: 2:2.

Gruff Walt Michaels from Swoyersville, Pennsylvania explained his view of football to the *New York Times* in 2011, nearly 20 years after his association with the NFL ended, "What has changed about football? Nothing. If you hit people, you can win." It's not surprising that the old linebacker tended to be more popular with his defensive players.

Michaels played linebacker in the league for a dozen years and played in five Pro Bowls. He went directly into coaching after retiring from the Browns by coaching the defense for the Raiders in 1962. When Al Davis took over in 1963, he fired Michaels and

Michaels, Walter E. (Walt)									
Year	Team	Games	Wins	Losses	Ties	%	P Wins	P Losses	P %
1977	Jets	14	3	11	0	.214	0	0	.000
1978	Jets	16	8	8	0	.500	0	0	.000
1979	Jets	16	8	8	0	.500	0	0	.000
1980	Jets	16	4	12	0	.250	0	0	.000
1981	Jets	16	10	5	1	.656	0	1	.000
1982	Jets	9	6	3	0	.667	2	1	.667
6 years		87	39	47	1	.454	2	2	.500

asked for his playbook, starting a lifelong feud between the two. Walt was hired that year by Weeb Ewbank to coach the Jets' defense and even suited up for one game when the squad was overwhelmed by injuries. Michaels coached the Jets defense for the next decade and had an interesting angle to the team's greatest triumph. In the Jets upset victory over the Colts in Super Bowl III, Walt's brother Lou was on the losing side and missed a couple field goals for Baltimore. Walt left the Jets in 1973 when Ewbank announced his successor would be his son-in-law Charley Winner. Michaels joined the staff of his former Browns' teammate Mike McCormack in Philadelphia for three years before returning to the Jets as Lou Holtz's defensive coach.

Holtz lasted less than a full season, and Walt was named his replacement in 1977. Over the next six years, Michaels rebuilt the Jets into a contending team again. The strength of the team was its pass rushing front four popularly called the Sack Exchange. On offense, Michaels first had to sort through a quarterback controversy between two young signal callers, Matt Robinson and Richard Todd. Although Robinson seemed to have won the competition in 1979, he made the mistake of lying to Walt about an injury. Michaels could not abide duplicity. The next year Robinson was traded to Denver, and Todd was the Jets undisputed quarterback.

Not everyone favored Michaels' fault finding approach. Former Jets receiver Richard Caster told the *New York Times* that his former coach, "makes a habit of dwelling on mistakes" and that made the team apprehensive and tentative. Tackle Marvin Powell responded, "Walt Michaels is the most constant person around here. As far as some guys not being able to deal with it, I think that's emotional immaturity on their part." However, Michaels himself did not handle pressure well. In one game against the Raiders, a bartender claiming to be Jets' owner Leon Hess was able to get through to the team's locker room on the phone at halftime. Michaels was convinced it was Al Davis pulling a prank and let it get under his skin. There were also repeated reports of Walt drinking too heavily and the team being concerned about that.

Michaels' career culminated in the strike season of 1982. Linebacker Greg Buttle told the *Times*, "Walt showed he was for the players during the strike, the way he talked about us, and he showed he was for the players when practices started, when he didn't make

us hit." In that year's expanded playoffs, New York made it all the way to the AFC championship that was played on a spongy field that was practically underwater in Miami. Michaels' was furious after the game that Dolphins' coach Don Shula, who he had long disliked, had not had the field covered with a tarp in the stormy days before the game. Miami won 14–0 on the strength of linebacker A.J. Duhe's three interceptions of Todd passes and went to the Super Bowl. On the flight home, a disgruntled and possibly inebriated Michaels reportedly was shouting about Shula and the field conditions to team officials. The next day, he refused to attend the squad's final meeting that was mandatory for the players. Two weeks later he stepped down as coach, saying that it was time to take a break from football, causing speculation that he was paid off to go away quietly by the team.

In short order, Michaels returned to the sideline as the coach of the New Jersey Generals of the USFL in 1984 and coached the team to a 25–13 record in the next two years behind quarterbacks Brian Sipe and Doug Flutie as well as star runner Herschel Walker. When the league folded, though, so did Walt's coaching career. He complained about being blackballed by the NFL in 1987 and never coached again in the league. However, the combination of his foreboding personality and the rumors of his problems with pressure situations would not make him an attractive candidate for a potential employer. His last connection to football was his involvement with the Helsinki team in the International League of American Football in 1989. He has been retired ever since.

MICHELOSEN, JOHN P. 2/13/1916–10/20/1982. Pittsburgh. QB; did not play professionally. *Apprenticeship:* College asst.—2 years; pro asst.—4 years. *Roots:* Jock Sutherland. *Branches:* Mike Nixon. *Coordinators/Key Assistants:* Walt Kiesling coached the line and Chuck Cherundolo ran the defense. *Hall of Fame Players:* Jack Butler, Ernie Stautner. *Primary Quarterbacks:* None. *Tendencies:* • His teams scored 16.4 points and allowed 18.5 per game • His teams ran 63.2% of the time, which was 112% of the league average • 14 rookie starters in four years • Winning Full Seasons to Losing Full Seasons: 1:2.

Born near Pittsburgh in Ambridge, Pennsylvania, John Michelosen would be closely associated with his

Michelosen, John P.									
Year	Team	Games	Wins	Losses	Ties	%	P Wins	P Losses	P %
1948	Steelers	12	4	8	0	.333	0	0	.000
1949	Steelers	12	6	5	1	.542	0	0	.000
1950	Steelers	12	6	6	0	.500	0	0	.000
1951	Steelers	12	4	7	1	.375	0	0	.000
4 years		48	20	26	2	.438	0	0	.000

hometown region and, in particular, with local hero Jock Sutherland throughout his career. Michelosen played quarterback, i.e., blocking back, in Sutherland's single wing attack at the University of Pittsburgh from 1935 to 1937. During that time, the Panthers went 30–2 and won two national championships. Having won the demanding Sutherland's respect, John became Jock's backfield coach for life the next year after graduating.

When Sutherland left Pitt to coach the Brooklyn Dodgers in the NFL in 1940, Michelosen went with him. When Jock went into the Navy in 1942, John did as well and was a flight trainer and football coach during the war. When the Steelers hired Sutherland as head coach in 1946, he brought along his loyal lieutenant Michelosen. Sutherland said of his assistant, "I can't think of a more knowledgeable or more qualified assistant coach. There isn't a single phase of football in which John does not have a thorough understanding and the ability to teach it to others. As long as I'm coaching, there will always be a place on my staff for a man with the capabilities of John Michelosen." Unfortunately, Jock was stricken with a brain tumor and died in 1948, so Art Rooney made the expected move and hired his acolyte as the new Steelers' head coach.

At just 32, though, Michelosen was not ready. Chet Smith of the *Pittsburgh Press* said later to the *Saturday Evening Post*, "John became Jock's shadow. Jock would walk out on the field in that long stride of his and John would be two steps behind, watching to see what Jock would do. If Jock put his hands in his pockets, John put his hands in his pockets. I don't know if Michelosen ever practiced Sutherland's Scotch burr, but I'd be surprised if he didn't." Jim Boston of the Steelers' front office told Rob Ruck for *Rooney* that the players had reservations, "These guys didn't take too kindly to the discipline they might have taken from Jock. Scrimmage in the morning, scrimmage in the afternoon—five days a week. This was bruising, workmanlike football. You had to be a tough guy to play for the Pittsburgh Steelers." The constant scrimmaging in pads beat up the players for the games. Defensive lineman Ernie Stautner told Ray Didinger for *Pittsburgh Steelers*, "It was as if John knew people talked about Jock being tough so he had to prove he could be tougher." The Steelers did have a solid defense throughout Michelosen's tenure, but they were the last team in the league to run the single wing offense. Michelosen had two natural T formation quarterbacks

on his roster in Jim Finks and Joe Gasparella, but refused to switch from Sutherland's offense even though some say that Jock himself would have modernized the attack had he lived.

In four years, the team never rose above mediocrity, so Rooney fired Michelosen after the 1951 season. The Steelers then instituted the T formation under new coach Joe Bach in 1952. Michelosen was hired as Red Dawson's backfield coach with the Pitt Panthers that year and learned the T himself. When Dawson's health forced him to step down after the 1954 season, John replaced him as head coach at his alma mater. From 1955 to 1965, Michelosen's Panthers posted a 56–49–7 record and used the T formation. Among the players he coached at Pitt were two future NFL coaches: Mike Ditka and Marty Schottenheimer. In 1966, John was hired as a scout by the 49ers and eventually became the team's personnel director before he retired.

MILLER, HENRY J. (HEINE) 1/1/1893–6/9/1964.
Penn. Played E for the Buffalo All-Americans from 1920 to 1921 and the Milwaukee Badgers in 1925. *Apprenticeship:* College coach—15 years (14 as head coach). *Roots:* None. *Branches:* None. *Coordinators/Key Assistants:* None. *Hall of Fame Players:* None. *Primary Quarterbacks:* Davey O'Brien. *Record:* Reportedly **Co-Coach** (with Bert Bell). *Tendencies:* • His team scored 10.1 points and allowed 19.2 per game • His team ran 46.7% of the time, which was 72% of the league average • One starting quarterback in one year; 100% of starts to primary quarterback • Two rookie starters in one year • Winning Full Seasons to Losing Full Seasons: 0:1.

While Heine Miller is listed as an assistant coach in the Eagles' Media Guide and Bert Bell is denoted as Philadelphia's 1940 head coach in all NFL reference materials, there is a rationale for including Miller here as the Eagles co-coach in 1940. When Bell hired him in December 1939, both the AP and UPI wire services stated he was the team's new co-coach. The local *Philadelphia Bulletin* also noted Heine was co-coach, with Miller claiming, "Possibly it's the way Bell has presented the professional picture to me by making it look attractive, both financially and from a working standpoint. I am familiar with the National League setup and know many of the players personally, especially the Eagles." Robert Lyons in his biography of Bell, *Any Given Sunday*, quotes Bill Mackrides, then a 15-year-old water boy and later a backup quarterback for the Eagles saying, "Bert would sit in the stands

Miller, Henry J. (Heine)									
Year	*Team*	*Games*	*Wins*	*Losses*	*Ties*	*%*	*P Wins*	*P Losses*	*P %*
1940	Eagles	11	1	10	0	.091	0	0	.000
1 year		11	1	10	0	.091	0	0	.000

during practice and Heine was the coach on the field ... [Bell] was the coach in name only."

In any case, Miller, a native of Williamsport, Pennsylvania, had a long history with both football and with his friend Bert Bell. The two men were teammates first at Haverford Prep and then at Penn, with Bell at quarterback and Miller at end. At Penn, Heine was a two-time All-American in the span from 1915 to 1919, with time out for military service during World War I. Miller began his pro football career in 1919, playing for the Massillon Tigers and the Detroit Heralds in the year before the NFL was formed. In 1920, he played for the independent Union Club of Phoenixville as well as Buffalo in the first incarnation of the NFL. In 1921, Heine not only played for Buffalo, but also the Union Athletic Association in Philadelphia. He was hired by the independent Frankford Yellow Jackets in 1922 and was team captain while spending two years with the club. He ended his playing career in 1925 with one game for the Milwaukee Badgers while also beginning his coaching career at Temple University.

Miller initiated the modern era of Temple University football and advanced the team from beating the likes of tiny Blue Ridge College 110–0 in 1927 to competing with the biggest football programs in the country by 1932. His reward was to be replaced by the legendary Pop Warner in 1933, although Heine stayed on staff coaching the ends for one year. In 1934, Miller moved across town to coach St. Joseph's through the 1939 season. His record at Temple was 50–15–8 and at St. Joe's 26–24–5. As detailed above, Bell hired his old friend for the Eagles in 1940 in some capacity. That year's Eagles' team, though, was probably the worst team in franchise history even with 5'6" passing sensation Davey O'Brien. A year later, Bell and Pittsburgh owner Art Rooney entered into a complicated franchise transaction that left Alex Thompson owning the team in Philadelphia and Bell and Rooney co-owning the team in Pittsburgh. Heine declined to follow Bell across the state, so Bell began 1941 as the Pittsburgh coach.

Miller coached West Chester to a 5–3–1 record in 1942, but the school then discontinued football for the war. He coached at Penn Charter Prep in 1944 and then retired from coaching to focus on his insurance business. Five years later, he retired to Longport, NJ, a seashore suburb of Atlantic City, where he spent the last 15 years of his life.

MILLER, ROBERT N. (RED) 10/31/1927– Western Illinois G/LB; did not play professionally. *Apprenticeship:* College asst.— 5 years; pro asst.—17 years. *Roots:* Lou Saban, Jack Faulkner, Mac Speedie, Charley Winner, Don McCafferty, John Sandusky (i), Chuck Fairbanks. *Branches:* Rod Dowhower, Bill Belichick. *Coordinators/Key Assistants*: Babe Parilli then Rod Dowhower were the key offensive coaches, while Joe Collier ran the defense. *Hall of Fame Players:* None. *Primary Quarterbacks:* Craig Morton. *Tendencies:* • His teams scored 18.6 points and allowed 15 per game • His teams ran 53.8% of the time, which was the league average • Four starting quarterbacks in four years; 74% of starts to primary quarterback • Three rookie starters in four years • Winning Full Seasons to Losing Full Seasons: 3:0.

Red Miller was born in Macomb, Illinois, and attended college there at Western Illinois. Miller was such an impressive guard/linebacker and leader that he was the team's MVP for three years in a row from 1947 to 1949 and elected team captain as a senior. Upon graduation, Red went directly into coaching on the high school level in Illinois from 1950 to 1954. In 1955, he moved up to the college level as an assistant at nearby Carthage College and subsequently returned to his alma mater in 1957 as an assistant to head coach Lou Saban.

When Saban was hired as the Patriots' first head coach in 1960, he brought half his WIU staff with him, including Miller. Red then followed Lou to Buffalo in 1962, but left for Denver a year later. Miller coached the Broncos line for three years before taking the same job on Charley Winner's staff in St. Louis in 1966. Red was so effective with the Cardinals that all five of his starting linemen were named to the Pro Bowl at least once in his five years in town. When Winner was fired in 1971, Red was hired by Don McCafferty in Baltimore. With the extreme turmoil in the Colts front office, Miller departed in 1973 to take charge of the Patriots' offense under new head coach Chuck Fairbanks.

New England's revitalization advanced Red's profile in the league. Meanwhile in Denver, head coach John Ralston had built the first winning team in franchise history, but lost the respect of his players in the process. The Broncos won five of their last six games in 1976. The only game they lost, and the only time Denver gave up more than 30 points all season, was against Miller's high-scoring Patriot offense. In

Miller, Robert N. (Red)

Year	Team	Games	Wins	Losses	Ties	%	P Wins	P Losses	P %
1977	Broncos	14	12	2	0	.857	2	1	.667
1978	Broncos	16	10	6	0	.625	0	1	.000
1979	Broncos	16	10	6	0	.625	0	1	.000
1980	Broncos	16	8	8	0	.500	0	0	.000
4 years		62	40	22	0	.645	2	3	.400

the off-season, the Broncos named Red head coach, and he had immediate spectacular success. After bringing in discredited veteran quarterback Craig Morton, Denver swept to its first Super Bowl in 1977. Red told the *New York Times*, "Instead of rebuilding from 1–13 or 2–12 as many head coaches must do, my coaches and I inherited a team coming off the most successful season in the history of the franchise. We had some very talented players. Overall, we had a squad that needed a player here or some improvement there to become a championship team." One source informed the *Los Angeles Times* that Ralston, "constantly preached good defense, desire and togetherness — a total team effort. But whereas Ralston preached it, Miller is getting it done."

Miller called the plays for Morton and was an early proponent of a steady rotation of defensive linemen and running backs throughout each game to keep everyone fresh and involved. He told the *Los Angeles Times*, "We want everybody going like hell every down — which is hard to do when you're out there for 60 minutes — and we want everybody playing because this is a team game. Every guy should feel he's part of things. My approach to this game is team unity. I don't care much for individual records. What we want are team results."

With that fast success, the Broncos stirred fan interest to a mile-high altitude and helped to solidify the traditionally marginal franchise in Denver for good — even with Morton and the Broncos' complete meltdown in Super Bowl X against the Cowboys. After the 1977 12–2 high point, though, Miller could not duplicate that crest of achievement, although his defense finished in the top five in fewest points allowed three times. Two 10–6 seasons were followed by an 8–8 record in 1980, and both Miller and GM Fred Gehrke were fired by new owner Edgar Kaiser in 1981. Two years later, Red returned to the local sidelines as head coach of the Denver Gold in the USFL, but was fired with the team at 4–7 in midseason after a series of rancorous incidents with team ownership. Miller once told the *Washington Post*, "Football is an emotional game. I like to show some emotion myself. I like to see the Broncomania." He had an enormous impact on the Broncos' franchise, but never coached again, instead becoming a stockbroker for Dean Witter.

MILLNER, WAYNE V. 1/31/1913–11/19/1976. Notre Dame. Played E for the Redskins from 1936 to 1941 and in 1945. *Apprenticeship:* Pro asst.— 7 years. *Roots:* Ray Flaherty, Turk Edwards, Clem Crowe, Bo McMillin. *Branches:* Jim Trimble. *Coordinators/Key Assistants:* Jim Trimble coached the defense. *Hall of Fame Players:* Chuck Bednarik, Pete Pihos, Steve Van Buren. *Primary Quarterbacks:* Adrian Burk. *Record:* **Hall of Fame Player; Interim Coach.**

Born in Roxbury, Massachusetts, Wayne Millner made a national name for himself as an end for Notre Dame from 1933 to 1935. In an early "Game of the Century" against Ohio State in 1935, Millner caught two touchdown passes from tailback Bill Shakespeare, including the game-winner in the closing seconds to cap a stirring fourth quarter comeback. Selected in the eighth round of the first NFL draft in 1936, Wayne played his entire pro career for the Redskins. Washington's coach Ray Flaherty informed owner George Preston Marshall, "With that Yankee playing end, please accept my resignation if the Redskins do not win the championship this year." While the team reached the title game in 1936, they lost. In Millner's second season, though, rookie tailback Sammy Baugh led the team to the championship, with the "big Yankee" catching two touchdown passes in the title game. On this basis, Wayne was not only elected to the College Football Hall of Fame but also, in 1968, to the Pro Football Hall of Fame. As a pro, though, Millner caught just 124 passes for 12 scores and was an odd choice for Canton.

Wayne served in the Navy during the war and returned for one last season as a Redskin in 1945, while doubling as an assistant coach. He remained as an assistant in Washington from 1946 to 1948 and then moved to Chicago to join Ray Flaherty's staff with the AAFC Hornets in 1949. When the league folded, he worked on Clem Crowe's Baltimore staff in 1950. After the initial Colts' franchise went bankrupt in 1951, Millner was hired by incoming Eagles' Coach Bo McMillin as an assistant. Two games into the season, McMillin was diagnosed with stomach cancer and had to step down. Wayne was promoted to interim head coach but was replaced by defensive coach Jim Trimble at the end of an uninspiring year. He returned to Washington as an assistant coach from 1952 to 1957 before joining old teammate Sammy Baugh's staff at Hardin-Simmons in 1958. For the next four years, Millner sold cars before returning to football as a scout in 1963. For several years, Wayne scouted for the Redskins, Colts and Eagles until returning once more to the sideline in 1974 as an assistant to former Redskin Jack Pardee for the Florida Blazers of the World Football League. He died two years later.

Millner, Wayne V.									
Year	Team	Games	Wins	Losses	Ties	%	P Wins	P Losses	P %
1951	Eagles	10	2	8	0	.200	0	0	.000
1 year		10	2	8	0	.200	0	0	.000

MODZELEWSKI, RICHARD B. (DICK)

2/16/1931– Maryland. Played DT for the Redskins, Steelers, Giants, Browns from 1953 to 1966. *Apprenticeship:* Pro asst.—10 years. *Roots:* Blanton Collier, Nick Skorich, Forrest Gregg. *Branches:* Raymond Berry. *Coordinators/Key Assistants*: None. *Hall of Fame Players:* Paul Warfield. *Primary Quarterbacks:* Terry Luck. *Record:* **Interim Coach.**

A year behind his brother Ed, Dick Modzelewski was known as "Little Mo," but was the bigger star in the family. The brothers from West Natrona, Pennsylvania played together for the University of Maryland in 1950 and 1951, but never got to team up in the pros. Fullback Ed graduated in 1952 and was drafted in the first round by Pittsburgh that year; tackle Dick was a two-time All-American who won the Outland Trophy as a senior in 1952 and was drafted in the second round by the Redskins in 1953. He considered jumping to the CFL in 1954, but then was traded to Pittsburgh in 1955. Unfortunately, his brother Ed was traded from Pittsburgh to Cleveland in the meantime. Dick spent just one year in Pittsburgh before being traded to the Giants in 1956. New York won the championship that year and played in six title games in the eight seasons he spent anchoring the Giants' defensive line.

Giants' coach Allie Sherman thought Dick was getting too old and traded him again in 1964 to the Browns who were looking for a stabilizing force on their line. Cleveland won the championship that year, and Dick was named "Brown of the Year" by the local Touchdown Club. The Browns returned to the title game in 1965, and Modzelewski played one more season after that before retiring. In his 14-year career, the steady tackle never missed a game, playing in 180 consecutive ones. Mo spent the 1967 season scouting for Cleveland and then joined their coaching staff in 1968. He then spent 10 years as a Browns' assistant under three coaches: Blanton Collier, Nick Skorich and Forrest Gregg. Gregg named him defensive coordinator in 1975, and when Forrest resigned with one game to play in 1977, Mo moved up to head coach for his last game in Cleveland. That game was a one-point loss to Seattle behind rookie quarterback Terry Luck who never played in the NFL again.

Modzelewski returned to the Giants as defensive coordinator in 1978 and then quickly moved on to Cincinnati in 1979 as defensive line coach. Gregg took over the team the following year and led the Bengals to the Super Bowl for the 1981 season. Two years later, the team was in decline, and Gregg was fired. He returned to his former team, the Packers, as head coach and brought in Dick as defensive coordinator. After four years without success, Gregg was fired again, so Mo hooked on with the Lions as defensive line coach from 1988 to 1989 and then retired.

MOELLER, GARY O.

1/26/1941– Ohio State. LB; did not play professionally. *Apprenticeship:* College coach — 28 years (8 as head coach); pro asst.— 5 years. *Roots:* Bobby Ross. *Branches:* Jim Zorn. *Coordinators/Key Assistants*: Sylvester Croom ran the offense, and Larry Peccatiello handled the defense. *Hall of Fame Players:* None. *Primary Quarterbacks:* Charley Batch.

Gary Moeller from Lima, Ohio was associated with Bo Schembechler for nearly 25 years on the football field. Gary played linebacker for Ohio State from 1961 to 1963 when Woody Hayes was the coach and Schembechler his top assistant. Moeller coached high school football from 1964 to 1966 before joining Schembechler's staff at the Miami University in 1967. When Bo took over the Michigan program in 1969, Gary followed him as defensive coach. Moeller left Michigan in 1977 when he was named head coach at Illinois, but in three years only compiled a 6–24–3 record. He then returned to Michigan in 1980. Over the next decade, Gary served as the Wolverines' quarterbacks coach, defensive coordinator and offensive coordinator as Bo's top assistant. When Schembechler stepped down in 1990, it was no surprise that he named the well-schooled Moeller as his successor.

From 1990 to 1994, Moeller's Wolverines posted a 44–13–3 record, won four of five bowl games and were ranked in the top ten three times. Unfortunately his college career came crashing down abruptly in May 1995 when he was arrested for being drunk and disorderly in an incident in which he punched a police officer. Within a week, Gary resigned. He admitted being embarrassed, but denied he had a drinking problem, claiming, "I con-

Modzelewski, Richard B. (Dick)									
Year	Team	Games	Wins	Losses	Ties	%	P Wins	P Losses	P %
1977	Browns	1	0	1	0	.000	0	0	.000
1 year		1	0	1	0	.000	0	0	.000

Moeller, Gary O.									
Year	Team	Games	Wins	Losses	Ties	%	P Wins	P Losses	P %
2000	Lions	7	4	3	0	.571	0	0	.000
1 year		7	4	3	0	.571	0	0	.000

sider myself a dedicated football coach. I am proud of my career and what I have accomplished in Michigan. I still have my family and dignity."

David Shula hired Moeller to coach the tight ends in Cincinnati that year, and Gary joined Bobby Ross' staff in Detroit in 1997 as assistant head coach. Ross was not able to attain the same success he had in San Diego and resigned in 2000 with the Lions at 5–4. Moeller was promoted on an interim basis and told the *New York Times*, "My plan, if I had it my way, was that I wanted to be a pro coordinator or a head coach again. I never gave up on that." Lions' quarterback Charlie Batch added, "Coach Moeller has a little more fire, a few different ways of motivating us. He has a way of talking to you one on one that gets through."

Detroit finished the year 4–3 under Moeller, and Gary wanted to keep the job. However, the Lions hired Matt Millen as GM, and he blew everything up in an attempt to remake the team in his own incompetent image. Moeller spent 2001 as the Jaguars defensive coordinator and 2002 and 2003 as the Bears linebackers coach before retiring in 2004.

MOLESWORTH, KEITH (RABBIT OR MOLEY)

10/20/1905–3/12/1966. Monmouth. Played QB for the Bears from 1931 to 1937. *Apprenticeship:* College asst.— 8 years; pro asst.—1 year; semipro head coach — 5 years. *Roots:* Joe Bach. *Branches:* Ray Richards. *Coordinators/Key Assistants*: Otis Douglass coached the line, and Ray Richards the defense. *Hall of Fame Players:* Gino Marchetti. *Primary Quarterbacks:* Fred Enke. *Tendencies:* • His team scored 15.2 points and allowed 29.2 per game • His team ran 50.7% of the time, which was 99% of the league average • Four starting quarterbacks in one year; 67% of starts to primary quarterback • Three rookie starters in one year • Winning Full Seasons to Losing Full Seasons: 0:1.

On Keith Molesworth's death, *Baltimore News American* sports editor John Steadman wrote, "Genuine — one of the greatest words in our vocabulary — was created to express the pure qualities of a man of the type of Keith Molesworth. He didn't know what it was to be deceitful or spiteful or hurtful." A native of Washington, Iowa, the esteemed Molesworth was a multisport star who lettered in football, baseball and basketball at Monmouth College in Illinois from 1923 to 1927. He would go on to play and coach both football and baseball at the professional level for the next two decades.

In 1928, Molesworth joined the independent

Portsmouth Spartans as a small but speedy halfback and backfield coach. After two seasons of double duty, Keith left Portsmouth to play for the competing Ironton Tanks under coach Greasy Neale in 1930. The main motivating factor in the switch was that the elusive halfback had stolen off with Portsmouth Coach Hal Griffen's girl. A year later, Keith was signed by the Bears and then converted to T formation quarterback in 1932. In his six seasons as a Bear quarterback, the team went to four championship games and won two NFL titles. Concurrent to his football career, Molesworth spent his summers from 1929 to 1937 playing shortstop in the minor leagues, batting .279 over his career.

Keith ended his playing career in both sports in 1938 when he joined the Naval Academy as backfield coach. He served in that capacity through 1945 and then took a job managing the Columbia Reds of the Sally League in 1946 before leaving for Hawaii where he coached the Warriors of the Pacific Coast Football League from 1946 to 1948. Under Molesworth, the Warriors posted a 20–7 record and won two league titles despite 15 players being entangled in a gambling scandal in 1947 and being banned from the league. He returned stateside in 1949 to coach the Richmond Rebels of the Eastern Football League from 1949 to 1950 and won two more titles. That was four consecutive championships across two different minor leagues from 1947 to 1950 and a 34–11–1 record for the full five-year stretch.

Molesworth returned to the NFL in 1952 as the backfield coach of the Steelers, having been hired to install the T formation in Pittsburgh at long last. Keith was tabbed a year later to be the first coach of the new Baltimore Colts franchise. The Colts' GM was Don Kellett who had been Molesworth's double play partner for Syracuse of the International League in 1937. Keith announced, "If anybody doesn't want to play football, we don't want them. I assure you they're going to be in shape." Although Baltimore was inheriting the roster of the failed Dallas Texans, the team was an expansion team and performed accordingly by going 3–9 in 1953. After losing their last seven games, though, owner Carroll Rosenbloom brought in Weeb Ewbank from Paul Brown's Cleveland staff as head coach and kicked Keith upstairs. From the front office, Molesworth helped build the Colts back-to-back champions of 1958–1959 and was heavily recruited in 1960 by the new American Football League and by three of its teams — the Raiders, Patriots and Bills. In-

Molesworth, Keith (Rabbit or Moley)									
Year	*Team*	*Games*	*Wins*	*Losses*	*Ties*	*%*	*P Wins*	*P Losses*	*P %*
1953	Colts	12	3	9	0	.250	0	0	.000
1 year		12	3	9	0	.250	0	0	.000

stead, Keith stayed with the Colts and ran the player personnel department for the team from 1954 to 1966, keeping a steady stream of talent flowing into Baltimore for Ewbank and Don Shula. Cutting his grass in March 1966, Molesworth had a sudden heart attack and died.

MORA, JAMES E. (JIM) 5/24/1935– Occidental. TE; did not play professionally. *Apprenticeship:* College coach —16 years (3 as head coach); pro asst.— 5 years; USFL head coach — 3 years. *Roots:* Jack Patera, Ron Meyer. *Branches:* Rick Venturi (i), Vince Tobin (USFL), Dom Capers, Jim Haslett, Jim Mora, Jr. *Co-ordinators/Key Assistants*: For the Saints, Carl Smith ran the offense, while Steve Sidwell then Monte Kiffin then Rick Venturi handled the defense; for the Colts, Tom Moore ran the offense, while Rusty Tillman then Vic Fangio handled the defense. *Hall of Fame Players:* Marshall Faulk, Ricky Jackson and Willie Roaf. *Primary Quarterbacks:* Bobby Hebert, Jim Everett, Peyton Manning. *Tendencies:* • His teams scored 21.8 points and allowed 20.4 per game • His teams ran 46.1% of the time, which was 102% of the league average • Seven starting quarterbacks in 15 years; 75% of starts to primary quarterbacks • 36 rookie starters in 15 years • Winning Full Seasons to Losing Full Seasons: 7:5.

Born in Glendale, California, Jim Mora played tight end for nearby Occidental College from 1955 to 1957 and caught passes from the team's quarterback and co-captain, Jack Kemp. While Kemp went from Occidental to a series of NFL training camps, co-captain Mora graduated to a Marine boot camp in 1957. Jim spent three years in the Marines and then began his coaching career as an assistant at his alma mater in 1960. Four years later in 1964, he was named the school's head coach and compiled an 18–9 record at Occidental from 1964 to 1966.

Mora jumped from Division III to Division I in 1967 when John Ralston hired him as an assistant at Stanford, replacing Rod Rust. Ralston was running a finishing school for future NFL coaches in Palo Alto. Bill Walsh had been on staff through 1965 and Dick Vermeil and Mike White were still there when Mora arrived. Ralston once said of Mora, "I think he has the executive ability to run General Motors. He's highly intelligent, disciplined, with a great grasp of what it takes to succeed." Jim only stayed at Stanford for one season before moving on to Colorado in 1968. Six years later, he returned to California as part of Dick Vermeil's first staff at UCLA in 1974. One year after that, Mora headed north to coach the defense for new Washington Huskies' coach Don James from 1975 to 1977; Mora had coached with James at Colorado.

Mora at last ascended to the NFL as the Seahawks' defensive line coach from 1978 to 1981. He left Seattle for New England and a promotion to defensive coordinator in 1982 before receiving his first professional head coaching offer with the Philadelphia Stars of the new USFL in 1983. Not only did Mora coach the Stars for all three years of the USFL's existence, but he led the team to all three league championship games, losing the first, but winning the ensuing two. Working with Stars' GM Carl Peterson, a former Vermeil associate, Jim assembled a 48–13–1 team that proved to be a forerunner to the teams he would coach in the NFL. In particular, the Stars featured a strong running attack and aggressive defense.

When the USFL folded, Mora was hired by the woeful New Orleans Saints as head coach in 1986. The Saints had never had a winning season, but Mora led them to a 12–3 record in his second year and compiled a 93–74 record in 11 years in New Orleans. The team was led by USFL-refugee Bobby Hebert at quarter-

Mora, James E. (Jim)									
Year	Team	Games	Wins	Losses	Ties	%	P Wins	P Losses	P %
1986	Saints	16	7	9	0	.438	0	0	.000
1987	Saints	15	12	3	0	.800	0	1	.000
1988	Saints	16	10	6	0	.625	0	0	.000
1989	Saints	16	9	7	0	.563	0	0	.000
1990	Saints	16	8	8	0	.500	0	1	.000
1991	Saints	16	11	5	0	.688	0	1	.000
1992	Saints	16	12	4	0	.750	0	1	.000
1993	Saints	16	8	8	0	.500	0	0	.000
1994	Saints	16	7	9	0	.438	0	0	.000
1995	Saints	16	7	9	0	.438	0	0	.000
1996	Saints	8	2	6	0	.250	0	0	.000
1998	Colts	16	3	13	0	.188	0	0	.000
1999	Colts	16	13	3	0	.813	0	1	.000
2000	Colts	16	10	6	0	.625	0	1	.000
2001	Colts	16	6	10	0	.375	0	0	.000
15 years		231	125	106	0	.541	0	6	.000

back, the rushing combo of Dalton Hilliard and Reuben Mayes and the Dome Patrol Pro Bowl linebacking corps of Ricky Jackson, Pat Swilling, Vaughan Johnson and former Philadelphia/Baltimore Star Sam Mills. What New Orleans could never do though was win a playoff game, losing in the first round in all four trips to the postseason. After 1992, Saints GM Jim Finks left and the talent stopped flowing. New Orleans sunk to mediocrity and then got off to a 2–6 start in 1996. By that point, Mora was so frustrated that he resigned shortly after peevishly spitting out, "We couldn't do diddly poo offensively. We couldn't make a first down. We couldn't run the ball; we didn't try to run the ball. We couldn't complete a pass. We sucked."

Mora was known for his bluntness with the media. After a close loss to the rival 49ers in 1987, he went on a tirade that concluded, "I'm pissed off right now. You bet your ass I am. I'm sick of coulda, woulda, shoulda, coming close, if only." During the preseason in 1989, he spoke for beleaguered coaches everywhere when he patronized the media and the fans by asserting, "You think you know, but you don't know. And you never will." He could be tough on players as well. Nose guard Tony Elliott told the *Washington Post*, "He's a disciplinarian and he expects a lot out of you on and off the field." Mora maintained to the *New York Times*, "I've always tried to be honest with the players, fair with them, consistent with them. If they know where they stand with you, they can accept certain things they may not like or agree with."

After spending 1997 as a TV analyst, Jim was hired to coach the Indianapolis Colts in 1998, Peyton Manning's rookie season. While that first season was rough at 3–13, Mora reversed the numbers in 1999 with a 13–3 finish. The Colts made the playoffs in both 1999 and 2000, but again Mora could not get past the first round. When the team declined in 2001, Mora gave his most famous rant of all following a loss to San Francisco on November 25 that dropped them to 4–6. Manning threw four interceptions that day, and Mora was apoplectic about it after the game. After a reporter asked him about the team's chances to reach the playoffs, Jim was incredulous, "Playoffs?! Don't talk about — playoffs?! You kidding me?! Playoffs?! I just hope we can win a game. Another game." That explosion continues to be mocked and imitated a

decade later. However at the time, his quarterback was not pleased at being called out in public. While Mora was officially fired for not agreeing to fire his defensive coordinator Vic Fangio at the end of the year, angering the sensitive franchise quarterback did not help.

Mora remains in the public eye through his son Jim, a two-time NFL coach, and through various broadcasting stints. As an analyst, he caused problems for his son in 2006 when he referred to his son's quarterback, Michael Vick, as a "coach killer," but nothing deters him from always speaking his mind.

Mora, James L. (Jim) 11/16/1961– Washington. DB; did not play professionally. *Apprenticeship:* College asst.—1 year; pro asst.—19 years. *Roots:* Don Coryell, Al Saunders, Dan Henning, Jim Mora, Sr., Steve Mariucci, Dennis Erickson. *Branches:* Emmitt Thomas (i), Tom Cable, Dennis Allen. *Coordinators/Key Assistants:* For the Falcons, Greg Knapp ran the offense, while Ed Donatell handled the defense; for the Seahawks, Knapp again ran the offense, while Gus Bradley handled the defense. *Hall of Fame Players:* None. *Primary Quarterbacks:* Mike Vick, Matt Hasselbeck. *Tendencies:* • His teams scored 19.7 points and allowed 21.8 per game • His teams ran 49.2% of the time, which was 110% of the league average • Four starting quarterbacks in five years; 94% of starts to primary quarterbacks • Eleven rookie starters in five years • Winning Full Seasons to Losing Full Seasons: 1:2.

Son of an NFL coach, Jim Mora the younger was born in Los Angeles and followed his father into the family business, although generally with less success. Like the elder Mora, Jim comes at the game from the defensive side of the ball. He was a defensive back at the University of Washington from 1980 to 1983 and then spent 20 years coaching defense before getting his first head coaching offer.

Mora began his coaching career as a graduate assistant at his alma mater in 1984; in fact, both father and son spent time as assistants under Don James. After just one year, though, Mora moved up to the pro game by joining Don Coryell's staff in San Diego. Mora coached for the Chargers from 1985 to 1991, under three head coaches. In 1992, he joined his father's Saints' staff as the secondary coach. After his dad quit during the 1996 season, Jim coached the sec-

Mora, James L. (Jim)									
Year	Team	Games	Wins	Losses	Ties	%	P Wins	P Losses	P %
2004	Falcons	16	11	5	0	.688	1	1	.500
2005	Falcons	16	8	8	0	.500	0	0	.000
2006	Falcons	16	7	9	0	.438	0	0	.000
2009	Seahawks	16	5	11	0	.313	0	0	.000
5 years		64	31	33	0	.484	1	1	.500

ondary of the 49ers from 1997 to 1998 and then was promoted to defensive coordinator in 1999. He served in that capacity in San Francisco from 1999 to 2003 under Steve Mariucci and then Dennis Erickson.

Jim was hired as head coach of the Falcons in 2004 and had immediate success with Michael Vick at quarterback. In 2004, the Falcons made it to the NFC Championship game where they lost to the Eagles. Unlike his father, Jim was noted as being a players' coach. Vick did not match up well with Mora's West Coast offensive coordinator Greg Knapp, though, and the team dropped back to mediocrity in the next two years. Toward the end of 2006, Jim's Falcons' tenure imploded. In November, his father labeled Vick a "coach killer" on a radio interview. A month later, Jim proved like-father-like-son when he stuck his own foot in his mouth in a radio interview with Hugh Millen, a former teammate at Washington. Mora jokingly told Millen on the air that he would take the head coaching job of the Huskies in a heartbeat no matter what was happening with the Falcons. This disloyalty did not sit well with owner Arthur Blank who fired Mora a month later.

Mike Holmgren hired Jim as his defensive coordinator in Seattle in 2007 and then indicated in 2008 that Mora would be his successor after Mike retired at the end of the year. That lame duck season was a disappointing one for Holmgren, and he left Mora with a team in decline. Jim probably would have survived his 5–11 first season had not the celebrated coach of USC, Pete Carroll, become available in 2010. As it was, Mora was fired on January 8 and Carroll hired January 11. Jim told the *Seattle Times*, "I'm disappointed I wasn't able to get a chance to see this thing through because I'm confident I could have turned it around." Mora spent the next two years working as an analyst for the NFL Network until accepting the head coaching position at UCLA for the 2012 season.

MORNHINWEG, MARTIN (MARTY) 3/29/1962–
Montana QB; did not play professionally. *Apprenticeship:* College asst.—10 years; pro asst.—6 years. *Roots:* Mike Holmgren, Steve Mariucci. *Branches:* None. *Coordinators/Key Assistants:* Mornhinweg ran his own offense before turning it over to Maurice Carthon, while Vince Tobin then Kurt Schottenheimer handled the defense. *Hall of Fame Players:* None. *Primary Quarterbacks:* Joey Harrington. *Tendencies:* • His teams

scored 18 points and allowed 27.3 per game • His teams ran 35.8% of the time, which was 82% of the league average • Four starting quarterbacks in two years; 38% of starts to primary quarterback • Six rookie starters in two years • Winning Full Seasons to Losing Full Seasons: 0:2.

Marty Mornhinweg, from Edmond, Oklahoma, was a 5'9" scrambling quarterback for Mike Holmgren at Oak Grove High School in San Jose from 1978 to 1980. He then started for four years at the University of Montana. Despite setting several school passing records, the undersized signal caller went undrafted by the NFL. He spent the next year as an assistant at his alma mater and then 1986–1987 as a graduate assistant at Texas-El Paso before giving Arena Football a shot in 1987. Marty blew out his knee for the Denver Dynamite in 1987 and returned to coaching with Northern Arizona in 1988. He moved on to Southeast Missouri State from 1989 to 1990, Missouri from 1991 to 1993 and back to Northern Arizona as offensive coordinator in 1994.

Marty's high school coach brought him to Green Bay in 1995 and promoted him to quarterbacks coach in 1996. When former Packers' quarterbacks coach Steve Mariucci was named head coach of the 49ers in 1997, he imported Marty as offensive coordinator. While the 49ers offense performed well, Mornhinweg' hidden dark legacy in San Francisco according to Charles P. Pierce in *Moving the Chains* was steering the team away from Michigan senior and Bay Area native Tom Brady for the 2000 draft. In that same year, Matt Millen took over as GM in Detroit and attempted to remake the underperforming Lions from scratch. Millen hired Mornhinweg as Detroit's head coach in 2001, and Marty announced, "The bar is high; the goal for this organization is to win Super Bowls."

However, both men were overmatched by their positions. After being upset at one of the team's first practices in training camp, Mornhinweg stormed off on his motorcycle in an obviously staged bit of false machismo. The result was a team that lost its first 12 games in 2001 and its last eight in 2002. The defense finished in the bottom two of the league in points allowed for each season; the Lions' offense was 26th in scoring in both years, despite throwing the ball two-thirds of the time, 18% more than the league average.

What Marty is most remembered for in his two-year stint was an overtime game against the Bears in November 2002 when he directed his captains to take

Mornhinweg, Martin (Marty)									
Year	Team	Games	Wins	Losses	Ties	%	P Wins	P Losses	P %
2001	Lions	16	2	14	0	.125	0	0	.000
2002	Lions	16	3	13	0	.188	0	0	.000
2 years		32	5	27	0	.156	0	0	.000

the wind rather than the ball if they won the coin flip for the sudden death period. Predictably, the Bears kicked the game-winning field goal on the opening possession without the Lions ever touching the ball. Mornhinweg was still defending the decision five years later to *Delaware Online*, "The people who were there and know all the information ... know it was the right call. It was the right call then, it's the right call now, and it's the right call 10 years from now."

Marty was not fired immediately after the 2002 season, but once Steve Mariucci became available, Millen dropped Morninweg for Marty's former boss. Mornhinweg caught on with another colleague from Green Bay, Andy Reid, who hired Marty as a senior assistant in 2003 and promoted him to offensive coordinator in 2006. With the resurrection of Michael Vick's career in Philadelphia in 2010, Mornhinweg has drawn a lot of praise and may even surface as a head coaching candidate again.

MORRIS, RAHEEM 9/3/1976– Hofstra. DB; did not play professionally. *Apprenticeship:* College asst.— 5 years; pro asst.—6 years. *Roots:* Jon Gruden. *Branches:* None. *Coordinators/Key Assistants*: Greg Olson ran the offense, while Jim Bates then Morris handled the defense. *Hall of Fame Players:* None. *Primary Quarterbacks:* Josh Freeman. *Tendencies:* • His teams scored 18.2 points and allowed 25.3 per game • His teams ran 41% of the time, which was 95% of the league average • Three starting quarterbacks in three years; 83% of starts to primary quarterback • 13 rookie starters in three years • Winning Full Seasons to Losing Full Seasons: 1:2.

Out of Irvington, New Jersey, Raheem Morris played safety at Hofstra from 1994 to 1997 and has been on a fast track ever since. He began his coaching career as a graduate assistant at his alma mater in 1998, coached the secondary for Cornell in 1999 and then returned to Hofstra to coach the defensive backs there from 2000 to 2001. Jon Gruden brought Morris in as defensive quality control coach in 2002, the year the Bucs won the Super Bowl. By 2004, he was assisting Mike Tomlin in coaching the Bucs' secondary. Raheem left Tampa in 2006 to become the defensive coordinator at Kansas State where he got to watch a sophomore quarterback named Josh Freeman.

One year later, Morris returned to Tampa as the secondary coach. In December 2008, the Bucs an-

nounced that Raheem would succeed the esteemed Monte Kiffin as defensive coordinator when Kiffin joined his son's staff at Tennessee. A month later, things changed dramatically after the team dropped its last four games and missed the playoffs. Tampa fired head coach Jon Gruden and promoted Morris all the way to head coach. Cornerback Ronde Barber told *Sports Illustrated*, "He's a proverbial from-the-bottom-floor-to-the-top guy. It's nice to see him get where he wants to be, even if it's a little bit sooner than he anticipated."

There was no doubt that Raheem was in charge. When he quickly lost trust in offensive coordinator Jeff Jagodzinski in September 2009, he fired him before the last exhibition game and replaced him with Greg Olson. Although the Bucs lost their first seven games, Morris didn't lose his confidence. After the bye week, Raheem anointed rookie quarterback Josh Freeman from Kansas State the starter, and the team won its first game of the season. Unhappy with the defense, he fired veteran defensive coordinator Jim Bates two weeks later and asserted full control of the defense. The next season, Tampa nearly made the playoffs with Freeman playing a starring role by leading the team to five fourth quarter comebacks, accounting for half of the Bucs 10 wins on the year. Morris acted as a bold leader much in the mold of his former superiors in Tampa—Jon Gruden and Mike Tomlin. However, he was also a players' coach who had discipline problems that undermined the team in his third year. The Bucs dropped 10 games in a row giving up the most points in the league and losing seven games by more than two touchdowns. As expected, Morris was fired at year's end. He signed on with Mike Shanahan to coach the Redskins defensive backs in 2012.

MULARKEY, MICHAEL R. (MIKE) 11/19/1961– Florida. Played TE for the Vikings and Steelers from 1983 to 1991. *Apprenticeship:* College asst.—1 year; pro asst.—10 years. *Roots:* Sam Wyche, Bill Cowher. *Branches:* Eric Studesville (i). *Coordinators/Key Assistants*: Tom Clements handled the offense, while Jerry Gray ran the defense. *Hall of Fame Players:* None. *Primary Quarterbacks:* Drew Bledsoe. *Tendencies:* • His teams scored 20.8 points and allowed 20.3 per game • His teams ran 47.7% of the time, which was 106% of the league average • Three starting quarterbacks in two years; 50% of starts to primary quarterback • Four

Morris, Raheem									
Year	Team	Games	Wins	Losses	Ties	%	P Wins	P Losses	P %
2009	Bucs	16	3	13	0	.188	0	0	.000
2010	Bucs	16	10	6	0	.625	0	0	.000
2011	Bucs	16	4	12	0	.250	0	0	.000
3 years		48	17	31	0	.354	0	0	.000

rookie starters in two years • Winning Full Seasons to Losing Full Seasons: 1:1.

Miami's Mike Mularkey switched from quarterback to tight end at the University of Florida where he played from 1979 to 1982. A ninth round pick of the 49ers in 1983, he was cut in training camp, but was picked up by Minnesota. Mike fashioned a nine-year career as a backup tight end in the NFL, playing for Bud Grant and Jerry Burns on the Vikings from 1983 to 1987 and for Chuck Noll in Pittsburgh from 1988 to 1991. As a player, he caught just 102 balls in 114 games with a season high of 32 catches in 1990. A year after retiring from playing, Mularkey coached the line for Concordia College in 1993. Subsequently, Sam Wyche hired him as tight ends coach in Tampa in 1994. After two years with the Bucs, Mike switched to the Steelers under Bill Cowher in 1996. In Pittsburgh, Mularkey coached the tight ends for five years and then was promoted to offensive coordinator in 2001. Working with Kordell Stewart and Tommy Maddox, Mike twice had the Steelers in the top 10 in scoring between 2001 and 2003. While opening up the passing game, he continued Cowher's affection for gadget plays in an imaginative offense.

Mularkey's success in Pittsburgh was noticed by Buffalo GM Tom Donahoe, who previously worked for the Steelers. He hired Mike as the Bills' head coach in 2004 and the club reached the brink of the playoffs that year with a 9–7 record behind Drew Bledsoe. In that first year, Buffalo finished seventh in scoring and eighth in fewest points allowed. In 2005, though, the club released Bledsoe and drafted J.P. Losman in the first round. Mularkey split the quarterbacking between Losman and Kelly Holcomb, but neither was any good. Both the offense and defense dropped to 24th in scoring as the Bills sunk to 5–11. Donahoe was fired and replaced by returning octogenarian Marv Levy.

Mularkey was not happy with the direction of the franchise and felt he did not have enough input to improve his chances on the field so he shocked everyone by resigning. Linebacker Takeo Spikes told ESPN Radio, "I don't really understand what's going on but I thought he did some things well and there were a lot of things a lot of the guys didn't agree with. I don't think he was a bad coach."

Mike returned to his hometown and was hired by Nick Saban as the Dolphins' offensive coordinator in 2006 who said, "It was clear that his teams always played hard and were well-coached in all aspects of the game. He instilled in his players a sense of belief in his system, and those leadership skills will serve him well in his new role." However, in Miami, Mularkey was working with Joey Harrington, Daunte Culpepper and Cleo Lemon at quarterback and the Dolphins finished 29th in scoring. Saban left for Alabama in 2007 and was replaced by Cam Cameron who demoted Mike to tight ends coach and ran the offense himself on the 1–15 team.

Mularkey escaped to Atlanta as offensive coordinator under Mike Smith in 2008. There he established a consistent run-oriented offense behind quarterback Matt Ryan and runner Michael Turner and rehabilitated his image as a potential NFL head coach. Mike received a second chance when he was hired by the Jaguars as head coach for 2012.

MUNCHAK, MICHAEL A. (MIKE) 3/6/1960– Penn State. Played G for the Oilers/Titans from 1982 to 1993. *Apprenticeship:* Pro asst.—17 years. *Roots:* Jack Pardee, Jeff Fisher. *Branches:* None. *Coordinators/Key Assistants:* Chris Palmer ran the offense, while Jerry Gray handled the defense. *Hall of Fame Players:* None. *Primary Quarterbacks:* Matt Hasselbeck. *Record:* **Hall of Fame Player.** *Tendencies:* • His team scored 20.3 points and allowed 19.8 per game • His team ran 38.2% of the time, which was 89% of the league average • One starting quarterbacks in one year; 100% of starts to primary quarterback • Three rookie starters in one year • Winning Full Seasons to Losing Full Seasons: 1:0.

The epitome of a hard-working offensive lineman, Mike Munchak of Scranton, Pennsylvania played for Penn State under the legendary Joe Paterno from 1978 to 1981 and was a second team All-American. Drafted first by the Oilers in 1982, Mike played guard in Houston for 12 years, went to nine Pro Bowls, was

Mularkey, Michael R. (Mike)									
Year	Team	Games	Wins	Losses	Ties	%	P Wins	P Losses	P %
2004	Bills	16	9	7	0	.563	0	0	.000
2005	Bills	16	5	11	0	.313	0	0	.000
2 years		32	14	18	0	.438	0	0	.000

Munchak, Michael A. (Mike)									
Year	Team	Games	Wins	Losses	Ties	%	P Wins	P Losses	P %
2011	Titans	16	9	7	0	.563	0	0	.000
1 year		16	9	7	0	.563	0	0	.000

All Pro four times and was elected to the Hall of Fame in 2001.

Munchak went directly from the trenches to the sideline, retiring in 1994 to join the Oilers' coaching staff. After three years as offensive quality control, Mike was named line coach in 1997 and remained in that position on Jeff Fisher's staff for Oilers and Titans for 14 years, regularly molding solid and steady offensive lines. When Fisher resigned in 2011 after 17 years as head coach, Munchak was named his replacement in his 30th year with the franchise, declaring, "I can't tell you how excited I am to be the next head coach of the Tennessee Titans. [Joe Paterno] is probably the guy I've learned the most from — his discipline, the way he ran the team. He commanded the room and the practice field. He was very hands-on and involved. I'm hoping to instill some of the things I learned from him here."

Given the number of players that Paterno sent to the NFL and the number of times that he was courted to move to the NFL, it is surprising that Munchak is the first Paterno-coached Nittany Lion to become an NFL head coach. When Paterno was forced out at Penn State late in the year, Munchak was linked to the job. However, Mike indicated he preferred to stay in Tennessee where he led the Titans to a winning record in his first year while surprisingly throwing the ball 11% more than the league average. Whether he can approach the success of either Paterno at Penn State or Jeff Fisher in Tennessee will be his challenge.

NEALE, ALFRED E. (GREASY) 11/5/1891–11/2/1973. West Virginia Wesleyan. Played E for Canton, Dayton and Massillon before the NFL was formed. *Apprenticeship:* College coach — 23 years (16 as head coach); semipro head coach —1 year. *Roots:* None. *Branches:* Charley Ewart. *Coordinators/Key Assistants:* John Kellison coached the line, Larry Cabrelli the ends and Charley Ewart the backs. *Hall of Fame Players:* Chuck Bednarik, Pete Pihos, Steve Van Buren, Alex Wojciehowicz. *Primary Quarterbacks:* Tommy Thompson. *Record:* **Hall of Fame Coach**; NFL

Championships 1948, 1949. *Tendencies:* • His teams scored 23 points and allowed 16.6 per game • His teams ran 67.3% of the time, which was 111% of the league average • Three starting quarterbacks in 10 years; 70% of starts to primary quarterback • 22 rookie starters in 10 years • Winning Full Seasons to Losing Full Seasons: 7:2.

Greasy Neale was a multisport figure who achieved the unique trifecta of playing in a World Series, coaching a Rose Bowl game and coaching an NFL championship team. He also was his team's leading scorer in basketball in college and an able golfer and bridge player as well. Neale grew up in Parkersburg, West Virginia where he was given the odd nickname of Greasy as a child. He was a three-sport athlete at West Virginia Wesleyan from 1912 to 1914 and also played some minor league baseball in Canada in 1914. He fully began his professional career in 1915 as an outfielder for three teams in the minor leagues. He moved up to the majors with the Cincinnati Reds in 1916 and played for them through 1922, with a return appearance in 1924. Overall, he batted .259, but in the tainted 1919 World Series, Neale batted .357 for the victorious Reds. He also spent 21 games with the Phillies in 1921. Simultaneously, Greasy began playing professional football for the Canton Bulldogs in 1917 on the recommendation of his former Wesleyan teammate John Kellison. The ever-loyal Kellison would go on to serve as Neale's line coach at every coaching stop except for West Virginia. Greasy then coached and

Head-to-Head:

Hall of Fame Opponent	Regular Season	Postseason
Paul Brown	0–2	0–0
Jimmy Conzelman	2–2	1–1
Ray Flaherty	0–4	0–0
George Halas	1–5	0–0
Curly Lambeau	2–3	0–0
Steve Owen	10–9–1	0–0
Total	15–25–1	1–1

Neale, Alfred E. (Greasy)

Year	Team	Games	Wins	Losses	Ties	%	P Wins	P Losses	P %
1941	Eagles	11	2	8	1	.227	0	0	.000
1942	Eagles	11	2	9	0	.182	0	0	.000
1943	Eagles	10	5	4	1	.550	0	0	.000
1944	Eagles	10	7	1	2	.800	0	0	.000
1945	Eagles	10	7	3	0	.700	0	0	.000
1946	Eagles	11	6	5	0	.545	0	0	.000
1947	Eagles	12	8	4	0	.667	1	1	.500
1948	Eagles	12	9	2	1	.792	1	0	1.000
1949	Eagles	12	11	1	0	.917	1	0	1.000
1950	Eagles	12	6	6	0	.500	0	0	.000
10 years		111	63	43	5	.590	3	1	.750

played for the Dayton Triangles in 1918 and played for the Massillon Tigers in 1919.

His football coaching career began at this same time by serving as the head coach for 2–4–1 Muskingum College in 1915 before moving on to his alma mater from 1916 to 1917, posting a 10–8 record. He then coached Marietta to a 13–1 record from 1919 to 1920, missing the first two games of 1919 because of the World Series. Neale took over the Washington & Jefferson team in 1921 and produced an undefeated season in his first year. He only spent two seasons there, but led the Presidents to the 1922 Rose Bowl where the tiny Pennsylvania college tied mighty California 0–0. On the strength of his 16–3–2 two-year record, Greasy was hired to coach the Virginia Cavaliers in 1923 and compiled a 28–22–5 record from 1923 to 1928. He also coached Virginia's baseball team but resigned from both jobs in 1929 to become third base coach on the St. Louis Cardinals baseball team. Neale dropped down to the minors in 1930 to managed a baseball team in Clarksburg before returning to football that fall as coach of the Ironton Tanks, a powerful independent team in Ohio. Tank's tailback Glenn Presnell told Chris Willis in *Old Leather,* "He was an innovator with the Tanks. He started looping his linemen, which was a new innovation at the time, but quite common now. Instead of charging straight ahead, Neale had us looping around to try and fool the blockers on offense." Greasy even appeared in one game with Ironton at age 39.

Greasy subsequently was hired by West Virginia as head football coach in 1931, but could coax only a 12–16–3 record from the Mountaineers from 1931 to 1933. His most famous pupil at WVU was Ben Schwartzwalder who would later coach Syracuse throughout the 1950s and 1960s. Neale moved on to Yale in 1934 and spent the next seven years in New Haven as Ducky Pond's backfield coach. Although Greasy was originally considered for the head coaching job, the Elis would only hire a Yale alumnus as head coach. Finally, in 1941 Neale got his opportunity to coach in the NFL when Yale alumnus Lex Thompson purchased the Philadelphia franchise and hired him as head coach. The Eagles were a weak team that had never had a winning season. The only player Greasy inherited who would still be on the team when it reached the title game seven years later was Tommy Thompson, a one-eyed, slow-footed single wing tailback. What made Neale's task even tougher was that Uncle Sam started drafting all able-bodied men for World War II the next year. Slowly and steadily, Greasy assembled the team he wanted, but the final pieces wouldn't arrive until the war ended and such players as new ace T formation quarterback Tommy Thompson, halfback Bosh Pritchard, halfback Russ Craft, end Pete Pihos and fullback Joe Muha came home.

Neale had a gruff and crude exterior on the foot-ball field that shocked some of his players at first. However, he reached out to them and became part of their lives as a friend. Linebacker Alex Wojciehowicz told Myron Cope for *The Game that Was,* "Greasy had a dual personality, which to me is what a successful coach must have. He's got to be a no-good son of a gun on the field and a great guy off the field. On the field, Greasy was God Almighty. Off the field, a terrific man." Greasy and his club got along so well that Eagle players would openly argue with Neale on the field without him losing any control over the direction of the team. Sometimes when Neale would lose his temper, certain players like Piggy Barnes would imitate Greasy's wife and wag their fingers at him, saying, "Now Earle, be careful." His players were continually amazed at Neale's perceptiveness in picking out flaws in their play and relied on him to make them better. He was so close to them that someone like quarterback Thompson could cajole Greasy into closing down practice early so they could go play golf together.

As a coach, Neale moved quickly to learn the Bears T formation by obtaining a copy of the newsreel footage of Chicago's 73–0 thrashing of the Redskins in the 1940 title match. Greasy ran that film back and forth hours a day for months in Thompson's office to implement what he saw as the offense of the future. He told *Sports Illustrated,* "I made some alterations, of course, gave it some outside running strength. It was the T adapted to our horses that won us three division titles and our two NFL championships." Guard Bucko Kilroy maintained that while the Bears relied on deception, the Eagles T was more of a power running offense. With Neale signaling in plays from the sidelines using baseball-style signals, Philadelphia ran more than two-thirds of the time, 11% more than the league average. Defensively, he was an innovator who devised the 5–4–2 "Eagle "defense to counter that same T formation, and the foundation of his championship teams was their defense. Greasy is also credited with developing such now common practices as man-to-man pass defense, the nine-man goal line defense, the fake reverse and the triple reverse.

Neale's decade in Philadelphia saw one of the greatest transformations in NFL history. Greasy's Eagles were in the top two in scoring five times and in points allowed four times, leading each category twice. The Eagles of the 1940s were a boisterous, hard-hitting crew that overpowered teams on both offense and defense. After losing the 1947 championship game to the Cardinals on an icy field in Chicago, Philadelphia won the 1948 and 1949 titles, both time by shutouts. Each game was played in bad weather—1948 in a blizzard against the Cardinals and 1949 in a rainstorm against the Rams. The ever-confident and buoyant Neale raised the possibility of a three-peat to the *Philadelphia Inquirer,* "I don't see why our boys can't do it again. Who is there to beat us?"

After three consecutive championship game appearances, 1950 was a major letdown for the Eagles right from the start when the All America Football Conference champion Cleveland Browns crushed Philadelphia 35–10 on opening day. The team rallied to win their next five games, but without a healthy Steve Van Buren to rely on, they lost five of their last six as the aging banged-up offense could not get the job done—although only one loss was by more than six points. Things came to a head late in the year after a 7–3 loss to the Giants when James Clark, head of the "100 Brothers" syndicate that had purchased the team in 1949, barged in the locker room to berate Neale in front of his players. Greasy told him off and was let go at the end of the disappointing season. While Neale probably was loyal to his aging veterans a bit too long, it was a sad end to a triumphant era in Eagle football.

Greasy's place in the hearts of his players was expressed at the time by tackle Al Wistert who wrote in a letter to the coach that was partially reprinted in Neale's three-part life story run in *Collier's* in 1951, "Greasy is fair, square and honest, he will never let a friend or player down when that person really needs help.... My father was killed when I was five years old. For many years I wondered what sort of man my dad would have been. I know now. My dad would have been an awful lot like Greasy Neale, I'm sure—as strong in his convictions as the Rock of Gibraltar, as honest as the day is long, yet tolerant and forgiving.... I'll never forget your teachings, Greasy for I feel that I'm a better man today for having known you." In retirement, Neale lived in New York and Florida and kept a close eye on his protégé Allie Sherman who had played backup quarterback for the Eagles in the 1940s before being named head coach of the Giants in 1961. Neale was elected to the College Football Hall of Fame in 1967 and the Pro Football Hall of Fame in 1969. He died at age 81 in 1973.

NEVERS, ERNEST A. (ERNIE) 6/11/1902–5/3/1976. Stanford. Played FB for the Duluth Eskimos from 1926 to 1927 and the Chicago Cardinals from 1929 to 1931. *Apprenticeship:* None. *Roots:* None. *Branches:* Phil Handler. *Coordinators/Key Assistants:* Phil Handler coached the line. *Hall of Fame Players:* Johnny Blood

McNally, Walt Kiesling. *Primary Quarterbacks:* None. *Record:* **Hall of Fame Player**; Began as **Player-Coach**. *Tendencies:* • His teams scored 9.8 points and allowed 15.8 per game • His teams ran 56.5% of the time, which was 88% of the league average • Eleven rookie starters in four years • Winning Full Seasons to Losing Full Seasons: 1:3.

Ernie Nevers was born in Willow River, Minnesota, but his family moved to Santa Rosa, California when he was a senior in high school. He was such a star performer, that Santa Rosa renamed its football field Nevers Field in 1925. By that time, Ernie was an All-American fullback at Stanford, whose renowned coach, Pop Warner, retooled his single wing offense to a double wing to take full advantage of Nevers' skills. Warner would later compare Ernie to the other great player he coached, Jim Thorpe, "Nevers could do everything Thorpe could do and Ernie always tried harder. Ernie gave 60 minutes of himself in every game." Indeed, Nevers played the 1925 Rose Bowl against Notre Dame's Four Horsemen with broken bones in both ankles.

In 1926, Ernie turned pro, but in three sports, not just one. He began a disappointing three-year pitching career with the St. Louis Browns in which he would compile a 6–12 record with a 4.64 ERA; he also gave up two of Babe Ruth's 60 home runs in 1927. In basketball, he played for the Chicago Bruins of the American Basketball League in 1926. However, he made his greatest impact on the football field. Nevers was the NFL's answer to Red Grange who had formed his own professional league in 1926. Ernie signed with his old friend Ole Haugsrud who was running the Duluth Eskimos coached by Dewey Scanlon. With Nevers, Duluth embarked on a 29-game national barnstorming tour that emulated the Bears' famous tour with Grange in 1925. Even more remarkable was the fact that Ernie missed only 26 minutes out of those 29 games. After a second year with Duluth in which he also served as coach, Nevers returned to Stanford as an assistant coach in 1928.

The Cardinals brought him back to the NFL in 1929, reuniting him with Duluth's Haugsrud and Scanlon, and Ernie set a record that still stands on Thanksgiving of that year when he scored six touchdowns and 40 points in a victory over the Bears.

Nevers, Ernest A. (Ernie)									
Year	Team	Games	Wins	Losses	Ties	%	P Wins	P Losses	P %
1927	Duluth Eskimos (defunct)	9	1	8	0	.111	0	0	.000
1930	Cardinals	13	5	6	2	.462	0	0	.000
1931	Cardinals	8	5	3	0	.625	0	0	.000
1939	Cardinals	11	1	10	0	.091	0	0	.000
4 years		41	12	27	2	.317	0	0	.000

Nevers also played minor league baseball that year for the San Francisco Missions. Scanlon was fired in 1930, so Ernie served as the Cardinals player-coach from 1930 to 1931 with moderate success. He went back to Stanford in 1932 as an assistant coach again through the 1935 season. Lafayette hired Nevers as head coach in 1936, but after a 1–8 season he was released. Ernie spent 1937–1938 as Iowa's backfield coach before Charley Bidwill hired him as the new Cardinals' head coach in 1939, saying, "As a coach, he has had extensive experience in both professional and college football and he established himself firmly in the affection of Cardinal followers when he starred for and coached the team." His tenure in Chicago was brief and got off to a bad start when he threw Cardinals' star receiver Gaynell Tinsley off the practice field before the season. Tinsley decided he'd rather take a 50% cut in pay and coach high school football than deal with Nevers and sat out the year. The 1–10 Cards finished last both in scoring and points allowed, and Ernie mailed his resignation to Bidwill in February 1940.

Nevers worked for a distiller for the next two years and then joined the Marines where he served as a captain from 1942 to 1945. Although he had plans to seek an NFL team for San Francisco after the war that didn't come to fruition. Rather, he worked as the backfield coach of the Chicago Rockets of the All America Football Conference for part of 1946 before leaving football. In the ensuing years, he worked in public relations for a winery and later became the vice president of the California Clippers of the National Professional Soccer League in 1967. In addition, Ernie officiated local football games and served as the 49ers' radio analyst for several years. Both his son Gordy and grandson Tom played minor league baseball. He died in San Rafael at the age of 73 in 1976.

NIXON, MICHAEL R. (MIKE) 11/21/1911–9/22/2000. Pittsburgh. Played HB for the Pittsburgh Pirates in 1935 and Brooklyn Dodgers in 1942. *Apprenticeship*: College asst.— 6 years; pro asst.—14 years. *Roots*: Mike Getto, Jock Sutherland, John Michelosen, Joe Kuharich. *Branches*: Bill McPeak, Abe Gibron, Ernie Hefferle. *Coordinators/Key Assistants*: For both teams, Nixon handled his own offense and relied on Torgy Torgeson to run the defense. *Hall of Fame Players*: John Henry Johnson. *Primary Quarterbacks*: Ralph

Guglielmi, Bill Nelsen. *Tendencies:* • His teams scored 14.9 points and allowed 27.8 per game • His teams ran 54% of the time, which was 103% of the league average • Five starting quarterbacks in three years; 71% of starts to primary quarterbacks • Ten rookie starters in three years • Winning Full Seasons to Losing Full Seasons: 0:3.

Born in the Pittsburgh suburb of Masontown, Mike Nicksick was another protégé of the renowned coach Jock Sutherland. Jock was so influential in his life that Mike changed his name to "Nixon" on Jock's recommendation that it would make him more palatable as a potential coach for ethnic-averse Southern colleges in the 1940s.

Nixon played halfback for Sutherland at Pitt from 1932 to 1934 and was an All-American in his senior year. He spent one year playing for the hometown Pirates in the NFL before returning to his alma mater in 1936 as an assistant coach. He also briefly played third base in the minor leagues at this time. When Jock left for the NFL himself in 1939, Nixon stayed at Pitt for a year and then switched to West Virginia as an assistant from 1940 to 1941. In 1942, he joined another Pitt alumnus, Mike Getto, in Brooklyn as backfield coach and also was forced to suit up at halfback for three games because the team was short of manpower.

Nixon went into the Navy from 1943 to 1945 until returning to football in 1946 as an assistant to Sutherland with the Steelers. Nixon remained on the Steelers' staff for six seasons: two under Sutherland and then four under his successor John Michelosen, another Pitt alum. During this time, Mike also served as a state senator from 1948 to 1950. When Michelosen was fired in 1952, Nixon moved on to the Cardinals as an assistant to Joe Kuharich. Nixon had gotten to know Kuharich when Joe served as Sutherland's line coach on the Steelers in 1946. Nixon would work on Kuharich's staff for the next seven years, one in Chicago and six for the Washington Redskins.

When Kuharich resigned from Washington to take the coaching job at his alma mater, Notre Dame, in 1959, Nixon was promoted to head coach. Mike said of his volatile boss, George Preston Marshall, "I have been around this organization six years and I think I know the Old Man pretty well. I like him, and I consider him to be a reasonable man." As for the team, Nixon's response was succinct, "Great potential;

Nixon, Michael R. (Mike)									
Year	*Team*	*Games*	*Wins*	*Losses*	*Ties*	*%*	*P Wins*	*P Losses*	*P %*
1959	Redskins	12	3	9	0	.250	0	0	.000
1960	Redskins	12	1	9	2	.167	0	0	.000
1965	Steelers	14	2	12	0	.143	0	0	.000
3 years		38	6	30	2	.184	0	0	.000

no depth." Mike was a dapper man on the sidelines, wearing a bow tie like Sid Gillman. He was also known for being a very nice guy who was much easier on the players than Kuharich, probably too nice. After just four wins in two years, though, Nixon was fired. He came back to Pittsburgh one more time in 1961 when Buddy Parker hired him as an assistant. Mike coached the Steelers' backs for four years until Parker abruptly quit two weeks before the start of the 1965 season. Owner Art Rooney offered Mike the job, but at the same time asked him not to take it. Rooney liked Nixon and told him that if he couldn't turn around the aging team in a year, he would be let go. Rooney even offered him lifetime employment elsewhere in the organization instead of the head coaching job. Still, Nixon wanted to coach his hometown team.

As expected, 1965 was a complete disaster on the field. Nixon summed up the season before he was fired at year's end, "I came into the situation under adverse conditions. We had 24 new players and 23 players were injured. You can't win when you have such injuries, especially to your quarterback and key offensive linemen. This season was a tragedy." In three years as a head coach, Nixon's teams were last in scoring all three years and last in points allowed two times.

Nixon was hired in 1966 as an assistant on the Eagles under Joe Kuharich again. When Kuharich was fired in 1969, Mike took a scouting job with Cleveland that led to his being named director of college scouting in 1974. He remained in that position until retiring in the 1980s.

NOLAN, MICHAEL (MIKE) 3/7/1959– Oregon. DB; did not play professionally. *Apprenticeship:* College asst.—6 years; pro asst.—18 years. *Roots:* Dan Reeves, Norv Turner, Al Groh, Brian Billick. *Branches:* Mike McCarthy, Mike Singletary, Jim Tomsula (i). *Coordinators/Key Assistants*: Mike McCarthy then Norv Turner then Jim Hostler, then Mike Martz ran the offense, while Billy Davis then Greg Manusky handled the defense. *Hall of Fame Players:* None. *Primary Quarterbacks:* Alex Smith. *Tendencies:* • His teams scored 16.6 points and allowed 25.5 per game • His teams ran 44.8% of the time, which was 101% of the league average • Eight starting quarterbacks in four years; 55% of starts to primary quarterback • Eleven rookie starters in four years • Winning Full Seasons to Losing Full Seasons: 0:3.

Baltimore's Mike Nolan was born into his profession, being the son of former NFL player and coach Dick Nolan. Mike played safety at Oregon for Rich Brooks, who had coached the secondary for Dick on the 49ers, and then served as a graduate assistant for the Ducks' football team in 1981 to begin his coaching career. He moved on in 1982 to become the linebackers coach at Stanford under Paul Wiggin, who also previously coached under Mike's father with the 49ers. After two years in Palo Alto, Nolan spent 1984 at Rice and 1985–1986 at LSU under Bill Arnsparger.

Mike was given a leg up to the pros by Dan Reeves in 1987. Reeves had played for the Cowboys when Dick Nolan was Tom Landry's first lieutenant in Dallas. Mike spent six years as the linebackers coach in Denver and was one of just two coaches, along with former Dallas safety Charley Waters, to survive a purge of the defensive coaches by Reeves in 1989. When Reeves was named head coach of the Giants in 1993, he brought Nolan with him as defensive coordinator.

Reeves left for Atlanta in 1997 and offered Mike the defensive coordinator job, but Nolan wanted to push out on his own after 10 years together. He joined the Redskins' staff of another former Oregon alumnus, Norv Turner, from 1997 to 1999. After Turner was fired, Mike took the defensive coordinator position under Al Groh with the Jets, but Groh bolted after just one season. Nolan then returned to his hometown of Baltimore in 2001 as the receivers coach for the defending champions. Defensive coordinator Marvin Lewis subsequently left in 2002, and Brian Billick promoted Nolan over defensive line coach Rex Ryan to succeed Lewis.

Three years later, Mike was hired as head coach of the 49ers, 37 years to the day after San Francisco hired his father as head coach. Mike credited his father's influence, "He was the one who taught me that football was a people business and not just an Xs and Os business." He added, "It's been proven again and again in this league that you can turn around programs very fast. It's reasonable to think we can turn things around very quickly." Unfortunately, Nolan's tenure was doomed from his first bad decision. Holding the number one overall draft selection in 2005, Mike was faced with a choice between quarterbacks Alex Smith or Aaron Rodgers as the top pick. He went with Smith who has proved ordinary at best while the local hero,

Nolan, Michael (Mike)									
Year	Team	Games	Wins	Losses	Ties	%	P Wins	P Losses	P %
2005	49ers	16	4	12	0	.250	0	0	.000
2006	49ers	16	7	9	0	.438	0	0	.000
2007	49ers	16	5	11	0	.313	0	0	.000
2008	49ers	7	2	5	0	.286	0	0	.000
4 years		55	18	37	0	.327	0	0	.000

Rodgers, has gone on to become a star in Green Bay. Nolan told *Sports Illustrated*, "Nobody ever made us an offer for the pick, but if someone had thrown a lot at us, I'd have made a trade." Nolan compounded his error by changing his offensive coordinator each year and never giving Smith any continuity. Ultimately, his 49ers were a failure on both sides of the ball, finishing in the bottom three in scoring twice and in points allowed two times as well.

The most memorable thing about Mike's stint in San Francisco was his successful lobbying of the league in 2006 to allow him to honor his father by wearing a business suit on the field. Nolan insisted, "My father always projected an image of authority, and I wanted to honor him — the way he lived his life and his whole career as a coach." Nolan and Jags' coach Jack Del Rio wore suits manufactured by the league's official clothier, Reebok, in 2006 and 2007. Mike was fired in midseason 2008. He has gone on to serve as the defensive coordinator for Denver in 2009, Miami in 2010 and Atlanta in 2012.

NOLAN, RICHARD C. (DICK) 3/26/1932–11/11/2007. Maryland. Played DB for the Giants, Cardinals and Cowboys from 1954 to 1962. *Apprenticeship:* Pro asst.—6 years. *Roots:* Tom Landry. *Branches:* Ed Hughes, Ken Meyer, Paul Wiggin, Dick Stanfel (i), Jim Shofner (i), Rich Brooks. *Coordinators/Key Assistants:* For the 49ers, Ed Hughes then Dick Stanfel ran the offense, while Nolan then Paul Wiggin handled the defense; for the Saints, Ed Hughes ran the offense, while Paul Wiggin handled the defense. *Hall of Fame Players:* Bob Hayes, Jim Johnson, Dave Wilcox. *Primary Quarterbacks:* John Brodie, Steve Spurrier, Archie Manning. *Tendencies:* • His teams scored 20.3 points and allowed 20.7 per game • His teams ran 49.4% of the time, which was 92% of the league average • Seven starting quarterbacks in 11 years; 80% of starts to primary quarterbacks • 22 rookie starters in 11 years • Winning Full Seasons to Losing Full Seasons: 4:6.

Pittsburgh's Dick Nolan physically resembled rebellious actor James Dean, but professionally was Tom Landry's most devoted acolyte. He played halfback for Maryland before being drafted in the fourth round by the Giants in 1954, Landry's first year as defensive coach. Dick was converted to defensive back in New York and was a steady performer in the Giants' secondary from 1954 to 1956. Traded to the Cardinals in 1957, he was reacquired by New York in 1958 to play with the team for another four years. Frank Gifford said of him to *Sports Illustrated*, "He didn't have the physical talent to do it all. He just willed himself. He was tough — as good as there comes in that respect." He was so popular that his face adorned a Times Square billboard for Camel cigarettes for several years.

In 1962, he rejoined Landry in Dallas where Tom had gone in 1960 as the Cowboys first head coach. Dick was a player-coach for the team that year, but retired from playing in 1963 to focus on coaching. Over the next five years, Nolan was Landry's top assistant on defense, in charge of implementing Tom's Flex defense. "Everything I know in football I've learned from Tom Landry," he later told Red Smith for the *New York Times*. The Cowboys' success drew attention to Dick's work, and he was named head coach of the underachieving 49ers in 1968. Quarterback John Brodie recalled to the *San Francisco Chronicle*, "The chemistry began to change when Dick Nolan showed up. He was tough as any man I've ever known when it comes to effort expended." Linebacker Dave Wilcox added to the *Chronicle*, "Dick was a defensive strategist. He changed the attitude of the 49ers from what had been going on there for a while. It was a lot more detailed than what we had done prior to him coming to the team." After two mediocre years implementing his system, San Francisco started a three-year run of division titles in 1970. Unfortunately each year they fell to Dallas in the playoffs as Nolan could not get past his mentor.

Dick told the *New York Times*, "Our defensive thoughts are very similar, very much like what I was

Year	Team	Games	Wins	Losses	Ties	%	P Wins	P Losses	P %
1968	49ers	14	7	6	1	.536	0	0	.000
1969	49ers	14	4	8	2	.357	0	0	.000
1970	49ers	14	10	3	1	.750	1	1	.500
1971	49ers	14	9	5	0	.643	1	1	.500
1972	49ers	14	8	5	1	.607	0	1	.000
1973	49ers	14	5	9	0	.357	0	0	.000
1974	49ers	14	6	8	0	.429	0	0	.000
1975	49ers	14	5	9	0	.357	0	0	.000
1978	Saints	16	7	9	0	.438	0	0	.000
1979	Saints	16	8	8	0	.500	0	0	.000
1980	Saints	12	0	12	0	.000	0	0	.000
11 years		156	69	82	5	.458	2	3	.400

Nolan, Richard C. (Dick)

taught when I worked under him as a player. Though I do it all my way, I've learned a lot from him. I was influenced by his beliefs and philosophy. We both play basically man-for-man and variations off a 4–3 lineup. I also use the multiple offense, but I don't use all the formations in every game like Tom does." Defensive end Cedric Hardman described the edge Landry had over Nolan in those three playoff losses to Tom Danyluk for *The Super '70s*, "He outcoached Dick in those games. I'm not saying that in a demeaning fashion.... Nolan was an introvert in those years and Tom was his closest friend. He talked to Landry all the time except for when we were getting ready to play the Cowboys. During that week, Dick didn't have anybody to talk to."

The last loss in 1972 when San Francisco gave up a 15-point fourth quarter lead to a vintage Roger Staubach comeback was the worst defeat of all, and the team never recovered from that. Brodie and other key players were aging. In Nolan's last three years by the Bay, he did not post a winning season, and he was fired after the 1975 campaign. In 1976, Dick's only connection to football was serving as an assistant coach at the annual College All Star Game, but he returned to the NFL in 1977 as the linebackers coach for the Saints under Hank Stram. Nolan then replaced Stram as head coach in 1978 with owner John Mecom grumbling, "The ex-coach came to me and told me he needed this man [Nolan] to take charge of the defense. And then all he did was sit in the corner. His impact was very limited." Dick delivered the Saints first non-losing season in 1979 with Archie Manning winning Offensive Player of the Year for leading the team to an 8–8 finish. Although it looked like New Orleans was finally headed in the right direction, everything went to hell the following season when the Saints dropped their first 12 games. Nolan was fired and his friend and line coach Dick Stanfel stepped in as interim coach. Allegedly decimated by rampant player drug use, this version of the Saints became known as the "Aints " with fans showing up at the Superdome wearing paper bags over their heads. Stanfel blistered the desultory club in his first team meeting by telling them that they "buried the best man they will ever know."

Nolan was hired by Ed Biles as defensive coordinator of the Oilers in 1981, but Houston ran a 3–4 defense, while Nolan had only run the 4–3 defense. A year later, Tom Landry brought Dick back to Dallas, and his second Cowboy stint extended beyond Landry's coaching tenure into the first two years of Jimmy Johnson. In 1991, Nolan retired from the NFL, but tried one season in the Arena League, leading the San Antonio Force to a 2–8 record in 1992. By then his son Mike was beginning to make a name for himself as a defensive coach in the pros. Mike eventually became the head coach of the 49ers like his dad,

but without his father's success. In Dick's final years, he was ravaged by Alzheimer's disease and prostate cancer and he died at the age of 75 in 2007 while his son was coaching the 49ers.

NOLL, CHARLES H. (CHUCK) 1/5/1932– Dayton. Played G/LB for the Browns from 1953 to 1959. *Apprenticeship:* Pro asst.—9 years. *Roots:* Sid Gillman, Don Shula. *Branches:* Bud Carson, Rod Rust, Tony Dungy, John Fox. *Coordinators/Key Assistants:* Noll ran his own offense then Tom Moore then Joe Walton handled it, while Walt Hackett then Dan Radakovich then Bud Carson then George Perles then Woody Widenhofer then Tony Dungy then Rod Rust then Dave Brazil ran the defense. *Hall of Fame Players:* Mel Blount, Terry Bradshaw, Dermonti Dawson, Joe Greene, Jack Ham, Franco Harris, Jack Lambert, John Stallworth, Lynn Swann, Mike Webster, Rod Woodson. *Primary Quarterbacks:* Terry Bradshaw, Bubby Brister, Mark Malone. *Record:* **Hall of Fame Coach;** Super Bowl Championships 1974, 1975, 1978, 1979. *Tendencies:* • His teams scored 21.2 points and allowed 18.2 per game • His teams ran 53.9% of the time, which was 107% of the league average • 13 starting quarterbacks in 23 years; 75% of starts to primary quarterbacks • 49 rookie starters in 23 years • Winning Full Seasons to Losing Full Seasons: 15:7.

Cleveland's Chuck Noll had as pure a pedigree as any head coach ever had when he was named head coach of the Steelers in 1968. After graduating from Dayton in 1953, he was drafted in the 20th round by his hometown team and played seven years under Paul Brown as a messenger guard on offense and linebacker on defense. He was such a quick study that Brown later said, "Chuck could have called the plays without any help from me, that's the kind of football student he was." On the Browns, Noll appeared in four title games and played for two championship teams. At 28, Noll retired as a player and joined Sid Gillman's first

Head-to-Head:		
Hall of Fame Opponent	Regular Season	Postseason
George Allen	1–0	0–0
Paul Brown	8–4	0–0
Weeb Ewbank	2–0	0–0
Joe Gibbs	0–3	0–0
Sid Gillman	3–1	0–0
Bud Grant	2–3	1–0
Tom Landry	4–3	2–0
Marv Levy	4–4	0–0
Vince Lombardi	0–1	0–0
John Madden	2–4	3–2
Don Shula	4–7	1–2
Hank Stram	2–2	0–0
Bill Walsh	2–2	0–0
Total	34–34	7–4

Chargers' coaching staff in 1960, being responsible for the defensive backfield. With the Chargers, Chuck coached in five AFL title games in six years with one victory. After Noll left for Don Shula's Colts' staff in 1966, Gillman never made the playoffs again. However, as Shula's defensive coach for three years, Noll oversaw a defense that finished third, second and first in points allowed. Baltimore, of course, swept to Super Bowl III in 1968 as massive favorites over the Jets, only to be unceremoniously upset by the AFL champions.

The day after that ignominious defeat, Noll was interviewed by the Rooneys for the Pittsburgh job and impressed them with his wide and deep knowledge of the Steelers and their problems on the field. The relatively anonymous Noll was not a popular choice with fans when he was hired; Chuck's choice for his first draft pick, Joe Greene, was even less popular and was greeted by newspaper headlines of "Joe Who?" Noll knew what he was doing, though, because the foundation of the 1970's Steel Curtain was Greene. With his background in defense, Chuck asserted, "I knew what you had to do to win. Number one, you had to not lose." Twice, Noll's Steelers allowed the fewest points in the league and six times finished in the top three.

Building slowly through the draft, Noll didn't have his first winning season until 1972, but over the remaining eight years of that decade, Pittsburgh went 86–27–1 and won four Super Bowls as the team of the 1970s. The coach repeatedly battled with his franchise

quarterback, Terry Bradshaw, visibly berating Terry on the sidelines at times and benching him for Terry Hanratty or Joe Gilliam at others. Chuck favored the run in general and ran the ball seven percent more than the league average, but he could be flexible. Once the pass defense rules changed in 1978 to free up the passing game, Noll unleashed Bradshaw to go to the air more often; Pittsburgh dropped from running the ball 61% of the time in 1978 to 52% in 1979 as the team won its final Super Bowl. After Bradshaw retired, though, Noll again put more emphasis on the run. That 1970s team is arguably the greatest team in NFL history, and their progression can be seen in their four Super Bowls.

Pittsburgh first made the playoffs in 1972 and won Noll's first postseason game in spectacular fashion on Franco Harris' "Immaculate Reception" against the rival Raiders, but then lost to the Dolphins the next week. In 1973, the Steelers lost to the Raiders in the first round of the playoffs, but the next year beat the Raiders in Oakland in the AFC championship to meet Minnesota in the Super Bowl. Pittsburgh's run-heavy offense and sledgehammer defense simply overpowered the Vikings that year. The Steelers repeated in 1975 by again beating Oakland in the AFC championship (this time on an icy field in freezing weather) before defeating the Cowboys in the Super Bowl. In that Super Bowl best remembered for Lynn Swann's athletic catches of Bradshaw's downfield passes, Noll

Noll, Charles H. (Chuck)

Year	Team	Games	Wins	Losses	Ties	%	P Wins	P Losses	P %
1969	Steelers	14	1	13	0	.071	0	0	.000
1970	Steelers	14	5	9	0	.357	0	0	.000
1971	Steelers	14	6	8	0	.429	0	0	.000
1972	Steelers	14	11	3	0	.786	1	1	.500
1973	Steelers	14	10	4	0	.714	0	1	.000
1974	Steelers	14	10	3	1	.750	3	0	1.000
1975	Steelers	14	12	2	0	.857	3	0	1.000
1976	Steelers	14	10	4	0	.714	1	1	.500
1977	Steelers	14	9	5	0	.643	0	1	.000
1978	Steelers	16	14	2	0	.875	3	0	1.000
1979	Steelers	16	12	4	0	.750	3	0	1.000
1980	Steelers	16	9	7	0	.563	0	0	.000
1981	Steelers	16	8	8	0	.500	0	0	.000
1982	Steelers	9	6	3	0	.667	0	1	.000
1983	Steelers	16	10	6	0	.625	0	1	.000
1984	Steelers	16	9	7	0	.563	1	1	.500
1985	Steelers	16	7	9	0	.438	0	0	.000
1986	Steelers	16	6	10	0	.375	0	0	.000
1987	Steelers	15	8	7	0	.533	0	0	.000
1988	Steelers	16	5	11	0	.313	0	0	.000
1989	Steelers	16	9	7	0	.563	1	1	.500
1990	Steelers	16	9	7	0	.563	0	0	.000
1991	Steelers	16	7	9	0	.438	0	0	.000
23 years		342	193	148	1	.566	16	8	.667

made a very odd decision with 1:28 to play. Pittsburgh faced a fourth-and-nine at the Cowboys 42 with a four point lead. Instead of punting, Noll trusted his defense more than his punt team and ran a futile running play to turn the ball over on downs. The Steel Curtain bailed him out with an interception to close out the win, but it was a gutsy call.

Injuries derailed the team in 1976 and 1977, but Pittsburgh returned to the Super Bowl against the Cowboys in 1978 and again outlasted a Roger Staubach fourth quarter comeback to win their third title. By 1979, the Steel Curtain was clearly slipping but the offense took up the slack to drive the team to its fourth championship on the strength of Terry Bradshaw's bombs to John Stallworth against the Rams. Beginning in 1980, though, the stars began to age and break down and were not adequately replaced through the draft. In Chuck's final 12 years as coach, the team reached 10 victories only once, although he may have done some of his best coaching with that mediocre talent. In particular, the 1989 Steelers were outscored 92–10 in their first two games, but recovered to go to the playoffs that year.

Above all, the low key Noll considered himself a teacher and detail-oriented organizer like his first mentor, Paul Brown. Chuck once said, "Basically, I am a private person. My thing is preparation and teaching and that's not a good story. I'm not a one-liner kind of guy. I'm not a comedian." He did not feel the need to try to motivate his players and did not have many rules off the field. He was detached and, some said, aloof and dour, but his personality and approach were best illustrated by the plaque he kept on his desk that quoted from Pope John XXIII, "See everything. Overlook a great deal. Improve a little."

Noll did his best to stay out of the limelight during his coaching career; he was a rarity among coaches in that he never had a television show. He continued that style after he retired in 1992 when he essentially dropped out of sight, content to pursue his expanse of interests, including wine, books, sailing, classical music and bird watching far out of the public eye. Because of this personal reticence, he is not as well recalled as the handful of other coaches with comparable accomplishments.

NORTH, JOHN P. 6/17/1921–7/6/2010. Vanderbilt. Played E for the Baltimore Colts from 1948 to 1950. *Apprenticeship:* College asst.—11 years; pro asst.—8

years. *Roots:* Joe Schmidt, J.D. Roberts. *Branches:* None. *Coordinators/Key Assistants:* Lamar McHan was the key offensive coach, while Bob Cummings handled the defense. *Hall of Fame Players:* None. *Primary Quarterbacks:* Archie Manning. *Tendencies:* • His teams scored 11.6 points and allowed 21.9 per game • His teams ran 55.5% of the time, which was 99% of the league average • Three starting quarterbacks in three years; 88% of starts to primary quarterback • Eleven rookie starters in three years • Winning Full Seasons to Losing Full Seasons: 0:2.

John North from Gilliam, Louisiana enrolled at Vanderbilt in 1941, but interrupted his college years to enlist in the Marines in 1943. He served overseas for three years and won a Purple Heart for being wounded helping to retake a Pacific Island. Returning to Vanderbilt after the war, John was named All-American in 1947. Although the Redskins had drafted him in 1945, he signed with the Colts of the All America Football Conference in 1948 and played end for them through their move to the NFL in 1950. North then coached high school ball for three years until he was hired as an assistant at Tennessee Tech in 1954. Two years later, he joined Blanton Collier's celebrated staff at Kentucky and stayed through 1961 when Collier was fired. Charley McClendon hired John for LSU in 1962, and he worked there for three years.

In 1965, North moved up to the pros by joining Joe Schmidt's staff in Detroit. John coached the Lions' receivers for eight years before being hired by J.D. Roberts in 1973 to be the Saints' offensive coordinator. However, midway through the preseason, New Orleans fired Roberts and promoted North to head coach. John announced, "I'm elated over the opportunity to get this thing going. It's going to take a little time. We have some good football players, but we don't have enough of them yet."

Three weeks later, though, after the Saints lost their opener to Atlanta 62–7, North was not so elated, "When you play like this, the Little Sisters of the Poor could beat you. They call themselves professional football players? You've got to be kidding me." Falcons' center Jeff Van Note felt that the Saints flat out quit in the first quarter. Saints' safety Tommy Myers later recalled to the *Atlanta Journal,* "Coach North came in and said, 'Don't any of you ever ask to be traded again. I just put the whole bunch of you on waivers and nobody wanted any of you guys.'"

North, John P.									
Year	Team	Games	Wins	Losses	Ties	%	P Wins	P Losses	P %
1973	Saints	14	5	9	0	.357	0	0	.000
1974	Saints	14	5	9	0	.357	0	0	.000
1975	Saints	6	1	5	0	.167	0	0	.000
3 years		34	11	23	0	.324	0	0	.000

North did get the team to show some improvement over the previous year's 2–11–1 record by posting back-to-back 5–9 records in 1973 and 1974, but when the team started 1975 1–5, he was fired. Leeman Bennett, who had coached with North on the Lions, hired John as an assistant in Atlanta in 1976, and the two were together for the next seven years on the Falcons. After Bennett was fired in 1983, North caught on as the quarterbacks coach for the New Orleans Breakers of the USFL in 1983 and then retired from football to sell real estate. He lived to the age of 89.

O'CONNOR, FRED 9/1/1939– East Stroudsberg State. Did not play professionally. *Apprenticeship:* College asst.—9 years; pro asst.—4 years; WFL asst.—1 year. *Roots:* Jack Pardee, Pete McCulley (i). *Branches:* Les Steckel, Frank Gansz. *Coordinators/Key Assistants:* O'Connor ran the offense, while Dan Radakovich handled the defense. *Hall of Fame Players:* O.J. Simpson. *Primary Quarterbacks:* Scott Bull. *Record:* **Interim Coach**.

Fred O'Connor from Oceanside, New York began his coaching career as the backfield coach at C.W. Post from 1965 to 1969 and then spent one-year terms at Villanova, Maryland, Southern Mississippi and back to Villanova in 1973 before joining Jack Pardee's staff on the Florida Blazers in the World Football League in 1974. Pardee brought Fred with him when he was named head coach of the Bears in 1975. As backfield coach, O'Connor was Walter Payton's first pro position coach and famously remarked, "The first time I saw Walter Payton in the locker room, I though God must have taken a chisel and said, 'I'm going to make me a halfback'" Fred stayed with Pardee for three years in Chicago, although when Sid Gillman was hired as offensive coordinator in 1977, he and Fred differed as to the team's offensive approach with O'Connor favoring a more conservative attack.

Pardee left Chicago for Washington in 1978, while O'Connor took a job as Pete McCulley's offensive coach in San Francisco in the second turbulent year of the Joe Thomas regime. With the team in complete disarray, Thomas fired McCulley nine games into the season and promoted Fred to interim coach of the 1–8 team. O'Connor posted a 1–6 record the rest of the way but was forced to go with receiver Freddie Solomon and defensive back Bruce Threadgill at quarterback in the season finale after both Steve DeBerg and Scott Bull went down to injuries. Still, O'Connor maintained after the season, "The whole situation can be rectified with just a little stability. The situation is the result of a lot of organizational instability over a number of years."

O'Connor rejoined Pardee as the Redskins backfield coach in 1979 and left when Jack was fired in 1981. Fred spent that year as the offensive coordinator of the Montreal Alouettes in Canada. He was out of football, working for Xerox in 1982 and 1983 and then resurfaced as the athletic director at Catholic University from 1984 to 1990, hiring himself as football coach in 1987. In a three-year stint as head coach at Catholic, O'Connor compiled a 17–13 record. He resigned from both posts in 1990, telling the *Washington Times*, "Of course my ultimate goal is returning to the NFL because it's the Mecca of coaching." That never worked out. Fred was out of football and semi-retired for the decade of the 1990s. In 2000, he joined Howard Schnellenberger's staff for the football startup program at Florida Atlantic University and spent seven years coaching there. Since 2006, he has worked as FAU's color analyst on radio. He was diagnosed with cancer in 2011.

OWEN, STEPHEN J. (STEVE) 4/21/1898–5/17/1964. Phillips. Played T for the Kansas City Blues, Hartford Blues, Kansas City Cowboys, Cleveland Bulldogs and New York Giants from 1924 to 1931 and in 1933. *Apprenticeship:* None. *Roots:* None. *Branches:* Ray Flaherty, Jim Lee Howell, Tom Landry, Allie Sherman. *Coordinators/Key Assistants:* Ray Flaherty was his first assistant; his brother Bill Owen then Red Smith were his main line coaches; Allie Sherman installed the T formation; Jim Lee Howell coached the ends; Tom Landry was a player-coach of the defense. *Hall of Fame Players:* Roosevelt Brown, Ray Flaherty, Benny Friedman, Frank Gifford, Mel Hein, Arnie Herber, Cal Hubbard, Tuffy Leemans, Ken Strong, Emlen Tunnell, Arnie Weinmeister. *Primary Quarterbacks:* Charlie Conerly. *Record:* **Hall of Fame Coach**; NFL Championships 1934, 1938. *Tendencies:* • His teams scored 16.7 points and allowed 14 per game • His teams ran 67.4% of the time, which was 108% of the league average • Five starting quarterbacks in six T formation years; 78% of starts to primary quarterback • 69 rookie starters in 23 years • Winning Full Seasons to Losing Full Seasons: 15:6.

Steve Owen was born in Cleo Springs in the Oklahoma Territory—before it was a state. He attended Phillips College between 1916 and 1921 as part of its Student Army Training Corps. After finishing

O'Connor, Fred									
Year	Team	Games	Wins	Losses	Ties	%	P Wins	P Losses	P %
1978	49ers	7	1	6	0	.143	0	0	.000
1 year		7	1	6	0	.143	0	0	.000

at Phillips, he worked in the oil fields and on a cattle ranch while also wrestling on the side. In 1924, the 5'10" 235-pound tackle returned to football with the Kansas City Blues and played for three other teams in the next two years before coach Leroy Andrews sold him to the Giants in 1926. Owen was a talented player and team captain who was named All-Pro in 1927 when the Giants won their first NFL championship. Two years later, owner Tim Mara bought the Detroit franchise to bring its celebrated passer Benny Friedman and coach Leroy Andrews to New York. One other Detroit Panther coming to the Giants was Steve's younger brother Bill who would play guard for the Giants for eight years, three times as an All-Pro. Bill also coached the Giants' Jersey City farm team from 1938 to 1940 and 1946–1947, winning three league titles and serving his brother as an assistant coach in between those stints.

With Leroy Andrews in charge from 1929 to 1930, the Giants went 26–5–1, but finished second each year to Green Bay. At the end of the 1930 season, Owen and Friedman led a players' revolt against Andrews who was ousted for the last two games of the year. Tim Mara then hired Owen as coach for 1931, claiming, according to Dave Klein in *The New York Giants*, "What I needed was a man's man. What I wanted was a man who could manage other men, a man other men would respect."

Steve would last for 23 years as coach and would establish the fundamental precepts of Giants football — a tough defense, a ball control offense and a reliable kicking game. George Halas once praised Owen by noting, "Steve was the first to stress the importance of defense and the advantage of settling for field goals instead of touchdowns. Every team strives today to do what Owen was doing twenty years ago." Four times, his Giants allowed the fewest points in the league and finished in the top three 10 times; 16 times, his teams were in the top three in turnover differential. The garrulous Owen was popular with the New York press and stated in his autobiography, "Coaching is a matter of fundamentals, the hardest kind of work and an understanding of human relations."

Owen was innovative with Xs and Os; he asserted in his book *My Kind of Football*, "I like to set up defenses. Defense is half the game, and neglecting it is just plain foolish. Mistakes cost you close games to

Head-to-Head:

HOF Opponent	Regular Season	Postseason
Paul Brown	4–4	0–1
Jimmy Conzelman	3–2	0–0
Ray Flaherty	8–5–1	0–0
George Halas	5–8	1–3
Curly Lambeau	14–12–2	1–2
Greasy Neale	9–10–1	0–0
Total	43–41–4	2–6

Owen, Stephen J. (Steve)

Year	Team	Games	Wins	Losses	Ties	%	P Wins	P Losses	P %
1931	Giants	14	7	6	1	.536	0	0	.000
1932	Giants	12	4	6	2	.417	0	0	.000
1933	Giants	14	11	3	0	.786	0	1	.000
1934	Giants	13	8	5	0	.615	1	0	1.000
1935	Giants	12	9	3	0	.750	0	1	.000
1936	Giants	12	5	6	1	.458	0	0	.000
1937	Giants	11	6	3	2	.636	0	0	.000
1938	Giants	11	8	2	1	.773	1	0	1.000
1939	Giants	11	9	1	1	.864	0	1	.000
1940	Giants	11	6	4	1	.591	0	0	.000
1941	Giants	11	8	3	0	.727	0	1	.000
1942	Giants	11	5	5	1	.500	0	0	.000
1943	Giants	10	6	3	1	.650	0	1	.000
1944	Giants	10	8	1	1	.850	0	1	.000
1945	Giants	10	3	6	1	.350	0	0	.000
1946	Giants	11	7	3	1	.682	0	1	.000
1947	Giants	12	2	8	2	.250	0	0	.000
1948	Giants	12	4	8	0	.333	0	0	.000
1949	Giants	12	6	6	0	.500	0	0	.000
1950	Giants	12	10	2	0	.833	0	1	.000
1951	Giants	12	9	2	1	.792	0	0	.000
1952	Giants	12	7	5	0	.583	0	0	.000
1953	Giants	12	3	9	0	.250	0	0	.000
23 years		268	151	100	17	.595	2	8	.200

teams, which, because of good defense, can take advantage of errors." During his time, the Giants were known for the special defenses Steve would devise to control superstars like Don Hutson and Sammy Baugh. In fact the "Umbrella" defense he drew up the first time New York faced the Browns in 1950 was the foundation on which Tom Landry devised the base 4–3 defense. Moreover, Owen was the first to keep his troops fresh by substituting virtually an entire unit each quarter and was the first to regularly elect to kick-off when winning the opening coin toss so that his defense could get on the field first. Owen also ran his own version of the single wing, the A formation, in which the line would be unbalanced to one side and the backfield weighted to the opposite side. And he always had a solid kicking game.

The team struggled a bit in Steve's first two years as coach but by 1933, the Giants became a perennial contender for the championship. From 1933 to 1946, New York compiled a 99–48–11 record and went to eight of the first 14 NFL title games. Much like later proponents of overly conservative football, though, Owen's Giants lost six of those eight championship matches. The first postwar year of 1946 brought not only Steve's final trip to a title game, but also scandal as Frankie Filchock and Merle Hapes were later suspended for having contact with gamblers before the championship game and not reporting it to authorities. From that point on, Owen's teams were just 41–40–3.

Time began to pass him by. He had to be pushed hard to move to the T formation and was one of the last coaches to do so, saying, "Offenses are like ladies hats. They run in cycles and always come back to basic principles. Maybe I'm just old-fashioned, but I haven't seen anything new in 15 years and that goes for the T formation or anything else you see." 1940s halfback George Franck told Baker and Corbett for *The Most Memorable Games in Giants History*, "Steve Owen only knew how to coach linemen and didn't like backfield coaching. He had no idea how to coach speed, and I was a speed guy."

In addition, Stout Steve was a disciplinarian who was described by his older players as being "good-hearted" and "down-to-earth." However, more modern players didn't look as kindly on his grumpy attitude. In his autobiography *The Whole Ten Yards*, Frank Gifford vividly remembered Owen as, "a fat snarly Oklahoman who dipped snuff—the juice would dribble onto his dirty rubber jacket—and stuck rigidly to

his 'old ways' of doing things." Owen, after all, felt, "This is essentially a game played by two men down in the dirt. The fellow who hits first and the hardest will usually be the winner."

Wellington Mara remembered the firing of Steve Owen, who never had a written contract in his 23 years as the Giants' head coach, as one of the worst days of his life. Owen himself never got over it. He coached the defense for George Sauer at Baylor in 1955 and then did the same for the Eagles in 1956 and 1957. Steve returned to the head coaching ranks in Canada in 1959 with Toronto and subsequently Calgary in 1960 and Saskatchewan from 1961 to 1962. Overall, he went 23–35–4 in Canada, but won Coach of the Year honors in 1962 for coaxing a winning season out of Saskatchewan. At the age of 65, Owen coached a semipro Syracuse team to an 0–12 record in 1963 before rejoining the Giants as a scout shortly before his death in 1964. He was elected to the Hall of Fame posthumously.

PALM, MYRON H. (MIKE) 11/26/1899–4/8/1974. Penn State. Played HB for the New York Giants in 1925 and 1926 and the Cincinnati Reds in 1933. *Apprenticeship:* College asst.—6 years. *Roots:* Al Jolley. *Branches:* None. *Coordinators/Key Assistants:* None. *Hall of Fame Players:* None. *Primary Quarterbacks:* None. *Record:* **Interim Player-Coach.**

Born in St. James, Minnesota, Mike Palm starred at Penn State in 1922 and 1923 and scored the Nittany Lions' only points in their 14–3 loss to USC in the 1923 Rose Bowl. In that game, he also set a Rose Bowl record with a 75-yard punt. In 1924, Georgetown coach Lou Little hired Palm as backfield coach and Mike worked there through 1929. He also appeared in three games at halfback for the New York Giants in 1925 and 1926 while he was coaching in D.C. Little was named head coach at Columbia in 1930, but Palm was passed over as his successor with the Hoyas. Mike also interviewed at Auburn and Penn State that year, but was turned down by each place, so he spent the next three years in the sporting goods industry.

Palm returned to the NFL in 1933 as a player and assistant coach for the expansion Cincinnati Reds. After the Reds got off to an 0–5–1 start under Al Jolley, Mike was appointed head coach for the balance of the season. Palm junked Jolley's Notre Dame Box offense and switched some players to different positions with the result being the Reds finishing the year on a 3–1 streak. Mike did not stay in Cincinnati the next year,

Palm, Myron H. (Mike)									
Year	Team	Games	Wins	Losses	Ties	%	P Wins	P Losses	P %
1933	Cincinnati Reds (defunct)	4	3	1	0	.750	0	0	.000
1 year		4	3	1	0	.750	0	0	.000

though. Rather, he went back to the college ranks in 1934 as an assistant at West Virginia and then moved on to coach the backs at Harvard in 1935.

In 1936, Palm returned to the professional game by buying into the new American Football League (AFL II) as co-owner of the Brooklyn Tigers with former Giants' star Harry Newman. Mike coached the team while Newman played, but Brooklyn never won a game and moved to Rochester by the end of the year. Palm and Newman continued in Rochester in 1937, but both the team and league folded by year's end. Mike's two-year coaching record in the AFL was just 3–9–2. He was out of football for the next few years until Steve Owen hired him as the Giants' backfield coach in 1941. Mike then went into the Navy during the war, but returned as New York's backfield coach in 1945 and 1946. In 1947, he moved back to Washington D.C. and opened Mike Palm's Tavern near the Library of Congress and the House office building. In fact, Palm's Tavern became known as the "Congressional Relaxitorium" in the post-war era for its regular clientele of congressmen and staffers. Palm moonlighted as an assistant coach at Georgetown again in 1948, but after that devoted himself to his restaurant for the rest of his life. His wife maintained the eatery through 1981, seven years after Mike's death.

PALMER, CHRIS 9/23/1949– Southern Connecticut State. QB; did not play professionally. *Apprenticeship:* College coach–15 years (4 as head coach); CFL asst.—1 year; USFL asst.—2 years; pro asst.—9 years. *Roots:* Jack Pardee, Bill Parcells, Tom Coughlin. *Branches:* Romeo Crennel, Ken Whisenhunt, Tony Sparano. *Coordinators/Key Assistants*: Palmer then Pete Carmichael, Sr., ran the offense, while Bob Slowik then Romeo Crennel handled the defense. *Hall of Fame Players:* None. *Primary Quarterbacks:* Tim Couch. *Tendencies:* • His teams scored 11.8 points and allowed 26.8 per game • His teams ran 37.7% of the time, which was 87% of the league average • Four starting quarterbacks in two years; 66% of starts to primary quarterback • 21 rookie starters in two years • Winning Full Seasons to Losing Full Seasons: 0:2.

When Mike Munchak hired Chris Palmer as the Titans' offensive coordinator in 2011, the new head coach noted, "The quarterback situation, we don't know what that's going to be. [Palmer's] been around a lot of great quarterbacks. He's done a great job developing a lot of guys in the league. He has a great de-

meanor for it." Indeed, Chris has helped develop Drew Bledsoe, Mark Brunell, Tony Romo and Eli Manning in the NFL, yet had less luck with protégés Tim Couch and David Carr. In Tennessee, he will work to bring Titans' rookie Jake Locker up to speed.

A native of Brewster, New York, Chris Palmer has taken a long and winding path through the coaching business. He played quarterback for Southern Connecticut State from 1968 to 1971 and then began his coaching career as an assistant at the University of Connecticut from 1972 to 1974. After a year at Lehigh and seven at Colgate, Palmer jumped to the CFL in 1983 as the Montreal Concordes' line coach. A year later, he joined Walt Michaels' New Jersey Generals' staff in the USFL, ascending to offensive coordinator in 1985.

Chris got his first opportunity as a head coach with the University of New Haven in 1986 where he installed the Run-and-Shoot offense. After posting a 16–4 record in two seasons, Palmer took over the Boston University program in 1988, but went just 8–14 in two years there. His Run-and-Shoot background brought him to the NFL in 1990 as the Oilers' receivers coach for the next three years. In 1993, Chris became a "Parcells' Guy" when he joined the Patriots' staff. After Parcells left New England, Palmer was hired by another former Parcells' assistant when Tom Coughlin, who named him Jacksonville's offensive coordinator in 1997. Two years later, the Browns were restarting as an expansion franchise and Vikings offensive coordinator Brian Billick was the top coordinator on their wish list, but Billick declined to be interviewed in Cleveland because he was interested in the Ravens' job. Rebuffed by Billick, the Browns turned to Palmer who realistically commented to *New York Times*, "When you're close to 50, your options start to dry up."

Palmer's main problem in Cleveland was that while he was telling *Sports Illustrated*, "No organization can fill all its needs in one year. It just takes time," GM Dwight Clark was telling the *New York Times*, "We need to be competitive in Year 2 or Year 3. We have higher expectations than the people outside this building." However, Clark and team president Carmen Policy, who both came over from the 49ers, were not supplying Chris much in terms of talent. They tried to rely on some seasoned veterans and a rookie quarterback, but the formula did not work because the veterans were washed up and top-drafted quarterback Tim Couch was overmatched and would never develop into a quality NFL signal caller. The

Palmer, Chris									
Year	Team	Games	Wins	Losses	Ties	%	P Wins	P Losses	P %
1999	Browns	16	2	14	0	.125	0	0	.000
2000	Browns	16	3	13	0	.188	0	0	.000
2 years		32	5	27	0	.156	0	0	.000

Browns lost their first game to Pittsburgh 43–0, which made Palmer's the worst NFL coaching debut since Weeb Ewbank's Colts lost to the Rams 48–0 in 1954. In his second season, Palmer told *Sports Illustrated*, "By the end of last season, we had seven rookies starting. Hopefully, they'll continue their growth, along with the others. What I've tried to tell everyone is that there's no substitute for learning on the field." With the offense scoring just 10 points per game and the defense giving up 26 in that second season, Chris was fired and out of football for a year.

A glutton for punishment, Palmer signed on as the expansion Houston Texans' offensive coordinator in 2002 and over the next four years got to work with another overall number one draft selection in David Carr who ultimately would flop as an NFL quarterback. When the Texans' entire coaching staff was fired in 2006, Chris was hired by the Cowboys as quarterbacks coach on Bill Parcells' staff. A year later, he moved on to the Giants as quarterbacks coach under Tom Coughlin again and won a Super Bowl ring. Palmer left New York after the 2009 season to become the head coach and GM of the Hartford Colonials of the developmental United Football League for one year until Munchak brought him back to the NFL in 2011.

PARCELLS, DUANE C. (BILL) 8/22/1941– Wichita State. LB; did not play professionally. *Apprenticeship:* College coach —15 years (1 as head coach); pro asst.— 4 years. *Roots:* Ray Perkins, Ron Erhardt. *Branches:* Bill Belichick, Ray Handley, Tom Coughlin, Chris Palmer, Al Groh, Romeo Crennel, Sean Payton, Eric Mangini, Tony Sparano, Todd Haley, Todd Bowles

(i). *Coordinators/Key Assistants:* For the Giants, Ron Erhardt ran the offense, while Parcells then Bill Belichick handled the defense; for the Patriots, Ray Perkins ran the offense, while Al Groh then Bill Belichick handled the defense; for the Jets, Ron Erhardt then Charlie Weis ran the offense, while Bill Belichick handled the defense; for the Cowboys, Maurice Carthon then Sean Payton then Todd Haley ran the offense, while Mike Zimmer handled the defense. *Hall of Fame Players:* Harry Carson, Curtis Martin, Lawrence Taylor, Andre Tippett. *Primary Quarterbacks:* Phil Simms, Drew Bledsoe, Vinny Testaverde. *Record:* Super Bowl Championships 1986, 1990. *Tendencies:* • His teams scored 21 points and allowed 18.9 per game • His teams ran 46.4% of the time, which was 102% of the league average • 19 starting quarterbacks in 19 years; 74% of starts to primary quarterbacks • 60 rookie starters in 19 years • Winning Full Seasons to Losing Full Seasons: 13:5.

Bill Parcells, the pride of Englewood, New Jersey, once told the *New York Times*, "One of the things I've always prided myself on is that if I did go someplace, when I left there it was a better operation." That was a true statement. After his initial NFL coaching foray with the Giants, Parcells took over four losing franchises and made them better. The Patriots had gone 14–50 in the four years before Parcells, including 2–14 the year before; he took them to a Super Bowl, and they have only had one losing season in the 15 years since he left. The Jets had gone 18–46 in the four years before Parcells and 1–15 in the year before; he took them to an AFC championship game and they have had just three losing seasons in the 12 years since then.

Parcells, Duane C. (Bill)									
Year	Team	Games	Wins	Losses	Ties	%	P Wins	P Losses	P %
1983	Giants	16	3	12	1	.219	0	0	.000
1984	Giants	16	9	7	0	.563	1	1	.500
1985	Giants	16	10	6	0	.625	1	1	.500
1986	Giants	16	14	2	0	.875	3	0	1.000
1987	Giants	15	6	9	0	.400	0	0	.000
1988	Giants	16	10	6	0	.625	0	0	.000
1989	Giants	16	12	4	0	.750	0	1	.000
1990	Giants	16	13	3	0	.813	3	0	1.000
1993	Patriots	16	5	11	0	.313	0	0	.000
1994	Patriots	16	10	6	0	.625	0	1	.000
1995	Patriots	16	6	10	0	.375	0	0	.000
1996	Patriots	16	11	5	0	.688	2	1	.667
1997	Jets	16	9	7	0	.563	0	0	.000
1998	Jets	16	12	4	0	.750	1	1	.500
1999	Jets	16	8	8	0	.500	0	0	.000
2003	Cowboys	16	10	6	0	.625	0	1	.000
2004	Cowboys	16	6	10	0	.375	0	0	.000
2005	Cowboys	16	9	7	0	.563	0	0	.000
2006	Cowboys	16	9	7	0	.563	0	1	.000
19 years		303	172	130	1	.569	11	8	.579

The Cowboys had gone 23–41 in the four years before Parcells; he brought them back to the playoffs for the first time in five years and they have had just one losing season in the five years since. The Dolphins had gone 20–44 in the four years before Parcells became GM, including 1–15 the year before; his handpicked coach Tony Sparano won 11 games with the team in the first season. Parcells has not won a Super Bowl since his time with the Giants, but he did turn around four downtrodden franchises. It is no wonder that before he quit New England, he memorably said, "If I'm going to be asked to cook the meal, I'd like to be able to pick the groceries."

Bill played linebacker at Wichita State and was drafted in the seventh round by Detroit in 1963 but was cut during training camp. The next year he began his coaching career at Hastings College as the linebackers coach. In 1965, he returned to his alma mater and then moved on to West Point in 1966. In his four years with Army, Parcells and rising basketball coach Bobby Knight became fast friends and have remained so ever since. The two crusty coaches appear to have much in common in their dealings with both with the players and the media. After leaving Army, Bill coached at Florida State from 1970 to 1972, Vanderbilt from 1973 to 1974 and Texas Tech from 1975 to 1977 (the latter two stops were under head coach Steve Sloan) before being named head coach at the Air Force Academy in 1978. Air Force went 3–8 that year, and Bill resigned to become the defensive coordinator of the Giants under Ray Perkins in 1979. Perkins caught passes from Steve Sloan when they were teammates at Alabama, so Parcells was not unfamiliar. However, because of family pressure, Parcells quit the Giants before the season started and spent the year working in real estate and hating it in Colorado. Ron Erhardt rescued Bill by hiring him as linebackers coach in New England in 1980 and then Perkins called him back to the Giants as defensive coordinator in 1981. Both Perkins and Erhardt would work for Parcells in the future.

After two years coaching a New York defense that was led by Lawrence Taylor, Bill got his break when Perkins quit to replace his mentor Bear Bryant at Alabama. By now, Parcells was known affectionately as the "Big Tuna" to the players, but the players' coach nearly was fired after winning just three games in his first year. He rededicated himself to succeed on his terms and turned the team around in his second season. After flirting with Scott Brunner, Bill committed himself to the much more talented Phil Simms at quarterback, and the Giants' glory years of smash-mouth football were born. Over the next seven years, New York went to the playoffs five times and won two Super Bowls behind the amalgamation of a marauding defense, dependable special teams and a pounding offensive attack. Five times his defense finished in the top three in fewest points allowed. His greatest

triumph came in 1990 when Simms was hurt late in the year and Bill rode backup quarterback Jeff Hostetler past the back-to-back champion 49ers on a late field goal to reach the Super Bowl. At that point Bill turned to offensive coordinator Ron Erhardt and said of the upcoming championship against the high flying Buffalo Bills, "Shorten the game," in other words, keep the ball out of the Bills' hands. In that memorable Super Bowl, the less talented Giants held the ball for more than two thirds of the game and eked out a thrilling championship by the narrow margin of a wide right missed field goal at the closing gun.

While some detractors point out that Parcells never won a Super Bowl without defensive genius Bill Belichick at his side, Parcells was clearly the ringmaster on this team. He told the *Times*, "I've always coached the same way. I really believe that players do what you make them do and they don't do what you don't make them do." Forever known as a motivator in the Lombardi mold, he added, "My feeling on players is this — if you find one thing to motivate them that might be all you need." Parcells was famous for the mind games he played with moody superstar Lawrence Taylor to draw out his Hall of Fame talent. Cowboys quarterback Tony Romo later marveled to *Sports Illustrated*, "It's amazing how deep he was able to get into your head."

Due to a heart condition, Parcells retired for the first time after the second Super Bowl and worked as a broadcaster in 1991 and 1992. He was courted by both Tampa and Green Bay in 1992 but stayed retired. Ray Perkins warned him of the meddling ownership in Tampa. Packers' GM Ron Wolf was an old friend of Bill's but probably held too much control for Parcells. Wolf later wrote of Bill in *The Packer Way*, "I like his honesty, his love of the history and integrity of the game and his intelligence." Finally, Parcells returned to coaching in 1993 with the woeful Patriots. In four years, he had them in the Super Bowl where they lost to the Wolf's Packers coached by Mike Holmgren. However, Bill did not even fly home with the team after the game. He and owner Robert Kraft were deeply divided over the direction of the organization, though, and Parcells resigned to take over the Jets. Kraft tried to block the move, and, after much wrangling, acquired four draft choices from New York for Bill's services.

Parcells transformed Rich Kotite's 1–15 team into a Super Bowl contender, but stepped down as coach of the Jets after three years and tried to appoint longtime acolyte Bill Belichick the new coach. However, Belichick felt trapped and bolted from the press conference to sign to coach the Patriots in 2000, while another assistant, Al Groh, took over the Jets. Parcells retired for the second time in 2001 and again worked as a TV analyst before taking over the Cowboys in 2003, but not before turning down the Bucs a second time in 2002. Bill rebuilt Dallas into a powerful perennial contender and even uncovered their quarterback of the future, undrafted free agent Tony Romo from obscure Eastern Illinois. Unfortunately, he was unable to win a playoff game in Dallas, though. Parcells retired for a third time in 2007, but then came back in 2008 as the Dolphins Vice President of Football Operations, helping to stabilize another floundering franchise before retiring for the fourth time.

Parcells lived by the dictum that success is never final, but failure can be. He put tremendous pressure on himself and his players to succeed and tended to burn out quickly at his later stops as a coach and GM. Even in New York, Bill was ready to jump to Atlanta in 1987, but the commissioner squelched the move since the restless Parcells was still under contract to the Giants. While not all his players bought into Bill's program, most did, and several followed him from team to team in his nomadic path. These tough and gritty players became known as "Parcells' Guys" and were one of the greatest legacies of one of the NFL's greatest coaches.

PARDEE, JOHN P. (JACK) 4/19/1936– Texas A&M. Played LB for the Rams and Redskins from 1957 to 1964 and 1966–1972. *Apprenticeship:* College asst.—1 year; pro asst.—1 year; WFL head coach—1 year. *Roots:* George Allen. *Branches:* Fred O'Connor (i), Joe Walton, Richie Petitbon, Jeff Fisher, Kevin Gilbride, Chris Palmer, Gregg Williams, Mike Munchak. *Coordinators/Key Assistants:* For the Bears, Fred O'Connor then Sid Gillman ran the offense, while Pardee ran his own defense; for the Redskins, Joe Walton ran the offense, while Doc Urich handled the defense; for the Oilers, Kevin Gilbride ran the offense, while Jim Eddy, then Buddy Ryan then Jeff Fisher handled the defense. *Hall of Fame Players:* Ken Houston, Art Monk, Warren Moon, Mike Munchak, Alan Page, Walter Payton, John Riggins. *Primary Quarterbacks:* Bob Avellini, Joe Theismann, Warren Moon. *Tendencies:* • His teams scored 19.8 points and allowed 18.2 per game • His teams ran 47.3% of the time, which was 94% of the league average • Ten starting quarterbacks in 11 years;

81% of starts to primary quarterbacks • 22 rookie starters in 11 years • Winning Full Seasons to Losing Full Seasons: 6:3.

For a man who once declared to the *Washington Post*, "I don't need to coach to live," Jack Pardee had a long and varied career coaching football. Jack was a head coach in the college ranks and in four different professional leagues — the WFL, NFL, USFL and CFL. Born in Exira, Iowa, Pardee moved with his family to Christoval, Texas, when he was nine. In the wide expanses of central Texas, he played six-man football in high school because the schools in that area were too small to support 11-man teams. He went on to Texas A&M where he was one of the famed "Juction Boys," as the survivors of Bear Bryant's punishing 10-day summer football boot camp of 1954 were known. Jack starred at fullback and linebacker for the Aggies from 1954 to 1956 before being drafted by the Rams in the second round in 1957.

Pardee played linebacker for the Rams from 1957 to 1970, aside from 1965 when he retired to work as an assistant coach at his alma mater one year after undergoing surgery on his arm for melanoma. Jack's last five years with Los Angeles were under Coach George Allen, and Allen then traded for Pardee to join the Over the Hill Gang in Washington when George was named head coach of the Redskins in 1971. Jack spent two more seasons as a player and one as an assistant coach before taking his first head coaching job with the Florida Blazers of the World Football League in 1974. Even though the Blazers went 14–6 and made it all the way to the championship game, neither Pardee nor the players were getting paid. After that desperate experience, Jack leaped at the chance to coach the Bears in 1975. His arrival coincided with the drafting of Walter Payton, and Pardee built his offense around Payton as the feature back. Jack brought in Sid Gillman as offensive coach in 1977, but Sid left after a year, frustrated by the conservative nature of Pardee's offense.

As it turned out, Jack left after the 1977 season as well. Once George Allen was fired in Washington,

Pardee, John P. (Jack)									
Year	*Team*	*Games*	*Wins*	*Losses*	*Ties*	*%*	*P Wins*	*P Losses*	*P %*
1975	Bears	14	4	10	0	.286	0	0	.000
1976	Bears	14	7	7	0	.500	0	0	.000
1977	Bears	14	9	5	0	.643	0	1	.000
1978	Redskins	16	8	8	0	.500	0	0	.000
1979	Redskins	16	10	6	0	.625	0	0	.000
1980	Redskins	16	6	10	0	.375	0	0	.000
1990	Oilers	16	9	7	0	.563	0	1	.000
1991	Oilers	16	11	5	0	.688	1	1	.500
1992	Oilers	16	10	6	0	.625	0	1	.000
1993	Oilers	16	12	4	0	.750	0	1	.000
1994	Oilers	10	1	9	0	.100	0	0	.000
11 years		164	87	77	0	.530	1	5	.167

Pardee resigned in Chicago to take over in his old haunts. Surprisingly, the Bears did not stand in his way despite Chicago making the playoffs in that year for the first time in 14 years. With the Redskins from 1978 to 1980, Jack faced a team in transition as the aging Over the Hill Gang began to retire, voluntarily or by force. Joe Theismann took over at quarterback for Billy Kilmer, and Pardee was forced to cut a lot of old friends. Kicker Mark Moseley told Thom Loverro for *Hail Victory*, "Guys like Ron McDole, who rode to work with Pardee every day. He had to cut Ron, and that was hard for him. That was his downfall in Washington, that he was such a nice guy that some of the guys who weren't real dedicated to the game took advantage of him and got away with a lot of stuff, and it really began to disrupt the team." In addition, Jack was feuding with GM Bobby Beathard who wanted the coach to rely more on the team's young draft picks. After a three-year record of 24–24, Pardee was fired and complained to the *Washington Post*, "When I took the Redskin job three years ago, the coach was the man primarily responsible for everything. Now, the owner of the team has exercised his prerogative to go in a different direction. Now, the primary responsibility lies with the general manager. The conditions of the job are not now what they were when I started. Don't tell me to win but then say, 'But you have to do it this way'"

Jack spent the 1981 season as Don Coryell's defensive coordinator in San Diego but without much success, so he dropped out of football to work in the oil business from 1982 to 1983, telling the *Washington Post*, "Football just isn't that much fun anymore. I felt once that I couldn't live without football. Now, I feel I can be very comfortable without it." Once he found he could live without it, though, he got back into it. In 1984 the Houston Gamblers were formed as an expansion team in the USFL and were looking for a local figure to coach the team. They hired Jack, and he shocked everyone by installing the Run-and-Shoot offense in Houston with gunslinger quarterback Jim Kelly running it. Former Bears' quarterback Bob Avellini marveled at Pardee's new offense to *Sports Illustrated*, "I never thought Jack Pardee had it in him." Actually, Pardee became a total convert to the Run-and-Shoot. After the Gamblers and the USFL folded in 1986, Jack was named head coach across town at the University of Houston in 1987. Running the same offense, Pardee produced a winning team, 22–11–1 from 1987 to 1989, and a Heisman Trophy winner in Andre Ware.

Although Jack was happy at the university, he returned to the pros in 1990 when Oilers' owner Bud Adams waved a big contract at him. While the Oilers went to the playoffs each year from 1990 to 1993, they went 1–4 in the postseason as the better defenses could cope with Houston's gimmicky Run-and-Shoot passing attack. The 1992 season ended with the Bills

miraculous comeback from a 35–3 second half deficit to beat the Oilers in overtime. Pardee brought in Buddy Ryan to coach the defense in 1993, but that blew up in his face when Ryan slugged offensive coordinator Kevin Gilbride on the sideline during the penultimate game of the 1993 season because he disliked Gilbride's pass-heavy play calling. The team made a quick exit in the playoffs that year. Both Ryan and starting quarterback Warren Moon departed the following season, Houston lost nine of its first 10 games, and Jack was fired. He later told *Sports Illustrated*, "I can't say I regret it, but I wasn't entirely comfortable leaving the [college] program for the NFL. I had much more fun coaching college. Were I to have the choice again, I'd probably stay [in college]."

Jack surfaced in 1995 with a new team and league, the Birmingham Barracudas in the newly expanded Canadian Football League. Boasting a wide-open passing attack, the Barracudas compiled a 10–8 record in their only year of existence. In 1996, the CFL shrunk back down and Pardee's coaching career ended. Since then, he has worked on his Texas ranch, no longer needing to coach to live.

PARKER, RAYMOND (BUDDY) 12/16/1913– 3/22/1982. North Texas and Centenary. Played FB for the Lions and Cardinals from 1935 to 1943. *Apprenticeship:* Pro asst.— 6 years. *Roots:* Phil Handler, Jimmy Conzelman. *Branches:* George Wilson, Buster Ramsey, Nick Skorich, Bill McPeak, Harry Gilmer. *Coordinators/Key Assistants:* For the Lions, George Wilson was the key offensive coach, while Buster Ramsey ran the defense; for the Steelers, Harry Gilmer then Mike Nixon were the key offensive coaches, while Thurman McGraw then Torgy Torgeson were the key defensive coaches. *Hall of Fame Players:* Jack Butler, Jack Christiansen, Lou Creekmur, Len Dawson, John Henry Johnson, Yale Lary, Bobby Layne, Joe Schmidt, Ernie Stautner, Charley Trippi, Doak Walker. *Primary Quarterbacks:* Bobby Layne, Ed Brown. *Record:* NFL Championships 1952, 1953. *Tendencies:* • His teams scored 22.8 points and allowed 20 per game • His teams ran 55.8% of the time, which was 104% of the league average • 12 starting quarterbacks in 15 years; 72% of starts to primary quarterbacks • 57 rookie starters in 15 years • Winning Full Seasons to Losing Full Seasons: 10:4.

Hailing from Slaton, Texas, Buddy Parker was one of the most colorful coaches in league history and became an early proponent of trading draft picks for veterans, a practice later perfected by George Allen. Parker shared Allen's immense distaste for losing as well, sometimes going into the blackest of alcohol-fueled black moods after a loss and always cutting off his necktie ritualistically with a pocketknife in frustration. A mercurial man, Buddy resigned abruptly from each of his three NFL head coaching positions.

Parker began as a fullback for little Centenary College in Louisiana from 1932 to 1934, playing on two undefeated teams. As an NFL rookie for Detroit in 1935, Parker played on the first Lions' championship team and scored a touchdown in the title game against the Giants. After two years in Detroit, Buddy joined the Cardinals in 1937 and played for them for the next seven years. Retiring in 1944, Parker became the backfield coach of the merged Card-Pitts under co-coaches Phil Handler and Walt Kiesling. Buddy remained on staff in 1945 under Handler and then from 1946 to 1948 when Jimmy Conzelman returned to coach the Cards a second time and led them to back-to-back title games in 1947 and 1948. Conzelman gave up coaching after that, but the Cardinals' management could not pick between Handler, who had coached the team to one win during three War years as coach, or Parker, so the two were named co-coaches. With the team at 2–4 halfway through the season, Handler was kicked upstairs and Parker was made sole head coach. The Cardinals responded with a 4–1–1 second half, but Buddy had had enough of Chicago's meddling front office and quit, saying, "I'm tired of being a head coach. The duties are too demanding and it's tough for a young coach to beat the old pro hands."

Parker returned to Detroit in 1950 as Bo McMillin's backfield coach, but there was a mutiny brewing among the up-and-coming Lions. McMillin was fired at year's end and wrote an open three-page letter in which he intimated that someone, meaning Parker, had been politicking for his job. It was true that the team's trio of young Texas stars, Bobby Layne, Doak Walker and Cloyce Box, naturally aligned with their fellow Texan and went to management after the season to say they were unhappy with McMillin and that they could "win with Parker."

Win they did, going to three straight NFL title games against Paul Brown's Cleveland Browns from 1952 to 1954 and winning the first two. Parker kept things simple. He had few rules and no curfew off the field. On the field, he ran a basic but effective offense with the one new feature being the two-minute drill expertly run by Layne, and four times the Lions were first or second in the league in scoring. Meanwhile, old friend Buster Ramsey ran a tough, opportunistic defense that four times finished in the top three in fewest points allowed. Buddy was a serious devotee of film study and was noted for his ability to make adjustments at halftime to help the Lions pull out comeback victories. While McMillin deserves credit for building the 1950s' Lions, it was Parker who made them winners. In 1955, Layne was banged up with injuries and the team dropped into the second division, although Parker's book, *We Play to Win* came out that year. Bouncing back in 1956, Detroit was poised to win another Western Division crown when Layne was knocked out of the year's end showdown with the Bears on a blatantly cheap shot by Chicago's Ed Meadows.

All the while, Buddy worked on one-year contracts until 1957 when the team signed him for two years. However, he had long feuded with management and suddenly quit during training camp that year, announcing at a Meet the Lions dinner, "This team of ours has been the worst I've ever seen in training. I don't want to get involved in another losing season so I'm leaving Detroit. As a matter of fact, I'm leaving tonight." He then added, "When you get to a situation where you can't handle football players, it's time to get out." Three weeks later, he attributed his departure to "the division of opinion that developed among the directors and myself."

A couple of weeks after that, Buddy was back in business as the new head coach of the lowly Pittsburgh

Parker, Raymond (Buddy)

Year	Team	Games	Wins	Losses	Ties	%	P Wins	P Losses	P %
1949	Cardinals	12	6	5	1	.542	0	0	.000
1951	Lions	12	7	4	1	.625	0	0	.000
1952	Lions	12	9	3	0	.750	2	0	1.000
1953	Lions	12	10	2	0	.833	1	0	1.000
1954	Lions	12	9	2	1	.792	0	1	.000
1955	Lions	12	3	9	0	.250	0	0	.000
1956	Lions	12	9	3	0	.750	0	0	.000
1957	Steelers	12	6	6	0	.500	0	0	.000
1958	Steelers	12	7	4	1	.625	0	0	.000
1959	Steelers	12	6	5	1	.542	0	0	.000
1960	Steelers	12	5	6	1	.458	0	0	.000
1961	Steelers	14	6	8	0	.429	0	0	.000
1962	Steelers	14	9	5	0	.643	0	0	.000
1963	Steelers	14	7	4	3	.607	0	0	.000
1964	Steelers	14	5	9	0	.357	0	0	.000
15 years		188	104	75	9	.577	3	1	.750

Steelers. Parker coached the Steelers for the next nine years, but his best year was 1962 when the 9–5 club finished second in the division. While Buddy went 4–1 against Paul Brown in Detroit, he struggled to a 4–8 mark against his rival as a Steeler. Parker made a flurry of trades to bring in veterans for draft picks, including old favorite Bobby Layne, and his Pittsburgh teams were tough and competitive, but ultimately not winners. Receiver Jimmy Orr told Jim Wexell for *Pittsburgh Steelers*, "Buddy Parker was one helluva football coach. You have to give him credit for that. Buddy Parker never got his credit compared to the other coaches that I see around. He won two championships. He always had a competitive team, even in Pittsburgh when the talent was pretty thin."

Buddy made one last bold move to try to salvage the Steelers in 1964. He traded All-Pro receiver Buddy Dial to Dallas for a top draft pick and selected Texas defensive tackle Scott Appleton with that pick to shore up the defense and drafted Pitt receiver Paul Martha to replace Dial. None of it worked out. Appleton signed with the AFL instead and was never very good anyway, Martha was a bust, and even Dial was a disappointment in Dallas. Parker got more and more frustrated. After one preseason game, he tried to put the whole team on waivers. In the 1965 preseason, he rashly tried to trade two good young defensive linemen, Chuck Hinton and Ben McGee, to Philadelphia for veteran backup quarterback King Hill, but young Dan Rooney asserted himself and disallowed the trade. Buddy then quit, announcing two weeks before the season opener, "I can't win with these stiffs."

He never coached again, but instead worked in real estate for the last 17 years of his life and died after surgery for a ruptured ulcer in 1982. Oddly, his brother R.W. was also a coach who made headlines in 1959 by hastily resigning from his position at Southwest Texas. It must have run in the family.

PATERA JOHN A. (JACK) 8/1/1933– Oregon.
Played LB for the Colts, Cardinals and Cowboys from 1955 to 1961. *Apprenticeship:* Pro asst. —13 years. *Roots:* Harland Svare, George Allen, Allie Sherman, Bud Grant. *Branches:* Jim Mora, Sr. *Coordinators/Key Assistants:* Sam Borghosian then Jerry Rhome ran the offense, while Bob Hollway then Larry Peccatielo then Jackie Simpson handled the defense. *Hall of Fame Players:* Carl Eller, Steve Largent. *Primary Quarterbacks:* Jim Zorn *Tendencies:* • His teams scored 19.9 points and allowed 25.2 per game • His teams ran 47.4% of the time, which was 89% of the league average • Three starting quarterbacks in seven years; 90% of starts to primary quarterback • 23 rookie starters in seven years • Winning Full Seasons to Losing Full Seasons: 2:4.

Born in Bismarck, North Dakota, Jack Patera was raised in Portland, Oregon where he was recruited by John McKay to play tackle at the University of Oregon from 1951 to 1954. Drafted in the fourth round by the Colts in 1955, Jack was converted to linebacker and spent three years in Baltimore before being traded to the Cardinals in 1958. Two years later, he was selected by Dallas in the expansion draft, but injured his knee and appeared in just four games in two years before retiring in 1962. A year later at age 29, he began his coaching career as the Rams defensive line coach. Under Patera, the Rams front four took on its own formidable persona as the Fearsome Foursome and served as the backbone of the team, particularly after George Allen took over as head coach in 1966.

Patera moved on to the Giants in 1968 and then to Minnesota in 1969. With the Vikings, Patera again helped develop a front four with a distinct personality — the Purple People Eaters — and got to go to three Super Bowls. With his background of being with a winner and knowledge of the challenges of an expansion team, Jack was hired as the first head coach of the Seahawks in 1976. That same year, fellow Oregon Duck John McKay took over the other expansion team in Tampa, but Patera had much more initial success in Seattle. In free agent quarterback Jim Zorn and Hall of Fame receiver Steve Largent, he established an exciting, gambling team that posted a winning record in year three.

The early Seahawks pulled out all the stops with gadget plays, unexpected onside kicks and fake punts and field goals to give themselves an edge despite being an undermanned expansion team. In retrospect, Jack told the *Seattle Post-Intelligencer*, "I was probably more creative than most coaches. It wasn't really a gamble

Patera John A. (Jack)									
Year	Team	Games	Wins	Losses	Ties	%	P Wins	P Losses	P %
1976	Seahawks	14	2	12	0	.143	0	0	.000
1977	Seahawks	14	5	9	0	.357	0	0	.000
1978	Seahawks	16	9	7	0	.563	0	0	.000
1979	Seahawks	16	9	7	0	.563	0	0	.000
1980	Seahawks	16	4	12	0	.250	0	0	.000
1981	Seahawks	16	6	10	0	.375	0	0	.000
1982	Seahawks	2	0	2	0	.000	0	0	.000
7 years		94	35	59	0	.372	0	0	.000

if it was well-scouted. I did things other people hadn't explored." He told former Seahawk receiver Steve Raible for *Steve Raible's Tales from the Seahawks Sideline*, "There's nothing but optimism in any coach's mind no matter where he is." He added, "People always told me how the best years of your life are going to be the first two or three years of an expansion team because there's just an enthusiasm that is never going to be there again."

For Patera that was true. After back-to-back 9–7 seasons in years three and four, Seattle declined rather than improved. Trading the rights to the top pick in 1976 [Tony Dorsett] to Dallas for a flock of mediocre players did not help. Neither did drafting overweight Stanford backup tackle Andre Hines by mistake with the top pick in 1980. While Seattle scored points, they could not stop their opponents — six times the Seahawks finished in the bottom five in points allowed. As the team failed to improve, the fans and media put the heat on Patera who once had been known as "Smilin' Jack." Seattle GM John Thompson told Tom Danyluk for *The Super 70s*, "Jack's biggest failure was his inability to get along with local media.... He didn't like the media and, as a result, the press was very, very tough on him." Indeed, Patera once held a seven-second press conference after a game. After that game, he sat down, asked whether there were any questions and when that was greeted by giggles from the press corps, stormed out.

Both Patera and Thompson were fired during the player strike in 1982. Jack never coached again. He got involved in a number of businesses and investments that did not work out, eventually got divorced after 44 years of marriage, ballooned up to 350 pounds and led a private life in a rural area.

PAYTON, PATRICK S. (SEAN) 12/29/1963– Eastern Illinois. Played QB for the Bears in 1987. *Apprenticeship:* College asst.— 9 years; pro asst.— 9 years. *Roots:* Ray Rhodes, Jim Fassel, Bill Parcells. *Branches:* Dennis Allen. *Coordinators/Key Assistants:* Doug Marone then Pete Carmichael, Jr., handled the offense, while Gary Gibbs then Gregg Williams ran the defense. *Hall of Fame Players:* None. *Primary Quarterbacks:* Drew Brees. *Record:* Super Bowl Championship 2009. *Tendencies:* • His teams scored 28.1 points and allowed

21.8 per game • His teams ran 39.2% of the time, which was 89% of the league average • One starting quarterback in six years; 100% of starts to primary quarterback • 18 rookie starters in six years • Winning Full Seasons to Losing Full Seasons: 4:1.

Sean Payton from San Mateo, California, was a record-setting passer at Eastern Illinois from 1983 to 1986, but the 5'11" quarterback went undrafted by the NFL. Payton tried desperately to extend his playing career in 1987. He was cut by the Chiefs in training camp, played for the Chicago Bruisers of the Arena Football League and was one of the replacement player "Spare Bears" in Chicago during the NFL players' strike. In 1988, he even went to England to play in a beer-sponsored semipro league before beginning his coaching career later in the year at San Diego State. Sean coached at San Diego State from 1988 to 1989, at Indiana State from 1990 to 1991, back to San Diego from 1992 to 1993 as Marshall Faulk's running backs coach, at Miami of Ohio from 1994 to 1995 as offensive coordinator and at Illinois as quarterbacks coach in 1996.

Payton made the jump to the NFL in 1997 when Ray Rhodes hired him as the Eagles' quarterbacks coach. Two years later, Jim Fassel brought Sean to New York as the Giants quarterbacks coach and then promoted him to offensive coordinator in 2000. When the offense flagged in 2002, Fassel took over the play calling responsibilities for the team, so Sean left at season's end to become the quarterbacks coach for the Cowboys under Bill Parcells. The period of 2003–2005 was Payton's post-graduate work in coaching as he learned from Parcells. Sean was offered the Raiders' head coaching position in 2004 but turned it down. After being rejected by Green Bay in 2006, though, he took on the daunting challenge of becoming the head coach of the post–Hurricane Katrina New Orleans Saints. Not only were the Saints an historically dysfunctional franchise that had won just one post-season game in 40 years, but the city itself was a reclamation project in the aftermath of Katrina. New Orleans needed not only a football coach but a community leader as well. Payton filled both roles.

Sean transformed a 3–13 team to a 10–6 division winner that went to the NFC Conference championship. The key move for Payton was signing free

Payton, Patrick S. (Sean)									
Year	*Team*	*Games*	*Wins*	*Losses*	*Ties*	*%*	*P Wins*	*P Losses*	*P %*
2006	Saints	16	10	6	0	.625	1	1	.500
2007	Saints	16	7	9	0	.438	0	0	.000
2008	Saints	16	8	8	0	.500	0	0	.000
2009	Saints	16	13	3	0	.813	3	0	1.000
2010	Saints	16	11	5	0	.688	0	1	.000
2011	Saints	16	13	3	0	.813	1	1	.500
6 years		96	62	34	0	.646	5	3	.625

agent quarterback Drew Brees to run his inventive offense. However, GM Mickey Loomis told *Sports Illustrated* that hiring Sean was the key move for the franchise. "If we don't sign Sean, then we probably don't get Drew to come. In hiring Sean, we got the best offensive mind in the NFL, and we got one of the best quarterbacks. He's made all of this work." According to Brees' book *Coming Back Stronger*, Payton told him, "We're going to take everything you like and everything you're good at and we're going to install it. We're going to put it in our offense. We're going to develop it together."

While the offense has been a league leader all along, the Saints' defense was too porous for Payton's first three years. In 2009, Sean hired Gregg Williams as defensive coordinator, even lowering his own salary so the team could meet Williams' demands. That investment paid off immediately when Williams' blitz-heavy approach transformed the defense into an opportunistic, quarterback-hunting, playmaking force. Meeting the Colts in the Super Bowl, Payton never relinquished his aggressive stance and shocked Indianapolis by starting the second half with an onside kick that gave New Orleans momentum and control of the game as they won the first Super Bowl championship in franchise history. Payton's team has twice led the league in scoring and four times in yards, and in 2011 set a new NFL record for most yards in a season with 7,474 while Brees broke Dan Marino's record for most passing yards in one year with 5,476. However, the defense failed in the postseason in both 2010 and 2011. Payton was suspended for 2012 because of the Saints' Bounty Scandal.

PEPPLER, ALBERT P. (PAT) 4/16/1922– Michigan State. Did not play professionally. *Apprenticeship:* College asst.— 9 years. *Roots:* None. *Branches:* None. *Coordinators/Key Assistants*: Bill Nelsen ran the offense. *Hall of Fame Players:* None. *Primary Quarterbacks:* None. *Record:* **Interim Coach.**

Born in Shorewood, Wisconsin, Pat Peppler enrolled at Michigan State in 1941 and then served in World War II. Returning to MSU in 1946, Peppler starred on the basketball and baseball teams from 1946 to 1948. Upon graduation, he coached high school football from 1949 to 1953 before being hired as an assistant at North Carolina State in 1954. Pat spent eight years under Earle Edwards at NC State until leaving to join the staff at Wake Forest in 1962. Wake Forest finished that season 0–10, but Peppler landed

on his feet when Vince Lombardi hired him as the champion Packers' director of player personnel in January 1963.

Peppler ran the front office in Green Bay for the next nine years until leaving to replace Joe Thomas in Miami in 1972. He was part of the Packers' three-peat from 1965 to 1967 and the Dolphins consecutive Super Bowl victories in 1972 and 1973, gaining the reputation as a builder of winning teams. He later told the *Milwaukee Journal-Sentinel*, "I was fortunate to work with two great coaches like Shula and Lombardi in my career." That reputation earned him the GM job for the Falcons in 1975. However, in Atlanta, Pat inherited a coach, Marion Campbell, that owner Rankin Smith valued much more highly than Peppler did. After a 4–10 1975 season, the Falcons began 1976 1–4, and Peppler met with Smith. According to Al Thomy, a reporter for the *Atlanta Constitution*, Smith told Pat, "You're the next coach. You've been telling me how Marion couldn't coach; let's see how you do."

Peppler told the *Los Angeles Times*, "What little I know about football is due to the fact that Lombardi made his personnel man stay with the team. I was on the practice field every day for nine years in Green Bay and I was on the phones with the other coaches every Sunday." Pat added, "My coaches coach the Falcons. All I do is make a few suggestions." Atlanta won three of its first six games under Peppler and beat Tom Landry's Cowboys in November after which Pat couldn't resist cracking, "See what happens since Rankin Smith had more time to devote to the team?" Smith had recently been asked to step down as chairman of the board of his insurance firm because he was spending too much time on football. Atlanta then lost its last three games, including a 59–0 beatdown by the Rams in the season finale, and Peppler was ousted by Smith.

Pat then served as assistant GM for the Oilers from 1977 to 1980 and followed Bum Phillips to New Orleans in 1981, working in the front office until Phillips was fired in 1985. After retiring from football, Peppler worked for a company that built sports stadiums.

PERKINS, WALTER R. (RAY) 12/6/1941– Alabama. Played WR for the Colts from 1967 to 1971. *Apprenticeship:* College asst.—1 year; pro asst.— 5 years. *Roots:* Chuck Fairbanks, Don Coryell. *Branches:* Bill Parcells, Richard Williamson, Bill Belichick. *Coordinators/Key*

Peppler, Albert P. (Pat)									
Year	Team	Games	Wins	Losses	Ties	%	P Wins	P Losses	P %
1976	Falcons	9	3	6	0	.333	0	0	.000
1 year		9	3	6	0	.333	0	0	.000

Assistants: For the Giants, Perkins then Ron Erhardt ran the offense, while Ralph Hawkins then Bill Parcells handled the defense; for the Bucs, Richard Williamson ran the offense, while Doug Graber then Fred Bruney handled the defense. *Hall of Fame Players:* Harry Carson, Lawrence Taylor. *Primary Quarterbacks:* Phil Simms, Scott Brunner, Vinny Testaverde. *Tendencies:* • His teams scored 17.3 points and allowed 22.3 per game • His teams ran 45.1% of the time, which was 93% of the league average • Nine starting quarterbacks in eight years; 81% of starts to primary quarterbacks • 35 rookie starters in eight years • Winning Full Seasons to Losing Full Seasons: 1:7.

Ray Perkins was born in Mt. Olive, Mississippi, but raised in nearby Petal. Attending Alabama under Bear Bryant, Perkins caught passes from Joe Namath, Steve Sloan and Ken Stabler from 1964 to 1966. The Tide won back-to-back national championships in his sophomore and junior seasons, and Ray was an All-American and team captain as a senior. Drafted in the seventh round by Baltimore in 1967, he spent five years catching passes from Johnny Unitas and won a Super Bowl in 1970. After suffering a knee injury, Perkins retired in 1972 and went into real estate.

In 1973, Ray joined the staff at Mississippi State and a year later was hired by Chuck Fairbanks as an assistant coach with the Patriots. After four years in New England, Perkins became the Chargers offensive coordinator in 1978 under Tommy Prothro and then Don Coryell at mid season. The Giants hired him as head coach in 1979, with owner Wellington Mara pointing out that Ray was the third offensive coordinator hired by Prothro to become an NFL head coach, as he followed in the footsteps of Dick Vermeil and Bill Walsh. Unfortunately, Perkins' career would never approach either of those two coaching icons.

Ray was a talented organizer who helped turn around a Giants' franchise that had been sleeping for a decade and a half. He also was an impersonal disciplinarian who favored three-a-day practices, but the Giants seemed to be buying into his program. However, he could show excitement at times such as when the Giants' clinched a playoff berth for the first time in 18 years on a Joe Danelo overtime field goal in 1981,

and Ray carried Danelo off the field in celebration. That all ended a year later when Bear Bryant announced he was stepping down as Alabama's coach and Perkins was approached to replace the coach he most respected.

Perkins told the *New York Times*, "I am leaving the Giants with mixed emotions. This new job does me great honor, being my alma mater and a great university in the part of the country where I was raised. My two children were born there. And it's an honor to follow the greatest coach of all time." New York then lost two of their last three games and missed the playoffs in the 1982 strike season. His greatest legacy to the Giants was that he hired both Bill Parcells and Bill Belichick to his coaching staff. Perkins told a reporter in 1983, "I like the relationship between player and coach that's peculiar to college. College men are easier to motivate than professionals." However, it's not so easy to follow a legend. Despite a 32–15–1 record and three winning seasons in four, Perkins was under increasing heat in Tuscaloosa and bolted back to the pros in 1987. Perkins was replaced at Alabama by former Colts' teammate Bill Curry.

Ray signed a lucrative contract with Tampa to coach the Bucs, and owner Hugh Culverhouse crowed that he'd found "my Vince Lombardi." Again, it did not work out as hoped. Perkins traded quarterback Steve Young to San Francisco and drafted Vinny Testaverde who turned out to be a confused interception machine. The Bucs never won more than five games in Ray's four seasons there, and popular banners in the stands recommended "Jerk the Perk" and "Throw Ray in the Bay." The players would probably have agreed with those sentiments. Perkins even got into a fight with Bucs' tackle Ron Heller at halftime in one 1987 game. Heller was exhorting his teammates, "don't quit," but Perkins just heard the word "quit" and went after the lineman who out weighed him by 100 pounds. Ray was fired after the 1990 season.

Perkins was out of football for a year, but then returned as head coach at Arkansas State in 1992. After a 2–9 season, Ray rejoined Parcells as an assistant coach in New England from 1993 to 1996, spent 1997 as Joe Bugel's offensive coordinator in Oakland and

Perkins, Walter R. (Ray)

Year	Team	Games	Wins	Losses	Ties	%	P Wins	P Losses	P %
1979	Giants	16	6	10	0	.375	0	0	.000
1980	Giants	16	4	12	0	.250	0	0	.000
1981	Giants	16	9	7	0	.563	1	1	.500
1982	Giants	9	4	5	0	.444	0	0	.000
1987	Buccaneers	15	4	11	0	.267	0	0	.000
1988	Buccaneers	16	5	11	0	.313	0	0	.000
1989	Buccaneers	16	5	11	0	.313	0	0	.000
1990	Buccaneers	13	5	8	0	.385	0	0	.000
8 years		117	42	75	0	.359	1	1	.500

then retired in 1998. Perkins came back in 1999 as the tight ends coach in Cleveland under Chris Palmer for two years and then retired for good in 2001.

PETERSON, WILLIAM E. (BILL) 5/14/1923– 8/5/1993. Ohio Northern. Did not play professionally. *Apprenticeship:* College coach —17 years (12 as head coach). *Roots:* None. *Branches:* Dan Henning. *Coordinators/Key Assistants:* King Hill ran the offense, while Jackie Simpson then Burnie Miller handled the defense. *Hall of Fame Players:* Elvin Bethea, Ken Houston, Charlie Joiner. *Primary Quarterbacks:* Dan Pastorini. *Tendencies:* • His teams scored 12.7 points and allowed 29.1 per game • His teams ran 48.6% of the time, which was 87% of the league average • Two starting quarterbacks in two years; 89% of starts to primary quarterback • Three rookie starters in two years • Winning Full Seasons to Losing Full Seasons: 0:1.

Bill Peterson's only contender for the title of "Mr. Malaprop" among NFL coaches was Joe Kuharich, but Peterson packed a lot of fractured communication into a short 19-game NFL coaching career, while Joe had 11 years to mouth off quizzically. Bill was quoted professing, "You guys pair off in groups of threes then line up in a circle." And "They gave me a standing observation." And "You guys line up alphabetically by height." And "We're going to throw the ball come high or hell water." And "We're not going to take this standing down." And "Men, when they play the national anthem, I want you standing on your helmets with the sideline under your arm." Another time, he told his players he was going to lead them in the Lord's Prayer and began, "Now I lay me down to sleep." Defensive end Elvin Bethea recalled in his autobiography *Smashmouth*, "Coach Peterson gave us a few laughs. We laughed at him, not with him" However, Peterson had enough self awareness in retirement to joke to one reporter that he was keeping busy by "writing my own dictionary."

Peterson was born in Toronto, Ohio, and knew hardship as a young man. His father died when Bill was 12, and he slowly worked his way through high school and college while working on the family farm and then as a house man in a campus fraternity. After graduating at age 26 from Ohio Northern where he played end, Peterson coached high school football in Ohio from 1946 to 1954. In 1955, Paul Dietzel hired

Bill as the line coach for LSU, which won a national championship in 1958. Florida State hired Peterson as its head coach in 1960, but FSU was a relatively new football program with no winning tradition. Outmanned by most of his rivals, Peterson took a strategic approach to overcome his disadvantage. He began attending San Diego Charger training camps to learn Sid Gillman's advanced passing offense and imported former Charger backup quarterback Don Breaux as a coach. Breaux was followed on staff by Dan Henning, Joe Gibbs, Ken Meyer, Bill Parcells, Don James and Bobby Bowden.

Peterson's Seminoles boasted their first All-American in 1964 with Fred Biletnikoff who caught passes from Steve Tensi, a quarterback drafted by Gillman in 1965. Bowden said on Bill's death, "He meant so much to Florida State, especially bringing the pro passing game into college football." Peterson also recruited the first black Florida State player, J.T. Thomas, in 1970, his final season in Tallahassee. During his 11 years at FSU, Bill compiled a 63–42–11 record before moving on to Rice in 1971. Peterson stayed there for just one 3–7–1 season, and then signed a "lifetime" contract as head coach of the Oilers in 1972. That year, Houston posted it only win in week three against the Jets behind second year quarterback Dan Pastorini; it would be the only victory Bill would ever celebrate in the NFL. Houston lost the last 11 games of 1972 and the first five in 1973 before newly hired GM Sid Gillman personally replaced Bill, saying, "The reasons are quite obvious. His record was 1–18."

Peterson never coached again, but continued to be paid on his "lifetime" contract for several years. In 1976, he was hired as an aide to Florida House Speaker Don Tucker, but the appointment was contingent on not negating his contract with Houston. In the late 1970s, Bill did some work as color analyst on FSU games and then served as athletic director at Central Florida from 1981 to 1985. In retirement, he worked as a fundraiser for the Seminoles once again.

PETITBON, RICHARD A. (RICHIE) 4/18/1938– Tulane. Played S for the Bears, Rams and Redskins from 1959 to 1972. *Apprenticeship:* Pro asst.—19 years. *Roots:* Sid Gillman, Bum Phillips, Jack Pardee, Joe Gibbs. *Branches:* Emmitt Thomas (i). *Coordinators/Key Assistants:* Rod Dowhower ran the offense, while Emmitt Thomas handled the defense. *Hall of Fame Players:*

Peterson, William E. (Bill)									
Year	Team	Games	Wins	Losses	Ties	%	P Wins	P Losses	P %
1972	Oilers (Titans)	14	1	13	0	.071	0	0	.000
1973	Oilers (Titans)	5	0	5	0	.000	0	0	.000
2 years		19	1	18	0	.053	0	0	.000

Darrell Green, Art Monk. *Primary Quarterbacks:* Mark Rypien. *Tendencies:* • His team scored 14.4 points and allowed 21.6 per game • His team ran 40.9% of the time, which was 91% of the league average • Three starting quarterbacks in one year; 63% of starts to primary quarterback • Four rookie starters in one year • Winning Full Seasons to Losing Full Seasons: 0:1.

New Orleans native Richie Petitbon played quarterback at Tulane and was a second round draft pick of the Bears in 1959. Converted to safety in the pros, Richie was a hard hitting All Pro who lasted 14 years in the league and played under George Allen at all three of his NFL stops. At age 35, he spent the 1973 season on Injured Reserve before finally retiring in 1974 to take a coaching position with Houston under Sid Gillman. After Gillman left, Petitbon continued on Bum Phillips staff for three years before former Ram and Redskin teammate Jack Pardee was named as head coach of the Redskins in 1978 and hired Richie as the secondary coach. When Joe Gibbs replaced Pardee in 1981, Petitbon was promoted to defensive coordinator and remained so for the next 12 years, winning three Super Bowl rings. Defensive end Charles Mann maintained to Thom Loverro for *Hail Victory* that the Washington defense never got its just due, "The defensive line had to beat their man. Because we did that pretty consistently, Richie could play sound fundamental defense and didn't have to gamble. That is not to say that Richie didn't bring the heat, didn't bring corner blitzes and the dogs, but we didn't do it too much. And because we didn't, people don't remember us as a great defense."

Petitbon told the *Washington Post* that he was only ever interested in three head coaching jobs, "New Orleans [in 1985] because I was born there. Chicago, because I played there, and I love Chicago. And here [Washington]. I love this town. That's it." In 1993, he was passed over for the Bears' job, but was hired to replace the retiring Joe Gibbs two months later. He joked to the *Post*, "Somebody must have been looking after me on that Chicago deal because right now, you'd have a suicide on your hands." Unfortunately, Gibbs was getting out at just the right time; the veteran team was about to crumble. With the team at 1–5, defensive

end Jason Buck attempted to defend his coach to the *Post*, "Nothing has changed since he became head coach. Everyone loves playing for him. We've just got to find a way to play better." What had changed was that the team had aged and slipped from 14th to 25th in scoring and from eighth to 23rd in points allowed. Richie was clearly a players coach, unable to crack the whip and make the major changes that needed to occur and was fired after just one year. Petitbon retired from football in 1994. Two years later, Ted Marchibroda tried to hire him to coach the defense in Baltimore, and Mike Ditka did the same in New Orleans in 1997, but Richie resisted and never returned to the NFL. His older brother John also played in the NFL as a defensive back with the Browns, Packers and Dallas Texans, in the 1950s.

PETRINO, ROBERT (BOBBY) 3/10/1961– Carroll (MT). QB; did not play professionally. *Apprenticeship:* College coach — 21 years (4 as head coach); pro asst.— 3 years. *Roots:* Tom Coughlin. *Branches:* Emmitt Thomas (i), Hue Jackson. *Coordinators/Key Assistants:* Hue Jackson ran the offense, while Mike Zimmer handled the defense. *Hall of Fame Players:* None. *Primary Quarterbacks:* Joey Harrington. *Tendencies:* • His team scored 14.2 points and allowed 23.5 per game • His team ran 39% of the time, which was 90% of the league average • Three starting quarterbacks in one year; 77% of starts to primary quarterback • Five rookie starters in one year • Winning Full Seasons to Losing Full Seasons: 0:1.

Bobby Petrino from Lewistown, Montana was essentially an interim coach in the NFL, but managed to generate a great deal of anger from players and coaches in his brief stint as the Falcons' head coach. His NFL career has similarities to Lou Holtz's from a generation before. Both were heralded for their work at mid level college programs — Holtz at NC State and Petrino at Louisville. Both racked up 3–10 records in their only NFL seasons; both vehemently denied rumors that they were leaving to return to the college ranks. Both quit their teams before the season ended, and both high-tailed it to Fayetteville in December to coach Arkansas.

Petitbon, Richard A. (Richie)									
Year	Team	Games	Wins	Losses	Ties	%	P Wins	P Losses	P %
1993	Redskins	16	4	12	0	.250	0	0	.000
1 year		16	4	12	0	.250	0	0	.000

Petrino, Robert (Bobby)									
Year	Team	Games	Wins	Losses	Ties	%	P Wins	P Losses	P %
2007	Falcons	13	3	10	0	.231	0	0	.000
1 year		13	3	10	0	.231	0	0	.000

Petrino played quarterback at Carroll College in Montana from 1980 to 1982 and went immediately into coaching at his alma mater in 1983. He jumped to Weber State in 1984, came back to Carroll in 1985, returned to Weber in 1987, and then moved on to Idaho in 1989, Arizona State in 1992, Nevada in 1994, Utah State in 1995 and finally Louisville as offensive coordinator in 1998. He made his first leap to the NFL in 1999 as Tom Coughlin's quarterbacks coach in Jacksonville and was promoted to offensive coordinator in 2001. After this three-year stint with the Jaguars, Bobby returned to the college ranks in 2002 as the offensive coordinator at Auburn before being named head coach at Louisville in 2003.

In four years at Louisville, Petrino compiled a 41–9 record with a dynamic spread passing attack. Falcons' owner Arthur Blank was excited to hire him as head coach in 2007, "Bobby knows how to motivate, he knows how to teach, he knows how to get the best out of his athletes. He'll push Mike Vick to even higher levels." Blank also concluded, "Bobby has the potential to be here a very long time, which is important to me." However, when Vick was lost to his dogfighting criminality, Petrino's offense was left in the hands of Byron Leftwich, Joey Harrington and Chris Redman. The Falcons would finish the year 29th in scoring and 29th in points allowed, but would not finish with Petrino. Rather, Bobby pinned a four-sentence note up in the locker room for the players to find on December 11 to inform them he had quit. Warrick Dunn wrote in *Running for My Life*, "Coach Petrino didn't know how to relate to professional players from the get-go. He alienated the veterans and was aloof with just about everyone in the organization."

Former Falcons' defensive coordinator Mike Zimmer was much harsher when asked about it three years later by the *Cincinnati Enquirer*, "He came in and said he resigned, said he would talk to us all at a later date, walked out of the office, and no one has ever talked to him since. Not that anybody wanted to. He's a gutless bastard. Quote that. I don't give a shit. He is a coward. Put that in quotes. He ruined a bunch of people's lives, a bunch of people's families, kids, because he didn't have enough nuts to stay there and finish the job. That's the truth. Most people in football have enough courage about them and enough fight to stick through something and not quit halfway through the year. It is cowardly."

Petrino has gone 34–17 in his first four years at Arkansas.

PHELAN, JAMES M. (JIMMY) 12/5/1892–11/14/1974. Notre Dame. QB; did not play professionally. *Apprenticeship:* College head coach — 27 years. *Roots:* None. *Branches:* None. *Coordinators/Key Assistants:* For the Dons, Mel Hein then Marty Kordick coached the line, while Earl Martineau then Dutch Clark coached the backs; for the Yanks, Nick Susoeff coached the ends; for the Texans, Cecil Isbell coached the backs, and Will Walls coached the line. *Hall of Fame Players:* Art Donovan, Len Ford, Gino Marchetti. *Primary Quarterbacks:* Glenn Dobbs, Bob Celeri. *Tendencies:* • His teams scored 18.7 points and allowed 28.7 per game • His teams ran 50.2% of the time, which was 89% of the league average • Eight starting quarterbacks in four years; 76% of starts to primary quarterbacks • 22 rookie starters in four years • Winning Full Seasons to Losing Full Seasons: 0:3.

The ESPN, Total Football and Neft & Cohen football encyclopedias all have Jimmy Phelan's coaching record wrong; all credited the 1951 New York Yanks to Red Strader as head coach, but Strader was fired before the season and the 60-year-old Phelan was given the thankless task of coaching the dreadful Yanks franchise in its last year before folding. It was the second time Jimmy would succeed Strader. Sadly, things would get worse still as his lengthy career in football reached its conclusion.

Phelan grew up in Portland, Oregon and played quarterback for Jesse Harper at Notre Dame from 1915 to 1917 when Knute Rockne was still an assistant coach. During World War I, Jimmy served as a pilot for the Army Air Corps and began his coaching career in 1920 as the head coach at Missouri where he compiled a 13–

Phelan, James M. (Jimmy)

Year	Team	Games	Wins	Losses	Ties	%	P Wins	P Losses	P %
1948	Los Angeles Dons (AAFC)	14	7	7	0	.500	0	0	.000
1949	Los Angeles Dons (AAFC)	12	4	8	0	.333	0	0	.000
1951	New York Yanks (defunct)	12	1	9	2	.167	0	0	.000
1952	Dallas Texans (defunct)	12	1	11	0	.083	0	0	.000
4 years		50	13	35	2	.280	0	0	.000

3 record in two years. He moved on to Purdue in 1922 and introduced the "Old Oaken Bucket" tradition for the annual cross-state showdown with Indiana. From 1922 to 1929, Phelan's Boilermakers went 35–22–5. Jimmy returned to his native Great Northwest in 1930 as the coach at Washington for the next decade. Phelan led the Huskies to the 1937 Rose Bowl and posted a 65–37–8 record from 1930 to 1941. In 1942, he took over the St. Mary's Gaels after Coach Red Strader went into the service. In six years at the small school, the team finished 24–25–1, but were nationally known because of Jimmy's biggest star, 5'10" Hawaiian halfback Herm "Squirmin' Herman" Wedemeyer.

As a college coach, Phelan generally ran the Notre Dame Box offense and originated the weak side spinner and end around plays in that offense. He also was among the first to signal in defensive calls using his fingers. While Jimmy once told a coaching convention, "You can't lose to a team that can't score on you," he is more remembered as an offense-minded coach. When he was hired by the Los Angeles Dons of the All America Football Conference in 1948, Phelan sold T formation quarterback Charley O'Rourke to Baltimore a month later because he intended on running a spread single wing with Glenn Dobbs instead. That offense did not prove very successful, though, and the Dons were not serious contenders in either of their last two seasons.

Jimmy was out of work when the team and league folded in 1950, but was called back to coaching when Red Strader (see above) was fired by the New York Yanks during training camp in 1951. Presented with 5'10" Bob Celeri as his best passer, Phelan devised a spread offense that was a forerunner to the shotgun formation later developed by Red Hickey. However, neither Celeri nor the Yanks were very talented, and the team won just one game all year before folding. A new franchise was created in 1952 for some Dallas investors. These Dallas Texans inherited the Yanks' weak roster and rehired Phelan to coach the team. Jimmy traded the team's top draft choice, Les Richter, to the

Rams for 11 players, but only one of the 11, Tom Keane, played in the NFL after 1952.

This time, Phelan's team didn't even make it through a full season before the owners pulled out. Attendance was so poor that Phelan once told the players that rather being introduced on the field, they should go up into the stands and shake hands with each fan. The Texans were taken over by the league and finished the year as a road team. When the Dallas investors pulled out, Phelan cancelled practice so that the players could race to the bank to cash their checks while there was still money in the team's account. Hall of Famer Art Donovan told the *Coffin Corner*, "We had a good time in spite of everything mostly because of Phelan." Donovan expanded on Jimmy to *Pro! Magazine*, "He cared about the game. If he thought you were laying down, he wouldn't stand for it. But football had passed him by." Dallas won just one game in Phelan's swan song as a coach. He retired in 1953 and went into real estate development in Sacramento, eventually serving three terms on the Sacramento Board of Commissioners. He moved to Honolulu in 1974 and died there later that same year at age 81.

PHILLIPS, OAIL A. (BUM) 9/29/1923– Stephen F. Austin. Did not play professionally. *Apprenticeship:* College coach — 7 years (1 as head coach); pro asst.— 5 years. *Roots:* Sid Gillman, Charlie Waller. *Branches:* Ed Biles, Wade Phillips, Joe Bugel, Richie Petitbon. *Coordinators/Key Assistants:* For the Oilers, King Hill ran the offense, while Ed Biles handled the defense; for the Saints, King Hill ran the offense, while Wade Phillips handled the defense. *Hall of Fame Players:* Elvin Bethea, Earl Campbell, Dave Casper, Ricky Jackson. *Primary Quarterbacks:* Dan Pastorini, Ken Stabler. *Tendencies:* • His teams scored 18.4 points and allowed 19.9 per game • His teams ran 54.1% of the time, which was 105% of the league average • 11 starting quarterbacks in 11 years; 66% of starts to primary quarterbacks • 31 rookie starters in 11 years • Winning Full Seasons to Losing Full Seasons: 5:5.

Phillips, Oail A. (Bum)									
Year	Team	Games	Wins	Losses	Ties	%	P Wins	P Losses	P %
1975	Oilers (Titans)	14	10	4	0	.714	0	0	.000
1976	Oilers (Titans)	14	5	9	0	.357	0	0	.000
1977	Oilers (Titans)	14	8	6	0	.571	0	0	.000
1978	Oilers (Titans)	16	10	6	0	.625	2	1	.667
1979	Oilers (Titans)	16	11	5	0	.688	2	1	.667
1980	Oilers (Titans)	16	11	5	0	.688	0	1	.000
1981	Saints	16	4	12	0	.250	0	0	.000
1982	Saints	9	4	5	0	.444	0	0	.000
1983	Saints	16	8	8	0	.500	0	0	.000
1984	Saints	16	7	9	0	.438	0	0	.000
1985	Saints	12	4	8	0	.333	0	0	.000
11 years		159	82	77	0	.516	4	3	.571

Bum Phillips was the definition of a players' coach. He had few rules and no curfew. He told *Sports Illustrated*, "My idea of discipline is not *makin'* guys do something. It's *gettin'*'em to do it. There's a difference in bitchin' and coachin'. Some places the whole damn practice is a constant gripe. All negative stuff. The first thing you know is your people tune you out. Then it becomes a challenge to make them do somethin' they should be doin' on their own all along. The only discipline that lasts is self-discipline."

Born in Orange, Texas, Bum started out at Lamar Junior College in 1941 and then went into the Marines during the war. When he was discharged, he finished his education at Stephen F. Austin from 1946 to 1948. Two years later he went into high school coaching in Texas, working at Nederland High School from 1950 to 1956. In 1957, Bum joined Bear Bryant's staff at Texas A&M for one year before returning to the high school level in Jacksonville and Amarillo through 1961. Texas Western hired Phillips as its head coach in 1962, but he left after one 4–5 season to go back to the high school level once more. Finally in 1965, Bum left high school football for good when he joined Bill Yeoman's staff as defensive coordinator at the University of Houston. Two years later, Sid Gillman brought him to the pros as the Chargers defensive coordinator from 1967 to 1970. After Sid stepped down in San Diego, Phillips coached at SMU from 1971 to 1972 and Oklahoma State in 1973 before Gillman recalled him to the NFL as the Oilers' defensive coordinator in 1974. When Sid left a year later, Bum was named head coach in Houston and presided over one of the most memorable eras in franchise history.

Bum strolled the sidelines in his cowboy hat and cowboy boots with no head set, more the team's leader than strategist. The "Luv Ya Blue" period under Phillips featured a hard-hitting Oilers' team that continually fell just short against their division rivals the Steelers. In January 1980 after having lost to Pittsburgh in two successive AFC Conference championships, Phillips told a crowd of 70,000 supporters in the Astrodome, "Last year we knocked on the door. This year we beat on it. Next year we're going to kick the son of a bitch in." It was down home, fiery confidence like that that players loved about Bum ... plus, as Ed Biles told *Sports Illustrated*, "Bum would rather release a player than yell at him."

Those Oilers were a spirited bunch, but they did not have the talent of the Steelers. Quarterback Dan Pastorini was a good leader, but he did not have the tools or weapons of Terry Bradshaw. Instead, the offense was built around the power running of Hall of Famer Earl Campbell. Phillips' 3–4 defense was the strength of the club, but that was not as good as Pittsburgh's either. Houston did not get the chance to "kick the door down" in 1980, though. On Pastorini's request, Phillips had traded the quarterback to Oakland

in the offseason for Ken Stabler and then lost to the Raiders in the first round of the playoffs. Pittsburgh missed the playoffs entirely. Despite posting an 11-win season that year, Phillips had serious conflicts with GM Ladd Herzeg. The team was aging and management was pushing for changes such as the hiring of an offensive coordinator. Bum resisted and was fired. Linebacker Robert Brazile commented, "It's got to be a joke. All that Bum Phillips has done for this team. Maybe some players or someone else should get fired but never him. He was a father, not only a coach, to most players, He treated us like men."

Phillips was hired shortly thereafter by the Saints and took most of the Oilers' staff with him, including his son Wade. In New Orleans, Bum would eventually reacquire some of his favorite players like Campbell and Stabler, but never posted a winning season with the Saints and quit at the end of 1985, with Wade finishing the year as interim coach. After that, Bum retired to his horse ranch. He worked as color analyst for the Oilers in their last five years in Houston from 1990 to 1994 and has since involved himself with any Texas team where his son Wade coaches.

PHILLIPS, WADE A. 6/21/1947– Houston. LB; did not play professionally. *Apprenticeship:* College asst.— 4 years; pro asst.—17 years. *Roots:* Bum Phillips, Buddy Ryan, Dan Reeves. *Branches:* Jim Fassel, Tony Sparano, Jason Garrett, Todd Bowles (i), Dennis Allen. *Coordinators/Key Assistants:* For the Broncos, Jim Fassel ran the offense, while Charlie Waters handled the defense; for the Bills, Joe Pendry ran the offense, while Ted Cottrell handled the defense; for the Cowboys, Jason Garrett ran the offense, while Brian Stewart then Phillips handled the defense. *Hall of Fame Players:* Earl Campbell, John Elway, Shannon Sharpe, Bruce Smith, Thurman Thomas, Gary Zimmerman. *Primary Quarterbacks:* John Elway, Doug Flutie, Tony Romo. *Tendencies:* • His teams scored 22.6 points and allowed 20.5 per game • His teams ran 43.6% of the time, which was 99% of the league average • Nine starting quarterbacks in 11 years; 78% of starts to primary quarterbacks • 12 rookie starters in 11 years • Winning Full Seasons to Losing Full Seasons: 6:1.

Wade Phillips is one of the most dependable defensive coordinators of the last 30 years in the NFL. As a head coach, he has had just one losing full season, but was fired from each of his three non-interim coaching positions after just a few years because the team seemed to be underachieving.

Wade was born in Orange, Texas, the same town as his father Bum. Wade played for his father both in high school and at the University of Houston where he was played linebacker and set the school record for career tackles from 1966 to 1968. The next season, he began his coaching career at his alma mater as a graduate assistant. Wade then coached high school football

Phillips, Wade A.

Year	Team	Games	Wins	Losses	Ties	%	P Wins	P Losses	P %
1985	Saints	4	1	3	0	.250	0	0	.000
1993	Broncos	16	9	7	0	.563	0	1	.000
1994	Broncos	16	7	9	0	.438	0	0	.000
1998	Bills	16	10	6	0	.625	0	1	.000
1999	Bills	16	11	5	0	.688	0	1	.000
2000	Bills	16	8	8	0	.500	0	0	.000
2003	Falcons	3	2	1	0	.667	0	0	.000
2007	Cowboys	16	13	3	0	.813	0	1	.000
2008	Cowboys	16	9	7	0	.563	0	0	.000
2009	Cowboys	16	11	5	0	.688	1	1	.500
2010	Cowboys	8	1	7	0	.125	0	0	.000
11 years		143	82	61	0	.573	1	5	.167

from 1970 to 1972 before joining his dad's defensive staff at Oklahoma State in 1973. Wade stayed a second season at OSU and then one at Kansas before rejoining his father as the Oilers' defensive line coach in 1976. When Bum was replaced in Houston by his defensive coordinator Ed Biles, he moved on to New Orleans and hired Wade as his new defensive coordinator. Wade ran the Saints' defense for five years and then took over as interim coach in 1985 when his dad stepped down with four games to play.

The following season, Phillips took the defensive coordinator position under Buddy Ryan and got to learn the 46 defense, but clearly was subordinate to Ryan with the Eagles' defense over the three years they were together. In 1989, Wade was hired by Dan Reeves in Denver to replace longtime coordinator Joe Collier. Linebacker Karl Mecklenburg told *Sports Illustrated,* "Joe Collier's defense was calculus. Wade's is Algebra. Wade got his best players and let them play." The Broncos went from 20th to first in points allowed that year and went to the Super Bowl. Four years later, Reeves was fired after the 1992 season due to his troubles getting along with quarterback John Elway, and the Bronco players were pleased that easy-going Phillips was hired as the new coach. They were so pleased that they responded with a 16–16 record from 1993 to 1994, and Wade was fired. He would later tell the *New York Times,* "There is a lot of distance between me and Denver. I appreciated the opportunity. I learned some things. But I think all Denver had to do was wait a couple years. The foundation was being laid. It would have all worked out." And it did work out, but with Mike Shanahan guiding back-to-back Super Bowl titles a few years later.

Wade was hired by Marv Levy in Buffalo as defensive coordinator in 1995 and three years later was promoted to head coach when Levy retired in 1998. With the Bills, Phillips became embroiled in a quarterback controversy between the popular Doug Flutie, who was too short and too old, but just won games, and youthful Rob Johnson, who was overly mechanical and sacked more regularly than flour.

Eventually, Phillips went with the younger Johnson, and it was the downfall of the team and the coach. Fired after the 2000 season, Phillips was again hired by Dan Reeves, this time in Atlanta in 2002. A year later, Reeves stepped down with three games to play and Wade stepped in as interim coach once more.

Marty Schottenheimer next hired Phillips as the Chargers' defensive coordinator in 2004 and San Diego's defense improved each year, but the team could not reach the Super Bowl. After finishing 14–2 in 2006, both coordinators left and Schottenheimer was fired. Chargers' offensive coordinator Cam Cameron was named head coach of the Dolphins, and Wade replaced Bill Parcells as the Cowboys' head coach. Parcells had accumulated a lot of talent, and the easy-going Phillips was seen by Jerry Jones as just the right guy to take the team to the Super Bowl, but Dallas proved to be overrated. In 2009, Phillips finally won his first playoff game as a head coach after four losses, but lost the next week to Minnesota to start his Dallas demise. In 2010, things fell apart completely with the Cowboys; the team's lack of discipline and toughness was clear in its 1–7 start, and Wade was replaced by Jason Garrett in mid season. Across the state though, was a Houston Texans' team with the worst pass defense in the league. The Texans hired Wade as defensive coordinator in 2011 to help them reach the postseason for the first time with a vastly improved defense. Houston is his ninth NFL stop; coaching is a hard life for families. When Phillips was in Denver, he told the *New York Times* about his son, "Well, Wesley's 10. I think I'll encourage him to be anything but a coach." However, Wesley was also a Phillips. He joined the Cowboys staff under his father in 2007 and became assistant offensive line coach the year after his father was fired.

POOL, HAMPTON J. 3/11/1915–5/26/2000. Stanford. Played E for the Bears from 1940 to 1943 and the Miami Seahawks in 1946. *Apprenticeship:* Pro asst.—4 years; college asst.—2 years. *Roots:* Jack Meagher (i), Jim Crowley (i), Joe Stydahar. *Branches:*

Ray Richards, Red Hickey. *Coordinators/Key Assistants*: Red Hickey and Mel Hein were key assistants for the Rams. *Hall of Fame Players:* Tom Fears, Elroy Hirsch, Night Train Lane, Les Richter, Andy Robustelli, Norm Van Brocklin, Bob Waterfield. *Primary Quarterbacks:* Norm Van Brocklin. *Tendencies:* • His teams scored 26.3 points and allowed 23.5 per game • His teams ran 55.4% of the time, which was 107% of the league average • Three starting quarterbacks in four years; 81% of starts to primary quarterback • 15 rookie starters in four years • Winning Full Seasons to Losing Full Seasons: 3:0.

Born in San Miguel, California, Hamp Pool was one of the great innovators in the history of the NFL, but too often had trouble getting along with his players and other coaches. He played end for California in 1934, Army in 1935 and Stanford between 1936 and 1939. At Palo Alto, Hamp also was on the track team. He was drafted by the Bears in the ninth round in 1940 and spent four years in Chicago catching passes from Sid Luckman before going into the Navy in 1944.

After the war, Pool signed as a player/assistant coach with the new Miami Seahawks of the All America Football Conference. The Seahawks were an underfunded and undermanned catastrophe, and head coach Jack Meagher quit after just six games. Pool took over as head coach and managed to guide Miami to two of its three wins on the season before the team folded at the end of the year. He returned to Chicago in 1947 as Jim Crowley's assistant on the AAFC's Chicago Rockets. Many sources list Hamp Pool as the coach of the Rockets for the last few games of that season, but contemporary newspaper accounts indicate Crowley was still in charge right to the club's closing trip to Los Angeles. In fact, Pool resigned from the Rockets before Halloween when the team was 0–8.

Staying in his home state, Pool coached at San Jose State in 1948 and San Bernadino Valley in 1949 before being hired as an assistant coach on the Rams under former Bears' teammate Joe Stydahar. Linebacker Don Paul told Mickey Herskowitz for *The Golden Age of Pro Football*, "Joe was a big happy guy, a nice guy. He was good with the press. Pool was the guy who worked his butt off and handled the offense and defense." While Clark Shaughnessy is credited with splitting out multiple receivers wide, Pool is often recognized as the coach who converted the second halfback position into the flanker receiver position. In Los Angeles, he also started alternating the Rams Hall of Fame quarterbacks, Bob Waterfield and Norm Van Brocklin, by quarter. In addition, Hamp was an early designer and practitioner of zone defense in the NFL. After Los Angeles won the 1951 NFL title, an insecure Stydahar came to believe that Pool was after his job and took control of the defense away from Hamp in 1952.

The Rams lost the season opener to the Browns that year, and Stydahar was quoted in the papers saying, "There has been dissension between Pool and myself. I believe a coaching staff should work hand in hand." A day later, Stydahar was forced out as coach, and Pool, who earlier had said he would not accept the head coaching job "under any circumstances," was named coach. "Someone had to step into the breach and take over," he said. The Rams rolled right along as a top contender for the next two years with Hamp in charge. Pool liked his two-quarterback setup and he liked to give his weekly game plans catchy names, such as "Rush 'em, Ram 'em, Ruin 'em." He started the practice of grading players according to performance charts to encourage steady improvement. Pool was a contentious coach who began to have serious troubles with the team by 1954. Linebacker Paul added to Herskowitz, "Hamp was a gung-ho winner who you could learn to detest as you won the championship."

In October 1954, most of Pool's assistant coaches told him they would not be back the following season. In December, Ram players were grumbling and one was quoted as saying, "If Pool stays, there are going to be some very good players who won't be back next year. All we want to do is win the championship, but we've gotten to the point where we don't think we can do it with Hamp Pool." Four coaches resigned immediately after the season finale, and Pool himself quit five days later.

Hamp coached the College All Star team for the next two summers and wrote a book, *Fly T Football,* which was published in 1957. That year he moved north to coach the Toronto Argonauts in Canada, and his key assistant was Joe Thomas who as a general manager would go on to build playoff teams in Min-

Pool, Hampton J.

Year	Team	Games	Wins	Losses	Ties	%	P Wins	P Losses	P %
1946	Miami Seahawks (AAFC)	8	2	6	0	.250	0	0	.000
1952	Rams	11	9	2	0	.818	0	1	.000
1953	Rams	12	8	3	1	.708	0	0	.000
1954	Rams	12	6	5	1	.542	0	0	.000
5 years		43	25	16	2	.605	0	1	.000

nesota, Miami and Baltimore. Pool coached Toronto through 1959, turning down the Eagles job in 1958, but could only manage a 12–30 record. In 1960, new Rams' coach Bob Waterfield brought Hamp back to Los Angeles as his offensive assistant. Pool coached under Waterfield for three years until a second players' revolt in 1962 led to his second exit from the Rams. The 1960s' players found his demeanor too demanding and his offense too antiquated.

Hamp spent 1963 as a Rams' scout and then formed his own Quadra Scouting Agency in 1964 and worked for the Rams, Cowboys, 49ers and Chargers for the next few decades.

PROCHASKA, RAYMOND E. (RAY) 8/9/1919–3/9/1997. Nebraska. Played E for the Rams in 1941. *Apprenticeship:* College asst.—7 years; CFL asst.—3 years; pro asst.—4 years. *Roots:* Pop Ivy. *Branches:* None. *Coordinators/Key Assistants:* None. *Hall of Fame Players:* Larry Wilson. *Primary Quarterbacks:* Sam Etcheverry. *Record:* **Interim Co-Coach** with Chuck Drulis and Ray Willsey.

Ray Prochaska spoke for all ambitious career assistant coaches when he told the *Los Angeles Times,* "I've never been at the right place at the right time. Otherwise, I would have been a head coach a long time ago." As it was, Prochaska coached football for 38 years, but was only a co-head coach for two games on an interim basis in 1961.

Born in Ulysses, Nebraska, Ray played end for Nebraska from 1938 to 1940 and for the Cleveland Rams in 1941 before going into the military during World War II. After being discharged, Prochaska returned to his alma mater in 1947 as an assistant coach. Aside from 1949, he coached on the Huskers' staff through the 1954 season. Ray went north in 1955 to coach the line for Pop Ivy in Edmonton. After winning three Grey Cups in four years, Ivy was hired to coach

the Chicago Cardinals in 1958 and brought Prochaska with him.

Ivy's inventive spread offense did not transfer to the NFL very well, and he resigned in frustration with two games to go in the 1961 season. The Cardinals, by now in St. Louis, appointed the triumvirate of Prochaska and defensive coaches Chuck Drulis and Ray Willsey to supervise the last pair of games of the year. The Cards won both games, but then hired Wally Lemm as the new coach in 1962. Prochaska and Drulis stayed with the Cardinals under Lemm, while Willsey moved on to join the Redskins' staff. During his years with the Cardinals, four members of Ray's St. Louis line went to the Pro Bowl.

When Lemm was fired in 1966, Prochaska was hired by George Allen to coach the Rams' line. Over the next seven years as the Rams' line coach under Allen and then Tommy Prothro, Ray coached five linemen who played in at least one Pro Bowl. Chuck Knox took over the Rams in 1973, and Prochaska was promoted to offensive coordinator of the ball control "Ground Chuck" offense. Ray would spend the rest of his coaching career working under Knox in Los Angeles from 1973 to 1977, Buffalo from 1978 to 1982 and Seattle from 1983 to 1985. In failing health at age 66 in 1986, Prochaska retired from coaching. In retrospect, he admitted to the *Los Angeles Times,* "The only job I really went after was at St. Louis a few years ago [in 1974]. I wanted it real bad. I originally talked to people in Houston and I was scared I would get that job because I wanted the St. Louis job." Ray lost out to Don Coryell that time.

PROTHRO, JAMES T. (TOMMY) 7/20/1920–5/14/1995. Duke. QB; did not play professionally. *Apprenticeship:* College coach—26 years (16 as head coach). *Roots:* None. *Branches:* Dick Vermeil, Bill Walsh, Rich Brooks. *Coordinators/Key Assistants:* For

Prochaska, Raymond E. (Ray)									
Year	Team	Games	Wins	Losses	Ties	%	P Wins	P Losses	P %
1961	Cardinals	2	2	0	0	1.000	0	0	.000
1 year		2	2	0	0	1.000	0	0	.000

Prothro, James T. (Tommy)									
Year	Team	Games	Wins	Losses	Ties	%	P Wins	P Losses	P %
1971	Rams	14	8	5	1	.607	0	0	.000
1972	Rams	14	6	7	1	.464	0	0	.000
1974	Chargers	14	5	9	0	.357	0	0	.000
1975	Chargers	14	2	12	0	.143	0	0	.000
1976	Chargers	14	6	8	0	.429	0	0	.000
1977	Chargers	14	7	7	0	.500	0	0	.000
1978	Chargers	4	1	3	0	.250	0	0	.000
7 years		88	35	51	2	.409	0	0	.000

the Rams, Dick Vermeil was the key offensive coach, while Tom Catlin ran the defense; for the Chargers, George Dickson then Dick Coury then Bill Walsh then Max Coley then Ray Perkins ran the offense, while Jackie Simpson handled the defense. *Hall of Fame Players:* Fred Dean, Charlie Joiner, Deacon Jones, Tom Mack, Merlin Olsen, Jack Youngblood. *Primary Quarterbacks:* Roman Gabriel, Dan Fouts. *Tendencies:* • His teams scored 17.5 points and allowed 20 per game • His teams ran 54.5% of the time, which was 98% of the league average • Eight starting quarterbacks in seven years; 76% of starts to primary quarterbacks • 27 rookie starters in seven years • Winning Full Seasons to Losing Full Seasons: 1:4.

While Tommy Prothro had great success as a college coach, he could not duplicate that in the pros. However, he had a serious impact on three franchises as a builder with a nose for recognizing talent. One observer told the *Los Angeles Times*, "Set Tommy down by a Coke machine, give him a deck of cards, a movie projector and a roomful of yellow tablets to scribble on, and he could live in Arabia, or even Cincinnati."

Tommy's father, Doc Prothro, played major league baseball throughout the 1920s for the Senators, Red Sox and Reds before going into managing. Tommy was born in Memphis and showed talent at both baseball and football. Meanwhile, Doc worked his way up from managing in the minor leagues to being named manager of the Phillies in 1939. Philadelphia was a talentless ball club, and Doc compiled a gruesome 138–320 record from 1939 to 1941 while Tommy was an All-American blocking back for George McAfee at Duke. Doc returned to Memphis in 1942 and bought into the local minor league Chicks; Tommy began his coaching career as an assistant at Western Kentucky that year before going into the Navy for the war.

After being discharged, Tommy was hired by Red Sanders as an assistant at Vanderbilt in 1946. Three years later, Sanders, known for exclaiming, "Winning isn't everything, it's the only thing," moved to Los Angeles to coach UCLA and brought Tommy with him. Tommy stayed on Sanders staff through the Bruins' 1954 national championship season and then was hired by Oregon State as head coach in 1955. Prothro coached the Beavers for 10 years from 1955 to 1964, posted a 63–37–2 record, went to one Rose Bowl and developed one Heisman Trophy winner in rollout quarterback Terry Baker. In 1965, Tommy was lured back to UCLA as head coach. From 1965 to 1970, he coached the Bruins to a 41–18–3 record, went to one Rose Bowl and developed one Heisman Trophy winner in rollout quarterback Gary Beban.

When Rams' owner Dan Reeves finally fired George Allen for good in 1971, he did not look far to replace him, turning to Prothro whose Bruins shared the Los Angeles Coliseum with the Rams and USC

Trojans. Allen's veteran team was unhappy with the change, but Prothro remarked to the *New York Times*, "I heartily support players being loyal to their coach. Ones who are disloyal to one coach are likely to be disloyal to the next one. I don't particularly care to have the affection of the players, but I like to have their respect." The trouble was that the Rams were an aging team that was slipping on the field. Prothro was there only two years, but he did manage to bring in such future standouts as Jack Youngblood, Larry Brooks, Isiah Robertson, Dave Elmendorf and Lawrence McCutcheon in an effort to transform the squad. That transformation saw full fruition under Tommy's successor Chuck Knox.

Prothro sued the Rams for firing him without cause after Reeves' death and eventually won a settlement with new owner Carroll Rosenbloom in 1973. A year later, Tommy returned to the league, taking over the drug-addled San Diego franchise, cleaning house and building the foundation of Don Coryell's highflying Chargers of the late 1970s. Unfortunately, Prothro was never able to produce a winning team himself, though. He once noted to reporters, "I was better younger. The longer you're a head coach, the less you know about football. That's right. You're too busy dealing with alumni, dealing with owners, dealing with press, dealing with problems."

Perhaps his greatest legacy was the coaches who worked for him. Dick Vermeil served under Prothro both for UCLA and the Rams. He told the *Los Angeles Times*, "He has a tremendous mind, and he's a genius at designing daily practice schedules that noticeably improve everybody every day. There's nobody I respect more." Prothro hired Bill Walsh as his offensive coach in 1976 when Walsh was being badmouthed throughout the league by Paul Brown. Walsh felt that Prothro's ethics in looking out for the best interests of his staff members contrasted sharply with Brown and served as an inspiration for how Walsh would treat his own assistants. For his part, Prothro always maintained that he was a teacher above all.

Tommy had an odd quirk of carrying a brief case on the sideline, but in his next position, he found a use for it. Prothro took over as personnel director of the Browns in 1979 and helped build a playoff contender in Cleveland in his three years there. In retirement, Prothro was a celebrated bridge player and was elected to the College Football Hall of Fame in 1991. He died four years later.

RALSTON, JOHN R. 4/26/1927– California. LB; did not play professionally. *Apprenticeship:* College coach —16 years (13 as head coach). *Roots:* None. *Branches:* None. *Coordinators/Key Assistants*: Max Coley ran the offense, while Joe Collier handled the defense. *Hall of Fame Players:* Floyd Little. *Primary Quarterbacks:* Charley Johnson, Steve Ramsey. *Ten-

Ralston, John R.

Year	Team	Games	Wins	Losses	Ties	%	P Wins	P Losses	P %
1972	Broncos	14	5	9	0	.357	0	0	.000
1973	Broncos	14	7	5	2	.571	0	0	.000
1974	Broncos	14	7	6	1	.536	0	0	.000
1975	Broncos	14	6	8	0	.429	0	0	.000
1976	Broncos	14	9	5	0	.643	0	0	.000
5 years		70	34	33	3	.507	0	0	.000

dencies: • His teams scored 22.1 points and allowed 20.8 per game • His teams ran 53.3% of the time, which was 96% of the league average • Four starting quarterbacks in five years; 96% of starts to primary quarterbacks • Eleven rookie starters in five years • Winning Full Seasons to Losing Full Seasons: 3:2.

John Ralston was born in Oakland, but grew up in Norway, Michigan. Right out of high school in 1944, he went into the Marines for the duration of World War II. After the war, Ralston played linebacker for Pappy Waldorf at California from 1948 to 1950 and then coached high school football from 1951 to 1955. He returned to his alma mater as an assistant in 1956 for three years before being named head coach at Utah State in 1959. From 1959 to 1962, John posted a 31–11–1 record at USU and developed such future NFL stars as Merlin Olson, Bill Munson, Len Rohde and Lionel Aldridge.

In 1963, Ralston moved on to Stanford where coaches must contend with higher academic standards in building a winning team. In Palo Alto, John hired some of the best young coaches around as assistants. Bill Walsh later recalled to the *San Francisco Chronicle*, "We were just enjoying working under John. Those weren't serious football days — Stanford football wasn't assertive. We had tough days on the field, but John changed that with an intense recruiting program." Walsh was joined on the staff by Dick Vermeil, Rod Rust, Mike White and, later, Jim Mora. Eventually, Ralston built a team that won consecutive Rose Bowls in 1971 and 1972; the first behind Heisman Trophy winner Jim Plunkett and the second behind unheralded successor at quarterback, Don Bunce.

Ralston was a rah-rah, positive-focused, motivational coach who had been trained by the Dale Carnegie Institute. When John made the leap to the NFL in 1972, he found that the pros don't always buy into that approach or his strong emphasis on conditioning. He took over the lowly Denver Broncos, a franchise that had never had a winning season in its first 12 years. Ralston led the improved Broncos to three winning seasons from 1972 to 1976, including a best ever 9–5 in 1976 right before he was fired. He would later tell a reporter, "I screwed up in Denver. The year after I was fired, Red Miller was in the Super Bowl."

How do you screw up with a 9–5 record? Ralston had turned over the team's roster in five years, but didn't engender loyalty from his players. Guard Mike Current told *Sports Illustrated* in 1972, "John will take more time for everything. He's very precise. We've been trained more like college players than pros. In many cases it's been good because we got back to some fundamentals, but a lot of the players have resented the little things. The more I see of John Ralston, the more he reminds me of Woody Hayes. He's not as obstinate and overbearing, but things are going to be done his way." Four years later, Current was one of the "Dirty Dozen" group of team leaders, including Lyle Alzado, Billy Thompson, Haven Moses, Tom Jackson, Riley Odoms and Otis Armstrong, that instigated a petition that 75% of the team signed to advocate for Ralston's ouster. Perhaps John's biggest mistake was in not finding a franchise quarterback. After veteran Charley Johnson retired, the team was left with career backup Steve Ramsey who was unable to generate enough offense.

Vermeil hired Ralston as offensive coordinator for the Eagles in 1978, and Bill Walsh brought him to San Francisco's front office from 1979 to 1980. John later joined the USFL in 1983, compiling a 9–12 record as the head coach of the Oakland Invaders for 1983 and the beginning of 1984. In 1985, he was named president of the USFL's Portland Breakers until the league folded in 1986. His next move was as GM of the San Jose Golddiggers, a women's professional volleyball team. A year later, Ralston was named the GM of the Sacramento Bees team tennis squad, and then he did some scouting for Seattle from 1989 to 1990. In 1990, he coached the Moscow Bears American football team in Russia and then scouted football players in Europe for NFL Europe in 1991.

John slowed down a bit in 1992 when he helped care for his son who died from AIDS that year, but leaped back into coaching in 1993 at San Jose State where he only attained a 11–34 record from 1993 to 1996. One of his assistants there was former Bronco Rubin Carter who told the Associated Press, "As a player, I considered myself part of his family. He made you feel that way. Being a coach on his staff, I can see what type of a sensitive person he is. He gives players a chance to express themselves, both athletically and as people." As SJS, he did uncover quarterback Jeff Garcia, who Bill Walsh would eventually sign for the

49ers. After stepping aside in 1997, Ralston worked in the athletic department at San Jose for the next decade, despite suffering a stroke in 2005, receiving a pacemaker and undergoing hip replacement surgery. He was elected to the College Football Hall of Fame in 1992.

RAMSEY, GARRARD S. (BUSTER) 3/16/1920–9/16/2007. William & Mary. Played G for the Cardinals from 1946 to 1951. *Apprenticeship:* Pro asst.—10 years. *Roots:* Curly Lambeau, Buddy Parker. *Branches:* Harvey Johnson. *Coordinators/Key Assistants:* Floyd Reid and Tommy O'Connell were the key offensive coaches, while Harvey Johnson handled the defense with Ramsey. *Hall of Fame Players:* Billy Shaw. *Primary Quarterbacks:* Johnny Green. *Tendencies:* • His teams scored 21.1 points and allowed 23 per game • His teams ran 46.2% of the time, which was 99% of the league average • Six starting quarterbacks in two years; 39% of starts to primary quarterback • 23 rookie starters in two years • Winning Full Seasons to Losing Full Seasons: 0:2.

Buster Ramsey was pure Tennessee. He was born in Townsend and died in Signal Mountain and favored both the "Tennessee Waltz" and Tennessee Moonshine. He was an All-American guard at William & Mary in 1942 and was drafted by the Cardinals in the 14th round in 1943, but went into the Navy from 1943 to 1945. After the war, Buster spent six years playing for the Cardinals where he got to know assistant coach Buddy Parker who had a similar volatile personality. Ramsey began his coaching career while still playing for the Cards in 1951. He was traded to Detroit for halfback Jerry Kraft in 1952, and Parker named him as the Lions' defensive coach. With the fiery combination of Parker and Ramsey, Detroit went to three straight NFL title games from 1952 to 1954. Buster had such success in molding Detroit's rugged defense into an early proponent of the 4–3 that he was said to be the highest paid assistant coach in the league.

Parker left Detroit for Pittsburgh in 1957, but Ramsey continued to coach the Lions' defense under new coach George Wilson and won another title in 1957. Buster was considered for the Cardinals head coaching job the next year, but lost out to Pop Ivy. Lions' Hall of Fame cornerback Dick LeBeau remembered Ramsey's to the *Pittsburgh Post-Gazette*, "He was a pressure guy. He liked to bring guys [on the blitz]." In 1960, former Lions' minority owner Ralph Wilson purchased the new American Football League

franchise in Buffalo and signed Ramsey as the Bills' first head coach. Buster later told the *Knoxville News-Sentinel*, "When I say I took over at Buffalo, I mean that literally. I had to order the uniforms, hire my assistants, arrange for a practice place ... just do everything. After the 1961 season, Ralph and I had a falling-out."

That initial Bills' team had a fair-to-middling defense, but a terrible offense that couldn't score any points. Ramsey went through six starting quarterbacks in two years. Halfback Willmer Fowler told Jeffrey Miller for *Rockin' the Rockpile*, "He had an excellent defensive mind—he could defense any team we played. He was tough, there was no question about it, but he was a good coach. He was not an offensive coach at all, he was strictly defense." In 1961, Buster allegedly slugged New York quarterback Al Dorow on the sideline, but he was just as unpredictable with his own team, too. One time he punched Bills' linebacker Archie Matsos and another time fired all his coaches on the team plane home after a loss.

Once he was let go by Buffalo, Ramsey rejoined Parker as the Steelers' defensive coach from 1962 to 1964. Buddy fired Chuck Cherundolo to make room for Buster. In spring 1965, Ramsey retired from football. "Coaching from 1952 through 1964 had left me a nervous wreck," he recalled to the Knoxville paper, "so I retired to this farm which I bought with championship money from those great Detroit and Chicago teams." In retirement, Ramsey raised cattle and served on both the County Commission and the local board of education. He died at age 87.

RAUCH, JOHN 8/20/1927–6/10/2008. Georgia. Played QB for the New York Bulldogs, New York Yanks and Philadelphia Eagles from 1949 to 1951. *Apprenticeship:* College asst.—11 years; pro asst.—3 years. *Roots:* Al Davis. *Branches:* John Madden, Bill Walsh. *Coordinators/Key Assistants:* Rauch handled his own offense, while Charlie Sumner was the key defensive coach; for the Bills, Rauch ran his own offense, while Richie McCabe handled the defense. *Hall of Fame Players:* Fred Biletnikoff, George Blanda, Willie Brown, Billy Shaw, Art Shell, O.J. Simpson, Gene Upshaw. *Primary Quarterbacks:* Daryle Lamonica, Dennis Shaw. *Tendencies:* • His teams scored 23.9 points and allowed 20.7 per game • His teams ran 45.7% of the time, which was 92% of the league average • Eight starting quarterbacks in five years; 56% of starts to

Ramsey, Garrard S. (Buster)									
Year	Team	Games	Wins	Losses	Ties	%	P Wins	P Losses	P %
1960	Bills	14	5	8	1	.393	0	0	.000
1961	Bills	14	6	8	0	.429	0	0	.000
2 years		28	11	16	1	.411	0	0	.000

primary quarterbacks • 18 rookie starters in five years • Winning Full Seasons to Losing Full Seasons: 3:2.

Born in Philadelphia, John Rauch played quarterback at Georgia from 1945 to 1948 and led the Bulldogs to a 36–8–1 record with four bowl game wins. He was the second overall pick in the 1949 NFL draft, but lasted just three years in the league, primarily backing up Bobby Layne for the Bulldogs and George Ratterman for the Yanks. In three years, John completed just 41% of his passes and then retired to go into coaching as an assistant at Florida in 1952. He moved on to Tulane in 1954, his alma mater in 1955, Army in 1959 and returned to Tulane in 1962 before Al Davis hired him to coach the Raiders' backfield in 1963. Rauch spent three years under Davis and was promoted to head coach in 1966 when Al became the AFL Commissioner. Oakland hired Bill Walsh to take Rauch's assistant's slot that year.

Although Rauch and Davis had worked together for three years, the relationship changed when Davis returned as managing general partner in 1967. Even though, John had been handpicked by Al to coach the Raiders, Rauch began to feel that Davis was overly intrusive and second-guessed him too much. After he left the Raiders, John said of Davis, "We couldn't get along. He wouldn't let me be myself. A lot of people said it was his team. Well, it wasn't." That year, Oakland acquired Daryle Lamonica, the "Mad Bomber" from Buffalo, and he made the offense fly. In 1967 and 1968, the Raiders led the league in scoring and went 13–1 and 12–2 while going to Super Bowl II. In the future, both Davis and Rauch would take credit for the Lamonica trade as part of their bitter relationship.

Years later, Bill Walsh recalled to reporter Rich Pagano, "Rauch was an excellent technician and he knew Davis' system very well." Walsh added, "John was a marvelous man, great sense of humor, worked very well with people. He had a brilliant football mind." Walsh also credited Rauch with his own development, "I learned so much of my football from John Rauch, the whole system of offense that is now termed the West Coast Offense, much of it originated through John Rauch." Rauch's linebackers coach and successor as head coach, John Madden, pointed out to Pagano, "It was the passing game and the distribution of receivers where John was so effective. John believed strongly that you don't only have your two wide receivers and your tight end, but you also keep your backs involved to where everyone is a receiver. John was always a believer that you not only had deep threats with your receivers, but you also had deep threats with your backs."

Rauch did not always have much of a relationship with his players, though. When he was named head coach in Oakland, he said, "This is pro football, a cold world, where we're interested in one thing — winning." John was big on meetings, long practices and lots of rules. At Super Bowl II, he told the *New York Times*, "This game is not a game of individuals, although individual effort may count on a single play." The downside of that according to one Bills' player who later spoke to the *Times* was that, "John's kind of players are robots with no feelings whatsoever." Raiders' Hall of Fame center Jim Otto summed up Rauch in his eponymous autobiography, "He really knew offense, but he also knew defense. He was a true football coach. Nevertheless, Rauch ran into problems because of a fragile ego. He was very insecure. He didn't feel appreciated on the Raiders."

So a discontent Rauch quit Oakland in 1969 and signed on as head coach of the 1–13 Buffalo Bills. The only good thing in Buffalo was that their ineptitude that year earned them the top overall draft choice — O.J. Simpson. As it turned out, though, that advantage turned into a liability for John. Rauch was so insistent that his backs be totally involved in all aspects of the offense and that workloads be shared that he underutilized the best running back in the league since Jim Brown. Rauch stubbornly told the press, "I'm not going to build my offense around one back, no matter how good he is." Simpson was an unhappy, unproductive player who gained less than 1,200 yards rushing on just 300 carries in his first two seasons. Rauch then took umbrage at owner Ralph Wilson defending some of his players in the press and quit during training camp in 1971.

John did some scouting for the Packers in 1971 and then caught on as an assistant in Philadelphia for two years. In 1973, he was named head coach of the Toronto Argonauts in Canada. In two years with Toronto, he posted a mediocre 10–9–2 record. Rauch spent 1975 on Marion Campbell's staff in Atlanta and

Rauch, John									
Year	Team	Games	Wins	Losses	Ties	%	P Wins	P Losses	P %
1966	Raiders	14	8	5	1	.607	0	0	.000
1967	Raiders	14	13	1	0	.929	1	1	.500
1968	Raiders	14	12	2	0	.857	1	1	.500
1969	Bills	14	4	10	0	.286	0	0	.000
1970	Bills	14	3	10	1	.250	0	0	.000
5 years		70	40	28	2	.586	2	2	.500

1976 as John McKay's first offensive coordinator in Tampa. He quit the Bucs at the end of the year and worked as a high school coach in 1977 before getting out of football entirely to sell insurance. John returned to the game in 1983 as the director of operations of the Tampa Bay Bandits in the USFL, but that lasted just two years. Rauch retired from football for good in 1985 and lived on to the age of 80.

REEVES, DANIEL E. (DAN) 1/19/1944– South Carolina. Played HB for the Cowboys from 1965 to 1972. *Apprenticeship:* Pro asst.— 9 years. *Roots:* Tom Landry. *Branches:* Mike Shanahan, Wade Phillips, Chan Gailey, Mike Nolan, Emmitt Thomas (i), Dennis Allen. *Coordinators/Key Assistants:* For the Broncos, Rod Dowhower then Mike Shanahan then Chan Gailey then George Henshaw ran the offense, while Joe Collier then Wade Phillips handled the defense; for the Giants, George Henshaw ran the offense, while Mike Nolan handled the defense; for the Falcons, George Sefcik then Reeves then Pete Mangurian ran the offense, while Rich Brooks then Don Blackmon then Wade Phillips handled the defense. *Hall of Fame Players:* Tony Dorsett, John Elway, Shannon Sharpe, Lawrence Taylor. *Primary Quarterbacks:* John Elway, Chris Chandler, Dave Brown. *Tendencies:* • His teams scored 20.1 points and allowed 20 per game • His teams ran 46.9% of the time, which was 103% of the league average • 18 starting quarterbacks

in 23 years; 72% of starts to primary quarterbacks • 31 rookie starters in 23 years • Winning Full Seasons to Losing Full Seasons: 12:9.

Dan Reeves was a coach of distinction. The only coach to win more regular season games than Reeves' 190 without winning a championship is Marty Schottenheimer with 200. Dan, along with Schottenheimer, Chuck Knox and Bill Parcells, are the only coaches to lead at least three different franchises to the playoffs. In the playoffs, he, Bud Grant and Marv Levy are the only coaches with four Super Bowl losses.

Born in Rome, Georgia, Reeves played quarterback up north for South Carolina from 1962 to 1964. Tom Landry converted the weak-armed passer to a slowish halfback adept at the option-pass, similar to the Packers' Paul Hornung. Dan started for the Cowboys in 1966 and 1967 before being injured in 1968 and replaced the following year by the more talented Calvin Hill. Even on the bench, Reeves was a team leader. His roommate, fullback Walt Garrison once said, "Rooming with Dan was damn near like rooming with one of the coaches, because he probably helped me learn more about football than the coaches did." By 1971, Reeves indeed was a player/assistant coach under Landry. When Dan retired from playing in 1973, though, he left the team entirely to go into the construction business. A year later, he was back in Dallas as the running backs coach and would stay on board for seven more years.

Reeves, Daniel E. (Dan)									
Year	*Team*	*Games*	*Wins*	*Losses*	*Ties*	*%*	*P Wins*	*P Losses*	*P %*
1981	Broncos	16	10	6	0	.625	0	0	.000
1982	Broncos	9	2	7	0	.222	0	0	.000
1983	Broncos	16	9	7	0	.563	0	1	.000
1984	Broncos	16	13	3	0	.813	0	1	.000
1985	Broncos	16	11	5	0	.688	0	0	.000
1986	Broncos	16	11	5	0	.688	2	1	.667
1987	Broncos	15	10	4	1	.700	2	1	.667
1988	Broncos	16	8	8	0	.500	0	0	.000
1989	Broncos	16	11	5	0	.688	2	1	.667
1990	Broncos	16	5	11	0	.313	0	0	.000
1991	Broncos	16	12	4	0	.750	1	1	.500
1992	Broncos	16	8	8	0	.500	0	0	.000
1993	Giants	16	11	5	0	.688	1	1	.500
1994	Giants	16	9	7	0	.563	0	0	.000
1995	Giants	16	5	11	0	.313	0	0	.000
1996	Giants	16	6	10	0	.375	0	0	.000
1997	Falcons	16	7	9	0	.438	0	0	.000
1998	Falcons	16	14	2	0	.875	2	1	.667
1999	Falcons	16	5	11	0	.313	0	0	.000
2000	Falcons	16	4	12	0	.250	0	0	.000
2001	Falcons	16	7	9	0	.438	0	0	.000
2002	Falcons	16	9	6	1	.594	1	1	.500
2003	Falcons	13	3	10	0	.231	0	0	.000
23 years		357	190	165	2	.535	11	9	.550

Reeves was approached by some teams about their head coaching vacancies, but did not leave Landry until 1981 when he was named head coach of the Broncos. In Denver, Dan made a trade with San Francisco to import Steve DeBerg to challenge his former Cowboys' teammate 38-year-old Craig Morton at quarterback that year, but DeBerg could not unseat Morton until the strike season of 1982 when the team dropped to 2–7. Fortunately, help was on the way in 1983 when the league's top draft pick John Elway refused to sign with the Colts who selected him, so Denver was able to trade for the future Hall of Famer to be its franchise quarterback.

Reeves had his greatest coaching success in Denver, with three trips to the Super Bowl and eight winning seasons in 12 years. Elway was a big part of that, but the two men grew increasingly distant over the decade they were together. Offensive coach Mike Shanahan was caught in the middle of this clash while leaning towards his star quarterback. At their first Super Bowl together in 1987, Reeves told the *New York Times*, "We both had to mature. I had to learn some things as a coach and he had to learn some as a quarterback." Despite leading the team to the playoffs six times under Reeves, Elway was frustrated by the coach's conservative offense that often left the quarterback having to scramble to pull out victories at the last minute. Reeves' Broncos were never a great team in terms of personnel. They never had a great running back, the wideouts and line were just so so and the defense, while three times finishing in the league's top three in fewest points allowed, was undersized. Essentially, Elway carried the Broncos for a decade.

As such, each trip to the Super Bowl became more one-sided. Against the Giants in 1987, Denver was in the game till halftime; against the Redskins, they competed through the first quarter; against the 49ers in 1990, they were never in the game. Dan told the *Times*, "A lot of coaches called me and said they would have loved to be in my position. I said about the middle of the third quarter, I would have given it to any of them." Elway made it clear to owner Pat Bowlen that he and Reeves could no longer coexist in 1993, so Dan was fired.

Reeves landed on his feet as the new coach of the Giants four weeks later. New York GM George Young had originally considered hiring Dan in 1979, but went with Ray Perkins instead. 14 years later, the time was right, and 1993 was a great year for Reeves and the Giants. He kept the team in contention for the division title right to the last week before losing out to the Cowboys. The coach told the *Times*, "I think if you look at it, John Elway and I both proved that we didn't need each other to be successful, but I think it also proved that both of us need a lot of people around us to be successful." Behind quarterback Phil Simms and the league's top scoring defense, New York won 11

games that year, but then Simms was cut in the off-season as a salary cap casualty. The remainder of Dan's time in New York was one of decline as he relied on the failed quarterbacks that Young drafted, Dave Brown and Kent Graham, as well as his own draft bust from Denver, Tommy Maddox. Because the coach and GM were in conflict over the draft and other personnel matters, Reeves left after the 1996 season.

Hired by Atlanta in 1997, Dan brought his trademarked discipline, order and attention to detail to his home state and remade the Falcons into a Super Bowl team a year later behind a pounding running attack and opportunistic defense as well as adequate passing from injury-prone journeyman quarterback Chris Chandler. That team was known for its "Dirty Bird" dance after victories, and when Atlanta beat Minnesota in the NFC Championship, Reeves did his own version of the shuffle, just weeks removed from undergoing heart surgery. Receiver Tim Dwight told *Sports Illustrated*, "He's back on the sideline a month after open-heart surgery. He's old school. There's not much we wouldn't do for this guy."

Unfortunately in Super Bowl trip number four he ran into his old nemesis John Elway coached by his "disloyal" former assistant Mike Shanahan. Reeves couldn't resist opening up old wounds by saying, "The biggest problem I had was when John Elway had a problem with me, and you're coaching his position, why did I not know that prior to reading that in the paper." Shanahan fired back, "It was a tough relationship from the second year, from the first year. Everybody in this town knows that." Shanahan and Elway had the better team and the last laugh, handily beating Reeves' Falcons for their second consecutive championship.

While Atlanta immediately declined, Reeves got a second chance when the team drafted Mike Vick in 2001. Vick led Atlanta to a winning season in his second year as a pro, but then got hurt in 2003, and Reeves resigned before the year was out. Dan was up for the 49ers offensive coordinator slot in 2009, but that, as well as a consultant's role with the Cowboys that year, fell through, and he has remained retired.

REID, ANDREW W. (ANDY) 3/19/1958– Brigham Young. T; did not play professionally. *Apprenticeship:* College asst.—10 years; pro asst.—7 years. *Roots:* Mike Holmgren. *Branches:* Brad Childress, John Harbaugh, Steve Spagnuolo, Leslie Frazier, Ron Rivera, Pat Shurmur. *Coordinators/Key Assistants*: Rod Dowhower then Brad Childress then Marty Mornhinweg ran the offense, while Jim Johnson then Sean McDermott then Juan Castillo handled the defense. *Hall of Fame Players:* None. *Primary Quarterbacks:* Donovan McNabb, Michael Vick. *Tendencies:* • His teams scored 23.4 points and allowed 19 per game • His teams ran 41.3% of the time, which was 94% of the league average • Nine starting quarterbacks in 13 years; 81% of starts to primary quarterbacks • 29 rookie starters in 13 years • Winning Full Seasons to Losing Full Seasons: 9:2.

Andy Reid is very much the son of his football "father" Mike Holmgren in style, demeanor and success. Despite being the winningest coach in Eagles' history, however, Reid's popularity in Philadelphia is on the weak side. Andy's clear preference for the passing game over the running game does not match the smashmouth style favored by the fans, and his reticence to interact with the fans and local media does nothing for his Philly reputation.

Reid played tackle at pass-happy Brigham Young and then spent a season on the coaching staff as a graduate student under new offensive coordinator Mike Holmgren in 1982. Reid moved on the following year to become offensive line coach at San Francisco State, where Holmgren had last coached before BYU. Andy coached the offensive line at SFS from 1983 to 1985, Northern Arizona in 1986, Texas El Paso from 1987 to 1988 and Missouri from 1989 to 1991 before being tapped in 1992 to join Holmgren's first Packers' staff as the tight ends/assistant offensive line coach. Remarkably, five of Holmgren's first-year assistants would become NFL head coaches. Reid spent five years coaching tight ends and linemen before moving up to quarterbacks' coach for Brett Favre in 1997 and 1998. The Packers thought so highly of Reid that they also named him assistant head coach so that another team couldn't hire him away as offensive coordinator. The 3–13 Eagles bypassed the coaching chain in 1999, though, and hired Andy as head coach with final say on football personnel decisions.

Reid inherited a terrible, undisciplined team that had scored only 161 points while giving up 344 the previous year. Starting quarterback choices were dazed Bobby Hoying, weak-armed Koy Detmer or fragile Rodney Peete. Yet, Andy won a playoff game in his

second season and became a consistent winner. It was an amazing turnaround fueled by low-key free agent signings, smart drafts and good coaching. It began with his first draft.

During the run-up to the 1999 draft, Eagle fans clamored loudly for the team to select Texas running back Ricky Williams with the second overall pick in the draft. A local talk radio station even bused a group of vociferous fans known as the "Dirty Thirty" to the draft to cheer for Williams' selection. However, Reid knew he needed a quarterback to run his West Coast Offense and picked Syracuse quarterback Donovan McNabb instead to a vigorous chorus of boos from that fan group. Once Reid picked McNabb, the fans clamored for him to play immediately. Andy again did things his way. He signed longtime Packer backup Doug Pederson to an overly generous free agent contract to break in the offense for the team and to mentor the rookie quarterback. Despite fan belligerence, Reid held off on starting McNabb until he felt the rookie was ready in the second half of the 1999 season.

The next year began a five-year streak of making the playoffs that included four straight appearances in the NFC Championship game. Three times in that stretch Philadelphia finished second in the NFL in fewest points allowed. One thing that was holding the team back was a lack of a big-time receiver, though, and the fans were frustrated with Reid's insistence that his mediocre receiving corps was adequate. Andy shocked everyone in 2004 by signing egotistical receiver Terrell Owens, and TO helped the Birds reach the Super Bowl that season before blowing up the team with divisive behavior in 2005. McNabb had a series of injuries and the team started to get old in some spots, so Reid began turning over the roster in 2007. The Eagles snuck back into the NFC title game in 2008, however, the ending was a familiar one — they lost. When the team got steamrolled by Dallas in the last game of the 2009 season and again the following

Reid, Andrew W. (Andy)

Year	Team	Games	Wins	Losses	Ties	%	P Wins	P Losses	P %
1999	Eagles	16	5	11	0	.313	0	0	.000
2000	Eagles	16	11	5	0	.688	1	1	.500
2001	Eagles	16	11	5	0	.688	2	1	.667
2002	Eagles	16	12	4	0	.750	1	1	.500
2003	Eagles	16	12	4	0	.750	1	1	.500
2004	Eagles	16	13	3	0	.813	2	1	.667
2005	Eagles	16	6	10	0	.375	0	0	.000
2006	Eagles	16	10	6	0	.625	1	1	.500
2007	Eagles	16	8	8	0	.500	0	0	.000
2008	Eagles	16	9	6	1	.594	2	1	.667
2009	Eagles	16	11	5	0	.688	0	1	.000
2010	Eagles	16	10	6	0	.625	0	1	.000
2011	Eagles	16	8	8	0	.500	0	0	.000
13 years		208	126	81	1	.608	10	9	.526

week in the opening playoff game, it was clearly a sign that something had to change. Reid boldly traded the only regular starting quarterback he had ever had to arch division rival Washington and turned the team over to McNabb's heir Kevin Kolb for a new start in 2010. As it turned out, though, Kolb was injured and replaced by disgraced former prison inmate Michael Vick who Reid had signed in 2009 in a clear commitment to second chances in life — a commitment especially strong after the coach's two sons both served jail time for a series of unsavory actions.

Andy Reid is seen as a cautious organization man, and the Eagles are a very frugal team who do not pay for past performance. Over the years, Reid has consistently made the wrenching decision to unload a popular veteran leader who was passing his peak: McNabb, Brian Westbrook, Brian Dawkins, Jeremiah Trotter, Hugh Douglass, Troy Vincent and Duce Staley. By firmly subscribing to his principles, Reid built a solid squad and has maintained it at a top level for a decade. Andy loves the big play and sometimes completely forgoes the run in his play calling. While he is sometimes justly criticized time management blunders and for not making in-game adjustments — particularly in championship games, Andy has proven to be a very clever play caller who always is willing to throw in change ups and gadget plays to keep the offense from getting stale.

With the passing of the McNabb era, Reid faced a formidable challenge to maintain his regular season success with a new signal caller who had a somewhat different skill set. With Vick playing quarterback better than he ever had despite essentially a three-year layoff from the NFL while McNabb struggled in Washington, the 2010 season demonstrated what a skilled quarterback mentor Andy Reid is. However, of Super Bowl winning coaches, only Bill Cowher waited as long to win his first as Reid has thus far. Feeling the heat, Andy again loaded up for a Super Bowl run with some high profile free agent signings in the 2011 off season. Unfortunately, the so-called "Dream Team" blundered through an 8–8 season, plagued by 38 turnovers, the second worst total in the league. With an inconsistent offense and rudderless defense, the Eagles surrendered a fourth quarter lead in five games, and Reid found himself serenaded by

chants of "Fire Andy" from disgruntled Philly fans. Although Andy was retained for the 2012 season, the pressure to win a Super Bowl continues to build in Philadelphia.

RHODES, RAYMOND E. (RAY) 10/20/1950– TCU and Tulsa. Played WR/DB for the Giants and 49ers from 1974 to 1980. *Apprenticeship:* Pro asst.—14 years. *Roots:* Bill Walsh, George Seifert, Mike Holmgren. *Branches:* Jon Gruden, Bill Callahan, Sean Payton, Mike McCarthy, Joe Vitt (i), Emmitt Thomas (i). *Coordinators/Key Assistants*: For the Eagles, Jon Gruden then Dana Bible ran the offense, while Emmitt Thomas handled the defense; for the Packers, Sherm Lewis ran the offense, while Emmitt Thomas handled the defense. *Hall of Fame Players:* Richard Dent, Art Monk. *Primary Quarterbacks:* Rodney Peete, Ty Detmer, Brett Favre. *Tendencies:* • His teams scored 19 points and allowed 21.7 per game • His teams ran 43% of the time, which was 98% of the league average • Six starting quarterbacks in five years; 70% of starts to primary quarterbacks • 15 rookie starters in five years • Winning Full Seasons to Losing Full Seasons: 2:2.

Born in tiny Mexia, Texas, Ray Rhodes came up the hard way. He once asserted to the *New York Times*, "I feel more comfortable as an underdog. This has been my life. I had to fight and claw for everything I've gotten — nobody has given me anything." He was a 10th round draft pick of the Giants in 1974 and spent three years with them as a wide receiver before being converted to defensive back in 1977. Three years later, he was traded to San Francisco where he came under the influence of Bill Walsh. After one season as a 49er, Rhodes joined the team's coaching staff, tutoring the defensive backs for the next decade and winning four Super Bowl rings. When offensive coordinator Mike Holmgren was named head coach of the Packers in 1992, he hired Ray as his defensive coordinator. After two years, Ray was homesick for San Francisco and returned to the 49ers as defensive coordinator in time to win a fifth ring in 1994.

With this background, he was hired by the Eagles in 1995, to replace Rich Kotite who had taken Buddy Ryan's talented team and dismantled it. Rhodes went about completely revamping the club by bringing in

Rhodes, Raymond E. (Ray)									
Year	Team	Games	Wins	Losses	Ties	%	P Wins	P Losses	P %
1995	Eagles	16	10	6	0	.625	1	1	.500
1996	Eagles	16	10	6	0	.625	0	1	.000
1997	Eagles	16	6	9	1	.406	0	0	.000
1998	Eagles	16	3	13	0	.188	0	0	.000
1999	Packers	16	8	8	0	.500	0	0	.000
5 years		80	37	42	1	.469	1	2	.333

scores of free agents and aging retreads. In addition to signing big name runner Ricky Watters in that first year, Rhodes also imported three starting offensive linemen, several defensive linemen, linebackers Bill Romanowski, and Kurt Gouveia and quarterback Rodney Peete. Rhodes tried to restructure the Eagles as a very scrappy, hungry team, but was unable to get through to shifty, wifty quarterback Randall Cunningham. With the team sitting at 1–3, Randall was benched. New starter Rodney Peete did not have the skills that Randall did, but he was a leader with heart who led Philadelphia on a 9–3 stretch that got them into the playoffs for the first time in three years.

Many more free agents would follow in the ensuing three years, but the most significant free agents were receiver Irving Fryar, cornerback Troy Vincent and fullback Kevin Turner in 1996, center Steve Everitt, linebacker Darrin Smith and kicker Chris Boniol in 1997. Defensive end Hugh Douglass was also acquired in 1998 via trade. However, Rhodes success in the draft was spotty. His first round picks were the disappointing Mike Mamula, the long-term project Jermayne Mayberry, the flop Jon Harris and the blue chipper Tra Thomas. Aside from second round picks Bobby Taylor in 1995 and Dawkins in 1996, the rest of Rhodes' picks were projects. Some would eventually be successful in Philadelphia like Duce Staley, Jeremiah Trotter and Ike Reese. Others would develop elsewhere, but most would simply languish like Jason Dunn, Barrett Brooks, Chris T. Jones, and Bobby Hoying. It was no way to build a team.

After Rhodes initial success when his fiery leadership was being compared by some to Vince Lombardi, the team declined rapidly. Ron Jaworski told *Sports Illustrated*, "One year, that stuff's good for one year. Sometimes not even that long." When a coach amps up his pregame speeches to the twilight zone level of comparing the opposing team to a band of rapists about to attack the players' wives, he's going to be tuned out. Ray was shown to be a tough guy fraud who could not develop talent, could not fix ongoing special teams' problems and could not manage quarterbacks. Rhodes had tried unsuccessfully to obtain Packer backup quarterback Mark Brunell in 1995 but settled for Ty Detmer as a free agent in 1996. Early in the 1996 season, starter Rodney Peete hurt his knee and Detmer at last got his chance. Things couldn't have gone better at first as the Eagles won Ty's first four starts, but in the second half of the year both Det-

mer and the Eagles unraveled. The team made the playoffs, but played poorly in being shut out by San Francisco. In 1997, Detmer just barely won the starting job in training camp and the team went from Detmer to Peete to Bobby Hoying in the next two dismal seasons before Rhodes was fired.

Meanwhile, Mike Holmgren left Green Bay, and GM Ron Wolf was presented with a dilemma: the Packers had been pushing offensive coordinator Sherm Lewis as a great head coaching candidate to several teams, but Wolf did not think he was right for Green Bay. On top of that, Lewis was black, so that if he was passed over by his own team that would not sit well with many Packer players. So Wolf brought Rhodes back to Green Bay as head coach as the tough new sheriff in town. Rhodes retained Lewis on offense and brought Emmitt Thomas with him as defensive coordinator so that for the first time in the NFL a head coach and both coordinators were all black.

Unfortunately, Rhodes had no control over the team. While he would get upset, he would not enforce discipline on or off the field. Wolf told Chuck Carlson for *Tales from the Packers Sideline*, "The players just didn't respond to Ray. The team had no life and it had to change." So after one 8–8 season, Rhodes was fired, with Wolf drawing some racially tinged criticism from Jesse Jackson that ultimately did not amount to much. Subsequently, Rhodes worked as defensive coordinator for the Redskins in 2000, the Broncos from 2001 to 2002 and the Seahawks from 2003 to 2005 until he suffered a stroke. After recovering, Ray returned to Seattle for two more years as a defensive assistant and then moved on to Houston in 2008 and Cleveland in 2011.

RICE, HOMER C. 9/9/1937– Centre. QB; did not play professionally. *Apprenticeship:* College coach — 9 years (4 as head coach); pro asst.—1 year. *Roots:* Bill Johnson. *Branches:* Chuck Studley (i), Frank Gansz. *Coordinators/Key Assistants*: Boyd Dowler was the key offensive coach, while Howard Brinker handled the defense. *Hall of Fame Players:* None. *Primary Quarterbacks:* Ken Anderson. *Tendencies:* • His teams scored 19.4 points and allowed 21.9 per game • His teams ran 52.1% of the time, which was 97% of the league average • Two starting quarterbacks in two years; 96% of starts to primary quarterback • Eight rookie starters in two years • Winning Full Seasons to Losing Full Seasons: 0:1.

The developer of the "Total Person Concept"

Rice, Homer C.									
Year	Team	Games	Wins	Losses	Ties	%	P Wins	P Losses	P %
1978	Bengals	11	4	7	0	.364	0	0	.000
1979	Bengals	16	4	12	0	.250	0	0	.000
2 years		27	8	19	0	.296	0	0	.000

while athletic director at Georgia Tech, Dr. Homer Rice was driven and goal-oriented, but took a different approach to success than most NFL coaches. Perhaps that's why he only spent two years in the league. Rice was born in Bellevue, Kentucky, and was an All-State quarterback in high school in 1944. Although he was offered a scholarship to Georgia Tech at the time, he enlisted in the Navy instead and served in the Philippines during the war. After the war, he enrolled at Centre College in Kentucky and also played baseball as a catcher in the Dodgers' chain.

Homer graduated in 1950 and went right into coaching at the high school level. From 1951 to 1961 he amassed a 102–9–7 record coaching in Kentucky and Tennessee high schools before joining Blanton Collier's staff at the University of Kentucky in 1962 where he worked with quarterback Rick Norton. Rice moved on to Oklahoma in 1966 and then was named head coach at the University of Cincinnati in 1967 where he developed quarterback Greg Cook. After two years and a disappointing 8–10–1 record, Homer was named athletic director at North Carolina in 1969 and ran that program for seven years. In 1976, Rice moved on to Rice University as athletic director and football coach. While he tutored future NFL star Tommy Kramer there, Homer only compiled a 4–18 record in two seasons.

Rice left for the Bengals as Bill Johnson's offensive coordinator in 1978. Johnson was in his third season as Paul Brown's replacement, but when the team got off to a 0–5 start with quarterback Kenny Anderson sidelined with an injury, Brown fired Johnson and named Rice the interim coach. Brown and Rice shared some history together. In the 1950s when he was coaching high school, Rice used to attend the Cleveland Browns' training camp to learn from Paul Brown. In addition, Homer's starting quarterback at the University of Cincinnati, Greg Cook, was drafted by Brown in 1968.

Brown extended Rice's contract after the team won four of its first eight games under Homer. However, Rice was not cut out to be a pro coach, and the team flopped in 1979 despite the return of Anderson behind center. Guard Dave Lapham later told reporters that the team lacked discipline and toughness under Rice, "We had 45 or so guys going in 45 or so directions. That's what we had. Guys out of shape. Hey, by the end of the season, your weight is supposed

to be down. Ours? We had guys 30, 40 pounds heavier than they were when the season started." Paul Brown fired Homer at season's end and said, "It was obvious we weren't getting it done. I'd go out week after week hopeful, but things began to happen so much of the time. Something always seemed to be happening to us. These little things have got to be controlled." Rice admitted, "Paul Brown did what he thought was right, and I believe in him."

Homer landed on his feet as the athletic director at Georgia Tech in 1980 and had a very successful 18-year tenure presiding over a model college athletic program. During his time at Tech, Rice earned his doctorate from Columbia Pacific and developed concepts on leadership on which he wrote a series of books. In all, Homer has written four books on football, particularly focusing on his own triple option offense, and four on leadership, including two since he retired from Tech in 1997 at the age of 70.

RICHARDS, RAY 7/16/1906–9/18/1974. Nebraska. Played G/T for the Frankford Yellow Jackets in 1930 and for the Chicago Bears and Detroit Lions from 1933 to 1936. *Apprenticeship:* Semipro asst.— 2 years; college coach —14 years (2 as head coach); pro asst.— 4 years. *Roots:* Joe Stydahar, Hampton Pool, Keith Molesworth. *Branches:* Wally Lemm, Chuck Drulis (i). *Coordinators/Key Assistants*: Otis Douglass and John Kellison coached the line, Tommy Thompson then Charlie Trippi coached the backs, Ray Nowaskey coached the ends and Wally Lemm and Chuck Drulis coached the defense. *Hall of Fame Players:* Night Train Lane, Charlie Trippi. *Primary Quarterbacks:* Lamar McHan. *Tendencies:* • His teams scored 18.4 points and allowed 20.4 per game • His teams ran 61.7% of the time, which was 105% of the league average • Three starting quarterbacks in three years; 92% of starts to primary quarterback • Seven rookie starters in three years • Winning Full Seasons to Losing Full Seasons: 1:2.

Kicker and broadcaster Pat Summerall fondly recalled Cardinals' Coach Ray Richards in his book *Giants,* "Richards was a real gentleman and very low-key, although he was in no way inspirational. He had a good knowledge of the game." In other words, another fine assistant coach who was ill matched as a head coach.

Richards was born in Liberty, Nebraska, and was

Richards, Ray

Year	Team	Games	Wins	Losses	Ties	%	P Wins	P Losses	P %
1955	Cardinals	12	4	7	1	.375	0	0	.000
1956	Cardinals	12	7	5	0	.583	0	0	.000
1957	Cardinals	12	3	9	0	.250	0	0	.000
3 years		36	14	21	1	.403	0	0	.000

an All-American tackle for the Huskers during his senior year in 1929. Ray spent 1930 playing for the Frankford Yellow Jackets in the NFL before beginning a tour as a professional wrestler. He returned to football in 1933 with the Chicago Bears, moved on to the Lions in 1934 and then returned to the Bears in 1935. After one game with Chicago in 1936, Richards joined the independent Los Angeles Bulldogs as a player/assistant coach under Gus Henderson.

In 1937, Ray was hired as the line coach for the UCLA Bruins and remained there for 11 seasons before moving on to nearby Pepperdine in 1948. A year later, he was promoted to head coach at Pepperdine and posted an 8–10 record there over two seasons. Richards then joined the staff of former Bears' teammate Joe Stydahar as the Rams' line coach in 1951. Stydahar quit in 1952, and Ray moved on to Baltimore as former Bear Keith Molesworth's line coach in 1953. He rejoined Stydahar in Chicago in 1954 as the Cardinals' line coach before replacing his friend as the team's head coach in 1955. Stydahar issued a statement saying, "Richards and I are the best of friends. He's a very capable coach. I wish him a lot of luck and hope he wins the championship." Richards noted his new challenge, "Our main task will be getting everybody to pull together again and to find a quarterback who can throw the long pass."

His quarterback was the inconsistent, skittish second-year man Lamar McHan, and the team showed little improvement in 1955. Richards tried a new offense in 1956, though, and the Cards got off to a 5–1 start and stayed in the divisional race all year. That year Ray installed the Split-T offense that was popular in the college ranks and had success with it because it fit the skill level of his running quarterback who lacked a reliable passing touch. The coach told *Sports Illustrated*, "He's really a wonderfully accurate passer and this year, with all the passing developing off our Split-T running plays, he hasn't been rushed hard." Richards also followed Paul Brown's lead that year and installed a radio in his quarterback's helmet to call plays from the sideline although Commissioner Bert Bell outlawed that practice by midseason.

After a loss to the Giants in week seven, the season came apart the next week in Pittsburgh when a nervous McHan asked Richards to not start him that week. Ray started McHan, pulled him when he struggled and then put him in again in the loss to the Steel-

ers. After the game, Richards was taken to the hospital with a gall bladder attack, and McHan was suspended and fined $3,000 by the team's assistant coaches because he had changed plays sent in from the bench and refused to reenter the game at one point. McHan met with Richards a few days later and was reinstated with the fine being rescinded, but the team would win just two of its last four games.

The Cardinals declined from second to 11th in defense in 1957, losing seven of the last eight games of the year. While Owner Walter Wolfner told Richards the job was his as long as he wanted it, Ray was forced out at the year's end. He coached the line for the Packers in 1958 and then retired from football entirely. Richards later ran a chemical company for several years.

RILEY, MICHAEL J. (MIKE) 7/6/1953– Alabama. DB; did not play professionally. *Apprenticeship:* College coach—15 years (2 as head coach); CFL coach—7 years (4 as head coach); WLAF head coach—2 years. *Roots:* None. *Branches:* None. *Coordinators/Key Assistants:* Geep Chryst then Norv Turner ran the offense, while Joe Pascale handled the defense. *Hall of Fame Players:* None. *Primary Quarterbacks:* Jim Harbaugh, Doug Flutie. *Tendencies:* • His teams scored 18.1 points and allowed 22.4 per game • His teams ran 39.5% of the time, which was 91% of the league average • Six starting quarterbacks in three years; 69% of starts to primary quarterbacks • Four rookie starters in three years • Winning Full Seasons to Losing Full Seasons: 0:2.

Born in Wallace, Idaho, Mike Riley grew up in Corvallis, Oregon, where his dad, Bud Riley, coached the defense at Oregon State under Dee Andros. Mike played quarterback and led Corvallis High to the state title before being recruited to Alabama where he played defensive back for Bear Bryant from 1971 to 1974 and was part of the 1973 national championship team. Riley went directly into coaching after graduation, working at California in 1975, Whitworth College in Washington in 1976 and Linfield College in Oregon from 1977 to 1982.

Mike moved up to the CFL in 1983 as an assistant with Winnipeg for three years and then returned to the collegiate ranks at Colorado in 1986. Named head coach at Winnipeg in 1987, Riley compiled a 40–32 record over the next four years and won

Year	Team	Games	Wins	Losses	Ties	%	P Wins	P Losses	P %
Riley, Michael J. (Mike)									
1999	Chargers	16	8	8	0	.500	0	0	.000
2000	Chargers	16	1	15	0	.063	0	0	.000
2001	Chargers	16	5	11	0	.313	0	0	.000
3 years		48	14	34	0	.292	0	0	.000

two Grey Cup Championships. In 1991, he was hired as the head coach of the San Antonio Riders of the developmental World League of American Football and posted an 11–9 record in two seasons. Once again he returned to college coaching in 1993 as John Robinson's offensive coordinator at USC, where he tutored future NFL quarterback Rob Johnson.

After a four-year stint with the Trojans, Riley went home in 1997 as the head coach of the long-dormant Oregon State Beavers. Under Mike, the team began to show improvement in two seasons with an 8–14 record, but he left two years later to become the Chargers' head coach in 1999. San Diego had a strong defense, but had won just five games the previous year primarily due to the atrocious quarterbacking of rookie Ryan Leaf and backup Craig Whelihan. Riley imported veteran quarterbacks Jim Harbaugh and Erik Kramer in 1999 and posted a .500 record in his first year. The divisive Leaf returned from an injury in 2000, and both the offense and defense collapsed. The resultant 1–15 record nearly cost Mike his job, but he returned in 2001 with new quarterbacks Doug Flutie and Drew Brees. The Chargers got off to a 5–2 start before ending the season on a nine-game losing streak that cost the coach his job. Riley's Chargers endured losing streaks of 11, nine and six games during his three-year stint.

Mike spent 2002 on Jim Haslett's Saints' staff before being rehired as OSU's head coach in 2003. Over the next nine years, Riley's Beavers went 64–59, including a 5–1 record in bowl games. When he was fired by San Diego, Mike was asked what he had accomplished and said, "I don't know, but I did it my way. I treated people the way I wanted to, and I coached the team the way I wanted to. I feel good about that." Riley is clearly in his preferred element as a college coach. Recently asked about coaching in the NFL, he said simply, "I wouldn't do it again."

RINGO, JAMES S. (JIM) 11/21/1931–11/19/2007. Syracuse. Played C for the Packers and Eagles from 1953 to 1967. *Apprenticeship:* Pro asst.— 8 years. *Roots:* Jim Dooley, Abe Gibron, Lou Saban. *Branches:* None. *Coordinators/Key Assistants:* Ringo ran his own offense, while Richie McCabe and Jimmy Carr handled the defense. *Hall of Fame Players:* Joe Delamielleure, O.J. Simpson. *Primary Quarterbacks:* Joe Ferguson. *Record:* **Hall of Fame Player.** *Tendencies:* • His teams scored 12.7 points and allowed 26 per game • His teams ran

47.7% of the time, which was 83% of the league average • Two starting quarterbacks in two years; 70% of starts to primary quarterback • Seven rookie starters in two years • Winning Full Seasons to Losing Full Seasons: 0:2.

Jim Ringo was a native of Orange, New Jersey and went on to play center for Ben Schwartzwalder at Syracuse from 1950 to 1952. Drafted by the Packers in the seventh round in 1953, the 6'1" and sub-230 pound lineman was so small that he left training camp after just two weeks because he felt he wasn't big enough to compete. Prompted to return by his wife and father, Ringo began a 15-year career in which he was All-Pro seven times, played in 10 Pro Bowls, set an NFL record for consecutive games played with 182, and was elected to the Hall of Fame in 1981. Jim relied on his intelligence, intensity, and quickness to become the best center of his era. He was fortunate also that he joined the league just as the position of middle guard was being phased out by the advent of the middle linebacker. Ringo's quickness and smarts were great assets in blocking the faster, more active middle linebacker.

Ringo played in Green Bay for 11 years until he was traded in 1964 to Philadelphia for the last four years of his career. An apocryphal story took hold that Jim brought in an agent to negotiate his 1964 contract with Vince Lombardi, and the volatile coach reacted by asking the agent to step outside for five minutes. When the agent returned, Lombardi informed him that he was negotiating with the wrong team — Ringo had been traded to Philadelphia. The story reputedly demonstrated Lombardi's iron control, but was patently false. Jim was traded along with former first round draft choice fullback Earl Gros to the Eagles for linebacker Lee Roy Caffey and the Eagles' 1965 first round draft choice that would be used for All-American halfback Donny Anderson. A deal of this magnitude and involving this much talent could not be thrown together spontaneously in a five-minute phone call. Ringo actually requested a trade to the East Coast where he lived to be closer to his family and business interests.

After four years with the Eagles, Ringo retired in 1968 and was out of football for a year. He returned to the NFL in 1969 as the Bears' line coach, but had actually begun his coaching career by helping out with spring practice at his alma mater for several years while he was playing professionally. Three years later, Lou

Ringo, James S. (Jim)									
Year	Team	Games	Wins	Losses	Ties	%	P Wins	P Losses	P %
1976	Bills	9	0	9	0	.000	0	0	.000
1977	Bills	14	3	11	0	.214	0	0	.000
2 years		23	3	20	0	.130	0	0	.000

Saban hired him in Buffalo to build a line for O.J. Simpson in 1972. That Buffalo line became known as "The Electric Company" because it turned on the "Juice" as Simpson was called. Hall of Fame guard Joe DeLamielleure told Sal Maiorana for *Memorable Stories of Buffalo Bills Football,* "Ringo was a great line coach, we had a great scheme and we'd do it over and over. We only ran about four different plays. I think it would work today. You have to have guards who can run. Everybody on that line could run a 5.0 flat except for Dave Foley.... That was the key to our line. We were like the Green Bay Packers of the 60s. That's all it was. Jim Ringo came in and put the Green Bay sweep in."

While that line helped O.J. set league rushing records, the team was never a serious Super Bowl contender under Saban. In 1976 with the roster deteriorating, Saban stepped down with the Bills at 2–3. Ringo replaced him, but later told the *Express-Times* of Pennsylvania's Lehigh Valley," One day Lou looked around the locker room and didn't see anybody [good]. That's why he quit. I did my best to fill in. I was in the wrong place at the wrong time." Two games later, starting quarterback Joe Ferguson went down to injury and was replaced by Gary Marangi who would never win an NFL start. Buffalo lost the last nine games under Jim in 1976, including a Thanksgiving loss to Detroit in which Simpson ran for a record 273 yards. The losing streak would reach 13 games in 1977 before Ringo would win his first game as a head coach.

Jim was fired at the end of his second season. He was hired by New England as line coach in 1978 and promoted to offensive coordinator in 1979. He later served as the line coach for the Rams in 1982 and the Jets in 1983–1984 before returning to Buffalo as offensive coordinator in 1985. He retired from the game in 1989.

RIVERA, RONALD E. (RON) 1/7/1962– California. Played LB for the Bears from 1984 to 1992. *Apprenticeship:* Pro asst.—14 years. *Roots:* Dave Wannstedt, Andy Reid, Lovie Smith, Norv Turner. *Branches:* None. *Coordinators/Key Assistants:* Rob Chudzinski ran the offense, while Sean McDermott handled the defense. *Hall of Fame Players:* None. *Primary Quarterbacks:* Cam Newton. *Tendencies:* • His team scored 25.4 points and allowed 26.8 per game • His team ran 44.5% of the time, which was 104% of the league average • One starting quarterbacks in one year; 100% of starts to primary quarterback • Five rookie starters

in one year • Winning Full Seasons to Losing Full Seasons: 0:1.

The son of a U.S. army officer, Ron Rivera was born in Fort Ord, California. He played linebacker for California and was drafted in the second round of the 1984 NFL draft by the Bears, but didn't become a starter for Chicago until 1988. He spent his entire career with the Bears playing under veteran defensive coordinators Buddy Ryan and Vince Tobin and retired in 1993. After four years as a Chicago-area TV analyst, Rivera began his coaching career on Dave Wannstedt's Bears' staff in 1997. He moved on to the Eagles in 1999 before returning to the Bears as Lovie Smith's defensive coordinator in 2004. In the wake of Chicago's surprise Super Bowl run in 2006, a longstanding personal conflict with Smith led to Ron being dismissed. He signed on as the linebackers coach in San Diego in 2007 and was promoted to defensive coordinator a year later. The Chargers' defense improved each year under Rivera until leading the league in fewest yards allowed in 2010.

Rivera took over the 1–15 Carolina Panthers, saying, "When you get into playing, you strive for one thing; that's to be a Super Bowl champion. When you get into coaching, you strive to be a Super Bowl-winning head coach. That's what my goal is." He also emphasized the importance of the quarterback position, "If there is one thing I've been fortunate to be around the last four years is a franchise quarterback in Philip Rivers."

Ron acted on that need for a quarterback with his first draft pick, Cam Newton, and turned the offense over to the rookie for Rivera's first game with the Panthers. Newton rewarded Ron's confidence with explosive performances right from the start, and the team did show marked improvement in 2011. Rivera's task now is to surround his franchise quarterback with championship quality teammates.

ROBERTS, JOHN D. (J.D.) 10/24/1932– Oklahoma. G; did not play professionally. *Apprenticeship:* College asst.— 8 years; pro asst.—1 year; semipro head coach — 2 years. *Roots:* Tom Fears. *Branches:* John North, Ken Shipp (i). *Coordinators/Key Assistants:* Ken Shipp then John North ran the offense, while Jim Champion and Marv Matuszak were the key defensive coaches. *Hall of Fame Players:* None. *Primary Quarterbacks:* Archie Manning. *Tendencies:* • His teams scored 16.2 points and allowed 25.7 per game • His teams ran 45.9% of the time, which was 85% of the

Rivera, Ronald E. (Ron)									
Year	Team	Games	Wins	Losses	Ties	%	P Wins	P Losses	P %
2011	Panthers	16	6	10	0	.375	0	0	.000
1 year		16	6	10	0	.375	0	0	.000

league average • Three starting quarterbacks in three years; 69% of starts to primary quarterback • 19 rookie starters in three years • Winning Full Seasons to Losing Full Seasons: 0:2.

J.D. Roberts was just 5'10" and his weight dropped from 230 to 185 pounds during his time playing guard for Bud Wilkinson's Oklahoma Sooners from 1951 to 1953, but he was both an All-American and the Outland Trophy winner as a senior. Upon graduation, the Oklahoma City native entered the Marines and was not drafted by the NFL. J.D. began his coaching career in 1957 as an assistant at the University of Denver and returned to his alma mater a year later, again under Wilkinson. Roberts once said of his college coach, "I learned from him. After getting out of the Marines, I was on his staff as an assistant. He hated mistakes, and the mental part was harder than the physical challenge."

Roberts moved on to the Naval Academy in 1960, Auburn in 1961 and the University of Houston in 1962. After three years with the Cougars, J.D. quit coaching in 1965, but returned in 1968 as an assistant on Tom Fears' Saints' staff. A year later, he took over the New Orleans farm team, the Richmond Roadrunners of the Atlantic Coast Football League and led it to a 7–5 record. Richmond changed its name to Saints in 1970 and then lost their coach to the parent club halfway through the season. Fears was fired with the team mired at 1–5–1, and Roberts replaced him. While Richmond, in the midst of a 2–10 season, threatened to sue New Orleans for stealing their coach, J.D. was not worth the fuss.

In Roberts' first game, kicker Tom Dempsey set an NFL record with a 63-yard gamewinning field goal against the Lions in the closing seconds. It would be the high point of his coaching career. A year later, Roberts cut Dempsey. Despite drafting Archie Manning in 1971, the Saints were a terrible team with no real prospects of improving. On top of the lack of talent, there was a clear disparity between the former Marine coaching the team and the 1970s players. J.D. later told the *Tulsa World*, "I had a bunch of long-haired draft-dodgers."

The experience of coaching the Saints soured Roberts on the coaching profession, and he never coached again after New Orleans fired him following the 1972 season. J.D. became successful in the oil and gas business and was heavily involved in alumni activities for Oklahoma.

ROBINSON, JOHN A. 7/25/1935– Oregon. E; did not play professionally. *Apprenticeship:* College coach — 22 years (7 as head coach); pro asst.—1 year. *Roots:* John Madden. *Branches:* Norv Turner, Jeff Fisher. *Coordinators/Key Assistants:* Jimmy Raye then Bruce Snyder then Ernie Zampese ran the offense, while Fritz Shurmur then Jeff Fisher handled the defense. *Hall of Fame Players:* Eric Dickerson, Jackie Slater, Jack Youngblood. *Primary Quarterbacks:* Jim Everett. *Tendencies:* • His teams scored 21.6 points and allowed 21 per game • His teams ran 49.7% of the time, which was 107% of the league average • Seven starting quarterbacks in nine years; 56% of starts to primary quarterback • 14 rookie starters in nine years • Winning Full Seasons to Losing Full Seasons: 6:3.

Although hailing from Chicago, John Robinson grew up alongside John Madden in Daly City, California, with the two friends dreaming big dreams that

Roberts, John D. (J.D.)									
Year	Team	Games	Wins	Losses	Ties	%	P Wins	P Losses	P %
1970	Saints	7	1	6	0	.143	0	0	.000
1971	Saints	14	4	8	2	.357	0	0	.000
1972	Saints	14	2	11	1	.179	0	0	.000
3 years		35	7	25	3	.243	0	0	.000

Robinson, John A.									
Year	Team	Games	Wins	Losses	Ties	%	P Wins	P Losses	P %
1983	Rams	16	9	7	0	.563	1	1	.500
1984	Rams	16	10	6	0	.625	0	1	.000
1985	Rams	16	11	5	0	.688	1	1	.500
1986	Rams	16	10	6	0	.625	0	1	.000
1987	Rams	15	6	9	0	.400	0	0	.000
1988	Rams	16	10	6	0	.625	0	1	.000
1989	Rams	16	11	5	0	.688	2	1	.667
1990	Rams	16	5	11	0	.313	0	0	.000
1991	Rams	16	3	13	0	.188	0	0	.000
9 years		143	75	68	0	.524	4	6	.400

came true for both of them with Madden going into the Pro Football Hall of Fame and Robinson elected to the College Football Hall of Fame. In January 1977, both coaches achieved their greatest triumphs in Pasadena's Rose Bowl Stadium: Robinson's USC Trojans winning the Rose Bowl on New Year's Day and Madden's Raiders winning the Super Bowl at the same site eight days later.

Robinson played end for Oregon from 1955 to 1957, briefly appearing in the 1958 Rose Bowl. After graduation, John served in the Army and then began his coaching career as an assistant at his alma mater from 1960 to 1971. In 1972, he moved to Los Angeles as John McKay's offensive coach at USC for three years before joining his friend John Madden's staff in Oakland in 1975. The next year he returned to USC to replace the revered McKay who was hired to coach Tampa in the NFL. Over the next seven years, Robinson led the Trojans to a 67–14–3 record, including three Rose Bowl victories, two Heisman Trophy winners in Charles White and Marcus Allen and one national championship in 1978.

John retired in 1983, but then was named head coach of the Rams that same year. His approach in the pros was the same as in college as he told *Sports Illustrated*, "My concept of the game is physical football. Play defense well. Run the ball well. You've got to do those things." While Robinson did not have the ultimate success with the Rams he did at USC, he still made the playoffs six times in nine years. His pal Madden marveled to *Sports Illustrated*, "It is amazing what he has done without a quarterback in a league that everyone says requires a quarterback. John took what he had — the running game and special teams — and did them as well as they've been done in a long time. And he did it by knowing people, by seeing their strengths and weaknesses, getting them doing what they can do best. Bill Walsh, say, plays football like a game of chess. John plays it like a game of people." Of course, Walsh's 49ers beat Robinson's Rams eight of 12 times in six seasons and won two Super Bowls in that time.

Robinson's biggest star on the Rams was Eric Dickerson, but the two had a falling out and the Hall of Fame runner was traded in 1987. By this time, big-armed Jim Everett was on board as the team's quarterback and Robinson allowed offensive coordinator Ernie Zampese to open up the offense. Finishing second and third in the league in scoring led to playoff

trips in 1988 and 1989, but then both Everett and the Rams fell off drastically for John's last two seasons at the helm.

Robinson retired in 1992, but then returned to USC for a second stint as head coach in 1993. Over the next five years, the Trojans went 37–21–1 for a combined mark at USC of 104–35–4. Again, John retired in 1998, only to return as head coach of UNLV in 1999. He was less successful with the Running Rebels, posting a substandard 28–42 record from 1999 to 2004. He stepped down as coach in 2005, but ultimately could not stay away. In 2010 at age 75, he began helping out the local high school team in San Marcos. He once told the *New York Times*, "What I enjoy about coaching is getting a guy to do what he can do. A lot of times people want to be something they are not. Heck, I was a kid once. I know how I wanted to run this fast or always have this or that as my play. But I like my guy doing what he can do. Sometimes that's a tough lesson to learn."

ROBISKIE, TERRY J. 11/12/1954– Louisiana State. Played RB for the Raiders and Dolphins from 1977 to 1981. *Apprenticeship:* Pro asst.—18 years. *Roots:* Tom Flores, Mike Shanahan, Norv Turner. *Branches:* Todd Bowles (i), Chuck Pagano. *Coordinators/Key Assistants:* None. *Hall of Fame Players:* Darrell Green, Deion Sanders, Bruce Smith. *Primary Quarterbacks:* Luke McCown. *Record:* **Interim Coach.**

Fiery New Orleans native Terry Robiskie starred at running back for LSU from 1974 to 1976 and then joined the Oakland Raiders as an eighth round draft pick in 1977. Despite never being more than a backup and special teams player in the NFL, Robiskie later recalled to Canton's *The Repository*, "I believed in John Madden. If John would have said, 'We're going to jump off the Golden Gate Bridge,' I would have jumped. I learned from John Madden. I learned what it was to be everything I'd ever dreamed of being in my life ... not only as a coach, but as a human being."

Robiskie began his coaching career with the Raiders in 1982 and worked his way up from running backs to special teams to tight ends ultimately to offensive coordinator in 1989 under Art Shell. Terry coached the Raiders' offense for four years before being replaced by Tom Walsh in 1993. He also was interviewed for head coaching vacancies in Green Bay in 1992 and his alma mater in 1994, but did not get either

Robiskie, Terry J.									
Year	Team	Games	Wins	Losses	Ties	%	P Wins	P Losses	P %
2000	Redskins	3	1	2	0	.333	0	0	.000
2004	Browns	6	1	5	0	.167	0	0	.000
2 years		9	2	7	0	.222	0	0	.000

job. In 1994, Robiskie joined Norv Turner's Redskins' staff as receivers coach. He was promoted to passing game coordinator in 2000. Washington got off to a 7–6 start and owner Daniel Snyder had seen enough of Turner's mediocrity. Dan called Robiskie at 12:30 at night and had Terry come in to tell him that he was replacing Turner with former college coach Pepper Rodgers who would need Robiskie to call the plays. Terry angrily refused, upset that he was being passed over for head coach, and went home. Snyder called him back an hour later and had him come back again, but still was unable to persuade Robiskie to accept the new arrangement. Terry went home again. An hour later Snyder called and summoned him a third time; this time, he offered Robiskie the interim coaching position.

Terry was named coach later that morning, and defensive end Bruce Smith told the *Washington Post*, "If I'm in an alley and I'm in a fight, I want to look over my shoulder and see Terry Robiskie." Under Robiskie, the Redskins won one of their three final games and Terry was dismissed. He joined Butch Davis' staff in Cleveland in 2001 as receivers coach. When the team started 2004 3–7, Davis was fired, and Robiskie got his second chance to be an interim coach. He told *The Repository*, "I really believe a big part of coaching is motivating. I don't have any hesitation to say I can get that done. I think one of the greatest qualities in any coach is to be a teacher, and I think I can be a tremendous teacher of the game. I'll say to [owner Randy Lerner], 'Give me a year. I believe I can motivate my kids to play. I believe I can teach 'em how to play and teach them how to win.'"

In that light, *Sports Illustrated* reported that Robiskie brought a shovel into the locker room before his first game as Browns' head coach and asked his players, "If I were digging a hole to hell and going to fight the devil and had nothing but this bucket of ice to fight him with, would you go with me?" His motivated players then went out and lost 42–15 to the Patriots. The undermanned Browns went 1–5 under Robiskie, and he was replaced by Romeo Crennel in 2005. Terry stayed on staff in Cleveland for two more years before leaving for the Dolphins in 2007. Since 2008, he has coached the Falcon receivers. His son Brian has played wide receiver for the Browns since 2009.

ROGERS, DARRYL 5/28/1935– Fresno State. WR; did not play professionally. *Apprenticeship:* College coach — 24 years (19 as head coach). *Roots:* None. *Branches:* Wayne Fontes. *Coordinators/Key Assistants:* Bob Baker ran the offense, while Wayne Fontes handled the defense. *Hall of Fame Players:* None. *Primary Quarterbacks:* Eric Hipple, Chuck Long. *Tendencies:* • His teams scored 17.3 points and allowed 22.6 per game • His teams ran 44.7% of the time, which was 95% of the league average • Five starting quarterbacks in four years; 78% of starts to primary quarterbacks • Eight rookie starters in four years • Winning Full Seasons to Losing Full Seasons: 0:4.

Los Angeles native Darryl Rogers had a decent college coaching career, but was a complete failure in the pros. Rogers played end and defensive back for Fresno State from 1955 to 1957 and began his college coaching career as an assistant at Cal State Hayward in 1961. After five years there, he was named head coach at his alma mater in 1966 and posted a 43–32–1 record over the next seven years at FSU. He switched to San Jose State in 1973 and went 22–9–3 from 1973 to 1975, earning himself a Big Ten job in 1976 when Michigan State hired him as head coach. Over the next four years, the Spartans finished 24–18–2. Rumors spread that Rogers was leaving for Arizona State, but Darryl denied them right up until leaving for Arizona State in 1980. He coached ASU from 1980 to 1984 and compiled a 37–18–1 record. Rumors spread that he was leaving for the pros, but Darryl denied them right up until leaving for the Lions' job in 1985. His overall college record was 126–77–7, but he only went to one bowl game in 19 years.

With the Lions, his coaching progression ended. Detroit did not just become a bad organization under Matt Millen in the new millennium; they have been poorly run for 50 years. Billy Sims retired right before Rogers arrived and left the team without any weapons on offense. Relying on Eric Hipple and then draft bust Chuck Long at quarterback produced an anemic fading offense that scored fewer points each year, while the defense was never better than mediocre. Rogers did manage to bump up Monte Clark's 4–11–1 team to a 7–9 record in his first year, but that would be his high point in Detroit. As the Lions slipped from seven to five to four win seasons, speculation ramped up that Darryl would be fired. In 1987 with the team at 2–9,

Rogers, Darryl

Year	Team	Games	Wins	Losses	Ties	%	P Wins	P Losses	P %
1985	Lions	16	7	9	0	.438	0	0	.000
1986	Lions	16	5	11	0	.313	0	0	.000
1987	Lions	15	4	11	0	.267	0	0	.000
1988	Lions	11	2	9	0	.182	0	0	.000
4 years		58	18	40	0	.310	0	0	.000

owner William Ford, who had been publicly criticizing his team, made a surprise visit to the Silverdome to assure the team and the public that Rogers would not lose his job at the end of the season. Allegedly, Rogers commented sarcastically, "What does it take to get fired around here?" Darryl did tell the *Detroit Free Press* later that year, "To be honest, a .500 season next year would be a hell of an effort."

Rogers did not come close to that modest goal. With the team at 2–9 again in 1988, Ford fired him. Darryl resurfaced in 1991 as the head coach of the Winnipeg Blue Bombers in Canada, but managed just a 9–9 record before being let go. He was announced as the head coach of the Arkansas Miners of the Professional Spring Football League in 1992, but the league never got off the ground. Rogers never coached again.

RONZANI, EUGENE B. (GENE) 3/28/1909–9/14/1975. Marquette. Played HB and QB for the Bears from 1933 to 1938 and 1944–1945. *Apprenticeship:* College asst.—1 year; pro asst.—3 years; semipro head coach—4 years. *Roots:* George Halas. *Branches:* Hugh Devore, Scooter McLean, Chuck Drulis (i). *Coordinators/Key Assistants*: Scooter McLean coached the backs, while Tarzan Taylor coached the line, and Chuck Drulis coached the defense. *Hall of Fame Players:* Tony Canadeo, Jim Ringo. *Primary Quarterbacks:* Tobin Rote. *Tendencies:* • His teams scored 20.9 points and allowed 29.3 per game • His teams ran 47.8% of the time, which was 89% of the league average • Three starting quarterbacks in four years; 83% of starts to primary quarterback • 32 rookie starters in four years • Winning Full Seasons to Losing Full Seasons: 0:3.

Gene Ronzani played and coached under one legend in Chicago, George Halas, and replaced another, Curly Lambeau, in Green Bay. Born in the town of Iron Mountain in Michigan's Upper Peninsula, Ronzani went to college in Wisconsin at Marquette where he was the first athlete to win nine letters from 1930 to 1932. Ronzani played basketball and track, but starred on the gridiron as an All-American back. Halas signed Gene for the Bears in 1933 and he was a steady performer for Chicago over the next six years. In 1939, he retired from playing to become head coach of the Newark Bears, Chicago's farm team. From 1939 to 1941, he led Newark to a 14–13–2 record. Newark shut down for the war, and Gene was recalled to

Chicago as a player in 1944 and 1945. After the war, the Bears reconstituted their farm team in Akron in 1946, again with Ronzani in charge. Akron finished the year 8–3, and Gene moved back to Chicago as an assistant coach for the next three years.

When the Packers ousted Lambeau in 1950, they turned to their chief rival, the Bears, for his replacement. Ronzani was a highly respected assistant in the league, and he hired a coaching staff of all former Bears. His biggest legacy in Green Bay, though, was the hiring of Chicago native Jack Vainisi as talent scout. Vainisi's drafts ultimately would provide Vince Lombardi with a nearly ready made championship team when he was named head coach at the end of the decade. Ronzani was not so fortunate.

The Packers were a very weak team in 1950, and Gene's efforts to rebuild the talent base were only partially successful. When he was fired with two games to play in 1953, he told the *Chicago Tribune*, "If I was the cause of our failure, they now can prove it. I'm glad to be out of it." He added, "All one has to do is compare us man for man with other teams to discover it is not a great club. Maybe next year or the year after, with a few additions, it will be." Being more specific, he noted, "We have no powerful fullback, no real break away runners in the backfield and lack experience in some spots. Also the Packers are not a big team. It is, however, a much better team than the one I took over in 1950."

Hall of Fame halfback Tony Canadeo told Richard Whittingham for *What a Game They Played*, "Ronzani knew a helluva lot about football. He was trying desperately to rebuild the football team and that was a pretty tough job." He tried to be innovative by installing a precursor to the Shotgun offense for running quarterback Tobin Rote. Ronzani also brought the first black players to Green Bay, with end Bob Mann being the very first in 1950, and changed the team colors from blue and gold to green and gold, a change that remains in place to this day. The team's poor record in conjunction with coaching turnover and some player dissension led to his firing after a dismal Thanksgiving loss to Detroit in 1953 that involved a second half collapse. Gene spent 1954 as the Steelers' backfield coach and then got out of coaching. Iron Mountain had a Gene Ronzani Day in 1969 to celebrate their favorite son; he died six years later.

Ronzani, Eugene B. (Gene)									
Year	*Team*	*Games*	*Wins*	*Losses*	*Ties*	*%*	*P Wins*	*P Losses*	*P %*
1950	Packers	12	3	9	0	.250	0	0	.000
1951	Packers	12	3	9	0	.250	0	0	.000
1952	Packers	12	6	6	0	.500	0	0	.000
1953	Packers	10	2	7	1	.250	0	0	.000
4 years		46	14	31	1	.315	0	0	.000

Ross, Robert J. (Bobby) 12/23/1936– Virginia Military Institute. QB: did not play professionally. *Apprenticeship:* College coach — 23 years (15 as head coach); pro asst. — 4 years. *Roots:* Marv Levy. *Branches:* Gary Moeller (i), John Fox, Jim Zorn. *Coordinators/ Key Assistants:* For the Chargers, Jack Reilly then Ralph Friedgen ran the offense, while Bill Arnsparger then Dave Adolph handled the defense; for the Lions, Sylvester Croom ran the offense, while Larry Peccatiello handled the defense. *Hall of Fame Players:* Barry Sanders. *Primary Quarterbacks:* Stan Humphries, Charlie Batch. *Tendencies:* • His teams scored 20.8 points and allowed 19.9 per game • His teams ran 43.7% of the time, which was 99% of the league average • Ten starting quarterbacks in nine years; 72% of starts to primary quarterbacks • 14 rookie starters in nine years • Winning Full Seasons to Losing Full Seasons: 4:1.

Bobby Ross was a ramrod-straight disciplinarian with a natural affinity for military institutions who is somewhat underappreciated for his significant coaching accomplishments. Born in Richmond, Bobby stayed in state to play quarterback at the Virginia Military Institute from 1956 to 1958. He served in the Army as a Lieutenant from 1960 to 1962 and then coached high school football for the next two years. In 1965, Ross returned to his alma mater as an assistant coach before moving on to Marv Levy's staff at William and Mary in 1967. He spent four years at William and Mary, one at Rice and one at Maryland until earning his first head coaching position at The Citadel in 1973.

Ross had little success at The Citadel; a 24–31 record over five years ultimately reunited him with Levy as the Chiefs' special teams coach in 1978. He switched to running backs coach in 1980 and resigned in 1982 to become head coach at Maryland. Over the next five years in College Park, Bobby posted a 39–19–1 record and developed future NFL quarterbacks Boomer Esiason, Frank Reich and Stan Gelbaugh. He traveled south to Georgia Tech in 1987 and slowly rebuilt that program from 2 wins in his first year to an undefeated National Championship season in 1990.

His five-year record at Tech was 31–26–1 when Chargers' GM Bobby Beathard offered Ross his first NFL head coaching job in 1992.

San Diego was coming off a 4–12 record. The Chargers began Bobby's first season 0–4 but ended it on an 11–1 tear that powered the team into the playoffs. Two years later, San Diego reached the Super Bowl where they were blasted 49–26 by a superior 49ers' club. Ross' Chargers' team was driven by a pounding running attack and a tough defense, yet strong-armed quarterback Stan Humphries let loose with the occasional bomb as well. Two years after the Super Bowl entry, though, conflicts surfaced with discontented players and with management. Bobby resigned following the 1996 season, saying, "Bobby Beathard felt our philosophical differences could not be overcome. I was surprised by that." While Ross never had a losing season in San Diego, the franchise would not have another winning season for eight years.

Bobby landed with Detroit the next year and improved the Lions' record from 5–11 to 9–7 in 1997. Defensive problems led to the team sliding to just five wins in 1998 and then Hall of Fame runner Barry Sanders dropped a bomb shell in the offseason by unexpectedly retiring. Sanders had never fully embraced the militaristic Ross style, so Bobby was blamed by some for Sanders' retirement. Ross complained to the *New York Times*, "I have coached football nearly all my life and to have to answer those kinds of questions about my character and my motives, it's insulting. You'd think I just rolled out of bed today and have no history with coaching and with players. It's nonsense the way that is happening, how I'm being crucified for a guy that just doesn't want to play football anymore."

Again Ross began to lose control of his team and with Matt Millen hired as the team's new GM in 2000, Bobby could see the writing on the wall. He resigned after nine games in 2000, telling ESPN, "I just don't have the energy level that you've got to have for the job, however you want to put it." Ross got his energy level back during three years of retirement and took on a new challenge in 2004 by coaching Army.

Ross, Robert J. (Bobby)

Year	Team	Games	Wins	Losses	Ties	%	P Wins	P Losses	P %
1992	Chargers	16	11	5	0	.688	1	1	.500
1993	Chargers	16	8	8	0	.500	0	0	.000
1994	Chargers	16	11	5	0	.688	2	1	.667
1995	Chargers	16	9	7	0	.563	0	1	.000
1996	Chargers	16	8	8	0	.500	0	0	.000
1997	Lions	16	9	7	0	.563	0	1	.000
1998	Lions	16	5	11	0	.313	0	0	.000
1999	Lions	16	8	8	0	.500	0	1	.000
2000	Lions	9	5	4	0	.556	0	0	.000
9 years		137	74	63	0	.540	3	5	.375

From 2004 to 2006, Ross's record at West Point was a slight 9–25, but it was a marked improvement from the previous three years record for the team of 4–32. At the age of 70, Bobby retired for good in 2007.

Rush, Clive H. 2/14/1931–8/22/1980. Miami (OH). Played E for the Packers in 1953. *Apprenticeship:* College coach —10 years (3 as head coach); pro asst.— 6 years. Roots: Weeb Ewbank. *Branches:* John Mazur. *Coordinators/Key Assistants:* John Mazur ran the offense, while John Meyer was a key defensive coach. *Hall of Fame Players:* None. *Primary Quarterbacks:* Mike Taliaferro. *Tendencies:* • His teams scored 16.3 points and allowed 23.1 per game • His teams ran 50.3% of the time, which was 102% of the league average • Two starting quarterbacks in two years; 86% of starts to primary quarterback • Three rookie starters in two years • Winning Full Seasons to Losing Full Seasons: 0:1.

Clive Rush had perhaps the saddest and most bizarre head coaching tenure in NFL history and ultimately would pass away before reaching age 50. Born in De Graff, Ohio, Rush played end for Woody Hayes in state at Miami University through 1952 and then spent one season with the Green Bay Packers. In 1954, he began his coaching career at Dayton before moving on to Ohio State as Hayes' top assistant for three years. Subsequently, Clive coached under Bud Wilkinson at Oklahoma in 1958 and then returned to OSU in 1959 until getting his shot as a head coach at Toledo in 1960. Posting a meager 8–20 record at Toledo through 1962, Rush left in 1963 to become Weeb Ewbank's offensive coach with the Jets. Clive played a key role in developing Joe Namath as a professional quarterback, and Joe said in the aftermath of New York's triumph in Super Bowl III, "I hope [Clive] doesn't take the job with the Patriots. He's too damn good a football coach for us to lose. I want him to stay with the Jets as long as I'm here." Ewbank noted to the *New York Times*, "I told Clive when I hired him that when I retire, I would do everything in my power to make him the coach."

Patriots' owner Billy Sullivan went to that Super Bowl game hoping to hire a coordinator from the winning team, either Chuck Noll of the Colts or Rush from the Jets. When the Jets upset Baltimore, Sullivan hired Rush and left Noll for Pittsburgh. The first omen that things were not going to work out well for the Pats came at Clive's first press conference in Boston when he was electrocuted by a loose microphone wire.

His first comment after getting over the shock was, "I heard the Boston press are tough, but I didn't think they were this tough."

What was really tough, though, was winning just five of his 21 games as Boston's head coach. Instead, his tenure was known for a series of odd incidents:

• He insisted the team's bus driver drive the wrong way up a one way road.
• He tried to call Commissioner Pete Rozelle from the field telephone during one game.
• Suspicious of the team's locker room being bugged, he announced in a loud voice new position assignments to confuse the imagined eavesdroppers.
• He fired quarterback Tom Sherman for his negative comments to the press.
• He instituted the Black Power Defense in one game by putting 11 black players on defense at one time, but had to employ some offensive players to fill out the scheme since the Patriots didn't have 11 black defensive players.

After the 1969 season, Rush checked into Massachusetts General Hospital suffering from nervous exhaustion. As the 1970 season was about to begin, he cut two defensive backs and had the PA announcer at Harvard Stadium intone, "Will Bob Gladieux please report to the locker room." Gladieux, who had been cut from the team earlier, happened to be in the stands and was rehired on the spot to play that day. Center Jon Morris told Baker and Corbett for *The Most Memorable Games in Patriots History*, "Clive Rush had some serious problems. He suffered from depression. He was an alcoholic. He had this idea in mind that because he worked for Paul Brown in Ohio, he was the next great coach coming down the line. He didn't have a clue. He couldn't deal with his demons, and we as players and fans suffered for it."

Clive resigned in November, announcing, "I'll never coach this football team again. If you want to know why I resigned, you'll have to ask [minority owner] Dave Marr." George Allen hired Rush for his Redskins' staff in March 1971, but Clive resigned six weeks later. He got out of football and sold insurance, but concluded, "I tried to fall in love with insurance, but I couldn't." He returned to coaching in 1976 with the Merchant Marine Academy. Although Rush led the school to an 8–1 record that year, he was fired at season's end because of player unrest. Subsequently, Clive ran a car dealership and became the regional di-

Rush, Clive H.

Year	Team	Games	Wins	Losses	Ties	%	P Wins	P Losses	P %
1969	Patriots	14	4	10	0	.286	0	0	.000
1970	Patriots	7	1	6	0	.143	0	0	.000
2 years		21	5	16	0	.238	0	0	.000

rector for Groliers, the company that published the *Encyclopedia Americana*. He died from a sudden heart attack at age 49 in 1980.

RUST, RODNEY A. 8/2/1928– Iowa State. LB; did not play professionally. *Apprenticeship:* College coach —13 years (6 as head coach); CFL asst.— 3 years; pro asst.—14 years. *Roots:* Dick Vermeil, Marv Levy, Ron Meyer, Raymond Berry, Frank Gansz. *Branches:* None. *Coordinators/Key Assistants:* Jimmy Raye ran the offense, while Charley Sumner handled the defense. *Hall of Fame Players:* Andre Tippett. *Primary Quarterbacks:* Tommy Hodson, Marc Wilson. *Tendencies:* • His team scored 11.3 points and allowed 27.9 per game • His team ran 40.1% of the time, which was 87% of the league average • Three starting quarterbacks in one year; 75% of starts to primary quarterbacks • Five rookie starters in one year • Winning Full Seasons to Losing Full Seasons: 0:1.

Rod Rust was born in Webster City, Iowa, and played center and linebacker for Iowa State from 1947 to 1949. He went directly into coaching and worked in that profession for more than 50 years at all levels, but only spent one year as an NFL head coach. Rod coached high school football in Iowa for the decade of the 1950s until Marv Levy gave him his first break by hiring Rust as an assistant at New Mexico in 1960. Following three years with Levy and four with John Ralston at Stanford, Rod was named head coach at North Texas State in 1967. He posted a modest 29–32–1 record from 1967 to 1972, but did prepare Mean Joe Greene for the NFL during his tenure.

In 1973, Rust reunited with Levy in Canada as the defensive coordinator of the Montreal Alouettes. Three years later, he joined another veteran of Ralston's Stanford staff, Dick Vermeil, as Dick's defensive coordinator in Philadelphia in 1976. By 1978, Rod was back with Levy a third time, this time as defensive coordinator in Kansas City. After a five-year stint, he moved on to New England in 1983 as Ron Meyer's defensive coordinator. When Meyer tried to scapegoat Rust by firing him midway through 1984, the players revolted and Meyer found himself replaced by Raymond Berry. The low key Rust was immediately reinstated by the Patriots, and the team went to the Super Bowl a year later.

Rust returned to Kansas City in 1988 and moved on to Pittsburgh in 1989 until at last winning the dubious reward of being named head coach of the sinking Patriots in 1990. Rod's one year as head coach was a complete disaster. At 61, he was the second oldest coach in the league, and things quickly spun out of control on and off the field. One receiver, Irving Fryar, was arrested on a weapons charge; another, Hart Lee Dykes, was beaten in a nightclub. Reporter Lisa Olson was verbally accosted by several naked Patriot players in the locker room after practice and sued the team for sexual harassment. Meanwhile, the team was an undisciplined mess on the field as well, finishing last in scoring behind quarterbacks Marc Wilson and Tommy Hodson and next to last in points allowed. Rust was put out of his coaching misery at the end of the worst season in franchise history, a 1–15 record. His simple take was, "There were a whole lot of factors that made it an unusual year. I don't consider getting to coach a professional team a birthright. It's something you may have a chance to do and you may not. My turn was a brief one, that's all."

In 1992, Rod returned to coaching with the Giants, but his more passive style of defense did not mesh with the aggressive Giant defenders. Rust coached at Lehigh in 1994, with the Falcons from 1995 to 1996, with Montreal from 1997 to 1998, with the 49ers in 1999 and back with Montreal as head coach in 2001 After one 9–9 season in the CFL, Rod returned to the Giants from 2002 to 2004 under Jim Fassel and concluded his career with Winnipeg in 2005. He retired at last at the age of 77. Pittsburgh linebacker coach David Brazil best summed up the soft spoken cerebral Rust once to the *New York Times*, "He gets a lot of respect because of his intelligence."

RUTIGLIANO, SAN (SAM) 7/1/1932– Tennessee, Tulsa. E; did not play professionally. *Apprenticeship:* College asst.— 3 years; pro asst.—11 years. *Roots:* Lou Saban, John Mazur, Chuck Fairbanks, Charley Winner, Ken Shipp (i), Hank Stram. *Branches:* Marty Schottenheimer, Jim Shofner, Rich Kotite, Dick MacPherson. *Coordinators/Key Assistants:* Jim Shofner then Paul Hackett then Larrye Weaver then Joe Scannella ran the offense, while Chuck Weber then Marty Schottenheimer handled the defense. *Hall of Fame Players:* Joe DeLamielleure, Ozzie Newsome. *Primary Quarterbacks:* Brian Sipe. *Tendencies:* • His teams scored 19.8 points and allowed 21.3 per game • His teams ran 45.2% of the time, which was 89% of the league average • Two starting quarterbacks in seven years; 78% of starts to primary quarterback • 14 rookie starters in seven years • Winning Full Seasons to Losing Full Seasons: 3:2.

Rust, Rodney A.									
Year	Team	Games	Wins	Losses	Ties	%	P Wins	P Losses	P %
1990	Patriots	16	1	15	0	.063	0	0	.000
1 year		16	1	15	0	.063	0	0	.000

Rutigliano, San (Sam)

Year	Team	Games	Wins	Losses	Ties	%	P Wins	P Losses	P %
1978	Browns	16	8	8	0	.500	0	0	.000
1979	Browns	16	9	7	0	.563	0	0	.000
1980	Browns	16	11	5	0	.688	0	1	.000
1981	Browns	16	5	11	0	.313	0	0	.000
1982	Browns	9	4	5	0	.444	0	1	.000
1983	Browns	16	9	7	0	.563	0	0	.000
1984	Browns	8	1	7	0	.125	0	0	.000
7 sections		97	47	50	0	.485	0	2	.000

Sam Rutigliano's life changed in 1962 when he fell asleep at the wheel and had a car accident in which his four-year-old daughter was killed. While he had been brought up Catholic, Sam's accident caused him and his wife to develop a much closer relationship with God that would color his perception of life and affect his coaching approach as well. Excitable defensive end Lyle Alzado told *Sports Illustrated*, "If you can't get along with Sam, then you'd better look in the mirror, because it's you, not him."

Rutigliano was born in the same Sheepshead Bay section of Brooklyn in which both Vince Lombardi and Joe Paterno were born and went to the same high school that Al Davis attended. He began his college career at Tennessee but ultimately graduated from Tulsa in 1955. After coaching high school football in New York from 1956 to 1963, Sam moved up to the University of Connecticut in 1964 as an assistant. Two years later, he joined Lou Saban's Maryland staff, but the nomadic Saban quit Maryland after just one year to take over the Denver Broncos in 1967 and brought Rutigliano with him. Sam coached in Denver from 1967 to 1970, in New England from 1971 to 1973, in New York with the Jets from 1974 to 1975 and in New Orleans from 1976 to 1977.

At last in 1978, Rutigliano got his chance as a head coach when Art Modell hired him to coach the Browns. He was a daring, offensive-minded coach who once replied to a Cleveland reporter who questioned his play call at the goal line, "Fasten your seat belt. I like to throw from there, and I'll go for it on fourth down, too — from anywhere on the field." He expanded on his offensive approach to *Sports Illustrated*, "The biggest mistake coaches make is saying, 'We're going to establish the run' or 'establish the pass.' You try to establish first downs. You keep the ball moving. And the clock. You do it in the most intelligent way you can."

Rutigliano placed full faith in his exciting, gunslinger quarterback Brian Sipe, and the result was a team that wouldn't quit until the final whistle, a team that pulled out so many games in the closing minutes that they became known as the "Kardiac Kids." Sam's Browns compiled a 28–20 record in his first three years and won the AFC Central Division in 1980, but that was the high point of his NFL coaching career. In the divisional round of the playoffs that year, the Browns lost to the Raiders when Sipe threw a terrible end zone interception at the end of the game on a play called "Red Right 88." It was the pivotal moment of Rutigliano's NFL tenure. Although he warmly greeted a distraught Sipe on the sideline after the play and told him he loved him, Sam's Browns would go 19–31 from this point on. Sipe slumped for the next two years before reviving some in 1983, but then left for the USFL in 1984. The Browns started 1–7 that year behind quarterback Paul McDonald, although the defense had grown quite formidable. At that point, Rutigliano was replaced by his defensive coordinator Marty Schottenheimer. Sam told the press, "Let's look at it as a fresh start. Today I've become the number one fan of the Cleveland Browns. I think I was treated fairly."

From 1985 to 1988, Rutigliano worked as an ESPN analyst and ran a football camp in Italy. In 1989, he became the first-ever football coach at Liberty University, a school founded by Christian evangelist Jerry Falwell. Sam coached Liberty to a 67–53 record from 1989 to 1999 before leaving to work for NFL Europe for the next five years. Since 2005, he has served as a local football analyst in Cleveland. When asked what his greatest accomplishment was, Sam usually referred to the Inner Circle, a group he formed when coaching the Browns to allow players with drug problems to come forward for help anonymously without risking their livelihoods. At the time, drug abuse was rampant in the league, but the NFL had no apparatus in place for dealing with the problem. Rutigliano was a pioneer in this area.

RYAN, JAMES D. (BUDDY) 2/16/1934– Oklahoma State. DL; did not play professionally. *Apprenticeship:* College asst.—6 years; pro asst.—18 years. *Roots:* Weeb Ewbank, Charley Winner, Ken Shipp (i), Bud Grant, Neill Armstrong, Mike Ditka. *Branches:* Rich Kotite, Wade Phillips, Jeff Fisher, Rex Ryan. *Coordinators/Key Assistants:* For the Eagles, Ted Plumb then Rich Kotite ran the offense, while Wade Phillips then Jeff Fisher handled Buddy's defense; for the Cardinals, Dave Atkins ran the offense, while Ronnie Jones handled the defense. *Hall of Fame Players:* Reggie White. *Pri-*

mary Quarterbacks: Randall Cunningham, Dave Krieg. *Tendencies:* • His teams scored 20 points and allowed 20.5 per game • His teams ran 45.2% of the time, which was 99% of the league average • Nine starting quarterbacks in seven years; 73% of starts to primary quarterbacks • 23 rookie starters in seven years • Winning Full Seasons to Losing Full Seasons: 3:3.

Ron Jaworski wrote in *The Games That Changed the Game*, "Buddy Ryan and I were hardly the best of friends. He didn't always treat me with respect. I thought his behavior was often unprofessional, and I still don't think he has a clue about offensive football. But I know a genius when I see one. Defensively, Buddy was exactly that. And I recognize his influence every Sunday, in every game, with every team." Ryan was the boastful and bullying defensive coach who devised the vaunted 46 defense that the 1985 Bears used as perhaps the most devastating defense in NFL history. When Buddy finally gained his own head coaching assignment, he was not able to duplicate the degree of success he did as a two-time Super Bowl winning assistant coach.

Ryan was born in Frederick, Oklahoma, and served as a staff sergeant in Korea at age 18. During his tour, he played for the 4th Army championship team in Japan before returning to the State to play guard for Oklahoma State from 1953 to 1955. After a year working in the Southwest oil fields, Buddy began his coaching career at the high school level in Texas from 1957 to 1961. In 1962, he joined the staff at the University of Buffalo where he tutored future Jets' defensive end Gerry Philbin. Ryan moved on to Vanderbilt in 1966 and Pacific in 1967 prior to being hired by Weeb Ewbank to coach the Jets defensive line in 1968, just in time for New York's historic Super Bowl upset win over the Colts.

Buddy spent eight years in New York, but left when Lou Holtz was hired to coach the team in 1976. Joining the Vikings' staff, he worked under Minnesota defensive coordinator Neill Armstrong who was his position coach when he played for Oklahoma State. Two years later, Armstrong was named head coach of the Bears, and he brought Ryan with him as defensive coordinator. While Armstrong's Bears featured a pop-gun offense, Ryan's defense was in the top ten in fewest points allowed for three straight years. Moreover, Buddy engendered a strong allegiance with his defensive players. When it became clear that Armstrong would be fired at the end of the 1981 season, Safety Gary Fencik and defensive tackle Alan Page drafted a letter to George Halas that the entire defense signed to implore the team owner to retain the defensive staff. Halas did just that—hiring Mike Ditka to replace Armstrong, but keeping Ryan and his assistants to coach the defense.

Needless to say, bull-headed Ditka and bombastic Ryan clashed right from the start and barely spoke as time went on, but the team became a playoff contender with Ditka's serviceable offense and Ryan's fearsome defense that put eight men in the box and aimed to decapitate the quarterback on every play. The 46 is heavy on blitzes from linebackers and safeties and strong against the run. His defense aimed not only at stopping the other team, but on getting turnovers and even on scoring. The weakness to the scheme is that the cornerbacks are on their own which gives the offense a chance for big plays. That defense was such a sensation that Ryan at last attracted attention for head coaching vacancies, and Buddy was hired by the Eagles immediately after the Bears manhandled the Patriots 46–10 in the Super Bowl in January 1986. Ryan was actually Philadelphia's third choice for head coach after Jim Mora and 26-year-old David Shula, but Buddy didn't let that deter him from being himself. Ditka later said that Ryan's contract wouldn't have been renewed in Chicago anyway.

Buddy inspired loyalty from his boys by being loyal and generous to them both during and after their careers. Fencik told the *New York Times*, "He was tough and you had to earn his respect. Once you did, Buddy would do anything for you." Former Bear safety Doug Plank, whose number 46 named Buddy's famous defensive scheme, even sat on the Eagles sideline during the first Ryan-Ditka Eagle-Bear game in 1986. Buddy stuck up for his players: he encouraged them all to stay on strike together in 1987 and welcomed contract holdout Keith Jackson back to town with limousine service in 1990. Meanwhile, he was surly and dismissive to the men who held the purse

Ryan, James D. (Buddy)									
Year	Team	Games	Wins	Losses	Ties	%	P Wins	P Losses	P %
1986	Eagles	16	5	10	1	.344	0	0	.000
1987	Eagles	15	7	8	0	.467	0	0	.000
1988	Eagles	16	10	6	0	.625	0	1	.000
1989	Eagles	16	11	5	0	.688	0	1	.000
1990	Eagles	16	10	6	0	.625	0	1	.000
1994	Cardinals	16	8	8	0	.500	0	0	.000
1995	Cardinals	16	4	12	0	.250	0	0	.000
7 years		111	55	55	1	.500	0	3	.000

strings; he referred to Eagles' owner Norman Braman contemptuously as "that guy in France" and called the general manager the "illegitimate son" of the owner.

Ryan was an obnoxious braggart, but it all only made him more popular with his team and a large proportion of the fans who loved the unbridled fury the Eagles exhibited in such games as the Bounty Bowl against the Cowboys when Buddy allegedly set a bounty on the Cowboys' kicker and the Body Bag Game against Washington in which eight Redskins were carried off the field. He insulted legendary coaches Don Shula, Tom Landry and Jimmy Johnson and slighted respected defensive coordinators Bud Carson and Fritz Shurmur. He made definitive snap judgments about players and dismissed those who didn't measure up with cutting remarks that could be quite cruel. He called fullback Michael Haddix "a reject guard from the USFL" and said of 1,000-yard rusher Earnest Jackson, "I'd trade him for a six-pack, and it wouldn't even have to be cold."

Buddy was a skilled personnel evaluator and assembled a lot of talent in Philadelphia, but his defense was the spirit of the team. His offense lagged behind and drew little interest from Ryan. He left undisciplined young quarterback Randall Cunningham on his own, just hoping that the spectacular scrambler would deliver enough big plays to win the game. He never developed an offensive line or a running game, and the offense suffered as a result. The Eagles' 46 was a fearsome defense to watch on most occasions, however, it could fly out of control and be bested by the better teams. Joe Montana threw four fourth quarter TD passes to beat the Eagles in 1989, and Buddy never did win a playoff game. Ryan could be excused for the flukey Fog Bowl postseason loss to Ditka's Bears in 1988. However, in the first round defeats of 1989 and 1990, the Birds were badly outplayed by the Rams and Redskins and Buddy outcoached by Fritz Shurmur and Joe Gibbs. When Ryan benched Cunningham, the owner's favorite, for one series in that Redskins' playoff loss, it marked the end for the blustering coach.

After Buddy was fired within days of that loss, there was a great outcry from players and fans, but the defense actually got better the next year under new coordinator Bud Carson. Ryan hired on as the coordinator for the underachieving Oilers in 1993, but his tenure there was noteworthy chiefly for him punching offensive coach Kevin Gilbride during a game and for

his defense allowing ancient Joe Montana to lead the Chiefs to a comeback victory over Houston in the playoffs. Buddy got another shot as head coach in 1994 with Arizona and crowed to local fans, "You've got a winner in town." However, the magic was gone. Ryan brought in a number of his former defensive stars, hired his two sons as defensive assistants, but still went 12–20 in two seasons. The final straw was when Buddy left the field with time still remaining in a loss to Dallas. He was fired after the 1995 season and retired to his horse farm. Having effectively burned every bridge he could in the NFL, he never coached again, but lives on most clearly through the careers of his two sons, Jets' head coach Rex and Cowboys' defensive coordinator Rob, as well as in the aggressive influence he had on the strategy of modern defensive football.

RYAN, REX 12/13/1962– Southwestern Oklahoma State. DE; did not play professionally. *Apprenticeship:* College asst.—11 years; pro asst.—12 years. *Roots:* Buddy Ryan, Brian Billick, John Harbaugh. *Branches:* None. *Coordinators/Key Assistants:* Brian Schottenheimer ran the defense, while Mike Pettine handled the defense. *Hall of Fame Players:* None. *Primary Quarterbacks:* Mark Sanchez. *Tendencies:* • His teams scored 23 points and allowed 18.8 per game • His teams ran 50.3% of the time, which was 116% of the league average • Two starting quarterbacks in three years; 98% of starts to primary quarterback • Four rookie starters in three years • Winning Full Seasons to Losing Full Seasons: 2:0.

Rex Ryan is just as brash, both in words and defensive scheming, as his father Buddy was, but there is a less belligerent tone to Rex. While Buddy truly seemed to despise his competitors like Tom Landry and Jimmy Johnson, Rex admits his respect for a great coach like Bill Belichick even as he makes clear he came to beat Belichick, not "kiss his rings." In his first three seasons as the Jets' coach, Rex has already had much more postseason success than his father ever did as a head coach. Buddy, Rex and Rex's twin brother Rob all have earned Super Bowl rings, but only as assistant coaches. In fact, Rob's came while working on Belichick's staff. Rex is working on being the first in the family to win one as a head coach.

Rex and Rob were born in Ardmore, Oklahoma, while Buddy was coaching at the University of Buffalo. Although their parents divorced, the rambunctious

Ryan, Rex

Year	Team	Games	Wins	Losses	Ties	%	P Wins	P Losses	P %
2009	Jets	16	9	7	0	.563	2	1	.667
2010	Jets	16	11	5	0	.688	2	1	.667
2011	Jets	16	8	8	0	.500	0	0	.000
3 years		48	28	20	0	.583	4	2	.667

twins remained close to their father and came to live with him when they were teenagers. Both brothers played on the defensive line at Southwestern Oklahoma State from 1981 to 1984, but began their coaching careers separately. Rex got his start at Eastern Kentucky in 1987. He moved on to New Mexico Highlands in 1989 and Morehead State in 1990. Four years later, Buddy was named head coach of the Cardinals and hired both his sons to his defensive staff in 1994. Buddy was fired after two years, so Rex returned to the college ranks as defensive coordinator for Cincinnati in 1996 and 1997 and Oklahoma in 1998. In 1999, he was hired by Kansas State, but left a few weeks later to join the Ravens as defensive line coach. Passed over for defensive coordinator when Marvin Lewis left in 2002, he was later promoted to that position in 2005 and spent a full decade coaching in Baltimore before the Jets hired him as head coach in 2009.

In his first two years as head coach, he played Belichick's Patriots, his chief rival, evenly and directed the Jets to consecutive AFC championship games, both times as a wild card entry playing all road games. Ryan transformed the New York defense into one of the best in the league, against both the run and the pass. He is known for his clever blitzing schemes, but linebacker coach Bob Sutton explained to the *New York Times*, "You could take this [defensive playbook] and give it to somebody else, and it wouldn't work. It's the other things he gives you besides the phrases and diagrams in a playbook that makes the playbook effective. Some say he's too brash. But he's just telling you what he really believes. The guy has some tremendous leadership skills." Former Ravens' defensive end Rob Burnett told *Sports Illustrated*, "Coaches are mostly pains in the ass. Rex has a humanity to him that most coaches don't have. It's rare for guys to want to win for their coach in this league. But we would have jumped on a grenade for that guy."

Like many defensive-oriented coaches, Ryan favors a "ground and pound" attack that is heavy on running the ball, particularly since his offense is run by a young and aggravatingly inconsistent quarterback in Mark Sanchez. However, the Jets do have playmakers and have been able to score points in Ryan's tenure. Rex is also known for smart adjustments during games and claimed to the *Times* he is able to see the whole field as he watches a game from the sideline, "Most coaches can see two or three guys. When they tested

me, my creative thing was the highest ever tested, and so was my problem solving. But I can't spell! But creative problem solving, that's what a coach is."

Ryan likes to boast of what his team is going to do ahead of time, and, by putting pressure on himself, he takes it off of his players. He is content to declare that an upcoming game with the rival Patriots is between him and Belichick. NPR commentator Frank Deford made the insightful point that Rex is the perfect coach for the boisterous, narcissistic players of today; he mirrors their attitude and inspires them to play at their very best. However, what happens when the boasts are proven hollow? In year three, cracks began to show on the field, and the 8–8 Jets dropped their last three games to miss the playoffs. Ryan will need to make changes to regain control of his team going forward.

RYMKUS, LOUIS J. (LOU) 11/6/1919–10/31/1998. Notre Dame. Played T for the Redskins in 1943 and the Browns from 1946 to 1951. *Apprenticeship:* College asst.—1 year; CFL asst.—1 year; pro asst.—6 years. *Roots:* Lisle Blackbourn, Sid Gillman. *Branches:* Wally Lemm, Mac Speedie. *Coordinators/Key Assistants:* Mac Speedie was the key offensive coach, while Wally Lemm ran the defense. *Hall of Fame Players:* George Blanda. *Primary Quarterbacks:* George Blanda. *Record:* AFL championship 1960. *Tendencies:* • His teams scored 27.5 points and allowed 20.9 per game • His teams ran 48.6% of the time, which was 101% of the league average • Two starting quarterbacks in two years; 74% of starts to primary quarterback • 19 rookie starters in two years • Winning Full Seasons to Losing Full Seasons: 1:0.

Lou Rymkus' father was shot outside the grocery store he owned in Royalton, Illinois when Lou was seven. A few years later, his mother moved the family to Chicago where Lou attended high school and was recruited to Notre Dame. For the Fighting Irish, he was an All-American tackle and team MVP during his undergraduate years from 1940 to 1942. Rymkus was a seventh round pick of the Redskins and played one year in the NFL before entering the Navy. He was stationed at the Great Lakes Naval Station during the war and played football there under Paul Brown. Brown then signed Lou for the fledgling Cleveland Browns of the new All America Football Conference in 1946, and Lou spent six years playing in Cleveland.

Rymkus, Louis J. (Lou)									
Year	Team	Games	Wins	Losses	Ties	%	P Wins	P Losses	P %
1960	Oilers (Titans)	14	10	4	0	.714	1	0	1.000
1961	Oilers (Titans)	5	1	3	1	.300	0	0	.000
2 years		19	11	7	1	.605	1	0	1.000

As a sidelight, he spent the summer of 1948 as an umpire for the All-American Girls Professional Baseball League.

Rymkus retired in 1952 and spent one year as an assistant coach at Indiana. Lou went north in 1953 and served as Bob Snyder's line coach on the Calgary Stampeders in Canada. He returned to the NFL in 1954, serving as the Packers' line coach from 1954 to 1957 and the Rams' line coach under Sid Gillman from 1958 to 1959. Rymkus did not get along with Gillman, so when he lost out to Sid for the Chargers head coaching job in 1960 even though the team's GM was Lou's former Notre Dame coach Frank Leahy, his enmity for Gillman increased further. Rymkus was hired as the first head coach of the Houston Oilers and met up with Gillman and the Chargers in the AFL's first championship game. Rymkus had beaten out Gillman for the services of quarterback George Blanda, and Blanda led the Oilers over the Chargers 24–16 for that first league title with three touchdown passes.

Things quickly turned sour in Houston the following season. Rymkus was a gruff, humorless perfectionist who grated on the players. Backup quarterback Jacky Lee told *Sports Illustrated*, "If you smiled, it was like you had committed a crime. If a guy laughed, Lou would stop practice and lecture us on being hard-nosed. You don't get that way from lectures." In the fifth game of the year with the team at 1–3 and rumors spreading of Rymkus about to be fired, Blanda lined up to kick a game-tying field goal against the Patriots when one of his teammates urged him to miss the field goal on purpose so Lou would be fired. Blanda angrily responded to the suggestion and converted the attempt. Rymkus was fired anyway. Owner Bud Adams told the press, "I questioned some of Coach Lou Rymkus' strategy and asked to see some game films. I studied them and decided we needed a coaching change." Lou reportedly asked Adams, "Why didn't you help me coach last year when we won the title?" Under Wally Lemm, the team rebounded and won a second straight AFL title.

Over the next three years, Rymkus did some scouting for the Bears while also doing some public relations work in the oil industry. He returned to coaching in 1965 with the Oilers as line coach under Bones Taylor. He was one of two former Oiler head coaches on Taylor's staff along with Sammy Baugh in a highly unusual move that lasted just one season until Wally Lemm returned as head coach again in 1966. Both Rymkus and Baugh joined the coaching staff of Harry Gilmer in Detroit that year, but the Lions' staff was fired at year's end. In 1967, Lou was named head coach and general manager of the Akron Vulcans minor league team, but that lasted just one 1–3 season. He spent 1968 coaching high school football and 1969 working for a trucking firm while coaching the West Texas Rufnecks to a 7–4 record in the Continental Football League until the Colts hired him as line coach in 1970. He slid into a scouting position by the end of the year and then got out of football entirely. He later sold cars and worked a series of other jobs in the Houston area and died there at the age of 78 in 1998.

SABAN, LOUIS H. (LOU) 10/13/1921–3/29/2009. Indiana. Played LB for the Browns from 1946 to 1949. *Apprenticeship:* College coach — 9 years (7 as head coach). *Roots:* None. *Branches:* Mike Holovak, Joe Collier, John Mazur, Jerry Smith, Jim Ringo, Red Miller, Sam Rutigliano, Dick MacPherson. *Coordinators/Key Assistants:* For the Patriots, Mike Holovak was the key offensive coach, while Joe Collier was the

Saban, Louis H. (Lou)									
Year	Team	Games	Wins	Losses	Ties	%	P Wins	P Losses	P %
1960	Patriots	14	5	9	0	.357	0	0	.000
1961	Patriots	5	2	3	0	.400	0	0	.000
1962	Bills	14	7	6	1	.536	0	0	.000
1963	Bills	14	7	6	1	.536	0	1	.000
1964	Bills	14	12	2	0	.857	1	0	1.000
1965	Bills	14	10	3	1	.750	1	0	1.000
1967	Broncos	14	3	11	0	.214	0	0	.000
1968	Broncos	14	5	9	0	.357	0	0	.000
1969	Broncos	14	5	8	1	.393	0	0	.000
1970	Broncos	14	5	8	1	.393	0	0	.000
1971	Broncos	9	2	6	1	.278	0	0	.000
1972	Bills	14	4	9	1	.321	0	0	.000
1973	Bills	14	9	5	0	.643	0	0	.000
1974	Bills	14	9	5	0	.643	0	1	.000
1975	Bills	14	8	6	0	.571	0	0	.000
1976	Bills	5	2	3	0	.400	0	0	.000
16 years		201	95	99	7	.490	2	2	.500

key defensive coach; for the Bills' first stint, John Mazur ran the offense, while Joe Collier handled the defense; for the Broncos, Hunter Enis was the key offensive coach, while Dick MacPherson then Joe Collier handled the defense; for the Bills' second stint, Jim Ringo ran the offense, while Jim Dooley then John Ray handled the defense. *Hall of Fame Players:* Joe DeLamielleure, Floyd Little, Billy Shaw, O.J. Simpson. *Primary Quarterbacks:* Butch Songin, Jack Kemp, Steve Tensi, Joe Ferguson. *Record:* AFL Championships 1964, 1965. *Tendencies:* • His teams scored 21.2 points and allowed 21.8 per game • His teams ran 53.5% of the time, which was 103% of the league average • 19 starting quarterbacks in 16 years; 67% of starts to primary quarterbacks • 86 rookie starters in 16 years • Winning Full Seasons to Losing Full Seasons: 7:6.

The peripatetic Lou Saban was head coach at 10 different colleges on varying levels and compiled a 94–99–4 college record, very similar to his 97–101–7 record for three professional franchises. That is not to mention his time coaching high school, semipro and Arena football. He once said, "I've coached at all levels, covered the gamut, and I've never really seen any difference. My coaching techniques are pretty much the same, with some adjustments for what younger players can and can't do." As for his overall losing record, Sam Rutigliano, a former Saban assistant, told *Sports Illustrated*, "Smart coaches with bad players always get beat by the dummies with good players." Rutigliano maintained, "Lou has done a great job wherever he has been. He has the ability to simplify all things, to get right to the core of what he has to do to win."

Born in Brookfield, Illinois, Lou was captain and team MVP at Indiana under Bo McMillin and graduated in 1943. During the war, he served as a Chinese interpreter in the Army and subsequently joined Paul Brown's Cleveland Browns in 1946. With Cleveland, he was the team captain on defense and twice was All Pro in the All America Football Conference. When the Browns merged into the NFL in 1950, Saban retired and was hired to coach Cleveland's Case Institute of Technology, while moonlighting as a Browns' radio announcer in 1952. In three years, Case went 10–14–1 but decided to deemphasize football, so Lou took an assistant's job at the University of Washington in 1953 and moved on to Northwestern the following year. He was promoted to head coach in 1955, but posted a disappointing 0–8–1 record and was fired. He returned to football in 1957 as the head coach at Western Illinois where he racked up an impressive 20–5–1 record in three years, earning Lou his first pro job as the head coach of the new Boston Patriots of the startup American Football League in 1960.

Saban brought two of his WIU assistants, Red Miller and Joe Collier, with him to Boston and the pair would go on to become two of the most accomplished assistant coaches in league history; each had less success as a head coach in the league though. Lou later complained to the *Boston Globe*, "We were the last team. All the good players were gone.... We had to take what was left over. We had tryouts in the city of Boston from one end to the other. We had bricklayers, we had carpenters, we had stoker men ... you name it, we had it." Saban was fired one third of the way into the 1961 season, but was hired as a scout by the Buffalo Bills. He was named head coach of the team in 1962 and would have his greatest coaching triumphs over the next four years in Buffalo.

Lou built the Bills into a team that mirrored the NFL's champion Packers with a ball control offense and the best defense in the league. He snookered Sid Gillman out of quarterback Jack Kemp and brought powerful fullback Cookie Gilchrist down from Canada, and the two were the twin pillars of the offensive attack. Even after Saban suspended, reinstated and ultimately traded the recalcitrant Gilchrist after the 1964 season in which Buffalo led the league in scoring, the team rumbled on. The defense twice allowed the fewest points in the AFL and was hard-hitting and solid at each level: line, linebackers and secondary. The Bills tied for the Eastern Division in 1963, but lost a playoff to the Patriots. The next two years, though, they were the class of the East and twice beat the favored Chargers in the championship game. With that, Saban abruptly quit, saying, "There can be little left to conquer in professional football." In reality, owner Ralph Wilson was trying to take some responsibilities away from his coach, and Lou would not stand for it.

Saban coached Maryland for one year and then took over the lowly Denver Broncos in 1967. While Denver did show some improvement over the next five years, they were still a losing team when he resigned during the 1971 season. Floyd Little emerged as a star on the team, but did not enjoy playing for Saban who was very tough on him. In Denver, Lou went through nine starting quarterbacks, even giving undersized African American Marlin Briscoe a shot in 1968 when Steve Tensi and two others was injured. Although Briscoe showed more talent than anyone else, Saban traded him to Buffalo the next year.

Briscoe was converted to receiver by the Bills and was still in Buffalo when Saban returned to the Queen City as head coach in 1972, but not for long. Lou traded him to Miami. In his second stint in Buffalo, Saban took advantage of the one prime asset he had, runner O.J. Simpson, and unleashed the most ground intensive attack in the league, running the ball 64% of the time, 15% more than the league average. The Bills did post three winning seasons and go to the playoffs one year, but were never a serious Super Bowl challenger. With the team going into a decline, Lou quit five games into the 1976 season. He would never return to the NFL, but had plenty of coaching left in his system.

Saban coached Miami to a 9–13 record from 1977 to 1978 and recruited quarterback Jim Kelly to the school. He then coached Army to a 2–8–1 record in 1979 and quit because he saw no chance of ever winning. New York Yankees' owner George Steinbrenner, who had once worked as an assistant to Saban at Northwestern, hired Lou in 1980 and for the next three years Saban helped run Tampa Downs Race Track and the Yankees. He left in 1983 to take over as the second ever head coach at Central Florida. Fired in midseason 1984, his record at CFU was 6–12. After a year in retirement, Lou coached high school football in the Carolinas from 1986 to 1989 and then semipro football in 1990. He led small college Peru State in Nebraska to a 7–4 record in 1991 and then retired again. In 1994 he returned once more, coaching the Milwaukee Mustangs of the Arena League for four games (all losses) and then initiating the football program at Alfred State University in New York. From 1995 to 2000, Lou coached SUNY Canton to a 34–16 record and then concluded his coaching career with Chowan University in North Carolina from 2001 to 2002. On that frustrating 2–13 mark, Saban retired from coaching for good at the age of 81. He died seven years later. Booker Edgerson who played for Saban at Western Illinois, Buffalo and Denver, summed up his old coach to reporters, "Lou Saban was a great teacher. He could have built any program — football, baseball, basketball, whatever."

SABAN, NICHOLAS L. (NICK) 10/31/1951– Kent State. DB; did not play professionally. *Apprenticeship:* College coach — 22 years (11 as head coach); pro asst.— 6 years. *Roots:* Jerry Glanville, Bill Belichick. *Branches:* Scott Linehan, Jason Garrett. *Coordinators/ Key Assistants*: Scott Linehan then Mike Mularkey ran the offense, while Will Muschamp then Dom Capers handled the defense. *Hall of Fame Players:* None. *Primary Quarterbacks:* Gus Frerotte, Joey Harrington. *Tendencies:* • His teams scored 18.1 points and allowed 18.8 per game • His teams ran 41.1% of the time, which was 91% of the league average • Five starting quarterbacks in two years; 81% of starts to primary quarterbacks • Three rookie starters in two years • Winning Full Seasons to Losing Full Seasons: 1:1.

Despite being reviled as a duplicitous snake by Miami Dolphins fans, Nick Saban is one of the great

college coaches of contemporary times, having won three national championships with two different SEC schools. Saban was born in Fairmont, West Virginia, and played defensive back under Don James at Kent State through 1971. He immediately began his coaching career at his alma mater in 1972 and coached there through 1976. In 1977, he left for Syracuse and then moved on to West Virginia in 1978 and Ohio State in 1980. In 1982 he joined the staff at Navy where he met Bill Belichick's father Steve.

George Perles hired Saban to coach the defense at Michigan State in 1983. Five years later, Nick took his first NFL job as the secondary coach on the Oilers in 1988, but left in 1990 for his first head coaching position with Toledo in 1990. Saban led the Rockets to a 9–2 record that year, but jumped the next year to the Browns to become Bill Belichick's defensive coordinator. When Belichick was fired in 1995, Saban replaced the retiring George Perles at Michigan State. From 1995 to 1999, he led the Spartans to a 34–24–1 record before leaving for LSU in 2000. From 2000 to 2004, Nick coached the Tigers to a 48–16 record that included a 13–1 national championship year in 2003.

Miami hired Saban in 2005 to restore a franchise that had been slipping for years. LSU athletic director Skip Bertman told the *New York Times* that Saban would succeed in the NFL where others like Steve Spurrier had failed, "Steve Spurrier was a great college coach, but Nick has a much different intensity level than him. It's an intensity that he got from Belichick." Saban himself later told the *Times*, "I'm not a tough guy. The word I would use, it would be demanding. There is a certain standard and sometimes you need to help them reach those standards."

Saban is a sideline screamer, and managed to patch together an improved 9–7 team in his first season with journeyman quarterback Gus Frerotte. His fatal error in 2006, though, was in passing on free agent quarterback Drew Brees to acquire washed up, overweight Daunte Culpepper and draft bust Joey Harrington to quarterback the Dolphins. The offense dropped to 29th in scoring, and Nick got the message that this pro thing might be tougher than it looks. Despite vehement denials throughout December that he was about to quit Miami to become head coach of Alabama, he did just that two days after the end of the season. While the decision left Miami in a tough spot, Saban landed on his feet in Alabama. He won a second national championship in 2009 and a third in

Saban, Nicholas L. (Nick)									
Year	Team	Games	Wins	Losses	Ties	%	P Wins	P Losses	P %
2005	Dolphins	16	9	7	0	.563	0	0	.000
2006	Dolphins	16	6	10	0	.375	0	0	.000
2 years		32	15	17	0	.469	0	0	.000

2011 while going 55–12 in his first five years with the Crimson Tide.

SANDUSKY, JOHN 12/28/1925–3/5/2006. Villanova. Played T for the Browns and Packers from 1950 to 1955. *Apprenticeship:* College asst.— 2 years; pro asst.—14 years. *Roots:* Weeb Ewbank, Don Shula, Don McCafferty. *Branches:* Red Miller, Hank Bullough. *Coordinators/Key Assistants*: None. *Hall of Fame Players:* Ted Hendricks, John Unitas. *Primary Quarterbacks:* Marty Domres. *Record:* **Interim Coach.**

Philadelphia native John Sandusky epitomized the loyal assistant coach, spending 28 years with former Browns' teammate Don Shula, 26 as an assistant coach. Sandusky graduated from Villanova and played tackle for six seasons in Cleveland before ending his career in Green Bay in 1956. He began his coaching career at his alma mater the following year and then joined Weeb Ewbank's Colts' staff in 1959. He would coach the line for the Colts for the next 14 years under Ewbank through 1962, under Shula through 1969 and under Don McCafferty through the beginning of 1972. The Colts in that time won an NFL title in 1959 and a Super Bowl in 1970.

By 1972, the team was getting very old and was led by 39-year-old legendary quarterback Johnny Unitas. New general manager Joe Thomas set about completely remaking the team with no regard for the past. He ordered McCafferty to bench Unitas and play younger backup quarterback Marty Domres early that season. When McCafferty refused, Thomas fired the coach and promoted Sandusky as his replacement. Sandusky told the press, "Don is like my brother. I lived with him 11 years as a roommate. For 16 years I've wanted to be a head coach, but I never wanted it under these circumstances. But it's done and I'll do my damnedest to do a good job."

Thomas' broom continued to sweep clean at the year's end and Sandusky was fired and Unitas traded. Sandusky joined Mike McCormack's Eagles' staff in his hometown for the next three years. When McCormack was fired in 1976, Sandusky was hired by Shula

to replace departed line coach Monte Clark and would spend the next 19 years reliably coaching the Dolphins' line for Shula. At the age of 69, John retired in 1995. He subsequently returned to coaching by helping out a local high school as line coach in 1998 and 1999 and died seven years later at the age of 80. His son Gerry is the voice of the Ravens in Baltimore.

SAUNDERS, ALAN K. (AL) 2/1/1947– San Jose State DB; did not play professionally. *Apprenticeship:* College asst.—13 years; pro asst.— 4 years. *Roots:* Don Coryell. *Branches:* Gunther Cunningham, Jim Mora, Jr. *Coordinators/Key Assistants*: Dave Levy then Jerry Rhome ran the offense, while Ron Lynn handled the defense. *Hall of Fame Players:* Dan Fouts, Charlie Joiner, Kellen Winslow. *Primary Quarterbacks:* Dan Fouts, Mark Malone. *Tendencies:* • His teams scored 16.7 points and allowed 21.1 per game • His teams ran 44.2% of the time, which was 93% of the league average • Eight starting quarterbacks in three years; 59% of starts to primary quarterbacks • Ten rookie starters in three years • Winning Full Seasons to Losing Full Seasons: 1:1.

A native of London, England, Al Saunders has made a long career of American football. Al played defensive back and wide receiver for San Jose State from 1966 to 1968 and began his coaching career with USC in 1970. He moved on to Missouri in 1972, Utah State in 1973 and California in 1976. Saunders served as the Golden Bears' offensive coordinator through 1981 and then held the same job for Tennessee in 1982 before jumping to the NFL as Don Coryell's receivers coach in 1983.

When the Chargers got off to a 1–7 start in 1986, Coryell stepped down and was replaced by Saunders who improved the team to 3–5 in the second half of the year. San Diego sprinted to an 8–1 start in 1987, aided by a 3–0 record in October by the Chargers' replacement players in this strike season. Winning primarily with defense and special teams, San Diego could not maintain that pace and dropped its last six games to miss the playoffs. The offense finished 27th

Sandusky, John									
Year	Team	Games	Wins	Losses	Ties	%	P Wins	P Losses	P %
1972	Colts	9	4	5	0	.444	0	0	.000
1 year		9	4	5	0	.444	0	0	.000

Saunders, Alan K. (Al)									
Year	Team	Games	Wins	Losses	Ties	%	P Wins	P Losses	P %
1986	Chargers	8	3	5	0	.375	0	0	.000
1987	Chargers	15	8	7	0	.533	0	0	.000
1988	Chargers	16	6	10	0	.375	0	0	.000
3 years		39	17	22	0	.436	0	0	.000

in the league in scoring with 253 points behind 36-year-old Dan Fouts, so Saunders imported Mark Malone and Babe Laufenberg in 1988 and the offense scored 231 points, still 27th in the league. The Chargers endured another six-game losing streak that year, and the distant and aloof Saunders was fired at the end of the year and would never be an NFL head coach again.

Al spent the next decade on Marty Schottenheimer's staff as receivers' coach/assistant head coach in Kansas City from 1989 to 1998. He subsequently joined the Vermeil/Martz "Greatest Show on Turf" offense in the same position from 1999 to 2000 before uniting with Vermeil in Kansas City as offensive coordinator from 2001 to 2005. Saunders had learned much from Coryell about two tight end sets and three receiver bunch formations that he would use over his career as a respected offensive coordinator, but his 700-page playbook was questioned at times for its overly dense complexity. When Vermeil retired, Al became the highest paid assistant coach in the league as the Redskins' offensive coordinator from 2006 to 2007. He returned to the Rams under Scott Linehan in 2008 and then worked for the Ravens from 2009 to 2010 until being hired by Hue Jackson in Oakland as offensive coordinator, reuniting with former Washington quarterback Jason Campbell.

SCHISSLER, PAUL J. 11/11/1893–4/17/1968. Doane. Did not play professionally. *Apprenticeship:* College coach —17 years (14 as head coach). *Roots:* None. *Branches:* None. *Coordinators/Key Assistants*: None. *Hall of Fame Players:* Red Badgro, Walt Kiesling. *Primary Quarterbacks:* None. *Tendencies:* • His teams scored 6.8 points and allowed 10.6 per game • His teams ran 70.6% of the time, which was 98% of the league average • 27 rookie starters in four years • Winning Full Seasons to Losing Full Seasons: 0:4.

Paul Schissler began his coaching career while still in college himself, coaching Hastings High School from 1913 to 1914 as he attended Doane College in Crete, Nebraska, 75 miles away. In 1915, Schissler coached his alma mater to a 5–3 record and then moved on to coach St. Viator in Illinois to a 6–2 mark in 1916. The Portland, Oregon native coached high school basketball back in Nebraska in 1917 and then served as an assistant football coach at the state university from 1918 to 1920; Paul also coached the Cornhusker baseball and basketball teams during this period.

In the fall of 1921, Schissler moved on to coach Lombard College in Illinois for the next three years. Lombard went 19–1–1 in that time, even holding the Notre Dame's mighty Four Horsemen to two touchdowns in 1923. That notoriety helped earn Paul the head coaching position at Oregon Agricultural College in 1924, and he coached that school now known as Oregon State to a 48–30–2 record through the 1932 season. Clearly influenced by Knute Rockne and the Fighting Irish, Schissler ran a modified Notre Dame Box offense throughout his career.

In 1933, Paul took over the Chicago Cardinals and struggled to a 1–9–1 record. Overturning the roster completely with rookies in 1934, he transformed the Cards to a respectable 5–6 team in his second season. One of the 1933 players who was ousted was star halfback Joe Lillard, an African American. Lillard had gotten into fights in the first three games of the year, and Schissler told the *Brooklyn Eagle*:

> I felt sorry for Lillard. He was a fine fellow, not as rugged as most in the pro game, but very clever. But he was a marked man, and I don't mean that just the Southern boys took it out on him either; after a while whole teams, Northern and Southern alike, would give Joe the works, and I'd have to take him out. Somebody started it, it seemed, and everybody would join in. But that wasn't the worst. It got so my Cardinals were a marked team because we had Lillard with us, and how the rest of the league took it out on us! We had to let him go for our own sake, and for his, too!

Paul quit Chicago at the end of the 1934, though, because he was supposed to receive a percentage of the team's profits and there were none. Due to the Cardinals rapid transformation, the struggling Brooklyn Dodgers quickly hired Schissler as head coach in 1935. Paul improved the 4–7 Dodgers to 5–6–1 in his first year, but the team dropped to 3–8–1 in 1936, and Schissler was replaced by Potsy Clark. Halfback Joe

Schissler, Paul J.									
Year	Team	Games	Wins	Losses	Ties	%	P Wins	P Losses	P %
1933	Cardinals	11	1	9	1	.136	0	0	.000
1934	Cardinals	11	5	6	0	.455	0	0	.000
1935	Brooklyn Dodgers (defunct)	12	5	6	1	.458	0	0	.000
1936	Brooklyn Dodgers (defunct)	12	3	8	1	.292	0	0	.000
4 years		46	14	29	3	.337	0	0	.000

Maniaci told Roger Godin for *The Brooklyn Football Dodgers*, "Schissler was a very good coach. He coached fundamentals, he was a gentleman, sincere in his teaching, and he tried to teach everything he knew about the game."

Paul founded the Hollywood Bears in 1938 and helped form the California Football League that year. Two years later, the Bears were the featured team in the Pacific Coast Football League with black stars Kenny Washington, Jackie Robinson and Woody Strode. In 1942, Schissler went into the Air Force and coached the March Field Flyers from 1942 to 1944 with ace passer Jack Jacobs. Paul returned to the Bears in 1945, but sold the team the following year, having coached them to a 26–5–1 record over four seasons.

Schissler was hired by the *Los Angeles Times* in 1946 as the director of special events. Over the next 15 years, he organized an annual charity game between the Redskins and Rams, operated the Riverside Grand Prix auto race and, most significantly, started the NFL's annual Pro Bowl game in 1951. This regular interaction with the NFL made him a secondary nominee for league commissioner after Bert Bell died. Paul drew some votes on the second ballot as a compromise entrant, but did not become a consensus candidate. He had a major stroke in 1963 and moved back to Nebraska where he died from a second stroke five years later in 1968 at the age of 74.

Schmidt, Joseph P. (Joe) 1/19/1932– Pittsburgh. Played LB for the Detroit Lions from 1953 to 1965. *Apprenticeship:* Pro asst.—1 year. *Roots:* Harry Gilmer. *Branches:* Chuck Knox, John North, Leeman Bennett. *Coordinators/Key Assistants*: Bill McPeak ran the offense, while Jim David handled the defense. *Hall of Fame Players:* Lem Barney, Dick LeBeau, Charley Sanders. *Primary Quarterbacks:* Greg Landry, Bill Munson. *Record:* **Hall of Fame Player.** *Tendencies:* • His teams scored 20.9 points and allowed 17.5 per game • His teams ran 57.3% of the time, which was 109% of the league average • Four starting quarterbacks in six years; 83% of starts to primary quarterbacks • Ten rookie starters in six years • Winning Full Seasons to Losing Full Seasons: 4:2.

Even in an era of standout middle linebackers, Joe Schmidt stood out as an eight-time All Pro and four-time team MVP. The Pittsburgh native first starred at the University of Pittsburgh from 1950 to 1952, but was not drafted by the Lions until the seventh round in 1953 because he weighed just 195 pounds in college. In Detroit, he bulked up to 220 pounds and became a starter on the defending champions in his rookie year. By 1956, he was a team captain and maintained that leadership role for 10 years. Retiring after the 1965 season, Schmidt moved directly onto the coaching staff in 1966.

After Harry Gilmer was fired in 1967, Joe was promoted to replace him. Perhaps because he was the youngest and least experienced coach in the league, Schmidt assembled a knowledgeable, experienced staff that included former NFL coach Bill McPeak and future NFL coaches Chuck Knox, Leeman Bennett and J.D. North. Reflecting the head coach's background, the Lions finished in the top five for fewest points allowed four times under Joe and ran a ball control offense that kept the ball on the ground almost 10% more than the league average. Although he had been immensely popular as a player, Schmidt soon found out that being a head coach is a different story. In 1968, he was booed for the first time by the home fans when he ordered his offense to run out the clock in a tie game against the Packers. By then, he had acquired two quarterbacks, Bill Munson by trade and Greg Landry through the draft, that he would alternate for the next three years before Landry won the job outright in 1971.

After two losing seasons, Joe turned it around in 1969 and led Detroit to the first of four straight winning seasons and the first of four straight second place finishes in the Central Division. Schmidt's Lions made the playoffs just once, in 1970 as a wild card team, and lost that sole postseason game to the Cowboys by the baseball score of 5–2. Detroit was good but never quite good enough under Joe. The 1971 season was marred by the death on the field of Lions' wide receiver Chuck Hughes in a game against the Bears. The following year marked another second place finish and brought public criticism of the team by owner William Clay Ford. At year's end, Schmidt had had enough, saying, "The job no longer is fun; I don't enjoy coaching anymore. It has gotten to be more burden than fun." He had met one goal in that he left the Lions a

Schmidt, Joseph P. (Joe)									
Year	*Team*	*Games*	*Wins*	*Losses*	*Ties*	*%*	*P Wins*	*P Losses*	*P %*
1967	Lions	14	5	7	2	.429	0	0	.000
1968	Lions	14	4	8	2	.357	0	0	.000
1969	Lions	14	9	4	1	.679	0	0	.000
1970	Lions	14	10	4	0	.714	0	1	.000
1971	Lions	14	7	6	1	.536	0	0	.000
1972	Lions	14	8	5	1	.607	0	0	.000
6 years		84	43	34	7	.554	0	1	.000

better team than when he took over, and only Monte Clark and Wayne Fontes have won at least as many games in Detroit in the past 40 years. The year after quitting football, Joe was elected to the Pro Football Hall of Fame and later was inducted in the College Football Hall of Fame in the year 2000.

SCHNELLENBERGER, HOWARD L. 3/16/1934– Kentucky. Played TE in the CFL. *Apprenticeship:* College asst.—7 years; pro asst.—7 years. *Roots:* George Allen, Don Shula. *Branches:* Pete McCulley (i). *Coordinators/Key Assistants*: Pete McCulley was the key offensive coach, while Dick Voris then Don Doll were the key defensive coaches. *Hall of Fame Players:* Ted Hendricks. *Primary Quarterbacks:* Marty Domres. *Tendencies:* • His teams scored 14.6 points and allowed 24.8 per game • His teams ran 61.8% of the time, which was 108% of the league average • Two starting quarterbacks in two years; 71% of starts to primary quarterback • Six rookie starters in two years • Winning Full Seasons to Losing Full Seasons: 0:1.

Howard Schnellenberger trained under the finest coaches on both the college and professional levels and has had an impressive career himself as a college head coach and program builder. His one foray as an NFL head coach did not end well, although that was due more to forces beyond his control than to his own actions. Schnellenberger was born in Saint Meinrad, Indiana, but grew up seventy miles away in Louisville where he played high school football and basketball with Hall of Fame halfback Paul Hornung. Howard moved across the state to play tight end at Kentucky for Blanton Collier from 1953 to 1956 and then spent two seasons with the Toronto Argonauts in Canada.

In 1959, Schnellenberger began his coaching career at his alma mater under Collier. Two years later, he traveled south to join Bear Bryant's staff at Alabama and coached there during the Namath era from 1961 to 1965. Howard jumped to the NFL in 1966 as George Allen's ends coach with the Rams and left in 1970 to join Don Shula's first staff in Miami. He ran the Dolphins' offense for three years before being hired as the head coach of the Colts in 1973 in the afterglow of Miami's undefeated 1972 season.

Schnellenberger was hired in Baltimore by volatile GM Joe Thomas who previously had been the personnel director in Miami. Schnellenberger announced, "I'm not predicting we'll be in the playoffs, but we'll be making every effort to be in the playoffs."

Thomas intended to completely revamp the veteran Colts and had just traded Johnny Unitas to the Chargers while drafting Bert Jones to replace him. Jones told Tom Danyluk for *The Super 70s*, "I think Howard Schnellenberger was a fabulous football coach but he was thrust into a terrible situation. During his first year, it was a terrible team he inherited. The only way you could figure out who the players were was to look at their numbers and then check the roster. There was no continuity." Thomas then added to the turmoil by firing two defensive assistants after the 1973 season.

Schnellenberger was tutoring Jones and blending his playing time with that of veteran Marty Domres in an effort to win games. Impatient owner Robert Irsay grew frustrated with this deliberate approach. Impulsively, he visited the sideline during the third game of the 1974 season and ordered Howard to yank Domres for Jones. Reportedly, Schnellenberger cursed Irsay on the field for interfering during the game, and Irsay angrily left the sideline to tell Thomas that he was the new coach. Afterwards, Schnellenberger said that he was about to make the quarterback change when Irsay butted in to demand the move. "If I had made the move then, I would have lost all stature with the team. A head coach has to have the authority to play the people he thinks are best. If he can't he may as well not be the coach."

Howard returned to Miami as Shula's offensive coordinator from 1975 to 1978 and then took over the Miami Hurricanes' program in 1979. In five years, he posted a 41–16 record, won the school's first national championship and established the foundation of the dominant college football program of the next decade or more. In May 1984, he followed that championship by signing to be the new coach of a South Florida USFL team to be moved from Washington. However, that franchise move fell through, so Schnellenberger departed Florida to restart the football program at Louisville. Despite compiling just a 54–56–2 record from 1985 to 1994, Howard did revive the program and produce two nationally ranked teams. In 1995, he was hired by the Oklahoma Sooners, but left after just one 5–5–1 season.

After two years out of football selling investment bonds, Schnellenberger returned to coaching in 1998 when he agreed to the challenge of founding a startup football program at Florida Atlantic University. The team did not begin playing games until 2001, but in ten years, he has led them to a 58–74 record and ad-

Schnellenberger, Howard L.									
Year	Team	Games	Wins	Losses	Ties	%	P Wins	P Losses	P %
1973	Colts	14	4	10	0	.286	0	0	.000
1974	Colts	3	0	3	0	.000	0	0	.000
2 years		17	4	13	0	.235	0	0	.000

vanced the program from NCAA Division IAA to Division IA. As Howard told the *New York Times*, "I've never been in a position in my coaching career to just let the thing happen. I've had to dream the dream, enunciate the dream and shout it from the mountain top — to invigorate those that were going to come with me to have a chance of making it happen."

SCHOTTENHEIMER, MARTIN E. (MARTY)

9/23/1943– Pittsburgh. Played LB for the Bills and Patriots from 1965 to 1970. *Apprenticeship:* WFL asst.—1 year; pro asst.—10 years. *Roots:* Bill Arnsparger, John McVay, Monte Clark, Sam Rutigliano,. *Branches:* Lindy Infante, Bill Cowher, Tony Dungy, Gunther Cunningham, Herman Edwards, Mike McCarthy, Cam Cameron, Tony Sparano, Hue Jackson. *Coordinators/Key Assistants:* For the Browns, Joe Pendry then Lindy Infante then Marc Trestman ran the offense, while Tom Bettis then Dave Adolph handled the defense; for the Chiefs, Joe Pendry then Paul Hackett then Jimmy Raye ran the offense, while Bill Cowher then Dave Adolph then Gunther Cunningham handled the defense; for the Redskins, Jimmy Raye ran the offense, while Kurt Schottenheimer handled the defense; for the Chargers, Cam Cameron ran the offense, while Dale Lindsey then Wade Phillips handled the defense. *Hall of Fame Players:* Marcus Allen, Joe DeLamielleure, Darrell Green, Joe Montana, Ozzie Newsome, Bruce Smith, Derrick Thomas, Mike Webster. *Primary Quarterbacks:* Bernie Kosar, Steve DeBerg, Joe Montana, Steve Bono, Drew Brees.

Tendencies: • His teams scored 21.8 points and allowed 18.7 per game • His teams ran 48.1% of the time, which was 107% of the league average • 20 starting quarterbacks in 21 years; 62% of starts to primary quarterbacks • 39 rookie starters in 21 years • Winning Full Seasons to Losing Full Seasons: 15:2.

Marty Schottenheimer has been one of the premier builders in NFL history, but his patented style of "Marty Ball" has inevitably failed in the postseason, leaving the native of Canonsburg, Pennsylvania with a somewhat mixed legacy. On the one hand, defensive tackle Bill Maas told Ray Didinger for *Game Plans for Success,* "I didn't know what the NFL was all about until Marty came to Kansas City. I never knew how unorganized we were until I saw how Marty did things. He put the whole thing together for us." Marty did the same construction job in both Cleveland and San Diego, but his postseason record of 5–13 means he never led any team, no matter how talented, to the Super Bowl.

Schottenheimer graduated from the University of Pittsburgh in 1965 and was drafted by Buffalo in the seventh round of the AFL draft and by Baltimore in the fourth round of the NFL draft. He signed with the Bills and won the AFL title in his rookie year; it would be his only connection to a championship team in an NFL career that would span 39 years. Marty was a mediocre linebacker with the Bills for four years and the Patriots for two. He was traded to the Steelers and then the Colts in 1971, but was cut in training camp. For the next three years, Schottenheimer sold real

Year	Team	Games	Wins	Losses	Ties	%	P Wins	P Losses	P %
1984	Browns	8	4	4	0	.500	0	0	.000
1985	Browns	16	8	8	0	.500	0	1	.000
1986	Browns	16	12	4	0	.750	1	1	.500
1987	Browns	15	10	5	0	.667	1	1	.500
1988	Browns	16	10	6	0	.625	0	1	.000
1989	Chiefs	16	8	7	1	.531	0	0	.000
1990	Chiefs	16	11	5	0	.688	1	1	.500
1991	Chiefs	16	10	6	0	.625	0	1	.000
1992	Chiefs	16	10	6	0	.625	0	1	.000
1993	Chiefs	16	11	5	0	.688	2	1	.667
1994	Chiefs	16	9	7	0	.563	0	1	.000
1995	Chiefs	16	13	3	0	.813	0	1	.000
1996	Chiefs	16	9	7	0	.563	0	0	.000
1997	Chiefs	16	13	3	0	.813	0	1	.000
1998	Chiefs	16	7	9	0	.438	0	0	.000
2001	Redskins	16	8	8	0	.500	0	0	.000
2002	Chargers	16	8	8	0	.500	0	0	.000
2003	Chargers	16	4	12	0	.250	0	0	.000
2004	Chargers	16	12	4	0	.750	0	1	.000
2005	Chargers	16	9	7	0	.563	0	0	.000
2006	Chargers	16	14	2	0	.875	0	1	.000
21 years		327	200	126	1	.613	5	13	.278

Schottenheimer, Martin E. (Marty)

estate while trying to figure out what to do next. He also spent time hanging around the office of Broncos defensive coordinator Joe Collier, trying to find a way back into the game. In 1974, Collier put Marty in touch with Dick Coury who was the head coach of the Portland Storm of the World Football League. Coury signed him as a linebacker and when Schottenheimer hurt his shoulder, Marty offered to coach the team's linebackers.

After the season, Marty got in touch with Giants' coach Bill Arnsparger who could not offer him a job at the time, but asked him to prepare a report on the talent in the WFL. Arnsparger so liked the detailed report that Schottenheimer wrote that he hired him as linebackers coach in 1975. Two years later, he was promoted to defensive coordinator under Arnsparger's successor John McVay. Marty next coached the linebackers for Detroit in 1978 and 1979 and then was named defensive coordinator in Cleveland in 1980. When Sam Rutigliano began to lose control of the team in 1984, Schottenheimer was promoted to head coach at midseason. The next year, the Browns drafted quarterback Bernie Kosar who led them to the playoffs for the next four years. As with all Marty's teams, Cleveland had a solid defense, smart special teams, seldom turned the ball over and played a conservative offense that emphasized field position and ball control. Seven times in his career, his teams finished in the top three in turnover differential.

Cleveland went to consecutive AFC championship games in 1986 and 1987, but lost both contests to John Elway's Broncos in two thrillers that weren't decided till the very end. Both games took on a name in league history. 1986 was "The Drive" because of Elway's 98-yard game-tying drive to force overtime in which Elway led a second drive to the game-winning field goal. 1987 was "The Fumble" when Bernie Kosar led the Browns on a furious comeback that culminated with normally reliable halfback Ernest Byner fumbling the ball away at the goal line in the closing minutes. A year later, Browns' owner Art Modell grew disappointed with Cleveland's conservative offense and demanded Schottenheimer hire an offensive coordinator. When Marty refused, the two agreed to part company.

Schottenheimer was hired by the Chiefs in 1989, and they had not had any consistent success since Hank Stram left 15 years before. Over ten years in Kansas City, Marty led the team to nine winning seasons and seven trips to the postseason, but could not reach the Super Bowl, even in the two years the club finished 13–3. The Chiefs did reach the AFC championship in 1993 during Joe Montana's first season in town, but Joe got hurt right after the first half and did not finish the game in Buffalo. Marty's Chiefs were known for their fierce pass rush led by defensive end Neil Smith and linebacker Derrick Thomas and their

air-tight secondary, but once again a mediocre offense doomed the team to ultimate defeat.

After experiencing his first losing season in Kansas City, Schottenheimer stepped down in 1999 and spent two years as a TV analyst for ESPN. He returned to coaching in 2001 with the Washington Redskins, but was very ill-matched with star-driven Redskins' owner Dan Snyder and was fired after one 8–8 season. A month later, Marty was named head coach of the Chargers and built his strongest team yet with San Diego winning 12 games behind Drew Brees in 2004 and 14 behind Philip Rivers in 2006. However, the Chargers lost in the first round of the playoffs in both years, perishing primarily due to an overly cautious approach that focused more on trying not to lose than trying to win. Perhaps because he had been in continual conflict with San Diego GM A.J. Smith and owner Alex Spanos, Marty followed a peculiar course in the 2006 off season. Despite being barred by the team from hiring relatives, Schottenheimer attempted to hire his brother Kurt as the team's defensive coordinator, thereby forcing Smith to fire him but leaving the team on the hook for Marty's $4-million salary.

Schottenheimer won 200 regular season games, more than any other coach who never reached a Super Bowl. His brother Kurt coached special teams and defense in the league for a couple decades, and his son Brian was the Jets' offensive coordinator for several years. Unable to remain on the sideline for god, Marty coached the Virginia Destroyers of the developmental United Football League in 2011 and won his first ever league championship as a coach. Ultimately, though, Schottenheimer is likely to remain the most successful coach outside the Hall of Fame due to his postseason failures.

SCHWARTZ, JAMES (JIM) 6/2/1966– Georgetown. LB; did not play professionally. *Apprenticeship:* College asst.— 4 years; pro asst.—13 years. *Roots:* Ted Marchibroda, Jeff Fisher. *Branches:* None. *Coordinators/Key Assistants:* Scott Linehan ran the offense, while Gunther Cunningham handled the defense. *Hall of Fame Players:* None. *Primary Quarterbacks:* Matthew Stafford, Shaun Hill. *Tendencies:* • His teams scored 22.9 points and allowed 26 per game • His teams ran 38.7% of the time, which was 90% of the league average • Four starting quarterbacks in three years; 81% of starts to primary quarterbacks • Nine rookie starters in three years • Winning Full Seasons to Losing Full Seasons: 1:2.

Born in Halethorpe, Maryland, outside of Baltimore, Jim Schwartz graduated from Georgetown with a degree in Economics with Honors in 1989. At Georgetown, he also was a four-year letterman as an undersized linebacker on the Hoyas football team and subsequently went immediately into coaching as an assistant at Maryland in 1989. Schwartz moved on to

Minnesota in 1990, North Carolina Central in 1991 and Colgate in 1992 before being hired as a scout by Bill Belichick in Cleveland from 1993 to 1995. That connection won him a spot on Ted Marchibroda's Baltimore Ravens' staff from 1996 to 1998. Jim joined Jeff Fisher in Tennessee in 1999 and was promoted to defensive coordinator in 2001. Over eight seasons, Schwartz had to rebuild the Titans' defense twice and they finished the 2008 season second in fewest points allowed.

The highly respected and analytical Schwartz was then hired by Detroit in 2009 to take over the 0–16 Lions, a franchise that had gone 31–97 in the last eight years. Jeff Fisher told the press, "In his eight years as our defensive coordinator, Jim has clearly put his stamp on that side of the ball. He is competitive, a tremendous communicator and motivator and, in our opinion, he has been ready for this next step for several years." Schwartz told reporters, "I can't speak of the past, I'm here right now. I'm not here to exorcise any ghosts." However, he did acknowledge the team's dismal past by adding, "Quarterback is the trump card of all positions in the NFL. It's probably time to find a replacement for Bobby Layne."

As with many defensive coaches, though, Schwatz's primary focus is, "You've got to be big and strong and be able to run and stop the run. I think you need to be built that way." Indeed, Jim has gone in that direction, drafting defensive linemen Ndamukong Suh and Nick Fairley with top picks in 2010 and 2011 and making defensive end Kyle Vanden Bosch his first free agent signing. Along with 2008's top pick, quarterback Matthew Stafford, the new blood began to assert itself at the end of 2010 when the team ended the year with four straight wins. 2011 was a continuation of that pattern with Detroit making the playoffs for the first time in 12 years. Although the chippy, immature Lions have shown too much of a propensity for drawing stupid penalties, Schwartz seems primed for a nice run as head coach in the revived Motor City.

SCOTT, TOM 1/7/1920–6/1978. West Point. E; did not play professionally. *Apprenticeship:* College asst.— 1 year; pro asst.—1 year. *Roots:* Mal Stevens (i). *Branches:* None. *Coordinators/Key Assistants:* None. *Hall of Fame Players:* None. *Primary Quarterbacks:* None. *Record:* **Interim Coach.**

Despite being listed in the standard football encyclopedias as the Brooklyn Dodgers' co-coach with Cliff Battles for the second half of the 1946 All America Football Conference season, Tom Scott actually was merely the interim coach of the team for just one game.

The 6'3" 215-pound Highland Falls, New York native played end on the freshman team at NYU in 1939 when Dr. Mal Stevens was head coach. He transferred to West Point in the next year and played for Army in 1942 before injuring his knee and helped out as a coach in 1943. During the war, Scott served in an anti-aircraft unit all across Europe.

Following his post-war discharge, Tom tried out for the Dodgers in the new AAFC, but when his knee problem flared up in training camp, he was added to the coaching staff by Coach Mal Stevens. Stevens soon found that coaching the dreadful Dodgers was interfering with his medical practice and abruptly resigned less than six hours before the team's seventh game on October 25.

Scott was put in charge of the team that day, and the Dodgers knocked off feeble Miami 30–7. The team announced that Stevens' former assistant at NYU, Fred Linehan, would be taking over in a few days. However, Linehan withdrew from his appointment on the 29th, so Brooklyn had to scramble to hire Cliff Battles, who had coached at Columbia and in the Marines, as head coach on November 1, one day prior to their next game against Chicago. Reporters questioned Scott whether he'd been offered the head coaching job, "No, I haven't been asked to take over on that basis. That would be silly. I'm only 26 and have had just one year of coaching experience, that in

Schwartz, James (Jim)									
Year	Team	Games	Wins	Losses	Ties	%	P Wins	P Losses	P %
2009	Lions	16	2	14	0	.125	0	0	.000
2010	Lions	16	6	10	0	.375	0	0	.000
2011	Lions	16	10	6	0	.625	0	1	.000
3 years		48	18	30	0	.375	0	1	.000

Scott, Tom									
Year	Team	Games	Wins	Losses	Ties	%	P Wins	P Losses	P %
1946	Brooklyn Dodgers (AAFC)	1	1	0	0	1.000	0	0	.000
1 year		1	1	0	0	1.000	0	0	.000

the service. Of course, someday I hope to qualify, but right now I know I'm not ripe for such a job. When the new man is named, I'll string along as assistant."

Scott continued as an assistant to Battles for the rest of 1946 and all of 1947. Battles was fired in 1948 and replaced by Carl Voyles. Scott never coached in the pros again and died at the age of 58 in 1978.

Seifert, George G. 1/22/1940– Utah. LB; did not play professionally. *Apprenticeship:* College coach —16 years (3 as head coach); pro asst.— 9 years. *Roots:* Bill Walsh. *Branches:* Mike Holmgren, Jeff Fisher, Ray Rhodes, Gary Kubiak. *Coordinators/Key Assistants:* For the 49ers, Mike Holmgren then Mike Shanahan then Marc Trestman ran the offense, while Bill McPherson then Ray Rhodes then Pete Carroll handled the defense; for the Panthers, Gil Haskell then Bill Musgrave then Richard Williamson ran the offense, while John Marshall handled the defense. *Hall of Fame Players:* Richard Dent, Chris Doleman, Ricky Jackson, Ronnie Lott, Joe Montana, Jerry Rice, Deion Sanders, Reggie White, Rod Woodson, Steve Young. *Primary Quarterbacks:* Joe Montana, Steve Young, Steve Beuerlein. *Record:* Super Bowl Championships 1989, 1994. *Tendencies:* • His teams scored 25.2 points and allowed 18 per game • His teams ran 42.5% of the time, which was 94% of the league average • Seven starting quarterbacks in 11 years; 82% of starts to primary quarterbacks • 23 rookie starters in 11 years • Winning Full Seasons to Losing Full Seasons: 8:2.

George Seifert has gotten remarkably little respect for a coach who won nearly two-thirds of his games and led two teams to Super Bowl triumphs. When he took over the defending champion 49ers following the retirement of Hall of Fame coach Bill Walsh, he was put in the awkward position of needing to win a repeat title to not be a disappointment. However, unlike Phil Bengtson following Vince Lombardi or Ray Handley following Bill Parcells, Seifert did just what he was supposed to do and won a championship in his first year. One near parallel to his situation was Don Mc-

Cafferty following Don Shula in Baltimore and winning it all in his first year. However, Shula had not won a title with the Colts, and McCafferty's tenure as head coach was very brief. A more similar circumstance was Tom Flores following Hall of Fame coach John Madden and winning two Super Bowls in his first five years with the Raiders. Flores even had a failed second NFL coaching stop that devalued his already lightly regarded Bay Area accomplishments much like Seifert would in Carolina. Despite the similarities, though, there is no exact parallel to George Seifert's singular head coaching career.

Seifert was born in San Francisco and grew up a 49ers fan, even working as an usher at Kezar Stadium at one point in his youth. Leaving the Bay Area for college, George played guard and linebacker at the University of Utah from 1958 to 1961 under Ray Nagel. He returned to his alma mater in 1964 as an assistant coach and then took over the moribund program at tiny Westminster College in Utah in 1965, posting an 0–3 record. The next year he moved to Iowa as an assistant to Nagel again before returning to the West Coast in 1967 at Oregon. Seifert was on the Oregon staff from 1967 to 1971 and then coached the secondary at Stanford from 1972 to 1974. Hired as the head coach at Cornell in 1975, he could manage just a 3–15 record in two years and was dismissed. In 1977, he returned to Stanford to join Bill Walsh's staff and stayed in Palo Alto even after Walsh took over the 49ers.

Walsh hired George to rebuild and coach the 49er secondary in 1980. The following season, San Francisco had three rookie starting defensive backs yet won the Super Bowl. After three years as secondary coach, Seifert was promoted to defensive coordinator in 1983, and the team won a second championship in 1984 when the defense completely shut down Miami's Dan Marino in the Super Bowl, with Seifert outshining former 49er coordinator Chuck Studley who coached the Dolphin defense. George was an early proponent of the mass substitution patterns now

Seifert, George G.

Year	Team	Games	Wins	Losses	Ties	%	P Wins	P Losses	P %
1989	49ers	16	14	2	0	.875	3	0	1.000
1990	49ers	16	14	2	0	.875	1	1	.500
1991	49ers	16	10	6	0	.625	0	0	.000
1992	49ers	16	14	2	0	.875	1	1	.500
1993	49ers	16	10	6	0	.625	1	1	.500
1994	49ers	16	13	3	0	.813	3	0	1.000
1995	49ers	16	11	5	0	.688	0	1	.000
1996	49ers	16	12	4	0	.750	1	1	.500
1999	Panthers	16	8	8	0	.500	0	0	.000
2000	Panthers	16	7	9	0	.438	0	0	.000
2001	Panthers	16	1	15	0	.063	0	0	.000
11 years		176	114	62	0	.648	10	5	.667

common to the game and was an underrated defensive coach. The team's practice sessions pitted him against Walsh's imaginative offense. Defensive back Ronnie Lott told *Sports Illustrated*, "You had a genius and a perfectionist, two guys who didn't want the other to see his weaknesses. It brought out the best in all of us."

After Walsh led San Francisco to a third championship in 10 years, he walked away from the pressurized cauldron of coaching and turned the team over in 1989 to Seifert, his top aide. Stepping into the vortex, George remained calm and composed while leading the 49ers to a repeat championship in his first season and then came within a Roger Craig fumble late in the 1990 NFC championship against the Giants of having the chance at a three-peat title versus Buffalo in Super Bowl XXVI.

Seifert was so even tempered and quiet that he was accused of having no personality, but his players grew to appreciate him. Cornerback Eric Davis told *Sports Illustrated*, "When I looked at George, I'd see the stone-faced guy on TV who never smiled and never talked to anyone. He seemingly had no relationship with any of the players. He would ride me so hard it made me wonder if I'd stolen money from him. I didn't like him at first, but eventually he brought out in me what he was trying to bring out, and I earned my stripes." Another defensive back, Eric Wright, summarized the coach to the *New York Times*, "George is a really nice man. He is a very good person and a very intelligent person. He is a workaholic and a loner." Receiver Jerry Rice added to the *Times*, "The players had mixed feelings about Bill [Walsh] because he did not communicate with everyone. He would pick his players and let them get the message to the rest of the team. George communicates with everyone, and everyone appreciates that."

Despite his placid exterior, Seifert was driven. One-time offensive coordinator Mike Holmgren was astonished at his attention to detail, telling *Sports Illustrated*, "There were times we'd pass each other in the hallway, and he's just whisk right by as if I didn't exist. Who knows where his mind was. If you didn't know him, you'd think he was a little standoffish." In addition, Seifert had several superstitious quirks that amused his players. He would never step on the 49ers emblem on the field; he would not leave his office without patting a book; he had to blow on a lifesaver three times before eating it; and he had to be the last person to leave the locker room before a game.

In that 1990 NFC championship loss to the Giants, quarterback Joe Montana was seriously injured and the team transitioned to Steve Young, acquired by Walsh, in 1991. Even when Montana returned in late 1992, it was now Young's team. Seifert made the wrenching decision to cut ties with the legendary four-time Super Bowl quarterback, and Joe was traded to

Kansas City. Young led the 49ers to back-to-back NFC title clashes in 1992 and 1993, but lost both to Jimmy Johnson's Cowboys. Fickle 49er fans favored Johnson to replace Seifert in a poll by 85% to 15%.

Seifert continued to overhaul the team each year and other legends like Ronnie Lott departed, but the retooled 49ers won a fifth Super Bowl in 1994. Still, when that was followed by consecutive losses to Mike Holmgren's Packers in the divisional round of the playoffs in 1995 and 1996, San Francisco GM Carmen Policy moved to hire former Green Bay assistant Steve Mariucci as the team's offensive coordinator and explicit heir apparent to Seiferrt in 1997. George found that scenario untenable and resigned. In eight seasons, he had never won fewer than 10 games, yet was driven out of the organization. Five times his offense led the league in scoring and three other times were in the top three; four times his defense was in the top three in fewest points allowed.

Seifert was out of football for two years, but returned in 1999 as head coach of the struggling Carolina Panthers. While he coaxed mediocre 8–8 and 7–9 seasons out of the Steve Beurlein-led Panthers in his first two years, George was fired after a 1–15 2001 season. In his defense, Seifert did bring in several stars like Steve Smith, Kris Jenkins and Dan Morgan who would propel Carolina to the Super Bowl in 2003 under Coach John Fox. George never returned to coaching and has not gotten the respect he is due.

SHANAHAN, MICHAEL E. (MIKE) 8/24/1952–

Eastern Illinois. QB; did not play professionally. *Apprenticeship:* College asst.— 9 years; pro asst.— 4 years. *Roots:* Dan Reeves. *Branches:* Art Shell, Terry Robiskie (i), Gary Kubiak. *Coordinators/Key Assistants:* For the Raiders, Tom Walsh ran the offense, while Charlie Sumner handled the defense; for the Broncos, Gary Kubiak then Rick Dennison ran the offense, while Greg Robinson then Ray Rhodes then Larry Coyer then Jim Bates then Bob Slowik handled the defense; for the Redskins, Kyle Shanahan ran the offense, while Jim Haslett handled the defense. *Hall of Fame Players:* Marcus Allen, John Elway, Mike Haynes, James Lofton, Howie Long, Shannon Sharpe, Gary Zimmerman. *Primary Quarterbacks:* Jay Schroeder, John Elway, Brian Griese, Jake Plummer, Donovan McNabb, Rex Grossman. *Record:* Super Bowl Championships 1997, 1998. *Tendencies:* • His teams scored 23.4 points and allowed 21.1 per game • His teams ran 45.7% of the time, which was 103% of the league average • 17 starting quarterbacks in 18 years; 74% of starts to primary quarterbacks • 38 rookie starters in 18 years • Winning Full Seasons to Losing Full Seasons: 9:5.

A common criticism of Mike Shanahan is that after Hall of Fame quarterback John Elway retired, the Broncos were never serious contenders again. It is true that the drop off was steep from Shanahan's Elway years when Denver averaged 12 wins per year and won two Super Bowls to the post–Elway decade when the team averaged nine wins a year and won just one play-off game. However, aside from founding fathers George Halas and Curly Lambeau, the only coaches who won championships with multiple quarterbacks were Weeb Ewbank, Bill Parcells, Joe Gibbs and George Seifert. Even revered coaches like Don Shula and Tom Landry who had a series of top quarterbacks, only won it all with one signal caller.

The closest equivalents to the pair of Shanahan/Elway were Paul Brown/Otto Graham and Chuck Noll/Terry Bradshaw. It should be noted that Brown's post–Graham Cleveland teams dropped from winning 84% of their games to 62% and lost their only two postseason games, while Noll's post–Bradshaw Steelers slipped from winning two-thirds of their games to less than half and went just 2–3 in the playoffs.

In his book, *Think Like a Champion*, Shanahan quotes Elway discussing his favorite coach, "He made me the player I am. I couldn't have done it without him." Shanahan and Elway had a special bond formed over several years working together that culminated in the shared high point of each man's career: consecutive Super Bowl triumphs in 1997 and 1998.

Like Elway, Mike began as a quarterback, but the Oak Park, Illinois native was just 5'9" and ruptured a kidney and almost died during his junior year at Eastern Illinois in 1973. He began his coaching career directly after graduation by working under Barry Switzer at Oklahoma in 1975. He then spent 1976–1977 at Northern Arizona, 1978 as offensive coordinator at his alma mater, 1979 as offensive coordi-

nator at Minnesota and from 1980 to 1983 as Florida's offensive coordinator under Charley Pell. Dan Reeves hired Shanahan in 1984 to be Denver's offensive coordinator in Elway's second season, and Mike and John hit it off immediately even as Elway and Reeves began to clash.

After two unsuccessful Super Bowl trips with the Broncos, Shanahan accepted the Raiders' head coaching position, but that would prove to be the bitterest experience of his coaching life. Mike sparred with owner Al Davis right from the start and was clearly an outsider in the Raider family. At the end of 1988, Shanahan fired defensive coordinator Charlie Sumner and defensive backs coach Willie Brown, both long-time Raiders. Sumner told the press, "I really think I'm being made the fall guy and I think this was a set-up deal from the beginning." Firing the defensive coordinator has become a regular practice for Shanahan throughout his career; he went through five defensive coordinators during the post–Elway decade in Denver. When the Raiders got off to a 1–3 start in 1989, Davis fired Mike and then refused to pay him all that had been agreed to in his contract, beginning a feud that would last over 20 years. According to the *New York Times*, a few years later when Shanahan was coaching the 49ers offense, San Francisco played the Raiders. Before the game, Mike spotted Davis on the field and ordered quarterback Elvis Grbac to fire a pass at Al's head.

Reeves rehired Shanahan in Denver, and the team made another failed Super Bowl trip in 1989. When San Francisco's offensive coordinator Mike Holmgren was named head coach in Green Bay in 1992, the 49ers hired Shanahan to take his place, and

Shanahan, Michael E. (Mike)									
Year	Team	Games	Wins	Losses	Ties	%	P Wins	P Losses	P %
1988	Raiders	16	7	9	0	.438	0	0	.000
1989	Raiders	4	1	3	0	.250	0	0	.000
1995	Broncos	16	8	8	0	.500	0	0	.000
1996	Broncos	16	13	3	0	.813	0	1	.000
1997	Broncos	16	12	4	0	.750	4	0	1.000
1998	Broncos	16	14	2	0	.875	3	0	1.000
1999	Broncos	16	6	10	0	.375	0	0	.000
2000	Broncos	16	11	5	0	.688	0	1	.000
2001	Broncos	16	8	8	0	.500	0	0	.000
2002	Broncos	16	9	7	0	.563	0	0	.000
2003	Broncos	16	10	6	0	.625	0	1	.000
2004	Broncos	16	10	6	0	.625	0	1	.000
2005	Broncos	16	13	3	0	.813	1	1	.500
2006	Broncos	16	9	7	0	.563	0	0	.000
2007	Broncos	16	7	9	0	.438	0	0	.000
2008	Broncos	16	8	8	0	.500	0	0	.000
2010	Redskins	16	6	10	0	.375	0	0	.000
2011	Redskins	16	5	11	0	.313	0	0	.000
18 years		276	157	119	0	.569	8	5	.615

the 49ers led the league in scoring for the next three years through 1994. Denver owner Pat Bowlen told the *New York Times* he tried to hire Mike as head coach in 1993, but Shanahan refused, "I think the best thing that happened to Mike and this organization was that he stayed in San Francisco for a few more years. When I finally did hire him, he was very well rounded." After San Francisco won the Super Bowl in 1994, Mike accepted Bowlen's renewed offer and took over as the Broncos' head coach.

In Denver, Shanahan improved the quality of Elway's surrounding cast and built a powerful cutback running game based on a zone blocking scheme that took a lot of pressure off Elway in that he no longer had to try to win games all by himself. Three times Denver finished in the top two in scoring. The blocking was so consistently good that Shanahan plugged in one 1,000-yard rusher after another during his 14 years in Denver, although the best was Terrell Davis who ran for over 2,000 yards in leading the Broncos to a second consecutive Super Bowl win in 1998. Shanahan out coached Mike Holmgren to upset the favored Packers in 1997 and in 1998 upended the Falcons coached by his former boss and his quarterback's bête noir, Dan Reeves. Elway then retired on top, while Shanahan spent the next ten years finding Brian Griese, Jake Plummer and Jay Cutler wanting as Elway's replacements.

Shanahan essentially ran all personnel matters for the Broncos, but his drafts were dismal and his free agent signings disappointing. Former Denver guard Mark Schlereth said after Mike was unexpectedly fired by Bowlen in 2009, "The reason Mike is not coaching the Broncos anymore is his personnel decisions."

Shanahan took a year off from coaching before agreeing to take over the Redskins in 2010. In Washington, Mike brought in his son Kyle from the Texans to serve as offensive coordinator, but the "Shanaclan" had problems in 2010 with newly-acquired quarterback Donovan McNabb and that made for one ugly situation; Shanahan's bullying of recalcitrant defensive lineman Albert Haynesworth made for another. In 2011, McNabb and Haynesworth were gone, and Mike placed the team in the shaky hands of backup quarterbacks Rex Grossman and John Beck with predictably sorry results. With Bruce Allen, George Allen's son, on hand as general manager, there is hope that personnel decisions will be better handled than they were in Denver, but there is much room for im-

provement. On the field, Shanahan is as he ever was, a master of organization. As quarterback Steve Young noted in Mike's book, "Discipline is something Mike Shanahan thrives on. His whole attitude is: I will out prepare you; I will not be stopped; I will do everything and more to make sure that my men are ready."

SHAUGHNESSY, CLARK D. 3/6/1892–3/15/1970. Minnesota. FB, T, E; did not play professionally. *Apprenticeship:* College coach — 32 years (31 as head coach); pro asst.—1 year. *Roots:* George Halas, Turk Edwards. *Branches:* Joe Stydahar, Red Hickey. *Coordinators/Key Assistants*: Joe Stydahar was his line coach and Red Hickey coached the ends. *Hall of Fame Players:* Tom Fears, Elroy Hirsch, Norm Van Brocklin, Bob Waterfield. *Primary Quarterbacks:* Bob Watrfield. *Tendencies:* • His teams scored 28.6 points and allowed 21.2 per game • His teams ran 53% of the time, which was 91% of the league average • Two starting quarterbacks in two years; 88% of starts to primary quarterback • Two rookie starters in two years • Winning Full Seasons to Losing Full Seasons: 2:0.

Clark Shaughnessy is a member of the College Football Hall of Fame for his 32 years as a creative college coach, and has been proposed at times as a candidate for the Pro Football Hall of Fame for his innovative work, primarily as an assistant coach and advisor with the pros.

Shaughnessy was born in St. Cloud, Minnesota, and played fullback at Minnesota from 1911 to 1913 for Henry L. Williams who was known for the presnap "Williams' Shift." He began his 50-year coaching career the very next year as Williams' assistant at his alma mater. After just one year, Clark was named head coach at Tulane and coached the Green Wave from 1915 to 1920, stepped down in 1921 and then resumed at Tulane from 1922 to 1926. Overall, he amassed a 59–28–7 record with Tulane and then moved across town to take over Loyola in 1927, compiling a 38–16–6 mark through 1932.

Shaughnessy fatefully returned to the Midwest in 1933, replacing the renowned Amos Alonzo Stagg at the University of Chicago and making friends with George Halas. While Clark struggled to a 17–34–4 record with Chicago as the university deemphasized football, he took on an advisor's role with the Bears, working with Halas and former Bears' coach Ralph Jones to retool the T formation. Halas credited Shaughnessy with devising counter plays away from

Shaughnessy, Clark D.									
Year	*Team*	*Games*	*Wins*	*Losses*	*Ties*	*%*	*P Wins*	*P Losses*	*P %*
1948	Rams	12	6	5	1	.542	0	0	.000
1949	Rams	12	8	2	2	.750	0	1	.000
2 years		24	14	7	3	.646	0	1	.000

the man in motion as well as a series of end runs. Others credit him with increasing the splits between offensive linemen, brush blocking, the hand-to-hand center snap and deceptive ball handling practices. Shaughnessy once described his approach to offense: "We'll coil up the defense in as small an area as possible, then run around it or throw over it. We'll shuttle tackles and ends back and forth along the line laterally, shift the guards sometimes in an unbalanced line and sometimes in a balanced line. Shuttling tackles and ends, shifting guards and setting a man in motion — away from the play — will force the defense out of a set position. It will make old set defenses obsolete!"

In 1940, Clark left Chicago for Stanford and immediately transformed a 1–7–1 team into 10–0 Rose Bowl champs behind tricky T formation ball handler Frankie Albert. He even found time to draw up some new counter plays for the Bears to use in that year's title game in which Chicago beat Washington 73–0. After going 16–3 in two years at Stanford, Clark took over the Maryland program in 1942, led the Terps to a 7–2 record and then assumed control of the Pittsburgh Panthers in 1943 — just as the school deemphasized football for the war. Following a disappointing 10–17 record from 1943 to 1945, he returned to Maryland in 1946. His advisory role with the Bears lasted till 1942 when Halas went into the Navy. Co-coaches Hunk Anderson and Luke Johnsos despised him and locked him out of Chicago's facilities at that point. Anderson later wrote in his autobiography, "We didn't know how much usurpation of credit Clark Shaughnessy inspired on his own behalf. It was in working with Shaughnessy in later years that Luke Johnsos, Paddy Driscoll and I were to learn that Shaughnessy was a charlatan." Anderson found Shaughnessy to be a grandstander who claimed recognition for plays that he didn't create. Continuing his dabbling in the pro game, Shaughnessy worked on the side as a consultant for the Redskins beginning in 1944, primarily installing the T formation in Washington.

Clark led Maryland to a 3–6 record and was fired when he refused to give up his side job with the Redskins. Shaughnessy stayed with Washington for one more season and then took a similar position with the Rams in 1948. He quickly impressed owner Dan Reeves with his strategic acumen and won himself a fast promotion. During training camp, Rams' coach Bob Snyder was fired and replaced by Clark just as the team was boarding a flight to Hawaii for a preseason game.

In Los Angeles, Clark is credited with developing the modern three-receiver Pro Set by regularly splitting out halfback Elroy Hirsch as a receiver. However, Hirsch actually was used more as a regular halfback by Shaughnessy; his transition to flanker occurred in 1950 under head coach Joe Stydahar and offensive

strategist Hampton Pool. In Clark's second season, the Rams met Philadelphia in the 1949 title game but could do nothing in a 14–0 game that was played in a rainstorm and was highlighted by Eagles' halfback Steve Van Buren rumbling for a record 196 yards in the slop. In the aftermath, Shaughnessy was shocked in February when he was fired and replaced by his assistant coach Stydahar. The Rams cited "internal friction" because neither the players nor coaches could get along with their imperious and obfuscatory coach. Clark sneered at his successor, "When Stydahar gets through coaching the Rams, I can take any high school team in the country and beat them." In reality, Stydahar led the team to a championship in 1951.

By then, Shaughnessy was an assistant coach with the Bears, causing Chicago's defensive coach Hunk Anderson to retire from coaching. Clark coached the Bears' defense through 1962. In that time, he played a role in developing the middle linebacker position in the 4–3 defense and originated some of the common terminology used in defensive play calling. Shaughnessy used both zone and man-to-man defense and employed an overly complicated system that Bear defenders disliked. Linebacker George Connor, an Anderson man, told Jeff Davis for *Papa Bear*, "Shaughnesy didn't know diddly-shit about defense! He was a phony all the way."

Shaughnessy was clearly a difficult man to get along with. He was a milkshake drinker who neither drank nor smoked, but was aloof with a superior attitude and a penchant for cutting, sarcastic comments. Safety Richie Petitbon charitably told ESPN, "He could be sharp tongued, abrupt and impatient, but I feel like a lot of people who think on a higher level in any [endeavor] are like that." After being shunted aside for George Allen in 1962, Shaughnessy retired from coaching in 1963 only to return to coach Hawaii to a 1–8–1 record in 1965. He died in 1970 at the age of 78 and his old friend Halas eulogized him, "He had one of the great inventive minds in the game. Clark was a master strategist and organizer, and it was my privilege to have him as a technical advisor. I shall miss him tremendously."

SHAW, LAWRENCE T. 3/28/1899–3/19/1977. Notre Dame. T; did not play professionally. *Apprenticeship:* College coach — 20 years (13 as head coach). *Roots:* None. *Branches:* Eddie Erdelatz, Nick Skorich, Phil Bengtson, Jerry Williams. *Coordinators/Key Assistants:* Al Ruffo and Jim Lawson were key offensive assistants, while Eddie Erdelatz then Phil Bengtson handled the defense. *Hall of Fame Players:* Chuck Bednarik, John Henry Johnson, Sonny Jurgensen, Tommy McDonald, Hugh McElhenny, Leo Nomellini, Joe Perry, Bob St. Clair, Y.A. Tittle, Norm Van Brocklin. *Primary Quarterbacks:* Frankie Albert, Y.A. Tittle, Norm Van Brocklin. *Record:* NFL Championship 1960. *Tendencies:* • His teams scored 25.4 points and allowed 19.8 per game • His teams ran 58.3% of the time, which was 105% of the league average • Six starting quarterbacks in 12 years; 98% of starts to primary quarterbacks • 47 rookie starters in 12 years • Winning Full Seasons to Losing Full Seasons: 10:2.

Buck Shaw was a 175-pound All-American tackle who played for Knute Rockne at Notre Dame from 1919 to 1921. The Mitchellville, Iowa native originally began his college years at Creighton in 1918, but the flu epidemic wiped out the football schedule, so Shaw transferred to the Fighting Irish. Rockne recommended Buck to North Carolina State in 1924, and he coached the Wolfpack to a 2–6–2 season before leaving for Nevada the next year. From 1925 to 1928, Shaw managed a meek 10–20–3 record and was dismissed. He joined former Notre Dame teammate Clipper Smith as an assistant at Santa Clara in 1929 and served as Clipper's line coach there for the next seven years. When Clipper left in 1936, Shaw was promoted to head coach of the Broncos and compiled a 47–10–4 record in Santa Clara from 1936 to 1942, while sending several players on to pro football.

Santa Clara dropped football for the war in 1943, so Shaw spent the next two years working as an Army trainer on campus. In 1945, he returned to coaching with California, but compiled just a 4–5–1 record with the Golden Bears that year until accepting the head coaching job with the new San Francisco 49ers of the fledgling All America Football Conference in 1946. Buck led the 49ers for their first nine years of existence, posting a winning record in every year but 1950 when San Francisco joined the NFL after the two leagues merged. Although the 49ers won more than 70% of their games in the AAFC, they could never get past Paul Brown's Cleveland Browns. The most famous story about the dignified Shaw is that in one game against the Browns, Graham was playing on a gimpy knee, but Buck forbid his players from going after Otto's injury as an affront to good sportsmanship. Unfortunately, San Francisco lost that day.

Despite having a top tier T formation quarterback in Frankie Albert who threw 29 TD passes in 1948 and 27 in 1949, Shaw favored the running game. San Francisco set a league record by rushing for 3,663 yards in 1948 and later developed the "Million Dollar Backfield" of four Hall of Famers: Y.A. Title, Joe Perry, Hugh McElhenny and John Henry Johnson. Three times the team led the league in scoring and was second another time. However, the 49ers never were a complete enough club to win it all or even to reach an NFL championship game. Following another near miss in 1954, San Francisco owner Tony Morabito fired Shaw, saying, "He has been given 100 percent authority, not 99 percent, but 100. Four out of the past five years, the 49ers have either folded completely or lost the big one. I think it's time we tried something else."

Buck returned to private business in 1955, but then took over the startup football program at the Air Force Academy from 1956 to 1957. He led the new team to a 9–8–2 record in those first two years and subsequently was hired by Philadelphia Eagles' GM Vince McNally, a Notre Dame alumnus from Shaw's time in South Bend. Buck had arranged to be a half-year coach in his years with the 49ers and at Air Force and told the press that would continue in Philadelphia, "My arrangements with the Eagles are such that my coaching duties will not interfere with my business interests in San Francisco. I will coach about 5 1/2 months of the year, delegating to a top flight assistant much of the off season detail work."

Shaw told McNally he wouldn't take the job without an established quarterback on the team; he was not interested in training Sonny Jurgensen. McNally swung the deal for Van Brocklin, and Buck, known as the "Silver Fox" for his shock of gray hair, came aboard. Since Van Brocklin asserted so much control over the offense and was such a forceful leader for the whole team, much has been made that Van Brocklin and not Shaw was the real coach of the team.

Shaw, Lawrence T.									
Year	Team	Games	Wins	Losses	Ties	%	P Wins	P Losses	P %
1946	49ers	14	9	5	0	.643	0	0	.000
1947	49ers	14	8	4	2	.643	0	0	.000
1948	49ers	14	12	2	0	.857	0	0	.000
1949	49ers	12	9	3	0	.750	1	1	.500
1950	49ers	12	3	9	0	.250	0	0	.000
1951	49ers	12	7	4	1	.625	0	0	.000
1952	49ers	12	7	5	0	.583	0	0	.000
1953	49ers	12	9	3	0	.750	0	0	.000
1954	49ers	12	7	4	1	.625	0	0	.000
1958	Eagles	12	2	9	1	.208	0	0	.000
1959	Eagles	12	7	5	0	.583	0	0	.000
1960	Eagles	12	10	2	0	.833	1	0	1.000
12 years		150	90	55	5	.617	2	1	.667

However, Shaw's soft spoken style was that of a delegator and very much the model of the contemporary head coach. He had been the same way in San Francisco, deferring a great deal to clever quarterback Frankie Albert. In Philadelphia, Van Brocklin and offensive coach Charlie Gauer took care of the offense, and defensive coach Jerry Williams handled the defense. Ultimately though, Buck was in control. Shaw was moving bodies in and out of Philadelphia through trades and signings at a constant pace as he tried to improve the quality of team as fast as possible.

At the outset, the team seemed to go backwards. After Hugh Devore's 4–8 1957 record, Shaw's 2–9–1 mark in 1958 was a disappointment. Following the ninth loss, he told the team, "This has never happened to me before. It will never happen again. If you don't have any pride, I do. I'll be here again next year, but some of you may not. We'll win if I have to use three teams — one coming, one going and one playing." Buck kept the steady stream of players flowing through as he pieced together a championship team. The Birds jumped to a 7–5 second place finish in 1959 and both Shaw and Van Brocklin announced 1960 would be their last year. They and 60-minute man Chuck Bednarik made it a memorable swan song with a 10–2 team record and a triumph over Vince Lombardi's Packers in the 1960 championship game. Shaw indeed retired from football immediately, a champion at last.

Two years later, Santa Clara named their new football field Buck Shaw Stadium in honor of the revered coach. Although the school dropped football in 1992, Buck Shaw Stadium still serves as the home to the college soccer team. In retirement, Buck did some scouting on the side and was inducted into the College Football Hall of Fame in 1972. He died in 1977 from cancer.

SHELL, ARTHUR (ART) 11/26/1946– Maryland Eastern Shore. Played T for the Raiders from 1968 to 1982. *Apprenticeship:* Pro asst.— 7 years. *Roots:* Tom Flores, Mike Shanahan. *Branches:* Mike White, Gunther Cunningham, Jim Haslett, John Fox, Chuck Pagano. *Coordinators/Key Assistants*: For his first stint, Tom Walsh ran the offense, while Dave Adolph then Gunther Cunningham then John Fox handled the de-

fense; in his second stint, Tom Walsh then John Shoop ran the offense, while Rob Ryan handled the defense. *Hall of Fame Players:* Marcus Allen, Eric Dickerson, Mike Haynes, Howie Long, Ronnie Lott. *Primary Quarterbacks:* Jay Schroeder, Jeff Hostetler. *Record:* **Hall of Fame Player.** *Tendencies:* • His teams scored 17.4 points and allowed 18.8 per game • His teams ran 47.4% of the time, which was 105% of the league average • Seven starting quarterbacks in seven years; 70% of starts to primary quarterbacks • Ten rookie starters in seven years • Winning Full Seasons to Losing Full Seasons: 4:2.

Art Shell was the first black head coach in the NFL since Fritz Pollard in 1925 and was the last Raiders' coach of Al Davis' glory years. In the decade and a half since Shell was fired the first time, the team slid to the bottom and went through nine head coaches, including a second stint for Shell himself. The only success the team had in that period was driven by Jon Gruden's remaking of the team for a few years before Al reasserted himself as Raider in Chief.

Shell was born in Charleston, South Carolina, and played football at Maryland State, a predominantly black school now known as Maryland Eastern Shore. The 6'5" 265-pound tackle was drafted in the third round by Oakland in 1968 and played with the Raiders for the next 15 years, teaming up with guard Gene Upshaw on the left side of the line to form an impregnable wall for Raider quarterbacks and runners. Both men eventually were elected to the Hall of Fame. Shell, who had served as a volunteer assistant line coach at the University of California in 1981 and 1982, moved directly onto the Raiders' coaching staff in 1983 as the team's line coach. When Al Davis fired Mike Shanahan just four games into the 1989 season, he turned to Art to replace the non–Raider intruder, "Art's quiet, but he's got something Madden had: he's a great communicator, a great teacher. Art's a bright guy, a clean guy. And he played with all our great quarterbacks: Lamonica, Blanda, Stabler and Plunkett. He knows Raider football. Going into the 90's, he's the guy I want to restore the identity of this franchise."

The truest part of Davis' comment is that Shell had played with all the great Raider quarterbacks — past tense. While the Raiders were still a talented team

Shell, Arthur (Art)

Year	Team	Games	Wins	Losses	Ties	%	P Wins	P Losses	P %
1989	Raiders	12	7	5	0	.583	0	0	.000
1990	Raiders	16	12	4	0	.750	1	1	.500
1991	Raiders	16	9	7	0	.563	0	1	.000
1992	Raiders	16	7	9	0	.438	0	0	.000
1993	Raiders	16	10	6	0	.625	1	1	.500
1994	Raiders	16	9	7	0	.563	0	0	.000
2006	Raiders	16	2	14	0	.125	0	0	.000
7 years		108	56	52	0	.519	2	3	.400

in 1989 and went to the AFC championship in 1990, they had a hole at quarterback throughout his tenure. In that championship game, the Raiders lost to Buffalo 51–3 behind inconsistent, big-armed Jay Schroeder. Schroeder was challenged by spaced-out Todd Marinovich and eventually supplanted by weak-armed, game-manager Jeff Hostetler in 1993. Shell would get in some trouble ironically in 1994 for denigrating Hostetler on the sideline in racial terms as "white" quarterback. By then the team was mediocre at best, and Shell was fired at year's end.

Art continued to work as a line coach in the league for several seasons. From 1995 to 1996, he was employed by the Raiders' traditional rival, the Chiefs, and from 1997 to 2000 by the Falcons. In 2001, he took a senior vice president's position with the league overseeing a variety of operations, but five years later, Davis rehired Art as the Raiders' coach. It was history repeating itself as farce. Shell appeared disinterested and lost. He hired Tom Walsh as offensive coordinator. Walsh had served the same role in the first Shell stint, but had been out of the league ever since. Wideout Randy Moss did however little he felt like doing, while receiver Jerry Porter fell into a needless feud with Shell and ultimately was suspended. The team's defense was middle of the pack, but the offense was last in the league, averaging a mere 10.5 points per game with Aaron Brooks and Andrew Walter at quarterback. At the end of 2006, Davis polled his players on Shell's fate after a 2–14 season, and found no support for the coach of this disorganized mess. Art was fired and has not coached in the NFL again.

SHERMAN, ALEXANDER (ALLIE) 2/10/1923– Brooklyn. Played QB for the Eagles from 1943 to 1947. *Apprenticeship:* Semipro head coach —1 year; pro asst.— 7 years; CFL head coach — 3 years. *Roots:* Steve Owen, Jim Lee Howell. *Branches:* Harland Svare, Alex Webster, Jack Patera. *Coordinators/Key Assistants*: Sherman ran his own offense, while Harland Svare then Andy Robustelli then Pop Ivy handled the defense. *Hall of Fame Players:* Roosevelt Brown, Frank Gifford, Sam Huff, Hugh McElhenny, Andy Robustelli, Fran Tarkenton, Y.A. Tittle. *Primary Quarterbacks:* Y.A.

Tittle, Earl Morrall, Fran Tarkenton. *Tendencies:* • His teams scored 23.7 points and allowed 24.3 per game • His teams ran 49.9% of the time, which was 99% of the league average • Seven starting quarterbacks in eight years; 87% of starts to primary quarterbacks • 21 rookie starters in eight years • Winning Full Seasons to Losing Full Seasons: 3:2.

Brooklyn-born Allie Sherman was the first left-handed T formation quarterback in NFL history. At just 5'8", his size was always an issue, but he relied on his brains to advance nearly to the top in professional football.

Allie first learned the T at Brooklyn College where he played from 1940 to 1942. He then joined Greasy Neale's Eagles in 1943 at the age of 19. In his role as backup quarterback, Sherman threw just 135 passes over the next five years before serving as player-coach of the Eagles' farm team, the Patterson Panthers in 1948. In the process, he clearly gained his coach's respect. Neale frequently insisted he was the "smartest man in football," and recommended Sherman to his coaching friend Steve Owen when Steve was installing the T formation with the Giants in 1949.

Allie coached the Giants' backfield for five years under Owen. When Jim Lee Howell replaced Owen as head coach in 1954, Sherman took a head coaching job with Winnipeg in Canada, while Vince Lombardi was hired as New York's offensive coach. Sherman returned to the Giants as a scout in 1956 and subsequently replaced Lombardi as offensive coach once Vince left for Green Bay in 1959. Two years later, Howell stepped down, and the Giants tried to get Lombardi out of his Packer contract just two years into his tenure there. Commissioner Pete Rozelle vetoed that possibility, though, and Sherman was hired, once more the second choice behind Lombardi.

Sherman's Giants won the Eastern Conference his first three years, and he was named Coach of the Year in 1961 and 1962, although his Giants lost to Lombardi's Packers in his first two title games and to George Halas' Bears in 1963. Still, Allie was riding high at this early point in his career as the "Littlest Giant." He had gotten his dream job and was lionized in the press and by the fans for his innovative passing

Sherman, Alexander (Allie)									
Year	Team	Games	Wins	Losses	Ties	%	P Wins	P Losses	P %
1961	Giants	14	10	3	1	.750	0	1	.000
1962	Giants	14	12	2	0	.857	0	1	.000
1963	Giants	14	11	3	0	.786	0	1	.000
1964	Giants	14	2	10	2	.214	0	0	.000
1965	Giants	14	7	7	0	.500	0	0	.000
1966	Giants	14	1	12	1	.107	0	0	.000
1967	Giants	14	7	7	0	.500	0	0	.000
1968	Giants	14	7	7	0	.500	0	0	.000
8 years		112	57	51	4	.527	0	3	.000

game and exciting offensive approach. At the outset, he successfully dealt with a potentially nasty quarterback controversy between holdover Charley Conerly and newly acquired veteran Y.A. Title and had revitalized a Giant team that was picked to finish in the middle of the pack in his first year. Four times Sherman's team finished in the top three in scoring.

Afraid that his aging team was on the verge of collapse, though, Sherman began trading away some veteran stars, particularly on defense, while others retired. The problem was that he did not get much value back in his trades and did not have comparable talent on hand to replace the veteran stars. While in his first year he had brought in Tittle, receivers Del Shofner and Joe Walton and cornerback Erich Barnes at little cost, now he was dumping key players like Don Chandler, Rosey Grier and Dick Modzelewski. The worst move was trading icon Sam Huff for nonentities Dick James and Andy Stynchula in 1964, which was the year everything turned sour for Sherman with a 2–10–2 finish. After a 33–8–1 record in his first three seasons, Sherman's teams went 24–43–3 in the next seven years.

While acquiring Earl Morrall in 1965 and Fran Tarkenton in 1967 helped the team to three .500 seasons, the club was a shell of its former greatness. In 1966, New York won just one game and gave up a record 501 points, 36 per game. Allie was prickly and defensive and had troubles getting along with both his players and assistant coaches. One person from the Giants told the *New York Times* in 1969, "He's an intelligent man, but he can't relate his intelligence to football." Finally, amidst a host of "Good Bye Allie" chants and signs from fans and after an embarrassing loss to the cross-town Jets in a 1969 preseason game, Sherman was fired with five years still remaining on his contract. He would never coach again, but kept active. In 1970, he tried to buy the Jets franchise with partners Bob Tisch (who would later buy half the Giants) and Steve Ross and later was involved with groups interested in buying the Redskins and the 49ers. In the 1970s, he worked for Warner Cable, on Wall Street, with the New York Cosmos soccer team and even announced his interest in the Eagles' head coaching position in 1976. In the 1980s and 1990s he worked for ESPN and turned around a dysfunctional

New York City Off Track Betting operation from 1995 to 1997.

SHERMAN, MICHAEL F. (MIKE) 12/19/1954– Central Connecticut State. T/DE; did not play professionally. *Apprenticeship:* College asst.—16 years; pro asst.— 3 years. *Roots:* Mike Holmgren. *Branches:* Joe Philbin. *Coordinators/Key Assistants:* Tom Rossley ran the offense, while Ed Donatell then Bob Slowik then Jim Bates handled the defense. *Hall of Fame Players:* None. *Primary Quarterbacks:* Brett Favre. *Tendencies:* • His teams scored 24 points and allowed 20.3 per game • His teams ran 42.5% of the time, which was 96% of the league average • One starting quarterbacks in six years; 100% of starts to primary quarterback • 15 rookie starters in six years • Winning Full Seasons to Losing Full Seasons: 5:1.

Mike Sherman was born in Norwood, Massachusetts, and grew up in the Boston area as a Green Bay Packers' fan during the Lombardi era. His mother later recalled to the *Milwaukee Journal Sentinel* that all he wanted for Christmas one year was the two-volume set, *Vince Lombardi on Football*; he was a decent enough lineman to play at Central Connecticut State from 1974 to 1977, but he was destined to be a coach.

Sherman coached high school football for three years after graduation before joining Jackie Sherrill's staff at Pittsburgh as a graduate assistant from 1981 to 1982. He subsequently coached the line at Tulane from 1983 to 1984 and Holy Cross from 1985 to 1987 until he was promoted to Holy Cross' offensive coordinator in 1988. Mike moved up to the big time in 1989 as the line coach at Texas A&M and coached there through 1996, with a one-year interlude at UCLA in 1994.

Sherman continued up the ladder in 1997 by becoming the tight ends coach for the defending champion Green Bay Packers. When head coach Mike Holmgren left Green Bay to take over the Seahawks in 1999, he brought Sherman with him as offensive coordinator. The Packers replaced Holmgren with Ray Rhodes, but were dissatisfied with the results and fired him a year later. GM Ron Wolf brought Sherman in for an interview and hired him as head coach for 2000. When Wolf retired a year later, Sherman was named GM as well.

Mike was taking over a veteran club that was led

Sherman, Michael F. (Mike)									
Year	Team	Games	Wins	Losses	Ties	%	P Wins	P Losses	P %
2000	Packers	16	9	7	0	.563	0	0	.000
2001	Packers	16	12	4	0	.750	1	1	.500
2002	Packers	16	12	4	0	.750	0	1	.000
2003	Packers	16	10	6	0	.625	1	1	.500
2004	Packers	16	10	6	0	.625	0	1	.000
2005	Packers	16	4	12	0	.250	0	0	.000
6 years		96	57	39	0	.594	2	4	.333

by larger-than-life gunslinger quarterback Brett Favre. For the next six years, Sherman did his best to reign in the on-the-field excesses of Favre by adopting a power running approach that sometimes utilized six large offensive linemen at a time to clear the way for runner Ahman Green. For the most part, it was a successful style, but in the playoffs there were problems. In 2001, Favre's six interceptions paved the way to a loss to the Rams. In 2002, Sherman's team was the first Packers' team to ever lose a home playoff game when Mike Vick led Atlanta to victory. In 2003, Green Bay lost to Philadelphia in a game they dominated after Sherman decided to punt on fourth and inches. The result was the Eagles converting a fourth-and-26 to force overtime and an ugly Favre interception leading to a sudden death loss. In 2004, Vikings receiver Randy Moss pretended to moon the crowd at Lambeau in an upset of the Pack, a second home postseason loss.

Sherman was fairly easy-going, but perhaps the most memorable moment of his career came after a game with Tampa during which Bucs' defensive tackle Warren Sapp took a cheap shot at Packers' tackle Chad Clifton following an interception and knocked him out for the year. Sherman angrily charged at Sapp after the game, but was mocked and pushed away.

When Sherman was replaced as GM by Ted Thompson in 2005, he knew his days were numbered. A combination of key injuries and a team weakened by Mike's bad drafting led to a 4–12 season, and Sherman was fired. Gary Kubiak, who Sheman had worked with at Texas A&M, hired Mike as offensive coordinator in 2006. After two years, Mike returned to Texas A&M, but this time as head coach. In five years, he went 25–25 and was fired in 2011 three days before the team received a bowl bid. A month later, Joe Philbin, who was hired by Sherman in Green Bay, hired Mike to be the Dolphins' offensive coordinator for 2012.

SHIPKEY, THEODORE E. (TED) 9/23/1904–7/18/1978. Stanford. E; did not play professionally. *Apprenticeship:* College head coach —12 years; semipro head coach — 2 years. *Roots:* Dud DeGroot. *Branches:* None. *Coordinators/Key Assistants:* None. *Hall of Fame Players:* None. *Primary Quarterbacks:* None. *Record:* **Interim Co-Coach** (with Mel Hein).

Ted Shipkey is best remembered for scoring the only touchdown for Stanford in the 1925 Rose Bowl,

a 27–10 loss to Notre Dame. Two years later, he played in a second Rose Bowl, a 7–7 tie with Alabama in 1927 when Stanford won the national championship. Shipkey grew up in Orange County, California and was a two-time All-American end in Palo Alto where his position coach at one point was Dudley DeGroot who later would play a key role in Ted's career.

Shipkey went into coaching immediately in 1927 at Sacramento Junior College. At Sacramento, he coached football, basketball and track from 1927 to 1929. In 1930, he moved on to Arizona State, coaching the football team and the basketball team. From 1930 to 1932, ASU went 13–10–2 in football and played in the school's first home night game to escape the desert heat. In 1933, Ted returned to his hometown to coach Los Angeles City College to a 7–2 record and then coached the semipro Hollywood Braves in 1934 and 1935.

Ted's next football coaching assignment was with New Mexico in 1937. There, Shipkey compiled a 30–17–2 mark from 1937 to 1941 and led the Lobos to their first bowl game. He was said to be hardnosed and demanding, but also imaginative. Years later, UNM halfback Finlay MacGillivray recalled the coach to the *Albuquerque Journal*, "Shipkey was a very innovative coach with a wide-open offense. He brought a pro-type offense that we called the Shipkey Spread. He'd split the linemen, forcing opponents into open spaces and constantly switched backfield formations. It's likened to today's pro shotgun. He was way ahead of his time as far as college football was concerned."

During the war, Shipkey was a major in the Army Air Corps and coached the Flying Kellys at Kirkland Field in Arizona. After the war, Ted was hired as an assistant by Dud DeGroot, the new head coach of the new Los Angeles Dons of the new All America Football Conference in 1946. The Don's had only middling success, and DeGroot did not get along with team owner Ben Lindheimer. The owner wanted to get a better idea of what was going on with his team in 1947, so he dispatched his daughter Marge to attend team meetings. Before a road game with the New York Yankees, she ordered DeGroot to the stands and took the field with the team herself, having assistants Shipkey and Mel Hein run the game. Ted told the *New York Times* on November 18, two days after the Yankees game, "We took over this morning and the team is in fine spirits. We went through a snappy practice."

Shipkey, Theodore E. (Ted)									
Year	Team	Games	Wins	Losses	Ties	%	P Wins	P Losses	P %
1947	Los Angeles Dons (AAFC)	3	2	1	0	.667	0	0	.000
1 year		3	2	1	0	.667	0	0	.000

When the team returned to Los Angeles, DeGroot officially quit and was very upset that his assistants did not follow him out the door in solidarity, but instead agreed to co-coach the team for its final games. Ted stayed on the staff when Jimmy Phelan was hired as the new head coach in 1948. A year later, Shipkey took his final coaching job with Montana where he posted a 12–16 record from 1949 to 1951. Ted left coaching in 1952 to go into business with his brother; he died in 1978 at the age of 73.

SHIPP, KENNETH (KEN) 2/3/1929– Middle Tennessee State. Did not play professionally. *Apprenticeship:* College asst.—16 years; CFL asst.—1 year; pro asst.— 8 years. *Roots:* Charley Winner, J.D. Roberts. *Branches:* Sam Rutigliano, Buddy Ryan. *Coordinators/Key Assistants*: None. *Hall of Fame Players:* Joe Namath, John Riggins. *Primary Quarterbacks:* Joe Namath. *Record:* **Interim Coach**.

Born in Murfreesboro, Tennessee, Ken Shipp starred as a halfback there both in high school and then in college at Middle Tennessee State. After a long coaching career in the college and pro ranks, Shipp continued to live and run his business in the area and in 2011 committed $1-million dollars to a scholarship fund at MTSU.

Ken graduated from MTSU in 1951 and immediately joined the coaching staff at his alma mater. He moved on to Trinity College in Texas in 1954 and Florida State in 1958 before spending one season as an assistant to Perry Moss on the Montreal Alouettes in Canada. Shipp returned to the States in 1961 at Tulsa and recruited the All-American passing combination of Jerry Rhome and Howard Twilley to the school, but left in 1963 for South Carolina where he worked with studious quarterback Dan Reeves. From 1964 to 1967, he was on the staff at the University of Miami and then jumped to the pros by joining Charley Winner's Cardinals' staff in St. Louis. After Winner was fired, Ken became offensive coordinator for the New Orleans Saints in 1971, and quarterback Archie Manning recalled his deliberate, pipe-smoking first offensive coach in his autobiography, *Manning*, "I was fortunate to have him as a coach. Ken never took shortcuts, never tried to cover up, never let you go into a situation unprepared."

However, the Saints were a terrible team, and the coaching staff was axed after a 2–11–1 season in 1972. Shipp was hired by Weeb Ewbank with the Jets in 1973 and reunited with Charley Winner (Weeb's son-in-law) in 1974. With the team struggling at 2–7 in 1975, Winner was replaced by Shipp. Ken told reporters, "I can't do anything about the personnel I have. I can't make any trades now. But maybe I can do something about their minds." Four weeks in, it was clear that was a pipe dream. In a game against San Diego on Monday Night Football, Shipp benched Joe Namath for the first quarter because of curfew violations. After that 24–16 loss to the 2–11 Chargers, Ken was disappointed in his team, "They wouldn't even play before a national TV audience. They let the worst rushing team on the National Football League rush for 249 yards against them."

Shipp was dismissed at the end of the season and moved on to the Lions' staff where he tutored a young coach named Bill Belichick. Belichick would remember Shipp's kindness and send Ken a thank you note after winning the Super Bowl a quarter century later. Belichick told ESPN, "Ken was really smart. He had an answer to everything. No matter what the situation was, no matter what the defense did, or we'd see something on film. The offense was very thorough. It was very simple, but there were a lot of variations." After just one year in Detroit, Ken spent 1977–1978 with the Oilers and then was a volunteer coach at Texas in 1980 before finishing his coaching career at South Carolina in 1981. He subsequently went into the storage business.

SHOFNER, JAMES (JIM) 12/18/1935– Texas Christian Played DB for the Browns from 1958 to 1963. *Apprenticeship:* College coach — 6 years (3 as head coach); pro asst.— 20 years. *Roots:* Jack Christiansen, Dick Nolan, Ken Meyer, Sam Rutigliano, Ed Biles, Tom Landry, Gene Stallings, Bud Carson. *Branches:* None. *Coordinators/Key Assistants*: Shofner handled his own offense, while Jim Vechiarella ran the defense. *Hall of Fame Players:* Ozzie Newsome. *Primary Quarterbacks:* Bernie Kosar. *Record:* **Interim Coach**.

Shipp, Kenneth (Ken)									
Year	Team	Games	Wins	Losses	Ties	%	P Wins	P Losses	P %
1975	Jets	5	1	4	0	.200	0	0	.000
1 year		5	1	4	0	.200	0	0	.000

Shofner, James (Jim)									
Year	Team	Games	Wins	Losses	Ties	%	P Wins	P Losses	P %
1990	Browns	7	1	6	0	.143	0	0	.000
1 year		7	1	6	0	.143	0	0	.000

Jim Shofner from Grapevine, Texas was Texas Christian's leading ball carrier and was selected in the first round of the 1958 NFL draft by the Cleveland Browns. Jim spent six years as a cornerback in Cleveland and intercepted 20 passes. He retired in 1964 to return to his alma mater as an assistant coach for three years. Shofner returned to the pros in 1967 on the staff in San Francisco and stayed with the 49ers for seven years until he was courted by his alma mater again, this time to be head coach. Jim coached TCU from 1974 to 1976, but won just two games in three years. He posted a 2–29 record there before being dismissed and returning to the 49ers in 1977. The following season, Shofner came back to Cleveland as Sam Rutigliano's offensive coach where he worked with the Kardiac Kids as the comeback Browns were called. Quarterback Brian Sipe once said, "Jim was the best quarterback coach I ever had. He has a good football mind. He's one of the most levelheaded persons I've ever been around. He was at his best in the fourth quarter of tight games."

Shofner moved on to work as offensive coordinator for the Oilers from 1981 to 1982, the Cowboys from 1983 to 1985 and the Cardinals from 1986 to 1989. In 1990, Bud Carson brought him back to Cleveland for a third time, but the team was old and banged up. Carson was fired after a 2–7 start and replaced by Jim who lost his first two games as head coach. After that second loss, though, Shofner told the press, "I have a feeling we may not lose again. I just feel that way. I don't know how you can feel any other way."

Unfortunately, feelings are not reality. The Browns lost all but one game under Shofner, and he was forced to admit after he was fired, "Obviously, I wasn't the answer. Certainly I inherited a lot of circumstances. You can say there are all these reasons why, and maybe they're legitimate. But it still adds up to the same thing: I didn't get it done." Jim worked as a scout for Cleveland in 1991 before joining Marv Levy's staff in Buffalo where he replaced Ted Marchibroda as offensive coordinator in 1992. While the Bills continued to be successful with Shofner running the offense, he ran into conflict with quarterback Jim Kelly as the K-Gun no-huddle attack was deemphasized, and Kelly was given less control over the offense. In

1997, Shofner was transferred to the scouting department and never coached in the league again.

SHULA, DAVID D. 5/28/1959– Dartmouth. Played WR for the Colts in 1981. *Apprenticeship:* Pro asst.— 10 years. *Roots:* Don Shula, Jimmy Johnson, Sam Wyche. *Branches:* None. *Coordinators/Key Assistants:* Mike Pope then Bruce Coslet ran the offense, while Ron Lynn then Larry Peccatiello handled the defense. *Hall of Fame Players:* Anthony Munoz. *Primary Quarterbacks:* Jeff Blake, David Klingler. *Tendencies:* • His teams scored 17.1 points and allowed 22.9 per game • His teams ran 42.3% of the time, which was 95% of the league average • Five starting quarterbacks in five years; 79% of starts to primary quarterbacks • 17 rookie starters in five years • Winning Full Seasons to Losing Full Seasons: 0:4.

With David Shula and his brother Mike, we see both the good and bad sides to following a famous father into the game. While David and Mike were given coaching opportunities they never would have had without being the sons of legend Don Shula, they were also placed under more intense scrutiny than others might in those same positions.

David was born in Lexington, Kentucky, but raised on the sidelines of his father's teams in Baltimore and Miami. He played wide receiver at Dartmouth where he caught passes from Jack Kemp's son Jeff and then played one year in the NFL with the Baltimore Colts in 1981. At age 23, he joined his father's Dolphins' staff during the 1982 season while on break from law school and moved up to offensive coordinator of the team within a few years. In 1986, Eagles' owner Norman Braman, who had a house in Miami and knew the Shulas, offered 26-year-old David the head coaching job in Philadelphia. However, negotiations eventually broke down, and Philadelphia hired Buddy Ryan instead.

While laid-back David had some rapport with the Miami receivers, he did not get along very well with headstrong quarterback Dan Marino. When new Dallas coach Jimmy Johnson asked Don Shula's permission in 1989 to hire his former defensive coach Dave Wannstedt, then on Miami's staff, Don gave the ok as long as he hired David as offensive coordinator as well so David would get some experience away from

Shula, David D.									
Year	Team	Games	Wins	Losses	Ties	%	P Wins	P Losses	P %
1992	Bengals	16	5	11	0	.313	0	0	.000
1993	Bengals	16	3	13	0	.188	0	0	.000
1994	Bengals	16	3	13	0	.188	0	0	.000
1995	Bengals	16	7	9	0	.438	0	0	.000
1996	Bengals	7	1	6	0	.143	0	0	.000
5 years		71	19	52	0	.268	0	0	.000

his father. In Dallas, though, things did not go well for David. He did not appreciate receiver Michael Irvin and urged Johnson to trade the difficult Hall of Fame team leader. He also underutilized runner Emmitt Smith so that the offense sputtered and David failed to win the respect of his players. Tight end Rob Awalt told Jeff Pearlman for *Boys Will Be Boys*, "It's bad enough when your team stinks, but when your offensive coordinator can't get out of his own way, it's brutal."

Johnson demoted David, so he left to become the receivers coach under Sam Wyche in Cincinnati. A year later, Paul Brown's son Mike hired Don Shula's son David to become the youngest coach in NFL history at 32. The next five seasons were an unmitigated disaster with the Bengals in the fumbling hands of the sons of football geniuses. David set the league mark for being the coach who got to 50 losses the fastest, doing it in just 69 games. He was fired two weeks and two losses later. One of those 50 losses was to his father's Dolphins in 1994 in a historic father-son contest. Even though it was clear that David did not have the personality or skill to be an NFL head coach, it should be pointed out that Mike Brown did him no favors in accumulating talent. Relying on David Klingler as your quarterback of the future assures a dim outlook.

David was forever diminished by his Cincinnati experience and never coached again. Since 1997, he has been heavily involved in running his father's successful steakhouse chain.

SHULA, DONALD F. (DON) 1/4/1930– John Carroll. Played DB for the Browns, Colts and Redskins from 1951 to 1957. *Apprenticeship:* College asst.—2 years; pro asst.—3 years. *Roots:* George Wilson. *Branches:* Charley Winner, Chuck Noll, Don McCafferty, John Sandusky (i), Howard Schnellenberger, Bill Arnsparger, Monte Clark, Dan Henning. *Coordinators/Key Assistants*: For the Colts, Don McCafferty was the key offensive coach, while Chuck Noll then Bill Arnsparger handled the defense; for the Dolphins, Howard Schnellenberger then Bill McPeak then Schnellenberger again then Dan Henning then Wally English then David Shula then Gary Stevens ran the offense, while Bill Arnsparger then Vince Costello then Mo Scarry then Arnsparger again then Chuck Studley then Tom Olivadotti handled the defense. *Hall of Fame Players:* Raymond Berry, Nick Buoniconti, Larry Csonka, Bob Griese, Ted Hendricks, Jim Langer, Larry Little, John Mackey, Gino Marchetti, Dan Marino, Lenny Moore, Jim Parker, Dwight Stephenson, John Unitas, Paul Warfield. *Primary Quarterbacks:* John Unitas, Bob Griese, Dan Marino. *Record:* **Hall of Fame Coach;** Super Bowl Championships 1972, 1973. *Tendencies:* • His teams scored 23.6 points and allowed 17.8 per game • His teams ran 49.6% of the time, which was the league average • 12 starting

quarterbacks in 33 years; 78% of starts to primary quarterbacks • 85 rookie starters in 33 years • Winning Full Seasons to Losing Full Seasons: 27:2.

Not only is Don Shula the NFL's all time winningest coach with 328 regular season and 347 total victories, but it is unlikely that anyone will challenge that record. Given the high-pressure nature of the league and the ever-changing character of the game, it is hard to imagine a coach remaining at the top of the sport for 33 years like Shula did. Even though Shula was not always the greatest big-game coach, there is no denying the large shadow his career casts on the profession.

Don was born in Grand River, Ohio, and played halfback at John Carroll University in Cleveland from 1948 to 1950. He was a ninth round draft pick of the local Cleveland Browns in 1951 and he and college teammate Carl Taseff were the only two rookies to make the squad that year. Shula played two seasons as a defensive back there under Paul Brown with Blanton Collier as his position coach. Don was one of ten Browns traded to Baltimore in 1953 for five Colts, most notably tackle Mike McCormack, in the largest trade in league history. A year later, the Colts hired Browns' assistant Weeb Ewbank as head coach who allowed the studious Shula to call the defensive signals on the field during his four years in Baltimore. Don was traded to Washington in 1957 and played one last year in the NFL before taking an assistant coaching job at Virginia under Dick Voris in 1958. He moved on to Kentucky under Blanton Collier in 1959 and then became the defensive coach of the Lions in 1960. Shula favored the zone defense, and his Detroit defense was the toughest in the league in the early 1960s. When Colts' owner Carroll Rosenbloom grew restless with Ewbank in 1963, he replaced him with the 33-year-old Shula.

Shula would never have a losing season in Baltimore and led the Colts to two championship games,

Head-to-Head:		
Hall of Fame Opponent	Regular Season	Postseason
George Allen	3–4–1	1–0
Paul Brown	2–0	1–0
Weeb Ewbank	7–1	0–1
Joe Gibbs	3–1	0–1
Bud Grant	4–2–1	2–0
George Halas	5–4	0–0
Tom Landry	5–2	0–1
Marv Levy	7–14	0–3
Vince Lombardi	4–6	0–1
John Madden	2–2	1–2
Chuck Noll	7–4	2–1
Hank Stram	2–0	1–0
Bill Walsh	2–1	0–1
Total	53–39–2	8–11

Shula, Donald F. (Don)

Year	Team	Games	Wins	Losses	Ties	%	P Wins	P Losses	P %
1963	Colts	14	8	6	0	.571	0	0	.000
1964	Colts	14	12	2	0	.857	0	1	.000
1965	Colts	14	10	3	1	.750	0	1	.000
1966	Colts	14	9	5	0	.643	0	0	.000
1967	Colts	14	11	1	2	.857	0	0	.000
1968	Colts	14	13	1	0	.929	2	1	.667
1969	Colts	14	8	5	1	.607	0	0	.000
1970	Dolphins	14	10	4	0	.714	0	1	.000
1971	Dolphins	14	10	3	1	.750	2	1	.667
1972	Dolphins	14	14	0	0	1.000	3	0	1.000
1973	Dolphins	14	12	2	0	.857	3	0	1.000
1974	Dolphins	14	11	3	0	.786	0	1	.000
1975	Dolphins	14	10	4	0	.714	0	0	.000
1976	Dolphins	14	6	8	0	.429	0	0	.000
1977	Dolphins	14	10	4	0	.714	0	0	.000
1978	Dolphins	16	11	5	0	.688	0	1	.000
1979	Dolphins	16	10	6	0	.625	0	1	.000
1980	Dolphins	16	8	8	0	.500	0	0	.000
1981	Dolphins	16	11	4	1	.719	0	1	.000
1982	Dolphins	9	7	2	0	.778	3	1	.750
1983	Dolphins	16	12	4	0	.750	0	1	.000
1984	Dolphins	16	14	2	0	.875	2	1	.667
1985	Dolphins	16	12	4	0	.750	1	1	.500
1986	Dolphins	16	8	8	0	.500	0	0	.000
1987	Dolphins	15	8	7	0	.533	0	0	.000
1988	Dolphins	16	6	10	0	.375	0	0	.000
1989	Dolphins	16	8	8	0	.500	0	0	.000
1990	Dolphins	16	12	4	0	.750	1	1	.500
1991	Dolphins	16	8	8	0	.500	0	0	.000
1992	Dolphins	16	11	5	0	.688	1	1	.500
1993	Dolphins	16	9	7	0	.563	0	0	.000
1994	Dolphins	16	10	6	0	.625	1	1	.500
1995	Dolphins	16	9	7	0	.563	0	1	.000
33 years		490	328	156	6	.676	19	17	.528

but lost both despite being heavily favored in each. His strict, disciplinarian approach was a stark contrast with Ewbank's more even-tempered manner. Hall of Fame quarterback Johnny Unitas told *Sports Illustrated*, "Don made a lot of enemies among the players. He was a good coach. But the way he handled some players left a lot of bad taste around here." Shula retooled the aging Colts and had them in the NFL title game in his second year, but lost it 27–0 to the underdog Browns coached by Blanton Collier. The next year, both Unitas and backup quarterback Gary Cuozzo got hurt, so Shula finished the season with half back Tom Matte playing quarterback and just narrowly lost a playoff to the Packers.

In 1968, Unitas was injured in the preseason, but Shula traded for journeyman Earl Morrall who he transformed into the NFL MVP on a 13–1 team. Led by a defense that allowed just 144 points, Baltimore bulldozed to Super Bowl III as 18-point favorite over Weeb Ewbank's AFL champion Jets, but then were upset 16–7 in a devastating loss to Shula and to an embarrassed Rosenbloom. Neither Shula nor the team could shake it off in 1969. Defensive end Bubba Smith told *Sports Illustrated*, "Last year, we started losing. Shula went crazy. He had this thing about Vince Lombardi. He wanted to be better than Lombardi, so he did a lot of screaming."

At the end of the 1969 season, Dolphins' owner Joe Robbie signed Shula as Miami's head coach, but he remained under contract to Baltimore. Even though Rosenbloom was sick of Shula, he still extracted a number one draft choice in return for letting Don go to Miami. The Dolphins were a four-year old expansion team that had never won more than five games in any year, but Shula drove them to a 10–4 season and the playoffs in his first year. In his second year, the team reached the Super Bowl where they were overpowered by Tom Landry's veteran Cowboys, and in year three, Miami went 17–0, still the only perfect season champions in league history. Shula exulted at the time, "It's hard to compare this team with other great teams of the past, but this team has gone into an area that no other has gone into before. In the past, there was always the feeling of not having achieved the ultimate. This is the ultimate." It's not hard to understand why Shula and that Dolphin team still celebrate the demise of the last undefeated team each season. Miami then repeated as champions in 1973.

Shula built the offense around the power running attack of Larry Csonka, Jim Kiick and Mercury Morris with occasional deep passes from Bob Griese to Paul Warfield, a Hall of Fame receiver obtained in a trade with Cleveland. The defense was transformed by fast young defenders directed by middle linebacker Nick Buoniconti in a clever zone defense that utilized the precursor of the 3–4 defense called the 53 Defense after the uniform number of linebacker/defensive end hybrid Bob Matheson. Although the players were largely anonymous, this No-Name defense featured two great safeties in Dick Anderson and Jake Scott and such quality defensive linemen as Manny Fernandez, Bill Stanfill and Vern Den Herder.

Miami missed a shot at a three-peat by losing to Oakland in the Sea of Hands game in 1974 and would not return to the playoffs again till 1978. By then the defense had transitioned to the swarming Killer Bees, led by seven defenders whose last names began with letter B. The offense lagged behind with Bob Griese retiring in 1980, but led by the "WoodStrock" quarterback duo of David Woodley and Don Strock, the Dolphins reached the Super Bowl again in the strike year of 1982, losing to Joe Gibbs' Redskins. A year later, Miami drafted Dan Marino and began a new era of Dolphin football. Shula showed how flexible a coach he could be by adjusting the offense to Marino's strengths and the more liberal passing rules. From 1970 to 1982, the Dolphins ran the 59% of the time, 10% more than the league average; from 1983 to 1995, the club ran the ball just 41% of the time, 10% less than the league average.

While the Shula/Marino Dolphins were an explosive team, they were also deeply flawed. They did reach the Super Bowl in Dan's second year, 1984, but were decimated by Bill Walsh's 49ers. Neither Shula nor Marino ever returned to the Super Bowl. Shula's drafting was lackluster, and Miami never built another top quality defense after assistant coach Bill Arnsparger left in 1984. On offense, Shula could never construct a decent enough running game to take some of the focus off Marino's arm so that when Miami played the better teams in the playoffs, the Dolphins did not measure up. Shula's postseason record in Miami

through 1982 was 11–7, but was just 6–7 in the Marino era.

Shula always had Hall of Fame quarterbacks. He went from Unitas to Griese to Marino with just a two-year WoodStrock interlude. He also had a series of talented backups from Gary Cuozzo to Earl Morrall to Don Strock. Despite his 2–5 mark in championship games, Shula won more postseason games than any coach other than Tom Landry. Over his long career, Shula's teams led the league in scoring four times and finished in the top three 11 times. Five times, his defenses allowed the fewest points and nine times finished in the top three.

He served the league for decades on the Competition Committee and coincidentally always had one of the least penalized teams in the league. Both of Don's sons went into coaching. David had a failed tenure as the youngest NFL head coach in history for the Bengals and lost to Don in the only game they coached against one another. Mike has served as an NFL assistant for over 20 years and was head coach at Alabama with moderate success from 2003 to 2006.

Don retired in 1995, two years after he broke George Halas' record for coaching wins. Two years later, he deservedly was elected to the Hall of Fame. As for his influences, Shula told the *Washington Post*, "Paul Brown was the greatest influence on me, especially in the teaching aspect of coaching. In football, it's not what you know but what your ballplayers know that counts." Shula coached in the NFL for 33 consecutive seasons, another record and told *Sports Illustrated*, "I never even heard the term burnout until Dick Vermeil left. Dick was so high-strung, so sensitive; he put so much into it that it just ate him up. Not that other people don't put a lot into it, or me either, for that matter. I just don't carry things away with me like others might. You can't let it influence the way you live your life." In retirement, he and his son David have operated a growing chain of steakhouses nationwide, with ever-competitive Don still going strong in his 80s.

SHURMUR, PATRICK (PAT) 4/14/1965– Michigan State. C; did not play professionally. *Apprenticeship:* College asst.—11 years; pro asst.—12 years. *Roots:* Andy Reid, Steve Spagnuolo. *Branches:* None. *Coordinators/ Key Assistants:* Shurmur ran his own offense, while Dick Jauron handled the defense. *Hall of Fame Players:* None. *Primary Quarterbacks:* Colt McCoy. *Tendencies:* • His team scored 13.6 points and allowed 19.2 per

Shurmur, Patrick (Pat)									
Year	Team	Games	Wins	Losses	Ties	%	P Wins	P Losses	P %
2011	Browns	16	4	12	0	.250	0	0	.000
1 year		16	4	12	0	.250	0	0	.000

game • His team ran 40.5% of the time, which was 94% of the league average • Two starting quarterbacks in one year; 81% of starts to primary quarterbacks • 9 rookie starters in one year • Winning Full Seasons to Losing Full Seasons: 0:1.

Born in Ann Arbor, Pat Shurmur grew up outside Detroit and was Coach George Perles' very first recruit after he took the Michigan State job in 1983. Four years later, Pat was team captain and starting center on the Spartans' 1988 Rose Bowl team. Shurmur graduated that year, briefly tried working for IBM and then joined Perles' staff as an assistant during the fall. He stayed on staff at MSU for 10 years, even after Nick Saban replaced Perles in 1995. Pat moved on to Stanford in 1998 as offensive line coach, but stayed for just one year before making the jump to the NFL in 1999.

That year, Andy Reid hired Shurmur as tight ends coach and assistant offensive line coach for Philadelphia. Reid had coached with Pat's uncle Fritz on Mike Holmgren's staff in Green Bay for several seasons. Like Shurmur, Reid played and coached offensive line in college before being hired as a tight ends coach in the pros. Shurmur, like Reid, next was promoted to quarterbacks coach. Pat was Donovan McNabb's position coach from 2002 to 2008 in Philadelphia.

Shurmur got his chance to advance in 2009 when another former Eagles' assistant, Steve Spagnuolo, was hired as the Rams' head coach and hired Pat as his offensive coordinator. The Rams were in a deep downturn and finished last in scoring and last in wins in 2009. With the overall number one draft choice, though, they selected quarterback Sam Bradford, and the following year improved to 26th in scoring and won seven games. The Rams still did not have any quality receivers so Shurmur had Bradford rely entirely upon short passes and the power running of Steven Jackson.

Meanwhile in Cleveland, Mike Holmgren had taken over as team president. He gave incumbent coach Eric Mangini one year to demonstrate he was on the right track. When the team showed no improvement in 2010, Holmgren fired Mangini and went looking for a coach schooled in the West Coast Offense that Holmgren preferred. Shurmur fit the bill and spent his first year working with a new quarterback, slightly built Colt McCoy, who seemed to have the right tools to run that offense. The key for Holmgren is to surround McCoy, or Brandon Weeden, with enough talent that Shurmur can transform the Browns into a consistently winning team.

SINGLETARY, MICHAEL (MIKE) 10/9/1958– Baylor. Played LB for the Bears from 1981 to 1992. *Apprenticeship:* Pro asst.— 6 years. *Roots:* Brian Billick, Mike Nolan. *Branches:* Jim Tomsula (i). *Coordinators/Key Assistants:* Mike Martz then Jimmy Raye ran the offense, while Greg Manusky handled the defense. *Hall of Fame Players:* None. *Primary Quarterbacks:* Alex Smith, Shaun Hill. *Record:* **Hall of Fame Player.** *Tendencies:* • His teams scored 19.5 points and allowed 20.1 per game • His teams ran 41% of the time, which was 94% of the league average • Four starting quarterbacks in three years; 78% of starts to primary quarterbacks • Four rookie starters in three years • Winning Full Seasons to Losing Full Seasons: 0:1.

As a middle linebacker, Mike Singletary was a fiery, wide-eyed exploding ball of intensity who broke 16 helmets in college and drove the Bears' fearsome 46 defense to the top in the pros. He once told *Sports Illustrated* that his favorite part of the game was, "The national anthem. I sing loud enough for the guys to hear me. And you know why? Because this is the greatest country in the world. It gives you the opportunity to compete. Goodness, I love that opportunity."

Born in Houston, the ultracompetitive Singletary played linebacker at Baylor from 1978 to 1980 and was a two-time All American. Selected in the second round of the 1981 draft by the Bears, Mike had to improve his pass defense to earn the respect of his demanding defensive coach Buddy Ryan, but worked so hard that he became one of Buddy's favorite players and one of the greatest middle linebackers in NFL history.

Singletary retired after a 12-year career in 1993 and spent the next decade as a motivational religious speaker traveling the country. In 2003, he got back into the game as the linebackers coach for the Baltimore Ravens under head coach Brian Billick and defensive coordinator Mike Nolan. Two years later, Nolan was hired as head coach of the 49ers and brought Singletary along as linebackers coach and assistant head coach, although Billy Davis was Nolan's first defensive coordinator.

Nolan was unable to rebuild the 49ers into a winning team and was replaced by his linebackers coach halfway through his fourth season. In his first game

Singletary, Michael (Mike)									
Year	Team	Games	Wins	Losses	Ties	%	P Wins	P Losses	P %
2008	49ers	9	5	4	0	.556	0	0	.000
2009	49ers	16	8	8	0	.500	0	0	.000
2010	49ers	15	5	10	0	.333	0	0	.000
3 years		40	18	22	0	.450	0	0	.000

as head coach, Singletary clearly demonstrated that his personality was markedly different from the more staid Nolan. Furious that the team was too lethargic in the first half of the game against the Seahawks, Singletary dropped his trousers in the locker room to show his team they were getting spanked by Seattle. Then he banished tight end Vernon Davis from the field after Davis was flagged for a stupid penalty in the fourth quarter. Finally, Mike delivered a postgame rant, declaring, "I want winners. I want people who want to win!"

He explained his outlook to *Sports Illustrated,* "Greatness is not about someone who has the ability to be great. Greatness shows up when someone might not have the ability but finds a way to succeed. They outwork their opponents. They outhit their opponents. They outfight their opponents. They want it more. Don't give me the guy who's supposed to be all-world and you've got to try to talk him into something. Give me the guy who has maybe just enough talent to be on the field but thinks he's great, and who's willing to do whatever he can do to contribute to make the team better."

It was clear there was a new, slightly off kilter sheriff in town, and the 49ers did finish the season 5–4 under Mike, winning him a contract extension. The team continued on a .500 pace in 2009, before collapsing in 2010 to just five wins. The motivational speeches can only take a team so far without accompanying coaching competence. Singletary continued Nolan's tradition of annually changing offensive coordinators, which impeded quarterback Alex Smith's progress. He was also impulsive in his use of quarterbacks, switching back and forth from Alex Smith to Troy Smith in 2010 without much direction. Finally, Troy Smith and the coach got into a screaming match on the sideline after an interception against the Rams, and it was clear to everybody that Mike was in over his head and had lost control of his team. He was fired before the last game of the year.

Singletary joined the staff of his former Bears' teammate Leslie Frazier in Minnesota in 2011, again as assistant head coach/linebackers coach. While he may never be an NFL head coach again, Singletary was a great player who was elected to the College Football Hall of Fame in 1995 and the Pro Football Hall of Fame in 1998. Moreover, he is a fine man whose values are the bedrock of the NFL.

SKORICH, NICHOLAS L. (NICK) 6/26/1921–10/2/2004. Cincinnati. Played G for the Steelers from 1946 to 1948. *Apprenticeship:* College head coach —1 year; pro asst.— 7 years. *Roots:* Walt Kiesling, Buddy Parker, Scooter McLean, Buck Shaw. *Branches:* Jerry Williams, Forrest Gregg, Dick Modzelewski (i). *Coordinators/Key Assistants:* For the Eagles, Charley Gauer then Sonny Grandelius ran the offense, while Jerry Williams handled the defense; for the Browns, Ray Prochaska then Jerry Smith then Dick Wood ran the offense, while Howard Brinker then Rich McCabe handled the defense. *Hall of Fame Players:* Chuck Bednarik, Gene Hickerson, Sonny Jurgensen, Leroy Kelly, Tommy McDonald. *Primary Quarterbacks:* Sonny Jurgensen, Mike Phipps *Tendencies:* • His teams scored 19.6 points and allowed 22 per game • His teams ran 50.9% of the time, which was 94% of the league average • Five starting quarterbacks in seven years; 75% of starts to primary quarterbacks • 18 rookie starters in seven years • Winning Full Seasons to Losing Full Seasons: 4:3.

Nick Skorich from Bellaire, Ohio, was a 5'9" 200-pound "watchcharm" guard for the University of Cincinnati from 1941 to 1943 and was drafted in his senior year by both the Pittsburgh Steelers and Uncle Sam. Skorich spent the next three years in the Navy before joining Pittsburgh in 1946. Legendary single wing coach Jock Sutherland was the new Steeler head coach that year and took a liking to Nick, claiming, "Someday, this young man will be a great coach."

Skorich was injured in 1948 and retired from playing. He coached high school football from 1949 to 1952 and then coached Rensselaer Polytechnic Institute to a 1–6–1 record in 1953. The Steelers rehired Nick in 1954 as line coach and he remained in Pittsburgh for the next four years. Skorich moved on to Green Bay in 1958 and could have stayed on staff under new coach Vince Lombardi in 1959, but chose to join Buck Shaw in Philadelphia instead. Neither team won more than two games that year. Two years later, the Eagles beat Lombardi's Packers in the NFL

Year	Team	Games	Wins	Losses	Ties	%	P Wins	P Losses	P %
1961	Eagles	14	10	4	0	.714	0	0	.000
1962	Eagles	14	3	10	1	.250	0	0	.000
1963	Eagles	14	2	10	2	.214	0	0	.000
1971	Browns	14	9	5	0	.643	0	1	.000
1972	Browns	14	10	4	0	.714	0	1	.000
1973	Browns	14	7	5	2	.571	0	0	.000
1974	Browns	14	4	10	0	.286	0	0	.000
7 years		98	45	48	5	.485	0	2	.000

Skorich, Nicholas L. (Nick)

championship game, and both Shaw and star quarterback Norm Van Brocklin retired following the game.

Van Brocklin was under the impression that he was to succeed Shaw as coach, but Philadelphia instead promoted Skorich to head coach and unsuccessfully tried to coax Van Brocklin into returning as a player. With the Dutchman gone, Skorich turned to fifth-year backup Sonny Jurgensen at quarterback and he led the team to seven wins in its first eight games in 1961. However, in the ninth game, key defensive back Tom Brookshier had his leg severely broken, and the defense that had allowed just 16 points per game to that point gave up 29 per game for the last six weeks. Philadelphia split those last six games to drop into second place. Skorich's luck got even worse. The Eagles then played the Lions in the meaningless postseason Runner-Up Bowl, and Jurgensen suffered such a bad shoulder separation in it that he was not the same for the next two years. On top of that, Jurgensen and backup quarterback King Hill staged a joint training camp holdout in 1963. The ultimate result for the team was consecutive 10-loss seasons.

Skorich commonly was described as a "gentleman" with a similar demeanor to former coach Buck Shaw. He rarely, if ever, lit into players. With the Eagles' decline in fortunes, however, he lost control of the team. Following the Kennedy assassination in late November, an off-field fight between Eagle defenders Ben Scotti and John Mellekas was so brutal that both men ended up in the hospital. Philadelphia dropped its last eight games of the season, and Nick was fired by new owner Jerry Wolman in the off season.

Blanton Collier hired Skorich as the Browns' line coach in 1964, and Nick became his top lieutenant over the next seven years in Cleveland. By 1970, Collier's hearing problem got so bad that he turned over his head set to Skorich for the last two games of the year. Collier later told Dan Coughlin for *Crazy, with the Papers to Prove It* that Nick's tactical errors in those games alarmed him, "I knew right then that Nick should not be head coach. Art [Modell] gave him the job anyway when I retired."

Upon being hired by Cleveland, Skorich announced, "I intend to be here a long time — about 10 years." Considering that he was just the third head coach in team history, that was not an overly cocky prediction, but it was wildly optimistic. The aging Browns made the playoffs in Nick's first two years as the team made the transition at quarterback from veteran Bill Nelsen to draftee Mike Phipps. By year three,

though, it was clear that Phipps was too inconsistent and unreliable and by year four the team's defense collapsed. Skorich was fired following the 1974 season, but landed in the league office as assistant supervisor of NFL officials. He worked for the league through 2001 until retiring at age 80. He died three years later.

SMITH, JEROME (JERRY) 9/9/1930– Wisconsin. Played LB for the 49ers and Packers from 1952 to 1953 and in 1956. *Apprenticeship:* College asst.—1 year; pro asst.—12 years. *Roots:* Lou Saban, Tom Fears. *Branches:* None. *Coordinators/Key Assistants:* None. *Hall of Fame Players:* Floyd Little. *Primary Quarterbacks:* Steve Ramsey. *Record:* Interim Coach.

Jerry Smith switched back and forth from coaching offensive and defensive line during his 25-year career as an NFL assistant coach. The Dayton, Ohio native played guard for Wisconsin from 1949 to 1951 as part of their "Hard Rocks" line. An eighth round draft pick of the 49ers, he played guard and linebacker in San Francisco for two seasons and then went into the Army for 1954 and 1955. Returning the 49ers in 1956, he was traded at midseason to Green Bay and finished his NFL career there.

Smith began his coaching career in his hometown as an assistant at the University of Dayton in 1959. A year later, Lou Saban hired him to coach the Patriots' defensive line. After Saban was fired and resurfaced in Buffalo, Jerry joined the Bills' staff in 1962 as defensive line coach. He later switched to offense after Red Miller left for St. Louis. Smith left Buffalo after seven years and spent two years with the Saints before rejoining Saban as offensive line coach and offensive coordinator for Denver in 1971.

Nine games into the season, Saban stepped down as coach and promoted Smith to head coach for the balance of the year. Jerry told the press, "I'm proud Lou selected me. He's a big man, a man who fascinated me by the job he has done. We have a tremendous organization and I don't think we are far away from a .500 season." Smith finished out the season, but by then Saban was gone from the organization, so Jerry was fired.

Smith subsequently coached the defensive line for Houston in 1972, the offensive line for Cleveland in 1973, the defensive line for the Colts from 1974 to 1976, the defensive line for San Diego from 1977 to 1983 and special teams for Arizona in 1985. He later did some scouting for Kansas City. Jerry's head coach for the Chargers was Don Coryell who once praised

Smith, Jerome (Jerry)									
Year	Team	Games	Wins	Losses	Ties	%	P Wins	P Losses	P %
1971	Broncos	5	2	3	0	.400	0	0	.000
1 year		5	2	3	0	.400	0	0	.000

Smith to the *Los Angeles Times*, "He's the best defensive line coach I've known. He's got real pride and a competitive spirit. He makes his players want to excel."

SMITH, LOVIE L. 5/8/1958– Tulsa. DB; did not play professionally. *Apprenticeship:* College asst.—13 years; pro asst.—8 years. *Roots:* Tony Dungy, Mike Martz. *Branches:* Perry Fewell (i), Ron Rivera. *Coordinators/Key Assistants*: Terry Shea then Ron Turner then Mike Martz ran the offense, while Ron Rivera then Bob Babich then Rod Marinelli handled the defense. *Hall of Fame Players:* None. *Primary Quarterbacks:* Kyle Orton, Rex Grossman, Jay Cutler. *Tendencies:* • His teams scored 20.6 points and allowed 19.4 per game • His teams ran 44.8% of the time, which was 102% of the league average • Ten starting quarterbacks in eight years; 78% of starts to primary quarterbacks • 14 rookie starters in eight years • Winning Full Seasons to Losing Full Seasons: 4:3.

Although born in Gladewater, Texas, Lovie Smith was raised in nearby Big Sandy where he played linebacker on three consecutive state championship teams in high school. In college at Tulsa, Smith shifted to defensive back and was a second team All-American in 1979, but did not pursue pro football. Instead, Lovie coached high school football from 1980 to 1982 before returning to his alma mater as an assistant coach from 1983 to 1986. He moved on to Wisconsin in 1987, Arizona State in 1988, Kentucky in 1992, Tennessee in 1993 and Ohio State in 1995. Finally, in 1996 he moved up to the pros as the linebackers coach on Tony Dungy's first staff at Tampa Bay.

Dungy, of course, served as a mentor to Smith and thoroughly trained him in the Cover 2 Defense. Both Dungy and Smith are soft-spoken men but have a commanding demeanor that earns players' respect. Lovie later told the *New York Times*, "I think what guys like Tony Dungy show men is be yourself. Just believe in what you know and just stay with that through the storms and different things like that, and you can get the job accomplished." In 2001, Mike Martz was looking to transform the Rams' defense that was last in points allowed the previous season. Martz hired Smith as defensive coordinator, and Lovie's de-

fense gave up 198 fewer points in 2001, while the Rams went to the Super Bowl where they lost to the Patriots. Even though the St. Louis slipped a bit in the ensuing two years, Smith's reputation grew, and he was hired as the Bears head coach in 2004.

In Chicago, Smith explained his Dungy-like affirming manner to the *New York Times*, "Guys want to know that you believe in them. And then they'll do anything for you. After a while, it grows on you. That's what I see here. We have a positive approach to coaching football." Lovie tightened the Bears' defense and shored up their special teams and two years later rode those two units to the Super Bowl. The offense continued to be a work in progress. Smith favored a ground-oriented attack largely because of the limitations of quarterbacks Rex Grossman and Kyle Orton, although Smith repeatedly stressed how much he believed in his quarterbacks. While the error-prone Grossman had his best year in 2006, he ultimately committed too many mistakes for kick returner Devin Hester and the Bears' stout defense to overcome in the Super Bowl.

That historic championship game matched the first two African American coaches to reach the big game, with Dungy's Colts besting his pupil Smith's Bears. However, both men did honor to their sport in this landmark game. Despite that success, though, Smith's inability to create a consistent offense has led to several mediocre seasons and to him continually being on the coaching hot seat. Once the Bears obtained highly ranked quarterback Jay Cutler in 2009 and then matched him with Mike Martz as offensive coordinator in 2010, the offense was supposed to reach new heights. However, the inconsistency of Cutler and the often impractical game plans of Martz continued the usual fitfulness of the attack even as the Bears reached the NFC championship game in 2010. The offense was improved in 2011 until injuries to Cutler and runner Matt Forte derailed the season.

SMITH, MAURICE F. (CLIPPER) 10/15/1898– 3/18/1894. Notre Dame. G; did not play professionally. *Apprenticeship:* College head coach—23 years. *Roots:* None. *Branches:* None. *Coordinators/Key*

Smith, Lovie L.									
Year	Team	Games	Wins	Losses	Ties	%	P Wins	P Losses	P %
2004	Bears	16	5	11	0	.313	0	0	.000
2005	Bears	16	11	5	0	.688	0	1	.000
2006	Bears	16	13	3	0	.813	2	1	.667
2007	Bears	16	7	9	0	.438	0	0	.000
2008	Bears	16	9	7	0	.563	0	0	.000
2009	Bears	16	7	9	0	.438	0	0	.000
2010	Bears	16	11	5	0	.688	1	1	.500
2011	Bears	16	8	8	0	.500	0	0	.000
8 years		128	71	57	0	.555	3	3	.500

Assistants: Doggie Julian coached the backs. *Hall of Fame Players:* None. *Primary Quarterbacks:* Frank Dancewicz, Roy Zimmerman. *Tendencies:* • His teams scored 14.3 points and allowed 26.2 per game • His teams ran 58.7% of the time, which was 99% of the league average • Four starting quarterbacks in two years; 83% of starts to primary quarterbacks • Four rookie starters in two years • Winning Full Seasons to Losing Full Seasons: 0:2.

There were two unrelated Clipper Smiths who coached college football in the first half of the twentieth century. Both began as guards under Knute Rockne: Maurice playing in South Bend from 1917 to 1920, and John playing from 1925 to 1927. John was an All-American and is a member of the College Football Hall of Fame but had a shorter and less successful coaching career than Maurice who was a teammate of George Gipp at Notre Dame. Neither played professional football, but Maurice, a native of Maneno, Illinois, eventually coached it in Boston.

Rockne recommended Maurice for his head coaching job at tiny Columbia College in Oregon right after graduation. Maurice coached Columbia from 1921 to 1924 until moving up to Gonzaga in Washington where he compiled a 23–9–5 record from 1925 to 1928. Traveling down the West Coast, Smith next coached Santa Clara to a 38–22–4 record from 1929 to 1935 before turning the team over to his line coach, Buck Shaw, a former teammate at Notre Dame. Clipper subsequently succeeded Harry Stuhldreher, still another Fighting Irish alumnus, at Villanova in 1936. Over the next seven years, he led the Wildcats to a 41–17–3 record until the school deemphasized football in 1943 for the war. Smith then took 25 of his players and joined the Marines.

After the war, Clipper coached the University of San Francisco to a 3–6 record in 1946 before taking over the NFL's Boston Yanks in 1947. Boston was a very weak team that had been formed during the war.

Smith ran his own version of the T formation featuring multiple spinners and a "butterfly" formation. He relied on Roy Zimmerman and Notre Dame alumnus Boley Dancewicz at quarterback, but the team finished last and next-to-last in scoring in 1947 and 1948, while the defense was second rate as well. After two fruitless seasons, Clipper resigned and accepted one last coaching position at Lafayette in 1949. However, Smith posted just a 4–21 record a there from 1949 to 1951 before leaving football for the insurance business. He died at age 85 in 1984.

SMITH, MICHAEL (MIKE) 6/13/1959– East Tennessee State. LB; did not play professionally. *Apprenticeship:* College asst.—17 years; pro asst.—9 years. *Roots:* Brian Billick, Jack Del Rio. *Branches:* None. *Coordinators/Key Assistants*: Mike Mularkey ran the offense, while Brian Van Gorder handled the defense. *Hall of Fame Players:* None. *Primary Quarterbacks:* Matt Ryan. *Tendencies:* • His teams scored 24.5 points and allowed 20.1 per game • His teams ran 46.4% of the time, which was 106% of the league average • Two starting quarterbacks in four years; 97% of starts to primary quarterback • Eight rookie starters in four years • Winning Full Seasons to Losing Full Seasons: 4:0.

Although born in Chicago, Mike Smith grew up in Florida and played linebacker for East Tennessee from 1977 to 1981. He tried out for Winnipeg in the CFL but was cut, so he immediately began his coaching career at San Diego State in 1982. In his four years in San Diego, he got to know tight ends coach Brian Billick and that would later help him both professionally and personally. Mike moved on to Morehead State in 1986 and Tennessee Tech in 1987. He coached at Tech for 12 years, eventually moving up to defensive coordinator, before jumping to the NFL in 1999 as a member of Brian Billick's first Baltimore Ravens' staff; as a further tie, he later married Billick's sister-in-law.

Smith won a Super Bowl ring in Baltimore in

Smith, Maurice F. (Clipper)									
Year	*Team*	*Games*	*Wins*	*Losses*	*Ties*	*%*	*P Wins*	*P Losses*	*P %*
1947	Boston Yanks (defunct)	12	4	7	1	.375	0	0	.000
1948	Boston Yanks (defunct)	12	3	9	0	.250	0	0	.000
2 years		24	7	16	1	.313	0	0	.000

Smith, Michael (Mike)									
Year	*Team*	*Games*	*Wins*	*Losses*	*Ties*	*%*	*P Wins*	*P Losses*	*P %*
2008	Falcons	16	11	5	0	.688	0	1	.000
2009	Falcons	16	9	7	0	.563	0	0	.000
2010	Falcons	16	13	3	0	.813	0	1	.000
2011	Falcons	16	10	6	0	.625	0	1	.000
4 years		64	43	21	0	.672	0	3	.000

2000 and then was promoted to linebackers coach in 2002 to replace Jack Del Rio who became defensive coordinator in Carolina. A year later, Del Rio was named head coach of Jacksonville and hired Mike as his defensive coordinator. Smith spent five years with the Jaguars and the team finished in the top ten in fewest points allowed for the last four seasons. Although Smith tends to be anonymous and understated just like his name, he gained a strong reputation as a defensive coach and was named head coach of the Atlanta Falcons in 2008. Former Raven defensive back Rod Woodson said of Smith, "There are a lot of coaches who can put X's and O's on the board, but they can't teach a guy why they did it. But Mike can do that. He will be a good teacher."

Atlanta was coming off a catastrophic season in 2007 when quarterback Mike Vick was arrested for running a dog fighting ring and new coach Bobby Petrino quit the team before the season was done. Working with new GM Thomas Dimitroff, Smith turned over the roster and remade the attitude in Atlanta. The key moves were acquiring workhorse runner Michael Turner and drafting quarterback Matt Ryan to transform the offense into ball control machine, while installing a tight Cover 2 defense. The Falcons improved from 4–12 to 11–5 in Smith's first year and made the playoffs. Even though the team slipped to 9–7 in 2009, it was still the first time in franchise history that the Falcons had recorded consecutive winning seasons. Smith followed that with a 13–3 season in 2010 in which Atlanta had the top record in the NFC. Unfortunately, the team underperformed in the playoffs for a second time despite losing just one game at home during the regular season.

Mike is a players' coach who memorably mixed it up with former Falcon defensive back DeAngelo Hall on the sideline after a late hit on Matt Ryan by Redskin LaRon Landry in a 2008 game. Falcons' safety Thomas DeCoud said afterward, "It's great to have a coach who gets fired up on the sideline and gets mad about things and wears his heart on his sleeve pretty much when he's coaching a football game." The challenge for Smith and the Falcons is to take the next step to become a force in the playoffs after three one-and-done appearances. However, the team has holes on defense and questions remain about the postseason cool of quarterback "Matty Ice."

SNYDER, ROBERT A. (BOB) 2/6/1913–1/4/2001. Ohio. Played QB for the Rams from 1937 to 1938 and the Bears from 1939 to 1941 and in 1943. *Apprenticeship:* College asst.—1 year; pro asst.— 2 years. *Roots:* Adam Walsh. *Branches:* Joe Stydahar. *Coordinators/Key Assistants*: Joe Stydahar coached the line. *Hall of Fame Players:* Bob Waterfield. *Primary Quarterbacks:* Bob Waterfield. *Tendencies:* • His team scored 21.6 points and allowed 17.8 per game • His team ran 61% of the time, which was 104% of the league average • One starting quarterback in one year; 100% of starts to primary quarterback • Two rookie starters in one year • Winning Full Seasons to Losing Full Seasons: 0:0.

Born in Freemont, Ohio, Bob Snyder grew up and lived most of his life in Toledo. He played quarterback for Ohio University and missed fewer than 10 minutes of playing time for the Bobcats from 1933 to 1935. Bob began his professional career with Pittsburgh of the second American Football League in 1936 before joining the NFL with the expansion Cleveland Rams in 1937. Snyder attracted the attention of George Halas in 1938 when he led the Rams over the Bears twice within two weeks.

Halas acquired Snyder as the Bears' backup quarterback and placekicker for 1939. Working with Halas and consultant Clark Shaughnessy, Bob became an expert at the intricacies of the T formation, so that when he retired in 1942, he was named freshman football coach at Notre Dame. With Snyder's primary focus being to install the T formation in South Bend, he worked extensively with two future Heisman Trophy winners in Angelo Bertelli and Johnny Lujack. Bob then returned to the Bears as a player in 1943 before retiring for good after Chicago won another title that year.

After spending 1944 aiding the war effort by working for Thompson Aircraft while coaching high school football on the side, Snyder was hired as an assistant coach for the Rams in 1945. Bob tutored rookie quarterback Bob Waterfield in the T, and the Rams won the championship in their last year in Cleveland. Snyder accompanied the team to Los Angeles in 1946 and then was named head coach in 1947 at age 34, replacing Adam Walsh. While the defense improved under Bob, the offense surprisingly slipped and the team finished at .500 in 1947.

Snyder brought in his mentor Clark Shaughnessy in 1948 to shore up the offense, but Shaughnessy struck up a quick rapport with owner Dan Reeves and got himself appointed head coach during the preseason. Snyder was reported to have resigned due to health concerns with his ulcers, but actually he was

Snyder, Robert A. (Bob)									
Year	Team	Games	Wins	Losses	Ties	%	P Wins	P Losses	P %
1947	Rams	12	6	6	0	.500	0	0	.000
1 year		12	6	6	0	.500	0	0	.000

fired moments before the Rams boarded a flight to Hawaii to play a preseason game. Shaughnessy told the *Los Angeles Times*, "It is very unfortunate that Bob's physical condition would not permit him to continue. I've enjoyed working with him. He's a fine young coach and can do a wonderful job for someone when he regains his health."

Bob "recovered" sufficiently to coach the backfield at USC that season. He then coached in Green Bay during Curly Lambeau's final season of 1949 before taking over as head coach at Toledo in 1950. Snyder resigned from that post after a 4–5 season and did not return to coaching until 1953 for Calgary in Canada. The Stampeders posted a dismal 3–12–1 record that year, and Bob caused an uproar upon his departure by alleging that there was widespread use of Benzedrine tablets by Canadian football players throughout the league. Snyder then worked as an assistant at Villanova in 1954, for the Steelers in 1955 and 1956 and for West Virginia in 1958.

After another break from coaching, Bob moved into the world of minor league football. He helped form the semipro Toledo Tornado in 1961 and led them to a 22–16–1 record from 1962 to 1964. Snyder began the 1965 season as an assistant in Fort Wayne but then was named head coach of the Wheeling Ironmen, where he compiled a lowly 7–28 record from 1965 to 1967. His final coaching stop was with the Indianapolis Capitols in 1968, and he led them to an 8–4 record. Bob also ran a restaurant in Toledo and later worked as a radio executive. Author Robert Peterson reportedly teamed with Snyder on his autobiography called *The Football Takes Funny Bounces*, but it was never published. A double amputee suffering from diabetes, Bob died in 2001 at the age of 87.

SPAGNUOLO, STEVEN C. (STEVE) 12/21/1959–
Springfield. WR; did not play professionally. *Apprenticeship:* College asst.—16 years; NFL Europe asst.—2 years; pro asst.—10 years. *Roots:* Andy Reid, Tom Coughlin. *Branches:* Pat Shurmur. *Coordinators/Key Assistants:* Pat Shurmur then Josh McDaniels ran the offense, while Ken Flajole handled the defense. *Hall of Fame Players:* None. *Primary Quarterbacks:* Sam Bradford. *Tendencies:* • His teams scored 12.1 points and allowed 25.4 per game • His teams ran 40.8% of the time, which was 94% of the league average • Six starting quarterbacks in three years; 54% of starts to

primary quarterback • Nine rookie starters in three years • Winning Full Seasons to Losing Full Seasons: 0:3.

Steve Spagnuolo was born in Whitinsville, Massachusetts, and played wide receiver for Springfield College from 1978 to 1980. He then spent the next two years as a graduate assistant at the University of Massachusetts before serving a one-year internship in the player personnel department of the Redskins where he met future Rams' GM Billy Devaney. In 1984 he returned to the college coaching ranks as an assistant at Lafayette and worked his way up to defensive coordinator by 1990. Two years later, he left to coach the defensive line of the Barcelona Dragons of the developmental World League of American Football in 1992 and then came back to the collegiate level again in 1993 at Maine. Steve moved on to Rutgers in 1994 and Bowling Green in 1996 before returning to NFL Europe in 1998 as the defensive coordinator of the Frankfort Galaxy. A year later, he joined Andy Reid's first staff in Philadelphia and then worked his way up from defensive assistant to defensive backs coach to linebackers coach in eight years with the Eagles as he studied under defensive mastermind Jim Johnson.

In 2007, Spagnuolo was hired as defensive coordinator of the Eagles' divisional rivals, the Giants. Steve transplanted Jim Johnson's aggressive defensive approach to New York and the result was a shocking Super Bowl upset of the undefeated New England Patriots. The upset was powered by Spagnuolo's inventive pass rushes that knocked Patriot quarterback Tom Brady off his game and kept the contest close enough for Eli Manning to pull it out at the end. Steve was heavily courted for head coach by the Redskins in the aftermath of the Super Bowl, but withdrew his name from consideration because he didn't like owner Daniel Snyder's heavy-handed moves such as hiring the team's coordinators before hiring the head coach.

The Giants' defense had another good season under Spagnuolo in 2008, and Steve interviewed for head coaching vacancies with Denver, Detroit, Cleveland and the Jets, but accepted the head coaching position in St. Louis where Billy Devaney was GM. Giants' Coach Tom Coughlin commented, "I'm very happy for Steve. We've been very, very aggressive on defense and we've been able to have two very successful years back-to-back." In Steve's first season with the Rams, the team actually declined slightly from 2–14

Spagnuolo, Steven C. (Steve)									
Year	Team	Games	Wins	Losses	Ties	%	P Wins	P Losses	P %
2009	Rams	16	1	15	0	.063	0	0	.000
2010	Rams	16	7	9	0	.438	0	0	.000
2011	Rams	16	2	14	0	.125	0	0	.000
3 years		48	10	38	0	.208	0	0	.000

to 1–15, but then drafted Oklahoma quarterback Sam Bradford and improved to 7–9 and playoff contention in 2010. Bradford was impressive as a rookie, but had no talented receivers on hand. The team's improvement was fueled primarily by the defense jumping from 31st to 12th in points allowed. However, both the offense and defense improved by more than 100 points in that one season.

Disappointment marked 2011. Offensive coordinator Pat Shurmur left to become head coach of Cleveland. He was replaced by Josh McDaniels who introduced a new scheme for Bradford, but the Rams foolishly did nothing to improve their subpar receiving corps until acquiring Brandon Lloyd in midseason. Furthermore, the team suffered injuries on both sides of the ball and did not have the depth to withstand the losses. The result was a ruinous season that ended with Spagnuolo's firing. He was hired in 2012 to replace Gregg Williams as the Saints defensive coordinator.

SPARANO, ANTHONY (TONY) 10/7/1961– New Haven. C; did not play professionally. *Apprenticeship:* College coach —15 years (5 as head coach); pro asst.— 9 years. *Roots:* Chris Palmer, Marty Schottenheimer, Tom Coughlin, Bill Parcells, Wade Phillips. *Branches:* Todd Bowles (i). *Coordinators/Key Assistants*: Dan Henning then Brian Daboll ran the offense, while Paul Pasqualoni then Mike Nolan handled the defense. *Hall of Fame Players:* None. *Primary Quarterbacks:* Chad Pennington, Chad Henne. *Tendencies:* • His teams scored 20.2 points and allowed 21.1 per game • His teams ran 45.6% of the time, which was 105% of the league average • Four starting quarterbacks in four years; 84% of starts to primary quarterbacks • Ten rookie starters in four years • Winning Full Seasons to Losing Full Seasons: 1:3.

Tony Sparano is distinctive on the sideline for always wearing dark glasses, but it is not for style; he does it because his eyes were burned by hot grease in a restaurant kitchen when he was 17. Sparano was born in West Haven, Connecticut, and played center for New Haven University from 1979 to 1982. Two years later, he joined the coaching staff at his alma mater as the offensive line coach under head coach Chris Palmer. Tony followed Palmer to Boston University in 1988 as line coach and then served as offensive co-

ordinator from 1989 to 1993 until returning once again to New Haven in 1994 — this time as head coach. From 1994 to 1998, Sparano posted an impressive 41–14–1 record at his old school.

In 1999, Sparano jumped to the NFL on Chris Palmer's first staff for the expansion Browns. Tony was Cleveland's quality control coach that year and offensive line coach in 2000. Subsequently, Marty Schottenheimer hired him as tight ends coach for the Redskins in 2001 and then Tom Coughlin hired him in the same capacity in 2002. For the third year in a row, Sparano's head coach was fired in 2003, but Tony landed with Bill Parcells that year as line coach. Parcells said that, "Tom [Coughlin] told me that Tony was one of the two best assistants he'd ever had. And it didn't take long to figure out what he was talking about." Having earned Parcells' respect, Sparano had the added title in Dallas of assistant head coach by 2007.

When Bill "retired" from the Cowboys in 2008, he moved on to his next challenge as team president of the 1–15 Miami Dolphins. In his utter revamping of the franchise, he brought in Sparano as head coach and things could not have gone better in year one. In 2008, the Dolphins improved to 11–5 and a playoff berth; the only other 10-win turnaround season was the 1999 Colts coached by Jim Mora and quarterbacked by Peyton Manning. Sparano's first team was quarterbacked by the clever but fragile Chad Pennington and introduced the single wing-like Wildcat formation to the offense.

However, when Pennington was injured in 2009, the team was put in the hands of inconsistent draftee Chad Henne and dropped to consecutive 7–9 seasons. It did not help that the Dolphins lost seven of eight home games that year and were just 10–14 playing in Miami during Tony's first three seasons. New owner Stephen Ross blatantly flirted with Stanford coach Jim Harbaugh in the 2011 offseason, but Harbaugh signed with the 49ers. Ross hurriedly made up with Sparano, but it was clear that Tony was a lame duck heading into the season and would need a second great turnaround year to save his job.

That turnaround did not occur and Tony was fired with three games to play in 2011. Part of the problem was the team's inadequate talent, but the players also seemed to tune Sparano out as time went on. For-

Sparano, Anthony (Tony)									
Year	Team	Games	Wins	Losses	Ties	%	P Wins	P Losses	P %
2008	Dolphins	16	11	5	0	.688	0	1	.000
2009	Dolphins	16	7	9	0	.438	0	0	.000
2010	Dolphins	16	7	9	0	.438	0	0	.000
2011	Dolphins	13	4	9	0	.308	0	0	.000
4 years		61	29	32	0	.475	0	1	.000

mer Miami runner Ricky Williams commented, "I think a team takes on the personality of a head coach. Tony goes through a lot of effort to show us the things it takes to win football games. He spends a lot of time saying 'if you do these things, you'll win.' Sometimes I feel he does it too much. My opinion is if you have the right attitude that you're going to win, that all that other stuff takes care of itself." Sparano landed with the Jets for 2012, replacing Brian Schottenheimer as offensive coordinator.

SPEEDIE, MAC C. 1/12/1920–3/12/1993. Utah. Played E for the Browns from 1946 to 1952. *Apprenticeship:* Pro asst.— 5 years. *Roots:* Lou Rymkus, Jack Faulkner. *Branches:* Ray Malavasi, Red Miller. *Coordinators/Key Assistants:* Red Miller was the key offensive coach, and Ray Malavasi was the key defensive coach. *Hall of Fame Players:* Willie Brown. *Primary Quarterbacks:* Mickey Slaughter, John McCormick. *Tendencies:* • His teams scored 15.9 points and allowed 29.3 per game • His teams ran 45.2% of the time, which was the league average • Three starting quarterbacks in three years; 73% of starts to primary quarterbacks • Ten rookie starters in three years • Winning Full Seasons to Losing Full Seasons: 0:2.

Mac Speedie was born in Odell, Illinois, but grew up in Utah. As a child he suffered from Perthes disease and was forced to wear leg braces for four years. Even as an adult, one of his legs was longer than the other. However, he was a multisport athlete in high school who tied a national record in the 120-meter high hurdles. He starred as an end for the University of Utah from 1940 to 1942 and then went into the Army for the duration of the war. While in the service, he caught the eye of Paul Brown when playing against Brown's Great Lakes Naval Station team, and Paul subsequently signed Mac for the first-year Cleveland Browns in 1946.

The fleet 6' 3" 200-pound Speedie was a great receiver for Cleveland. Three times he led his league in receptions and twice in yards. He was a three-time consensus All-Pro, a member of the NFL's All-Decade team for the 1940s and a three-time finalist for the Hall of Fame. Still, he was too much of a free spirit for the buttoned-down Brown. The two regularly clashed over salary issues and discipline matters; Speedie even brought a skunk he called "Paul" to training camp in 1952. Halfback Ken Carpenter told

Andy Piascik for *The Greatest Show in Football*, "He was one of the ones Paul picked on quite a bit. He'd get on Speedie's case for no particular reason, but he knew he could get on certain players and it's not going to hurt their play any." By 1953, Mac was 33 years old and decided to try to cash in on his football talents while he still could and jumped from the NFL to play for Saskatchewan in Canada. The spiteful Brown never spoke to Speedie again and referred to him dismissively as "the one who went to Canada."

Mac played two years for the Roughriders and was All League both seasons. In 1955, he signed with British Columbia, but broke his leg in his first game and retired from football. After five years in the investment business, Speedie was lured back to football by former Browns' teammate Lou Rymkus, head coach of the new Houston Oilers of the startup American Football League in 1960. Speedie coached the Oiler ends, but when Rymkus was fired during the 1961 season, Mac resigned in support of his friend. He was hired the next year to coach the ends for Jack Faulkner in Denver. In his five years as an end coach in the AFL, Speedie coached the first two pass receivers to catch 100 passes in a season: Lionel Taylor and Charley Hennigan. Hennigan told *Sports Illustrated*, "He's the reason I'm in the game. Everybody else wanted to cut me. He told me if I went, so did he."

When Denver management grew impatient with Faulkner after four games in 1964, Speedie was appointed head coach, but the Broncos were a hopeless case in the 1960s. In that decade, Denver had the worst record of the original eight AFL franchises by 24 games with their overall 39–97–4 record. Mac slightly improved the offense, but after two losing seasons and dropping the first two games in 1966, he was fired as coach. The Broncos bumped Speedie up into the front office and he spent the next 17 years scouting for the team. He died from a heart attack at age 73 in 1993.

SPURRIER, STEVEN O. (STEVE) 4/20/1945– Florida. Played QB for the 49ers and the Bucs from 1967 to 1976. *Apprenticeship:* College coach — 20 years (15 as head coach); USFL head coach — 3 years. *Roots:* None. *Branches:* Marvin Lewis, Hue Jackson. *Coordinators/Key Assistants:* Hue Jackson ran the offense, while Marvin Lewis then George Edwards handled the defense. *Hall of Fame Players:* Darrell Green, Bruce Smith. *Primary Quarterbacks:* Patrick Ramsey. *Ten-*

Speedie, Mac C.									
Year	Team	Games	Wins	Losses	Ties	%	P Wins	P Losses	P %
1964	Broncos	10	2	7	1	.250	0	0	.000
1965	Broncos	14	4	10	0	.286	0	0	.000
1966	Broncos	2	0	2	0	.000	0	0	.000
3 years		26	6	19	1	.250	0	0	.000

dencies: • His teams scored 18.6 points and allowed 23 per game • His teams ran 42.5% of the time, which was 96% of the league average • Four starting quarterbacks in two years; 50% of starts to primary quarterback • Four rookie starters in two years • Winning Full Seasons to Losing Full Seasons: 0:2.

Although he was born in Miami Beach and primarily is known for his superlative playing and coaching at the University of Florida, Steve Spurrier actually grew up all across the South. The son of a Presbyterian minister, Steve lived in North Carolina, Georgia and Virginia before attending high school in Johnson City, Tennessee where he was All-State in football, baseball and basketball.

Spurrier enrolled at the University of Florida and was a two-time All-American quarterback who won the Heisman Trophy as a senior in 1966. Steve was drafted in the first round in 1967 by San Francisco. Miami player personnel director Joe Thomas later admitted that he was relieved when San Francisco selected Spurrier because he intended on drafting the much more studious Bob Griese rather than Spurrier, the lackadaisical in-state hero. Steve played without distinction for the 49ers for nine years, primarily as a punter and backup quarterback. He finished his desultory playing career as the starter for the historically bad expansion Tampa Bay Bucs in their first year of 1976.

Spurrier began his coaching career in 1978 as quarterbacks coach at his alma mater. A year later, he moved on to Georgia Tech in the same role and then joined Duke as offensive coordinator in 1980. Steve then was given his first opportunity to be a head coach by the Tampa Bay Bandits of the USFL in 1983 and posted a 35–21 record in three seasons. His Bandits were an offense-oriented team that relied on the passing of the veteran quarterback who followed Spurrier at Gainesville and broke his records — John Reaves.

After the league folded, Steve was hired as head coach at Duke in 1987. Despite Duke's limited football heritage, Spurrier coaxed a 20–13–1 record out of the Blue Devils from 1987 to 1989. In 1990, though, he was "called home" and named head coach at Florida. Over the next 12 years, Steve crafted an explosive "Fun 'n' Gun" offense that led the Gators to a 122–27–1 record and a national championship in 1996. While reviled by some who criticized the arrogant "old ball coach's" predilection for running up the score, Steve was a hero in the Sunshine State once again.

Even though Spurrier consistently had resisted overtures from the pros, by 2002 he was open to a new challenge and signed a five-year $25-million contract with owner Dan Snyder to coach the Washington Redskins. After a successful preseason, Steve quickly discovered that coaching in the NFL was not the same easy experience that the college game was.

In his devotion to the pass, Spurrier deemphasized the use of Pro Bowl runner Stephen Davis in 2002 and cut him in 2003. Unfortunately, Steve's Fun 'n' Gun attack fizzled against pro defenses, particularly when he tried to run it with former Gator quarterbacks Shane Matthews and Danny Wuerffel. However, it wasn't much more effective when draft pick Patrick Ramsey was under center. By the middle of 2003, Spurrier turned the playcalling over offensive coordinator Hue Jackson, saying, "If I have to bench the play-caller, then I can do that. So I benched myself."

Spurrier's biggest problem as a pro coach was the same one he had as a pro player: he lacked total dedication and didn't work at his craft as hard as his opponents. One Redskins' assistant anonymously told *Sports Illustrated*, "Steve was bored by blocking schemes to protect the quarterback, so all he'd ever say was 'Block 'em up. Gotta block 'em up.' You can't ask the line coach to do that without getting other offensive coaches involved — and being involved yourself."

Steve resigned after just two years in Washington. Following a year out of football, he returned to football as coach of the South Carolina Gamecocks in 2005 yet has managed just a middling 55–35 record in seven seasons in Columbia through 2011.

STALLINGS, EUGENE C. (GENE) 3/2/1935– Texas A&M. E; did not play professionally. *Apprenticeship:* College coach —14 years (7 as head coach); pro asst.— 14 years. *Roots:* Tom Landry. *Branches:* Hank Kuhlmann (i), Jim Shofner (i). *Coordinators/Key Assistants*: Jim Shofner ran the offense, while Stallings handled his own defense. *Hall of Fame Players:* None. *Primary Quarterbacks:* Neil Lomax. *Tendencies:* • His teams scored 19.5 points and allowed 23.6 per game • His teams ran 42.8% of the time, which was 92% of the league average • Six starting quarterbacks in four years; 69% of starts to primary quarterback • Nine rookie starters in four years • Winning Full Seasons to Losing Full Seasons: 0:4.

Born in Paris, Texas, Gene Stallings was recruited

Spurrier, Steven O. (Steve)

Year	Team	Games	Wins	Losses	Ties	%	P Wins	P Losses	P %
2002	Redskins	16	7	9	0	.438	0	0	.000
2003	Redskins	16	5	11	0	.313	0	0	.000
2 years		32	12	20	0	.375	0	0	.000

to play end at Texas A&M where he was one of Bear Bryant's "Junction Boys," as the survivors of Bryant's brutal summer of 1954 football boot camp were called. Stallings remained a follower of Bryant and his disciplinarian approach throughout his football career in both college and the pros.

In fact, Stallings began his coaching career immediately after graduation by joining Bryant's staff at Alabama in 1958. In seven years as a defensive assistant in Tuscaloosa, the Crimson Tide won two national championships. At the age of 29, Gene returned to his alma mater as head coach in 1965. However, he posted just one winning season in his seven-year stint at A&M and compiled a 27–45–1 record before being fired in 1972.

That year, Stallings was hired by Tom Landry to coach the defensive backs in Dallas. He performed that role for 14 years until the St. Louis Cardinals hired him as head coach in 1986. Gene told the press, "I'm sorry Coach Bryant couldn't be here. I know somewhere he's smiling." Stallings' martial style was not welcomed by everyone. Star runner Ottis Anderson was traded during the 1986 season and later complained, "He treated all the players like dogs. What he said to other human beings in team meetings was unbelievable. But I think he used to criticize black players more severely."

Unable to record a winning season in either two years in St. Louis or two in Phoenix after the franchise was uprooted in 1988, Gene announced late in 1989 he would not return in 1990. At that point, Cardinals' GM Larry Wilson abruptly fired him with five games to go. Cardinals' tackle Luis Sharpe responded, "It was handled in a terrible manner. A class man was handled in a very classless way."

From that degradation, though, Stallings rose to his greatest triumph. He was named head coach at Alabama in 1990, replacing Bill Curry. Over the next seven years, the Crimson Tide went 70–16–1, finished in the top five three times and won the school's first national championship (in 1992) since Bear Bryant retired. Following an 11th ranked 11–3 season in 1996,

Gene stepped down as coach and retired from football. Since then he has worked as a cattle rancher and served on several corporate boards as well as being a member of the Texas A&M Board of Regents. For many years, he has been involved with children with disabilities in tribute to his Downs' Syndrome son John who died in 2008. Stallings was elected to the College Football Hall of Fame as a coach in 2010.

STANFEL, RICHARD A. (DICK) 7/20/1927– San Francisco. Played G for the Lions and Redskins from 1952 to 1958. *Apprenticeship:* College asst.— 5 years; pro asst.—17 years. *Roots:* Joe Kuharich, Jerry Williams, Dick Nolan, Hank Stram. *Branches:* None. *Coordinators/Key Assistants:* None. *Hall of Fame Players:* None. *Primary Quarterbacks:* Archie Manning. *Record:* **Interim Coach.**

San Francisco native Dick Stanfel was perhaps the premier NFL guard of the 1950s and spent more than 30 years as a respected offensive line coach in the league. Stanfel once told the *San Francisco Chronicle*, "I told every player, 'If you can get it done, I don't care if you stand on your head. But if you can't get it done, you'd better damn well do it my way.'"

After graduating high school, Dick spent two years in the Army before attending college in his hometown at the University of San Francisco where he played under Joe Kuharich from 1948 to 1950. Stanfel graduated from USF the year before the Dons undefeated 1951 season, but nonetheless played with such future NFL stars as Gino Marchetti, Ollie Matson and Bob St. Clair in college.

Dick was drafted in the second round by Detroit in 1951, but missed that season after suffering a knee injury in the College All Star game. He joined the Lions in 1952 and played in three straight NFL title games from 1952 to 1954. In 1953, Stanfel even was voted team MVP, an unusual honor for an offensive lineman. Kuharich, his college coach, acquired Dick for the Redskins in 1956, and Stanfel played three years in Washington before retiring with knee and ankle in-

Stallings, Eugene C. (Gene)									
Year	Team	Games	Wins	Losses	Ties	%	P Wins	P Losses	P %
1986	Cardinals	16	4	11	1	.281	0	0	.000
1987	Cardinals	15	7	8	0	.467	0	0	.000
1988	Cardinals	16	7	9	0	.438	0	0	.000
1989	Cardinals	11	5	6	0	.455	0	0	.000
4 years		58	23	34	1	.405	0	0	.000

Stanfel, Richard A. (Dick)									
Year	Team	Games	Wins	Losses	Ties	%	P Wins	P Losses	P %
1980	Saints	4	1	3	0	.250	0	0	.000
1 year		4	1	3	0	.250	0	0	.000

juries at age 32 to follow Kuharich to Notre Dame as line coach. Dick spent four years under Kuharich in South Bend before moving on to California to coach the line for Marv Levy in 1963. By 1964, Kuharich was back in the NFL with Philadelphia and hired Stanfel again as his line coach. Dick spent seven years in Philadelphia, outlasting Kuharich, and then returned to the Bay Area as Dick Nolan's line coach and offensive coordinator in 1971. Following Nolan's dismissal in 1976, Stanfel was hired by Hank Stram in New Orleans. Two years later, Nolan replaced Stram but neither established coach was able to succeed with the Saints.

In fact, the Saints became widely known as the "Aints" in 1980, dropping their first 12 games and costing Nolan his job. Stanfel was elevated to interim head coach and did manage to lead the team to one win in its final four games, but the club was a mess on and off the field. Stanfel even had to suspend one defensive lineman, Don Reese, for fighting with another, Derland Moore. In the offseason, Dick was hired by Neill Armstrong to coach the offensive line for the Bears and stayed on staff after Mike Ditka was hired in Chicago; he held that position for a dozen years until Ditka was fired in 1993. Stanfel retired at that point, but returned to New Orleans and coaching in 1997 when Ditka was hired to coach the Saints. Dick retired for good in 1999. Despite a brief seven-year playing career, Stanfel was a five-time All-Pro and a member of the NFL's All-Decade team for the 1950s. He was the Seniors' Committee Hall of Fame finalist in 1993 and again in 2012.

STARR, BRYAN B. (BART) 1/9/1934– Alabama. Played QB for the Packers from 1956 to 1971. *Apprenticeship:* Pro asst.—1 year. *Roots:* Dan Devine. *Branches:* Dick LeBeau. *Coordinators/Key Assistants:* Paul Roach then Zeke Bratkowski then Bob Schnelker ran the offense, while Dave Hanner then John Meyer handled the defense. *Hall of Fame Players:* James Lofton, Jan Stenerud. *Primary Quarterbacks:* Lynn Dickey, David Whitehurst. *Record:* **Hall of Fame Player.** *Tendencies:* • His teams scored 17.4 points and allowed 20.8 per game • His teams ran 50.2% of the time, which was 96% of the league average • Six starting quarterbacks in nine years; 86% of starts to primary quarterbacks • 15 rookie starters in nine years • Winning Full Seasons to Losing Full Seasons: 2:5.

A native of Montgomery, Alabama, Bart Starr was a high school All-American quarterback who went to Alabama and led the team to bowl games as a freshman and sophomore, but injured his back as a junior; as a senior, he was relegated to the bench when new coach J.B. "Ears" Whitworth decided to emphasize underclassmen. As a result, Starr was a lowly 17th round draft choice for Green Bay in 1956, but Bart made the team as Tobin Rote's backup. Vince Lombardi arrived in 1959, yet he did not decide on Bart as his permanent starting quarterback until late in 1960, when Starr led Green Bay to its first Western Division crown in 16 years. Although the Packers lost the championship game to the Eagles that year, 1960 would be the last time either Starr or Lombardi would lose a playoff game. Starr's Packers won each of the next nine postseason games in the decade to win five championships, with Bart achieving the highest postseason quarterback rating in NFL history at 104.5 and the lowest interception percentage of any postseason quarterback who threw at least 200 passes.

Starr was a master at calling plays, reading defenses and switching off to audibles at the line of scrimmage. Cool under pressure, his signature play was the deep pass on short yardage third and fourth down plays, where Bart would fake to the halfback or fullback and pass to an open receiver downfield. Because Lombardi's offense was a ball-control running offense, though, Starr did not throw enough to accumulate the big passing numbers of others. What is often forgotten is that Green Bay's overpowering running attack had dissipated by the second half of the decade. For the three consecutive championships in the latter part of the 1960s, the Packer offense relied more on Bart's brains and his arm. Those Packers were not always the most talented team on the field in those championship years, but they always won. Besides Lombardi, the primary reason was because Starr consistently excelled and drove his team to victory.

Starr, Bryan B. (Bart)

Year	Team	Games	Wins	Losses	Ties	%	P Wins	P Losses	P %
1975	Packers	14	4	10	0	.286	0	0	.000
1976	Packers	14	5	9	0	.357	0	0	.000
1977	Packers	14	4	10	0	.286	0	0	.000
1978	Packers	16	8	7	1	.531	0	0	.000
1979	Packers	16	5	11	0	.313	0	0	.000
1980	Packers	16	5	10	1	.344	0	0	.000
1981	Packers	16	8	8	0	.500	0	0	.000
1982	Packers	9	5	3	1	.611	1	1	.500
1983	Packers	16	8	8	0	.500	0	0	.000
9 years		131	52	76	3	.408	1	1	.500

After his playing career ended, Bart spent 1972 coaching the quarterbacks under Dan Devine, and the Packers won a division title that year behind inconsistent young signal caller Scott Hunter. Starr and Devine clashed over play calling in the postseason loss to Washington, though, and Bart resigned. After working as a TV analyst and running his automobile dealership for two years, he was summoned back to Green Bay in 1975 as head coach. He accepted the job with a quote from Winston Churchill ("To every man there comes in his lifetime that special moment when he is tapped..."); nine years later he would bow out with a quote from Teddy Roosevelt ("It's not the critic that counts..."). In between was a disappointing, dispiriting tenure that sullied Starr's reputation as a winner and accomplished little else. In 1979, he told the *New York Times* that he should have begun his coaching career differently, "I would have been an assistant under the great coaches in the game — the Shulas, the Knoxes, the Grants, the Allens."

Not only did Devine leave a depleted roster, but also had traded away several top draft picks in unsuccessfully trying to find a decent quarterback. By the time Starr gained some coaching experience and built an explosive passing offense, the defense turned into a sieve. Green Bay finished fifth in scoring in both 1982 and 1983, but was third from the bottom in points allowed in 1983, and Bart was fired on the heels of an 8–8 season. It was a mistake for the team to offer the job to the inexperienced Starr, and it was a mistake for him to accept it. Regrettably, it was a mistake that went on for nine years. In addition to the losing, Starr had discipline problems with his players and personality issues with the media covering the team.

Starr subsequently moved to Phoenix and was involved with a group that fruitlessly sought to bring an NFL franchise to Arizona. Eventually, he returned to Alabama where he has worked in the health care and real estate fields. The Packers retired his number and he was elected to the Hall of Fame in 1977. In a fitting legacy, Athletes in Action instituted the Bart Starr Award in 1988 to honor an NFL player of strong character and leadership on and off the field each year.

STECKEL, LESLIE T. (LES) 7/1/1946– Kansas. RB; did not play professionally. *Apprenticeship:* College asst.—6 years; pro asst.—6 years. *Roots:* Pete McCulley (i), Fred O'Connor (i), Bud Grant. *Branches:* Raymond Berry, Jerry Burns. *Coordinators/Key Assistants*: Jerry Burns ran the offense, while Floyd Reese

handled the defense. *Hall of Fame Players:* Jan Stenerud. *Primary Quarterbacks:* Tommy Kramer. *Tendencies:* • His team scored 17.3 points and allowed 30.3 per game • His team ran 42.7% of the time, which was 91% of the league average • Three starting quarterbacks in one year; 56% of starts to primary quarterback • Two rookie starters in one year • Winning Full Seasons to Losing Full Seasons: 0:1.

Les Steckel was born in Whitehall, Pennsylvania, outside Allentown and contracted polio when he was five. He eventually overcame that disease to fashion a life of faith in sports and the military. While at the University of Kansas, Les was a Golden Gloves boxing champion and then enlisted in the Marines after graduating in 1968. Steckel served a tour of duty in Vietnam and later played on the Marines football team when he returned stateside. Upon his discharge in 1972, Les signed up for the Marine Reserves and served the corps another 30 years while establishing himself as a football coach.

Steckel worked first as an assistant at the University of Colorado from 1972 to 1976 and then spent 1977 at the Naval Academy. He moved up to the NFL in 1978 when former Naval Academy assistant Pete McCulley hired him in San Francisco. A year later, Les joined Bud Grant's staff in Minnesota. When Grant stepped down in 1984, the Vikings bypassed longtime offensive coordinator Jerry Burns to tap Steckel as Grant's successor. Right away, the team knew things had changed. Grant relied on light workouts to preserve his veteran team's strength throughout the season. By contrast, Steckel ran training camp like boot camp, even beginning it with an obstacle course challenge. His language was salted with military-like jargon with acronyms like ABC — Attitude, give your Best, Commitment — which is what he wanted from the players. He struck that attitude when explaining to *Sports Illustrated* why he called six consecutive safety blitzes in a preseason game, "You don't change your game plan just because the enemy sneaks up on you in the middle of the river. Only unstable, wishy-washy people make excuses. I wanted to see how my cornerbacks would perform in adversity."

Minnesota dropped from 8–8 to 3–13 in 1984, and the vastly unpopular Steckel was fired — replaced by a returning Bud Grant. To be fair, the Vikings were an aging, mediocre team in decline, but Steckel's approach was a complete failure. Linebacker Scott Studwell summarized the team's relief when Les was let go, "He tried to run a professional team with a high

Steckel, Leslie T. (Les)									
Year	Team	Games	Wins	Losses	Ties	%	P Wins	P Losses	P %
1984	Vikings	16	3	13	0	.188	0	0	.000
1 year		16	3	13	0	.188	0	0	.000

school attitude. Les dug himself an awful big hole and couldn't climb out of it."

Steckel moved on to coach on Raymond Berry's Patriots' staff from 1985 to 1988 and at Brown University in 1989. Les returned to active duty in the Reserves at one point while he continued to look for coaching jobs. Finally in 1991, Colorado coach Bill McCartney offered him an assistant's position. Two years later, Steckel got back in the NFL on Dan Reeves' Broncos' staff and then moved on to Jeff Fisher's Houston Oilers staff in 1995. By 1997, Les was the offensive coordinator for the run-oriented Tennessee Oilers and served through the Tennessee Titan's Super Bowl loss to the Rams to conclude the 1999 season. Tony Dungy hired Les to spruce up the Bucs lackluster ground-oriented attack in 2000, but replaced him with Clyde Christiansen just one year later. Steckel spent 2003 coaching running backs in Buffalo and then 2004 coaching high school. Since 2005, he has been the president of the Fellowship of Christian Athletes.

STEPHENSON, GEORGE K. (KAY) 12/17/1944– Florida. Played QB for the Chargers in 1967 and the Bills in 1968. *Apprenticeship:* College asst.— 2 years; WFL asst.—1 year; pro asst.— 6 years. *Roots:* Chuck Knox. *Branches:* Hank Bullough, Jerry Glanville, Dick Jauron. *Coordinators/Key Assistants:* Jim Ringo ran the offense, while Bob Zeman then Don Lawrence then Hank Bullough handled the defense. *Hall of Fame Players:* Joe DeLamielleure, Bruce Smith. *Primary Quarterbacks:* Joe Ferguson. *Tendencies:* • His teams scored 16.1 points and allowed 25.1 per game • His teams ran 39.3% of the time, which was 83% of the league average • Three starting quarterbacks in three years; 75% of starts to primary quarterback • Seven rookie starters in three years • Winning Full Seasons to Losing Full Seasons: 0:1.

Kay Stephenson backed up Heisman Trophy winner Steve Spurrier at Florida from 1964 to 1966 and never got a chance to play. As would be expected, the native of De Funiak, Florida went undrafted, yet he made the San Diego Chargers as a free agent. A year later, he was in Buffalo and even got a chance to start three games after the Bills' first three quarterbacks were injured. Kay had tryouts with Atlanta and Oakland in 1969, but was not able to stick in the NFL.

Stephenson coached at Rice in 1971 and 1972 and

then coached high school football in 1973. In 1974, he made one last attempt to extend his playing career with the Jacksonville Sharks of the WFL where he also served as an assistant coach. Stephenson lost his starting job and retired from playing that year, but served as the director of player personnel for the reorganized Jacksonville Express in 1975. Kay returned to the NFL in 1977 as a member of Chuck Knox's Rams staff and then followed Knox to Buffalo in 1978. When Knox quit the Bills five years later, Owner Ralph Wilson unexpectedly promoted Stephenson to head coach in 1983.

Kay led Buffalo to an 8–8 season that year, but the bottom dropped out in 1984 when the Bills won just 2 games. In the off season, Stephenson asserted, "We emerged from 1984 wiser, tougher and more determined than ever to restore a winning personality to the Buffalo Bills." Sloppy nose tackle Fred Smerlas later sneered to the *New York Times* that Stephenson was a "Barbie Doll" and, "He wanted everything to be perfect. If everyone slept right and ate right, you'd win. That's what he thought." However, after the team lost its first four games in 1985, Stephenson was replaced by his defensive coordinator Hank Bullough. GM Bill Polian, who had come to Buffalo in 1984, later attributed the Bills' slide to a series of poor drafts and the club's losing Joe Cribbs and draftee Jim Kelly to the USFL. He noted that when he came to Buffalo, "There was a feeling of negativism." Polian would change all that, but by then Kay was selling real estate.

Stephenson got back into the game in 1990 when he was hired to coach the Sacramento Surge in the upcoming World League of American Football that opened in 1991. Behind scrambling quarterback David Archer, Kay led the Surge to the league title in 1992. He then moved on to the Canadian game by taking over as head coach of the Sacramento Gold Miners in 1993 and brought Archer with him. Stephenson coached the Gold Miners for two years and stayed with the team when it relocated to San Antonio as the Texans in 1995. When the CFL retrenched from its American experiment in 1996, Kay was out of work. He spent 1997 as an assistant at the University of Arkansas and then was named head coach of Edmonton in the CFL in 1998. Once more he signed Archer as his quarterback, but was fired after one 9–9 season. Overall, Stephenson compiled a 36–35–1 record in

Stephenson, George K. (Kay)									
Year	Team	Games	Wins	Losses	Ties	%	P Wins	P Losses	P %
1983	Bills	16	8	8	0	.500	0	0	.000
1984	Bills	16	2	14	0	.125	0	0	.000
1985	Bills	4	0	4	0	.000	0	0	.000
3 years		36	10	26	0	.278	0	0	.000

the CFL and 13–9 in the WLAF. He has not coached since then, but has penned a regular column on football for the *Pensacola News Journal* since 2003.

Stevens, Marvin A. (Mal) 4/14/1900–12/6/1979. Washburn and Yale. QB/HB; did not play professionally. *Apprenticeship:* College coach — 18 years (13 as head coach). *Roots:* None. *Branches:* Tom Scott (i). *Coordinators/Key Assistants:* Tom Scott coached the ends; Hank Reese coached the line. *Hall of Fame Players:* None. *Primary Quarterbacks:* Glenn Dobbs. *Record:* **Interim Coach.**

Dr. Mal Stevens combined his dual interests in sports and medicine by coaching football while also serving as a practicing physician for many years. Born in Osborne, Kansas, Stevens served in the Army Air Corps in 1918 prior to beginning his college career at Washburn in Topeka where he lettered in football (as a quarterback), baseball, basketball, track and tennis from 1919 to 1921. He subsequently transferred to Yale, for whom he played halfback, in 1923 and was hired as the Eli's backfield coach in 1924. Mal served on Tad Jones' staff for four years and then was named head coach in 1928. All during that time, Stevens was attending Yale's medical school and graduated in 1929. Following his graduation, Mal joined the medical school faculty as an assistant professor for surgery, gynecology and obstetrics while coaching the football team to a 16–11–8 record from 1928 to 1932.

Stevens moved to New York City in 1933, but maintained a private practice in both New Haven and New York and taught at both institutions for the next several years. That year, he served as the freshman football coach at NYU and then was named head coach in 1934. Mal coached NYU from 1934 to 1941 and compiled a 33–34–2 record before entering the Navy Medical Corps as a Lieutenant Commander in charge of orthopedic surgery in 1942. During his four years of service, he also coached the football team at the Sampson, New York Naval Training Station in 1942 before going overseas. Gary L. Bloomfield quoted the coach in *Duty, Honor, Victory* as emphasizing the importance of football to the war effort, "Football strategy is being used all over the world today in tactics designed to outsmart the enemy — so football training should be invaluable to the training of our armed forces. Most of the great admirals and generals — Halsey, Eisenhower and MacArthur, for instance — were football players. The individual strategy and thinking as a result of football training and conditioning make for faster and clearer decisions."

When the war ended, Stevens was hired as head coach of the new Brooklyn Dodgers in the startup All America Football Conference in 1946. He was also given a 10% stake in the team. The team was formed after the NFL's Brooklyn Dodgers were brought into the AAFC as the New York Yankees by owner Dan Topping who also owned both the baseball Yankees and Yankee Stadium. The new Dodgers were owned by William Cox, a Yale alumnus who had previously owned the New York franchise in the third American Football League in 1941 and had purchased the Philadelphia Phillies baseball team in 1943.

Despite the presence of triple-threat single wing tailback Glenn Dobbs, though, the Dodgers were a terrible team. After just six games, Stevens bowed out just six hours before the seventh game of the year. Mal stated that it was impossible to do justice to both his medical practice and to football, so he gave up coaching. He did serve as the team doctor of both the baseball and football Yankees in 1947 and in 1951 was appointed to the New York Medical Advisory Board for the New York State Athletic Commission overseeing boxing. He served in that capacity for several years, but more importantly was well known as a bone specialist and polio researcher who was the Eastern Director of the Sister Elizabeth Kenny Institute and Clinic for Infantile Paralysis in Jersey City, New Jersey for 13 years. He was inducted in the College Football Hall of Fame in 1974 and died five years later.

Strader, Norman P. (Red) 12/21/1902–5/26/1956. St. Mary's. Played FB for the Cardinals in 1927. *Apprenticeship:* College coach — 14 years (6 as head coach); pro asst. — 3 years. *Roots:* Ray Flaherty. *Branches:* Frankie Albert, Red Hickey, Phil Bengtson, Bill Johnson. *Coordinators/Key Assistants:* Frankie Albert was the key offensive coach, while Phil Bengtson ran the defense. *Hall of Fame Players:* John Henry Johnson, Hugh McElhenny, Leo Nomellini, Joe Perry, Bob St. Clair, Y.A. Tittle, Arnie Weinmeister. *Primary Quarterbacks:* George Ratterman, Dom Panciera, Y.A. Tittle. *Tendencies:* • His teams scored 21.3 points and allowed 23 per game • His teams ran 59% of the time, which was 103% of the league average • Five starting quarterbacks in four years; 78% of starts to primary quarterbacks • 15 rookie starters in four years • Winning Full Seasons to Losing Full Seasons: 2:1.

Stevens, Marvin A. (Mal)									
Year	Team	Games	Wins	Losses	Ties	%	P Wins	P Losses	P %
1946	Dodgers (AAFC)	6	1	4	1	.250	0	0	.000
1 year		6	1	4	1	.250	0	0	.000

Bicoastal Red Strader was born in Newton, New Jersey, but grew up in Modesto, California and spent most of his professional life on either coast. Red played fullback at St. Mary's under Slip Madigan from 1923 to 1925 and was a third team All-American as a senior. He also starred on the baseball team as a catcher and attended spring training with the Cleveland Indians in 1926 before playing minor league baseball for one year. In the fall, Strader played for the Chicago Bulls of Red Grange's American Football League. A year later, he played for the Chicago Cardinals for one year prior to being named head coach of Regis College in Denver Colorado in 1928. Red posted a 14–14 record at Regis from 1928 to 1931 and also coached the baseball team there.

Strader returned to his alma mater as the backfield coach under Madigan in 1932 and worked on Slip's staff for the next eight years. Finally, in 1940 Madigan stepped down, and Red was elevated to the top job. In two years, he compiled a 10–7 record and installed the T formation at St. Mary's. With the outbreak of World War II, Strader joined the Navy and rose to Lieutenant Commander while coaching teams on three separate naval bases. At the conclusion of the war, Red was hired as Ray Flaherty's backfield coach on the fledgling New York Yankees of the new All America Football Conference in 1946. During this time, he also served as a bird dog scout for the baseball Yankees, with both teams being owned by Dan Topping. The powerful football Yankees used Flaherty's single wing attack to go to consecutive AAFC championship games in 1946 and 1947, but lost both times to the Cleveland Browns. Flaherty's edgy personality grated on the players, though, so when the team lost three of its first four games in 1948, he was forced to resign. Under Strader, the team split its remaining 10 games, and Red's contract was extended. He converted the Yankees to a T formation team in 1949, and New York posted an 8–4 mark despite being saddled with ineffective rookie quarterbacks Don Panciera and Gil Johnson.

The AAFC was merged into the NFL in 1950 and the Yankee players were dissolved and divided amongst the New York Giants and the former New York Bulldogs, now renamed the Yanks. Strader had a verbal agreement with Yanks owner Ted Collins to coach the new squad in 1950. Led by quarterback George Ratterman and defensive back Spec Sanders, the Yanks went 7–5 and finished in third place that year. The following year, Ratterman departed for Canada and Strader had heart problems in June. Collins asked the coach to sign a letter that indicated he was in sufficient shape that the strain of coaching would not imperil his health and that Collins was absolved of any responsibility. When Red failed to do so, he was dismissed as coach at the beginning of training camp and replaced by Jimmy Phelan, the same coach who replaced him at St. Mary's a decade earlier.

Since Strader had no written contract, he was forced to sue Collins for the salary agreed to for 1951 and in his affidavit parenthetically attacked the NFL draft as "illegal." He was out of football that year and eventually won a judgment against Collins 1952. He then was hired by the 49ers as a scout and worked in that role until the team decided to replace low key head coach Buck Shaw with the more intense and organized Red Strader in 1955. Red's tenure as San Francisco head coach lasted just one losing season, however. Owner Tony Morabito fired the coach, citing player dissatisfaction. "They played under Mr. Strader, not for him. They just weren't compatible." Strader fired back, "I've been coaching for 25 years and one of my strong points always has been getting the most out of my players. If there was incompatibility, why did they give me the game ball after the final game?" Years later, team captain Clay Matthews confirmed to Matt Maiocco in the book *San Francisco 49ers* that there indeed was dissension, "All of the gripes and things that happened, I had to present to management." Five months later, Strader was dead, having suffered a heart attack in his sleep. That December, Red's widow sued the 49ers for her late husband's contracted salary. Following three years of wrangling, she settled with the team for $18,000 in December 1959.

STRAM, HENRY L. (HANK) 1/3/1924–7/4/2005. Purdue. HB; did not play professionally. *Apprenticeship:* College asst.—12 years. *Roots:* None. *Branches:*

Strader, Norman P. (Red)									
Year	Team	Games	Wins	Losses	Ties	%	P Wins	P Losses	P %
1948	Yankees (AAFC)	10	5	5	0	.500	0	0	.000
1949	Yankees (AAFC)	12	8	4	0	.667	0	1	.000
1950	New York Yanks (defunct)	12	7	5	0	.583	0	0	.000
1955	49ers	12	4	8	0	.333	0	0	.000
4 years		46	24	22	2	.543	0	1	.000

Ed Hughes, Tom Bettis (i), Sam Rutigliano, Dick Stanfel (i), Rich Kotite. *Coordinators/Key Assistants:* For the Chiefs, Tom Catlin then Tom Bettis ran the defense; for the Saints, Doug Shively was the key defensive coach; Stram always ran his own offense. *Hall of Fame Players:* Bobby Bell, Buck Buchanan, Len Dawson, Willie Lanier, Jan Stenerud, Emmitt Thomas. *Primary Quarterbacks:* Len Dawson, Cotton Davidson, Mike Livingston. *Record:* **Hall of Fame Coach**; Super Bowl Championship 1969; AFL Championship 1962. *Tendencies:* • His teams scored 23.2 points and allowed 18.6 per game • His teams ran 53.6% of the time, which was 102% of the league average • 11 starting quarterbacks in 17 years; 85% of starts to primary quarterbacks • 50 rookie starters in 17 years • Winning Full Seasons to Losing Full Seasons: 11:5.

Hank Stram at 5'7" was a dapper, animated bantam rooster on the sideline, bedecked in sharp business suits with team-color vests and tasseled loafers. The attention to detail displayed by his wardrobe was reflected by his team's exacting performance on the field. With the Chiefs, Stram emphasized intricate offensive and defensive designs and execution, and his team was an innovative leader throughout his tenure.

Stram played single wing tailback for Purdue in 1942 and then joined the military from 1943 to 1945. After his discharge, Hank returned to Purdue as a T formation halfback in 1946 and 1947. Upon graduation, he was added to the Boilermakers' coaching staff and coached the backfield there through the 1955 season. Hank also coached the Purdue baseball team from 1951 to 1955. Probably his greatest impact at Purdue, though, was recruiting Len Dawson to the university and that would later pay off in Kansas City as well.

Stram's second coaching stop was as an assistant at SMU in 1956. While there, he just missed coaching future AFL and Chiefs' founder Lamar Hunt who was on the Mustangs the year before. Stram moved on to Notre Dame in 1957 and the University of Miami in 1959 before Hunt invited him to become the first head coach of the Dallas Texans of the AFL in 1960. Ultimately, Hank would be the only man to coach all ten full seasons of the rebel league's existence and would win three AFL titles.

Even though Stram's Dallas Texans were clearly

Head-to-Head:

Hall of Fame Opponent	Regular Season	Postseason
George Allen	1–0	0–0
Paul Brown	4–4	0–0
Weeb Ewbank	7–5	1–0
Sid Gillman	13–10–1	0–0
Bud Grant	0–3	1–0
Tom Landry	0–1	0–0
Vince Lombardi	0–0	0–1
John Madden	3–7–2	1–1
Chuck Noll	2–2	0–0
Don Shula	0–2	0–1
Total	30–34–3	3–3

Stram, Henry L. (Hank)

Year	Team	Games	Wins	Losses	Ties	%	P Wins	P Losses	P %
1960	Dallas Texans (Chiefs)	14	8	6	0	.571	0	0	.000
1961	Dallas Texans (Chiefs)	14	6	8	0	.429	0	0	.000
1962	Dallas Texans (Chiefs)	14	11	3	0	.786	1	0	1.000
1963	Chiefs	14	5	7	2	.429	0	0	.000
1964	Chiefs	14	7	7	0	.500	0	0	.000
1965	Chiefs	14	7	5	2	.571	0	0	.000
1966	Chiefs	14	11	2	1	.821	1	1	0500
1967	Chiefs	14	9	5	0	.643	0	0	.000
1968	Chiefs	14	12	2	0	.857	0	1	.000
1969	Chiefs	14	11	3	0	.786	3	0	1.000
1970	Chiefs	14	7	5	2	.571	0	0	.000
1971	Chiefs	14	10	3	1	.750	0	1	.000
1972	Chiefs	14	8	6	0	.571	0	0	.000
1973	Chiefs	14	7	5	2	.571	0	0	.000
1974	Chiefs	14	5	9	0	.357	0	0	.000
1976	Saints	14	4	10	0	.286	0	0	.000
1977	Saints	14	3	11	0	.214	0	0	.000
17 years		238	131	97	10	.571	5	3	.625

more successful than Tom Landry's expansion Cowboys that also started in 1960, the Texans struggled at the gate in Big D. Hank's first two teams finished in second place in the West and were held back by mediocre quarterbacking from Cotton Davidson. In 1962, though, Lenny Dawson won his release from the Browns after five years of sitting on the bench in the NFL and was signed by Stram. However, Hank was shocked at how far Dawson's skills had deteriorated and worked hard to reinvigorate the Purdue alumnus' career throughout the preseason. By the start of the 1962 season, Dawson was himself again and his 29 touchdown passes led Dallas to the league title that year. Dawson was perfect for Stram's innovative offense, and he and Hank teamed together for 13 years.

Stram was an innovator on both offense and defense right from the start. Even from the earliest days in Dallas, the team used a 3–4 defense at times and mixed man-to-man and zone coverage schemes. In addition to exploiting bump-and-run coverage, Stram later would develop the "Stack" defense in which each linebacker was hidden directly behind a defensive lineman and both "over" and "under" shifts of the defensive tackles so that one was lined up over the center. On offense, he utilized a two tight end formation as early as 1962 and also designed a moving pocket to allow Dawson to avoid a strong pass rush. Hank regularly applied a variety of shifts from multiple formations — at one point he put the tight end in the I formation as a precursor to the latter day H back. Stram once told the New York Times, "The creation of formations has a purpose. We have what we call a dictator offense. We dictate to the defense by making them do what we want them to do. And we do it by creating formations." On a personnel level, he was color blind, freely employing several African American players as well as the first black middle linebacker in league history, Willie Lanier. Even Hank's huddle was different — arranged like a choir with the taller lineman standing with their backs to the defense and the skill players bent over in front of them, all facing the quarterback.

Despite the 1962 championship, though, the underappreciated Texans moved to Kansas City and became the Chiefs in 1963. Over the next three years, the Chiefs were a bit inconsistent on the field and had to overcome a series of player tragedies. Runner Stone Johnson died from a neck injury suffered in the 1963 preseason; tight end Fred Arbanas was blinded in one eye in 1964; and fullback Mack Lee Hill died on the operating table in 1965. Finally in 1966, everything came together, and the Chiefs whipped Buffalo in the AFL championship game to earn a berth in the very first Super Bowl against the vaunted Green Bay Packers. Although they were denounced as the champions of a "Mickey Mouse" league, Kansas City stayed fairly

even with Green Bay for the first half until coming undone from mistakes in the second half. Angry that Packers' coach Vince Lombardi downgraded the Chiefs in his postgame comments, Kansas City took it out on the Bears the following August by beating Chicago 66–14 in the first preseason game between the two leagues, while Stram set about to improve his club.

The Chiefs were superseded by the Raiders as the power team from the West over the next couple of years, but, led by a rugged defense, emerged from the 1969 playoffs as the AFL's representative in last Super Bowl before the leagues fully merged in 1970. Prior to the matchup with the Vikings, Hank told the Washington Post that the 1969 team was much better than the 1966 one, "We're much better defensively now. We have better size, better speed and more strength. We're about the same offensively." The Chiefs then went out and proved that assessment in a game that demonstrated that the Jets defeat of the Colts the previous year was no fluke; the two leagues were equal rivals. What's more, the vocal Stram was the first coach ever wired by NFL Films for a championship game and provided a memorable running commentary for the highlight film that solidified Kansas City's dominance in the public's perception. Hank's buoyant personality and unique expressions ("Just keep matriculating the ball down the field, boys!") made him a media star.

As a world champion, Stram drew a forum in which he crowed that his offense was the "Offense of the Seventies." He told Sports Illustrated, "Well, the 70s will be the decade of difference — different offensive sets, different defensive formations. What we try to do is to create a moment of hesitation, a moment of doubt in the defense. It will be a decade of experiment. I think football teams reflect the personality of coaches, and I like to think my personality is reflected in the variety of the Chiefs' attack and defense. I like to see Hank Stram in the stacked defense and the 18 different offensive sets we use and the 300 and something plays we can run off those sets."

Unfortunately, Stram would only lead the Chiefs to one more postseason game in his remaining five years in Kansas City despite signing a 10-year contract extension in 1972. For all his innovations, Hank was at heart a players' coach. Hall of Fame linebacker Bobby Bell told Bob Carroll for Football When the Grass Was Real, "He had a way with players. He was very personal with them, very concerned about them. He's always been that way. Even today, he contacts all the players." Receiver Otis Taylor added to Carroll, "We called him 'The Mentor.' He laid down the rules, but in a friendly way. Things were going to get done his way.... Sometimes during practice you'd wonder if the man had a heart. Then you'd be coming in and he'd have the clubhouse man pick up some barbecue — Kansas City's a great barbecue town — and two or three kegs of beer. Three or four hundred dollars' worth. And he'd say, 'Hey, guys, it's on me.' You'd want to kill him one minute, and then you'd say, well, the guy's all right." Sadly though, the team got old, and the great veterans were not adequately replaced in a timely manner. Hank's drafts were terrible and he made some awful trades, including Curley Culp and a number one pick for John Matuszak and then another number one pick for the forgettable George Seals. Following years of decline, Stram was fired after a 5–9 season in 1974.

Hank went into broadcasting for a year before returning to the NFL in 1976 as the coach of the dysfunctional New Orleans Saints. However, he was given just two years to turn the team around and then was fired in 1978. His Saints were the first team to lose to the second-year Tampa Bay Bucs, and the embarrassed coach reportedly burned the tape of that game. With his coaching career concluded, Stram went on to have a long successful broadcasting career on both television and radio. He was both entertaining and informative and continued in this role through Super Bowl XXX following the 1995 season.

Hank once said, "You can't win unless you have good people with great attitude. They are the ones who won the games. I didn't win any games. You never saw a coach make a tackle anywhere. My philosophy was to get the best players and then try to do something new with them." Those inventive schemes that Stram devised allowed his colorful teams to twice lead the league in scoring and seven times finish in the top three, while four times allowing the fewest points and seven times finishing in the top three in that area. He was elected to the Pro Football Hall of Fame in 2003, two years before his death due to complications from diabetes.

STUDESVILLE, ERIC 5/29/1967– Wisconsin-Whitewater. DB; did not play professionally. *Apprenticeship:* College asst.—6 years; pro asst.—14 years. *Roots:* Dave Wannstedt, Dick Jauron, Jim Fassel, Mike Mularkey, Perry Fewell (i), Josh McDaniels. *Branches:* None. *Coordinators/Key Assistants:* None.

Hall of Fame Players: None. *Primary Quarterbacks:* Tim Tebow. *Record:* **Interim Coach.**

Eric Studesville was born in Madison, Wisconsin, and played defensive back for the University of Wisconsin at Whitewater, a small branch campus of the state school. He began his coaching career as a graduate assistant at the University of Arizona in 1991. He moved on to North Carolina in 1992, Wingate in 1994 and Kent State from 1995 to 1996. During the summer of 1996, Eric spent training camp with the Bears as part of the team's minority internship program. Chicago then hired Studesville as a quality control coach under Dave Wannstedt in 1997.

Wannstedt was fired in 1999, but Eric remained on the staff under Dick Jauron as running backs coach. In 2001, he moved on to the Giants as the running backs coach under Jim Fassel. When Fassel was dismissed three years later, Studesville took over as Mike Mularkey's running backs coach in Buffalo. Mularkey resigned in 2006, but was replaced by Dick Jauron and Studesville stayed on staff. After Jauron was fired during the 2009 season, Eric was hired as Josh McDaniels' running backs coach in Denver in 2010 and was promoted to interim head coach 12 games into the season. In his four-game trial, Studesville gave Tim Tebow his first chance to play and the team won one of four games. The Broncos brought in John Fox as head coach in 2011, but retained Studesville in his familiar role tutoring the running backs.

STUDLEY, CHARLES B. (CHUCK) 1/17/1929– Illinois. G; did not play professionally. *Apprenticeship:* College coach —12 years (7 as head coach); pro asst.— 15 years. *Roots:* Paul Brown, Bill Johnson, Homer Rice, Bill Walsh, Ed Biles. *Branches:* None. *Coordinators/Key Assistants:* None. *Hall of Fame Players:* Elvin Bethea, Earl Campbell, Dave Casper, Bruce Matthews, Mike Munchak. *Primary Quarterbacks:* Oliver Luck. *Record:* **Interim Coach.**

Chuck Studley was born in Maywood, Illinois, and captained the 1952 Illinois Rose bowl team as a guard. After three years coaching high school football, Chuck returned to his alma mater as an assistant coach in 1955. One of his key projects in Champaign was

Studesville, Eric									
Year	Team	Games	Wins	Losses	Ties	%	P Wins	P Losses	P %
2010	Broncos	4	1	3	0	.250	0	0	.000
1 year		4	1	3	0	.250	0	0	.000

Studley, Charles B. (Chuck)									
Year	Team	Games	Wins	Losses	Ties	%	P Wins	P Losses	P %
1983	Oilers (Titans)	10	2	8	0	.200	0	0	.000
1 year		10	2	8	0	.200	0	0	.000

working with Ray Nitschke at linebacker and that created a long lasting legacy for Studley.

Chuck spent five years coaching at Illinois before earning his first head coaching assignment at Massachusetts in 1960. After leading the team to a 7–2 record that year, Studley took over the program at the University of Cincinnati in 1961. From 1961 to 1966, Chuck compiled a 27–33 record with the Bearcats and was dismissed. He did some scouting for the Cowboys, Rams and 49ers from 1967 to 1968 and then joined Paul Brown's Bengals' staff in 1969 as the defensive line coach.

During the 1970s, Studley became very friendly with offensive assistant Bill Walsh in Cincinnati and the two coaches would often ride to work together. When Walsh was named head coach in San Francisco in 1979, he hired Chuck as his defensive coordinator. Three years later, the 49ers were in the Super Bowl where they defeated their former team, the Bengals. The 49ers stumbled badly in the 1982 strike season, and Walsh considered quitting. Studley then jumped to Houston as the Oilers' defensive coordinator. One version of the story is that Walsh deliberately feinted leaving to Studley so that Chuck would leave without Walsh having to fire him because Bill had lost faith in his defensive coach.

Unfortunately, Houston's Ed Biles was struggling as he entered his third year as head coach. The team dropped the last seven games of 1982 and then started 1983 by losing its first six. Biles was then replaced by Studley who greeted the announcement by saying, "I didn't look up interim, but I think it means temporary. If we continue to play inconsistently, its adios at the end of the season." Houston dropped four more games before winning one for Chuck who noted, "It's only one win, it isn't redemption." Studley could do little with the veteran club and had a rancorous conflict with runner Earl Campbell. After posting a 2–8 record with rag-armed quarterbacks Oliver Luck and Gifford Nielsen, Chuck was dismissed.

Getting fired by the Oilers was a blessing in that Studley landed the job of defensive coordinator in Miami in 1984 and went to the Super Bowl that year where the opponent was Bill Walsh's 49ers. Chuck downplayed the possible advantage of knowing his opponent's moves by telling the Los Angeles Times,

"People seem to think that because Bill and I spent 11 seasons together, it gives me some kind of inside track. But the most predictable thing about Bill Walsh is his unpredictability." The 49ers won that game easily and over the next two years it became clear that Miami's defense could not keep pace with its offense. After the club dropped to 26th in points allowed in 1986, Chuck was demoted to linebackers coach. Two years later, he left Miami to finish his NFL coaching career as the Bengals' defensive line coach from 1989 to 1991. Ten years into his retirement, Studley made a brief return to coaching in 2002 when he helped out at a Cincinnati high school. That year, he summed up the great coaches with whom he had worked to the Cincinnati Post, "I learned more technical football from Bill Walsh than anybody else. He forced me to think. Don Shula was a tough, demanding disciplinarian. Paul [Brown] was at the end of his career and he didn't really coach that much, but he had great coaches with him." One of whom was Chuck Studley.

STYDAHAR, JOSEPH L. (JOE) 3/16/1912–3/23/1977. Pittsburgh and West Virginia. Played T for the Bears from 1936 to 1942 and 1945–1946. *Apprenticeship*: Pro asst.— 3 years. *Roots*: Bob Snyder, Clark Shaughnessy. *Branches*: Hampton Pool, Ray Richards, Red Hickey. *Coordinators/Key Assistants*: For the Rams, Hampton Pool handled the offense and defense; for the Cardinals, Ray Richards coached the line and was his key lieutenant. *Hall of Fame Players*: Tom Fears, Elroy Hirsch, Night Train Lane, Ollie Matson, Andy Robustelli, Charlie Trippi, Norm Van Brocklin, Bob Waterfield. *Primary Quarterbacks*: Norm Van Brocklin, Bob Waterfield, Lamar McHan. *Record*: **Hall of Fame Player**; NFL Championship 1951. *Tendencies*: • His teams scored 25.3 points and allowed 26.3 per game • His teams ran 48.2% of the time, which was 90% of the league average • Six starting quarterbacks in five years; 73% of starts to primary quarterbacks • 31 rookie starters in five years • Winning Full Seasons to Losing Full Seasons: 2:2.

In Stuart Leuthner's *Iron Men*, Pat Summerall described Joe Stydahar, his coach with the Chicago Cardinals, as the type of man's man "who could smoke a cigar, chew tobacco and drink whiskey at the same

Stydahar, Joseph L. (Joe)

Year	Team	Games	Wins	Losses	Ties	%	P Wins	P Losses	P %
1950	Rams	12	9	3	0	.750	1	1	.500
1951	Rams	12	8	4	0	.667	1	0	1.000
1952	Rams	1	0	1	0	.000	0	0	.000
1953	Cardinals	12	1	10	1	.125	0	0	.000
1954	Cardinals	12	2	10	0	.167	0	0	.000
5 years		49	20	28	1	.418	2	1	.667

time." Stydahar was a large man for his playing time at 6'4" and 260-pounds and was known as Jumbo Joe. The son of a coal miner, Stydahar was born in Kaylor, Pennsylvania, but grew up in Shinnston, West Virginia. In 1932, he started his college career at Pitt, but was poached by West Virginia coach Greasy Neale at the beginning of his freshman year. Joe played tackle for the Mountaineers from 1933 to 1935 and then was the first lineman ever drafted when the Bears selected him in the first round of the initial NFL draft in 1936.

With Chicago, Stydahar was a four-time All-Pro whose career was interrupted by two years of naval service from 1943 to 1944. When he returned to the Bears in 1945, he was 33 years old and starting to slip; he retired after one last championship in 1946. The next season, Joe joined the Rams to coach the line for head coach Bob Snyder, a former Bear teammate. Snyder brought in another former Bear associate in 1948, Clark Shaughnessy, and ended up losing his job to Shaughnessy during training camp. Stydahar coached the line for two years under the cantankerous Shaughnessy and then was promoted to head coach in a surprise move in 1950. Shaughnessy was shocked and commented that with Stydahar coaching the Rams, "I could take any high school team in the country and beat them."

For his part, Joe had planned on leaving the Rams to coach the line in Green Bay because, "Mr. Shaughnessy ran the Rams like a one-man show. He wouldn't let anybody do anything. I didn't learn a thing and I wanted to move." Stydahar also asserted that he would be installing a Bear offense, "The primary principle of Halas' offense is that the running attack must go." As such, he brought in another former Bear, Hampton Pool, to serve as the team's chief strategist on both offense and defense. Linebacker Don Paul recalled to Mickey Herskowitz in *The Golden Age of Pro Football* that while Pool sculpted the game plans the head coach attended to other responsibilities, "Joe was a big, happy guy, a nice guy. He was good with the press."

Of course, Joe could be a temperamental guy as well. After one preseason game he fined 28 of his players a total of $7,900, a huge amount in those days. And then he rescinded the fines right before the start of the season. The Rams had two Hall of Fame quarterbacks at that time in Bob Waterfield and Norm Van Brocklin. Stydahar's solution was to alternate the two by quarter, an arrangement that both proud signal callers resented, but the team was a powerhouse—particularly on offense. While the Rams did have the strong running attack that Joe had called for originally, they were more noted for their revolutionary three-receiver Pro Set passing offense that enabled them to lead the league in scoring and reach the title game in both 1950 and 1951. In 1951, Los Angeles won the championship when Norm Van Brocklin, held out of

the first three quarters of the title game against Cleveland because he was in Stydahar's dog house, entered the game in the fourth quarter and threw a 73-yard touchdown pass to win it.

All the while, though, Joe grew to distrust his assistant coach Pool and came to believe that Pool was trying to undermine him with ownership. In fact, Stydahar checked into the Scripps Clinic in La Jolla after the championship and was found to be suffering from "marked mental tension." The perceived dissension continued into 1952 when Joe essentially told owner Dan Reeves it was either him or Pool. After losing the season opener to the Browns, Stydahar claimed he was fired, while Reeves said that the coach resigned. In either case, Pool replaced him as the Rams head coach. Years later, Joe ruefully observed, "I used my pride instead of my mind. I thought I was so big I couldn't be replaced. Nobody's that big—not in football, not in anything."

Stydahar caught on as former teammate Gene Ronzani's line coach in Green Bay for the rest of the 1952 season and then was named head coach of the Cardinals in 1953. After winning just three games in two years, Joe was dismissed in 1955 and retired from football. Aside from a two-year stint as the Bears defensive line coach from 1963 to 1964, Stydahar spent the rest of his life working for a container company in the Chicago area. He made the news in 1957 when he saved a family of four from a burning building. Joe was elected to the Hall of Fame in 1967 and died ten years after that. George Halas remembered him as, "a man of outstanding character and loyalty."

SUTHERLAND, JOHN B. (JOCK) 3/21/1889–4/11/1948. Pittsburgh. G; did not play professionally. *Apprenticeship:* College head coach—20 years. *Roots:* None. *Branches:* Mike Getto, John Michelosen, Joe Kuharich, Mike Nixon. *Coordinators/Key Assistants:* For the Dodgers, Mike Getto coached the line, while John Michelosen coached the backs; for the Steelers, Joe Kuharich then Frank Walton coached the line, while Michelosen and Mike Nixon handled the backs, and Frank Souchak then Joe Skladany coached the ends. *Hall of Fame Players:* Bill Dudley, Bruiser Kinard, Ace Parker. *Primary Quarterbacks:* None. *Tendencies:*
• His teams scored 16 points and allowed 13.8 per game
• His teams ran 69.9% of the time, which was 111% of the league average • 19 rookie starters in four years
• Winning Full Seasons to Losing Full Seasons: 3:0.

Ramrod straight Scotsman Jock Sutherland was a cold, dour lifelong bachelor, yet one of the greatest football coaches of all time. He won more than 80% of his games in college and was elected to the College Football Hall of Fame in 1951. He once forcefully summarized his outlook by saying, "The only permanent satisfaction is to attain your objective by facing difficulty squarely and overpowering it." Born in poverty in the town of Coupar Angus in Scotland, Sutherland emigrated to the United States in his teens. He worked his way through the Oberlin Academy and then enrolled at the University of Pittsburgh's Dentistry School in 1914.

It was at Pitt that Jock first saw the game of American football, and he played guard for the Panthers from 1915 to 1917. There he learned the single wing attack from the man who invented it, Glenn "Pop" Warner. In those three years, Pitt did not lose a game and won national championships in 1915 and 1916. Sutherland became a U.S. citizen in 1917 and served in the military in 1918 during World War I.

The following year, Jock played a few games for the professional Massillon Tigers and also began his coaching career at Lafayette. In five years, he posted a 33–8–2 record at that Pennsylvania school. When Warner left Pittsburgh for Stanford in 1924, Sutherland was the natural replacement and outdid his mentor over the next 15 years. From 1924 to 1938, Jock's Panthers compiled a 111–20–12 record with 79 shutouts. The school went to four Rose Bowls and won national championships in 1929, 1931, 1936 and 1937. Even Warner was impressed, noting, "Jock put more power and punch into the single wing than any other coach." His brutal ground attack became known as the "Sutherland Scythe" for the way it cut through defenses, and his blocking schemes were later adapted by Vince Lombardi in designing the famous Green Bay Packers' Power Sweep. Like Lombardi, Sutherland emphasized blocking and tackling fundamentals and precise execution, but Jock lacked Vince's warmth in his dealings with his players.

Pitt's administration decided to deemphasize football at the school in 1939, and Sutherland resigned in protest. Art Rooney tried to hire him to coach the Pirates, as the Steelers were then known, but was not able to persuade the coach to sign. Jock did join the NFL in 1940, but in Brooklyn, where he transformed a 4–6–1 Dodgers' team to an 8–3 contender in one year. In his second season, Sutherland led the Dodgers to a 7–4 record and another second place finish in the East. When War came though, Sutherland's love of country trumped his devotion to football. Jock convinced the Navy to accept the 53-year-old coach into the service. Sutherland attained the rank of Lieutenant Commander and served from 1942 to 1945.

Within weeks of his discharge from the Navy, Sutherland signed a five-year contract to coach the Steelers. Co-owner Bert Bell crowed, "He's the man we've been wanting right along. We are confident he'll produce a winning team." That he did, turning the 2–8 Steelers into a 5–5–1 team in 1946 and an 8–4 contender in 1947. He did so by driving his team with little relief. In training camp he put oatmeal in the water to discourage water consumption, practiced for five hours a day and scrimmaged in pads every day. As a result, only five Steelers weighed more than 210 pounds for the 1946 season.

Sutherland clashed regularly with independent-minded star tailback Bill Dudley. Dudley later told Richard Whittingham for *What a Game They Played*, "Sutherland was the best coach I ever played for. He knew what it took to win; he knew how to get the job done. Despite the fact that we didn't get along, he was the person, I believe, who made me the league's most valuable player that year, looking at it in retrospect. He got me to go out and play some intense football." After that first year, however, Dudley quit football, unwilling to endure any more of his style of coaching. Echoing that sentiment, former Brooklyn Dodger wingback Ralph Kercheval recalled to Roger Godin in *The Brooklyn Football Dodgers*, "He enjoyed this head knocking business that I thought was a little bit ridiculous."

Sutherland's 1947 Steelers tied the Eagles for the Eastern crown but then went on strike in the week before the playoff game because they wanted to be paid for the extra week of practice. Jock was no help in smoothing over this difficulty, and the team lost to Philadelphia 21–0. It was the last game Jock would ever coach. The next spring Sutherland was found wandering in a Kentucky field, able only to say, "I am Jock Sutherland." He was taken to a Pittsburgh hospital and died four days later from a brain tumor. Eight Steelers (Chuck Cherundolo, Steve Lach, Charley Mehelic, Ralph Calcagni, Val Jansante, Jack Wylie, Red Moore and Frank Sinkovitz) served as his pallbearers.

Sutherland, John B. (Jock)									
Year	Team	Games	Wins	Losses	Ties	%	P Wins	P Losses	P %
1940	Dodgers (defunct)	11	8	3	0	.727	0	0	.000
1941	Dodgers (defunct)	11	7	4	0	.636	0	0	.000
1946	Steelers	11	5	5	1	.500	0	0	.000
1947	Steelers	12	8	4	0	.667	0	1	.000
4 years		45	28	16	1	.633	0	1	.000

SVARE, HARLAND J. 11/15/1930– Washington State. Played LB for the Rams in 1953 and the Giants from 1954 to 1960. *Apprenticeship:* Pro asst.— 3 years. *Roots:* Jim Lee Howell, Allie Sherman, Bob Waterfield. *Branches:* Ron Waller (i), Forrest Gregg, Jack Patera. *Coordinators/Key Assistants:* For the Rams, Don Heinrich then Vic Schwenk were the key offensive coaches, while Svare ran his own defense; for the Chargers, Bob Schnelker ran the offense, while Svare handled his own defense. *Hall of Fame Players:* Dan Fouts, Deacon Jones, John Mackey, Ollie Matson, Tommy McDonald, Merlin Olsen, Les Richter, John Unitas. *Primary Quarterbacks:* Roman Gabriel, Bill Munson, John Hadl. *Tendencies:* • His teams scored 17.8 points and allowed 24.7 per game • His teams ran 48.9% of the time, which was 93% of the league average • Six starting quarterbacks in seven years; 79% of starts to primary quarterbacks • 23 rookie starters in seven years • Winning Full Seasons to Losing Full Seasons: 0:4.

Born in Clarkfield, Minnesota, Harland Svare played for Washington State from 1950 to 1952 and was a 17th round draft pick of the Los Angeles Rams in 1953. After just one year in Los Angeles, though, the linebacker was traded to the New York Giants where he became a fixture on the renowned defense developed by assistant coach Tom Landry. Svare was such a team leader that when Landry left to become head coach in Dallas in 1960, Harland assumed his defensive coaching responsibilities in New York. Svare continued playing through the 1960 season and then devoted 1961 solely to being an assistant coach.

Following a series of conflicts with Giants' head coach Allie Sherman, Harland returned to the Rams in 1962 as Bob Waterfield's defensive coach. After the team won just one of its first eight games that year, Waterfield quit and Svare was elevated to head coach — then the youngest in league history, just one month shy of his 32nd birthday. Harland later noted to the *New York Times* that Waterfield told him at the time, "Yeah, I'm leaving. I'm going hunting, and if you had any sense, you'd leave, too, and go hunting with me." Waterfield was actually giving him good advice. In three and a half years with the Rams, the team was at the bottom of the league in both offense and defense each year. Three years in a row, Los An-geles drafted a quarterback with its first pick, but Svare couldn't commit to Roman Gabriel or Bill Munson or Terry Baker. In retrospect, he told the *Los Angeles Times*, "I hadn't had enough experience [leading] people. I was immature. I was inconsistent, too inconsistent."

Svare was fired in 1966 and stayed out of football that year. He returned to the game as the Giants' defensive coach again in 1967, but soon found that he still couldn't get along with Allie Sherman. Harland lasted two years in New York until leaving in 1969 to reunite with former Giants' assistant Vince Lombardi in Washington. Svare continued to coach the defense after Lombardi died in 1970 and then was named general manager of the Chargers in 1971.

With four games to go in 1971, Svare fired legendary coach Sid Gillman and returned to the sideline himself. In San Diego, Harland attempted to follow the pattern of his successor with the Rams, George Allen, by trading away draft picks for veterans, but found that to be a tricky proposition. Although he obtained fading stars Deacon Jones, John Mackey, Dave Costa, Cid Edwards, Lionel Aldridge, Tim Rossovich, Duane Thomas and ultimately Johnny Unitas, the club did not improve. There was also dissension between the coaches and the players and, most significantly, rampant drug use among the players. Svare lost control of the Chargers and eventually replaced himself as head coach with assistant Ron Waller in 1973. He then replaced Waller with Tommy Prothro in 1974. That year, Harland was fined $40,000 by the league for the team's violations of the NFL's drug policy. Svare admitted, "I was not aware of the severity of the problem. I really didn't believe it, but I was responsible. I accept the discipline."

Prothro worked to clean up the mess, and Svare was fired at the end of the 1975 season. Harland blamed his demise in San Diego on a book due to come out that year called *The Nightmare Season* written by Dr. Arnold Mandell that detailed heavy use of amphetamines by San Diego's players. Svare never worked in the NFL again. He later ran a health clinic with a program based on proper posture and muscle development.

Svare, Harland J.									
Year	Team	Games	Wins	Losses	Ties	%	P Wins	P Losses	P %
1962	Rams	6	0	5	1	.083	0	0	.000
1963	Rams	14	5	9	0	.357	0	0	.000
1964	Rams	14	5	7	2	.429	0	0	.000
1965	Rams	14	4	10	0	.286	0	0	.000
1971	Chargers	4	2	2	0	.500	0	0	.000
1972	Chargers	14	4	9	1	.321	0	0	.000
1973	Chargers	8	1	6	1	.188	0	0	.000
7 years		74	21	48	5	.318	0	0	.000

SWITZER, BARRY 10/5/1937– Arkansas. C/LB; did not play professionally. *Apprenticeship:* College coach — 28 years (16 as head coach). *Roots:* None. *Branches:* Dave Campo, Butch Davis, Jim Bates (i). *Coordinators/Key Assistants*: Ernie Zampese ran the offense, while Butch Davis then Dave Campo handled the defense. *Hall of Fame Players:* Troy Aikman, Michael Irvin, Deion Sanders, Emmitt Smith. *Primary Quarterbacks:* Troy Aikman. *Record:* **Super Bowl Championship 1995**. *Tendencies:* • His teams scored 22.5 points and allowed 17.2 per game • His teams ran 48.3% of the time, which was 110% of the league average • Four starting quarterbacks in four years; 95% of starts to primary quarterback • Eight rookie starters in four years • Winning Full Seasons to Losing Full Seasons: 3:1.

Barry Switzer called his autobiography, *Bootlegger's Boy*, and the native of Crossett, Arkansas, rose from humble and somewhat seedy origins to become one of the greatest college coaches of all time. His legacy as an NFL coach is a bit more debatable.

Switzer played center and linebacker at Arkansas from 1957 to 1959 and then returned to his alma mater as an assistant coach on Frank Broyles staff from 1961 to 1965. In Fayetteville, he coached future Cowboys' owner Jerry Jones and future Cowboys' coach Jimmy Johnson, both members of the 1964 national championship team. Barry moved on to Oklahoma in 1966 to join a fellow Razorback assistant Jim Mackenzie who was named head coach that year. Sadly, Mackenzie died after just one year and was replaced by Chuck Fairbanks in 1967, but Switzer stayed on staff as a key offensive coach. By 1970 with the Sooners struggling with the Veer offense, Switzer began advocating a switch to the Wishbone attack utilized by Texas. While the team initially struggled with the change, a year later they were a Wishbone powerhouse. Back-to-back 11–1 seasons took Fairbanks to the pros, and Switzer was named his replacement in 1973.

Over the next 16 years, Switzer's Sooners posted a 157–29–4 record and won national championships in 1974, 1975 and 1985. Oklahoma was known for attracting top talent and running up big scores every Saturday. Barry was popular with his players, particularly the black players who felt a special kinship with this profane country boy from the wrong side of the tracks. He gave them wide leeway, too much leeway as it turned out after several players were implicated in felonies and the NCAA eventually slapped the Sooners with three years' probation in 1989 soon after Switzer resigned as head coach.

Switzer got out of coaching and kept busy with various business activities until Jones and Johnson had their famous falling out in the aftermath of winning consecutive Super Bowls in Dallas. When those two agreed to part company, Jones immediately hired Switzer as the Cowboys' coach in 1994. In some ways, Barry was the perfect coach to step into this situation. His ego was under control; he neither tried to pass himself off as a master strategist, nor tried to make any major changes to the team's style of play while his easy-going manner was a relief to the players after five years under the whip of Johnson. Tight end Jay Novacek told Jeff Pearlman for *Boys Will Be Boys*, "He changed the pace when the pace needed to be adjusted." Receiver Michael Irvin told *Sports Illustrated* in the wake of the Cowboys Super Bowl win in January 1996, "Sometimes doing nothing is the right thing to do. When you walk into a situation and everything's great, it shows more power and more intelligence to do nothing. Most coaches would have made you feel their power. They would have made a move just to make a move and would have screwed up everything."

That 1995 season was the same year that Switzer was excoriated by the national media for twice calling the same unsuccessful dive play on a fourth-and-one at his own 29 with two minutes to play in a game against the rival Eagles. The Super Bowl win over the Steelers washed away the stench of that call, but things began to fall apart in 1996. Switzer's lax style allowed the team to drift completely out of control as is colorfully documented in Pearlman's book. In 1997, even Barry added to the negative headlines by getting stopped at the airport with a gun in his luggage. The team built by Johnson was allowed to completely deteriorate under Switzer's watch in much the same way that the Oklahoma Sooners did. Years later, Barry pled ignorance, "Coaches pay a tremendous price for the actions of their athletes. We are held accountable for their actions. That's what the media and administration do. Is it fair? You judge it."

Switzer, Barry									
Year	Team	Games	Wins	Losses	Ties	%	P Wins	P Losses	P %
1994	Cowboys	16	12	4	0	.750	1	1	.500
1995	Cowboys	16	12	4	0	.750	3	0	1.000
1996	Cowboys	16	10	6	0	.625	1	1	.500
1997	Cowboys	16	6	10	0	.375	0	0	.000
4 years		64	40	24	0	.625	5	2	.714

Taylor, Hugh W. (Bones) 7/6/1923–11/1/1992. Northeast Louisiana; Tulane; Oklahoma City College. Played E for the Redskins from 1947 to 1954. *Apprenticeship:* College coach — 4 years (2 as head coach); pro asst.— 5 years. *Roots:* Sammy Baugh, Sid Gillman. *Branches:* None. *Coordinators/Key Assistants:* Former Oiler head coaches Sammy Baugh and Lou Rymkus coached the offense, while Walt Schlinkman handled the defense. *Hall of Fame Players:* George Blanda. *Primary Quarterbacks:* George Blanda. *Tendencies:* • His team scored 21.3 points and allowed 30.6 per game • His team ran 35.8% of the time, which was 79% of the league average • Two starting quarterbacks in one year; 86% of starts to primary quarterback • Two rookie starters in one year • Winning Full Seasons to Losing Full Seasons: 0:1.

At 6' 4" and 194 pounds, Bones Taylor was built like a more recent deep threat receiver — Randy Moss. In his eight years with the Redskins, Taylor only caught 272 passes, but he averaged 19.4 yards per catch and scored 58 touchdowns as Sammy Baugh's favorite target at the end of the Hall of Fame quarterback's career.

Bones was born in Wynne, Arkansas, and had a nomadic college tenure. He began at Northeast Louisiana from 1941 to 1942 and then transferred to Tulane in 1943. However, after a two-year stint in the Navy, Taylor finished his college years at Oklahoma City College in 1946. He made the Redskins as an undrafted free agent in 1947 and played in Washington through the 1954 season. He completed his playing career with one season in Ottawa playing Canadian football.

Taylor went directly into coaching, joining the staff at Florida State in 1956 before taking the head coaching position at Arkansas State in 1958. After compiling a modest 7–11 record in two years there, Bones reunited with his old friend and teammate, Baugh, who had been named the first head coach of the New York Titans in the new American Football League in 1960. Taylor coached the Titan ends for two years under Baugh and one under his successor Bulldog Turner before moving on to Sid Gillman's Chargers' staff in 1963. Bones later explained, "I went to San Diego for one reason. Sid Gillman is the master of team organization — the best in the business."

The Chargers won the AFL title that year, but Taylor moved on to Houston in 1964 when Sammy Baugh took over as the Oilers' head coach. One year later, Baugh was replaced by Taylor as head coach, and accepted the demotion to assistant coach on Bones' staff along with another former Oilers' head coach, Lou Rymkus. Unfortunately, Taylor was no more successful in Houston in 1965 than Baugh had been in 1964. The Oiler defense was terrible, and Bones was feuding with his 37-year-old quarterback George Blanda who he found to be fading, selfish and unwilling to "grow old gracefully." The coach announced, "I learned one thing in my first year as a head coach. You can't let a player dictate to you. Lou Saban didn't take it from Cookie Gilchrist in Buffalo. Cookie was gone as soon as the season was over. I don't plan on taking it from George Blanda." Taylor issued an ultimatum to club owner Bud Adams that the quarterback or the coach had to go. Blanda laughed when he heard about that, telling the press, "I guess it will be him because I have a no-trade clause." Four days later, Bones was fired.

Taylor subsequently coached the Steelers' receivers from 1966 to 1968 and served as the head coach of the minor league Spokane Shockers in 1969, posting a 5–7 mark. Bones retired from coaching and later worked in the school system of his hometown of Wynne for several years.

Thomas, Emmitt E. 6/3/1943– Bishop. Played DB for the Chiefs from 1966 to 1978. *Apprenticeship:* College asst.— 2 years; pro asst.— 27 years. *Roots:* Joe Gibbs, Richie Petitbon, Norv Turner, Denny Green, Ray Rhodes, Dan Reeves, Jim Mora, Jr., Bobby Petrino. *Branches:* Hue Jackson. *Coordinators/Key Assistants:* None. *Hall of Fame Players:* None. *Primary Quarterbacks:* Chris Redman. *Record:* **Hall of Fame Player; Interim Coach.**

Born in Angleton, Texas, Emmitt Thomas played quarterback and wide receiver at Bishop College, a black school in Dallas. Undrafted by either league, Thomas made the Chiefs as a defensive back in 1966.

Taylor, Hugh W. (Bones)									
Year	Team	Games	Wins	Losses	Ties	%	P Wins	P Losses	P %
1965	Oilers (Titans)	14	4	10	0	.286	0	0	.000
1 year		14	4	10	0	.286	0	0	.000

Thomas, Emmitt E.									
Year	Team	Games	Wins	Losses	Ties	%	P Wins	P Losses	P %
2007	Falcons	3	1	2	0	.333	0	0	.000
1 year		3	1	2	0	.333	0	0	.000

He was a four-time All-Pro and intercepted 58 passes for Kansas City from 1966 to 1978.

Upon his retirement, Thomas went right into coaching as an assistant at Central Missouri State from 1979 to 1980. In 1981, he joined Jim Hanifan's staff in St. Louis and coached for the Cardinals through 1985. Joe Gibbs then brought Emmitt to Washington to coach wide receivers in 1986 and eventually switched him to the other side of the ball to coach the defensive backs.

Emmitt left Washington in 1995 to become the Eagles' defensive coordinator under new coach Ray Rhodes. Thomas' defenses relied heavily on blitzing and bump-and-run coverage. They were so effective that he was interviewed for the Giants and Rams head coaching positions in 1997. When Rhodes moved on to Green Bay in 1999, Emmitt came with him. With the Packers, Rhodes, Thomas and offensive coordinator Sherman Lewis marked the first instance in NFL history of a team having African Americans at head coach and both coordinator positions.

Rhodes was fired in 2000, but Emmitt and Sherman Lewis stayed in the Central Division, taking the same positions with Dennis Green in Minnesota. After Green was fired, Thomas took the assistant head coach/defensive backs coaching job with Dan Reeves in Atlanta in 2002. He stayed on under Jim Mora, Jr., and then Bobby Petrino. When Petrino bugged out before the end of his first season of 2007, Emmitt was given his only chance to be a head coach — for three games with a demoralized team. In 2008, new head coach Mike Smith retained Thomas on staff. Two years later, Emmitt returned to the Chiefs at long last. He was elected to the Hall of Fame in 2008, thirty years after he retired from playing. Thomas' son Derek is the head basketball coach at Western Illinois.

THOMAS, JOSEPH 3/18/1921–2/11/1983. Ohio Northern. E; did not play professionally. *Apprenticeship:* College asst.— 6 years; pro asst.— 3 years; CFL asst.— 3 years. *Roots:* Sid Gilman, Weeb Ewbank. *Branches:* Pete McCulley (i). *Coordinators/Key Assistants:* Pete McCulley was the key offensive coach. *Hall of Fame Players:* None. *Primary Quarterbacks:* Bert Jones. *Record:* **Interim Coach.**

Hailing from Warren, Ohio, Joe Thomas originally hoped to play professional baseball. However, after playing end on the football team and catcher on the baseball team at Ohio Northern from 1940 to 1942, Joe went into the Navy. He was stationed at the Great Lakes Naval Station for the next three years and

felt he was too old to start in the low minors when he was discharged from the service.

Thomas coached high school football in 1946 and 1947 and then was hired as an assistant at Depauw in 1948. Four years later, he moved on to Indiana. Two years after that, Weeb Ewbank hired Joe as the Colts' defensive coach in 1954. Thomas then joined Sid Gillman's first Rams' staff in the same capacity in 1955. Following two years in Los Angeles, Joe was hired by former Rams' coach Hampton Pool as the defensive coach of the Toronto Argonauts in Canada in 1957.

In those days, part of the duties of assistant coaches was scouting players. Thomas demonstrated such an affinity for finding talent that he was the first employee hired by the expansion Minnesota Vikings in 1960. Joe thought he had a chance to be named their first head coach, but that prize went to Norm Van Brocklin in 1961. Instead, Thomas was the team's player personnel director through 1965 season, accumulating a lot of talent that Bud Grant would eventually utilize when he became the team's second coach in 1967.

Joe set out building a second expansion team in 1966 — the Miami Dolphins — and supplemented his drafting of such stars as Larry Csonka and Bob Griese by trading for such Hall of Famers as Larry Little, Nick Buoniconti and Paul Warfield. It wasn't until initial coach George Wilson was replaced by Don Shula in 1970, though, that the talent began to shine.

Thomas left Miami to become the general manager of the Colts in February 1972, right before the Dolphins undefeated season. He had brokered the deal in which Robert Irsay bought the Rams and then traded the franchise to Carroll Rosenbloom for the Colts franchise and ended up running the team. After a mediocre first season in Baltimore, Thomas decided it was time to blow up the veteran club in 1973 and made eight trades in 11 days, dumping the aging Colts' stars. Joe later told the *New York Times,* "But somebody had to do the dirty work and tell the players they were through with pro football. I had to do that with John Unitas."

In that first season, Thomas had ordered Coach Don McCafferty to bench Unitas and play younger backup Marty Domres. When McCafferty refused, Joe replaced him with line coach John Sandusky who benched Unitas. At year's end, he replaced Sandusky with Miami assistant Howard Schnellenberger. He then traded Unitas and drafted Bert Jones. Owner Irsay grew impatient with Schnellenberger's measured

Thomas, Joseph									
Year	Team	Games	Wins	Losses	Ties	%	P Wins	P Losses	P %
1974	Colts	11	2	9	0	.182	0	0	.000
1 year		11	2	9	0	.182	0	0	.000

development of Jones, went on the field in week three and demanded the coach to switch from Domres to Jones. Schnellenberger cursed out his boss who then left the field and after the game told his GM that he was the new coach. Bert Jones told Stephen Norwood for *Real Football*, "That was total disarray. Half the coaching staff quit. I love Joe, and he had a great ability to find a ballplayer. But he wasn't a coach."

Thomas never wanted that job and resigned as head coach in December, saying, "The main thing is that no man can do a good job of handling both full-time jobs of head coach and general manager. One or both has to suffer." All his tumultuous rebuilding began to come to fruition when Ted Marchibroda was hired as head coach in 1975. Thomas' revamped Baltimore Colts won three straight division titles, but he was fired before the final one because he became the fall guy in an ugly power struggle involving Irsay, himself and Marchibroda.

Soon after, Joe was hired as general manager of the 49ers in 1977 by Eddie DeBartolo, the new owner in San Francisco. By this point, Thomas' ego had gotten so large that he thought of himself as an infallible master builder of NFL teams. Joe was an utter cataclysm for the 49ers, though. Years earlier, he had boasted to *Sports Illustrated*, "It's embarrassing, but I guess I never made a bad trade." He clearly invalidated that doubtful claim in San Francisco by acquiring a washed up O.J. Simpson for five draft picks — a 1, two 2's, a 3 and a 4. From the start, Thomas clashed with incumbent coach Monte Clark, a former Dolphins' assistant who refused to give up the personnel powers in his contract. Joe fired Clark and replaced him with Ken Meyer in 1977. In 1978, he replaced Meyer with Pete McCulley who he then fired in midseason and replaced with Fred O'Connor. At the end of 1978, DeBartolo fired both coach and GM and brought in Bill Walsh to resuscitate the franchise.

Thomas unsuccessfully tried to assemble a group to obtain a new NFL franchise over the next two years and then was rehired in 1981 by Miami as a vice president in charge of player contracts. Joe died suddenly of a heart attack in 1983 at the age of 61.

TICE, MICHAEL P. (MIKE) 2/2/1959– Maryland. Played TE for the Seahawks and Vikings from 1981 to

1993 and in 1995. *Apprenticeship:* Pro asst.— 6 years. *Roots:* Denny Green. *Branches:* Scott Linehan. *Coordinators/Key Assistants*: Scott Linehan then Steve Loney ran the offense, while Willie Shaw then George Leary then Ted Cottrell handled the defense. *Hall of Fame Players:* None. *Primary Quarterbacks:* Daunte Culpepper. *Tendencies:* • His teams scored 23.4 points and allowed 23.9 per game • His teams ran 42.7% of the time, which was 96% of the league average • Five starting quarterbacks in five years; 82% of starts to primary quarterback • 17 rookie starters in five years • Winning Full Seasons to Losing Full Seasons: 2:1.

Mike Tice's time in Minnesota was one of turmoil, on field disappointment and off field embarrassment. Tice loosely presided over the Viking franchise spinning out of control. "He's like one of the players," runner Michael Bennett once told the *New York Times*, and that was Mike's downfall as a head coach.

Tice was a 6'8" 230-pound quarterback from Bayshore, New York, who preceded Boomer Esiason at Maryland but had trouble holding onto the starting job. After he was benched in 1979, a frustrated Tice told the *Washington Post*, "If education had been the most important thing to me, I would have gone to an Ivy League school. But football has always been the most important thing. I came to Maryland to play big-time football."

Undrafted as a quarterback, Mike signed as a free agent with Seattle in 1981 and was converted to tight end. Tice played tight end for the Seahawks from 1981 to 1988, for the Redskins in 1989, for Seattle again from 1990 to 1991 and for the Vikings in 1992, 1993 and 1995. In his 14-year career as a backup tight end, Mike caught just 107 passes in 110 games. His younger brother John also played tight end, catching 158 passes in ten years with the Saints.

Mike went directly from player to assistant coach with Minnesota in 1996 and advanced from tight ends coach to offensive line coach over the next six years. 2001 began a very sour run for the Vikings. In January, they were beaten by 34 points in the NFC championship after having been favored in the game. In July, 300-pound offensive tackle Korey Stringer collapsed and died from heat exhaustion in training camp. Stringer's wife Kelci later told *Sports Illustrated*, "Korey and Mike Tice needed each other. Mike promised him

Tice, Michael P. (Mike)									
Year	Team	Games	Wins	Losses	Ties	%	P Wins	P Losses	P %
2001	Vikings	1	0	1	0	.000	0	0	.000
2002	Vikings	16	6	10	0	.375	0	0	.000
2003	Vikings	16	9	7	0	.563	0	0	.000
2004	Vikings	16	8	8	0	.500	1	1	.500
2005	Vikings	16	9	7	0	.563	0	0	.000
5 years		65	32	33	0	.492	1	1	.500

the kind of accolades that would get him into the Pro Bowl if Korey helped [forge a strong offensive line] that would get Mike a head job. It was a lot of pressure. It was a lot more serious." With the Vikings playing that season under a dark cloud, Coach Dennis Green's final year as a head coach in Minnesota was a sloppy one, and Mike replaced him as head coach for the season finale.

Tice was named the fulltime coach just days after the season ended, but his five-year tenure was fraught with underachievement and ugliness. Mike began by stressing the "Randy Ratio" to get his best player, the mercurial Randy Moss, more involved in the offense. "There were only five games last year when we threw the ball to Randy on 40 percent of our throws, and we were 4–1 in those games. This year our offense will be built around Randy Moss." Unfortunately in September, Moss was arrested for intentionally bumping a traffic officer with his car, and the season went downhill from there with quarterback Daunte Culpepper throwing more interceptions than touchdowns.

In 2003, sexual assault charges were filed against two members of the organization, while the team started the season 6–0 before collapsing to a 3–7 finish. Minnesota missed the playoffs by losing the last game to Arizona on a last-second fourth down 28-yard touchdown pass from Josh McCown to Nate Poole.

In 2004, Culpepper had a brilliant year throwing for over 4,700 yards and for 39 touchdowns, but the team backed into the playoff by losing their last two games to finish 8–8. The defense was an ongoing problem; Minnesota never finished higher than 19th in points allowed during Tice's tenure. The Vikings did win one playoff game that year, but that was marred by Randy Moss pretending to moon the Packer fans in Lambeau Field.

There was an utter meltdown in 2005. Tice was fined $100,000 by the league in March for scalping Super Bowl tickets. Running back Onterrio Smith was caught at the Minneapolis Airport in April with the "Whizzinator," a device used to falsify drug tests. Moss was traded to Oakland, and Culpepper got hurt during the season. In October, several players, including Culpepper, were implicated in the "Love Boat" scandal in which four Vikings were charged with "lewd or las-

civious conduct" aboard a chartered boat cruise. Allegations included live sex acts, prostitution and drug use. Mercifully for Minnesota fans, Tice was dismissed by new owner Zygi Wilf immediately following the 2005 season finale. Mike then was hired by former Viking teammate Jack Del Rio as assistant head coach in Jacksonville in 2006 and spent four years with the Jaguars. Since 2010, he has coached the Bears' offensive line under Lovie Smith.

TOBIN, VINCENT M. 9/29/1943– Missouri. DB; did not play professionally. *Apprenticeship:* College asst.—10 years; CFL asst.—6 years; USFL asst.—3 years; NFL asst.—10 years. *Roots:* Jim Mora (USFL), Mike Ditka, Ted Marchibroda. *Branches:* Jim Fassel. *Coordinators/Key Assistants*: Jim Fassel then Dick Jamieson then Marc Trestman ran the offense, while Dave McGinnis handled the defense. *Hall of Fame Players:* None. *Primary Quarterbacks:* Jake Plummer. *Tendencies:* • His teams scored 17.9 points and allowed 24.6 per game • His teams ran 39.3% of the time, which was 89% of the league average • Five starting quarterbacks in five years; 56% of starts to primary quarterback •15 rookie starters in five years • Winning Full Seasons to Losing Full Seasons: 1:3.

Born in Burlington Junction, Missouri, Vince Tobin followed his brother Bill to the University of Missouri. Vince was a starting defensive back under Dan Devine as a senior in 1964 and then joined the coaching staff as a graduate assistant in 1965. Tobin spent 1966 and 1967 as a part of President Johnson's Youth Corps, but left his government job for coaching in 1968 when he returned to Mizzou.

From 1968 to 1976, Vince coached at his alma mater, the last six years as defensive coordinator. In 1977, he traveled north to become defensive coordinator of the BC Lions of the CFL under another Missouri alumnus, Vic Rapp. After six years there, Tobin returned to the U.S. as Jim Mora's defensive coordinator with the Philadelphia Stars of the USFL. When that league folded, Vince decided against accompanying Mora to New Orleans. Rather, he took on the challenge of following the popular Buddy Ryan as defensive coordinator of the defending champion Chicago Bears in 1986. Of course, Chicago's GM was his brother Bill Tobin.

Tobin, Vincent M.

Year	Team	Games	Wins	Losses	Ties	%	P Wins	P Losses	P %
1996	Cardinals	16	7	9	0	.438	0	0	.000
1997	Cardinals	16	4	12	0	.250	0	0	.000
1998	Cardinals	16	9	7	0	.563	1	1	.500
1999	Cardinals	16	6	10	0	.375	0	0	.000
2000	Cardinals	7	2	5	0	.286	0	0	.000
5 years		71	28	43	0	.394	1	1	.500

Under Tobin, the Bears' defense remained formidable, but not as frighteningly fearsome as Ryan's squad was. After Ditka was dismissed in 1993, Vince was out of football for a year until he was hired by Ted Marchibroda as the defensive coordinator in Indianapolis where brother Bill was now the GM. Two years later, Vince was named head coach of the Cardinals — once again following a Buddy Ryan regime. This time, though, Ryan was not leaving a championship quality team in his wake.

The bland Tobin was known in Arizona as "Coach Beige." In Tobin's five years there, the team posted just one winning season, 1998. That year, the Cardinals went 9–7 and made the playoffs — even winning a postseason game for the first time in the last 50 years for the franchise. However, that team was more lucky than good, relying on some late-game comebacks by Jake Plummer to pull out games. The Cardinals never finished above 24th in the league in points allowed or 18th in scoring during Vince's tenure.

Tobin was fired at midseason in 2000 and replaced by his defensive coach Dave McGinniss who said, "What happened to Vince, I feel responsible for like I think all of our players and all of our assistant coaches do." Long snapper Trey Junkin added, "You've got 53 guys in there that got a great coach fired." For his part, Tobin said, "I'm disappointed that we didn't win more ball games, but I'm not disappointed in the way we conducted ourselves. When we got here four years ago, the Arizona Cardinals were probably the laughingstock of the NFL. Everything was in disarray. The offense hated the defense, and the defense hated the offense. The front office wasn't talking. We gave it a good go."

Tobin was hired by the Lions as defensive coordinator in 2001, but was fired after just one year. Following two years out of football, Vince then was hired as a special assistant to Mike Sherman in Green Bay in 2004 to help with game issues like clock management. One year later, he was let go and retired to his home in Phoenix.

TODD, RICHARD S. (DICK) 10/2/1914–11/9/1999. Texas A&M. Played HB for the Redskins from 1939 to 1942 and 1945–1948. *Apprenticeship:* College asst.— 2 years; pro asst.—1 year. *Roots:* Herman Ball. *Branches:* None. *Coordinators/Key Assistants:* None. *Hall of Fame Players:* Sammy Baugh, Bill Dudley. *Primary Quarterbacks:* Sammy Baugh. *Record:* **Interim Coach.**

Born in Thrall, Texas, Dick Todd was a 5'10"

170-pound scatback who scored 49 touchdowns and 318 points in his senior year at Crowell High School in 1934. Altogether, he scored 664 points in his four years as a schoolboy athlete. He then played for Texas A&M through 1938 and was drafted in the fifth round by the Redskins in 1939. Over the next four years, Todd was a key weapon for Sammy Baugh in Washington, both running the ball and catching passes out of the backfield. Dick went into the Navy in 1943, was discharged in 1946 and returned to the Redskins from 1946 to 1948 until retiring from playing.

Todd coached the backfield at his alma mater in 1949 and 1950 and was offered the head coaching job in 1951, but turned it down because he did not want to neglect his Texas ranch. Instead, Dick was hired for the less demanding job of coaching the backs in Washington in 1951. After the Redskins dropped their first three games, head coach Herman Ball was fired. Owner George Preston Marshall wanted to hire former Bears' assistant Hunk Anderson as the new head coach, but was blocked from doing so by George Halas. So Marshall turned to Todd, and Dick led Washington to a respectable 5–4 record for the rest of the season. Not everyone loved him, though. Center Harry Ulinski, who had played under autocratic Bear Bryant at Kentucky, left for Canada in 1952. He later told Thom Loverro for *Hail Victory*, "Dick Todd was a great athlete, but as a coach he tried that college rah-rah stuff on a bunch of veterans, many of whom were in World War II, and they weren't going to take it. His comments were belittling."

Todd returned to coach the team in 1952, but was fired by Marshall over a dispute during the preseason. Dick told the *Washington Post*, "I told the players when I took over last year that either I would run the team my way or I wouldn't coach. I told the coaches the same thing this year. It was a choice between being a man or a mouse." Todd returned to his ranch, but later coached at SMU in 1953 and 1954 and was named head coach at Midwestern University in Texas in 1955. He posted a 5–15 record there in two years and then left coaching again. He returned once more as an assistant to Sammy Baugh with the New York Titans in 1960, but left after one year. In 1961, his 17-year-old son Denny died from a cerebral hemorrhage after a football injury. Dick never coached again. He died in 1999 at the age of 85.

TOMLIN, MICHAEL 3/15/1972– William & Mary. WR; did not play professionally. *Apprenticeship:* Col-

Todd, Richard S. (Dick)									
Year	*Team*	*Games*	*Wins*	*Losses*	*Ties*	*%*	*P Wins*	*P Losses*	*P %*
1951	Redskins	9	5	4	0	.556	0	0	.000
1 year		9	5	4	0	.556	0	0	.000

lege asst.—6 years; pro asst.—6 years. *Roots:* Tony Dungy, Jon Gruden, Brad Childress. *Branches:* None. *Coordinators/Key Assistants*: Bruce Arians ran the offense, while Dick LeBeau handled the defense. *Hall of Fame Players:* None. *Primary Quarterbacks:* Ben Roethlisberger. *Record:* **Super Bowl Championship 2008**. *Tendencies:* • His teams scored 22.6 points and allowed 15.9 per game • His teams ran 45.7% of the time, which was 105% of the league average • Three starting quarterbacks in five years; 90% of starts to primary quarterback • Seven rookie starters in five years • Winning Full Seasons to Losing Full Seasons: 5:0.

Mike Tomlin's vibrant personality and clear record of accomplishment propelled him on a fast track to become an NFL head coach at the age of 34 in 2007. Tomlin was a teammate of safety Darren Sharper at William & Mary, but while Sharper went on to have a 15-year playing career in the league, Mike went directly into coaching. He started as the wide receivers coach at VMI in 1995, was a graduate assistant at Memphis in 1996 and moved on to Arkansas State as receivers coach in 1997. A year later, he switched to coaching the defensive backs and then took the same position with the University of Cincinnati in 1999. In his first year there, the Bearcats' secondary improved from 111th to 16th in the nation. That drew the notice of Tony Dungy in Tampa, and he hired Tomlin to coach the Bucs secondary in 2001.

Tomlin was retained by Jon Gruden who replaced Dungy in 2002 and spent five years in Tampa before Brad Childress hired Mike as defensive coordinator in Minnesota in 2006. One year later, Bill Cowher stepped down in Pittsburgh after 15 years as head coach. It was widely expected that the Steelers' would choose between two respected Steeler assistants—offensive coordinator Ken Whisenhunt or assistant head coach Russ Grimm. Instead, owner Dan Rooney surprised everyone by selecting Tomlin to be just the third Steelers' head coach in 38 years. Rooney told the *New York Times*, "He strikes me as being young, but I know he can do the job. Chuck Noll and Bill Cowher were young when we hired them. They're all different in certain ways, but they're all very similar in others." Tight end Heath Miller later explained the similarities to Cowher to the *Pittsburgh Post-Gazette*, "They're very similar in their passion for the game,

their work ethic and the energy they bring to it; it's kind of contagious. But the thing I admired right away about Coach Tomlin was that he was himself; he was his own coach, and he knew how he wanted to coach."

While Tomlin was very clear on how he wanted to run things, he also displayed a winning flexibility right from the outset when he retained revered defensive coordinator Dick LeBeau despite the fact that Mike was a defensive coach whose background was in running a 4–3 Cover 2 scheme not the 3–4 Zone Blitz style of LeBeau. That decision has paid off with two Super Bowl trips in Tomlin's first four years, powered by a defense that finished first or second in points allowed three times in that period. Offensively, Mike favors a strong running attack, but has worked to establish a dangerous deep passing attack as well behind improvisational quarterback Ben Roethlisberger.

Tomlin is tough, demanding, upfront and vocal. Players respond to his forcefulness and his honesty with them and play hard for him. Mike does not put up with any nonsense, but is not an unfeeling automaton on the sideline. Above all else, he has maintained Pittsburgh's physical style of football so much that the competition with the equally physical Baltimore Ravens has become the league's best rivalry in the last five years.

Under Tomlin, the Steelers have made the playoffs in every season but one, have reached two Super Bowls that both went down to the final minute of play and won the championship in 2008. At 37, Mike was the youngest coach ever to win a Super Bowl when Pittsburgh beat Arizona that year on Roethlisberger's last minute touchdown strike to Santonio Holmes. Since then, Tomlin has sustained the Steelers success despite such side issues as Roethlisberger's injury problems and sexual harassment troubles and volatile linebacker James Harrison's periodic outbursts. Mike once noted the challenge of coaching in the NFL to *Sports Illustrated*, "None of us is ready. I wasn't. What you need to know, you have to experience. I'm the type who never anticipates transition being easy. In fact, I anticipate it being miserable. But with that misery can come great gain if you embrace the change."

TOMSULA, JAMES (JIM) 4/14/1968– Middle Tennessee State; Catawba. DL; did not play pro-

Tomlin, Michael									
Year	Team	Games	Wins	Losses	Ties	%	P Wins	P Losses	P %
2007	Steelers	16	10	6	0	.625	0	1	.000
2008	Steelers	16	12	4	0	.750	3	0	1.000
2009	Steelers	16	9	7	0	.563	0	0	.000
2010	Steelers	16	12	4	0	.750	2	1	.667
2011	Steelers	16	12	4	0	.250	0	1	.000
5 years		80	55	25	0	.688	5	3	.625

fessionally. *Apprenticeship:* College asst.—7 years; NFL Europe coach—9 years (1 as head coach); pro asst.—4 years. Roots: Mike Nolan, Mike Singletary. *Branches:* None. *Coordinators/Key Assistants:* None. *Hall of Fame Players:* None. *Primary Quarterbacks:* Alex Smith. *Record:* **Interim Coach.**

Born in West Homestead, Pennsylvania, Jim Tomsula is a former "Mr. Pittsburgh" who could bench press 500-pounds and squat press over 800 and has come up the hard way in coaching. He played defensive line at Middle Tennessee State and then transferred to Catawba. Following graduation, Tomsula was hired by his alma mater as strength and conditioning coach in 1989. After one year he left to coach high school football and then returned to the college ranks as the defensive line coach at Charleston Southern University from 1992 to 1996. Jim coached the defensive line at Catawba in 1997 and then got involved in NFL Europe in 1998.

Tomsula coached the defensive line for the England Monarchs in 1998 and the Scottish Claymores from 1999 to 2003 before being promoted to defensive coordinator for the Berlin Thunder in 2004. He was elevated to head coach of the Rhein Fire in 2006 and led the team to a 6–4 record. Mike Nolan then hired him to coach the defensive line for the 49ers in 2007. Jim stayed on staff after Mike Singletary replaced Nolan in 2008. When Singletary was fired with one game to play in 2010, Tomsula was promoted to interim head coach since he was the only assistant with head coaching experience. He modestly greeted the press by introducing himself, "I'm a football coach. I'm Jim Nobody from Nowhere." Defensive end Justin Smith said of Tomsula, "He works you, now, but he'll make it fun. He's a great teacher, a great guy to be around." Jim drew many compliments for his positive attitude and the way he prepared the 49ers for their season finale in which they pummeled Arizona 38–7.

Tomsula realized that he had no chance at being named the permanent coach, but refreshingly reasoned, "My family is not going to starve, and if my wife has stayed with me for the last 19 years, she's not going anywhere. So I'm good." New coach Jim Harbaugh retained the popular Tomsula on staff in 2011.

TRIMBLE, JAMES W. (JIM) 5/29/1918–5/23/2006. Indiana. T; did not play professionally. *Apprenticeship:* College coach—5 years (3 as head coach); pro asst.—1 year. Roots: Bo McMillin, Wayne Millner. *Branches:* None. *Coordinators/Key Assistants:* Charley Gauer was the key offensive coach, while Trimble handled his own defense. *Hall of Fame Players:* Chuck Bednarik, Pete Pihos, Steve Van Buren. *Primary Quarterbacks:* Adrian Burk, Bobby Thomason. *Tendencies:* • His teams scored 23.7 points and allowed 19.7 per game • His teams ran 48.4% of the time, which was 91% of the league average • Two starting quarterbacks in four years; 100% of starts to primary quarterbacks • 20 rookie starters in four years • Winning Full Seasons to Losing Full Seasons: 3:1.

Jungle Jim Trimble was a 6'2" 250-pound rough-edged former steel worker from McKeesport, Pennsylvania who played tackle for Bo McMillin at Indiana from 1939 to 1941 and then went into the Navy for the duration of the war. In 1946, Jim was named line coach at Wichita State and two years later was elevated to head coach and athletic director at the school. From 1948 to 1950, Trimble's Shockers went 13–14–3.

In 1951, Jim was hired by Bo McMillin, the new coach of the Philadelphia Eagles, to coach the line and the defense. McMillin subsequently had to step down after just two games because of cancer and assistant Wayne Millner was named interim coach. Millner resigned at the end of the disappointing 4–8 season, and the 34-year-old Trimble replaced him as head coach in 1952. Over the next four seasons, the Eagles finished second to the Browns in the East three times. Philadelphia had a rugged defense and two exciting receivers in Pete Pihos and Bobby Walston, but an inconsistent quarterbacking duo of Bobby Thomason and Adrian Burk and no running game. After the team slipped to fourth place in 1955, Jim was fired.

Tomsula, James (Jim)

Year	Team	Games	Wins	Losses	Ties	%	P Wins	P Losses	P %
2010	49ers	1	1	0	0	1.000	0	0	.000
1 year		1	1	0	0	1.000	0	0	.000

Trimble, James W. (Jim)

Year	Team	Games	Wins	Losses	Ties	%	P Wins	P Losses	P %
1952	Eagles	12	7	5	0	.583	0	0	.000
1953	Eagles	12	7	4	1	.625	0	0	.000
1954	Eagles	12	7	4	1	.625	0	0	.000
1955	Eagles	12	4	7	1	.375	0	0	.000
4 years		48	25	20	3	.552	0	0	.000

Trimble was not out of work long. He was named head coach of Canada's Hamilton Tiger-Cats in 1956. From 1956 to 1962, Jim posted a 60–36–2 record in Hamilton and led the team to five Grey Cup Championship games. In each of those five title games, he faced the Winnipeg Blue Bombers coached by Bud Grant who had played under Trimble in Philadelphia. Hamilton won the Grey Cup in 1957, and Jim boasted before the 1958 game that "we're gonna waffle 'em. We're going to put lumps on them. Front and back." Unfortunately, Winnipeg beat Hamilton in 1958, 1959, 1961 and 1962.

When the Montreal Alouettes offered Jim a sizeable raise to switch teams in 1963, he did, but never had much success in Montreal. From 1963 to 1965, the Alouettes finished 17–25 and won no postseason games. Trimble was fired after the 1965 season during which he got into a fist fight with a reporter. Jim once said, "If I can't be the best football coach in the business, then I'll quit and be the best ditch-digger." He spent the next year working with part-time inventor friend Joel Rottman to develop and market a Y-shaped one-post goal post to replace the conventional H-shaped two-post goal used at all levels of the game. All 16 NFL teams adopted the new style post in 1967.

That year, Jim returned to the NFL as the line coach of the Giants under Allie Sherman. In 1969, he moved into the front office as the team's director of player personnel and held that position through 1981 when he retired at the age of 63. Trimble continued to work for the Giants as a consultant and super scout into the 1990s and died in 2006 at the age of 87.

TUCKER, MEL 1/4/1972– Wisconsin. DB; did not play professionally. *Apprenticeship:* College asst.—7 years; pro asst.—7 years. *Roots:* Romeo Crennel, Jack Del Rio. *Branches:* None. *Coordinators/Key Assistants:* None. *Hall of Fame Players:* None. *Primary Quarterbacks:* Blaine Gabbert. *Record:* **Interim Coach.**

Cleveland native Mel Tucker played defensive back at Wisconsin from 1992 to 1995. He began his coaching career two years later at Michigan State under Nick Saban in 1997. A year later, Mel moved on to

Miami of Ohio and then reunited with Saban at LSU in 2000. Tucker returned to his home state in 2001 when he joined Jim Tressell's staff at Ohio State as defensive backs coach. He moved up to defensive coordinator by 2004 and then jumped to the NFL in 2005.

Romeo Crennel hired Mel as defensive backs coach, and, again, Tucker moved up to defensive coordinator in his fourth year, 2008. After Crennel was fired in 2009, Tucker was hired by Jack Del Rio as defensive coordinator in Jacksonville. Even as the Jaguars slogged through a disappointing 2011 season behind overmatched rookie quarterback Blaine Gabbert, the defense leaped into the top 10 in points and yards allowed. When owner Wayne Weaver, decided that nine years was enough of Del Rio, he hired Tucker as the team's interim coach as he prepared to sell it. Once the season and sale were completed, Mike Mularkey was hired as head coach and Tucker returned to his defensive coordinator position in Jacksonville.

TURNER, CLYDE D. (BULLDOG) 3/10/1919– 10/30/1998. Hardin-Simmons. Played C/LB for the Bears from 1940 to 1952. *Apprenticeship:* College asst.—1 year; pro asst.—5 years. *Roots:* George Halas, Paddy Driscoll. *Branches:* None. *Coordinators/Key Assistants:* George Sauer was a key offensive coach, while John Dell Isola handled the defense. *Hall of Fame Players:* Don Maynard. *Primary Quarterbacks:* Johnny Green. *Record:* **Hall of Fame Player.** *Tendencies:* • His team scored 19.9 points and allowed 30.2 per game • His team ran 36.2% of the time, which was 77% of the league average • Three starting quarterbacks in one year; 57% of starts to primary quarterback • Two rookie starters in one year • Winning Full Seasons to Losing Full Seasons: 0:1.

Although Bulldog Turner was born in Plains, Texas, he grew up in Sweetwater where he was two years behind Sammy Baugh in high school. Turner attended Hardin-Simmons in nearby Abilene and was a Little All-American during his playing years from 1937 to 1939. Detroit owner George Richards courted Turner and ordered Lions' coach Gus Henderson to draft him first in 1940. When Henderson drafted

Tucker, Mel										
Year	Team	Games	Wins	Losses	Ties	%	P Wins	P Losses	P %
2011	Jaguars	5	2	3	0	.400	0	0	.000
1 year		5	2	3	0	.400	0	0	.000

Turner, Clyde D. (Bulldog)										
Year	Team	Games	Wins	Losses	Ties	%	P Wins	P Losses	P %
1962	New York Titans (Jets)	14	5	9	0	.357	0	0	.000
1 year		14	5	9	0	.357	0	0	.000

Doyle Nave instead, he was fired. Turner was picked by the Bears in the first round, but Richards didn't give up. He told Turner not to sign with George Halas of the Bears, and he would get Bulldog a job for a year and then sign him for Detroit.

When the league found out about this chicanery, Richards was fined and soon after sold the team. Turner eventually signed with the Bears and had a 13-year Hall of Fame career at center and linebacker in Chicago. Bulldog was a smart player of whom teammate Hugh Gallerneau once said, "Bulldog knew what every player should do in his position on any given play." After he retired from playing in 1953, the Bears retired his number 66.

Turner joined George Sauer's coaching staff at Baylor for one year and then returned to Chicago as an assistant from 1954 to 1958. Bulldog went back to his cattle ranch in 1959, but was brought back to coaching in 1962 when financially-strapped New York Titans' owner Harry Wismer demoted head coach Sammy Baugh to assistant coach to try to force him to quit so Wismer would not have to make good on Sammy's three-year contract. Eventually, Wismer and Baugh worked out their difficulties, and Turner took over as head coach, but his boss, GM George Sauer, was also the team's backfield coach.

Turner announced, "We'll still be basically a spread-formation team." However, Turner lacked a quality quarterback to continue running Baugh's wide open offense, so the Titans were next to last in scoring and last in points allowed. Furthermore, Wismer was out of money and failed to meet the payroll so the league had to front the team the money to pay the players who raced to the bank each week to cash their dubious checks. In this environment, it's remarkable the Titans managed to win five games. With new ownership in 1963, Bulldog was dismissed and replaced by Weeb Ewbank for the newly-christened Jets.

Turner left football for good and returned to his cattle ranch once again. He was elected to the College Football Hall of Fame in 1960 and the Pro Football Hall in 1966.

TURNER, NORVAL E. (NORV) 5/17/1952– Oregon. QB; did not play professionally. *Apprenticeship:* College asst.—10 years; pro asst.—9 years. *Roots:* John Robinson, Jimmy Johnson. *Branches:* Mike Martz, Terry Robiskie (i), Mike Nolan, Cam Cameron, Emmitt Thomas (i), Ron Rivera, Chuck Pagano. *Coordinators/Key Assistants*: For the Redskins, Cam Cameron then Mike Martz then Gregg Olson were the key offensive coaches, while Ron Lynn then Mike Nolan then Ray Rhodes handled the defense; for the Raiders, Jimmy Raye ran the offense, while Rob Ryan handled the defense; for the Chargers, Clarence Shelmon ran the offense, while Ted Cottrell then Ron Rivera then Greg Manusky handled the defense. *Hall of Fame Players:* Darrell Green, Jerry Rice, Deion Sanders, Bruce Smith. *Primary Quarterbacks:* Gus Frerotte, Brad Johnson, Kerry Collins, Philip Rivers *Tendencies:* • His teams scored 23.1 points and allowed 22 per game • His teams ran 43 % of the time, which was 98% of the league average • 11 starting quarterbacks in 14 years; 78% of starts to primary quarterbacks • 30 rookie starters in 14 years • Winning Full Seasons to Losing Full Seasons: 6:5.

Norv Turner's reputation as an offensive coach is pristine; his reputation as a head coach is not. Turner is only the second NFL coach (with Lou Saban) to coach two hundred games in the league and lose more games than he won. Saban's case is mitigated by his winning two championships, but Norv has won no titles and instead inspires fans to create negative web sites like firenorv.com.

Turner was born in Camp Lejeune, North Carolina, but grew up in Martinez, California. As a quar-

Turner, Norval E. (Norv)									
Year	Team	Games	Wins	Losses	Ties	%	P Wins	P Losses	P %
1994	Redskins	16	3	13	0	.188	0	0	.000
1995	Redskins	16	6	10	0	.375	0	0	.000
1996	Redskins	16	9	7	0	.563	0	0	.000
1997	Redskins	16	8	7	1	.531	0	0	.000
1998	Redskins	16	6	10	0	.375	0	0	.000
1999	Redskins	16	10	6	0	.625	1	1	.500
2000	Redskins	13	7	6	0	.538	0	0	.000
2004	Raiders	16	5	11	0	.313	0	0	.000
2005	Raiders	16	4	12	0	.250	0	0	.000
2007	Chargers	16	11	5	0	.688	2	1	.667
2008	Chargers	16	8	8	0	.500	1	1	.500
2009	Chargers	16	13	3	0	.813	0	1	.000
2010	Chargers	16	9	7	0	.563	0	0	.000
2011	Chargers	16	8	8	0	.500	0	0	.000
14 years		221	107	113	1	.480	4	4	.500

terback at Oregon from 1971 to 1974, Norv originally backed up Dan Fouts and didn't start until his senior year. Fouts later joked, "We had two kinds of passes at Oregon: a spiral and a Norval." Turner began his coaching career as a graduate assistant at his alma mater in 1975 and then joined John Robinson's staff at USC in 1976, first coaching wide receivers and then defensive backs until moving up to quarterbacks in 1981. Robinson left in 1983, but Turner stayed on staff and was promoted to offensive coordinator in 1984. He reunited with Robinson as the Rams' receivers coach from 1985 to 1990 where he fell under the sway of offensive coordinator Ernie Zampese who had worked under Don Coryell both for San Diego State and the San Diego Chargers.

When Turner left the West Coast in 1991 to become offensive coordinator of Jimmy Johnson's Dallas Cowboys, he brought the Coryell-Zampese offense with him. Cowboy quarterback Troy Aikman credited Turner as being "instrumental in my development as a player." Dallas won consecutive Super Bowls in 1992 and 1993, making Norv the hot coordinator for head coaching vacancies. Turner signed with the Redskins in 1994 and rebuilt the fallen champions into a thoroughly mediocre team in his seven years in Washington.

His first draft choice, quarterback Heath Shuler, turned out to be a bust who was replaced by seventh round pick Gus Frerrote, and the offense was never better than so-so. The same could be said for the defense. Moreover, distractions caused the team to question Norv's leadership qualities, whether it was the ugly incident when receiver Michael Westbrook assaulted runner Stephen Davis or the postgame berating given Turner by new owner Dan Snyder after a 38–20 loss to Dallas in 1999 that left Norv with red eyes when he returned to the locker room.

Snyder fired Turner with three games to play in 2000, and Norv spent 2001 as the offensive coordi-

nator of the Chargers before taking the same position in Miami from 2002 to 2003 under former Dallas colleague Dave Wannstedt. Turner got a second chance as head coach in 2004 with the Oakland Raiders. He greeted the news by telling the press, "I belong here. When I got off the plane the other night, I felt like I was coming home." However, the Raiders won just nine games in the next two years as Turner struggled with plodding quarterback Kerry Collins, incorrigible receiver Randy Moss, a bad defense and a difficult owner in Al Davis.

Having lost control of a bad team, Norv was fired in 2006 and moved across the bay to become the 49ers offensive coordinator. A year later, Chargers' GM A.J. Smith shocked the football world by replacing coach Marty Schottenheimer with two-time loser Turner. Norv noted to the *New York Times*, "The offensive system that the Chargers run, I installed in 2001." However, under the unassuming and unimposing Turner, the well-stocked Chargers have underachieved. Almost each year they start out poorly, rally to reach the postseason and then check out of the playoffs fairly quickly. His teams lack toughness and direction. Like his brother Ron who once coached the Bears' offense, Norv is a born coordinator. Mike Martz, who worked under Turner in Washington, told the *San Diego Union-Tribune*, "What I got from Norv is the ability to call plays. There isn't a better play-caller in the league. He's understated, but brilliant." That brilliance does not extend to the fuller responsibilities of a head coach. Most observers were surprised that Turner was retained for 2012 on the heels of still another disappointing season out of the playoffs for the Chargers in 2011.

Van Brocklin, Norman M. (Norm)
3/15/1926–5/2/1983. Oregon. Played QB for the Rams and Eagles from 1949 to 1960. *Apprenticeship:* None. *Roots:* None. *Branches:* Harry Gilmer, Marion Camp-

Year	Team	Games	Wins	Losses	Ties	%	P Wins	P Losses	P %
1961	Vikings	14	3	11	0	.214	0	0	.000
1962	Vikings	14	2	11	1	.179	0	0	.000
1963	Vikings	14	5	8	1	.393	0	0	.000
1964	Vikings	14	8	5	1	.607	0	0	.000
1965	Vikings	14	7	7	0	.500	0	0	.000
1966	Vikings	14	4	9	1	.321	0	0	.000
1968	Falcons	11	2	9	0	.182	0	0	.000
1969	Falcons	14	6	8	0	.429	0	0	.000
1970	Falcons	14	4	8	2	.357	0	0	.000
1971	Falcons	14	7	6	1	.536	0	0	.000
1972	Falcons	14	7	7	0	.500	0	0	.000
1973	Falcons	14	9	5	0	.643	0	0	.000
1974	Falcons	8	2	6	0	.250	0	0	.000
13 years		173	66	100	7	.402	0	0	.000

bell, Fred Bruney (i). *Coordinators/Key Assistants*: For the Vikings, Van Brocklin ran his own offense, while Harry Gilmer then Marion Campbell handled the offense; for the Falcons, Van Brocklin ran his own offense, while Marion Campbell handled the defense. *Hall of Fame Players:* Carl Eller, Hugh McElhenny, Fran Tarkenton. *Primary Quarterbacks:* Fran Tarkenton, Bob Berry. *Record:* **Hall of Fame Player**. *Tendencies:* • His teams scored 19.8 points and allowed 22.8 per game • His teams ran 54.8% of the time, which was 105% of the league average • Ten starting quarterbacks in 13 years; 75% of starts to primary quarterbacks • 49 rookie starters in 13 years • Winning Full Seasons to Losing Full Seasons: 3:7.

Tempestuous, acerbic Norm Van Brocklin was known as the Brat as a player by opponents and teammates alike. Hampton Pool, who coached Van Brocklin with the Rams, once said of him, "Soon he'll break every existing record — if some lineman doesn't break his neck first." Born in Eagle Butte, South Dakota, his family moved to California when Norm was three. At 17, he forged his mother's signature on his enlistment papers and joined the Navy in 1943. Discharged three years later, Van Brocklin enrolled at the University of Oregon under the G.I. Bill and was named All American in 1948. Since he was able to complete all his degree requirements in three years — perhaps aided by his wife who was his former Biology lab instructor, Van Brocklin was eligible for the NFL draft and was taken by Los Angeles in the fourth round.

Norm's gifts were obvious from the start. While he could not run at all, his arm was strong and accurate with great touch and timing on both long and short passes. In addition, he was an outstanding punter. He did not play much as a rookie backup for Hall of Famer Bob Waterfield, but new coach Joe Stydahar instituted an unusual platoon system for his quarterbacks in 1950. Waterfield would take the first and third quarters, and Van Brocklin would play the second and fourth periods.

The Rams won the 1951 title match against the Browns on a 73-yard fourth quarter touchdown bomb from Van Brocklin to Tom Fears. In an off year for Van Brocklin, the Rams returned to the title game in 1955, but Cleveland intercepted six of the Dutchman's passes and pummeled Los Angeles. The Rams' coach by this time was Sid Gillman who did not get along with Van Brocklin. After three years, Norm told Ram GM Pete Rozelle that he'd be happy to go anywhere but Philadelphia, so the cooperative Rozelle worked out a deal with the Eagles.

Once the Eagles traded for Van Brocklin they were able to convince the highly-respected Buck Shaw to coach the team. They still had to convince Van Brocklin not to retire. Commissioner Bert Bell got involved with the negotiations and assured Van Brocklin

that once the elderly Shaw retired after three years, he would be named the next Eagles' coach. It was a gentleman's agreement; nothing was committed to paper. The Eagles were a bad team under Hugh Devore in 1957, but Shaw rebuilt the team in three years. Relying heavily on the leadership of Van Brocklin on offense, Philadelphia beat Green Bay in the 1960 championship game.

Shaw and Van Brocklin capped their triumph by both retiring, but Norm soon found he was not being offered the coaching job he had been promised. The Eagles wanted to keep him solely as a player, but the betrayed Van Brocklin announced that he was accepting an offer to become the coach of the expansion Minnesota Vikings since the Eagles had reneged on their promise to him. Van Brocklin went on to coach seven years in Minnesota and another seven in Atlanta without consistent success.

The Vikings slowly rose to an 8–5–1 record in 1964, but Van Brocklin clashed openly with his scrambling quarterback Fran Tarkenton. In 1966, Norm resigned in frustration on November 15 only to rejoin the team a day later, saying he was a "fighter, not a quitter." He signed a new five-year contract a few weeks later. By season's end though, Tarkenton had had enough and wrote a letter to Vikings' management saying he wanted out. Even after Van Brocklin again resigned, Fran still forced a trade to New York. The sarcastic, caustic Dutchman spent 1967 as a broadcaster before taking over the Falcons three games into the 1968 season. Once again, Norm improved the team on the field, but made no friends in the clubhouse or the press box. Center Ken Mendenhall told Stephen Norwood for *Real Football*, "Guys were pretty fearful of him. He went into some real tirades as a coach. I knew some guys who played for him for a long period of time, and it was the most miserable experience they had had." In 1974, guard Andy Mauer told his local Medford, Oregon newspaper, "I think the Falcons have everything you need to win a championship. It's just a matter of the players getting old enough where they will ignore Van Brocklin." Mauer was traded before the next season, Van Brocklin's last.

As for the press, Norm famously said before undergoing brain surgery in 1979, "I want the brain of a sportswriter because I want one that hasn't been used." Another time he objected to a microphone thrust in his face by barking, "Don't put that thing in my mouth, Sonny, or you'll be wearing it in a different part of your anatomy." In November 1974 he challenged reporter Ron Hudspeth to a fist fight during a press conference; a day later he was dismissed.

Van Brocklin ran his pecan farm in Georgia from 1975 to 1978, but did interview for openings with the Eagles and at Oregon in 1975 and 1976. Norm worked as an assistant under Pepper Rodgers at Georgia Tech in 1979, but that was his last connection to the game.

He was elected to the Hall of Fame in 1971 and died in 1983 following a stroke.

VENTURI, RICK J. 2/23/1946– Northwestern. QB/DB; did not play professionally. *Apprenticeship:* College coach —12 years (3 as head coach); pro asst.— 10 years. *Roots:* Frank Kush, Hal Hunter (i), Rod Dowhower, Ron Meyer, Ted Marchibroda, Bill Belichick, Jim Mora. *Branches:* Jim Haslett. *Coordinators/Key Assistants*: For the Colts, Leon Burtnett ran the offense; for the Saints, Carl Smith ran the offense. *Hall of Fame Players:* Eric Dickerson, Willie Roaf. *Primary Quarterbacks:* Jeff George, Jim Everett. *Record:* **Interim Coach.**

Despite his father and brother being successful high school coaches, Rick Venturi's experience as a head coach was more similar to that of the biblical Job. As such, Rick was head coach for 52 games in college and the pros but won just three of them — one at each of his three stops.

Born in Taylorville, Illinois, Venturi played quarterback and defensive back for Alex Agase at Northwestern from 1965 to 1967. Agase thought highly enough of Rick that he added him to his Northwestern staff in 1968 and brought Venturi along when he was named coach of Purdue in 1973. After five years as an assistant at Northwestern and four at Purdue under Agase, Rick struck out on his own in 1977 to coach the defensive backs at Illinois. One year later, Venturi was hired as head coach at his alma mater.

With its academic requirements, Northwestern has struggled to maintain a major college football program. The Wildcats tied Illinois 0–0 in Rick's debut, but then lost the remaining ten games in 1978. NU beat Wyoming 27–22 in the second game of 1979 and then lost the remaining nine games of that year and all 11 in 1980. That streak of 20 losses would eventually grow to 34, but not under Venturi; he was fired after the 1980 season, having been outscored 1,270 to 358 in his three-year tenure. He commented to the *Chicago Tribune*, "It's over. It's history, and there were painful lessons learned. A fresh start is all I'm looking for now."

Outcast coach Frank Kush hired Rick to work training camp for the Hamilton Tiger-Cats of the CFL in 1981, but Venturi essentially was out of football that year. When Kush was named head coach of the Colts in 1982, though, he remembered Rick and hired him as linebackers coach. Venturi would spend the next 27 years in the NFL. He moved up to defensive coor-

dinator in 1984, but dropped back to linebackers after Kush left. Rick stayed with the Colts for 13 years and got his second chance as a head coach in 1991 when he was named interim coach of the 0–5 Colts after Ron Meyer was fired. Venturi led the Colts to a 28–27 win over the Jets in his fifth game and exclaimed to *Sports Illustrated*, "Except for some personal family things, this is the best feeling I've ever had in my life, no doubt." After that brief high, the Colts lost the last six games of the season and Rick went back to being linebackers coach.

Venturi worked for Bill Belichick in Cleveland in 1994 and 1995 before joining Jim Mora's Saints' staff in 1996. When Mora quit at midseason, Rick was made interim coach again because he had head coaching experience despite its dubious quality. The Saints won just one of eight games under Venturi, but he told the *Mobile Register*, "Actually, we have done a damn good job. It just didn't translate into wins. I would like to have a pro job on a level playing field where you organize it from the beginning, have everything in place like you want it and go from there." Rick remained in New Orleans for nine more years under Mike Ditka and then Jim Haslett before following Haslett to the Rams: Haslett as defensive coordinator and Venturi as linebackers coach. When Haslett became the Rams' interim head coach in midseason 2008, Rick was promoted to defensive coordinator. Both men were fired at the end of the season. Venturi has since retired from coaching.

VERMEIL, RICHARD A. (DICK) 10/30/1936– San Jose State. QB; did not play professionally. *Apprenticeship:* Junior college coach — 4 years (1 as head coach); college coach — 7 years (2 as head coach); pro asst.— 4 years. *Roots:* George Allen, Tommy Prothro. *Branches:* Fred Bruney (i), Rod Rust, Mike Martz, Joe Vitt (i). *Coordinators/Key Assistants*: For the Eagles, John Idzik then John Ralston then Sid Gilman was the key offensive coach, while John Mazur then Marion Campbell handled the defense; for the Rams, Jerry Rhome then Mike Martz ran the offense, while Bud Carson then Peter Giunta and John Bunting handled the defense; for the Chiefs Al Saunders ran the offense, while Greg Robinson then Gunther Cunningham handled the defense. *Hall of Fame Players:* Marshall Faulk and Willie Roaf. *Primary Quarterbacks:* Ron Jaworski, Tony Banks, Kurt Warner, Trent Green. *Record:* Super Bowl Championship 1999. *Tendencies:* • His teams scored 22.7 points and allowed

Venturi, Rick J.									
Year	*Team*	*Games*	*Wins*	*Losses*	*Ties*	*%*	*P Wins*	*P Losses*	*P %*
1991	Colts	11	1	10	0	.091	0	0	.000
1996	Saints	8	1	7	0	.125	0	0	.000
2 years		19	2	17	0	.105	0	0	.000

Vermeil, Richard A. (Dick)

Year	Team	Games	Wins	Losses	Ties	%	P Wins	P Losses	P %
1976	Eagles	14	4	10	0	.286	0	0	.000
1977	Eagles	14	5	9	0	.357	0	0	.000
1978	Eagles	16	9	7	0	.563	0	1	.000
1979	Eagles	16	11	5	0	.688	1	1	.500
1980	Eagles	16	12	4	0	.750	2	1	.667
1981	Eagles	16	10	6	0	.625	0	1	.000
1982	Eagles	9	3	6	0	.333	0	0	.000
1997	Rams	16	5	11	0	.313	0	0	.000
1998	Rams	16	4	12	0	.250	0	0	.000
1999	Rams	16	13	3	0	.813	3	0	1.000
2001	Chiefs	16	6	10	0	.375	0	0	.000
2002	Chiefs	16	8	8	0	.500	0	0	.000
2003	Chiefs	16	13	3	0	.813	0	1	.000
2004	Chiefs	16	7	9	0	.438	0	0	.000
2005	Chiefs	16	10	6	0	.625	0	0	.000
15 years		229	120	109	0	.524	6	5	.545

19.6 per game • His teams ran 48.5% of the time, which was 102% of the league average • Seven starting quarterbacks in 15 years; 93% of starts to primary quarterbacks • 27 rookie starters in 15 years • Winning Full Seasons to Losing Full Seasons: 7:7.

Hailing from Calistoga, California, the emotional Dick Vermeil has had success coaching at every level from high school to the pros. He was a backup quarterback at San Jose State from 1956 to 1958 and then went directly into high school coaching in 1959. In 1961, he moved up a level as an assistant at Foothills Junior College. After three years, he was named head coach at Napa Junior College and led the team to a 7–2 record in 1964. Dick then joined John Ralston's all star staff at Stanford in 1965 and stayed in Palo Alto for four years.

Rams' coach George Allen hired Vermeil in 1969 to be the first special teams coach in NFL history. One year later, Dick joined Tommy Prothro's staff at UCLA and then followed Prothro back to the Rams in 1971. Vermeil stayed with the Rams through the 1973 season and then was named UCLA's head coach in 1974. A year later, Dick led the Bruins to the Rose Bowl where they upset Ohio State. With a two-year mark of 15–5–3, he was happy at UCLA and, partly out of loyalty to his staff, resisted the initial overtures from Eagles' owner Leonard Tose and GM Jim Murray to come to Philadelphia. However, Vermeil met with Tose and took the head coaching job. What he inherited in Philadelphia was a mess. The team was riddled with drug problems and dissension. They had just finished 4–10, had not had a winning record in 9 years and had not been to the postseason in 15. As for reinforcements, he had no draft choice higher than a third rounder for his first four years because his predecessor had traded them away for faded veterans. Dick ruthlessly weeded out any suspected drug users and built a tough new Eagles team through trades (Ron Jaworski and Claude

Humphrey), free agents (Herman Edwards and Woody Peoples), and low draft picks (Wilbert Montgomery, Carl Hairston and Dennis Harrison) in conjunction with the core players who remained (Bill Bergey, Jerry Sisemore and Harold Carmichael).

Vermeil worked 20-hour days and slept on a cot in his office three nights a week. During his first training camp, he once complained that a fireworks extravaganza celebrating the nations' Bicentennial was a disruption and wanted it stopped. Vermeil pushed his players as hard as he pushed himself. Harold Carmichael told the *Washington Post*, "Dick's the type of motivating coach. He's a demanding hard worker. He gives you everything you need to know. He works his coaches hard. We can't go into a game saying we weren't prepared." Vermeil's offense was conservative and run-based, but he did bring in Sid Gillman as an assistant to open up the passing attack with Jaworski and polish the Polish Rifle's skills. The strength of the team was the defense that twice led the league in fewest points allowed and three other times finished in the top ten.

Year by year, the team steadily improved: a winning record and the playoffs in 1978, beating Dallas in 1979 and reaching the Super Bowl in 1980. The Super Bowl itself was a disappointment as the favored Eagles came on the field nervous and tense and were easily beaten by the relaxed and loose Raiders. After that, the team declined just as steadily. By 1982, some players had had enough of the intensity. All Pro defensive tackle Charlie Johnson complained and was traded. He told the *New York Times*, "I felt the training and preparation was really tough. There was a lot of pounding, a lot of contact. The body could never heal." The 1982 players' strike disturbed team chemistry, and Tose made it worse by blasting the players after a loss when they came back. By season's end, Vermeil quit coaching claiming to be "emotionally burned out." He noted, "I'm my own worst enemy. I'm far too intense, far too emotional."

Dick became a college football analyst on TV for the next 14 years while occasionally flirting with NFL coaching openings. The most serious flirtation was with the Eagles in 1995 after Jeff Lurie had purchased the team, but the negotiations fell apart at the last minute over control issues. Vermeil finally took the coaching job with the downtrodden Rams in 1997, but had trouble winning over the players to his heavy practice schedule. After two losing seasons, Dick was under a threat of win or else in 1999 when he hired Mike Martz to coach the offense, signed quarterback Trent Green to run it, traded for runner Marshall Faulk and drafted receiver Torry Holt. Despite losing Green in the preseason, the Rams' full throttle offense won the Super Bowl that year with unheralded backup Kurt Warner quarterbacking the "Greatest Show on Turf." However, with offensive coach Mike Martz a hot commodity, the Rams pressured Vermeil to step aside and retire. He did, but quickly regretted it. Chiefs GM Carl Peterson, Dick's former assistant with UCLA and the Eagles, had no trouble luring him to Kansas City in 2001.

With the Chiefs, Vermeil acquired Green again and quickly developed another high-octane offense that twice led the league in points and finished second another season. However, the Chiefs' defense never finished higher than 16th, so the team reached the postseason just once in five years before Dick retired to his winery in 2006

Vermeil's strengths are also his weaknesses. Intensity and loyalty are fine qualities, but they, too, can be overdone. After the Super Bowl debacle with the Eagles where his overworked team was too tired and tight to perform, Vermeil loosened up enough with the Rams to win it all. His offense evolved from the conservative play selection in Philadelphia to the aggressive attack of the Rams and Chiefs. However, his extreme loyalty to players and coaches who weren't performing may have held his teams back.

Vitt, Joseph 8/23/1954– Towson State. LB; did not play professionally. *Apprenticeship:* Pro asst.— 27 years. *Roots:* Chuck Knox, Ray Rhodes, Dick Vermeil, Mike Martz. *Branches:* None. *Coordinators/Key Assistants*: Steve Fairchild ran the offense, while Larry Marmie handled the defense. *Hall of Fame Players:* Marshall Faulk. *Primary Quarterbacks:* Jamie Martin. *Record:* **Interim Coach.**

Joe Vitt, the pride of Blackwood, New Jersey, was a 5'10" 190-pound linebacker with plenty of Jersey attitude at Towson State from 1974 to 1977. A year after graduating, he landed a job as strength coach for the nearby Baltimore Colts in 1979. It was the start of 30+ years as an NFL coach.

Three years later, Chuck Knox hired Joe as strength coach in Seattle but soon moved him to secondary coach. Vitt was in Seattle with Knox from 1982 to 1991 and then accompanied Chuck to Los Angeles in 1992 when Knox began his second stint as Rams' coach. In the next three seasons, he got to know fellow assistant Mike Martz, and their relationship would continue in coming years.

After Knox was cashiered by the Rams, Joe was hired as linebackers coach for Ray Rhodes on the Eagles in 1995. Most profitably in Philadelphia, he made friends with another Rhodes' assistant, Sean Payton. Again, Vitt followed his head coach to a second stop when Rhodes landed in Green Bay in 1999. Rhodes and Vitt coached the Packers for just one year; both were dismissed in 2000, but Joe signed on with Dick Vermeil in Kansas City that year.

Four years later, Rams' coach Mike Martz hired Vitt away from the Chiefs. However, the Greatest Show on Turf was no more, and Martz had lost his luster in town. When Mike had to step away from coaching in week six of the 2005 season due to a heart problem, Joe was named interim coach. Even when Martz was fully recovered, though, the Rams' front office would not permit him to return, and Mike was dismissed at season's end.

As head coach, Vitt did a credible job, leading the fading team to a 4–7 record. He told the press, "I've had a ball. The biggest fear I've had is having to talk to you guys everyday." Still, Joe was released when the season concluded. Meanwhile, Sean Payton landed the Saints' head coaching job and hired Vitt to coach the linebackers and to serve as assistant head coach — Payton's most trusted advisor.

Payton revitalized the franchise with Vitt at his side, winning the first championship in team history. While Joe was named in allegations involving the disbursement of pain killers for Payton in 2009, the case disappeared into arbitration, and he remained Sean's number one guy. Indeed, when Payton tore up his knee after a player rolled in to him on the sideline in 2011, Vitt assumed Sean's sideline spot for three games while the injured Payton retreated to the safety of the booth above the field. Vitt will serve as interim coach

Vitt, Joseph									
Year	Team	Games	Wins	Losses	Ties	%	P Wins	P Losses	P %
2005	Rams	11	4	7	0	.364	0	0	.000
1 year		11	4	7	0	.364	0	0	.000

in 2012 while Payton is suspended from the Saints' Bounty Scandal, despite Joe being suspended for six games himself.

Voyles, Carl M. 8/11/1898–1/11/1982. Oklahoma State. E; did not play professionally. *Apprenticeship:* College coach — 27 years (13 as head coach). *Roots:* None. *Branches:* None. *Coordinators/Key Assistants:* Horace Hendrickson coached the backs, Steve Hokuff the ends and A.H. Werner handled the line. *Hall of Fame Players:* None. *Primary Quarterbacks:* Bob Hoernschemeyer (Single Wing TB). *Tendencies:* • His team scored 18.1 points and allowed 27.6 per game • His team ran 49.9% of the time, which was 85% the league average • Eight rookie starters in one year • Winning Full Seasons to Losing Full Seasons: 0:1.

Born in McCloud, Oklahoma, Carl "Dutch" Voyles attended Oklahoma A&M, where he played football in 1917 and 1919 and basketball from 1919 to 1921. He spent 1918 in the military during World War I. Voyles went directly into coaching at Southwestern Oklahoma Teachers' College in 1922 and delivered a 19–15–1 record from 1922 to 1925.

Carl got his big break in coaching when the legendary Bob Zuppke hired him as the freshman coach at Illinois in 1926. Five years later, Voyles moved on to Duke in 1931, where, in addition to his duties as an assistant football coach, he also coached the track team. Carl spent eight years at Duke until he was offered the head coaching job at William & Mary in 1939.

From 1939 to 1943, Voyles compiled a 29–7–3 record with the Indians. When the school dropped football for World War II, Carl moved on to Auburn in 1944, but had less success in Alabama than Virginia. Voyles posted a 15–22 record with the Tigers through 1947. Quarterback Travis Tidwell recalled in Phillip Marshall's *Stadium Stories: Auburn Tigers,* "Coach Voyles was a hard-nosed guy. We would scrimmage until dark and after. It didn't matter how tired we were. We kept going. They didn't let you have any water in those days either. He believed in blood-and-guts football."

Auburn fired Voyles with two games remaining in 1947, but he landed in Brooklyn in 1948 when Bob Zuppke recommended him to Branch Rickey of the baseball Dodgers who had taken control of the football Dodgers of the All America Football Conference. The Dodgers were one of the weakest teams in the league

and did not improve under Carl. Tackle Ralph Sazio, who had played for Voyles at William & Mary, explained to Roger Godin in *The Brooklyn Football Dodgers,* "He was very persistent, a very dedicated man, certainly [a] very stable person.... He was what we call a single wing formation man.... He knew that system, but maybe it was a bit outdated when you ... started to play against some of the competition that we had in the league."

By 1949, the ever-frugal Rickey had seen enough financial loss and merged the Dodgers into the cross town New York football Yankees. He announced that the New York-Brooklyn team would be coached by Yankees' coach Red Strader with Voyles as his assistant. However, most of the better Dodger players were sent to the Chicago Hornets to beef up that weak AAFC franchise, and Carl was made a vice president of the baseball Dodgers to fulfill his contract.

Voyles left Brooklyn in 1950 to coach the Hamilton Tiger-Cats in Canada. From 1950 to 1955, Carl led the Cats to a 48–27–1 record and won the Grey Cup championship in 1953. That same year, Voyles tussled with the Bears' George Halas by trying to sign away Chicago quarterback George Blanda for Hamilton, but was foiled. After the 1955 season, Carl stepped down and went into real estate in the Toronto area for the next several years. In the 1960s and 1970s, Ralph Sazio, who had served as an assistant coach to Voyles in Hamilton, moved up in that organization from head coach to GM and ultimately to team vice president. Sazio made sure to employ his mentor as a scout throughout that period, and Carl also did some scouting for Buffalo. He died in 1983 at the age of 82.

Waller, Charles F. (Charlie) 12/26/1921–9/5/2009. Georgia. QB/HB; did not play professionally. *Apprenticeship:* College asst.—15 years; pro asst.—4 years. *Roots:* Sid Gillman. *Branches:* Bum Phillips. *Coordinators/Key Assistants:* Waller ran his own offense, while Bum Phillips handled the defense. *Hall of Fame Players:* Lance Alworth, Ron Mix. *Primary Quarterbacks:* John Hadl. *Tendencies:* • His teams scored 23 points and allowed 19.2 per game • His teams ran 47.1% of the time, which was 91% of the league average • Two starting quarterbacks in two years; 74% of starts to primary quarterback • Six rookie starters in two years • Winning Full Seasons to Losing Full Seasons: 0:1.

Voyles, Carl M.

Year	Team	Games	Wins	Losses	Ties	%	P Wins	P Losses	P %
1948	Brooklyn Dodgers (AAFC)	14	2	12	0	.143	0	0	.000
1 year		14	2	12	0	.143	0	0	.000

A native of Griffin, Georgia, Charlie Waller played quarterback and halfback for Oglethorpe University from 1939 to 1941 and captained the team as a senior. Upon graduation, he went into the Navy for the duration of the war and took up high school coaching after being discharged in 1946. Following consecutive state championships at Decatur High in 1949 and 1950, Waller was hired by Shug Jordan as backfield coach at Auburn in 1951. Four years later, he moved on to Texas in 1955 and then went on to Clemson in 1957.

Charlie spent nine years at Clemson before being hired by Sid Gillman in 1966 to coach the Chargers' backfield. Gillman's ulcer caused him to step down from coaching nine games into the 1969 season, although he remained the team's GM, and Waller was promoted to head coach. Charlie finished the season 4–1 and set out to try some new things in 1970. In training camp, he experimented with the 3–4 defense and gave young quarterback Marty Domres a full shot to unseat veteran John Hadl.

Unfortunately, San Diego was still a third place club in the West, unable to truly compete with the Raiders and the Chiefs. In December following the team's disappointing 5–6–3 performance, Gillman announced he was feeling better and would return to the sidelines in 1971 with Waller going back to being backfield coach.

Charlie decided that was untenable and joined George Allen in Washington as offensive coordinator. Waller balanced competing quarterbacks Sonny Jurgensen and Billy Kilmer, and the Redskins went to the Super Bowl in 1972. Allen liked to bring in veterans of all backgrounds and even acquired the supremely disgruntled runner Duane Thomas in 1973. Waller did his best to reach the troubled Thomas, but in August 1974 Thomas attacked Waller after a confrontation and then was cut. A week later, though, Thomas apologized and was reinstated on the team. Duane was cut for good the following August, but Charlie remained with the Redskins through 1977.

When Allen signed to coach the Rams in 1978 after being fired by Washington, Waller came with

him. Regrettably, Allen was fired during the preseason and replaced by assistant Ray Malavasi who made no staff changes for the season at that late date. However, all was not well. Waller and backfield coach Max Coley even got into a fist fight during a game plan meeting in August. At the end of the season, Malavasi cleaned house and hired his own staff.

Charlie then was out of football until George Allen rehired him in 1982 to coach the offense for the Chicago Blitz in the USFL. Waller later coached for Oakland and Memphis in the USFL before retiring to Florida in 1986. He died in 2009 at age 87.

WALLER, RONALD B. (RON) 2/14/1933– Maryland. Played HB for the Rams from 1955 to 1958 and the Chargers in 1960. *Apprenticeship*: Semipro coach — 6 years (3 as head coach); pro asst.— 2 years. *Roots*: Harland Svare. *Branches*: None. *Coordinators/Key Assistants*: None. *Hall of Fame Players*: Dan Fouts, Deacon Jones. *Primary Quarterbacks*: Wayne Clark. *Record*: **Interim Coach.**

Sometimes called the "All American Dollar," Ron Waller was a bit of a hustler who was willing to try anything to get ahead. He once reflected to the *Los Angeles Times*, "I had a glamorous marriage and a big ego. I also had some misplaced values. I thought I had to be a multimillionaire by the time I was 40. Well, I've matured some. I realize that the satisfaction is in the job, not the rewards of the job."

Waller was born in Hastings, Florida, and was a star schoolboy athlete in Delaware who played for the University of Maryland from 1952 to 1954. Drafted in the second round by Los Angeles, Waller led the Rams in rushing and made the Pro Bowl as a rookie in 1955. That same year, Ron married Post Cereal heiress Marjorie Durant who was a champion swimmer and an aspiring actress that appeared in three movies in the 1950s. Waller's playing career with the Rams ended with a knee injury in 1958, so his wife's grandmother encouraged him to move into the management side of the game. Ron gathered some backers and attempted to buy the Chicago Cardinals in 1958 with the plan of moving them to Miami, but was

Waller, Charles F. (Charlie)									
Year	*Team*	*Games*	*Wins*	*Losses*	*Ties*	*%*	*P Wins*	*P Losses*	*P %*
1969	Chargers	5	4	1	0	.800	0	0	.000
1970	Chargers	14	5	6	3	.464	0	0	.000
2 years		19	9	7	3	.553	0	0	.000

Waller, Ronald B. (Ron)									
Year	*Team*	*Games*	*Wins*	*Losses*	*Ties*	*%*	*P Wins*	*P Losses*	*P %*
1973	Chargers	6	1	5	0	.167	0	0	.000
1 year		6	1	5	0	.167	0	0	.000

spurned in his bid. Next, he tried to break into the world of boxing promotion in 1959. By 1960, the struggling promoter was offered the chance to buy the Los Angeles franchise of the fledgling American Football League, but had doubts of the league's feasibility; instead, the Chargers' franchise was purchased by Ron's Santa Monica neighbor, Barron Hilton. Waller came out of retirement to appear in two games as a Los Angeles Charger that year, but then retired for good.

Ron's Hollywood marriage ended in 1961 and over the next five years he tried running a public relations firm, a liquor store, a bowling alley and a catering company. In 1966, he gave up on the West Coast and returned to Delaware to head a school for delinquent girls. On the side, he served as an assistant coach for the minor league Wilmington Clippers that season. He took over as the team's head coach in 1967 and led them to a 2–7 record before being named head coach of the Harrisburg Capitols in 1968. After a 3–8 season, he returned to the assistants' ranks with the Atlantic Coast Football League champion Pottstown Firebirds in 1969 and 1970. Waller finished his six-year run in the ACFL by steering the Norfolk Neptunes to a 9–3 mark in 1971. He told the *Los Angeles Times*, "You do it all in the minors. I was a coach, general manager, director of ticket sales and PR man. I am as familiar with front office intrigue as I am with diagramming plays."

Ron returned to the Chargers as special teams coach in 1972 under Harland Svare. When the team started 1973 1–6–1, Svare, who was also the team's GM, kicked himself upstairs and named Waller the interim coach. Ron's biggest move was relegating 40-year-old Johnny Unitas to the taxi squad. Waller favored razzle dazzle play calling, but the 1973 Chargers were a drug-addled mess. Despite leading San Diego to just a 1–5 record, Ron told reporters he was interested in returning in 1974, "If I were the owner, I would get the individual best suited for the job. Of course, if Ron Waller was available, I'd probably hire him."

Not surprisingly, Ron was fired at the end of the year. He then was named head coach of the Philadelphia Bell of the new World Football League in 1974 and led the team to a 9–11 record. The following August, he resigned during the preseason after a dispute with Philadelphia's owner. Waller coached the Southern California Rhinos of the California Football

League to a 5–5 record in 1977 and then became the director of player personnel for the Chiefs from 1978 to 1982. Ron served under former Chiefs' coach Marv Levy as offensive coordinator for the USFL's Chicago Blitz in 1984 and then returned to Kansas City as a scout from 1986 to 1991. He also scouted for the Rams in the 1990s.

WALSH, ADAM J. 12/4/1901–1/13/1985. Notre Dame. C; did not play professionally. *Apprenticeship:* College coach — 20 years (12 as head coach). *Roots:* None. *Branches:* Bob Snyder, Red Conkright (i). *Coordinators/Key Assistants:* Bob Snyder coached the backs, while Red Conkright coached the line. *Hall of Fame Players:* Bob Waterfield. *Primary Quarterbacks:* Bob Waterfield. *Record:* **NFL Championship 1945.** *Tendencies:* • His teams scored 24.8 points and allowed 18.7 per game • His teams ran 59.7% of the time, which was 94% of the league average • One starting quarterbacks in two years; 100% of starts to primary quarterback • Five rookie starters in two years • Winning Full Seasons to Losing Full Seasons: 2:0.

Adam Walsh was born in Churchville, Iowa, but his family moved to California in 1908. Walsh graduated from Hollywood High School and enrolled at Notre Dame in 1921. Adam played center on the famous Seven Mules line that blocked for the fabled Four Horsemen backfield from 1922 to 1924. Walsh was so well respected that he was team captain and an All-American as a senior.

Many years later, Walsh recalled to the *Des Moines Register*, "I swore that I'd never coach. I had taken mechanical engineering at Notre Dame and that's what I wanted for my future. But during Easter vacation of my senior year, I found myself coaching Santa Clara in spring practice." Adam was named head coach for the fall and led the Broncos to a 17–18–2 record from 1925 to 1928. He left Santa Clara in 1929 to become line coach at Yale and stayed there through the 1933 season. Walsh moved on to Harvard as line coach in 1934 and then was named head coach at Bowdoin College in Maine in 1935 where he posted a 34–16–6 record from 1935 to 1942. When the college dropped football for the war, Adam returned to his alma mater and coached the line in South Bend in 1943 and 1944.

In the meantime, Adam's brother Charles (known as "Chile") had taken over as the general manager of the Cleveland Rams in 1944. When Rams'

Walsh, Adam J.									
Year	Team	Games	Wins	Losses	Ties	%	P Wins	P Losses	P %
1945	Rams	10	9	1	0	.900	1	0	1.000
1946	Rams	11	6	4	1	.591	0	0	.000
2 years		21	15	5	1	.738	1	0	1.000

coach Aldo Donelli joined the military in 1945, Chile offered the Rams head coaching job first to Bears' assistant Luke Johnsos before turning to his brother. Adam took over the Rams in 1945 and installed the T formation with rookie quarterback Bob Waterfield. With spectacular passing, kicking, running and punting from Waterfield, Cleveland hosted the NFL championship game that December. On a freezing day, Walsh persuaded Redskins coach Dudley DeGroot that as a point of honor neither team should wear sneakers because only Washington had them and that would constitute an unfair advantage on the icy field.

The Rams won the game 15–14, with the margin being a safety awarded when a Sammy Baugh pass from his own end zone hit the goal post. However, there was fallout for both teams: DeGroot was fired for his honorable stance toward footwear, while Cleveland had no opportunity to celebrate its first NFL title because the Rams moved to Los Angeles in the offseason. Walsh coached the first Los Angeles Ram team in 1946 that included, Kenny Washington and Woody Strode, the first black players in the league since 1933. Adam then unexpectedly resigned at the end of 1946 and was followed soon after by his brother who quit as GM a month later.

Adam returned to Bowdoin in 1947, telling the *Los Angeles Times*, "Yes, I turned down lots of money in both professional leagues and also rejected offers from other colleges to return to Bowdoin." He coached at the school from 1947 to 1958 and compiled a much weaker 29–51–3 record in his second stint there. In addition, Walsh was elected a Maine state representative as a Democrat for two terms from 1953 to 1960 and also served as minority leader in the state legislature. President Kennedy appointed Adam U.S. Marshall for Maine in 1961 and Walsh functioned in that role through 1966. He was elected to the College Football Hall of Fame in 1968. Suffering from lung cancer, Adam died on a plane to Providence in 1985 at the age of 83

WALSH, CHARLES F. (CHILE) 2/4/1903–
9/4/1971. Notre Dame. E; did not play professionally. *Apprenticeship:* College coach — 6 years (4 as head coach). *Roots:* None. *Branches:* None. *Coordinators/Key Assistants:* None. *Hall of Fame Players:* None. *Primary Quarterbacks:* None. *Record:* Interim Coach.

Born in Des Moines, Iowa, Chile Walsh moved

with his family to California in 1908. Like his older brother, Adam, Chile graduated from Hollywood High School and enrolled at Notre Dame to play under Knute Rockne. By the time Chile played end for the Fighting Irish from 1925 to 1927, Adam had already begun his coaching career at Santa Clara.

Like Adam, Chile took up coaching right out of South Bend. Chile served as the ends coach for St. Louis University in 1928 and 1929 under Notre Dame alumnus Hunk Anderson before being named head coach there in 1930. From 1930 to 1933, he led the school to a 22–9–2 record and then got involved with an independent professional team in the area — the St. Louis Gunners.

The Gunners were a high level independent club, but were clearly not of NFL quality. However, when the NFL's Cincinnati Reds were about to fold during the 1934 season, they were purchased by St. Louis and merged into the Gunners who then finished out the Reds' remaining three scheduled league games with Walsh as head coach. St. Louis beat Pittsburgh 6–0 in their first game, but lost 40–7 to Detroit and 21–14 to Green Bay to conclude the NFL season. The league then revoked the St. Louis franchise, and the team folded in 1935.

Walsh joined a Florida real estate and hotel management firm in 1935 but returned to coaching in 1940 when another former St. Louis Gunners' coach, Jimmy Conzelman, was named head coach of the Cardinals and hired Chile to coach the ends. Walsh left Chicago for Cleveland in 1942 to coach the ends for Dutch Clark on the Rams. When Clark resigned in 1943, Chile was named his successor, but the Rams suspended operations for the year due to the war. The team resumed operations in 1944 with Walsh as the club's general manager and vice president. Since owner Dan Reeves was still in the service, Chile ran the Rams and hired Buff Donelli to coach the team in 1944. After Donelli went into the military in 1945, Chile turned to his brother Adam who led Cleveland to the NFL title in his first year.

The Rams moved to Los Angeles in 1946 to open up the West Coast for the NFL. Under pressure from the Los Angeles Coliseum Commission, Chile also hired the league's first black players since 1933, although neither Kenny Washington nor Woody Strode had a major impact on the team in 1946. In December, Adam quit as the Rams' coach; a month later, Chile

Walsh, Charles F. (Chile)									
Year	Team	Games	Wins	Losses	Ties	%	P Wins	P Losses	P %
1934	St. Louis Gunners (defunct)	3	1	2	0	.333	0	0	.000
1 year		3	1	2	0	.333	0	0	.000

resigned as GM after several differences with Reeves. Walsh told reporters that he had realized two great dreams with the Rams: being the GM of a championship club and bringing major league football to his hometown of Los Angeles. Chile went into private business and never returned to the NFL. He died in 1971 at the age of 68.

WALSH, WILLIAM E. (BILL) 11/30/1931–7/30/2007. San Jose State. QB/TE; did not play professionally. *Apprenticeship:* College coach — 9 years (2 as head coach); semipro head coach —1 year; pro asst.—10 years. *Roots:* John Rauch, Paul Brown, Tommy Prothro. *Branches:* Chuck Studley (i), Sam Wyche, George Seifert, Bruce Coslet, Mike Holmgren, Denny Green, Ray Rhodes, Mike White. *Coordinators/Key Assistants*: Sam Wyche then Paul Hackett then Mike Holmgren were the key offensive coaches, while Chuck Studley then George Seifert handled the defense. *Hall of Fame Players:* Fred Dean, Ronnie Lott, Joe Montana, Jerry Rice, O.J. Simpson, Steve Young. *Primary Quarterbacks:* Joe Montana, Steve DeBerg. *Record:* **Hall of Fame Coach**; Super Bowl Championships 1981, 1984, 1988 *Tendencies:* • His teams scored 24.4 points and allowed 18.8 per game • His teams ran 46.3% of the time, which was 96% of the league average • Seven starting quarterbacks in ten years; 89% of starts to primary quarterbacks • 21 rookie starters in ten years • Winning Full Seasons to Losing Full Seasons: 7:3.

Head-to-Head:		
Hall of Fame Opponent	Regular Season	Postseason
Joe Gibbs	4–1	0–1
Bud Grant	1–2	0–0
Tom Landry	3–2	1–0
Marv Levy	1–0	0–0
Chuck Noll	2–2	0–0
Don Shula	1–2	1–0
Total	12–9	2–1

Bill Walsh had a unique vision and perspective among football coaches. He once told the *San Francisco Chronicle*, "If I have any talent, it's in the artistic end of football. The variation of movement of 11 players and the orchestration of that facet of football is beautiful to me." He left a lasting legacy as an innovative strategist, talented team builder and influential leader throughout the game despite serving as a head coach for just ten years in the NFL. Ultimately, Walsh was a haunted perfectionist. Tackle Keith Fahnhorst once sorrowfully summarized his coach to *Sports Illustrated*, "He was the type who had everything, but he could never enjoy it."

Bill was born in Los Angeles, but his family lived in Oregon for a number of years before he returned to California to graduate from Hayward High School in the Bay Area. Although he played running back in high school, he was a left-handed quarterback for San Mateo Junior College in 1950 and 1951. Transferring to San Jose State in 1952, Walsh was converted to tight end by Coach Bob Bronzan. At San Jose, Bill not only played two years of football, but was also an intramural boxing champion. After graduation, he spent a hitch in the Army at Fort Ord and then returned to his alma mater as a graduate assistant from 1955 to 1956. When he left in 1957 to coach high school football, he had Bronzan's written recommendation claiming, "I predict Bill Walsh will become the outstanding football coach in the United States."

Walsh coached high school for three years until Marv Levy hired him as the defensive coach for California in 1960. Three years later, Bill moved on to Stanford where he served under John Ralston from 1963 to 1965. In 1966, Al Davis hired Bill as the backfield coach for the Raiders on John Rauch's staff. Despite spending just one year in Oakland, Walsh absorbed Davis' commanding passing offense before leaving in 1967 to take the head coaching position for the semipro San Jose Apaches. Bill led the Apaches to an 8–4 record and then was hired by coaching legend Paul Brown to coach the offense for the expansion Cincinnati Bengals in 1968.

Walsh, William E. (Bill)									
Year	Team	Games	Wins	Losses	Ties	%	P Wins	P Losses	P %
1979	49ers	16	2	14	0	.125	0	0	.000
1980	49ers	16	6	10	0	.375	0	0	.000
1981	49ers	16	13	3	0	.813	3	0	1.000
1982	49ers	9	3	6	0	.333	0	0	.000
1983	49ers	16	10	6	0	.625	1	1	.500
1984	49ers	16	15	1	0	.938	3	0	1.000
1985	49ers	16	10	6	0	.625	0	1	.000
1986	49ers	16	10	5	1	.656	0	1	.000
1987	49ers	15	13	2	0	.867	0	1	.000
1988	49ers	16	10	6	0	.625	3	0	1.000
10 years		152	92	59	1	.609	10	4	.714

In Cincinnati, Walsh installed a Davis-like downfield passing attack with sensational rookie quarterback Greg Cook in 1969, but when Cook's career was destroyed by a shoulder injury, Bill had to adjust. His best remaining quarterback was Virgil Carter who was undersized and lacked a strong arm, but also was smart, mobile and able to deliver accurate short passes. What Walsh devised that year later became known as the West Coast Offense, although a better name would be the Cincinnati Offense or, best of all, the Walsh Offense. That offense has permeated the NFL in the intervening four decades.

The Walsh Offense is a ball-control passing approach. It relies on a mobile quarterback to take short drop backs, quickly go through a progression of reads of his receivers' timed routes and to hit the open one in stride to allow the receiver to make additional yardage after the catch. The offense spreads the field horizontally, making the defense cover the whole field, accumulates first downs and keeps the clock moving. Walsh later described three key distinctions of the offense to the *New York Times*, "I think we're willing to settle for a little less yardage on passes than some teams are. Two, our willingness to throw to the second and third receivers. And three, to look downfield for the great individual play." In 1970, Carter led the third-year Bengals to a division title in this new offense, and the Bengals finished in the top ten in yards in five of the next six years with young quarterback Ken Anderson replacing Carter. Bill came to believe that he was the heir apparent to Paul Brown, but when Brown finally stepped down in 1976, he appointed crusty line coach Tiger Johnson his replacement. Walsh was devastated and left Cincinnati.

Brown reacted in a petty manner and talked down Walsh throughout the league, but Bill landed the offensive coordinator position on the Chargers under Tommy Prothro in 1976 and tutored struggling Dan Fouts in the fundamentals of quarterbacking. One year later, Walsh was offered his first major head coaching job by Stanford. He later lauded Prothro for encouraging him to take it and better himself in contrast to Paul Brown's self-centered attitude to assistants. Bill led Stanford to a 17–7 record and two bowl wins from 1977 to 1978.

Nearby, the San Francisco 49ers were being deconstructed by egomaniacal GM Joe Thomas. By 1979, owner Eddie DeBartolo had had enough — he fired Thomas and coach Fred O'Connor and put Walsh in total control of the football operations. The job that Walsh did in transforming the 2–14 49ers into a Super Bowl champion in three years cannot be praised enough. Walsh quickly proved himself a master of the draft, not only in finding talent but in correctly slotting the perceived value of that talent so that he made a regular practice of trading higher picks for additional lower picks. In this method, he was able to get more of the players he had targeted to start with. He was the first coach to truly work the draft in this way and did it throughout his decade in San Francisco. For example, in 1986, he made eight draft trades and ended up selecting eight future starters to help overturn an aging two-time Super Bowl team.

His key moves at the beginning were choosing quarterback Joe Montana in the third round in 1979 and obtaining pass rusher Fred Dean and middle linebacker Jack Reynolds through trades. Walsh once noted to the *San Francisco Chronicle* that his greatest contributions to the game had to do with preparation: "the format of practice and contingency planning." That preplanning was best seen in Bill's innovation of scripting the first 15–25 plays so that he could make better play calls during the excitement of the game itself. The 1981 49ers had no rushing attack worth mentioning, but rode Montana's mastery of the Walsh Offense and a surprising defense led by three rookie defensive backs to beat Paul Brown's Bengals in the Super Bowl. After the 1982 team was derailed by drug problems, Walsh retooled by 1984 and led the 49ers to a 15–1 season that was culminated by beating record-setting passer Dan Marino and the Dolphins in the Super Bowl.

Bill became so well known for his offensive inventiveness that the 49ers were often thought of as a "finesse team." However, Walsh also put a strong, hard hitting defense on the field led by safety Ronnie Lott. While the 49er offense led the league in scoring once and was second another year, the defense finished in the top three in points allowed five times. Even though the handsome, silver-haired coach on the sideline appeared to be a charming sophisticate, Bill also reveled in his toughness. Assistant coach Fred Van Appen told the *San Francisco Chronicle*, "He's not always the distinguished, patriarchal guy television viewers are used to seeing on the sidelines. He's a very competitive guy, and he can be scathing, especially in the heat of battle. There have been times when I would have gladly split his skull with an axe. Then again, he's the greatest."

Lott told *Sports Illustrated*, "He used to be a players' coach. He'd crack jokes, be sarcastic. But he started to change after the second Super Bowl. The media started calling him a genius and prying into his private life. He was really distant after that." After San Francisco lost in the first round of the playoffs in each of the next three years, the "genius" of Walsh was beginning to lose its luster to owner DeBartolo and to fickle fans. Bill then pulled off the key trade that would extend the 49ers' dynasty for a second decade when he obtained quarterback Steve Young from Tampa in 1987. Bill grimly explained his dilemma to *Sports Illustrated*, "In the pros, I felt great affection for the players, but I couldn't demonstrate it. I was the employer. If I were to keep a player on too long out of friendship, I would be compromising the interests of the entire venture."

Pushed by Young and fully recovered from injuries in 1988, Montana led San Francisco to a third Super Bowl triumph, again over the Bengals. Overwhelmed by the pressures of coaching at the highest level, Bill abruptly retired. His hand-picked successor, George Seifert, led the team to a second straight championship in 1989 and back to the NFC championship game in 1990 before Montana was succeeded by Young who won his own Super Bowl four years later.

Walsh worked as a television analyst for three years, but missed coaching. He returned to Stanford in 1992 and compiled a 17–17–1 record there from 1992 to 1994. He stepped down in 1995 and was out of football for the next few years, aside from some consulting for the 49ers in 1996. In 1999, Bill was welcomed back to the San Francisco organization as vice president and general manager to help extract the team from the "salary cap hell" they had slipped into by overpaying for talent. Walsh overturned the roster, brought in former San Jose State quarterback Jeff Garcia and the club quickly returned to the postseason by 2001. With this success, Bill stepped back into a consulting role for the next three years. He moved on to a consulting role with Stanford from 2004 to 2006. At that point, his health began to fail and he died from leukemia in 2007 at the age of 75.

Walsh told the *San Jose Mercury News* in 2002 that he regretted his initial departure from the 49ers, "I never should have left. I'm still disappointed in myself for not continuing. There's no telling how many Super Bowls we might have won." While there is some poignancy to that remark, it can also be seen as a slight to his successor by a man with a very large ego. Ironically, the success of Seifert and several other Walsh-trained coaches may be Bill's greatest heritage. Jim Harbaugh, who got to know Walsh when coaching at Stanford, emphasized Bill's effect on all coaches to *Sports Illustrated*, "He created the modern-day practice, the modern-day weekly schedule, the way to run a meeting, the way to manage an organization. And when it comes to football expertise, he's the most respected man who's ever coached the game, period." Furthermore, Walsh made a point of extending opportunities to African American coaches by establishing a minority coaching fellowship in 49er training camps that Tony Dungy, Marvin Lewis and many others utilized. The program, now run by the league, is ongoing and is named the Bill Walsh Minority Coaching Fellowship Program.

WALTON, JOSEPH F. (JOE) 2/15/1935– Pittsburgh. Played E for the Redskins and Giants from 1957 to 1963. *Apprenticeship:* Semipro asst.— 3 years; pro asst.—14 years. *Roots:* Alex Webster, George Allen, Jack Pardee, Walt Michaels. *Branches:* Bud Carson, Rich Kotite. *Coordinators/Key Assistants*: Rich Kotite ran the offense, while Joe Gardi then Bud Carson then Ralph Hawkins handled the defense. *Hall of Fame Players:* None. *Primary Quarterbacks:* Ken O'Brien. *Tendencies:* • His teams scored 21.3 points and allowed 22.3 per game • His teams ran 45.5% of the time, which was 97% of the league average • Six starting quarterbacks in seven years; 64% of starts to primary quarterback • 16 rookie starters in seven years • Winning Full Seasons to Losing Full Seasons: 3:4.

Like Joe Namath, Joe Walton was born in Beaver Falls, Pennsylvania, and culminated his pro career with the New York Jets. However, Walton is not a hero of Jets' fans like Broadway Joe. Center Joe Fields recalled to Mark Cannizzaro for *New York Jets*, "I don't think he'll be remembered too fondly by the players or the fans. He inherited a healthy patient, a team that came within one game of the Super Bowl. All we needed was a little exploratory surgery to get better, but Joe cut everything up and killed the patient."

Walton began as an All-American end at the University of Pittsburgh who played for the Panthers from 1954 to 1956. Drafted in the second round by the Redskins, he spent four years in Washington, where his father Frank had played guard for three years in the 1930s and 1940s. Obtained by the Giants in 1961, Joe was an undersized, but fierce and reliable tight end for the best passing attack in the league for the next three years in New York. He caught 17 touchdown passes in that time and was called by his quarterback Y.A. Tittle, "the best third down receiver in the game, bar none."

When Joe retired in 1964, he became a scout for the Giants during the next three years. From 1967 to 1969, he worked as an assistant coach for the Giants'

Walton, Joseph F. (Joe)									
Year	*Team*	*Games*	*Wins*	*Losses*	*Ties*	*%*	*P Wins*	*P Losses*	*P %*
1983	Jets	16	7	9	0	.438	0	0	.000
1984	Jets	16	7	9	0	.438	0	0	.000
1985	Jets	16	11	5	0	.688	0	1	.000
1986	Jets	16	10	6	0	.625	1	1	.500
1987	Jets	15	6	9	0	.400	0	0	.000
1988	Jets	16	8	7	1	.531	0	0	.000
1989	Jets	16	4	12	0	.250	0	0	.000
7 years		111	53	57	1	.482	1	2	.333

farm clubs in Westchester and Long Island and then joined Alex Webster's staff in New York in 1969. When Webster was dismissed after the 1973 season, Walton returned to Washington as the running backs coach for George Allen. After Allen left, Joe was promoted to offensive coordinator under Jack Pardee in 1978. From 1978 to 1980, he helped develop Joe Theismann into a starting quarterback for the Redskins.

Pardee was replaced by Joe Gibbs in 1981, and Walton came back to New York, this time as offensive coordinator with the Jets. After two seasons, Joe was promoted to head coach when Walt Michaels abruptly retired under a strange cloud following the bitter AFC championship loss to the Dolphins in the mud in 1982. Walton favored a fairly complex offense. He explained what he preferred to the *New York Times*, "The use of more formations, motion, situation substitutions. You combat what the defense is doing to you, but you must be basically sound and balanced. I believe in the running game and the short-pass game."

His tenure as the Jets' head coach was a rocky six-year rollercoaster, though. Defensive end Marty Lyons told Mark Cannizzaro for *New York Jets*, "He was a great offensive coordinator, but it was hard for him to make that transition from coordinator to head coach. He had a difficult time relating to the players." Joe transitioned from Richard Todd to Ken O'Brien at quarterback in 1985 and promoted Rich Kotite to offensive coordinator and brought in Zeke Bratkowski as quarterback coach that same year. In this period of change, the Jets made the playoffs in both 1985 and 1986. Unfortunately, they lost in the first round in 1985, while in 1986 O'Brien came up with a dead arm in December and the Jets dropped their last five games to back into the postseason. Indeed, the team's record for the last quarter of the season during Joe's seven years in New York was a paltry 9–19.

With both the players and the fans in near revolt, Walton was fired after the 1989 season. He spent the next two years as Chuck Noll's offensive coordinator in Pittsburgh, but when Noll retired in 1992, Joe was

out of football that year. In 1993, he was recruited by a former Pitt teammate to become the first-ever head coach at Robert Morris University and has been there ever since. Walton led the Colonials to Division IAA championships in 1999 and 2000 and has compiled a 106–79–1 record at the school through the 2011 season. In Joe's honor, Robert Morris University named its new football field Joe Walton Stadium in 2005.

WANNSTEDT, DAVID R. (DAVE) 5/21/1952– Pittsburgh. T; did not play professionally. *Apprenticeship:* College asst.—14 years; pro asst.—4 years. *Roots:* Jimmy Johnson. *Branches:* Dave McGinnis, Jim Bates (i), Eric Studesville (i), Ron Rivera, Greg Schiano. *Coordinators/Key Assistants:* For the Bears, Ron Turner then Matt Cavanaugh ran the offense, while Bob Slowik handled the defense; for the Dolphins, Chan Gailey then Norv Turner then Chris Foerster ran the offense, while Jim Bates handled the defense. *Hall of Fame Players:* Richard Dent, Thurman Thomas. *Primary Quarterbacks:* Erik Kramer, Jay Fiedler. *Tendencies:* • His teams scored 18.9 points and allowed 19.3 per game • His teams ran 48.7% of the time, which was 110% of the league average • 12 starting quarterbacks in 11 years; 62% of starts to primary quarterbacks • 18 rookie starters in 11 years • Winning Full Seasons to Losing Full Seasons: 6:4.

Born in Baldwin, Pennsylvania, Dave Wannstedt played tackle for the University of Pittsburgh when Heisman Trophy winner Tony Dorsett played for the Panthers. Dave was drafted in the 15th round by Green Bay in 1974, but injured his neck and spent the season on injured reserve. The next year he began his coaching career as a graduate assistant at his alma mater under Johnny Majors. Wannstedt stayed at Pitt through the 1978 season, even after Jackie Sherrill succeeded Majors in 1977 and brought in Jimmy Johnson as one of his assistants; subsequently Dave and Jimmy would become a coaching team throughout their coaching careers.

In fact, when Johnson was named head coach at

Wannstedt, David R. (Dave)									
Year	Team	Games	Wins	Losses	Ties	%	P Wins	P Losses	P %
1993	Bears	16	7	9	0	.438	0	0	.000
1994	Bears	16	9	7	0	.563	1	1	.500
1995	Bears	16	9	7	0	.563	0	0	.000
1996	Bears	16	7	9	0	.438	0	0	.000
1997	Bears	16	4	12	0	.250	0	0	.000
1998	Bears	16	4	12	0	.250	0	0	.000
2000	Dolphins	16	11	5	0	.688	1	1	.500
2001	Dolphins	16	11	5	0	.688	0	1	.000
2002	Dolphins	16	9	7	0	.563	0	0	.000
2003	Dolphins	16	10	6	0	.625	0	0	.000
2004	Dolphins	9	1	8	0	.111	0	0	.000
11 years		169	82	87	0	.485	2	3	.400

Oklahoma State in 1979, Dave came along as defensive line coach. Four years later in 1983, Wannstedt left Johnson to coach the USC defensive line, but he reunited with Johnson in 1986 as the defensive coordinator for the Miami Hurricanes. The two were together for the school's 1987 national championship, and the Hurricanes lost just two games in the three years the intense Johnson and more laid back Wannstedt joined forces in Miami.

Johnson was named head coach of the Dallas Cowboys in 1989 and promptly hired Dave as his defensive coordinator. In four years, Johnson transformed the Cowboys into a Super Bowl champion, and Wannstedt cashed in by becoming the first member of Jimmy's staff to gain his own head coaching position in the NFL in 1993 when he was hired by the Bears. Dave had been seriously pursued by the division rival Giants as well, but did not want to compete so directly with his close friend Johnson in Dallas.

In Chicago, Wannstedt replaced Mike Ditka and told the press, "I'm sure some of the fans will wonder if I'm tough enough to be in Chicago. I'm tough enough, and I'm looking forward to the challenge. I'm a hands-on coach, enthusiastic, emotional. A players' coach. I need the respect and like to have good rapport with players." With the Bears, he was a .500 coach for the first four seasons before everything fell apart. Those first four seasons balanced two 9–7 seasons with two 7–9 ones. The Bears did make the playoffs in Dave's second year, but they were never a very good team. Relying on quarterbacks like Steve Walsh, Steve Stenstrom and Erik Kramer, the team finished 24th or worse in scoring in five of Wannstedt's six years in Chicago. Wannstedt personnel problems sunk his chances with the Bears. His drafts were poor, as were his free agent signings and trades, highlighted by the dealing of a number one draft pick for washout quarterback Rick Mirer and the signing of linebacker Bryan Cox who flopped in his two years as a Bear. Following consecutive 4–12 seasons, Wannstedt was fired in 1999.

At that point, Jimmy Johnson was struggling in his second NFL stop with the Dolphins and brought in Dave to coach the defense in 1999. Miami limped into the playoffs that year and were battered 62–7 by Jacksonville in the divisional round. Both quarterback Dan Marino and Coach Johnson called it quits after that humiliation. Johnson then handpicked Wannstedt as his successor. Despite having to replace Marino with Jay Fiedler at quarterback, the Dolphins made the postseason in Dave's first two years in Miami by relying on a strong running game and a sturdy defense. In three of his first four years, the defense finished in the top four in fewest points allowed. Wannstedt kept trying to replace Fiedler at quarterback, but the succession of free agent Ray Lucas, free agent Brian Griese and trade acquisition A.J. Feeley could do no better. When the defense imploded in 2004 in conjunction with the sudden retirement of unpredictable running back Ricky Williams, the Dolphins lost seven of their first eight games, and Dave stepped down as coach.

The following season, Wannstedt returned to his alma mater again, this time as head coach. From 2005 to 2010, he led the Panthers to a 42–31 record (oddly the same as his tally with the Dolphins), but no BCS bowl invitations and was forced out as coach. Dave returned to the NFL in 2011 as the assistant head coach/linebackers coach of the Buffalo Bills under Chan Gailey who had been one of Dave's offensive coordinators with the Dolphins. In 2012, Gailey promoted him to defensive coordinator.

WATERFIELD, ROBERT S. (BOB) 7/26/1920– 3/25/1983. UCLA. Played QB for the Rams from 1945 to 1952. *Apprenticeship:* Pro asst.—1 year. *Roots:* Sid Gillman. *Branches:* Harland Svare, Tom Fears. *Coordinators/Key Assistants:* Hampton Pool ran the offense, while Don Paul then Harland Svare handled the defense. *Hall of Fame Players:* Deacon Jones, Ollie Matson, Merlin Olsen, Les Richter. *Primary Quarterbacks:* Zeke Bratkowski. *Record:* **Hall of Fame Player.** *Tendencies:* • His teams scored 19.5 points and allowed 23.9 per game • His teams ran 48.2% of the time, which was 93% of the league average • Four starting quarterbacks in three years; 56% of starts to primary quarterback • 12 rookie starters in three years • Winning Full Seasons to Losing Full Seasons: 0:2.

Bob Waterfield was the quintessential All-American. In addition to being a top flight passer, "Waterbuckets" was a good runner, a big-legged punter and accurate placekicker as well as a solid defensive back. Born in Elmira, New York, his family moved to Van Nuys, California when he was a boy, and Bob enrolled at UCLA in 1938. He dropped out in 1939 and missed 1940 because he was declared ineligible, but starred as a triple threat quarterback in UCLA's modified T formation in 1941 and 1942. Waterfield led the Bruins to

Waterfield, Robert S. (Bob)									
Year	Team	Games	Wins	Losses	Ties	%	P Wins	P Losses	P %
1960	Rams	12	4	7	1	.375	0	0	.000
1961	Rams	14	4	10	0	.286	0	0	.000
1962	Rams	8	1	7	0	.125	0	0	.000
3 years		34	9	24	1	.279	0	0	.000

the 1943 Rose Bowl and then went into the Army, although he was discharged the following year due to a knee problem. In the meantime, he married his high school sweetheart, aspiring move star Jane Russell, and then returned for his senior year at UCLA in 1944. Drafted by the Cleveland Rams, Bob was an immediate sensation as a rookie in 1945, leading the Rams to the NFL title.

Waterfield had a short, Hall of Fame playing career with the Rams from 1945 to 1952 and led the team to four NFL championship games. Beginning with the 1950 season, though, he had to compete for playing time with another future Hall of Famer in Norm Van Brocklin. For Bob's last three years, the two ace quarterbacks alternated quarters with Waterfield playing the first and third and Van Brocklin the second and fourth each game. Following the 1952 season, Bob retired from playing to devote himself to his other interests that included a restaurant, oil investments and a film production company in partnership with his wife.

Waterfield returned to the Rams in 1958 as an offensive coach under Sid Gillman but left after one year because he did not see eye-to-eye with the head coach. When Gillman was dismissed in 1960, Bob was a popular choice with the public to succeed him as head coach. However, much like another inexperienced quarterback legend elevated to head coach through popular acclaim a decade later (Bart Starr in Green Bay), Waterfield was wholly unprepared for the job. Furthermore, Bob's personality was ill suited to being a head coach. He was a shy, stoic loner who loved the solitary pursuits of hunting and fishing. He showed his testy side right from the opening press conference when he announced, "I don't think this team is as good as everyone thinks it is." When a reporter asked him how he would handle difficult players, Waterfield snapped, "That's a good question. How the hell should I know? I'll let you know in six months."

The Rams were indeed a weak club, and Bob's impatient juggling of quarterbacks did not help. Frank Ryan later told *Sports Illustrated*, "Waterfield came in and he didn't know what to do. He'd sort of been elected by popular demand, and he didn't have enough coaching experience. I had a tremendous personal feeling for Waterfield that I hadn't had for any other coach. If I could have climbed mountains for him, I

would have. He was very fair at first. He said I was going to be his quarterback. So he started me in the preseason stuff, and I played the first half of the first exhibition game, and I played lousy. I didn't play again until four games into the league season."

Although signed to a five-year contract, Waterfield quit eight games into the 1962 season with the team at 1–8. His life was a sad one after that. In 1964, he tutored the quarterbacks and kickers during training camp in Denver where former Ram assistant Jack Faulkner was coach. He announced to the press in 1967 that he was open to coaching, but received no offers and remained a scout for the Rams. In addition, Waterfield's marriage to Jane Russell ended after 25 years in 1968 in a very public divorce. Moreover, his son Robert was convicted of involuntary manslaughter in 1977 and sentenced to nine months in county jail for accidentally killing a man while firing a gun at a bar sign after having downed 24 beers. Bob was elected to Hall of Fame in 1965 and died of respiratory failure in 1983 at the age of 62.

WEBSTER, ALEXANDER (ALEX) 4/19/1931– North Carolina State. Played HB/FB for the Giants from 1955 to 1964. *Apprenticeship:* Pro asst.— 2 years. *Roots:* Allie Sherman. *Branches:* Joe Walton. *Coordinators/Key Assistants*: Joe Walton was the key offensive coach, while Norb Hecker then Jim Garrett handled the defense. *Hall of Fame Players:* Fran Tarkenton. *Primary Quarterbacks:* Fran Tarkenton, Norm Snead *Tendencies:* • His teams scored 19.3 points and allowed 22 per game • His teams ran 50.3% of the time, which was 93% of the league average • Three starting quarterbacks in five years; 89% of starts to primary quarterbacks • Nine rookie starters in five years • Winning Full Seasons to Losing Full Seasons: 2:3.

Alex Webster coached the Giants during a long period of dormancy. In fact, his two winning seasons in 1970 and 1972 were the only winning seasons the franchise had between 1964 and 1980. Not coincidentally, those were also the two years that oft-injured running back Ron Johnson ran for more than 1,000 yards to provide some balance to the passing of quarterback Fran Tarkenton.

Webster, a native of Kearny, New Jersey, played for North Carolina State from 1950 to 1952. Drafted

Webster, Alexander (Alex)									
Year	Team	Games	Wins	Losses	Ties	%	P Wins	P Losses	P %
1969	Giants	14	6	8	0	.429	0	0	.000
1970	Giants	14	9	5	0	.643	0	0	.000
1971	Giants	14	4	10	0	.286	0	0	.000
1972	Giants	14	8	6	0	.571	0	0	.000
1973	Giants	14	2	11	1	.179	0	0	.000
5 years		70	29	40	1	.421	0	0	.000

in the 11th round by the Redskins, Alex was tried as a defensive back and was cut. He headed north to Montreal where he became a star in the CFL and led the league in rushing in 1954. The Giants sent a scout to check out Montreal's quarterback Sam Etcheverry, but he came back with Webster. Big Red was a reliable Giants' hero for the next decade. Originally a halfback, he switched to fullback in 1961 under Allie Sherman and experienced his two best years before age began to catch up to him in 1963. He retired after the 1964 season as New York's all-time leading rusher.

Alex went into private business for two years, but returned to the team as running backs coach under Sherman in 1967. As the fans grew increasingly angry with Sherman and his failure to turn the club around, the Giants decided to part company with Allie late in the preseason of 1969 and turned to Webster as his successor. Tackle Steve Wright wrote in *I'd Rather Be Wright*, " The assistants did all the planning and funneled their ideas through him. He was more of a cheerleader, a figurehead. He would get up in front and say OK we gotta do this or we gotta do that, or I'm proud of you guys, or I'm teed off at you guys, and then the rest of the coaches would take over."

Under Webster, the Giants were up and down on both offense and defense, and he was never given a lot of talent with which to work. Fran Tarkenton handled the quarterbacking for three years but then was traded back to Minnesota while Norm Snead and Randy Johnson took over calling signals. Some criticized Alex for being too easy on his players, and he later responded to the *Washington Post*, "I wasn't soft. I took the players the way I would want the coach to take me. I used to tell them, 'You're making good money, better than the average guy. I want to treat you like men. I don't want to baby-sit you.' Now that I think about it, I should have kicked them..." A 2–11–1 1973 season made it clear that Webster did not have the answer to restoring the Giants to greatness, and he was fired. He later worked for former teammate Ralph Guglielmi's computer forms business.

WHELCHEL, JOHN E. (BILLICK) 4/1/1898–11/5/1973. Naval Academy. QB; did not play professionally. *Apprenticeship:* College coach–10 years (2 as head coach). *Roots:* None. *Branches:* Herman Ball. *Coordinators/Key Assistants*: Herman Ball coached the line, and Wilbur Moore coached the backs. *Hall of Fame Players:* Sammy Baugh. *Primary Quarterbacks:* Sammy Baugh. *Record:* **Interim Coach.**

Vice Admiral John "Billick" Whelchel was born in Hogansville, Georgia, but grew up in Washington D.C. where he was a multisport athlete. When he attended the Naval Academy from 1916 to 1919, Billick played on the football, baseball and basketball teams. He immediately joined the football coaching staff upon graduation and remained on staff through 1924, returning in 1926 to coach the freshman team. From 1927 to 1929, Whelchel was stationed on the USS *Florida* and coached their football squad. Transferred to the Norfolk Navy Yard, he coached the team there from 1930 to 1933. At that point, he was assigned to the USS *Idaho* and once again coached football on board from 1934 to 1936. Billick returned to the Academy in 1941 and served as backfield coach that season before succeeding Swede Larson as head coach in 1942. He led Navy to a 5–4 record in 1942 and an 8–1 record and the Lambert Trophy as the top team in the East in 1943. Moreover, he beat Army both years.

Whelchel reported to the Pacific theater in 1944 and took command of the USS *San Francisco* in 1945, winning the Legion of Merit with a Gold Star and a Bronze Star. After the war, he was assigned to Pearl Harbor and was promoted to Rear Admiral in 1947 and Vice Admiral in 1949 when he retired from the Navy.

Meanwhile, Redskins' owner George Preston Marshall was unhappy with his head coach Turk Edwards and was looking for someone to instill more discipline in the team. He first offered the job to Bear Bryant, but the Bear could not get out of his contract at Kentucky. So Marshall turned to the shocking choice of Billick Whelchel. Sammy Baugh told Myron Cope for *The Game That Was*, "Marshall thought the admiral would put a lot of discipline in the ball club. Well, he showed up, and he looked like anything but an admiral. He was just a kind of average-looking guy, not very impressive. And the funny thing was, he turned out to be a real nice fellow. All the players liked him, although he wasn't as up on his football as he should have been."

Reporters were skeptical of his football knowledge and questioned Whelchel about his knowledge of the T formation at his opening press conference. Billick replied, "In 1943, we brought the Chicago Bears' Keith Molesworth to Navy to teach us something about the T formation. We used several T formation plays that year and won eight out of nine games. Then, too, I learned considerable about the T as I studied the plays of several opponents like Notre Dame."

As it turned out, Whelchel got along better with

Whelchel, John E. (Billick)									
Year	*Team*	*Games*	*Wins*	*Losses*	*Ties*	*%*	*P Wins*	*P Losses*	*P %*
1949	Redskins	7	3	3	1	.500	0	0	.000
1 year		7	3	3	1	.500	0	0	.000

the players than with the owner. By week seven, he had had enough of the meddlesome Marshall. Trailing the Steelers 14–7 at halftime that week, Billick told his players, "Gentlemen, this is my last game as coach of the Redskins. You are a fine group of men and a good football team. I wish you all the success in the world in your future games. Washington will be proud of you." After a pause, he added, "I'd like to win this last game." The Redskins obliged him by scoring 20 points in the final quarter. Three weeks later, Whelchel was arrested for being drunk and disorderly at a party celebrating a win by the minor league Richmond Rebels coached by his friend Molesworth. The old admiral worked in real estate and farming in future years and died in 1973 at the age of 75.

WHISENHUNT, KENNETH M. (KEN) 2/28/1962– Georgia Tech. Played TE for the Falcons from 1985 to 1988, the Redskins in 1990 and the Jets from 1991 to 1992. *Apprenticeship:* College asst.— 2 years; pro asst.—10 years. *Roots:* Ted Marchibroda, Chris Palmer, Al Groh, Bill Cowher. *Branches:* Todd Haley. *Coordinators/Key Assistants*: Todd Haley then Mike Miller ran the offense, while Clancy Pendergast then Bill Davis then Ray Horton handled the defense. *Hall of Fame Players:* None. *Primary Quarterbacks:* Kurt Warner. *Tendencies:* • His teams scored 22.6 points and allowed 24.2 per game • His teams ran 36.9% of the time, which was 85% of the league average • Six starting quarterbacks in five years; 53% of starts to primary quarterback • Nine rookie starters in five years • Winning Full Seasons to Losing Full Seasons: 2:1.

Hailing from Augusta, Ken Whisenhunt had clear Georgia beginnings. He was an All-ACC tight end at Georgia Tech, was drafted in the 12th round by the Falcons and played four years in Atlanta before moving on to the Redskins and then the Jets. In a lackluster career as a backup tight end, Whisenhunt appeared in 74 games over seven seasons and caught 62 passes. He was not done, though, he later told the *New York Times*, "When I was finished after the 1993 season, there was something missing. After being involved with it for so long, when Saturday and Sunday rolled around and football was going on and you weren't involved, there was a void there."

Ken joined the staff at Vanderbilt in 1995 to coach tight ends and special teams. Two years later, he moved up to Ted Marchibroda's staff in Baltimore as tight ends coach. Two years after that, he signed on to Chris Palmer's first staff in Cleveland as special teams coach. In 2000, Whisenhunt was back to coaching tight ends with the Jets and then switched to the Steelers in 2001. In 2004 when offensive coordinator and former tight ends coach Mike Mularkey left to become head coach in Buffalo, Ken was promoted to offensive coordinator in Pittsburgh just in time to work with rookie quarterback Ben Roethlisberger. Whisenhunt and Roethlisberger made a good team and the Steelers finally won a Super Bowl for Coach Bill Cowher and runner Jerome Bettis in 2005.

With the Steelers' offense known for its imagination despite its ball control basis, Ken became a hot coordinator in the league, interviewing for head coaching vacancies with the Rams and Raiders. One year later, Cowher stepped down after 15 years as head coach, leaving two heirs apparent: Whisenhunt and assistant head coach/line coach Russ Grimm. However, Dan Rooney surprised the football world by instead tapping Mike Tomlin to replace Cowher. Ken also interviewed in Miami, Atlanta and Arizona before taking the Cardinals job in 2007. He brought Grimm along with him to the desert, telling *Sports Illustrated*, "Russ and I had a great run in Pittsburgh, but it's not hard to fall in love with this area. When your only decision in the morning is which short-sleeved shirt you're going to wear, you know life is sweet."

The Cardinals were a historically bad franchise that had had just three winning seasons in the last 30 years. While Arizona had a young touted quarterback in Matt Leinart, Whisenhunt soon became convinced that his best chance to win was with discarded veteran Kurt Warner throwing the ball to Larry Fitzgerald and Anquan Boldin early and often. Indeed, Whisenhunt's Cardinals have thrown the ball nearly two-thirds of the time, 15% more than the league average.

Despite giving up 56 points to the Jets, 48 to Eagles and 47 to the Patriots, the 2008 Cardinals managed to win their division with a 9–7 record. Even though the team was widely viewed as imposters that would quickly disappear from the playoffs, Arizona won three straight games by scoring more than 30 points each time and reached the Super Bowl to face

Whisenhunt, Kenneth M. (Ken)

Year	Team	Games	Wins	Losses	Ties	%	P Wins	P Losses	P %
2007	Cardinals	16	8	8	0	.500	0	0	.000
2008	Cardinals	16	9	7	0	.563	3	1	.750
2009	Cardinals	16	10	6	0	.625	1	1	.500
2010	Cardinals	16	5	11	0	.313	0	0	.000
2011	Cardinals	16	8	8	0	.500	0	0	.000
5 years		80	40	40	0	.500	4	2	.667

Mike Tomlin's Steelers. The powerful Steelers were favored, but Warner led the Cardinals back to take a lead in the closing minutes only to have Ben Roethisberger pull the game out in the closing seconds.

Arizona returned to the playoffs in 2009, but collapsed in 2010 following Warner's retirement. As Whisenhunt tries to build a complete team, his biggest deficiency remains at quarterback. In 2011, he traded starting cornerback Dominique Rodgers-Cromartie and a second round pick to Philadelphia for the Kevin Kolb, but the oft-injured Kolb was generally outplayed by inaccurate, undrafted quarterback John Skelton. New defensive coordinator Ray Horton improved the defense in 2011, but Whisenhunt's future may depend on the ultimate success of his quarterback.

WHITE, MICHAEL K. (MIKE) 1/4/1936– California. E/HB; did not play professionally. *Apprenticeship:* College coach — 28 years (14 as head coach); pro asst.— 7 years. *Roots:* Bill Walsh, Art Shell. *Branches:* John Fox. *Coordinators/Key Assistants:* Joe Bugel ran the offense, while John Fox then Fred Whittingham handled the defense. *Hall of Fame Players:* None. *Primary Quarterbacks:* Jeff Hostetler. *Tendencies:* • His teams scored 21.5 points and allowed 19.5 per game • His teams ran 44.3% of the time, which was 102% of the league average • Three starting quarterbacks in two years; 75% of starts to primary quarterback • Two rookie starters in two years • Winning Full Seasons to Losing Full Seasons: 0:1.

Born in Berkeley, Mike White played football, rugby, basketball and track at the University of California from 1955 to 1957 and was team captain of the football team as a senior. As a graduate assistant, he immediately joined the Golden Bears' coaches in 1958 and stayed on staff through 1963. White left to become John Ralston's offensive coordinator at Stanford in 1964 where he recruited and tutored Jim Plunkett. Ralston was named head coach of the Denver Broncos in 1972 and Mike was seen as his successor at Stanford. However, when his downtrodden alma mater offered Mike the head coaching position, he accepted that assignment instead.

Over the next six years, White did a remarkable job in the demanding environment of Cal. He brought in such stars as Steve Bartkowski, Chuck Muncie and Wesley Walker and produced three winning teams and an overall record of 35–30–1. Still, he had conflicts with strict athletic director Dave Maggard who objected to some of White's improprieties with the football program and to the team being accused of playing dirty football by USC. Maggard fired Mike in 1978, but White remained in the Bay Area as Pete McCulley's line coach on the 49ers. A year later, Bill Walsh took over the 49ers, but kept Mike on staff; the two had worked together at Stanford and were friends. Walsh once told the *Los Angeles Times*, "He was a dynamic guy, just terrific. He had a lot of charisma and charm, as you might guess. He had a magnetic personality, and he was a terrific coach."

A year later, the smooth talking White was back in the college ranks as the head coach for the Fighting Illini (or "Biting Illini" as they sometimes would be called after Michigan State again accused a Mike White team of dirty play). Mike coached Illinois from 1980 to 1987, developed star quarterbacks Dave Wilson, Jack Trudeau and Tony Eason, led the team to five winning seasons and a Rose Bowl berth while compiling an overall 46–41–3 record. White's tenure was marred by the team being put on two years' probation by the NCAA for recruiting violations in 1984, and the program declined after that.

Mike was fired in 1988 and spent the next two years working for a scouting combine before joining the Raiders as quarterbacks coach under Art Shell in 1990. In 1993, he switched to offensive line coach. When Shell was fired in 1995, White politicked for the job with Al Davis and was hired. Davis noted, "I've known Mike White for 40 years. I watched him grow, become an assistant coach. His history, his records, are tremendously unique. I think he comes extremely qualified; he has a vibrant personality."

Mike brought a West Coast-style offense of short passes to the Raiders despite Al Davis' well known penchant for the bombs-away Vertical Offense. All was well for the first 10 weeks when Oakland got off to an 8–2 start. After a few injuries, though, the team dropped its last six games of the season and Davis tightened the leash. He began faxing plays to White and his not-so-helpful personnel moves included signing free agent busts Larry Brown and Russell Maryland. Following a 7–9 season in 1996, White was fired.

The next year, Mike joined the Rams' staff of another old colleague from Stanford, Dick Vermeil. White coached under Vermeil in St. Louis for three years and then retired with him. When Vermeil came back to coach the Chiefs in 2001, he hired Mike as Kansas City's director of football administration. Ver-

White, Michael K. (Mike)									
Year	Team	Games	Wins	Losses	Ties	%	P Wins	P Losses	P %
1995	Raiders	16	8	8	0	.500	0	0	.000
1996	Raiders	16	7	9	0	.438	0	0	.000
2 years		32	15	17	0	.469	0	0	.000

meil and White both retired again in 2006. Since then, Mike has been involved heavily with alumni activities at California.

WIGGIN, PAUL D. 11/18/1934– Stanford. Played DE for the Browns from 1957 to 1967. *Apprenticeship:* Pro asst.—7 years. *Roots:* Dick Nolan. *Branches:* Tom Bettis (i). *Coordinators/Key Assistants:* Chet Franklin then Bob Schnelker ran the offense, while Vince Costello then Tom Bettis handled the defense. *Hall of Fame Players:* Buck Buchanan, Len Dawson, Willie Lanier, Jan Stenerud, Emmitt Thomas (i). *Primary Quarterbacks:* Mike Livingston *Tendencies:* • His teams scored 19 points and allowed 25.7 per game • His teams ran 52% of the time, which was 94% of the league average • Three starting quarterbacks in three years; 74% of starts to primary quarterback • Nine rookie starters in three years • Winning Full Seasons to Losing Full Seasons: 0:2.

Paul Wiggin was born in Modesto, California, and played guard and tackle for Stanford from 1954 to 1956. He was an All-American as a senior. Drafted as a future pick by the Browns in 1956, Paul joined Cleveland in 1957, was converted to defensive end and moved right into the starting lineup. Wiggin played 11 years for the Browns and went to two Pro Bowls as a consistently solid performer on the defensive line.

Upon retiring from playing in 1968, Paul was hired by Dick Nolan in San Francisco to coach the 49ers' defensive line, which quickly became one of the best in the league. After seven years with Nolan, Wiggin got his opportunity to be a head coach in 1975 with Kansas City, where he replaced Hank Stram, the only coach the team had ever had. Wiggin told the press, "I do not see the Chiefs being in such dire straits that we would need to slough off a year or two and just play youngsters. I'm not going to sit here and tell you I think we will go to the Super Bowl. If this team were going to the Super Bowl, I would not be here."

In fact, the aging Chiefs were a below average team that had finished 5–9 in Stram's last season and would repeat that record in each of the next two years

under Wiggin. Quarterback Len Dawson was playing his last few games and replacements Mike Livingston and Tony Adams were inadequate. The defense was even worse. The most memorable event of Wiggin's tenure in Kansas City occurred during training camp in 1976 when the coach had to rush wild defensive end John Matuszak to the hospital while pounding on his chest after Tooz had keeled over from drinking too much beer and wine with his sleeping pills.

When the club got off to a 1–6 start in 1977, Paul was fired on Halloween. He told the press, "I did a damn good job. Hey, I'm a damn good man. And when I'm handing out Halloween candy to the kids tonight and when I'm cleaning out my desk tomorrow, I'm going to hold my head up. I'm not embarrassed about what happened here." For their part, the Kansas City players issued a statement that said, "Every man on this football team feels a deep sense of guilt for the actions that were taken. It is our fault that we lost a fine man and a great individual — Paul Wiggin. One of the great crimes in life is to have someone else suffer the consequences of your own actions. We feel this is the case today."

Wiggin reunited with Nolan in New Orleans in 1978 as defensive coordinator, but that was a losing situation. In 1980, he returned to his alma mater as head coach. Despite recruiting John Elway, Stanford went just 16–28 from 1980 to 1983 under Paul. Again, the biggest memory was a negative one: The Play, when California beat Stanford on a five-lateral kickoff return while the band marched on the field in the closing seconds. Wiggin went into scouting with the Vikings in 1984. Over the years he advanced to the director of player personnel with the team and in retirement still serves as a scouting consultant with the franchise in 2011.

WILKIN, WILBUR B. (WILLIE) 4/21/1916– 5/16/1973. St. Mary's. Played T for the Redskins from 1938 to 1943 and the Chicago Rockets in 1947. *Apprenticeship:* None. *Roots:* None. *Branches:* None. *Coordinators/Key Assistants:* Co-coach with Bob Dove

Wiggin, Paul D.

Year	Team	Games	Wins	Losses	Ties	%	P Wins	P Losses	P %
1975	Chiefs	14	5	9	0	.357	0	0	.000
1976	Chiefs	14	5	9	0	.357	0	0	.000
1977	Chiefs	7	1	6	0	.143	0	0	.000
3 years		35	11	24	0	.314	0	0	.000

Wilkin, Wilbur B. (Willie)

Year	Team	Games	Wins	Losses	Ties	%	P Wins	P Losses	P %
1946	Rockets (AAFC)	6	3	2	1	.583	0	0	.000
1 year		6	3	2	1	.583	0	0	.000

(ends) and Ned Mathews (backs). *Hall of Fame Players:* Elroy Hirsch. *Primary Quarterbacks:* None. *Record:* **Interim Player Co-Coach** (with Bob Dove and Ned Mathews).

Wee Willie Wilkin was one of the biggest players of his era at 6'4" and 260-pounds (at least) and was a two-time All-Pro at tackle in six years with the Redskins. Surprisingly, this giant player was undrafted in 1938. A native of Bingham Canyon, Utah, Wilkin played for little St. Mary's College in California from 1935 to 1937 and was discovered by Washington coach Ray Flaherty when the champion Redskins barnstormed through the West Coast in 1937. Willie actually played for the team during that winter tour, but spent the summer working in a silver mine in Mexico before reporting to Washington in 1938.

In 1943, Wilkin was inducted into the Marines and was stationed at the El Toro base in California where he played under Coach Dick Hanley in 1944 and 1945. Hanley was named head coach of the Chicago Rockets of the new All America Football Conference in 1946 and brought several of his El Toro players with him to Chicago, including Wilkin who jumped leagues from the NFL. Unfortunately, Hanley could not get along with owner John Keeshin and was fired after just two games. At that point, Keeshin put Hanley's assistants Pat Boland and Ernie Nevers on paid leave and turned the team over to a triumvirate of player coaches: end Bob Dove, halfback Ned Mathews and tackle Wilkin. The Rockets posted a winning record over the next six weeks, but Keeshin then brought back line coach Boland as head coach for the remainder of the year.

Willie finished the season with the Rockets and then retired from the game. He became a high school math and social studies teacher who worked extensively with special education children and was noted for his patience and gentle manner. He worked several years in Monterey, California, where he also coached the line for the football team, before eventually moving to Deer Lodge, Montana. Sadly, Wilkin's later years were filled with tragedy. In 1965, his twin sons John and Chris were killed at the age of 22 in a car crash; John had played tackle at Stanford in 1963. In 1970, Willie had a brain tumor removed successfully, but two years later was stricken with stomach cancer and that killed him at age 57 in 1973. Shortly before he died, Wilkin touchingly told Jim Castiglia of the NFL Alumni Association, "I'm not worried about my illness. But since the twins went, I'm a lonesome man. Jim, tell some of my Washington friends that Wee Willie would appreciate a letter, a card, anything."

WILKINSON, CHARLES B. (BUD) 4/23/1916– 2/9/1994. Minnesota. G/QB; did not play professionally. *Apprenticeship:* College coach — 23 years (17 as head coach). *Roots:* None. *Branches:* None. *Coordinators/Key Assistants*: Harry Gilmer was a key offensive coach, while Tom Bettis handled the defense. *Hall of Fame Players:* Dan Dierdorf, Roger Wehrli. *Primary Quarterbacks:* Jim Hart. *Tendencies:* • His teams scored 17.5 points and allowed 20.1 per game • His teams ran 51.4% of the time, which was 96% of the league average • Two starting quarterbacks in two years; 97% of starts to primary quarterback • Six rookie starters in two years • Winning Full Seasons to Losing Full Seasons: 0:2.

Calm and upright in all things, Bud Wilkinson was one of the most successful college coaches of all time, the winner of three national championships and an inductee in the College Football Hall of Fame. However, this national hero's time in pro football proved to be brief and forgettable.

A native of Minneapolis, Wilkinson played both ice hockey and football at the University of Minnesota from 1934 to 1936. He played guard as a sophomore and junior and then switched to quarterback as a senior. In those three years, Bernie Bierman's Golden Gophers went 23–1 and won three straight national championships. Bud went on to play in the College All Star Game the summer of 1937 and led the Stars to a 6–0 win over the NFL champion Packers. Rather than go into pro football, though, Wilkinson opted to work for his father's bank that year.

Drawn back to the gridiron, Bud joined the coaching staff at Syracuse in 1938. After four years with the Orangemen, Wilkinson returned to his alma mater as an assistant in 1942. The following year, he went into the Navy and coached, along with Jim Tatum under Don Faurot at the Iowa Pre-Flight School. Faurot was the creator of the Split-T option-style offense and taught it to both of his assistants. Bud was assigned to an aircraft carrier for the next two years, but after the war, took a job as Tatum's assistant at Oklahoma. Just one year later, Tatum left for Maryland, and Wilkinson succeeded him with the Sooners.

Wilkinson, Charles B. (Bud)									
Year	Team	Games	Wins	Losses	Ties	%	P Wins	P Losses	P %
1978	Cardinals	16	6	10	0	.375	0	0	.000
1979	Cardinals	13	3	10	0	.231	0	0	.000
2 years		29	9	20	0	.310	0	0	.000

In Bud's 17 years as head coach at Oklahoma from 1947 to 1963, he led the team to an overall 145–29–4 record. The Sooners won national championships in 1950, 1955 and 1956 and produced a record-setting 47-game winning streak from 1953 to 1957. Players whose eligibility ran from 1954 to 1956, like Hall of Famer Tommy McDonald, never lost a game in college. As a coach, Wilkinson was soft spoken but inspired respect and loyalty from his players and staff. He broke the color line at OU by recruiting black half back Prentice Gautt in 1956 and was an innovator on the field as well. On offense, Bud relied on the Split-T; on defense, he employed a 3–4 alignment known as the Oklahoma Defense.

From 1948 to 1958, Oklahoma lost as many as two games in only one season and posted a 107–8–2 record. Wilkinson's complete mastery of the college game began to slip in his last five years though. He was being pulled in other directions. President Kennedy named Wilkinson to the President's Council on Physical Fitness and he took the responsibility seriously. From 1959 to 1963, the Sooners compiled a winning 31–19–1 record that was nonetheless far below Bud's standards. Wilkinson stepped down in 1964 and embarked on a run for the U.S. Senate as a Republican, but was defeated in a close race during Democrat Lyndon Johnson's landslide victory as President.

In 1965, Bud began a new career as the lead analyst for ABC College Football coverage. Wilkinson as a broadcaster was like Wilkinson the coach — restrained, courteous and analytical. He worked for ABC for 13 years, but also drew criticism from some who found his style too bland. Finally in 1978, Bud decided to get back into coaching by replacing Don Coryell with the St. Louis Cardinals. At age 62, after a 15-year layoff and in the new environment of pro football, it was clearly a challenge. Cowboys tackle Ralph Neely who played for Wilkinson's last Oklahoma teams told *Sports Illustrated*, "I personally think the odds are against him. The game has changed so much in the last 15 years that it won't be easy. And if he thinks the game hasn't changed and that the players haven't changed, he's in for a rude awakening. The old-time mid-'60s methods won't work. He treated his players like gentlemen and expected the same from them; I don't know how well that will work with some guys in the pros."

As it turned out, Wilkinson's insurmountable difficulties were with ownership, not the players. Quarterback Jim Hart told Tom Danyluk for *The Super 70s*, "He tried to do some things that were innovative, things like running the no-huddle, putting the tight end into a full-house backfield to disguise the strong side. But the media attacked him for it. 'The game has passed him by,' they said. 'Look at all the crazy things he's doing.'" Bud also switched the Cardinals to the 3–4 defense, but his strategic moves could not counter the Cardinals' lack of talent.

Wilkinson had increasing conflicts with owner Bill Bidwill. The final dispute was over former first round draft pick Steve Pisarkiewicz. Bidwill insisted the coach play Pisarkiewicz at quarterback instead of Hart. However, because Bud knew that Pisarkiewicz could not play at this level, He refused and was fired with three games to go in 1979. Wilkinson dryly told the press, "I feel the fans of the team and the players themselves deserve to have the players on the field with the best chance of winning the game. That might have been a mistake on my part."

Pisarkiewicz started the last three games of the season and was cut the next year. Wilkinson returned to broadcasting with ESPN for a few more years and then retired. He died in 1994 at the age of 77.

WILLIAMS, GREGG 7/15/1958– Truman State and Northeast Missouri State. QB; did not play professionally. *Apprenticeship:* College asst.— 2 years; pro asst.—11 years. *Roots:* Jack Pardee, Jeff Fisher. *Branches:* None. *Coordinators/Key Assistants:* Mike Sheppard then Kevin Gilbride ran the offense, while Jerry Gray handled the defense. *Hall of Fame Players:* None. *Primary Quarterbacks:* Drew Bledsoe *Tendencies:* • His teams scored 18.5 points and allowed 22.8 per game • His teams ran 40.1% of the time, which was 91% of the league average • Three starting quarterbacks in three years; 67% of starts to primary quarterback • Eleven rookie starters in three years • Winning Full Seasons to Losing Full Seasons: 0:2.

This native of Excelsior Springs, Missouri has made a career of attacking quarterbacks despite having been one at Northeast Missouri State in the late 1970s. Gregg Williams began his football journey by coaching high school ball in Missouri from 1980 to 1987. Gregg then got his first big break in 1988 when Jack Pardee brought him in as a graduate assistant at the University of Houston from 1988 to 1989. When Pardee was

Williams, Gregg

Year	Team	Games	Wins	Losses	Ties	%	P Wins	P Losses	P %
2001	Bills	16	3	13	0	.188	0	0	.000
2002	Bills	16	8	8	0	.500	0	0	.000
2003	Bills	16	6	10	0	.375	0	0	.000
3 years		48	17	31	0	.354	0	0	.000

named head coach of the Oilers in 1990, he hired Williams as a defensive assistant. Over the next seven years, Gregg moved up to special teams and then linebackers coach under Pardee's successor Jeff Fisher and subsequently was elevated to defensive coordinator for the Tennessee Oilers in 1997.

Williams guided Tennessee's defense for four years and developed an aggressive approach that owed a great deal to his having coached under Buddy Ryan when Ryan was the team's defensive coordinator in 1993 and under Fisher who was a follower of Ryan as well. In 2001, Gregg interviewed for the open Buffalo job. Despite everyone expecting the Bills to hire Marvin Lewis, the defensive coordinator of the Super Bowl champion Ravens, Buffalo picked Williams. By this time, the Bills were embarked on a decade of decline from the 1990s Super Bowl teams. Gregg switched the team to a 4–3 defense and tried to rebuild Buffalo by dumping aging veterans, however, the drop off in talent was too great. After a 3–13 first season, Buffalo obtained Drew Bledsoe from the Patriots, and Bledsoe's competent quarterbacking enabled the team to go 8–8 in 2002. Bledsoe had his limitations, though, so the team slipped to 6–10 in 2003, and Williams was fired. While the defense was improving, the offense was not, and Gregg had repeated problems with game management decisions.

Williams was hired by Redskins owner Daniel Snyder to be Joe Gibbs' defensive coordinator in 2004 and had a mostly successful four-year run in Washington. Gregg often displays a large ego and marches to his own drummer. In 2007 after star safety Sean Taylor was killed, Williams started the next game with just ten men on the field as a tribute to the fallen safety. Gregg was bypassed as head coach when Gibbs retired in 2008 but landed in Jacksonville for one year as defensive coordinator. In 2009, Saints' coach Sean Payton decided that Williams was so important to his team's chances that Payton took a pay cut to afford to bring in Gregg to coach the defense. That gamble paid off with a Super Bowl championship for New Orleans with Williams' aggressive defense providing enough support for Payton's high-octane offense to win it all. However, Williams' risky, heavy blitzing approach led directly to the Saints early postseason departures in both 2010 and 2011, and he was dismissed. Then, the NFL suspended him indefinitely in 2012 for his lead role in the Saints' Bounty Scandal.

WILLIAMS, JEROME R. (JERRY) 11/1/1923–12/31/1998. Idaho and Washington State. Played DB/HB for the Rams from 1949 to 1952 and the Eagles from 1953 to 1954. *Apprenticeship:* College head coach — 3 years; pro asst.— 6 years; CFL coach — 5 years (4 as head coach). *Roots:* Buck Shaw, Nick Skorich. *Branches:* Ed Khayat, Marv Levy, Dick Stanfel (i). *Coordinators/Key Assistants*: Charley Gauer ran the offense, while Williams handled his own defense. *Hall of Fame Players:* None. *Primary Quarterbacks:* Norm Snead. *Tendencies:* • His teams scored 17.5 points and allowed 26.4 per game • His teams ran 47.9% of the time, which was 94% of the league average • Four starting quarterbacks in three years; 84% of starts to primary quarterback • Ten rookie starters in three years • Winning Full Seasons to Losing Full Seasons: 0:2.

A native of Spokane, Jerry Williams first enrolled at the University of Idaho in 1942 but then went into the Army Air Corps in 1943 to serve as a combat pilot in the Pacific during the war. After his discharge, Williams returned to his home state to play for Washington State from 1946 to 1948. Although only 5'10" and 175 pounds, Jerry was very fast and was drafted in the seventh round by the Rams in 1949. Called "Jittery Jerry" by the media, Williams started at safety as a 26-year-old rookie and over four years in Los Angeles picked off 15 passes. In his second year with the Rams, Jerry began working as an assistant coach for the University of Idaho during spring practice. When the Idaho head coaching job opened in 1953, Williams was considered for the position. Instead, the Rams traded him to the Eagles for a draft pick.

The Eagles shifted Jerry to offense as a change-of-pace runner, a fast return man and a shifty receiver out of the backfield. After two seasons in Philadelphia, Jerry retired from playing to take the head coach's position at the University of Montana. From 1954 to 1957, Montana went just 6–21 so Williams was fired. He returned to Philadelphia to coach the defense under new Eagles' coach Buck Shaw in 1958 and also was charged with the team's "off-season detail work" since Shaw only worked 6-months a year as coach. Jerry improved the rank of the Eagles' pass defense to second in the league by 1960 and was credited for creating the five defensive back "nickel" defense that George Allen later fully developed. In 1961, Shaw was succeeded at head coach by offensive assistant Nick

Williams, Jerome R. (Jerry)									
Year	Team	Games	Wins	Losses	Ties	%	P Wins	P Losses	P %
1969	Eagles	14	4	9	1	.321	0	0	.000
1970	Eagles	14	3	10	1	.250	0	0	.000
1971	Eagles	3	0	3	0	.000	0	0	.000
3 years		31	7	22	2	.258	0	0	.000

Skorich who kept Williams as defensive coach until both were fired at the end of 1963.

Jerry subsequently worked as an assistant coach for the Calgary Stampeders in 1964, was promoted to head coach in 1965 and was named CFL Coach of the Year in 1967 when he led Calgary to the CFL title game. Eagles' GM Pete Retzlaff hired Williams as Philadelphia's head coach in 1969 over Calgary's objections to losing a coach who posted a 40–23–1 record in four seasons through 1968. At the press conference, Retzlaff noted that Williams had been associated with winning teams in 14 of the 17 years he had played or coached professional football. What he didn't specify was that the three losing seasons had all occurred in Philadelphia. Williams told the press, "I still believe that if you can stop the other team's passing attack, you'll win the ball game. I feel if the other team cannot stop your passing attack, you'll win. I think pass first and run second."

Unfortunately, Jerry had Norm Snead at quarterback. Not only were the Eagles players substandard as demonstrated by their 2–12 record in 1968, but Retzlaff's drafts were weak and his trade record was abysmal. Williams was a very smart man with a law degree from Temple, but was not much of a motivator and lost control of the team over his three-year tenure. Defensive end Gary Pettigrew expounded to *Sports Illustrated*, "Jerry is the first coach I know who's been willing to discuss the change in the athlete that's happening in American sports. When he came around and asked me what goes with the long hair, I told him the stupid-athlete syndrome is passing. More and more you're going to find athletes who are interested in things other than sports — who, in a sense, are contemporary men interested in the environment, in government, in changing social mores. If you're going to get respect from them, I told him, then you'll have to treat them as individuals. The first coach who realizes there are changes — and understands those changes — will be a new kind of winner."

However, after finishing last with 4–9–1 and 3–10–1 records in his first two seasons, Jerry was an old kind of loser, and there was a lot of talk that owner Leonard Tose was getting ready to fire Williams. When given a reprieve, Jerry noted, "Every football coach has to feel like the first mate on the titanic. I feel I'm at my best in icy water." Philadelphia then began 1971 by losing to the Bengals 37–14, the Cowboys 42–7 and the 49ers 31–3, so Tose fired Williams in an ugly

scene. Just that week, Jerry had fined several players for lack of effort, yet he claimed that he was dismissed just as the players and coaches were looking forward to upsetting the Vikings to turn their season around. Williams added, "Unfortunately, I was working for a man who is without courage or character. I was offered a sizeable sum of money to resign, but to accept a bribe of that nature is to lower myself to his depths."

Williams hooked on as Nick Skorich's receivers coach in Cleveland for the rest of the season before returning to Canada where he won the Grey Cup with the Hamilton Tiger Cats in 1972. From 1972 to 1975, Jerry compiled a 30–29–1 record with Hamilton, but was dismissed following consecutive losing seasons. From 1976 to 1980, he ran a ranch in Arizona and then returned to coaching as an assistant in Calgary in 1981 when he finished the season as the interim coach, winning one of the last four games. Retiring in 1982, Jerry began a charter flight service in Arizona. His brother William H. Williams played quarterback for Idaho after World War II and rose to become Chief Justice on the Washington State Supreme Court from 1983 to 1985.

WILLIAMSON, RICHARD A. 4/13/1941– Alabama. E; did not play professionally. *Apprenticeship:* College coach —18 years (6 as head coach); pro asst.— 8 years. Roots: Ray Perkins. *Branches:* None. *Coordinators/Key Assistants:* Williamson then Hank Kuhlmann ran the offense, while Fred Bruney then Floyd Peters handled the defense. *Hall of Fame Players:* None. *Primary Quarterbacks:* Vinny Testaverde. *Tendencies:* • His teams scored 13.3 points and allowed 22.2 per game • His teams ran 40.2% of the time, which was 89% of the league average • Three starting quarterbacks in two years; 79% of starts to primary quarterback • Seven rookie starters in two years • Winning Full Seasons to Losing Full Seasons: 0:1.

Born in Fort Deposit, Alabama, Richard Williamson played end for Bear Bryant at the University of Alabama from 1960 to 1962 and caught Joe Namath's first touchdown pass as a senior. The next year, Williamson joined the Tide's coaching staff and worked under Bryant for five years from 1963 to 1967. He left to work for Frank Broyles at Arkansas in 1968, but returned to the Bear's staff in 1970 before bouncing back to Broyles in 1972 for a three-year stint.

Richard got his opportunity to be a head coach with Memphis State in 1975 and led the Tigers to a

Williamson, Richard A.										
Year	Team	Games	Wins	Losses	Ties	%	P Wins	P Losses	P %
1990	Buccaneers	3	1	2	0	.333	0	0	.000
1991	Buccaneers	16	3	13	0	.188	0	0	.000
2 years		19	4	15	0	.211	0	0	.000

32–34 record from 1975 to 1980. While he posted winning seasons in his first three years, the next three were all losing ones, so Williamson was fired. After being out of football, Richard spent 1982 running the Bluebonnet Bowl in Houston and then was hired to coach the Chiefs' receivers in Kansas City under John Mackovic in 1983. Following four years in Kansas City, Williamson reunited with another former Alabama receiver, Ray Perkins, in Tampa Bay. Richard had been Ray's position coach at Alabama and spent four years as his assistant with the Bucs.

When Tampa fired Perkins with three games to play in 1990, Williamson was named interim coach. Richard's easygoing, friendly coaching manner was in distinct contrast to the belligerent Perkins and was welcomed by the players. However, it was still a surprise that the generally anonymous Williamson was given a one-year deal as head coach in 1991 rather than the team hiring either Buddy Ryan or Bill Belichick who both were available. The Bucs were the youngest team in the league and showed some progress on defense; they were ranked 11th in the league in yards given up, although they were still 25th in points allowed that year. On offense, Richard could do little with the interception-prone Vinny Testaverde at quarterback and the team finished 26th in scoring. By season's end, owner Hugh Culverhouse was courting Bill Parcells as head coach, so he fired Williamson, but then was jilted by the fickle Parcells. Richard's reaction was, "We didn't win enough games. I think I could have turned it around in another year. If I had been in [Culverhouse's] shoes, I would have kept me. But I wasn't in his shoes."

Williamson was hired to coach the receivers by David Shula in Cincinnati in 1992 and then left in 1995 to join the staff of the new Carolina Panthers expansion franchise in 1995. Richard would spend the next 15 years coaching for the Panthers under three head coaches: Dom Capers, George Seifert and John Fox. Under Seifert, Williamson served for a time as offensive coordinator, but the bulk of his tenure in Carolina was as the team's receivers coach, tutoring Steve Smith and Muhsin Muhammad. He retired in 2010 at age 68.

WILLSEY, RAYMOND (RAY) 9/30/1928– California. Played QB/DB in the CFL. *Apprenticeship:* College asst.—6 years; CFL asst.—1 year; pro asst.— 2 years. *Roots:* Pop Ivy. *Branches:* None. *Coordinators/ Key Assistants:* None. *Hall of Fame Players:* Larry Wil-

son. *Primary Quarterbacks:* Sam Etcheverry. *Record:* **Interim Co-Coach** (with Chuck Drulis and Ray Prochaska).

Canadian Ray Willsey was born in Regina, Saskatchewan, but was raised in California. After high school, he served in the Navy and then attended Santa Ana Junior College from 1949 to 1950 before transferring to California in 1951. Ray played defensive back and quarterback under Pappy Waldorf in 1951 and 1952 and subsequently signed with the Edmonton Eskimos of the CFL in 1953. Willsey spent three years playing Canadian football and also served as an assistant coach in 1954 under Pop Ivy. In addition, Ray did some coaching at his alma mater in 1954 and 1955.

In 1956, Willsey became a full time assistant coach under Darrell Royal at the University of Washington. Ray followed Royal to Texas in 1957 and stayed for three years until Ivy hired him to coach the Cardinals' secondary in 1960. When Ivy abruptly resigned in frustration after 12 games in 1961, the team appointed a triumvirate of assistant coaches, Willsey, Chuck Drulis and Ray Prochaska, to handle the final two games of the season—and the coaching committee won both. When St. Louis hired Wally Lemm as its new head coach in 1962, Drulis and Prochaska remained on staff, but Willsey moved on to the Redskins as defensive coach in 1962.

Two years later, Ray returned to his alma mater as head coach and, in a difficult recruiting period for Cal, managed to post three winning seasons between 1964 and 1971. His best year was 1968 when Willsey switched all of his best players to the defense and posted a 7–3–1 record. Following the 1971 season, Ray resigned after the school was placed on NCAA probation for playing ineligible receiver Isaac Curtis that year. Willsey compiled a 40–42–1 overall record at Berkeley during those years of student unrest.

Following a year out of football, Ray returned to the NFL in 1973 as Don Coryell's defensive coordinator with the Cardinals. When Coryell left in 1978, so did Willsey who was signed by the Raiders to coach their secondary in 1978. Over the next 10 years, Ray earned two Super Bowl rings in Oakland before he was let go in 1988. That year he coached the Arena League Los Angeles Cobras to a 5–6–1 record and then coached the Arena Maryland Commandos to an 0–4 mark in 1989. Subsequently, Willsey left Arena football to become involved with the NFL's European developmental league. He served as the defensive coordinator of the London Monarchs in 1991 and then was

Willsey, Raymond (Ray)									
Year	Team	Games	Wins	Losses	Ties	%	P Wins	P Losses	P %
1961	Cardinals	2	2	0	0	1.000	0	0	.000
1 year		2	2	0	0	1.000	0	0	.000

promoted to head coach in 1992 but compiled just a 2–7–1 record. The World League disbanded for 1993 and 1994, but when it resurfaced in 1995, Ray was on board as the defensive coordinator of the Scottish Claymores for the next two years. He was part of championship teams in both 1991 and 1996. In 1997, he moved to the league administration and served as the director of personnel for NFL Europe for the next several years until retiring in the new millennium.

WILSON, GEORGE W. 2/3/1914–11/23/1978. Northwestern. Played E for the Bears. *Apprenticeship:* Pro asst.—10 years. *Roots:* George Halas, Bo McMillin, Buddy Parker. *Branches:* Don Shula. *Coordinators/Key Assistants:* For the Lions, Red Cochran then Scooter McLean was the key offensive coach, while Buster Ramsey then Les Bingaman handled the defense; for the Dolphins, John Idzik ran the offense, while Les Bingaman handled the defense. *Hall of Fame Players:* Nick Buoniconti, Jack Christiansen, Lou Creekmur, Larry Csonka, Frank Gatski, Bob Griese, John Henry Johnson, Night Train Lane, Yale Lary, Bobby Layne, Dick LeBeau, Larry Little, Ollie Matson, Hugh McElhenny, Joe Schmidt. *Primary Quarterbacks:* Earl Morral, Milt Plum, Bob Griese. *Record:* NFL Championship 1957 *Tendencies:* • His teams scored 19.3 points and allowed 21.3 per game • His teams ran 48.4% of the time, which was 94% of the league average • Ten starting quarterbacks in 12 years; 54% of starts to primary quarterbacks • 37 rookie starters in 12 years • Winning Full Seasons to Losing Full Seasons: 5:7.

Chicago native George Wilson starred at nearby Northwestern from 1934 to 1936 and then signed with the home town Bears in 1937. George had a ten-year career with Chicago that was highlighted by his devastating block that obliterated two Redskins on Bill Osmanski's 68-yard touchdown on the second play of the 1940 NFL title game that the Bears won 73–0.

Wilson retired in 1947 and spent the next two years coaching under George Halas in Chicago. In 1949, though, he moved to Detroit to join Bo McMillin's staff, coaching the Lions' ends. When fellow assistant Buddy Parker replaced McMillin in 1951, Wilson took on even more of a key role with the offense of the two-time champions during the next six years. The volatile Parker abruptly quit during the 1957 preseason, announcing at a booster club dinner, "This team of ours has been the worst I've ever seen in training. I don't want to get involved in another losing season so I'm leaving Detroit." The Lions were coming off a 9–3 season, but Parker had longstanding conflicts with the team's ownership.

Wilson's first order of business was sorting out Detroit's quarterback situation. Bobby Layne was the veteran starter, but the Lions had acquired Tobin Rote from the Packers as an insurance policy against Layne being injured. During the season, Wilson generally alternated starts between the two quarterbacks and usually employed both signal callers in each game. When Layne broke his leg in the penultimate game of the year, the acquisition of Rote seemed a stroke of genius. Rote led the Lions to a victory in the season finale against the Bears and a comeback win over the 49ers in a playoff game before engineering a crushing 59–14 triumph over the Browns in the title game George said of his club after the game, "The big thing about them was they never quit. I guess this is the fightingest team I ever saw." However, with an NFL championship in his first year as head coach, Wilson had already peaked.

At the beginning of 1958, George traded Layne to Pittsburgh where Parker had become head coach, unleashing the Curse of Bobby Layne on Lions' fans. Detroit posted losing seasons in 1958 and 1959, and Wilson dumped both Rote and fullback John Henry Johnson, implying they were clubhouse lawyers who "weren't giving top performance." On the whole, though, the easy-going coach was popular with his players. Linebacker Joe Schmidt told Stuart Leuthner for *Iron Men* that George was "a motivator." One

Wilson, George W.									
Year	*Team*	*Games*	*Wins*	*Losses*	*Ties*	*%*	*P Wins*	*P Losses*	*P %*
1957	Lions	12	8	4	0	.667	2	0	1.000
1958	Lions	12	4	7	1	.375	0	0	.000
1959	Lions	12	3	8	1	.292	0	0	.000
1960	Lions	12	7	5	0	.583	0	0	.000
1961	Lions	14	8	5	1	.607	0	0	.000
1962	Lions	14	11	3	0	.786	0	0	.000
1963	Lions	14	5	8	1	.393	0	0	.000
1964	Lions	14	7	5	2	.571	0	0	.000
1966	Dolphins	14	3	11	0	.214	0	0	.000
1967	Dolphins	14	4	10	0	.286	0	0	.000
1968	Dolphins	14	5	8	1	.393	0	0	.000
1969	Dolphins	14	3	10	1	.250	0	0	.000
12 years		160	68	84	8	.450	2	0	1.000

anonymous Lions defender told *Sports Illustrated*, "He thinks like a player. We respect him and like him and we'll play our guts out for him." Wilson himself told the same magazine, "These players are men. I try to treat them like men."

Wilson obtained quarterback Jim Ninowski from Cleveland in 1960, but after two years in which Ninowski threw nine touchdowns and 36 interceptions, it was clear that the offense was holding back the rugged defense that had led the Lions to consecutive second place finishes. So in 1962, George sent Ninowski back to Cleveland for Milt Plum who was in Paul Brown's doghouse. The offense did improve, but when an errant Plum pass against Vince Lombardi's Packers cost Detroit a victory early in the year, there was a near mutiny by the defense in the locker room. The blitz-happy Lions finished second to Green Bay in 1962 despite clobbering the Packers in the Thanksgiving Day rematch for the third straight season. Their meager consolation each year was playing in the meaningless Bert Bell Playoff Bowl against the second place team from the Eastern Conference. Detroit won all three times.

The Lions descended into mediocrity over the next two years. In response, frustrated owner William Ford fired all of Wilson's assistants following the 1964 season. George countered by quitting. He landed with the Redskins as an assistant coach in 1965 and then was named the very first coach of the expansion Miami Dolphins in 1966. Wilson did about as well as could be expected in slowly building the Dolphins up from nothing, but never had a winning season. He was fired in February 1970 and replaced by Don Shula, who once had worked as a Lions' assistant under George. Wilson's son George Jr., who quarterbacked a few games for the 1966 team, later expressed resentment to the *Miami Herald* that, "When [George Sr.] first got there he asked for five years to build a winner and they gave him four."

Wilson senior also clearly harbored bitterness about his reputation. In 1969, he spouted, "I'm tired of all this Lombardi business. Everyone makes him out to be such a great coach. Given the same material, I'll beat him every time." Two years later when Miami went to the Super Bowl in Don Shula's second year, Wilson angrily vented to the press again, "As far as I'm concerned, he took a ready-made team. I was fired just when the team was ready to go." George added, "Shula was making $7,000 a year as an assistant at Kentucky when I hired him at Detroit for $14,000. I also helped

him get the Baltimore Colts head coaching job. I practically wrote his contract for him." Both Lombardi and Shula took the high road and did not to respond in kind to Wilson's bile. After all, when Shula took over, he introduced eight new starters to the 1970 Dolphins. Moreover, guard Larry Little told Tom Daynluk for *The Super 70s* that the atmosphere under Wilson was more like a country club, "A lot of the ingredients for a winning team were already there. Shula's job was to refine it."

Wilson never coached again. He worked in real estate and construction in Florida for several years until retiring to his home town of Chicago where he died in 1978 from a heart attack at the age of 64.

WILSON, LAWRENCE F. (LARRY) 3/24/1938– Utah. Played S for the Cardinals from 1960 to 1972. *Apprenticeship:* None. *Roots:* None. *Branches:* None. *Coordinators/Key Assistants*: None. *Hall of Fame Players:* Dan Dierdorf, Roger Wehrli. *Primary Quarterbacks:* Steve Pisarkiewicz. *Record:* **Hall of Fame Player; Interim Coach.**

Quarterback Bobby Layne once claimed the slightly-built Larry Wilson, "may have been the toughest guy, pound for pound, who ever played this game." In 1965, he played two games with casts on both hands and even intercepted a pass doing so. Giants coach Allie Sherman marveled at his hustle, "Wilson is the goingest player I ever saw. He never stops."

Born in Rigby, Idaho, Wilson played halfback from 1957 to 1959 for Utah where he once scored five touchdowns in a game. Drafted by the Cardinals in the seventh round in 1960, Larry went directly into the starting lineup at free safety. A five-time All-Pro, Wilson was particularly noted for his reckless charges up the middle on safety blitzes. Although the Bears' Hunk Anderson claimed to have invented the safety blitz in the 1940s using George McAfee on the Bears, it was Wilson who popularized the play throughout the 1960s.

In 1968, he considered retiring at age 29 to become head coach at his alma mater, telling the press, "My long range ambition always has been to go into coaching." Wilson decided against it then and again in 1974 when he was a candidate for the same position. Instead, when Larry retired from playing in 1973, he was named the Cardinals' director of scouting. In 1977, he was promoted to director of personnel, but made a brief detour into coaching in 1979. That year, Owner Bill Bidwill ordered Coach Bud Wilkinson to play

Wilson, Lawrence F. (Larry)									
Year	Team	Games	Wins	Losses	Ties	%	P Wins	P Losses	P %
1979	Cardinals	3	2	1	0	.667	0	0	.000
1 year		3	2	1	0	.667	0	0	.000

young quarterback Steve Pisarkiewicz, but Bud refused and was fired. Wilson was dispatched to the locker room to coach the final three games of the season with Pisarkiewicz under center. Although Pisarkiewicz played poorly, the Cardinals managed to win two of the games. By the start of 1980, however, Larry was back in the front office, Pisarkiewicz was in Green Bay and Jim Hanifan was coaching the team.

Wilson was promoted in 1988 to vice president and general manager and then shed the GM duties in 1994. He retired from football in 2003 after 30 years in the front office and 43 years with the Cardinals. He was elected to the Hall of Fame in 1978.

WINNER, CHARLES H. (CHARLEY) 7/2/1924– Southeast Missouri State and Washington (MO). HB; did not play professionally. *Apprenticeship:* College asst.—5 years; pro asst.—12 years. *Roots:* Weeb Ewbank, Don Shula. *Branches:* Rick Forzano, Ken Shipp (i), Leeman Bennett, Red Miller, Sam Rutigliano, Buddy Ryan. *Coordinators/Key Assistants:* For the Cardinals, Red Miller ran the offense, while Winner handled his own defense; for the Jets, Ken Shipp ran the offense, while Dick Voris handled the defense. *Hall of Fame Players:* Joe Namath, John Riggins, Jackie Smith, Roger Wehrli, Larry Wilson. *Primary Quarterbacks:* Jim Hart, Joe Namath. *Tendencies:* • His teams scored 21.7 points and allowed 22.8 per game • His teams ran 51.6% of the time, which was the league average • Four starting quarterbacks in seven years; 73% of starts to primary quarterbacks • 16 rookie starters in seven years • Winning Full Seasons to Losing Full Seasons: 3:2.

Charley Winner was an excellent assistant coach who was unprepared to handle the special difficulties that he would encounter as a head coach. Born in Somerville, New Jersey, Winner was a 5'7" 150-pound halfback who enrolled at Southeast Missouri State as a freshman in 1942. A year later, he was in the Army Air Corps where ultimately he flew 17 bombing missions during the war. Shot down in 1945, he was captured and spent eight weeks as a prisoner of war in Germany until the war ended. Following his discharge, Charley played for Washington University in St. Louis from 1946 to 1948. During his junior and

senior years, the Washington coach was Weeb Ewbank. Ewbank left to join Paul Brown's staff in Cleveland in 1949, while Winner spent the year as an assistant at his alma mater. The two would be reunited in 1950 when Charley married Weeb's daughter Nancy and took an assistant's job at Case Tech in Cleveland.

Winner spent four years at Case, but when Ewbank was named head coach of the Colts in 1954, he hired Charley as an assistant. Within a few years, Winner was in charge of the Baltimore defense and was part of two NFL championship teams under his father-in-law. Even after Ewbank was fired in 1963, Charley remained the team's defensive coach under new head coach Don Shula, who had once played under Winner. Shula later said, "I thought for sure I'd have to fire him because of the loyalty thing, but Charley told me he'd have no trouble being loyal to me, and it turned out he was a very hard-working individual."

In 1965, Winner was named head coach of the St. Louis Cardinals, but didn't realize exactly what he was getting into. Despite having three winning seasons in five under Charley, the team was deeply troubled. In the front office, the Bidwill brothers who owned the team did not act in concert. In the locker room there was widespread discontent. Linebacker and self-fashioned intellectual Dave Meggyesy was involved in antiwar and civil rights issues and published a controversial book, *Out of Their League*, slamming the league and the game in 1970. Of highest significance, the Cardinals had a festering racial divide that exploded onto the pages of *Sports Illustrated* in 1968. To his credit, Winner made several moves to combat this problem and improved the situation immensely. Black tackle Ernie McMillan told the *New York Times* in 1973, "He inherited the Cardinals' racial situation; he didn't create it. I think he learned a lot from it. Basically, he's a good man. And he's even more aware now."

On the field, Winner struggled to build a defense and to sort through a quarterback controversy involving veteran Charley Johnson and a young Jim Hart. Hart told Tom Danyluk for *The Super 70s*, "The older players did not really like him. They thought he wasn't decisive enough, especially with the quarterback position. I don't blame them. I would've probably felt

Winner, Charles H. (Charley)									
Year	Team	Games	Wins	Losses	Ties	%	P Wins	P Losses	P %
1966	Cardinals	14	8	5	1	.607	0	0	.000
1967	Cardinals	14	6	7	1	.464	0	0	.000
1968	Cardinals	14	9	4	1	.679	0	0	.000
1969	Cardinals	14	4	9	1	.321	0	0	.000
1970	Cardinals	14	8	5	1	.607	0	0	.000
1974	Jets	14	7	7	0	.500	0	0	.000
1975	Jets	9	2	7	0	.222	0	0	.000
7 years		93	44	44	5	.500	0	0	.000

that way if I was one of those veterans. However, it's pretty hard for me to pan Charley because he went out on a limb by making me his starter." By 1970, the defense was improved, Johnson was gone and Hart was fully entrenched at quarterback. The team got off to an 8–2–1 start, but lost its last three games to miss the playoffs. Winner subsequently was fired because of the team's late season collapse.

Charley was hired as defensive coordinator by George Allen in Washington in 1971. Two years later, he reunited with his father-in-law on the Jets in 1973. Once Weeb stepped down in 1974, Winner was named his successor. Quarterback Joe Namath once called Charley, "the most enthusiastic coach I've ever been around." However, enthusiasm could not alter the downward trajectory the Jets were on since their Super Bowl III triumph five years before. Although the offense featured runner John Riggins and receivers Jerome Barkum and Richard Caster, its success depended wholly on the health of Namath, and Broadway Joe was too hobbled by a series of past injuries to play at his best. The defense was a complete mess. It allowed the third most points in 1974 and the most in the league in 1975. Nine games into the 1975 season, the Jets were on a six-game losing streak, so owner Phil Iselin fired Winner "to save the team." The team then won just one of its final five games under Charley's successor Ken Shipp.

Winner coached under Bill Johnson and Homer Rice in Cincinnati from 1976 to 1979 and then was out of football for a year. He returned in 1981 as director of player personnel for the Dolphins, working with Don Shula once again. Charley worked in Miami for a dozen years until retiring in 1992

Wray, James R. Ludlow (Lud) 2/7/1894–7/24/1967. Pennsylvania. Played C for the Buffalo All-Americans from 1920 to 1921. *Apprenticeship:* College coach — 8 years (1 as head coach). *Roots:* None. *Branches:* None. *Coordinators/Key Assistants:* None. *Hall of Fame Players:* Cliff Battles, Turk Edwards. *Primary Quarterbacks:* None. *Tendencies:* • His teams scored 7.8 points and allowed 12.2 per game • His teams ran 68.7% of the time, which was 94% of the league average • 26 rookie starters in three years • Winning Full Seasons to Losing Full Seasons: 0:3.

Lud Wray was the first coach to lead two expansion teams in their initial season; he has since been followed in that distinction by Paul Brown and Dom Capers. Also like Brown, Wray had an ownership interest in the second team. Yet, that did not ensure success or a long career for the gruff former center known as "Rough and Ready" in college.

Wray was born into a well-to-do Philadelphia family and grew up a close friend of future commissioner Bert Bell. He and Bell both played for the Penn Quakers and played on Penn's 1917 Rose Bowl team before serving in France during World War I. Wray returned to Penn as a senior in 1918, while Bell returned to the Quakers in 1919 and then joined the team's coaching staff in 1920. Wray continued his playing career in the professional ranks in 1919 with the Massillon Tigers and the Buffalo Prospects. From 1920 to 1921, Lud played for the NFL's Buffalo All-Americans, while moonlighting with two independent teams: the Union Club of Phoenixville in 1920 and the Union Quakers of Philadelphia in 1921. In 1922, he finished his playing days with the Frankford Yellow Jackets in his home town and then reunited with Bell on Lou Young's coaching staff at Penn; not so coincidentally, Young was another former Quaker teammate of the two.

As a coach, Wray was a tobacco-chewing screamer who favored vigorous scrimmaging in pads. His favorite expression was, "Wear 'em down." However, this old school football approach did not appeal to everyone. In 1928, halfback Marty Brill transferred to Notre Dame to get away from Wray, and Bert Bell left Penn to move across town to Temple University as an assistant because he disagreed with his friend's methods. Wray eventually succeeded Young as Penn's head coach in 1930 and posted a 5–4 record but was fired in December. John Arthur Brown, a member of the school's Athletic Council, told the *New York Times*, "I have known Mr. Wray since he was four years old and have always known him to be honest and courageous. He was a splendid and fearless football player. Apparently, he has a lot of enemies in the university among the graduates, some of the players, the alumni and the public. How many of the players were opposed to his methods I am unable to say. We were not dealing in that primarily, but suffice to say, there

Wray, James R. Ludlow (Lud)									
Year	Team	Games	Wins	Losses	Ties	%	P Wins	P Losses	P %
1932	Boston Braves (Redskins)	10	4	4	2	.500	0	0	.000
1933	Eagles	9	3	5	1	.389	0	0	.000
1934	Eagles	11	4	7	0	.364	0	0	.000
1935	Eagles	11	2	9	0	.182	0	0	.000
4 years		41	13	25	3	.354	0	0	.000

was friction." Lud responded to his dismissal with the biblical quotation, "Sufficient unto the day is the evil thereof."

Partly on Bell's recommendation, George Preston Marshall hired Wray in 1932 as the first coach of the Boston Braves, who would later become the Washington Redskins. Lud held mass tryouts of over 100 players and was embarrassed when eight of the players he cut were signed by the Providence Steamroller who then steamrolled the Braves in a preseason game. Wray hired six of the players back before the season began and led the team to a respectable 4–4–2 record in its first season.

A year later, Bell brought in Wray as a co-investor in assuming the debts of the bankrupt Frankford Yellow Jackets in order to purchase the expansion Philadelphia Eagles' franchise. With Bell operating as general manager and Wray as coach, the Eagles were a bad team from 1933 to 1935 that accumulated its own debt of $80,000. Bell restructured the team financially in 1937 and offered Wray a pay cut of two-thirds of his salary as a coach. When Lud refused, Bell assumed the coaching reigns as well. As the Eagles sunk even lower in the coming years, Wray coached at St. Joseph's prep school in Philadelphia during 1936 and 1937 until joining Manhattan College in 1938 as line coach. He moved on to Holy Cross as line coach in 1941 and then to Villanova in the same role in 1944.

Lud eventually reconciled with Bell and in 1945 was named line coach under Jim Leonard in Pittsburgh, where Bell was then co-owner with Art Rooney. Both Leonard and Wray were fired in 1946 when the Steelers hired Jock Sutherland. Lud later rejoined Leonard as line coach at Villanova during Leonard's stint as head coach there from 1949 to 1950. Wray then formed his own insulation and asbestos business while also coaching at Camden Catholic High School in New Jersey during the 1950s until suffering a stroke in 1959. He died in 1967 at age 73.

WYCHE, SAMUEL D. (SAM) 1/5/1945– Furman. Played QB for the Bengals, Redskins, Lions and Cardinals from 1968 to 1972 and 1974 and 1976. *Apprenticeship:* College coach — 2 years (1 as head coach); pro asst. — 4 years. *Roots:* Bill Walsh. *Branches:* Bruce Coslet, David Shula, Dick LeBeau, Mike Mularkey. *Coordinators/Key Assistants*: For the Bengals, Wyche then Bruce Coslet ran the offense, while Dick LeBeau handled the defense; for the Bucs, Wyche ran his own offense, while Floyd Peters then Rusty Tillman handled the defense. *Hall of Fame Players:* Anthony Munoz. *Primary Quarterbacks:* Boomer Esiason, Craig Erickson. *Tendencies:* • His teams scored 20.6 points and allowed 22.9 per game • His teams ran 47.9% of the time, which was 105% of the league average • 11 starting quarterbacks in 12 years; 71% of starts to primary quarterbacks • 27 rookie starters in 12 years • Winning Full Seasons to Losing Full Seasons: 3:7.

Bill Walsh once said of his former assistant Sam Wyche, "He's a dynamic, creative man. The things that most coaches aren't, he is." Indeed, Wyche, an amateur magician, was known for being unconventional throughout his life and that quality infused his coaching career for both good and bad. While he led one team to a Super Bowl, he was also derided as "Wicky Wacky" by detractors for his not always successful innovations.

Sam was born in Atlanta and played quarterback for Furman University from 1963 to 1965 despite starting as a non-scholarship, walk-on player. He fractured a vertebra as a senior and was not drafted by the NFL, so he played a year with the semipro Wheeling Ironmen in 1966 and then spent 1967 as a graduate assistant at South Carolina. When the Bengals were formed in 1968, Sam made the team as a backup and started just nine games in three years in Cincinnati. Acquired by George Allen in 1971, Wyche spent the next three years in the Redskins' organization behind Sonny Jurgensen and Billy Kilmer. When Joe Theismann joined the team in 1974, Sam moved on to De-

Year	Team	Games	Wins	Losses	Ties	%	P Wins	P Losses	P %
	Wyche, Samuel D. (Sam)								
1984	Bengals	16	8	8	0	.500	0	0	.000
1985	Bengals	16	7	9	0	.438	0	0	.000
1986	Bengals	16	10	6	0	.625	0	0	.000
1987	Bengals	15	4	11	0	.267	0	0	.000
1988	Bengals	16	12	4	0	.750	2	1	.667
1989	Bengals	16	8	8	0	.500	0	0	.000
1990	Bengals	16	9	7	0	.563	1	1	.500
1991	Bengals	16	3	13	0	.188	0	0	.000
1992	Buccaneers	16	5	11	0	.313	0	0	.000
1993	Buccaneers	16	5	11	0	.313	0	0	.000
1994	Buccaneers	16	6	10	0	.375	0	0	.000
1995	Buccaneers	16	7	9	0	.438	0	0	.000
12 years		191	84	107	0	.440	3	2	.600

troit before finishing his playing career on the Cardinals in 1976

Bill Walsh tried to entice Wyche to join his staff at Stanford in 1977, but instead Sam worked in sporting goods and as a broadcaster of Furman football in 1977 and 1978. In 1979, though, Walsh was named head coach of the 49ers and hired Sam as an assistant to help tutor young quarterbacks Steve DeBerg and Joe Montana. San Francisco's success burnished Wyche's resume, and he was named head coach of Indiana in 1983. Following a 3–8 season though, Sam left to become head coach of the Bengals in 1984. Owner Paul Brown later remembered his former backup quarterback to *Sports Illustrated*, "All of the players had to keep their playbooks neat. Sam's asides, the little things you write, were done as a coach would do them. Every year, I kept the best one. I kept Sam's."

In Cincinnati, Wyche transitioned the team from his former teammate Ken Anderson at quarterback to outspoken rookie Boomer Esiason. As Esiason gained experience, Sam began to move increasingly to a No-Huddle Offense. By 1986, the transition was complete and the Bengals went 10–6. Wyche told Tim Layden for *Blood Sweat and Chalk*, "A big part of the thinking behind the no-huddle was saying to your opponent, 'We're going to take away your normal recovery time. By the end of the game, you're going to be too tired to compete.'" Meanwhile on defense, Dick LeBeau was experimenting with the groundbreaking Zone Blitz Defense. Although the creative Bengals backslid during the strike year of 1987, in 1988 the club led the NFL in scoring, won 12 games and reached the Super Bowl where they lost in the closing seconds to Bill Walsh and Joe Montana's 49ers. Former Redskin teammate Ron McDole remarked to the *Washington Post*, "I just couldn't picture Sam as a head coach. It seemed he always had his tongue in his cheek. Watching the games and watching him on the sidelines, I see so much of the old Sam.... He's still mesmerizing people."

The Bengals suffered a letdown in 1989, and the team became more known for Sam's actions than their play. That year, he carried on a running feud with obnoxious Oilers' coach Jerry Glanville that culminated with Cincinnati running up the score to embarrass the Oilers 61–7 in December. The week before that incident, Wyche grabbed a microphone on the sideline after Bengals' fans had thrown snowballs on the field to protest an officials' call and admonished the home

crowd, "You don't live in Cleveland; you live in Cincinnati." The Bengals returned to the playoffs in 1990, but Sam again garnered headlines by barring a female reporter's access to the club's locker room. The team completely collapsed in 1991, and Sam was fired. Overall, his Bengals finished in the top four in scoring four times in his eight seasons as head coach.

On that record, Wyche was named head coach of the Bucs in 1992 after Bill Parcells turned Tampa down. Parcells knew enough to avoid a bad situation; Sam, however, slowly did begin to improve the franchise for Tony Dungy, his successor in 1996, to build a winner. Wyche worked as a TV analyst for the next four years but had surgery on his vocal chords in 2000. He helped coach high school football in 2002 and 2003, assisted his former backup quarterback Turk Schonert who was offensive coordinator in Buffalo in 2005 and then returned to being a volunteer high school coach from 2006 to 2008. In addition, Sam has worked as a college football broadcaster since 2006 and has served on the County Council in Pickens County South Carolina since 2008. His younger brother Bubba played quarterback for the University of Tennessee, in the CFL and in the WFL.

ZORN, JAMES A. (JIM) 5/10/1953– California Polytechnic—Pomona. Played QB for the Seahawks, Packers and Bucs from 1976 to 1985 and 1987. *Apprenticeship:* College asst.—9 years; pro asst.—11 years. *Roots:* Dennis Erickson, Bobby Ross, Gary Moeller (i), Mike Holmgren. *Branches:* None. *Coordinators/Key Assistants*: Sherman Smith then Sherman Lewis ran the offense, while Greg Blache handled the defense. *Hall of Fame Players:* None. *Primary Quarterbacks:* Jason Campbell. *Tendencies:* • His teams scored 16.6 points and allowed 19.8 per game • His teams ran 43.5% of the time, which was 99% of the league average • One starting quarterbacks in two years; 100% of starts to primary quarterback • Two rookie starters in two years • Winning Full Seasons to Losing Full Seasons: 0:1.

Left handed Jim Zorn was a free thinker, willing to try almost anything as a player and as a coach. While that led to some excitement during his playing career, it did not translate to head coaching success.

Zorn was born in Whitier, California, and played quarterback for California Polytechnic at Pomona from 1972 to 1974. He went undrafted and tried to catch on in the NFL as a free agent but was cut by

Zorn, James A. (Jim)									
Year	Team	Games	Wins	Losses	Ties	%	P Wins	P Losses	P %
2008	Redskins	16	8	8	0	.500	0	0	.000
2009	Redskins	16	4	12	0	.250	0	0	.000
2 years		32	12	20	0	.375	0	0	.000

both the Cowboys and the Rams in 1975. Signed by the expansion Seahawks in 1976, he was a good match for Coach Jack Patera's free-wheeling approach that employed a grab-bag of trick plays to overcome their lack of talent. Zorn was a scrambler who kept plays alive to keep Seattle in games and forged a connection with Hall of Fame receiver Steve Largent to light up the Northwest skies with footballs.

Zorn eventually was pushed aside by another free agent quarterback, Dave Krieg, in 1983 and moved on to Green Bay as a backup in 1985. After a year with Winnipeg of the CFL in 1986, Jim returned to the NFL in 1987 as a replacement player in Tampa for one game. He subsequently began his coaching career as quarterbacks coach for Boise State from 1988 to 1991 and then was offensive coordinator at Utah State from 1992 to 1994 and quarterbacks coach at the University of Minnesota in 1995 and 1996.

Zorn returned to the NFL as a traveling quarterbacks coach in 1997. He was with the Seahawks from 1997 to 1998, with the Lions from 1999 to 2000 and back with the Seahawks from 2001 to 2007. Seattle head coach Mike Holmgren told the *Seattle Post-Intelligencer* that he liked Jim's "enthusiasm and knowledge. You put those two things together and it's kind of contagious." Zorn interviewed with the Redskins in January 2008 and was hired as the team's new offensive coordinator despite the fact that Washington did not have a head coach since Joe Gibbs had retired recently. A month later, Washington owner Dan Snyder promoted Jim to head coach once he saw how difficult it was to hire a desirable head coach with an untried offensive coordinator already on staff.

In Washington, Zorn did things his way as long as he was able. He utilized many of the same peculiar drills he had instituted in Seattle, such as having the quarterbacks play dodge ball to improve their footwork and use a Slip'n' Slide to teach them how to slide. When the team got off to an 8–2 start, all was great. After losing the last six games of the year, though, Jim began to have trouble with veterans such as Clinton Portis and was put on a short leash by Snyder. When the Redskins began the 2009 season 2–4, Snyder hired Sherman Lewis as assistant coach to call the plays for the team and completely destroyed Zorn's credibility with the players.

While the Redskins went 4–4 under that arrangement, Jim was fired at year's end. He tutored Joe Flacco as Baltimore's quarterbacks coach in 2010, but then was fired at the end of the year, with some speculating that offensive coordinator Cam Cameron thought Flacco was getting too close to Zorn. Jim moved on to Kansas City as quarterbacks coach in 2011.

II. Pre–1933 Coaches

ABBOTT, LAFAYETTE (FAYE OR HACK)
8/16/1895–1/21/1965. Kenyon College and then Syracuse for Buck O'Neill. Played B/E for Dayton from 1921 to 1929. *Hall of Fame Players:* None. *Record:* **Player-Coach.**

Clearport, Ohio native Faye Abbott had a bifurcated college career. Before World War I, he served as captain of the Kenyon College team in both 1916 and 1917. After the war, Abbott enrolled at Syracuse, where he played alongside All-American guard and future NFL star Joe "Doc" Alexander, but was dismissed from school in 1921 due to his grades. One newspaper account noted "Abbott has a brilliant business offer in the west." Evidently, that offer was to sign with the Dayton Triangles. The Triangles began as an independent team in 1916 and were a charter member of the American Professional Football Association in 1920. Abbott joined the team in 1921 and spent the rest of the decade playing for them. The Triangles deteriorated throughout the 1920s to the point that when Abbott took over as coach, they were a traveling team, too weak to draw a home crowd in Dayton. Faye's coaching record of 0–13 is the worst in NFL history. To make it worse, Dayton was shut out in 11 of those 13 losses and was outscored 267–16. In fact, Abbott's Triangles scored in just one game in 1928 and just one in 1929. After that debacle, the franchise was sold to investors from Brooklyn, and Dayton vanished from the NFL landscape. Abbott later served as an NFL lineman.

ALEXANDER, JOSEPH A. (DOC) 4/1/1898–9/12/1975. Syracuse for Buck O'Neill and Chick Meehan. Played C/G/T for the Rochester Jeffersons and

New York Giants from 1921 to 1927. *Hall of Fame Players:* None. *Record:* **Player-Coach.**

The son of Russian immigrants, Doc Alexander was born in Silver Creek, New York and played five varsity seasons from 1916 to 1920 for Syracuse while he attained his medical degree and twice was named All-American at guard. Graduating to the Rochester Jeffersons of the NFL in 1921, Doc was chosen as an All Pro for his first two seasons, but in his three years in Rochester, including one as a player-coach, the Jeffersons won only two games. In between, Alexander spent the 1923 season playing for the independent Frankford Yellow Jackets. When Tim Mara founded the Giants in 1925, Doc was the first player he signed, and he also served as a playing assistant coach under head coach Bob Folwell. When Folwell left to coach the Philadelphia Quakers in Red Grange's American Football League in 1926, Alexander succeeded him as Giants' coach. With Doc's medical practice becoming more active, he stepped down as coach in 1927, but continued to play for the Giants that year in which they won their first NFL championship. Doc retired after the 1927 season to devote his full attention to medicine and became a specialist in lung disease, working in several New York City hospitals for nearly 50 years until his death in 1975 at the age of 77. He briefly returned to football from 1935 to 1938 when he worked as an assistant coach under Benny Friedman at City College of New York. Alexander then replaced Friedman as head coach at CCNY in 1942 when Friedman went into the Navy and posted a 1–7–1 record before stepping down. Alexander was elected to both the College Football Hall of Fame and the International Jewish Sports Hall of Fame.

Abbott, Lafayette (Faye or Hack)

Year	Team	Games	Wins	Losses	Ties	%	Rank	Points	Allowed
1928	Dayton Triangles	7	0	7	0	.000	10	9	131
1929	Dayton Triangles	6	0	6	0	.000	12	7	136
2 years		13	0	13	0	.000		16	267

Alexander, Joseph A. (Doc)

Year	Team	Games	Wins	Losses	Ties	%	Rank	Points	Allowed
1922	Rochester Jeffersons	5	0	4	1	.000	15	13	76
1926	New York Giants	13	8	4	1	.667	6	147	51
2 years		18	8	8	2	.500		160	127

Andrews, Leroy B. 6/27/1986–7/1978. Pittsburg State (KS) for Garfield Weede. Played G for the St. Louis All Stars, Kansas City Blues and Cowboys and Cleveland Bulldogs from 1923 to 1927. *Hall of Fame Players:* Red Badgro, Ray Flaherty, Benny Friedman, Joe Guyon, Walt Kiesling, Ernie Nevers. *Record:* Began as **Player-Coach.**

Only Hall of Fame coaches George Halas (with his co-coach Dutch Sternaman), Curly Lambeau, Guy Chamberlin and Jimmy Conzelman won more games than Leroy Andrews in the pre–1933 NFL, but Andrews never won a championship and is largely forgotten today. Leroy was a 225-pound guard from Kansas who was a member of the Great Lakes Naval Training station team that won the 1919 Rose Bowl. Also on that squad were George Halas, Paddy Driscoll, Jimmy Conzelman and Hal Erickson. Leroy got started as the player-coach and general promoter of the Kansas City Blues that evolve into the Kansas City Cowboys. Hall of Fame coach Steve Owen, who played under Andrews in Kansas City and New York, claimed in his autobiography, *My Kind of Football,* that Leroy ran the team "on a shoestring," often struggling to meet payroll and sometimes borrowing money from players just to keep the team going until the next good payday. The Kansas City teams were primarily traveling teams, and Andrews had his players come into town all duded up in western apparel — chaps, cowboy boots and cowboy hats — to attract attention. Andrews favored large linemen like himself but had limited success in his three years in Kansas City. Moving on to Cleveland in 1927, Leroy hitched his star to passing sensation Benny Friedman and accompanied Benny from Cleveland to Detroit to New York in three years. He brokered the deal that brought Friedman to New York, insisting that the Giants purchase not only Benny, but the entire Wolverine team along with their coach. Because of Friedman, Andrews' teams led the league in scoring for four consecutive seasons from 1927 to 1930.

Despite going 24–5–1 in two seasons at the helm of the Giants and finishing second to the Packers both years, Leroy was fired at the end of the 1930 season. Two incidents are often recounted as his downfall. First, he was given the job of signing NYU football star Ken Strong to a contract in 1929 and lowballed Strong by offering him half of what the Maras had authorized Andrews to spend, presumably to make a good show with the boss. Consequently, Strong signed with the rival Staten Island Stapletons and tormented the Giants for the next few years. Second, Friedman and Owen led a players' revolt against Andrews at the end of the 1930 season. Friedman later claimed that Andrews was cracking under the pressure of having to face Knute Rockne in an upcoming exhibition game against a Notre Dame All Star team, but that sounds like a cover story. Friedman and Owen were named co-coaches for the final two games in 1930, and Owen was appointed head coach the following season. Andrews moved on to the Chicago Cardinals, but was fired after losing on opening day 13–3 to the Portsmouth Spartans. Leroy claimed to have resigned, but the *Chicago Tribune* reported that 17 Cardinal players went to the owner and pleaded that he bring back Ernie Nevers as coach because they favored Nevers' double wing attack over Andrews' single wing. Andrews told reporters, "I expect to be back in the National Professional league as coach of another team next season." Although he was mentioned as a possible head coach of the fledgling Cincinnati Reds franchise in 1933, Andrews never coached in the league again.

Armstrong, John A. 8/10/1897–4/30/1960. Dubuque for John Chalmers. Played B for the Rock

Andrews, Leroy B.

Year	Team	Games	Wins	Losses	Ties	%	Rank	Points	Allowed
1924	Kansas City Blues	9	2	7	0	.222	15	46	124
1925	Kansas City Cowboys	8	2	5	1	.286	13	65	97
1926	Kansas City Cowboys	11	8	3	0	.727	4	76	53
1927	Cleveland Bulldogs	13	8	4	1	.667	4	209	107
1928	Detroit Wolverines	10	7	2	1	.778	3	189	76
1929	New York Giants	15	13	1	1	.929	2	312	86
1930	New York Giants	15	11	4	0	.733	2	308	98
1931	Chicago Cardinals	1	0	1	0	.000	4	3	13
8 years		82	51	27	4	.654		1208	654

Armstrong, John A.

Year	Team	Games	Wins	Losses	Ties	%	Rank	Points	Allowed
1924	Rock Island Independents	9	5	2	2	.714	5	88	38
1 year		9	5	2	2	.714		88	38

Island Independents from 1923 to 1925. *Hall of Fame Players:* Joe Guyon. *Record:* **Player-Coach.**

Armstrong was a local hero in Iowa. Having been a star athlete at Dubuque, he later coached football for Columbia College there, owned and managed a minor league baseball club in town and ran a recreation hall that offered bowling and billiards to the community. Just 5'8" and 170-pounds, he played three years in the NFL for the Rock Island Independents (about an hour away from Dubuque) and unofficially led the league in passing yards and interceptions thrown in 1923. The following season he served as the team's player-coach and led the Independents to a fifth place finish. He was replaced as coach by teammate Rube Ursella in 1925 and both Armstrong and the Independents left the league the following year. Johnny coached Rock Island to a 2–6–1 record in Red Grange's AFL in 1926; it was his final year in pro football.

BARR, WALLACE A. (SHORTY) 11/30/1897–4/26/1957. Wisconsin for John Richards • Played B for the Racine Legion, Milwaukee Badgers and Racine Tornadoes from 1923 to 1926. *Hall of Fame Players:* None. *Record:* **Interim Player-Coach.**

At 5'8" and 195-pounds, Milwaukee's Shorty Barr was generally described as "rotund," but was known as an able field general who played at Wisconsin with Ralph Scott and Gus Tebell who also coached in the NFL. Barr won the starting Badger quarterback slot as a freshman in 1918 before serving in World War I. After the war, Barr returned to Wisconsin to quarterback the Badgers for three more years before moving on to play for the Racine Legion in 1923. In his rookie year, Barr threw for three touchdown passes against the Packers on October 28th and in a game against the Cardinals on November 25 accounted for six points for Racine and four for Chicago by running for one touchdown and being tackled for two safeties. The second safety was a deliberate sacrifice to preserve the lead late in the final three minutes of the game and characterized Barr's heady approach to football. After 1924, Racine shut down and

Barr joined the Milwaukee Badgers for 1925. When Racine reformed in 1926, Barr was named player-coach and lasted three games before being replaced by teammate Wally McIlwain for the Tornadoes final two NFL games. Barr had been coaching Racine three nights a week that year while also working as an assistant coach at Carroll College. In retirement, Barr was a prominent Milwaukee attorney who frequently officiated local football games and served on the area draft board during World War II.

BARRY, NORMAN C. 12/25/1897–10/13/1988. Notre Dame for Knute Rockne. Played HB for the Chicago Cardinals, Green Bay Packers and Milwaukee Badgers from 1921 to 1922. *Hall of Fame Players:* Paddy Driscoll. *Record:* NFL Championship 1925.

Chicago-native Norm Barry spent 13 years at Notre Dame, attending elementary school, high school, college and law school there. Norm was George Gipp's friend and teammate on the Fighting Irish, and, in fact, threw a 55-yard touchdown pass to Gipp against Northwestern in 1920 that was the final scoring play of Gipp's career. In 1921, the 5'10" 170-pound Barry joined another former teammate, Curly Lambeau, in Green Bay, and then also played for the Cardinals and the Milwaukee Badgers in the next two years. In 1925, Cardinals coach Arnie Horween became ill, and Barry was hired to take his place. He was the first non-playing coach in team history. Barry added Red Dunn to the backfield and remade the line, and Chicago went from averaging nine points a game in 1924 to nearly 17 in 1925. The Cardinals won a disputed NFL championship that year after the league-leading Pottsville Maroons were suspended at the end of the season. That same year, Barry coached De La Salle High School to the Chicago city championship as well. Years later, Norm told the *Chicago Tribune*, "It wasn't as difficult as it sounds. The Cardinals only practiced two or three times a week, and I had able help from Dr. Eddie Anderson running practices and Fred Gillies who coached the line. I could spend part of my day at De La Salle and then take care of the Cardinal duties. Coaching was more

Barr, Wallace A. (Shorty)									
Year	Team	Games	Wins	Losses	Ties	%	Rank	Points	Allowed
1926	Racine Tornadoes	3	1	2	0	.333	16	8	36
1 year		3	1	2	0	.333		8	36

Barry, Norman C.									
Year	Team	Games	Wins	Losses	Ties	%	Rank	Points	Allowed
1925	Chicago Cardinals	14	11	2	1	.846	1	230	65
1926	Chicago Cardinals	12	5	6	1	.455	10	74	98
2 years		26	16	8	2	.667		304	163

casual then." Financial problems forced Cardinals' owner Chris O'Brien to sell his star Paddy Driscoll to the cross town Bears in 1926, and the Cardinals slumped badly, dropping back to scoring just six points per game. Barry then was replaced by Guy Chamberlin for the 1927 season. While Barry continued to coach high school ball in Chicago, he had a long career as a successful attorney, state legislator from 1942 to 1954 and Superior Court judge from 1954 to 1978. His son, Jack, played end for Notre Dame under Frank Leahy.

BATTERSON, GEORGE W. (DIM) 10/3/1881–12/3/1935. No College. Did not play in the NFL. *Hall of Fame Players:* None.

Having played local semi-pro football in the early years of the 20th century, Buffalo's Dim Batterson became a prominent high school coach in his hometown and won three consecutive city titles from 1918 to 1920. He spent one season as the head coach at the University of Buffalo, but only managed a 1–5 record in 1922. He later worked as an assistant coach for the Buffalo Bisons — perhaps the first non-playing assistant in NFL history. Dim was promoted to head coach in 1927 but presided over the staggering franchise's demise. After five consecutive losses, Batterson resigned, citing lack of cooperation from the players and meddling from the ownership. Club officials then disbanded the team due to financial losses. Although the franchise was reinstated in 1929, it would only last one more season. Batterson went into real estate in suburban Tonawanda in the ensuing years.

BEHMAN, RUSSELL K. (BULL) 1/15/1900–3/24/1950. Lebanon Valley and Dickinson College for Glenn Killinger. Played T/G for the Frankford Yellow Jackets from 1924 to 1925 and 1927–1931. *Hall of Fame Players:* None. *Record:* **Player-Coach.**

Although just 5'10", Steelton, Pennsylvania's Bull Behman actually was a large player for his era, weighing in the neighborhood of 215-pounds. He starred first on the line at Lebanon Valley College in

1920 and 1921, and also played some games for the independent Frankford Yellow Jackets at that time under an assumed name to preserve his college eligibility. Behman then captained the football squad at little Dickinson College for two years under Glenn Killinger who called him "one of the greatest college lineman in the country." Behman signed with Frankford for their first NFL season in 1924 and spent his entire NFL career with the Yellow Jackets. He was a two-time All Pro lineman who also punted and place-kicked. In 1926, he jumped to the Philadelphia Quakers of Red Grange's AFL and captained them to the league title before both the team and league folded.

Behman returned to Frankford in 1927 and was named player-coach two years later. Behman led the team to a third place finish in his first year as coach, but the team lost several veterans who were not ably replaced due to financial pressures that management faced, so Bull was replaced as coach by George Gibson late in the 1930 season. Gibson came from the disbanded Minneapolis franchise along with several Red Jacket teammates, and the merged squads won two of five games to close the year. Behman returned as coach for the Yellow Jackets final inept season in 1931 before Frankford relinquished its NFL franchise deep in debt. Behman went on to work as a labor organizer and a prison guard until his death at the age of 50.

BERRYMAN, ROBERT N. (PUNK) 12/13/1893–5/20/1988. Penn State for Bill Hollenback and Dick Harlow. Did not play in the NFL. *Hall of Fame Players:* None.

Philadelphia's Punk Berryman starred as All-American halfback at Penn State from 1912 to 1915 and went into coaching immediately upon graduation. In 1916, he coached Gettysburg College to a 5–4 record and then moved on to Lafayette in 1917 where his team managed a 3–5 mark. Over the next several years, Berryman worked as an assistant coach at Iowa, Dickinson and Colgate, with a brief stop at a Philadelphia high school, before he was named head coach of the Frankford Yellow Jackets in 1924, their first season in

Batterson, George W. (Dim)									
Year	Team	Games	Wins	Losses	Ties	%	Rank	Points	Allowed
1927	Buffalo Bisons	5	0	5	0	.000	12	8	123
1 year		5	0	5	0	.000		8	123

Behman, Russell K. (Bull)									
Year	Team	Games	Wins	Losses	Ties	%	Rank	Points	Allowed
1929	Frankford Yellow Jackets	18	9	4	5	.692	3	129	128
1930	Frankford Yellow Jackets	13	2	10	1	.167	9	100	315
1931	Frankford Yellow Jackets	8	1	6	1	.143	9	13	99
3 years		40	12	20	7	.375		242	542

the NFL. The soft-spoken Berryman led the fledgling team to an 11–2–1 record that was good for third place in the league. It was also just good enough to get sacked, as Frankford brought in three-time championship coach Guy Chamberlin for the 1925 season. Berryman spent the season coaching the Millville Football and Athletic Club independent team in South Jersey. He resurfaced a year later coaching another new franchise, the Brooklyn Lions, but this time was not so successful. The Lions were shut out in six of their 11 games and merged with the Brooklyn Horsemen of the AFL to form the *Brooklion* Horsemen for the last three games of the season. Berryman never coached in the league again.

BIERCE, BRUCE W. (SCOTTY) 9/3/1896–4/26/1982. Akron for Fred Sefton. Played E for the Akron Pros, Buffalo All-Americans, Cleveland Indians and Cleveland Bulldogs from 1920 to 1925. *Hall of Fame Players:* Fritz Pollard. *Record:* **Player-Coach.**

Although born in Kearney, Nebraska, Scotty Bierce grew up in Akron. Bierce and his high school teammate Art Haley continued on to the University of Akron together and both later played for the Akron Pros in the NFL. The 5'9" 164-pound Bierce played for the Pros during the first three years of the NFL and was part of a championship team in Akron in 1920 and then again in 1924 with the Cleveland Bulldogs. In 1925, Scotty returned to Akron as player-coach and coached his former Pros teammate Fritz Pollard in Akron's penultimate NFL season. After football, Bierce became a prominent Akron lawyer and established in his will the Bruce W. "Scotty" Bierce Athletic Scholarship at his alma mater.

BRANDY, JOSEPH H. (JOE) 11/6/1897–7/20/1971. Notre Dame for Knute Rockne. QB. Did not play in the NFL. *Hall of Fame Players:* None.

World War I veteran Joe Brandy quarterbacked Knute Rockne's first two unbeaten teams at Notre Dame in 1919 and 1920. While George Gipp was the team's star, Brandy was the team leader and play-caller who once ordered Gipp off the field for questioning his play-calling. According to the *New York Times,* Rockne said of Joe, "He has greater possibilities as a coach than any player I have known." Brandy signed on as coach of St. Thomas College in St. Paul, Minnesota in 1921 and spent five years there where he coached future pro football Hall of Famer Walt Kiesling. In his fourth year at St. Thomas, Joe also took on coaching the NFL's Minneapolis Marines, succeeding Harry Mehre — another Notre Dame alumnus who was Brandy's assistant at St. Thomas. Despite his forceful personality, Brandy had no success with the Marines, and the team folded at the end of the season. Two years later, Brandy got out of coaching altogether, although he had compiled a 23–7–1 record at St. Thomas. He returned to his hometown of Ogdensburg, New York and got married. His banker father-in-law helped Joe buy the local newspaper in 1926, and he ran it for the next 16 years. He later bought a radio station in the area.

BRENKERT, WAYNE D. 3/5/1898–8/1/1979. Washington & Jefferson for Greasy Neale. Played HB for the Akron Pros from 1923 to 1924. *Hall of Fame Players:* None. *Record:* **Player-Coach.**

Future NFL coaches Wayne Brenkert and Hal Erickson were the star halfbacks on the remarkable 1921 Washington & Jefferson team that went to the Rose Bowl and held mighty California to a scoreless tie. Washington & Jefferson was a small Pennsylvania school of just 450 students at the time, but future Hall of Fame coach Greasy Neale led the team to an undefeated season in which the Presidents came within a

Berryman, Robert N. (Punk)

Year	Team	Games	Wins	Losses	Ties	%	Rank	Points	Allowed
1924	Frankford Yellow Jackets	14	11	2	1	.846	3	326	109
1926	Brooklyn Lions	11	3	8	0	.273	14	60	150
2 years		25	14	10	1	.583		386	259

Bierce, Bruce W. (Scotty)

Year	Team	Games	Wins	Losses	Ties	%	Rank	Points	Allowed
1925	Akron Pros	8	4	2	2	.667	4	65	51
1 year		8	4	2	2	.667		65	51

Brandy, Joseph H. (Joe)

Year	Team	Games	Wins	Losses	Ties	%	Rank	Points	Allowed
1924	Minneapolis Marines	6	0	6	0	.000	16	14	108
1 year		6	0	6	0	.000		14	108

disputed penalty call on Brenkert's 35-yard touchdown run against the Golden Bears of winning the Rose Bowl. The popular 5'10" 170-pound Brenkert was a Detroit native who signed with the Akron Pros upon graduation. When coach Dutch Hendrian was fired after an 0–5 start, Wayne was named coach for the last two games of 1923 and continued as an unsuccessful player-coach in 1924. Brenkert manufactured theater equipment after retiring.

Brewer, Edward Brooke (Untz)
11/21/1894–2/11/1970. Maryland for Curly Byrd. Played HB for the Akron Pros in 1922. *Hall of Fame Players:* None. *Record:* Player-Coach.

Born in the nation's capitol, Untz Brewer was a 5'6" 160-pound sprinter who ran either a 9.6 or 9.8 100-yard dash according to various accounts. Brewer went from prestigious St. Alban's Prep to the University of Maryland where he starred on the football and track teams in 1916, 1920 and 1921. From 1917–1919, Brewer was in the Army. After graduating from Maryland with a degree in Chemistry, Untz was signed as player-coach of the Akron Pros, replacing Fritz Pollard. Brewer was no Pollard on the field, though, and Untz's NFL career lasted just one season. In 1923, Brewer worked as an assistant coach at George Washington, while also coaching a local semi-pro team called the Mercurys. Brewer coached other D.C.-area semipro teams and spent 18 years officiating local high school and college games. In 1941, he made a public appeal to be considered for the open position of head coach at his alma mater, but that came to nothing. Brewer worked as an advertising salesman for newspapers.

Brickley, Charles E. (Charley) 11/24/1891–12/28/1949/ Harvard for Percy Haughton. Did not play in the NFL. *Hall of Fame Players:* None.

Boston's Charley Brickley is a fabled name in the early history of football, mostly for his drop-kicking prowess. At Harvard, Brickley set a college football mark with five field goals to defeat Yale in 1913 and graduated from Harvard in 1915 having kicked a record number of field goals in a season (13) and career (34). Brickley coached Johns Hopkins in 1915 and Boston College in 1916 and 1917, achieving a 6–2 record in each season. In 1917, Charley was also brought in as a player-coach ringer for the Massillon Tigers in their grudge match with the Canton Bulldogs. Unfortunately, Massillon lost a warm up game against the Akron Pros under Brickley and then also lost to Jim Thorpe's Bulldogs with Charley not being much of a factor. The Tigers quickly dropped Brickley and replaced him with Stan Cofall on Knute Rockne's recommendation; Cofall led Massillon to a 6–0 upset of Canton in the rematch a week later.

Brickley's coaching career in the NFL was extremely short and embarrassing. He formed the New York Brickley Giants in 1921, and his team lost to Buffalo 55–0 in October and then 17–0 to the 2–5 Cleveland Indians in December. Although he continued with occasional kicking exhibitions, Brickley never coached again. He worked as a stockbroker and salesman and twice was indicted on stock transaction illegalities; he was convicted of four such counts in 1928. He died at 58 in 1949.

Brill, Martin (Marty) 3/13/1906–4/30/1973. Pennsylvania and Notre Dame for Knute Rockne. Did not play professionally. *Hall of Fame Players:* Ken Strong. *Record:* **Interim Coach.**

Marty Brill's father owned the prosperous J.G. Brill Company that manufactured railroad cars in St. Louis. Marty started out in the backfield at the University of Pennsylvania, but he and future Baltimore

Brenkert, Wayne D.

Year	Team	Games	Wins	Losses	Ties	%	Rank	Points	Allowed
1923	Akron Pros	2	1	1	0	.500	16	8	20
1924	Akron Pros	8	2	6	0	.250	13	59	132
2 years		10	3	7	0	.300		67	152

Brewer, Edward Brooke (Untz)

Year	Team	Games	Wins	Losses	Ties	%	Rank	Points	Allowed
1922	Akron Pros	10	3	5	2	.375	10	146	95
1 year		10	3	5	2	.375		146	95

Brickley, Charles E. (Charley)

Year	Team	Games	Wins	Losses	Ties	%	Rank	Points	Allowed
1921	New York Brickley Giants	2	0	2	0	.000	18	0	72
1 year		2	0	2	0	.000		0	72

Colts' owner Carroll Rosenbloom were so unhappy with the Quakers' gruff line coach Lud Wray that they agreed to transfer to Notre Dame. While Rosenbloom changed his mind about transferring and later quit the team at Penn, Brill starred as an All-American halfback on the undefeated Fighting Irish teams in 1929 and 1930. In fact, when Notre Dame played Penn in 1930, Brill's father offered him $1,000 for each touchdown he scored. Marty reached the end zone three times that day in a 60–20 rout and earned $3,000 in government bonds that unfortunately were worth nothing six weeks later.

Upon graduation, Brill took a job as assistant coach at Columbia. While there, the struggling Staten Island Stapletons fired their coach Hinkey Haines and hired Brill to moonlight as a pro coach. Brill managed a .500 record with a weak team in 1931 but spent 1932 solely at Columbia. From 1933–1939, Marty was the head coach at La Salle in Philadelphia and attained a 32–23–6 record. After Clipper Smith and Slip Madigan turned down the head position at Loyola Marymount in California, Brill was offered that job and told the *Los Angeles Times*, "My boys will be treated just as I wanted to be treated when I was playing." He went 8–12 there in two seasons to conclude his college coaching career. Brill then coached Santa Ana and Oakland in the Pacific Coast Football League to a combined 2–7 record in 1943 and 1944. He later worked as a sales manager for a liquor distributor in California for several years.

BRYAN, JOHN F. (JOHNNY) 2/28/1897–7/1/1966. Dartmouth and Chicago for Amos Alonzo Stagg. Played QB for the Chicago Cardinals, Chicago Bears and Milwaukee Badgers from 1922 to 1927. *Hall of Fame Players:* Johnny Blood. *Record:* **Player-Coach.**

Johnny Bryan's coach at the University of Chicago, the venerated Amos Alonzo Stagg, so despised professional football that he threatened to take away the varsity letters of Bryan and a few other former Maroons who had graduated and turned pro. Stagg claimed to the *Chicago Tribune*, "Professionalism is a worm at the very core of character development."

Bryan took issue with his former coach's public pronouncements, and Stagg fired back that Johnny never actually graduated from Chicago and was upset because he was no longer welcome on the university's athletic field. Stagg never took away Johnny's letter, but the Windy City native's career was instructive of some of the looseness of the pro game in the early days.

The 5'8" 170-pound Bryan was an able quarterback and tailback for the Cardinals and Bears from 1922 to 1924. In 1925, though, Bryan was player-coach for all six of the Milwaukee Badger games, while concurrently appearing in six games for the Bears and serving as Red Grange's understudy during the Bears' postseason barnstorming tour. When the Cardinals were looking around for a patsy to beat up on to increase their winning percentage at the end of the season, they scheduled a game against Milwaukee nearly three weeks after the Badgers had played their final game. To put enough bodies on the field, Milwaukee owner Ambrose McGurk signed four players from Englewood High School in Chicago to play under assumed names, and the new Badgers lost 59–0. When NFL President Joe Carr later found out about this shady subterfuge, he fined the club $500 and ordered McGurk to sell the team.

Carr approved the sale of the team to boxing promoter Frank Mulkern and Bryan who continued as the team's player-coach in 1926. Bryan managed to sign star Marquette end Lavie Dilweg, but still the Badgers could only manage a 2–7 record. Meanwhile, Johnny appeared in three more games with the Bears that season. Bryan withdrew Milwaukee from the NFL in 1927 and sold Dilweg to Green Bay but continued to be involved in various ventures in Milwaukee over the next few years. He ran a new independent team sponsored by Otto Haderer in 1930, operated another squad in a Wisconsin semipro league in 1931 and even attempted to organize a pro basketball team in 1931. Johnny died at the age of 55 in 1966.

CHAMBERLIN, BERLIN G. (GUY) 1/16/1894–4/4/1967. Nebraska Wesleyan and Nebraska for Jumbo Stiehm. Played E for Chicago Staleys, Canton Bull-

Brill, Martin (Marty)									
Year	Team	Games	Wins	Losses	Ties	%	Rank	Points	Allowed
1931	Staten Island Stapletons	7	3	3	1	.500	7	50	59
1 year		7	3	3	1	.500		50	59

Bryan, John F. (Johnny)									
Year	Team	Games	Wins	Losses	Ties	%	Rank	Points	Allowed
1925	Milwaukee Badgers	6	0	6	0	.000	16	7	191
1926	Milwaukee Badgers	9	2	7	0	.222	15	41	66
2 years		15	2	13	0	.133		48	257

dogs, Cleveland Bulldogs, Frankford Yellow Jackets, Chicago Cardinals from 1920 to 1927. *Hall of Fame Players:* Pete Henry, Link Lyman. *Record:* **Hall of Fame Player-Coach**; NFL Championships 1922, 1923, 1924, 1926.

Guy Chamberlin was perhaps the greatest winner the game has ever known. He played on three undefeated teams in college and three in the pros. The record of the teams on which he played up to his final year of 1927 was 111–13–11, a 12-year average performance of 9–1–1. Chamberlin did not even play high school football in Blue Springs, Nebraska because his school was too small. He started college at little Nebraska Wesleyan, where the 6' 210-pound halfback attracted the attention of Nebraska head coach Jumbo Stiehm who brought him to Lincoln in 1914. Stiehm moved Chamberlin to end in 1915, and Guy scored 16 touchdowns in eight games and helped the Huskers beat Notre Dame 20–19 that year. After graduation, Chamberlin taught high school science and coached the football team in 1916 before going into the Army in 1917.

When Chamberlin was discharged in 1919, he began his pro football career by signing with Jim Thorpe's Canton Bulldogs who went undefeated in that last year before the NFL was organized. George Halas signed Guy in 1920 for the Decatur Staleys, and the next year the Chicago Staleys won the league title. Halas later would call Chamberlin the "best two-way end I've ever seen." Guy returned to Canton in 1922 as player-coach and quickly rebuilt the Bulldogs by keeping just five players from the 1921 team that finished 5–2–3. The 1922 Bulldogs went undefeated, shutting out nine opponents and allowing just 15 points on the season. The following season, Canton again finished without a loss, shut out eight opponents and allowed just 19 points. With an expensive payroll, though, the team was losing money and was sold to Cleveland promoter Sam Deutsch who already owned the NFL's Cleveland Indians. Chamberlin brought six Bulldog teammates with him to the new team and won his third consecutive NFL championship as a coach (and fourth consecutive as a player) with the new Cleveland Bulldogs. Deutsch sold the Bulldog franchise back to some Canton businessmen in 1925, but Chamberlin moved on to Frankford to coach the Yellow Jackets.

While Chamberlin said of himself, "I was an easy-going sort of guy except when I was in a football uniform," he was known as a real taskmaster as a coach. His practices sometimes ran 3½ hours as his players perfected their execution of a concise playbook, just like Lombardi's Packers would decades later. Frankford guard Bill Hoffman told the *Philadelphia Daily News* in 1991, "We only had a dozen plays. A couple of off-tackle runs and sweeps. Four or five passes, including a screen. A reverse and an end-around. That was it, but we practiced those plays over and over until we could run them in our sleep." Hall of Fame tackle Link Lyman once described that reverse to NFL Films, "We had this play where [Chamberlin] came around on an end-reverse, and sometimes he would get the ball on an end sweep, or we'd fake it to him and hand it to the fullback up the middle. Other times, our fullback Louie Smyth would drop back and hit me on a tackle-eligible down the field."

Despite the fact that the 1924 Yellow Jackets had finished 11–2–1, Chamberlin again remade the squad and kept just six incumbent players in 1925. Frankford shot out of the gate with a 9–1 start in 1925, but key injuries led to the team going just 4–6 down the stretch. Because of Pennsylvania's Blue Laws, Frankford could not play home games on Sundays, so they would frequently work out scheduling deals in which they would play in Philadelphia on Saturday and then take a train to play a second game on Sunday. The Yellow Jackets regularly played more games than any other team in the league, and it took a toll on the players. Even so, Frankford shut out ten opponents in both 1925 and 1926 and won the NFL championship in the latter season — Chamberlin's fourth title as a coach and fifth as a player. In fact, Chamberlin played an essential roll in the key victory of the season over the Bears in December by blocking an extra point that proved to be the difference in the 7–6 game.

The day after the 1926 season ended, however, Frankford Athletic Association President Theodore Holden resigned under pressure, and Chamberlin left shortly after to sign with the financially-strapped Chicago Cardinals for what would prove to be the only losing season of Guy's career. After Chicago, Chamberlin returned to Nebraska where he ran a farm, served as a state livestock inspector and worked

Chamberlin, Berlin G. (Guy)

Year	Team	Games	Wins	Losses	Ties	%	Rank	Points	Allowed
1922	Canton Bulldogs	12	10	0	2	1.000	1	184	15
1923	Canton Bulldogs	12	11	0	1	1.000	1	246	19
1924	Cleveland Bulldogs	9	7	1	1	.875	1	229	60
1925	Frankford Yellow Jackets	20	13	7	0	.605	6	190	169
1926	Frankford Yellow Jackets	17	14	1	2	.933	1	236	49
1927	Chicago Cardinals	11	3	7	1	.300	9	69	134
6 years		81	58	16	7	.784		1154	446

for the state reformatory. He was elected to the College Football Hall of Fame in 1962 and the Pro Football Hall of Fame in 1965. In the year he died, 1967, Nebraska instituted the Guy Chamberlin Trophy that has been awarded to the outstanding senior Husker every year since.

CHECKAYE, SEVERIN J. (COONIE OR COONEY)
1/6/1893–11/18/1970. No College. Played BB for the Muncie Flyers from 1920 to 1921. *Hall of Fame Players:* None. *Record:* **Player-Coach.**

Along with his brother Toad, Coonie Checkaye was a local gridiron legend in Indiana during the prehistoric 1910's decade. The 5'9" 185-pound Coonie starred at quarterback for the independent Fort Wayne Friars in 1915 and 1916, and both brothers played with the Wabash Athletic Association in 1917. Coonie organized the Muncie Flyers in 1919 in his hometown, and the team became a charter member of the APFA in 1920. Coached by Ken Huffine, the Flyers played only one league game that first year and lost 45–0. Coonie took over as player-coach in 1921, but broke his leg in the second game. Consequently, the team dropped out of the league for good having never scored a point in league competition. Coonie kept the Flyers alive as an independent team through 1925 — first as the Congerville Flyers and then the Jonesboro Flyers. He later worked for Republic Iron and Steel.

CHEVIGNY, JOHN E. (JACK)
8/14/1906–2/19/1945. Notre Dame for Knute Rockne. Did not play professionally. *Hall of Fame Players:* Walt Keisling.

The famous "Win one for the Gipper" tale prominently features Jack Chevigny, a star halfback from 1926 to 1928 for Notre Dame. The story goes that the Irish were trailing Army at halftime in 1928 when Knute Rockne recounted George Gipp's last wish that sometime when the team was struggling Rockne should pep the boys up by imploring them to win one for the late Gipper. In the second half, Chevigny scored the tying touchdown against the cadets and reportedly shouted, "There's one for the Gipper." The Irish went on to score again, win the game and

birth an American legend that would animate a future U.S. President. The next year, Rockne kept the inspirational Chevigny around to coach the backs, and the Hammond, Indiana native filled that role for three years under Rockne and then Hunk Anderson until the Cardinals hired him as head coach in 1932. Not surprisingly, Chevigny installed the Notre Dame offense in Chicago. He claimed, "I'm going to develop the fastest and best balanced backfield in the circuit." For most of the season, that backfield included Joe Lillard, one of the last two black players in the NFL before the color line was drawn in 1934. The Cardinals got off to a 2–1–2 start in 1932, but then lost their last five games of the year by scoring just 22 points in the second half of the season. Lillard was suspended by Chevigny for the last two games of the year for missing a team meeting and for a clash in attitudes.

Chevigny left the Cardinals for Notre Dame's sister institution, St. Edwards, in Austin, Texas and produced a 7–2 team there in 1933. The University of Texas took note of that and signed Jack to coach the Longhorns in 1934. Not only did Texas go 7–2–1 that year, but they also beat Chevigny's alma mater. At the end of the year, the coach was presented with a pen engraved, "To Jack Chevigny, a Notre Dame boy who beat Notre Dame." Unfortunately, Texas won just four games in 1935 and two the following year, leading to Jack resigning at a banquet for the seniors prior to the last game of 1936. Chevigny went into the oil business, and then joined the Marines. In the war, Jack died while leading one of the first waves of soldiers onto the beaches of Iwo Jima in the 1945 island invasion. As an odd postscript to Chevigny's life, that engraved pen from Texas turned up seven months later on deck of the U.S. Missouri, carried by one of the Japanese envoys signing the treaty that ended the war. An American official took the pen to return to Jack's sister and had it re-engraved, "To Jack Chevigny, a Notre Dame boy who gave his life for his country in the spirit of Notre Dame."

CLARK, GEORGE M. (POTSY) (SEE SECTION I)

Checkaye, Severin J. (Coonie or Cooney)									
Year	Team	Games	Wins	Losses	Ties	%	Rank	Points	Allowed
1921	Muncie Flyers	2	0	2	0	.000	18	0	28
1 year		2	0	2	0	.000		0	28

Chevigny, John E. (Jack)									
Year	Team	Games	Wins	Losses	Ties	%	Rank	Points	Allowed
1932	Chicago Cardinals	10	2	6	2	.250	6	72	114
1 year		10	2	6	2	.250		72	114

Cofall, Stanley B. (Stan) 5/5/1894–
9/21/1962. Notre Dame for Jess Harper. Played WB
for the Cleveland Tigers in 1920. *Hall of Fame Players:*
None. *Record:* **Interim Player-Coach.**

Stan Cofall scored 30 touchdowns in three years
as a 5'11" 190-pound halfback for Notre Dame and
struck up a friendship with assistant coach Knute
Rockne during that time. Cofall and Rockne later
played together for the Massillon Tigers in 1917 when
player-coach Cofall led the Tigers over their archrivals,
the Canton Bulldogs. Stan then served in the Army
under Dwight Eisenhower during World War I and
became one of the founders of the American Professional Football Association in 1920, even serving as
the league's first Vice President. Cofall's team, the
Cleveland Tigers, did not score a point in their first
three games, and Stan abruptly left the APFA altogether, with Al Pierotti taking over the coaching in
Cleveland.

What appears to have happened is that in late
October, Cofall met chorus girl Irene Held while she
was filming some scenes in a Cleveland movie studio
and fell in love. When Held's stage show moved to
Philadelphia, so did Stan. Four weeks later, they were
married. Cofall finished 1920 playing for the independent Union Club of Phoenixville in Philadelphia.
Irene told the local *Evening Public Ledger* that her husband was going to give up football. However, over the
next few years, Cofall played for three independent
teams — the Holmesburg AC, the Union Quakers and
the Pottsville Maroons — while coaching at Roman
Catholic High School. In 1925, he was named head
coach at Loyola College in Baltimore, and, after a three
year record of 10–16–1, took over at Wake Forest but
could only manage a 2–6–2 record in Carolina in
1928. Cofall left coaching and returned to his native
Cleveland to start his own company, Stanco Oil. Stan
later purchased the National Solvent Corporation,
founded the Cleveland Touchdown Club and chaired
the Cleveland Boxing Commission for many years.
He divorced Irene in 1953 and remarried. In later life,
he had heart problems and died from a heart attack
at the age of 67, survived by his second wife and three
children from Irene.

**Conzelman, James G. (Jimmy) (see Sec-
tion I)**

Cornsweet, Albert C. (Al) 7/16/1906–
10/16/1991. Brown for Tuss McLaughry. Played FB for
the Cleveland Indians in 1931. *Hall of Fame Players:*
None. *Record:* **Player-Co-Coach** (with Hoge Workman).

The 5'7" 180-pound Cornsweet, was the fullback
and captain on Brown University's "Iron Men" team
of 1926 that beat Yale and Dartmouth without making
a substitution during the game. Al was an Honorable
Mention All-American for those undefeated Brown
Bears, and, over the next couple years, also lettered in
lacrosse, track and wrestling. The brainy Cornsweet
was a member of Phi Beta Kappa and a Rhodes
Scholar who spent 1929–1930 at Oxford. Upon returning to the U.S., Al signed with his hometown
Cleveland Indians as player and coach. This latest version of football Indians also included one of his teammates from Brown, Dave Mishel, making them, in a
manner of speaking, the first Cleveland "Browns." The
Indians lasted just one unsuccessful season before folding. Cornsweet worked at the University of North
Carolina while getting his Ph.D. and experimented
with the use of gasoline as an anesthetic. Al enlisted
in the Navy in 1941 and served as a clinical psychologist
during the war. He later became the Chief Clinical
Psychologist for the Veterans' Administration.

Coughlin, Francis E. (Frank) 2/28/1896–
9/8/1951. Notre Dame for Knute Rockne. Played T
for the Detroit Tigers, Rock Island Independents and
Green Bay Packers in 1921. *Hall of Fame Players:* Ed
Healey. *Record:* **Interim Player-Coach.**

The 1919 undefeated Notre Dame team that featured George Gipp was filled with leaders. It included
eight future college or professional coaches in addition
to Frank Coughlin: Hunk Anderson, Slip Madigan,
Clipper Smith, Buck Shaw, Eddie Anderson, Joe
Brandy, Norm Barry and Dutch Bergman. The strap-
ping 6'3" 220-pound tackle Frank Coughlin had
served aboard a minesweeper in World War I and was
named Notre Dame team captain for 1920 in place of

Cofall, Stanley B. (Stan)									
Year	*Team*	*Games*	*Wins*	*Losses*	*Ties*	*%*	*Rank*	*Points*	*Allowed*
1920	Cleveland Tigers	3	0	2	1	.000	10	0	14
1 year		3	0	2	1	.000		0	14

Cornsweet, Albert C. (Al)									
Year	*Team*	*Games*	*Wins*	*Losses*	*Ties*	*%*	*Rank*	*Points*	*Allowed*
1931	Cleveland Indians	10	2	8	0	.200	8	45	137
1 year		10	2	8	0	.200		45	137

Gipp. Rock Island owner Walter Flanigan signed the Chicago native to play tackle and coach the Independents in 1921, but then replaced him with Jimmy Conzelman during game two. Coughlin moved on to play for Detroit and the Packers that year. Coughlin did not stay with pro football long, but became St. Joseph County prosecutor in 1923 and served as assistant Attorney General of Indiana under Governor Ralph Gates from 1945 to 1949. He continued in that position in the Henry Schricker administration until Frank died at age 55 in 1951.

DAUGHERTY, RUSSELL S. (RUSS OR PUG) 1/31/1902–3/17/1971. Illinois for Bob Zuppke. Played HB for the Frankford Yellow Jackets in 1927. *Hall of Fame Players:* Link Lyman. *Record:* **Interim Player-Co-Coach** (with Charley Rogers, Ed Weir and Swede Youngstrom).

Streater, Illinois native Pug Daugherty blocked for Red Grange at Illinois. As a senior, the 5'10" 175-pound halfback took Grange's place as the Illini's lead ball carrier after Red turned pro. Pug also captained the Illini basketball team and coached high school basketball. Daugherty signed with the NFL champion Frankford Yellow Jackets in 1927. However, head coach Guy Chamberlin already had left the team, and the father-son duo of Charley and Tom Moran was hired to replace him. After a 2–5–1 start, though, the Morans were replaced by a quartet of player-coaches according to the record book. However, veteran Swede Youngstrom was already the line coach and was given the lead responsibility in the transition. Furthermore, Daugherty and Rogers were both rookies, with Pug appearing in just two games during the season. By going 4–1–2 at home, Youngstrom steadied the team and managed a 6–9–3 finish in 1927. The following year, Weir is listed as the sole coach, and both Daugherty and Youngstrom were gone from the NFL for

good. Frankford bounced back to 11–3–2 that year. Pug coached basketball at Rice Institute from 1927 to 1930 with a 17–37 record and subsequently took a job with the highway department. He served in the Navy during World War II and then ran a farm in California before dying of leukemia at age 69 in 1971.

DELL, HERBERT E. (HERB) 1/28/1889–1/10/1964. No college. Did not play professionally. *Hall of Fame Players:* None.

The Columbus Panhandles had been owned and operated by league president Joe Carr since 1904, beginning as a semipro independent team. The core of the team over that time was the Nesser family, seven football-playing brothers. Even as late as 1921, the Panhandles employed five brothers, plus brother Ted's son Charlie, a nephew and a brother-in-law. However, that year was the club's fifth straight losing season, and four of the brothers, including Ted, the coach, retired. Carr brought in his friend Herb Dell who had officiated many Columbus games over the years, to coach the team in 1922, but the Panhandles failed to win a game with only one Nesser (Frank) remaining. Carr disbanded the team to concentrate fully on running the league and sold a new Columbus Tigers franchise to a local group of investors. Dell continued to work in the NFL as an official.

DEPLER, JOHN C. (JACK) 1/6/1899–12/5/1970. Illinois for Bob Zuppke. Played C/T for the Hammond Pros in 1921 and the Orange Tornadoes and in 1929. *Hall of Fame Players:* None. *Record:* Began as **Player-Coach.**

Stocky Jack Depler won All-American notice as a center from 1918 to 1920 with Illinois and captained the team as a senior. After spending one year with the Hammond Pros, the 5'10" 220-pound Depler retired from playing to serve as the line coach at Columbia

Coughlin, Francis E. (Frank)

Year	Team	Games	Wins	Losses	Ties	%	Rank	Points	Allowed
1921	Rock Island Independents	2	0	1	1	.000	5	10	14
1 year		2	0	1	1	.000		10	14

Daugherty, Russell S. (Russ or Pug)

Year	Team	Games	Wins	Losses	Ties	%	Rank	Points	Allowed
1927	Frankford Yellow Jackets	10	4	4	2	.500	7	65	86
1 year		10	4	4	2	.500		65	86

Dell, Herbert E. (Herb)

Year	Team	Games	Wins	Losses	Ties	%	Rank	Points	Allowed
1922	Columbus Panhandles	8	0	8	0	.000	15	24	174
1 year		8	0	8	0	.000		24	174

under Buck O'Neill in 1922 and stayed there for seven years under three different head coaches. In 1929, Jack returned to the NFL as coach and sometime-player with the Orange Tornadoes, a new NFL franchise born from the ashes of the Duluth Eskimos. Depler had played for and coached the Tornadoes the previous season when they were an independent team. Jack did not have much luck in the NFL with the Tornadoes, though.

The following season, he joined with William V. Dwyer to purchase the failed Dayton franchise and move it to Brooklyn with Depler as coach. In contrast to the well-regarded Depler, Big Bill Dwyer was a notorious bootlegger who had served two years in prison for his liquor smuggling. Dwyer also owned the New York Americans of the National Hockey League and later operated racetracks. Depler brought home a winning team in his first season coaching the brand new Dodgers, but little went right in 1932, and Jack left professional football. Dwyer signed Benny Friedman as player-coach and gate attraction in 1932 and then sold the Brooklyn franchise to Chris Cagle and Shipwreck Kelly the year after. Depler coached briefly under Bob Zuppke at his alma mater and then went into hotel management in New York and San Francisco. Eventually, Jack retired to his hometown of Lewistown, Illinois in 1963 and died there seven years later.

Doherty, John L. (Mel) 4/21/1896–7/17/1942. Marietta? Played C for the Cincinnati Celts in 1921. *Hall of Fame Players:* None. *Record:* **Player-Coach**.

The Cincinnati Celts were an active semipro team for a decade before joining the APFA in 1921 but quickly found themselves out of their depth in the league. The Celts were a traveling team that never played a league game in Cincinnati and were shut out in three of four games. The only game they won was against the Muncie Flyers who then promptly disbanded. The *ESPN Pro Football Encyclopedia* lists Mel Doherty, born in 1894, as the team's player-coach, while *Total Football* lists Bill Doherty, born in 1883.

David Neft's *The Football Encyclopedia* lists Bill as the 38-year-old center and coach, with Mel as an end/wingback. There is not much to be found about either Doherty, but I'm betting on Mel being John Mellon Doherty.

This Mel Doherty was a bandleader and football coach from Cincinnati who was born in 1894, played football for the Great Lakes Training Station in 1917 and 1918 and then was an assistant coach for Xavier University. Unfortunately, his obituary does not mention anything about the Celts, but they were not even covered by the *Cincinnati Enquirer* when they were active, so that conceivably was not something that would be noted. Mel Doherty was a popular bandleader in town throughout the 1920s before he eventually became a salesman for the Hudepohl Brewery. He had two sons, Lawrence and Jerry. According to the *Cincinnati Times Star* obituary for his father, Jerry was part of a dance team with "Doris Kuppelkoff, who now is in Hollywood under the name Doris Dawn." The dance partner the paper was referring to actually was Cincinnati's Doris Kappelhoff who became better known as Doris Day.

Driscoll, John L. (Paddy) (see Section I)

Edwards, Howard E. (Cap or Horse) 9/5/1888–11/23/1944. Notre Dame for Jess Harper. Played G/T for the Canton Bulldogs, Toledo Maroons, Cleveland Indians and Cleveland Bulldogs from 1920 to 1924. *Hall of Fame Players:* Pete Henry, Link Lyman. *Record:* **Player-Coach**.

Cap Edwards was part of the sorrowful contingent that traveled to Kansas City in April 1931 to retrieve the remains of fabled coach Knute Rockne and bring them back to South Bend for burial. The 6' 207-pound Edwards was a star tackle from South Bend who captained Notre Dame in 1909. After graduation, he coached West Virginia Wesleyan in 1911 before signing on as an assistant coach under Jess Harper at Notre Dame in 1913. That year the passing combi-

Depler, John C. (Jack)									
Year	Team	Games	Wins	Losses	Ties	%	Rank	Points	Allowed
1929	Orange Tornadoes	12	3	5	4	.375	6	35	80
1930	Brooklyn Dodgers	12	7	4	1	.636	4	154	59
1931	Brooklyn Dodgers	14	2	12	0	.143	9	64	199
3 years		38	12	21	5	.364		253	338

Doherty, John L. (Mel)									
Year	Team	Games	Wins	Losses	Ties	%	Rank	Points	Allowed
1921	Cincinnati Celts	4	1	3	0	.250	13	14	117
1 year		4	1	3	0	.250		14	117

nation of Gus Dorais to Knute Rockne became a national sensation, and Rockne and Edwards became lifelong friends. Edwards was very active in the early days of professional football throughout the teens, playing for Akron in 1914, Canton from 1915 to 1917 and also Fort Wayne in 1915 and 1916. At times, both Dorais and Rockne were his teammates; at others, Dorais played while Edwards or another Notre Dame alumnus pretended to be the Rock to satisfy fans who came to see him.

Edwards himself was a top tackle who played a decade as a professional, both before and after the formation of the APFA. As a coach, his assignments shadowed Guy Chamberlin's. Chamberlin replaced Cap as Canton's coach in 1922 and led the Bulldogs to consecutive championships, while Edwards toiled in Toledo and Cleveland in 1922 and 1923. When Chamberlin took over as coach of the merged Bulldogs and Indians in 1924, he again was replacing Edwards. Again, Chamberlin led the Bulldogs to the title, but this time with Edwards on the roster. Chamberlin moved on to Frankford in 1925, and Edwards took over as coach of the diminished Cleveland Bulldogs for one season before retiring to his South Bend manufacturing firm. He also did some officiating of league games.

ERICKSON, HAROLD A. (HAL) 3/10/1899–1/28/1963. St. Olaf and Washington & Jefferson for Greasy Neale. Played HB for the Milwaukee Badgers, Chicago Cardinals and Minneapolis Red Jackets from 1923 to 1930. *Hall of Fame Players:* None. *Record:* **Player-Coach.**

Hal Erickson joined with Wayne Brenkert to

form an unbeatable halfback duo at Washington and Jefferson that propelled the Greasy Neale-led Presidents to the 1922 Rose Bowl where they tied California 0–0. It was Hal's second trip to Pasadena, though. Four years earlier, he was part of the Great Lakes Naval Training Station team that beat the Mare Island Marines 19–7 in the 1918 Rose Bowl. The 5′9″ 193-pound Erickson signed with the Milwaukee Badgers in 1923 and had a long career in the NFL. As a rookie, Hal also served as an assistant coach at DePauw University, and then was given the coaching position with Milwaukee the following season. In 1925, Johnny Bryan replaced Erickson as player-coach, and Hal signed with the Cardinals who went on to win the NFL title that year. In the postseason, Erickson played with the Bears on their Red Grange barnstorming tour of the U.S. Hal spent three years in Chicago and then two more in his native Minnesota with Minneapolis before leaving football. Erickson subsequently went into the insurance business and rose to become President of Security National Life Insurance.

FALCON, GUILFORD W. (GUIL OR HAWK) 12/15/1892–7/28/1982. No College. Played FB for the Chicago Tigers, Hammond Pros, Canton Bulldogs, Toledo Maroons, Rochester Jeffersons and Akron Pros from 1920 to 1925. *Hall of Fame Players:* None. *Record:* **Owner-Player-Coach.**

Guil Falcon never attended college, but had a long career in professional football as player, coach and owner and sometimes all three at once. He went from Evanston High School to the Evanston North Ends as an 18-year-old in 1911 and played for several professional teams over the next decade and a half, in-

---

Edwards, Howard E. (Cap or Horse)

Year	Team	Games	Wins	Losses	Ties	%	Rank	Points	Allowed
1921	Canton Bulldogs	10	5	2	3	.714	4	106	55
1923	Cleveland Indians	7	3	1	3	.750	5	52	49
1925	Cleveland Bulldogs	14	5	8	1	.385	12	75	135
3 years		31	13	11	7	.542		233	239

Erickson, Harold A. (Hal)

Year	Team	Games	Wins	Losses	Ties	%	Rank	Points	Allowed
1924	Milwaukee Badgers	13	5	8	0	.385	12	142	188
1 year		13	5	8	0	.385		142	188

Falcon, Guilford W. (Guil or Hawk)

Year	Team	Games	Wins	Losses	Ties	%	Rank	Points	Allowed
1920	Chicago Tigers	8	2	5	1	.286	11	49	63
1922	Toledo Maroons	9	5	2	2	.714	4	94	59
1923	Toledo Maroons	8	3	3	2	.500	10	35	66
3 years		25	10	10	5	.500		178	188

cluding Evanston and Wabash in the years before the NFL. A 5'10" 220-pound hard-charging fullback, Falcon brought his own Chicago Tigers into the fledgling APFA in 1920 where the team competed against the Cardinals for the Windy City's football fans. Legend has it that when the two teams played in November, Falcon and Cardinals' owner Chris O'Brien made a winner-take-all bet that the loser would clear out of town. While the Tigers did lose 6–3 and folded at the end of the year, the story is most likely apocryphal. Falcon continued to play in the league until his mid-thirties and also coached in Toledo for two seasons.

FAUSCH, FRANKLIN L. (FRANK) 6/13/1895–7/19/1968. Kalamazoo for Ed Mather and Ralph Young. Did not play in the NFL. *Hall of Fame Players:* None. *Record:* **Owner-Coach.**

Born in Goshen, Indiana, Frank Fausch played fullback for Kalamazoo College and then for the semi-pro Evansville Ex-Collegians in 1920. Fausch also owned a storage battery company in the area and in 1921 joined with some other prominent Evansville businessmen and professionals to form the American Football Association, an ownership group, with Frank as president, general manager and coach. Fausch then traveled to Chicago and posted the APFA franchise fee to found the Evansville Crimson Giants. He coaxed most of his former Ex-Collegian players to try out for the new team but added several players from outside Evansville as well. Due to scheduling problems and bad weather, though, Evansville ended up playing only half of its 10 games against league opponents and lost a great deal of money over the course of its initial season. Fausch lost control of the team to a rebellious "Committee of Five" near the end of the year, but regained charge in 1922. Despite a challenge by the newly-reformed Ex-Collegians team in Evansville,

Fausch maintained his league franchise. However, the Crimson Giants essentially became a road team, drawing little local support for a weak product on the field. Fausch made no effort to renew the franchise in 1923.

FISH, JACK 5/1/1892–6/29/1971. Seton Hall. Did not play professionally. *Hall of Fame Players:* none. *Record:* **Interim Coach.**

Boston-native Jack Fish was a celebrated athlete at Seton Hall in football, basketball and baseball. A star catcher, he declined offers to join Jersey City and Toronto of the International League in 1913 to finish college, and then unsuccessfully tried out for the Baltimore Terrapins of the Federal League in 1914. During the war, Fish coached an Army football team in Paris and afterwards coached football, baseball and basketball at St. Benedict's Prep in Newark and Seton Hall Prep before becoming Athletic Director at Cathedral Prep in Trenton.

After the Newark Tornadoes lost their second game 32–0 in 1930, angry general manager Eddie Simandi fired Coach Al McGall and replaced him with Fish. However, Jack would not last the year either, winning just one game in seven. After the team's second 32–0 loss of the season in game number nine, Simandi was talking about firing the coach again. Fish resigned instead and was replaced by guard Andy Salata who had coached the line under both Fish and McGall. Fish's successor was outscored 54 to 7 in the final three games, and the franchise folded at the end of the year.

FOLWELL, ROBERT C. JR. (BOB) 2/17/1885–1/8/1928. Pennsylvania under Carl Williams. Did not play professionally. *Hall of Fame Players:* Jim Thorpe.

Bob Folwell had a hard bark but achieved success wherever he coached in both the college ranks and the

Fausch, Franklin L. (Frank)									
Year	*Team*	*Games*	*Wins*	*Losses*	*Ties*	*%*	*Rank*	*Points*	*Allowed*
1921	Evansville Crimson Giants	5	3	2	0	.600	6	89	46
1922	Evansville Crimson Giants	3	0	3	0	.000	15	6	88
2 years		8	3	5	0	.375		95	134

Fish, Jack									
Year	*Team*	*Games*	*Wins*	*Losses*	*Ties*	*%*	*Rank*	*Points*	*Allowed*
1930	Newark Tornadoes	7	1	5	1	.167	11	38	91
1 year		7	1	5	1	.167		38	91

Folwell, Robert C. Jr. (Bob)									
Year	*Team*	*Games*	*Wins*	*Losses*	*Ties*	*%*	*Rank*	*Points*	*Allowed*
1925	New York Giants	12	8	4	0	.667	4	122	67
1 year		12	8	4	0	.667		122	67

pros. A native South Jerseyan from Mullica Hill, Folwell played football and wrestled at Penn and then went directly into coaching at a series of Eastern colleges. Bob went 22–4–1 in three seasons at Lafayette from 1909 to 1911; 36–5–3 from 1912 to 1915 at Washington & Jefferson; 27–10–2 from 1916 to 1919 at his alma mater; and 24–12–3 from 1920 to 24 at Navy. His teams played in the 1917 and 1924 Rose Bowls as the best squads from the East. He was an innovative strategist who is sometimes credited as the first coach to use the screen pass. At Penn, Folwell coached future NFL coaches Bert Bell and Lud Wray, but was fired in 1920 by the Faculty Committee on Athletics because he "did little character building." Folwell responded, "I challenge any man in the world to prove that my actions during the last season have reflected [badly] on the University of Pennsylvania in any way. If Penn is through with me, I am through with football, but I am not going to quit under fire." Navy was happy to hire Bob two months later. He had four winning seasons there and split the annual showdowns with Army, but was forced out after one losing season.

Dr. Harry March, general manager of the fledgling New York Giants' franchise, signed the crusty Folwell as coach in 1925. Bob greeted the challenge by telling the press, "As for entertaining the public, I am sure professional football can be made to flourish in New York as it has in the West. I know of no greater thrill in professional sport than the sight of 22 highly trained experts engaged in a game of football. It is my plan to organize a football machine in New York on the same basis that I would a college team, and when it is realized that instead of having only one or two stars for a nucleus, I will have a skilled man with four years of college training in each position, it should mean that the public should see some spectacular football." After losing their opening three games, Folwell's Giants rallied to win eight of their last nine to finish fourth in the NFL. However, Folwell jumped to more lucrative pastures closer to home in 1926, signing to coach the Philadelphia Quakers in Red Grange's rival American Football League.

That year the Quakers streaked to the AFL title over the favored New York Yankees that featured Grange himself. The Quakers were one of just four AFL teams still operational at the end of the year, but were full of confidence. They started challenging the leading teams in the NFL to a postseason game, but

were turned down by everyone until the seventh place Giants accepted. In a major embarrassment for both the league and for Folwell himself, the middle-of-the-pack Giants shellacked the champion Quakers 31–0 on December 12 at the Polo Grounds. With the team and league disbanded, Bob got a job coaching the minor league Atlantic City Roses in 1927. Bothered by a hip problem since coaching the Quakers, though, Folwell underwent surgery in Philadelphia in January 1928. Due to complications, he died shortly after at the age of 42. Folwell's abrasiveness was not always appreciated by his players, but he was a winner wherever he went.

FORSYTH, WALTER S. (JACK) 5/4/1892–12/19/1966. Rochester. Did not play in the NFL. *Hall of Fame Players:* None.

Hometown hero Jack Forsyth played halfback for the University of Rochester and captained both the football and hockey teams there in 1913. He went on to coach high school football in the area before taking over the independent Rochester Jeffersons in 1919 and leading them to a 6–2–1 record. Forsyth continued as coach when the Jeffs joined the APFA in 1920, but the team's 6–3–2 record included just one game against an APFA opponent — they lost 17–6 to the Buffalo All-Americans on October 31. (For that first season, non-league games were included in the standings and are thus reflected in Forsyth's totals above.) The following season only league games counted, and the decline in fortunes is clear for a fringe team like Rochester. In 1922, Rochester's star center Doc Alexander took over as player-coach, and Forsyth moved on to coach the Rochester Mechanics Institute. Jack became a prominent attorney in the area and later got involved in local politics.

FRIEDMAN, BENJAMIN (BENNY) 3/18/1905–11/24/1982. Michigan under Fielding Yost. Played QB for Cleveland Bulldogs, Detroit Wolverines, New York Giants, Brooklyn Dodgers from 1927 to 1934. *Hall of Fame Players:* Red Badgro. *Record:* **Hall of Fame Player; Player-Coach.**

Benny Friedman was the greatest passer by far in the early days of the NFL and a great proponent of offensive football. The teams for which he played led the league in scoring four consecutive seasons from 1927 to 1930. Benny was the first passer to throw 20 touchdown passes in a season and is the only NFL

Forsyth, Walter S. (Jack)									
Year	Team	Games	Wins	Losses	Ties	%	Rank	Points	Allowed
1920	Rochester Jeffersons	11	6	3	2	.667	7	156	57
1921	Rochester Jeffersons	5	2	3	0	.400	10	85	76
2 years		16	8	6	2	.571		241	133

player to ever lead the league in both touchdown passes and rushing touchdowns in the same season. In fact, he led his team in both rushing and passing for his first five years in the league. Born in Cleveland and an All-American player at Michigan, the stellar passer developed a following everywhere he played. The 5'10" 183-pound Friedman was a major gate attraction in the 1920s, so much so that the Giants purchased the entire Detroit Wolverine franchise to obtain Benny's services in 1929. Friedman was spectacular in New York, leading the Giants to a 33–11–2 record with two second-place finishes in three years. However, Benny wanted more and began to push for owning a piece of the club, but Tim Mara would never agree to that.

Friedman signed with the less glamorous Brooklyn Dodgers in 1932 as player-coach, but the team was weak, and Benny had some injury issues, so the Dodgers could only manage a 3–9 record. Aside from two games that Friedman served as co-coach with Steve Owen in 1930 for the Giants after the two led a rebellion against coach Leroy Andrews, that one season in Brooklyn was the extent of Friedman's NFL coaching career. He also coached the backfield at Yale in 1932 and 1933 and was named head coach at City College in 1934, while he finished his playing career in Brooklyn. Benny had a 27–31–4 record at CCNY from 1934 to 1941 before entering the Navy during the war.

After the war, Friedman was named as Athletic Director at Brandeis University in 1949 and served in that capacity until 1963. While there, he coached the football team to a 38–35–4 record from 1951 to 1959. Benny ran a kids football camp for years after that until he lost his leg due to diabetes in 1979. Three years later, he committed suicide. Friedman was at the time a member of the College Football Hall of Fame and the International Jewish Sports Hall of Fame, but was not inducted into the Pro Football Hall of Fame until 2005 because of his widely perceived uncompromising arrogance and glory-seeking.

GARRETT, ALFRED T. (BUDGE) 4/17/1893– 6/11/1950. Rutgers for George Foster Sanford. Played E/G/FB for the Akron Pros in 1920 and the Milwaukee Badgers in 1922. *Hall of Fame Players:* Fritz Pollard. *Record:* **Interim Player-Coach.**

Muskogee's Budge Garrett was raised on a Creek Indian reservation in Oklahoma before attending prestigious Peddie Prep in New Jersey where he captained the football team in 1913. The 5'9" 200-pound Garrett matriculated at Rutgers and played there from 1914 to 1917 and then captained the team in 1919. He received All-American notice in 1915, while his more famous teammate Paul Robeson achieved All-American status in both 1917 and 1918.

Garrett worked as assistant coach at Rutgers while he finished his master's degree there. He signed with Akron in 1920 and played with the very first league champions that year. In 1922, Budge was hired to play for and coach the new Milwaukee Badger franchise. Adding Garrett's Akron teammate Fritz Pollard as well as his old Rutgers teammate Paul Robeson gave the Badgers a solid base, and the team got off to a 2– 1–3 start before Budge broke his leg against Oorang Indians on November 19. Garrett's playing and coaching career was over, and Milwaukee lost its last three games under new coach Jimmy Conzelman. Budge remained an active Rutgers alumnus throughout his life, teaching business management courses on the Newark campus, and also served on the board of the Peddie School for 15 years. He worked for several years as the Director of Training at Western Electric in Kearny, New Jersey before dying from a heart attack at the age of 57.

GIBSON, GEORGE F. 10/2/1905–8/19/2004. Minnesota under Doc Spears. Played G for the Minneapolis Red Jackets and Frankford Yellow Jackets in 1930. *Hall of Fame Players:* None. *Record:* **Player-Coach.**

In his only NFL season, George Gibson was player-coach for two teams, one of which went bankrupt and the other of which folded a year later. The Kendaia, New York native was team captain and a two-time All-American at Minnesota where he was Bronko Nagurski's roommate. In 1929 while taking

Friedman, Benjamin (Benny)									
Year	*Team*	*Games*	*Wins*	*Losses*	*Ties*	*%*	*Rank*	*Points*	*Allowed*
1930	New York Giants	2	2	0	0	1.000	2	27	6
1932	Brooklyn Dodgers	12	3	9	0	.250	6	63	131
2 years		14	5	9	0	.357		90	137

Garrett, Alfred T. (Budge)									
Year	*Team*	*Games*	*Wins*	*Losses*	*Ties*	*%*	*Rank*	*Points*	*Allowed*
1922	Milwaukee Badgers	6	2	1	3	.667	11	45	15
1 year		6	2	1	3	.667		45	15

graduate courses at Minnesota, George also served as the line coach for both his alma mater and the Minneapolis Red Jackets; a year later, he replaced another former Gopher, Herb Joesting, as player-coach. Joesting remained a Red Jackets' player, but the team won just one game in 1930, matching their total under Joesting. When the team went bankrupt, the struggling Frankford Yellow Jackets hired Gibson to replace Bull Behman as player-coach for the remainder of 1930. Gibson brought nine of his Red Jacket teammates with him to Philadelphia, and the combined Red and Yellow "Jacket" players won two of their remaining five games.

Gibson spurned an offer from Curly Lambeau to play for the Packers in 1931 in order to return to Minnesota and work on his doctorate in geology. Frankford brought back Bull Behman as player coach in 1931 and won just one game in their final season, with luckless Herb Joesting in the Yellow Jacket backfield. After earning his PhD in 1934, Gibson coached and taught geology at Carleton College in Minnesota until 1938 before spending two years working in Egypt. In 1941, he moved to Midland, Texas where he spent the next 64 years working as an oil company geologist. He continued to support his alma mater by endowing a Chair in Hydrogeology and by donating over $600,000 to the Gibson-Nagurski Football Complex for the gridiron Gophers. He lived to be 98 and worked almost to the end of his life with the help of hearing aids and a powerful magnifying glass. His sister was married to agronomist Norman Borlaug who won the Nobel Peace Prize in 1970 for his work in increasing the food supply worldwide.

Gillies, Frederick M. (Fred) 12/9/1895–5/8/1974. Cornell under Albert Sharpe. Played T for the Chicago Cardinals from 1920 to 1926 and in 1928. *Hall of Fame Players:* Jim Thorpe. *Record:* **Player-Coach.**

Chicago-native Fred Gillies received some All-American notice while at Cornell in 1916, but put football aside after his 1918 graduation to fly planes for the Navy during World War I. Returning to his home

town, the 6'3" 215-pound tackle was a mainstay on the Cardinal line throughout the 1920s, and even served as the line coach for Chicago during the 1925 championship season. Fred began his career in the steel industry at this time as well; he worked there during the week and played pro football on Sundays. Gillies was never an All Pro, but he earned the respect of both teammates and competitors in the NFL with his solid play. When former Cardinals' coach Arnie Horween was coaching Harvard from 1926 to 1930, Fred would travel to Boston each year on his vacation to help out his friend and former teammate. George Halas of the cross-town Bears thought so highly of Gillies that he paid him a $1-a-year honorarium as an advisory line coach for many years. Unfortunately, Fred's one year as head coach of the Cardinals was a disaster, with the team being outscored 107–7 in a reduced six-game schedule. Financially-strapped, longtime owner Chris O'Brien sold his depleted franchise to David Jones after the season, and that ended Gillies NFL career.

Gillies continued to coach a local semipro team throughout the 1930s and survived a plane crash in 1932 that took the life of pioneer aviator and airplane manufacturer, Eddie Stinson. Stinson, who had learned to fly with the Wright Brothers, was demonstrating a new model when he struck a flag pole and the plane crashed on a golf course. Fred broke his leg so severely in the crash that he wore a brace the rest of his life. Nonetheless, Gillies was a stalwart civic leader in the Chicago community and quickly rose in the steel industry. Ultimately, Fred retired as Chairman and CEO of Acme Steel in 1960, but continued on as a prominent GOP fundraiser until he died at age 79.

Gillo, Henry C. (Hank) 10/5/1894–9/6/1948. Colgate under Laurence Bankert. Played HB for the Hammond Pros, Racine Legion, Milwaukee Badgers and Racine Tornadoes from 1920 to 1926. *Hall of Fame Players:* None. *Record:* **Player-Coach.**

Milwaukee's Hank Gillo was a pile-driving fullback for Colgate at 5'10" and 195-pounds. Gillo captained the 1918 squad and was a third team Walter Camp All-American prior to serving as a flyer in

Gibson, George F.									
Year	Team	Games	Wins	Losses	Ties	%	Rank	Points	Allowed
1930	Frankford Yellow Jackets	5	2	3	0	.400	9	20	63
	Minneapolis Red Jackets	9	1	7	1	.125	10	27	165
1 year		14	3	10	1	.231		47	228

Gillies, Frederick M. (Fred)									
Year	Team	Games	Wins	Losses	Ties	%	Rank	Points	Allowed
1928	Chicago Cardinals	6	1	5	0	.167	9	7	107
1 year		6	1	5	0	.167		7	107

World War I. With the formation of the APFA in 1920, Hank was hired as player-coach of the Hammond Pros, but the team was more like a semipro team in quality and was outscored 22–7 per game. Gillo spent five more years in the league with three other teams, but only as a player. He played in just one league game with Hammond in 1921 before jumping to the independent Racine Legion, closer to home. Perhaps the biggest highlight of Hank's career came on December 4, 1921 when Racine met Green Bay in a non-league game billed as the Wisconsin professional championship. The Packers held a 3–0 lead for the whole game until Gillo tied the game with a 40-yard drop-kick field goal with three minutes to play.

The next year, Racine joined the NFL, and Hank unofficially led the league with 52 points scored. He also became the first NFL kicker to boot three field goals in a game that year against Rochester. In October of the next year against Akron, he became the first to kick a 50-yard field goal in a league game. Once his football career ended, Gillo became a high school biology teacher and football coach in Milwaukee for the next 20 years until he died from a heart attack at the age of 53. There was an odd postscript to his life 11 years later. Hank's 29-year-old son Robert H. Gillo went to court in 1959 to legally change his name to Paul V. Banner because his long-deceased father was so well known that Robert did not want to live in his shadow.

GOLEMBESKI, ANTHONY E. (ARCHIE)
5/25/1900–3/9/1976. Holy Cross under Cleo O'Donnell. Played E/G/C for the Providence Steam Roller in 1925, 1926 and 1929. *Hall of Fame Players:* Fritz Pollard. *Record:* **Player-Coach.**

Although born in Kentucky, Archie Golembeski lived almost his entire life in Worcester, Massachusetts. A 1923 graduate of Holy Cross in Worcester, Golem-beski joined the independent Providence Steam Roller in 1924, the year before the team joined the NFL. Just 5'10" and 185-pounds, he played end, guard and center for Providence, while also coaching both the Steam Roller and the Providence College Friars as well. Golembeski gave up pro coaching after just one year, but continued to coach the Friars through 1933 and compiled a 27–34–12 record in football and 8–8 in one season as the college's basketball coach. Archie retired from the Steam Roller in 1927. New coach Jimmy Conzelman then posted back-to-back 8-win seasons, including winning the 1928 NFL championship. Golembeski came back to play one last season in 1929, but the team slipped to four wins that year.

Archie was still coaching at Providence College then and also working as the Phys. Ed. Director for Worcester's Polish Parish. In 1934, Golembeski left Providence to become Athletic Director at the Worcester Academy prep school. He later ran a prosperous Worcester clothing store called Archie's Men's Shop for many years.

GRIFFEN, HAROLD W. (HAL OR TUBBY)
3/1/1902–12/31/1947. Iowa under Howard Jones and Burt Ingwersen. Played C/T for the Green Bay Packers in 1928 and Portsmouth Spartans in 1930 and 1932. *Hall of Fame Players:* None. *Record:* **Player-Coach.**

Sioux City's 6'1" 247-pound Griffen was a big man for his time. Coming out of Iowa, Hal played first with the New York Yankees of Red Grange's AFL in 1926. Griffen spent 1928 in Green Bay, and then was hired to coach the brand new Portsmouth Spartans. The Spartans were founded as an independent town team to compete against other Ohio town teams. By twice beating Greasy Neale's powerful Ironton Tanks in 1929, Hal made a name for himself and for the Spartans who then joined the NFL in 1930. Unfortunately, Griffen let his star player, Keith

Gillo, Henry C. (Hank)									
Year	*Team*	*Games*	*Wins*	*Losses*	*Ties*	*%*	*Rank*	*Points*	*Allowed*
1920	Hammond Pros	7	2	5	0	.286	11	41	154
1 year		7	2	5	0	.286		41	154

Golembeski, Anthony E. (Archie)									
Year	*Team*	*Games*	*Wins*	*Losses*	*Ties*	*%*	*Rank*	*Points*	*Allowed*
1925	Providence Steam Roller	12	6	5	1	.545	10	111	101
1 year		12	6	5	1	.545		111	101

Griffen, Harold W. (Hal or Tubby)									
Year	*Team*	*Games*	*Wins*	*Losses*	*Ties*	*%*	*Rank*	*Points*	*Allowed*
1930	Portsmouth Spartans	14	5	6	3	.455	7	176	161
1 year		14	5	6	3	.455		176	161

Molesworth, go before the 1930 season, and Ironton quickly signed the scrappy signal caller. Carl Becker reported in his book, *Home and Away,* that the rumor at the time was that Molesworth stole his coach's girl and married her. Without Molesworth, Portsmouth finished its initial NFL season with a respectable 5–6–3 record, but Hal was replaced in 1931 by Potsy Clark who led the team to an 11–3 record. Griffen did eventually marry another girl from the area and played briefly for the Spartans again in 1932 before ending his football career.

Hal had worked for the U.S. Justice Department investigating stolen cars one summer, but he struggled to find work in the off seasons during the Depression. When Griffen got an offer from the Post Office for a regular government job in Alaska in April 1933, he and his wife headed north to Nome. For the next 15 years, they ran a trading post in isolated Dillingham, Alaska. However, on New Year's Eve 1947, Griffen and a visiting friend died of asphyxiation when their coal stove went out. Hal's wife, Avis, was discovered alive two days later and taken to the hospital in Anchorage where she had a lengthy stay recovering from extensive frostbite to her arms. Although Avis originally planned to go back to her trading post, she instead returned to her mother's home near Portsmouth in 1948.

Grigg, Cecil B. (Tex) 2/15/1891–9/6/1968. Austin College. Played HB for the Canton Bulldogs, Rochester Jeffersons, New York Giants and Frankford Yellow Jackets from 1920 to 1927. *Hall of Fame Players:* None. *Record:* **Player-Coach.**

Born in Nashville, Tex Grigg started playing for Austin College in 1912 before he even had finished high school, but didn't graduate college until 1919, after spending two years in France during World War I. The 5'11" 191-pound Grigg joined the Canton Bulldogs that fall and played with them through 1923. He started out alongside three notable Indians in the backfield, Jim Thorpe, Joe Guyon and Pete Calac, and finished his time in Canton playing for Guy Chamberlain's back-to-back champions of 1922–1923. After gaining All Pro recognition in 1923, Tex left the champions for Rochester and did not win a game for the

next two years in upstate New York. He even served as player-coach in 1925, the Jeffersons last season in the NFL. After a year in New York and one game for Frankford, Grigg retired from the pro game to become the Athletic Director and Head Coach at his alma mater. Tex was in Austin from 1928 to 1933, and then left for Rice Institute where he served as backfield coach from 1934 to 1966. In his long tenure at Rice, he also coached the baseball team for a dozen years and led the track team. He once commented to a reporter, "I'm the luckiest person in the world because I got to make my living the way I wanted to, by doing what I enjoyed the most—playing and coaching sports."

Haines, Henry L. (Hinkey) 12/23/1898–1/9/1979. Lebanon Valley College and Penn State under Hugo Bezdek. Played HB for the New York Giants and Staten Island Stapletons from 1925 to 1929 and in 1931. *Hall of Fame Players:* Ken Strong. *Record:* **Interim Player-Coach.**

Hinkey Haines came from a prominent family and picked up his unusual nickname in boarding school. His father was the mayor of Haines' hometown of Red Lion, Pennsylvania and went on to serve in the U.S. Congress from 1931 to 1939 and from 1941 to 1943. Hinkey was an exceptional athlete and a popular public figure. He starred first at Lebanon Valley College in 1916 and 1917 and then served in the Army during the war. Upon returning to the States, Haines enrolled at Penn State and graduated in 1920. For the next dozen years, Hinkey played professional baseball and football for a living. On the baseball diamond, he was an outfielder for a string of minor league teams throughout the 1920s, but did spend the 1923 season as a .160-hitting backup on the champion New York Yankees. On the Yankees, he befriended Babe Ruth, and when he was sent back to the minors, roomed with Lou Gehrig.

On the gridiron, Haines was a 5'10" 170-pound star half back on the independent Union Quakers and Frankford Yellow Jackets in the early years of the '20s' before joining the New York Giants for their first season of 1925. Haines was the Giants' first star and

Grigg, Cecil B. (Tex)									
Year	Team	Games	Wins	Losses	Ties	%	Rank	Points	Allowed
1925	Rochester Jeffersons	7	0	6	1	.000	16	26	111
1 year		7	0	6	1	.000		26	111

Haines, Henry L. (Hinkey)									
Year	Team	Games	Wins	Losses	Ties	%	Rank	Points	Allowed
1931	Staten Island Stapletons	4	1	3	0	.250	7	29	59
1 year		4	1	3	0	.250		29	59

first gate attraction. The outgoing celebrity was in his element in New York. He ran around with stars like Jimmy Durante and Al Jolson, pulled publicity stunts like catching a football thrown from the top of a building and even had a song written about his exploits. On the field, he was a fast and shifty runner and a heady player as well. In the Giants' 1927 showdown with the Bears, the key play turned out to be the fake punt that Haines called and converted deep in his own territory. New York won 13–7 that day and went on to win the championship, giving Hinkey two New York championships in two different sports.

Haines moved on to the Staten Island Stapletons in 1929 and then retired from football, while continuing to play baseball in the minors. Two years later, the Stapes brought him back as player-coach. After going just 1–3 in October, Hinkey retired from football for good, with the Stapes bringing in Columbia assistant coach Marty Brill as coach for the rest of the season. Haines played minor league baseball for a couple more years and then worked as an NFL official for 20 years from 1934 to 1954. In later years, he owned an auto dealership, acted in television commercials and local theater and worked for the IRS.

HALAS, GEORGE S. (SEE SECTION I)

HANLEY, WILLIAM J. (BO) 7/10/1891–11/23/1954. Marquette. Did not play professionally. *Hall of Fame Players:* None. *Record:* Co-Coach (with Earl Potteiger).

All of the football encyclopedias list Bo Hanley as the Kenosha Maroons coach in their only year of existence, 1924. Each lists his name as Edward Louis Hanley and indicates he was a Marquette alumnus who also played wingback for the Detroit Heralds in 1920. The only part that is true, though, is that a man named Bo Hanley coached Kenosha in 1924. There were actually four Hanley brothers, three of whom played football at Marquette, and two of whom went by the nickname Bo. Unfortunately, Edward was not one of the four. There was an Edward L. Hanley from Milwaukee who was born in 1887 and died in 1980, but there is no evidence that he was a Marquette athlete. Parenthetically, another contemporaneous Edward T. Hanley, who attended the University of Pittsburgh, played fullback for Akron and Massillon in the days before the NFL, but he is not Bo either.

The three athletic Hanley brothers of Marquette consisted of William, a tackle known as Bo who lived

from 1890 to 1954, George, also a tackle known as Bo who was born in 1896, and Cornelius, a quarterback who was born in 1897. William was the more famous Bo. He was captain of the 1910 team, coached at the Colorado School of Mines in 1912 and returned to Marquette as assistant coach in 1913. In a Marquette yearbook piece lauding Red Dunn in 1923, they describe him as the greatest Hilltopper since the legendary first Bo Hanley over a decade prior. William, got his medical degree and, after the war, began his practice in Kenosha in 1920. It makes sense that the fledgling Kenosha Maroons would hire Bo as their coach since he was a local football legend and prominent Kenosha citizen. Not that it did much good; the Maroons did not win a game in the NFL and disbanded in November. Bo later moved back to Milwaukee in 1938 where he died in 1954 after a six-month illness.

So, Bo number one was a 30-year-old former tackle in 1920. He was not the Hanley who played wingback for the Detroit Heralds that season. Bo number two also was a tackle and played service ball during the war. He became an attorney and subsequently served two terms as Sheriff in Milwaukee, although he left under a cloud of some shady business dealing. He also did not play wingback for the Heralds. Now, let's look at brother number three, Cornelius Patrick. He was wounded in France during the war and coached Marquette's prep school in 1919. He then attended law school at the University of Detroit in 1920, with newspaper accounts listing him as playing for the Heralds at the time. It appears then that two Hanley brothers were part of the NFL in its earliest days, although the Heralds' Hanley may have been Edward T. who attended Pitt. In later life, Cornelius ran for local judgeships twice, despite having served six months in jail in 1931 for contempt of court.

HANSEN, HAROLD F. (HAL) 11/30/1894–6/1977. Minnesota under Henry L. Williams. Played HB for the Packers in 1923?. *Hall of Fame Players:* Ken Strong.

There are at least four players named Hal Hansen or Hanson who were active in the early years of the NFL. Three of them played in the NFL; three of them played for the University of Minnesota, and two were teammates in the Twin Cities. The non–Minnesotan, Harold William Hanson (1895–1973), played center and guard with the University of South Dakota and then with the Rock Island Independents (1921) and Minneapolis Marines (1923). He is erroneously

Hanley, William J. (Bo)									
Year	Team	Games	Wins	Losses	Ties	%	Rank	Points	Allowed
1924	Kenosha Maroons	5	0	4	1	.000	16	12	117
1 year		5	0	4	1	.000		12	117

credited with being the final coach of the Staten Island Stapletons in 1932. The three Golden Gopher Hal's include Harlan C. Hansen who lettered in 1915 and 1916 as a lineman, Harold Frederick Hansen who lettered as a halfback in 1916 and Harold Walter Hanson who was a two-time All-American guard from 1925 to 1927 and played for the Frankford Yellow Jackets and Minneapolis Marines from 1928 to 1930. Harlan played a game in the backfield for the Packers in 1923, although he was a lineman at Minnesota.

Harold F., though, starred at running back for the Gophers in 1916, completed his degree in 1918 and coached St. Thomas College to a 1–1 record that same fall. From 1919 to 1920, he coached the football team at Hamline College in Minnesota, posting a 9–3–1 mark, and then worked as an assistant coach at his alma mater through 1923. In April 1924, Harold F. was hired by Georgia Tech to coach the backfield in football, the basketball team and the freshman track team. Tech's star halfback was Doug Wycoff who subsequently signed with the Newark Bears of Red Grange's American Football League in 1926 — signing on as the Newark head coach was Harold F. Hansen.

The Bears were a weak and underfinanced team that disbanded with a 0–3–2 AFL record, but not before defeating the independent Staten Island Stapletons 33–0. Stapletons' owner Dan Blaine then hired the whole Bears' team to blend with his team to finish the 1926 season. In 1927, the 5'10" 200-pound Hansen continued as the head coach and sometime-player of the Stapletons that featured star runner Doug Wycoff. Wycoff took over as player-coach from 1928 to 1930, and the Stapes entered the NFL in 1929. Wycoff jumped to the Giants in 1931, so Blaine brought in Hinkey Haines as coach to start the year. The next year, Wycoff returned to Staten Island, and so did Hal Hansen as coach. To complicate things further, that 1932 team featured still another Hanson, Thomas (Swede) Hanson, a halfback from Temple University who later had some good years with the Eagles. The Stapes got off to a terrible 1–6–2 start, so Hansen cut five players before the final home stand of the year and finished up at 2–7–3. Staten Island dropped out of the NFL in 1932, but continued for

one final year as an independent with Wycoff again serving as player-coach. Hal Hansen disappeared from the league. He died in Annandale, Virginia.

HEGARTY, JOHN E. (JACK) 6/9/1888–Deceased. Holy Cross and Georgetown under Frank Gargan. Did not play professionally. *Hall of Fame Players:* None.

Jack Hegarty was part of a well-known family from Newburyport, Massachusetts. He attended Exeter and Dean Academy prep schools and then enrolled at Holy Cross in 1909. The next year, he transferred to Georgetown and starred on the football team as an end and tackle; he was team captain in 1912, but broke his ankle so severely that he never played again. After graduation, Jack spent the 1914 and 1915 seasons coaching at what is now called North Carolina State and compiled a 5–6–2 record. He subsequently returned to Washington and did some semi-pro coaching until 1921 when he was named coach of the newly-minted Washington Senators football team — the first D.C. representative in the NFL. Hegarty put together a team of mostly local talent that played against several semi-pro teams before finally playing their first league game in late November, when they lost to Canton. Washington only scheduled four league games in 1921, losing twice to Canton, beating Cleveland and, on a snowy December 5, forfeiting to Rochester. With a small crowd on hand that day, Washington could not afford to pay the required $800 guarantee to the visiting Jeffersons and forfeited the game 1–0. That loss is generally not recorded in league standings, but league president Joe Carr would not allow the Senators to continue their franchise without paying the guarantee to Rochester.

Washington dropped out of the NFL in 1922, but continued as an independent team without Hegarty for another year. Jack's only other involvement with professional football was putting together a local All-Star team to face the barnstorming Red Grange Bears in 1925. Hegarty became a dentist and is not to be confused with Jack Hagarty who played for Georgetown from 1923 to 1925 and coached the school from 1931 to 1948. Later in life, Hegarty

Hansen, Harold F. (Hal)									
Year	Team	Games	Wins	Losses	Ties	%	Rank	Points	Allowed
1932	Staten Island Stapletons	12	2	7	3	.222	8	77	173
1 year		12	2	7	3	.222		77	173

Hegarty, John E, (Jack)									
Year	Team	Games	Wins	Losses	Ties	%	Rank	Points	Allowed
1921	Washington Senators	3	1	2	0	.333	12	21	43
1 year		3	1	2	0	.333		21	43

unsuccessfully contested the distribution of his father's estate from 1941 to 1943. That estate of $55,000 went entirely to Jack's brother and sister.

HELDT, JOHN C. (JACK) 12/2/1899–10/25/1975. Iowa under Howard Jones. Played G/C for the Columbus Tigers in 1923 and 1926. *Hall of Fame Players:* None. *Record:* **Player-Coach.**

The 5'9" 210-pound Heldt was an All-Western Conference (Big Ten) center for Iowa in 1922 despite missing time due to lumbago. On the unbeaten 1922 Hawkeyes, Heldt played alongside All-American Duke Slater. The next year, Heldt was hired to coach Ohio University. The current media guide for Ohio lists "F.B. Heldt" as the coach, but the school's yearbook for 1924 identifies John C. as the coach. The Bobcats went 3–5–1 that year, and Jack also appeared in one game professionally with the Columbus Tigers. Heldt resigned from Ohio University, but in 1926 was hired by the Tigers as player-coach for what turned out to be their final cheerless year in the NFL.

Heldt disappeared from view for a quarter century, but turned up in a horrifying news story on September 8, 1951. Somehow having fallen asleep on the train tracks, he found himself trapped beneath a Pacific Electric boxcar in Gardena, California with his head inches from the locomotive's wheels. Jack's body was so severely twisted around the brake rods that his leg was dislocated, and he also suffered a fractured skull. It took two hours to free Heldt, as workmen had to jack up the 50,000-pound car to be able to lift him out. He told police that he was a salesman who had no recollection of anything that happened after he left a local gambling hall. Jack lived for another quarter century after this bizarre accident.

HENDRIAN, OSCAR G. (DUTCH) 1/19/1896– 12/13/1953. Depauw, Detroit, Pittsburgh and Princeton under Bill Roper. Played HB for the Akron Pros, Canton Bulldogs, Green Bay Packers, New York Giants and Rock Island Independents from 1923 to 1925. *Hall of Fame Players:* None. *Record:* **Interim Player-Coach.**

Detroit-native Dutch Hendrian attended four colleges as an itinerant athlete. Dutch passed through Depauw and Detroit Mercy and then joined the Marines during World War I. After the war, the 5'9" 182-pound Hendrian spent one year at Pittsburgh and finally landed at Princeton. Akron hired him in 1923 as player coach, but Dutch only lasted the first five games, all losses, before jumping to the champion Canton Bulldogs for the second half of the season. He showed up in Green Bay the next year with his German shepherd in tow, and the dog was on the sidelines for all the Packers' games that year, even showing up in the front row of the team picture. Hendrian began the 1925 season with the Rock Island Independents, but soon left to become the New York Giants' first-ever starting quarterback, albeit in the single-wing.

Hendrian moved out to Hollywood and appeared in roughly 150 movies from 1930 to 1951. Mostly, he was employed as an extra in B-movies or in such stirring roles as "Henchman" in the film "Nevada" or "Plug Ugly" in "Punch Drunks." Dutch did get to play Hunk Anderson for the movie, "Knute Rockne All-American" in 1940 and worked with Gary Cooper, Jimmy Cagney, Humphrey Bogart, the Marx Brothers and the Three Stooges in his acting career.

HENRY, WILBUR F. (PETE OR FATS) 10/31/1897– 2/7/1952. Washington & Jefferson under David Morrow. Played T for the Canton Bulldogs, New York Giants and Pottsville Maroons from 1920 to 1923 and 1925–1928. *Hall of Fame Players:* Walt Kiesling, Johnny Blood McNally. *Record:* **Hall of Fame Player; Player-Coach; Co-Coach** (with Harry Robb, 1926).

Pete Henry's rotund, flabby appearance in old photographs does not belie the talent that made him a member of both the College and Pro Football Halls of Fame. The 5'11" 245-pound Henry was an unmoveable wall at tackle and also one of the finest kickers and punters of his era. A three-time All-American at Washington & Jefferson from 1917 to 1919, the Mansfield, Ohio native also lettered in baseball, basketball and track. Pete went directly from college to the Canton Bulldogs, where, along with fellow Hall of Famers Link Lyman and Guy Chamberlin, he anchored the

Heldt, John C. (Jack)									
Year	*Team*	*Games*	*Wins*	*Losses*	*Ties*	*%*	*Rank*	*Points*	*Allowed*
1926	Columbus Tigers	7	1	6	0	.143	19	26	93
1 year		7	1	6	0	.143		26	93

Hendrian, Oscar G. (Dutch)									
Year	*Team*	*Games*	*Wins*	*Losses*	*Ties*	*%*	*Rank*	*Points*	*Allowed*
1923	Akron Pros	5	0	5	0	.000	16	17	54
1 year		5	0	5	0	.000		17	54

line for the two-time NFL champions. Notably, he drop-kicked a 45-yard field goal in 1922 and supposedly set a league record in 1923 with a 94-yard punt.

The Bulldogs were sold and moved to Cleveland in 1924, but Henry, the pride of Mansfield, Ohio, refused to go and instead spent the season playing for the independent Pottsville Maroons. When Canton rejoined the NFL in 1925, he returned to the Bulldogs and was named co-coach along with Harry Robb the following year. The Bulldogs were running on fumes by then, however, and won just one game in 1926 before disbanding. Pete played four games with the Giants in 1927, but had some problems with a sprained ankle. He was dropped from the team and signed on with Pottsville in October. In 1928, Henry again became player-coach for a terrible team about to fold. Pottsville won just two games that year and moved to Boston to become the Bulldogs the following year. Rather than become a new breed of Bulldog, Pete was hired by his alma mater to coach track, basketball and work as an assistant football coach. In 1931, he was named Athletic Director and went on to serve as football coach from 1942 to 1945, posting a 4–9 record. Henry had his leg amputated due to diabetes in 1948, but continued to work at Washington & Jefferson until his death from the disease in 1952.

HESS, WALTER B. (WALLY) 10/28/1894–8/30/1963. Indiana under Clarence Childs and Jumbo Stiehm. Played HB for the Hammond Pros from 1920 to 1925. *Hall of Fame Players:* Fritz Pollard. *Record:* **Player-Coach.**

Hammond's own Wally Hess played for the Pros in six of their seven NFL seasons, serving as player-coach for three of them. The 5'9" 177-pound halfback starred at quarterback for Indiana University as a sophomore in 1916, but was refused his letter and had his football eligibility rescinded for having played with the Hammond Clabbys that December. The Clabbys were operated by the Hammond Clabby Athletic Association and were a forerunner to Doc Young's Hammond Pros that became a charter member of the APFA in 1920. On the outs with Indiana, Hess continued with the Clabbys in 1917 and joined the Pros when they entered the APFA. The Pros were not a very strong team, though, as Hess' 3–12–3 cumulative coaching record indicates. The one thing notable about Hess' years as coach was that he coached four pioneer African American players: Inky Williams, John Shelbourne, Sol Butler and Fritz Pollard. Pollard claimed in later years that he was the Hammond coach in 1923 and 1924.

HICKS, MAX 7/1/1884–11/12/1944. Geneva College. Played E for the Hammond Pros in 1920–1921. *Hall of Fame Players:* None. *Record:* **Player-Coach.**

The 175-pound Hicks played in one game as an end for Hammond in 1920 and another in 1921. He took over as coach from Hank Gillo in 1921 and managed to lead the team to a 3–0 victory over Evansville in October. He attended Geneva College in Beaver Falls, Pennsylvania, later famous as the hometown of Joe Namath.

HIGGINS, AUSTIN G. 11/29/1897–3/3/1976. No College. Played C/E for the Louisville Brecks. *Hall of Fame Players:* None. *Record:* **Player-Coach.**

The Louisville Brecks dated their origins to a team sponsored by the Louisville Breckinridge Club in 1899. In 1921, Brecks owner Aaron Hertzman paid

Henry, Wilbur F. (Pete or Fats)									
Year	Team	Games	Wins	Losses	Ties	%	Rank	Points	Allowed
1926	Canton Bulldogs	13	1	9	3	.100	20	46	161
1928	Pottsville Maroons	10	2	8	0	.200	8	74	134
2 years		23	3	17	3	.150		120	295

Hess, Walter B. (Wally)									
Year	Team	Games	Wins	Losses	Ties	%	Rank	Points	Allowed
1922	Hammond Pros	6	0	5	1	.000	15	0	69
1923	Hammond Pros	7	1	5	1	.167	15	14	59
1924	Hammond Pros	5	2	2	1	.500	10	18	45
3 years		18	3	12	3	.200		173	

Hicks, Max									
Year	Team	Games	Wins	Losses	Ties	%	Rank	Points	Allowed
1921	Hammond Pros	5	1	3	1	.250	13	17	45
1 year		5	1	3	1	.250		17	45

the franchise fee to join the APFA, and league President Joe Carr hoped they would function as a traveling team to fill in open scheduling dates for other league teams. That first year, though, the Brecks only played two league games: losing 21–0 at Evansville in October and losing 6–0 to Columbus in Louisville in December. In between those contest, the team went 4–2 against a series of independent teams. The 5'9" 168-pound Higgins played center and end as well as coached the team. He continued to play for the Brecks for the next two seasons, but never coached in the league again. Higgins was a local player who never went to college.

HOEFFEL, JOSEPH M. (JOE) 10/31/1890– 4/15/1964. Wisconsin under John Richards and Bill Juneau. Did not play professionally. *Hall of Fame Players:* Curly Lambeau.

One of the most memorable lines of dialogue in movie history occurs in "The Man Who Shot Liberty Valance," John Ford's meditation on the reliability of what we know of the old West — "When the legend becomes fact, print the legend." That is certainly the case concerning who was the first coach of the Green Bay Packers. Conventional wisdom is that Curly Lambeau was the only coach the team had from its founding as an independent team in 1919 through its acceptance into the APFA in 1921 until Curly was fired after the 1949 season. It's the legend, but it's not the truth.

The first to point that out was Larry Names with the publication of the first volume of his four-volume *The History of the Green Bay Packers* by tiny Angel Press in 1987. Names extensively studied primary documents to conclude that on the team's founding in 1919, Green Bay West High School coach Bill Ryan was named coach with Lambeau team captain. Names also argued that two years later when the Packers joined the APFA, Green Bay High School East coach Joe Hoeffel was the coach with, again, Lambeau as team captain. Only after Green Bay applied for reinstatement into the NFL in 1922 did Lambeau assume the head coaching job. There was no publicity for the Names' book, though, and the story went nowhere in 1987.

14 years later, veteran Packers' beat man Cliff Christl of the *Milwaukee Journal-Sentinel* did his own research and came to the same conclusions as Names did. Christl ran the story in the *Journal-Sentinel* and at least managed to get a reaction from the team, league and Hall of Fame. However, the response was to "print the legend." Packer President Bob Harlan told Christl, "[Lambeau] ran everything. Now what his title was and what a title meant at that particular time, I'm really not comfortable saying. But he was the one running the show. Considering what he did, I'm a little reluctant to take away any significance to his career." What Harlan said is true in that the job of head coach was of less importance in those days, but *Green Bay Press-Gazette* stories from 1921 credit Hoeffel with running practices, designing plays and making game substitutions like other coaches of the time. Still, to this day, the Packers make no mention of Hoeffel (or Ryan for that matter) in their annual Media Guide.

So who was Joe Hoeffel? Hoeffel was captain of the unbeaten 1912 Wisconsin team. That year he was named a second team All-American at end by Walter Camp. Hoeffel returned to his hometown of Green Bay in 1916 and was named coach of East High School where he coached a star back named Earl Lambeau. Three years later, he was offered the position of head coach of the newly established Packers, but turned down the offer. In 1921, though, Hoeffel became the team's first coach in the APFA. After this long forgotten and ignored interlude, Joe went into the family business and lived the rest of his life in Green Bay. His son, Joseph Jr. became a doctor. His grandson, Joseph M. Hoeffel III, served as a U.S. Congressman from Pennsylvania from 1999 to 2005. He has also run unsuccessfully for U.S. Senate and the Pennsylvania governorship. He is an Eagles' fan.

HORWEEN, ARNOLD (ARNIE) 7/7/1898– 8/5/1985. Harvard under Percy Haughton. Played FB for the Racine Cardinals and Chicago Cardinals from 1921 to 1924. *Hall of Fame Players:* Paddy Driscoll. *Record:* **Player-Coach.**

Chicago-native Arnie Horween was Harvard's

Higgins, Austin G.								
Year	Team	Games	Wins	Losses	Ties	%	Rank	Points	Allowed
1921	Louisville Brecks	2	0	2	0	.000	18	0	27
1 year		2	0	2	0	.000		0	27

Hoeffel, Joseph M. (Joe)								
Year	Team	Games	Wins	Losses	Ties	%	Rank	Points	Allowed
1921	Green Bay Packers	6	3	2	1	.600	6	70	55
1 year		6	3	2	1	.600		70	55

two-time captain when he played in the backfield with his older brother Ralph. Both brothers joined the Navy in World War I and returned to Harvard in 1919. Both brothers joined the Cardinals in 1921, but played under the last name "McMahon" so that their mother wouldn't be upset that her Ivy League–educated sons had sunk to playing professional football. Ralph played for three years with the Cardinals, while the 5'11" 206-pound Arnie stayed for four, including two as player-coach and then retired.

In 1926, Harvard hired brought him back to coach the football team, but Horween could manage just a 20-17-3 record from 1926 to 1930—although he did win three of five matches with Yale. As a coach, Horween was said to have an even disposition. The *New York Times* said of him in 1927, "His quiet, unassuming and business-like manner makes him a difficult mark for the anvil chorus. There is always the feeling that he is working to the best of his ability on a difficult job. Above all, he has won the respect of his athletic pupils." However, that Crimson "anvil chorus" did catch up with Arnie for his mediocre record, and he landed back in Chicago where he eventually took over the Horween Leather Company, founded by his father in 1905. That family business is still going today, with one of its steadiest clients being the NFL. Horween Leather has supplied the leather for the footballs used by the NFL since the early 1940s and uses its own "Tanned in Tack" process. Arnie ran the company from 1949 to 1984 and died just a year after retiring. He also served as a trustee for the Chicago Symphony and a member of the board of overseers at Harvard.

HUFFINE, KENNETH W. (KEN) 12/22/1897–9/26/1977. Purdue for Butch Scanlon. Played FB for the Muncie Flyers, Fort Wayne Friars, Chicago Staleys and Dayton Triangles from 1920 to 1925. *Hall of Fame Players:* None. *Record:* **Player-Coach.**

The first day of league games for the American Professional Football Association, as the NFL was originally called, was on Sunday, October 3, 1920. There were two games between league members that day. One was Columbus playing at Dayton, and the other featured Muncie playing at Rock Island. Because Dayton is in the Eastern Time Zone and Rock Island the Central, the Dayton contest is often considered the NFL's first game. However, we do not know the start times of either game, so the Muncie Flyers, coached by Ken Huffine, may very well have played in the league's first game. It was not a memorable day for either Huffine or the Flyers, though. From his fullback position, Ken had three punts blocked in the first quarter; two were returned for touchdowns, and the third led directly to a touchdown that put the Flyers down 21–0. They would go on to lose 45–0 and drop out of football within a week.

Better things were in store for the 6'3" 208-pound Huffine. The Hammond, Indiana native had been a three-year letterman and an All-Conference selection at Purdue from 1916 to 1919, with a break for serving in World War I. He fled the collapsing Flyers to join the independent Fort Wayne Friars in 1920 and then signed with the Chicago Staleys in 1921. George Halas' Staleys won the league title that year. From the champion Staleys, though, Huffine moved on to the Dayton Triangles for three years of steadily declining fortunes until his retirement. Afterwards, Ken had a long career at Johns-Manville, moving up to plant supervisor and then to a vice presidency in the company. His one-game coaching career still stands as the worst per game scoring differential in league history, tied only by the one-game career of Tonawanda's Tam Rose.

HUGHITT, ERNEST F. (TOMMY) 12/27/1892–12/27/1961. Michigan under Fielding Yost. Played QB/HB for the Buffalo All-Americans and Buffalo Bisons from 1920 to 1924. *Hall of Fame Players:* None. *Record:* **Player-Coach.**

Tommy Hughitt was born in British Columbia and came east to star as an All American quarterback for Fielding Yost at Michigan in 1913. The 5–8" 159-pound Hughitt was a triple-threat back who could run, pass and kick as well as play all the backfield positions. In 1916, Tommy signed with Youngstown Patricians and played with that independent team

Horween, Arnold (Arnie)

Year	Team	Games	Wins	Losses	Ties	%	Rank	Points	Allowed
1923	Chicago Cardinals	12	8	4	0	.667	6	161	56
1924	Chicago Cardinals	10	5	4	1	.556	8	90	67
2 years		22	13	8	1	.619		251	123

Huffine, Kenneth W. (Ken)

Year	Team	Games	Wins	Losses	Ties	%	Rank	Points	Allowed
1920	Muncie Flyers	1	0	1	0	.000	14	0	45
1 year		1	0	1	0	.000		0	45

through 1917. At the same time, he was coaching the University of Maine to a 6–7–3 mark from 1915 to 1916, while moonlighting with the semipro Buffalo All Stars in 1917. He played for the Buffalo Niagras in 1918 and then helped run the Buffalo Prospects in 1919, while appearing in a few more games with Youngstown.

When the APFA started in 1920, Hughitt joined the Buffalo All-Americans and served as player-coach of both that team and its successor, the Buffalo Bisons, through the 1924 season when he retired at 32. Tommy was a taskmaster who stressed fundamentals as a coach. Under Hughitt, Buffalo had claims to the league title in both 1920 and 1921. If they had beaten the Akron Pros in the 1920 season closer, they could have claimed the title, but the game ended in a 0–0 tie. In 1921, Buffalo was undefeated until team owner Frank Mc-Neil booked an away game against the Staleys at the last minute, just one day after the scheduled season finale against Akron. Buffalo lost 10–7 to Chicago; the Staleys claimed the league championship in the first of a long series of football disappointments for the Queen City.

Tommy remained in Buffalo after football and eventually became a city councilman. Meanwhile, he kept his hand in pro football by serving as a game official for 20 years in the NFL and four years in the All America Football Conference. Hall of Famer Marion Motley later credited Hughitt as putting a stop to the physical abuse that the African American star was enduring on the field when breaking the color barrier.

IMLAY, TALMA W. (TUT) 3/20/1902–3/20/1976. California under Andy Smith. Played HB for the Los Angeles Buccaneers in 1926 and the New York Giants in 1927. *Hall of Fame Players:* None. *Record:* **Player-Co-Coach** (with Brick Muller).

The 5'8" 165-pound Imlay captained the undefeated 1925 University of California team and threw for the first touchdown in the inaugural East-West Shrine Game on December 26 of that year. That touchdown pass was caught by Brick Muller, a former California star end who was an assistant coach during Imlay's time. The two Golden Bears' stars teamed up the following year to be player-co-coaches for the Los Angeles Buccaneers, although Imlay was likely more of an assistant to Muller. Los Angeles was actually a road team that never played a game west of Kansas City. The Bucs were well-stocked with West Coast stars, though, and finished sixth in the 22-team league with a 6–3–1 record.

Born in Panguitch, Utah, Imlay was a slippery halfback who also was skilled as a passer, receiver and punt returner. He was named All Pro with the Bucs, but with the demise of the team in 1927, Tut jumped to the Giants to play for the NFL champs in his second and final season in the league. Imlay rose to the rank of Colonel in the Air Force after leaving football. He also served as the county assessor for Salinas, California.

JOESTING, HERBERT W. (HERB) 4/17/1905–10/2/1963. Minnesota under Doc Spears. Played HB for the Minneapolis Red Jackets, Frankford Yellow Jackets and the Chicago Bears from 1929 to 1932. *Hall of Fame Players:* None. *Record:* **Player-Coach**.

The 6'2" 194-pound Joesting was known as the "Owatonna Thunder Bolt" while starring at fullback

Hughitt, Ernest F. (Tommy)

Year	Team	Games	Wins	Losses	Ties	%	Rank	Points	Allowed
1920	Buffalo All-Americans	11	9	1	1	.900	3	258	32
1921	Buffalo All-Americans	12	9	1	2	.900	2	211	29
1922	Buffalo All-Americans	10	5	4	1	.556	9	87	41
1923	Buffalo All-Americans	12	5	4	3	.556	8	94	43
1924	Buffalo Bisons	11	6	5	0	.545	9	120	140
5 years		56	34	15	7	.694		770	285

Imlay, Talma W. (Tut)

Year	Team	Games	Wins	Losses	Ties	%	Rank	Points	Allowed
1926	Los Angeles Buccaneers	10	6	3	1	.667	6	67	57
1 year		10	6	3	1	.667		67	57

Joesting, Herbert W. (Herb)

Year	Team	Games	Wins	Losses	Ties	%	Rank	Points	Allowed
1929	Minneapolis Red Jackets	10	1	9	0	.100	11	48	185
1 year		10	1	9	0	.100		48	185

for the University of Minnesota from 1925 to 1927. In 1926, Herb tied Red Grange's Big Ten record of 13 touchdowns scored and was an All-American that year and the next.

Joesting worked in a bank after graduation before signing with the NFL's Minneapolis Red Jackets as player-coach in 1929. After a 1–9 season, Herb was replaced as coach by fellow Golden Gopher alum George Gibson, but once again the Red Jackets won just one game in 1930 before disbanding. Herb and several other players on the team joined the struggling Frankford Yellow Jackets to close out the 1930 season.

Frankford was also a tottering franchise, though. The team announced in September 1931 that Joesting would be the team's player-coach and would utilize the "Minnesota System" of Coach Doc Spears. However, Bull Behman ended up as the Frankford coach, while Joesting played for a one-win team for the third time. The Yellow Jackets folded for good in November, and Herb was acquired by the Bears to team with Red Grange and former Minnesota teammate Bronko Nagurski in the Chicago backfield. The Bears won the championship in 1932 in Joesting's final season. In retirement, Herb worked at the Minnesota Motor Vehicle Department for the next 30 years. He died of a heart attack at the age of 58 while out driving with his wife.

JOLLEY, ALVIN J. (AL) (SEE SECTION I)

JONES, RALPH R. (CURLY) 9/22/1880–7/26/1951.
No College. Did not play professionally. *Hall of Fame Players:* Red Grange, Bill Hewitt, Link Lyman, Bronko Nagurski, George Trafton. *Record:* NFL Championship 1932.

Ralph Jones was a man who left a lasting legacy in two sports and successfully coached a third as well, yet he is little remembered today. Born in 1880 in Marion County, Indiana, Jones grew up in Indianapolis where he attended Shortridge High School. While a student at Shortridge, Ralph formed a basketball team, played on it and coached it, making him the first high school basketball coach in Indiana. He moved on to coaching the local YMCA, then Butler University in 1903, Wabash College from 1904 to 1908, Crawfordsville High School from 1904 to 1912 and Purdue basketball from 1909 to 1912. Jones won a state basketball title with Crawfordsville in 1911 and

also coached football there and at Wabash and Purdue. It is no wonder that Jones was the 2011 Centennial Award winner of the Indiana Basketball Hall of Fame and is sometimes called the Father of Indiana High School Basketball.

In 1913, Jones was hired by Illinois as basketball coach, baseball coach and freshman football coach. While there, he led the Illini to the 1915 Helms National Championship. At this time, Ralph also came to know future Chicago Bears' owners George Halas and Dutch Sternaman, not only from freshman football, but baseball and basketball as well. Halas even clinched the 1918 conference basketball title for Illinois with a buzzer beater shot against Wisconsin. Jones had an 85–34 record in basketball at Illinois. He served two years as Athletic Director there before leaving in 1920 for Lake Forest Academy, a Chicago-area prep school where Ralph posted a 94–9 record in basketball and lost just six football games from 1921 to 1929.

Meanwhile, the Bears were struggling on the field and off. In 1929, Chicago finished ninth in a 12-team league with a 4–9–2 record, while Halas and Sternaman feuded over control of the team. As a compromise, they agreed to hire their old mentor, Ralph Jones, as coach, telling the press, "We believe our hope for development of a winning team would be increased if we could turn the squad over to a professional coach." Boy, did they find one. Jones promised his former students an NFL title within three years. He took the basic T-formation offense that Halas had learned from Bob Zuppke at Illinois and completely revamped it. Jones spaced the guards and tackles a yard apart rather than a foot, and the ends two yards off the tackles in order to spread out the defense. He brought the quarterback directly under center to ease the center's duties and to increase in the ball handling deception of the quarterback. He put a man in motion, usually Red Grange, on every play to challenge the defense further. He also assigned numbers to line gaps and to backfield positions to make play-calling easier.

Jones improved the Bears to third place finishes in 1930 and 1931, before winning the promised championship in year three with a 7–1–6 record by beating the Portsmouth Spartans in the NFL's first championship game on a shortened indoor field in Chicago Stadium. That game itself led to serious rule changes for the league in 1933. Hash marks were introduced

Jones, Ralph R. (Curly)									
Year	Team	Games	Wins	Losses	Ties	%	Rank	Points	Allowed
1930	Chicago Bears	14	9	4	1	.692	3	169	71
1931	Chicago Bears	13	8	5	0	.615	3	145	92
1932	Chicago Bears	14	7	1	6	.875	1	160	44
3 years		41	24	10	7	.706		474	207

to move the ball in from the sidelines, the passing game was liberalized so that the passer did not have to be five yards behind the line of scrimmage to throw the ball, and the league was split into two conferences, with the championship game made an annual event. But by then Jones was gone. Halas bought out Sternaman and returned to the sidelines in Chicago; Ralph took over as athletic director, football and baseball coach at Lake Forest College and served from 1933 to 1948. At age 68, Ralph retired to Estes Park, Colorado where he died three year later. Overall, he was 25–10–7 with the Bears, 52–31–10 in football with Lake Forest College and 306–60 in high school and college basketball. Although just 5'7" tall and soft-spoken, Ralph Jones was a giant of the coaching profession; he was a man that George Halas lauded for his stature and integrity, a man who changed the face of two sports.

KENDRICK, JAMES M. (JIM) 8/22/1893–11/17/1941. Texas A&M under Charley Moran and E.H.W. Harlan. Played E for the Toledo Maroons, Canton Bulldogs, Louisville Brecks, Chicago Bears, Hammond Pros, Buffalo Bisons, Rochester Jeffersons, Rock Island Independents, Buffalo Rangers and New York Giants from 1922 to 1927. *Hall of Fame Players:* None. *Record:* **Player-Coach.**

Born in Hillside, Texas, Jim Kendrick played for nine teams in six years in the NFL during his generally peripatetic life. The 6' 197-pound end was All Conference in his senior year at Texas A&M. After graduation, he joined the Texas National Guard in 1916 and served in France during the war. In 1920, Kendrick became assistant football coach at Baylor. Two years later, he began his NFL career with the Toledo Maroons in 1922, but ended that season playing for the champion Canton Bulldogs. The following season, Jim served as player-coach for the Louisville Brecks in their inept final season, while simultaneously working as assistant football coach and head baseball coach at Centre College. He continued with his college coaching responsibilities the following year while playing for the Chicago Bears and played

minor league baseball in Florida as well. 1925 was even more active for Kendrick who played one game for Rock Island, one for Rochester, two for Hammond and then seven for the Buffalo Bisons.

The Bisons won just one game that year, which led them to make a radical change in 1926. Kendrick was hired to coach the team and stock it with the best players from the Southwest. Jim said of the renamed Buffalo Rangers, "Here I have 14 husky young fellows who have never been east of the Mississippi River. They are boys who know football, for in the Texas universities you have to fight for a place on the team and then fight all the time to keep it. There's no baby, silk-pillow football in the West or Southwest. These boys want to see something of the world before they set down to kick a living or a fortune out of life."

The Rangers did play appreciably better in 1926, and Kendrick indicated the Texas Plan would continue the next year, "We will be goin' back to where the air is balmy, the weather God's kind and there's no snow to freeze your nose and toes.... I hate to leave you folks, for Buffalo and all its people have been mighty kind to me and my boys.... The boys are all solid on Buffalo and the men who backed us. They'll all be glad to come back again next year."

While Kendrick and his team did make a post-season barnstorming tour of the Southwest, they did not return to Buffalo in 1927. Jim ended up playing for the Giants during their championship run that year, both starting and ending his NFL career on title teams. Kendrick went on to coach at St. Mary's in San Antonio, work for the Civilian Conservation Corps, run an oil business and serve as a college official in the 1930s. He died of a stroke at the age of 48.

KEOGH, JOHN J. (JACK) 6/17/1886–2/13/1955. Amherst and Pennsylvania under Andy Smith. Did not play professionally. *Hall of Fame Players:* None.

Raised in Massachusetts and a graduate of Amherst, Jack Keogh came to Philadelphia in 1910 to attend the University of Pennsylvania Dental School. While at Penn, Keogh was a 145-pound quarterback who later joined the staff as the freshman football

Kendrick, James M. (Jim)

Year	Team	Games	Wins	Losses	Ties	%	Rank	Points	Allowed
1923	Louisville Brecks	3	0	3	0	.000	19	0	90
1926	Buffalo Rangers	10	4	4	2	.500	9	53	62
2 years		13	4	7	2	.364		53	152

Keogh, John J. (Jack)

Year	Team	Games	Wins	Losses	Ties	%	Rank	Points	Allowed
1926	Hartford Blues	10	3	7	0	.300	13	57	99
1 year		10	3	7	0	.300		57	99

coach under Bob Folwell in 1918. Jack was a fireball on the sidelines, cheering on his freshmen and screaming about the opponent's transgressions, even in practice sessions against the varsity. He continued in his coaching position for several years under both John Heisman and former Penn teammate Lou Young. However, by 1925 Lou Young had had enough of Keogh's overly competitive nature and let Jack go as coach of the first-year men.

The next year, Keogh was hired to coach the Hartford Blues, a new franchise in the NFL set to play in a bicycle track in West Hartford. As an example of how different the league was in the 1920s, Keogh was hired with the understanding that he would remain in Philadelphia working in his dental practice three days a week, while coaching the Blues the rest of the week. Rookie Penn State lineman Ernie McCann doubled as line coach. Keogh told the press at the outset, "I don't want the fans of Hartford and vicinity to expect too much in our first season, but we will do our best. When they see the opposition, they will know the caliber of the men now in professional football." That turned out to be a pretty fair assessment of Hartford's only year in the NFL. 37 players appeared for the Blues while Keogh went through all available players trying to find a winning combination, but the team still ended up at 3–7.

Keogh returned to his dental practice with just one more brief foray into coaching with the Valley Forge Military Academy in 1928 before he gave up the sport. By all accounts, the lively Keogh had a thriving dental practice in which he would entertain patients in the waiting room by dancing, singing and playing the violin. After he retired in 1951, Jack returned to Holyoke, Massachusetts where he died four years later.

KOPPISCH, WALTER F. (WALT OR WALLY)
6/6/1901–11/2/1952. Columbia under Buck O'Neill and Percy Haughton. Played HB for the Buffalo Bisons in 1925 and New York Giants in 1926. *Hall of Fame Players:* None. *Record:* **Player-Coach.**

The speedy Walt Koppisch excelled on both the track and the gridiron. The 5'10" 180-pound halfback led his high school to the Buffalo city championship three times. At Columbia, he was the metropolitan area champion at the quarter-mile, captain of the football team and a gridiron All-American in his senior year. One of his backfield mates was future baseball Hall of Famer Lou Gehrig, and Walt joined Lou on the college baseball team, too, as a star outfielder.

With the retirement of local institution Tommy Hughitt, the Bisons brought in Koppisch to serve as player-coach in his rookie year. Koppisch tried to put together a team of dedicated role players and told the *Buffalo Courier,* "These men have all subscribed to the idea of remaining in Buffalo all through the season. They have been practicing for two weeks, twice daily, and their condition will be perfect. This is my hobby and my theory, that a group of first-class players, knowing football and in first-class condition can beat an aggregation of stars who meet to play but once a week."

Unfortunately, Wally's theory did not hold up and the under-skilled Bisons won just won game. Koppisch himself was in an auto accident on October 22 and only appeared in one of the team's remaining four games. Wally spent the following season with the Giants and retired to be a stockbroker, later taking on former teammate Lou Gehrig as a partner. Koppisch died at the age of 51 in 1952. Two years later, his classmates from the Columbia class of 1924 remembered him by dedicating the new football scoreboard as the Walter Koppisch Memorial Scoreboard. He was elected to the College Football Hall of Fame in 1981.

KRAEHE, OLIVER R. (OLLIE)
8/22/1898–12/19/1966. Washington (MO). Played G/C for the Rock Island Independents in 1922 and the St. Louis All-Stars in 1923. *Hall of Fame Players:* None. *Record:* **Owner-Player-Coach.**

St. Louis-native Ollie Kraehe was a teammate of the celebrated Jimmy Conzelman at Washington University and captained the team after Conzelman graduated. Kraehe was a 5'10" 180-pound lineman who also played guard for the basketball team. He spent part of the 1922 season with Rock Island and then organized his own hometown team for the 1923 NFL season, serving as owner, coach and player for the St.

Koppisch, Walter F. (Walt or Wally)									
Year	Team	Games	Wins	Losses	Ties	%	Rank	Points	Allowed
1925	Buffalo Bisons	9	1	6	2	.143	15	33	113
1 year		9	1	6	2	.143		33	113

Kraehe, Oliver R. (Ollie)									
Year	Team	Games	Wins	Losses	Ties	%	Rank	Points	Allowed
1923	St. Louis All-Stars	7	1	4	2	.200	14	14	39
1 year		7	1	4	2	.200		14	39

Louis All-Stars. The team was mostly made up of local talent and was not very good, winning just one game and losing $3,600 for the year before permanently disbanding. Years later, Ollie told football historian Bob Carroll, "There were some players who didn't want their parents to know they were in the game, and some of them used fictitious names. Also, there were some who pretended to be All-Americans from the East just to get a chance to play."

The players weren't the only pretenders, though. Kraehe had an end who called himself Dolly Gray, the name of an All-American from Princeton, In need of cash, Kraehe sold Gray to the Packers. Once Curly Lambeau saw Gray play one game for Green Bay, though, he confronted Ollie about the mysterious Dolly Gray. Kraehe told Lambeau that it was all a joke and returned the money. With the collapse of his team, Ollie's days in the NFL ended. Instead, he became a very successful real estate developer.

LAIRD, JAMES T. (JIM) 9/10/1897–8/16/1970. Colgate under Laurence Bankart. Played FB/G for the Rochester Jeffersons, Buffalo All-Americans, Canton Bulldogs, Providence Steam Roller and Staten Island Stapletons from 1920 to 1922, 1925–1928 and in 1931. *Hall of Fame Players:* None. *Record:* **Player-Coach.**

Born in Montpelier, Vermont, Jim Laird would go wherever someone was paying him to play football. The 6' 194-pound fullback left Colgate University in February 1920 after he was declared ineligible for football because he appeared in a professional game played in Buffalo in November 1919. So in 1920, Laird moved on to the APFA, playing nine games with Rochester and one with Buffalo. The following year he appeared in six games for Rochester, one for Buffalo and one for Canton in league games, plus four for the independent Union Quakers and at least one for the New York Brickley Giants. Jim settled in Buffalo in 1922, playing the whole season with the All-Americans while coaching high school in the city.

Laird dropped out of the NFL in 1923 when he was hired to coach Norwich University. He led Norwich to a 6–18 record over three years, but also began

playing for the independent Providence Steam Roller in 1924. He stayed with the team when it entered the NFL in 1925 and took over as player-coach in 1926. After a mediocre 5–7–1 season, Jim was replaced by Jimmy Conzelman who led the team to an NFL title two years later with Laird still at fullback. Jim retired from the NFL again in 1929, but came back at age 34 for one last year with Staten Island in 1931. He returned to Norwich as coach in 1932 and later worked as recreation director at a state prison in Connecticut.

LAMBEAU, EARL L. (CURLY) (SEE SECTION I)

LYONS, LEO V. 3/11/1892–5/18/1976. No College. Did not play in the NFL. *Hall of Fame Players:* None. *Record:* **Owner-Coach.**

In his later years, Leo Lyons was called the "honorary historian of the league" and even drew a small annual stipend from the NFL from the 1960s until his death. He would haunt the league's annual meetings talking about the old days to anyone who would listen. After all, Leo had been there since before the beginning. At the age of 16 in 1908, Lyons began playing end for the semi-pro Rochester Jeffersons, named for their origins on Jefferson Avenue; two years later he was running the team, and at some point in the teens became their owner. When the APFA was founded in the Hupmobile showroom in August 1919, Leo could not attend, but sent a letter expressing his interest. He attended the follow-up meeting in September and secured a spot in the league for the Jeffs.

Leo stopped playing in 1919, but did everything he could to hold the team together and promote professional football in Rochester. All he could manage in six years, though, were two league wins. In the two years, Lyons acted as coach, they didn't win a game and were outscored 180–13. He later complained that he was caught in a vicious circle: attendance was poor, so he couldn't pay for top players, and without top players, fans wouldn't come out. Leo was so dedicated that he lost his house in 1921 due to the financial losses of the team. Finally, in 1924, Lyons made a deal with local sportsman Johnny Murphy to hand over man-

Laird, James T. (Jim)

Year	Team	Games	Wins	Losses	Ties	%	Rank	Points	Allowed
1926	Providence Steam Roller	13	5	7	1	.417	11	89	103
1 year		13	5	7	1	.417		89	103

Lyons, Leo V.

Year	Team	Games	Wins	Losses	Ties	%	Rank	Points	Allowed
1923	Rochester Jeffersons	4	0	4	0	.000	19	6	141
1924	Rochester Jeffersons	3	0	3	0	.000	16	7	39
2 years		7	0	7	0	.000		13	180

aging the team in return for an influx of cash. Murphy withdrew from the team at the end of the year, another losing one, and Leo continued to run the Jeffs for one last season in 1925. Lyons even made a run at signing Red Grange that year in one last desperate attempt to preserve football in Rochester. After the team folded, Leo manufactured paint in the area, while maintaining friendships with the other founding fathers of the NFL and keeping up with the history of the league until his death at age 84.

MAHRT, LOUIS R. (LOU) 7/30/1904–8/7/1982.
Dayton under Harry Baujan. Played QB for the Dayton Triangles from 1926 to 1927. *Hall of Fame Players:* None. *Record:* **Player-Coach.**

The Mahrt brothers represented a remarkable football dynasty in Dayton football. Al was the oldest, born in 1893. He starred in football and basketball at St. Mary's, as the University of Dayton was originally called, from 1911 to 1914. He then played quarterback for the professional Dayton Triangles from 1916 to 1917 and then from 1919 to 1922, leading the Triangles to a 13–9–4 record in their first three years in the NFL. After Al left, though, the team never had another winning season. He later rose to become a Vice President at Mead in Dayton, and had a Chair in Accounting at his alma mater bequeathed in his name by his brother-in-law. Second brother Armin, born in 1897, played halfback at Dayton before transferring to West Virginia. He played professionally with the Triangles and Pottsville. Third brother John, born 1899, played end for both the Flyers and the Triangles.

Lou was the youngest brother. Like Al, Lou played quarterback on the Flyers football team. In fact, Al and Lou were the first pair of brothers to be elected captain for the University of Dayton. Upon graduation in 1926, Lou followed family tradition and signed with the Triangles. He and Armin were teammates for two years, the second of which Lou served as player-coach. Unfortunately, the team went 2–10–2 in those two seasons, but would never win a game after the passing of the Mahrts from football in 1927. Lou went on to become an attorney and also chaired the local War Price and Rationing Board during World War II.

MARSHALL, WILLIAM H. (BILLY) 10/24/1887–
Deceased. Detroit. Did not play professionally. *Hall of Fame Players:* None. *Record:* **Owner-Coach.**

When the University of Detroit decided against fielding a football team in 1905, their halfback, Billy Marshall, took matters into his own hands and founded the Detroit Heralds as an amateur team. The Heralds continued on and dropped its amateur status in 1911. Under Marshall's guidance, the Heralds became the first independent team to wear numbers on their jerseys in 1913 and steadily improved on the field to the point where it was an unofficial member of the APFA in the league's initial season of 1920. However, the team was slipping on the field and encountered major financial setbacks when a couple of November games were cancelled due to bad weather. The next season, Detroit officially joined the APFA, but with some changes. Marshall brought in new investors, changed the team's name to Tigers to echo the baseball team and brought in University of Detroit All-American tackle Tillie Voss as vice president. Unfortunately, the Tigers declined on the fold and went bankrupt, ending their connection the NFL.

McGALL, ALBERT H. (AL) 7/14/1881–9/8/1941.
Stevens Technology Institute. Did not play professionally. *Hall of Fame Players:* None. *Record:* **Interim Coach.**

Mahrt, Louis R. (Lou)									
Year	*Team*	*Games*	*Wins*	*Losses*	*Ties*	*%*	*Rank*	*Points*	*Allowed*
1927	Dayton Triangles	8	1	6	1	.143	10	15	57
1 year		8	1	6	1	.143		15	57

Marshall, William H. (Billy)									
Year	*Team*	*Games*	*Wins*	*Losses*	*Ties*	*%*	*Rank*	*Points*	*Allowed*
1920	Detroit Heralds	8	2	3	3	.400	9	53	82
1921	Detroit Tigers	7	1	5	1	.167	16	19	109
2 years		15	3	8	4	.273		72	191

McGall, Albert H. (Al)									
Year	*Team*	*Games*	*Wins*	*Losses*	*Ties*	*%*	*Rank*	*Points*	*Allowed*
1930	Newark Tornadoes	2	0	2	0	.000	11	6	32
1 year		2	0	2	0	.000		6	32

Al McGall played on both the football and track teams at Stevens Tech in Hoboken, New Jersey, where he graduated in 1907. He went on to coach both sports as well as to use his engineering skills to earn a patent on a dynamically balanced football that placed the air valve at the nose of the ball. McGall coached the Stevens' football team from 1915 to 1924 and had unbeaten seasons in 1915 and 1916. From 1925 to 1928, Al held two coaching positions simultaneously. He coached the independent Orange Tornadoes football team, while also serving as assistant track coach at Yale where he helped develop Olympic pole vaulter Sabin Carr. In 1929, the Tornadoes joined the NFL, but center John Depler was appointed player-coach, leaving McGall out. The following season, Depler became co-owner of the new Brooklyn Dodgers franchise, and the Tornadoes moved to Newark. Manager Eddie Simandi brought McGall back as coach, but Depler had taken his best players with him to Brooklyn. With a weak team, Newark got off to a bad start, losing 13–6 to Portsmouth and then being crushed 32–0 by the Giants at home. Simandi was furious and replaced McGall with local prep school coach Jack Fish before the third game of the season. Although McGall is credited with three losses in the record books, he actually only coached two league games.

Al went on to coach track at his alma mater and then at Muhlenberg College in Pennsylvania in the 1930s, until he died from a heart attack before the start of track season in 1941. McGall's devoted track athletes went to the school's athletic director and requested that no coach replace Al that year; they were so imbued with his teaching that they preferred to follow team captain Ernest Fellows. Indeed, the following year Fellows was named track coach after his graduation.

McIlwain, Wallace W. (Wally)

McIlwain, Wallace W. (Wally) 1/20/1903–6/30/1963. Illinois under Bob Zuppke. Played WB for the Racine Tornadoes in 1926. *Hall of Fame Players:* None. *Record:* **Interim Player-Coach.**

Chicago's Wally McIlwain was a sprinter who played in the backfield with Red Grange for two years at Illinois, but was the only member of the backfield not to be named All-Conference. Coach Zuppke said,

"If it hadn't been for Grange, McIlwain would have been a famous halfback in his own right." Wally finished at Illinois the year before Red, but entered the pros the year after Grange. The 5' 9" 173-pound rookie wingback took over as coach of the awful Racine Tornadoes after Shorty Barr retired in mid–October. After being outscored 36–8 in three games under Barr, the Tornadoes were outscored 56–0 in their final two games under McIlwain. Not surprisingly, the team folded. McIlwain went on to work for International Harvester and co-found the Highland Park Boy Scouts. He never played or coached in the NFL again.

Mehre, Harry J. (Horse)

Mehre, Harry J. (Horse) 9/19/1901–9/27/1978. Notre Dame under Knute Rockne. Played C for the Minneapolis Marines from 1922 to 1923. *Hall of Fame Players:* None. *Record:* **Player-Coach.**

Harry Mehre played center for both Notre Dame's football and basketball teams. In basketball, he was a two-time captain of the team. In football, the Huntington, Indiana native played alongside All-American Hunk Anderson and with the legendary George Gipp on back-to-back undefeated national championship teams in 1919 and 1920. Harry's professional football career was short as he played for the Minneapolis Marines from 1922 to 1923. In that second season, though, Mehre coached the Marines while also serving as line coach at St. Thomas College in Saint Paul and then as the school's basketball coach. One of Harry's pupils on the football team was future Hall of Famer Walt Kiesling.

In 1924, though, Mehre became a southerner. University of Georgia coach George Woodruff brought down former Rockne pupils Mehre, Jim Crowley and Frank Thomas as assistant coaches, and all three would go on to have successful college coaching careers. Mehre succeeded Woodruff as head football coach in 1928 and went 59–34–6 in ten seasons while also serving as athletic director. Having lost the support of rabid Bulldog boosters, though, Harry resigned in 1938 to become athletic director and football coach at Mississippi where he spent eight years and attained a

McIlwain, Wallace W. (Wally)								
Year	Team	Games	Wins	Losses	Ties	%	Rank	Points	Allowed
1926	Racine Tornadoes	2	0	2	0	.000	16	0	56
1 year		2	0	2	0	.000		0	56

Mehre, Harry J. (Horse)								
Year	Team	Games	Wins	Losses	Ties	%	Rank	Points	Allowed
1923	Minneapolis Marines	9	2	5	2	.286	13	48	81
1 year		9	2	5	2	.286		48	81

39–26–1 record. After the war, Mehre stepped down as coach. He became an executive at a soft drink company who moonlighted as a popular football columnist with the *Atlanta Journal*.

MORAN, CHARLES B. (UNCLE CHARLEY)

2/22/1878–6/14/1949. Tennessee and Bethel (TN). Did not play professionally. *Hall of Fame Players:* Link Lyman. *Record:* **Interim Coach.**

Born in Nashville, Charley Moran is most famous for his self assured dictum as a major league umpire: "It may be fair and it may be foul. But it ain't nothing' until I call it." Charley made his living in two sports, baseball and football. He played and coached football at Tennessee in 1897 and then transferred to Bethel College, a small Christian school in the same state. After graduation, Moran was hired by Pop Warner as an assistant at Carlisle Indian School where he got to coach the legendary Jim Thorpe. Charley also began playing minor league baseball at this time, earning a brief stint with the St. Louis Cardinals as a pitcher in 1903. His 5.25 earned run average got him sent back to the minors where he switched to catcher after his arm went dead. Charley returned to the Cardinals as a backstop in 1908, but batted just .175 in another short trial.

Again, Moran returned to the minors, but he was also hired by Texas A&M in 1909 to coach their football team. Over the next six years, the Aggies went 38–8–4 while Charley's baseball playing days came to an end in 1914. His next career move was becoming a minor league umpire in 1915. That finally got Moran to the big leagues for good in 1918. He would spend the next 22 summers umpiring in the majors and called five World Series: 1927, 1929, 1932, 1938 and 1939. With his autumns free, though, he got back to coaching college football, too. His next coaching job came about accidentally. Charley was visiting his son Tom at Centre College in Kentucky in 1919 when the experienced mentor was offered the football job. Within three years, the underdog "Praying Colonels," behind quarterback Bo McMillin, upset a top-ranked Harvard team to gain national attention Moran coached at the tiny school through 1923 and racked

up a 42–6–1 record. His next stop was Bucknell from 1924 to 1926 with a 19–10–2 record.

Charley left Bucknell to try pro football. In 1927, the Frankford Yellow Jackets were defending NFL champions, but let unhappy coach Guy Chamberlin go. Moran signed to replace him, but also drew his first World Series assignment that year, which would force him to miss the first two games of the season. Charley put his son Tom in charge of getting the team ready for the season and of running the team for the first two games. In the record books, Charley is given credit for coaching Frankford for the first eight games of 1927, but actually just coached games three through eight. With the team mired at 2–5–1, Moran resigned under fire and was replaced by a committee of players. His final brush with coaching came from 1930 to 1933 at Catawba College in North Carolina, and his 22–11–5 record there gave Charley an overall 121–35–12 college football coaching tally. In 1939, he retired from sports to become a tobacco farmer and died ten years later of a heart attack at age 71.

MORAN, THOMAS M. (TOM)

1899–7/4/1933. Centre (KY) under his father Charley Moran. Played B for the Giants in 1925. *Hall of Fame Players:* Link Lyman. *Record:* **Interim Coach.**

Tom Moran played guard under his father, Charley Moran, at Centre College when the "Praying Colonels" knocked off mighty Harvard in 1921. Tom coached at Carson-Newman College in Tennessee in 1922. Over the next few years, he played minor league baseball and had tryouts with the St. Louis Cardinals as a pitcher and the Pittsburg Pirates as an outfielder. He also appeared in one NFL game as a 5'8" 175-pound blocking back for the Giants in their inaugural season of 1925. When Moran's father was named coach of Frankford to succeed Guy Chamberlin for the 1927 season, Charley brought in Tom to run things while he finished up his umpiring duties. Those duties included the Yankees-Pirates World Series that lasted until October 8, meaning that Tom was actually the acting head coach for the first two games of the Yellow Jacket's season. The team announced that, "Those of you who have witnessed practice know that Tom

Moran, Charles B. (Uncle Charley)									
Year	Team	Games	Wins	Losses	Ties	%	Rank	Points	Allowed
1927	Frankford Yellow Jackets	6	2	4	0	.333	7	84	74
1 year		6	2	4	0	.333		84	74

Moran, Thomas M. (Tom)									
Year	Team	Games	Wins	Losses	Ties	%	Rank	Points	Allowed
1927	Frankford Yellow Jackets	2	0	1	1	.000	7	3	6
1 year		2	0	1	1	.000		3	6

knows his onions and he also has a most amiable disposition and you can expect perfect harmony in the team." Official sources list Charley as the team's head coach for the first eight games, but that is wrong.

After the 1926 championship season, Frankford fans were not pleased with the team's bad start, and the Moran's were gone by Halloween. Tom became a tobacco buyer, but in the early 1930s began to have health problems. The problems became so debilitating that Tom shot himself on the Fourth of July, 1933 at the age of just 33.

MULLER, HAROLD P. (BRICK) 6/12/1901–5/17/1962. California under Andy Smith. Played E for the Los Angeles Buccaneers in 1926. *Hall of Fame Players:* None. *Record:* **Player-Co-Coach** (with Tut Imlay).

Brick Muller earned his sobriquet for his brick-red hair, but "Brick" was also appropriate for his rugged playing style. Known as a fierce tackler and tough blocker from the end position, Muller was also a winner. The Dunsmuir, California native won a silver medal in the high jump at the 1920 Olympics and never lost a game in three years at Cal from 1920 to 1922. He was a two-time All-American and earned the MVP in the 1921 Rose Bowl for a legendary performance that included throwing a 53-yard cross field touchdown pass, recovering three fumbles and making several tackles in Cal's 28–0 upset of Ohio State.

From 1923 to 1925, Muller served as Cal's end coach while he attended Medical School. In December of 1925, he played in the inaugural East-West Shrine Game and scored the first touchdown in the game. The following season the fledgling Los Angeles Buccaneers paid Brick $15,000 to serve as the team's player-coach with the assistance of another Golden Bear alum, Tut Imlay. The Bucs were a traveling team that never played a game west of Kansas City, but finished sixth in the 22-team NFL that year with a 6–

3–1 year before barnstorming in California during the winter. Muller returned to Cal as end coach in 1927 and stayed for another three-year stint. He went on to become a family doctor and orthopedic surgeon. During World War II, Brick was a Major at the Army Medical School, and in 1956, he served as the team physician for the American Olympic team. He died at the age of 60.

MURPHY, JOHNNY Unknown. Rochester. Did not play professionally. *Hall of Fame Players:* None. *Record:* **Interim Owner-Coach** (see Jerry Noonan).

Johnny Murphy was a local basketball fixture in Rochester in the 1920s and 1930s. Murphy was captain and played guard for the University of Rochester at the beginning of the Roaring Twenties and then coached the team for the remainder of the decade. At the same time, Johnny played and coached the local professional squad, the Centrals. In 1924, he expanded his sports interests by heading a syndicate that purchased managing control of the Jeffersons from Leo Lyons in October. Although the original press clipping from the *Rochester Evening Journal* said that Jeffs' end Jerry Noonan would serve as coach, official records list Murphy as the unfortunate mentor who led the team that was outscored 117–0 in its final four league games of the season. The Jeffersons only lasted for one more year, but Murphy's professional basketball team continued into the mid–1930s. As Rochester's Mr. Basketball, he wrote an occasional column in the Rochester paper, "Food for Basketball Bugs," with Nibs Neiman.

NESSER, ALFRED L. (AL OR NAPPY OR WHITEY) 6/6/1893–3/11/1967/ No College. Played G/C/E for the Akron Pros, Cleveland Bulldogs, Akron Indians and New York Giants from 1920 to 1928 and the Cleveland Indians in 1931. *Hall of Fame Players:* None. *Record:* **Interim Player-Coach.**

Muller, Harold P. (Brick)									
Year	*Team*	*Games*	*Wins*	*Losses*	*Ties*	*%*	*Rank*	*Points*	*Allowed*
1926	Los Angeles Buccaneers	10	6	3	1	.667	6	67	57
1 year		10	6	3	1	.667		67	57

Murphy, Johnny									
Year	*Team*	*Games*	*Wins*	*Losses*	*Ties*	*%*	*Rank*	*Points*	*Allowed*
1924	Rochester Jeffersons	4	0	4	0	.000	16	0	117
1 year		4	0	4	0	.000		0	117

Nesser, Alfred L. (Al or Nappy or Whitey)									
Year	*Team*	*Games*	*Wins*	*Losses*	*Ties*	*%*	*Rank*	*Points*	*Allowed*
1926	Akron Indians	2	0	1	1	.000	16	6	13
1 year		2	0	1	1	.000		6	13

Seven of the eight Nesser brothers, born between 1876 and 1898, played professional football for the Columbus Panhandles. Ironically, the one brother who did not play because he did not care for the game, Pete, was the largest, weighing in at over 300-pounds. Although some of the Nessers began playing with Columbus when the team was firmly established in 1907, six of the seven were still playing when Columbus became a charter member of the APFA in 1920. Oddly, only the youngest, Ray, never played in the league. In fact, the oldest, John, was the oldest player in NFL history at 45 until George Blanda topped him in the 1970s. The brothers were not known for their finesse; Knute Rockne once said of the brothers, "getting hit by a Nesser is like falling off a moving train." Arguably the toughest of the brothers was Al, who played his entire 22-year career without a helmet and without shoulder pads.

Al played for the Panhandles from 1910 to 1917 before jumping to Akron where he spent most of his NFL career. At 6' 2" 195-pounds, he was a rugged lineman and played on the first league champions in 1920. With a slight sidestep into Cleveland in 1925, Nesser spent seven years of league ball in Akron and ten years altogether. Al began the 1926 season as player-coach, but was replaced as coach by team owner Frank Nied after just two games. In the inflated atmosphere of 22 NFL and eight AFL teams, Akron could no longer compete and folded in November. Nesser joined the Cleveland Panthers of Red Grange's AFL in October, but by the end of the month, they, too, had folded. He then finished that season with the Giants and played on their championship team of 1927. Al spent one more season in New York and then played semi-pro ball for a couple of years before finishing his NFL career in 1931 at the age of 38 with the Cleveland Indians. Nesser continued on playing semipro ball until he was 45 and then took up boxing. His ring career spanned several bouts that ended with Al knocking out his opponent in the first round until one challenger knocked out his teeth and won in a TKO. Nesser also worked as a plumber.

NESSER, THEODORE (TED) 4/5/1883–6/7/1941. No College. Played C/G/T for the Columbus Panhandles from 1920 to 1921. *Hall of Fame Players:* None. *Record:* **Player-Coach.**

Ted was the third of the seven football-playing Nesser brothers and was the first to play professionally. The 5'10" 225-pound lineman played for the Ohio state champion Massillon Tigers from 1904 to 1906. Ted joined the Columbus Panhandles when Joe Carr reorganized the club in 1907 and spent the next 15 years with the team. Born in Denison, Ohio, he also had very brief stints in Akron and Canton. In all years but 1909 and 1918, Ted also coached the Panhandles. As a coach, he is remembered for originating the triple pass play and the short kickoff; as a player, he played every position on the field and may have been the best of all the brothers.

By the time Columbus joined the APFA, they had little left but the Nessers and won just three games in those first two years. The Nessers were known more for their brawn than speed and were like a swarm on the field. In fact, the 1921 Panhandles featured not only five Nesser brothers (Frank, Fred, John, Phil and Ted), but also Ted's son, Charlie, and his nephew, Ted Hopkins. When Columbus played Akron, sixth brother Al was also on the field on the opposing team. That Panhandles team was the first instance in league history of a father coaching his son and the only instance of a father playing alongside his son on the same team. However, both father and son were out of the league the next year, leaving brother Frank as the last Nesser to play in the league for the 1923 Panhandles. Both Ted and Charlie worked for the Pennsylvania Railroad. Ted was a boilermaker at the Pennsy from 1902 to 1941 until he had a heart attack and died at work.

NEVERS, ERNEST A. (ERNIE) (SEE SECTION I)

NIED, FRANCIS T. (FRANK) 8/14/1894–5/13/1969. No College. Did not play professionally. *Hall of Fame Players:* Fritz Pollard. *Record:* **Interim Owner-Coach**

Frank Nied was a sportsman by birth. His father laid out Akron's League Park in 1906, and that stadium

Nesser, Theodore (Ted)									
Year	*Team*	*Games*	*Wins*	*Losses*	*Ties*	*%*	*Rank*	*Points*	*Allowed*
1920	Columbus Panhandles	10	2	6	2	.250	13	41	121
1921	Columbus Panhandles	9	1	8	0	.111	17	47	222
2 years		19	3	14	2	.176		88	343

Nied, Francis T. (Frank)									
Year	*Team*	*Games*	*Wins*	*Losses*	*Ties*	*%*	*Rank*	*Points*	*Allowed*
1926	Akron Indians	6	1	3	2	.250	16	17	76
1 year		6	1	3	2	.250		17	76

housed minor league baseball and professional football throughout the first half of the twentieth century. Frank started out as a clerk in an Akron cigar store in 1917 and within a couple of years had not only purchased the cigar store, but also half of the Akron Indians football team. Fellow Akron businessman Art Ranney, a former University of Akron athlete, partnered with Nied to buy the team. Nied and Ranney then attended the founding meetings of the APFA, and the renamed Akron Pros became a charter member of the league in 1920. The independent Akron squad was a solid team; Nied and Ranney then signed swift Fritz Pollard, and they won the first APFA championship in 1920. For that, Akron was awarded a silver loving cup provided by the Brunswick-Balke-Collender company at the league meetings in April 1921.

Akron finished third in 1921 with Pollard listed as co-coach with Elge Tobin, making him the first black coach in league history. Nied told the team that if they didn't want to listen to Pollard, "they could leave right then." Nied and Ranney were especially solicitous of their African American star, allowing him to change for games in the cigar store and driving him to and from the park. Pollard jumped to Milwaukee in 1922. Replacing him with Untz Brewer then Dutch Hendrian then Wayne Brenkert led to three straight losing seasons. Nied brought Pollard back in 1925 as a player, with Scotty Bierce as coach, and the Pros went 4–2–1. Nied changed the team's name back to Indians for 1926, but Akron's final season in the NFL was a disaster. Even with the 32-year-old Pollard, the team was slipping and could not draw fans . Nied replaced new coach Al Nesser after two games, but the Indians would only win one game all year under Frank. Nied and Ranney suspended operations at the end of the year and folded the team the following year.

Meanwhile, Nied's cigar business was thriving and became a hangout for the local sporting set. Nied even installed the first Western Union baseball ticker in town so that his customers could follow the Indians' games. Nied himself was also involved with horse racing and auto racing concerns in the area. In time, he became known as the "Mayor of Mill Street" before selling his cigar store in 1947 and moving to St. Petersburg, Florida to retire. He died 22 years later at the age of 74. Sadly, the 1920 Championship Loving Cup has never been found.

NOONAN, GERARD M. (JERRY) 7/31/1898–8/24/1971. Notre Dame and Fordham. Played B/E for

the New York Brickley Giants and Rochester Jeffersons in 1921, 1923 and 1924. *Hall of Fame Players:* None. *Record:* **Interim Player-Coach** (see also Johnny Murphy).

There were two Jerry Noonans born in 1898: Gerald was born on October 13 and died in San Francisco in November 1967; Gerard was born on July 31 and died in Los Angeles in August 1971. All of the football encyclopedias list the first as the NFL's Jerry Noonan and that he attended Fordham and Notre Dame. Archival notes from Notre Dame indicate that their Jerry Noonan was one of 11 siblings from a prominent family in Bayonne, New Jersey. His father Thomas was a state judge; his mother sang for the Metropolitan Opera. Two of his sisters acted in the movies under the stage names Molly O'Day and Sally O'Neill. He attended Notre Dame in 1916–1917 and then went in the service. After the war, Jerry played for Fordham where he played both football and hockey in 1920. In 1921, he appeared in games for both the Brickley Giants and the Rochester Jeffersons. A Jerry Noonan also played quarterback for Northwestern's freshman team in 1919 and for Santa Clara in 1922.

In 1924, Rochester sportsman Johnny Murphy purchased managing control of the Jeffersons from Leo Lyons in October. According to the original press clipping from the *Rochester Evening Journal*, Jerry was to serve as coach, although official records list Murphy as the unfortunate mentor who led the team that was outscored 117–0 in its final four league games of the season. The Jeffersons only lasted for one more year, and neither Murphy nor Noonan was a part of the team in its ultimate demise.

One Jerry Noonan was involved in a more personal sort of demise, though. According to a lurid trail of *Los Angeles Times* stories over the next decade, Molly O'Day and Sally O'Neill's brothers did not apply glory to the Noonan name. Between 1928 and 1936, Jerry was implicated in stock market swindles in Wisconsin, Texas, New York, Colorado and California, as well as passing bad checks in California. Between 1928 and 1932, his brother Jack was arrested for drunkenness, assault with a deadly weapon, burglary and forgery. He had his middle finger amputated after a fight and broke out of jails in Wyoming, Iowa and California. Brother Victor was arrested in connection to New Jersey and New York stock swindles in 1932, and brother Thomas was arrested for non-support of his five children that same year.

Noonan, Gerard M. (Jerry)									
Year	Team	Games	Wins	Losses	Ties	%	Rank	Points	Allowed
1924	Rochester Jeffersons	4	0	4	0	.000	16	0	117
1 year		4	0	4	0	.000		0	117

OWEN, STEPHEN J. (STEVE) (SEE SECTION I)

PIEROTTI, ALBERT F. (AL) 10/24/1895–2/12/1964. Washington & Lee. Played C/G/T for the Akron Pros, Cleveland Tigers, New York Brickley Giants, Milwaukee Badgers and Racine Legion from 1920 to 1924, the Providence Steam Roller in 1927 and the Boston Bulldogs in 1929. *Hall of Fame Players:* None. *Record:* **Interim Player-Coach.**

Boston-native Al Pierotti captained both the football and basketball teams at Washington & Lee in 1916 and 1917, while also starring in baseball and track. After the war, Pierotti pitched in the minor leagues from 1919 to 1922 and earned two cups of coffee with his hometown Boston Braves in 1920 and 1921 (ERA: 4.05). Al had more luck on the gridiron, though. In 1920, he played for both the Akron Pros and the Cleveland Tigers in the newly established APFA. Once Stan Cofall left the Tigers in midseason, Pierotti took over the coaching duties with middling success. The 5'10" 204-pound lineman played mostly at center throughout his career. He played for New York in 1921 and then for Milwaukee and Racine from 1922 to 1924.

In the meantime, Al finally earned his degree from Washington & Lee and then went on to Harvard Law School. When Red Grange's American Football League put a franchise in Boston, Pierotti returned to pro football in 1926. He came back to the NFL the following season with the nearby Providence Steam Roller, and then finished his football career with Boston's first NFL team, the Bulldogs, in 1929. The muscular Pierotti earned some more sports paychecks from professional wrestling in the 1930s, but eventually retired to become a high school teacher and coach in Massachusetts. He died at the age of 68.

POLLARD, FREDERICK D. (FRITZ) 1/27/1894–5/11/1986. Bates, Northwestern, Harvard and Brown under Edward N. Robinson. Played HB/QB for the Akron Pros, Milwaukee Badgers and Hammond Pros from 1920 to 1923 and 1925–1926. *Hall of Fame Players:* None. *Record:* **Hall of Fame Player; Player-Coach** (Co-Coach with Elge Tobin, 1921).

The slight 5' 9" 165-pound Pollard left a very long shadow in football history. A speedy, elusive tailback, the Chicago native was one of the best players of his era and the first black NFL coach. Fritz was a high school track champion as well as football star and enrolled at Brown University where he was a two-time All-American leading the Bears to the 1916 Rose Bowl as a freshman. He also spent very brief periods with Bates, Northwestern, Harvard and Dartmouth that year. While in Rhode Island, he coached the backfield for the independent Providence Steam Roller on the side. Pollard was declared ineligible for football in 1918 because he had let his grades slip and went into the Army. During the war, he was stationed near Philadelphia and coached the football team at Lincoln University, an historically black college.

Frank Nied and Art Ranney then signed Fritz for the Akron franchise in the newly formed APFA in 1920. Elge Tobin was the coach, but years later, Pollard claimed to the *New York Times* that, "When I came they were still using some old plays. So I said why don't we try some of the stuff we had been doing at Brown. The owner, Frank Nied, told everybody that if they didn't want to listen to me, they could leave right then." While Tobin is listed as the sole coach in the Pros championship season of 1920, he and Pollard are listed as co-coaches in 1921. Akron was not a hospitable place for Fritz, though. He had to get dressed for games at Nied's cigar store and get driven to the field where he was booed and called names by his own fans. The Pros lost three of their last four games in 1921, and the disgruntled owners released Pollard who signed on with the new Milwaukee Badgers franchise.

Milwaukee was close to his Chicago home and enabled Fritz to start his own Chicago brokerage firm. Budge Garrett is listed as the Badgers coach, but Pollard claimed that he was Garrett's co-coach. After Garrett broke his leg in mid-season, though, management brought in Jimmy Conzelman as the new coach for the last three games of 1922. Pollard signed with Hammond in 1923 and later maintained he was the team's coach from 1923 to 1925. At that same time, Fritz was

Pierotti, Albert F. (Al)									
Year	Team	Games	Wins	Losses	Ties	%	Rank	Points	Allowed
1920	Cleveland Tigers	5	2	2	1	.500	10	28	32
1 year		5	2	2	1	.500		28	32

Pollard, Frederick D. (Fritz)									
Year	Team	Games	Wins	Losses	Ties	%	Rank	Points	Allowed
1921	Akron Pros	12	8	3	1	.727	3	148	31
1925	Hammond Pros	1	0	1	0	.000	14	0	14
2 years		13	8	4	1	.667		148	45

coaching Wendell Phillips High School in Chicago and playing for the independent Gilberton Cadamounts in the Pennsylvania coal regions through 1924. Wally Hess is given credit as the Hammond coach in 1923 and 1924, although Pollard was undoubtedly involved to some extent. Pollard is listed as the team's coach for one game in 1925, before he moved on to play for his old friend Pierce Johnson, who owned the Providence Steam Roller, new to the NFL in 1925. Fritz finished 1925 back with Akron and then played one last season in the Rubber City.

Pollard pursued a number of interests after the NFL. He owned a brokerage firm, a black newspaper, a black movie studio and also worked as a theatrical agent and tax consultant. In addition he organized two independent all-black football teams the Chicago Black Hawks from 1929 to 1932 and the Harlem Brown Bombers from 1935 to 1938. Both teams featured Joe Lillard and several other prominent African American players not permitted to play in the NFL at the time. Concurrently, Pollard's son Fritz Jr. won a bronze medal in the 1936 "Jesse Owens" Olympics. Some of the business ventures went belly up, and Pollard's first marriage fell apart, but he lived to be 92 and eventually began to receive some belated notoriety for his truly significant accomplishments before he died. Still, he was not elected to the Hall of Fame until 2005, 19 years after his death.

POTTEIGER, WILLIAM E. (EARL OR DUTCH OR POTTY) 2/11/1893–4/7/1959. Ursinus and Albright. Played HB for the Buffalo All-Americans, Chicago Cardinals, Milwaukee Badgers, Kenosha Maroons and New York Giants from 1920 to 1922 and 1924–1928. *Hall of Fame Players:* Ray Flaherty, Joe Guyon, Pete Henry and Cal Hubbard. *Record:* **Player-Coach** (Co-Coach with Bo Hanley, 1924); NFL Championship 1927.

This 5'7" 170-pound two-sport star was feisty and quick with his fists. As a minor league baseball player in 1913–1917, 1919 and 1926–1927, a minor league baseball manager in 1926, 1927 and 1932 and also as a semipro player-manager throughout the 1920s, Potteiger got into frequent scraps. Notably, he beat up a teammate and his team owner in 1919, punched out an opposing pitcher in 1923 and slugged an umpire in 1924. In fact, a fight derailed the best chance for the speedy centerfielder to reach the major

leagues. In 1915, his contract was sold to the Philadelphia A's, but Earl could not play because his arm became infected from being bitten during an on-field fracas while playing semipro football.

Potteiger played football for the independent Conshohocken Athletic Club and the Union Club of Phoenixville from 1914 until joining the APFA's Buffalo All-Americans in 1920. Earl spent most of the next decade playing for six NFL teams. He only appeared in 21 games during that time and started just five, but found a home in New York. He joined the Giants in their first season, 1925, and was named coach in 1927. Potteiger had been a player-co-coach with Bo Hanley in Kenosha in 1924, and the Maroons were outscored by over 100 points. The 1927 Giants proved to be the opposite of that experience. Featuring four future Hall of Fame players, they were a powerful team that allowed just 20 points in a 13-game season and won the NFL championship. Earl did not have much time to celebrate, though; a series of injuries derailed the Giants in their title defense during 1928. Losing a ton of money, the Maras bought the Detroit franchise to bring in drawing card and star passer Benny Friedman. Friedman was accompanied by his Detroit coach Leroy Andrews, so Potteiger's NFL career abruptly ended.

In later life, Earl worked in speakeasies and roadhouses and was arrested for transporting a truckload of beer during Prohibition. He went on to manage a garage, work in a factory and labor in road construction before opening a tavern in his hometown of Pottstown in 1949. He was married three times and allegedly also fathered an illegitimate child.

RAUCH, RICHARD H. (DICK) 7/15/1893–10/9/1970. Penn State under Hugo Bezdek. Played C/G/T for the Pottsville Maroons, New York Yankees and Boston Bulldogs in 1925, 1928 and 1929. *Hall of Fame Players:* Red Badgro, Pete Henry and Mike Michalske. *Record:* **Player-Coach.**

Dick Rauch posthumously received some notice in recent years with the publication of David Fleming's book, *Breaker Boys*, on the disputed 1925 NFL championship awarded to the Cardinals over Rauch's Pottsville Maroons. Rauch is celebrated in the book as an innovative coach with wide ranging interests from poetry to ornithology. The Harrisburg, Pennsylvania native played on the line at Penn State both

Potteiger, William E. (Earl or Dutch or Potty)									
Year	*Team*	*Games*	*Wins*	*Losses*	*Ties*	*%*	*Rank*	*Points*	*Allowed*
1924	Kenosha Maroons	5	0	4	1	.000	16	12	117
1927	New York Giants	13	11	1	1	.917	1	197	20
1928	New York Giants	13	4	7	2	.364	6	79	136
3 years		31	15	12	4	.556		288	273

before and after World War I and then was hired as a Nittany Lion assistant coach in 1921. Dick moved on to a similar position at Colgate in 1923.

In 1924, Rauch signed to play and coach for the independent coal region team in Pottsville. Dick drove them to the Anthracite League championship that year, and they joined the NFL in 1925.

Fleming makes the case that Rauch insisted that all the players live together in town and attend daily practice. He stressed pre-game scouting, was a proponent of the pass (particularly the screen pass), ran a double wing offense and regularly substituted for his players to negate injury and keep them fresh. Rauch emphasized the importance of speed, deception and execution as opposed to just pure physical power. The Maroons dressed 15 players per game, but had another 10 at practice, in essence an early taxi squad. One advantage the team had was that they often got to play teams that had just played the Frankford Yellow Jackets the day before since Philadelphia Blue Laws prevented Frankford from playing on Sundays. Pottsville went 5–1 in day-after games in 1925. The Maroons finished the season with the league's best record and had beaten the Cardinals in Chicago late in the season, but were not awarded the championship because they were suspended from the league for playing an unauthorized game in Frankford's territory in December. The controversy flared up again in 1963, 1978 and in 2007, but each time the NFL's original ruling was reaffirmed.

Pottsville won another 10 games in 1926, but slipped the next year, and Rauch moved on to coach the New York Yankees in 1928 with little success. Dick's final NFL coaching assignment came in 1929 when the Pottsville franchise was sold and moved to Boston. Rauch coached the Bulldogs in their only season before leaving football. According to Fleming, he became a nationally recognized government ornithologist.

ROBB, HARRY D. 5/11/1897–12/1971. Columbia under Bob Folwell and Penn State under Hugo Bezdek. Played QB for the Canton Bulldogs from 1921 to 1923 and from 1925 to 1926. *Hall of Fame Players:* Pete Henry. *Record:* **Player-Coach** (Co-Coach with Pete Henry, 1926).

The highly respected Harry Robb was elected captain of the football squads at both Columbia and Penn State. His college career from 1916 to 1919 was wrapped around his service during World War I when he was commissioned a lieutenant and transferred to Columbia for 1918. The Pitcairn, Pennsylvania native finished his college years at Penn State and then coached Catholic University in Washington, DC in 1920. Harry began his professional career in 1921 with Canton and spent his entire five-years in the NFL with the Bulldogs. The signal caller won All Pro honors in both 1922 and 1923 while the Bulldogs were winning back-to-back championships. When the team was purchased and moved to Cleveland in 1924, Robb signed with his former Penn State teammate Dick Rauch who was coaching the independent Pottsville Maroons in 1924. The following year, Pottsville moved up to the NFL, but Harry returned to Canton as player-coach for the reinstated Bulldogs. However, the new Bulldogs were a poor team, and Robb had little success coaching them for two seasons.

Robb worked for the Timken Roller Bearing Company of Pittsburgh for 39 years, working up from grinder to Division Sales Manager. He also spent several seasons as a college and NFL official. In fact, he worked the NFL title games in 1940, 1945 and 1947 as an umpire. Suffering in poor health, Harry ended his own life with a shotgun blast to the chest at age 74.

ROBINSON, EDWARD N. (EDDIE OR COACH ROBBIE) 10/15/1873–3/10/1945. Brown under Wallace Moyle. Did not play professionally. *Hall of Fame Players:* None.

Rauch, Richard H. (Dick)									
Year	Team	Games	Wins	Losses	Ties	%	Rank	Points	Allowed
1925	Pottsville Maroons	12	10	2	0	.833	2	270	45
1926	Pottsville Maroons	14	10	2	2	.833	3	155	29
1927	Pottsville Maroons	13	5	8	0	.385	8	80	163
1928	New York Yankees	13	4	8	1	.333	7	103	179
1929	Boston Bulldogs	8	4	4	0	.500	4	98	73
5 years		60	33	24	3	.579		706	489

Robb, Harry D.									
Year	Team	Games	Wins	Losses	Ties	%	Rank	Points	Allowed
1925	Canton Bulldogs	8	4	4	0	.500	11	50	73
1926	Canton Bulldogs	10	1	9	0	.100	20	46	161
2 years		18	5	13	0	.278		96	234

Sometimes called the "father of Brown football," Eddie Robinson was similar to Walter Camp at Yale in that regard. Indeed, Robinson was selected by Camp as a third team All-American while playing halfback for Brown in 1895. The following year, the Lynn, Massachusetts native began his coaching career that would span over a quarter of a century with a two-year spell at Nebraska. In 1898, Robinson returned to Brown for his first of three stints at his alma mater. Eddie coached there from 1898 to 1901, 1904–1907 and 1910–1925. He also spent 1902 coaching Maine. His overall coaching record was 157–88–13, with a 140–82–12 tally at Brown. Robinson was a soft-spoken and friendly man who eschewed pep talks but was beloved by his players. Perhaps his most famous player was Fritz Pollard who led Brown to the 1916 Rose Bowl. After 1925, Brown's third consecutive four-loss season, Eddie was "not reengaged" as coach by the Faculty Committee on Student Organization. Six years later, the Providence Steam Roller engaged the 58-year-old local legend as the team's head coach in what would prove to be their last year in the NFL. Robinson died of pneumonia in 1945 at the age of 73; he was elected to the College Football Hall of Fame in 1955.

ROGERS, CHARLES S. (CHARLEY) 1903–6/26/1986. Pennsylvania under Lou Young. Played TB for the Frankford Yellow Jackets from 1927 to 1929. *Hall of Fame Players:* Link Lyman. *Record:* **Interim Player-Co-Coach** (with Russ Daugherty, Ed Weir and Swede Youngstrom).

At just 5'10" and 167-pounds, Charley Rogers was a speedy open-field runner who played in the shadow of Red Grange. Rogers starred at the University of Pennsylvania where his backfield coach was Bert Bell. In the 1925 showdown between powerhouses Illinois and Penn, Grange ran wild and led the Illini to a 24–2 victory, while Rogers was stuck in the mud. He secretly got married to a local sportswriter, Helen Morton, before the 1926 season and gained 1,100 yards for the Quakers. That year, Charley tried to form a team of college All-Americans to barnstorm professionally just as Grange did the year before, but ran into too many obstacles and dropped the idea. Rogers left Penn and turned pro in 1927 anyway, signing with the local Frankford Yellow Jackets.

Charley led the team in rushing as a rookie and was part of the committee of player coaches that took over after Charlie Moran resigned as coach in midseason. Swede Youngstrom had been line coach and was initially in charge during the transition. Ed Weir continued as head coach in 1928. Rogers finished second on the team in rushing that year, and played little in 1929. He was hired as an assistant football coach and track coach at the University of Delaware in 1930 and became head coach the following season. Charley had a three-year record with the Blue Hens of 12–9–4. He died at the age of 83.

ROSE, WALTER S. (TAM) 12/5/1888–10/2/1961. Syracuse under Buck O'Neill. Played HB for the Tonawanda Kardex in 1921. *Hall of Fame Players:* None. *Record:* **Player-Coach**.

Aside from his college years, Tam Rose spent his entire life in Tonawanda, New York. The 5'11" 170-pound halfback majored in Agriculture at Syracuse and was the three-time captain of the Orange football team from 1915 to 1916. Rose founded the local independent Tonawanda Kardex — named after the area office supplies company, American Kardex — in 1916 and was their player-coach for the team's entire six-year existence. Tonawanda joined the NFL in 1921, but played just one league game, a 45–0 loss to the mediocre Rochester Jeffersons. That one-game 45–0 differential tied Rose with Muncie's Ken Huffine for

Robinson, Edward N. (Eddie or Coach Robbie)									
Year	*Team*	*Games*	*Wins*	*Losses*	*Ties*	*%*	*Rank*	*Points*	*Allowed*
1931	Providence Steam Roller	11	4	4	3	.500	6	78	127
1 year		11	4	4	3	.500		78	127

Rogers, Charles S. (Charley)									
Year	*Team*	*Games*	*Wins*	*Losses*	*Ties*	*%*	*Rank*	*Points*	*Allowed*
1927	Frankford Yellow Jackets	10	4	4	2	.500	7	65	86
1 year		10	4	4	2	.500		65	86

Rose, Walter S. (Tam)									
Year	*Team*	*Games*	*Wins*	*Losses*	*Ties*	*%*	*Rank*	*Points*	*Allowed*
1921	Tonawanda Kardex	1	0	1	0	.000	18	0	45
1 year		1	0	1	0	.000		0	45

the worst average spread for any NFL coach in history. The team folded that year. Rose died in Tonawanda forty years later.

Ruetz, George G. (Babe) 9/23/1893–5/24/1927. No college. Did not play in the NFL. *Hall of Fame Players:* None.

Representing the local American Legion post, 285-pound George Ruetz traveled to Canton, Ohio in 1922 and paid the franchise fee for the new Racine Legion team. Racine's Ruetz had played football throughout the area over the past decade and ran the team on and off the field. He brought in star players like Hank Gillo and Shorty Barr, and the Legion performed decently on the field for three years, but could not survive financially. Nine years ahead of his time, Ruetz proposed in 1924 that the league be divided into East and West conferences that would meet annually in a championship game, but his idea was ignored. Racine dropped out of the NFL in 1925 and the franchise was sold to outside investors who returned the franchise to the NFL in 1926, but without Ruetz.

George ran a grocery store in Racine and had two sons who went on to play pro football. His son Howard played tackle for the Packers from 1951 to 1953. His son Joe went to Notre Dame and played guard for the Chicago Rockets of the AAFC in 1946 and 1948. Joe would later go on to be athletic director at Stanford and hire Bill Walsh as the Cardinal's coach. George did not see either son play, though; he died at age 33 in 1927.

Sachs, Leonard D. (Lenny) 8/7/1897–10/27/1942. American College of Physical Education (Depaul). Played E for the Chicago Cardinals, Milwaukee Badgers, Hammond Pros and Louisville Colonels from 1920 to 1926. *Hall of Fame Players:* None.

Lenny Sachs was an institution in his hometown of Chicago for basketball and was well known for his football exploits as well. Lenny did not enroll in college till after serving in the Navy during the World War I. In his college years, though, Sachs played end for the Cardinals from 1920 to 1922 while also coaching high school basketball. The following year, the 5'8" 176-pound Sachs graduated college, played for the Milwaukee Badgers and began coaching basketball at Loyola-Chicago. Sachs' football career wound down, with him splitting 1924 between Milwaukee and Hammond and 1925 between Hammond and the Cardinals. In 1926, Chicago investors bought the Louisville franchise and tried running it as a traveling team out of Chicago with Sachs as coach. After being outscored 108–0, the team folded, and Sachs devoted himself to the hardwood. Lenny coached at Loyola for 19 years and amassed a 224–129 record with a fast-break offense and a 2–2–1 zone defense. In 1935, he earned a graduate degree from Loyola and became the school's athletic director. The ever-busy Sachs moonlighted as football coach at the all-black Wendell Phillips High School beginning in the late 1930s and died from a heart attack on school grounds at the age of 44 in 1942. He was survived by a wife and small daughter.

Salata, Andrew J. (Andy) 9/30/1905–7/22/1983. Pittsburgh under Jock Sutherland. Played G for the Orange Tornadoes and the Newark Tornadoes from 1929 to 1930. *Hall of Fame Players:* None. *Record:* **Interim Player-Coach**

Andy Salata starred as a "watch charm" guard for

Ruetz, George G. (Babe)

Year	Team	Games	Wins	Losses	Ties	%	Rank	Points	Allowed
1922	Racine Legion	11	6	4	1	.600	6	122	56
1923	Racine Legion	10	4	4	2	.500	10	86	76
1924	Racine Legion	10	4	3	3	.571	7	69	47
3 years		31	14	11	6	.560		277	179

Sachs, Leonard D. (Lenny)

Year	Team	Games	Wins	Losses	Ties	%	Rank	Points	Allowed
1926	Louisville Colonels	4	0	4	0	.000	21	0	108
1 year		4	0	4	0	.000		0	108

Salata, Andrew J. (Andy)

Year	Team	Games	Wins	Losses	Ties	%	Rank	Points	Allowed
1930	Newark Tornadoes	3	0	3	0	.000	11	7	54
1 year		3	0	3	0	.000		7	54

Jock Sutherland at Pitt where he played in the 1928 Rose Bowl. The 5'10" 188-pound Kingston, Pennsylvania native signed with the Orange Tornadoes and accompanied the team when it moved to Newark in 1930. As one of the few holdovers, Salata was named line coach under Al McGall in 1930. When McGall was fired two games into the season and replaced by Jack Fish, Salata continued as guard and line coach. When Fish was fired seven games later, Salata took over for the last three games of Newark's NFL tenure, all losses. Andy retired from football and opened a dental practice.

SCANLON, DEWEY 8/16/1899–9/24/1944. Valparaiso under Earl Goheen and William Shadoan. Played BB for the Duluth Eskimos in 1926. *Hall of Fame Players:* Walt Kiesling, Johnny Blood McNally and Ernie Nevers. *Record:* **Player-Coach** (for one game in 1926) and **Owner-Coach.**

Duluth-native Dewey Scanlon played quarterback around town and at Valparaiso University for several years. In the early 1920s, Scanlon got together with M.C. Gebert from the Duluth-Kelley Hardware Store to form the semipro Duluth Kelleys football team. The two obtained an NFL franchise in 1923 and brought in Bears' star Joey Sternaman to coach the team and play quarterback. Gebert dropped out at the end of the season, so Scanlon bought the team as a cooperative with his players in 1924. Sternaman left the team, and Scanlon assumed the coaching duties for the next three years. In 1926, Scanlon and partner Ole Haugsrud bought the team back for $1. Haugsrud signed his former high school teammate Ernie Nevers to a personal contract out of Stanford, and the newly christened Duluth Eskimos not only played 14 NFL games but an additional 15 in a postseason barnstorming tour. Dewey himself appeared in one game, his only NFL playing time. Since the team was structured around Nevers, Scanlon installed the double wing offense of Stanford coach Pop Warner.

Nevers took over as coach in 1927, but the team dropped out of the league in 1928. Haugsrud and Scanlon sold the franchise to Eddie Simandi of Orange, NJ for $2,000 in 1929. Many of the players, though, including Nevers had been signed to personal contracts to Haugsrud. When Ole and Dewey were hired by the new Cardinals' owner David Jones to run the 1929 Cardinals, Nevers and Walt Kiesling, among others, came along. Scanlon coached the team for just one season before being replaced by Nevers again. He later worked at a local shipyard. He died at 45 from a fall down the front stairs at his sister's home.

SCOTT, RALPH V. 9/26/1894–8/15/1936. Wisconsin under John R. Richards. Played T/G for the Chicago Staleys, Chicago Bears and the New York Yankees from 1921 to 1925 and 1927. *Hall of Fame Players:* Red Badgro, Red Grange and Mike Michalske. *Record:* **Player-Coach.**

The stocky 6'2" 235-pound Scott was a Westerner who spent some time as a ranch hand in Montana. Born in Dewey, Wisconsin, he was an All-American for the Badgers and served in World War I from 1917 to 1919. In the war, Scott was wounded in the foot and also gassed on the battlefield. Ralph returned to Wisconsin in 1920 and then turned pro with the Chicago Staleys in 1921. He spent an anonymous five seasons on George Halas' line, but when Red Grange and his agent C.C. Pyle blew into town in November 1925, Ralph's life changed.

In 1926, Scott, Pyle, Grange and a friend rented a 10-room house in Hollywood while Grange made a movie and Pyle and Grange planned out their new American Football League for the fall. Grange recounted playing a cruel practical joke on the innocent Scott by persuading him that 5,000 students at his alma mater had signed a petition demanding that Scott be named coach. Grange and his pals had Scott so convinced that Ralph was designing plays for the Badgers and talking about how much salary to request. In his autobiography, Grange dimly concluded, "Scott usually had a good sense of humor, but he was crushed

Scanlon, Dewey

Year	Team	Games	Wins	Losses	Ties	%	Rank	Points	Allowed
1924	Duluth Kelleys	6	5	1	0	.833	4	56	16
1925	Duluth Kelleys	3	0	3	0	.000	16	6	25
1926	Duluth Eskimos	14	6	5	3	.545	8	113	81
1929	Chicago Cardinals	13	6	6	1	.500	4	154	83
4 years		36	17	15	4	.531		329	205

Scott, Ralph V.

Year	Team	Games	Wins	Losses	Ties	%	Rank	Points	Allowed
1927	New York Yankees	16	7	8	1	.467	6	142	174
1 year		16	7	8	1	.467		142	174

in this instance." Although Pyle first tried to sign Bear tackle Ed Healey as coach of Grange's New York Yankees, Healey found Pyle too sleazy. Healey turned him down and pleaded with the naïve Scott to do so, too. However, Ralph took the job and led the Yankees to a 10–5 record in the AFL and then remained coach when the team switched to the NFL in 1927. Still, many considered Grange the team's unofficial coach that the players looked to for substitutions and key play calls. In 1928, Scott's football career was over, but he was chasing after Pyle, having to sue the agent for nearly $5,000 in back pay while Pyle was sponsoring a much ballyhooed, disastrous cross-country race. Eventually, Scott's health declined. After having a leg amputated, a depressed Scott asphyxiated himself in a car in Billings, Montana at the age of 41.

SIES, DALE H. (HERB) 1/2/1893–10/17/1954. Pittsburgh under Pop Warner. Played G for the Cleveland Tigers, Dayton Triangles and Rock Island Independents from 1920 to 1924. *Hall of Fame Players:* None. *Record:* **Player-Coach**

Herb Sies teamed with the legendary Jock Sutherland as the All-American guard tandem of Pop Warner's 1917 Pittsburgh Panthers. Pitt was undefeated that season with five shutouts, but lost out on the national championship to John Heisman's Georgia Tech squad. Pitt won the national title in 1915, 1916 and 1918, but the 1917 team, known as the "Fighting Dentists" because most of the team was in dental school, finished second in the polls. Sies also played for the Massillon Tigers that year. The Ames, Iowa native went into the Army during World War I and then into professional football with Cleveland in 1920. The 6'1" 203-pound Sies played on three teams in the NFL over his five-year career. He succeeded Jimmy

Conzelman as player-coach of Rock Island in 1923, the same year Dale was named a second team All Pro. After one more season in the league, Sies retired. Dale went on to become a Division Manager for Pennzoil in Chicago. He died from a heart attack at the age of 61.

STERNAMAN, EDWARD C. (DUTCH) 2/9/1895–2/1/1973. Illinois under Bob Zuppke. Played QB for the Chicago Bears from 1920 to 1927. *Hall of Fame Players:* Guy Chamberlin, Jimmy Conzelman, Paddy Driscoll, Red Grange, Ed Healey, Link Lyman and George Trafton. *Record:* **Player-Co-Coach** (with George Halas); NFL championship 1921.

The axiom that history is written by the victors is certainly true of the Chicago Bears. It is clear that George Halas formed the Decatur Staleys in 1920 and then moved to Chicago with $5,000 in seed money from A. E. Staley of the Staley Starch Company to maintain the Chicago Staleys in 1921. However, when the Staleys became the Bears in 1922, Springfield's Dutch Sternaman put up half the money with Halas to be a full partner. Sternaman was co-founder, co-owner and co-coach, but the only mention one finds of Dutch in the Bears media guide or in the standard football encyclopedias is as a Bears' player. Sternaman sold out to Halas in 1931 and was erased from their team history.

Dutch and Halas both played football for Bob Zuppke at Illinois. Sternaman was in Champaign from 1916 to 1919 and was team captain as a senior. By that time, Halas was playing baseball for the Yankees and football for the Hammond Pros. In assembling the Staleys, Halas naturally drew heavily from his alma mater for players, including Sternaman. Two years later when Halas needed money to establish the Bears

Sies, Dale H. (Herb)									
Year	*Team*	*Games*	*Wins*	*Losses*	*Ties*	*%*	*Rank*	*Points*	*Allowed*
1923	Rock Island Independents	8	2	3	3	.400	12	84	62
1 year		8	2	3	3	.400		84	62

Sternaman, Edward C. (Dutch)									
Year	*Team*	*Games*	*Wins*	*Losses*	*Ties*	*%*	*Rank*	*Points*	*Allowed*
1920	Decatur Staleys	13	10	1	2	.846	2	164	21
1921	Decatur Staleys	11	9	1	1	.864	1	128	53
1922	Chicago Bears	12	9	3	0	.750	2	122	44
1923	Chicago Bears	12	9	2	1	.792	2	123	35
1924	Chicago Bears	11	6	1	4	.727	2	136	55
1925	Chicago Bears	17	9	5	3	.618	7	158	96
1926	Chicago Bears	16	12	1	3	.844	2	216	63
1927	Chicago Bears	14	9	3	2	.714	3	149	98
1928	Chicago Bears	13	7	5	1	.577	5	182	85
1929	Chicago Bears	15	4	9	2	.333	9	119	227
10 Years		124	84	31	19	.754		1497	777

in 1922, he asked Sternaman who accepted. Papers were signed, money was pooled and the Chicago Bears were formed. Both men played for the team and coached it; both signed the players' paychecks each week. Dutch's brother Joey told Richard Whittingham for *What a Game They Played*, "My brother and Halas shared everything then. They were co-owners, co-coaches, they both played."

Joey was one of the main reasons for the split between the two men. Joey was the Bears' quarterback in 1922, 1924 and 1925. In 1926 when Red Grange formed his rival American Football League, Joey left the Bears and formed his own AFL team, the Chicago Bulls. Halas not only saw Joey's challenge on the field as a threat, but also suspected divided loyalties in Dutch, especially in some scheduling issues. In his autobiography, Halas wrote, "My biggest problem was personal. My relationship with Dutch Sternaman was worsening. Mutual trust had almost vanished. The split hurt the team. I developed plays. Dutch would drill them into the backfield, I into the line. I was steadily moving toward an open game with a sixty-forty division between running and passing. Sternaman wanted a tight game. The consequence was that I would tell the team to do this and Sternaman would tell them to do that."

That situation continued for a couple more years. By the end of 1929, Halas wrote, "The time had come for Dutch and me to stop coaching, or, more accurately, miscoaching. We had to put coaching under one mind." The two agreed to bring in Ralph Jones who had been their freshman football coach at Illinois as coach. Meanwhile, some investments turned bad for Dutch, and he needed cash. He offered Halas the opportunity to buy him out in 1931. Halas had to borrow money from several friends to raise the cash, but by July 1932, the team was all his. Dutch became a non-person in Bears history. After selling out to Halas, Sternaman operated his gas station business and eventually developed his own petroleum products firm. At one point, he also served as the business manager of the Chicago Black Hawks hockey team. He passed away on his brother Joey's birthday in 1973 at the age of 77.

STERNAMAN, JOSEPH T. (JOEY) 2/1/1900–3/10/1988. Illinois under Bob Zuppke. Played QB for the Chicago Bears and Duluth Kelleys from 1922 to 1925 and 1927–1930. *Hall of Fame Players:* None. *Record:* **Player-Coach.**

Springfield's Joey Sternaman followed his brother to Illinois and to the Bears, but he had a mind of his own and didn't follow his brother everywhere. Joey was proud, feisty and smart, an ideal signal caller. The 5'6" 152-pound quarterback, according to one sportswriter, was a cross between "a bantam rooster and a pit bulldog." He played three years at Illinois, but then was kicked off the team in 1921 for moonlighting in an All Star game and getting paid. In 1922, Joey joined the Bears, where he played with his brother Dutch and George Halas, co-owners of the team. A year later, Joey jumped on an offer to play and coach the brand new Duluth Kelleys. He spent the season in Minnesota perfecting the quarterback option and bootleg plays. Returning to Chicago in 1924, he was part of the Bears' all–Illinois starting backfield of the Sternaman brothers, Laurie Walquist and Oscar Knop. That season, Joey and Dutch became the first brothers in NFL history to score in the same game and to play quarterback in the same season. Joey even led the league in scoring with 75 points in 1924.

After another successful season as the Bear quarterback, Sternaman took another gamble in 1926 by joining in with his Bear teammate Red Grange's new American Football League. This time Joey was not only player and coach, but owner as well. His new team was the Chicago Bulls who competed directly with his brother's team and the Cardinals. Joey took an aggressive approach and outbid the defending champion Cardinals for the lease to Comiskey Park. He also made a serious run at signing their star player Paddy Driscoll, but Halas and brother Dutch managed to secure Paddy's services from the struggling Cardinals. The Bulls finished a disappointing 5–6–3 in their only season. Joey emerged from the AFL broke and rejoined the Bears for a third go-round. He held the Bears' starting quarterback job for three more years, but in 1930 at the age of thirty, Joey lost his job to rookie Carl Brumbaugh under new coach Ralph Jones. Sternaman retired at the end of the year and began a business making cast iron incinerator pipe. It was reported in the *Chicago Tribune* that Joey rarely was invited to team reunions until he complained to Halas about it in 1979, and the two finally reconciled. Sternaman died at age 88, outlasting his brother by 15 years and Halas by five.

STINCHCOMB, GAYLORD R. (PETE) 6/24/1895–8/24/1973. Ohio State under John Wilce. Played QB/HB for the Chicago Staleys, Chicago Bears,

Sternaman, Joseph T. (Joey)									
Year	Team	Games	Wins	Losses	Ties	%	Rank	Points	Allowed
1923	Duluth Kelleys	7	4	3	0	.571	7	35	33
1 year		7	4	3	0	.571		35	33

Cleveland Indians and Columbus Tigers from 1921 to 1923 and the Louisville Colonels in 1926. *Hall of Fame Players:* None. *Record:* **Interim Player-Coach.**

Born in Sycamore, Ohio, Pete Stinchcomb's years at Ohio State were sandwiched around his 1918 service in the Navy during World War I. After the war, the 5' 8" 157-pound Stinchcomb returned to Columbus as the Buckeye quarterback. For his senior year of 1920, though, Pete moved to halfback to accommodate underclassman Hoge Workman, and the Workman-to-Stinchcomb combination led Ohio State to an undefeated season and a berth in the 1921 Rose Bowl, where they were beaten by Brick Muller's California Bears. Stinchcomb was an All-American on the gridiron but also played basketball and track for OSU and was the NCAA champion at the long jump in 1921. Later that year, he began his professional football career as a starting halfback on George Halas' league champion Staleys. He stayed in Chicago for two seasons, drawing some All Pro recognition both years. In 1923, Pete returned to Ohio as player-coach of the Columbus Tigers, but his glory days were over. He lost his starting job to Bob Rapp and was sold to Cleveland on November 14 to be delivered after the two teams played on the 18th. Stinchcomb appeared in one game for Cleveland and retired. He came back in 1926 to play for the Louisville Colonels that were actually a traveling team run out of Chicago. Then retiring for good, Pete went on to run the Linworth Homes company, a successful construction firm. He was elected to the College Football Hall of Fame in 1973 but passed away before the induction ceremonies.

STORCK, CARL (SCUMMY) 1/22/1887–3/13/1950. George Williams College. Did not play in the NFL. *Hall of Fame Players:* None. *Record:* **Owner-Coach.**

Chris Willis' recent biography of early NFL President Joe Carr is aptly entitled *The Man Who Built the NFL,* but also makes clear that Carr had help in building the league. Carr's able assistant throughout his 18-year tenure was Carl Storck, owner of the Dayton Triangles as well as Secretary, Treasurer, Vice President and, eventually, President of the NFL. Storck was a stout, 250-pound former lineman known for his jovial, friendly nature. After graduating college in 1917, he joined the hometown Triangles as assistant manager. When manager Mike Redelle went into the service in 1918, Carl filled his position. Two years later, he and Redelle bought the team, and Storck attended the APFA's organizing meetings. Carl was elected Secretary and Treasurer of the league in 1921 and took over as Triangles coach in 1922. As the league grew, though, Dayton became less and less able to compete with the larger cities. Storck's team won four games in 1922 and then just four more in his last four years as coach after stars Al Mahrt and Herb Sies left the team. In the last three years of the decade after Storck gave up coaching the team, the Triangles managed just one win. Carl sold the sinking franchise to Brooklyn investors in 1930 but continued to run the Dayton Wings minor league baseball team in the 1930s. All through that time, Carl went on with his unpaid league duties while working as a foreman in the Inspection and Packing department at National Cash Register and then as Assistant Works Manager of Delco Products of General Motors.

When Joe Carr died suddenly in 1939, Storck took over as acting president of the NFL. While he was generally liked by the team owners, they did not see Carl as a long-term solution at president. In 1940, they stripped away some of his control of game officials and offered the presidency to *Chicago Tribune* sports editor Arch Ward who turned them down. The next year, the owners rewrote the league's constitution to create the new, more powerful position of commissioner and offered that to Ward. Arch again demurred but instead recommended Notre Dame coach Elmer Layden, one of Rockne's legendary Four Horsemen.

On April 3, 1941, Storck announced he was leaving his sick bed after seven weeks of suffering from

Stinchcomb, Gaylord R. (Pete)									
Year	Team	Games	Wins	Losses	Ties	%	Rank	Points	Allowed
1923	Columbus Tigers	7	3	4	0	.429	8	82	35
1 year		7	3	4	0	.429		82	35

Storck, Carl (Scummy)									
Year	Team	Games	Wins	Losses	Ties	%	Rank	Points	Allowed
1922	Dayton Triangles	8	4	3	1	.571	7	80	62
1923	Dayton Triangles	8	1	6	1	.143	16	16	95
1924	Dayton Triangles	8	2	6	0	.250	13	45	148
1925	Dayton Triangles	8	0	7	1	.000	16	3	84
1926	Dayton Triangles	6	1	4	1	.200	16	15	82
5 years		38	8	26	4	.235		159	471

nervous exhaustion to fight the move at the league meetings. He told reporters, "For 15 years I worked for nothing. Two years ago when I became president, I didn't quit my job with General Motors because I was afraid something like this would happen." The next day, Storck surprised everyone by resigning for "the best interests of the league." He did not go quietly, though, telling the *Dayton Herald*, "I'll never take orders from a man I do not respect. I am convinced that Layden is not qualified to handle the job, due mostly to his lack of administrative experience in professional sports.... Layden was steamrolled into his job when George Halas, Chicago Bears' president, and Arch Ward, *Chicago Tribune* sports editor, saw an opportunity to put it across." All of which turned out to be true. Storck ultimately had a stroke and died in a nursing home in 1950 at the age of 57, but his family maintained he died from a broken heart from being betrayed by his colleagues in his life's work.

TALBOTT, NELSON S. (BUD) 6/10/1892–7/6/1952. Yale under Arthur Howe, Howard Jones and Frank Hinkey. Did not play in the NFL. *Hall of Fame Players:* None.

Born in Dayton, Ohio, Bud Talbott was a two-time All-American tackle at Yale. The 6'1" 190-pound Talbott was team captain in 1914 and then an assistant coach in 1915. In 1916, he helped form the Dayton Triangles back in his hometown. Bud joined the Army in 1917 and went on to serve his country in World War I, World War II and the Korean War, ultimately rising to the rank of Brigadier General. He returned to Dayton to coach the Triangles from 1919 to 1921, including their first two seasons in the APFA, before he resigned as a result of business pressures. Bud was president of his family's Talbott Corporation that manufactured everything from ice cream cones to steel. He also served as vice president of Maxon Construction and as a director for several large corporations, including TWA. Bud's brother, Harold E. Talbott, was Secretary of the Air Force under Eisenhower, and Bud's grandson, Strobe Talbott, was Deputy Secretary of State under Clinton.

TEBELL, GUSTAVE K. (GUS) 9/6/1897–5/28/1969. Wisconsin under John R. Richards. Played E for the Columbus Tigers from 1923 to 1924. *Hall of Fame Players:* None. *Record:* **Interim Player-Coach**.

At Wisconsin, Gus Tebell was a 5'10" 178-pound end who was named All-American in 1922. The St. Charles, Illinois native was also All Conference in basketball. Gus joined the Columbus Tigers in 1923 and added coaching duties for the last three games after player-coach Pete Stinchcomb was sold to Cleveland. Tebell earned some All Pro notice that rookie season, but played just one game for Columbus in 1924 before leaving to assist Buck Shaw in coaching North Carolina State. When Shaw left the following season, Tebell was named head coach. Gus spent five seasons in Raleigh coaching both football and basketball. He won a conference title in both sports, but his overall football coaching record was just 21–25–2. In 1930, the University of Virginia hired Tebell as its basketball coach and assistant football coach. In Charlottesville, Gus coached the basketball team from 1930 to 1951, the baseball team from 1931 to 1943 and from 1945 to 1955 and the football team from 1934 to 1936. He only achieved a 6–18–4 record in football, but went 240–190 in basketball. From 1951 to 1962, Tebell was the school's athletic director as well. Gus was not only popular on campus, but also in the town. He was elected twice as Charlottesville's Mayor in the 1940s and served on city council in the 1950s.

THORPE, JAMES F. (JIM) 5/28/1888–3/28/1953. Carlyle Indian Industrial School. Played TB for the Canton Bulldogs, Cleveland Indians, Oorang Indians, Rock Island Independents and New York Giants from 1920 to 1926 and the Chicago Cardinals in 1928. *Hall of Fame Players:* Joe Guyon and Pete Henry. *Record:* **Hall of Fame Player; Player-Coach**.

Widely acclaimed the greatest American athlete of the first half of the 20th century, the 6'1" 190-pound Thorpe excelled in football, track and baseball, and even played some professional basketball. He was raised on a Sac and Fox Indian Reservation in Oklahoma until he was sent away to school, first to the

Talbott, Nelson S. (Bud)									
Year	*Team*	*Games*	*Wins*	*Losses*	*Ties*	*%*	*Rank*	*Points*	*Allowed*
1920	Dayton Triangles	9	5	2	2	.714	6	150	54
1921	Dayton Triangles	9	4	4	1	.500	8	96	67
2 years		18	9	6	3	.600		246	121

Tebell, Gustave K. (Gus)									
Year	*Team*	*Games*	*Wins*	*Losses*	*Ties*	*%*	*Rank*	*Points*	*Allowed*
1923	Columbus Tigers	3	2	0	1	1.000	8	37	0
1 year		3	2	0	1	1.000		37	0

Haskell Indian Nations University in Kansas and then to the Carlisle Indian Industrial School in Pennsylvania. At Carlisle, he competed on both the track and football teams coached by Pop Warner from 1907 to 1912, while spending his summers playing minor league baseball. Jim was an All-American in football in 1908, 1911 and 1912 as well as a sensation in the 1912 Stockholm Olympics, where he won gold medals in both the decathlon and pentathlon. Part of sports folklore is that Sweden's King Gustav V congratulated Thorpe by intoning, "You, sir, are the greatest athlete in the world." To which Jim innocently replied, "Thanks, King."

In 1913, word got out that Thorpe had played professional baseball and thus had violated the genteel rules of amateurism propagated by the Olympics. As a result, Thorpe's medals were stripped from him. Jim never understood the reason or got over the disappointment from this bureaucratic imposition into athletics. At any rate, he turned professional with a vengeance in 1913, beginning a seven-year major league baseball career with the New York Giants. Playing with the Giants, Reds and Braves through 1919, Thorpe's mediocre .252 anticipated a similar future athlete. Like Bo Jackson, Thorpe had spectacular skills, but lacked the consistency to be a great baseball player. Football, Jim's favorite sport, was a different story.

Thorpe signed with the Canton in 1915 and played for the Bulldogs through their 1920 entry into the APFA. With his all-around rugged excellence on offense and defense, he led Canton to consensus championships in 1916, 1917 and 1919. As the most famous football personality in the nation, Jim was elected APFA President in 1920, although he was merely a figurehead and was replaced by able administrator Joe Carr in 1921. Now 33 and starting to slip as a player, Thorpe jumped to Cleveland as player-coach in 1921. Coming off a 3–5 season, he befriended a Larue, Ohio dog kennel owner named Walter Lingo. Lingo proposed that he sponsor an All-Indian NFL traveling team called the Oorang Indians to publicize his business and that Jim organize the team and be its player-coach. While the players had a great deal of alcohol-fueled fun off the field, they won just four games in two years. Thorpe was not much of a coach, and Oorang was more carnival than football, with the players doing tricks with the kennel's Airedales to entertain

fans at halftime. When Oorang folded, Jim joined Rock Island as a player only in 1924 and then signed with the fledgling New York Giants football team in 1925.

Thorpe continued playing for different non-league teams, including a Florida contingent that faced Red Grange's barnstorming Bears in 1926. Grange later wrote of the aging Thorpe in the *Saturday Evening Post*, "Jim was old, fat and slow, yet he could still hit hard." Thorpe played his last NFL game on Thanksgiving 1928 with the Chicago Cardinals in a 34–0 loss to the cross town Bears, but continued playing semipro football, baseball and basketball for a couple more years.

Once his athletic career ended, Thorpe struggled to survive, depending somewhat on playing bit parts in Hollywood movies, most often as an Indian in Westerns. His life story was glorified and airbrushed in a 1951 movie, *Jim Thorpe — All American*, that starred Burt Lancaster. Thorpe's personal life was marked by alcoholism, divorce and strained relations with his eight children until his death in 1953. His wife wanted Oklahoma to erect a memorial to house her husband's body, but was rebuffed, so she made a deal with a struggling Pennsylvania town to change its name to Jim Thorpe and receive his remains. Jim had never set foot in Mauch Chunk, Pennsylvania, but there he has rested since 1954. Thorpe's Olympic medals were posthumously reinstated in 1983, but his strange legacy continues even today as his children sue Jim Thorpe, Pennsylvania to have their father's remains returned to his native Oklahoma.

TOBIN, ELZA W. (ELGIE OR YEGG) 5/8/1886–9/4/1953. West Virginia under Clarence W. Russell and Penn State under Bill Hollenback. Played G/BB for the Akron Pros from 1920 to 1921. *Hall of Fame Players:* Fritz Pollard. *Record:* **Player-Coach** (Co-coach with Fritz Pollard, 1921); NFL Championship 1920.

Elgie Tobin first played college football in 1907 for West Virginia, and then didn't resurface until 1912 when he began a three-year run at Penn State. By 1914, Tobin was the Nittany Lion captain and led the team to a 4–0–1 start that culminated with a 13–13 tie of mighty Harvard. When the team returned to State College, Pennsylvania, they were greeted by an overly fueled bonfire in their honor. Tobin was given the

Thorpe, James F. (Jim)								
Year	Team	Games	Wins	Losses	Ties	%	Rank	Points	Allowed
1920	Canton Bulldogs	13	7	4	2	.636	8	208	57
1921	Cleveland Indians	8	3	5	0	.375	11	95	58
1922	Oorang Indians	9	3	6	0	.333	11	69	190
1923	Oorang Indians	11	1	10	0	.091	18	50	157
4 years		41	14	25	2	.359		422	462

torch to light the fire, but was blown off his feet in an explosion and severely burned in igniting it. Tobin missed most of the rest of the year, and the Lions lost three of their last four.

For the next five years, Tobin played for the independent Youngstown Patricians while coaching the line for West Virginia. In 1920, he was signed by Frank Nied to be player-coach of the Akron Pros in the brand new APFA. Behind the spectacular play of Fritz Pollard, Tobin led the Pros to the first league championship that year. Years later, Pollard contended to the *New York Times*, "I was really the coach that year, but the book lists Elgie Tobin as coach. When I got there, they were using a lot of old-fashioned plays, and I showed them some of the plays we had used at Brown, like the unbalanced line and reverses and all that." Pollard's claim is buttressed by the fact that the two are listed as co-coaches the following season in which Akron finished third in the league. By 1922, though, both were gone from Akron. Tobin got involved with a group trying to get an NFL team for Youngstown, where he lived, but that came to nothing. He also was player-coach of the semipro Elco Sterlings near his hometown of Roscoe, Pennsylvania in the early 1920s. Throughout the 1920s, Tobin played, coached and officiated semipro football in the Youngstown area while working at Republic Iron and Steel and at a local gas station.

TOLLEFSON, RUSSELL I. (TOLLE) 9/27/1891–5/13/1962. Minnesota under Doc Williams. QB/T; did not play professionally. *Hall of Fame Players:* None.

Born in Minneapolis, Russell Tollefson played quarterback for the University of Minnesota in 1912 and 1913. Three years later, he served as player-coach

for the independent Minneapolis Marines and led them to an undefeated season in 1916. Tollefson left Minneapolis to coach Grinnell College in Iowa in 1917 and produced another undefeated season. Over the next two years, though, Grinnell dropped to a 2–6–1 record. Tolle" returned to coach the Marines in 1922. He did not have much luck in league games, but was undefeated outside the NFL that year. Tollefson quit coaching and became an attorney. He was disbarred in Minnesota in 1931 and later moved to California. He died in Glendale at the age of 70.

URSELLA, REUBEN J. (RUBE) 1/11/1890–2/1/1980. No College. Played B for the Rock Island Independents, Minneapolis Marines, Akron Indians, Hammond Pros from 1920 to 1921 and 1924–1926 and the Minneapolis Red Jackets in 1929. *Hall of Fame Players:* Ed Healey. *Record:* **Player-Coach.**

The University of Minnesota's football media guide lists Rube Ursella as one of the Golden Gophers who went on to play in the NFL, however, he is not listed as a letterman. Instead, Ursella began playing professional football with the independent Minneapolis Marines in his hometown at the age of 17 in 1907. Rube was a triple threat quarterback who spent a dozen seasons as the Marines' star signal caller before Walter Flanigan, the owner of the Rock Island Independents, lured him to Illinois in 1919 as player-coach. Ursella brought along several of his Minneapolis teammates and his offensive system to make Rock Island an instant power. In fact, Rube scored 99 points himself. When the APFA formed a year later, the Independents were a charter member with Rube still their player-coach. In 1921, Minneapolis joined the league, and Ursella went back to his hometown team. The

Tobin, Elza W. (Elgie or Yegg)

Year	Team	Games	Wins	Losses	Ties	%	Rank	Points	Allowed
1920	Akron Pros	11	8	0	3	1.000	1	151	7
1921	Akron Pros	12	8	3	1	.727	3	148	31
2 years		23	16	3	4	.842		299	38

Tollefson, Russell I. (Tolle)

Year	Team	Games	Wins	Losses	Ties	%	Rank	Points	Allowed
1922	Minneapolis Marines	4	1	3	0	.250	13	19	40
1 year		4	1	3	0	.250		19	40

Ursella, Reuben J. (Rube)

Year	Team	Games	Wins	Losses	Ties	%	Rank	Points	Allowed
1920	Rock Island Independents	9	6	2	1	.750	4	201	49
1921	Minneapolis Marines	4	1	3	0	.250	13	37	41
1925	Rock Island Independents	11	5	3	3	.625	8	99	58
3 years		24	12	8	4	.600		337	148

Marines were not what they once were, however, and Rube dropped out of the league in 1922. He returned to the NFL in Rock Island with the aging Jim Thorpe in 1924 and resumed his player-coach duties in 1925. After splitting the 1926 season between Hammond and Akron, Ursella played for a number of independent teams before ending his NFL career back in his hometown again as a 39-year-old sometime starter on the 1–9 Minneapolis Red Jackets. Rube's professional football career spanned over 20 years, and, along the way, he also played minor league baseball in the Northern League for several seasons. He lived to the age of 90.

WEAVER, JAMES R. (RED) 7/19/1897–11/23/1968. Centre under Charlie Moran. Played C for the Columbus Tigers in 1923. *Hall of Fame Players:* None.

Born in Garland, Texas, Red Weaver was childhood friends with Bo McMillin and accompanied him to Centre College in Kentucky, where the two lifted the little school to national prominence. Red was a two-time All-American at center from 1918 to 1920, snapping the ball to McMillin. The 5'10" 185-pound Weaver was also a noted kicker who booted 90 straight point-after-touchdowns in college. He graduated the year before McMillin engineered Centre's greatest triumph by beating Harvard and immediately became the coach at West Virginia Tech in 1921. Red played one season with Columbus in the NFL in 1923 and then coached the Tigers for the next two years after that. In 1926, Weaver jumped to Red Grange's AFL to play for the Cleveland Panthers, but finished the season trying to get back pay from the owners for himself and his teammates before the Panthers folded in November. Weaver's last major coaching job was with the University of Charleston in West Virginia from 1932 to 1933, but his squads won just one game in two years. Red died at the age of 71 in Mayfield, Kentucky.

WEIR, SAMUEL E. (ED) 3/14/1903–5/15/1991. Nebraska under Fred Dawson and Ernest Bearg. Played T/E for the Frankford Yellow Jackets from 1926 to 1928. *Hall of Fame Players:* Link Lyman. *Record:* **Player-Coach** (Interim co-coach with Russ Daugherty, Charley Rogers and Swede Youngstrom in 1927).

The 6' 190-pound Weir was strong, fast, powerful and clever. Born in Superior, Nebraska, he was a two-time All-American tackle at the University of Nebraska between 1923–1925 who is remembered as one of the first lineman to practice blitzing. Weir signed with Frankford, coached by Husker legend Guy Chamberlin, in 1926 and won a championship in his rookie year. Chamberlin left in some sort of management dispute and was replaced by Uncle Charley Moran in 1927, but the personable Moran resigned on November 5 with the defending champions' record at 2–5–1. Veteran Swede Youngstrom was put in charge of a committee of player-coaches including Weir and two rookie backs, Charley Rogers and Pug Daugherty. Youngstrom retired at the end of the 6–9–3 1927 season, and Ed was named player-coach for 1928.

Weir drove the Yellow Jackets to a second-place 11–3–2 record in 1928 that hinged on a showdown with Providence, the eventual champion, on November 17. Frankford was so upset by the calls of the game's umpire that the team lodged an official protest with league President Joe Carr over a questionable out-of-bounds ruling on a Frankford touchdown and over shortened quarters. The *New York Times* claimed it was the first such protest in NFL history. Nothing came of the protest, but if Frankford had beaten rather than tied the Steam Roller that day, the two teams would have had the same winning percentage at the end of the year — with Frankford having the advantage head-to-head. It was Ed Weir's lost championship.

In 1929, Ed was called back to Lincoln to work as an assistant coach on both the football and track teams. As a student, Weir had competed in the high hurdles in track as well. In 1939, Weir was named head coach of the track team. He coached track at Nebraska until 1955 and won 10 conference titles. At that point, the humble and effective Weir was named assistant athletic director and served in that capacity until 1968.

Weaver, James R. (Red)									
Year	Team	Games	Wins	Losses	Ties	%	Rank	Points	Allowed
1924	Columbus Tigers	8	4	4	0	.5	10	91	68
1925	Columbus Tigers	9	0	9	0	.000	16	28	124
2 years		17	4	13	0	.235		119	192

Weir, Samuel E. (Ed)									
Year	Team	Games	Wins	Losses	Ties	%	Rank	Points	Allowed
1927	Frankford Yellow Jackets	10	4	4	2	.500	7	65	86
1928	Frankford Yellow Jackets	16	11	3	2	.786	2	175	84
2 years		26	15	7	4	.682		240	170

When Nebraska dedicated a new track stadium in 1974, it was named Ed Weir Stadium, after one of the greatest of all Husker athletes. No less than Knute Rockne called Weir one of the greatest tackles he had ever seen when Weir was leading Nebraska to two wins in three years over Notre Dame's famed Four Horsemen backfield. Indeed, Ed was the first Nebraska football player elected to the College Football Hall of Fame in 1951.

WIGGS, HUBERT T. 9/29/1893–10/18/1977. Vanderbilt under Dan McGugin. Played FB for the Louisville Brecks from 1921 to 1923. *Hall of Fame Players:* None. *Record:* **Player-Coach.**

At Vanderbilt, the 5'8" 180-pound Hubert Wiggs started at fullback as a freshman in 1915 until a faculty committee declared him ineligible for his grades. Born in Tullahoma, Tennessee, he was back on the team in 1917 and 1919, but spent 1918 and part of 1919 on Paris Island as a drill instructor in the Marines during World War I. Wiggs appeared in seven of the nine league games Louisville played in three years; furthermore, he coached the team to its only NFL victory in 1922 over the execrable Evansville Crimson Giants that were about to fold in November. Hubert later worked as an accountant for the K & I Railroad. He died at the age of 86 in New Albany, Indiana, right across the Ohio River from Louisville

WORKMAN, HARRY H. (HOGE) 9/25/1899– 5/20/1972. Ohio State under John Wilce. Played TB for the Cleveland Bulldogs in 1924 and for the Cleveland Indians and New York Giants in 1931–1932. *Hall of Fame Players:* None. *Record:* **Player-Co-Coach** (with Al Cornsweet).

The November 26, 1920 Huntingdon (WV) High School alumni football game was dubbed the "Workman Day Celebration." Five Workman brothers took part including Hoge and Noel who played quarterback and end respectively on that year's Ohio State Buckeye team that would meet California in the 1921 Rose Bowl. That year, the 5'11" 170-pound Hoge was a freshman already noted for his passing not only to his brother Noel but also to All-American Pete Stinch-

comb. As a senior in 1923, Hoge was named All-American himself.

Workman also starred on the baseball diamond. However, after recording an 8.50 earned run average pitching for the Boston Red Sox in the summer of 1924, Workman joined the NFL's Cleveland Bulldogs that fall. He started all but one game at tailback for the league champions before retiring to become head football coach at Redlands University, a Baptist college in California. Workman stayed on the coast for just one year, though. When brother Noel gave up his coaching position at Simpson College in Iowa to coach Iowa State, Hoge resigned from Redlands to replace Noel at Simpson, telling reporters, "I'm leaving Redlands and this conference with the greatest regret, and I am simply going because the opportunity is greater and there is more money." He spent three years at Simpson before leaving to assist his brother at Iowa State in 1929, but the two brothers could manage just one win in two years. At the age of 32, Hoge resumed his NFL career after an eight-year gap in 1931; this time as player-co-coach with Al Cornsweet for Cleveland's latest doomed franchise. The 2–8 1931 Indians lasted just one season before folding. Workman joined the Giants in 1932, but was released after one game when New York acquired Bo Molenda from Green Bay. He died at age 72 in Florida.

WRAY, JAMES R. LUDLOW. (LUD) (SEE SECTION I)

WYCOFF, STEPHEN D. (DOUG) 9/16/1903– 10/27/1981. Georgia Tech under Bill Alexander. Played FB for the New York Giants, Staten Island Stapletons and Boston Redskins in 1927, 1929–1932 and 1934. *Hall of Fame Players:* Ken Strong. *Record:* **Player-Coach.**

Although Doug Wycoff was a southerner born in St. Louis, he spent most of his professional football career bouncing among several teams in the New York area, particularly the Staten Island Stapletons. The 6' 206-pound triple-threat fullback was a two-time All-American at Georgia Tech in 1924–1925. Doug also played on Tech's baseball, basketball and track teams, but football was his favorite.

Wiggs, Hubert T.

Year	Team	Games	Wins	Losses	Ties	%	Rank	Points	Allowed
1922	Louisville Brecks	4	1	3	0	.250	13	13	140
1 year		4	1	3	0	.250		13	140

Workman, Harry H. (Hoge)

Year	Team	Games	Wins	Losses	Ties	%	Rank	Points	Allowed
1931	Cleveland Indians	10	2	8	0	.200	8	45	137
1 year		10	2	8	0	.200		45	137

Wycoff signed with the Newark Bears of Red Grange's American Football League in 1926. The Bears were coached by Georgia Tech's backfield coach, Hal Hansen, who also played a bit in the backfield. By October, Newark was unable to pay its players and dropped out of the league with a 0–3–2 record. However, the Bears did manage to batter the independent Staten Island Stapletons so badly that Staten Island owner Dan Blaine hired the Bears' players for his own team. Missing paychecks, Wycoff was disillusioned by his Newark experience. He told the press that pro football was a "bust," and that "there is no chance of building up any team spirit among the professionals."

Despite asserting that he was done with pro football, Doug returned in 1927 with the New York Giants before shifting back to Staten Island as player-coach of the independent Stapletons in 1928. Blaine moved his Stapes to the NFL in 1929, with Wycoff continuing as player-coach through 1930. Doug jumped back to the Giants in 1931 and then rotated back to Staten Island, again under Hal Hansen, in 1932. That was the Stapletons final year in the NFL, but Wycoff remained with the club in 1933 as it struggled along as an independent team once more. All through his career, Doug regularly was among team leaders in rushing, passing and scoring. In 1934, he again rebounded to the NFL with the Boston Redskins. His final year playing football was 1936 with the New York Yankees of the short-lived second American Football League, where he paired with former Stapes' teammate Ken Strong.

Wycoff went into professional wrestling in 1935 and later said of it, "Wrestling! What a game. I did a couple of years at it. The roughest, toughest sport I know." Never one to shy away from a football startup, though, Doug partnered with restaurateur Harvey Hester in 1944 to work toward establishing a franchise in the proposed All America Football Conference. Two years later, that came to fruition with the ill-fated Miami Seahawks that primarily employed southern players. Done in by bad weather and weak talent, Miami barely lasted the season before being taken over by the league. For a change, Wycoff found himself on the management side of a failing franchise that was unable to pay its players. It was his last foray in pro football.

YOUNG, ALVA A. (DOC) 12/18/1881–8/9/1942. Indiana and New York University. Did not play professionally. *Hall of Fame Players:* None. *Record:* **Owner-Coach.**

Doc Young was a personable sportsman in the early years of the twentieth century. He played professional baseball, promoted boxing matches, owned race horses and was a founder of the NFL. The Hamilton County, Indiana native received his medical degree in 1905 from Indiana and did some post-graduate work at NYU in 1915. That same year, Young began acting as the trainer and team doctor of the independent Hammond Clabbys football club and continued until World War I when he served in the U.S. Army Medical Corps in Texas.

After the war, Doc became co-owner of the new Hammond Pros that featured George Halas in 1919. A year later, Young joined Halas and others to form the American Professional Football League. Hammond was largely a traveling team best known for regularly featuring one or two black players in the 1920s and, unfortunately, for winning few games — only five in seven years in the league. As the Pros wheezed to their end, Doc assumed the coaching responsibilities for their last two years in the NFL. Historian Bob Carroll noted in *The Coffin Corner* that Young was known to tell his players, "Go out there looking nice, boys, even if you cannot play so good. People like to see a team look nice at the kickoff."

After the Pros folded, Doc's time was filled with his practice and his horses. He even developed and marketed vitamin supplements for horses. However, that love for horses eventually cost Young his life. In 1942, he contracted pneumonia from working late hours with a sick horse. Pneumonia led to the heart problems that killed him later that year at 61.

Wycoff, Stephen D. (Doug)								
Year	Team	Games	Wins	Losses	Ties	%	Rank	Points	Allowed
1929	Staten Island Stapletons	10	3	4	3	.429	6	89	65
1930	Staten Island Stapletons	12	5	5	2	.500	6	95	112
2 years		22	8	9	5	.471		184	177

Young, Alva A. (Doc)								
Year	Team	Games	Wins	Losses	Ties	%	Rank	Points	Allowed
1925	Hammond Pros	4	1	3	0	.250	14	23	73
1926	Hammond Pros	4	0	4	0	.000	21	3	56
2 years		8	1	7	0	.125		26	129

YOUNGSTROM, ADOLPH F. (SWEDE) 5/24/1897–8/5/1968. Dartmouth under Doc Spears. Played G/T/E/C for the Buffalo All-Americans, Canton Bulldogs, Buffalo Bisons and Frankford Yellow Jackets from 1920 to 1927. *Hall of Fame Players:* Link Lyman. *Record:* **Interim Player-Co-Coach** (with Russ Daugherty, Charley Rogers and Ed Weir).

The 6'1" 187-pound Youngstrom was one of the top guards in the NFL's first decade. He was a three-time All Pro especially celebrated for his kick blocking prowess. The Waltham, Massachusetts native played for Dartmouth from 1914 to 1917 where he teamed with Ed Healey and Gus Sonnenberg on the Big Green line. Swede joined the Navy during World War I, but in 1919, he returned to Dartmouth and earned All-American status on the basis of his blocking nine punts that year.

The college All-American joined the professional Buffalo All-Americans in 1920 and reportedly blocked 11 punts that year and nine more in 1921. Youngstrom was one of eight Buffalo players who were double-dipping in 1921 by also playing with the independent Union Quakers of Philadelphia on Saturdays. After league President Joe Carr stepped in to stop that, Swede was one of just three of the eight players who continued playing for Buffalo. Actually, Youngstrom stayed in Buffalo for four more seasons, all the while working as line coach with NYU on the side. In 1925, new inexperienced coach Walter Koppisch had Youngstrom to double as Buffalo's line coach, too. Swede signed with Frankford in 1926 and at last enjoyed a championship season in which he contributed two touchdowns off of blocked punts. The next season, the defending champs had a new coach, Charley Moran, and Swede again doubled as line coach. When Moran resigned with the team floundering at 2–5–1, Youngstrom was put in charge of a four-player committee of player-coaches to lead the team. Frankford played .500 ball the rest of the season, and Swede retired. From 1929 to 1933 he coached the line for his alma mater, but when Red Blaik was hired as head coach in 1934, Youngstrom left football. In retirement, he sold real estate and served as a review appraiser for the state of Massachusetts.

Youngstrom, Adolph F. (Swede)									
Year	Team	Games	Wins	Losses	Ties	%	Rank	Points	Allowed
1927	Frankford Yellow Jackets	10	4	4	2	.500	7	65	86
1 year		10	4	4	2	.500		65	86

APPENDIX: RANKING THE COACHES

The entries in this book explain who each coach was, delineate his coaching style and approach, outline obstacles he encountered and demonstrate how successful he ultimately was. However, the essential question remains: how good was he in relation to his peers? Who was better? Who was worse? In the results-oriented profession of NFL coaching, the only goal is winning. Each coach is hired to win, and that's the metric against which to rank these men.

In order to quantify how much of a winner each coach was, I have designed a simple algorithm to rank NFL coaches by their results: Multiply each coach's regular season winning percentage by 100, multiply the percentage of seasons that they made the postseason by 10; add the number of Super Bowl or championship game appearances; multiply championships by four; then add all four elements together for the Coach's Results Score. For example, if we look at Vince Lombardi, his regular season winning percentage of .728 × 100 = 72.8 points; his teams reached the postseason six of 10 seasons, so .600 × 10 = 6 points; his teams reached six NFL title games or Super Bowls for 6 more points; finally, his teams won five championships multiplied times four = 20 more points. Lombardi's total then is 104.8 (or 104.79 to be more precise). Only Paul Brown has scored higher among coaches. And only George Halas joins those two with a score over 100. In this scale, anything over 70 is very good, over 80 is great, and over 90 is the pantheon.

I originally ranked all post–1932 coaches who worked at least one full season. However, recognizing the importance of longevity in establishing a meaningful record, here I have only listed the rankings for those who coached at least 55 games in the NFL/AAFC/AFL, roughly half of the post–1932 non-interim coaches. Rankings are not as firmly established for those who coached less than that. It does not take long to establish a truly awful legacy, though. While Bert Bell is the lowest ranked coach in the list, 23 coaches who coached at least one full season but fewer than 55 games scored lower on this results scale. To satisfy the reader's morbid curiosity, I have included a list of those catastrophic coaches as well

Obviously in fully evaluating coaches, one would be smart to include originality, innovativeness and the overall impact of their tactical and strategic advances to the profession. Those unmeasurables are discussed in the textual entries, but this numeric ranking is based solely on results. To that point, Don Coryell is one of the most influential coaches in the history of the game for his passing game enhancements, but this scale only gauges how his team fared on the field because that is a coach's top priority. In that light, Coryell's 61.47 is a fair evaluation — good, but not great. After all, his teams never advanced to a Super Bowl and only made the playoffs in six of 14 seasons. Lasting influence is a strong argument to be put forward when deliberating Coryell's potential Hall of Fame induction, but not here.

These ranking do not pertain very well to the pioneer coaches listed in Section II of this book, so I have ranked the top 15 in wins separately here, simply by wins and then by winning percentage.

Results Scores for Coaches Who Coached at Least 55 Games

(*denotes Hall of Fame)

Name	Years	Games	W/L %	Years in Playoffs	% of Years in Playoffs	Title Game Appear	Champs	Results Score
Paul Brown*	25	326	.667	15	.60	11	7	111.72
Vince Lombardi*	10	136	.728	6	.60	6	5	104.79
George Halas*	40	497	.671	9	.23	9	6	102.35
Curly Lambeau*	33	380	.624	8	.24	7	6	95.79
Don Shula*	33	490	.676	19	.58	7	2	88.31
John Madden*	10	142	.750	8	.80	1	1	88.00
Bill Belichick	17	272	.643	10	.59	5	3	87.22
Ray Flaherty*	11	122	.676	6	.55	6	2	87.08
Joe Gibbs*	16	248	.621	10	.63	4	3	84.35
Bill Walsh*	10	152	.609	7	.70	3	3	82.86

Name	Years	Games	W/L %	Years in Playoffs	% of Years in Playoffs	Title Game Appear	Champs	Results Score
Mike Tomlin	5	80	.688	4	.80	2	1	82.75
Chuck Noll*	23	342	.566	12	.52	4	4	81.80
George Seifert	11	176	.648	7	.64	2	2	81.14
Blanton Collier	8	112	.688	5	.63	2	1	81.00
Tony Dungy	13	208	.668	11	.85	1	1	80.29
Steve Owen*	23	268	.595	10	.43	8	2	79.86
Tom Landry*	29	418	.605	18	.62	5	2	79.73
John Harbaugh	4	64	.688	4	1.00	0	0	78.75
George Allen*	12	168	.705	7	.58	1	0	77.37
Mike McCarthy	6	96	.656	4	.67	1	1	77.29
Jim Lee Howell	7	84	.655	3	.43	3	1	76.76
Sean Payton	6	96	.646	4	.67	1	1	76.25
Barry Switzer	4	64	.625	3	.75	1	1	75.00
Bill Cowher	15	240	.623	10	.67	2	1	74.96
Mike Smith	4	64	.672	3	.75	0	0	74.69
Mike Holmgren	17	272	.592	12	.71	3	1	73.25
Bill Parcells	19	303	.569	10	.53	3	2	73.19
Red Miller	4	62	.645	3	.75	1	0	73.02
Greasy Neale*	10	111	.590	3	.30	3	2	73.01
Bud Grant*	18	259	.620	12	.67	4	0	72.64
Jimmy Johnson	9	144	.556	6	.67	2	2	72.22
Tom Coughlin	16	256	.555	9	.56	2	2	71.09
Hank Stram*	17	238	.571	5	.29	3	2	71.08
Mike Shanahan	18	276	.569	7	.39	2	2	70.77
Buddy Parker	15	188	.577	3	.20	3	2	70.71
Jimmy Conzelman*	15	167	.572	3	.20	3	2	70.19
Mike Martz	6	85	.624	4	.67	1	0	70.02
Buck Shaw	12	150	.617	2	.17	2	1	69.33
Andy Reid	13	208	.608	9	.69	1	0	68.74
Sid Gillman*	18	228	.550	6	.33	6	1	68.38
Marty Schottenheimer	21	327	.613	13	.62	0	0	67.51
Weeb Ewbank*	20	266	.502	4	.20	3	3	67.19
Tom Flores	12	184	.527	5	.42	2	2	66.88
Mike Sherman	6	96	.594	4	.67	0	0	66.04
Mike Ditka	14	216	.560	7	.50	1	1	66.02
Potsy Clark	10	118	.593	1	.10	1	1	65.32
Brian Billick	9	144	.556	4	.44	1	1	65.00
Marv Levy*	17	255	.561	8	.47	4	0	64.78
John Rauch	5	70	.586	2	.40	1	0	63.57
Jon Gruden	11	176	.540	5	.45	1	1	63.52
Dick Vermeil	15	229	.524	6	.40	2	1	62.40
Wade Phillips	11	143	.573	5	.45	0	0	61.89
Lou Saban	16	201	.490	4	.25	2	2	61.50
Don Coryell	14	195	.572	6	.43	0	0	61.47
Dan Reeves	23	357	.535	9	.39	4	0	61.41
Chuck Knox	22	334	.558	11	.50	0	0	60.84
Dennis Green	13	207	.546	8	.62	0	0	60.74
Bobby Ross	9	137	.540	5	.56	1	0	60.57
Lovie Smith	8	128	.555	3	.38	1	0	60.22
Jerry Burns	6	95	.547	3	.50	0	0	59.74
Raymond Berry	6	87	.552	2	.33	1	0	59.51
Allie Sherman	8	112	.527	3	.38	3	0	59.43
John Robinson	9	143	.524	6	.67	0	0	59.11
Jeff Fisher	17	262	.542	6	.35	1	0	58.73
Jim Mora	15	231	.541	6	.40	0	0	58.11
Wally Lemm	10	135	.500	3	.30	1	1	58.00
Ray Malavasi	6	85	.518	3	.50	1	0	57.76
Jack Pardee	11	164	.530	5	.45	0	0	57.59
Jim Fassel	7	112	.522	3	.43	1	0	57.52
Chuck Fairbanks	6	85	.541	2	.33	0	0	57.45
Joe Schmidt	6	84	.554	1	.17	0	0	57.02
Brad Childress	5	74	.527	2	.40	0	0	56.70
Steve Mariucci	9	139	.518	4	.44	0	0	56.24

Name	Years	Games	W/L %	Years in Playoffs	% of Years in Playoffs	Title Game Appear	Champs	Results Score
Art Shell	7	108	.519	3	.43	0	0	56.14
John Fox	10	160	.506	4	.40	1	0	55.63
Ken Whisenhunt	5	80	.500	2	.40	1	0	55.00
Bum Phillips	11	159	.516	3	.27	0	0	54.30
Buddy Ryan	7	111	.500	3	.43	0	0	54.29
Ron Meyer	9	104	.519	2	.22	0	0	54.15
Wayne Fontes	9	133	.496	4	.44	0	0	54.07
Pete Carroll	6	96	.490	3	.50	0	0	53.96
Mike Holovak	9	108	.523	1	.11	0	0	53.43
Marvin Lewis	9	144	.483	3	.33	0	0	51.60
Norv Turner	14	221	.486	4	.29	0	0	51.50
Nick Skorich	7	98	.485	2	.29	0	0	51.33
Sam Rutigliano	7	97	.485	2	.29	0	0	51.31
Dave Wannstedt	11	169	.485	3	.27	0	0	51.25
Mike Tice	5	65	.492	1	.20	0	0	51.23
Jack Del Rio	9	139	.489	2	.22	0	0	51.14
Joe Walton	7	111	.482	2	.29	0	0	51.06
Jerry Glanville	9	129	.465	4	.44	0	0	50.96
Jim Mora	4	64	.484	1	.25	0	0	50.94
Ray Rhodes	5	80	.469	2	.40	0	0	50.88
George Wilson	12	160	.450	1	.08	1	1	50.83
Dan Devine	4	56	.482	1	.25	0	0	50.71
John Ralston	5	70	.507	0	.00	0	0	50.71
Gary Kubiak	6	96	.490	1	.17	0	0	50.63
Ted Marchibroda	12	186	.470	4	.33	0	0	50.38
Tony Sparano	4	61	.475	1	.25	0	0	50.04
Charley Winner	7	93	.500	0	.00	0	0	50.00
Red Hickey	5	55	.500	0	.00	0	0	50.00
Forrest Gregg	11	161	.469	2	.18	1	0	49.71
Neill Armstrong	4	64	.469	1	.25	0	0	49.38
John Mackovic	4	64	.469	1	.25	0	0	49.38
Chan Gailey	4	64	.438	2	.50	0	0	48.75
Walt Michaels	6	87	.454	2	.33	0	0	48.74
Dick Nolan	11	156	.458	3	.27	0	0	48.56
Herman Edwards	8	128	.422	4	.50	0	0	47.19
Dutch Clark	6	66	.470	0	.00	0	0	46.97
Red Strader	5	58	.448	1	.20	0	0	46.83
Sam Wyche	12	191	.440	2	.17	1	0	46.65
Pop Ivy	6	76	.434	1	.17	1	0	46.09
Monte Clark	8	119	.433	2	.25	0	0	45.78
Leeman Bennett	8	119	.420	3	.38	0	0	45.77
Jim Haslett	7	108	.435	1	.14	0	0	44.95
Jim Hanifan	7	93	.425	1	.14	0	0	43.90
Butch Davis	4	58	.414	1	.25	0	0	43.88
Rich Kotite	6	96	.417	1	.17	0	0	43.33
Dick Jauron	10	142	.423	1	.10	0	0	43.25
Eric Mangini	5	80	.413	1	.20	0	0	43.25
Alex Webster	5	70	.421	0	.00	0	0	42.14
Bart Starr	9	131	.408	1	.11	0	0	41.95
Joe Kuharich	11	142	.419	0	.00	0	0	41.90
Dennis Erickson	6	96	.417	0	.00	0	0	41.67
Vince Tobin	5	71	.394	1	.20	0	0	41.44
Jack Christiansen	5	67	.410	0	.00	0	0	41.04
Tommy Prothro	7	88	.409	0	.00	0	0	40.91
Gene Stallings	4	58	.405	0	.00	0	0	40.52
June Jones	4	58	.379	1	.25	0	0	40.43
Norm Van Brocklin	13	173	.402	0	.00	0	0	40.17
Lindy Infante	6	96	.375	1	.17	0	0	39.17
Bruce Coslet	9	124	.379	1	.11	0	0	39.01
Romeo Crennel	5	67	.388	0	.00	0	0	38.81
Dom Capers	8	128	.375	1	.13	0	0	38.75
Jack Patera	7	94	.372	0	.00	0	0	37.23
Ray Perkins	8	117	.359	1	.13	0	0	37.15

Name	Years	Games	W/L %	Years in Playoffs	% of Years in Playoffs	Title Game Appear	Champs	Results Score
John McKay	9	133	.335	3	.33	0	0	36.79
Mike McCormack	6	81	.364	0	.00	0	0	36.42
Walt Kiesling	9	90	.361	0	.00	0	0	36.11
Jim Dooley	4	56	.357	0	.00	0	0	35.71
Dan Henning	7	112	.344	0	.00	0	0	34.38
Bill Austin	4	56	.330	0	.00	0	0	33.04
Mike Nolan	4	55	.327	0	.00	0	0	32.73
Bill McPeak	5	70	.321	0	.00	0	0	32.14
Harland Svare	7	74	.318	0	.00	0	0	31.76
Darryl Rogers	4	58	.310	0	.00	0	0	31.03
Marion Campbell	9	115	.300	0	.00	0	0	30.00
Joe Bugel	5	80	.300	0	.00	0	0	30.00
Dave McGinnis	4	57	.298	0	.00	0	0	29.82
David Shula	5	71	.268	0	.00	0	0	26.76
Bert Bell	6	58	.190	0	.00	0	0	18.97

23 Coaches Who Coached Fewer Than 55 Games and Scored Below the Bert Bell Line (Table Above)

Name	Results Score	Wins	Losses	Ties	Name	Results Score	Wins	Losses	Ties
Les Steckel	18.75	3	13	0	Charlie Ewart	12.50	1	10	1
Mike Nixon	18.42	6	30	2	Marty Feldman	11.76	2	15	0
Hank Bullough	18.18	4	18	0	Scooter McLean	11.71	1	12	1
Rod Dowhower	17.24	5	24	0	Phil Handler	11.53	4	34	0
Luby DiMeolo	16.67	2	10	0	Harvey Johnson	9.62	2	23	1
Marty Mornhinweg	15.63	5	27	0	Hugo Bezdek	7.14	1	13	0
Chris Palmer	15.63	5	27	0	Jim Crowley	7.14	1	13	0
Norb Hecker	14.52	4	26	1	Ed McKeever	7.14	1	13	0
Carl Voyles	14.29	2	12	0	Cam Cameron	6.25	1	15	0
Heine Miller	13.64	1	10	1	Rod Rust	6.25	1	15	0
Pete Cawthon	13.33	2	13	0	Bill Peterson	5.26	1	18	0
Jim Ringo	13.04	3	20	0					

Top 15 Pioneer Coaches Ranked by 1920–1932 Wins

Name	Seasons	Games	Wins	Losses	Ties	%	Champs
Curly Lambeau	12	143	93	33	15	.703	3
George Halas/ Dutch Sternaman	10	135	84	31	20	.696	1
Guy Chamberlin	6	81	58	16	7	.759	4
Jimmy Conzelman	9	99	53	32	14	.606	1
Leroy Andrews	8	82	51	27	4	.646	0
Tommy Hughitt	5	56	34	15	7	.670	0
Dick Rauch	5	60	33	24	3	.575	0
Ralph Jones	3	41	24	10	7	.671	1
Potsy Clark	2	26	17	5	4	.731	0
Paddy Driscoll	3	29	17	8	4	.655	0
Dewey Scanlon	4	36	17	15	4	.528	0
Elgie Tobin	2	23	16	3	4	.783	1
Norm Barry	2	26	16	8	2	.654	1
Ed Weir	2	26	15	7	4	.654	0
Earl Potteiger	3	31	15	12	4	.548	1

BIBLIOGRAPHY

Books

Adler, Brad. *Coaching Matters: Leadership and Tactics of the NFL's Ten Greatest Coaches.* Washington, D.C.: Brassey's, 2003.

Allen, Jennifer. *Fifth Quarter: The Scrimmage of a Football Coach's Daughter.* New York: Random House, 2000.

Anderson, Heartley, with Emil Klosinski. *Notre Dame, Chicago Bears and Hunk: Football Memoirs in Highlight.* Oviedo, FL: Florida Sun-Gator, 1976.

Baker, Jim, and Bernard Corbett. *The Most Memorable Games in Giants History: The Oral History of a Legendary Team.* New York: Bloomsbury, 2010.

_____. *The Most Memorable Games in Patriots History: The Oral History of a Legendary Team.* New York: Bloomsbury, 2011.

Barber, Phil. *The Official Vince Lombardi Playbook: His Classic Plays & Strategies, Personal Photos & Mementos: Recollections from Friends & Former Players.* Guilford, CT: Lyons Press, 2009.

Barnes, Howard L. *A Documentary Scrap Book of Football in Frankford.* Philadelphia: Historical Society of Frankford, 1985.

Bayliss, Skip. *The Boys.* New York: Simon & Schuster, 1993.

_____. *God's Coach: The Hymns, Hype and Hypocrisy of Tom Landry's Cowboys.* New York: Simon & Schuster, 1990.

_____. *Hell-Bent: The Crazy Truth about the "Win or Else" Dallas Cowboys.* New York: HarperCollins, 1996.

Becker, Carl M. *Home and Away: The Rise and Fall of Professional Football on the Banks of the Ohio, 1919–1934.* Athens: Ohio University Press, 1998.

Bengtson, Phil, with Todd Hunt. *Packer Dynasty.* Garden City, NY: Doubleday, 1969.

Benjey, Tom. *Keep A-Goin': The Life of Lone Star Dietz.* Carlisle, PA: Tuxedo Press, 2006.

Bennett, Tom. *The NFL's Official Encyclopedic History of Professional Football.* New York: Macmillan, 1977.

_____. *The Pro Style.* Englewood Cliffs, NJ: Prentice-Hall, 1976.

Bethea, Elvin, and Mark Adams. *Smash Mouth: My Football Journey from Trenton to Canton.* Champaign, IL: Sports Publishing, 2005.

Bisheff, Steve. *Los Angeles Rams.* New York: Macmillan 1973.

Bloomfield, Gary L. *Duty, Honor, Victory: America's Athletes in World War II.* Guilford, CT: Lyons Press, 2003.

Bowden, Mark. *Bringing the Heat.* New York: Knopf, 1994.

Boyer, Mary Schmitt. *Browns Essential: Everything You Need to Know to Be a Real Fan.* Chicago: Triumph Books, 2006.

Brees, Drew, with Chris Fabry. *Coming Back Stronger: Unleashing the Hidden Power of Adversity.* Carroll Stream, IL: Tyndale House, 2010.

Brown, Paul, with Jack Clary. *PB: The Paul Brown Story.* New York: Atheneum, 1979.

Buford, Kate. *Native American Son: The Life and Sporting Legend of Jim Thorpe.* New York: Knopf, 2010.

Callahan, Tom. *The GM: The Inside Story of a Dream Job and the Nightmares That Go with It.* New York: Crown, 2007.

Cannizzaro, Mark. *New York Jets: The Complete Illustrated History.* Minneapolis: MVP Books, 2011.

Cantor, George. *Paul Brown: The Man Who Invented Modern Football.* Chicago: Triumph Books, 2008.

Carlson, Chuck. *Tales from the Packers Sideline: A Collection of the Greatest Stories Ever Told.* Champaign, IL: Sports Publishing, 2003.

Carroll, Bob. *When the Grass Was Real: Unitas, Brown, Lombardi, Sayers, Butkus, Namath and All the Rest: The Ten Best Years of Pro Football.* New York: Simon & Schuster, 1993.

_____., Michael Gershman, David Neft, and John Thorn. *Total Football: The Official Encyclopedia of the National Football League.* New York: HarperCollins, 1999.

Carroll, John M. *Fritz Pollard: Pioneer in Racial Advancement.* Urbana: University of Illinois Press, 1992.

_____. *Red Grange and the Rise of Modern Football.* Urbana: University of Illinois Press, 1999.

Claassen, Harold (Spike). *The History of Professional Football.* Englewood Cliffs, NJ: Prentice-Hall, 1963.

Cohane, Tim. *Great College Football Coaches of the Twenties and Thirties.* New Rochelle, NY: Arlington House 1973.

Cohen, David. *Rugged and Enduring: The Eagles, the Browns and 5 Years of Football.* Philadelphia: Xlibris, 2001.

Cohen, Richard M., Jordan A. Deutsch, Roland T. Johnson, and David S. Neft. *The Scrapbook History of Pro Football.* Indianapolis: Bobbs-Merrill, 1976.

Cope, Myron. *The Game That Was: An Illustrated Account of the Tumultuous Early Days of Pro Football.* New York: Crowell, 1974.

Coughlin, Dan. *Crazy, with the Papers to Prove It: Stories about the Most Unusual, Eccentric and Outlandish People I've Known in Four Decades as a Sports Journalist.* Cleveland: Gray & Co., 2010.

Coughlin, Tom, with Brian Curtis. *A Team to Believe In: Our Journey to the Super Bowl Championship.* New York: ESPN Books, Ballantine, 2008.

Crippen, Kenneth R. *The Original Buffalo Bills: A History of the All-America Football Conference Team 1946–1949.* Jefferson, NC: McFarland, 2010.

Curran, Bob. *Pro Football's Rag Days.* Englewood Cliffs, NJ: Prentice-Hall, 1969.

Curry, Bill. *Ten Men You Meet in the Huddle: Lessons from a Football Life.* New York: ESPN Books, 2008.

Daley, Arthur. *Pro Football's Hall of Fame.* New York: Grosset and Dunlap, 1968, c1963.

Daly, Dan, and Bob O'Donnell. *The Pro Football Chronicle: The Complete (Well, Almost) Record of the Best Players, the Greatest Photos, the Hardest Hits, the Biggest Scandals, and the Funniest Stories in Pro Football.* New York: Collier Books, 1990.

Danyluk, Tom. *The Super '70s: Memories from Pro Football's Greatest Era.* Chicago: Mad Uke, 2005.

Danzig, Allison. *The History of American Football: Its Great Teams, Players, and Coaches.* Englewood Cliffs, NJ: Prentice-Hall, 1956.

Davis, Jeff. *Papa Bear: The Life and Legacy of George Halas.* New York: McGraw-Hill, 2004.

_____. *Rozelle: Czar of the NFL.* New York: McGraw-Hill, 2008

Dent, Jim. *Monster of the Midway: Bronko Nagurski, the 1943 Chicago Bears, and the Greatest Comeback Ever.* New York: Thomas Dunne, 2003.

Devine, Dan, with Michael R. Steele. *Simply Devine: Memoirs of a Hall of Fame Coach*. Champaigne, IL: Sports Publishing, 2000.

Didinger, Ray. *The Eagles Encyclopedia*. Philadelphia: Temple University Press, 2005.

_____. *Game Plans for Success: Winning Strategies for Business and Life from Ten Top NFL Head Coaches*. Boston: Little, Brown, 1995.

_____. *Pittsburgh Steelers*. New York: Macmillan, 1974.

Ditka, Mike, with Don Pierson. *Ditka: An Autobiography*. Chicago: Bonus Books, 1986.

Donaldson, Jim. *Stadium Stories: New England Patriots*. Guilford, CT: Insiders' Guide, 2005.

Donovan, Arthur J., with Bob Drury. *Fatso: How Football Was When Men Were Really Men*. New York: William Morrow, 1987.

Dowling, Tom. *Coach: A Season with Lombardi*. New York: Norton, 1970.

Duncan, Jeff. *Tales from the Saints Sideline*. Champaign, IL: Sports Publishing, 2004.

Dungy, Tony, with Nathan Whitaker. *Quiet Strength: A Memoir*. Carol Stream, IL: Tyndale House, 2007.

Dunn, Warrick, with Don Yaeger. *Running for My Life: My Journey in the Game of Football*. New York: HarperCollins, 2008.

Eisenberg, John. *Cotton Bowl Days: Growing Up with Dallas and the Cowboys in the 1960s*. New York: Simon & Schuster, 1997.

_____. *That First Season: How Vince Lombardi Took the Worst Team in the NFL and Set It on the Path to Glory*. Boston: Mariner Books, 2010.

Eskenazi, Gerald. *There Were Giants in Those Days*. New York: Grosset and Dunlap, 1976.

Eyring, Donna. *Cowher Power*. Chicago: Triumph Books, 2006.

Felger, Michael. *Tales from the Patriots Sideline*. Champaign, IL: Sports Publishing, 2004.

Fleder, Rob, ed. *Sports Illustrated: The Football Book*. New York: Time Inc. Home Entertainment, 2005.

Fleming, David. *Breaker Boys: The NFL's Greatest Team and the Stolen 1925 Championship*. New York: ESPN Books, 2007.

Flynn, George, ed. *Vince Lombardi on Football*. Greenwich, CT: New York Graphic Society and Wallyn, 1973.

_____. *The Vince Lombardi Scrapbook*. New York: Grossett and Dunlap, 1976.

Forbes, Gordon. *Dick Vermeil: Whistle in His Mouth, Heart on His Sleeve*. Chicago: Triumph Books, 2009.

_____. *Tales from the Eagles Sidelines*. Champaign, IL: Sports Publishing, 2002.

Freedman, Lew. *Game of My Life: Chicago Bears*. Champin, IL: Sports Publishing, 2006.

Garraty, John A., and Mark C. Carnes, gen. eds. *American National Biography*. New York: Oxford University Press, 1999.

Georgatos, Dennis. *Stadium Stories: San Francisco 49ers*. Guilford, CT: Insiders' Guide, 2005.

Gifford, Frank, with Harry Waters. *The Whole Ten Yards*. New York: Random House, 1993.

Gillette, Gary, Matt Silverman, Pete Palmer, Ken Pullis and Sean Lahman. *The ESPN Pro Football Encyclopedia*. New York: Sterling, 2007.

Godin, Roger A. *The Brooklyn Football Dodgers: The Other "Bums."* Haworth, NJ: St. Johann Press, 2003.

Golenbock, Peter. *Cowboys Have Always Been My Heroes: The Definitive Oral History of America's Team*. New York: Warner Books, 1997.

Goodman, Murray, and Leonard Lewin. *My Greatest Day in Football*. New York: Barnes, 1948.

Grange, Red. *The Red Grange Story: An Autobiography*. Urbana: University of Illinois Press, 1953.

Green, Dennis, with Gene McGivern. *Dennis Green: No Room for Crybabies*. Champaign, IL: Sports Publishing, 1997.

Green, Jerry. *Super Bowl Chronicles: A Sportswriter Reflects on the First 25 Years of America's Game*. Grand Rapids: Masters Press, 1991.

Green, Tim. *The Dark Side of the Game: My Life in the NFL*. New York: Warner Books, 1996.

Greenberg, Murray. *Passing Game: Benny Friedman and the Transformation of Football*. New York: Public Affairs, 2008.

Grossi, Tony. *Tales from the Browns' Sideline*. Champaign, IL: Sports Publishing, 2004.

Gruden, Jon, with Vic Carucci. *Do You Love Football?! Winning with Heart, Passion, and Not Much Sleep*. New York: HarperCollins, 2003.

Gullickson, Denis J. *Vagabond Halfback: The Life and Times of Johnny Blood McNally*. Madison: Trails Books, 2006.

Halas, George, with Gwen Morgan and Arthur Veysey. *Halas by Halas*. New York: McGraw-Hill, 1979.

Halberstam, David. *The Education of a Coach*. New York: Hyperion, 2005.

Hanifan, Jim, with Rob Rains. *Beyond X's and O's: My Thirty Years in the NFL*. Champaign, IL: Sports Publishing, 2003.

Harris, David. *The Genius: How Bill Walsh Reinvented Football and Created an NFL Dynasty*. New York: Random House, 2008.

_____. *The League: The Rise and Decline of the NFL*. New York: Bantam Books, 1986.

Herskowitz, Mickey. *The Golden Age of Pro Football: NFL Football in the 1950s*. Dallas: Taylor, 199.

Izenberg, Jerry. *Championship: The Complete NFL Title Story*. New York: Four Winds Press, 1966.

James, Craig. *Game Day: A Rollicking Journey to the Heart of College Football*. Hoboken, NJ: Wiley, 2009.

Jaworski, Ron, with Greg Cosell and David Plaut. *The Games That Changed the Game: The Evolution of the Game in Seven Sundays*. New York: ESPN Books, 2010.

Johnson, Jimmy, with Ed Hinton. *Turning the Thing Around: Pulling America's Team Out of the Dumps—and Myself Out of the Doghouse*. New York: Hyperion, 1993.

King, Joe. *Inside Pro Football*. Englewood Cliffs, NJ: Prentice-Hall, 1958.

King, Peter. *Football: A History of the Professional Game*. New York: Bishop Books [Time Inc. Home Entertainment], 1997.

Klein, Dave. *The New York Giants: Yesterday, Today and Tomorrow*. Chicago: Regnery, 1973.

Klosinski, Emil. *Pro Football in the Days of Rockne*. New York: Carlton Press, 1970.

Knight, Jonathan. *Kardiac Kids: The Story of the 1980 Cleveland Browns*. Kent, OH: Kent State University Press, 2003.

Kramer, Jerry, with Dick Schaap. *Instant Replay: The Green Bay Diary of Jerry Kramer*. New York: World, 1968.

LaMarre, Tom. *Stadium Stories: Oakland Raiders: Colorful Tales of the Silver and Black*. Guilford, CT: Globe Pequot Press, 2003.

Landry, Tom, with Gregg Lewis. *Tom Landry: An Autobiography*. Grand Rapids: Zondervan, and New York: HarperCollins, 1990.

Layden, Tim. *Blood, Sweat and Chalk: The Ultimate Football Playbook: How the Great Coaches Built Today's Game*. New York: Sports Illustrated Books, 2010.

Lea, Bud. *The Magnificent Seven: The Championship Games That Built the Lombardi Dynasty*. Chicago: Triumph Books, 2002.

Leuthner, Stuart. *Iron Men: Bucko, Crazy Legs, and the Boys Recall the Golden Days of Professional Football*. New York: Doubleday, 1988.

Lombardi, Vince, with W.C. Heinz. *Run to Daylight*. Englewood Cliffs, NJ: Prentice-Hall, 1963.

Loverro, Thom. *Hail Victory: An Oral History of the Washington Redskins*. Hoboken, NJ: J. Wiley, 2006.

Lynch, Etta. *Tender Tyrant: the Legend of Pete Cawthon.* Canyon, TX: Staked Plains Press, 1976.

Lyons, Robert. *On Any Given Sunday: A Life of Bert Bell.* Philadelphia: Temple University Press, 2010.

MacCambridge, Michael. *America's Game: The Epic Story of How Pro Football Captured a Nation.* New York: Random House, 2004.

Madden, John, with Dave Anderson. *All Madden: Hey, I'm Talking Pro Football.* New York: HarperCollins, 1996.

_____, with _____. *Hey, Wait a Minute, I Wrote a Book.* New York: Villard Books, 1984.

_____, with _____. *One Knee Equals Two Feet (and Everything Else You Need to Know about Football).* New York: Villard Books, 1986.

_____, with _____. *One Size Doesn't Fit All.* New York: Villard Books, 1988.

Maiocco, Matt. *San Francisco 49ers: Where Have You Gone?* Champaign, IL: Sports Publishing, 2005.

Maiorana, Sal. *Buffalo Bills: The Complete Illustrated History.* Minneapolis: MVP Books, 2010.

_____. *Game of My Life: Memorable Stories of Buffalo Bills Football.* Champaign, IL: Sports Publishing, 2005.

Manning, Archie, with John Underwood. *Manning: A Father, His Sons and a Football Legacy.* New York: HarperEntertainment, 2000.

Maraniss, David. *When Pride Still Mattered: A Life of Vince Lombardi.* New York: Simon & Schuster, 1999.

March, Harry. *Pro Football, Its "Ups" and "Downs": A Lighthearted History of the Post Graduate Game.* Albany: J. B. Lyon, 1934.

Marshall, Phillip. *Stadium Stories: Auburn Tigers.* Guilford, CT: Insiders' Guide, 2005.

Maule, Tex. *The Game: The Official Picture History of the NFL and AFL.* New York: Random House, 1967.

Maxymuk, John. *Strong Arm Tactics: A History and Statistical Analysis of the Professional Quarterback.* Jefferson, NC: McFarland, 2008.

McClellan, Keith. *The Sunday Game: At the Dawn of Professional Football.* Akron: University of Akron Press, 1998.

McCullough, Bob. *My Greatest Day in Football: The Legends of Football Recount Their Greatest Moments.* New York: Thomas Dunne, 2001.

McGinn, Bob. *The Ultimate Super Bowl Book: A Complete Reference to the Stats, Stars, and Stories behind Football's Biggest Game—and Why the Best Team Won.* Minneapolis: MVP Books, 2009.

McGrane, Bill. *Bud: The Other Side of the Glacier.* New York: Harper Collins, 1986.

Meggyesy, Dave. *Out of Their League.* Berkeley, CA: 1970.

Miller, Jeff. *Going Long: The Wild 10-Year Saga of the Renegade American Football League in the Words of Those Who Lived It.* New York: Contemporary Books, 2003.

Miller, Jeffrey. *Rockin' the Rockpile: The Buffalo Bills of the American Football League.* Toronto: ECW Press, 2007.

Mullin, John. *Tales from the Chicago Bears Sidelines.* Champaign, IL: Sports Publishing, 2003.

Names, Larry. *The History of the Green Bay Packers: Book I: The Lambeau Years Part One.* Wautoma: Angel Press of Wisconsin, 1987.

_____. *The History of the Green Bay Packers: Book II: The Lambeau Years Part Two.* Wautoma: Angel Press of Wisconsin, 1989.

_____. *The History of the Green Bay Packers: Book III: The Lambeau Years Part Three.* Wautoma: Angel Press of Wisconsin, 1990.

_____. *The History of the Green Bay Packers: Book IV: The Shameful Years Part One.* Wautoma: Angel Press of Wisconsin, 1995.

Natali, Alan. *Brown's Town: 20 Famous Browns Talk Amongst Themselves.* Wilmington, OH: Orange Frazer Press, 2001.

Neft, David S., Richard M. Cohen, and Richard Korch. *The Football Encyclopedia: The Complete History of Professional Football from 1892 to the Present.* New York: St. Martin's, 1994.

Norwood, Stephen H. *Real Football: Conversations on America's Game.* Jackson: University Press of Mississippi, 2004.

O'Toole, Andrew. *Paul Brown: The Rise and Fall and Rise Again of Football's Most Innovative Coach.* Cincinnati: Clerisy Press, 2008.

Otto, Jim, with Dave Newhouse. *Jim Otto: The Pain of Glory.* Champaign, IL: Sports Publishing, 2000.

Owen, Steve, with Joe King. *My Kind of Football.* New York: D. McKay, 1952.

Parker, Buddy. *We Play to Win! The Inside Story of the Fabulous Detroit Lions.* Englewood Cliffs, NJ: Prentice-Hall, 1955.

Payton, Sean, with Ellis Henican. *Home Team: Coaching the Saints and New Orleans Back to Life.* New York: New American Library, 2010.

Pearlman, Jeff. *Boys Will Be Boys: The Glory Days and Party Nights of the Dallas Cowboys Dynasty.* New York: Harper, 2008.

Peterson, Bill, with Cecil A. Roberts. *Building from the Start.* Waco: Advertising and Marketing Associates, 1971.

Peterson, Robert. *Pigskin: The Early Years of Pro Football.* New York: Oxford University Press, 1997.

Piascik, Andy. *The Best Show in Football: The 1946–1955 Cleveland Browns, Pro Football's Greatest Dynasty.* Lanham, MD: Taylor Trade, 2007.

Pierce, Charles P. *Moving the Chains: Tom Brady and the Pursuit of Everything.* New York: Farrar, Straus and Giroux, 2006.

Plimpton, George. *One More July: A Football Dialogue with Bill Curry.* New York: Harper and Row, 1977.

_____. *Paper Lion.* New York: Harper and Row, 1966.

Pool, Hampton. *Fly T Football.* Englewood Cliffs, NJ: Prentice-Hall, 1957.

Poole, Gary Andrew. *The Galloping Ghost: Red Grange, an American Football Legend.* Boston: Houghton Mifflin, 2008.

Pluto, Terry. *Things I've Learned from Watching the Browns.* Cleveland: Gray & Company, 2010.

_____. *When All the World was Browns Town: Cleveland Browns and the Championship Season of 1964.* New York: Simon & Schuster, 1997.

Pope, Edwin. *Football's Greatest Coaches.* Atlanta: Tupper and Love, 1955.

Porter, David L., ed. *Biographical Dictionary of American Sports: Football.* New York: Greenwood Press, 1987.

_____. *Biographical Dictionary of American Sports: 1989–1992 Supplement for Baseball, Football, Basketball, and Other Sports.* New York: Greenwood Press, 1992.

_____. *Biographical Dictionary of American Sports: 1992–1995 Supplement for Baseball, Football, Basketball, and Other Sports.* New York: Greenwood Press, 1995.

Raible, Steve, and Mike Sando. *Steve Raible's Tales from the Seahawk Sidelines.* Champaign, IL: Sports Publishing, 2004.

Rathet, Mike, and Don R. Smith. *Their Deeds and Dogged Faith.* New York: Rutledge Books, 1984.

Richman, Michael. *The Redskins Encyclopedia.* Philadelphia: Temple University Press, 2008.

Richmond, Peter. *Badasses: The Legend of Snake, Foo, Dr. Death and John Madden's Oakland Raiders.* New York: Harper, 2010.

Romanowski, Bill, with Adam Schefter and Phil Towle. *Romo: My Life on the Edge: Living Dreams and Slaying Dragons.* New York: William Morrow, 2005.

Rooney, Jr., Art, with Roy McHugh. *Ruanaidh: the Story of Art Rooney and His Clan.* Pittsburgh: [self published?], 2008.

Rooney, Dan, with Andrew Masich. *My 75 Years with the Pittsburgh Steelers and the NFL.* New York: Da Capo, 2007.

Ross, Charles K. *Outside the Lines: African Americans and the Integration of the National Football League.* New York: New York University Press, 1999.

Ruck, Rob. *Rooney: A Sporting Life*. Lincoln: University of Nebraska Press, 2010.

Ryan, Rex, with Don Yaeger. *Play Like You Mean It: Passion, Laughs and Leadership in the World's Most Beautiful Game*. New York: Doubleday, 2011.

Sanders, Charlie, with Larry Paladino. *Tales from the Detroit Lions*. Champaign, IL: Sports Publishing, 2005

75 Seasons: The Complete Story of the National Football League 1920–1995. Atlanta: Turner, 1994.

Shanahan, Mike, with Adam Schefter. *Think Like a Champion*. New York: HarperBusiness, 1999.

Shmelter, Richard. *The Raiders Encyclopedia: All Players, Coaches, Games and More through 2009–2010*. Jefferson, NC: McFarland, 2011.

Smith, Myron J. *Pro Football: The Official Pro Football Hall of Fame Bibliography*. Westport, CT: Greenwood Press, 1993.

Smith, Robert. *Illustrated History of Pro Football*. New York: Grossett and Dunlap, 1977.

Stram, Hank, with Lou Sahadi. *They're Playing My Game*. Chicago: Triumph Books, 2006.

Strother, Shelby. *NFL Top 40: The Greatest Football Games of All Time*. New York: Viking, 1988.

Sullivan, George. *Touchdown! The Picture History of the American Football League*. New York: Putnam, 1967.

Summerall, Pat, with Michael Levin. *Giants: What I Learned About Life from Vince Lombardi and Tom Landry*. Hoboken, NJ: John Wiley & Sons, 2010.

Switzer, Barry, with Edwin Shrake. *Bootlegger's Boy*. New York: Morrow, 1990.

Taylor, Otis, with Mark Stallard. *Otis Taylor: The Need to Win*. Champaign, IL: Sports Publishing, 2003.

Tittle, Y.A., with Don Smith. *Y.A. Tittle: I Pass*. New York: Franklin Watts, 1965.

Wagner, Len. *Launching the Glory Years: The 1959 Packers— What They Didn't Tell Us*. Green Bay: Coach's Books [Jay Bengtson], 2001.

Walsh, Bill, with James A. Peterson. *Finding the Winning Edge*. Champaign, IL: Sports Publishing, 1998.

Wexell, Jim. *Pittsburgh Steelers: Men of Steel*. Champaign, IL: Sports Publishing, 2006.

Whittingham, Richard. *The Fireside Book of Pro Football*. New York: Simon & Schuster, 1989.

_____. *What a Game They Played*. New York: Harper and Row, 1974.

Wiebusch, John, ed. *A Game of Passion: The NFL Literary Companion*. Atlanta: Turner Pub., 1994.

_____. *Lombardi*. Chicago: Follett, 1971.

Willis, Chris. *The Columbus Panhandles: A Complete History of Pro Football's Toughest Team, 1900–1922*. Lanham, MD: Scarecrow Press, 2007.

_____. *The Man Who Built the National Football League: Joe F. Carr*. Lanham, Md.: Scarecrow Press, 2010.

_____. *Old Leather: An Oral History of Early Pro Football in Ohio, 1920–1935*. Lanham, Md.: Scarecrow Press, 2005.

Wolf, Ron, with Paul Attner. *The Packer Way: Nine Stepping Stones to Building a Winning Organization*. New York: St. Martin's Press, 1998.

Wright, Steve, with William Gildea and Kenneth Turan. *I'd Rather Be Wright: Memoirs of an Itinerant Tackle*. Englewood Cliffs, NJ: Prentice-Hall, 1974.

Ziemba, Joe. *When Football Was Football*. Chicago: Triumph Books, 1999.

Zimmer, Larry. *Stadium Stories: Denver Broncos: Colorful Tales of the Orange and Blue*. Guilford, CT: Pequot Press, 2004.

Zimmerman, David H. *Lambeau: The Man Behind the Mystique*. Hales Corners, WI: Eagle Books, 2003.

Zimmerman, Paul. *The New Thinking Man's Guide to Pro Football*. New York: Simon & Schuster, 1984.

Newspapers and Magazines

The following were checked extensively:
Chicago Tribune
The Coffin Corner
Los Angeles Times
New York Times
Sports Illustrated
Washington Post
Countless other newspapers were searched through the following aggregators:
Access World News
Google News Archive
The Library of Congress' Chronicling America: Historic American Newspapers
ProQuest Historical Newspapers.

Web Sites

College Football Data Warehouse (http://www.cfbdatawarehouse.com/)
College Football Hall of Fame (http://collegefootball.org/)
NFL.com (http://www.nfl.com/)
Pro Football Hall of Fame (http://www.profootballhof.com/)
Pro-Football-Reference.com (http://www.pro-football-reference.com/)
Professional Football Researchers Association (http://www.profootballresearchers.org/)

INDEX